# eGrade Plus

## www.wiley.com/college/russell

## Based on the Activities You Do Every Day

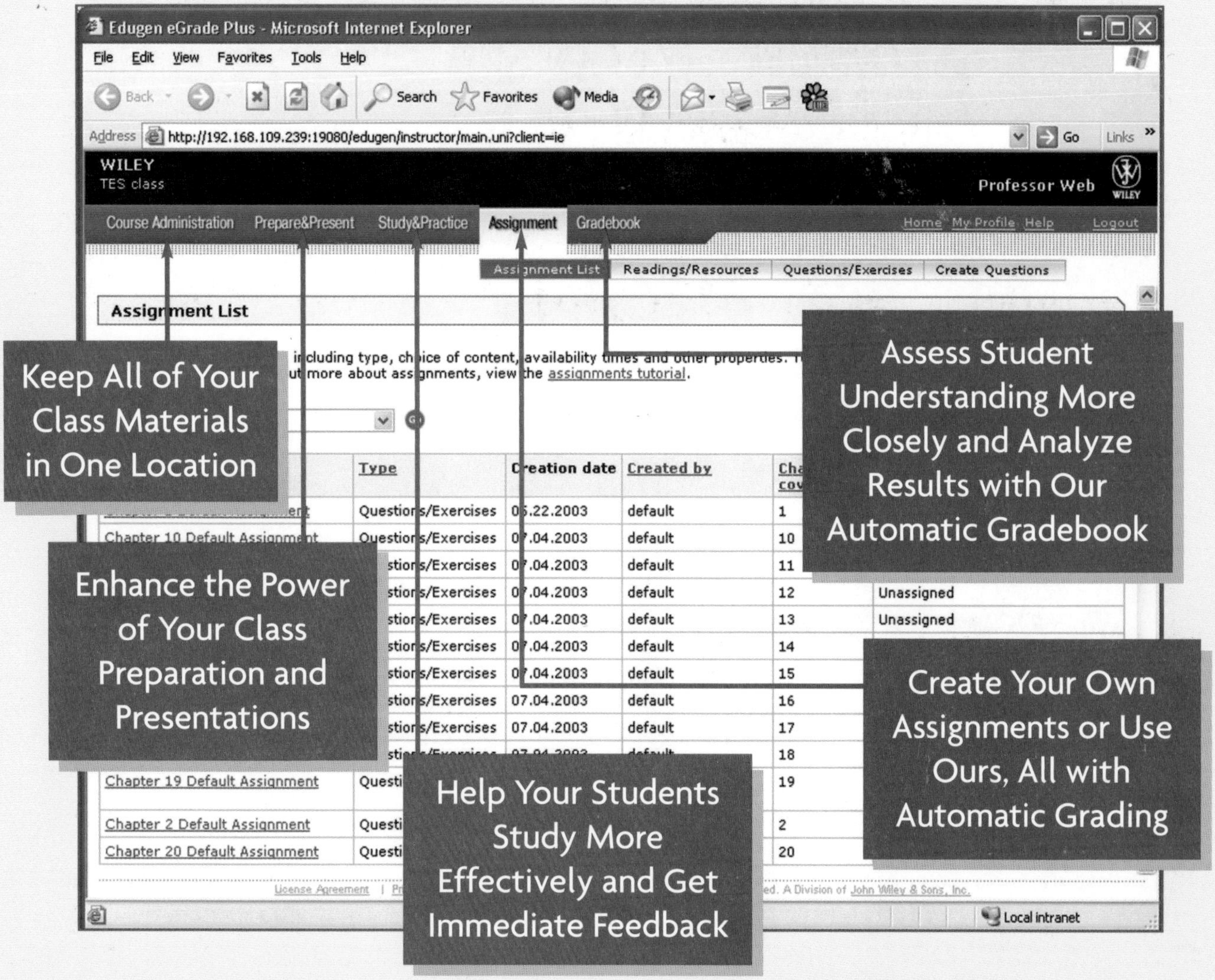

Keep All of Your Class Materials in One Location

Enhance the Power of Your Class Preparation and Presentations

Help Your Students Study More Effectively and Get Immediate Feedback

Assess Student Understanding More Closely and Analyze Results with Our Automatic Gradebook

Create Your Own Assignments or Use Ours, All with Automatic Grading

**All the content and tools you need, all in one location, in an easy-to-use browser format.**

**Choose the resources you need, or rely on the arrangement supplied by us.**

Now, many of Wiley's textbooks are available with eGrade Plus, a powerful online tool that provides a completely integrated suite of teaching and learning resources in one easy-to-use website. eGrade Plus integrates Wiley's world-renowned content with media, including a multimedia version of the text, PowerPoint slides, and more. Upon adoption of eGrade Plus, you can begin to customize your course with the resources shown here.

**See for yourself!**

**Go to www.wiley.com/college/egradeplus for an online demonstration of this powerful new software.**

# Students,
# eGrade Plus Allows You to:

## Study More Effectively

## Get Immediate Feedback When You Practice on Your Own

eGrade Plus problems link directly to relevant sections of the **electronic book content,** so that you can review the text while you study and complete homework online. Additional resources include **animated demo problems, practice quizzes** and **Excel templates.**

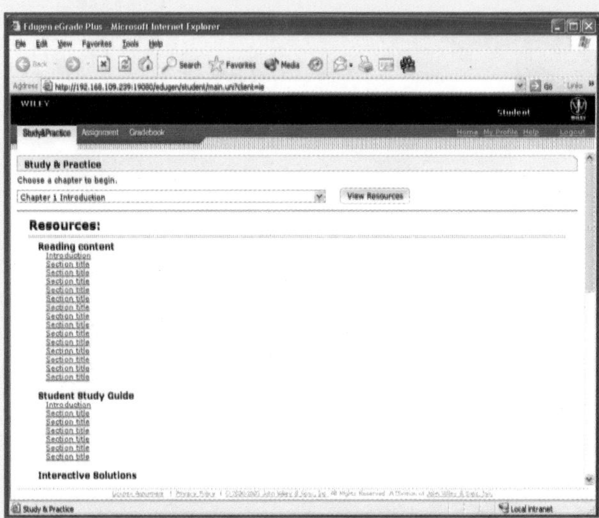


## Complete Assignments / Get Help with Problem Solving

An **Assignment** area keeps all your assigned work in one location, making it easy for you to stay "on task." In addition, many homework problems contain a **link** to the relevant section of the **multimedia book,** providing you with a text explanation to help conquer problem-solving obstacles as they arise. You will have access to a variety of **end of chapter problems** and **practice assignments,** as well as other resources for building your confidence and understanding.

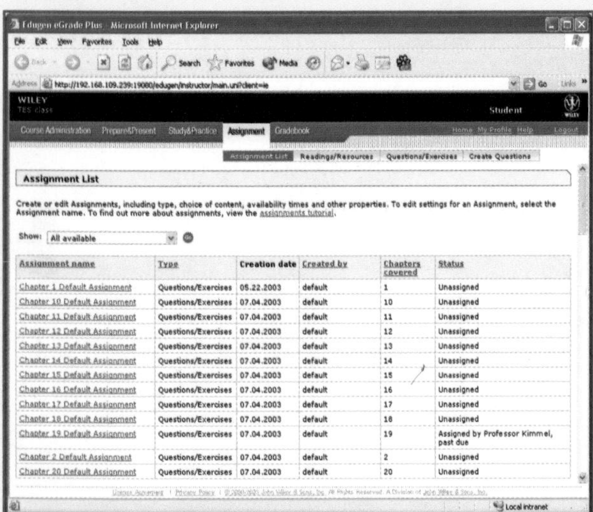


## Keep Track of How You're Doing

A **Personal Gradebook** allows you to view your results from past assignments at any time.

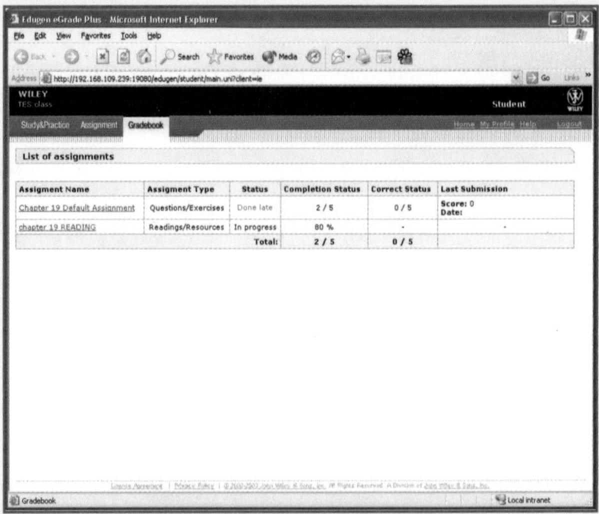


www.wiley.com/college/russell

# Operations Management

## *Quality and Competitiveness in a Global Environment*

5th Edition

**Roberta S. Russell**

Professor

*Virginia Polytechnic Institute and State University*

**Bernard W. Taylor III**

R. B. Pamplin Professor

*Virginia Polytechnic Institute and State University*

John Wiley & Sons, Inc

| | |
|---|---|
| **Acquisitions Editor:** | Beth Lang Golub |
| **Associate Editor:** | Lorraina Raccuia |
| **Editorial Assistant:** | Jennifer Snyder |
| **Production Editor:** | Janine Rosado |
| **Marketing Manager:** | Jillian Rice |
| **Design Director:** | Harry Nolan |
| **Illustration Editor:** | Anna Melhorn |
| **Senior Media Editor:** | Allison Morris |
| **Photo Editor:** | Ellinor Wagner |
| **Photo Researcher:** | Elyse Rieder |
| **Cover Design:** | Howard Grossman |
| **Interior Design:** | Fearn Cutler De Vicq De Cumptich |
| **Production Services:** | GGS Book Services, Atlantic Highlands |
| **Cover Photo:** | *(left, top to bottom)* Glen Allison/Getty Images/PhotoDisc, Inc; Tommaso di Girolamo/Age Fotostock America; Juan Silva/Getty Images/The Image Bank; Mark Segal/Digital Vision; S.L. Francisco Ontanon/Getty Images/The Image Bank; Bartomeu Amengual/Age Fotostock America; *(right)* C-Squared Studio/Getty Images/PhotoDisc, Inc. |

This book was set in Times Roman by GGS Book Services and printed and bound by Von Hoffmann. The cover was printed by Von Hoffmann.

This book is printed on acid free paper. ∞



ISBN 0-471-69209-3

**Library of Congress Cataloging-in-Publication Data**

Russell, Roberta S.
  Operations management/Roberta S. Russell, Bernard W. Taylor III.
    p. cm.
  ISBN 0-471-69209-3 (cloth)
  1. Production management. 2. Quality control. I. Taylor, Bernard W. II. Title.

TS155.R752 2005
658.5—dc22

2004059096

Printed in the United States of America

10 9 8 7 6 5 4 3 2 1

*To my children, Travis and Amy,*
*as they make their way in this world*

*To my mother, Jean V. Taylor*
*and in memory of my father, Bernard W. Taylor, Jr.,*
*with love and appreciation.*

# About the Authors

**Bernard W. Taylor III and Roberta S. Russell**

*Bernard W. Taylor III* is the Pamplin Professor of Management Science and Head of the Department of Business Information Technology in the Pamplin College of Business at Virginia Polytechnic Institute and State University. He received a Ph.D. and an M.B.A. from the University of Georgia and a B.I.E. from the Georgia Institute of Technology. He is the author of the book *Introduction to Management Science* (8th ed.) and co-author of *Management Science* (4th ed.), both published by Prentice Hall. Dr. Taylor has published over 80 articles in such journals as *Operations Research, Management Science, Decision Sciences, IIE Transactions, Journal of the Operational Research Society, Computers and Operations Research, Omega*, and the *International Journal of Production Research*, among others. His paper in *Decision Sciences* (with P. Y. Huang and L. P. Rees) on the Japanese kanban production system received the Stanley T. Hardy Award for its contribution to the field of production and operations management. He has served as President of the Decision Sciences Institute (DSI) as well as Program Chair, Council Member, Vice President, Treasurer, and as the Editor of *Decision Line*, the newsletter of DSI. He is a Fellow of DSI and a recipient of their Distinguished Service Award. He is a former President, Vice-President, and Program Chair of the Southeast Decision Sciences Institute and a recipient of their Distinguished Service Award. He teaches management science and production and operations management courses at both the undergraduate and graduate level. He has received the University Certificate of Teaching Excellence on four occasions, the Pamplin College of Business Certificate of Teaching Excellence Award, and the Pamplin College of Business Ph.D. Teaching Excellence Award at Virginia Tech.

*Roberta S. Russell* is a Professor of Business Information Technology in the Pamplin College of Business at Virginia Polytechnic Institute and State University. She received a Ph.D. from Virginia Polytechnic Institute and State University, an M.B.A. from Old Dominion University, and a B.S. degree from Virginia Polytechnic Institute and State University. Dr. Russell's primary research and teaching interests are in the areas of production and operations management, service operations management, scheduling, and quality. She has published in *Decision Sciences, IIE Transactions, International Journal of Production Research, Material Flow, Business Horizons, Annals of Operations Research, Computers and Operations Research*, and others. She is also co-author of the Prentice Hall book, *Service Management and Operations*. Dr. Russell is a member of DSI, ASQ, POMS and IIE and a certified fellow of APICS. She is Past Vice President of POMS, Past President of the Southwest Virginia Chapter of APICS and has held numerous offices in Southeast DSI. She has received the Pamplin College of Business Certificate of Teaching Excellence, the University Certificate of Teaching Excellence, and the MBA Association's Outstanding Professor Award. She is also listed in Outstanding Young Women of America and is a recipient of the Virginia Tech Outstanding Young Alumna Award.

# Brief Contents

# Contents

# Preface

## OUR COVER

*Rice feeds the world; Operations Management is what gets it from the ground to the table.*

Rice production is one of the biggest, most pervasive, and most important economic activities in the world. It is the primary food staple for about one-half the world's population. More rice is consumed throughout the world than even wheat or corn. So, what does operations management have to do with modern rice production? Everything.

From the paddy fields, to processing and packaging, and shipping to markets around the world; to your local supermarket and take-out restaurants, operations management provides the planning, coordination, and technical know-how needed to bring rice to your table. At each stage, operations management adds value to the rice production process, using the most modern techniques and tools available. In our Fifth Edition, we wanted to convey the global nature and pervasive impact of operations management and what better example to get us started than rice. To put it simply, rice feeds much of the world and operations management is what makes that possible.

Our new Fifth Edition is the most extensive and comprehensive we have ever written, with many new topics and features, and many parts rewritten and revised. This edition continues to offer a clear, concise, and organized approach to operations management, enhanced with many special features and examples to bring the topics to life. We wanted to convey the concepts in a way that is logical and easy to understand. We also wanted to get students excited about the many new, unique, and interesting changes occurring in service and manufacturing operations around the world.

This new edition is completely attuned to these new and recent developments, including global issues, supply chains, ebusiness, and information technology. We have conspicuously integrated these important changes with the more traditional topics in operations management and the major themes of the text including quality, strategy and competitiveness.

## MAJOR TEXT THEMES

### OPERATIONS STRATEGY: QUALITY AND COMPETITIVENESS

A company's plan for achieving a competitive edge is its strategy. The success of a strategic plan is determined by how well a company coordinates all of its internal processes, including operations, and brings them to bear on its goals, which typically focus on quality attributes. Throughout the book we try to show how the functions and processes described in each chapter fit into a company's strategic plan. In each chapter we emphasize the need for considering the overall strategic implications of particular operating decisions.

Although most firms express their goals in terms of customer satisfaction or level of quality, their underlying objective is to beat the competition. One way in which companies can gain a competitive edge is by deploying the basic functions of operations management in a more effective manner than their rivals. Therefore, we give literally dozens of examples that explain how companies deploy specific operations functions that achieve quality, provide a competitive edge, and make them successful. We begin our discussion of competitiveness in Chapter 1 and continue throughout the book with "Competitive Edge" boxes, describing how successful companies have gained a competitive edge through operations.

## GLOBAL OPERATIONS

Companies and organizations today must increasingly compete in a global marketplace. The establishment of new trade agreements between countries, innovations in information technology, and improvements in transport and shipping are just a few of the factors that have enabled companies to do business around the world. The opening of the global marketplace has only served to introduce more competitors and make competition tougher, thus making strategic planning and quality in operations even more important for achieving success. In this edition we have sought to introduce this global aspect of operations into our discussion at every opportunity. In each chapter we include examples that touch on the impact of global operations relative to the topic under discussion, and we discuss how globalization affects operating decisions.

## E-BUSINESS AND INFORMATION TECHNOLOGY

In this new edition we continue to emphasize information technology and the effect of the Internet and e-business on supply chains and operations management. Throughout the text we indicate how information technology and the Internet are changing how operations are managed. For example, in the first chapter the fundamentals of business-to-consumer and business-to-business e-commerce are discussed as well as the impact of e-business on operations management. In Chapter 2 we discuss strategy and the Internet, in Chapter 5 collaborative product commerce, in Chapter 6 e-manufacturing and advanced communications. A major portion of Chapter 10 discusses e-procurement, e-business and information in the supply chain. Chapter 13 presents Web-based ERP and related e-business software.

## SERVICES AND MANUFACTURING

We have attempted to strike a balance between manufacturing and service operations in this book. Traditionally, operations management was thought of almost exclusively in a manufacturing context. However, in the United States and other industrialized nations, there has been a perceptible shift toward service industries. Thus, managing service operations has become equally as important as managing manufacturing operations. In many cases, operations management processes and techniques are indistinguishable between service and manufacturing. However, in many other instances, service operations present unique situations and problems that require focused attention and unique solutions. We have tried to reflect the uniqueness of service operations by providing focused discussions on service operations when there is a clear distinction between operations in a service environment and by providing many examples that address service situations. For example, in Chapter 3 on quality management we specifically address the unique conditions of TQM in service companies, in Chapter 5 on product and service design we emphasize the differences in design considerations between manufacturing and services, in Chapter 13 we discuss aggregate planning in services, and in Chapter 17 we focus on how waiting lines impact on the quality of service.

## QUALITATIVE AND QUANTITATIVE PROCESSES

We have also attempted to strike a balance between the qualitative (or managerial) aspects of operations management and the quantitative aspects. In the contemporary world of operations management, the quantitative and technological aspects are probably more important than ever. The ability to manage people and resources effectively, to motivate, organize, control, evaluate, and to adapt to change, have become critical to competing in today's global markets. Thus, throughout this book we seek to explain and clearly demonstrate how the successful operations manager manages and how to use quantitative techniques and technology when they are applicable.

However, we attempt to present these quantitative topics in a way that's not overly complex or mathematically intimidating. Above all, we want to show how the quantitative topics fit in with, and complement, the qualitative aspects of operations management. We want you to be able to see both "the forest and the trees."

## CHANGES IN THE FIFTH EDITION

We have reorganized this new edition around two primary themes, quality and competitiveness, in a global operating environment. As a result, we have moved our chapters related to quality to the front of the book, and we have repositioned the chapters related to supply chain in the second part of the book. The first part of this new edition is called "Designing the Productive System," while the second part of the book is called "Operating the Productive System." This results in a logical text flow from establishing strategic goals that are closely related to and driven by quality, and designing the operating system to meet these goals in the first part of the book, to managing the supply chain and its many components to achieve the strategic goals in the second part.

A new feature that has been added for this edition are chapter opening diagrams that serve as "roadmaps" showing how each chapter relates to other chapters and fits in with the book's structure and major themes. Following is an example of the opening diagram for Chapter 3 on Quality Management.

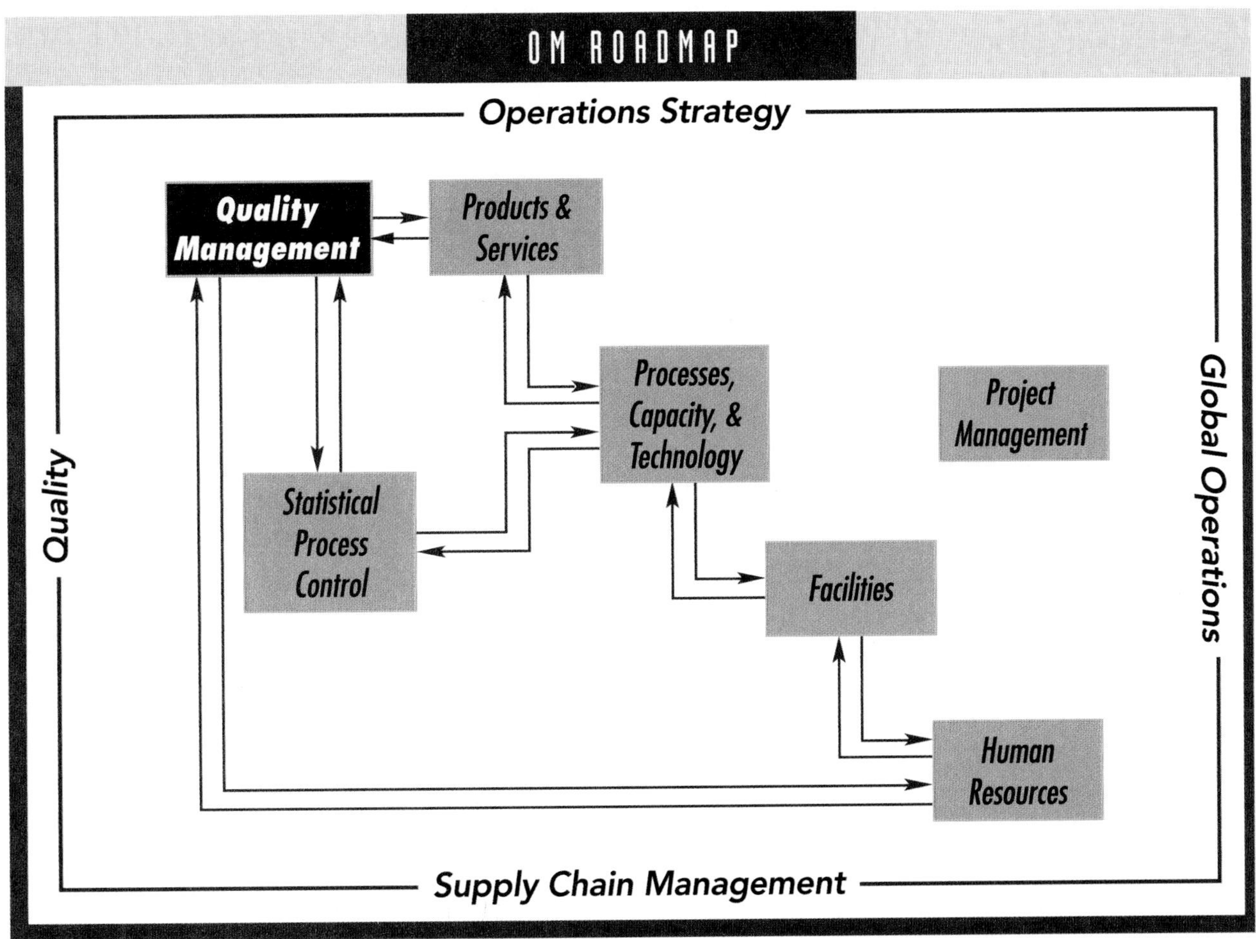


Notice that this diagram includes the topics in the first part of the book for "Designing the Productive System," and "Quality Management" is positioned in a key location that drives many of the other design topics. The bars along the outside that encompass the diagram represent the four major factors that impact on design issues—Quality, Strategy, Global Operations, and the Supply Chain. The bar at the bottom of the diagram for "Supply Chain Management" is also the link to the second part of the book. As you go through the chapters in the second part of the book, you will notice that the four major factors that impact on "Operating the Productive System" include Quality, Supply Chain Management, Global Operations, and Competitiveness.

We have placed increased emphasis on global issues throughout this new edition, starting in Chapters 1 and 2 where we discuss the implications of globalization for strategic planning and competitiveness. In Chapter 3, Quality Management, we have added new sections on "Kaizen and Continuous Improvement" and "Six Sigma" (including subsections on black and green belts, design for six sigma, and "breakthrough" strategies). The topic of "capacity" has been moved to the first part of the book in Chapter 6 (Processes, Technology, and Capacity) and Chapter 7 (Facilities).

Chapter 8 (Human Resources) covers a number of new topics, including employee motivation, cross training, job enrichment, empowerment, teamwork, flexible work schedules, telecommuting, compensation, gain sharing and profit sharing, managing workplace diversity, job design, and ergonomics. Work measurement, which is mainly a quantitative topic, has been moved out of the chapter and into a chapter supplement.

In Chapter 9 (Project Management) we switched to the "activity-on-node" network convention, which allows us to emphasize the Microsoft Project software. We have also included new sections on "Project Planning," "Scope Statement," "Responsibility Assignment Matrix," "Global Issues in Planning," and "Project Control" with discussions of time management, cost management, quality management, communication, and enterprise project management.

In the second part of the book, Chapter 10 (Supply Chain Management) has a number of new features. New sections on "Supply Chains for Service Providers" and "Value Chains" have been added, as well as a new section on the relationship between inventory and supply chains and an expanded discussion of the "bullwhip effect." Other new topics include radio frequency identification, reverse auctions, postponement, collaborative logistics, supply chain integration, measuring supply chain performance, and SCOR. The section on "Global Supply Chain" now includes discussions of the World Trade Organization, recent trends in globalization that focus on Mexico and China, and new sections on "Web-Based International Trade Logistics Systems" and the "Effects of 9/11 on Global Supply Chains." The "Transportation" problem has been moved to a Chapter 10 supplement, which now also includes the "Transshipment" problem.

Chapter 11 (Forecasting) now includes additional discussion of how the bullwhip effect impacts forecasting in the supply chain, and in Chapter 13 (Aggregate Planning) the section on yield management has been significantly expanded. In Chapter 14 (Resource Planning) lot sizing rules for MRP systems have been added, along with extensive coverage of ERP systems. In Chapter 15 (Lean Production) the discussion of lean production has been expanded, and the topic of lean services has been added. Chapter 16 (Scheduling) now includes examples of computerized scheduling systems, as well as an expanded section on the "Theory of Constraints." Chapter 17 (Waiting Lines) emphasizes the relationship between waiting lines and quality service, including a new section on the "Psychology of Waiting," and many new diagrams and figures have been added that illustrate the different waiting lines structures and how they relate to quality service.

## TEACHING AND LEARNING SUPPORT FEATURES

This text is accompanied by many features and supplements both in the text and online for students and instructors.

## PEDAGOGY IN THE TEXTBOOK

### Competitive Edge Boxes

These boxes are located in every chapter in the text. They describe the operations of a real world company, organization or agency related to specific topics in each chapter. They emphasize how companies effectively compete with operations management in the global marketplace. There are 53 of these boxes dispersed throughout the text, 31 of which are new to this edition. The descriptions of operations at actual companies in these boxes help the student understand how specific OM techniques and concepts are used by companies, which also make the topics and concepts easier to understand.

### OM Dialogue Boxes

These boxes, new to this edition, include dialogues with recent college business school graduates who are working in operations management in the real world. They describe how they apply various OM topics in the text in their own jobs and the value of their own OM training in college. This provides students with a perspective on the benefit of studying operations management now and its future benefit.

### Marginal Notes

Notes are included in the margins that serve the same basic function as notes that students themselves might write in the margin. They highlight important topics, making it easier for students to locate them; they summarize important points and key concepts, and provide brief definitions of key terms.

### Examples

The primary means of teaching the various quantitative topics in this text is through examples. These examples are liberally distributed throughout the text to demonstrate how problems are solved in a clear, straightforward approach to make them easier to understand.

### Solved Example Problems

At the end of each chapter, just prior to the homework questions and problems, there is a section with solved examples to serve as a guide for working the homework problems. These examples are solved in a detailed step-by-step manner.

### Summary of Key Formulas

These summaries at the end of each chapter and supplement include all of the key quantitative formulas introduced in the chapter in one location for easy reference.

### Summary of Key Terms

Located at the end of each chapter these summaries provide a list of key terms introduced in that chapter and their definitions in one convenient location for quick and easy reference.

### Homework Problems, Questions and Cases

Our text contains a large number of end-of-chapter exercises for student assignments. There are over 530 homework problems including 100 new problems, and 51 more advanced end-of-chapter case problems, 13 of which are new for this edition. In addition, over one-third of the problems carried over from the previous edition have been changed to provide new solutions. There are also 400 end-of-chapter discussion questions including 56 new questions. Answers to selected odd-numbered homework problems are included in the back of the book. As we mention in the following "Online Resources for Instructors" section, Excel spreadsheet solution files are available to the instructor for the majority of the end-of-chapter problems and cases.

## ONLINE RESOURCES FOR STUDENTS WWW.WILEY.COM/COLLEGE/RUSSELL

No other innovation has affected operations management in the past few years as much as computer technology and the Internet, and this is no less true in education. Therefore, we make full use of this technology as a learning and teaching medium in the courses we teach and in our text.

The text website contains animated demo problems, interactive applications and exercises, and direct links to other sources on the Internet. These various resources and learning tools are organized by chapter and are flagged in the textbook with a web icon. Here are some of the items found on the text website.

## SUMMARY OF KEY CONCEPTS

A brief summary of each chapter, highlighting the important concepts from the chapter, including a list of the interactive elements provided in that chapter.

## ANIMATED DEMO PROBLEMS

The website includes animated demo problems that clearly explain the problem-solving process by taking the student through complicated problems step-by-step. Students can click through the animated problems on their own as many times as they wish until they understand how the problem is solved.

## OTHER INTERNET RESOURCES, PRACTICE QUIZZES, AND VIRTUAL TOURS WWW.WILEY.COM/COLLEGE/RUSSELL

Students can link to the text website where an exciting set of Internet resources have been compiled. ***Web links*** for companies and concepts discussed in each chapter can be accessed online. These provide enrichment for those students who want to learn more about a topic, and serve as a valuable resource for student assignments and papers.

***Virtual Tours*** provided for each chapter bring operations management to life. Each tour is accompanied by a set of questions directly related to concepts discussed in the chapter.

***Internet Exercises*** provide up-to-date access to current issues in operations. These add immediacy to classroom discussions and ensure that operations management topics remain relevant to the student.

***Practice Quizzes*** are provided online where students can get immediate feedback on their progress.

## EXCEL FILES

Excel is used extensively throughout the text to solve various quantitative problems and many Excel illustrations are provided throughout the text.

**Exhibit 11.1**

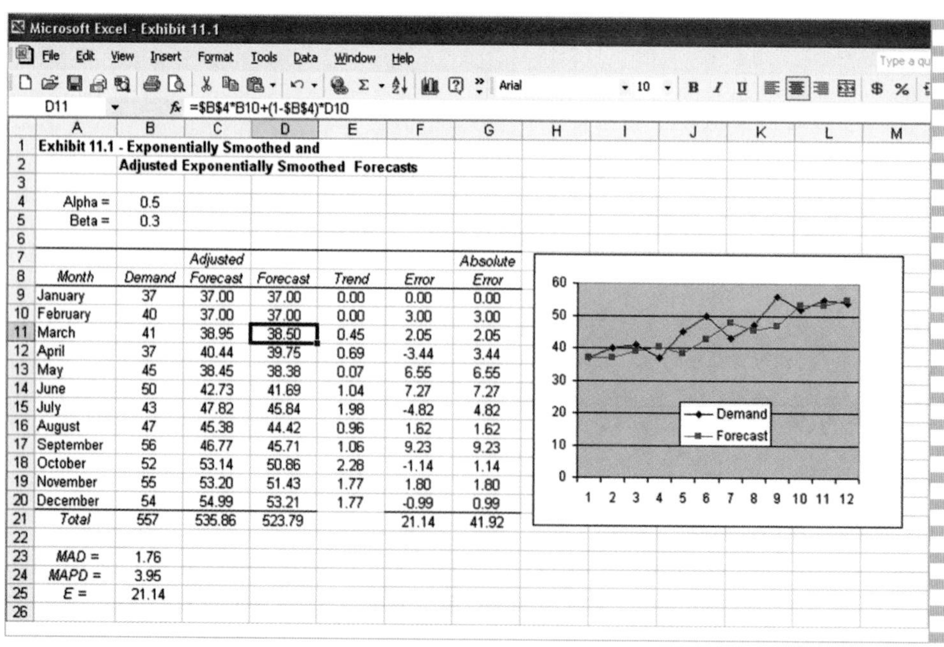
Microsoft Excel - Exhibit 11.1

D11 =$B$4*B10+(1-$B$4)*D10

Exhibit 11.1 - Exponentially Smoothed and Adjusted Exponentially Smoothed Forecasts

Alpha = 0.5
Beta = 0.3

| Month | Demand | Adjusted Forecast | Forecast | Trend | Error | Absolute Error |
|---|---|---|---|---|---|---|
| January | 37 | 37.00 | 37.00 | 0.00 | 0.00 | 0.00 |
| February | 40 | 37.00 | 37.00 | 0.00 | 3.00 | 3.00 |
| March | 41 | 38.95 | 38.50 | 0.45 | 2.05 | 2.05 |
| April | 37 | 40.44 | 39.75 | 0.69 | -3.44 | 3.44 |
| May | 45 | 38.45 | 38.38 | 0.07 | 6.55 | 6.55 |
| June | 50 | 42.73 | 41.69 | 1.04 | 7.27 | 7.27 |
| July | 43 | 47.82 | 45.84 | 1.98 | -4.82 | 4.82 |
| August | 47 | 45.38 | 44.42 | 0.96 | 1.62 | 1.62 |
| September | 56 | 46.77 | 45.71 | 1.06 | 9.23 | 9.23 |
| October | 52 | 53.14 | 50.86 | 2.28 | -1.14 | 1.14 |
| November | 55 | 53.20 | 51.43 | 1.77 | 1.80 | 1.80 |
| December | 54 | 54.99 | 53.21 | 1.77 | -0.99 | 0.99 |
| Total | 557 | 535.86 | 523.79 | | 21.14 | 41.92 |

MAD = 1.76
MAPD = 3.95
E = 21.14

Every Excel spreadsheet used to prepare the examples in the text is available on the text web site for students and instructors. They are organized by chapter and are listed by their exhibit number. On the facing page is an example of Exhibit 11.1 from Chapter 11 (Forecasting). Notice the file name is simply the Exhibit number, i.e., Exhibit 11.1.xls. Please look in each file carefully. In many cases several sheets in one file have been used to display different parts of a problem, such as a graphical solution as well as a numerical solution. Example files are also available for MS Project files in Chapter 9.

## ONLINE RESOURCES FOR INSTRUCTORS WWW.WILEY.COM/COLLEGE/RUSSELL

All Instructor's Resources are online.

- **Instructors Manual.** The Instructor's Manual updated by the authors features sample course syllabi, chapter outlines, teaching notes, exponential exercises, alternate examples to those examples provided in the text, pause and reflect questions for classroom discussion, practice quizzes, video guide, projects, and PowerPoint lecture slides, created by Beni Asllani of University of Tennessee at Chattanooga.
- **Test Bank and Computerized Test Bank.** The test bank created by Philip Fry of Boise State University, contains a variety of true/false, multiple choice, fill-in, short answer, and essay questions.
- **Instructor's Solutions Manual.** The Instructor's Solutions Manual, updated by the authors, features detailed answers to end-of-chapter questions, homework problems, and case problems.
- **WebCT and Blackboard.** Wiley now makes its class-tested online course content available in WebCT and Blackboard. Instructors receive easy-to-use design templates, communication, testing, and course management tools. To learn more, contact your local Wiley representative or go to www.wiley.com/college/russell for a quick preview of our online solutions.
- **eGrade plus.** eGrade Plus is a powerful online tool that provides instructors and students with an integrated suite of teaching and learning resources, including an online version of the text, in one easy-to-use website. To learn more about eGrade Plus, and view a demo, please visit www.wiley.com/college/egradeplus.
- **Business Extra Select** (www.wiley.com/college/bxs) Business Extra Select enables you to add copyright-cleared articles, cases, and readings from such leading business resources as INSEAD, Ivey, Harvard Business School Cases, *Fortune*, *The Economist*, *The Wall Street Journal*, and more. You can create your own custom CoursePack, combining these resources with content from Wiley's business textbooks, your own content such as lecture notes, and any other third-party content. Or you can use a ready-made CoursePack for Russell and Taylor's *Operations Management Fifth Edition*.

### OM Video Series

A collection of videos provides students and instructors with dynamic business examples directly related to the concepts introduced in the text. The Instructor's website contains a video guide with discussion questions for the 27 video segments that accompany this text. Please go to www.wiley.com/college/russell, then the Supplements section, to get information on how to order the videos.

### Excel Homework Solutions

New to this edition are files for the instructor, which provide Excel spreadsheet solutions for the majority of the end-of-chapter homework and case problems in the text (see the accompanying illustration). This new edition includes over 530 end-of-chapter homework problems and 51 case problems, and Excel solution files are provided on the text Website for many of these problems. In addition, Microsoft Project solution files are provided for most of the homework problems in Chapter 9 (Project Management).

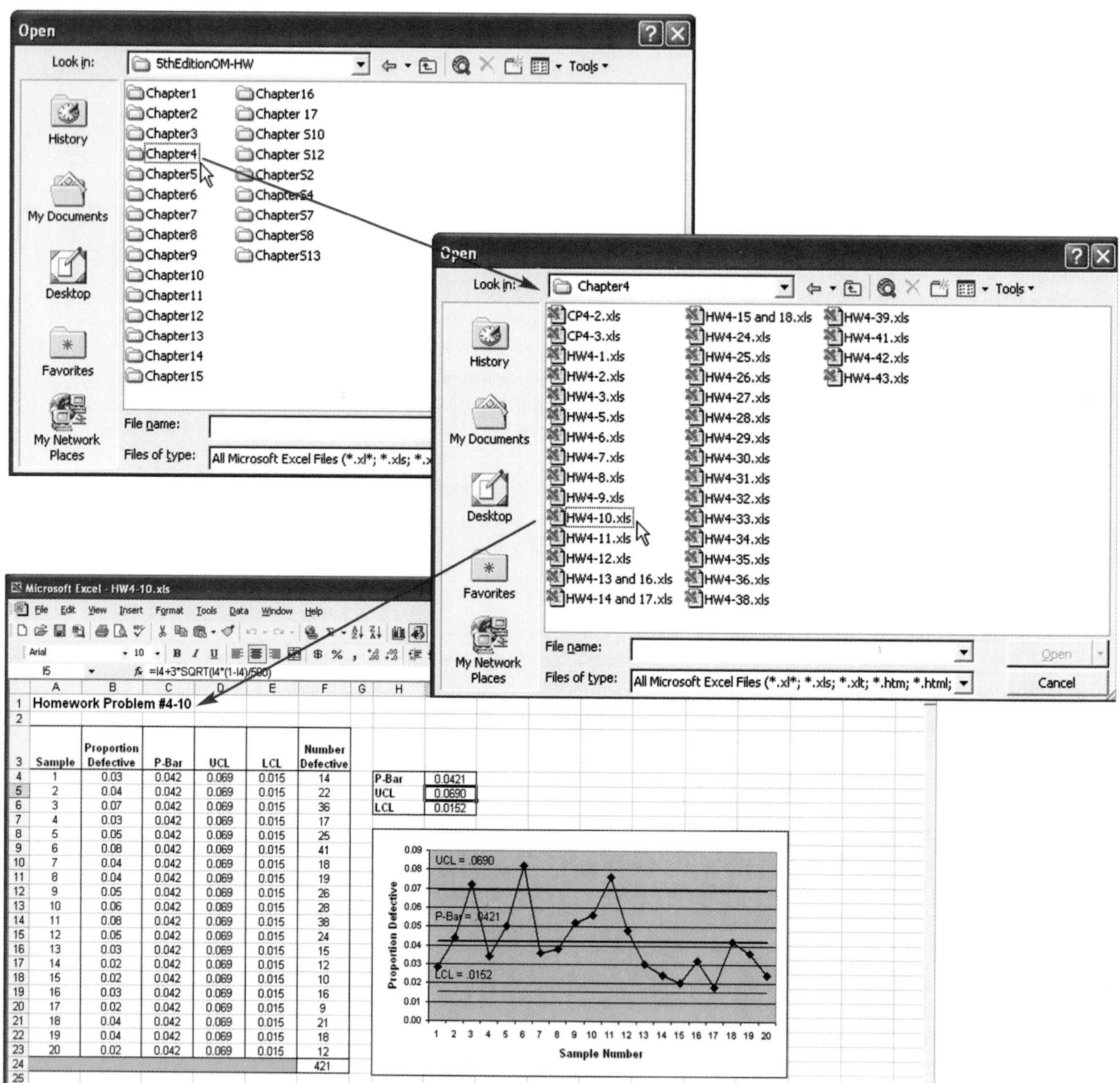


| Sample | Proportion Defective | P-Bar | UCL | LCL | Number Defective |
|---|---|---|---|---|---|
| 1 | 0.03 | 0.042 | 0.069 | 0.015 | 14 |
| 2 | 0.04 | 0.042 | 0.069 | 0.015 | 22 |
| 3 | 0.07 | 0.042 | 0.069 | 0.015 | 36 |
| 4 | 0.03 | 0.042 | 0.069 | 0.015 | 17 |
| 5 | 0.05 | 0.042 | 0.069 | 0.015 | 25 |
| 6 | 0.08 | 0.042 | 0.069 | 0.015 | 41 |
| 7 | 0.04 | 0.042 | 0.069 | 0.015 | 18 |
| 8 | 0.04 | 0.042 | 0.069 | 0.015 | 19 |
| 9 | 0.05 | 0.042 | 0.069 | 0.015 | 26 |
| 10 | 0.06 | 0.042 | 0.069 | 0.015 | 28 |
| 11 | 0.08 | 0.042 | 0.069 | 0.015 | 38 |
| 12 | 0.05 | 0.042 | 0.069 | 0.015 | 24 |
| 13 | 0.03 | 0.042 | 0.069 | 0.015 | 15 |
| 14 | 0.02 | 0.042 | 0.069 | 0.015 | 12 |
| 15 | 0.02 | 0.042 | 0.069 | 0.015 | 10 |
| 16 | 0.03 | 0.042 | 0.069 | 0.015 | 16 |
| 17 | 0.02 | 0.042 | 0.069 | 0.015 | 9 |
| 18 | 0.04 | 0.042 | 0.069 | 0.015 | 21 |
| 19 | 0.04 | 0.042 | 0.069 | 0.015 | 18 |
| 20 | 0.02 | 0.042 | 0.069 | 0.015 | 12 |
| | | | | | 421 |

# Acknowledgments

The writing and revision of a textbook, like any large project, requires the help and creative energy of many people, and this is certainly not the exception. We especially appreciate the confidence, support, help, and friendship of our new editor at Wiley, Beth Golub. We also thank the Wiley staff members who helped with our book including: Lorraina Raccuia, Associate Editor; Jennifer Snyder, Editorial Assistant; Allison K. Morris, Media Editor; Jillian Rice, Marketing Manager; Janine Rosado, Production Editor; Jeanine Furino, Production Manager; Harry Nolan, Design Director; Elle Wagnor, Photo Editor; and Anna Melhorn, Illustration Editor and numerous other people who work behind the scenes and whom we never saw or talked to. We would also like to thank Sandra Krausman at GGS Book Services for all her help during the editing and production process. We are indebted to the reviewers of the fifth edition including: Robert Aboolian, California State University San Marcos; Ajay Aggarwal, Millsaps College; Fred Anderson, Indiana University of Pennsylvania; Beni Asllani, University of Tennessee Chattanooga; Anteneh Ayanso, University of Connecticut, Storrs; Brent Bandy, University of Wisconsin, Oshkosh; Joe Biggs, California Polytechnic State University; Tom Bramorski, University of Wisconsin Whitewater; Kimball Bullington, Middle Tennessee State University; Cem Canel, University of North Carolina Wilmington; Janice Cerveny, Florida Atlantic University; Robert Clark, SUNY Stony Brook; Ajay Das, Baruch College CUNY; Kathy Dhanda, University of Portland; Susan Emens, Kent State University; Yee Fok, University of New Orleans; Phillip Fry, Boise State University; Mark Gershon, Temple University; Robert Greve, Oklahoma State University; Robert Frese, Maryville University; Jay Jayaram, University of South Carolina, Columbia; Vaidy Jayaraman, University of Miami; Serge Karalli, DePaul University; William Kime, University of New Mexico; Peter Klein, Ohio University; Howard Kraye, University of New Mexico, Albuquerque; John Kros, East Carolina University; Gopalan Kutty, Mansfield University; Bingguang Li, Albany State University; Royce Lorentz, Slippery Rock University; Sheldon Lou, California State University, San Marcos; Ken Mannino, Milwaukee School of Engineering; Lance Matheson, Virgina Tech; Duncan McDougall, Plymouth State University; Jaideep Motwani, Grand Valley State University; Hilary Moyes, University of Pittsburgh; Barin Nag, Towson University; Ozgur Ozluk, San Francisco State University; Amer Qureshi, University of Texas Arlington; Jim Robison, Sonoma State University; Raj Selladurai, Indiana University Northwest; Robert Setaputro, University of Wisconisin Milwaukee; Jacob Simons, Georgia Southern University; Marilyn Smith, Winthrop University; Donna Stewart, University of Wisconsin, Stout; Donald Stout, St. Martin's College; Dothang Truong, Fayetteville State University; Elizabeth Trybus, California State University Northridge; Ray Vankataraman, Pennsylvania State University, Erie; Timothy Vaughan, University of Wisconsin, Eau Claire; Mark Vrobelfski, Virginia Tech; Gustavo Vulcano, New York University; Kevin Watson, University of New Orleans; Michel Whittenberg, University of Texas Arlington; Hulya Yazici, University of Wisconsin, La Crosse; Jinfeng Yue, Middle Tennessee State University; and Xiaoqun Zhang, Pennsylvania State University, Harrisburg. They contributed numerous suggestions, comments, and ideas that dramatically improved and changed this edition. We offer our sincere thanks to these colleagues and hope that they can take some satisfaction in their contribution to our final product. We wish to thank our students who have class-tested, critiqued, and contributed to the first four editions and this fifth edition from a consumer's point of view. We thank graduate students Bryan Jorstad, Jay Pokorski, and Jay Teets for their many contributions to the final product. We are especially grateful to Tracy McCoy and Sylvia Seavey at Virginia Tech for their unstinting help, hard work, and patience.

R.S.R
B.W.T

# Photo Credits

**Chapter 1.** Page 2: (left) Courtesy Eveready Battery Company, Inc.; (top right) Tom McCarthy/Index Stock; (bottom right) Photo Edit. Page 5: Courtesy Roberta Russell. Page 21: Courtesy PSA Corporation Limited. Page 28: Courtesy Land's End, Inc. and Virtual Model, Inc.

**Chapter 2.** Page 32: Reprinted by permission of United Features Syndicate, Inc. Page 36: Randy Duchaine/Corbis Digital Stock. Page 42: (far right) Joel Benard/Masterfile; (top) Lonnie Duka/Allstock/Stone/Getty Images; (center) C.F. Martin & Co., Inc.; (bottom) Courtesy of Northrop Grumman Newport News. Page 44: (far right) Alamy Images; (top): John Coletti/Index Stock; (center) Gary Conner/PhotoEdit; (bottom) SuperStock, Inc. Page 47: Courtesy Don Hankinson, Lucent Technologies. Page 48: Roberta Russell.

**Chapter 3.** Page 78: (left) Courtesy National Institute of Standards and Measures; (right) Courtesy Motorola, Inc. Page 81: (top) Courtesy of Mercedes-Benz; (bottom) Courtesy Ford Motor Company. Page 82: Phil Schermeister/Network Aspen. Page 89: Pascal Le Sergretain/Getty Images News and Sport Services. Page 90: William Strode/Woodfin Camp & Associates. Page 95: Spencer Grant/PhotoEdit. Page 97: Tom Raymond/Pal's Sudden Service. Page 118: Courtesy Capstone Turbine Corp.

**Chapter 4.** Page 132: Richard Pasley Photography. Page 134: Courtesy Ford Motor Company. Page 141: Corbis/Bettmann. Page 145: Stone/Getty Images.

**Chapter 5.** Page 180: Courtesy General Motors Corp. Used with permission. Page 188: The New Yorker Collection, ©2004 Robert Leighton from cartoonbank.com. All rights reserved. Page 191: Courtesy General Motors Corp. Used with permission. Page 195: Courtesy Titleist and FootJoy Worldwide. Page 194: Courtesy H&M.

**Chapter 6.** Page 220: Justin Sullivan/Getty Images News and Sport Services. Page 224: (left) Courtesy Northrop Grumman Newport News; (right) Judi Baldwin/Northrup Grumman. Page 225: Stone/Getty Images. Page 226: (top) EPA/Landov, LLC; (bottom) Courtesy Ford Motor Company. Page 227: Courtesy Rockwell Automation. Page 232: Courtesy John Chiasson. Page 236: Roberta Russell.

**Chapter 7.** Page 258: Courtesy Ford Motor Company. Page 261: (top) John A. Wee. Page 261 (left): H. R. Branaz/Peter Arnold, Inc. Page 261 (right): Marianna Day Massey/Zuma/Corbis Digital Stock. Page 264: Courtesy The Boeing Corporation. Page 269: Chuck Keeler/Allstock/Stone/Getty Images. Page 270: (left) F. Charles Photography; (right): Courtesy Hedrich Blessing. Page 278: Courtesy Rowe's Furniture. Page 282: Courtesy Vought Aircraft Company, Northrop Grumman Corporation.

**Chapter 8.** Page 312: Courtesy U.S. Department of Commerce. Page 328: Murray Lee/Age Fotostock America, Inc. Page 334: Mike Dobel/Masterfile. Page 343: Jeff Greenberg/Unicorn Stock Photos.

**Chapter 9.** Page 360: Courtesy Disney Enterprises, Inc. Page 372: Photri-Microstock, Inc. Page 378: Gabriel Bouys/AFP/Getty Images.

**Chapter 10.** Page 410: Catherine Karnow/Woodfin Camp & Associates. Page 422: Courtesy Matrics, Inc. Page 438: Chris Sorensen Photography. Page 439: SuperStock, Inc. Page 449: Courtesy PSA Corporation, Ltd.

**Chapter 11.** Page 476: Corbis/Bettmann. Page 488: Fritz Hoffman/Image Works/Time Life Pictures/Getty Images. Page 495: PhotoDisc, Inc./Getty Images. Page 497: Alamy Images.

**Chapter 12.** Page 528: Francis Dean/The Image Works. Page 531: Courtesy The Goodyear Tire & Rubber Company. Page 534: Courtesy of Symbol Technologies, Inc.

**Chapter 13.** Page 580: Alamy Images. Page 581: Photo Courtesy Blandin Paper Company, Carlson & Kirwan, and Jeffrey Frey & Associates. Page 585: Hubert Camille/Allstock/Stone/Getty Images. Page 587: (left) Mark Gibson/Index Stock; (right) Kent Dufault/Index Stock.

**Chapter 14.** Page 644: Courtesy Cybex Controls. Page 658: (left) Paul Rio, Courtesy The New Orleans Marriott; (right) Tom Tracy/Photophile. Page 671: ©Scott Adams, reprinted by permission of United Features Syndicate, Inc.

**Chapter 15.** Page 684: Courtesy Bob Day, Solectron Corporation. Page 691: Courtesy Toyota Motor Manufacturing, Kentucky, Inc. Page 696: Kevin Fleming/Corbis-Bettmann. Page 702: Courtesy Toyota Motor Corp. Page 704: Courtesy Johnson Controls. Page 706: Taxi/Getty Images. Page 708: Stone/Getty Images.

**Chapter 16.** Page 718: Courtesy John Deere. Page 738: Myrleen Ferguson/PhotoEdit. Page 738: D.Young Wolff/PhotoEdit.

**Chapter 17.** Page 750: Jeff Greenberg/PhotoEdit. Page 758: Joe Raedle/Getty Images News and Sport Services. Page 760: Roy/EXPLORER/Photo Researchers. Page 764: Chad Ehlers/ Alamy Images. Page 772: David Young-Wolff/PhotoEdit.

# Part I Designing a Productive System

# Operations and Competitiveness

CHAPTER 1

Web resources for this chapter include

- Internet Exercises
- Online Practice Quizzes
- Virtual Tours
- Excel Worksheets
- Company and Resource Weblinks
- Animated Demo Problems
- Microsoft Project Exhibits

www.wiley.com/college/russell

## CHAPTER OUTLINE

In this chapter you will learn about . . .

- What Operations Managers Do
- The Operations Function
- The Evolution of Operations Management
- Operations Management and E-Business
- Globalization and Competitiveness
- Primary Topics in Operations Management
- Learning Objectives for This Course

## WHAT DO OPERATIONS MANAGERS DO?

Operations managers are the *improvement people*, the realistic, hard-nosed, make-it-work, get-it-done people. They perform a variety of tasks in many different types of businesses and organizations. Let's meet Rebecca Oesterle, production manager for Eveready Battery Company; Claire Thielen, management engineer for Memorial Hospitals Association; and Ada Liu, division manager for Li & Fung trading company.

Rebecca Oesterle began her career at Eveready analyzing and coordinating quality and productivity improvements for the production process. She later served as planner and scheduler of battery production, and project leader for the movement of assembly operations to Mexico. Now she manages the entire production process at the Maryville alkaline plant, coordinating the work of 13 supervisors and more than 500 production workers. Rebecca gets the product out the door for Eveready.

Claire Thielen facilitates continuous quality improvement projects and analyzes methods and systems for a large medical center. Her projects include determining staffing patterns and workflow for computerized booking systems; consolidating policies, procedures, and practices for the merger of two hospitals; analyzing demand for 911 services; designing clinical studies of new medication effectiveness; and conducting training sessions on process mapping and analysis. Claire ensures a smooth flow of operations for Memorial Hospitals.

Ada Liu coordinates global production and distribution for one of Li & Fung's major clients, Gymboree. Her 40-person staff in Hong Kong includes merchandising, raw material purchasing, quality assurance, technical support, and shipping. She has dedicated sourcing teams in China, the Philippines, and Indonesia and employees or contractors in 26 other countries. For an order of 10,000 garments, Ada might decide to buy yarn from a Korean producer, have it woven and dyed in Taiwan, and then have it shipped to Thailand for production, along with zippers and buttons made by a

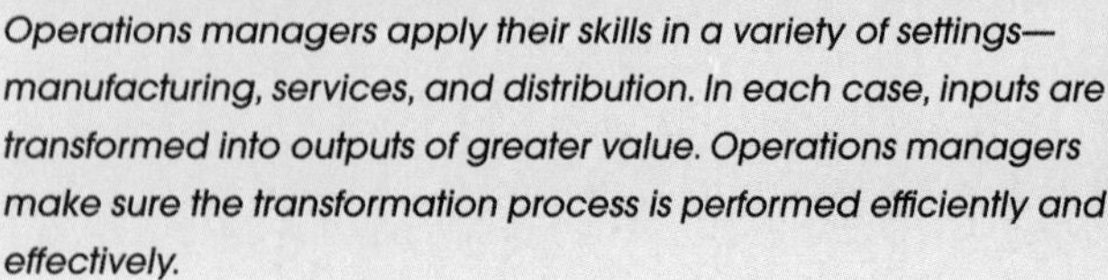

*Operations managers apply their skills in a variety of settings—manufacturing, services, and distribution. In each case, inputs are transformed into outputs of greater value. Operations managers make sure the transformation process is performed efficiently and effectively.*

Japanese firm in China. For quicker delivery, the order may be divided across five factories in Thailand. Five weeks after receipt of the order, 10,000 identical garments arrive in Gymboree stores across the United States and Europe. Ada is the supply chain expert for Gymboree.

*Sources:* Adapted from Joan Magretta, "Fast, Global, and Entrepreneurial: Supply Chain Management, Hong Kong Style," *Harvard Business Review* (September–October 1998):103–114; Katherine Aldred, "IE Gets Charge Out of Battery Production," *IIE Solutions* (July 1998):16–17; Katherine Aldred, "IE Marks a Difference One Person at a Time," *IIE Solutions* (April 1998): 14–15.

**Operations management:** the design, operation, and improvement of productive systems.

**Operations management** designs, operates and improves productive systems—systems for getting work done. The food you eat, the movies you watch, the stores in which you shop, and this book you are reading are provided to you by the people in operations. Operations managers are found in banks, hospitals, factories, and government. They design systems, ensure quality, produce products, and deliver services. They work with customers and suppliers, the latest technology, and global partners. They solve problems, reengineer processes, innovate, and integrate. Operations is more than planning and controlling; it's doing. Whether its superior quality, speed-to-market, customization, or low cost, excellence in operations is critical to a firm's success.

**Operations:** a function or system that transforms inputs into outputs of greater value.

**Operations** is often defined as a transformation process. As shown in Figure 1.1, inputs (such as material, machines, labor, management, and capital) are transformed into outputs (goods and services). Requirements and feedback from customers are used to adjust factors in the transformation process, which may in turn alter inputs. In operations management, we try to ensure that the transformation process is performed efficiently and that the output is of greater *value* than the sum of the inputs. Thus, the role of operations is to create value. The transformation process itself can be viewed as a series of activities along a *value chain* extending from supplier to customer. Any activities that do not add value are superfluous and should be eliminated.

The input–transformation–output process is characteristic of a wide variety of operating systems. In an automobile factory, sheet steel is formed into different shapes, painted and finished, and then assembled with thousands of component parts to produce a working automobile. In an aluminum factory, various grades of bauxite are mixed, heated, and cast into ingots of different sizes. In a hospital, patients are helped to become healthier individuals through special care, meals, medication, lab work, and surgical procedures. Obviously, "operations" can take many different forms. The transformation process can be

| | |
|---|---|
| *physical,* | as in manufacturing operations; |
| *locational,* | as in transportation or warehouse operations; |
| *exchange,* | as in retail operations; |
| *physiological,* | as in health care; |
| *psychological,* | as in entertainment; or |
| *informational,* | as in communication. |

Figure 1.1
**Operations as a Transformation Process**

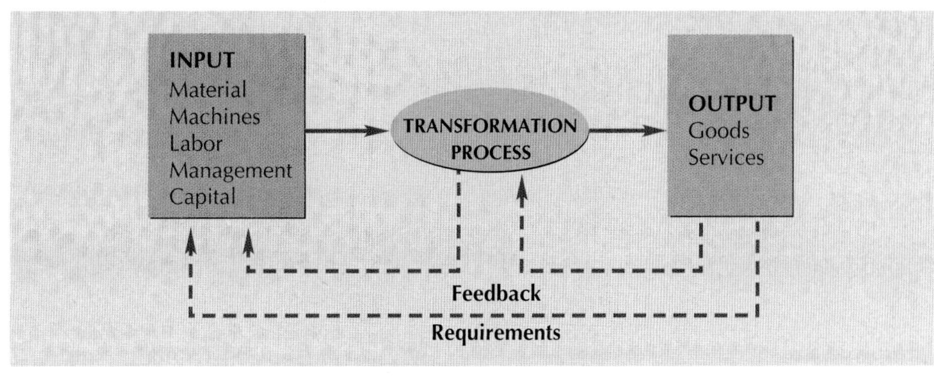

## THE OPERATIONS FUNCTION

Activities in operations management (OM) include organizing work, selecting processes, arranging layouts, locating facilities, designing jobs, measuring performance, controlling quality, scheduling work, managing inventory, and planning production. Operations managers deal with people, technology, and deadlines. These managers need good technical, conceptual, and behavioral skills. Their activities are closely intertwined with other functional areas of a firm.

The four primary functional areas of a firm are marketing, finance, operations, and human resources. As shown in Figure 1.2, for most firms, operations is the technical core or "hub" of the organization, interacting with the other functional areas and suppliers to produce goods and provide services for customers. For example, to obtain monetary resources for production, operations provides finance and accounting with production and inventory data, capital budgeting requests, and capacity expansion and technology plans. Finance pays workers and suppliers, performs cost analyses, approves capital investments, and communicates requirements of shareholders and financial markets. Marketing provides operations with sales forecasts, customer orders, customer feedback, and information on promotions and product development. Operations, in turn, provides marketing with information on product or service availability, lead-time estimates, order status, and delivery schedules. For personnel needs, operations relies on human resources to recruit, train, evaluate, and compensate workers and to assist with legal issues, job design, and union activities. Outside the organization operations interacts with suppliers to order materials or services, communicate production and delivery requirements, certify quality, negotiate contracts, and finalize design specifications.

As a field of study, operations brings together many disciplines and provides an integrated view of business organizations. Operations managers are in demand in business, industry, and government. Chief operating officers (COOs) run major corporations. Typical jobs for new college graduates include business process analyst, inventory analyst, project coordinator, unit supervisor, supply chain analyst, materials manager, quality assurance specialist, production scheduler, and logistics planner. Even if you do not pursue a career in operations, you'll be able to use the ideas you learn in this course to organize work, en-

Figure 1.2
**Operations as the Technical Core**

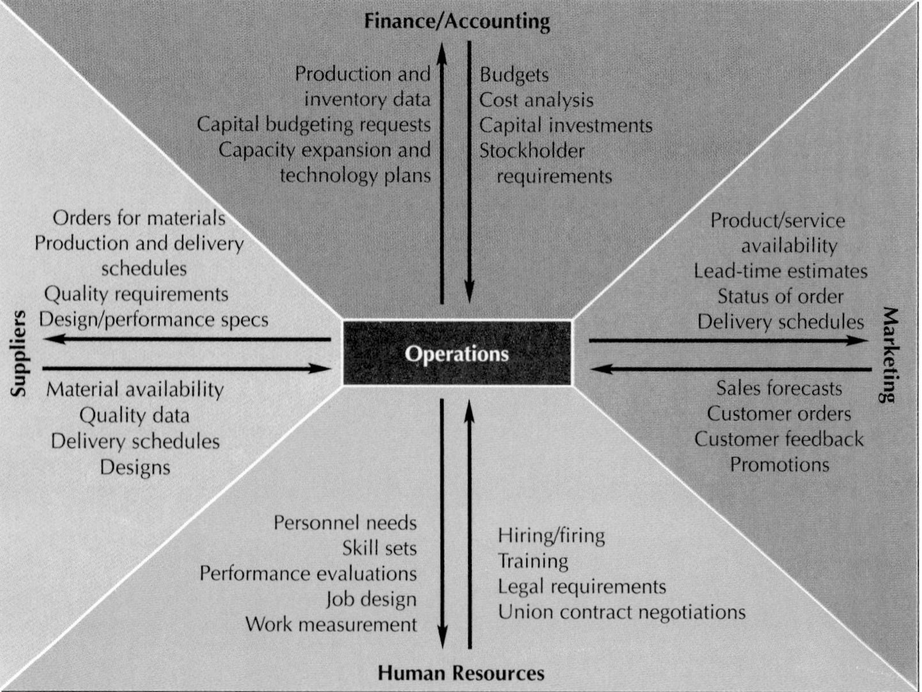

Figure 1.3
**The Relevance of Operations Management**

sure quality, and manage processes. Regardless of your major, you can apply some aspect of operations management to your future career—as did Mark, Nicole, John, Vignesh, Margie, and Anastasia who tell their stories in Figure 1.3 and the ***OM Dialogues*** dispersed throughout the text. Let's hear first from Mark Jackson, marketing manager for Pizza Hut (see page 6).

Now that you are aware of how operations might relate to your interests, let's take a brief look at how the field of OM has evolved to its present state.

## THE EVOLUTION OF OPERATIONS MANAGEMENT

Although history is full of amazing production feats—the pyramids of Egypt, the Great Wall of China, the roads and aqueducts of Rome—the widespread production of consumer goods—and thus, operations management—did not begin until the Industrial Revolution in the 1700s. Prior to that time, skilled craftspersons and their apprentices fashioned goods for individual customers from studios in their own homes. Every piece was unique, hand-fitted, and made entirely by one person, a process known as **craft production**. Although *craft production* still exists today, the availability of coal, iron ore, and steam power set into motion a series of industrial inventions that revolutionized the way work was performed. Great mechanically powered machines replaced the laborer as the primary factor of production and brought workers to a central location to perform tasks under the direction of an "overseer" in a place called a "factory." The revolution first took hold in textile mills, grain mills, metalworking, and machine-making facilities.

**Craft production:** the process of handcrafting products or services for individual customers.

***Mark Jackson,***
***Marketing Manager for Pizza Hut***

As regional marketing manager for Pizza Hut, I'm responsible for 21 stores. It's my job to make sure each store is operating properly and, when new products come out, to see that they are given the attention they deserve. I also coach managers and employees about their job and their relationship with the customer.

You would think that a marketing manager's job would be concerned solely with advertising, special promotions, store signage, customer service, and the like. But we also deal with quality, forecasting, logistics, and other operational issues. Marketing and operations are almost inseparable in services. We can come out with a new product and spend mega bucks advertising it, but if the product is not made or delivered properly, all is lost.

The most important aspect of quality is consistency—so that the customer gets the same pizza at any Pizza Hut from whichever cook happens to be on shift. We have exact standards and specifications for our products, and it's important that operating procedures be followed.

Scheduling is somewhat of a headache because of staff turnover and individual limitations on working hours. Some of that is alleviated in our new system where we allow employees to request days off up to six months in advance. They can put requests into the system when they clock in each day, and they can view upcoming schedules.

Our forecasting system keeps historical data on sales by hour and day of the week five years back. Forecasts are weighted averages of past demand—usually 60% of the past two weeks' sales and 40% of the past six weeks' sales. A manager can *freeze* the forecast and make manual adjustments, such as increasing demand during a home football game weekend or when a local festival is underway. Managers can also enter notes into the system when unusual occurrences affect demand, like a snowstorm. When the forecast is set, it generates a labor plan for the week, along with prep plans for salad, dough, breadsticks, and so forth. The labor plan just specifies the number of workers needed; it is up to the manager to do the detailed scheduling of individuals.

After quality, it's all about speed of delivery—whether to the customer's table or to the customer's home. We have initiatives such as *Ready for Revenue* where we pre-sauce and pre-cheese in anticipation of customer orders, and *Aces in Their Places* where we make sure the best people are scheduled and ready to go for peak demand periods. As for delivery, we keep track of percent of deliveries under 39 minutes and percent of deliveries to promise. We found we could significantly reduce the number of drivers needed (and keep the same customer satisfaction numbers) by promising delivery within 39 minutes rather than 30. We also are more efficient now that dispatching divides our delivery areas into delivery pods and uses computerized estimates of transit time.

**Division of labor:** dividing a job into a series of small tasks each performed by a different worker.

**Interchangeable parts:** the standardization of parts initially as replacement parts; enabled mass production.

Around the same time, Adam Smith's *Wealth of Nations* (1776) proposed the **division of labor**, in which the production process was broken down into a series of small tasks, each performed by a different worker. The specialization of the worker on limited, repetitive tasks allowed him or her to become very proficient at those tasks and further encouraged the development of specialized machinery.

The introduction of **interchangeable parts** by Eli Whitney (1790s) allowed the manufacture of firearms, clocks, watches, sewing machines, and other goods to shift from customized one-at-a-time production to volume production of standardized parts. This meant the factory needed a system of measurements and inspection, a standard method of production, and supervisors to check the quality of the worker's production.

Advances in technology continued through the 1800s. Cost accounting and other control systems were developed, but management theory and practice were virtually nonexistent.

**Scientific management:** the systematic analysis of work methods.

In the early 1900s an enterprising laborer (and later chief engineer) at Midvale Steel Works named Frederick W. Taylor approached the management of work as a science. Based on observation, measurement, and analysis, he identified the best method for performing each job. Once determined, the methods were standardized for all workers, and economic incentives were established to encourage workers to follow the standards. Taylor's philosophy became known as **scientific management**. His ideas were embraced and extended by efficiency experts Frank and Lillian Gilbreth, Henry Gantt, and others. One of Taylor's biggest advocates was Henry Ford.

Henry Ford applied scientific management to the production of the Model T in 1913 and reduced the time required to assemble a car from a high of 728 hours to $1\frac{1}{2}$ hours. A Model T chassis moved slowly down a conveyor belt with six workers walking alongside it, picking up parts from carefully spaced piles on the floor and fitting them to the chassis.[1] The short assembly time per car allowed the Model T to be produced in high volumes, or "en masse," yielding the name **mass production**.

**Mass production:** the high-volume production of a standardized product for a mass market.

American manufacturers became adept at mass production over the next 50 years and easily dominated manufacturing worldwide. The human relations movement of the 1930s, led by Elton Mayo and the Hawthorne studies, introduced the idea that worker motivation, as well as the technical aspects of work, affected productivity. Theories of motivation were developed by Frederick Herzberg, Abraham Maslow, Douglas McGregor, and others. Quantitative models and techniques spawned by the operations research groups of World War II continued to develop and were applied successfully to manufacturing and services. Computers and automation led still another upsurge in technological advancements applied to operations. These events are summarized in Table 1.1.

From the Industrial Revolution through the 1960s, the United States was the world's greatest producer of goods and services, as well as the major source of managerial and technical expertise. But in the 1970s and 1980s, industry by industry, U.S. manufacturing

Table 1.1
**Historical Events in Operations Management**

| Era | Events/Concepts | Dates | Originator |
|---|---|---|---|
| Industrial Revolution | Steam engine | 1769 | James Watt |
| | Division of labor | 1776 | Adam Smith |
| | Interchangeable parts | 1790 | Eli Whitney |
| Scientific Management | Principles of scientific management | 1911 | Frederick W. Taylor |
| | Time and motion studies | 1911 | Frank and Lillian Gilbreth |
| | Activity scheduling chart | 1912 | Henry Gantt |
| | Moving assembly line | 1913 | Henry Ford |
| Human Relations | Hawthorne studies | 1930 | Elton Mayo |
| | Motivation theories | 1940s | Abraham Maslow |
| | | 1950s | Frederick Herzberg |
| | | 1960s | Douglas McGregor |
| Operations Research | Linear programming | 1947 | George Dantzig |
| | Digital computer | 1951 | Remington Rand |
| | Simulation, waiting line theory, decision theory, PERT/CPM | 1950s | Operations research groups |
| | MRP, EDI, EFT, CIM | 1960s, 1970s | Joseph Orlicky, IBM and others |
| Quality Revolution | JIT (just-in-time) | 1970s | Taiichi Ohno (Toyota) |
| | TQM (total quality management) | 1980s | W. Edwards Deming, Joseph Juran |
| | Strategy and operations | | Wickham Skinner, Robert Hayes |
| | Business process reengineering | 1990s | Michael Hammer, James Champy |
| Globalization | World Trade Organization, European Union, and other trade agreements | 1990s 2000s | Numerous countries and companies |
| Internet Revolution | Internet, WWW | 1990s | ARPANET, Tim Berners-Lee |
| | ERP, supply chain management | | SAP, i2 Technologies, ORACLE, PeopleSoft |
| | E-commerce | 2000s | Amazon, Yahoo, eBay, and others |

[1]David Halberstam, *The Reckoning* (New York: William Morrow, 1986), pp. 79–81.

An emphasis on quality and the strategic role of operations.

superiority was challenged by lower costs and higher quality from foreign manufacturers, led by Japan. Several studies published during those years confirmed what the consumer already knew—U.S.-made products of that era were inferior and could not compete on the world market. Early rationalizations that the Japanese success in manufacturing was a cultural phenomenon were disproved by the successes of Japanese-owned plants in the United States, such as the Matsushita purchase of a failing Quasar television plant in Chicago from Motorola. Part of the purchase contract specified that Matsushita had to retain the entire hourly workforce of 1000 persons. After only two years, with the identical workers, half the management staff, and little or no capital investment, Matsushita doubled production, cut assembly repairs from 130% to 6%, and reduced warranty costs from $16 million a year to $2 million a year. You can bet Motorola took notice, as did the rest of American industry.

How did this come about? How did a country that dominated manufacturing for most of the twentieth century suddenly become no good at it? Quite simply, U.S. companies weren't paying attention. They thought mass production had solved the "problem" of production, so they delegated the function of manufacturing to technical specialists who ignored changes in the consumer environment and the strategic importance of operations. Decisions were made based on short-term financial goals rather than long-term strategic initiatives.

Mass production can produce large volumes of goods quickly, but it cannot adapt very well to changes in demand. Today's consumer market is characterized by product proliferation, shortened product life cycles, shortened product development times, changes in technology, more customized products, and segmented markets. Mass production did not "fit" that type of environment. Using a concept known as just-in-time, Japanese manufacturers changed the rules of production from mass production to **lean production**. Lean production prizes flexibility (rather than efficiency) and quality (rather than quantity). The *quality* mantra has since spread across the globe and is the underlying force for successful operations today.

**Lean production:** an adaptation of mass production that prizes quality and flexibility.

The renewed emphasis on quality and the *strategic importance* of operations made U.S. companies competitive again. Technology, together with changing political and economic conditions, has prompted an era of industrial *globalization* in which companies compete worldwide for both market access and production resources. The emergence of the Internet has energized this trend toward globalization.

Today, businesses use the Internet to communicate designs, contracts, and agreements; to schedule work and deliveries; to buy and sell from suppliers; to transfer funds; to share knowledge; and to transact business.

In the next few sections we'll explore operations management in the service sector, in an e-business environment, and in a global environment of increasing competitiveness.

## OPERATIONS MANAGEMENT IN THE SERVICE SECTOR

Operations management is just as applicable to services as it is to manufacturing. Services have work to be organized, quality to be assured, resources to allocate, and workers to schedule. Although the intangibility, perishability, and high customer contact of services makes operating decisions more difficult, the number of service outlets, flexibility of operation, and decentralized decision making create numerous opportunities for rapid process improvement. Service examples are used extensively throughout the text, and each chapter includes sections devoted to special considerations in services. It is interesting to note that the distinction between products and services has become increasingly blurred. Products are bundled with services (Internet service with your PC), and services are accompanied by *facilitating goods* (meals at a restaurant). Figure 1.4 shows a continuum from manufactured goods to pure services. We discuss the nature of services in more detail in Chapter 5 on Product and Service Design.

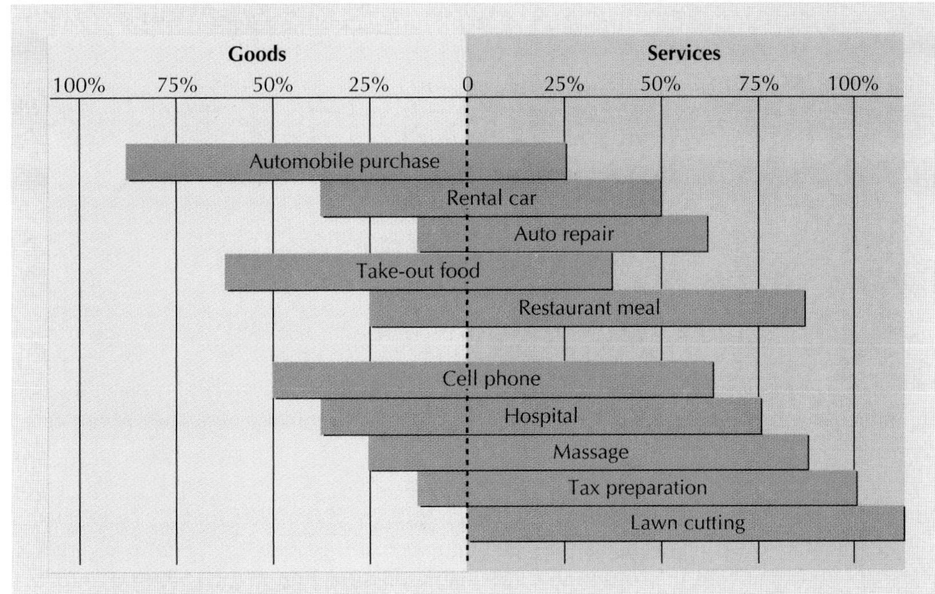


**Figure 1.4**

**A Continuum from Goods to Services**

*Source:* Adapted from Earl W. Sasser, R. P. Olsen, and D. Daryl Wyckoff, *Management of Service Operations* (Boston: Allyn Bacon, 1978), p. 11.

## OPERATIONS MANAGEMENT IN AN E-BUSINESS ENVIRONMENT

Trade that occurs over the Internet (or any computer network) is called *electronic commerce*, *e-commerce*, or *e-business*.[2] Electronic commerce can take the form of trade between businesses, between consumers, or between businesses and consumers (Figure 1.5). **Business-to-business (B2B)** trade typically involves companies and their suppliers, such as General Electric's Trading Process Network or Commerce One's Global Trading Web. **Business-to-consumer (B2C)** trade can take the form of online retailing, like Amazon, or online stockbrokerage, like E*Trade. *Consumer-to-business* (C2B) transactions reverse the normal flow of trade by having customers post what they want and having businesses accept or reject their offers. Priceline pioneered this type of trade, giving passengers the opportunity to bid on airline seats. *Consumer-to-consumer* transactions involve consumer auction sites like eBay. B2B transactions account for 90% of the dollar value of electronic commerce.

**Business-to-business (B2B):** electronic communication and trade among businesses.

**Business-to-consumer (B2C):** electronic communication and trade between businesses and consumers.

**Value chain:** the set of activities that create and deliver products to the customer.

Some businesses use the Internet primarily to conduct business directly with their customers (B2C), whereas others focus more on using it for conducting business with their suppliers and distributors (B2B). Companies that integrate both types of e-business into their operational structure and corporate strategy are said to have a fully integrated **value chain**. The Internet promotes a build-to-order environment in which the customer order initiates the manufacture of the product. From this perspective, we now have two flows in the value chain, an input flow (the customer order), and an output flow (the order fulfillment). A simple value

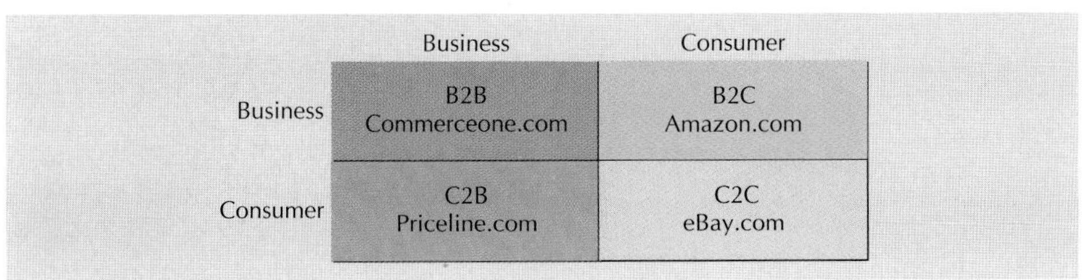


**Figure 1.5**

**Categories of E-Commerce**

[2]There is a slight distinction between e-commerce and e-business. Consumer trade is generally referred to as *e-commerce*, whereas business trade is more often thought of as *e-business*. In many cases, the terms are used interchangeably.

Figure 1.6
**An Integrated Value Chain**

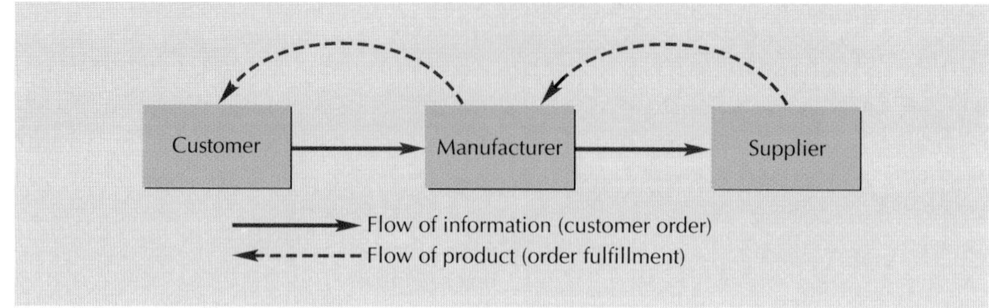


chain is shown in Figure 1.6. Dell, Cisco, IBM, and Ford are examples of companies that are able to take advantage of the Internet on both the input and the output side of the value chain.

OM enables B2C e-commerce.

The Internet highlights the scope of the operations function and its importance in company competitiveness. Operations management skills in order fulfillment, warehousing, logistics, and distribution "enable" B2C e-commerce. At the same time, B2B e-commerce plays an important role in streamlining the operations function in areas such as product design, procurement, and supply chain management.

B2B e-commerce streamlines OM.

When the World Trade Center was attacked on September 11, 2001, U.S. borders were closed and air travel was shut down. With the help of the Internet and a worldwide network of suppliers, Dell Computers was able to identify where production

Table 1.2
**The Impact of E-Business on Operations Management**

| Benefits of E-Business | Impact on Operations |
|---|---|
| **1.** Comparison shopping by customers | Customer expectations escalate; quality must be maintained and costs lowered |
| **2.** Direct contact with customers | No more guessing about demand; inventory costs go down; product and service design improves; build-to-order products and services are made possible |
| **3.** Business processes conducted online | Transaction costs are lower; customer support costs decrease; e-procurement saves big bucks |
| **4.** Access to customers worldwide | Demand increases; order fulfillment and logistics become major issues; production moves overseas |
| **5.** Middlemen are eliminated | Logistics change from delivering to a store or distribution center to delivering to individual homes; consumer demand is more erratic and unpredictable than business demand |
| **6.** Access to suppliers worldwide | Outsourcing increases; more alliances and partnerships among firms are formed; supply is less certain; global supply chain issues arise |
| **7.** Online auctions and e-marketplaces | Competitive bidding lowers the cost of materials; supply needs can be found in one location |
| **8.** Better and faster decision making | More timely information is available with immediate access by all stakeholders in the decision-making process; customer orders and product designs can be clarified electronically; electronic meetings can be held; collaborative planning is facilitated |
| **9.** IT synergy | Productivity increases as information can be shared more efficiently internally and between trading partners |
| **10.** Expanded supply chains | Order fulfillment, logistics, warehousing, transportation and delivery become the focus of operations management; risk is spread out; trade barriers fall |

would be disrupted for lack of supplies. It quickly ramped up production at its European and Asian plants and prioritized orders to fill the most important customers first. Dell was further able to look online and see which PC configurations could be assembled quickly with available supply and steered its customers in that direction. Companies that lost thousands of computers in the attack were able to depend on Dell to deliver. In contrast, Compaq was unable to ship $300 million worth of orders due to supply chain disruptions.

Table 1.2 summarizes the impact of e-business on operations management.

## GLOBALIZATION

Two thirds of today's businesses operate globally[3]—global markets, global operations, global financing, global supply chains. Globalization can take the form of selling in foreign markets, producing in foreign lands, purchasing from foreign suppliers, or partnering with foreign firms. Companies "go global" to take advantage of favorable costs, to gain access to international markets, to be more responsive to changes in demand, to build reliable sources of supply, and to keep abreast of the latest trends and technologies.

Falling trade barriers have paved the way for globalization. More countries than ever before have opened their borders to trade and investment. As shown in Figure 1.7, annual increases in world trade reached a peak of 26% in 2000. Fourteen major trade agreements were enacted in the 1990s.[4] The creation of the World Trade Organization (WTO) brought tariffs on manufactured goods down to 4% for most industrialized countries, opened up the heavily protected industries of agriculture, textiles, and telecommunications, and extended the scope of international trade rules to cover services, as well as goods. The European Union (EU) requires that strict quality and environmental standards be met before companies can do business with member countries.

Strategic alliances, joint ventures, licensing arrangements, research consortia, supplier partnerships, and direct marketing agreements among global partners have proliferated.

Figure 1.8 shows the hourly wage rates in U.S. dollars for production workers in seven countries from 1975 to 2002. U.S. labor rates have increased at a remarkably stable rate, while the labor rates of Japan, Germany, and the United Kingdom are more erratic.

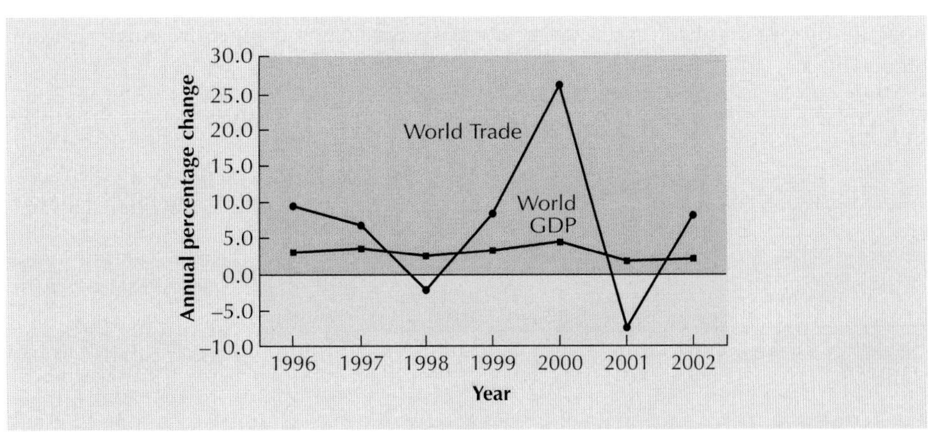


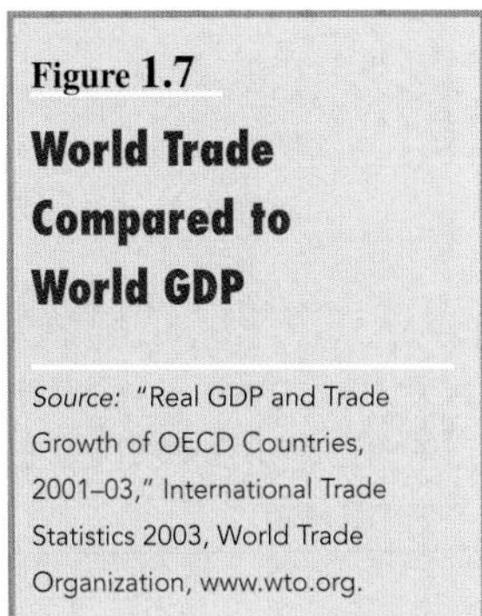

**Figure 1.7**

**World Trade Compared to World GDP**

*Source:* "Real GDP and Trade Growth of OECD Countries, 2001–03," International Trade Statistics 2003, World Trade Organization, www.wto.org.

[3]Gail Edmonson, "See the World, Erase Its Borders," *Business Week* (August 28, 2000), pp. 113–114.

[4]ANZCERTA—Australia New Zealand Closer Economic Relations Trade Agreement; APEC—Asian Pacific Economic Cooperation; ASEAN—Association of Southeast Asian Nations; ATPA—Andean Trade Preference Act; CACM—Central America Common Market; CEFTA—Central Europe Free Trade Agreement; EU—European Union; FTAA—Free Trade Area of the Americas; MERCOSUR—Mercado Commun del Sur (Latin American trade treaties); NAFTA—North American Free Trade Agreement; TAFTA—TransAtlantic Free Trade Area; SADC—Southern African Development Community; SAPTA—South Asian Area Preferential Trading Agreement; and WTO—World Trade Organization.

## THE COMPETITIVE EDGE

### It's a Global Workforce

Did you know that your phone call to Capital One may be routed to a customer service rep in New Delhi? or that your insurance claim may be sent to the Philippines for processing? that Microsoft's latest software was developed in Ireland? or that video-on-demand comes from Bangalore? More and more jobs in accounting, customer support, legal services, software design, R&D, and pharmaceutical development are shifting away from Europe and the United States to less developed countries. Improvements in information technology and telecommunications, along with worldwide financial and technology standards, have allowed companies to "scatter centers of excellence around the world." Some companies are seeking the 30 percent cost advantage in professional work; others are seeking skills that are unavailable at home or higher capacities to speed up work. Whatever the motivation, Forrester Research predicts that by 2015, 3.3 million jobs will move over seas. And it's not just low-paying clerical jobs.

Caltex Petroleum moved its headquarters from Dallas to Singapore, its accounting to Manila, and its Web development work to South Africa. Cognizant Technologies does sales and marketing work in New Jersey and virtually everything else in Madras and Calcutta. Bell Labs, Microsoft, and Motorola operate large research centers in India, while Verizon and Andersen employ thousands in the Philippines. Ireland is now the world's largest exporter of software, and China and Scandinavia are leaders in engineering expertise.

The Internet, interactive software, and telecom networks have made communications seamless and nationality irrelevant. It really is a global workforce.

*Source:* Adapted from Mark Clifford and Manjeet Kripalani, "Different Countries, Adjoining Cubicles," *Business Week* (August 28, 2000), pp. 182–184; Manjeet Kripalani and Pete Engardio, "The Rise of India," *Business Week* (December 8, 2003).

Wage rates in Germany are the highest at \$26.18 an hour, comparable to the U.S. rate of \$21.33. The low-wage countries are Taiwan at \$5.41, Mexico at \$2.38, and China with an extremely low \$0.50 an hour. Not surprisingly, much of the world has moved its manufacturing to China. But low-wage rates are not the only reason to expand globally.

China has become the world's factory.

China also has an enormous consumer market, and as its industrial base multiplies, so does its need for machinery and basic materials. As more companies move to China, so do their suppliers and their suppliers' suppliers. Although China has been the preferred location for the production of low-tech goods, such as toys and textiles, for years, the production of high-tech sophisticated products is a more recent phenomenon. Figure 1.9 shows the exports to and imports from China for the major economies of the world. Clearly, China has become a strategic manufacturing base for nearly every industry worldwide. Managing global operations and quality in a far-reaching supply chain is an added challenge for operations managers. Keeping domestic production competitive is an even bigger challenge.

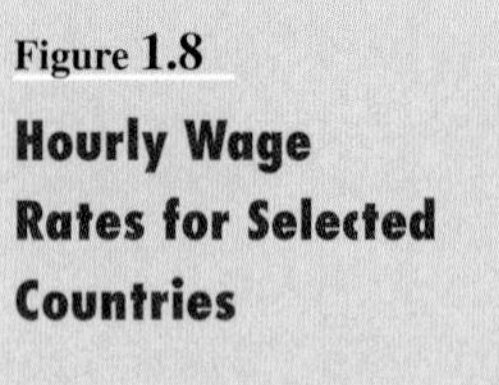

**Figure 1.8**
**Hourly Wage Rates for Selected Countries**

*Source:* "International Comparisons of Hourly Compensation Costs for Production Workers in Manufacturing," Bureau of Labor Statistics, U.S. Department of Labor, Updated September 30, 2003.

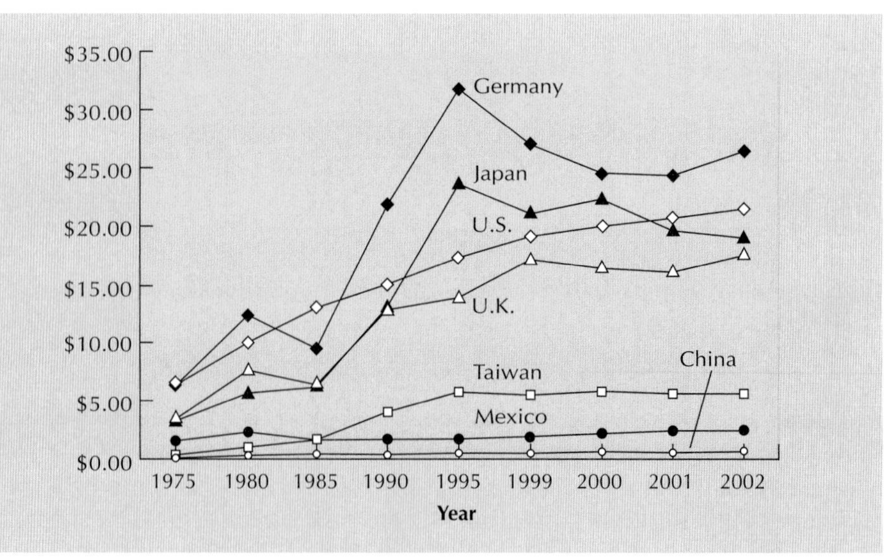

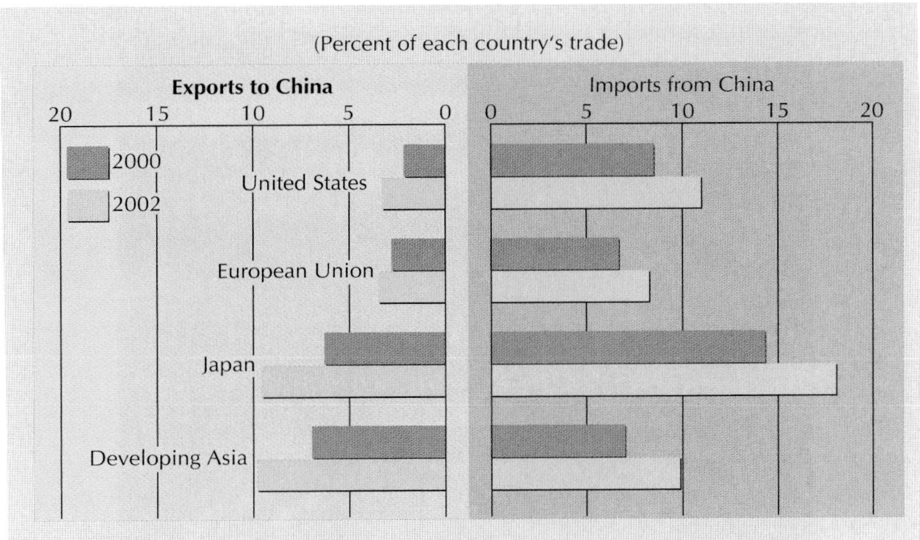


**Figure 1.9**

**Trade with China**

*Source:* "Share of China in Exports and Imports of Major Traders, 2000 and 2002," International Trade Statistics 2003, World Trade Organization, www.wto.org.

India excels in services.

Although we may think of globalization more in the context of products than services, there has been an enormous increase in the global outsourcing of services as well. It began with back-office work such as accounting, claims processing, and computer programming. Now it extends to customer service centers, brokerage firms, financial analysis, research and development, engineering, medical diagnosis, architectural design, and more advanced work in information technology. Global service work is performed in many countries throughout Asia, Eastern Europe, and Latin America; however, the biggest participant is India. India has an enormous resource of highly skilled engineers, scientists, and technically trained workers available at less than half the cost of those located in developed countries. Analysts predict that by 2015 roughly 3.3 million U.S. service jobs will move offshore.

Globalization yields new markets, technologies, and skills.

Global expansion may have been motivated to a large extent by cheap labor, but it has been sustained by the ability to access new markets, technologies, and skills. Design work performed closer to the foreign markets in which the consumer resides results in more successful product and service offerings. The diversity of ideas, expertise, and approaches to management enriches both foreign and domestic work. Experiments in product and process improvement can be initiated and tested in a multitude of environments. Technology transfer moves both east and west. Being able to access to the best talent, regardless of location, is a boon to businesses worldwide. Yet despite these benefits, globalization is not without risk.

## RISKS OF GLOBALIZATION

Globalization poses risks due to (1) cultural differences, (2) supply chain logistics, (3) safety, security, and stability, (4) quality problems, (5) corporate image, and (6) loss of capabilities.

Be aware of cultural differences.

Cultural differences can make it difficult to communicate, negotiate, and manage operations in other countries. For example, Asian firms consider it impolite to turn down a customer's request, no matter how unreasonable. They will just fail to deliver on time. Developing the kind of personal relationship necessary to do business in some countries can take two years or more. U.S. firms view such closeness as unnecessary and question the tactics as an attempt to gain concessions or stall negotiations.

When partners in a global effort are located at considerable distances from each other, the movement of goods both within and between the countries can be problematic. For example, rapid economic growth in Asia has stretched its transportation infrastructure to the limit. Bottlenecks in ports, on roads, and on railways delay the arrival of products in their markets. The markets themselves are highly fragmented, with distinct languages, customs,

*The arrival of the global marketplace has dramatically increased international trade and the logistics operations to support it. Shown here is Singapore's global port, where 16 million containers are processed annually from ship to rail car or tractor trailer for distribution. Its geographic location, highly skilled workforce, advanced telecommunications systems, and excellent financial services make Singapore an ideal hub for international business.*

trade barriers, and levels of development. In addition, distribution channels within regions are unorganized and inefficient. China's transportation infrastructure in particular is overtaxed, costly, and cumbersome. Ships and railroads are slow and inflexible; modern trucking networks are nonexistent at the less-then-truckload level; and cargo planes account for only 20% of China's aircraft.[5]

Shipments from long distances may incur substantial costs and require long transit times. Ninety-five percent of cargo tonnage that moves in and out of the U.S. is shipped by sea. Each year more than 7500 commercial vessels handle over six million cargo containers at U.S. ports, a number that is expected to double in 10 years. Customs problems, incomplete documents, and security issues can delay processing times by weeks or months. The availability of dock workers, shipping containers, and cargo space can also wreak havoc with shipping lead times. Lengthy transit times mean that companies must hold more inventory to last until the next shipment arrives. This cost is rarely considered in outsourcing decisions.

Cargo packed in standard shipping containers (as shown in the photo above) can be quickly transferred from ships to trucks or railcars without being opened. This rapid movement of goods cuts costs and speeds supply, but presents a huge security risk. The *Container Security Initiative* (CSI) requires prescreening of containers headed for the U.S. from more than 20 ports worldwide. This is a costly and time-consuming process. Ironically, if problems arise, it is the recipient firm that loses out because the recipient pays for the contents of the container in advance, insures its value, and assumes all risk of delay or damage.

The instability of governments, fluctuating currency rates, and poor economic conditions strongly impact a company's success with globalization. These factors continue to inhibit increased trade and localized operations in Latin America, the Middle East, and Eastern European countries. Threats of terrorism, health epidemics, and counterfeiting of products are additional safety and security risks.

Quality assurance is difficult.

The quality of products and services is easier to maintain when the production or delivery is closer to home. Standard tolerances and work methods are not applied worldwide. It is imperative, then, to communicate design specifications clearly and precisely. Engineers and quality control specialists may need to co-locate in suppliers' plants to oversee production. A new industry of third-party quality inspectors has arisen, in part because high shipping costs make returns of low-quality goods cost prohibitive.

[5]Much of the data in this section comes from Walter Quade, "A Beginners' Guide to the Asian Supply Chain," *Inside Supply Management* (March 2004), pp. 8–9.

## THE COMPETITIVE EDGE

### The Balancing Act at New Balance

Boston-based New Balance Corporation is a nonconformist in many ways. It refuses to hire superstars to endorse its product, it shuns style in favor of performance, it holds fast to its emphasis on running shoes, and it is committed to manufacturing at least some of its product in America. New Balance currently has five factories in the United States, the last of its kind for makers of athletic shoes. It also has wholly-owned subsidiaries in 13 countries and a number of licensees, joint ventures, and distributors all over the globe.

Of its domestic production, owner Jim Davis says "it's part of the company's culture to design and manufacture here." Producing close to their customers also allows quick turnarounds on new designs and order fulfillment. At New Balance's factory in Norridgewock, Maine, well-trained employees make $14 an hour working in small teams performing half-a-dozen different jobs and switching tasks every few minutes. They operate computerized sewing equipment and automated stitchers that allow one person to do the work of 20.

New Balance is able to remain competitive at home by creatively adapting new technologies to shoemaking, and constantly training their employees in teamwork and technical skills. Employees start with 22 hours of classroom training on teamwork and get constant training on the factory floor. They work in teams of five or six, sharing tasks and helping one another to make sure everything gets done. Many of the ideas for process improvement come from shop floor workers.

Says Davis, "In Asia, their labor is so inexpensive that they waste it. Ours is so dear that we come up with techniques to be very efficient." Borrowing technology from apparel manufacturers, New Balance purchased 70 see-and-sew machines for $100,000 each and set up on-site machine shops to grind the 30 templates needed for a typical shoe. Making each set of templates takes about a week, but they allow workers to produce a pair of shoes in 24 minutes, versus 3 hours in China. Labor cost per shoe is $4 an hour in Maine compared to $1.30 in China. The $2.70 labor cost differential is a manageable 4 percent of the $70 selling price.

Staying involved with the manufacturing process helps New Balance develop better designs, improve quality, and innovate their processes, capabilities the company would lose if it outsourced all of its production. But staying in one country is not advantageous either, especially when a 10% market share of athletic shoes in China would be the equivalent of 100 million customers. New Balance re-launched a China strategy in 2004 to prepare for the Beijing Olympic Games scheduled for 2008. To sell in China, it is necessary to produce there.

The company's earlier foray into outsourcing on the mainland was not a good experience. In one of the most notorious cases of counterfeiting, New Balance's own supplier flooded the market with unauthorized New Balance footwear and continued to do so even after the contract was canceled. New Balance spent millions of dollars in legal fees and lost millions more in sales without a satisfactory resolution to the problem. Today, the company has reduced the number of Asian suppliers and monitors them more closely. New Balance continues the balancing act between domestic and foreign production, and strives to produce closer to its markets, wherever in the world they might be.

*Sources:* Adapted from Aaron Bernstein, "Low-Skilled Jobs: Do They Have To Move?" *Business Week* (February 26, 2001); Gabriel Kahn, "A Sneaker Maker Says China Partner Became Its Rival," *The Wall Street Journal* (December 19, 2002), pp. A1, A8; "New Balance Shoots for Second in Local Market," *China Daily* (November 13, 2003); "A Balancing Act," *Business and Industry* (February 11, 2004), p. 22.

**A backlash against foreign investment.**

Opponents of globalization maintain that wealthy Western economies at worst take advantage of poorer economies and at best try to impose their way of life on countries that prefer to remain true to their roots. This backlash against foreign investment can affect sales, as well as the safety and security of employees and company assets. Similarly, companies that send jobs overseas may have trouble with workers, governments, and consumers in their own country. Differing views of social responsibility between countries and cultures can also present public relations problems for multinational corporations. Companies are increasingly held to task for the labor practices, living standards, human rights, and environmental standards of their suppliers. Companies that outsource work should plan on visiting supplier operations (or having a permanent presence there) not only to verify quality levels, but also to ensure that working conditions are acceptable.

**Loss of capabilities.**

Finally, as companies send operations overseas, they also send critical knowledge about products, processes, and technology. Such knowledge and capabilities are difficult to regain should relations sour or circumstances change. This is of particular concern to national security advocates.

Although the extent of globalization will vary from firm to firm and industry to industry, most companies find it necessary to have some degree of global presence to remain competitive. In the next few sections, we'll explore this concept of *competitiveness*.

## COMPETITIVENESS

**Competitiveness:** the degree to which a nation can produce goods and services that meet the test of international markets.

A global marketplace for products and services means more customers and more intense competition. In the broadest terms, we speak of competitiveness in reference to other *countries* rather than to other companies. That's because how effectively a nation competes in the global marketplace, affects the economic success of the nation and the quality of life for its citizens. The U.S. Department of Commerce defines **competitiveness** as "the degree to which a nation can produce goods and services that meet the test of international markets while simultaneously maintaining or expanding the real incomes of its citizens."[6] The most common measure of competitiveness is productivity. Increases in productivity allow wages to grow without producing inflation, thus raising the standard of living. Productivity growth also represents how quickly an economy can expand its capacity to supply goods and services.

### PRODUCTIVITY AS A MEASURE OF COMPETITIVENESS

**Productivity:** the ratio of output to input.

**Productivity** is calculated by dividing units of output by units of input.

$$\text{Productivity} = \frac{\text{Output}}{\text{Input}}$$

Output can be expressed in units or dollars in a variety of scenarios, such as sales made, products produced, customers served, meals delivered, or calls answered. *Single-factor productivity* compares output to individual inputs, such as labor hours, investment in equipment, material usage, or square footage. *Multifactor productivity* relates output to a combination of inputs, such as (labor + capital) or (labor + capital + energy + materials). Capital can include the value of equipment, facilities, inventory, and land. *Total factor productivity* compares the total quantity of goods and services produced with all the inputs used to produce them. These productivity formulas are summarized in Table 1.3.

**Table 1.3 Measures of Productivity**

***Single-Factor Productivity***

$$\frac{\text{Output}}{\text{Labor}} \qquad \frac{\text{Output}}{\text{Materials}} \qquad \frac{\text{Output}}{\text{Capital}}$$

***Multifactor Productivity***

$$\frac{\text{Output}}{\text{Labor} + \text{Materials} + \text{Overhead}} \qquad \frac{\text{Output}}{\text{Labor} + \text{Energy} + \text{Capital}}$$

***Total Factor Productivity***

$$\frac{\text{Goods and services produced}}{\text{All inputs used to produce them}}$$

[6]*Report of the President's Commission on Industrial Competitiveness*, chaired by John A. Young, President and CEO, Hewlett-Packard, 1985.

**Example 1.1**

**Calculating Productivity**

Osborne Industries is compiling the monthly productivity report for its Board of Directors. From the following data, calculate (a) labor productivity, (b) machine productivity, and (c) the multifactor productivity of dollars spent on labor, machine, materials, and energy. The average labor rate is \$15 an hour, and the average machine usage rate is \$10 an hour.

| | |
|---|---:|
| Units produced | 100,000 |
| Labor hours | 10,000 |
| Machine hours | 5,000 |
| Cost of materials | \$35,000 |
| Cost of energy | \$15,000 |

*Solution*

(a) $\text{Labor productivity} = \dfrac{\text{Output}}{\text{Labor hours}} = \dfrac{100{,}000}{10{,}000} = 10 \text{ units/hour}$

(b) $\text{Machine productivity} = \dfrac{\text{Output}}{\text{Machine hours}} = \dfrac{100{,}000}{5{,}000} = 20 \text{ units/hour}$

(c) $$\text{Multifactor productivity} = \frac{\text{Output}}{\text{Labor costs} + \text{Machine costs} + \text{Material costs} + \text{Energy costs}}$$

$$= \frac{100{,}000}{(10{,}000 \times \$15) + (5{,}000 \times \$10) + \$35{,}000 + \$15{,}000}$$

$$= \frac{100{,}000}{\$250{,}000} = 0.4 \text{ unit per dollar spent}$$

The Excel solution to this problem is shown in Exhibit 1.1.

**Exhibit 1.1**

**Osborne Industries**

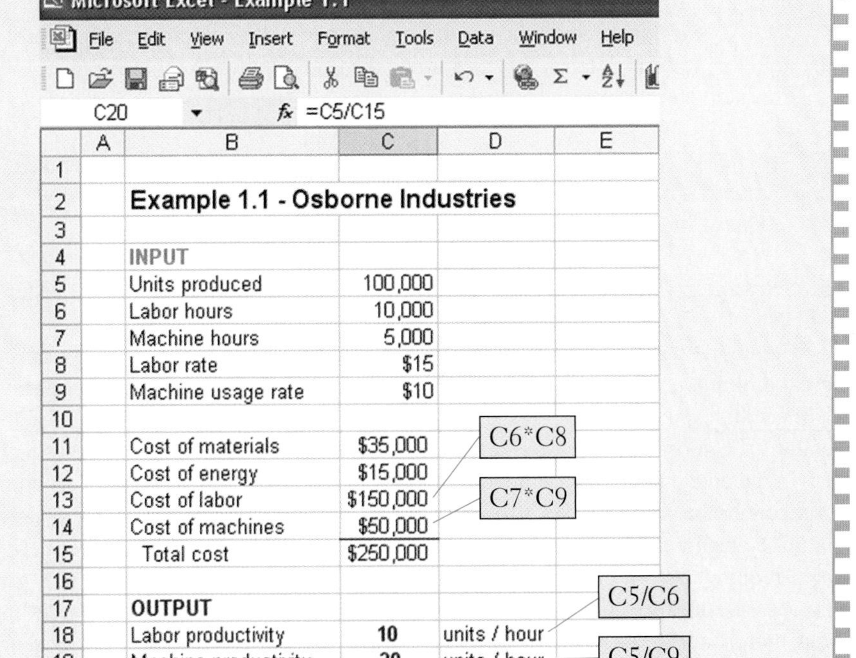

Microsoft Excel - Example 1.1

C20 = C5/C15

| | A | B | C | D |
|---|---|---|---|---|
| 1 | | | | |
| 2 | | **Example 1.1 - Osborne Industries** | | |
| 3 | | | | |
| 4 | | INPUT | | |
| 5 | | Units produced | 100,000 | |
| 6 | | Labor hours | 10,000 | |
| 7 | | Machine hours | 5,000 | |
| 8 | | Labor rate | \$15 | |
| 9 | | Machine usage rate | \$10 | |
| 10 | | | | |
| 11 | | Cost of materials | \$35,000 | |
| 12 | | Cost of energy | \$15,000 | |
| 13 | | Cost of labor | \$150,000 | |
| 14 | | Cost of machines | \$50,000 | |
| 15 | | Total cost | \$250,000 | |
| 16 | | | | |
| 17 | | **OUTPUT** | | |
| 18 | | Labor productivity | **10** | units / hour |
| 19 | | Machine productivity | **20** | units / hour |
| 20 | | Multifactor productivity | **0.40** | units / \$ |
| 21 | | | | |
| 22 | | | | |

Figure 1.10

**Changes in Productivity for Select Countries**

*Source:*
"International Comparisons of Manufacturing Productivity and Unit Labor Cost Trends, 2002," Bureau of Labor Statistics, U.S. Department of Labor, September 2003.
U.S. figures for 2002–2003 from "Major Sector Productivity and Costs Index," Bureau of Labor Statistics, U.S. Department of Labor, March 2004.

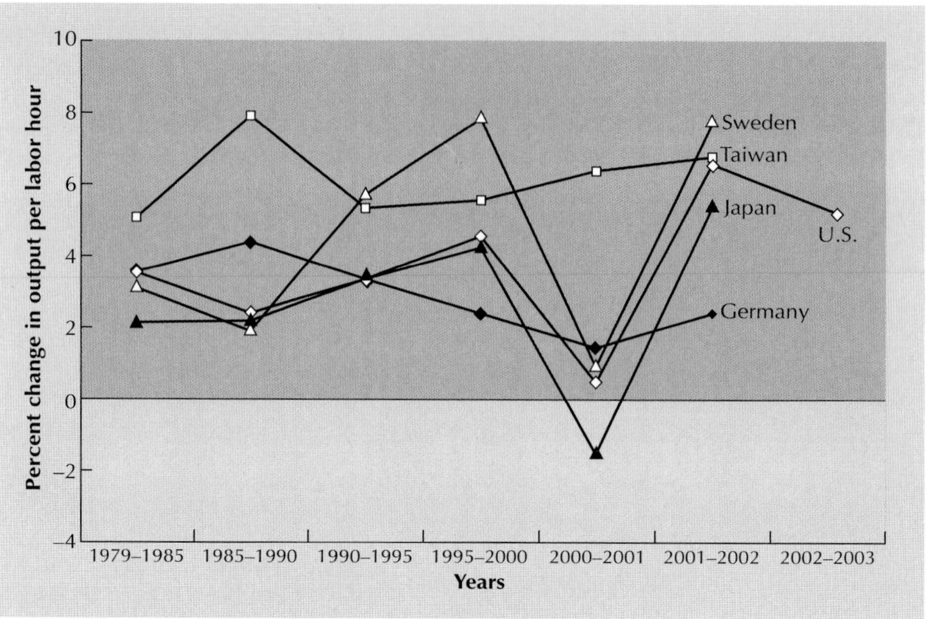


The most common input in productivity calculations is labor hours. Labor is an easily identified input to virtually every production process. In the United States, labor costs represent approximately two-thirds of the value of output produced.[7] Productivity is a relative measure. Thus, productivity statistics provided in government reports typically measure percent changes in productivity from month to month, quarter to quarter, year to year, or over a number of years.

Figure 1.10 shows percent changes in productivity in five-year increments from 1979 to 2000 and in yearly increments from 2000 to 2002 for select countries. The United States, Japan, and Sweden followed similar patterns over the years. Taiwan and Germany were more consistent, with Taiwan performing at higher than average levels of productivity and Germany at lower than average levels. The peak in 2000 reflected Internet-enabled productivity increases, while the precipitous drop in 2001 coincided with the dot-com bust and the 9/11 terrorist attacks. Let's examine the 2002 figures in more detail.

Productivity increases when firms:

1. *Become more efficient*—output increases with little or no increase in input,
2. *Expand*—both output and input grow with output growing more rapidly,
3. *Achieve breakthroughs*—output increases while input decreases,
4. *Downsize*—output remains the same and input is reduced, or
5. *Retrench*—both output and input decrease, with input decreasing at a faster rate.

Figure 1.11 shows the input and output data for the five countries. Sweden achieved breakthrough performance, Taiwan became more efficient, and the economies of the United States, Japan, and Germany retrenched. The drop in labor hours for these three countries is most likely due to increased global outsourcing and better use of technology.

In the end, a country's competitiveness is determined by the ability of its companies to compete in the world market. However, the ability of companies to compete is determined in large part by the business environment in which they operate. More productive companies require more highly skilled people, better information, more efficient government processes, improved infrastructure, better suppliers, more advanced research institutions, and more intense competitive pressure.[8] These are the types of factors measured in the

[7]"Major Sector Productivity and Cost Index," Bureau of Labor Statistics, U.S. Department of Labor, March 2004.

[8]Xavier Sala-I-Martin, *The Global Competitiveness Report 2003–2004*, World Economic Forum, January 2004, www.weforum.org.

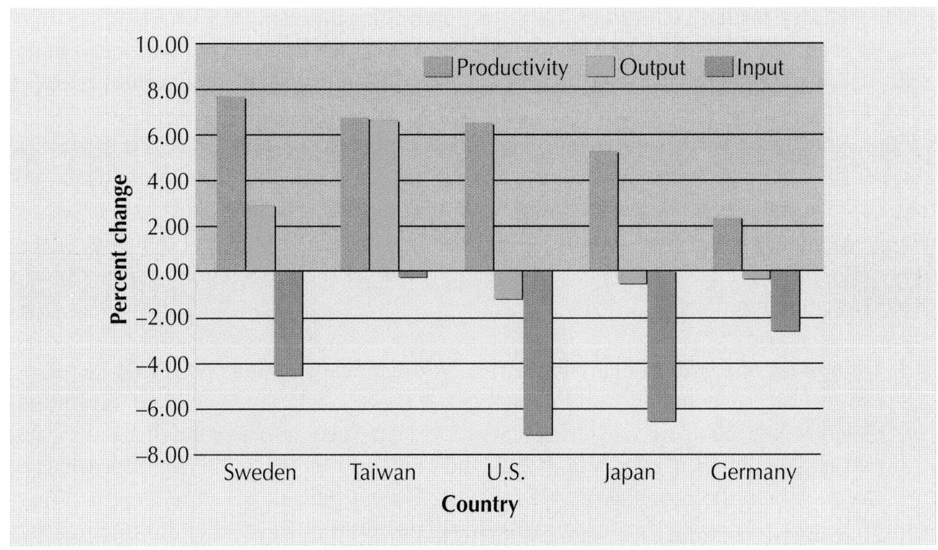


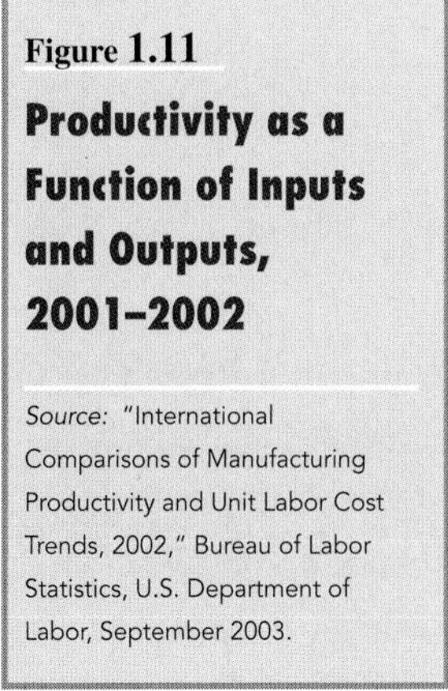
**Figure 1.11**
**Productivity as a Function of Inputs and Outputs, 2001–2002**

*Source:* "International Comparisons of Manufacturing Productivity and Unit Labor Cost Trends, 2002," Bureau of Labor Statistics, U.S. Department of Labor, September 2003.

Global Competitiveness Index, published each year by the World Economic Forum. The 2003 rankings are shown in Table 1.4. The rankings are based on two measures: (1) the sophistication of a company's operations and (2) the quality of the national business environment. Finland tops the list with the best overall environment for business and the most productive companies. The United States performs strongly in the technology area but is less effective in its public institutions. Five of the top 10 countries are Scandinavian. Taiwan and Singapore continue to be the most productive Asian countries.

## COMPETITIVE INDUSTRIES

Competitiveness can also be viewed from an industry or a firm perspective. Competition within industries is more intense when the firms are relatively equal in size; resources, products, and services are standardized; and industry growth is either slow (so that one company gains at the expense of another) or exponential (so that gaining a foothold in the market is a strategic imperative). Price wars, relentless advertising (such as nightly phone calls from long-distance carriers), the frequency of new product or service introduction, free trials (by software companies and Internet providers), low profit margins, and purchasing incentives (extended warranties, financial packages, switching bonuses, and so on) are evidence of competition within industries.

Industry competitiveness can be measured by the number of major players in an industry and the market share of the industry leader. By these measures, the most competitive industries worldwide are commercial banking, food and drug stores, and electronics, in

**Table 1.4**
**Global Competitiveness Ranking**

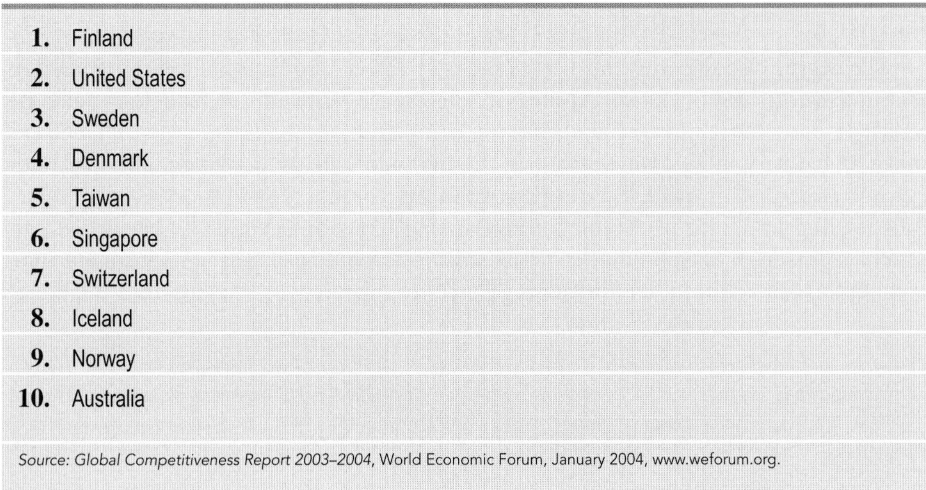

|  |  |
|---|---|
| 1. | Finland |
| 2. | United States |
| 3. | Sweden |
| 4. | Denmark |
| 5. | Taiwan |
| 6. | Singapore |
| 7. | Switzerland |
| 8. | Iceland |
| 9. | Norway |
| 10. | Australia |

*Source: Global Competitiveness Report 2003–2004*, World Economic Forum, January 2004, www.weforum.org.

which industry leaders, Citigroup, Carrefour, and Siemens, hold market shares of only 6%, 10%, and 12%, respectively. Contrast those industries with tobacco, diversified financials, and general merchandisers, in which Altria, GE, and Wal-Mart hold market shares of 64%, 42%, and 47%, respectively.

Industries with low barriers of entry are more competitive. Internet-based start-ups rise quickly since very little capital or physical facilities are needed to enter the industry, but they can also fall quickly when the number of competitors is more than the market can handle. Many of the **barriers to entry**[9]—economies of scale, capital requirements, access to supply and distribution channels, and learning curves—are operations-oriented. Let's explore them in more detail.

**Barriers to entry:** factors that make it difficult for new firms to enter an industry.

**Economies of scale:** as volume increases, the cost per unit decreases.

1. ***Economies of scale.*** In many industries, as the number of units produced increases, the cost of producing each individual unit decreases, which is known as **economies of scale**. New companies entering such an industry may not have the demand to support large volumes of production; thus, their unit cost would be higher. Economies of scale apply to the aggregation of buyers and sellers, as well as infrastructure. eBay's early presence on the Web captured so many customers that other online auction sites have found it difficult to compete.
2. ***Capital investment.*** Large initial investments in facilities, equipment, and training may be required to become a "player" in some industries. For example, opening a new hospital requires an enormous investment in facilities, equipment, and professional personnel; in contrast, a day-care center may operate out of an existing home with only minimal equipment, training, and licensing requirements. Similarly, creating a Web site and selling online require little capital investment.
3. ***Access to supply and distribution channels.*** Existing firms within an industry have established supply and distribution channels that may be difficult for new firms to replicate. For example, Wal-Mart's size, along with its information and distribution systems provide a strong competitive advantage. VISA will not allow its member banks to do business with American Express. In contrast, entertainment and education can be delivered over the Web to anyone anywhere. Direct sales over the Internet eliminates the need for a sales force and lets express-package-delivery companies handle distribution.
4. ***Learning curves.*** Lack of experience can be a barrier to entry in an industry with significant **learning curves**. For example, U.S. firms dominate the aerospace industry because of their experience and expertise in airplane design and construction. However, this may not always be the case, as component manufacturers in Korea and Japan are gaining valuable experience as suppliers to aerospace firms. Shipbuilders claim a 10% learning curve (and corresponding cost advantage) for each similar vessel built. Hospitals performing heart transplants exhibit an amazing 79% learning curve.[10] In contrast, Web services are notoriously easy to copy, requiring very little learning.

**Learning curve:** the rate at which performance improves with repetition.

## COMPETITIVE FIRMS

The degree of competitiveness in an industry affects product innovation, technological investment, and operations strategy for individual firms in the industry. It also determines the profitability of the average competitor. Sometimes structural changes make an industry more competitive and the individual firms less profitable. The Internet, for example, has made it more difficult to keep products and processes proprietary, thus tending to induce price competition among firms in an industry. Expanded geographical markets may provide a larger customer base, but they also bring in more competitors. In addition, the bargaining power of customers is enhanced through easy

[9]These are adapted from Michael Porter, *Competitive Advantage* (New York: Free Press, 1985).

[10]David Smith and Jan Larson, "The Impact of Learning on Cost: The Case of Heart Transplantation," *Hospital and Health Services Administration* (Spring 1989): 85–97. Learning curves are discussed in more detail in Chapter 17.

accessibility to companies, products, and comparisons. The same is true for companies and their suppliers.

As the business world becomes more competitive, firms must find their own path to sustainable competitive advantage. Effectively managed operations are important to a firm's competitiveness. How a firm chooses to compete in the marketplace is the subject of Chapter 2, on Operations Strategy. In the remaining section of this chapter, we present a brief overview of the primary topics in operations management and explain how this book is organized to cover those topics.

## AN OVERVIEW OF THE SCOPE OF OPERATIONS MANAGEMENT

There are many issues, concepts, and techniques associated with the field of operations management (OM). Figure 1.12 shows the primary decision-making areas of OM and how they relate to each other as a roadmap. The figure is loosely organized by the order in which similar decisions are made in a firm.

Notice that the diagram is divided into two major sections. The first section shows the decisions required for *designing* a productive system. Strategy drives the design of products and services, the selection of processes and technologies, the creation of facilities, and the acquisition of human resources. Quality management sets the standard under which these decisions are made, and project management helps manage and control the design process. The second section is concerned with *operating* the system designed in section one. The series of decisions involved in operating the supply chain, forecasting demand, managing inventory, planning production, allocating resources, and scheduling production are often incorporated in the term *supply chain management*. Companies can achieve competitiveness when both the design and operating decisions are driven by quality in the context of a global business environment.

As you might suspect, this text covers the various OM topics reflected in Figure 1.12. As a prelude to this course, we present a brief overview of these topics and indicate where they are presented in the text. Please note that your professor may elect to cover these topics in a different order than presented in the text. This is perfectly understandable in as much as decisions in operations management are extremely interrelated.

### STRATEGY

Strategy is only as good as the results it produces. Good results require that the corporate vision and strategic plan be converted into a series of consistent, achievable action plans to be deployed throughout the organization. Operations strategy must be consistent with corporate strategy and, in many cases, operations provides the distinctive competence on which a firm competes. For example, operations has taken center stage in the ability to execute strategy in the world of e-business. These topics are covered in **Chapter 2**, "Operations Strategy."

**Chapter 2:** Maintaining an operations strategy to support the firm's competitive advantage.

### QUALITY

Quality underlies all operational decisions. The level of quality a company seeks to achieve is a strategic decision that eventually determines how a product is made or a service is delivered. Designing products and services, designing and planning the production process, locating and developing the production facility, designing jobs and work activities, managing the supply chain, and planning and scheduling the flow of products throughout the system are all areas of operations management that depend on quality. For this reason, we have chosen to present the topic of quality early in the text immediately after operations strategy. Ensuring quality entails establishing a quality management system, using statistical quality control, improving customer service, and managing human resources wisely. These topics are presented in **Chapters 3 and 4** as "Quality Management," and "Statistical Process Control."

**Chapters 3 and 4:** Focusing on quality in operational decision making.

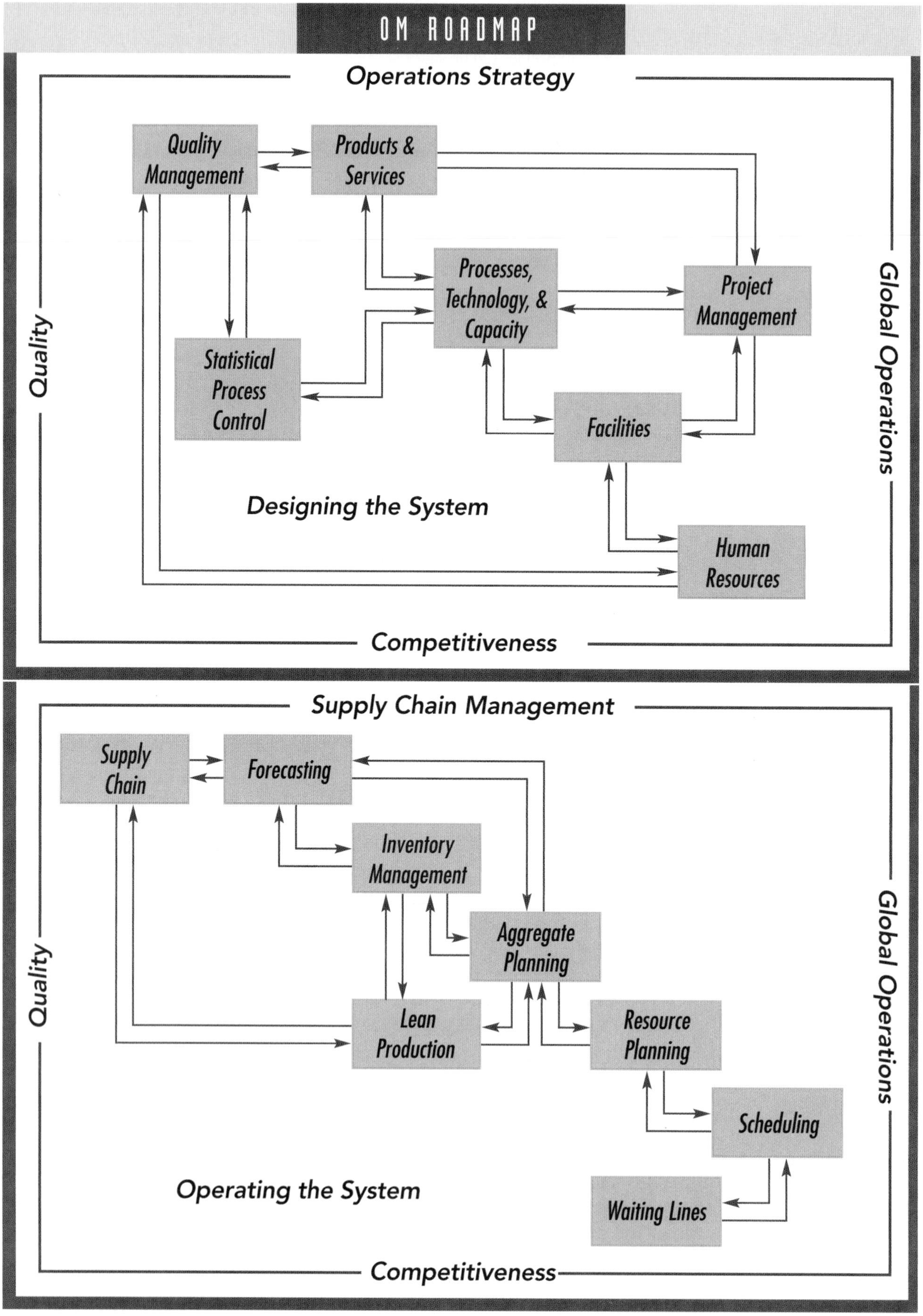

OM ROADMAP
Operations Strategy
Quality Management
Products & Services
Processes, Technology, & Capacity
Project Management
Statistical Process Control
Facilities
Human Resources
Designing the System
Quality
Global Operations
Competitiveness
Supply Chain Management
Supply Chain
Forecasting
Inventory Management
Aggregate Planning
Lean Production
Resource Planning
Scheduling
Waiting Lines
Operating the System
Quality
Global Operations
Competitiveness

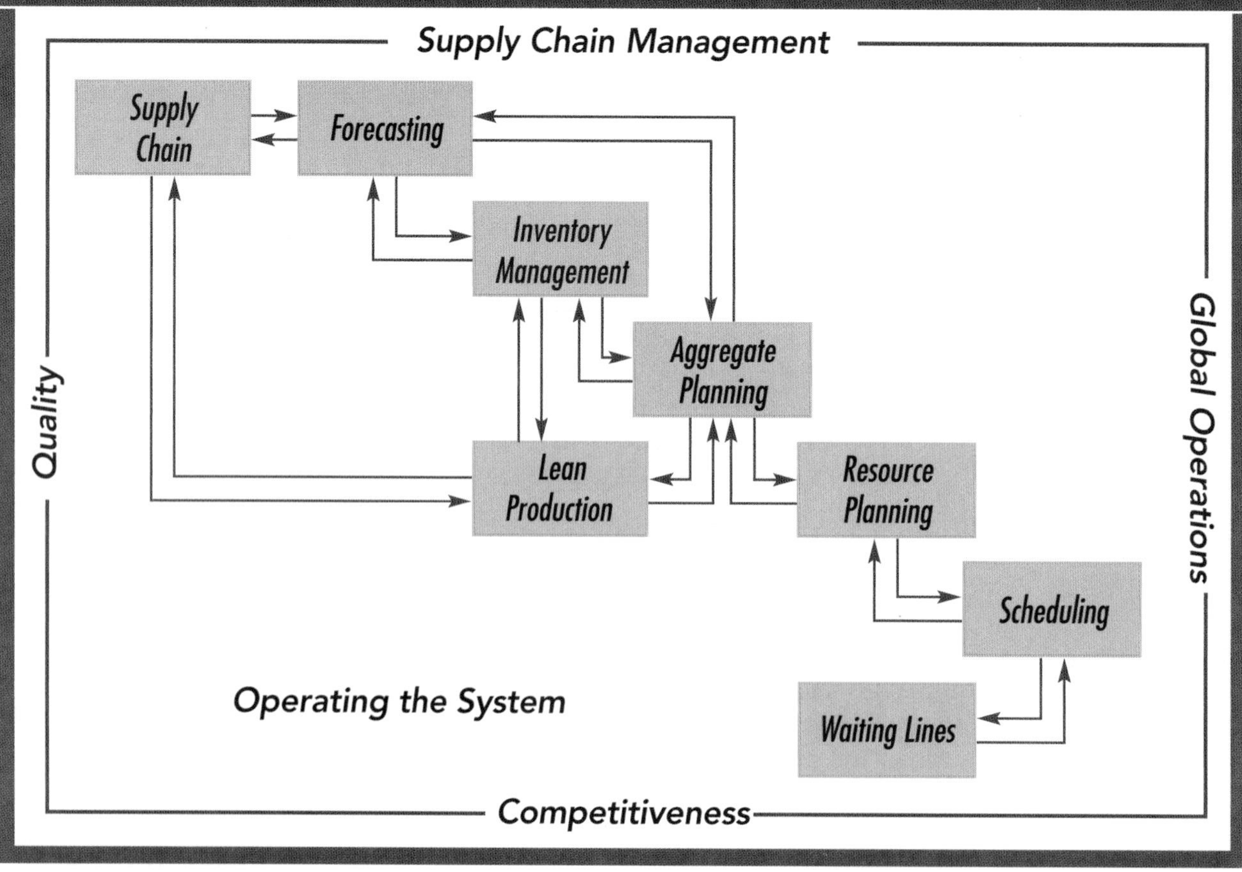

Figure 1.12
**OM Roadmap**

## PRODUCTS AND SERVICES

The traditional starting point for operations management is the design of products and services. The design process converts customer requirements into technical product or service characteristics. Although it is important that products and services meet customer requirements, it is also imperative that designs be as simple as possible to ensure higher quality and reasonable cost. The design process itself must be conducted in an efficient fashion, as time-to-market is a key measure of success. This topic is covered in **Chapter 5**, "Products and Services."

**Chapter 5:** Designing quality products and services.

## PROCESSES, TECHNOLOGY, AND CAPACITY

Once the product or service has been designed, the physical process for producing the product and providing the service must be prepared. Process planning involves deciding what tasks need to be done, what labor and equipment resources are needed, and how they are to be coordinated. Processes are planned, analyzed, and redesigned as required by changes in strategy and emerging technology. Process decisions lead directly to capacity decisions such as the number of facilities to operate and the size of those facilities. These topics are covered in **Chapter 6**, "Processes, Technology, and Capacity."

**Chapters 6 and 7:** Setting up the process so that it works smoothly and efficiently.

## FACILITIES

To be effective, processes must be physically housed in facilities that are laid out in an efficient fashion. Decision making focuses on how to organize work and arrange different parts of the production or service delivery process to ensure a smooth flow and minimal cycle time. **Chapter 7** on Facilities discusses these topics.

## HUMAN RESOURCES

A primary component of the production process is the work performed by people, alone, together, or with machines and equipment. *Human resources management*, the topic of **Chapter 8**, is the area of OM concerned with making sure that jobs meet the requirements of the production and service processes in the most efficient and effective manner possible.

**Chapter 8:** Designing jobs and work to produce quality products.

## PROJECT MANAGEMENT

Designing a product, deploying strategy, launching a new service, and building a facility are examples of projects that require careful coordination. Project management is a technique that breaks down complex processes, schedules activities, and ensures that the project is completed on time and on budget. This topic is presented in **Chapter 9**, "Project Management."

**Chapter 9:** Managing complex projects.

## THE SUPPLY CHAIN

Operating a production process or delivering a service often involves utilizing items or processes that are outsourced. It is not unusual for suppliers to account for 80 percent of product content. The number of suppliers and their locations around the globe make supply chain management an important aspect of operations management. A supply chain encompasses all the facilities, functions, and activities involved in producing and delivering a product or service, from the suppliers (and their suppliers) to the customer (and their customers). The topic is introduced in **Chapter 10**, "Supply Chain Management," and continued through subsequent chapters from forecasting to scheduling.

**Chapter 10:** Managing the supply chain.

## FORECASTING

Once the physical facility and production process are in place to produce a product or deliver a service, a host of planning decisions are required to determine how much to produce and when to produce it. These decisions are based on customer demand. Forecasting

**Chapter 11:** Predicting demand—how much to produce and when to produce it.

involves using a number of different methods and quantitative techniques to provide accurate estimates of demand, which are later used to make production decisions. This topic is covered in **Chapter 11**, "Forecasting."

## PLANNING AND SCHEDULING

**Chapters 12–17:** Planning and scheduling to meet demand.

Once management has determined how much product or service is needed to meet demand, production schedules that involve myriad decisions are developed. These decisions include how much material or how many parts to order, when material or parts should be ordered, how many workers to hire, and how these workers should be scheduled on jobs and machines. Decisions must also be made to ensure that the amount of inventory available at each stage of the production process is sufficient to avoid unnecessary delays and that the amount of final inventory is sufficient to meet customer demand. These decisions are facilitated by IT systems, such as enterprise resource planning, and management systems such as lean production. Production and service planning represent major areas of decision making in operations management. These topics are presented in **Chapters 12 through 17** as "Aggregate Planning," "Inventory Management," "Resource Planning," "Lean Production," "Scheduling," and "Waiting Lines."

# LEARNING OBJECTIVES OF THIS COURSE

The learning objectives of this course are threefold:

1. ***To gain an appreciation of the strategic importance of operations in a global business environment and to understand how operations relates to other business functions.*** Regardless of your major, as you pursue a career in business, you will need to understand the basic issues, capabilities, and limitations of the operations function. By the conclusion of this course, you will be able to describe the impact of operations on other functions within a firm, as well as on the competitive position of the firm. You will also be more aware of the global nature of operations.
2. ***To develop a working knowledge of the concepts and methods related to designing and managing operations.*** In this course, you will learn the basic steps involved in bringing a product to market from its design through production and delivery. You will also learn such skills as how to forecast demand, lay out a facility, manage a project, and schedule work.
3. ***To develop a skill set for quality and process improvement.*** From this course, you will gain the ability to conceptualize how systems are interrelated, to organize activities effectively, to analyze processes critically, to make decisions based on data, and to push for continual process improvement. These skills will serve you well in whatever career you choose.

# SUMMARY

Operations can be viewed as a transformation process that converts inputs into outputs of greater value. Operations is also a basic function of a firm and the technical core of an organization. Operations management involves deploying strategy, ensuring quality, designing products and services, selecting processes and technologies, arranging facilities, forecasting demand, planning the production process, and managing the supply chain. Operations plays a major role in maintaining competitiveness.

Globalization and management advances in information technology have dramatically broadened the business landscape. Efficiencies created by e-commerce, for both consumers and businesses, have sent operations expertise to the forefront of managerial excellence.

## SUMMARY OF KEY TERMS

**barriers to entry** factors such as economies of scale, capital investment, access to supply and distribution channels, and learning curves that make it difficult for a new firm to enter an industry.

**business-to-business (B2B)** electronic communication and transactions among business entities such as manufacturers, wholesalers, retailers, and suppliers.

**business-to-consumer (B2C)** electronic communication and transactions between businesses and their customers.

**competitiveness** the degree to which a nation can produce goods and services that meet the test of international markets.

**craft production** the process of handcrafting products or services for individual customers.

**division of labor** dividing a job into a series of small tasks each performed by a different worker.

**e-commerce** trade that occurs over a computer network, usually the Internet; more generally known as "e-business."

**economies of scale** an advantage that accrues from high-volume production; as the number of units produced increases, the cost of producing each individual unit decreases.

**lean production** an adaptation of mass production that prizes quality and flexibility.

**learning curve** the rate at which performance improves with repetition.

**mass production** the high-volume production of a standardized product for a mass market.

**operations** a function or system that transforms inputs into outputs of greater value.

**operations management** the design and operation of productive systems.

**productivity** the ratio of output to input.

**scientific management** the systematic analysis of work methods proposed by Frederick Taylor in the early 1900s.

**value chain** the set of activities that create and deliver products and services to the customer.

## QUESTIONS

**1-1.** What activities are involved in the operations function? How does operations interact with other functional areas?

**1-2.** What constitutes "operations" at (a) a bank, (b) a retail store, (c) a hospital, (d) a cable TV company?

**1-3.** Briefly describe how operations has evolved from the Industrial Revolution to the Internet Revolution.

**1-4.** What is competitiveness? How is it measured? How has the Internet affected competitiveness?

**1-5.** Investigate the role of government in improving industrial competitiveness. Begin with the U.S. Council on Competitiveness at www.compete.org. Find a similar site for at least one other country. Compare their priorities and initiatives.

**1-6.** Discuss four common barriers that firms may experience as they try to enter a new industry.

**1-7.** Describe the global activities of a corporation of your choice. How many foreign plants do they have? Where are they located? How much of their business is foreign? Are any global strategies evident?

**1-8.** Examine the climate for foreign investments in Europe, South America, and the Pacific Rim. What are the advantages of locating a production or distribution facility in each area?

**1-9.** Choose three trade agreements from the following list: ANZERTA, APEC, ASEAN, ATPA, CACM, CEFTA, FU, FTAA, MERCOSUR, NAFTA, TAFTA, SADC, SAPTA, WTO. Describe the treaties, how long they have been in effect, and if they've been renegotiated recently.

**1-10.** Examine *Fortune*'s Global 500 by industry. Which industries are the most competitive? Which industries are the least competitive? Are some industries dominated by certain countries? Which industries are the most profitable?

**1-11.** Choose an industry on which you will be the class "expert" for the duration of this course. Write an initial profile of major players, customers, structure, and competitive issues.

**1-12.** Find an interesting Web site related to the operations function in a firm with which you are familiar. Write a summary of what you find.

**1-13.** Look for articles related to operations management at *Fortune*, *Business Week*, or CNN. How do they relate to the primary topics discussed in this chapter?

**1-14.** Discuss the various ways in which trade is conducted over the Internet.

**1-15.** Describe how e-business has affected operations management.

**1-16.** The World Bank ranks countries in terms of globalization. Go to the research section of www.worldbank.com and choose four countries to compare.

**1-17.** The World Trade Organization has its advocates and its adversaries. Find out more about the organization by visiting its Web site at www.wto.org. What kinds of activities does the organization support? What rules and regulations does it enforce? Who are its member states, and how is membership achieved?

**1-18.** Cultural differences can make it difficult to do business in other countries. Executive Planet provides a guide to business culture for the executive world traveler. Go to www.executiveplanet.com and choose a country to explore. Share your discoveries with your professor and classmates in a one- to two-page write-up.

**1-19.** Much of the negotiation in trade agreements centers on ethical/legal issues such as intellectual property protection, bribery and payoffs, and copyright and patent infringement. Transparency International at www.transparency.org publishes a bribery index by country. Report on which countries and industries are most susceptible to bribery.

**1-20.** Ethics is easier when there are laws to fall back on. Search the Internet for information on the Foreign Corrupt Practices Act. Briefly describe what it entails. Then find two companies that explicitly state a code of conduct on their Web page, and in particular, reference the Foreign Corrupt Practices Act. How does each company approach the issue?

## PROBLEMS

**1-1.** Tried and True Clothing has opened four new stores in college towns across the state. Data on monthly sales volume and labor hours are given below. Which store location has the highest productivity?

| Store | Annandale | Blacksburg | Charlottesville | Danville |
|---|---|---|---|---|
| Sales volume | $40,000 | $12,000 | $60,000 | $25,000 |
| Labor hours | 250 | 60 | 500 | 200 |

**1-2.** Tried and True's accountant (from Problem 1-1) suggests that monthly rent and hourly wage rate also be factored into the productivity calculations. Annandale pays the highest average wage at $6.75 an hour. Blacksburg pays $6.50 an hour, Charlottesville $6, and Danville $5.50. The cost to rent store space is $1800 a month in Annandale, $2000 a month in Blacksburg, $1200 a month in Charlottesville, and $800 a month in Danville.

a. Which store is most productive?
b. Tried and True is not sure it can keep all four stores open. Based on productivity, which store would you close? What other factors should be considered?

**1-3.** At last year's bass tournament, Jim caught 12 bass in a four-hour period. This year he caught 15 in a six-hour period. In which year was he most productive? If the average size of the bass last year was 20 lb and the average size this year was 25 lb, would your decision change?

**1-4.** It is time for the annual performance review of Go-Com's account executives. Account values and hours spent each week acquiring and servicing accounts are shown below. Each agent works approximately 45 weeks out of the year, but the time spent on accounts each week differs considerably. How would you rate the performance of each individual? Which agent is most productive? Which agents show the most potential?

| Agents | Albert | Bates | Cressey | Duong |
|---|---|---|---|---|
| New accounts | $100,000 | $40,000 | $80,000 | $200,000 |
| Existing accounts | $40,000 | $40,000 | $150,000 | $100,000 |
| Labor hours | 40 | 20 | 60 | 80 |

**1-5.** The Bureau of Labor Statistics collects input and output data from various countries for comparison purposes. Labor hours are the standard measure of input. Calculate the output per hour from the following data. Which country is most productive?

| | Labor Hours | Units of Output |
|---|---|---|
| United States | 89.5 | 136 |
| Germany | 83.6 | 100 |
| Japan | 72.7 | 102 |

**1-6.** Omar Industries maintains production facilities in several locations around the globe. Average monthly cost data and output levels are as follows.

a. Calculate the labor productivity of each facility
b. Calculate the multifactor productivity of each facility
c. If Omar needed to close one of the plants, which one would you choose?

| Units (in 000s) | Cincinnati | Frankfurt | Guadalajara | Beijing |
|---|---|---|---|---|
| Finished goods | 10,000 | 12,000 | 5,000 | 8,000 |
| Work-in-process | 1,000 | 2,200 | 3,000 | 6,000 |

| Costs (in 000s) | Cincinnati | Frankfurt | Guadalajara | Beijing |
|---|---|---|---|---|
| Labor costs | $3,500 | $4,200 | $2,500 | $800 |
| Material costs | $3,500 | $3,000 | $2,000 | $2,500 |
| Energy costs | $1,000 | $1,500 | $1,200 | $800 |
| Transportation costs | $250 | $2,500 | $2,000 | $5,000 |
| Overhead costs | $1,200 | $3,000 | $2,500 | $500 |

**1-7.** Rushing yardage for three Heisman Trophy candidates is given below. Which candidate is the most productive running back?

| Candidates | Hall | Walker | Dayne |
|---|---|---|---|
| Rushing yards | 2110 | 3623 | 6925 |
| No. of carries | 105 | 875 | 1186 |
| No. of touchdowns | 15 | 20 | 70 |

**1-8.** Carpet City recorded the following data on carpet installations over the past week. Use the data to calculate the average rate at which carpet can be installed.

| Installation | 1 | 2 | 3 |
|---|---|---|---|
| Square yards | 1225 | 1435 | 2500 |
| No. of workers | 4 | 3 | 5 |
| No. of hours | 3 | 5 | 6 |

**1-9.** Merrifield Post Office is evaluating the productivity of its mail processing centers. The centers differ in the degree of automation, the type of work that can be performed, and the skill of the workers.

| Center | 1 | 2 | 3 |
|---|---|---|---|
| Pieces processed/hr. | 1000 | 2000 | 3000 |
| No. of workers/hr | 10 | 5 | 2 |
| Hourly wage rate | $5.50 | $10 | $12 |
| Overhead rate/hr | $10 | $25 | $50 |

a. Calculate the multifactor productivity for each center.
b. Workers in Center 1 are scheduled to receive a 10% pay raise next month. How will that affect productivity?
c. A new processing machine is available for Center 3 that would increase the output to 5000 pieces an hour at an additional overhead rate of $30 an hour. Should Merrifield install the new processing machine?

**1-10.** Posey Ceramics makes ceramic vases for a chain of department stores. The output and cost figures over the past four weeks are shown here. Labor costs $10 an hour, and materials are $4 a pound. Calculate the (a) labor productivity, (b) material productivity, and (c) multifactor productivity for each week. Comment on the results.

| Week | 1 | 2 | 3 | 4 |
|---|---|---|---|---|
| Units of output | 2000 | 4000 | 5000 | 7000 |
| No. of workers | 4 | 4 | 5 | 6 |
| Hours per week | 40 | 48 | 56 | 70 |
| Material (lbs) | 286 | 570 | 720 | 1000 |

## CASE PROBLEM 1.1

### *What Does It Take to Compete?*

Rubatex Corporation manufactures rubber and foam for a variety of products, including artificial turf, hosing and insulation, hockey helmet liners, scuba diving suits, sports sandals, and mouse pads. The company was purchased by an investment firm called American Industrial Partners (AIP) that has so far earned only a 1 percent return on its investment. Obviously, the company is having problems. Its sales are up but earnings down. In the first three months after acquisition, the company lost $2 million on $68 million in sales. Understandably, AIP wants to know why and is demanding aggressive action.

Employees at the Bedford, Virginia, plant say they know something's wrong. The plant is hot and dirty and crumbling, and they are working harder to produce items of poorer quality. Fewer than 7 of 10 orders are shipped on time, and 2% of sales are returned as defective. Built in 1924, the plant sprawls over 14 buildings, with only the offices and lunchroom air-conditioned. Equipment is old and outdated, much of it purchased in the 1940s. The 800 to 2000 workers at the Bedford plant are paid an average of $11.50 an hour, far above the minimum wage average for the area. In the mill room, workers get a 20-minute lunch break and two 10-minute breaks each 8-hour shift. They spend their day lifting and loading heavy bags of compounds into mixers and working with rubber stock that can reach temperatures of 300°F or more. At the end of the day, workers leave covered with chemical dust from the mixing compounds. The company says exposure to the chemical poses no cancer or health risks. The workers aren't so sure.

Recently, in an effort to increase productivity, workers in the mill area were asked to increase the amount of rubber made in a single batch and decrease the bake time. Batches that used to take 30 minutes to cook were scheduled for 15 minutes, and 15-minute batches were reduced to 12 minutes or less. Paradoxically, even though the workers were running about a third more batches than before, they produced less usable rubber.

Labor–management relations are not good. Management says it pays the workers well and expects top-notch performance. If productivity does not increase soon, AIP will be forced to lay off about a third of the Rubatex workforce and may eventually close down the Bedford plant. Cost estimates to update the plant exceed $6 million. AIP does not want to authorize additional investment in plant and equipment until worker commitment to improved productivity is ensured. Rubatex management vows to engineer a turnaround. They set goals for the plant to increase sales by 30%, institute mandatory overtime to increase output, and reduce health care benefits to retirees to save costs.

Bedraggled workers call a strike that lasts nine months. Only 324 workers are rehired when the strike draws to a close. Rubatex files chapter 11. The Executive Vice President of Rubatex Corporation explains, "With the exception of the Bedford, Virginia, facility, our operations continue to perform reasonably well and provide positive cash flow. We are a competitive company facing some significant challenges. Our capital structure has become unmanageable and we have been greatly affected by a nine-month strike at our Bedford plant and the continued disruption associated with operating in the absence of a labor contract at that location."

Three years later Rubatex closes the Bedford plant for good, and more than 900 retirees lose their retirement benefits in bankruptcy court.

1. Examine the responses by management to the problems of the Bedford plant. Why didn't they achieve the results expected?
2. What did Rubatex need to do at the Bedford plant to remain competitive?

*Sources:* Jeff Sturgeon, "Rubatex Building Road to Recovery," and Richard Foster, "Old Plant Takes Toll on Workers, Morale," *Roanoke Times and World News* (July 21, 1996); press release at www.rubatex.com (December 7, 2000); Duncan Adams, "Rubatex, Union Move Closer to Agreement," *Roanoke Times and World News* (March 16, 2001); Duncan Adams, "Bedford Rubatex Plant to Close, Lay Off 64 People," *Roanoke Times and World News* (February 3, 2004).

## CASE PROBLEM 1.2

### *Value-Added Operations at Lands' End*

Lands' End, headquartered in Dodgeville, Wisconsin, is the largest specialty catalogue company in the United States and one of the top sellers of clothes on the Internet today. The company's products include casual and tailored clothing for men, women, and children, shoes and accessories, soft luggage, and items for bed and bath. Fast, efficient operations allow Lands' End to offer convenient at-home shopping of quality merchandise at competitive prices.

Lands' End catalogues are known for descriptive product narratives that tell customers everything they could want to know about a garment and its construction. The company's toll-free phone lines for sales and customer service are open 24 hours a day, 364 days a year. More than 1000 phone lines handle about 50,000 calls each day—almost 100,000 calls daily in the weeks prior to Christmas. That doesn't include the 189,000 e-mails received and answered.

Lands' End uses the Internet to boost sales, provide customized service, stay in touch with its customers, and rid itself of excess inventory. With its expertise in warehousing, distribution, and order fulfillment, using the Internet to communicate with customers is a win–win situation.

The catalogue is a good tool for promoting the Web site, and the Web site can handle catalogue orders at lower cost with greater speed and accuracy. Customers get tailored reminders of special events and sales items via e-mail. And sites can be reconfigured to meet specific customer wants and needs. Customers can search by color, size, fabric, style, or price range, or they can browse through the latest offerings. Based on items placed in the shopping cart, the Web site can suggest additional items for purchase or offer special deals on accessory items. Prices can be changed automatically based on demand. Featured items can change, too—so the company is not caught highlighting a fashion flop.

Lands' End converts 10% of its Web visitors into buyers, twice as many as the industry average. They do this through live chats and personalized service—from remembering what you have purchased recently to meta models that try clothes on "your" body (see Exhibit 1.2). Not sure what you want? Start an instant messaging conversation with a *personal shopper*. Difficult to make a selection?

Exhibit 1.2
**Lands' End Virtual Model**

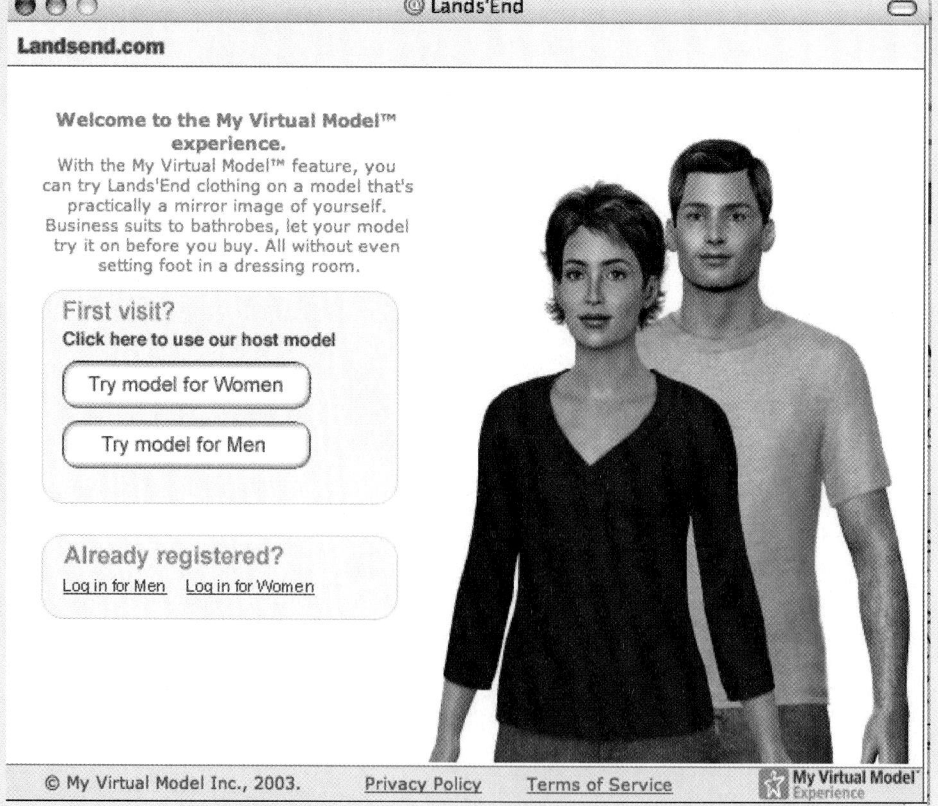

Order all three and return those you don't want postage free (as long as you use an affiliated credit card). Uncertain what size to order? Enter your measurements into *My Fit* and Lands' End will recommend a size and style. Or have Lands' End custom make shirts, blouses, and slacks. Want a friend's advice? Shop together simultaneously from separate computers and add the items to a single shopping bag.

Order fulfillment and delivery is a company specialty. In-stock orders leave Lands' End's Dodgeville distribution center (a structure the size of 16 football fields) the day after they are received. Standard delivery is two business days anywhere within the continental United States. Lands' End works directly with some of the best fabric mills and manufacturers in the world. Garments are produced to Lands' End's own quality specifications, not to less stringent industrywide specifications. In addition to its booming U.S. business, the company now does business in 75 countries, with facilities or special licensing agreements in Canada, the United Kingdom, Japan, and Germany.

**1.** Think about the operations function at Lands' End. What is involved in the transformation process? How does the company "add value" for its customers?
**2.** Examine the list of primary topics in OM. In which activities is Lands' End involved?
**3.** Gather information on Lands' End's competitors L.L. Bean and Eddie Bauer. Are there any obvious differences in their competitive strategies? Describe the Internet and global activities of each company.

*Source:* Rebecca Quick, "Getting the Right Fit—Hips and All," *The Wall Street Journal* (October 18, 2000), p. B1; "Lands' End Makes Big Strides Online," *Sunday Herald Times* (December 19, 1999), p. G1; Peter Gallanis, "Clicks and Bricks Apparel Sites Poised for Web Dominance," *DSN Retailing Today* (July 19, 2000), pp. 23–24; www.landsend.com

## REFERENCES


Baker, Stephen, and Manjeet Kripalani. "Software—Will Outsourcing Hurt America's Supremacy?" *Business Week* (March 1, 2004), pp. 84–95.

Carson, Iain. "Meet the Global Factory." *The Economist* (June 20, 1998), pp. 3–18.

Evans, Philip, and Thomas Wurster. *Blown to Bits*. Boston: Harvard Business School Press, 1999.

Dertouzos, Michael, Richard Lester, and Robert Solow. *Made in America*. Cambridge, MA: MIT Press, 1989.

Gates, Bill. *Business @ the Speed of Thought*. New York: Warner Books, 1999.

Hagel, John, and Marc Singer. *Net Worth*. Boston: Harvard Business School Press, 1999.

Haksever, Cenviz, Robert Murdick, Barry Render, and Roberta Russell. *Service Operations Management*. Upper Saddle River, NJ: Prentice Hall, 2000.

Hayes, Robert H., Gary P. Pisano, and David M. Upton. *Strategic Operations: Competing Through Capabilities*. New York: Free Press, 1996.

Hayes, Robert, and Steven Wheelwright. *Restoring Our Competitive Edge: Competing Through Manufacturing*. New York: John Wiley, 1984.

Hill, Sidney. "Strategic Sourcing: Getting Your Hands Around Direct Materials Procurement." *Manufacturing Systems* (January 1, 2001), p. 42.

Kalakota, R., and M. Robinson. *e-Business: Roadmap for Success*. Reading, MA: Addison-Wesley, 1999.

Kripalani, Manjeet, and Pete Engardio. "The Rise of India." *Business Week* (December 6, 2003).

Mandel, Michael, and Rich Miller. "Productivity—The Real Story." *Business Week* (November 5, 2001), pp. 36–38.

McAfee, Andrew. "The Economic Impact of the Internet Revolution: Manufacturing." The E-conomy Project. www.e-conomy.berkeley.edu.

Manufacturing Studies Board. *Towards a New Era in Manufacturing: The Need for a National Vision*. Washington, DC: National Academy Press, 1986.

Peters, Tom. *Thriving on Chaos*. New York: Alfred A. Knopf, 1987.

Porter, Michael. *Competitive Advantage*. New York: Free Press, 1985.

Porter, Michael. "Strategy and the Internet." *Harvard Business Review*. (March 2001), pp. 62–78.

Powell, Bill. "It's All Made in China Now." *Fortune* (March 4, 2002).

Quade, Walter. "Beginner's Guide to the Asian Supply Chain." *Inside Supply Management* (March 2004), pp. 8–9.

Rocks, David. "The Net as a Lifeline." *Business Week* (October 29, 2001), pp. EB16–EB23.

Skinner, Wickham. *Manufacturing: The Formidable Competitive Weapon*. New York: John Wiley, 1985.

Skinner, Wickham. "Three Yards and a Cloud of Dust: Industrial Management at Century End." *Production and Operations Management* 5(1; Spring 1996):15–24.

"Survey: Business and the Internet." *The Economist* (June 26, 1999), pp. B21–B40.

"Survey: E-Commerce." *The Economist* (February 26, 2000), pp. S6–S15.

Voss, Christopher. "Operations Management—from Taylor to Toyota—and Beyond." *British Journal of Management* 6(December 1995):S17–S29.

Womack, James, Daniel Jones, and Daniel Roos. *The Machine that Changed the World*. New York: Macmillan, 1990.

# Operations Strategy

CHAPTER 2

Web resources for this chapter include

- Internet Exercises
- Online Practice Quizzes
- Virtual Tours
- Excel Worksheets
- Company and Resource Weblinks
- Animated Demo Problems
- Microsoft Project Exhibits

www.wiley.com/college/russell

## CHAPTER OUTLINE

In this chapter, you will learn about . . .

- Strategy Formulation
- Competitive Priorities
- Operations' Role in Corporate Strategy
- Strategy and the Internet
- Strategic Decisions in Operations
- Strategy Deployment
- Issues and Trends in Operations

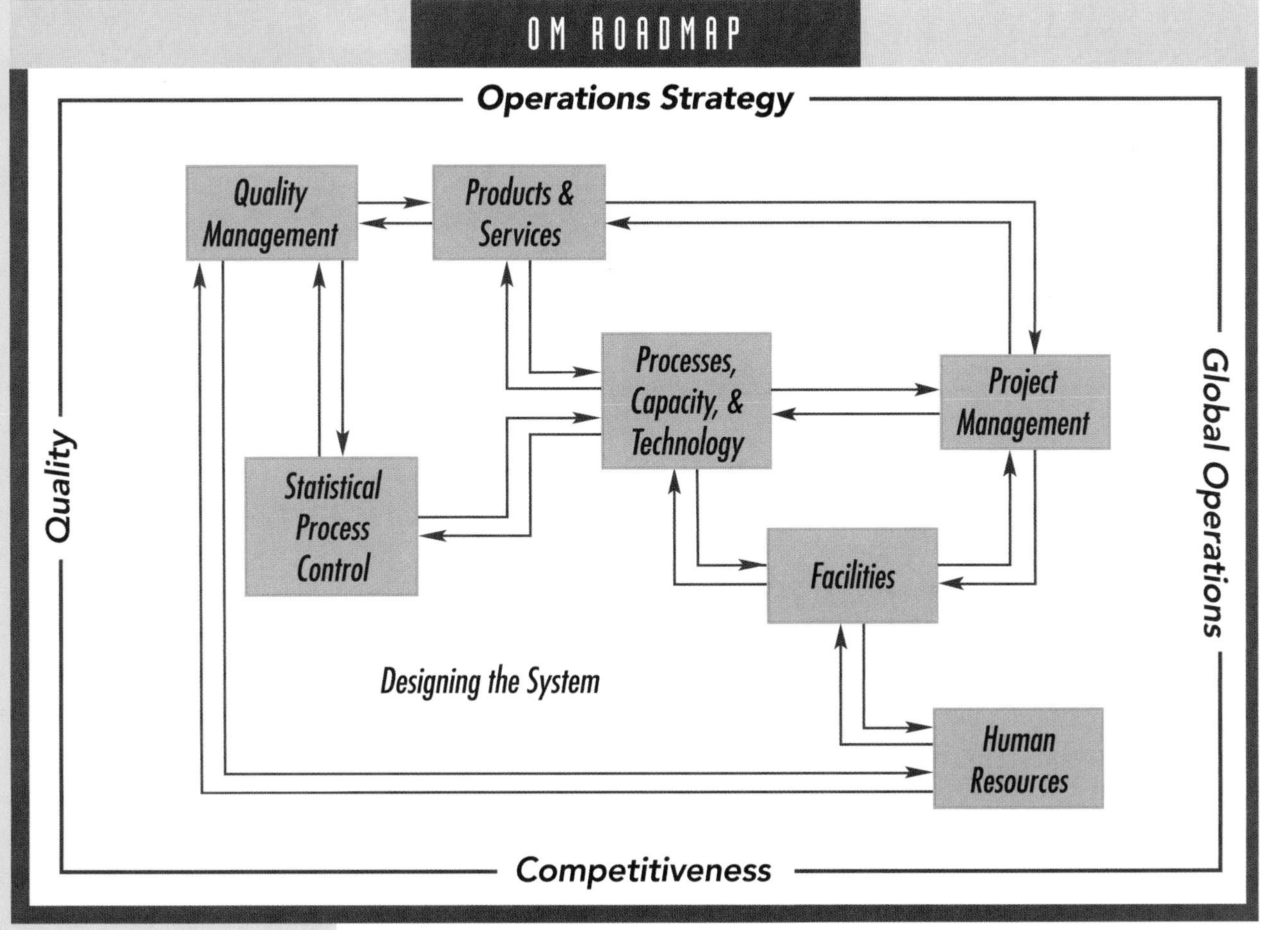

## SO YOU HAVE A MISSION STATEMENT . . . NOW WHAT?

Visioning is big in corporate America. Everyone from IBM to the Little League team has mission statements, visions, philosophies, and core values. Most mission statements began in the 1990s, when companies incorporated total quality, teamwork, and customer focus into their day-to-day operations—and they've multiplied rapidly since. Let's look at a few examples.

Some mission statements clarify what business a company is in—for Levi Strauss it's "branded casual apparel"; for Intel it's supplying "building blocks to the Internet economy"; for Binney & Smith (Crayola) it's "colorful visual expression"; for Currency Doubleday it's "ideas that link business with life's meaning"; for eBay it's "trading communities"; and for Merck it's "preserving and improving human life."

Other mission statements reflect the character of the company—Southwest Airline delivers its service "with a sense of warmth, friendliness, individual pride, and Company Spirit"; Ben and Jerry's creates "a new corporate concept of linked prosperity" that includes a social mission; Hanna Andersson wants to "enhance the richly textured experience of family and community"; and Ritz-Carlton proclaims "we are ladies and gentlemen serving ladies and gentlemen." Wal-Mart exists to "provide value to [its] customers," 3M "to solve problems," and Hewlett-Packard "to make a contribution."

Still others are short and focused—Motorola: "Total Customer Satisfaction"; and Delta Air Lines: "Worldwide Airline of Choice."

Finally, some mission statements signal a radical change in the way the company does business—General Electric: "Boundaryless . . . Speed . . . Stretch."

Mission statements are the "constitution" for an organization, the corporate directive. But they are no good, as Dilbert implies, unless they are supported by strategy and converted into action. And that's what this chapter is all about—converting missions to strategy to results.

Source: *Dilbert* reprinted by permission of United Feature Syndicate, Inc.

## STRATEGY FORMULATION

**Strategy** is how the mission of a company is accomplished. It unites an organization, provides consistency in decisions, and keeps the organization moving in the right direction. Strategy formulation consists of four basic steps:

**Strategy:** provides direction for achieving a mission.

1. ***Defining a primary task.*** The **primary task** represents the purpose of a firm—what the firm is in the business of doing. It also determines the competitive arena. As such, the primary task should not be defined too narrowly. For example, Norfolk Southern Railways is in the business of transportation, not railroads. Paramount is in the business of communication, not making movies. Amazon's business is providing the fastest, easiest, and most enjoyable shopping experience, while Disney's is making people happy! The primary task is usually expressed in a firm's *mission* statement. The mission may be accompanied by a **vision** statement that describes what the organization sees itself becoming.

**Primary task:** what is the firm in the business of doing.

**Vision:** what an organization sees itself becoming.

2. ***Assessing core competencies.*** **Core competency** is what a firm does better than anyone else, its *distinctive competence*. A firm's core competence can be exceptional service, higher quality, faster delivery, or lower cost. One company may strive to be first to the market with innovative designs, whereas another may look for success arriving later but with better quality.

   Based on experience, knowledge, and know-how, core competencies represent *sustainable competitive advantages*. For this reason, products and technologies are seldom core competencies. The advantage they provide is short-lived, and other companies can readily purchase, emulate, or improve on them. Core competencies are more likely to be *processes*, a company's ability to *do* certain things better than a competitor. Thus, while a particular product is not a core competence, the process of developing new products is. Consider Chaparral Steel for example. Chaparral management allows its competitors to tour its plants at will because "they can't take [what we do best] home with them."[1] Although Chaparral is known for its low cost and high technology, its core competency is not technology, but *the ability to transform technology rapidly into new products and processes*. By the time a competitor copies its current technology, Chaparral will have moved on to something else.

   Core competencies are not static. They should be nurtured, enhanced, and developed over time. Close contact with the customer is essential to ensuring that a competence does not become obsolete.

**Core competency:** what the firm does better than anyone else.

3. ***Determining order winners and order qualifiers.*** A firm is in trouble if the things it does best are not important to the customer. That's why it's essential to look toward customers to determine what influences their purchase decision.

   **Order qualifiers** are the characteristics of a product or service that qualify it to be considered for purchase by a customer. An **order winner** is the characteristic of a product or service that wins orders in the marketplace—the final factor in the purchasing decision. For example, when purchasing a DVD player, customers may determine a price range (order qualifier) and then choose the product with the most features (order winner) within that price range. Or they may have a set of features in mind (order qualifiers) and then select the least expensive DVD player (order winner) that has all the required features.

   Order winners and order qualifiers can evolve over time, just as competencies can be gained and lost. Japanese automakers initially competed on price but had to ensure certain levels of quality before the U.S. consumer would consider their product. Over time, the consumer was willing to pay a higher price (within reason) for the assurance of a superior-quality Japanese car. Price became a qualifier, but quality won the orders. Today, high quality, as a standard of the automotive industry, has become an order qualifier, and innovative design wins the orders.

**Order qualifiers:** what qualifies an item to be considered for purchase.

**Order winner:** what wins the order.

[1]The discussion of Chaparral Steel and core competencies is adapted from Dorothy Leonard-Barton, *Wellsprings of Knowledge* (Boston: Harvard University Press, 1996), Chapters 1 and 2.

It is important for a firm to meet the order qualifiers and excel on the order winner. Ideally, a firm's distinctive competence should match the market's order winner. If it does not, perhaps a segment of the market could be targeted that more closely matches the firm's expertise. Or the firm could begin developing additional competencies that are more in tune with market needs.

**Positioning:** how the firm chooses to compete.

4. ***Positioning the firm.*** No firm can be all things to all people. Strategic **positioning** involves making choices—choosing one or two important things on which to concentrate and doing them extremely well. A firm's positioning strategy defines how it will compete in the marketplace—what unique value it will deliver to the customer. An effective positioning strategy considers the strengths and weaknesses of the organization, the needs of the marketplace, and the positions of competitors.[2]

## COMPETITIVE PRIORITIES

Let's look at companies that have positioned themselves to compete on cost, quality, flexibility, and speed.

### COMPETING ON COST

Eliminate all waste.

Companies that compete on cost relentlessly pursue the elimination of all waste. In the past, companies in this category produced standardized products for large markets. They improved yield by stabilizing the production process, tightening productivity standards, and investing in automation. Today, the entire cost structure is examined for reduction potential, not just direct labor costs. High-volume production and automation may or may not provide the most cost-effective alternative.

Take the example of Lincoln Electric, a manufacturer that has reduced costs by $10 million a year for 10 years. One example of cost-cutting measures: Air currents from ducts behind a waterfall draw excess paint that has missed its mark during the painting process into a filtering system so that it can be reused. Skilled machine operators, working on a strict piece-rate system, earn around $80,000 a year. They make their own tools, maintain and repair the equipment themselves, and check their own quality. Called "million-dollar men," these workers have saved the company millions of dollars that would have been spent on automated equipment.

Southwest Airlines' strategy of low-cost, no frills air transportation forever changed the public's attitude about flying. The strategy is supported by carefully designed service, efficient operations, and committed personnel. Southwest uses only one type of airplane, the Boeing 737, to facilitate crew changes and to streamline training, record-keeping, maintenance, and inventory costs. Turnaround time between flights is 15 minutes. Since its flights are limited to short routes, all flights are direct. That means no baggage transfers and no meals to be served. There are no assigned seats and no printed boarding passes for flights. Boarding priority is a function of arrival time at any Southwest check-in facility (not just the departure gate). Southwest saves $30 million annually in travel agent commissions by requiring customers to contact the airline directly to book flights. The airline carefully selects employees and reinforces its commitment with a model profit-sharing plan. The result? Southwest flies more domestic passengers than any other airline in the United States and earns more money than all other U.S. airlines combined. Its on-time performance, baggage handling, and customer satisfaction are always among the best in the industry.

Companies that compete successfully on cost realize that low cost cannot be sustained as a competitive advantage if increases in productivity are obtained solely by short-term cost reductions. A long-term productivity "portfolio" is required that trades off current expenditures for future reductions in operating cost. The portfolio consists of investments in updated facilities and infrastructure; equipment, programs, and systems to streamline operations; and training and development that enhances the skills and capabilities of people.

[2]These factors can be depicted in a SWOT matrix, which lists the current strengths (S) and weaknesses (W) internal to the company, and the opportunities (O) and threats (T) external to the company.

## COMPETING ON QUALITY

Most companies approach quality in a defensive or reactive mode; quality is confined to minimizing defect rates or conforming to design specifications. To compete on quality, companies must view it as an opportunity to please the customer, not just a way to avoid problems or reduce rework costs.

Please the customer.

To please the customer, one must first understand customer attitudes toward and expectations of quality. One good source is the American Customer Satisfaction Index compiled each year by the American Society for Quality and the National Quality Research Center. Examining recent winners of the Malcolm Baldrige National Quality Award and the criteria on which the award are based also provides insight into companies that compete on quality.

The Ritz-Carlton Hotel Company is a Baldrige Award winner and a recognized symbol of quality. The entire service system is designed to understand the individual expectations of more than 500,000 customers and to "move heaven and earth" to satisfy them. Every employee is empowered to take immediate action to satisfy a guest's wish or resolve a problem. Processes are uniform and well defined. Teams of workers at all levels set objectives and devise quality action plans. Each hotel has a quality leader who serves as a resource and advocate for the development and implementation of those plans. Daily quality reports submitted from the 720 work systems track such measures as guest room preventive maintenance cycles, percentage of check-ins with no waiting, and time spent to achieve industry-best clean room appearance. Guest Incident Action Reports completed by every employee help to identify patterns of problems so that they can be resolved permanently. Guest Preference Reports are recorded in a sophisticated customer database for service delivery throughout the company. For example, if a guest in Atlanta likes fresh fruit and five different newspapers each morning, that wish is stored in the database and automatically fulfilled whether the guest's next stay occurs at a Ritz in Naples or Hong Kong. Ritz-Carlton provides exceptional service quality—one customer at a time.

## COMPETING ON FLEXIBILITY

Marketing always wants more variety to offer its customers. Manufacturing resists this trend because variety upsets the stability (and efficiency) of a production system and increases costs. The ability of manufacturing to respond to variation has opened up a new level of competition. **Flexibility** has become a competitive weapon. It includes the ability to produce a wide variety of products, to introduce new products and modify existing ones quickly, and to respond to customer needs. Examples of companies that compete on flexibility include Andersen Windows, Custom Foot Shoe Store, and National Bicycle.

**Flexibility:** the ability to adjust to changes in product mix, production volume, or design.

Andersen Windows, like most manufacturers, used to produce a limited range of standard products in large volumes. As customers demanded uniqueness, Andersen introduced more and more options to their standard windows—so many, in fact, that the number of products offered grew from 28,000 to 86,000. Thick catalogues allowed customers to combine thousands of options into truly unique windows. However, pricing became quite complex, and the rate of error in the finished product was high. Then, Andersen introduced an electronic version of its catalogue that can be used to add, change, or strip away features until the customer is pleased with the design. Special computer-aided design (CAD) programs are used by architects and builders to incorporate Andersen windows directly into their design. The computer then checks the window specs for structural soundness, generates a price quote, and transmits the order to an Andersen factory. At the factory, standard parts from inventory are used to assemble custom products, and bar codes keep track of the customer order as it moves through assembly. In five years, demand for Andersen windows has tripled, the number of different products offered has topped 188,000, and errors are down to 1 per 200 truckloads.

Shoe stores carry lots of inventory and yet customers are still turned away because a particular size or style of shoe is not in stock. Other styles are sold only with deep discounts. Custom Foot Shoe Store has an alternative business model for selling shoes. Handmade shoes begin with custom-sculpted models, called "lasts," that can cost hundreds of dollars and take 10 to 20 hours to construct. The entire shoemaking process takes

*Efficient operations can meet the demands of individual customers with a concept known as* mass customization. *For example, retail customers worldwide can design their own windows by computer and then send their creations to factories for manufacture and delivery within a month's time.*

about eight months and is very expensive. At Custom Foot Shoe Store, a customer's feet are scanned electronically to capture 12 different three-dimensional measurements. The measurements are sent to a factory in Italy, where a library of 3000 computerized lasts can be modified digitally instead of manually and then milled by a machine out of plastic. Custom shoes are mailed to the customer's home in weeks, and since the shoe store carries no inventory, the prices are comparable to off-the-shelf shoes.

National Bicycle Industrial Company fits bicycles to exact customer measurements. Bicycle manufacturers typically offer customers a choice among 20 or 30 different models. National offers 11,231,862 variations and delivers within two weeks at costs only 10% above standard models. Computerized design and computer-controlled machinery allow customized products to be essentially mass produced. The popular term for this phenomenon is **mass customization**. Mass customization takes advantage of both flexibility and speed.

**Mass customization:** the mass production of customized products.

## COMPETING ON SPEED

More than ever before, speed has become a source of competitive advantage. The Internet has conditioned customers to expect immediate response and rapid product shipment. Service organizations such as McDonald's, LensCrafters, and Federal Express have always competed on speed. Citicorp advertises a 15-minute mortgage approval, L.L. Bean ships orders the day they are received, and Wal-Mart replenishes its stock twice a week instead of the industry average of every two weeks. Now manufacturers are discovering the advantages of *time-based competition*, with build-to-order production and efficient supply chains.

In the fashion industry where trends are temporary, Gap's nine-month time-to-market can no longer compete with the two-month design-to-rack lead time of H&M, the Swedish retailer, or the two-week lead time of Zara of Spain. The Gap only introduces 20 new fashion lines a year compared to hundreds for H&M and Zara.

Saks Fifth Avenue sends suit measurements via the Internet to France, where a laser cuts the cloth and tailors begin their work. The suit is completed and shipped back to New York within four days. That's about the same amount of time required for alterations in most clothing stores. The standard for custom-made suits is 10 weeks.

In five days, Hewlett-Packard can produce electronic testing equipment that used to take four weeks to produce. General Electric has reduced the time of manufacture for circuit-breaker boxes from three weeks to three days and the manufacture of dishwashers from 6 days to 18 hours. Dell ships custom-built computers in two days, and Motorola now needs less than 30 minutes to build to order pagers that used to take three weeks!

**Fast moves, fast adaptations, tight linkages.**

Competing on speed requires an organization characterized by fast moves, fast adaptations, and tight linkages. Decision making is pushed down the organization as levels of management are collapsed and work is performed in cross-functional teams. Change is embraced and risk taking encouraged. Close contact is maintained with both suppliers and customers. Performance metrics reflect time, speed, and rate, in addition to cost and profit. Strategy is *time paced* to create a predictable rhythm for change. Intel's time-paced strategy involves doubling the capacity of computer chips every 18 months and adding a new fabrication facility every 9 months. Dell computer sets the pace for the entire industry.[3]

Forming alliances is one of the most effective avenues for competing on speed. The best example is the textile industry's *quick response* (QR) initiative, designed to improve the flow of information, standardize recording systems, and reduce turnaround time along the entire supply chain from fiber to textiles to apparel to retailing. Automotive, electronics, and equipment manufacturers encourage similar alliances within their respective industries with an initiative called "agile manufacturing." E-marketplaces and company-sponsored B2B sites are dramatically speeding up the time required to locate suppliers, negotiate contracts, and communicate purchasing needs.

## OPERATIONS' ROLE IN CORPORATE STRATEGY

Effective strategy can be achieved in two ways—by performing *different* activities from those of competitors or by performing the same activities *better*. Operations plays an important role in either approach. It can provide *support* for a differentiated strategy, and it can serve as a firm's *distinctive competence* in executing similar strategies better than competitors.

**Operations provides support for a differentiated strategy.**

The operations function helps strategy evolve by creating new and better ways of delivering a firm's competitive priorities to the customer. Once a firm's competitive priorities have been established, its operating system must be configured and managed to provide for those priorities. This involves a whole series of interrelated decisions. For example, moving to a low-wage country is not a sustainable advantage unless the firm is skilled at setting up and managing such facilities. Nor is new technology a competitive advantage if a firm cannot efficiently convert the technology into saleable products, or improve on the technology over time. Lincoln Electric shared its manufacturing methods and equipment designs with its competitors during World War II as part of the war effort. Industry production soared and costs dropped across the board. But soon after the war, Lincoln resumed its cost leadership position (still intact today) because it kept improving its processes, while others did not.[4] Wal-Mart, known for its tightly integrated strategy, excels in operations. Figure 2.1 shows how Wal-Mart's competitive priorities are supported by its operations strategy and structure.

[3]See Charles Fine, *Clockspeed: Winning Industry Control in the Age of Temporary Advantage* (Boston: MIT Press, 1999).

[4]Many of the ideas and examples in this section are from Robert H. Hayes and David Upton, "Operations-Based Strategy," *California Management Review* (Summer 1998), pp. 8–25.

Figure 2.1
**Operations Strategy at Wal-Mart**

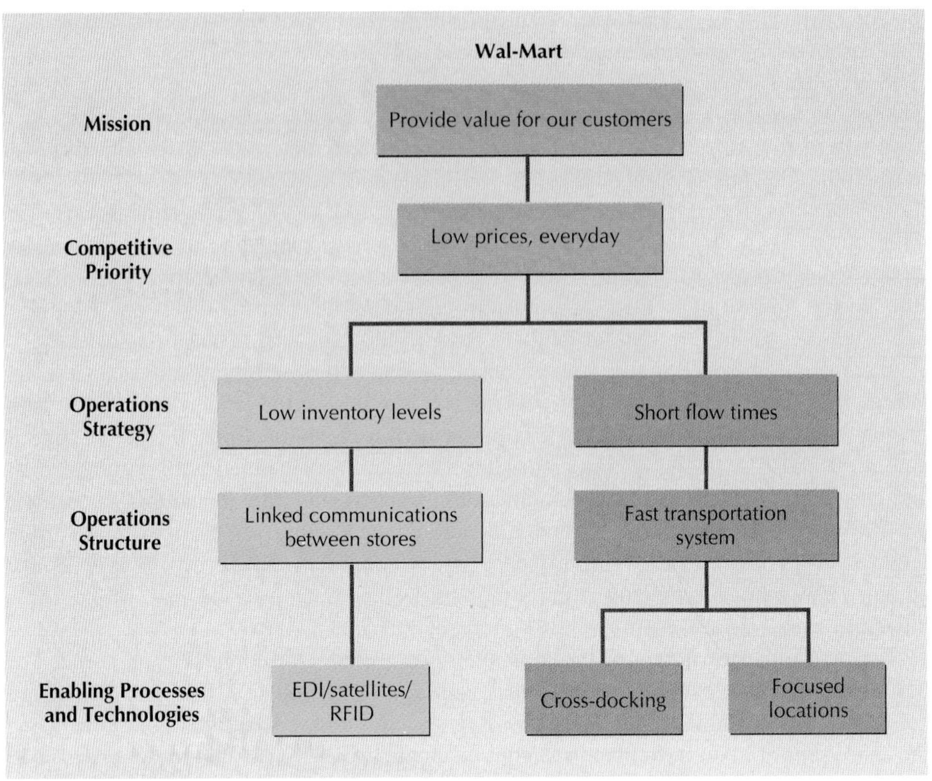


Operations can be a firm's distinctive competence.

Strategic advantages built on operations expertise are frequently underestimated or ignored by competitors. Competencies that take years to develop can emerge suddenly with considerable force. Small companies, especially in different geographical areas, can go about developing operating capabilities and translating them to competitive advantage in relative obscurity. Wal-Mart built its skills in retailing slowly over a dozen years in rural areas of the South before going head to head with the competition in large urban areas. KMart's substantial investment in computerized scanners and new procurement and inventory-control systems did not bring them up to speed with Wal-Mart. Employees did not understand the importance of data accuracy, nor did they have the proper training, motivation, or discipline to use the systems effectively. United Airlines tried to emulate Southwest's success by eliminating meals and baggage service, adding more direct routes, and buying Boeing 737s, but they could not replicate the fast turnarounds, on-time arrivals, committed employees, and cooperative customers. Southwest had built and nurtured those capabilities over time. Southwest also has the discipline to stick to its competitive priorities. For example, the company decided *not* to enter the lucrative Denver market because logistics at the Denver airport prevent quick turnarounds.

Reconfiguring an operating system to align with new strategic priorities takes not only time and resources, but also a change in corporate culture. That's why operations-based advantages are so difficult to replicate and slow to diffuse. As we will discover in Chapters 3 and 15, American automakers took more than a decade to implement Toyota's lean manufacturing techniques. Similarly, total quality management (TQM) burst onto the management scene more than 20 years ago, and companies are still trying to put it into action. Ever wonder why other companies have had difficulty copying Dell's well-documented direct sales model? Dell's Web site can be easily duplicated, but not its back-end expertise in purchasing, scheduling, and logistics, or its corporate culture of speed and constant change.

The phenomenon of *disruptive technologies*, proposed by Clay Christensen, explains how companies with less sophisticated technologies producing lower-margin products can enter a market unchallenged, then evolve to transform an industry.[5] Examples include the

[5]Clayton Christensen, Thomas Craig, and Stuart Hart, "The Great Disruption," *Foreign Affairs* (March/April 2001), pp. 80–95.

emergence of personal computers, tabletop copiers, and networking technologies associated with the Internet.

## STRATEGY AND THE INTERNET

With the meteoric rise and fall of dot-coms in the past five years, it is apparent that strategy is even more essential in an e-technology environment. The Internet can be used to create a distinctive business strategy, to strengthen a company's existing competitive advantages, and to bring new and traditional activities into a more tightly integrated system.

There are some businesses for which the Internet is uniquely suited. eBay was created to provide an efficient market where none previously existed. As an auctioneer, eBay does little more than provide rules, software, and a Web server. All the work is done by the buyers and sellers. Sellers pay the company for the privilege of setting up their own auctions. Buyers use eBay's site to place bids. The winning buyer and seller negotiate payment and shipping between them. eBay never touches the goods. There is basically no marginal cost for the service, and yet the company receives 7 to 18% of the negotiated sale price. Unlike traditional auctioneers, eBay has almost unlimited capacity and a huge market. Larger markets attract more sellers. Just as important as its size and reach is the "community" eBay has been able to create and sustain among its customers. Operating margins are from 20 to 35%.

Similarly, the Internet is essential to Cisco, a company that sells Internet operating systems (IOSs) and networking equipment. Cisco's integrated value chain is its competitive advantage. From direct sales and product configuration on its Web site, to electronic ordering and coordination of suppliers, Cisco uses the Internet more effectively than any other large company. Words such as "amazoned" or "napsterized" have entered the business lexicon to describe small start-ups that surprised industry stalwarts with new ways of doing business based on the dual capabilities of IT expertise and customer-focused operations.

**The Internet should complement competitive priorities.**

For most companies, the Internet complements, rather than cannibalizes, traditional business activities and competitive priorities. General Electric, for example, combined its strong manufacturing skills with networking technologies to create GE's Trading Process Network, an automated Web-based purchasing system. The system cut the average purchasing cycle and cost of purchases in half, but more importantly, it enabled a much larger group of suppliers to bid on jobs and customers to track their orders through the shop in real time. The transparency provided by the Internet showcased GE's operations expertise and brought them closer to their customers and suppliers. The "closeness" generates new ideas for meeting customer needs. GE's plastics business sells polymer pellets to customers who store them in silos. GE-installed sensors signal GE via the Internet when a silo is running low, triggering a reorder. The customer continues to do business with GE because it's easier. With better information about customer use, GE can schedule its own production processes more efficiently. The Internet allows GE to offer convenient, simple, precision fulfillment. GE estimates that its e-business plans will add an extra $1.6 billion to its earnings.[6]

Intel sells $2 billion a month over the Internet and purchases 80% of its direct materials online. Online sales replace the 19,000 sales-order faxes received daily before the company embarked on its e-business initiative. But efficiency of business processes is not the only reason Intel aims to become a "100% e-corporation." The company says the Internet is vital to serving its global customers and to maintaining its leading-edge reputation in technology. Walgreen's Web site, which allows customers to order prescriptions online for later pickup, has brought more customers into its existing stores and away from mail-order prescriptions. Catalogue companies can personalize their offerings and gather more useful customer information with online ordering, thereby increasing customer loyalty, purchasing frequency, and customer sales.

[6]Many of the examples in this section are taken from Larry Selden and Geoffrey Colvin, "Will Your E-Business Leave You Quick or Dead?" *Fortune* (May 28, 2001), pp. 112–124.

The Internet is the great equalizer.

Companies without a firm foundation in providing something special for their customers, however, gain only temporary benefits from the Internet. With the efficiencies of the Internet extending across industries, companies, and supply chains, Internet technology has become the great equalizer, allowing innovations to be enjoyed and copied with little investment in time or money. For example, the Internet allows automobile customers to gather extensive information and compare features, repair records, and prices for both new and used cars. Internet car dealers may be able to reach a larger market, but they can no longer differentiate their service through showrooms, salespersons, or service departments. When the basis for competition is reduced to price, the market cannot support the multitude of online dealers. That's one of the lessons from the dot-com shakedown. To truly benefit from the Net, a firm must provide a unique value to the customer. Companies with well-developed competitive advantages can gain efficiencies and closer customer contact through the Web. Companies that are not managed well offline are a disaster online. Trying to reengineer a company's processes while simultaneously going online doubles the likelihood of failure.

Provide a unique value.

Michael Porter suggests that dot-coms need more than technical capabilities to be successful.[7] They need a distinctive strategy for providing value to the customer, deep industry knowledge, and the ability to perform the physical functions necessary to support their strategic position. Established companies need to deploy the Internet throughout their value chain, look for innovative ways to bring together virtual and physical activities, and concentrate on markets or processes for which the Internet offers real advantages.

## STRATEGIC DECISIONS IN OPERATIONS

Strategic decisions in operations involve products and services, processes and technology, capacity and facilities, human resources, quality, sourcing, and operating systems. As shown in Figure 2.2, all these decisions should "fit" like pieces in a puzzle. A tight strategic fit means competitors must replicate the entire system to obtain its advantages. Thus, the competitive advantage from an integrated operating system is more sustainable than new products or technologies. Let's briefly discuss what is involved in strategic decisions for operations.

### PRODUCTS AND SERVICES

**Make-to-order:** producing to customer specifications after an order has been received.

The kinds of products and services offered by a company drive operations strategy. Products and services can be classified as make-to-order, make-to-stock, or assemble-to-order. **Make-to-order** products and services are designed, produced, and delivered to customer specifications in response to customer orders. Examples include wedding invitations, custom-built homes, custom-tailored clothes, charter airline flights, component parts, and most professional services (such as medical, legal, and financial services). Critical operations issues relate to satisfying the customer (since each customer wants something different) and minimizing the time required to complete the order.

Figure 2.2
**Operations Strategy**

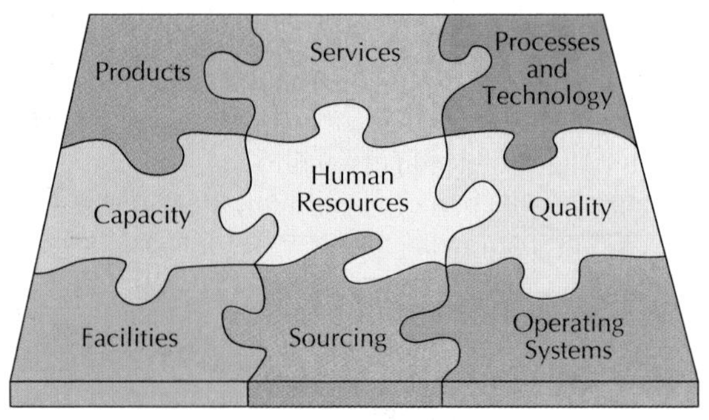


[7]Michael Porter, "Strategy and the Internet," *Harvard Business Review* (March 2001), pp. 62–78.

**Make-to-stock** products and services are designed and produced for "standard" customers in anticipation of demand. Shelves are prestocked with the items, and customers choose from among the products or services available for purchase. Examples include ready-to-wear apparel, books, televisions, airline flights, spec homes, and standard vacation packages. Critical operations issues are forecasting future demand and maintaining inventory levels that meet customer service goals.

**Make-to-stock:** producing in anticipation of demand.

**Assemble-to-order** products and services, also known as *build-to-order*, are produced in standard modules to which options are added according to customer specifications. Thus, components are made-to-stock and then assembled to order after the customer order has been received. Examples include computer systems, corporate training, and industrial equipment. The operations function is concerned with minimizing the inventory level of standard components, as well as the delivery time of the finished product.

**Assemble-to-order:** adding options according to customer specifications.

## PROCESSES AND TECHNOLOGY

Production processes can be classified into projects, batch production, mass production, and continuous production, as shown in Figure 2.3. We introduce the classifications here and discuss them more thoroughly in Chapter 6.

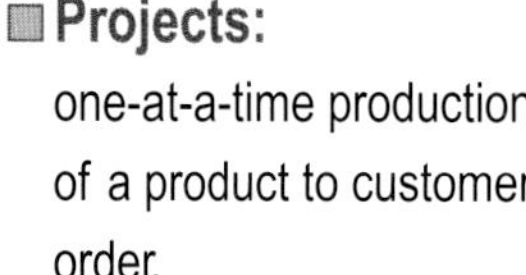

**Projects:** one-at-a-time production of a product to customer order.

A **project** takes a long time to complete, involves a large investment of funds and resources, and produces one item at a time to customer order. Examples include construction projects, shipbuilding, new-product development, and aircraft manufacturing.

**Batch production** processes many different jobs through the production system at the same time in groups or batches. Products are typically made to customer order, volume (in terms of customer order size) is low, and demand fluctuates. Examples of batch production include printers, bakeries, machine shops, education, and furniture making.

**Batch production:** processing many different jobs at the same time in groups (or batches).

**Mass production** produces large volumes of a standard product for a mass market. Product demand is stable, and product volume is high. Goods that are mass produced include automobiles, televisions, personal computers, fast food, and most consumer goods.

**Mass production:** producing large volumes of a standard product for a mass market.

**Continuous production** is used for *very* high-volume commodity products that are *very* standardized. The system is *highly* automated and is typically in operation continuously 24 hours a day. Refined oil, treated water, paints, chemicals, and foodstuffs are produced by continuous production.

**Continuous production:** producing very high-volume commodity products.

The process chosen to create the product or service must be consistent with product and service characteristics. The most important product characteristics (in terms of process choice) are degree of *standardization* and *demand volume*. Figure 2.3 shows a product-process matrix that matches product characteristics with process choice.

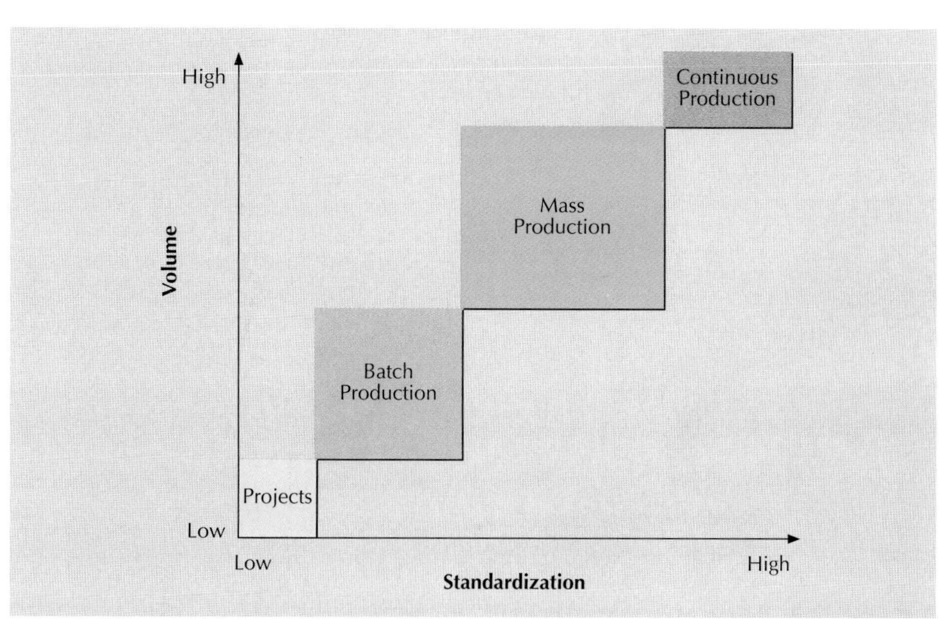


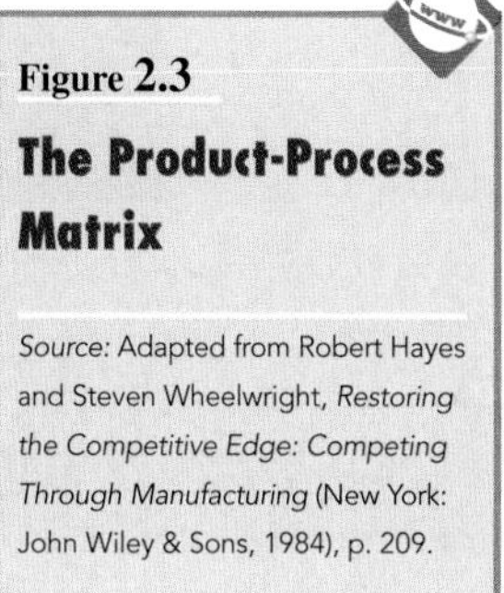
Figure 2.3
**The Product-Process Matrix**

*Source:* Adapted from Robert Hayes and Steven Wheelwright, *Restoring the Competitive Edge: Competing Through Manufacturing* (New York: John Wiley & Sons, 1984), p. 209.

*Continuous Production.* A paper manufacturer produces a continuous sheet of paper from wood pulp slurry, which is mixed, pressed, dried, and wound onto reels. Later, winders will cut the paper into customer-size rolls for wrapping and labeling. Production per day exceeds 1700 tons of paper.

More Standardized, Higher Volume

*Mass Production.* Here in a clean room a worker performs quality checks on a computer assembly line.

*Batch Production.* At Martin Guitars the bindings on the guitar frame are installed by hand and are wrapped with a cloth webbing until the glue is dried. The wrap procedure has been used for hundreds of years on bound instruments.

*Project.* The construction of the aircraft carrier USS Nimitz was a huge project that took almost 10 years to complete.

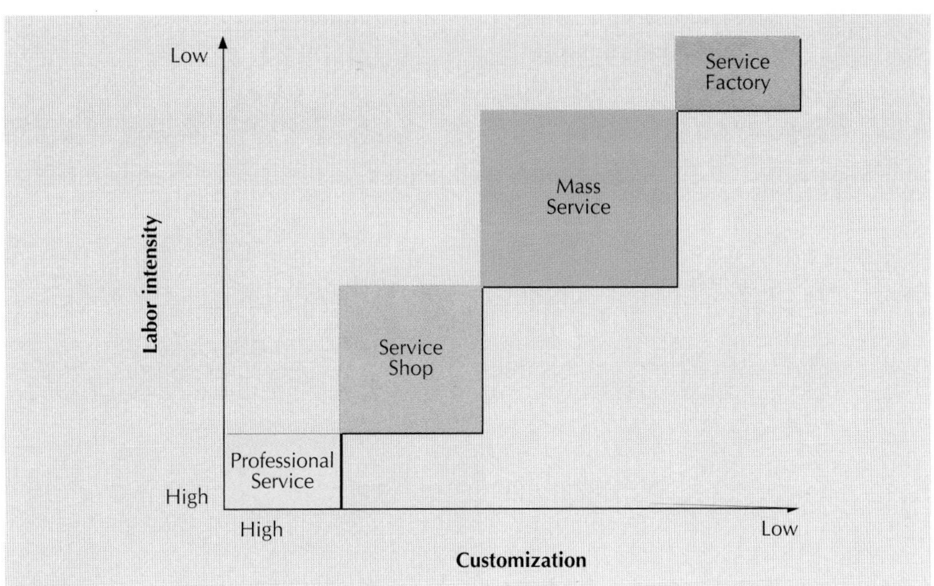


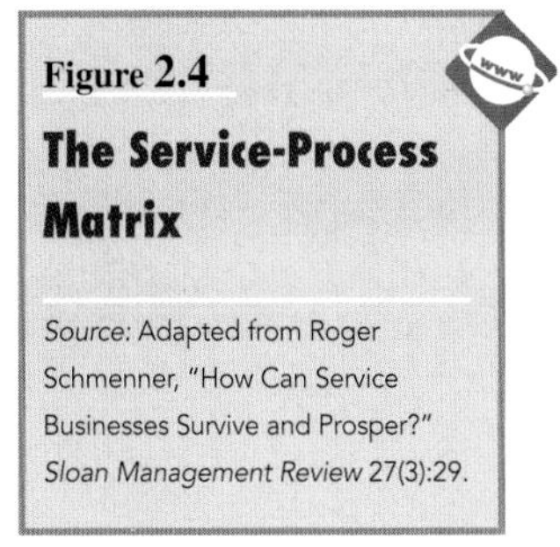


**Figure 2.4**

**The Service-Process Matrix**

*Source:* Adapted from Roger Schmenner, "How Can Service Businesses Survive and Prosper?" *Sloan Management Review* 27(3):29.

The best process strategy is found on the diagonal of the matrix. Companies or products that are off the diagonal have either made poor process choices or have found a means to execute a competitive advantage. For example, technological advancements in flexible automation allow Motorola to mass produce customized pagers. Volvo and Rolls Royce occupy a special market niche by producing cars in a crafted, customized fashion. Examples of poor process choice include Texas Instruments' attempt to produce consumer products for mass markets by the same process that had been successful in the production of scientific products for specialized markets, and Corning's production of low-volume consumer items, such as range covers, with the same continuous process used for other items formed from glass.

Although most services can be classified into the same types of processes as manufactured products, a more natural classification system for services emphasizes degree of *customization* (rather than standardization) and degree of *labor intensity* (rather than volume). Figure 2.4 shows a service-process matrix based on these two service characteristics. A *professional service*, such as accountant, lawyer, or doctor, is highly customized and very labor intensive. A *service shop*, such as schools and hospitals, is less customized and labor intensive but still attentive to individual customers. A *mass service*, such as retailing and banking, offers the same basic services to all customers and allows less interaction with the service provider. Services with the least degree of customization and labor intensity, such as airlines and trucking, are most like manufactured products and are thus best processed by a *service factory*.

## CAPACITY AND FACILITIES

Capacity decisions affect product lead times, customer responsiveness, operating costs, and a firm's ability to compete. Inadequate capacity can lose customers and limit growth. Excess capacity can drain a company's resources and prevent investments in more lucrative ventures. *When*, *how much*, and in *what* form to alter capacity are critical decisions.

Overall capacity must then be divided into individual facilities. Strategic decisions include determining whether demand should be met with a few large facilities or with several smaller ones, and whether facilities should focus on serving certain geographic regions, product lines, or customers.

Facility location can also be a strategic decision, especially when it concerns global expansion. If items are to be made as well as sold in foreign countries, what kind of relationship is needed with manufacturers in the foreign countries—licensing agreements, joint ventures, partnerships, alliances, mergers?

**Service Factory.** Electricity is a commodity available continuously to customers.

Less Labor Intensive,
Less Customized

**Mass Service.** A retail store provides a standard array of products from which customers may choose.

**Service Shop.** A professor interacts with a classroom of students. Although a lecture may be prepared in advance, its delivery is affected by the students in each class.

**Professional Service.** A doctor provides personal service to each patient based on extensive training in medicine.

## HUMAN RESOURCES

Strategic issues in human resources involve determining the skill levels and degree of autonomy required to operate the production system, outlining training requirements and selection criteria, and setting up policies on performance evaluations, compensation, and incentives. Will workers be salaried, paid an hourly rate, or paid a piece rate? Will profit sharing be allowed, and if so, on what criteria? Will workers perform individual tasks or work in teams? Will they have supervisors or work in self-managed work groups? How many levels of management will be required? Will extensive worker training be necessary? Should the workforce be cross-trained? What efforts will be made in terms of retention?

## QUALITY

Quality permeates virtually every strategic decision. What is the target level of quality for our products and services? How will it be measured? How will employees be involved with quality? What types of training are necessary? What will be the responsibilities of the quality department? What types of systems will be set up to ensure quality? How will quality awareness be maintained? How will quality efforts be evaluated? How will customer perceptions of quality be determined? How will decisions in other functional areas affect quality?

## SOURCING

A firm that sells the product, assembles the product, makes all the parts, and extracts the raw material is completely **vertically integrated**. But most companies cannot or will not make all of the parts that go into a product. A major strategic decision, then, is how much of the work should be done outside the firm. This decision involves questions of dependence, competency-building, and proprietary knowledge, as well as cost.

**Vertical integration:** the degree to which a firm produces the parts that go into its products.

On what basis should particular items be made in-house? When should items be outsourced? How should suppliers be selected? What type of relationship should be maintained with suppliers—arm's length, controlling, partnership, alliance? What is expected from the suppliers? How many suppliers should be used? How can the quality and dependability of suppliers be ensured? How can suppliers be encouraged to collaborate?

## OPERATING SYSTEMS

Operating systems execute strategic decisions on a day-to-day basis, so it is important that they be designed to support how the firm competes in the marketplace. The IT system must be able to support both customer and worker demands for rapid access, storage, and retrieval of information. Planning and control systems must be set up with timely feedback loops and consistent decision-making criteria. Inventory levels, scheduling priorities, and reward systems should align with strategic goals.

# STRATEGY DEPLOYMENT

"The difficulty is not in knowing what to do. It's doing it," said Kodak's CEO, George Fisher.[8] Implementing strategy can be more difficult than formulating strategy. Strategies unveiled with much fanfare may never be followed because they are hard to understand, too general, or unrealistic. Strategies that aim for results five years or so down the road mean very little to the worker who is evaluated on his or her daily performance. Different departments or functional areas in a firm may interpret the same strategy in different ways. If their efforts are not coordinated, the results can be disastrous.

[8]Michael Hammer, *Beyond Reengineering* (New York: HarperCollins, 1996), p. 193.

**Figure 2.5**

**Strategic Planning**

*Source:* Adapted from AT&T Quality Steering Committee, *Policy Deployment* (Indianapolis: AT&T Technical Publications Center, 1992).

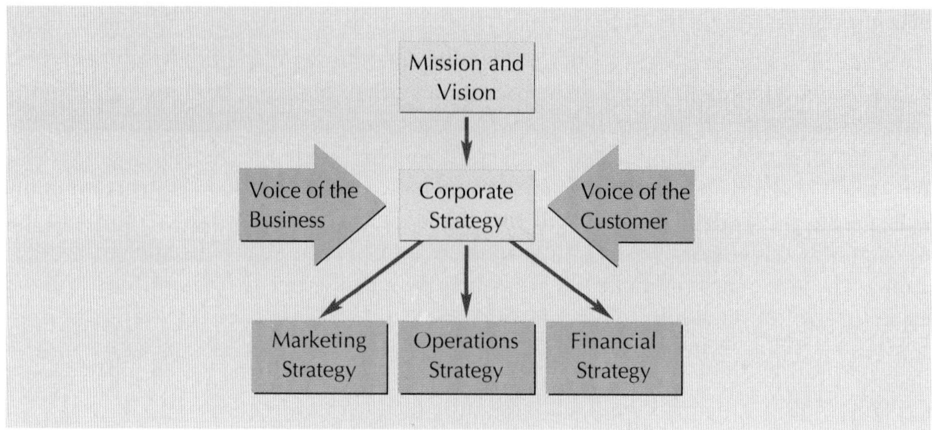


Consider Schlitz Brewing Company, whose strategy called for reduced costs and increased efficiency. Operations achieved its goals by dramatically shortening its brewing cycle—and, in the process, lost 6 of every 10 customers when the clarity and taste of the beer suffered. The efficiency move that was to make the company the most profitable in its industry instead caused its stock value to plummet from $69 per share to $5 per share. Let's examine the strategic planning process and explore more effective ways to deploy strategy.

## THE STRATEGIC PLANNING HIERARCHY

As shown in Figure 2.5, the strategic planning process involves a hierarchy of decisions. Senior management, with input and participation from different levels of the organization, develops a corporate strategic plan in concurrence with the firm's mission and vision, customer requirements (voice of the customer), and business conditions (voice of the business). The strategic plan focuses on the gap between the firm's vision and its current position. It identifies and prioritizes what needs to be done to close the gap, and it provides direction for formulating strategies in the functional areas of the firm, such as marketing, operations, and finance. It is important that strategy in each of the functional areas be internally consistent as well as consistent with the firm's overall strategy.

Companies struggling to align day-to-day decisions with corporate strategy have found success with two types of planning systems—policy deployment and the balanced scorecard.

## POLICY DEPLOYMENT

Policy deployment, also known as hoshin planning, is adapted from Japan's system of *hoshin kanri*, which is roughly translated from Japanese as "shining metal pointing direction"—a compass.

**Policy deployment:** a planning system that translates corporate strategy into measurable objectives.

**Policy deployment** tries to focus everyone in an organization on common goals and priorities by translating corporate strategy into measurable objectives throughout the various functions and levels of the organization. As a result, everyone in the organization should understand the strategic plan, be able to derive several goals from the plan, and determine how each goal ties into their own daily activities.

Suppose the corporate strategic plan of competing on speed called for a reduction of 50% in the length of the business cycle. Senior management from each functional area would assess how their activities contribute to the business cycle, confer on the feasibility of reducing the cycle by 50%, and agree on each person's particular role in achieving the reduction. Marketing might decide that creating strategic alliances with its distributors would shorten the average time to release a new product. Operations might try to reduce its purchasing and production cycles by reducing its supplier base, certifying suppliers, using e-procurement, and implementing a just-in-time (JIT) system. Finance might decide to eliminate unnecessary approval loops for expenditures, begin prequalifying sales

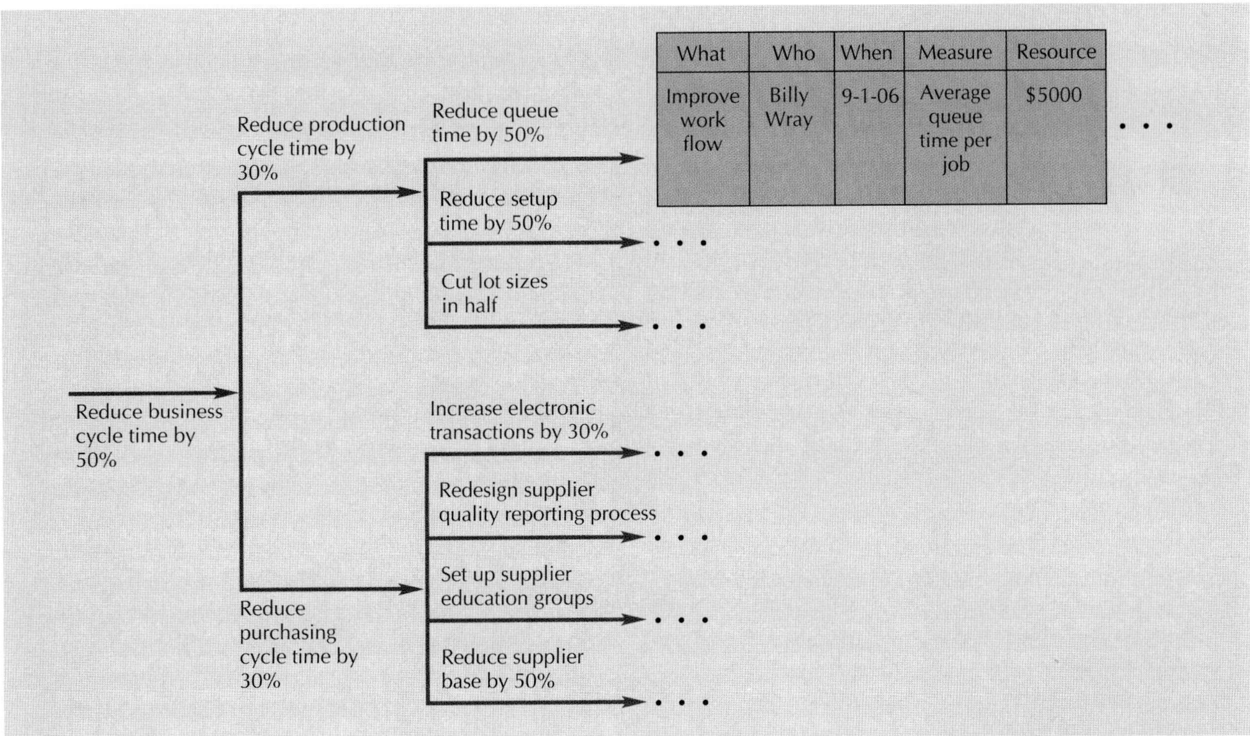


Figure 2.6
**Derivation of an Action Plan Using Policy Deployment**

prospects, and explore the use of electronic funds transfer (EFT) in conjunction with operations' JIT strategy.

The process for forming objectives would continue in a similar manner down the organization with the *means* of achieving objectives for one level of management becoming the *target*, or objectives, for the next level. The outcome of the process is a cascade of action plans (or **hoshins**) aligned to complete each functional objective, which will, in turn, combine to achieve the strategic plan.

**Hoshins:** the action plans generated from the policy deployment process.

Figure 2.6 shows the derivation of an action plan for reducing cycle time. For simplicity, only the top branch of the tree diagram is completed, in which Bill Wray is given $5000 to reduce the average queue time per job by 50%. In the following box, Nicole Sanders shares her experiences with policy deployment.

*Is your company pointed in one direction? AT&T uses the analogy of migrating geese to explain the concept of policy deployment. Naturalists believe the instinctive V-formation allows the geese to follow one leader and migrate in a cohesive unit toward their destination. Policy deployment does the same thing—it enables business leaders to mobilize the organization toward a common destination, aligning all employees behind a common goal and a collective wisdom.*

**_Nicole Sanders_**
**_Commodity Manager for Danaher Motion_**

Danaher Motion is a leading global manufacturer of motion control products that improve the efficiency and productivity of complex manufacturing operations. I am a commodity manager at Danaher, responsible for sourcing, purchasing, and e-procurement of all the electronics components that go into our products. I locate suppliers, negotiate contracts, manage supplier relations, and supervise the work of four buyers.

The job has changed quite a bit since I started working here. Until a year ago, we used forecasts from our material requirements planning (MRP) system to generate purchase orders. It would not be uncommon to purchase the same item from eight different vendors over the course of a year. Today our core supplier base has been reduced from 400 vendors to 10, and most of our parts (3000 to 4000 of them) use kanbans (standard order cards) to generate replenishment orders. We provide our suppliers with a six-month forecast of demand with weekly, then daily, updates. A supplier must be able to fill an order within five days with 100% good quality. We are in the process of moving 40% of our dollar spend to low-cost regions, such as China and Malaysia. The logistics of global supply is not as difficult for small products such as electronics. Shipments can be air freighted from China in a week's time, versus five weeks by ship. Increased moisture content of the product is a bigger problem than long lead times.

New suppliers submit bids to our RFQ (request for quote). Then we conduct site audits on probably three suppliers that had reasonable bids. We look at their business processes, their production operations, their bottlenecks, workflow, quality systems, and capability to deliver. A typical contract is for three to five years with built-in price reductions of 5% a year. The contract is very explicit including not only the negotiated price, but also required finished goods, raw material and work-in-process stocking levels, liability issues, forecasts of demand, logistics, inventory review cycles, kanban procedures (such as quantities per container), policies on rejects, repairs, and corrective action, air freighting, and dock dates. For the first few months, we'll perform 100% incoming inspection on goods from new suppliers and ask them to submit statistical process control data (which we call *part qualifying check sheets*). For the next few months, we'll sample, say 100 pieces, of a 500-piece shipment. If all goes well, after six months we accept the supplier shipments *dock to stock.*

Danaher is passionate about continually improving its operations and eliminating waste. We use kaizen (quality) teams for continuous improvement and policy deployment to focus our improvements on breakthrough achievements. Every year we have policy goals for *Quality, Delivery, Cost,* and *Innovation* (QDCI) that cascade down from corporate to department levels. I'm at level six, after the CEO, vice president of operations, global supply chain manager, plant manager, and purchasing manager. My buyers are at level seven. This year our quality objectives refer to reducing the number of returns and the efficient processing of those returns. On-time delivery goals are 85% to voice of the customer (i.e., to customer request, not our promise dates). Our purchase price reduction goal is $2 million for the year, and employees must participate in a number of kaizen events. Each of my buyers, for example, will be members of five kaizen teams and leader of one of them. My goal is to attain a Black Belt in Materials Kaizen.

You know, when I look back at what I learned in my operations management class, it's amazing how much what we talked about is actually used in the business world.

Note: *We will cover MRP (a software system for inventory control and production planning), kanbans (standard cards for withdrawing inventory and ordering production), and kaizen (continuous quality improvement) in Chapters 3, 14, and 15 later in the text.*

## BALANCED SCORECARD

**Balanced scorecard:** measuring more than financial performance.

The **balanced scorecard**, developed by Robert Kaplan and David Norton,[9] examines a firm's performance in four critical areas:

1. *Finances*—How should we look to our shareholders?
2. *Customers*—How should we look to our customers?
3. *Processes*—At which business processes must we excel?
4. *Learning and Growing*—How will we sustain our ability to change and improve?

[9]See Robert S. Kaplan and David P. Norton, "Transforming the Balanced Scorecard from Performance Measurement to Strategic Management." *Accounting Horizons* (March 2001), pp. 87–104; and Robert S. Kaplan and David P. Norton, "Having Trouble with Your Strategy? Then Map It," *Harvard Business Review* (September/October 2000), pp. 167–176.

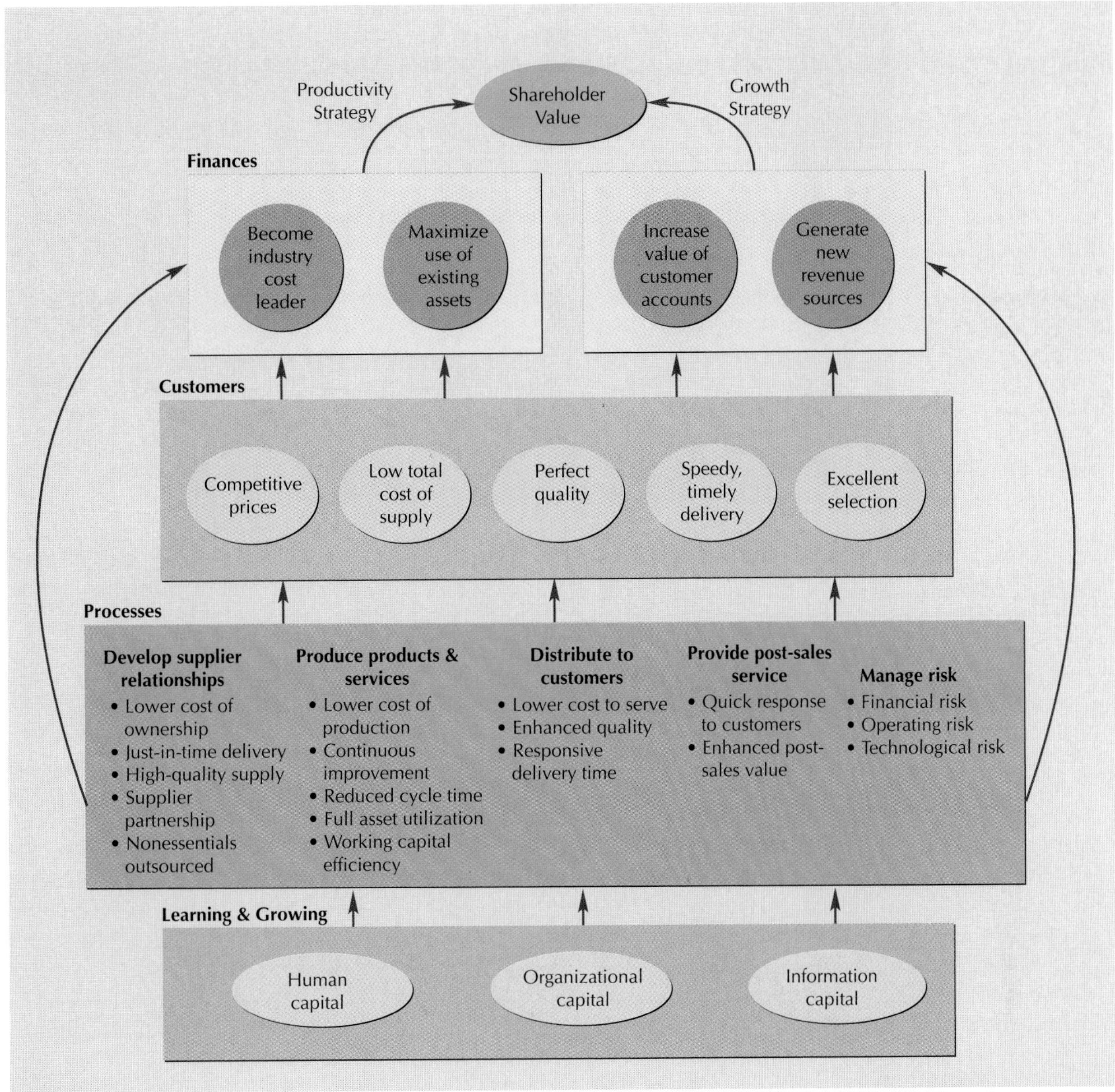


**Figure 2.7**

**A Strategy Map for Operations**

*Source:* Robert Kaplan and David Norton, *Strategy Maps: Converting Intangible Assets into Tangible Outcomes* (Boston: Harvard Business School Press, 2004), Figure 3-2, p. 67.

It's called a *balanced* scorecard because more than financial measures are used to assess performance. Operational excellence is important in all four areas. How efficiently a firm's assets are managed, products produced, and services provided affects the financial health of the firm. Identifying and understanding targeted customers helps determine the processes and capabilities the organization must concentrate on to deliver value to the customer. The firm's ability to improve those processes and develop competencies in new areas is critical to sustaining competitive advantage.

Figure 2.7 shows a generic strategy map for managing operations. Notice that all four areas of performance are included on the map, although the processes section is more detailed. The detail would look different for a map concerned with attracting new customers or designing new products. The organization's ability to learn and grow improves its processes, which affect both customers and company finances. Shareholder value is enhanced through both increased productivity and revenue growth.

Table 2.1 is a balanced scorecard worksheet. The worksheet selects areas of the strategy map to incorporate in annual objectives for the company. The objectives are then operationalized with **key performance indicators** (KPI). The goals for the year are given,

**Key performance indicators:** a set of measures that help managers evaluate performance in critical areas.

Table 2.1

**The Balanced Scorecard Worksheet**

| Dimension | | Objectives | Key Performance Indicator | Goal for 2006 | KPI Results to Date | Score | Mean Performance |
|---|---|---|---|---|---|---|---|
| Finances | Productivity | Become industry cost leader | % reduction in cost per unit | 20% | 10% | 50% | 65% |
| | Growth | Increase market share | Market share | 50% | 40% | 80% | |
| Customers | Quality | Zero defects | % good quality first pass | 100% | 80% | 80% | 87% |
| | Timeliness | On-time delivery | % of on-time deliveries | 95% | 90% | 95% | |
| Processes | Suppliers | Integrate into production | % orders delivered to assembly | 50% | 40% | 80% | 73% |
| | | Reduce inspections | % suppliers ISO 9000 certified | 90% | 60% | 67% | |
| | Products | Reduce time to produce | Cycle time | 10 mins. | 12 mins. | 83% | 52% |
| | | Improve quality | # warranty claims | 200 | 1000 | 20% | |
| | Distribution | Reduce transportation costs | % FTL shipments | 75% | 30% | 40% | 40% |
| | Post-sales Service | Improve response to customer inquiries | % queries satisfied on first pass | 90% | 60% | 67% | 67% |
| | Risk | Reduce inventory obsolescence | Inventory turnover | 12 | 6 | 50% | 50% |
| | | Reduce customer backlog | % order backlogged | 10% | 20% | 50% | |
| Learning & Growing | Humar capital | Develop quality improvement skills | # of six sigma Black Belts | 25 | 2 | 8% | 35% |
| | | | % trained in SPC | 80% | 50% | 63% | |
| | Information capital | Provide technology to improve processes | % customers who can track orders | 100% | 60% | 60% | 61% |
| | | | % suppliers who use EDI | 80% | 50% | 63% | |
| | Organizational capital | Create innovative culture | # of employee suggestions | 100 | 60 | 60% | 55% |
| | | | % of products new this year | 20% | 10% | 50% | |

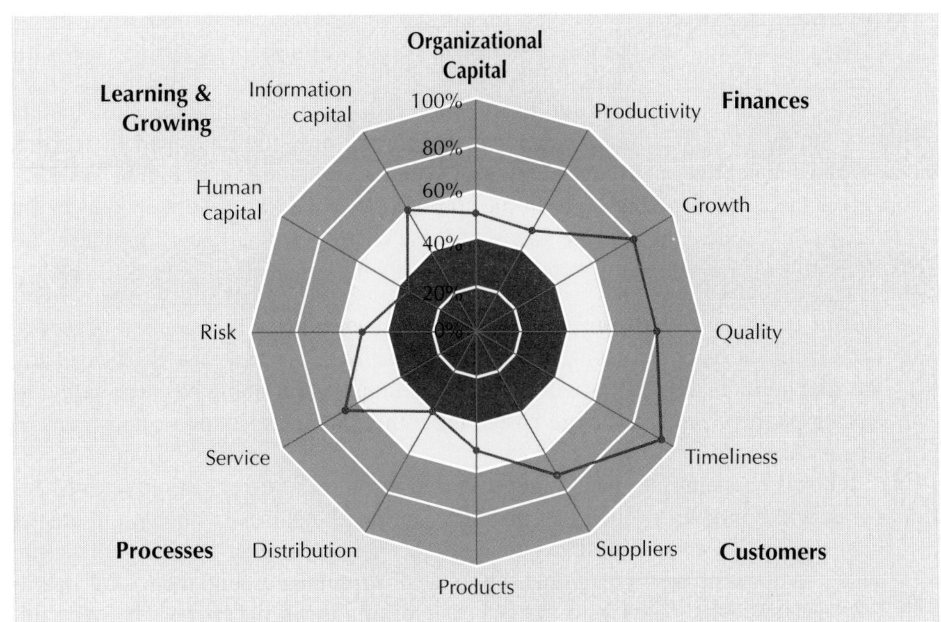


Figure 2.8

**A Radar Chart of the Balanced Scorecard for Operations**

and the KPI results are recorded. The score converts the different performance measures into percentage completed. For example, if the goal is to achieve 12 inventory turns a year and the company manages only six, then the goal is 50% achieved. The mean performance column averages the score for each dimension. The scorecard performance can be visualized in many ways, two of which are illustrated in Figures 2.8 and 2.9.

Figure 2.8 is a radar chart of the balanced scorecard. Goals 0% to 40% achieved appear in the red "danger" zone, 40% to 80% achieved are in the yellow "cautionary" zone, and 80% to 100% achieved are in the green "moving ahead" zone. In this example, the company is in the danger zone for human capital and distribution, but is doing well with growth, quality, timeliness, and service. Figure 2.9 shows the same information in an alternative format. The dashboard presents each scorecard perspective in a different graphic. The red zone is set at 25% or less goal achievement, yellow from 25% to 75%, and green in excess of 75%, although different limits can be set for each perspective. The company excels in growth, quality, and timeliness, and is not in danger on any measure. Note that different limits can be set for each gauge, and measures other than percentages can be used. Dashboards are popular ways for managers to quickly interpret the massive amounts of data collected each day and in some cases can be updated in real time.

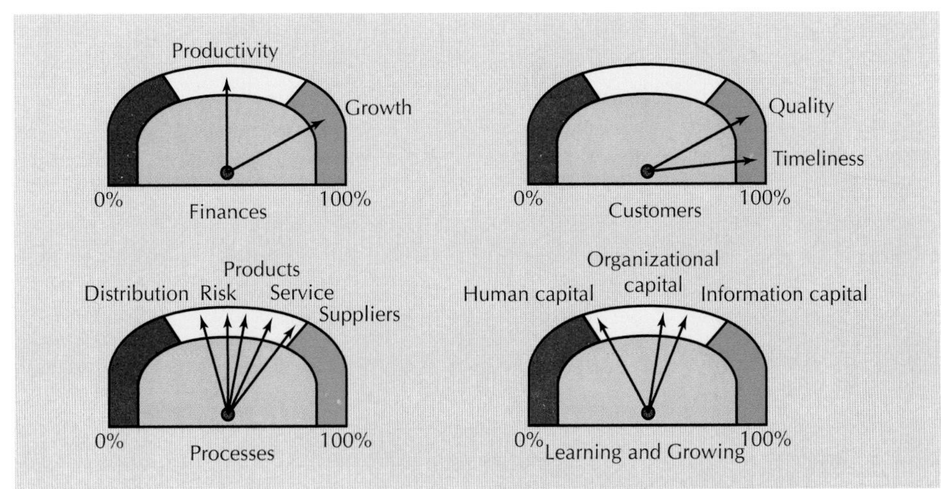


Figure 2.9

**A Dashboard for the Balanced Scorecard**

## ISSUES AND TRENDS IN OPERATIONS

Strategy, at both the corporate and functional levels, involves setting direction into an uncertain future. Thus, it is important for managers not only to understand the current business and competitive environment, but also to gain insight into future trends. Table 2.2 summarizes the changes taking place in the corporate world as we have moved from the twentieth to the twenty-first century. Many of these changes have a direct impact on the field of operations. The following trends are especially importants:[10]

1. ***Global markets, global sourcing, and global operations.*** The intensity of worldwide competition continues in spite of political instability and threats of terrorism. Shifting political alignments will provide opportunities for doing business with new trading partners. Look for more partnering rather than mergers and acquisitions of foreign firms.

   Global restructuring, newly industrialized economies, deregulation, and the Internet will continue to open new markets worldwide. No one country, culture, or company will dominate. Production will take place wherever in the world it can safely be done the best with global supply chains reaching around the world. Operations managers are faced with the task of breaking down the barriers between domestic and international operations, and providing global service for local needs.
2. ***Virtual companies.*** A new type of capitalism based on strategic alliances and cooperative specialization is emerging. The organizational structure of the twenty-first century no longer resembles a pyramid, but a web of autonomous business units, partners, spinoff companies, contractors, and freelancers. The boundaries of individual firms are becoming harder to define. Groups of individuals will form to meet a need, dissolve when the need is met, and reform to meet another need.

**Table 2.2 The Changing Corporation**

| Characteristic | 20th-Century Corporation | 21st-Century Corporation |
|---|---|---|
| *Organization* | The Pyramid | The Web |
| *Focus* | Internal | External |
| *Style* | Structures | Flexible |
| *Source of strength* | Stability | Change |
| *Structure* | Self-sufficiency | Interdependencies |
| *Resources* | Physical assets | Information |
| *Operations* | Vertical integration | Virtual integration |
| *Products* | Mass production | Mass customization |
| *Reach* | Domestic | Global |
| *Financials* | Quarterly | Real-time |
| *Inventories* | Months | Hours |
| *Strategy* | Top-down | Bottom-up |
| *Leadership* | Dogmatic | Inspirational |
| *Workers* | Employees | Employees, free agents |
| *Job expectations* | Security | Personal growth |
| *Motivation* | To compete | To build |
| *Improvements* | Incremental | Revolutionary |
| *Quality* | Affordable best | No compromise |

*Source:* Reprinted from John Byrne, "Management by Web," *Business Week* (August 28, 2000), p. 87 by special permission, copyright © 2000 by The McGraw-Hill Companies, Inc.

[10]We discuss many of these trends in later chapters. Supply chains and e-commerce are more thoroughly discussed in Chapter 10, as are labor issues in Chapter 8 and environmental issues in Chapter 5. Services are covered throughout the book, but particularly in Chapter 5. Technological advances are addressed primarily in Chapter 6.

3. ***Greater choice, more individualism.*** The days of mass production and mass consumption have passed. Mass customization will bring thousands of individualized products and services to the market at huge savings to producers, who no longer have to guess what people want. Customers will be viewed as partners, with the technology to design their own products to their particular specifications. The expected life of products will continue to decrease, as companies race to get breakthrough ideas to the market first.

**Customers want speed, variety, and service.**

4. ***Emphasis on service.*** Eighty-eight percent of jobs and 75% of the GDP in the United States are provided by the service sector. Many corporations we think of as successful manufacturing firms, such as General Motors and General Electric, generate more than half of their income from services. For both manufacturing and service firms, customer service is a competitive battleground that will continue to intensify. Companies will concentrate more on serving the customer rather than producing the product.
5. ***Speed and flexibility.*** With the Internet comes speed—speed of information, speed of actions, speed of communication, speed of delivery, and speed of innovation. From product cycles to employee turnover to decision making, everything is moving in fastforward. To adapt to the rapidly changing environment in which we work, our workers, managers, technologies, and production systems must be flexible.
6. ***Supply chains.*** Few companies will have the expertise or the inclination to create, make, and market their products by themselves. Companies will focus on what they do best and outsource the rest. Instead of *vertical integration* of operations within a company, *virtual integration* of outside suppliers is increasingly the norm. Managing these supply chains, or supply webs, is a major responsibility of operations managers.
7. ***C-commerce.*** *Collaborative commerce* (also known as *c-commerce*) is the ultimate benefit of e-commerce interactions. Doing business on the Internet has brought together suppliers, manufacturers, and customers. C-commerce occurs when business partners share data, collaborate on design decisions, synchronize activities, optimize events, solve problems together, and manage business processes across enterprises. C-commerce can improve the efficiency and effectiveness of operations by drastically reducing time to market, order fulfillment time, economies of scale, purchasing costs, and transaction costs. Operations management is an integral part of c-commerce success, especially in the areas of supply chain management, contract manufacturing, and transportation and distribution.

**Collaborative commerce occurs along the supply chain.**

8. ***Technological advances.*** Information technology, electronic commerce, and telecommunications will continue to advance at a rapid rate. Smart materials, intelligent sensors, biotechnology, artificial intelligence, and nanotechnology will dramatically change how people work, how products are made, and how firms compete. Technology has given us material that can mend itself, animals that are perfect clones, plants that can turn leaves into petals, and people who can design and manufacture products simultaneously from different locations around the globe. And that is just the beginning.
9. ***Knowledge.*** The competitive advantage of products, services, and technologies is short-lived. Companies must attract and retain the best thinkers to stay ahead of their competition. The ability to create, absorb, and utilize knowledge is the paramount skill of the new economy. Those in operations will need to foster *learning communities* that can share knowledge across physical and cultural boundaries. Countries that perform the best in the world market will have the best research and development (R&D), the best education system, the brightest people, and the savvy to use those assets to their fullest.

**Knowledge and the ability to learn to provide a competitive advantage.**

10. ***Environmental and social responsibilities.*** Companies and industries must increasingly consider the environmental impact of the design, manufacture, distribution, use, and disposal of their products and services. The impetus for environmental responsibility must come from government, industry, and customers. Social responsibilities are especially important as the markets and resources of developing nations become more available to global entities. At the same time, persuading companies to act socially responsible will be more difficult as legalities in the host country may have little effect on companies that compete and produce across national borders.

Decision making for the future can be scary at best. Fortunately, there are quantitative tools available for making decisions under uncertain conditions. The supplement to this chapter reviews several of them for us.

## SUMMARY

There is no one best way to design a product, make a product, manage operations, or serve customers. The "best way" depends on a firm's objectives, resources, competencies, and context (products and customers). Firms choose to compete in different ways. A firm's *strategy* defines how it will compete in the marketplace—its own best way.

Strategy formulation involves defining the primary task, assessing core competencies, determining order winners and order qualifiers, and positioning the firm. An effective strategy excels on the order winners, meets the order qualifiers, capitalizes on core competencies, and maintains focus. A competitive position is not sustainable unless the operating system that supports it is configured and managed effectively.

Corporate strategy drives functional strategy. Functional strategies must be consistent with and supportive of corporate strategy. Strategic decisions in the operations function involve products and services, processes and technology, capacity and facilities, human resources, quality, sourcing, and operating systems. *Policy deployment* is a planning system that helps align day-to-day operating decisions with the company's overall strategy. The *balanced scorecard* reinforces a firm's strategy by providing customer-oriented and process-oriented measures of performance, in addition to traditional financial measures.

## SUMMARY OF KEY TERMS

**assemble-to-order** products or services created in standard modules to which options are added according to customer specifications.

**balanced scorecard** performance assessment that includes metrics important to customers and employees, as well as financial metrics.

**batch production** a type of process that produces a variety of jobs in groups or batches.

**continuous production** a type of process used to produce very high-volume commodity products.

**core competencies** the essential capabilities that create a firm's sustainable competitive advantage.

**flexibility** in operations, the ability to adjust to changes in product mix, production volume, or product and process design.

**hoshins** the action plans generated from the policy deployment process.

**key performance indicators** a set of measures that help managers evaluate performance in critical areas.

**make-to-order** products or services made to customer specifications after an order has been received.

**make-to-stock** products or services created in anticipation of demand.

**mass customization** the mass production of customized products.

**mass production** a type of process that produces large volumes of a standard product or service for a mass market.

**order qualifiers** the characteristics of a product or service that qualify it to be considered for purchase.

**order winner** the characteristic of a product or service that wins orders in the marketplace.

**policy deployment** a planning system for converting strategy to measurable objectives throughout all levels of an organization.

**positioning** determining how a firm will compete in the marketplace.

**primary task** the task that is most central to the operation of a firm; it defines the business that a firm is in and is often expressed in a mission statement.

**project** a type of process that creates a product or service one at a time to customer order.

**strategy** a common vision that unites an organization, provides consistency in decisions, and keeps the organization moving in the right direction.

**vertical integration** the degree to which a firm produces the parts that go into a product.

**vision** what an organization sees itself becoming and how it intends to get there.

## QUESTIONS

**2-1.** Gather mission or vision statements from four different companies. What do they tell you about the organizations? Is their mission or vision reflected in the way they do business?

**2-2.** List and explain the four steps of strategy formulation. Follow the steps to outline a strategy for a company or organization with which you are familiar.

**2-3.** Explain the concept of core competencies in your own words. Provide examples of a core competency for a bank, a retail store, and an auto manufacturer.

**2-4.** What is your core competency? Make a list of the core competencies you will need to compete successfully in the job market. Design a strategy for developing the competencies that you do not have and capitalizing on the competencies that you do have.

**2-5.** What is the difference between an order winner and an order qualifier? Tell how you have used the two concepts in a purchasing decision.

**2-6.** Discuss the requirements from an operations perspective of competing on (a) quality, (b) cost, (c) flexibility, (d) speed,

(e) innovation, and (f) service. Give examples of manufacturing or service firms that successfully compete on each of the criteria listed.

**2-7.** What role should operations play in corporate strategy?

**2-8.** Name several strategic decisions that involve the operations function.

**2-9.** Explain the difference between make-to-stock, make-to-order, and assemble-to-order products and services. Give an example of each.

**2-10.** What are the four basic types of production processes? How do they differ? Give an example of each.

**2-11.** What two characteristics have the most influence on process choice for products? for services? How do the product-process and service-process matrices relate to operations strategy?

**2-12.** In what instances is higher education provided as (a) a professional service, (b) a service shop, (c) a mass service, and (d) a service factory?

**2-13.** Why do companies need policy deployment? What does it do?

**2-14.** What is the balanced scorecard? How does it relate to operations?

**2-15.** Examine the annual reports of a company of your choosing over three years. Use quotes from the reports to describe the company's overall strategy and its specific goals each year. How well do you think the company deploys its strategy?

**2-16.** Use either policy deployment or a balanced scorecard to map out a personal strategy for your future.

## CASE PROBLEM 2.1

### *Visualize This*

Visualize This (VT) is a small start-up company specializing in virtual reality and computer visualizations. Located in the research park of a major university, the company was founded by Isaac Trice, a university professor, and staffed with the brightest of his former students. By all accounts the technology is cutting edge. Facilities include a lab of 14 high-end computer workstations adjacent to a CAVE (computer-aided virtual environment) and a small office. A conference room and central lobby are shared with other tenants in the building. Originally the company had partnered with the Swedish firm Salvania to create virtual environments for medical and industrial design. Trice and his staff would develop the software for each application, create a visual database supported with engineering or medical data, and run design sessions for their clients in the CAVE. Salvania provided the capital, generated the clients, and handled the business end of the operations.

In its first two years of business, VT completed four projects. With each project, VT advanced its skills in visualization and developed customized tools to help its clients design intricate products. The clients were pleased but did not anticipate repeating the intensive design process for several years. Unfortunately, Salvania was unable to remain solvent and dissolved its partnership with Visualize This. VT was able to keep its workstations (whose salvage value was low), but gave up its rights to the CAVE and furloughed all but three employees. To stay afloat, VT needed new clients and a steady stream of income. Trice hit the streets and came back with the following possibilities:

- Designing computer-based training sessions for bank tellers of an international finance institution
- Conducting software certification for the sales staff of a large software vendor
- Designing virtual reality tours through history for a major museum
- Developing Web-based virtual models for a women's clothing retailer
- Creating virtual catalogues in which a customer can enlarge, rotate, and dissect a product online.

"This isn't what I had in mind for my company," Trice lamented as he shared the list with his employees. "I wanted to be developing the next generation of visualization tools in concert with the brightest minds in industry, not digitizing pictures of products and making them turn around, or teaching people to use software that's not even our own!"

That said, Trice and his staff of three began going through the list analyzing the pros and cons of each alternative.

1. Help Professor Trice formulate a strategy for his company by going through the steps of strategy formulation. For ideas, search the Internet for other companies that provide visualization solutions.
2. What capabilities does VT need to develop in order to pursue the strategy developed in question 1?
3. How can Trice reconcile his goals for the organization with the needs of the marketplace?
4. Compare the processes required to satisfy each customer on Trice's client list. Consider the mix of equipment and personnel, the length and scope of each project, and the potential for future business. How do the requirements differ from the projects already completed by VT?
5. Which projects would you recommend to VT? Why?

## CASE PROBLEM 2.2

### *Whither an MBA at Strutledge?*

Strutledge is a small private liberal arts school located within 50 miles of a major urban area in the southeast United States. As with most institutions of higher education, Strutledge's costs are rising, and its enrollments are decreasing. In an effort to expand its student base, build valuable ties with area businesses, and simply survive, the Board of Regents is considering establishing an MBA program.

Currently no undergraduate degree is given in business, although business courses are taught. The dean of the school visualizes the MBA as an interdisciplinary program emphasizing problem solving, communication, and global awareness. Faculty expertise would be supplemented by instructors from local industry. The use of local faculty would better connect the university with the business community and provide opportunities for employment of the program's graduates.

In terms of competition, a major state-funded university that offers an MBA is located in the adjacent urban area. Strutledge hopes that state budget cutbacks and perceptions of overcrowded classrooms and overworked professors at public institutions will open the door for a new entrant into the market. The Board of Regents also feels that the school's small size will allow Strutledge to tailor the MBA program more closely to area business needs.

Several members of the Board are concerned about recent reports of the dwindling value of an MBA and are wondering if a better niche could be found with another graduate degree, perhaps a masters in computer science or something in the education or health-care field.

1. What action would you recommend to the Board of Regents?
2. How should Strutledge go about making a strategic decision such as this?

## CASE PROBLEM 2.3

### *Weighing Options at the Weight Club*

The Weight Club started out as a student organization of 25 individuals who gathered together to discuss fitness goals and lift weights in the campus gym. When budget cutbacks cut gym hours and equipment availability, the students began to look elsewhere for a facility they could organize and control as they wished. They found an empty store in a small, abandoned strip mall, rented it for next to nothing, asked its members to pay dues, and began sponsoring weight-lifting contests to raise money for equipment. Off-campus now, they could recruit members from the town as well as the university. Their members had many talents, and they began sponsoring cheerleading training and other specialized training programs for athletes.

Growth of the student-run organization was phenomenal. Within six years the club had more than 4000 members from inside and outside of the university community. The facility itself extended over three additional storefronts in the now bustling mall, housing more than 50 pieces of aerobic equipment, two complete sets of Nautilus equipment for circuit training, an entire floor of free weights, a separate room for heavy weights, and a large exercise room for a full range of aerobic, step, kick boxing, and stretch and tone classes. Graduate students found the facility an excellent source of subjects for projects ranging from nutrition to exercise to lifestyle changes (after heart attacks, for instance). Members were often able to take advantage of these additional services "free of charge."

The Weight Club clientele began to change as more nonuniversity students joined (from moms in the morning hours to teenagers after school and businesspersons after work). This diversity brought with it numerous requests for additional services such as child care, personal trainers, children's classes, massages, swimming and running facilities, locker rooms and showers, food and drink, sportswear, gymnastics, hotel and corporate memberships, meetings, and sponsored events.

Currently, all members pay the same $25 monthly usage fee with no other membership fees or assessments for additional services (like exercise classes). The staff consists predominantly of student members, many of whom have financed their way through school by working at the Weight Club. The organization is run by a founding member of the original weight club, who will finally graduate this year. Two other founding members have already graduated but work full time in the area and help administer the club whenever they can, serving as an informal "board of directors." In general, this arrangement has worked well, although decisions are made by whoever is behind the desk at the time, and there is no long-range planning.

The Weight Club has no significant competition. The three remaining "administrators" wonder if they need to make any changes.

Help the Weight Club get a handle on its operations and plan for the future by creating a balanced scorecard. Make a list of possible objectives for the Weight Club in terms of finance, customers, processes, and development (i.e., learning and growing). Add key performance measures and set goals for the year. Visit an exercise facility near you for ideas as you complete this assignment.

## REFERENCES


AT&T Quality Steering Committee. *Policy Deployment: Setting the Direction for Change.* Indianapolis: AT&T Technical Publications Center, 1992.

Campbell, Andrew, and Marcus Alexander. "What's Wrong with Strategy?" *Harvard Business Review* (November–December 1997), pp. 42–51.

Christensen, Clayton. "Making Strategy: Learning by Doing." *Harvard Business Review* (November–December 1997), pp. 141–156.

Christensen, Clayton, Thomas Craig, and Stuart Hart. "The Great Disruption." *Foreign Affairs* (March/April 2001), pp. 80–95.

Collis, David, and Cynthia Montgomery. "Creating Corporate Advantage." *Harvard Business Review* (May–June 1998), pp. 71–83.

Courtney, Hugh, Jane Kirkland, and Patrick Viguerie. "Strategy Under Uncertainty." *Harvard Business Review* (November–December 1997), pp. 66–79.

Eisenhardt, Kathleen, and Shona Brown. "Time-Pacing: Competing in Markets that Won't Stand Still." *Harvard Business Review* (March–April 1998), pp. 59–69.

Gadiesh, Orit, and James Gilbert. "Profit Pools: A Fresh Look at Strategy." *Harvard Business Review* (May–June 1998), pp. 139–148.

Hammer, Michael. *Beyond Reengineering.* New York: HarperCollins, 1996.

Hayes, Robert H., and Gary P. Pisano. "Manufacturing Strategy: At the Intersection of Two Paradigm Shifts." *Production and Operations Management* 5(1; Spring 1996), 25–41.

Hayes, Robert, Gary Pisano, David Upton, and Steven Wheelwright. *Operations Strategy and Technology: Pursuing the Competitive Edge.* Hoboken, NJ: John Wiley, 2005.

Hayes, Robert H., Gary P. Pisano, and David M. Upton. *Strategic Operations: Competing Through Capabilities.* New York: Free Press, 1996.

Hayes, Robert H., and David M. Upton. "Operations-Based Strategy." *California Management Review* 40(4; Summer 1998), pp. 8–25.

Hill, Terry. *Manufacturing Strategy: Test and Cases*, 3rd ed. Homewood, IL: Irwin, 2000.

Jones, Patricia, and Larry Kahaner. *Say It and Live It: The 50 Corporate Mission Statements That Hit the Mark.* New York: Currency Doubleday, 1995.

Kaplan, Robert S., and David P. Norton. "Transforming the Balanced Scorecard from Performance Measurement to Strategic Management." *Accounting Horizons* (March 2001), pp. 87–104.

Kaplan, Robert, and David Norton. *Strategy Maps: Converting Intangible Assets into Tangible Outcomes.* Boston: Harvard Business School Press, 2004.

King, Bob. *Hoshin Planning: The Developmental Approach* Springfield, MA: GOAL/QPC, 1989.

Leonard-Barton, Dorothy. *Wellsprings of Knowledge: Building and Sustaining the Sources of Innovation.* Boston: Harvard Business School Press, 1995.

Porter, Michael. "What Is Strategy?" *Harvard Business Review* (November–December 1996), pp. 61–106.

Porter, Michael. "Strategy and the Internet." *Harvard Business Review* (March 2001), pp. 62–78.

Prahalad, C. K., and Venkat Ramaswamy. *The Future of Competition: Co-Creating Unique Value with Customers.* Boston: Harvard Business School Press, 2004.

Wheelwright, Steven, and H. Kent Bowen. "The Challenge of Manufacturing Advantage." *Production and Operations Management* 5(1; Spring 1996), pp. 59–77.

# Operational Decision-Making Tools: Decision Analysis

SUPPLEMENT 2

## CHAPTER OUTLINE

**In this supplement you will learn about . . .**

- **Decision Analysis (with and without probabilities)**

At the operational level hundreds of decisions are made in order to achieve local outcomes that contribute to the achievement of a company's overall strategic goal. These local outcomes are usually not measured directly in terms of profit, but instead are measured in terms of quality, cost-effectiveness, efficiency, productivity, and so forth. Achieving good results for local outcomes is an important objective for individual operational units and individual operations managers. However, all these decisions are interrelated and must be coordinated for the purpose of attaining the overall company goals. Decision making is analogous to a great stage play or opera, in which all the actors, the costumes, the props, the music, the orchestra, and the script must be choreographed and staged by the director, the stage managers, the author, and the conductor so that everything comes together for the performance.

*Quantitative methods* **are the tools of the operations manager.**

For many topics in operations management, there are quantitative models and techniques available that help managers make decisions. Some techniques simply provide information that the operations manager might use to help make a decision; other techniques recommend a decision to the manager. Some techniques are specific to a particular aspect of operations management; others are more generic and can be applied to a variety of decision-making categories. These different models and techniques are the "tools" of the operations manager. Simply having these tools does not make someone an effective operations manager, just as owning a saw and a hammer does not make someone a carpenter. An operations manager must know how to use decision-making tools. How these tools are used in the decision-making process is an important and necessary part of the study of operations management. In this supplement and others throughout this book, we examine several different aspects of operational decision making using these tools.

## DECISION ANALYSIS

**Decision analysis:** a set of quantitative decision-making techniques for decision situations in which uncertainty exists.

In this supplement we demonstrate a quantitative technique called **decision analysis** for decision-making situations in which uncertainty exists. Decision analysis is a generic technique that can be applied to a number of different types of operational decision-making areas.

Many decision-making situations occur under conditions of uncertainty. For example, the demand for a product may not be 100 units next week but may vary between 0 and 200 units, depending on the state of the market, which is uncertain. Decision analysis is a set of quantitative decision-making techniques to aid the decision maker in dealing with a decision situation in which there is uncertainty. However, the usefulness of decision analysis for decision making is also a beneficial topic to study because it reflects a structured, systematic approach to decision making that many decision makers follow intuitively without ever consciously thinking about it. Decision analysis represents not only a collection of decision-making techniques but also an analysis of logic underlying decision making.

### DECISION MAKING WITHOUT PROBABILITIES

A decision-making situation includes several components—the decisions themselves and the events that may occur in the future, known as *states of nature*. Future states of nature may be high or low demand for a product or good or bad economic conditions. At the time a decision is made, the decision maker is uncertain which state of nature will occur in the future and has no control over these states of nature.

**Payoff table:** a method for organizing and illustrating the payoffs from different decisions given various states of nature.

When probabilities can be assigned to the occurrence of states of nature in the future, the situation is referred to as *decision making under risk*. When probabilities cannot be assigned to the occurrence of future events, the situation is called *decision making under uncertainty*. We discuss the latter case next.

To facilitate the analysis of decision situations, they are organized into **payoff tables**. A payoff table is a means of organizing and illustrating the payoffs from the different decisions, given the various states of nature, and has the general form shown in Table S2.1.

| Decision | States of Nature *a* | *b* |
|---|---|---|
| 1 | Payoff 1a | Payoff 1b |
| 2 | Payoff 2a | Payoff 2b |

Table S2.1
**Payoff Table**

Each decision, 1 or 2, in Table S2.1 will result in an outcome, or **payoff**, for each state of nature that will occur in the future. Payoffs are typically expressed in terms of profit, revenues, or cost (although they may be expressed in terms of a variety of quantities). For example, if decision 1 is to expand a production facility and state of nature *a* is good economic conditions, payoff 1a could be $100,000 in profit.

**Payoff:** the outcome of the decision.

Once the decision situation has been organized into a payoff table, several criteria are available to reflect how the decision maker arrives at a decision, including maximax, maximin, minimax regret, Hurwicz, and equal likelihood. These criteria reflect different degrees of decision-maker conservatism or liberalism. On occasion they result in the same decision; however, they often yield different results. These decision-making criteria are demonstrated by the following example.

Decision-making criteria

Example S2.1
**Decision-Making Criteria under Uncertainty**

The Southern Textile Company is contemplating the future of one of its plants located in South Carolina. Three alternative decisions are being considered: (1) Expand the plant and produce lightweight, durable materials for possible sale to the military, a market with little foreign competition; (2) maintain the status quo at the plant, continuing production of textile goods that are subject to heavy foreign competition; or (3) sell the plant now. If one of the first two alternatives is chosen, the plant will still be sold at the end of the year. The amount of profit that could be earned by selling the plant in a year depends on foreign market conditions, including the status of a trade embargo bill in Congress. The following payoff table describes this decision situation.

| | **States of Nature** | |
|---|---|---|
| **Decision** | *Good Foreign Competitive Conditions* | *Poor Foreign Competitive Conditions* |
| Expand | $800,000 | $500,000 |
| Maintain status quo | 1,300,000 | −150,000 |
| Sell now | 320,000 | 320,000 |

Determine the best decision using each of the decision criteria.

1. Maximax
2. Maximin
3. Minimax regret
4. Hurwicz
5. Equal likelihood

*Solution*

1. Maximax

The decision is selected that will result in the maximum of the maximum payoffs. This is how this criterion derives its name—the maximum of the maxima. The **maximax criterion** is very optimistic. The decision maker assumes that the most favorable state of nature for each decision alternative will occur. Thus, for this example, the company

**Maximax criterion:** a decision criterion that results in the maximum of the maximum payoffs.

would optimistically assume that good competitive conditions will prevail in the future, resulting in the following maximum payoffs and decisions:

Expand: $800,000
Status quo: 1,300,000 ←Maximum
Sell: 320,000

Decision: Maintain status quo

**2.** Maximin

**Maximin criterion:** a decision criterion that results in the maximum of the minimum payoffs.

The **maximin criterion** is pessimistic. With the maximin criterion, the decision maker selects the decision that will reflect the maximum of the minimum payoffs. For each decision alternative, the decision maker assumes that the minimum payoff will occur; of these, the maximum is selected as follows:

Expand: $500,000 ←Maximum
Status quo: −150,000
Sell: 320,000

Decision: Expand

**3. Minimax Regret**

**Minimax regret criterion:** a decision criterion that results in the minimum of the maximum regrets for each alternative.

The decision maker attempts to avoid regret by selecting the decision alternative that minimizes the maximum regret. A decision maker first selects the maximum payoff under each state of nature; then all other payoffs under the respective states of nature are subtracted from these amounts, as follows:

| Good Competitive Conditions | Poor Competitive Conditions |
|---|---|
| $1,300,000 − 800,000 = 500,000 | $500,000 − 500,000 = 0 |
| 1,300,000 − 1,300,000 = 0 | 500,000 − (−150,000) = 650,000 |
| 1,300,000 − 320,000 = 980,000 | 500,000 − 320,000 = 180,000 |

These values represent the regret for each decision that would be experienced by the decision maker if a decision were made that resulted in less than the maximum payoff. The maximum regret for *each decision* must be determined, and the decision corresponding to the minimum of these regret values is selected as follows:

Expand: $500,000 ←Minimum
Status quo: 650,000
Sell: 980,000

Decision: Expand

**4.** Hurwicz

**Hurwicz criterion:** a decision criterion in which the decision payoffs are weighted by a coefficient of optimism, $\alpha$.

**Coefficient of optimism ($\alpha$):** a measure of a decision maker's optimism, from 0 (completely pessimistic) to 1 (completely optimistic).

A compromise is made between the maximax and maximin criteria. The decision maker is neither totally optimistic (as the maximax criterion assumes) nor totally pessimistic (as the maximin criterion assumes). With the **Hurwicz criterion**, the decision payoffs are weighted by a **coefficient of optimism**, a measure of the decision maker's optimism. The coefficient of optimism, defined as $\alpha$, is between 0 and 1 (i.e., $0 < \alpha < 1.0$). If $\alpha = 1.0$, the decision maker is completely optimistic; if $\alpha = 0$, the decision maker is completely pessimistic. (Given this definition, $1 - \alpha$ is the *coefficient of pessimism.*) For each decision alternative, the maximum payoff is multiplied by $\alpha$ and the minimum payoff is multiplied by $1 - \alpha$. For our investment example, if $\alpha$ equals 0.3 (i.e., the company is slightly optimistic) and $1 - \alpha = 0.7$, the following decision will result:

Expand: $800,000(0.3) + 500,000(0.7) = $590,000 ←Maximum
Status quo: 1,300,000(0.3) − 150,000(0.7) = 285,000
Sell: 320,000(0.3) + 320,000(0.7) = 320,000

Decision: Expand

**5.** Equal Likelihood

The **equal likelihood** (or **La Place**) **criterion** weights each state of nature equally, thus assuming that the states of nature are equally likely to occur. Since there are two states of nature in our example, we assign a weight of 0.50 to each one. Next, we multiply these weights by each payoff for each decision and select the alternative with the maximum of these weighted values.

| | | |
|---|---|---|
| Expand: | \$800,000(0.50) + 500,000(0.50) = \$650,000 | ←Maximum |
| Status quo: | 1,300,000(0.50) − 150,000(0.50) = 575,000 | |
| Sell: | 320,000(0.50) + 320,000(0.50) = 320,000 | |

Decision: Expand

The decision to expand the plant was designated most often by four of the five decision criteria. The decision to sell was never indicated by any criterion. This is because the payoffs for expansion, under either set of future economic conditions, are always better than the payoffs for selling. Given any situation with these two alternatives, the decision to expand will always be made over the decision to sell. The sell decision alternative could have been eliminated from consideration under each of our criteria. The alternative of selling is said to be *dominated* by the alternative of expanding. In general, dominated decision alternatives can be removed from the payoff table and not considered when the various decision-making criteria are applied, which reduces the complexity of the decision analysis.

■ **Equal likelihood (La Place) criterion:** decision criterion in which each state of nature is weighted equally.

Different decision criteria often result in a mix of decisions. The criteria used and the resulting decisions depend on the decision maker. For example, the extremely optimistic decision maker might disregard the preceding results and make the decision to maintain the status quo, because the maximax criterion reflects his or her personal decision-making philosophy.

## DECISION ANALYSIS WITH EXCEL

Throughout this book we will demonstrate how to solve quantitative models using the computer with Microsoft Excel spreadsheets. Exhibit S2.1 shows the Excel spreadsheet solutions for the different decision-making criteria in Example S2.1. The "call out" boxes displayed on and around the spreadsheet define the cell formulas used to compute the criteria values. For example, the spreadsheet formula used to compute the maximum payoff value for the decision to "Expand," **=MAX(C6:D6)**, is embedded in cell E6 and is also shown on the toolbar at the top of the spreadsheet. The formula for the Maximax decision, **=MAX(E6:E8)**, is embedded in cell C10.

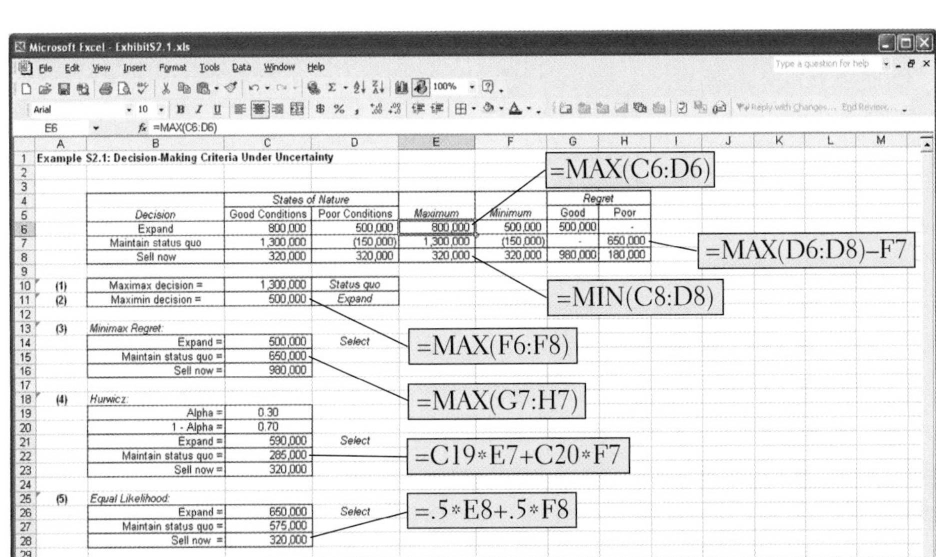

Microsoft Excel - ExhibitS2.1.xls

E6 =MAX(C6:D6)

Example S2.1: Decision-Making Criteria Under Uncertainty

| | Decision | States of Nature: Good Conditions | States of Nature: Poor Conditions | Maximum | Minimum | Regret: Good | Regret: Poor |
|---|---|---|---|---|---|---|---|
| | Expand | 800,000 | 500,000 | 800,000 | 500,000 | 500,000 | - |
| | Maintain status quo | 1,300,000 | (150,000) | 1,300,000 | (150,000) | - | 650,000 |
| | Sell now | 320,000 | 320,000 | 320,000 | 320,000 | 980,000 | 180,000 |
| (1) | Maximax decision = | 1,300,000 | *Status quo* | | | | |
| (2) | Maximin decision = | 500,000 | *Expand* | | | | |
| (3) | *Minimax Regret:* | | | | | | |
| | Expand = | 500,000 | *Select* | | | | |
| | Maintain status quo = | 650,000 | | | | | |
| | Sell now = | 980,000 | | | | | |
| (4) | *Hurwicz:* | | | | | | |
| | Alpha = | 0.30 | | | | | |
| | 1 - Alpha = | 0.70 | | | | | |
| | Expand = | 590,000 | *Select* | | | | |
| | Maintain status quo = | 285,000 | | | | | |
| | Sell now = | 320,000 | | | | | |
| (5) | *Equal Likelihood:* | | | | | | |
| | Expand = | 650,000 | *Select* | | | | |
| | Maintain status quo = | 575,000 | | | | | |
| | Sell now = | 320,000 | | | | | |



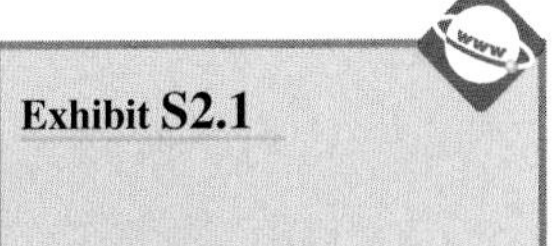

Exhibit S2.1

The Excel file for Exhibit S2.1 and the Excel files for all of the exhibits in the subsequent chapters in this text are contained on the text Web site. Students and instructors can download this file to see how the spreadsheet was constructed as well as the individual cell formulas. This spreadsheet can also be used as a guideline or template to solve the homework problems at the end of the chapter using Excel.

## DECISION MAKING WITH PROBABILITIES

Risk involves assigning probabilities to states of nature.

For the decision-making criteria we just used we assumed no available information regarding the probability of the states of nature. However, it is often possible for the decision maker to know enough about the future states of nature to assign probabilities that each will occur, which is decision making under conditions of *risk*. The most widely used decision-making criterion under risk is **expected value**, computed by multiplying each outcome by the probability of its occurrence and then summing these products according to the following formula:

**Expected value:** a weighted average of decision outcomes in which each future state of nature is assigned a probability of occurrence.

$$EV(x) = \sum_{i=1}^{n} p(x_i)x_i$$

where

$$x_i = \text{outcome } i$$
$$p(x_i) = \text{probability of outcome } i$$

**Example S2.2**
**Expected Value**

Assume that it is now possible for the Southern Textile Company to estimate a probability of 0.70 that good foreign competitive conditions will exist and a probability of 0.30 that poor conditions will exist in the future. Determine the best decision using expected value.

*Solution*

The expected values for each decision alternative are computed as follows.

$$\text{EV(expand)} = \$800{,}000(0.70) + 500{,}000(0.30) = \$710{,}000$$
$$\text{EV(status quo)} = 1{,}300{,}000(0.70) - 150{,}000(0.30) = 865{,}000 \quad \leftarrow \text{Maximum}$$
$$\text{EV(sell)} = 320{,}000(0.70) + 320{,}000(0.30) = 320{,}000$$

The decision according to this criterion is to maintain the status quo, since it has the highest expected value.

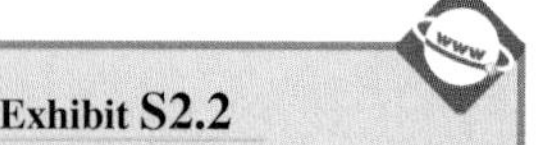

Exhibit S2.2

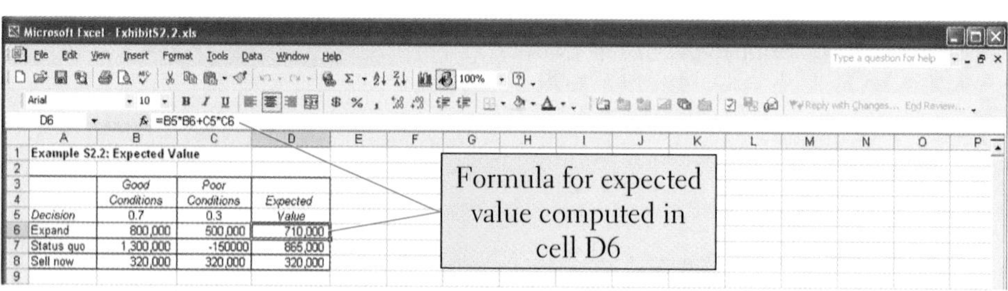


The Excel spreadsheet solution for Example S2.2 is shown in Exhibit S2.2. Note that the values contained in cells D6, D7, and D8 were computed using the expected value formulas embedded in these cells. For example, the formula for cell D6 is shown on the formula bar on the Excel screen.

## EXPECTED VALUE OF PERFECT INFORMATION

Occasionally, additional information is available, or can be purchased, regarding future events, enabling the decision maker to make a better decision. For example, a company could hire an economic forecaster to determine more accurately the economic conditions that will occur in the future. However, it would be foolish to pay more for this information than it stands to gain in extra profit from having the information. The information has some maximum value that is the limit of what the decision maker would be willing to spend. This value of information can be computed as an expected value—hence its name, the **expected value of perfect information (EVPI)**.

**Expected value of perfect information (EVPI):** the maximum value of perfect information to the decision maker.

To compute the expected value of perfect information, first look at the decisions under each state of nature. If information that assured us which state of nature was going to occur (i.e., perfect information) could be obtained, the best decision for that state of nature could be selected. For example, in the textile company example, if the company executives knew for sure that good competitive conditions would prevail, they would maintain the status quo. If they knew for sure that poor competitive conditions will occur, then they would expand.

The probabilities of each state of nature (i.e., 0.70 and 0.30) indicate that good competitive conditions will prevail 70% of the time and poor competitive conditions will prevail 30% of the time (if this decision situation is repeated many times). In other words, even though perfect information enables the investor to make the right decision, each state of nature will occur only a certain portion of the time. Thus, each of the decision outcomes obtained using perfect information must be weighted by its respective probability:

$$\$1{,}300{,}000(0.70) + (500{,}000)(0.30) = \$1{,}060{,}000$$

The amount of $1,060,000 is the expected value of the decision *given perfect information*, not the expected value of perfect information. The expected value of perfect information is the maximum amount that would be paid to gain information that would result in a decision better than the one made without perfect information. Recall from Example S2.2 that the expected-value decision without perfect information was to maintain the status quo and the expected value was $865,000.

The expected value of perfect information is computed by subtracting the expected value without perfect information from the expected value given perfect information:

$$\text{EVPI} = \text{expected value given perfect information} - \text{expected value without perfect information}$$

For our example, the EVPI is computed as

$$\text{EVPI} = \$1{,}060{,}000 - 865{,}000 = \$195{,}000$$

The expected value of perfect information, $195,000, is the maximum amount that the investor would pay to purchase perfect information from some other source, such as an economic forecaster. Of course, perfect information is rare and is usually unobtainable. Typically, the decision maker would be willing to pay some smaller amount, depending on how accurate (i.e., close to perfection) the information is believed to be.

## SEQUENTIAL DECISION TREES

**Sequential decision tree:** a graphical method for analyzing decision situations that require a sequence of decisions over time.

A payoff table is limited to a single decision situation. If a decision requires a series of decisions, a payoff table cannot be created, and a **sequential decision tree** must be used. We demonstrate the use of a decision tree in the following example.

**Example S2.3**

**A Sequential Decision Tree**

The Southern Textile Company is considering two alternatives: to expand its existing production operation to manufacture a new line of lightweight material; or to purchase land on which to construct a new facility in the future. Each of these decisions has outcomes based on product market growth in the future that result in another set of decisions (during a 10-year planning horizon), as shown in the following figure of a sequential decision tree. In this figure the square nodes represent decisions, and the circle nodes reflect different states of nature and their probabilities.

The first decision facing the company is whether to expand or buy land. If the company expands, two states of nature are possible. Either the market will grow (with a probability of 0.60) or it will not grow (with a probability of 0.40). Either state of nature will result in a payoff. On the other hand, if the company chooses to purchase land, three years in the future another decision will have to be made regarding the development of the land.

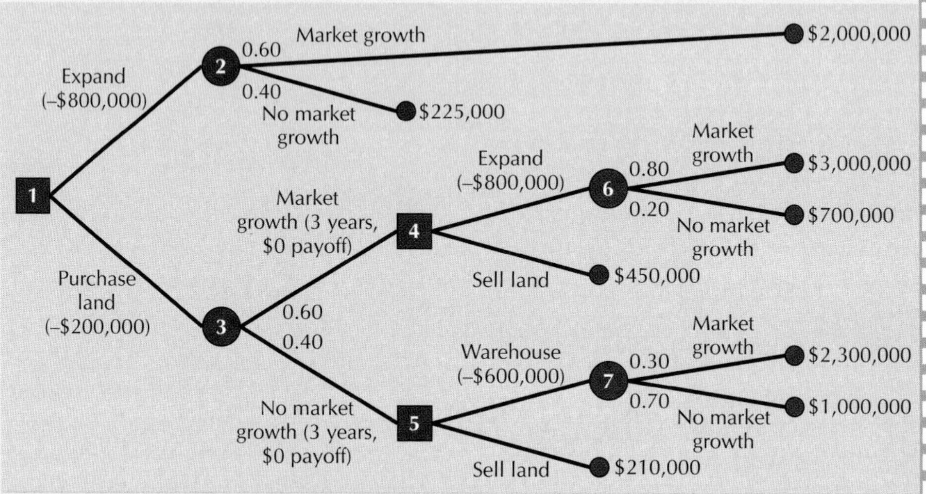


At decision node 1, the decision choices are to expand or to purchase land. Notice that the costs of the ventures ($800,000 and $200,000, respectively) are shown in parentheses. If the plant is expanded, two states of nature are possible at probability node 2: The market will grow, with a probability of 0.60, or it will not grow or will decline, with a probability of 0.40. If the market grows, the company will achieve a payoff of $2,000,000 over a 10-year period. However, if no growth occurs, a payoff of only $225,000 will result.

If the decision is to purchase land, two states of nature are possible at probability node 3. These two states of nature and their probabilities are identical to those at node 2; however, the payoffs are different. If market growth occurs for a three-year period, no payoff will occur, but the company will make another decision at node 4 regarding development of the land. At that point, either the plant will be expanded at a cost of $800,000 or the land will be sold, with a payoff of $450,000. The decision situation at node 4 can occur only if market growth occurs first. If no market growth occurs at node 3, there is no payoff, and another decision situation becomes necessary at node 5: A warehouse can be constructed at a cost of $600,000 or the land can be sold for $210,000. (Notice that the sale of the land results in less profit if there is no market growth than if there is growth.)

If the decision at decision node 4 is to expand, two states of nature are possible: The market may grow, with a probability of 0.80, or it may not grow, with a probability of 0.20. The probability of market growth is higher (and the probability of no growth is lower) than before because there has already been growth for the first three years, as shown by the branch from node 3 to node 4. The payoffs for these two states of nature at the end of the 10-year period are $3,000,000 and $700,000, respectively.

If the company decides to build a warehouse at node 5, two states of nature can occur: Market growth can occur, with a probability of 0.30 and an eventual payoff of $2,300,000, or no growth can occur, with a probability of 0.70 and a payoff of $1,000,000. The probability of market growth is low (i.e., 0.30) because there has already been no market growth, as shown by the branch from node 3 to node 5.

*Solution*

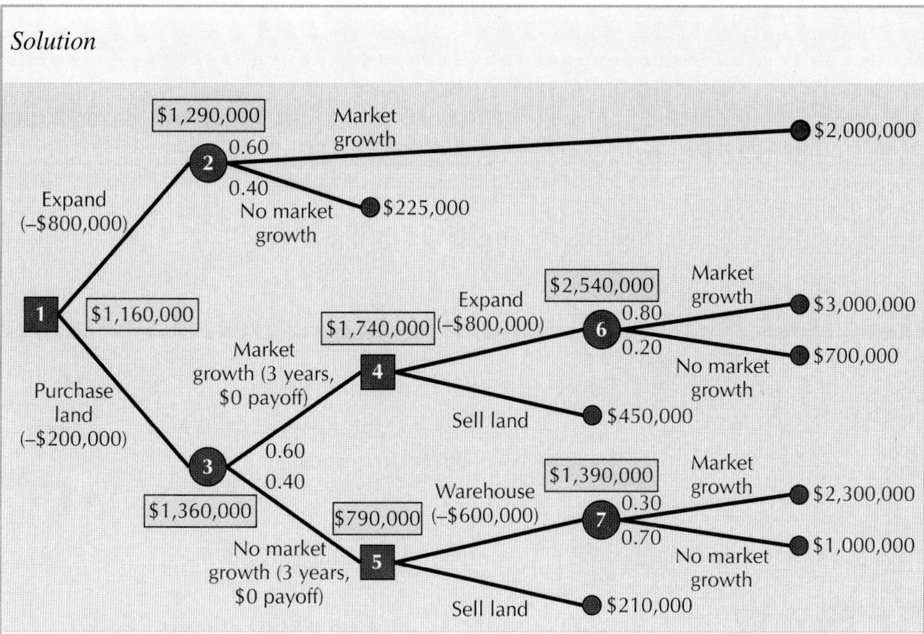


We start the decision analysis process at the end of the decision tree and work backward toward a decision at node 1.

First, we must compute the expected values at nodes 6 and 7:

$$\text{EV(node 6)} = 0.80(\$3{,}000{,}000) + 0.20(\$700{,}000) = \$2{,}540{,}000$$
$$\text{EV(node 7)} = 0.30(\$2{,}300{,}000) + 0.70(\$1{,}000{,}000) = \$1{,}390{,}000$$

These expected values (as well as all other nodal values) are shown in boxes in the figure.

At decision nodes 4 and 5, a decision must be made. As with a normal payoff table, the decision is made that results in the greatest expected value. At node 4 the choice is between two values: $1,740,000, the value derived by subtracting the cost of expanding ($800,000) from the expected payoff of $2,540,000, and $450,000, the expected value of selling the land computed with a probability of 1.0. The decision is to expand, and the value at node 4 is $1,740,000.

The same process is repeated at node 5. The decisions at node 5 result in payoffs of $790,000 (i.e., $1,390,000 − 600,000 = $790,000) and $210,000. Since the value $790,000 is higher, the decision is to build a warehouse.

Next, the expected values at nodes 2 and 3 are computed:

$$\text{EV(node 2)} = 0.60(\$2{,}000{,}000) + 0.40(\$225{,}000) = \$1{,}290{,}000$$
$$\text{EV(node 3)} = 0.60(\$1{,}740{,}000) + 0.40(\$790{,}000) = \$1{,}360{,}000$$

(Note that the expected value for node 3 is computed from the decision values previously determined at nodes 4 and 5.)

Now the final decision at node 1 must be made. As before, we select the decision with the greatest expected value after the cost of each decision is subtracted.

Expand: $1,290,000 − 800,000 = $490,000
Land: $1,360,000 − 200,000 = $1,160,000

Since the highest *net* expected value is $1,160,000, the decision is to purchase land, and the payoff of the decision is $1,160,000.

Decision trees allow the decision maker to see the logic of decision making by providing a picture of the decision process. Decision trees can be used for problems more complex than this example without too much difficulty.

## SUMMARY

In this supplement we have provided a general overview of decision analysis. To a limited extent, we have also shown that the logic of such operational decisions throughout the organization are interrelated to achieve strategic goals.

## SUMMARY OF KEY FORMULAS

*Expected Value*

$$EV(x) = \sum_{i=1}^{n} p(x_i)x_i$$

*Expected Value of Perfect Information*

EVPI = expected value given perfect information − expected value without perfect information

## SUMMARY OF KEY TERMS

**coefficient of optimism (α)** a measure of a decision maker's optimism, from 0 (completely pessimistic) to 1 (completely optimistic), used in the Hurwicz decision criterion.

**decision analysis** a set of quantitative decision-making techniques to aid the decision maker in dealing with decision situations in which uncertainty exists.

**equal likelihood (La Place) criterion** a decision criterion in which each state of nature is weighted equally.

**expected value** a weighted average of decision outcomes in which each future state of nature is assigned a probability of occurence.

**expected value of perfect information** the maximum value that a decision maker would be willing to pay for perfect information about future states of nature.

**Hurwicz criterion** a decision criterion in which the decision payoffs are weighted by a coefficient of optimism, α.

**maximax criterion** a decision criterion that results in the maximum of the maximum payoffs.

**maximin criterion** a decision criterion that results in the maximum of the minimum payoffs.

**minimax regret criterion** a decision criterion that results in the minimum of the maximum regrets for each alternative.

**payoff** the outcome of a decision.

**payoff table** a means of organizing and illustrating the payoffs from different decisions given various states of nature.

**sequential decision tree** a graphical method for analyzing decision situtations that require a sequence of decisions over time.

## SOLVED PROBLEM

Consider the following payoff table for three product decisions (A, B, and C) and three future market conditions (payoffs = $ millions).

| | MARKET CONDITIONS | | |
|---|---|---|---|
| DECISION | 1 | 2 | 3 |
| A | $1.0 | $2.0 | $0.5 |
| B | 0.8 | 1.2 | 0.9 |
| C | 0.7 | 0.9 | 1.7 |

• Animated Demo Problem

Determine the best decision using the following decision criteria.

1. Maximax
2. Maximin

### SOLUTION

*Step 1.* Maximax criterion

| | MAXIMUM PAYOFFS |
|---|---|
| A | $2.0 ←Maximum |
| B | 1.2 |
| C | 1.7 |

Decision: Product A

*Step 2.* Maximin criteria

| | MINIMUM PAYOFFS |
|---|---|
| A | 0.5 |
| B | 0.8 ←Maximum |
| C | 0.7 |

Decision: Product B

## PROBLEMS

**S2-1.** Telecomp is a U.S.-based manufacturer of cellular telephones. It is planning to build a new manufacturing and distribution facility in either South Korea, China, Taiwan, Poland, or Mexico. The cost of the facility will differ between countries and will even vary within countries depending on the economic and political climate, including monetary exchange rates. The company has estimated the facility cost (in $ millions) in each country under three different future economic/political climates as follows.

| | Economic/Political Climate | | |
|---|---|---|---|
| **Country** | *Decline* | *Same* | *Improve* |
| South Korea | 21.7 | 19.1 | 15.2 |
| China | 19.0 | 18.5 | 17.6 |
| Taiwan | 19.2 | 17.1 | 14.9 |
| Poland | 22.5 | 16.8 | 13.8 |
| Mexico | 25.0 | 21.2 | 12.5 |

Determine the best decision using the following decision criteria. (Note that since the payoff is cost, the maximax criteria becomes minimin and maximin becomes minimax.)

a. Minimin
b. Minimax
c. Hurwicz ($\alpha = 0.40$)
d. Equal likelihood

**S2-2.** A global economist hired by Telecomp, the U.S.-based computer manufacturer in Problem S2-1, estimates that the probability that the economic and political climate overseas and in Mexico will decline during the next five years is 0.30, the probability that it will remain approximately the same is 0.40, and the probability that it will improve is 0.30. Determine the best country to construct the new facility in and the expected value of perfect information.

**S2-3.** Landloc, a real estate development firm, is considering several alternative development projects. These include building and leasing an office building, purchasing a parcel of land and building a parking lot, buying and leasing a warehouse, building a shopping mall, and building and selling condominiums. The financial success of these projects depends on interest rate movement in the next five years. The various development projects and their five-year financial return ($ millions) given that interest rates will decline, remain stable, or increase are shown in the following payoff table.

| | Interest Rates | | |
|---|---|---|---|
| **Project** | *Decline* | *Stable* | *Increase* |
| Office building | 0.5 | 1.7 | 4.5 |
| Parking lot | 1.5 | 1.9 | 2.4 |
| Warehouse | 1.7 | 1.4 | 1.0 |
| Shopping mall | 0.7 | 2.4 | 3.6 |
| Condominiums | 3.2 | 1.5 | 0.6 |

Determine the best investment using the following decision criteria.

a. Maximax
b. Maximin
c. Equal likelihood
d. Hurwicz ($\alpha = 0.3$)

**S2-4.** In Problem S2-3 the Landloc real estate development firm has hired an economist to assign a probability to each direction interest rates may take over the next five years. The economist has determined that there is a 0.50 probability that interest rates will decline, a 0.40 probability that rates will remain stable, and a 0.10 probability that rates will increase.

a. Using expected value, determine the best project.
b. Determine the expected value of perfect information.

**S2-5.** Nicole Nelson has come into an inheritance from her grandparents. She is attempting to decide among several investment alternatives. The return after one year is dependent primarily on the interest rate during the next year. The rate is currently 7%, and she anticipates it will stay the same or go up or down by at most 2 points. The various investment alternatives plus their returns ($10,000s) given the interest rate changes are shown in the following table.

| | Interest Rates | | | | |
|---|---|---|---|---|---|
| **Investments** | *5%* | *6%* | *7%* | *8%* | *9%* |
| Money market fund | 1.7 | 2.8 | 3.0 | 3.6 | 4.5 |
| Stock growth fund | −5 | −3 | 3.5 | 5 | 7.5 |
| Bond fund | 5 | 4 | 3.5 | 3 | 2 |
| Government fund | 4 | 3.6 | 3.2 | 2.8 | 2.1 |
| Risk fund | −12 | −7 | 4.2 | 9.3 | 16.7 |
| Savings bonds | 3 | 3 | 3.2 | 3.4 | 3.5 |

Determine the best investment using the following decision criteria.

a. Maximax
b. Maximin
c. Equal likelihood
d. Assume that Nicole, with the help of a financial newsletter and some library research, has been able to assign probabilities to each of the possible interest rates during the next year as follows:

| Interest Rate | 5% | 6% | 7% | 8% | 9% |
|---|---|---|---|---|---|
| Probability | 0.1 | 0.2 | 0.4 | 0.2 | 0.1 |

Using expected value, determine her best investment decision.

**S2-6.** The Tech football coaching staff has six basic plays it runs every game. Tech has an upcoming game against State on Saturday, and the coaches know State employs five different defenses. The coaches have estimated the number of yards Tech will gain with each play against each defense, as shown in the following payoff table.

| | Defense | | | | |
|---|---|---|---|---|---|
| **Play** | *54* | *63* | *Wide Tackle* | *Nickel* | *Blitz* |
| Off tackle | 2 | −2 | 6 | 8 | −2 |
| Option | 3 | 7 | −1 | 10 | 16 |
| Toss Sweep | 5 | 14 | −5 | 6 | 12 |
| Draw | −2 | −3 | 2 | 8 | 7 |
| Pass | 10 | 20 | 12 | −7 | −6 |
| Screen | −5 | −3 | 8 | 7 | 16 |

a. If the coaches employ an offensive game plan, they will use the maximax criterion. What will their best play be?
b. If the coaches employ a defensive plan, they will use the maximin criterion. What will their best play be?
c. What will their best play be if State is equally likely to use any of its defenses?
d. The Tech coaches have reviewed game films and have determined the following probabilities that State will use each of its defenses.

| Defense | 54 | 63 | Wide Tackle | Nickel | Blitz |
|---|---|---|---|---|---|
| Probability | 0.40 | 0.10 | 0.20 | 0.20 | 0.10 |

Using expected value, rank Tech's plays from best to worst. During the actual game, Tech has a third down and 10 yards to go and the coaches are 60% certain State will blitz, with a 10% chance of any of the other four defenses. What play should Tech run, and is it likely Tech will make the first down?

**S2-7.** The Dynamax Company is going to introduce one of three new products: a widget, a hummer, or a nimnot. The market conditions (favorable, stable, or unfavorable) will determine the profit or loss the company realizes, as shown in the following payoff table.

| | Market Conditions | | |
|---|---|---|---|
| | *Favorable* | *Stable* | *Unfavorable* |
| **Product** | *0.2* | *0.5* | *0.3* |
| Widget | $160,000 | $90,000 | −$50,000 |
| Hummer | 70,000 | 40,000 | 20,000 |
| Nimnot | 45,000 | 35,000 | 30,000 |

a. Compute the expected value for each decision and select the best one.
b. Determine how much the firm would be willing to pay to a market research firm to gain better information about future market conditions.
c. Assume that probabilities cannot be assigned to future market conditions, and determine the best decision using the maximax, maximin, minimax regret, and equal likelihood criteria.

**S2-8.** The Midtown Market purchases apples from a local grower. The apples are purchased on Monday at $2.00 per pound, and the market sells them for $3.00 per pound. Any apples left over at the end of the week are sold to a local zoo for $0.50 per pound. The possible demands for apples and the probability for each are as follows.

| Demand (lb) | Probability |
|---|---|
| 20 | 0.10 |
| 21 | 0.20 |
| 22 | 0.30 |
| 23 | 0.30 |
| 24 | 0.10 |
| | 1.00 |

a. The market must decide how many apples to order in a week. Construct a payoff table for this decision situation and determine the amount of apples that should be ordered using expected value.
b. Assuming that probabilities cannot be assigned to the demand values, what would the best decision be using the maximax and maximin criteria?

**S2-9.** The manager of the greeting card section of Harvey's department store is considering her order for a particular line of holiday cards. The cost of each box of cards is $3; each box will be sold for $5 during the holiday season. After the holiday season, the cards will be sold for $2 a box. The card section manager believes that all leftover cards can be sold at that price. The estimated demand during the holiday season for the cards, with associated probabilities, is as follows:

| Demand (boxes) | Probability |
|---|---|
| 25 | 0.10 |
| 26 | 0.15 |
| 27 | 0.30 |
| 28 | 0.20 |
| 29 | 0.15 |
| 30 | 0.10 |

a. Develop the payoff table for this decision situation and compute the expected value for each alternative and identify the best decision.
b. Compute the expected value of perfect information.

**S2-10.** Assume that the probabilities of demand in Problem S2-9 are no longer valid; the decision situation is now one without probabilities. Determine the best number of cards to stock using the following decision criteria.
a. Maximin
b. Maximax
c. Hurwicz ($\alpha = 0.4$)
d. Minimax regret

**S2-11.** A machine shop owner is attempting to decide whether to purchase a new drill press, a lathe, or a grinder. The return from each will be determined by whether the company succeeds in getting a government military contract. The profit or loss from each purchase and the probabilities associated with each contract outcome are shown in the following payoff table. Compute the expected value for each purchase and select the best one.

| | Contract | No Contract |
|---|---|---|
| **Purchase** | **0.40** | **0.60** |
| Drill press | $40,000 | $−8,000 |
| Lathe | 20,000 | 4,000 |
| Grinder | 12,000 | 10,000 |

**S2-12.** The Extron Oil Company is considering making a bid for a shale oil development contract to be awarded by the federal government. The company has decided to bid $110 million. The company estimates that it has a 60% chance of winning the contract with this bid. If the firm wins the contract, it can choose one of three methods for getting the oil from the shale: It can develop a new method for oil extraction, use an existing (inefficient) process, or subcontract the processing out to a number of smaller companies once the shale has been excavated. The results from these alternatives are given as follows.

| Develop New Process | | |
|---|---|---|
| *Outcomes* | *Probability* | *Profit (millions)* |
| Great success | 0.30 | $600 |
| Moderate success | 0.60 | 300 |
| Failure | 0.10 | −100 |

| Use Present Process | | |
|---|---|---|
| *Outcomes* | *Probability* | *Profit (millions)* |
| Great success | 0.50 | $300 |
| Moderate success | 0.30 | 200 |
| Failure | 0.20 | −40 |

| Subcontract | | |
|---|---|---|
| *Outcomes* | *Probability* | *Profit (millions)* |
| Moderate success | 1.00 | $250 |

The cost of preparing the contract proposal is $2,000,000. If the company does not make a bid, it will invest in an alternative venture with a guaranteed profit of $30 million. Construct a sequential decision tree for this decision situation and determine whether the company should make a bid.

**S2-13.** The New England Bombers professional basketball team just missed making the playoffs last season and believes it only needs to sign one very good free agent to make the playoffs next season. The team is considering four players: Jamelle Morris, Rayneal O'Neal, Marvin Jackson, and Michael Gordon. Each player differs according to position, ability, and attractiveness to fans. The payoffs (in $ millions) to the team for each player based on their contract, profits from attendance, and team product sales for several different seasonal outcomes are provided in the following table.

| | Season Outcome | | |
|---|---|---|---|
| **Player** | *Loser* | *Competitive* | *Playoffs* |
| Morris | $−3.2 | $1.3 | $4.4 |
| O'Neal | −5.1 | 1.8 | 6.3 |
| Jackson | −2.7 | 0.7 | 5.8 |
| Gordon | −6.3 | −1.6 | 9.6 |

Determine the best decision using the following decision criteria.

a. Maximax
b. Maximin
c. Hurwicz ($\alpha = .25$)
d. Equal likelihood
e. The Bombers' management has determined the following probabilities of the occurrence of each future seasonal outcome for each player.

| | Probability | | |
|---|---|---|---|
| **Player** | *Loser* | *Competitive* | *Playoffs* |
| Morris | 0.15 | 0.55 | 0.30 |
| O'Neal | 0.18 | 0.26 | 0.56 |
| Jackson | 0.21 | 0.32 | 0.47 |
| Gordon | 0.30 | 0.25 | 0.45 |

Compute the expected value for each player and indicate which player the team should try to sign.

**S2-14.** Alex Mason has a wide-curving, uphill driveway leading to his garage. When there is a heavy snow, Alex hires a local carpenter, who shovels snow on the side in the winter, to shovel his driveway. The snow shoveler charges $30 to shovel the driveway. Following is a probability distribution of the number of heavy snows each winter.

| Heavy Snows | Probability |
|---|---|
| 1 | 0.12 |
| 2 | 0.19 |
| 3 | 0.24 |
| 4 | 0.22 |
| 5 | 0.13 |
| 6 | 0.08 |
| 7 | 0.02 |
| | 1.00 |

Alex is considering the purchase of a new self-propelled snowblower for $575 that would allow him, his wife, or his children to clear the driveway after a snow. Discuss what you think Alex's decision should be and why.

**S2-15.** The management of State Union Bank was concerned about the potential loss that might occur in the event of a physical catastrophe such as a power failure or a fire. The bank estimated that the loss from one of these incidents could be as much as $100 million, including losses due to interrupted service and customer relations. One project the bank is considering is the installation of an emergency power generator at its operations headquarters. The cost of the emergency generator is $900,000, and if it is installed no losses from this type of incident will be incurred. However, if the generator is not installed, there is a 10% chance that a power outage will occur during the next year. If there is an outage, there is a 0.04 probability that the resulting losses will be very large, or approximately $90 million in lost earnings. Alternatively, it is estimated that there is a 0.96 probability of only slight losses of around $2 million. Using decision tree analysis, determine whether the bank should install the new power generator.

**S2-16.** Alleghany Mountain Power and Light is an electric utility company with a large fleet of vehicles including automobiles, light trucks, and construction equipment. The company is evaluating four alternative strategies for maintaining its vehicles at the lowest cost, including (1) take no preventive maintenance at all and repair vehicle components when they fail; (2) take oil samples at regular intervals and perform whatever preventive maintenance is indicated by the oil analysis; (3) change the vehicle oil on a regular basis and perform repairs when needed; and (4) change the oil at regular intervals and take oil samples regularly, performing maintenance repairs as indicated by the sample analysis.

For autos and light trucks, strategy 1 (no preventive maintenance) costs nothing to implement and results in two possible outcomes: There is a .08 probability that a defective component will occur requiring emergency maintenance at a cost of $1,600, or there is .92 probability that no defects will occur and no maintenance will be necessary.

Strategy 2 (take oil samples) costs $40 to implement (i.e., take a sample), and there is a .08 probability that there will be a defective part and 0.92 probability that there will not be a defect. If there is actually a defective part, there is a 0.70 probability the sample will correctly identify it, resulting in preventive maintenance at a cost of $500. However, there is a 0.30 probability that the sample will not identify the defect and indicate everything is okay, resulting in emergency maintenance later at a cost of $1,600. On the other hand, if there are actually no defects, there is a 0.20 probability that the sample will erroneously indicate that there is a defect, resulting in unnecessary maintenance at a cost of $250. There is a 0.80 probability that the sample will correctly indicate there are no defects, resulting in no maintenance and no costs.

Strategy 3 (changing the oil regularly) costs $34.80 to implement and has two outcomes: a 0.04 probability of a defective component, which will require emergency maintenance at a cost of $1,600, and a 0.96 probability that no defects will occur, resulting in no maintenance and no cost.

Strategy 4 (changing the oil and sampling) costs $54.80 to implement and results in the same probabilities of defects and no defects as strategy 3. If there is a defective component, there is a 0.70 probability that the sample will detect it and $500 in preventive maintenance costs will be incurred. Alternatively, there is a 0.30 probability that the sample will not detect the defect, resulting in emergency maintenance at a cost of $1,600. If there is no defect, there is a 0.20 probability the sample will indicate there is a defect, resulting in an unnecessary maintenance cost of $250, and a 0.80 probability that the sample will correctly indicate no defects, resulting in no cost.

Develop a decision strategy for Blue Ridge Power and Light and indicate the expected value of this strategy.[1]

**S2-17.** In Problem S2-16, the decision analysis is for automobiles and light trucks. Alleghany Mountain Power and Light would like to reformulate the problem for its heavy construction equipment. Emergency maintenance is much more expensive for heavy equipment, costing $15,000. Required preventive maintenance costs $2000 and unnecessary maintenance costs $1200. The cost of an oil change is $200 and the cost of taking an oil sample and analyzing it is $50. All the probabilities remain the same. Determine the strategy the company should use for its heavy equipment.

**S2-18.** Tech is playing State in the last conference game of the season. Tech is trailing State 21 to 14 with 7 seconds left in the game, when they score a touchdown. Still trailing 21 to 20, Tech can either go for two points and win or go for one point to send the game into overtime. The conference championship will be determined by the outcome of this game. If Tech wins they will go to the Sugar Bowl, with a payoff of $9.2 million; if they lose they will go to the Gator Bowl, with a payoff of $1.5 million. If Tech goes for two points there is a .30% chance they will be successful and win (and a .70% chance they will fail and lose). If they go for one point there is a 0.98 probability of success and a tie and a 0.02 probability of failure. If they tie they will play overtime, in which Tech believes they have only a 20% chance of winning because of fatigue.

a. Use decision-tree analysis to determine if Tech should go for one point or two points.
b. What would Tech's probability of winning the game in overtime have to be to make Tech indifferent between going for one point or two points?

**S2-19.** Mary Decker is thinking of suing the manufacturer of her car because of a defect that she believes caused her to have an accident, and kept her out of work for a year. She is suing the company for $3.5 million. The company has offered him a settlement of $700,000, of which Mary would receive $600,000 after attorneys' fees. Her attorney has advised her that she has a 50% chance of winning her case. If she loses she will incur attorneys' fees and court costs of $75,000. If she wins she is not guaranteed of her full requested settlement. Her attorney believes that there is a 50% chance she could receive the full settlement, in which case Mary would get $2 million after her attorney takes his cut, and a 50% chance that the jury will award her a lesser amount of $1,000,000, of which Mary would get $500,000.

Using decision-tree analysis, decide if Mary should sue the manufacturer.

**S2-20.** State University has three health-care plans for its faculty and staff to choose from, as follows.

Plan 1—monthly cost of $32 with a $500 deductible; the participants pay the first $500 of medical payments for the year, the insurer pays 90% of all remaining expenses.

Plan 2—monthly cost of $5 but a deductible of $1200, with the insurer paying 90% of medical expenses after the insured pays the first $1200 in a year.

Plan 3—monthly cost of $24 with no deductible, the participants pay 30% of all expenses with the remainder paid by the insurer.

Tracy McCoy, an administrative assistant in the Management department, estimates that her annual medical expenses are defined by the following probability distribution.

| Annual Medical Expenses | Probability |
|---|---|
| $100 | 0.15 |
| 500 | 0.30 |
| 1,500 | 0.35 |
| 3,000 | 0.10 |
| 5,000 | 0.05 |
| 10,000 | 0.05 |

Determine which medical plan Tracy should select.

**S2-21.** The Orchard Wine Company purchases grapes from one of two nearby growers each season to produce a particular red wine. It purchases enough grapes to produce 3000 bottles of the wine. Each grower supplies a certain portion of poor-quality grapes that will result in a percentage of bottles being used as fillers for cheaper table wines according to the following probability distribution.

[1]This problem is based on J. Mellichamp, D. Miller, and O-J. Kwon, "The Southern Company Uses a Probability Model for Cost Justification of Oil Sample Analysis," *Interfaces* 23(3; May–June 1993), pp. 118–124.

| Percentage Defective | Probability of % Defective | |
|---|---|---|
| | Grower A | Grower B |
| 2 | 0.12 | 0.26 |
| 4 | 0.21 | 0.34 |
| 6 | 0.26 | 0.22 |
| 8 | 0.31 | 0.10 |
| 10 | 0.10 | 0.08 |

The two growers charge a different price for their grapes and because of differences in taste, the company charges different prices for their wine depending on which grapes they use. The annual profit from the wine produced from each grower's grapes for each percentage defective is as follows.

| Defective | Profit | |
|---|---|---|
| | Grower A | Grower B |
| 2% | $44,200 | $42,600 |
| 4 | 40,200 | 40,300 |
| 6 | 36,200 | 38,000 |
| 8 | 32,200 | 35,700 |
| 10 | 28,200 | 33,400 |

Use decision-tree analysis to determine from which grower the company should purchase grapes.

**S2-22.** Huntz Food Products is attempting to decide if it should introduce a new line of salad dressings called Special Choices. The company can test market the salad dressings in selected geographic areas or bypass the test market and introduce the product nationally. The cost of the test market is $150,000. If the company conducts the test market, it must wait to see the results before deciding whether or not to introduce the salad dressings nationally. The probability of a positive test market result is estimated to be 0.6. Alternatively, the company cannot conduct the test market and make the decision to introduce the dressings or not. If the salad dressings are introduced nationally and are a success, the company estimates it will realize an annual profit of $1,600,000 while if the dressings fail it will incur a loss of $700,000. The company believes the probability of success for the salad dressings is 0.50 if it is introduced without the test market. If the company does conduct the test market and it is positive, the probability of successfully introducing the salad dressings increases to 0.8. If the test market is negative and the company introduces the salad dressings anyway, the probability of success drops to 0.30.

Using decision-tree analysis, determine if the company should conduct the test market.

## CASE PROBLEM S2.1

### *Transformer Replacement at Mountain States Electric Service*

Mountain States Electric Service is an electrical utility company serving several states in the Rocky Mountain region. It is considering replacing some of its equipment at a generating substation and is attempting to decide whether it should replace an older, existing PCB transformer. (PCB is a toxic chemical known formally as polychlorinated biphenyl.) Even though the PCB generator meets all current regulations, if an incident occurred, such as a fire, and PCB contamination caused harm either to neighboring businesses or farms or to the environment, the company would be liable for damages. Recent court cases have shown that simply meeting utility regulations does not relieve a utility of liability if an incident causes harm to others. Also, courts have been awarding large damages to individuals and businesses harmed by hazardous incidents.

If the utility replaces the PCB transformer, no PCB incidents will occur, and the only cost will be that of the transformer, $85,000. Alternatively, if the company decides to keep the existing PCB transformer, then management estimates there is a 50–50 chance of there being a high likelihood of an incident or a low likelihood of an incident. For the case in which there is a high likelihood that an incident will occur, there is a 0.004 probability that a fire will occur sometime during the remaining life of the transformer and a 0.996 probability that no fire will occur. If a fire occurs, there is a 0.20 probability that it will be bad and the utility will incur a very high cost of approximately $90 million for the cleanup, whereas there is a 0.80 probability that the fire will be minor and a cleanup can be accomplished at a low cost of approximately $8 million. If no fire occurs, then no cleanup costs will occur. For the case in which there is a low likelihood of an incident occurring, there is a 0.001 probability that a fire will occur during the life of the existing transformer and a 0.999 probability that a fire will not occur. If a fire does occur, then the same probabilities exist for the incidence of high and low cleanup costs, as well as the same cleanup costs, as indicated for the previous case. Similarly, if no fire occurs, there is no cleanup cost.

Perform a decision-tree analysis of this problem for Mountain States Electric Service and indicate the recommended solution. Is this the decision you believe the company should make? Explain your reasons.

*Source:* This case was adapted from W. Balson, J. Welsh, and D. Wilson, "Using Decision Analysis and Risk Analysis to Manage Utility Environmental Risk," *Interfaces* 22(6; November–December 1992), pp. 126–139.

## CASE PROBLEM S2.2

### *Evaluating Projects at Nexcom Systems*

Nexcom Systems develops information technology systems for commercial sale. Each year it considers and evaluates a number of different projects to undertake. It develops a road map for each project in the form of a decision tree that identifies the different decision points in the development process from the initial decision to invest in a project's development through the actual commercialization of the final product.

The first decision point in the development process is whether or not to fund a proposed project for one year. If the decision is no, then there is no resulting cost; if the decision is yes, then the project proceeds at an incremental cost to the company. The company establishes specific short-term, early technical milestones for its projects after one year. If the early milestones are achieved, the project proceeds to the next phase of project development; if the milestones are not achieved, the project is abandoned. In its planning process, the company develops probability estimates of achieving and not achieving the early milestones. If the early milestones are achieved, then the project is funded for further development during an extended time frame specific to a project. At the end of this time frame, a project is evaluated according to a second set of (later) technical milestones. Again the company attaches probability estimates for achieving and not achieving these later milestones. If the late milestones are not achieved, the project is abandoned.

If the late milestones are achieved, this means that technical uncertainties and problems have been overcome and the company next assesses the project's ability to meet its strategic business objectives. At this stage the company wants to know if the eventual product coincides with the company's competencies, and if there appears to be an eventual, clear market for the product. It invests in a product "prelaunch" to ascertain the answers to these questions. The outcomes of the prelaunch are that either there is a strategic fit or there is not, and the company assigns probability estimates to each of these two possible outcomes. If there is not a strategic fit at this point, the project is abandoned and the company loses its investment in the prelaunch process. If it is determined that there is a strategic fit, than three possible decisions result. (1) The company can invest in the product's launch and a successful or unsuccessful outcome will result, each with an estimated probability of occurrence. (2) The company can delay the product's launch and at a later date decide whether to launch or abandon. (3) If it launches later, then the outcomes are success or failure, each with an esti-

| | Project | | | | |
|---|---|---|---|---|---|
| **Decision Outcomes/Event** | *1* | *2* | *3* | *4* | *5* |
| Fund—1 year | $200,000 | 380,000 | 270,000 | 230,000 | 400,000 |
| *P*(Early milestones—yes) | 0.72 | 0.64 | 0.84 | 0.56 | 0.77 |
| *P*(Early milestones—no) | 0.28 | 0.36 | 0.16 | 0.44 | 0.23 |
| Long-term funding | $690,000 | 730,000 | 430,000 | 270,000 | 350,000 |
| *P*(Late milestones—yes) | 0.60 | 0.56 | 0.65 | 0.70 | 0.72 |
| *P*(Late milestones—no) | 0.40 | 0.44 | 0.35 | 0.30 | 0.28 |
| Prelaunch funding | $315,000 | 420,000 | 390,000 | 410,000 | 270,000 |
| *P*(Strategic fit—yes) | 0.80 | 0.75 | 0.83 | 0.67 | 0.65 |
| *P*(Strategic fit—no) | 0.20 | 0.25 | 0.17 | 0.33 | 0.35 |
| *P*(Invest—success) | 0.60 | 0.65 | 0.70 | 0.75 | 0.83 |
| *P*(Invest—failure) | 0.40 | 0.35 | 0.30 | 0.25 | 0.17 |
| *P*(Delay—success) | 0.80 | 0.70 | 0.65 | 0.80 | 0.85 |
| *P*(Delay—failure) | 0.20 | 0.30 | 0.35 | 0.20 | 0.15 |
| Invest—success | $7,300,000 | 8,200,000 | 4,700,000 | 5,200,000 | 3,800,000 |
| Invest—failure | −2,000,000 | −3,500,000 | −1,500,000 | −2,100,000 | −900,000 |
| Delay—success | 4,500,000 | 6,000,000 | 3,300,000 | 2,500,000 | 2,700,000 |
| Delay—failure | −1,300,000 | −4,000,000 | −800,000 | −1,100,000 | −900,000 |

mated probability of occurrence. Also, if the product launch is delayed, there is always a likelihood that the technology will become obsolete or dated in the near future, which tends to reduce the expected return.

The table on the preceding page provides the various costs, event probabilities, and investment outcomes for five projects the company is considering.

Determine the expected value for each project and then rank the projects accordingly for the company to consider.

*Source:* This case was adapted from R. K. Perdue, W. J. McAllister, P. V. King, and B. G. Berkey, "Valuation of R and D projects Using Options Pricing and Decision Analysis Models," *Interfaces* 29, (6; November–December 1999), pp. 57–74.

## REFERENCES

Holloway, C. A. *Decision Making under Uncertainty*. Englewood Cliffs, NJ: Prentice Hall, 1979.

Howard, R. A. "An Assessment of Decision Analysis." *Operations Research* 28(1; January–February 1980), pp. 4–27.

Keeney, R. L. "Decision Analysis: An Overview." *Operations Research* 30(5; September–October 1982), pp. 803–838.

Luce, R. D., and H. Raiffa. *Games and Decisions*. New York: John Wiley, 1957.

Von Neumann, J., and O. Morgenstern. *Theory of Games and Economic Behavior*, 3rd ed. Princeton, NJ: Princeton University Press, 1953.

Williams, J. D. *The Complete Strategist*, rev. ed. New York: McGraw-Hill, 1966.

# Quality Management

CHAPTER 3

Web resources for this chapter include

- Internet Exercises
- Online Practice Quizzes
- Virtual Tours
- Excel Worksheets
- Company and Resource Weblinks
- Animated Demo Problems
- Microsoft Project Exhibits

www.wiley.com/college/russell

## CHAPTER OUTLINE

In this chapter you will learn about . . .

- The Meaning of Quality
- Total Quality Management
- Quality Improvement and the Role of Employees
- Strategic Implications of TQM
- Six Sigma
- TQM in Service Companies
- The Cost of Quality
- The Effect of Quality Management on Productivity
- Identifying Quality Problems and Causes
- Quality Awards and Setting Quality Standards
- ISO 9000

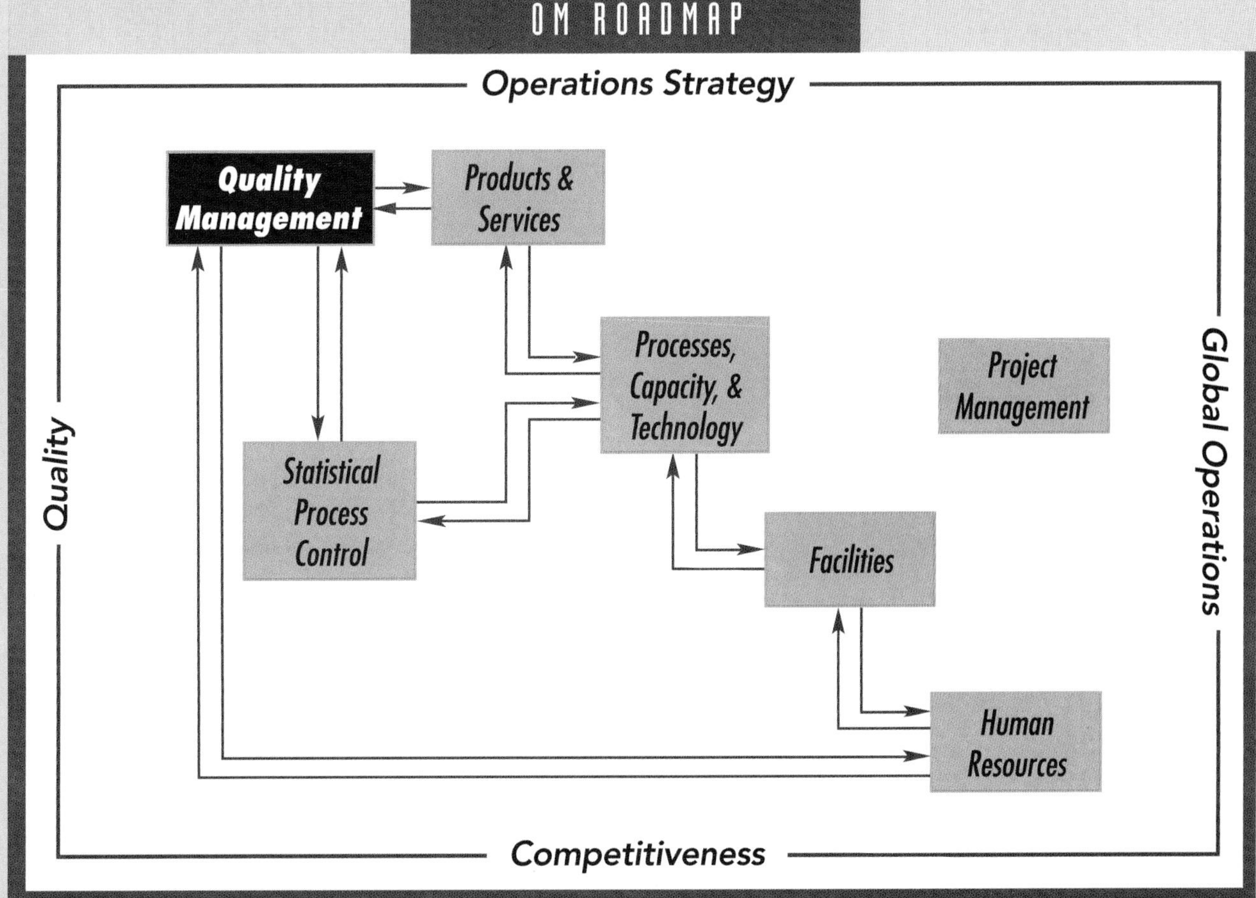

## MOTOROLA'S SIX SIGMA QUALITY

Motorola began in the late 1920s as a small manufacturer of car radios (hence the name ***Motorola***). It has grown to a corporation with more than 132,000 employees at 50 factories around the world, manufacturing such products as semiconductors, integrated circuits, paging systems, cellular telephones, computers, and satellite communications systems.

Motorola was an engineering-oriented company that focused on product development to create new markets. In the mid-1970s it changed its focus from products to customers, with an objective of total customer satisfaction. Motorola is now recognized as having one of the best quality management programs in the world. In 1988 it was among the first group of winners of the prestigious Malcolm Baldrige National Quality Award.

In 1987 Motorola announced its goal of "six sigma" quality. Six sigma quality is a statistical measure that equates to only 3.4 defects per million customer "opportunities" (in services and products), or nearly perfect quality. This goal effectively changed the focus of quality in the United States, where quality levels had traditionally been measured in terms of percentages or parts per hundred.

Motorola's six sigma has since become a benchmark standard that many other companies have adopted. Six sigma has become a recognized quality program based on the goal of virtually perfect quality. General Electric, Ford Motor Company, Johnson Controls, Xerox, Bank of America, and Honeywell are just a few of the companies that have adopted six sigma as the basis for their approaches to quality. Allied Signals (now Honeywell) has attributed savings of $1.5 billion to its six sigma program, and General Electric credits savings of $2 billion as a result of its six sigma program. Motorola estimates its savings at many billions, since it first adopted six sigma as its goal.

The companies that have adopted six sigma see it as the basis for a "best-in-class" philosophy and a long-term business strategy that measures quality improvement. The

*Motorola's six sigma symbol represents its commitment to producing quality products and customer satisfaction. Technically, six sigma performance is a level of statistical variation in product quality that translates to only a little over three defects for every million parts produced, or virtually no defects. Its goal of six sigma performance enabled Motorola, Inc., to be among the first U.S. companies to receive the coveted Malcolm Baldrige National Quality Award from the U.S. Department of Commerce. A quality management program based on the six sigma approach has been adopted by numerous companies that hope to survive in today's highly competitive global business environment.*

fundamental objective of six sigma is to focus on improvement and variance reduction in every process and transaction within a company. In this way, waste and cost are driven out as quality improves, and customer satisfaction and loyalty, and thus profits, are increased through the continuous improvement of quality.

*Source:* Motorola Web site, http://www.motorola.com.

We emphasize quality throughout this book in the context of all operational processes. In today's global business environment, quality cannot be underestimated or overlooked by any firm, regardless of its size or assets. Business leaders and CEOs cite quality as the most important strategic factor in the long-term profitability and success of their firms.

Why has quality become so important to businesses and consumers around the world? After World War II, when the consumption of goods and services expanded dramatically in the United States, quality was not a big concern to consumers or producers. Consumers purchasing U.S. goods and services assumed they were getting the best products available; that they were of good quality was accepted without question. "Made in Japan" stamped on inferior Japanese products was a term of derision. This began to change during the 1970s due mainly to foreign competition, especially from Japan, in markets for manufactured goods and electronic products. Consumers began to have more choices and more information to help them make these choices. This resulted in higher expectations for products and services. Consumers found that they could demand—and expect to receive—high-quality products that were reliable and priced affordably and competitively. In this new environment of increased competition from foreign companies, quality not only allows for product discrimination, it also has become a marketing weapon.

**Globalization and foreign competition began to change the business environment in the 1970s.**

Quality was not the sole reason for the initial Japanese success in the U.S. market. High-quality products from foreign firms such as Rolls Royce and Mercedes Benz automobiles and Hasselblad cameras had been available in the United States for years but had not altered consumers' preferences or perceptions. However, these products were expensive; Japanese products were not. The Japanese were uniquely able to establish the concept of *value*—the combination of price plus quality—and change their product-design philosophy such that the cost of achieving better quality was not prohibitive.

The Japanese achieved enhanced product quality by adapting many of the principles of quality management originally developed in the United States, combined with their own quality-focused management philosophies. As a competitive reaction, American firms focused attention on quality as possibly the most important factor in their long-term profitability and survival. They have learned what the Japanese discovered before them; that the things that must be done to improve quality will also make the company as a whole more efficient and productive, and thus more profitable. American firms in general, as well as companies from around the world, now rival, and sometimes exceed, Japanese companies in their commitment to, and achievement of, product and service quality.

**The key to foreign competition—producing quality products at competitive prices.**

## THE MEANING OF QUALITY

Asked "What is quality?" one of our students replied "getting what you pay for." Another student added that to her, quality was "getting *more* than you paid for!" The *Oxford American Dictionary* defines quality as "a degree or level of excellence." The "official" definition of quality by the American National Standards Institute (ANSI) and the American Society for Quality (ASQ) is "the totality of features and characteristics of a product or service that bears on its ability to satisfy given needs." Obviously quality can be defined in many ways, depending on who is defining it and to what product or service it is

**What is quality in the eye of the beholder?**

related. In this section we attempt to gain a perspective on what quality means to consumers and different people within a business organization.

## QUALITY FROM THE CONSUMER'S PERSPECTIVE

A business organization produces goods and services to meet its customers' needs. Quality has become a major factor in a customer's choice of products and service. Customers know that certain companies produce better-quality products than others, and they buy accordingly. That means a firm must consider how the consumer defines quality. The consumer can be a manufacturer purchasing raw materials or parts, a store owner or retailer purchasing products to sell, or someone who purchases retail products or services over the Internet. W. Edwards Deming, author and consultant on quality, says that "The consumer is the most important part of the production line. Quality should be aimed at the needs of the consumer, present and future." From this perspective, product and service quality is determined by what the consumer wants and is willing to pay for. Since consumers have different product needs, they will have different quality expectations. This results in a commonly used definition of quality as a service's or product's *fitness for its intended use*, or **fitness for use**; how well does it do what the consumer or user thinks it is supposed to do and wants it to do?

**Fitness for use:** is how well the product or service does what it is supposed to.

Products and services are designed with intentional differences in quality to meet the different wants and needs of individual consumers. A Mercedes and a Ford truck are equally "fit for use," in the sense that they both provide automobile transportation for the consumer, and each may meet the quality standards of its individual purchaser. However, the two products have obviously been designed differently for different types of consumers. This is commonly referred to as the **quality of design**—the degree to which quality characteristics are designed into the product. Although designed for the same use, the Mercedes and Ford differ in their performance, features, size, and various other quality characteristics.

**Quality of design:** involves designing quality characteristics into a product or service.

## DIMENSIONS OF QUALITY: MANUFACTURED PRODUCTS

*Dimensions of quality* for which a consumer looks.

The *dimensions of quality* for manufactured products a consumer looks include the following:[1]

1. ***Performance:*** The basic operating characteristics of a product; for example, how well a car handles or its gas mileage.
2. ***Features:*** The "extra" items added to the basic features, such as a stereo CD or a leather interior in a car.
3. ***Reliability:*** The probability that a product will operate properly within an expected time frame; that is, a TV will work without repair for about seven years.
4. ***Conformance:*** The degree to which a product meets preestablished standards.
5. ***Durability:*** How long the product lasts; its life span before replacement. A pair of L.L.Bean boots, with care, might be expected to last a lifetime.
6. ***Serviceability:*** The ease of getting repairs, the speed of repairs, and the courtesy and competence of the repair person.
7. ***Aesthetics:*** How a product looks, feels, sounds, smells, or tastes.
8. ***Safety:*** Assurance that the customer will not suffer injury or harm from a product; an especially important consideration for automobiles.
9. ***Other perceptions:*** Subjective perceptions based on brand name, advertising, and the like.

These quality characteristics are weighed by the customer relative to the cost of the product. In general, consumers will pay for the level of quality they can afford. If they feel they are getting what they paid for, then they tend to be satisfied with the quality of the product.

[1]Adapted from D. A. Garvin, "What Does Quality Really Mean?" *Sloan Management Review* 26(1; 1984), pp. 25–43.

*A Mercedes and a Ford pickup truck are equally "fit for use," but with different design dimensions for different customer markets that result in significantly different purchase prices.*

## DIMENSIONS OF QUALITY: SERVICES

Dimensions of service quality.

The dimensions of quality for a service differ somewhat from those of a manufactured product. Service quality is more directly related to time, and the interaction between employees and the customer. Evans and Lindsay[2] identify the following dimensions of service quality.

1. ***Time and timeliness:*** How long must a customer wait for service, and is it completed on time? For example, is an overnight package delivered overnight?
2. ***Completeness:*** Is everything the customer asked for provided? For example, is a mail order from a catalogue company complete when delivered?
3. ***Courtesy:*** How are customers treated by employees? For example, are catalogue phone operators at Lands' End nice and are their voices pleasant?

[2]J. R. Evans and W. M. Lindsay, *The Management and Control of Quality*, 3rd ed. (St. Paul, MN: West, 1996).

4. ***Consistency:*** Is the same level of service provided to each customer each time? Is your newspaper delivered on time every morning?
5. ***Accessibility and convenience:*** How easy is it to obtain the service? For example, when you call Lands' End or L.L.Bean does the service representative answer quickly?
6. ***Accuracy:*** Is the service performed right every time? Is your bank or credit card statement correct every month?
7. ***Responsiveness:*** How well does the company react to unusual situations, which can happen frequently in a service company? For example, how well is a telephone operator at L.L.Bean able to respond to a customer's questions about a catalogue item not fully described in the catalogue?

## QUALITY FROM THE PRODUCER'S PERSPECTIVE

Now we need to look at quality the way a producer or service provider sees it. We already know that product development is a function of the quality characteristics (i.e., the product's fitness for use) the consumer wants, needs, and can afford. Product or service design results in design specifications that should achieve the desired quality. However, once the product design has been determined, the producer perceives quality to be how effectively the production process is able to conform to the specifications required by the design referred to as the **quality of conformance**. What this means is quality during production focuses on making sure that the product meets the specifications required by the design.

**Quality of conformance:** is making sure the product or service is produced according to design.

Examples of the quality of conformance: If new tires do not conform to specifications, they wobble. If a hotel room is not clean when a guest checks in, the hotel is not functioning according to the specifications of its design; it is a faulty service. From this producer's perspective, good-quality products conform to specifications—they are well made; poor-quality products are not made well—they do not conform to specifications.

*L.L.Bean's first product was the Maine Hunting shoe, developed in 1912 by company founder, Leon Leonwood Bean, a Maine outdoorsman. He initially sold 100 pairs to fellow sportsmen through the mail, but 90 pairs were sent back when the stitching gave way. However, true to his word L.L.Bean returned their money and started over with an improved boot. In years to come L.L.Bean operated his business according to the following belief: "Sell good merchandise at a reasonable profit, treat your customers like human beings, and they will always come back for more." L.L.Bean also guarantees their products to "give 100% satisfaction in every way." If they don't, L.L.Bean will replace the item or refund the purchase price "at any time."*

Achieving quality of conformance depends on a number of factors, including the design of the production process (distinct from product design), the performance level of machinery, equipment and technology, the materials used, the training and supervision of employees, and the degree to which statistical quality-control techniques are used. When equipment fails or is maladjusted, when employees make mistakes, when material and parts are defective, and when supervision is lax, design specifications are generally not met. Key personnel in achieving conformance to specifications include the engineering staff, supervisors and managers, and, most important, employees.

Achieving quality of conformance involves design, materials and equipment, training, supervision, and control.

An important consideration from the consumer's perspective of product quality is product or service price. From the producer's perspective, an important consideration is achieving quality of conformance at an acceptable cost. Product cost is also an important design specification. If products or services cannot be produced at a cost that results in a competitive price, then the final product will not have acceptable value—the price is more than the consumer is willing to pay given the product's quality characteristics. Thus, the quality characteristics included in the product design must be balanced against production costs.

## THE MEANING OF QUALITY: A FINAL PERSPECTIVE

We approached quality from two perspectives, the consumer's and the producer's. These two perspectives are dependent on each other as shown in Figure 3.1. Although product design is customer-motivated, it cannot be achieved without the coordination and participation of the production process. When a product is designed without considering how it will be produced, it may be impossible for the production process to meet design specifications or it may be so costly to do so that the product or service must be priced prohibitively high.

Figure 3.1 depicts the meaning of quality from the producer's and consumer's perspectives. The final determination of quality is fitness for use, which is the consumer's view of quality. It is the consumer who makes the final judgment regarding quality, and so it is the consumer's view that must dominate.

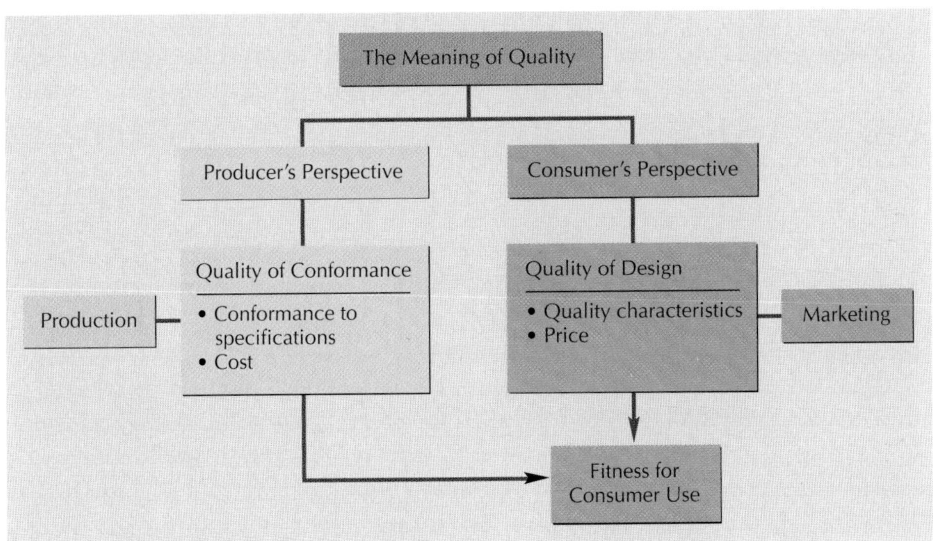


**Figure 3.1 The Meaning of Quality**

## TOTAL QUALITY MANAGEMENT

To make sure that products and services have the quality they have been designed for, a commitment to quality throughout the organization is required. This approach to the management of quality throughout the entire organization has evolved into what is referred to as total quality management or TQM.

## THE EVOLUTION OF TOTAL QUALITY MANAGEMENT

A handful of prominent individuals summarized in Table 3.1 have had a dramatic impact on the rise of quality awareness in the United States, Japan, and other countries. Of these "quality gurus" W. Edwards Deming has been the most prominent.

In the 1940s Deming worked at the Census Bureau, where he introduced the use of statistical process control to monitor the mammoth operation of key punching data from census questionnaires onto millions of punch cards. During World War II Deming developed a national program of 8- and 10-day courses to teach statistical quality-control techniques to over 10,000 engineers at companies that were suppliers to the military during the war. By the end of World War II he had an international reputation.

In the 1950s W. E. Deming began teaching quality control in Japan.

In 1950 Deming began teaching statistical quality control to Japanese companies. As a consultant to Japanese industries and as a teacher, he was able to convince them of the benefits of statistical quality control. He is a major figure in the Japanese quality movement, and in Japan he is frequently referred to as the father of quality control.

Deming's approach to quality management advocated continuous improvement of the production process to achieve conformance to specifications and reduce variability. He identified two primary sources of process improvement: eliminating common causes of quality problems, such as poor product design and insufficient employee training, and eliminating special causes, such as specific equipment or an operator. Deming emphasized the use of statistical quality-control techniques to reduce variability in the production process. He dismissed the use of final product inspection as coming too late to reduce product defects. Primary responsibility for quality improvement, he said, was employees' and management's. He promoted extensive employee involvement in a quality improvement program, and he recommended training for workers in quality-control techniques and methods.

**Table 3.1**
**Quality Gurus**

| Quality Guru | Contribution |
|---|---|
| Walter Shewart | Working at Bell Laboratories in the 1920s, he developed the technical tools such as control charts that formed the basis of statistical quality control; he and his colleagues at Bell Labs introduced the term *quality assurance* for their program to improve quality through the use of statistical control methods. |
| W. Edwards Deming | A disciple of Shewart, he developed courses during World War II to teach statistical quality-control techniques to engineers and executives of companies that were military suppliers; after the war he began teaching statistical quality control to Japanese companies, initiating their quality movement. |
| Joseph M. Juran | An author and consultant, he followed Deming to Japan in 1954; he focused on strategic quality planning within an annual quality program, setting goals for product quality and designing process to achieve those goals; quality improvement is achieved by focusing on projects to solve problems and securing breakthrough solutions. |
| Armand V. Feigenbaum | In his 1951 book, *Quality Control: Principles, Practices and Administration*, he introduced the concept of total quality control and continuous quality improvement as a companywide strategic commitment requiring the involvement of all functions in the quality process, not just manufacturing; discovered by Japanese in the 1950s at about the same time as Juran's visit; from 1958 to 1968 he was director of manufacturing operations and quality control at GE. |
| Philip Crosby | In his 1979 book, *Quality Is Free*, he emphasized that the costs of poor quality (including lost labor and equipment time, scrap, downtime and lost sales) far outweigh the cost of preventing poor quality; in his 1984 book, *Quality Without Tears*, he defined absolutes of quality management—quality is defined as conformance to requirements, quality results from prevention, the performance standard is "zero defects." |
| Kaoru Ishikawa | This Tokyo University professor promoted use of quality circles and developed the "fishbone" (cause and effect) diagram to diagnose quality problems; he emphasized the importance of the internal customer, that is, that a quality organization is first necessary in order to produce quality products or services. |

**Table 3.2**
**W. E. Deming's 14 Points**

1. Create a constancy of purpose toward product improvement to achieve long-term organizational goals.
2. Adopt a philosophy of preventing poor-quality products instead of acceptable levels of poor quality as necessary to compete internationally.
3. Eliminate the need for inspection to achieve quality by relying instead on statistical quality control to improve product and process design.
4. Select a few suppliers or vendors based on quality commitment rather than competitive prices.
5. Constantly improve the production process by focusing on the two primary sources of quality problems, the system and employees, thus increasing productivity and reducing costs.
6. Institute worker training that focuses on the prevention of quality problems and the use of statistical quality-control techniques.
7. Instill leadership among supervisors to help employees perform better.
8. Encourage employee involvement by eliminating the fear of reprisal for asking questions or identifying quality problems.
9. Eliminate barriers between departments, and promote cooperation and a team approach for working together.
10. Eliminate slogans and numerical targets that urge employees to achieve higher performance levels without first showing them how to do it.
11. Eliminate numerical quotas that employees attempt to meet at any cost without regard for quality.
12. Enhance worker pride, artisanry, and self-esteem by improving supervision and the production process so that employees can perform to their capabilities.
13. Institute vigorous education and training programs in methods of quality improvement throughout the organization, from top management down, so that continuous improvement can occur.
14. Develop a commitment from top management to implement the previous 13 points.

Deming's overall philosophy for achieving improvement is embodied in his 14 points, summarized in Table 3.2.

Deming is also credited for development of the *Deming Wheel*, or *plan–do–check–act (PDCA) cycle*, although it was originally formulated by Walter Shewhart and renamed by the Japanese. The Deming Wheel is a four-stage process for continuous quality improvement that complements Deming's 14 points, as shown in Figure 3.2.

The *Deming Wheel*—plan, do, check, act.

Deming's approach to quality embodied in his 14 points and PDCA cycle are the foundation for modern TQM programs.

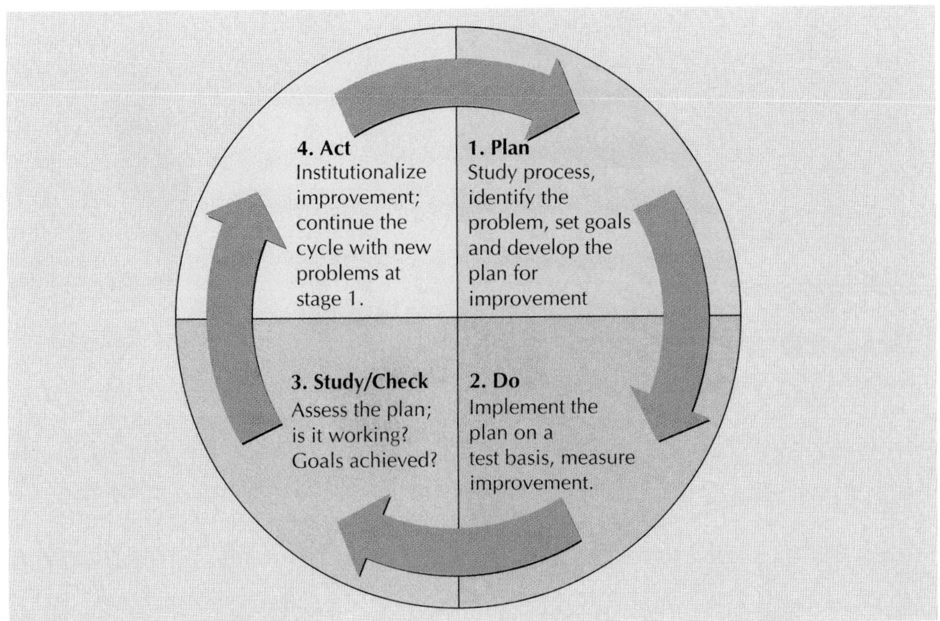


**Figure 3.2**
**The Deming Wheel (PDCA Cycle)**

## PRINCIPLES OF TOTAL QUALITY MANAGEMENT

**Total Quality Management TQM:** customer-oriented, leadership, strategic planning, employee responsibility, continuous improvement, cooperation, statistical methods, and training and education.

Although companies use different terms to refer to their approach to quality, they mean essentially the same thing and embody many of the same concepts: strategic goals, total commitment, continuous improvement, comprehensive focus, employee responsibility, job training, and so forth. **Total quality management** represents a set of management principles that focus on quality improvement as the driving force in all functional areas and at all levels in a company. These principles are:

1. The *customer* defines quality, and customer satisfaction is the top priority.
2. Top management must provide the *leadership* for quality.
3. Quality is a *strategic* issue and requires a strategic plan.
4. Quality is the responsibility of every *employee* at every level of the organization.
5. All functions of the company must focus on *continuous quality improvement* to achieve strategic goals.
6. Quality problems are solved through *cooperation* among employees and management.
7. Problem solving and continuous quality improvement use *statistical quality-control* methods.
8. *Training* and *education* of all employees is the basis for continuous quality improvement.

## TQM AND BUSINESS PARTNERS

Companies know that to satisfy customers requires not only their own commitment to quality, but also the support and resources of its business partners, or suppliers. This is especially true of companies that outsource many of their activities to suppliers. Companies and their suppliers must work together to meet the needs of the company's customers. In TQM a partnership exists between the supplier and its customer wherein the supplier is expected to manage its own quality effectively so that the company it supplies can count on the quality of the materials, parts, and services it receives. Companies that have adopted TQM do not expect to have to inspect materials and parts from their suppliers to see if defects exist; this defeats the purpose of their own quality program.

Many TQM companies have reduced their numbers of suppliers in order to have more direct influence over their suppliers' quality and delivery performance, which was one of Deming's 14 points. Called *single-sourcing*, it is based on the notion that if a company has a major portion of a supplier's business, then the supplier is more willing to meet the customer's quality standards. The company and supplier enter into a business relationship referred to as **partnering**, in which the supplier agrees to meet the company's quality standards, and in return the company enters into a long-term purchasing agreement with the supplier that includes a stable order and delivery schedule.

**Partnering:** a relationship between a company and its supplier based on mutual quality standards.

In order to ensure that its supplier meets its quality standards, a company will often insist that the supplier adopt a TQM program similar to its own, or a company's TQM program will include its suppliers. Still other companies require that their suppliers achieve ISO 9000 certification, an international quality standard that ensures a high industry standard of quality; some companies require their suppliers to follow Baldrige National Quality Award guidelines or even enter the Baldrige Award competition.

## TQM AND CUSTOMERS

At the other end of a company's spectrum from its suppliers is its direct relationship with its customers. An important component of any TQM program is the company's ability to measure customer satisfaction. The company needs to know if its TQM program is effective. Is the company meeting customer expectations? Is its products or services meeting their fitness for use definition? Is it what the customer wants, does the customer like it, does the customer need it, would the customer like it changed? TQM programs require that some form of measurement system be in place to answer these questions and provide data about the customer's level of satisfaction. It is a well-established fact of consumer be-

TQM requires a system to measure customer satisfaction, such as a survey.

## THE COMPETITIVE EDGE

### The Challenge of Becoming a Whirlpool Supplier in a TQM Environment

Whirlpool Corporation is the world's leading manufacturer of appliances. In 1993 the range appliance division of Whirlpool notified its suppliers that it was adopting TQM principles, and companies that wanted to be considered as future Whirlpool suppliers would also have to develop compatible quality improvement objectives. Whirlpool committed itself to continuous quality improvement and to exceed customer expectations for its products, and it expected its suppliers to enter into a business partnership with them to do likewise. At the same time Whirlpool wanted to decrease its number of suppliers. Whirlpool set specific strategic goals to increase customer choices by increasing its product output from 9 units per day to 30, and to increase its product availability from 80 to 95%. Furthermore, Whirlpool wanted to achieve a 10-fold reduction in the incidence of service calls to repair defective ranges in homeowners' kitchens from 200 house calls per 1000 ranges to 20 calls per 1000 ranges. To achieve this service-incidence rate reduction, Whirlpool set a goal for its suppliers of a maximum defect rate of less than 3.4 parts per million (i.e., the six sigma rate). Whirlpool also expected its suppliers to reduce the cost of their products and processes by a minimum of 5% each year as a result of continuous process improvement and to limit on-hand parts inventory at Whirlpool to a maximum two-day supply. Whirlpool offered potential suppliers no guidance on how to achieve these TQM-based goals, only that it expected its suppliers to do it.

Stanley Engineered Components (SEC), a small supplier of oven-door latches with annual sales of $15 to $20 million, had been a Whirlpool supplier for over 20 years. Whirlpool was SEC's largest customer, and its TQM-based demands provided SEC with a daunting challenge. In order to remain a Whirlpool supplier, SEC had to convince Whirlpool that it could help Whirlpool achieve its corporate TQM objectives. This would represent a major change in the way SEC did business and also expose it to enormous financial risks. It was a stable and successful company that had previously won orders on the basis of low price. If SEC was to remain as a Whirlpool supplier in a TQM environment, SEC would be subject to much greater uncertainty with a much greater risk of failure. Even if SEC invested in major changes, there was no assurance it would be selected as a Whirlpool supplier, and thus it could lose all of the money it would have to spend to even be considered. Losing Whirlpool business would result in a 20% loss of sales. Even if it were selected as a supplier, Whirlpool's goal of decreasing costs by 5% annually would mean continuously declining profits.

SEC answered this challenge by adopting TQM and using it to gain its own competitive advantage. SEC used a team approach to evaluating and improving its manufacturing processes, and as a result it reduced its defect rate from 63 parts per million to 3.4 parts per million by 1995. SEC achieved Whirlpool's annual 5% cost reduction goal by requiring its own suppliers to meet the same goal; SEC demanded of its suppliers what Whirlpool demanded of SEC. By adopting a flexible manufacturing program and acquiring an EDI system SEC was able to achieve Whirlpool's inventory goals while increasing output to meet Whirlpool's new production objectives. In 1995 SEC was selected by Whirlpool as a supplier. When General Electric, Whirlpool's primary competitor, adopted a similar TQM approach, SEC found itself positioned to gain its business as well. SEC also gained additional business from Whirlpool for other range parts. These gains for SEC were simultaneously losses for SEC's competitors. Between 1993 and 1997 SEC's sales to Whirlpool increased by 125%, its productivity increased by 76%, and it increased its sales to other customers by 25%.

*Source:* C. Roethlein and P. Mangiameli, "The Realities of Becoming a Long-Term Supplier to a Large TQM Customer," *Interfaces* 19(4;July–August 1999), pp. 71–81.

havior that unhappy customers will tell almost twice as many others about their quality problems as they will tell others about satisfactory products or services.

The most widely used means for measuring customer satisfaction is the customer survey. Applicants for the Baldrige National Quality Award are expected to provide measures of customer satisfaction, usually through customer surveys. For example, third-party customer satisfaction survey results for Baldrige National Quality Award winner Dana Corporation-Spicer Driveshaft Division, showed 80% overall customer satisfaction with their product quality and performance over a three-year period, which was over 10 points higher than their top competitor.

Total customer satisfaction is Motorola's overriding objective—the whole purpose of its six sigma philosophy of virtually zero defects. To help it better understand its customers' ever-changing requirements for its products and services, Motorola contracts with an independent survey firm to conduct regularly scheduled surveys with its customers around the world. This independent and customer-focused approach helps Motorola to measure how well it is meeting its customers' needs.

## TQM AND INFORMATION TECHNOLOGY

Ritz-Carlton Hotels gather data about their customers through various types of service contacts, and systematically enter these into a database, which holds a million files; thus, when the same customer subsequently checks into any of its hotels around the world, it can customize its service specifically to meet that customer's wants and needs. Gerber Baby Foods uses a unique coding system for each jar of its baby food and a sophisticated computer tracking system for all of its raw materials, produce, and finished goods that enables it to identify the chemical makeup of the soil in which the produce was planted, when it was planted, and when it was harvested, among other data. These are examples of how a sophisticated information technology system can enhance and promote quality.

In the human body the central nervous system monitors and controls all the other bodily functions. A healthy and successful business organization must have an active and functional central nervous system to monitor and control its functions, to receive information and translate that information into appropriate action and effective decisions. In a business this central nervous system is called an information technology (IT) system. When a company embarks on a TQM program or adopts some other quality initiative like six sigma, it needs to be aware of the IT requirements of such an undertaking. An IT system provides the infrastructure of hardware, networks, and software necessary to support a TQM program. If the company does not have an appropriate IT system in place, it will fail to reap all the benefits it expects from its quality program. This need has significantly expanded in recent years as a result of the huge increase of data and information sources available via the Internet.

# QUALITY IMPROVEMENT AND THE ROLE OF EMPLOYEES

Employee issues are universally perceived by companies to be one of the most important, if not *the* most important, consideration when initiating a quality-improvement program. Failure to address employee issues will usually lead to a failure of the total quality effort.

Job training and employee development are major features of a successful TQM program. Increased training in job skills results in improved processes that improve product quality. Training in quality tools and skills such as statistical process control enable employees to diagnose and correct day-to-day problems related to their job. This provides employees with greater responsibility for product quality and greater satisfaction for doing their part to achieve quality. When achievement is reinforced through rewards and recognition, it further increases employee satisfaction. At Ritz-Carlton first-year employees receive up to 310 hours of training, and their "Pride and Joy" program gives employees a role in designing their jobs. Marriott employees are trained to view breakdowns in service as opportunities for satisfying customers; for example, they may send a gift and note of apology to customers who have experienced a problem in the hotel.

In previous discussions of TQM, the importance of customer satisfaction as an overriding company objective was stressed. However, another important aspect of a successful TQM program is internal customer (e.g., employee) satisfaction. It is unlikely that a company will be able to make its customers happy if its employees are not happy. For that reason, many companies conduct employee satisfaction surveys just as they conduct customer surveys.

**Participative problem solving:** employees are directly involved in the quality-management process.

When employees are directly involved in the quality-management process, it is referred to as **participative problem solving**. Employee participation in identifying and solving quality problems has been shown to be effective in improving quality, increasing employee satisfaction and morale, improving job skills, reducing job turnover and absenteeism, and increasing productivity.

Participative problem solving is usually within an *employee-involvement (EI)* program, with a team approach. We will look at some of these programs for involving employees in quality management, including kaizen, quality circles, and process improvement teams.

*Mickey Mouse is not just a costumed character at the various Disney parks in the United States and abroad; he is a host who represents all the other costumed hosts and hostesses to Disney's thousands of "guests" each day. Every employee at a Disney park from janitors to Mickey has undergone extensive training to provide quality service to Disney's guests.*

## KAIZEN AND CONTINUOUS IMPROVEMENT

**Kaizen:** involves everyone in a process of continuous improvement.

**Kaizen** is the Japanese term for *continuous improvement*, not only in the workplace but also in one's personal life, home life, and social life. In the workplace, kaizen means involving everyone in a process of gradual, organized, and continuous improvement. Every employee within an organization should be involved in working together to make improvements. If an improvement is not part of a continuous, ongoing process, it is not considered kaizen.

Employees are most directly involved in kaizen when they are determining solutions to their own problems. Employees are the real experts in their immediate workspace. In its most basic form, kaizen is a system in which employees identify many small improvements on a continual basis and implement these improvements themselves. This is actually the application of the steps in the Deming Wheel (Figure 3.2) at its most basic, individual level. Employees identify a problem, come up with a solution, check with their supervisor, and then implement it. This works to involve all employees in the improvement process and gives them a feeling that they are really participating in quality improvement, which in turn keeps them excited about their jobs. Nothing motivates someone more than when they come up with a solution to their own problem. Small individual changes have a cumulative effect in improving entire processes, and with this level of participation improvement occurs across the entire organization. No companywide six sigma or TQM program can succeed without this level of total employee involvement in continuous improvement.

Employees at Dana Corporation's Spicer Driveshaft Division, North America's largest independent manufacturer of driveshafts and a 2000 Malcolm Baldrige National Quality Award winner, participate in a kaizen-type program. On average, each employee submits three suggestions for improvements per month and almost 80 percent of these ideas are implemented. The company also makes use of kaizen "blitzes" in which teams brainstorm, identify, and implement ideas for improvement, sometimes as often as every three or four weeks. Companywide, Dana Corporation employees implemented almost 2 million ideas in one year alone.

## QUALITY CIRCLES

One of the first team-based approaches to quality improvement was quality circles. Called quality-control circles in Japan when they originated during the 1960s, they were

*Quality circles like this one at a General Electric assembly plant are part of many TQM programs. They provide an organized format for allowing workers and supervisors to work together as a team to solve operational problems and improve quality.*

**Quality circle:** a group of workers and supervisors from the same area who address production problems.

introduced in the United States in the 1970s. A **quality circle** is a small, voluntary group of employees and their supervisor(s), comprising a team of about 8 to 10 members from the same work area or department. The supervisor is typically the circle moderator, promoting group discussion but not directing the group or making decisions; decisions result from group consensus. A circle meets about once a week during company time in a room designated especially for that purpose, where the team works on problems and projects of their own choice. These problems may not always relate to quality issues; instead, they focus on productivity, costs, safety, or other work-related issues in the circle's area. Quality circles follow an established procedure for identifying, analyzing, and solving quality-related (or other) problems. Figure 3.3 is a graphical representation of the quality circle process.

A group technique for identifying and solving problems is *brainstorming* to generate ideas. Free expression is encouraged, and criticism is not allowed. Only after brainstorming is completed are ideas evaluated.

## PROCESS IMPROVEMENT TEAMS

A *process improvement team* includes members from the interrelated functions or departments that make up a process.

*Process improvement teams*, also called quality improvement teams (QIT), focuses attention on business processes rather than separate company functions. It was noted previously that quality circles are generally composed of employees and supervisors from the same work area or department, whereas process improvement teams tend to be cross-functional or even cross-business between suppliers and their customers. A process improvement team would include members from the various interrelated functions or departments that constitute a process. For example, a process improvement team for customer service might include members from distribution, packaging, manufacturing, and human resources. A key objective of a process improvement team is to understand the process the team is addressing in terms of how all the parts (functions and departments) work together. The process is then measured and evaluated, with the goal of improving the process to make it more efficient and the product or service better. A key tool in helping the team understand how the process works is a *process flowchart*, a quality improvement tool we will discuss in greater detail in the section "Identifying Quality Problems and Causes."

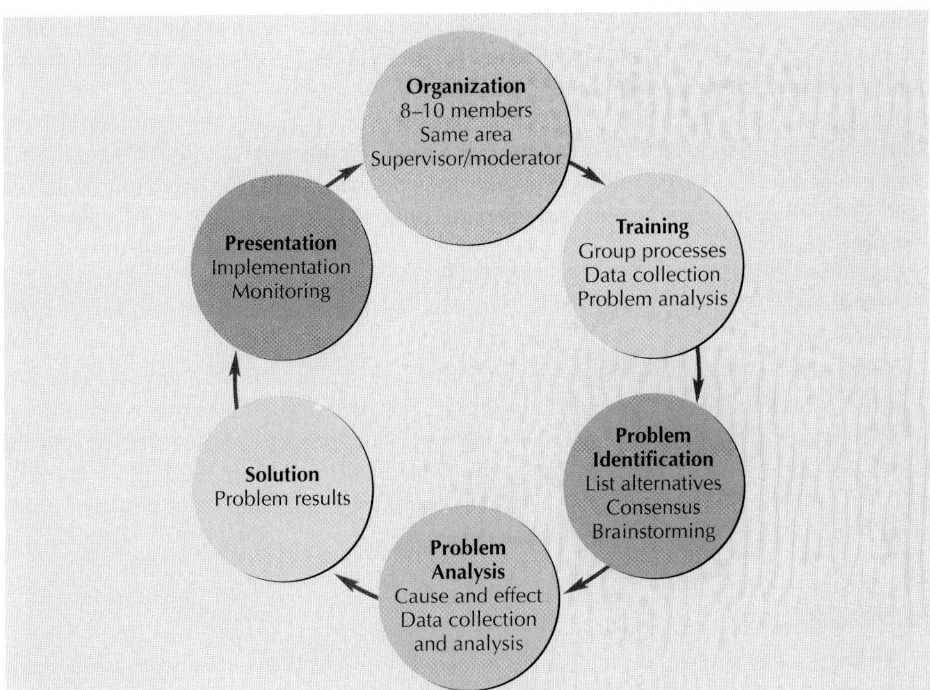


Figure 3.3
**The Quality Circle Process**

## STRATEGIC IMPLICATIONS OF TQM

**Quality is a key component of strategic planning.**

A *strategy* is a set of decisions a company makes that establishes a plan to achieve its long-term goals. A company's success in implementing its strategy, or strategic plan, through its operations is a key to its long-term competitiveness. In today's global business environment, since a company competes on quality, it is likely the most important aspect of its strategic plan. For some companies, their strategic plan is embodied in their quality management program or, at the very least, quality is a key part of a company's strategic plan. Alternatively, various studies have shown that the single biggest obstacle to the successful implementation of TQM is the lack of a strategic plan. In this section we will look at the relationship between strategy and TQM in companies in which quality is the driving force.

## LEADERSHIP

**Strong leadership is a key to a successful strategic plan and achieving goals for quality.**

*Strong leadership* is a key to successfully integrating quality into a company's strategic plan. Robert Galvin, the former CEO of Motorola, often made quality the first item on the agenda at his staff meetings. David Kearns, the president of Xerox, was the driving force behind the development of his company's quality strategy that resulted in the 1989 Baldrige Award for Xerox's Leadership Through Quality program. However, strong leadership is not only about making the decision that quality will be an important component of a company's strategy; it is also about creating a company environment that is conducive to quality management. Such an environment actively involves management and employees in the strategic planning process, promotes teamwork between and among managers and employees, makes employees responsible for quality, and encourages managers and employees to take risks and talk openly about quality. It also rewards employees for quality improvement. If this type of environment is not created, then the company's quality strategy is not likely to be successful.

## GOALS

Companies in which quality drives their competitive strategy have certain common characteristics. They have a clear *strategic goal, vision,* or *mission* that focuses on customer satisfaction through quality. Motorola's company objective of "Total Customer

Satisfaction," and AT&T Universal Card Services headquarters inscription, "Customers are the center of our universe," reflect their commitment to customer satisfaction and quality as part of their overall strategy or vision.

**Strategic plans should include a high goal for quality.**

High goals for quality are characteristic of the strategic plans for these companies. Motorola's six sigma goal of 3.4 defects per million products is a policy of virtually no defective items. AT&T Consumer Communication Services, which provides long-distance services to 80 million residential customers, has the goal of providing a perfect connection every time.

### PLANS

Strategic planning also includes a set of programs, or *operational plans and policies*, to achieve the company's goals. Establishing goals without telling employees how to achieve them will be fruitless. In a quality-management program, goals and objectives are established at all levels, and the means and resources for achieving these goals are provided to employees and managers. This may include new or improved processes, employee training, and quality tools and techniques.

### FEEDBACK

Strategic quality planning includes *a mechanism for feedback* to adjust, update, and make corrections in the strategic plan. Original quality goals may prove to be so easily attained that employees become complacent, or so impossible that employees become frustrated. Goals need to be continuously reevaluated and revised. The strategic plan also needs to be capable of quickly reflecting changing technology and market changes.

## SIX SIGMA

At the beginning of this chapter we talked about the origination of the six sigma quality program at Motorola and its adoption at Allied Signals and Honeywell (which subsequently merged under the name Honeywell). Each of these companies has credited six sigma with billions of dollars in savings, and these successes have led many other large and small companies to implement six sigma programs. As a result, six sigma has become the next major evolutionary step (i.e., "hot topic") in the quality field.

Fundamentally, six sigma is a very organized and detailed process for improving quality, and as such, it has been perceived both as the prime ingredient of a TQM system or as a TQM system with itself. Whichever the case, there is little doubt that six sigma is a direct descendant of the philosophy and principles of TQM we have discussed previously. In its simplest form, six sigma is based on Deming's PDCA cycle and Joseph Juran's assertion that "all quality improvement occurs on a project-by-project basis," with elements of kaizen-type employee involvement.[3] In this section we will provide a more detailed description of the basic components of six sigma. Figure 3.4 illustrates the elements of a six sigma program.

### THE SIX SIGMA GOAL—3.4 DPMO

**Six sigma:** measure of how much a process deviates from perfection.

**Six sigma** is a process for developing and delivering near perfect products and services. The word "sigma" is a familiar statistical term for the standard deviation, a measure of variability around the mean of a normal distribution. In six sigma it is a measure of how much a given product or process deviates from perfection, or zero defects. The main idea behind six sigma is that if the number of "defects" in a process can be measured, then it can be systematically determined how to eliminate them and get as close to zero defects as possible. In six sigma "as close to zero defects as possible" translates into a statistically based numerical goal of 3.4 defects per million opportunities (DPMO), which is the near

[3] J.M. Lucas, "The Essential Six Sigma," *Quality Progress* 35(1; 2002), pp. 27–31.

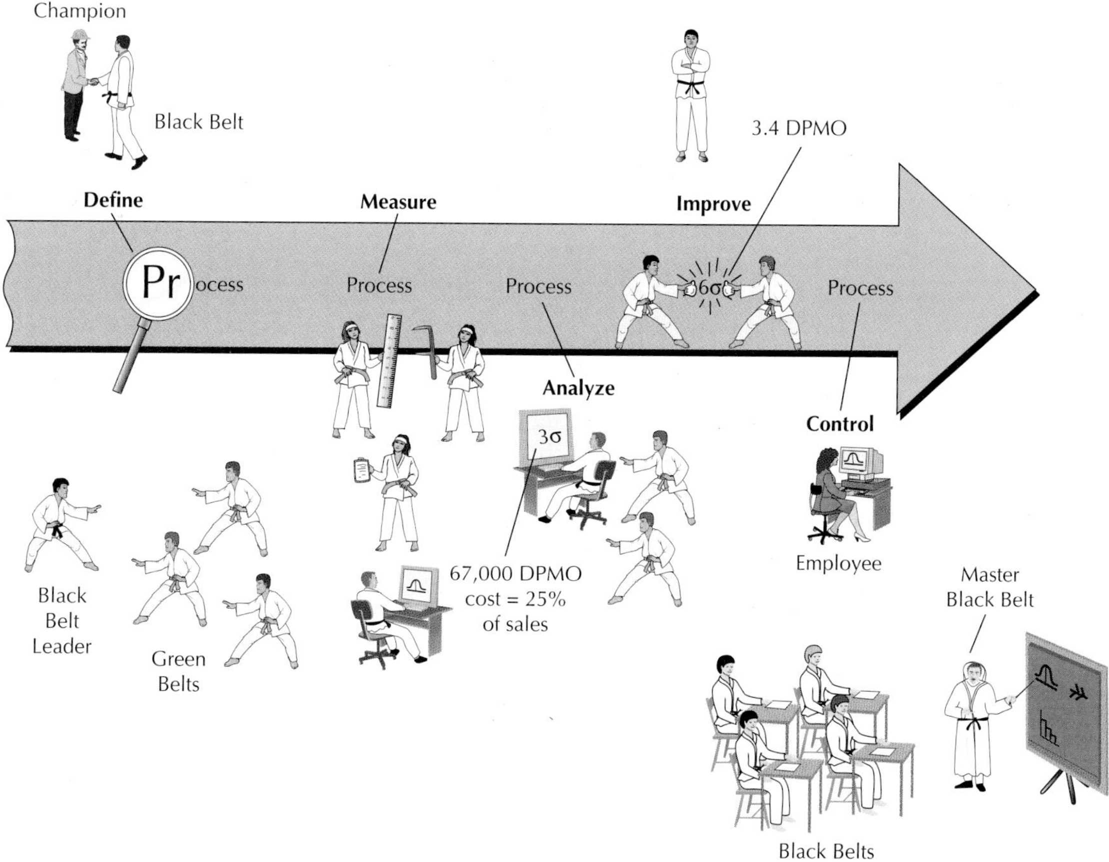


Figure 3.4
**Six Sigma**

elimination of defects from a process, product, or service. This is a goal far beyond the quality level at which most companies operate. Through the reduction of variation of all processes (i.e., achieving the six sigma goal), the overall performance of the company will be improved and significant overall cost savings will be realized.

## IMPROVEMENT PROJECTS

The first step in the six sigma process is the identification of improvement projects. These projects are selected according to business objectives and the goals of the company. As such, they normally have a significant financial impact. These projects are not one-time, unique activities as projects are typically thought of, but team-based activities directed at the continuing improvement of a process.

Once projects are identified, they are assigned a **champion** from upper management who is responsible for project success, providing resources and overcoming organizational barriers. Champions are typically paid a bonus tied to the successful achievement of six sigma goals.

**Champion:** an executive responsible for project success.

## THE BREAKTHROUGH STRATEGY: DMAIC

At the heart of six sigma is the **breakthrough strategy**, a five-step process applied to improvement projects. The five steps in the breakthrough strategy are very similar to Deming's four-stage PDCA cycle (Figure 3.2). The breakthrough strategy steps are define, measure, analyze, improve, and control (DMAIC) shown in Figure 3.4.

**Breakthrough strategy:** define, measure, analyze, improve, control.

*Define:* The process is defined, including who the customers are and what their problems are. It is improtant to know which quality attributes are most important to the customer, what the defects are, and what the process can deliver.
*Measure:* The process is measured, and data are collected.

*Analyze:* The data are analyzed in order to develop information that provides insight into the process, including the most important causes of the defects.
*Improve:* Solutions to problems are developed, changes are made to the process, and the results are measured to see if the defects have been eliminated. If not, more changes may be necessary.
*Control:* If the process is performing at the desired level of performance, it is monitored to make sure no unexpected and undesirable changes occur.

## BLACK BELTS AND GREEN BELTS

**Black Belt:** the project leader.

The project leader who implements the DMAIC steps is called a **Black Belt**. Black Belts hold full-time positions and are extensively trained in the use of statistics and quality-control tools, as well as project and team management. A Black Belt assignment normally lasts two years during which the Black Belt will lead 8 to 12 projects from different areas in the company, each lasting about one quarter. A Black Belt is certified after two successful projects. Black Belts are typically very focused change agents who are on the fast track to company advancement.

**Master Black Belt:** a teacher and mentor for Black Belts.

**Master Black Belts** monitor, review, and mentor Black Belts across all projects. They are primarily teachers who are selected based on their quantitative skills, and on their teaching and mentoring ability. As such, they are a resource for project teams and Black Belts. They also hold full-time positions and are usually certified after participating in about 20 successful projects, half while a Black Belt and half as a Master Black Belt.

**Green Belts** project team members.

Project team members are **Green Belts**, which is not a full-time position; they do not spend all of their time on projects. Green Belts receive similar training as Black Belts but somewhat less of it.

At General Electric employees are not considered for promotion to any management position without Black Belt or Green Belt training. It is part of the six sigma overall strategy that as Black Belts and Green Belts move into management positions they will continue to promote and advance six sigma in the company. A generally held perception is

### THE COMPETITIVE EDGE

### Six Sigma at Bank of America

Bank of America began its six sigma initiative in 2001 in response to a change in strategy from growth through acquisition and merger to growth through acquiring, retaining, and deepening customer relationships. Although the bank was a major financial institution with a national customer base of 27 million households, it was not well positioned to provide customers with the level of world-class service that would achieve this objective. Error-prone processes caused inefficient, poor-quality service, resulting in general customer dissatisfaction with hundreds of thousands of defects per million opportunities. Only 40% of Bank of America customers rated their banking experience a 9 to 10 on a 10-point customer "delight" scale. ("Delighted" customers score their satisfaction at 9 or 10, whereas "satisfied" customers give scores of 6, 7, or 8. Delighted customers are three times more likely than satisfied customers to open new accounts and four times more likely to recommend Bank of America to family and friends—key factors in achieving their strategic objectives for growth.)

Bank of America started by recruiting senior six sigma professionals (Black Belts and Master Black Belts) from companies like Motorola, Honeywell, and General Electric to establish a quality culture throughout the organization. Engineers helped business units focus on customer delight and define priorities; customer data were used to identify key business processes (i.e., deposits and payments); and process engineering teams worked across business lines to facilitate improvements that would cause maximum impact on customer delight. Metrics were defined to measure success, and six sigma tools were widely adopted so that the DMAIC steps would become the foundation of the bank's approach to business. Examples of results from Green Belt projects included a 70% reduction in missing items from customer statements; an 88% reduction in malfunctions in automated and electronic customer channels; and the improvement of CD and IRA service by reducing customer costs and response time for account requests from 3 days to 10 minutes. Overall, six sigma resulted in more than $2 billion in costs savings, an increase in customer delight across the company of more than 25%, and over a million new accounts in 2003 alone.

*Source:* M. H. Jones, Jr., "Six Sigma . . . at a Bank?" *Six Sigma Forum Magazine* (February 2004), pp. 13–17.

that companies that have successfully implemented six sigma have one Black Belt for every 100 employees and one Master Black Belt for every 100 Black Belts. This will vary according to the size of the company and the number of projects regularly undertaken.

In six sigma all employees receive training in the six sigma breakthrough strategy, statistical tools, and quality-improvement techniques. Employees are trained to participate on six sigma project teams. Because quality is considered to be the responsibility of every employee, every employee must be involved in, motivated by, and knowledgeable about six sigma.

## DESIGN FOR SIX SIGMA

An important element of the six sigma system is **design for six sigma (DFSS)**, a systematic methodology for designing products and processes that meet customer expectations and can be produced at six sigma quality levels. It follows the same basic approach as the breakthrough strategy with Master Black Belts, Black Belts, and Green Belts and makes extensive use of statistical tools and design techniques, training, and measurement. However, it employs this strategy earlier, up front in the design phase and developmental stages. This is a more effective and less expensive way to achieve the six sigma goal than fixing problems after the product or process is already developed and in place.

**Design for six sigma:** a systematic approach to designing products and processes that will achieve six sigma.

## TQM IN SERVICE COMPANIES

TQM evolved in manufacturing companies like Toyota, IBM, and Motorola. In the 1990s service companies began to realize that they could benefit from quality management. This is important because the service sector is the largest segment of the U.S. economy, employing almost three times as many people as manufacturing industries.

Service organizations and manufacturing companies both convert inputs into outputs—products or services—through a productive process. Both manufacturing and services use the same kinds of inputs—resources such as physical facilities, capital, materials, equipment, and people. In some instances the processes and products are similar. For example, both Ford and McDonald's produce a tangible, physical product (cars and hamburgers) assembled from component parts. However, in pure service industries such as law, hotels, entertainment, communication, engineering, education, clubs, real estate, banks, retail, health care, and airlines, the processes are less similar and the products are not as tangible. The "products" provided by these organizations are not typically a physical item that can be held or stored. The customer of a manufacturer tends to interact only at the output end of the production process. The customer of a service often interacts directly with the production process, consuming services like legal advice, a classroom lecture, or an airline flight as they are being produced. Services tend to be customized and provided at the convenience of the customer; for example, doctors prescribe individually to patients. In addition, services are labor-intensive, while manufacturing is more capital-intensive. Thus, human contact and its ramifications are an important part of the process of producing services.

Service defects are not always easy to measure because service output is not usually a trangible, physical item.

Services tend to be labor-intensive.

Manufactured products are physical items; they can be observed, held, felt, stored, and used again. If a manufactured item is defective, the defect can be felt or seen, and counted or measured. The improvement (or deterioration) in a product's quality can likewise be measured.

It's not the same for service. A service cannot be held, felt, stored, and used again. A service output is not always tangible; thus, it is not as easy to measure service defects. The dimensions of quality for manufactured items include things such as performance, features, reliability, conformance, and durability that can be quantitatively measured. The dimensions of service quality include timeliness, courtesy, consistency, accuracy, convenience, responsiveness, and completeness—all hard to measure beyond a subjective assessment by the customer. This does not mean that the potential for poor quality is any less in services. Each day thousands of travelers check into and out of Ritz-Carlton Hotels,

Services and manufacturing companies have similar inputs but different processes and outputs.

UPS handles and delivers millions of packages, and VISA processes millions of credit transactions worldwide. However, it is more difficult to assess defects in service and thus more difficult to measure customer satisfaction.

Disney World, for example, has had to develop a more extensive view of quality than a manufacturing company. In some ways, a theme park is similar to an assembly line except that Disney's rides have to work flawlessly all the time. However, the Disney experience is not just about defect-free rides. It is also about customer emotions and expectations, which are likely to vary widely. Customers have different tolerance levels for things that go wrong. When there is a long line at a ride, the issue is not just the length of the wait, but how a customer feels about waiting. Disney addresses this problem by being innovative; costumed characters entertain customers waiting in line. (See Chapter 17, "Waiting Lines.")

## QUALITY ATTRIBUTES IN SERVICES

Service organizations must often rely on talking directly with customers in the form of surveys or interviews—both subjective responses—to measure the attributes of quality.

### THE COMPETITIVE EDGE

#### Quick Service and Customer Satisfaction at Pal's Sudden Service

Pal's Sudden Service, 2001 Malcolm Baldrige Award winner in the small business category, is a privately owned, quick-service restaurant chain, with 17 locations within 60 miles of Kingsport, Tennessee. It is the first business in the restaurant industry to receive the Baldrige National Quality Award. Pal's competes directly with national fast-food chains; however, Pal's is the regional leader in all major areas of comparative performance—quality, service, speed, food health and safety, customer satisfaction, market share, sales, and profit. It has a market share of 19%, and in 2001 it had sales of approximately $17 million. Pal's distinguishes itself by offering competitively priced food of consistently high quality, delivered rapidly, cheerfully, and without error.

Pal's employs a business excellence process in which everything it does follows a process from new product development to hiring practices to work systems, and nothing is done without thoroughly understanding how a process impacts customer satisfaction. Benchmarking is a key element of the business excellence process. Managers are continually looking for benchmarking candidates and are pursuing useful data, the basis of sound planning and decision making. Customer, employee, and supplier feedback is a particularly important source of data, and it is gathered in formal and informal ways. For example, Pal's owner/operators spend part of every day "marketing by wandering around," asking customers and employees how a location is performing and soliciting ideas for improvement. They also go door to door within a 3-mile radius of their restaurants (where the majority of Pal's customers live), seeking customer input and determining satisfaction levels through surveys. The owner/operators record what they learn about sales, expenses, customers, staff, products, services, equipment, and suppliers in logs which, with ideas for improvement, they send to Pal's executives on a weekly basis. Pal's also uses balanced scorecard of performance measures for quality, service, cleanliness, value, people, and speed.

Achieving Pal's objective of the "quickest, friendliest, most accurate service available" is a challenge in an industry with annual employee turnover greater than 200%. However, Pal's turnover rate of 127%, which continues to fall, compared to its best competitor's turnover rate of 300% is a competitive advantage. Pal's has an extensive training program based on a four-step model: show it, do it, evaluate, and perform again. Training also includes instruction on effective listening skills. Cross-training is required of all staff to ensure their complete understanding of all production and service processes as well as quality standards. Since for most of its front-line workers (high school and college students) it is their first job, Pal's believes it has a responsibility to help its employees grow, develop knowledge and skills that can be applied in future jobs, and become better citizens.

Pal's customer satisfaction scores for quality averaged 98.5% in 2001 compared with 84.1% for its best competitor. Its order speed improved by 30% from 1995 to 2001, decreasing from 31 seconds to 20 seconds. This is almost four times faster than its best competitor, whose order speed increased from 73 to 76 seconds over the same period. Errors average less than one for every 2000 transactions, and its goal is one in 5000. Pal's has also received the highest health inspection scores not only in its market but in the entire state of Tennessee.

*Sources:* S. Daniels, "The Little Hot Dog Stand That Could," *Quality Progress* 35 (9; September 2002), pp. 66–71; and National Quality Program at the National Institute of Standards and Technology Web site http://www.quality.nist.gov.

*Employees at Pal's Sudden Service fast-food restaurant, mostly high school and college students, are committed to providing the "quickest, friendliest, most accurate service available." Fast-food restaurants are generally recognized as having high quality standards in terms of cleanliness and service. Pal's, the first business in the restaurant industry to win the Baldrige National Quality Award, is a recognized quality leader.*

Timeliness, or how quickly a service is provided, is an important dimension of service quality, and it is not difficult to measure. The difficulty is determining what is "quick" service and what is "slow" service. How long must a caller wait to place a phone catalogue order before it is considered poor service? The answer, to a large extent, depends on the caller's expectations: "too long" is not the same for everyone. Varying expectations make it difficult to determine an exact specification, such as the number of ounces in a carton of milk.

Timeliness is an important dimension of service quality.

Quality management in services must focus on employee performance related to intangible, difficult-to-measure quality dimensions. The most important of these quality dimensions is how quickly, correctly, and pleasantly employees are able to provide service. That is why service companies such as Federal Express, Lands' End, Avis, Disney, and Ritz-Carlton Hotels have well-developed quality-management programs that focus on employee performance, behavior, and training. These companies design their TQM programs to treat employees well, as if they were customers. Federal Express's slogan is "People, Service, Profits," and its treatment of employees, including its no layoff policy, is viewed as a TQM model or **benchmark** that other companies try to copy. Disney park employees are treated as "cast members," and Disney's mission is to keep cast members happy so they will make customers happy.

The principles of TQM apply equally well to services and manufacturing.

**Benchmark:** "best" level of quality achievement in one company that other companies seek to achieve.

McDonald's has a reputation for high-quality service resulting from its application of established TQM principles. Its food preparation process has been simplified into small autonomous units just as a manufacturing firm might do. It provides fresh food promptly on demand, which is essentially an inventory situation. Restaurant managers meet with customer groups on a regular basis and use questionnaires to identify quality "defects" in its operation. It monitors all phases of its process continuously from purchasing to restrooms to restaurant decor and maintenance in a total quality approach. It empowers all employees to make spot decisions to dispose of unfresh food or to speed service. The McDonald's workforce is flexible so that changes in customer traffic and demand can be met promptly by moving employees to different tasks. Food is sampled regularly for taste and freshness. Extensive use is made of information technology for scheduling, cash register operation, food inventory, cooking procedures, and food assembly processes—all with the objective of faster service. All of these quality-improvement procedures are standard and similar to quality-improvement techniques that could be found in a manufacturing firm.

## THE COMPETITIVE EDGE

### Ritz-Carlton Hotels: Two-Time Baldrige National Quality Award Winner

The Ritz-Carlton Hotel Company is the only two-time recipient of the Malcolm Baldrige National Quality Award in the service category, having won in 1992 and 1999. An independently operated division of Marriott International, Inc., it manages luxury hotels around the world. All have received four- or five-star ratings from the *Mobil Travel Guide* and diamond ratings from the American Automobile Association.

The goal for customer satisfaction is a defect-free experience for guests and 100% customer loyalty. The hotel employs a measurement system to chart progress toward elimination of customer problems, no matter how minor. To meet its goal of total elimination of problems, the Ritz-Carlton has identified over 1000 potential instances for a problem to arise during interactions with guests. To cultivate customer loyalty the hotel has instituted an approach of "Customer Customization," which relies on extensive data gathering. Information gathered during various types of customer contacts, such as responses to service requests by overnight guests or post-event reviews with meeting planners, are systematically entered into a database, which holds almost a million files. The database enables hotel staff worldwide to anticipate the needs of returning guests. The "Greenbook" is the Ritz-Carlton handbook of quality processes and tools, a nearly constant reference that is distributed to all employees. Any employee can spend up to $2000 to immediately correct a guest's problem or handle a complaint.

More than 85% of the company's 17,000 employees—known as "The Ladies and Gentlemen of the Ritz-Carlton"—are front-line hotel workers. The hotel's "pride and joy" program gives employees a larger role in the design of their jobs. First-year managers and employees receive 250 to 310 hours of training. As a result, the hotel's employee turnover rate, in an industry in which employee turnover is a chronic problem, declined annually from 1992 to 1999, and levels of employee satisfaction are moving upward.

In an independent customer survey, more than 80% of guests said they were extremely satisfied and 99% said they were satisfied with their overall Ritz-Carlton experience, compared with under 70% for their nearest luxury hotel competitor. Pretax return on investment and earnings nearly doubled between 1995 and 1999. In 1999 revenue per available room (the industry's measure of market share) exceeded the industry average by more than 300%.

*Source:* National Quality Program at the National Institute of Standards and Technology Web site, http://www.quality.nist.gov.

*Any of the "Ladies and Gentlemen of the Ritz-Carlton" can spend up to $2000 to immediately correct a guest's problem or handle a complaint. Its employees are the key factor in Ritz-Carlton's receipt of two Malcolm Baldrige National Quality Awards and the highest guest satisfaction level in the luxury hotel industry.*

Companies in service industries like fast-food restaurants, airlines, entertainment, and hotel lodging lose more customers because either their customer service is poor or their competitors are providing better service, than for any other reason, including price.

## THE COST OF QUALITY

According to legendary quality guru Armand Feigenbaum, "quality costs are the foundation for quality-systems economics." Quality costs have traditionally served as the basis for evaluating investments in quality programs. The costs of quality are those incurred to achieve good quality and to satisfy the customer, as well as costs incurred when quality fails to satisfy the customer. Thus, quality costs fall into two categories: the cost of achieving good quality, also known as the *cost of quality assurance*, and the cost associated with poor-quality products, also referred to as the *cost of not conforming* to specifications.

### THE COST OF ACHIEVING GOOD QUALITY

The costs of a quality-management program are *prevention costs* and *appraisal costs*. **Prevention costs** are the costs of trying to prevent poor-quality products from reaching the customer. Prevention reflects the quality philosophy of "do it right the first time," the goal of a quality-management program. Examples of prevention costs include:

**Prevention costs:** costs incurred during product design.

The *costs of preventing poor quality* include planning, design, process, training, and information costs.

*Quality planning costs*: The costs of developing and implementing the quality-management program.
*Product-design costs*: The costs of designing products with quality characteristics.
*Process costs*: The costs expended to make sure the productive process conforms to quality specifications.
*Training costs*: The costs of developing and putting on quality training programs for employees and management.
*Information costs*: The costs of acquiring and maintaining (typically on computers) data related to quality, and the development and analysis of reports on quality performance.

**Appraisal costs** are the costs of measuring, testing, and analyzing materials, parts, products, and the productive process to ensure that product-quality specifications are being met. Examples of appraisal costs include:

**Appraisal costs:** costs of measuring, testing, and analyzing.

*Costs of measuring quality* include inspection, testing, equipment, and operator costs.

*Inspection and testing*: The costs of testing and inspecting materials, parts, and the product at various stages and at the end of the process.
*Test equipment costs*: The costs of maintaining equipment used in testing the quality characteristics of products.
*Operator costs*: The costs of the time spent by operators to gather data for testing product quality, to make equipment adjustments to maintain quality, and to stop work to assess quality.

Appraisal costs tend to be higher in a service organization than in a manufacturing company and, therefore, are a greater proportion of total quality costs. Quality in services is related primarily to the interaction between an employee and a customer, which makes the cost of appraising quality more difficult. Quality appraisal in a manufacturing operation can take place almost exclusively in-house; appraisal of service quality usually requires customer interviews, surveys, questionnaires, and the like.

### THE COST OF POOR QUALITY

Costs associated with poor quality are also referred to as costs of nonconformance, or failure costs. The cost of failures is the difference between what it actually costs to produce a product or deliver a service and what it would cost if there were no failures. This is generally the largest quality cost category in a company, frequently accounting for 70 to 90% of total quality costs. This is where the greatest cost improvement is possible.

**Internal failure costs:** include scrap, rework, process failure, downtime, and price reductions.

The cost of poor quality can be categorized as *internal failure costs* or *external failure costs*. **Internal failure costs** are incurred when poor-quality products are discovered before they are delivered to the customer. Examples of internal failure costs include:

*Scrap costs*: The costs of poor-quality products that must be discarded, including labor, material, and indirect costs.
*Rework costs*: The costs of fixing defective products to conform to quality specifications.
*Process failure costs*: The costs of determining why the production process is producing poor-quality products.
*Process downtime costs*: The costs of shutting down the productive process to fix the problem.
*Price-downgrading costs*: The costs of discounting poor-quality products—that is, selling products as "seconds."

**External failure costs:** include complaints, returns, warranty claims, liability, and lost sales.

**External failure costs** are incurred after the customer has received a poor-quality product and are primarily related to customer service. Examples of external failure costs include:

*Customer complaint costs*: The costs of investigating and satisfactorily responding to a customer complaint resulting from a poor-quality product.
*Product return costs*: The costs of handling and replacing poor-quality products returned by the customer.
*Warranty claims costs*: The costs of complying with product warranties.
*Product liability costs*: The litigation costs resulting from product liability and customer injury.
*Lost sales costs*: The costs incurred because customers are dissatisfied with poor-quality products and do not make additional purchases.

Internal failure costs tend to be low for a service, whereas external failure costs can be quite high. A service organization has little opportunity to examine and correct a defective internal process, usually an employee–customer interaction, before it actually happens. At that point it becomes an external failure. External failures typically result in an increase in service time or inconvenience for the customer. Examples of external failures include a customer waiting too long to place a catalogue phone order; a catalogue order that arrives with the wrong item, requiring the customer to repackage and send it back; an error in a charge card billing statement, requiring the customer to make phone calls or write letters to correct it; sending a customer's orders or statements to the wrong address; or an overnight mail package that does not arrive overnight.

## MEASURING AND REPORTING QUALITY COSTS

Collecting data on quality costs can be difficult. The costs of lost sales, of responding to customer complaints, of process downtime, of operator testing, of quality information, and of quality planning and product design are all costs that may be difficult to measure. These costs must be estimated by management. Training costs, inspection and testing costs, scrap costs, the cost of product downgrading, product return costs, warranty claims, and liability costs can usually be measured. Many of these costs are collected as part of normal accounting procedures.

**Index numbers:** ratios that measure quality costs against a base value.

Management wants quality costs reported in a manner that can be easily interpreted and is meaningful. One format for reporting quality costs is with **index numbers**, or **indices**. Index numbers are ratios that measure quality costs relative to some base value, such as the ratio of quality costs to total sales revenue or the ratio of quality costs to units of final product. These index numbers are used to compare quality management efforts between time periods or between departments or functions. Index numbers themselves do not provide very much information about the effectiveness of a quality-management program. They usually will not show directly that a company is producing good- or poor-quality products. These measures are informative only when they are compared to some standard or other index. Some common index measures are:

**Labor index**: The ratio of quality cost to direct labor hours; it has the advantage of being easily computed (from accounting records) and easily understood, but it is not always effective for long-term comparative analysis when technological advances reduce labor usage.
**Cost index**: The ratio of quality cost to manufacturing cost (direct and indirect cost); it is easy to compute from accounting records and is not affected by technological change.
**Sales index**: The ratio of quality cost to sales; it is easily computed, but it can be distorted by changes in selling price and costs.
**Production index**: The ratio of quality cost to units of final product; it is easy to compute from accounting records but is not effective if a number of different products exist.

**Labor index:** the ratio of quality cost to labor hours.

**Cost index:** the ratio of quality cost to manufacturing cost.

**Sales index:** the ratio of quality cost to sales.

**Production index:** the ratio of quality cost to units of final product.

The following example illustrates several of these index numbers.

Example 3.1

**An Evaluation of Quality Costs and Quality Index Numbers**

The H&S Motor Company produces small motors (e.g., 3 hp) for use in lawnmowers and garden equipment. The company instituted a quality-management program in 2001 and has recorded the following quality cost data and accounting measures for four years.

| | Year | | | |
|---|---|---|---|---|
| | *2001* | *2002* | *2003* | *2004* |
| ***Quality Costs*** | | | | |
| Prevention | $27,000 | 41,500 | 74,600 | 112,300 |
| Appraisal | 155,000 | 122,500 | 113,400 | 107,000 |
| Internal failure | 386,400 | 469,200 | 347,800 | 219,100 |
| External failure | 242,000 | 196,000 | 103,500 | 106,000 |
| Total | $810,400 | 829,200 | 639,300 | 544,400 |
| ***Accounting Measures*** | | | | |
| Sales | $4,360,000 | 4,450,000 | 5,050,000 | 5,190,000 |
| Manufacturing costs | 1,760,000 | 1,810,000 | 1,880,000 | 1,890,000 |

The company wants to assess its quality-assurance program and develop quality index numbers using sales and manufacturing cost bases for the four-year period.

*Solution*

The H&S Company experienced many of the typical outcomes when its quality-assurance program was instituted. Approximately 78% of H&S's total quality costs are a result of internal and external failures, not unlike many companies. Failure costs frequently contribute 50 to 90% of overall quality costs. The typical reaction to high failure costs is to increase product monitoring and inspection to eliminate poor-quality products, resulting in high appraisal costs. This appeared to be the strategy employed by H&S when its quality-management program was initiated in 2001. In 2002 H&S was able to identify more defective items, resulting in an apparent increase in internal failure costs and lower external failure costs (as fewer defective products reached the customer).

During 2001 and 2002 prevention costs were modest. However, prevention is critical in reducing both internal and external failures. By instituting quality training programs, redesigning the production process, and planning how to build in product quality, companies are able to reduce poor-quality products within the production process and prevent them from reaching the customer. This was the case at H&S, because prevention costs increased by more than 300% during the four-year period. Since fewer poor-quality products are being made, less monitoring and inspection is necessary, and appraisal costs thus decline. Internal and external failure costs are also reduced because of a reduction in defective products. In general, an increase in expenditures for prevention will result in a decrease in all other quality-cost categories. It is also not uncommon for a quality-management program to isolate one or two specific quality problems that, when prevented, have a large impact on overall quality cost reduction. Quality problems are not usually evenly distributed throughout the product process; a few isolated problems tend to result in the majority of poor-quality products.

The H&S Company also desired to develop index numbers using quality costs as a proportion of sales and manufacturing costs, generally two of the more popular quality indexes. The general formula for these index numbers is

$$\text{Quality index} = \frac{\text{total quality costs}}{\text{base}}(100)$$

For example, the index number for 2001 sales is

$$\text{Quality cost per sale} = \frac{\$810{,}400(100)}{4{,}360{,}000}$$
$$= 18.58$$

The quality index numbers for sales and manufacturing costs for the four-year period are given in the following table.

| Year | Quality Sales Index | Quality Manufacturing Cost Index |
|---|---|---|
| 2001 | 18.58 | 46.04 |
| 2002 | 18.63 | 45.18 |
| 2003 | 12.66 | 34.00 |
| 2004 | 10.49 | 28.80 |

These index numbers alone provide little insight into the effectiveness of the quality-management program; however, as a standard to make comparisons over time they can be useful. The H&S Company quality index numbers reflect dramatically improved quality during the four-year period. Quality costs as a proportion of both sales and manufacturing costs improved significantly. Quality index numbers do not provide information that will enable the company to diagnose and correct quality problems in the production process. They are useful in showing trends in product quality over time and reflecting the impact of product quality relative to accounting measures with which managers are usually familiar.

## THE QUALITY–COST RELATIONSHIP

In Example 3.1 we showed that when the sum of prevention and appraisal costs increased, internal and external failure costs decreased. Recall that prevention and appraisal costs are the costs of achieving good quality, and internal and external failure costs are the costs of poor quality. In general, when the cost of achieving good quality increases, the cost of poor quality declines.

**The *cost of quality* is the difference between the price of nonconformance and conformance.**

Philip Crosby's fourth absolute from his 1984 book *Quality Without Tears*, explains that basically the dollar *cost of quality* is the difference between the price of nonconformance, the cost of doing things wrong (i.e., the cost of poor quality), and the price of conformance, the cost of doing things right (i.e., the cost of achieving good quality). He estimates that the cost of doing things wrong can account for 20 to 35% of revenues, while the cost of doing things right is typically 3 to 4%. As such, managers should determine where the cost of quality is occurring and find out what causes it.

## THE COMPETITIVE EDGE

### Reducing Quality Costs at Seagate Technology

Seagate Technology, headquartered in Scotts Valley, California (near San Jose), with 20 global plants, is a leading provider of information storage technology for the Internet, business, and consumer applications. When Seagate was founded in 1979, it was the first company to build 5.25-inch hard disk drives specifically for the personal computer. Its products now include disk drives for computer servers and consumer electronics, storage area network solutions, and server applications. As the demand for more storage capacity increases, Seagate strives to be first to market with products with improved head and disk technology to quickly store and retrieve more information on increasingly smaller disk space. Reducing the time for new product development by only one day can result in additional profits of as much as $4 million.

At Seagate the cost of poor quality includes the direct costs of finding and fixing defects as well as the hidden costs of failing to meet customer expectations, missing opportunities for increased efficiency, losses in market share, increases in production cycle time, labor associated with ordering replacement materials, and the cost of rework. For most companies the cost of poor quality is around 25% of sales, which at Seagate is over $1 billion annually. Since various studies indicate that approximately 70% of a products total cost is determined by its design, Seagate focuses on design for six sigma (DFSS). This allows it to cut costs in the most efficient manner possible: in development before the product is produced in volume. After the product reaches the production stage, the company focuses on improvement through six sigma projects. Black Belts lead customer focus teams supported by Green Belts through the DMAIC breakthrough strategy. Six sigma at Seagate technology has achieved annual savings of $500 million, and has reduced inventory by 40%, product development cycle time by 35% and production cycle time by 30%.

*Source:* S. Kumar and M. Gronseth, "The Seagate Story," *Qualityworld* 28 (11, November 2002), pp. 46–48.

Companies committed to TQM believe that the increase in sales and market share resulting from increased consumer confidence in the quality of their products offsets the higher costs of achieving good quality. Furthermore, as a company focuses on good quality, the cost of achieving good quality will be less because of the improvements in technologies, processes, and work methods that will result from the quality-improvement effort. These companies frequently seek to achieve 100% quality and *zero defects*.

The Japanese first recognized that the costs of poor quality had been traditionally underestimated. These costs did not take into account the customer losses that can be attributed to a reputation for poor quality. Costs of poor quality were hard to quantify, so they were ignored. The Japanese viewed the cost associated with a reputation for poor quality to be quite high. The traditional quality–cost relationship does not reflect the total impact of an effective quality management program on a company's performance. A General Accounting Office report on companies that were Baldrige Quality Award finalists has shown that corporationwide quality-improvement programs result in higher worker motivation, improved employee relations, increased productivity, higher customer satisfaction, and increased market share and profitability.

## THE BOTTOM LINE—PROFITABILITY

Quality improvement, as originally initiated by Japanese companies, was not intended to improve profitability but to gain customer focus and be more competitive. Quality management was considered to be a longer-term commitment than simply short-run cost savings and profits. However, quality management has been around now for about three decades, and researchers have begun to look at it to see if it has been profitable.

A survey of 26 Japanese Deming Quality Prize–winning companies committed to TQM showed that all gained higher-than-average results for different financial performance indicators. A number of studies of Baldrige Award winners in the United States have consistently shown that their financial performance exceeds industry averages.

In *Quality Is Free*, Philip Crosby states that, "Quality is not only free, it is an honest-to-everything profit maker."[4] Gary L. Tooker, CEO and vice chairman of Motorola, in response

[4]Philip Crosby, *Quality Is Free* (New York: McGraw-Hill, 1979).

to the question, "Is there a link between quality and profitability?" responded that "We've saved several billion dollars over the last year because of our focus on quality improvement and the six sigma initiative. . . . there is no doubt about the fact that it has enhanced our bottom line."[5]

This is only the tip of a mountain of conclusive evidence that *in the long run* quality improvement and profitability are closely related. As quality improves, the costs associated with poor quality decline. Quality improvements result in increased productivity. As the quality of a company's products or services improve, it becomes more competitive and its market share increases. Customers' perception of a company's products as being of high quality and its competitive posture enables the company to charge higher prices. Taken together, these things result in higher long-run profitability.

## THE EFFECT OF QUALITY MANAGEMENT ON PRODUCTIVITY

In the previous section we saw how an effective quality-management program can help to reduce quality-related costs and improve market share and profitability. Quality management can also improve productivity—the number of units produced from available resources.

### PRODUCTIVITY

**Productivity:** the ratio of output to input.

**Productivity** is a measure of a company's effectiveness in converting inputs into outputs. It is broadly defined as

$$\text{Productivity} = \frac{\text{output}}{\text{input}}$$

An output is the final product from a service or production process, such as an automobile, a hamburger, a sale, or a catalogue order. Inputs are the parts, material, labor, capital, and so on that go into the productive process. Productivity measures, depending on the outputs and inputs used, are labor productivity (output per labor-hour) and machine productivity (output per machine-hour).

*Quality impact on productivity:* Fewer defects increase output and quality improvement reduces inputs.

Improving quality by reducing defects will increase good output and reduce inputs. In fact, virtually all aspects of quality improvement have a favorable impact on different measures of productivity. Improving product design and production processes, improving the quality of materials and parts, and improving job designs and work activity will all increase productivity.

### MEASURING PRODUCT YIELD AND PRODUCTIVITY

**Yield:** a measure of productivity.

Product **yield** is a measure of output used as an indicator of productivity. It can be computed for the entire production process (or for one stage in the process) as follows:

$$\begin{aligned}\text{Yield} &= (\text{total input})(\%\text{ good units}) \\ &\quad + (\text{total input})(1 - \%\text{ good units})(\%\text{ reworked})\end{aligned}$$

or

$$Y = (I)(\%G) + (I)(1 - \%G)(\%R)$$

where

$$\begin{aligned}I &= \text{planned number units of product started in the production process} \\ \%\,G &= \text{percentage of good units produced} \\ \%\,R &= \text{percentage of defective units that are successfully reworked}\end{aligned}$$

In this formula, yield is the sum of the percentage of products started in the process (or at a stage) that will turn out to be good quality plus the percentage of the defective (rejected) products that are reworked. Any increase in the percentage of good products through improved quality will increase product yield.

Improved quality increases product yield.

[5]K. Bemowski, "Motorola's Fountain of Youth," *Quality Progress* 28(10; October 1995), pp. 29–31.

**Example 3.2**

**Computing Product Yield**

The H&S Motor Company starts production for a particular type of motor with a steel motor housing. The production process begins with 100 motors each day. The percentage of good motors produced each day averages 80% and the percentage of poor-quality motors that can be reworked is 50%. The company wants to know the daily product yield and the effect on productivity if the daily percentage of good-quality motors is increased to 90%.

*Solution*

$$\text{Yield} = (I)(\%\,G) + (I)(1 - \%\,G)(\%\,R)$$
$$Y = 100(0.80) + 100(1 - 0.80)(0.50)$$
$$= 90 \text{ motors}$$

If product quality is increased to 90% good motors, the yield will be

$$Y = 100(0.90) + 100(1 - 0.90)(0.50)$$
$$= 95 \text{ motors}$$

A 10 percentage-point increase in quality products results in a 5.5% increase in productivity output.

Now we will expand our discussion of productivity to include product manufacturing cost. The manufacturing cost per (good) product is computed by dividing the sum of total direct manufacturing cost and total cost for all reworked units by the yield, as follows:

$$\text{Product cost} = \frac{\text{(direct manufacturing cost per unit)(input)} + \text{(rework cost per unit)(reworked units)}}{\text{yield}}$$

or

$$\text{Product cost} = \frac{(K_d)(I) + (K_r)(R)}{Y}$$

where

$K_d$ = direct manufacturing cost per unit
$I$ = input
$K_r$ = rework cost per unit
$R$ = reworked units
$Y$ = yield

**Example 3.3**

**Computing Product Cost per Unit**

The H&S Motor Company has a direct manufacturing cost per unit of $30, and motors that are of inferior quality can be reworked for $12 per unit. From Example 3.2, 100 motors are produced daily, 80% (on average) are of good quality and 20% are defective. Of the defective motors, half can be reworked to yield good-quality products. Through its quality-management program, the company has discovered a problem in its production process that, when corrected (at a minimum cost), will increase the good-quality products to 90%. The company wants to assess the impact on the direct cost per unit of improvement in product quality.

*Solution*

The original manufacturing cost per motor is

$$\text{Product cost} = \frac{(K_d)(I) + (K_r)(R)}{Y}$$

$$\text{Product cost} = \frac{(\$30)(100) + (\$12)(10)}{90 \text{ motors}}$$
$$= \$34.67 \text{ per motor}$$

The manufacturing cost per motor with the quality improvement is

$$\text{Product cost} = \frac{(\$30)(100) + (\$12)(5)}{95 \text{ motors}}$$

$$\text{Product cost} = \$32.21 \text{ per motor}$$

The improvement in the production process as a result of the quality-management program will result in a decrease of $2.46 per unit, or 7.1%, in direct manufacturing cost per unit as well as a 5.5% increase in product yield (computed in Example 3.2), with a minimal investment in labor, plant, or equipment.

In Examples 3.2 and 3.3 we determined productivity measures for a single production process. However, it is more likely that product quality would be monitored throughout the production process at various stages. Each stage would result in a portion of good-quality, "work-in-process" products. For a production process with $n$ stages, the yield, $Y$ (without reworking), is,

$$Y = (I)(\%g_1)(\%g_2)\cdots(\%g_n)$$

where

I = input of items to the production process that will result in finished products
$g_i$ = good-quality, work-in-process products at stage $i$

Example 3.4

**Computing Product Yield for a Multi-stage Process**

At the H&S Motor Company, motors are produced in a four-stage process. Motors are inspected following each stage, with percentage yields (on average) of good-quality, work-in-process units as follows.

| Stage | Average Percentage Good Quality |
|---|---|
| 1 | 0.93 |
| 2 | 0.95 |
| 3 | 0.97 |
| 4 | 0.92 |

The company wants to know the daily product yield for product input of 100 units per day. Furthermore, it would like to know how many input units it would have to start with each day to result in a final daily yield of 100 good-quality units.

*Solution*

$$Y = (I)(\%g_1)(\%g_2)(\%g_3)(\%g_4)$$
$$= (100)(0.93)(0.95)(0.97)(0.92)$$
$$Y = 78.8 \text{ motors}$$

Thus, the production process has a daily good-quality product yield of 78.8 motors.

To determine the product input that would be required to achieve a product yield of 100 motors, $I$ is treated as a decision variable when $Y$ equals 100:

$$I = \frac{Y}{(\%g_1)(\%g_2)(\%g_3)(\%g_4)}$$

$$I = \frac{100}{(0.93)(0.95)(0.97)(0.92)}$$
$$= 126.8 \text{ motors}$$

To achieve output of 100 good-quality motors, the production process must start with approximately 127 motors.

## THE QUALITY–PRODUCTIVITY RATIO

Another measure of the effect of quality on productivity combines the concepts of quality index numbers and product yield. Called the **quality–productivity ratio** (QPR),[6] it is computed as follows:

**Quality–productivity ratio:** a productivity index that includes productivity and quality costs.

$$\text{QPR} = \frac{\text{good-quality units}}{(\text{input})(\text{processing cost}) + (\text{defective units})(\text{rework cost})}(100)$$

This is actually a quality index number that includes productivity and quality costs. The QPR increases if either processing cost or rework costs or both decrease. It increases if more good-quality units are produced relative to total product input (i.e., the number of units that begin the production process).

**Example 3.5**
**Computing the Quality–Productivity Ratio (QPR)**

The H&S Motor Company produces small motors at a processing cost of $30 per unit. Defective motors can be reworked at a cost of $12 each. The company produces 100 motors per day and averages 80% good-quality motors, resulting in 20% defects, 50% of which can be reworked prior to shipping to customers. The company wants to examine the effects of (1) increasing the production rate to 200 motors per day; (2) reducing the processing cost to $26 and the rework cost to $10; (3) increasing, through quality improvement, the product yield of good-quality products to 95%; and (4) the combination of 2 and 3.

*Solution*

The QPR for the base case is computed as follows.

$$\begin{aligned}\text{QPR} &= \frac{80 + 10}{(100)(\$30) + (10)(\$12)}(100)\\ &= 2.89\end{aligned}$$

*Case 1.* Increase input to production capacity of 200 units.

$$\begin{aligned}\text{QPR} &= \frac{160 + 20}{(200)(\$30) + (20)(\$12)}(100)\\ &= 2.89\end{aligned}$$

Increasing production capacity alone has no effect on the QPR; it remains the same as the base case.

*Case 2.* Reduce processing cost to $26 and rework cost to $10.

$$\begin{aligned}\text{QPR} &= \frac{80 + 10}{(100)(\$26) + (10)(\$10)}(100)\\ &= 3.33\end{aligned}$$

These cost decreases caused the QPR to increase.

*Case 3.* Increase initial good-quality units to 95 percent.

$$\begin{aligned}\text{QPR} &= \frac{95 + 2.5}{(100)(\$30) + (2.5)(\$12)}(100)\\ &= 3.22\end{aligned}$$

Again, the QPR increases as product quality improves.

*Case 4.* Decrease costs and increase initial good-quality units.

$$\begin{aligned}\text{QPR} &= \frac{95 + 2.5}{(100)(\$26) + (2.5)(\$10)}(100)\\ &= 3.71\end{aligned}$$

The largest increase in the QPR results from decreasing costs and increasing initial good-quality product through improved quality.

[6]E. E. Adam, J. E. Hershauer, and W. A. Ruch, *Productivity and Quality: Measurement as a Basis of Improvement*, 2nd ed. (Columbia, MO: Research Center, College of Business and Public Administration, University of Missouri, 1986).

## IDENTIFYING QUALITY PROBLEMS AND CAUSES

Seven quality-control tools for identifying quality problems and their causes.

Some of the most popular techniques for identifying the causes of quality problems are Pareto charts, process flowcharts, check sheets, histograms, scatter diagrams, statistical process control charts, and cause-and-effect diagrams. These well-known tools are sometimes known as the "magnificent seven," the "*seven QC tools*" and the seven process improvement tools. We discuss each in the following sections, and they are summarized in Figure 3.5 on the facing page.

### PARETO ANALYSIS

**Pareto analysis:** most quality problems result from a few causes.

**Pareto analysis** is a method of identifying the causes of poor quality. It was devised in the early 1950s by the quality expert Joseph Juran. He named this method after a nineteenth-century Italian economist, Vilfredo Pareto, who determined that a small percentage of the people accounted for most of the wealth. Pareto analysis is based on Juran's finding that most quality problems and costs result from only a few causes. For example, he discovered in a textile mill that almost 75% of all defective cloth was caused by only a few weavers, and in a paper mill he studied, more than 60% of the cost of poor quality was attributable to a single category of defects. Correcting the few major causes of most of the quality problems will result in the greatest cost impact.

Pareto analysis can be applied by tallying the number of defects for each of the different possible causes of poor quality in a product or service and then developing a frequency distribution from the data. This frequency distribution, referred to as a *Pareto diagram*, is a useful visual aid for focusing on major quality problems.

Consider a product for which the causes of poor quality have been identified as follows.

| Cause | Number of Defects | Percentage |
|---|---|---|
| Poor design | 80 | 64% |
| Wrong part dimensions | 16 | 13 |
| Defective parts | 12 | 10 |
| Incorrect machine calibration | 7 | 6 |
| Operator errors | 4 | 3 |
| Defective material | 3 | 2 |
| Surface abrasions | 3 | 2 |
| | 125 | 100% |

For each cause of poor quality, the number of defects attributed to that cause has been tallied over a period of time. This information is then converted into the Pareto chart shown in Figure 3.6 on page 110.

This Pareto chart identifies the major cause of poor quality to be poor design. Correcting the design problem will result in the greatest quality cost savings with the least expenditure. However, the other problems should not be ignored. TQM teaches us that total and continual quality improvement is the long-term goal. The Pareto diagram simply identifies the quality problems that will result in the greatest immediate impact on quality improvement.

### PROCESS FLOWCHARTS

A *flowchart* is a diagram of a job operation or process.

A **process flowchart** is a diagram of the steps in a job, operation, or process. It enables everyone involved in identifying and solving quality problems to have a clear picture of how a specific operation works and a common frame of reference. It also enables a process improvement team to understand the interrelationship of the departments and

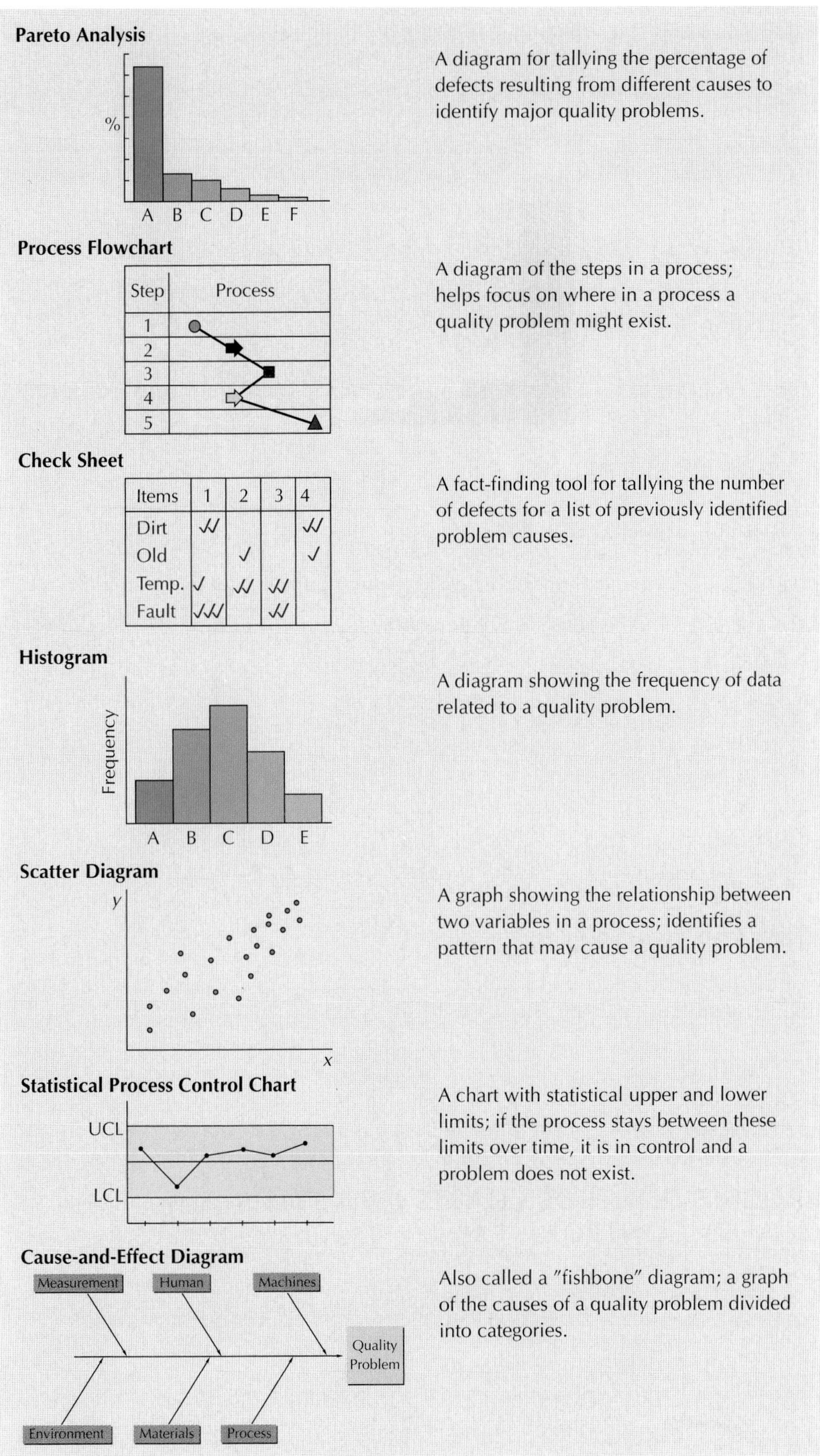


**Figure 3.5**
**The Seven Quality-Control Tools**

functions that constitute a process. This helps focus on where problems might occur and if the process itself needs fixing. Development of the flowchart can help identify quality problems by helping the problem solvers better understand the process. Flowcharts are described in greater detail in Chapter 6 ("Processes and Technologies") and Chapter 8 ("Human Resources in Operations Management").

**Figure 3.6**
**Pareto Chart**

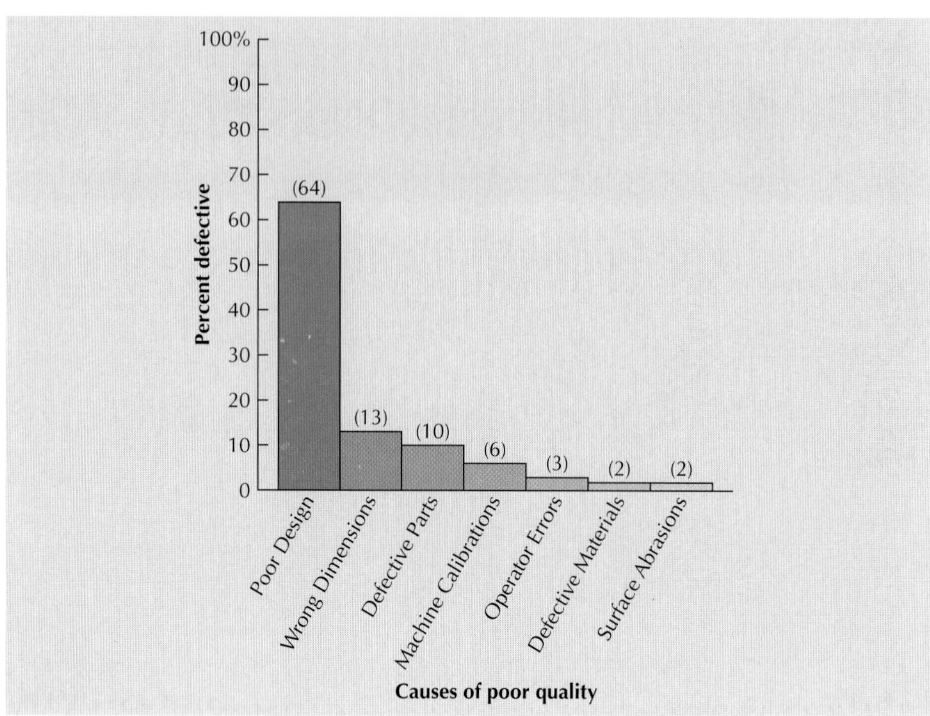


## CHECK SHEETS AND HISTOGRAMS

A *check sheet* is a list of causes of quality problems with the number of defects resulting from each cause used to develop a bar chart called a *histogram*.

Check sheets are frequently used in conjunction with histograms, as well as with Pareto diagrams. A *check sheet* is a fact-finding tool used to collect data about quality problems. A typical check sheet for quality defects tallies the number of defects for a variety of previously identified problem causes. When the check sheet is completed, the total tally of defects for each cause can be used to create a *histogram* or a Pareto chart.

## SCATTER DIAGRAMS

A *scatter diagram* is a graph showing how two process variables relate to each other.

*Scatter diagrams* graphically show the relationship between two variables, such as the brittleness of a piece of material and the temperature at which it is baked. One temperature reading should result in a specific degree of brittleness representing one point on the diagram. Many such points on the diagram visually show a pattern between the two variables and a relationship or lack of one. This diagram could be used to identify a particular quality problem associated with the baking process.

## PROCESS CONTROL CHARTS AND STATISTICAL QUALITY CONTROL

*Process control* involves monitoring a production process using statistical quality-control methods.

We discuss control charts and other statistical quality-control methods in Chapter 4, "Statistical Process Control." For now, it is sufficient to say that a control chart includes a horizontal line through the middle of a chart representing the process average or norm. It also has a line below this center line representing a lower control limit and a line above it for the upper control limit. Samples from the process are taken over time and measured according to some attribute. In its simplest form, if the measurement is within the two control limits, the process is said to be in control and there is no quality problem, but if the measurement is outside the limits, then a problem probably exists and should be investigated.

Statistical quality-control methods such as the process control chart are important tools for quality improvement. Employees in TQM companies at all levels, and especially in production, are provided with extensive training in statistical quality-control methods. This enables them to identify quality problems and their causes and to make suggestions for improvement.

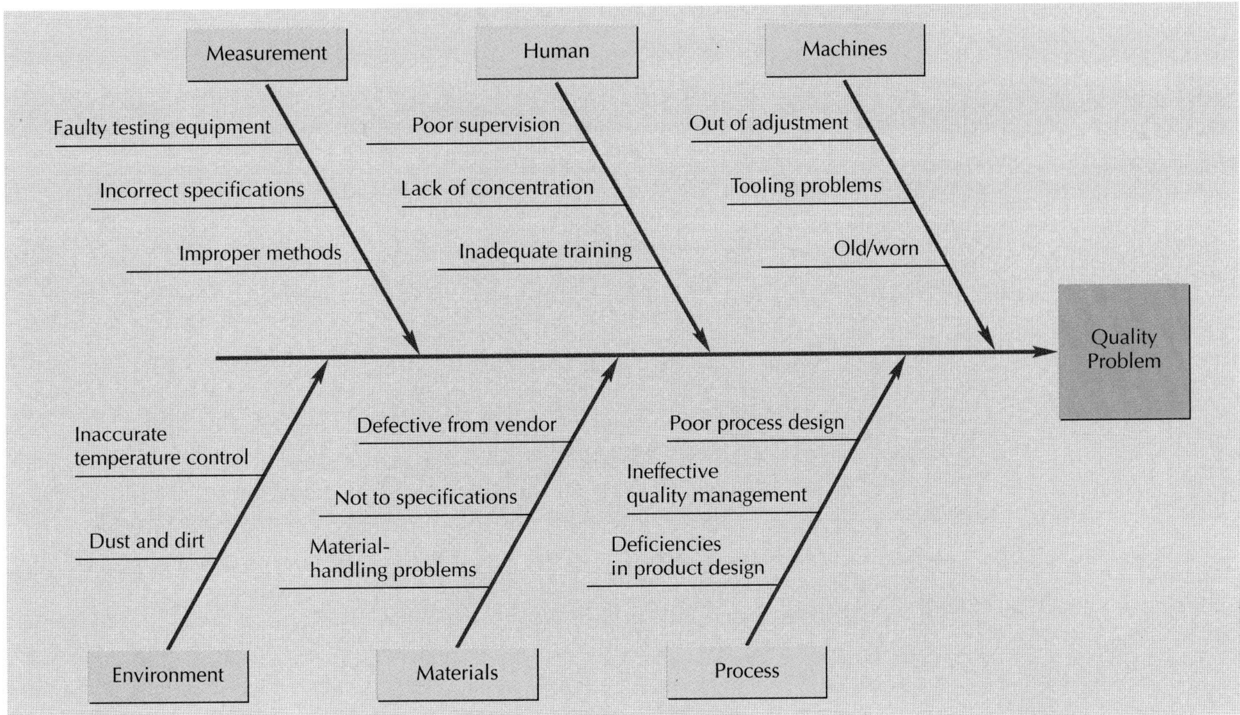


**Figure 3.7**
**A General Cause-and-Effect Diagram**

## CAUSE-AND-EFFECT DIAGRAMS

A **cause-and-effect diagram**, also called a "fishbone" or Ishikawa diagram, is a graphical description of the elements of a specific quality problem and the relationship between those elements. It is used to identify the causes of a quality problem so it can be corrected. Cause-and-effect diagrams are usually developed as part of participative problem solving to help a team of employees, supervisors, and managers identify causes of quality problems. This tool is a normal part of the problem-solving activity of quality circles and teams.

**Cause-and-effect diagram or fishbone diagram:** a chart showing the different categories of problem causes.

Figure 3.7 illustrates the general structure of the cause-and-effect diagram. The "effect" box at the end of the diagram is the quality problem that needs correction. A center line connects the effect box to the major categories of possible problem causes, displayed as branches off of the center line. The box at the end of each branch (or fishbone) describes the cause category. The diagram starts out in this form with only the major categories at the end of each branch. Individual causes associated with each category are attached as separate lines along the length of the branch during the brainstorming process. Sometimes the causes are rank-ordered along the branches in order to identify those that are most likely to affect the problem. The cause-and-effect diagram is a means for thinking through a problem and recording the possible causes in an organized and easily interpretable manner. The causes listed along the branches under each category in Figure 3.7 are generic, but for a specific quality problem with an actual product, the causes would be product- and problem-specific.

## QUALITY AWARDS AND SETTING QUALITY STANDARDS

The Baldrige Award, Deming Prize, and other award competitions have become valuable and coveted prizes to American companies eager to benefit from the aura and reputation for quality that awaits the winners. They have also provided widely used sets of guidelines to help companies implement an effective quality-management program, and winners provide quality standards, or "benchmarks," for other companies to emulate.

## THE MALCOLM BALDRIGE AWARD

The Baldrige Award was created in 1987 to stimulate growth of quality management in the United States.

The Malcolm Baldrige National Quality Award is given annually to one or two companies in each of five categories: manufacturing, services, small businesses (with less than 500 full-time employees), health care, and education. It was created by law in 1987 (named after former Secretary of Commerce Malcolm Baldrige, who died in 1987) to (1) stimulate U.S. companies to improve quality, (2) establish criteria for businesses to use to evaluate their individual quality-improvement efforts, (3) set as examples those companies that were successful in improving quality, and (4) help other U.S. organizations learn how to manage quality by disseminating information about the award winners' programs.

The award criteria focus on the soundness of the approach to quality improvement, the overall quality-management program as it is implemented throughout the organization, and customer satisfaction. The seven major categories of criteria by which companies are examined are leadership, information and analysis, strategic planning, human resource focus, process management, business results, and customer and market focus.

## THE COMPETITIVE EDGE

### Baldrige Quality Award Winners: What It Takes

Year 2002 Baldrige Award recipients, Motorola, Inc. Commercial, Government and Industrial Solutions Sector (manufacturing category); Branch-Smith Printing Division (small business category); and SSM Health Care (health-care category), reflect the level of quality achievement and organizational characteristics that are necessary to win this award. All three companies have a companywide commitment to quality and continuous improvement reflected in very high customer satisfaction ratings; they have a high degree of employee satisfaction; they are socially conscious and diverse; they consistently outperform their benchmark competitors; and they have usually won other awards.

Motorola Inc. Commercial, Government and Industrial Sector (CGISS), headquartered in Schaumburg, Illinois, is the world's leading supplier of two-way radio communications, including radio networks, systems, products, and services, with sales of almost $4 billion in 2001. Customers include fire, police, and public service organizations, governments, and businesses. It has 14,000 employees in facilities in the United States, Africa, Asia, Europe, Latin America, and the Middle East. CGISS uses "Performance Excellence Scorecards" to involve customers in the design, development, and implementation of products. From 1999 to 2002 overall customer satisfaction exceeded 88%, and customers rated CGISS best-in-class radio manufacturer with quality ratings over 21% higher than those of its closest competitor. Product defects were reduced to 52 DPMO (5.38 sigma), and employee productivity increased 32%.

Branch-Smith Printing Division, located in Forth Worth, Texas, is a fourth-generation family-owned business with 68 employees. It specializes in designing, printing, binding, and mailing multipage bound materials, including publications, magazines, catalogues, directories, and books. In 2001 Branch-Smith had over $10 million in sales. To stand out in a highly competitive business (with over 45,000 companies nationwide and over 1000 in the Dallas/Fort Worth area), Branch-Smith uses a systematic customer complaint process, customer satisfaction surveys, regular meetings with key customers, and individual customer plans. From 1996 to 2002, the company's ratings for customer satisfaction with product quality exceeded those of competitors, the company grew 72%, and its growth rate has exceeded the industry average. It involves employees in all aspects of process improvement, and it conducts an annual employee satisfaction survey. From 1996 to 2001, employee satisfaction increased from 67 to 86%, near its benchmark of 87% achieved by a previous Baldrige Award winner; and employee turnover dropped from over 40% to under 8%.

SSM Health Care is a St. Louis-based, private, not-for-profit health-care system sponsored by the Franciscan Sisters of Mary in St. Louis, Missouri. It owns, manages, and is affiliated with 21 acute care hospitals and three nursing homes in Illinois, Missouri, Oklahoma, and Wisconsin. With operating revenues of $1.7 billion, 5000 physician partners and 23,000 employees, SSM provides a wide range of medical services. SSM seeks ways to improve patient care as part of its continuous quality-improvement program. SSM requires each of its entities to engage in one or more community projects such as free dental care clinics and campaigns to reduce teen drinking and smoking. Since 1999 SSM has exceeded its charity care goal of contributing a minimum of 25% of its operating margin from the prior year. Through a systemwide "Passport" tool, employees develop goals that support organization goals. Its employee benefits package includes flextime, work-at-home options, extensive insurance coverage, wellness programs, tuition assistance, and student loan repayment programs. Its employee turnover rate decreased from 21% in 1999 to 13% in 2002.

*Source:* National Quality program at the National Institute of Standards and Technology Web site, http://www.quality.nist.gov.

The Baldrige Award has had a major influence on U.S. companies, thousands of which request applications from the government each year to obtain a copy of the award guidelines and criteria for internal use in establishing quality-management programs. Many companies have made the Baldrige criteria for quality their own, and have also demanded that their suppliers submit applications for the Baldrige Quality Award. Since its inception in 1987, it has been estimated that the economic benefits of the Baldrige award to the U.S. economy is almost $30 billion. Companies that have won the Baldrige Quality Award and have become known as leaders in quality include Motorola, Xerox, Cadillac, Milliken, Federal Express, Ritz Carlton, and IBM. These and other Baldrige Award winners have become models or benchmarks for other companies to emulate in establishing their own TQM programs.

## OTHER AWARDS FOR QUALITY

The creation and subsequent success of the Baldrige Award has spawned a proliferation of national, international, government, industry, state, and individual quality awards. Table 3.3 (on page 114) provides information about selected national and international quality awards. (Internet addresses for these awards can be found on the Chapter 3 web links page on the text Web site.) The American Society for Quality (ASQ) sponsors a number of national individual awards, including, among others, the Armand V. Feigenbaum Medal, the Deming Medal, the E. Jack Lancaster Medal, the Edwards Medal, the Shewart Medal, and the Ishikawa Medal.

Prominent international awards include the European Quality Award, the Canadian Quality Award, the Australian Business Excellence Award, and the Deming Prize from Japan. The countries from which these four awards are administered plus the United States account for approximately 75% of the world's gross national product. The European Quality Award, established in 1991 to recognize outstanding businesses in 16 European countries, is similar in criteria and scope to the Baldrige Award, as are most of the other international awards.

## THE COMPETITIVE EDGE

### The Chugach School District, A Baldrige Award Winner in Education

The first Baldrige Award winners in the education category created in 2001 were the Chugach School District in Alaska, the Pearl River School District in New York's Hudson River Valley, and the University of Wisconsin-Stout in Menomonie in northwest Wisconsin. All three winners implemented the Baldrige quality criteria for education: leadership; strategic planning; student, stakeholder, and market focus; information and analysis; faculty and staff focus; process management; and organizational, performance results. The educational winners demonstrated that customer satisfaction is as critical in education as it is in business, and high-quality performance is attainable in all settings, not just business.

The Chugach School District (CSD) serves 200-plus students throughout 22,000 square miles in south-central Alaska accessible only by air and water. Half the students are native Alaskans. The students receive educational services in one of three small villages accessible by small aircraft or from itinerant teachers who visit their wilderness homes. The Chugach program is based on an individual learning plan that helps each student take ownership of his or her education and tie it to goals related to life beyond high school. To graduate, students must pass performance exams in traditional subjects such as reading, math, and science, as well as nontraditional areas such as service learning, career development, personal, social, and health development, technology, and cultural awareness and expression. CSD teachers make extensive use of technology and the Internet rather than textbooks. Students and teachers have unlimited access to computers, and all assessment and student reporting is done electronically. Before implementing the Baldrige criteria for quality performance, the school district was plagued by high dropout rates, low test scores, and a heavy reliance on social services after leaving school. As a result of Chugach's quality initiatives in pursuit of the Baldrige Award, achievement tests increased by almost 300%, and the percentage of students taking college entrance exams increased from zero to 70%. The teacher turnover rate decreased from an average of 55% to 12% as a result of a performance-based pay component, flexible working conditions, job rotation, and a high degree of empowerment.

*Source:* S.E. Daniels, "First to the Top, *Quality Progress*, 35(5; May 2002), pp. 41–53.

| Award | Organization | Description |
|---|---|---|
| Malcolm Baldrige Award | National Institute of Standards and Technology | Small business, manufacturing, service, education, and health care |
| Deming Medal | American Society for Quality | Leader in quality |
| J.D. Powers Awards | J.D. Powers Associates | Customer satisfaction in a variety of industries |
| George M. Low Trophy | NASA | NASA suppliers |
| President's Quality Award | U.S. Office of Personnel Management | Federal government organizations |
| IIE Award for Excellence in Productivity Improvement | Institute of Industrial Engineers | Large and small manufacturing companies and large and small service companies |
| Distinguished Service Medal | American Society for Quality | Gold medal for individual distinction |
| International Asia Pacific Award | Asia Pacific Quality Organization | Winners of national quality awards |
| Australian Business Excellence Awards | Standards Australia International Limited | Excellence medal, gold, silver, and bronze . awards open to Australian companies |
| Gold Award for Quality | Joint Accreditation Scheme of Australia and New Zealand | ISO 9004—2000 criteria |
| Canada Awards for Excellence | National Quality Institute | Quality Award and Healthy Workplace Award |
| European Quality Awards | European Foundation for Quality Management (EFQM) | European organizations demonstrating excellence in quality |
| French Quality Award | French Quality Movement (FQM) | Award based on FQM guidelines |
| Hungarian Quality Development Center Award | Hungarian Quality Development Center | EFQM criteria for Hungary |
| German National Quality Award | German Society for Quality and Association of German Engineers | EFQM criteria for German companies |
| Hong Kong Award for Industry | Quality Trade and Industry Dept. | Companies based and operating in Hong Kong |
| Rajiv Ghandi National Award | Bureau of Indian Standards | Indian manufacturing and service organizations |
| Japan Quality Award | Japanese Quality Award Committee | Six companies in manufacturing, service, and small/medium businesses |
| Deming Prize | Union of Japanese Scientists and Engineers | Application prize, individual prize, and quality-control award for business units |
| Japan Quality Medal | Union of Japanese Scientists and Engineers | Deming Application Prize companies |
| Scottish Quality Award | Quality Scotland Foundation | EFQM criteria for Scotland |
| Swedish Quality Award | Swedish Institute for Quality | Baldrige or EQFM criteria for Sweden |
| Swiss Quality Award | Swiss Association for Promotion of Quality | EQFM criteria for Switzerland |
| UK Qualith Award for Business Excellence | British Quality Foundation | EFQM criteria for United Kingdom |

**Table 3.3**
**Selected National and International Quality Awards**

The President's Quality Award was established in 1989 to recognize federal government organizations that improve their overall performance and capabilities, demonstrate mature approaches to quality throughout the organization, and demonstrate a sustained trend in high-quality products and services that result in effective use of taxpayer dollars. 2002 winners include the 55th Wing, Offutt Air Force Base (Nebraska); the Federal Aviation Administration Logistics Center (Oklahoma City); and the National Imagery and Mapping Agency (Bethesda, Maryland).

J.D. Power and Associates is an independent, third-party, company that provides companies in the automotive, energy/communications, travel, financial, and home-building industries with feedback from their customers based on surveys that they conduct. They also annually present awards to companies that have excelled in their industry based on independently financed consumer opinion studies. Award-winning companies are allowed to license the use of J.D. Power and Associates awards in advertising. For example, their 2002 automotive performance award winner for the "most appealing premium midsize

## THE COMPETITIVE EDGE

### Quality Award Winners in Hungary

Hungary has become one of Europe's economic success stories since the fall of the Soviet Union. Gross domestic product (GDP) grew by 3.8% in 2001 and 3.8% in 2002, industrial production increased by 18.6% in 2000, and unemployment was around 5.6% in 2001 and 2002. A nationwide focus on quality is one of the primary reasons cited for this level of success while other European nations have floundered. Following are examples of several quality award-winning Hungarian companies that have achieved success by focusing on quality improvement.

Burton-Apta make refractory ceramic products and systems used in kilns that produce ceramics. In 1986 Shoji Shiba, a Japanese professor, introduced TQM to Hungary, and Burton-Apta learned about quality concepts and tools. In 1993 it achieved ISO 9000 certification and won the International Institute for Applied Systems Analysis-Shiba Award, which is similar to the Deming Award in Japan. In 1997 Burton-Apta won the Hungarian National Quality Award, and in 1998 it was a European Quality Award finalist and in 2000 the winner. In 2002 it achieved ISO 9001:2000 certification. A self-assessment program has helped Burton-Apta to continue to make quality improvements that have resulted in increased customer and employee satisfaction and market share despite economic downturns.

Herend Porcelain Manufacturing, a 176-year-old firm, introduced a quality-management system in 1993 based on ISO 9000 criteria. The company achieved ISO certification in 1995, and it also developed a TQM system based on employee and customer satisfaction. Its quality initiatives have resulted in increased market share. In 1996 the company won the first Hungarian National Quality Award.

Pick Szeged Salami and Meat Processing Company, founded in 1869, is the largest meat processing company in Hungary. Pick used TQM principles to develop an extensive team approach to quality improvement, including use of PDCA cycle for different business functions such as product development. The company achieved ISO 9000 certification in 1995 and later upgraded to ISO 9001:2000. It received the Hungarian National Quality Award in 1999.

Westel Mobile Communications Company Ltd., headquartered in Budapest with 1700 employees, is Hungary's leading provider of wireless communications service. Shortly after the company was founded in 1993, it developed a quality program based on Malcolm Baldrige Award criteria, and in 1995 it achieved ISO 9001 certification. In 1996 Westel became the first service company to win the Hungarian National Quality Award, and it received the European Quality Award in 2001. Westel makes extensive use of customer survey results and data analysis and market analysis to assess customer habits, needs, and characteristics as well as developing strategies for customer satisfaction and retention.

All of Hungary's quality award winners strive to be role models for other companies. All are socially conscious firms, with a commitment to the environment as well as society.

*Source:* P. Molnar, "Hungary's Journey to Business Excellence," *Quality Progress* 36(2; February 2003), pp. 55–64.

car" was the Toyota Avalon; their 2002 award winner for the "highest guest satisfaction among economy/budget hotel chains" was Microtel Inns and Suites.

## AMERICAN CUSTOMER SATISFACTION INDEX

The *American Customer Satisfaction Index (ACSI)* was established in 1994 through a partnership of the University of Michigan Business School, the American Society for Quality (ASQ), and the international consulting firm, CFI Group. The ACSI is funded in part by corporate subscribers who receive industry benchmarking data and company-specific information about financial returns from improving customer satisfaction.

ACSI measures customer satisfaction with the goods and services of 7 economic sectors, 39 industries (including e-commerce and e-business), and more than 200 companies and 70 federal and local government agencies. The ACSI reports scores on a 0 to 100 scale which are based on econometric modeling of data obtained from telephone interviews with customers. From random-digit-dial (RDD) telephone samples (and Internet samples for e-commerce and e-business), more than 65,000 consumers are identified and interviewed annually.

ACSI scores are posted on their Web site at www.theacsi.org. For example, in 2003 Amazon.com had an ACSI score of 88, the highest score ever recorded in any service industry. Dell was the leading company in the PC industry with a score of 78. Cadillac was the highest-scoring car company at 87, followed by BMW and Toyota, both at 85.

## ISO 9000

*ISO* is not an acronym for the International Organization for Standardization; it is a word, "ISO," derived from the Greek "isos" meaning "equal."

The International Organization for Standardization (ISO), headquartered in Geneva, Switzerland, has as its members the national standards organizations for more than 130 countries. The ISO member for the United States is the American National Standards Institute (ANSI). The purpose of ISO is to facilitate global consensus agreements on international quality standards. It has resulted in a system for certifying suppliers to make sure they meet internationally accepted standards for quality management. It is a nongovernment organization and is not a part of the United Nations.

ISO 9000 is a set of procedures and policies for the international quality certification of suppliers.

During the 1970s it was generally acknowledged that the word *quality* had different meanings within and among industries and countries and around the world. In 1979 the ISO member representing the United Kingdom, the British Standard Institute (BSI), recognizing the need for standardization for quality management and assurance, submitted a formal proposal to ISO to develop international standards for quality assurance techniques and practices. Using standards that already existed in the United Kingdom and Canada as a basis, ISO established generic quality standards, primarily for manufacturing firms, that could be used worldwide.

### STANDARDS

Standards are documented agreements that include technical specifications or other precise criteria to be used consistently as rules, guidelines, or definitions to ensure that materials, products processes, and services are fit for their purpose. For example, the format for credit cards and phone cards was derived from ISO standards that specify such physical features as the cards' thickness so that they can be used worldwide. Standards, in general, increase the reliability and effectiveness of goods and services used around the world and as a result make life easier for everyone.

The ISO 9000 series of quality-management standards, guidelines, and technical reports was first published in 1978, and it is reviewed at least every five years. It was most recently revised and updated in 2000. ISO 9000:2000, *Quality Management Systems—Fundamentals and Vocabulary*, is the starting point for understanding the standards. It defines the fundamental terms and definitions used in the ISO 9000 family of standards, guidelines, and technical reports. ISO 9001:2000, *Quality Management Systems—Requirements*, is the requirement standard a company uses to assess its ability to meet customer and applicable regulatory requirements in order to achieve customer satisfaction. ISO 9004:2000, *Quality Management Systems—Guidelines for Performance Improvements*, provides detailed guidance to a company for the continual improvement of its quality-management system in order to achieve and sustain customer satisfaction. The ISO 9000 family includes 10 more published standards and guidelines; however, these three are the most widely used and applicable to the majority of companies.

### CERTIFICATION

Many companies around the world require that companies they do business with (e.g., suppliers) have ISO 9000 certification. In that way, despite possible language, technology, and cultural differences, a company can be sure that the company it's doing business with meets uniform standards—that is, they are "on the same page." ISO 9001:2000 is the only standard in the ISO 9000 family that carries third-party *certification* (referred to as *registration* in the United States). A third-party company called a registrar is the only authorized entity that can award ISO 9000 certification. Registrars are accredited by an authoritative national body and are contracted by companies to evaluate their quality-management system to see if it meets the ISO 9001 standards; if the company does, it is issued an ISO 9000 certification, which is recognized around the world. More than 350,000 ISO certifications were issued between 1994 and 2000 for the 1994 editions of the ISO 9001 series by third-party organizations in 150 countries.

ISO 9001:2000 primarily serves as a basis for benchmarking a company's quality-management system. Quality management, in ISO terms, measures how effectively man-

## THE COMPETITIVE EDGE

### Global ISO 9001 Certification at Dow Corning

Dow Corning Corporation, a pioneer in the development of silicones, has more than 40 manufacturing and customer service locations and research facilities in seven countries, supplying more than 7000 products to over 25,000 customers in more than 100 countries. Dow Corning's sales in 2001 were $2.44 billion, with 62% coming outside of the United States. Its first sites achieved ISO 9000 registration in the late 1980s, and over time it acquired 26 separate registrations. Some locations had as many as four registrations for different functions. With the introduction of ISO 9000:2000, rather than upgrade all 26 registrations, Dow Corning decided to implement a new global quality-management system and acquire a global ISO registration for the entire company. The company had to overcome some hurdles to achieve its objective, including significant variations between different facilities that were not only of different sizes but that had also tailored their systems to meet local needs and regulations. The first step in eventually achieving a global ISO registration was to gain global registration at all of its facilities for the then current ISO 9000:1994. In order to accomplish this, a project team developed a global quality-management system that all company facilities would use. After achieving ISO 9000:1994 registration in 2002, the company began the upgrade process for ISO 9001:2000, which was completed in 2003. The new ISO standards emphasize customer awareness and continual improvement; Dow Corning's new quality-management system addressed the first requirement, and six sigma programs addressed the second. The benefits of Dow Corning's global approach to ISO registration include a reduction in audit costs of 60% and a dramatic reduction in the time required in dealing with third-party auditors. Another benefit is sharing best practices learned at one facility with other facilities across the company.

*Source:* S. Vanderhaeghe, "Quality at Dow Corning," *Qualityworld*, 12(12; December 2002), pp. 26–28.

agement determines the company's overall quality policy, its objectives, and its responsibilities, as well as its quality policy implementation. A company has to fulfill all of the requirements in ISO 9001:2000 to be certified (except for activities and functions it does not perform at all). Customer satisfaction is an explicit requirement. Thus, to be certified a company must identify and review customer requirements, ensure that customer requirements are met, and be able to measure and monitor customer satisfaction. The company must also be able to show that measuring and monitoring customer satisfaction leads to corrective and preventive actions when nonconformance (to the standards) is found—that is, continual improvement. This type of analysis of customer satisfaction requires a large amount of data collection and processing.

## IMPLICATIONS OF ISO 9000 FOR U.S. COMPANIES

Originally, ISO 9000 was adopted by the 12 countries of the European Community (EC)—Belgium, Denmark, France, Germany, Greece, Ireland, Italy, Luxembourg, the Netherlands, Portugal, Spain, and the United Kingdom. The governments of the EC countries adopted ISO 9000 as a uniform quality standard for cross-border transactions within the EC and for international transactions. The EC was soon joined by the countries of the European Free Trade Association (EFTA), including Austria, Finland, Iceland, Liechtenstein, Norway, Sweden, and Switzerland. In addition, Australia, Japan, and many other Pacific Rim countries plus South America and Africa adopted ISO 9000.

**Many overseas companies will not do business with a supplier unless it has ISO 9000 certification.**

These countries (especially those in the EC) were specifically acknowledging that they preferred suppliers with ISO 9000 certification. To remain competitive in international markets, U.S. companies had to comply with the standards in the ISO 9000 series. Some products in the EC, for example, are "regulated" to the extent that the products must be certified to be in ISO 9000 compliance by an EC-recognized accreditation registrar. Most of these products have health and safety considerations. However, companies discovered that to remain competitive and satisfy customer preferences, their products had to be in compliance with ISO 9000 requirements even if these products were not specifically regulated.

The United States exports more than $150 billion annually to the EC market, much of it to France, Germany, Italy, Spain, and the United Kingdom. More than half of these exports are affected in some way by ISO 9000 standards.

*Thousands of businesses have improved their operations by fully implementing a quality system based on the international standards known as ISO 9001:2000. When a company has met all the requirements of the standards, a registrar will certify/register them. This status is represented by a certificate, such as this sample.*

UNDERWRITERS LABORATORIES INC.

CERTIFICATE OF REGISTRATION

ISO 9000

**Capstone Turbine Corp.**

21211 Nordhoff Street
Chatsworth, CA 91311

with an off-site facility located at:

16640 Stagg Ave.
Van Nuys, CA 91406

Underwriters Laboratories Inc.® (UL) issues this certificate to the Firm named above, after assessing the Firm's quality system and finding it in compliance with

**ISO 9001:2000**

**EN ISO 9001:2000; BS EN ISO 9001:2000; ANSI/ASQ Q9001:2000**

for the following scope of registration

**3629 (US) : Electrical Industrial Apparatus, Not Elsewhere Classified**

**The design and manufacture of standard distributed power generation micro-turbines and accessories.**

**The off-site location located at Van Nuys, CA performs the following functions: manufacturing and assembly of recuperator cores.**

Further clarifications regarding the scope of this certificate and the applicability of ISO 9001:2000 requirements may be obtained by consulting the organization.

This quality system registration is included in UL's Directory of Registered Firms and applies to the provision of goods and/or services as specified in the scope of registration from the address(es) shown above. By issuance of this certificate the firm represents that it will maintain its registration in accordance with the applicable requirements. This certificate is not transferable and remains the property of Underwriters Laboratories Inc. ®.

File Number: A9549
Volume: 1
Issue Date: January 16, 2001
Revision Date: February 5, 2003
Renewal Date: February 5, 2006

S. Joe Bhatia
Executive Vice President and
Chief Operating Officer - International

Companies are also pressured within the United States to comply with ISO 9000 by more and more customers. For example, the U.S. Department of Defense, and specifically the Department of the Navy, as well as private companies like Du Pont, 3M, and AT&T, adopted ISO 9000. They recognized the value of these standards for helping to ensure top-quality products and services and required that their suppliers comply with ISO 9000.

## ISO 9000 ACCREDITATION

In ISO 9000 an accredited registrar, for a fee, assesses a company's quality-management system and determines if it is in compliance with the ISO 9001:2000 standard. Fees for first-time ISO 9001:2000 registration in the United States are estimated to range from $250,000 to $1 million, depending on the size of the company. If the company's quality-management system is in compliance with the standards, the registrar issues it a certificate and registers that certificate in a book that is widely distributed.

In the EC registration system, the third-party assessors of quality are referred to as *notified bodies*; that is, the 12 EC governments *notify* one another as to which organization in their country is the officially designated government-approved quality assessor. The notified bodies ultimately certify a company with a European Conformity (CE) mark. The CE mark must be on any product exported from the United States that is ISO 9000–regulated. It is illegal to sell a regulated product in a store in the EC without the CE mark. For a supplier in the United States to export regulated products to an EC country, it must be accredited by European registrars—notified bodies within the EC. However, more and more EC companies are requiring ISO 9000 certification for suppliers of products that fall in the unregulated categories, and eventually all products exported to the EC will probably require certification. It is also important that U.S. companies obtain accreditation with a notified body that has widespread positive recognition in the EC so that they will have broad access to markets in the EC.

The U.S. member of the ISO, the American National Standards Institute (ANSI), designated the American Society for Quality (ASQ), as the sponsoring organization for ISO 9000 in the United States. ASQ and ANSI created the Registrar Accreditation Board (RAB) to act as an accrediter of third-party registrars in the United States.

## ISO REGISTRARS

A registrar is an organization that conducts audits by individual auditors. Auditors are skilled in quality systems and the manufacturing and service environments in which an audit will be performed. The registrar develops an audit team of one or more auditors to evaluate a company's quality program and then report back to the registrar. An organization that wants to become a registrar must be accredited by RAB. Once RAB accredits a registrar, the registrar can then authorize its registered suppliers to use the RAB certificate in advertising, indicating compliance with ISO 9000.

ISO certification, or registration as it is called in the United States, is accomplished by a registrar through a series of document reviews and facility visits and audits. The registrar's auditors review a company's procedures, processes, and operations to see if the company conforms to the ISO quality-management system standards. The registrar looks at a variety of things, including the company's administrative, design, and production processes; quality system documentation; personnel training records; management reviews; and internal audit processes. The registration process might typically include an initial document review that describes the company's quality-management system, followed by the development of an audit plan and then the audit itself. This is usually followed by semiannual or annual surveillance audits to make sure the quality system is being maintained. The registration process can take from several weeks up to a year, depending on how ready the company is for registration. A RAB accredited registrar does not "help" the company attain certification either by giving advice or consulting.

## SUMMARY

In our discussion of quality management in this chapter, certain consistencies or commonalities have surfaced. The most important perspective of quality is the customer's; products and services must be designed to meet customer expectations and needs for quality. A total commitment to quality is necessary throughout an organization for it to be successful in improving and managing product quality. This commitment must start at the top and filter down through all levels of the organization and across all areas and departments. Employees need to be active participants in the quality-improvement process and must feel a responsibility for quality. Employees must feel free to make suggestions to improve product quality, and a systematic procedure is necessary to involve workers and solicit their input. Improving product quality is cost-effective; the cost of poor quality greatly exceeds the cost of attaining good quality. Quality can be improved with the effective use of statistical quality-control methods. In fact, the use of statistical quality control has been a pervasive part of our discussions on quality management, and it has been identified as an important part of any quality-management program. In the following chapter we concentrate on statistical quality-control methods and principles.

## SUMMARY OF KEY FORMULAS

*Quality Index Numbers*

$$\text{Quality index} = \frac{\text{total quality costs}}{\text{base}}(100)$$

*Product Yield*

$$Y = (I)(\%G) + (I)(1 - \%G)(\%R)$$

*Manufacturing Cost per Product*

$$\text{Product cost} = \frac{(K_d)(I) + (K_r)(R)}{Y}$$

*Multistage Product Yield*

$$Y = (I)(\%g_1)(\%g_2)\cdots(\%g_n)$$

*Quality-Productivity Ratio*

$$\text{QPR} = \frac{\text{good-quality units}}{(\text{input})(\text{processing cost}) + (\text{defective units})(\text{rework cost})}(100)$$

## SUMMARY OF KEY TERMS

**appraisal costs** costs of measuring, testing, and analyzing materials, parts, products, and the productive process to make sure they conform to design specifications.

**benchmark** a level of quality achievement established by one company that other companies seek to achieve (i.e., a goal).

**Black Belt** in a six sigma program, the leader of a quality improvement project; a full-time position.

**breakthrough strategy** in six sigma, a five-step process for improvement projects: define, measure, analyze, improve, and control.

**cause-and-effect diagram** a graphical description of the elements of a specific quality problem.

**champion** a member of top management who is responsible for project success in a six sigma program.

**cost index** the ratio of quality cost to manufacturing cost.

**design for six sigma** a systematic methodolgy to design products and processes that meet customer expectations and can be produced at six sigma quality levels.

**external failure costs** costs of poor quality incurred after the product gets to the customer; that is, customer service, lost sales, and so on.

**fitness for use** a measure of how well a product or service does what the consumer thinks it is supposed to do and wants it to do.

**Green Belt** in a six sigma program, a project team member, a part-time position.

**index numbers** ratios that measure quality costs relative to some base accounting values such as sales or product units.

**internal failure costs** costs of poor-quality products discovered during the production process—that is, scrap, rework, and the like.

**kaizen** involving everyone in the workplace, in a process of gradual, organized, and continuous improvement.

**labor index** the ratio of quality cost to direct labor hours.

**Master Black Belt** in a six sigma program, a teacher and mentor for Black Belts; a full-time position.

**Pareto analysis** a method for identifying the causes of poor quality, which usually shows that most quality problems result from only a few causes.

**participative problem solving** involving employees directly in the quality-management process to identify and solve problems.

**partnering** relationship between a company and its supplier based on mutual quality standards.

**prevention costs** costs incurred during product design and manufacturing that prevent nonconformance to specifications.

**production index** the ratio of quality cost to final product units.

**productivity** a measure of effectiveness in converting resources into products, generally computed as output divided by input.

**quality circles** a small, voluntary group (team) of workers and supervisors formed to address quality problems in their area.

**quality of conformance** the degree to which the product or service meets the specifications required by design during the production process.

**quality of design** the degree to which quality characteristics are designed into a product or service.

**quality–productivity ratio** a productivity index that includes productivity and quality costs.

**sales index** the ratio of quality cost to sales.

**six sigma** a measure of how much a given product or process deviates from perfection, or zero defects; the basis of a quality-improvement program.

**total quality control** a total, companywide systems approach to quality developed by Armand V. Feigenbaum.

**total quality management (TQM)** the management of quality throughout the organization at all management levels and across all areas.

**yield** a measure of productivity; the sum of good-quality and reworked units.

## SOLVED PROBLEMS

### 1. PRODUCT YIELD

A manufacturing company has a weekly product input of 1700 units. The average percentage of good-quality products is 83%. Of the poor-quality products, 60% can be reworked and sold as good-quality products. Determine the weekly product yield and the product yield if the good-product quality is increased to 92%.

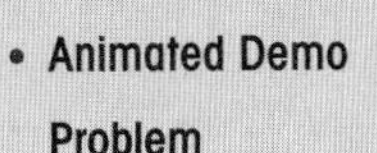
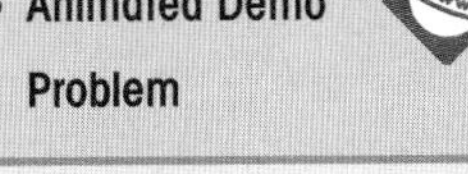

• Animated Demo Problem

**SOLUTION**

*Step 1.* Compute yield according to the following formula:

$$Y = (I)(G\%) + (I)(1 - \%G)(\%R)$$

$$Y = (1700)(0.83) + (1700)(0.17)(0.60)$$

$$= 1584.4 \text{ units}$$

*Step 2.* Increase %$G$ to 92%:

$$Y = (1700)(0.92) + (1700)(0.08)(0.60)$$

$$= 1645.6 \text{ units}$$

**2. QUALITY–PRODUCTIVITY RATIO**

A retail telephone catalogue company takes catalogue orders from customers and then sends the completed orders to the warehouses to be filled. An operator processes an average of 45 orders per day. The cost of processing an order is $1.15, and it costs $0.65 to correct an order that has been filled out incorrectly by the operator. An operator averages 7% bad orders per day, all of which are reworked prior to filling the customer order. Determine the quality–productivity ratio for an operator.

**SOLUTION**

Compute the quality-productivity ratio according to the following formulas:

$$\text{QPR} = \frac{\text{qood-quality units}}{(\text{input})(\text{processing cost}) + (\text{defective units})(\text{rework cost})}(100)$$

$$\text{QPR} = \frac{45}{(45)(\$1.15) + (3.15)(\$0.65)}(100)$$

$$= 83.65$$

# QUESTIONS

**3-1.** How does the consumer's perspective of quality differ from the producer's?

**3-2.** Briefly describe the *dimensions of quality*, for which a consumer looks in a product, and apply them to a specific product.

**3-3.** How does *quality of design* differ from *quality of conformance*?

**3-4.** How does the purchasing/sourcing area affect product quality in a total quality management system?

**3-5.** Define the two major categories of quality cost and how they relate to each other.

**3-6.** What is the difference between internal and external failure costs?

**3-7.** A defense contractor manufactures rifles for the military. The military has exacting quality standards that the contractor must meet. The military is very pleased with the quality of the products provided by the contractor and rarely has to return products or has reason for complaint. However, the contractor is experiencing extremely high quality-related costs. Speculate on the reasons for the contractor's high quality-related costs.

**3-8.** Consider your school (university or college) as a production system in which the final product is a graduate. For this system:

a. Define quality from the producer's and customer's perspectives.

b. Develop a fitness-for-use description for final product quality.

c. Give examples of the cost of poor quality (internal and external failure costs) and the cost of quality assurance (prevention and appraisal) costs.

d. Describe how quality circles might be implemented in a university setting. Do you think they would be effective?

**3-9.** Explain how the Japanese perspective on the cost of quality originally differed from the traditional American perspective.

**3-10.** Discuss the possible differences between the American and Japanese business environments and cultures that might make it difficult for American companies to duplicate successfully some of Japan's quality-management programs such as quality circles.

**3-11.** Describe how a quality-assurance program might affect the different organizational functions for a fast-food business such as McDonald's or Burger King.

**3-12.** Discuss how a quality-management program can affect productivity.

**3-13.** The Aurora Electronics Company has been receiving a lot of customer complaints and returns of a front-loading VCR that it manufactures. When a videotape is pushed into the loading mechanism, it can stick inside with the door open; the recorder cannot run, and it is difficult to get the tape out. Consumers will try to pull the tape out with their fingers or pry the tape out with an object such as a knife, pencil, or screwdriver, frequently damaging the VCR, tearing up the tape cartridge, or hurting themselves. What are the different costs of poor quality and costs of quality assurance that might be associated with this quality problem?

**3-14.** What are the different quality characteristics you (as a consumer) would expect to find in the following three products: a VCR, a pizza, running shoes?

**3-15.** AMERICARD, a national credit card company, has a toll-free, 24-hour customer service number. Describe the input for this system function and the final product. What quality-related costs might be associated with this function? What impact might a quality-management program have on this area?

**3-16.** A number of quality-management philosophies hold that prevention costs are the most critical quality-related costs. Explain the logic behind this premise.

**3-17.** Why is it important for companies to measure and report quality costs?

**3-18.** What traits of quality management are generally consistent among most current quality philosophies and trends?

**3-19.** Describe the primary contribution to quality management of each of the following: W.E. Deming, Joseph Juran, Phillip Crosby, Armand Feigenbaum, and Kaoru Ishikawa.

**3-20.** Describe the impact that the creation of the Malcolm Baldrige Award has had on quality improvement in the United States.

**3-21.** Write a one- to two-page summary of an article from *Quality Progress*, about quality management in a company or organization.

**3-22.** More companies probably fail at implementing quality-management programs than succeed. Discuss the reasons why a quality-management program might fail.

**3-23.** Select a service company or organization and discuss the dimensions of quality on which a customer might evaluate it.

**3-24.** Select two competing service companies that you are familiar with or can visit, such as fast-food restaurants, banks, or retail stores, and compare how they interact with customers in terms of quality.

**3-25.** Develop a hypothetical quality-improvement program for the class in which you are using this textbook. Evaluate the class according to the dimensions of quality for a service. Include goals for quality improvement and ways to measure success.

**3-26.** Identify a company or organization from which you have received poor-quality products or services, describe the nature of the defects, and suggest ways in which you might improve quality.

**3-27.** Identify a company or organization from which you have received high-quality products and describe the characteristics that make them high-quality.

**3-28.** Explain why strategic planning might benefit from a TQM program.

**3-29.** Why has ISO 9000 become so important to U.S. firms that do business overseas?

**3-30.** Go to the Baldrige Award Web site, http://www.quality.nist.gov and research several companies that have won the Malcolm Baldrige Award. Describe any common characteristics that the quality-management programs in those companies have.

**3-31.** The discussion in this chapter has focused on the benefits of implementing a quality-management program; however, many companies do not have such a program. Discuss the reasons why you think a company would not adopt a TQM program.

**3-32.** Access a Web site of a company that sells products to the general public on the Internet. Discuss the quality attributes of the site, and evaluate the quality of the Web site.

**3-33.** For an airline you have flown on list all of the quality "defects" you can recall. Discuss whether you think the airline exhibited overall good or poor quality. If it exhibited good quality, explain what made it so; if it exhibited poor quality, what actions do you think could be taken by the airline to improve quality?

**3-34.** Identify three Web sites that you think are poor-quality and three that are good-quality. What common characteristics are exhibited by the group of poor-quality sites? the group of good-quality sites? Compare the two groups.

**3-35.** The production and home delivery of a pizza is a relatively straightforward and simple process. Develop a fishbone diagram to identify potential defects and opportunities for poor quality in this process.

**3-36.** Most students live in a dormitory or apartment that they rent. Discuss whether this type of living accommodation is a product or service. Assess the quality of your living accommodation according to your previous response.

**3-37.** Develop a fishbone diagram for the possible causes of flight delays.

**3-38.** Observe a business with which you are familiar and interact with frequently, such as a restaurant or food service, a laundry service, your bank, or the college bookstore. Develop a Pareto chart that encompasses the major service defects of the business, identify the most significant service problems and suggest how quality could be improved.

**3-39.** County school buses are inspected every month for "defects." In a recent monthly inspection, 27 worn or torn seats were found, 22 buses had dirty floors, there were 14 cases of exterior scratches and chipped paint, there were 8 cracked or broken windows, the engines on 4 buses had trouble starting or were not running smoothly, and 2 buses had faulty brakes. Develop a Pareto chart for the bus inspections and indicate the most significant quality-problem categories. What does this tell you about the limitations of applying Pareto chart analysis. How might these limitations be overcome in Pareto chart analysis?

**3-40.** Joseph Juran created a "quality spiral" showing that each element of the business process, each function, not just the end product, is important. Describe how each of the following business process areas can impact on quality: marketing, engineering, purchasing/sourcing, human resources, and distribution.

**3-41.** Referring to Table 3.3, research the winner of an international quality award at one of the award Web sites and write a brief report.

**3-42.** Compare Pal's Sudden Service drive-in restaurant (described in the Competitive Edge box on page 96) with another food chain restaurant like McDonalds' or Burger King and speculate on why Pal's might have superior quality.

**3-43.** Go to the Malcolm Baldrige Award Web site, www.quality.nist.gov, and write a brief report on one of the most recent years' Baldrige Award winners similar to the "Competitive Edge" boxes in this chapter.

**3-44.** Write a brief summary on the application of quality management in a company from *Qualityworld*, a professional trade magazine published in the United Kingdom.

**3-45.** Develop a fishbone diagram for the possible causes of your car not starting.

**3-46.** Describe the differences between Black Belts, Green Belts, and Master Black Belts in a six sigma program.

**3-47.** Describe the steps in the six sigma breakthrough strategy for quality improvement.

**3-48.** Develop a quality-improvement project in a situation you are familiar with such as a current or former job, a part-time job, a restaurant, your college bookstore, your dorm or apartment, a local business, and so on, and describe how you would apply the steps of the six sigma breakthrough strategy.

**3-49.** Reference the Web site for the American Customer Satisfaction Index (ACSI) at www.theacsi.org and write a brief summary describing how the numerical ACSI value is determined. Also, select an industry or service sector and pick two companies, one with a high ACSI and one with a relatively low ACSI; using your own knowledge and research about the companies, explain why you think they have different ACSI values.

## PROBLEMS

**3-1.** Backwoods American, Inc., produces expensive water-repellent, down-lined parkas. The company implemented a total quality-management program in 2000. Following are quality-related accounting data that have been accumulated for the five-year period after the program's start.

| | Year | | | | |
|---|---|---|---|---|---|
| | 2000 | 2001 | 2002 | 2003 | 2004 |
| ***Quality Costs (000s)*** | | | | | |
| Prevention | $ 3.2 | 10.7 | 28.3 | 42.6 | 50.0 |
| Appraisal | 26.3 | 29.2 | 30.6 | 24.1 | 19.6 |
| Internal failure | 39.1 | 51.3 | 48.4 | 35.9 | 32.1 |
| External failure | 118.6 | 110.5 | 105.2 | 91.3 | 65.2 |
| ***Accounting Measures (000s)*** | | | | | |
| Sales | $2,700.6 | 2,690.1 | 2,705.3 | 2,810.2 | 2,880.7 |
| Manufacturing cost | 420.9 | 423.4 | 424.7 | 436.1 | 435.5 |

a. Compute the company's total failure costs as a percentage of total quality costs for each of the five years. Does there appear to be a trend to this result? If so, speculate on what might have caused the trend.

b. Compute prevention costs and appraisal costs, each as a percentage of total costs, during each of the five years. Speculate on what the company's quality strategy appears to be.

c. Compute quality-sales indices and quality-cost indices for each of the five years. Is it possible to assess the effectiveness of the company's quality-management program from these index values?

d. List several examples of each quality-related cost—that is, prevention, appraisal, and internal and external failure—that might result from the production of parkas.

**3-2.** The Backwoods American company in Problem 3-1 produces approximately 20,000 parkas annually. The quality-management program the company implemented was able to improve the average percentage of good parkas produced by 2% each year, beginning with 83% good-quality parkas in 2000. Only about 20% of poor-quality parkas can be reworked.

a. Compute the product yield for each of the five years.

b. Using a rework cost of $12 per parka, determine the manufacturing cost per good parka for each of the five years. What do these results imply about the company's quality-management program?

**3-3.** The Colonial House Furniture Company manufactures two-drawer oak file cabinets that are sold unassembled through catalogues. The company initiates production of 150 cabinet packages each week. The percentage of good-quality cabinets averages 83% per week, and the percentage of poor-quality cabinets that can be reworked is 60%.

a. Determine the weekly product yield of file cabinets.

b. If the company desires a product yield of 145 units per week, what increase in the percentage of good-quality products must result?

**3-4.** In Problem 3-3, if the direct manufacturing cost for cabinets is $27 and the rework cost is $8, compute the manufacturing cost per good product. Determine the manufacturing cost per product if the percentage of good-quality file cabinets is increased from 83% to 90%.

**3-5.** The Omega Shoe Company manufactures a number of different styles of athletic shoes. Its biggest seller is the X-Pacer running shoe. In 2002 Omega implemented a quality-management program. The company's shoe production for the past three years and manufacturing costs are as follows.

| | Year | | |
|---|---|---|---|
| | 2002 | 2003 | 2004 |
| Units produced/input | 32,000 | 34,600 | 35,500 |
| Manufacturing cost | $278,000 | 291,000 | 305,000 |
| Percent good quality | 78% | 83% | 90% |

Only one-quarter of the defective shoes can be reworked, at a cost of $2 apiece. Compute the manufacturing cost per good product for each of the three years and indicate the annual percentage increase or decrease resulting from the quality-management program.

**3-6.** The Colonial House Furniture Company manufactures four-drawer oak filing cabinets in six stages. In the first stage, the boards forming the walls of the cabinet are cut; in the second stage, the front drawer panels are wood-worked; in the third stage, the boards are sanded and finished; in the fourth stage, the boards are cleaned, stained, and painted with a clear finish; in the fifth stage, the hardware for pulls, runners, and fittings is installed; and in the final stage, the cabinets are assembled. Inspection occurs at each stage of the process, and the average percentages of good-quality units are as follows.

| Stage | Average Percentage Good Quality |
|---|---|
| 1 | 87% |
| 2 | 91% |
| 3 | 94% |
| 4 | 93% |
| 5 | 93% |
| 6 | 96% |

The cabinets are produced in weekly production runs with a product input for 300 units.

a. Determine the weekly product yield of good-quality cabinets.

b. What would weekly product input have to be in order to achieve a final weekly product yield of 300 cabinets?

**3-7.** In Problem 3-6, the Colonial House Furniture Company has investigated the manufacturing process to identify potential improvements that would improve quality. The company has identified four alternatives, each costing $15,000, as follows.

| Alternative | Quality Improvement |
|---|---|
| 1 | Stage 1: 93% |
| 2 | Stage 2: 96%, Stage 4: 97% |
| 3 | Stage 5: 97%, Stage 6: 98% |
| 4 | Stage 2: 97% |

a. Which alternative would result in the greatest increase in product yield?

b. Which alternative would be the most cost effective?

**3-8.** The Backwoods American company operates a telephone order system for a catalogue of its outdoor clothing products. The catalogue orders are processed in three stages. In the first stage, the telephone operator enters the order into the computer; in the second stage, the items are secured and batched in the warehouse; and in the final stage, the ordered products are packaged. Errors can be made in orders at any of these stages, and the average percentage of errors that occurs at each stage are as follows.

| Stage | % Errors |
|---|---|
| 1 | 12% |
| 2 | 8% |
| 3 | 4% |

If an average of 320 telephone orders are processed each day, how many errorless orders will result?

**3-9.** The total processing cost for producing the X-Pacer running shoe in Problem 3-5 is $18. The Omega Shoe Company starts production of 650 pairs of the shoes weekly, and the average weekly yield is 90%, with 10% defective shoes. One quarter of the defective shoes can be reworked at a cost of $3.75.

a. Compute the quality–productivity ratio (QPR).

b. Compute the QPR if the production rate is increased to 800 pairs of shoes per week.

c. Compute the QPR if the processing cost is reduced to $16.50 and the rework cost to $3.20.

d. Compute the QPR if the product yield is increased to 93% good quality.

**3-10.** Airphone, Inc., manufactures cellular telephones at a processing cost of $47 per unit. The company produces an average of 250 phones per week and has a yield of 87% good-quality phones, resulting in 13% defective phones, all of which can be reworked. The cost of reworking a defective telephone is $16.

a. Compute the quality-productivity ratio (QPR).

b. Compute the QPR if the company increased the production rate to 320 phones per week while reducing the processing cost to $42, reducing the rework cost to $12, and increasing the product yield of good-quality telephones to 94%.

**3-11.** Burger Doodle is a fast-food restaurant that processes an average of 680 food orders each day. The average cost of each order is $6.15. Four percent of the orders are incorrect, and only 10% of the defective orders can be corrected with additional food items at an average cost of $1.75. The remaining defective orders have to be thrown out.

a. Compute the average product cost.

b. In order to reduce the number of wrong orders, Burger Doodle is going to invest in a computerized ordering and cash register system. The cost of the system will increase the average order cost by $0.05 and will reduce defective orders to 1%. What is the annual net cost effect of this quality-improvement initiative?

c. What other indirect effects on quality might be realized by the new computerized order system?

**3-12.** Compute the quality–productivity ratio (QPR) for the Burger Doodle restaurant in parts (a) and (b) in Problem 3-11.

## CASE PROBLEM 3.1

### *Designing a Quality-Management Program for the Internet at D4Q*

Design for Quality (D4Q) is a consulting firm that specializes in the design and implementation of quality-management programs for service companies and organizations. It has had success designing quality programs for retail stores and catalogue order services. Recently D4Q was approached by a catalogue order company, BookTek Media, Inc., with the offer of a job. BookTek sells books, CDs, cassettes, DVDs, and videos through its mail-order catalogue operation. BookTek has decided to expand its service to the Internet. BookTek is experienced in catalogue telephone sales and has a successful quality-management program in place. Thus, the company is confident that it can process orders and make deliveries on time with virtually no errors.

A key characteristic of BookTek's quality-management program is the company's helpful, courteous, and informative phone representatives. These operators can answer virtually any customer question about BookTek's products, with the help of an information system. Their demeanor toward customers is constantly monitored and graded. Their telephone system is so quick that customers rarely have to wait for a representative to assist them. However, the proposed Internet ordering system virtually eliminates direct human contact with the customer. Since there will be no human contact, BookTek is concerned about how it will be able to make customers feel that they are receiving high-quality service. Furthermore, the company is unsure how its employees can monitor and evaluate the service to know if the customer thinks it is good or poor. The primary concern is how to make customers feel good about the company in such an impersonal, segregated environment. At this point BookTek is unconcerned with costs; management simply wants to develop the highest-quality, friendliest Web site possible.

D4Q indicated that it would like to take on the job, but while it is familiar with BookTek's type of catalogue order system, it is relatively unfamiliar with the Internet and how things are ordered on the Internet. It suggested that its first order of business might be to investigate what other companies were doing on the Internet.

Help D4Q develop a quality-management plan for BookTek. Include in your plan the quality dimensions and characteristics of an Internet ordering system specifically for BookTek's products, suggestions for achieving customer satisfaction, ways to measure defective service, and how to evaluate the success of the order system in terms of quality.

## * CASE PROBLEM 3.2 Due 9/24

### *TQM at State University*

As a result of several years of severe cuts to its operating budget by the state legislature, the administration at State University has raised tuition annually for the past five years. Five years ago getting an education at State was a bargain for both in-state and out-of-state students; now it is one of the more expensive state universities. An immediate repercussion has been a decline in applications for admission. Since a portion of state funding is tied to enrollments, State has kept its enrollments up at a constant level by going deeper into its pool of applications, taking some less-qualified students.

The increase in the cost of a State degree has also caused legislators, parents, and students to be more conscious of the value of a State education—that is, the value parents and students are receiving for their money. This increased scrutiny has been fueled by numerous media reports about the decreased emphasis on teaching in universities, low teaching loads by faculty, and the large number of courses taught by graduate students. This, in turn, has led the state legislature committee on higher education to call for an "outcomes assessment program" to determine how well State University is achieving its mission of producing high-quality graduates.

On top of those problems, a substantial increase in the college-age population is expected this decade, resulting from a "baby boom" during the 1990s. Key members of the state legislature have told the university administration that they will be expected to absorb their share of the additional students during the next decade. However, because of the budget situation, they should not expect any funding increases for additional facilities, classrooms, dormitory rooms, or faculty. In effect, they will be expected to do more with their existing resources. State already faces a classroom deficit, and faculty have teaching loads above the average of its peer institutions. Legislators are fond of citing a study that shows that if the university simply gets all the students to graduate within a four-year period or reduces the number of hours required for graduation, they can accommodate the extra students.

This entire scenario has made the university president, Fred McMahan, consider retirement. He has summarized the problems to his administration staff as "having to do more, better, with less." One of the first things he did to address these problems was to set up a number of task forces made up of faculty and administrators to brainstorm a variety of topics. Among the topics and problems these task forces addressed were quality in education, educational success, graduation rates, success rates in courses (i.e., the percentage of students passing), teaching, the time to graduation, faculty issues, student issues, facilities, class scheduling, admissions, and classroom space.

Several of the task forces included faculty from engineering and business. These individuals noted that many of the problems the university faced would benefit from the principles and practices of a total quality-management (TQM) approach. This recommendation appealed to Fred McMahan and the academic vice president, Anne Baker.

Discuss in general terms how TQM philosophy and practices might be instituted at State University.

## CASE PROBLEM 3.3

### *Quality Problems at the Tech Bookstores*

Tech is a major state university located in a small, rural college town. Tech Services is an incorporated university entity that operates two bookstores, one on campus and one off campus at a nearby mall. The on-campus store sells school supplies, textbooks, and school-licensed apparel and gifts and it has a large computer department. The off-campus store sells textbooks, school supplies, and licensed apparel and gifts and it has a large trade book department. The on-campus store has very limited parking, but it is within easy walking distance of the downtown area, all dormitories, and the football stadium and basketball arena. The off-campus store has plenty of parking, but it is not within walking distance of campus, although it is on the town bus line. Both stores compete with several other independent and national chain college bookstores in the town plus several school supply stores, apparel stores, computer stores, and trade bookstores. The town and university have been growing steadily over the past decade, and the football team has been highly ranked and gone to a bowl for eight straight seasons.

The Tech bookstores have a long-standing policy of selling textbooks with a very small markup (just above cost), which causes competing stores to follow suit. However, because textbooks are so expensive anyway most students believe the Tech bookstores gouge them on textbook prices. In order to offset the lack of profit on textbooks, the Tech bookstores sell all other products at a relatively high price. All "profits" from the stores are used to fund student-related projects such as new athletic fields and student center enhancements.

Tech Services has a Board of Directors made up of faculty, administrators, and students. The executive director, Mr. David Watson, reports to the Board of Directors and oversees the operation of the bookstores (plus all on-campus vending and athletic event vending). His office is in the on-campus store. Both bookstores have a store manager and an assistant store manager. There is one textbook manager for both stores, a trade book manager, a single school supplies and apparel manager, and a computer department manager, as well as a number of staff people, including a computer director and staff, a marketing director, a finance staff, a personnel director, a warehouse manager and secretaries. Almost all of the floor employees including cash register operators, sales clerks, stock people, delivery truck drivers, and warehouse workers, are part-time Tech students. Hiring Tech students has been a long-standing university policy in order to provide students with employment opportunities. The bookstores have a high rate of turnover among the student employees, as would be expected.

Several incidents have occurred at the off-campus store that have caused the Tech Services Board of Directors concern. In one incident a student employee was arrested for drug possession. In another incident a faculty customer and student employee got into a shouting match when the employee could not locate a well-known book on the bookstore computer system and the faculty member got frustrated over the time it was taking. In still another incident an alumnus who had visited the store after a football game sent a letter to the university president indicating that a student employee had been rude to him when he asked a question about the return policy for an apparel item he had purchased on the bookstore's Web site. When the student did not know the return policy, he told the customer in a condescending manner to come back later. The last incident was an offhand remark made by a local town resident to a Board member at a party about the difficulty she had completing a purchase at the mall store because the registers were unmanned, although she could see several employees talking together in the store.

Although sales and profits at the bookstore have been satisfactory and steady over the past few years, the Board of Directors is extremely sensitive to criticism about anything that might have the potential to embarrass the university. The Board of Directors suggested to Mr. Watson that he might consider some type of assessment of the service at the bookstores to see if there was a problem. Mr. Watson initially attempted to make random, surprise visits to the bookstores to see if he could detect any problems; however, there seemed to be a jungle telegraph system that alerted his employees whenever he entered a store, so he abandoned that idea. Next he decided to try two other things. First he conducted a customer survey during a two-week period in the middle of the semester at both stores. As customers left the store, he had employees ask them to respond to a brief questionnaire. Second, he hired several graduate students to pose as customers and make purchases and ask specific questions of sales clerks, and report on their experiences.

Selected results from the customer survey are on the table on the next page.

The only consistent responses from the graduate students posing as customers were that the student employees were sometimes not that familiar with store policies, how to operate the store computer systems, what products were available, and where products were located in the stores. When they didn't know something they sometimes got defensive. A few also said that students sometimes appeared lackadaisical and bored.

Using observations of the operation of your own college bookstores to assist you, answer the following questions.

**a.** Why do you think Mr. Watson organized the customer survey the way he did? What other things do you think he might have done to analyze the stores' quality problems?

**b.** Develop Pareto charts to help analyze the survey results.

**c.** How would you define quality at the bookstores?

**d.** Discuss what you believe are the quality problems the bookstores have?

**e.** What are the bookstores' costs of poor quality?

**f.** What actions or programs would you propose to improve quality at the bookstores?

**g.** What obstacles do you perceive might exist to hinder changes at the bookstores and quality improvement?

**h.** What benefits do you think would result from quality improvement at the bookstores?

| | CAMPUS STORE | | | | OFF-CAMPUS STORE | | | |
|---|---|---|---|---|---|---|---|---|
| | *Student* | | *Nonstudent* | | *Student* | | *Nonstudent* | |
| | **Yes** | **No** | **Yes** | **No** | **Yes** | **No** | **Yes** | **No** |
| Were employees courteous and friendly? | 572 | 93 | 286 | 147 | 341 | 114 | 172 | 156 |
| Were employees knowledgeable and helpful? | 522 | 143 | 231 | 212 | 350 | 105 | 135 | 193 |
| Was the overall service good? | 569 | 96 | 278 | 165 | 322 | 133 | 180 | 148 |
| Did you have to wait long for service? | 74 | 591 | 200 | 243 | 51 | 404 | 150 | 178 |
| Did you have to wait long to check out? | 81 | 584 | 203 | 240 | 72 | 383 | 147 | 181 |
| Was the item you wanted available? | 602 | 63 | 371 | 72 | 407 | 48 | 296 | 32 |
| Was the cost of your purchase(s) reasonable? | 385 | 280 | 398 | 45 | 275 | 180 | 301 | 27 |
| Have you visited the store's Web site? | 335 | 330 | 52 | 391 | 262 | 193 | 17 | 311 |

## CASE PROBLEM 3.4

### *Product Yield at Continental Luggage Company*

The Continental Luggage Company manufactures several different styles of soft- and hardcover luggage, briefcases, hanging bags, and purses. Their best-selling item is a line of hardcover luggage called the Trotter. It is produced in a basic five-stage assembly process that can accommodate several different outer coverings and colors. The assembly process includes constructing a heavy-duty plastic and metal frame; attaching the outer covering; joining the top and bottom and attaching the hinge mechanism; attaching the latches, lock, and handle; and doing the finishing work, including the luggage lining.

The market for luggage is extremely competitive, and product quality is a very important component in product sales and market share. Customers normally expect luggage to be able to withstand rough handling while retaining its shape and an attractive appearance and protecting the clothing and personal items inside the bag. They also prefer the bag to be lightweight and not cumbersome. Furthermore, customers expect the latches and locks to work properly over an extended period of time. Another key factor in sales is that the luggage must be stylish and visually appealing.

Because of the importance of quality, company management has established a process control procedure that includes inspection at each stage of the five major stages of the assembly process. The following table shows the percentage of good-quality units yielded at each stage of the assembly process and the percentage of bad units that can be reworked, on average.

| Assembly Stage | Average Percentage Good Quality | Average Percentage Reworked |
|---|---|---|
| 1 | 0.94 | 0.23 |
| 2 | 0.96 | 0.91 |
| 3 | 0.95 | 0.67 |
| 4 | 0.97 | 0.89 |
| 5 | 0.98 | 0.72 |

The first stage of the process is construction of the frame, and it is very difficult to rework the frame if an item is defective, which is reflected in the low percentage of reworked items.

Five hundred new pieces of luggage of a particular style and color are initiated through the assembly process each week. The company would like to know the weekly product yield and the number of input units that would be required to achieve a weekly yield of 500 units. Furthermore, the company would like to know the impact on product yield (given 500 initial starting units) if a quality-improvement program were introduced that would increase the average percentage of good-quality units at each stage by 1%.

## CASE PROBLEM 3.5

### *USEast Airlines*

Mike Shepard was traveling from Roanoke, Virginia, to Nashville, Tennessee, through Pittsburgh on USEast Airlines and had purchased an electronic ticket on the airline's Web site. When he checked in with an airline agent in Roanoke, she gave Mike a boarding pass from Roanoke to Pittsburgh and a second boarding pass for his connecting flight from Pittsburgh to Nashville. Mike uses a carry-on bag, so he proceeded directly to the gate, boarded his flight on time, and had an uneventful trip to Pittsburgh. Arriving on time in Pittsburgh, he ate a sandwich and went to the gate where he waited for his flight to Nashville to board. When his flight began to board, Mike stood nearby so he could get on the plane as soon as his row was called. From experience he knew that people who boarded a full flight late often could not find space in the overhead bin for their carry-on, and this appeared to be a full flight. When Mike handed his ticket to the gate attendant, she told him.

"I'm sorry sir, you can't board; your boarding pass is supposed to have a ticket coupon attached. The boarding pass does not verify that you have paid for your ticket."

Mike told her, "The boarding pass was all I was given in Roanoke. Anyway, how do you think I got from Roanoke to Pittsburgh if I didn't pay for my ticket?"

The attendant showed Mike his boarding pass which clearly said, "Not valid without flight coupon attached," and curtly told him to see the attendant at the gate desk and tell him he needed a ticket. Mike dutifully did as he was told; he walked to the desk 30 feet away and approached the attendant, who looked up at Mike. Mike explained what had happened and said that the boarding pass was all that he had been given by the agent in Roanoke. The attendant held out his hand for Mike's boarding pass and began working at his computer. Several minutes passed and the attendant returned the boarding pass to Mike with a copy of a ticket coupon stapled to the boarding pass, never having spoken a single word to Mike. Mike joined the end of the line boarding the plane and was the last to board. When he handed the boarding pass and ticket to the gate attendant, she tore the coupon off and said,

"Thank you, Mr. Shepard, you may board now."

Mike sucked up his courage and asked the attendant,

"Why did this happen? What I originally gave you was what I got in Roanoke, so why was I made to wait when it was the airline's fault?"

The attendant responded, "They just messed up down there in Roanoke. Half the time they hire inexperienced people who don't know what they're doing. We're the hub here in Pittsburgh, so all of our people are very experienced and are more efficient so we catch things like this. If your flight had originated here this would not have happened."

She offered Mike a quick smile to indicate the conversation was over, and Mike boarded his flight wondering if she was implying that he should have driven to Pittsburgh to catch his flight rather than in Roanoke where he was evidently doomed from the start.

On board the flight was full as Mike suspected, so there was no available space in the overhead bins to put his carry-on bag. The stewardess immediately approached Mike and informed him he would have to take a seat and she would take his bag and have it checked through to Nashville. The whole point of using a carry-on was so he would not have to check it through, so Mike crammed the soft-sided bag under the seat in front of him, which left him no room to stretch his legs out.

Mike then asked the attendant for a pillow; he has a bad back and he puts a pillow behind him for support. However, the attendant informed him that they were short on pillows on this flight and there were none available. Mike spent an uncomfortable two hours flying to Nashville.

In Nashville Mike picked up a car at the rental car agency, and when he opened his carry-on to get his sunglasses he found that they were broken from shoving his bag under the seat. The day was bright and sunny so by the time he arrived at his hotel he had a headache from squinting, his legs were cramped, and his back hurt.

After his visit in Nashville, Mike retraced his route to Roanoke through Pittsburgh, which was uneventful—for him. However, after he had settled into his seat in Pittsburgh for his flight to Roanoke, three elderly ladies got on. They sat down behind Mike, and they were obviously distressed. After it appeared everyone had boarded, one of the ladies approached the flight attendant and explained that two of their friends who were traveling with them were not on the plane and could she (the attendant) check on them. The flight attendant said she would. After about 15 minutes, it was obvious the flight had been delayed and was now running late when two more elderly ladies boarded. One of the ladies was angry, and the other was near tears. As they sat down just behind Mike he overhead their conversation about what had happened, a story all too familiar to him. When one of the ladies handed her boarding pass to the gate attendant, she was told that she should have an attached ticket coupon. She told the attendant that this was all she had been given by the ticket agent when he checked her bags when she arrived at the airport. She said the gate attendant acted like she was trying to sneak on board without paying.

The other lady said, "They were just plain rude! They acted like we were two addled old ladies who had never flown anywhere before and had somehow lost the ticket or forgotten we had bought it in the first place. Why, we travel all the time!"

Her friend said, "I asked the gate lady how she thought we got that far without paying for a ticket; they took our bags and there's security everywhere but she never did answer me. She just told us to go to the desk at the gate and if we had paid for our ticket they would issue us a coupon and we could board. Can you believe that? 'If we had paid for our ticket!' The nerve of her! Oh I was so mad!"

The plane then took off and arrived in Roanoke 15 minutes late—the same 15 minutes that the flight was delayed in Pittsburgh because the two old ladies could not board. Mike thought of a recent news article he had read that rated airlines according to on-time flights, a key airline performance indicator, and how the airlines had maintained their statistics were low because of abnormally bad weather conditions in the East during the past six months.

A few days after Mike got home he saw a friend, Vicki, who was a flight attendant for USEast. He related his story and that of the two elderly ladies to her in a humorous tone, and was somewhat taken aback by her defensive response.

"You don't understand, Mike, how hard it is. We're really just overwhelmed since 9/11. With the loss of business we've had to cut back and lay people off, and we just don't have enough people to cover everything. We've really been up against it; there's just a whole lot of pressure. I wish people would be more understanding about how much we have to do now and be a little more patient. And people aren't flying because they're scared so nobody knows when business is going to pick back up?"

Mike decided not to pursue this conversation, but he did wonder to himself if people were not flying because they were scared or because of other reasons.

Assess the airline's approach to quality and customer satisfaction based on Mike's experiences on his trip and consider the following questions.

1. In what ways does the airline appear deficient in its approach to quality?
2. What things could the airline adopt from the Baldrige Award-winning companies discussed in this chapter to improve their performance?
3. What specific measures would you suggest the airline take to improve customer service?
4. Is Vicki's claim that the airlines employees are overworked a valid reason for the airline's shortcomings in customer service?
5. Do you think the airline could use another airline to benchmark its performance? If yes, which airline? If not, what kind of service company could it use as a benchmark for outstanding quality performance?
6. Six sigma is most often used by manufacturing firms; do you think it could be applied to an airline like USEast?
7. Using the process of collecting boarding passes and tickets at the gate as a quality-improvement project, describe how the steps of the six sigma breakthrough strategy could be applied.
8. An airline like USEast often serves many small markets, like Roanoke, Virginia, and Asheville, North Carolina, where there is little or no competition. How do you think this fact influences how the airline addresses the issue of quality?
9. Identify some other quality problems that you have experienced traveling on airlines.
10. Construct a fishbone (cause-and-effect) diagram for the problem of the "missing flight coupon" described in this case.

## REFERENCES


Crosby, P. B. *Quality is Free*. New York: McGraw-Hill, 1979.

Deming, W. E. *Out of the Crisis*. Cambridge, MA: MIT Center for Advanced Engineering Study, 1986.

Evans, J. R., and W. M. Lindsay. *The Management and Control of Quality*. 3rd ed. St. Paul, MN: West, 1996.

Feigenbaum, A. V. *Total Quality Control*. 3rd ed. New York: McGraw-Hill, 1983.

Garvin, D. A. *Managing Quality*. New York: Free Press/Macmillan, 1988.

Ishikawa, K. *Guide to Quality Control*. 2nd ed. White Plains, NY: Kraus International Publications, 1986.

Juran, J. M. *Juran on Planning for Quality*. New York: Free Press/Macmillan, 1988.

Juran, J. M., and F. M. Gryna, Jr. *Quality Planning and Analysis*. 2nd ed. New York: McGraw-Hill, 1980.

Montgomery, D. C. *Introduction to Statistical Quality Control*. 2nd ed. New York: John Wiley, 1991.

*Profile of ISO 9000*. Needham Heights, MA: Allyn and Bacon, 1992.

Taguchi, G. *Introduction to Quality Engineering*. Tokyo: Asian Productivity Organization, 1986.

# Statistical Process Control

CHAPTER 4

Web resources for this chapter include

- Internet Exercises
- Online Practice Quizzes
- Virtual Tours
- Excel Worksheets
- Company and Resource Weblinks
- Animated Demo Problems
- Microsoft Project Exhibits

www.wiley.com/college/russell

## CHAPTER OUTLINE

In this chapter you will learn about . . .

- The Basics of Statistical Process Control
- Control Charts
- Control Charts for Attributes
- Control Charts for Variables
- Control Chart Patterns
- SPC with Excel
- Process Capability

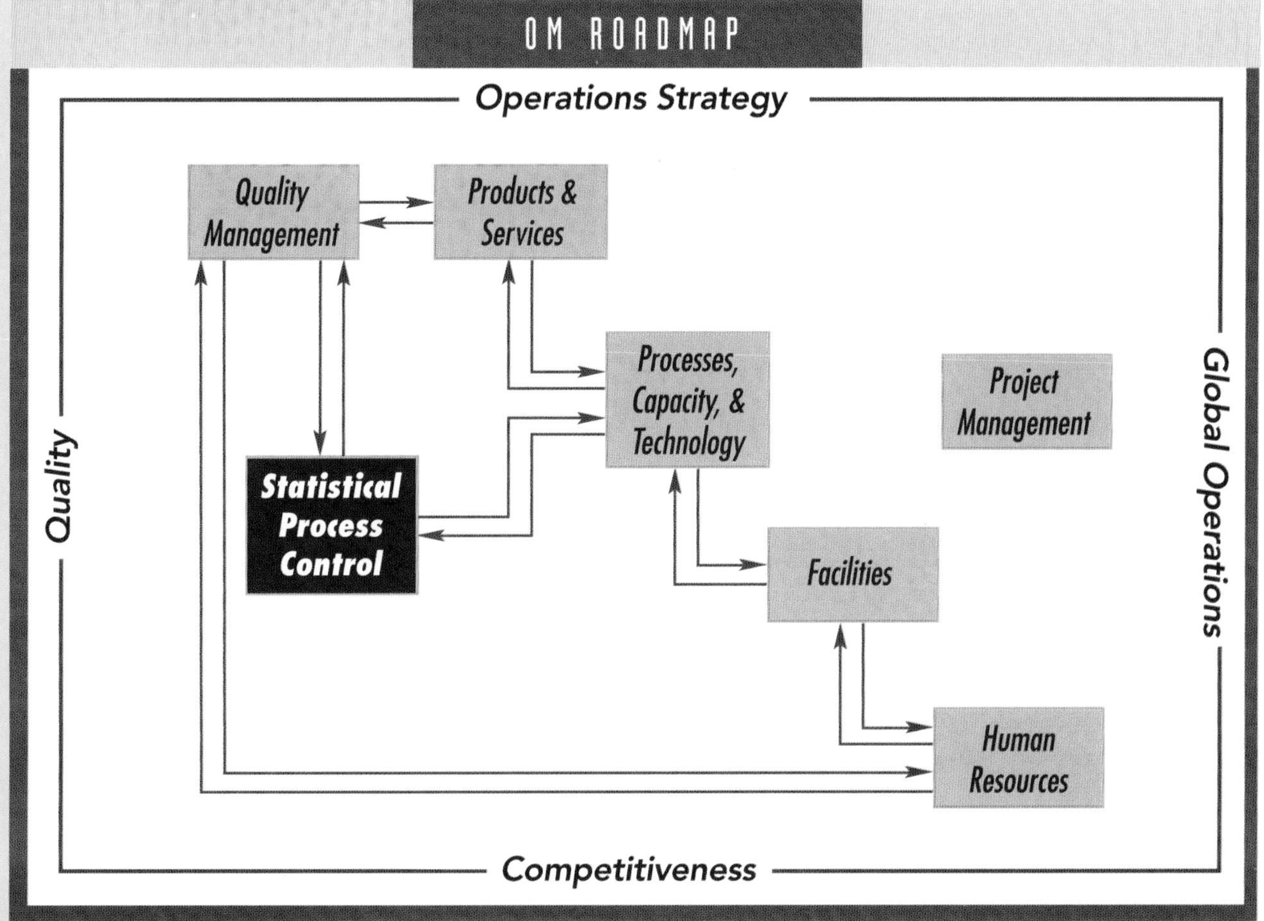

## ACHIEVING SIX SIGMA QUALITY WITH BLACK BELTS AT MOTOROLA AND GENERAL ELECTRIC

Six sigma is a statistical measure that translates to 3.4 defects per million opportunities. Since its conception by Motorola in 1987, numerous companies have adopted this standard as the goal of a quality program now universally known as six sigma in their drive to achieve near-perfect quality in all their products and services and, as a result improve profitability. However, the focus of the six sigma approach is not so much on eliminating defects as it is on providing a systematic method for improving processes, which is generally achieved by reducing process variability. If process variability is reduced, then defects, any source of customer irritation, will be eliminated and total customer satisfaction will result.

For most companies six sigma embodies a systematic approach to process improvement that includes the recognition, measurement, and analysis of problems in processes so that they can be improved and controlled. This approach relies very heavily on well-known quality tools for data collection and statistical analysis to identify the sources of process problems and errors. Chief among these tools is statistical process control.

At companies that have adopted a six sigma approach, like Motorola and General Electric, Black Belts are specially selected and trained in the use and application of quality tools such as statistical process control. However, all GE employees are trained in the use of statistical tools and techniques, both for individual use and to equip them to participate on six sigma teams.

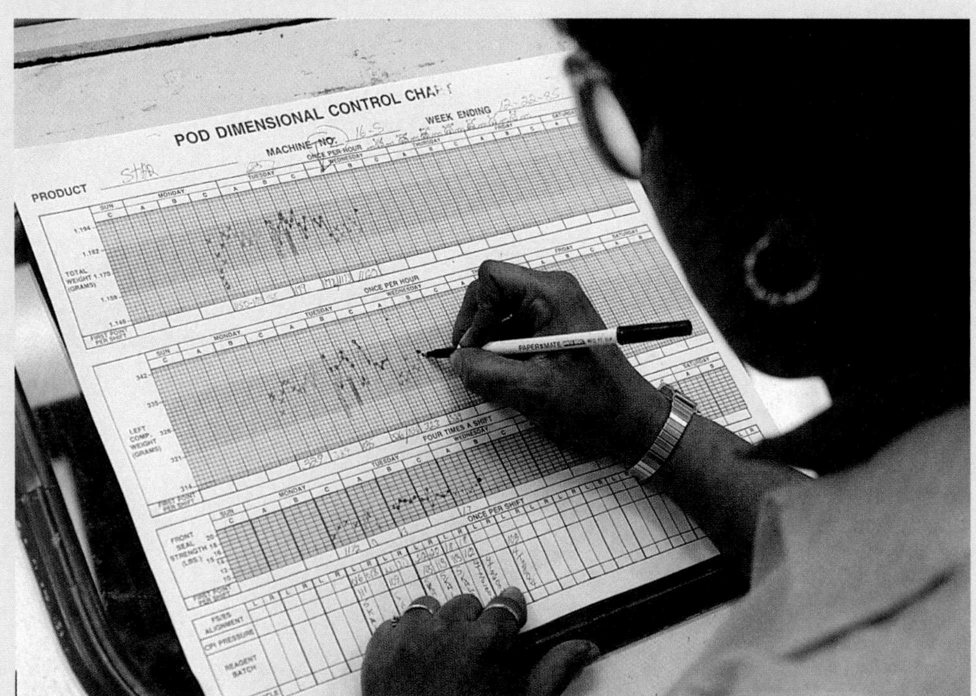


*A statistical control chart like this one is a graph to monitor a production process. Samples are taken from the process periodically, and the observations are plotted on the graph. If an observation is outside the upper or lower limits on the graph, it may indicate that something is wrong in the process; that is, it is not in control, which may cause defective or poor-quality items. By monitoring a process with a control chart, the employee and management can detect problems quickly and prevent poor-quality items from passing on through the remainder of the process and ending up as defective products that must be thrown away or reworked, thus wasting time and resources.*

After World War II, W. E. Deming, the quality expert and consultant, was invited to Japan by the Japanese government to give a series of lectures on improving product reliability. This was probably the single most important event that started the Japanese toward a global quality revolution. These lectures were based on statistical quality control, and they became a cornerstone of the Japanese commitment to quality management.

A major topic in statistical quality control is *statistical process control*. **Statistical process control (SPC)** is a statistical procedure using control charts to see if any part of a production process is not functioning properly and could cause poor quality. In TQM operators use SPC to inspect and measure the production process to see if it is varying from what it is supposed to be doing. If there is unusual or undesirable variability, the process is corrected so that defects will not occur. In this way, statistical process control is used to prevent poor quality before it occurs. It is such an important part of quality management that nearly all workers at all levels in committed TQM companies are given extensive and continual training in SPC. Conversely, in many companies the reason cited for failure to achieve high quality is the lack of comprehensive training for employees in SPC methods. U.S. companies successful in adopting TQM train all their employees in SPC methods and make extensive use of SPC for continuous process improvement.

**Statistical process control (SPC):** involves monitoring the production process to detect and prevent poor quality.

**Employee training in SPC is a fundamental principle of TQM.**

## THE BASICS OF STATISTICAL PROCESS CONTROL

Process control is achieved by taking periodic **samples** from the process and plotting these sample points on a chart, to see if the process is within statistical control limits. A sample can be a single item or a group of items. If a sample point is outside the limits, the process may be out of control, and the cause is sought so that the problem can be corrected. If the sample is within the control limits, the process continues without interference but with continued monitoring. In this way, SPC prevents quality problems by correcting the process before it starts producing defects.

**Sample:** a subset of the items produced to use for inspection.

No production process produces exactly identical items, one after the other. All processes contain a certain amount of variability that makes some variation between units inevitable. There are two reasons why a process might vary. The first is the inherent random variability of the process, which depends on the equipment and machinery, engineering, the operator, and the system used for measurement. This kind of variability is a result of natural occurrences. The other reason for variability is unique or special causes that are identifiable and can be corrected. These causes tend to be nonrandom and, if left unattended, will cause poor quality. These might include equipment that is out of adjustment, defective materials, changes in parts or materials, broken machinery or equipment, operator fatigue or poor work methods, or errors due to lack of training.

**All processes have variability—random and nonrandom (identifiable, correctable).**

## SPC IN TQM

In TQM employees use SPC to see if their process is in control—working properly. This requires that companies provide SPC training on a continuing basis that stresses that SPC is a tool operators can use to monitor their part of the production or service process *for the purpose of making improvements*. Through the use of statistical process control, employees are made responsible for quality in their area: to identify problems and either correct them or seek help in correcting them. By continually monitoring the production process and making improvements, the employee contributes to the TQM goal of continuous improvement and few or no defects.

**SPC is a tool for identifying problems in order to make improvements.**

The first step in correcting the problem is identifying the causes. In Chapter 3 we described several quality-control tools used for identifying causes of problems, including brainstorming, Pareto charts, histograms, check sheets, quality circles, and fishbone (cause-and-effect) diagrams.

When an operator is unable to correct a problem, the supervisor is typically notified who might initiate group problem solving. This group may be a quality circle, or it may be less formal, including other operators, engineers, quality experts, and the supervisor. This group will brainstorm the problem to seek out possible causes. They might use a fishbone diagram to assist in identifying problem causes. Sometimes experiments are conducted under controlled conditions to isolate the cause of a problem.

## QUALITY MEASURES: ATTRIBUTES AND VARIABLES

**Attribute:** a product characteristic that can be evaluated with a discrete response (good/bad, yes/no).

**Variable measure:** a product characteristic that is continuous and can be measured (weight, length).

The quality of a product or service can be evaluated using either an *attribute* of the product or service or a *variable measure*. An **attribute** is a product characteristic such as color, surface texture, cleanliness, or perhaps smell or taste. Attributes can be evaluated quickly with a discrete response such as good or bad, acceptable or not, or yes or no. Even if quality specifications are complex and extensive, a simple attribute test might be used to determine whether or not a product or service is defective. For example, an operator might test a light bulb by simply turning it on and seeing if it lights. If it does not, it can be examined to find out the exact technical cause for failure, but for SPC purposes, the fact that it is defective has been determined.

A **variable measure** is a product characteristic that is measured on a continuous scale such as length, weight, temperature, or time. For example, the amount of liquid detergent in a plastic container can be measured to see if it conforms to the company's product specifications. Or the time it takes to serve a customer at McDonald's can be measured to see if it is quick enough. Since a variable evaluation is the result of some form of measurement, it is sometimes referred to as a *quantitative* classification method. An attribute evaluation is sometimes referred to as a *qualitative* classification, since the response is not measured. Because it is a measurement, a variable classification typically provides more information about the product—the weight of a product is more informative than simply saying the product is good or bad.

## SPC APPLIED TO SERVICES

A service defect is a failure to meet customer requirements.

Control charts have historically been used to monitor the quality of manufacturing processes. However, SPC is just as useful for monitoring quality in services. The difference is the nature of the "defect" being measured and monitored. Using Motorola's definition—*a failure to meet customer requirements in any product or service*—a defect can be an empty soap dispenser in a restroom or an error with a phone catalogue order, as well as

*This Goodyear employee is using a dial caliper to measure variations in tire tread in a tire mold. The dial caliper is a mechanical device, or gauge, in which movable contacts touch the object to be measured and, using a gear train, translate the dimensions to the dial, where it can be read by the operator. Measurements from a gauge like this are accurate to within 0.001 inch. Digital gauges, which perform the same function electronically, are more accurate than a mechanical gauge. Measuring instruments like the dial caliper are used by operators to take sample measurements during the inspection process for use with a process control chart.*

a blemish on a piece of cloth or a faulty plug on a VCR. Control charts for service processes tend to use quality characteristics and measurements such as time and customer satisfaction (determined by surveys, questionnaires, or inspections). Following is a list of several different services and the quality characteristics for each that can be measured and monitored with control charts.

*Hospitals:* Timeliness and quickness of care, staff responses to requests, accuracy of lab tests, cleanliness, courtesy, accuracy of paperwork, speed of admittance and checkouts.
*Grocery stores:* Waiting time to check out, frequency of out-of-stock items, quality of food items, cleanliness, customer complaints, checkout register errors.
*Airlines:* Flight delays, lost luggage and luggage handling, waiting time at ticket counters and check-in, agent and flight attendant courtesy, accurate flight information, passenger cabin cleanliness and maintenance.
*Fast-food restaurants:* Waiting time for service, customer complaints, cleanliness, food quality, order accuracy, employee courtesy.
*Catalogue-order companies:* Order accuracy, operator knowledge and courtesy, packaging, delivery time, phone order waiting time.
*Insurance companies:* Billing accuracy, timeliness of claims processing, agent availability and response time.

## WHERE TO USE CONTROL CHARTS

Most companies do not use control charts for every step in a process. Although that might be the most effective way to ensure the highest quality, it is costly and time consuming. In most manufacturing and service processes, there are clearly identifiable points where control charts should be used. In general, control charts are used at critical points in the process where historically the process has shown a tendency to go out of control, and at points where if the process goes out of control it is particularly harmful and costly. For example, control charts are frequently used at the beginning of a process to check the quality of raw materials and parts, or supplies and deliveries for a service operation. If material and parts are bad to begin with, it is a waste of time and money to begin the production process with them. Control charts are also used before a costly or irreversible point in the process, after which the product is difficult to rework or correct; before and after assembly or painting operations that might cover defects; and before the outgoing final product or service is shipped or delivered.

## CONTROL CHARTS

**Control charts** are graphs that visually show if a sample is within statistical **control limits**. They have two basic purposes: to establish the control limits for a process and then to monitor the process to indicate when it is out of control. Control charts exist for attributes and variables; within each category there are several different types of control charts. We will present four commonly used control charts, two in each category: *p*-charts and *c*-charts for attributes and *mean* ($\bar{x}$) and *range* (*R*) control charts for variables. Even though these control charts differ in how they measure process control, they all have certain similar characteristics. They all look alike, with a line through the center of a graph that indicates the process average and lines above and below the center line that represent the upper and lower limits of the process, as shown in Figure 4.1 on page 136.

**Control chart:** a graph that establishes the control limits of a process.

**Control limits:** the upper and lower bands of a control chart.

**Types of charts: attributes, *p*, and *c*; variables, $\bar{x}$ and *R*.**

The formulas for conducting upper and lower limits in control charts are based on a number of standard deviations, "$z$," from the process average (e.g., center line) according to a normal distribution. Occasionally, $z$ is equal to 2.00 but most frequently is 3.00. A $z$ value of 2.00 corresponds to an overall normal probability of 95%, and $z = 3.00$ corresponds to a normal probability of 99.74%.

The normal distribution in Figure 4.2 on page 136 shows the probabilities corresponding to $z$ values equal to 2.00 and 3.00 standard deviations ($\sigma$).

Figure 4.1
**Process Control Chart**

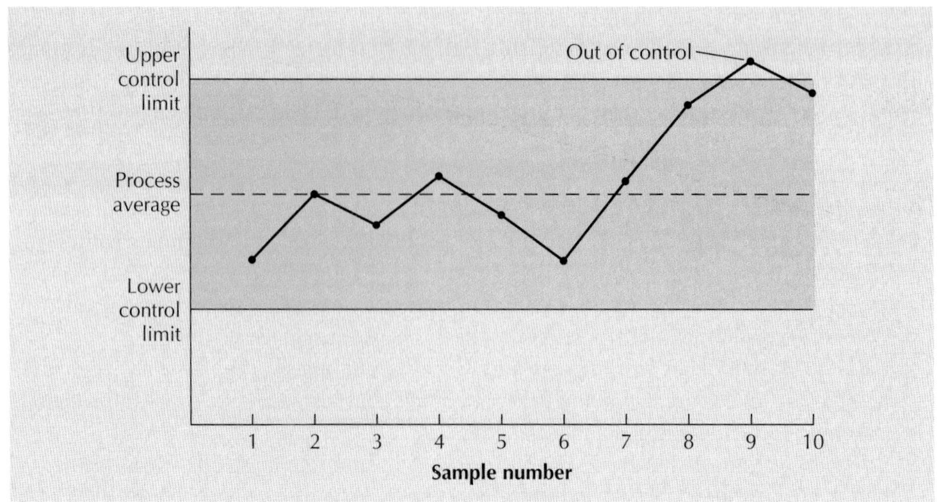


*Sigma limits* are the number of standard deviations.

The smaller the value of $z$, the more narrow the control limits are and the more sensitive the chart is to changes in the production process. Control charts using $z = 2.00$ are often referred to as having 2-sigma ($2\sigma$) limits (referring to two standard deviations), whereas $z = 3.00$ means 3-sigma ($3\sigma$) limits.

Management usually selects $z = 3.00$ because if the process is in control it wants a high probability that the sample values will fall within the control limits. In other words, with wider limits management is less likely to (erroneously) conclude that the process is out of control when points outside the control limits are due to normal, random variations. Alternatively, wider limits make it harder to detect changes in the process that are not random and have an assignable cause. A process might change because of a nonrandom, assignable cause and be detectable with the narrower limits but not with the wider limits. However, companies traditionally use the wider control limits.

Each time a sample is taken, the mathematical average of the sample is plotted as a point on the control chart as shown in Figure 4.1. A process is generally considered to be in control if, for example,

1. There are no sample points outside the control limits.
2. Most points are near the process average (i.e., the center line), without too many close to the control limits.
3. Approximately equal numbers of sample points occur above and below the center line.
4. The points appear to be randomly distributed around the center line (i.e., no discernible pattern).

A sample point can be within the control limits and the process still be out of control.

If any of these conditions are violated, the process may be *out of control*. The reason must be determined, and if the cause is not random, the problem must be corrected.

Sample 9 in Figure 4.1 is above the upper control limit, suggesting the process is out of control. The cause is not likely to be random since the sample points have been moving toward the upper limit, so management should attempt to find out what is wrong with the process and bring it back in control. Although the other samples display some degree of

Figure 4.2
**The Normal Distribution**

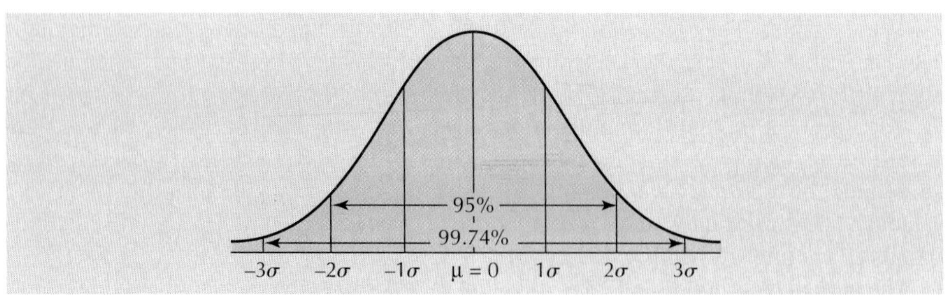

variation from the process average, they are usually considered to be caused by normal, random variability in the process and are thus in control. However, it is possible for sample observations to be within the control limits and the process to be out of control anyway, if the observations display a discernible, abnormal pattern of movement. We discuss such patterns in a later section.

After a control chart is established, it is used to determine when a process goes out of control and corrections need to be made. As such, a process control chart should be based only on sample observations from when the process is in control so that the control chart reflects a true benchmark for an in-control process. However, it is not known whether or not the process is in control until the control chart is first constructed. Therefore, when a control chart is first developed if the process is found to be out of control, the process should be examined and corrections made. A new center line and control limits should then be determined from a new set of sample observations. This "corrected" control chart is then used to monitor the process. It may not be possible to discover the cause(s) for the out-of-control sample observations. In this case a new set of samples is taken, and a completely new control chart constructed. Or it may be decided to simply use the initial control chart, assuming that it accurately reflects the process variation.

The development of a control chart.

## CONTROL CHARTS FOR ATTRIBUTES

The quality measures used in *attribute control charts* are discrete values reflecting a simple decision criterion such as good or bad. A ***p*-chart** uses the proportion of defective items in a sample as the sample statistic; a ***c*-chart** uses the actual number of defects per item in a sample. A *p*-chart can be used when it is possible to distinguish between defective and nondefective items and to state the number of defectives as a percentage of the whole. In some processes, the proportion defective cannot be determined. For example, when counting the number of blemishes on a roll of upholstery material (at periodic intervals), it is not possible to compute a proportion. In this case a *c*-chart is required.

***p*-chart:** uses the proportion defective in a sample.

***c*-chart:** uses the number of defective items in a sample.

### *p*-CHART

With a *p*-chart a sample of *n* items is taken periodically from the production or service process, and the proportion of defective items in the sample is determined to see if the proportion falls within the control limits on the chart. Although a *p*-chart employs a discrete attribute measure (i.e., number of defective items) and thus is not continuous, it is assumed that as the sample size ($n$) gets larger, the normal distribution can be used to approximate the distribution of the proportion defective. This enables us to use the following formulas based on the normal distribution to compute the upper control limit (UCL) and lower control limit (LCL) of a *p*-chart:

$$\text{UCL} = \bar{p} + z\sigma_p$$
$$\text{LCL} = \bar{p} - z\sigma_p$$

where

$z$ = the number of standard deviations from the process average
$\bar{p}$ = the sample proportion defective; an estimate of the process average
$\sigma_p$ = the standard deviation of the sample proportion

The sample standard deviation is computed as

$$\sigma_p = \sqrt{\frac{\bar{p}(1-\bar{p})}{n}}$$

where $n$ is the sample size.

Example 4.1 demonstrates how a *p*-chart is constructed.

**Example 4.1**

**Construction of a *p*-Chart**

The Western Jeans Company produces denim jeans. The company wants to establish a *p*-chart to monitor the production process and maintain high quality. Western believes that approximately 99.74% of the variability in the production process (corresponding to 3-sigma limits, or $z = 3.00$) is random and thus should be within control limits, whereas 0.26% of the process variability is not random and suggests that the process is out of control.

The company has taken 20 samples (one per day for 20 days), each containing 100 pairs of jeans ($n = 100$), and inspected them for defects, the results of which are as follows.

| Sample | Number of Defectives | Proportion Defective |
|---|---|---|
| 1 | 6 | .06 |
| 2 | 0 | .00 |
| 3 | 4 | .04 |
| 4 | 10 | .10 |
| 5 | 6 | .06 |
| 6 | 4 | .04 |
| 7 | 12 | .12 |
| 8 | 10 | .10 |
| 9 | 8 | .08 |
| 10 | 10 | .10 |
| 11 | 12 | .12 |
| 12 | 10 | .10 |
| 13 | 14 | .14 |
| 14 | 8 | .08 |
| 15 | 6 | .06 |
| 16 | 16 | .16 |
| 17 | 12 | .12 |
| 18 | 14 | .14 |
| 19 | 20 | .20 |
| 20 | 18 | .18 |
| | 200 | |

The proportion defective for the population is not known. The company wants to construct a *p*-chart to determine when the production process might be out of control.

*Solution*

Since *p* is not known, it can be estimated from the total sample:

$$\bar{p} = \frac{\text{total defectives}}{\text{total sample observations}}$$

$$= \frac{200}{20(100)}$$

$$= 0.10$$

The control limits are computed as follows:

$$\text{UCL} = \bar{p} + z\sqrt{\frac{\bar{p}(1-\bar{p})}{n}}$$

$$= 0.10 + 3.00\sqrt{\frac{0.10(1-0.10)}{100}} = 0.190$$

$$\text{LCL} = \bar{p} - z\sqrt{\frac{\bar{p}(1-\bar{p})}{n}}$$

$$= 0.10 - 3.00\sqrt{\frac{0.10(1-0.10)}{100}} = 0.010$$

The $p$-chart, including sample points, is shown in the following figure:

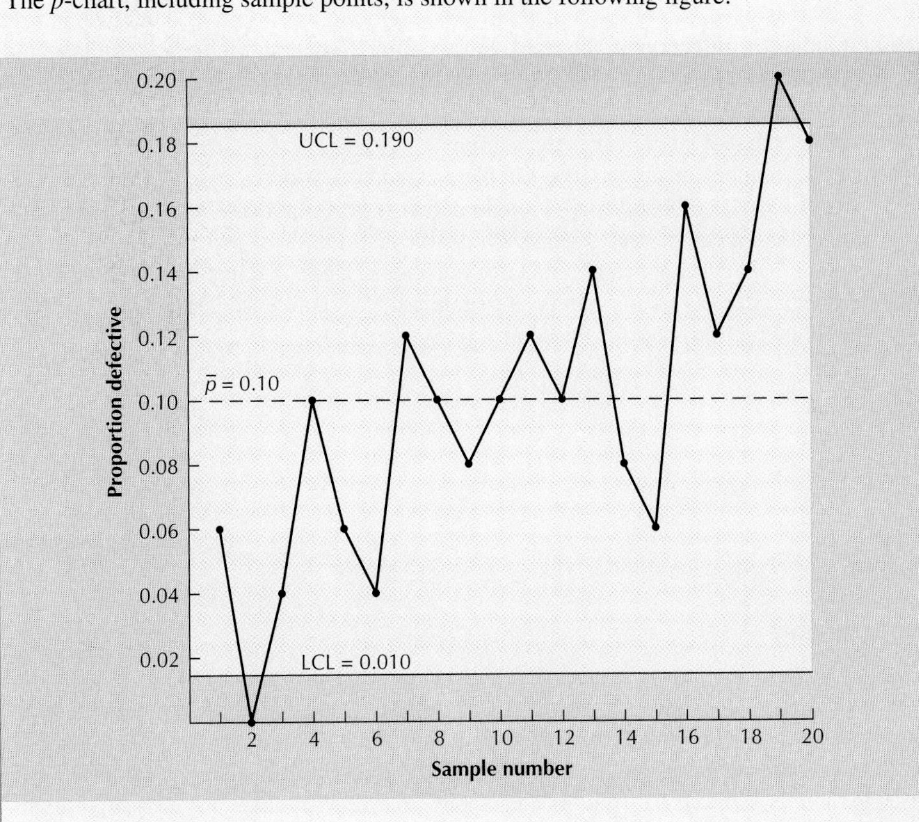


The process was below the lower control limits for sample 2 (i.e., during day 2). Although this could be perceived as a "good" result since it means there were very few defects, it might also suggest that something was wrong with the inspection process during that week that should be checked out. If there is no problem with the inspection process, then management would want to know what caused the quality of the process to improve. Perhaps "better" denim material from a new supplier that week or a different operator was working.

The process was above the upper limit during day 19. This suggests that the process may not be in control and the cause should be investigated. The cause could be defective or maladjusted machinery, a problem with an operator, defective materials (i.e., denim cloth), or a number of other correctable problems. In fact, there is an upward trend in the number of defectives throughout the 20-day test period. The process was consistently moving toward an out-of-control situation. This trend represents a pattern in the observations, which suggests a nonrandom cause. If this was the actual control chart used to monitor the process (and not the initial chart), it is likely this pattern would have indicated an out-of-control situation before day 19, which would have alerted the operator to make corrections. Patterns are discussed in a separate section later in this chapter.

This initial control chart shows two out-of-control observations and a distinct pattern of increasing defects. Management would probably want to discard this set of samples and develop a new center line and control limits from a different set of sample values after the process has been corrected. If the pattern had not existed and only the two out-of-control observations were present, these two observations could be discarded, and a control chart could be developed from the remaining sample values.

Once a control chart is established based solely on natural, random variation in the process, it is used to monitor the process. Samples are taken periodically, and the observations are checked on the control chart to see if the process is in control.

## c-CHART

A $c$-chart is used when it is not possible to compute a proportion defective and the actual number of defects must be used. For example, when automobiles are inspected, the number of blemishes (i.e., defects) in the paint job can be counted for each car, but a proportion cannot be computed, since the total number of possible blemishes is not known. In this case a single car is the sample.

Since the number of defects per sample is assumed to derive from some extremely large population, the probability of a single defect is very small. As with the $p$-chart, the normal distribution can be used to approximate the distribution of defects. The process average for the $c$-chart is the mean number of defects per item, $\bar{c}$, computed by dividing the total number of defects by the number of samples. The sample standard deviation, $\sigma_c$, is $\sqrt{\bar{c}}$. The following formulas for the control limits are used:

$$\text{UCL} = \bar{c} + z\sigma_c$$

$$\text{LCL} = \bar{c} - z\sigma_c$$

## THE COMPETITIVE EDGE

### Using Control Charts for Improving Health-Care Quality

In 2002 the National Health Service (NHS) in the United Kingdom began making extensive use of statistical control charts to improve service delivery. Control charts developed on Excel spreadsheets are now used to monitor service performance at NHS facilities that deal directly with patients. Initially, it was necessary for personnel to have a thorough understanding of control charts in order to implement their use of control charts throughout NHS. Employees attend a two-day SPC training course to which they are asked to bring 20 time-sequenced data points related to the processes they work with. During the first day attendees are provided with working knowledge of $X$- and $R$-charts. On the evening of the first day, participants construct control charts with the data they brought with them using a software program that performs the mathematical calculations. On the second day, participants make presentations on how they are using (or plan to use) control charts and how SPC impacts the culture of their operation. Deming's 14 points and principles of quality management are discussed, and the attendees consider how this information will influence their own operation and their use of control charts.

The range of applications for a health-care facility is surprisingly high, but most applications relate to waiting times. For example, applications include waiting time to see a nurse or other medical consultant, or to get medical results, although they can also be used to monitor administrative errors. A specific example is for "door to needle" times, which is the time it takes after a heart attack patient is registered into the hospital to receive an appropriate injection. Control charts are used to compare performance for this process at hospitals throughout the UK. However, a key difference in constructing this control chart as opposed to a control chart for a manufacturing process is in establishing the upper control limit. In this case the upper limit is not a statistical measure (based on three standard deviations) but a government-mandated target that 75% of heart patients receive treatment within 20 minutes of being received into the hospital. In some cases, control charts like this are being used to question the way the government sets such targets.

Statistical process control charts are also a popular tool for monitoring quality at Royal North Shore Hospital and Community Health Services, a 650-bed government referral teaching hospital and trauma center in Sydney, Australia. The hospital uses control charts to analyze patient satisfaction as well as other clinical data. One application of control charts has been for monitoring patient waiting times for elective clinical (i.e., operating room) procedures. The measure tracked was the number of patients waiting more than 30 days for a procedure. A Minitab statistical software package was used to develop control charts and track data points. The control charts indicated that the system was out of control, with an average of 160 patients waiting above the target time of 30 days. As a result, the hospital developed procedures to improve the waiting time process; specifically, a "waitlist" coordinator was appointed. Patient waiting times were reduced to an average of 50.7 patients waiting more than 30 days, a significant improvement, with a parallel reduction in variability. Control charts enabled the hospital to better understand the wait process, determine whether the process was in control, ascertain the outcome of improvement efforts, and predict future results. However, the primary result was that patient satisfaction improved.

*Sources:* M. Owen, "From Sickness to Health," *Qualityworld* 29 (8: August 2003), pp. 18–22; and H. E. Ganley and J. Moxey, "Making Informed Decisions in the Face of Uncertainty," *Quality Progress* 33 (10; October 2000); pp. 76–78.

*Checking cracker texture at a Nabisco plant as part of the quality-control process.*

Example 4.2

**Construction of a *c*-Chart**

The Ritz Hotel has 240 rooms. The hotel's housekeeping department is responsible for maintaining the quality of the rooms' appearance and cleanliness. Each individual housekeeper is responsible for an area encompassing 20 rooms. Every room in use is thoroughly cleaned and its supplies, toiletries, and so on are restocked each day. Any defects that the housekeeping staff notice that are not part of the normal housekeeping service are supposed to be reported to hotel maintenance. Every room is briefly inspected each day by a housekeeping supervisor. However, hotel management also conducts inspection tours at random for a detailed, thorough inspection for quality-control purposes. The management inspectors not only check for normal housekeeping service defects like clean sheets, dust, room supplies, room literature, or towels, but also for defects like an inoperative or missing TV remote, poor TV picture quality or reception, defective lamps, a malfunctioning clock, tears or stains in the bedcovers or curtains, or a malfunctioning curtain pull. An inspection sample includes 12 rooms, that is, one room selected at random from each of the twelve 20-room blocks serviced by a housekeeper. Following are the results from 15 inspection samples conducted at random during a one-month period:

| Sample | Number of Defects |
|---|---|
| 1 | 12 |
| 2 | 8 |
| 3 | 16 |
| 4 | 14 |
| 5 | 10 |
| 6 | 11 |
| 7 | 9 |
| 8 | 14 |
| 9 | 13 |
| 10 | 15 |
| 11 | 12 |
| 12 | 10 |
| 13 | 14 |
| 14 | 17 |
| 15 | 15 |
| | 190 |

The hotel believes that approximately 99% of the defects (corresponding to 3-sigma limits) are caused by natural, random variations in the housekeeping and room maintenance service, with 1% caused by nonrandom variability. They want to construct a *c*-chart to monitor the housekeeping service.

*Solution*

Because *c*, the population process average, is not known, the sample estimate, $\bar{c}$, can be used instead:

$$\bar{c} = \frac{190}{15} = 12.67$$

The control limits are computed using $z = 3.00$, as follows:

$$\text{UCL} = \bar{c} + z\sqrt{\bar{c}} = 12.67 + 3\sqrt{12.67} = 23.35$$
$$\text{LCL} = \bar{c} - z\sqrt{\bar{c}} = 12.67 - 3\sqrt{12.67} = 1.99$$

The resulting *c*-chart, with the sample points, is shown in the following figure:

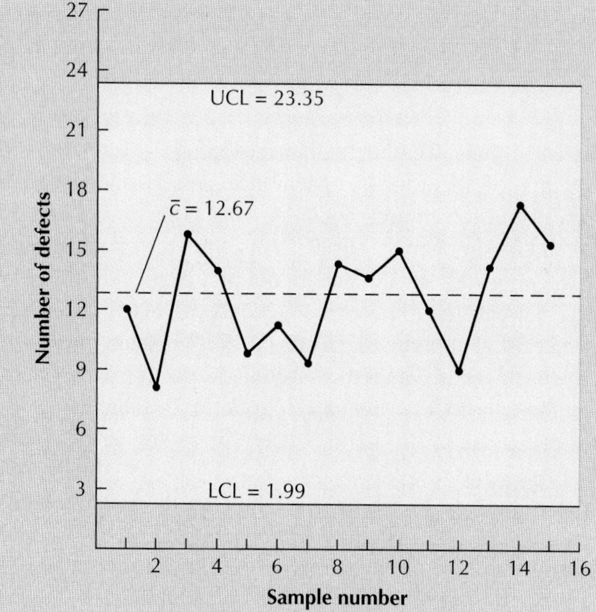


All the sample observations are within the control limits, suggesting that the room quality is in control. This chart would be considered reliable to monitor the room quality in the future.

## CONTROL CHARTS FOR VARIABLES

**Range (*R*-) chart:** uses the amount of dispersion in a sample.

**Mean ($\bar{x}$-) chart:** uses the process average of a sample.

Variable control charts are used for continuous variables that can be measured, such as weight or volume. Two commonly used variable control charts are the range chart, or *R*-chart, and the mean chart, or $\bar{x}$-chart. A **range (*R*-) chart** reflects the amount of dispersion present in each sample; a **mean ($\bar{x}$-) chart** indicates how sample results relate to the process average or mean. These charts are normally used together to determine whether a process is in control.

### MEAN ($\bar{x}$-) CHART

In a mean (or $\bar{x}$) control chart, each time a sample of a group of items is taken from the process, the mean of the sample is computed and plotted on the chart. Each sample mean ($\bar{x}$) is a point on the control chart. The samples taken tend to be small, usually around 4 or 5. The center line of the control chart is the overall process average, that is, the mean of the sample means.

The $\bar{x}$-chart is based on the normal distribution. It can be constructed in two ways depending on the information that is available about the distribution. If the standard deviation of the distribution is known from past experience or historical data, then formulas using the standard deviation can be used to compute the upper and lower control limits. If the standard deviation is not known, then a table of values based on sample ranges is available to develop the upper and lower control limits. We will first look at how to construct an $\bar{x}$-chart when the standard deviation is known.

The formulas for computing the upper control limit (UCL) and lower control limit (LCL) are

$$\text{UCL} = \bar{\bar{x}} + z\sigma_{\bar{x}}$$
$$\text{LCL} = \bar{\bar{x}} - z\sigma_{\bar{x}}$$

where

$$\bar{\bar{x}} = \text{process average} = \frac{\bar{x}_1 + \bar{x}_2 + \ldots + \bar{x}_n}{n}$$

$\sigma$ = process standard deviation

$\sigma_{\bar{x}}$ = standard deviation of sample means = $\sigma/\sqrt{n}$

$n$ = sample size

Example 4.3 illustrates how to develop an $\bar{x}$-chart using these formulas.

**Example 4.3**

**Constructing an $\bar{x}$-Chart**

The Goliath Tool Company produces slip-ring bearings, which look like flat doughnuts or washers. They fit around shafts or rods, such as drive shafts in machinery or motors. At an early stage in the production process for a particular slip-ring bearing, the outside diameter of the bearing is measured. Employees have taken 10 samples (during a 10-day period) of 5 slip-ring bearings (i.e., $n$ = 5) and measured the diameter of the bearing. The individual observations from each sample are shown as follows:

| | Observations (Slip-Ring Diameter, cm) | | | | | |
|---|---|---|---|---|---|---|
| **Sample $k$** | *1* | *2* | *3* | *4* | *5* | $\bar{x}$ |
| 1 | 5.02 | 5.01 | 4.94 | 4.99 | 4.96 | 4.98 |
| 2 | 5.01 | 5.03 | 5.07 | 4.95 | 4.96 | 5.00 |
| 3 | 4.99 | 5.00 | 4.93 | 4.92 | 4.99 | 4.97 |
| 4 | 5.03 | 4.91 | 5.01 | 4.98 | 4.89 | 4.96 |
| 5 | 4.95 | 4.92 | 5.03 | 5.05 | 5.01 | 4.99 |
| 6 | 4.97 | 5.06 | 5.06 | 4.96 | 5.03 | 5.01 |
| 7 | 5.05 | 5.01 | 5.10 | 4.96 | 4.99 | 5.02 |
| 8 | 5.09 | 5.10 | 5.00 | 4.99 | 5.08 | 5.05 |
| 9 | 5.14 | 5.10 | 4.99 | 5.08 | 5.09 | 5.08 |
| 10 | 5.01 | 4.98 | 5.08 | 5.07 | 4.99 | 5.03 |
| | | | | | | 50.09 |

From past historical data it is known that the process standard deviation is .08. The company wants to develop a control chart with 3-sigma limits to monitor this process in the future.

The process average is computed as

$$\bar{\bar{x}} = \frac{50.09}{10} = 5.01$$

The control limits are

$$\begin{aligned}\text{UCL} &= \bar{\bar{x}} + z\sigma_{\bar{x}} \\ &= 5.01 + 3(.08/\sqrt{10}) \\ &= 5.09\end{aligned}$$

$$\text{LCL} = \bar{\bar{x}} - z\sigma_{\bar{x}}$$
$$= 5.01 - 3(.08/\sqrt{10})$$
$$= 4.93$$

None of the sample means ($\bar{x}$) falls outside these control limits, which indicates that the process is *in control* and this is an accurate control chart.

In the second approach to developing an $\bar{x}$-chart, the following formulas are used to compute the control limits:

$$\text{UCL} = \bar{\bar{x}} + A_2\bar{R}$$
$$\text{LCL} = \bar{\bar{x}} - A_2\bar{R}$$

where $\bar{\bar{x}}$ is the average of the sample means and $\bar{R}$ is the average range value. $A_2$ is a tabular value that is used to establish the control limits. Values of $A_2$ are included in Table 4.1. They were developed specifically for determining the control limits for $\bar{x}$-charts and are comparable to three-standard deviation ($3\sigma$) limits. These table values are frequently used to develop control charts.

**Table 4.1** **Factors for Determining Control Limits for $\bar{x}$- and *R*-Charts**

| Sample Size $n$ | Factor for $\bar{x}$-Chart $A_2$ | Factors for *R*-Chart $D_3$ | $D_4$ |
|---|---|---|---|
| 2 | 1.88 | 0 | 3.27 |
| 3 | 1.02 | 0 | 2.57 |
| 4 | 0.73 | 0 | 2.28 |
| 5 | 0.58 | 0 | 2.11 |
| 6 | 0.48 | 0 | 2.00 |
| 7 | 0.42 | 0.08 | 1.92 |
| 8 | 0.37 | 0.14 | 1.86 |
| 9 | 0.34 | 0.18 | 1.82 |
| 10 | 0.31 | 0.22 | 1.78 |
| 11 | 0.29 | 0.26 | 1.74 |
| 12 | 0.27 | 0.28 | 1.72 |
| 13 | 0.25 | 0.31 | 1.69 |
| 14 | 0.24 | 0.33 | 1.67 |
| 15 | 0.22 | 0.35 | 1.65 |
| 16 | 0.21 | 0.36 | 1.64 |
| 17 | 0.20 | 0.38 | 1.62 |
| 18 | 0.19 | 0.39 | 1.61 |
| 19 | 0.19 | 0.40 | 1.60 |
| 20 | 0.18 | 0.41 | 1.59 |
| 21 | 0.17 | 0.43 | 1.58 |
| 22 | 0.17 | 0.43 | 1.57 |
| 23 | 0.16 | 0.44 | 1.56 |
| 24 | 0.16 | 0.45 | 1.55 |
| 25 | 0.15 | 0.46 | 1.54 |

*A conveyor of potato chips at a Frito-Lay plant. Periodically, samples of chips will be taken from the conveyor and tested for salt content, thickness, crispness, and other product variables. The sample results will be plotted on a control chart to see if the production process is in control. If not, it will be corrected before a large number of defective chips are produced, thereby preventing costly waste.*

**Example 4.4**

**An $\bar{x}$-Chart**

The Goliath Tool Company desires to develop an $\bar{x}$-chart using table values. The sample data collected for this process with ranges is shown in the following table.

| | Observations (Slip-Ring Diameter, cm) | | | | | | |
|---|---|---|---|---|---|---|---|
| **Sample *k*** | *1* | *2* | *3* | *4* | *5* | $\bar{x}$ | *R* |
| 1 | 5.02 | 5.01 | 4.94 | 4.99 | 4.96 | 4.98 | 0.08 |
| 2 | 5.01 | 5.03 | 5.07 | 4.95 | 4.96 | 5.00 | 0.12 |
| 3 | 4.99 | 5.00 | 4.93 | 4.92 | 4.99 | 4.97 | 0.08 |
| 4 | 5.03 | 4.91 | 5.01 | 4.98 | 4.89 | 4.96 | 0.14 |
| 5 | 4.95 | 4.92 | 5.03 | 5.05 | 5.01 | 4.99 | 0.13 |
| 6 | 4.97 | 5.06 | 5.06 | 4.96 | 5.03 | 5.01 | 0.10 |
| 7 | 5.05 | 5.01 | 5.10 | 4.96 | 4.99 | 5.02 | 0.14 |
| 8 | 5.09 | 5.10 | 5.00 | 4.99 | 5.08 | 5.05 | 0.11 |
| 9 | 5.14 | 5.10 | 4.99 | 5.08 | 5.09 | 5.08 | 0.15 |
| 10 | 5.01 | 4.98 | 5.08 | 5.07 | 4.99 | 5.03 | 0.10 |
| | | | | | | 50.09 | 1.15 |

The company wants to develop an $\bar{x}$-chart to monitor the process.

*Solution*

$\overline{R}$ is computed by first determining the range for each sample by computing the difference between the highest and lowest values as shown in the last column in our table of sample observations. These ranges are summed and then divided by the number of samples, $k$, as follows:

$$\overline{R} = \frac{\sum R}{k} = \frac{1.15}{10} = 0.115$$

$\overline{\overline{x}}$ is computed as follows:

$$\overline{\overline{x}} = \frac{\sum \overline{x}}{10} = \frac{50.09}{10} = 5.01 \text{ cm}$$

Using the value of $A_2 = 0.58$ for $n = 5$ from Table 4.1 and $\overline{R} = 0.115$, we compute the control limits as

$$\begin{aligned} \text{UCL} &= \overline{\overline{x}} + A_2\overline{R} \\ &= 5.01 + (0.58)(0.115) = 5.08 \\ \text{LCL} &= \overline{\overline{x}} - A_2\overline{R} \\ &= 5.01 - (0.58)(0.115) = 4.94 \end{aligned}$$

The $\overline{x}$-chart defined by these control limits is shown in the following figure. Notice that the process is on the UCL for sample 9; in fact, samples 4 to 9 show an upward trend. This would suggest that the process variability is subject to nonrandom causes and should be investigated.

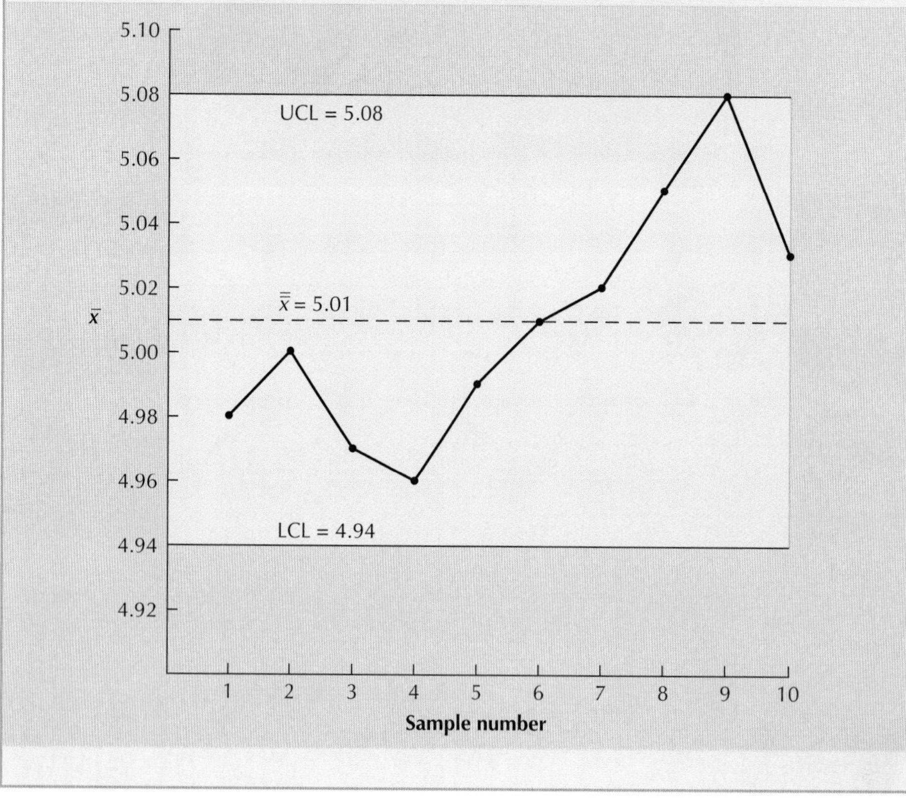


## RANGE ($R$-) CHART

**Range:** the difference between the smallest and largest values in a sample.

In an $R$-chart, the **range** is the difference between the smallest and largest values in a sample. This range reflects the process variability instead of the tendency toward a mean value. The formulas for determining control limits are

$$\begin{aligned} \text{UCL} &= D_4\overline{R} \\ \text{LCL} &= D_3\overline{R} \end{aligned}$$

$\overline{R}$ is the average range (and center line) for the samples,

$$\overline{R} = \frac{\sum R}{k}$$

where

$R$ = range of each sample
$k$ = number of samples

$D_3$ and $D_4$ are table values like $A_2$ for determining control limits that have been developed based on range values rather than standard deviations. Table 4.1 also includes values for $D_3$ and $D_4$ for sample sizes up to 25.

**Example 4.5**

**Constructing an R-Chart**

The Goliath Tool Company from Examples 4.3 and 4.4 wants to develop an $R$-chart to control process variability.

From Example 4.4, $\overline{R} = 0.115$; from Table 4.1 for $n = 5$, $D_3 = 0$ and $D_4 = 2.11$. Thus, the control limits are,

$$\text{UCL} = D_4\overline{R} = 2.11(0.115) = 0.243$$
$$\text{LCL} = D_3\overline{R} = 0(0.115) = 0$$

These limits define the $R$-chart shown in the following figure. It indicates that the process appears to be in control; any variability observed is a result of natural random occurrences.

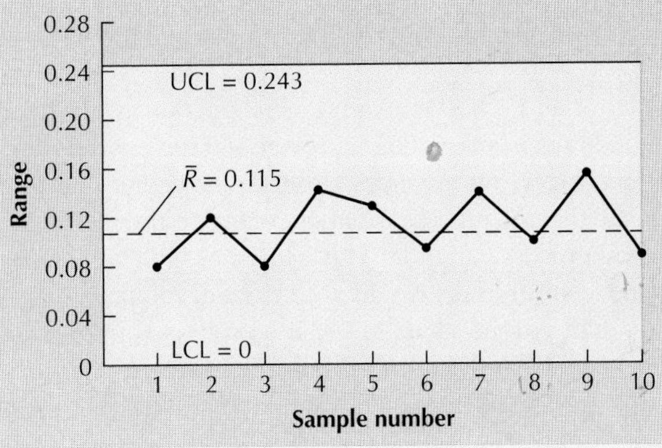


This example illustrates the need to employ the $R$-chart and the $\overline{x}$-chart together. The $R$-chart in this example suggests that the process is in control, since none of the ranges for the samples are close to the control limits. However, the $\overline{x}$-chart in Example 4.4 suggests that the process is not in control. In fact, the ranges for samples 8 and 10 were relatively narrow, whereas the means for these samples were relatively high. The use of both charts together provided a more complete picture of the overall process variability.

## USING $\overline{x}$- AND $R$-CHARTS TOGETHER

Both the process average and variability must be in control.

The $\overline{x}$-chart is used with the $R$-chart under the premise that both the process average and variability must be in control for the process to be in control. This is logical. The two charts measure the process differently. It is possible for samples to have very narrow ranges, suggesting little process variability, but the sample averages might be beyond the control limits.

For example, consider two samples, the first having low and high values of 4.95 and 5.05 centimeters, and the second having low and high values of 5.10 and 5.20 centimeters. The range of both is 0.10 centimeters, but $\overline{x}$ for the first is 5.00 centimeters and $\overline{x}$ for the second is 5.15 centimeters. The two sample ranges might indicate the process is in control and $\overline{x} = 5.00$ might be okay, but $\overline{x} = 5.15$ could be outside the control limit.

## THE COMPETITIVE EDGE

### Using Control Charts at Kentucky Fried Chicken

Kentucky Fried Chicken (KFC) Corporation, USA, is a fast-food chain consisting of 2000 company-owned restaurants and more than 3000 franchised restaurants with annual sales of more than $3 billion. Quality of service and especially speed of service at its drive-through window operations are critical in retaining customers and increasing its market share in the very competitive fast-food industry. As part of a quality-improvement project in KFC's South Central (Texas and Oklahoma) division, a project team established a goal of reducing customer time at a drive-through window from more than 2 minutes down to 60 seconds. This reduction was to be achieved in 10-second increments until the overall goal was realized. Large, visible electronic timers were used at each of four test restaurants to time window service and identify problem areas. Each week tapes from these timers were sent to the project leader, who used this data to construct $\bar{x}$- and $R$-control charts. Since the project goal was to gradually reduce service time (in 10-second increments), the system was not stable. The $\bar{x}$-chart showed if the average weekly sample service times continued to go down toward the 60-second goal. The $R$-chart plotted the average of the range between the longest and shortest window times in a sample, and was used for the traditional purpose to ensure that the variability of the system was under control and not increasing.

*Source:* U. M. Apte and C. Reynolds, "Quality Management at Kentucky Fried Chicken," *Interfaces* 25(3;1995), pp. 6–21.

Conversely, it is possible for the sample averages to be in control, but the ranges might be very large. For example, two samples could both have $\bar{x} = 5.00$ centimeters, but sample 1 could have a range between 4.95 and 5.05 ($R = 0.10$ centimeter) and sample 2 could have a range between 4.80 and 5.20 ($R = 0.40$ centimeter). Sample 2 suggests the process is out of control.

It is also possible for an $R$-chart to exhibit a distinct downward trend in the range values, indicating that the ranges are getting narrower and there is less variation. This would be reflected on the $\bar{x}$-chart by mean values closer to the center line. Although this occurrence does not indicate that the process is out of control, it does suggest that some nonrandom cause is reducing process variation. This cause needs to be investigated to see if it is sustainable. If so, new control limits would need to be developed.

Sometimes an $\bar{x}$-chart is used alone to see if a process is improving. For example, in the "Competitive Edge" box for Kentucky Fried Chicken, an $\bar{x}$-chart is used to see if average service times at a drive-through window are continuing to decline over time toward a specific goal.

In other situations, a company may have studied and collected data for a process for a long time and already know what the mean and standard deviation of the process are; all they want to do is monitor the process average by taking periodic samples. In this case it would be appropriate to use the mean chart where the process standard deviation is already known as shown in Example 4.3.

## CONTROL CHART PATTERNS

A pattern can indicate an out-of-control process even if sample values are within control limits.

**Run:** a sequence of sample values that display the same characteristic.

Even though a control chart may indicate that a process is in control, it is possible the sample variations within the control limits are not random. If the sample values display a consistent pattern, even within the control limits, it suggests that this pattern has a nonrandom cause that might warrant investigation. We expect the sample values to "bounce around" above and below the center line, reflecting the natural, random variation in the process that will be present. However, if the sample values are consistently above (or below) the center line for an extended number of samples or if they move consistently up or down, there is probably a reason for this behavior; that is, it is not random. Examples of nonrandom patterns are shown in Figure 4.3.

A pattern in a control chart is characterized by a sequence of sample observations that display the same characteristics—also called a **run**. One type of pattern is a sequence of

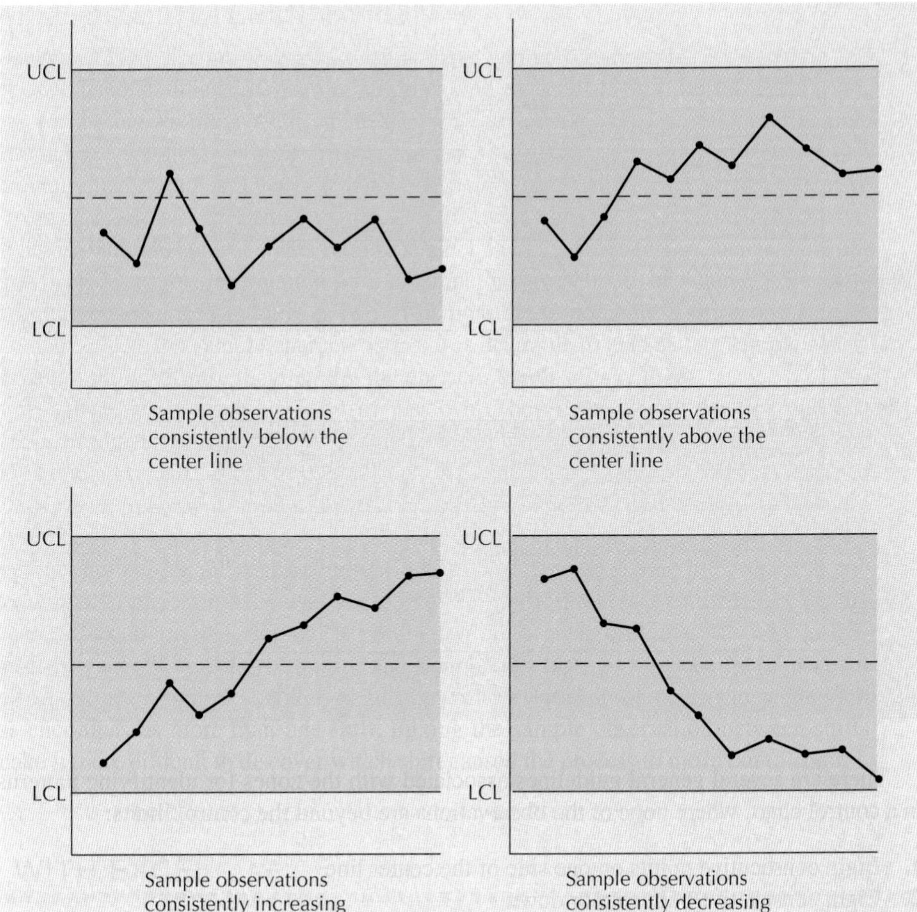


Figure 4.3
**Control Chart Patterns**

observations either above or below the center line. For example, three values above the center line followed by two values below the line represent two runs of a pattern. Another type of pattern is a sequence of sample values that consistently go up or go down within the control limits. Several tests are available to determine if a pattern is nonrandom or random.

One type of **pattern test** divides the control chart into three "zones" on each side of the center line, where each zone is one standard deviation wide. These are often referred to as 1-sigma, 2-sigma, and 3-sigma limits. The pattern of sample observations in these zones is then used to determine if any nonrandom patterns exist. Recall that the formula for computing an $\bar{x}$-chart uses $A_2$ from Table 4.1, which assumes 3 standard deviation control limits (or 3-sigma limits). Thus, to compute the dividing lines between each of the three zones for an $\bar{x}$-chart, we use $\frac{1}{3} A_2$. The formulas to compute these zone boundaries are shown on the next page.

**Pattern test:** determines if the observations within the limits of a control chart display a nonrandom pattern.

## THE COMPETITIVE EDGE

### Using $\bar{x}$-Charts at Frito-Lay

Since the Frito-Lay Company implemented statistical process control, it has experienced a 50% improvement in the variability of bags of potato chips. As an example, the company uses $\bar{x}$-charts to monitor and control salt content, an important taste feature in Ruffles potato chips. Three batches of finished Ruffles are obtained every 15 minutes. Each batch is ground up, weighed, dissolved in distilled water, and filtered into a beaker. The salt content of this liquid is determined using an electronic salt analyzer. The salt content of the three batches is averaged to get a sample mean, which is plotted on an $\bar{x}$-chart with a center line (target) salt content of 1.6%.

*Source:* Based on "Against All Odds, Statistical Quality Control," COMAP Program 3, Annenberg/CPB Project (Needham Heights, MA: Allyn and Bacon, 1988).

In TQM, 3-sigma limits do not provide good quality.

In 6-sigma quality, we have 3.4 defective PPM, or zero defects.

reasonable quality goal. If the process distribution is normally distributed and the natural control limits are three standard deviations from the process mean—that is, they are 3-sigma limits—then the probability between the limits is 0.9973. This is the probability of a good item. This means the area, or probability, outside the limits is 0.0027, which translates to 2.7 defects per thousand or 2700 defects out of one million items. However, according to strict TQM philosophy, this is not an appropriate quality goal. As Evans and Lindsay point out in the book *The Management and Control of Quality*, this level of quality corresponding to 3-sigma limits is comparable to "at least 20,000 wrong drug prescriptions each year, more than 15,000 babies accidentally dropped by nurses and doctors each year, 500 incorrect surgical operations each week, and 2000 lost pieces of mail each hour."[1]

As a result, a number of companies have adopted "6-sigma" quality. This represents product-design specifications that are twice as large as the natural variations reflected in 3-sigma control limits. This type of situation, where the design specifications exceed the natural control limits, is shown graphically in Figure 4.5*c*. The company would expect that almost all products will conform to design specifications—as long as the process mean is centered on the design target. Statistically, 6-sigma corresponds to only 0.0000002 percent defects or 0.002 defective parts per million (PPM), which is only two defects per billion! However, when Motorola announced in 1989 that it would achieve 6-sigma quality in five years they translated this to be 3.4 defects per million. How did they get 3.4 defects per million from 2 defects per billion? Motorola took into account that the process mean will not always exactly correspond to the design target; it might vary from the nominal design target by as much as 1.5 sigma (the scenario in Figure 4.5*d*), which translates to a 6-sigma defect rate of 3.4 defects per million. This value has since become the standard for 6-sigma quality in industry and business. Applying this same scenario of a 1.5-sigma deviation from the process mean to the more typical 3-sigma level used by most companies, the defect rate is not 2700 defects per million, but 66,810 defects per million.

As indicated, Figure 4.5*d* shows the situation in which the design specifications are greater than the process range of variation; however, the process is off center. The process is capable of meeting specifications, but it is not because the process is not in control. In this case a percentage of the output that falls outside the upper design specification limit will be defective. If the process is adjusted so that the process center coincides with the design target (i.e., it is centered), then almost all of the output will meet design specifications.

Determining process capability is important because it helps a company understand process variation. If it can be determined how well a process is meeting design specifications, and thus what the actual level of quality is, then steps can be taken to improve quality. Two measures used to quantify the capability of a process, that is, how well the process is capable of producing according to design specifications, are the capability ratio ($C_p$) and the capability index ($C_{pk}$).

## PROCESS CAPABILITY MEASURES

One measure of the capability of a process to meet design specifications is the *process capability ratio* ($C_p$). It is defined as the ratio of the range of the design specifications (the tolerance range) to the range of the process variation, which for most firms is typically $\pm 3\sigma$ or $6\sigma$.

$$C_p = \frac{\text{tolerance range}}{\text{process range}}$$

$$= \frac{\text{upper specification limit} - \text{lower specification limit}}{6\sigma}$$

If $C_p$ is less than 1.0, the process range is greater than the tolerance range, and the process is not capable of producing within the design specifications all the time. This is the situation depicted in Figure 4.5*a*. If $C_p$ equals 1.0, the tolerance range and the process range

[1]J. R. Evans and W. M. Lindsay, *The Management and Control of Quality*, 3rd ed. (Minneapolis: West, 1993), p. 602.

## THE COMPETITIVE EDGE

### Design Tolerances at Harley-Davidson Company

Harley-Davidson, once at the brink of going out of business, is now a successful company known for high quality. It has achieved this comeback by combining the classic styling and traditional features of its motorcycles with advanced engineering technology and a commitment to continuous improvement. Harley-Davidson's manufacturing process incorporates computer-integrated manufacturing (CIM) techniques with state-of-the-art computerized numerical control (CNC) machining stations. These CNC stations are capable of performing dozens of machining operations and provide the operator with computerized data for statistical process control.

Harley-Davidson uses a statistical operator control (SOC) quality-improvement program to reduce parts variability to only a fraction of design tolerances. SOC ensures precise tolerances during each manufacturing step and predicts out-of-control components before they occur. SOC is especially important when dealing with complex components such as transmission gears.

The tolerances for Harley-Davidson cam gears are extremely close, and the machinery is especially complex. CNC machinery allows the manufacturing of gear centers time after time with tolerances as close as 0.0005 inch. SOC ensures the quality necessary to turn the famous Harley-Davidson Evolution engine shift after shift, mile after mile, year after year.

are virtually the same—the situation shown in Figure 4.5*b*. If $C_p$ is greater than 1.0, the tolerance range is greater than the process range—the situation depicted in Figure 4.5*c*. Thus, companies would logically desire a $C_p$ equal to 1.0 or greater, since this would indicate that the process is capable of meeting specifications.

**Example 4.7**

**Computing $C_p$**

The Munchies Snack Food Company packages potato chips in bags. The net weight of the chips in each bag is designed to be 9.0 oz, with a tolerance of $\pm 0.5$ oz. The packaging process results in bags with an average net weight of 8.80 oz and a standard deviation of 0.12 oz. The company wants to determine if the process is capable of meeting design specifications.

*Solution*

$$C_p = \frac{\text{upper specification limit} - \text{lower specification limit}}{6\sigma}$$

$$= \frac{9.5 - 8.5}{6(0.12)}$$

$$= 1.39$$

Thus, according to this process capability ratio of 1.39, the process is capable of being within design specifications.

A second measure of process capability is the *process capability index* ($C_{pk}$). The $C_{pk}$ differs from the $C_p$ in that it indicates if the process mean has shifted away from the design target, and in which direction it has shifted—that is, if it is off center. This is the situation depicted in Figure 4.5*d*. The process capability index specifically measures the capability of the process relative to the upper and lower specifications.

$$C_{pk} = \text{minimum}\left[\frac{\bar{\bar{x}} - \text{lower specification}}{3\sigma}, \frac{\text{upper specification} - \bar{\bar{x}}}{3\sigma}\right]$$

If the $C_{pk}$ index is greater than 1.00, then the process is capable of meeting design specifications. If $C_{pk}$ is less than 1.00, then the process mean has moved closer to one of the upper or lower design specifications, and it will generate defects. When $C_{pk}$ equals $C_p$, this indicates that the process mean is centered on the design (nominal) target.

**Example 4.8**

**Computing $C_{pk}$**

Recall that the Munchies Snack Food Company packaged potato chips in a process designed for 9.0 oz of chips with a tolerance of ±0.5 oz. The packaging process had a process mean ($\bar{\bar{x}}$) of 8.80 oz and a standard deviation of 0.12 oz. The company wants to determine if the process is capable, and if the process mean is on or off center.

$$C_{pk} = \text{minimum}\left[\frac{\bar{\bar{x}} - \text{lower specification}}{3\sigma}, \frac{\text{upper specification} - \bar{\bar{x}}}{3\sigma}\right]$$

$$= \text{minimum}\left[\frac{8.80 - 8.50}{3(0.12)}, \frac{9.5 - 8.80}{3(0.12)}\right]$$

$$= \text{minimum}\,[0.83, 1.94]$$

$$= 0.83$$

Although the $C_p$ of 1.39 computed in Example 14.7 indicated that the process is capable (it is within the design specifications), the $C_{pk}$ value of 0.83 indicates the process mean is off center. It has shifted toward the lower specifications limit; that means underweight packages of chips will be produced. Thus, the company needs to take action to correct the process and bring the process mean back toward the design target.

## COMPUTING PROCESS CAPABILITY MEASURES WITH EXCEL

Exhibit 4.2 shows the Excel solution screen for the computation of the process capability ratio and the process capability index for Examples 4.7 and 4.8. The formula for the process capability index in cell D16 is shown on the formula bar at the top of the screen.

**Exhibit 4.2**

Microsoft Excel - Exhibit4.2.xls

D16 =MIN(((D12-(D13-D14))/(3*D15)),(((D13+D14)-D12)/(3*D15)))

**Examples 4.6 and 4.7: Process Capability**

*Process Capability Ratio:*

| | |
|---|---|
| Upper limit = | 9.5 |
| Lower limit = | 8.5 |
| Standard deviation = | 0.12 |
| $C_p$ = | 1.39 |

=(D6-D7)/(6*D8)

*Process Capability Index:*

| | |
|---|---|
| Process mean = | 8.80 |
| Design target = | 9.00 |
| Tolerance range = | 0.50 |
| Standard deviation = | 0.12 |
| $C_{pk}$ = | 0.83 |

see formula bar

## SUMMARY

Statistical process control is the main quantitative tool used in TQM. Companies that have adopted TQM provide extensive training in SPC methods for all employees at all levels. In a TQM environment employees have more responsibility for their own operation or process. Employees recognize the need for SPC for accomplishing a major part of their job, product quality, and when employees are provided with adequate training and understand what is expected of them, they have little difficulty using statistical process control methods.

## SUMMARY OF KEY FORMULAS

*Control Limits for* p-*Charts*

$$\text{UCL} = \bar{p} + z\sqrt{\frac{\bar{p}(1-\bar{p})}{n}}$$

$$\text{LCL} = \bar{p} - z\sqrt{\frac{\bar{p}(1-\bar{p})}{n}}$$

*Control Limits for* c-*Charts*

$$\text{UCL} = \bar{c} + z\sqrt{\bar{c}}$$

$$\text{LCL} = \bar{c} - z\sqrt{\bar{c}}$$

*Control Limits for* R-*Charts*

$$\text{UCL} = D_4\bar{R}$$

$$\text{LCL} = D_3\bar{R}$$

*Control Limits for* $\bar{x}$-*Charts*

$$\text{UCL} = \bar{\bar{x}} + A_2\bar{R}$$

$$\text{LCL} = \bar{\bar{x}} - A_2\bar{R}$$

*Process Capability Ratio*

$$C_p = \frac{\text{upper specification limit} - \text{lower specification limit}}{6\sigma}$$

*Process Capability Index*

$$C_{pk} = \text{minimum}\left[\frac{\bar{\bar{x}} - \text{lower specification}}{3\sigma}, \frac{\text{upper specification} - \bar{\bar{x}}}{3\sigma}\right]$$

## SUMMARY OF KEY TERMS

**attribute** a product characteristic that can be evaluated with a discrete response such as yes or no, good or bad.

***c*-chart** a control chart based on the number of defects in a sample.

**control chart** a graph that visually shows if a sample is within statistical limits for defective items.

**control limits** the upper and lower bands of a control chart.

**mean ($\bar{x}$-) chart** a control chart based on the means of the samples taken.

***p*-chart** a control chart based on the proportion defective of the samples taken.

**pattern test** a statistical test to determine if the observations within the limits of a control chart display a nonrandom pattern.

**process capability** the capability of a process to accommodate design specifications of a product.

**range** the difference between the smallest and largest values in a sample.

**range (*R*-) chart** a control chart based on the range (from the highest to the lowest values) of the samples taken.

**run** a sequence of sample values that display the same tendency in a control chart.

**sample** a portion of the items produced used for inspection.

**statistical process control (SPC)** a statistical procedure for monitoring the quality of the production process using control charts.

**tolerances** product design specifications required by the customer.

**variable measure** a product characteristic that can be measured, such as weight or length.

## SOLVED PROBLEMS

### 1. *p*-CHARTS

Twenty samples of $n = 200$ were taken by an operator at a workstation in a production process. The number of defective items in each sample were recorded as follows.

| SAMPLE | NUMBER OF DEFECTIVES | $p$ | SAMPLE | NUMBER OF DEFECTIVES | $p$ |
|---|---|---|---|---|---|
| 1 | 12 | 0.060 | 11 | 16 | 0.080 |
| 2 | 18 | 0.090 | 12 | 14 | 0.070 |
| 3 | 10 | 0.050 | 13 | 12 | 0.060 |
| 4 | 14 | 0.070 | 14 | 16 | 0.080 |
| 5 | 16 | 0.080 | 15 | 18 | 0.090 |
| 6 | 19 | 0.095 | 16 | 20 | 0.100 |
| 7 | 17 | 0.085 | 17 | 18 | 0.090 |
| 8 | 12 | 0.060 | 18 | 20 | 0.100 |
| 9 | 11 | 0.055 | 19 | 21 | 0.105 |
| 10 | 14 | 0.070 | 20 | 22 | 0.110 |

Management wants to develop a *p*-chart using 3-sigma limits. Set up the *p*-chart and plot the observations to determine if the process was out of control at any point.

#### SOLUTION

*Step 1.* Compute $\bar{p}$:

$$\bar{p} = \frac{\text{total number of defectives}}{\text{total number of observations}} = \frac{320}{(20)(200)} = 0.08$$

*Step 2.* Determine the control limits:

$$\text{UCL} = \bar{p} + z\sqrt{\frac{\bar{p}(1-\bar{p})}{n}} = 0.08 + (3.00)(0.019) = 0.137$$

$$\text{LCL} = \bar{p} - z\sqrt{\frac{\bar{p}(1-\bar{p})}{n}} = 0.08 - (3.00)(0.019) = 0.023$$

*Step 3.* Construct the $\bar{p}$-chart with $\bar{p} = 0.08$, UCL = 0.137, and LCL = 0.023. The process does not appear to be out of control.

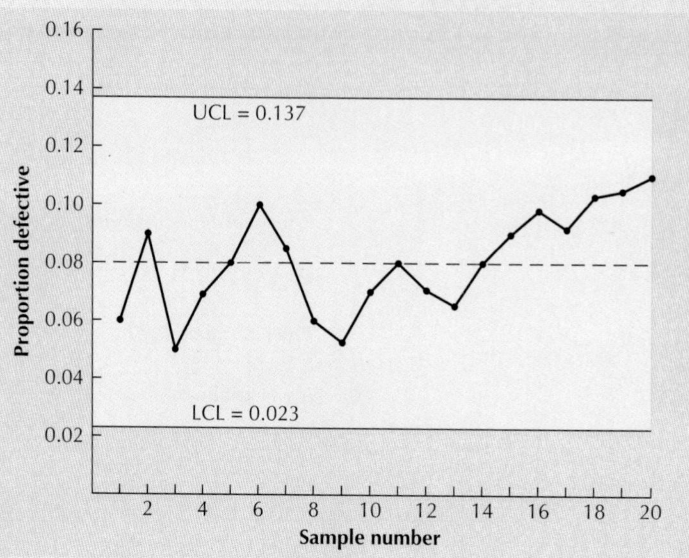


**2. PATTERN TESTS**

In the preceding problem, even though the control chart indicates that the process is in control, management wants to use pattern tests to further determine if the process is in control.

## SOLUTION

*Step 1.* Determine the "up-and-down" and "above-and-below" runs and zone observations. Construct the zone boundaries on the control chart as follows.

| SAMPLE | ABOVE/BELOW $\bar{p} = 0.08$ | UP/DOWN | ZONE |
|---|---|---|---|
| 1 | B | — | B |
| 2 | A | U | C |
| 3 | B | D | B |
| 4 | B | U | C |
| 5 | A | U | C |
| 6 | A | U | B |
| 7 | A | D | C |
| 8 | B | D | B |
| 9 | B | D | B |
| 10 | B | U | C |
| 11 | A | U | C |
| 12 | B | D | C |
| 13 | B | D | C |
| 14 | A | U | C |
| 15 | A | U | C |
| 16 | A | U | B |
| 17 | A | D | C |
| 18 | A | U | B |
| 19 | A | U | B |
| 20 | A | U | B |

(*Note*: Ties are broken in favor of A and U.)

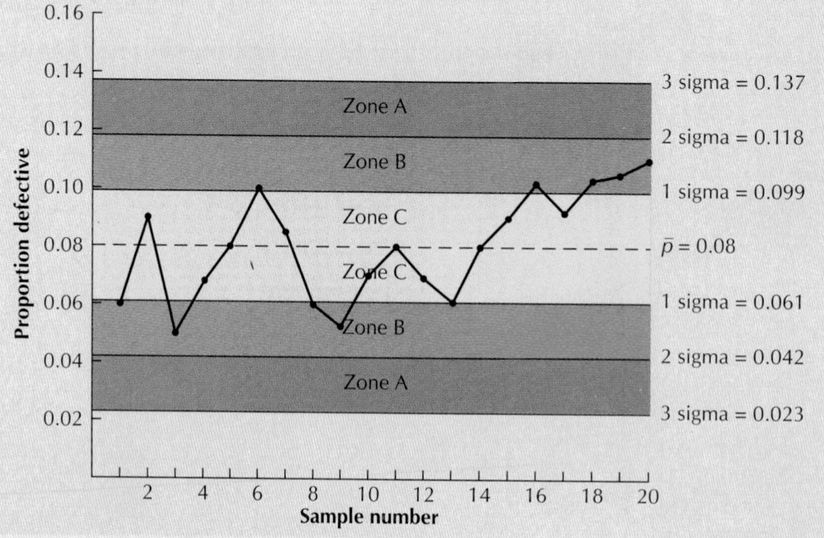


Because 4 of 5 consecutive points are in Zone B (i.e., points 16 to 20), it suggests that nonrandom patterns may exist and that the process may not be in control.

## QUESTIONS

**4-1.** Explain the difference between attribute control charts and variable control charts.

**4-2.** How are mean ($\bar{x}$-) and range ($R$-) charts used together?

**4-3.** What is the purpose of a pattern test?

**4-4.** What determines the width of the control limits in a process chart?

**4-5.** Under what circumstances should a $c$-chart be used instead of a $p$-chart?

**4-6.** What is the difference between tolerances and control limits?

**4-7.** Why have companies traditionally used control charts with 3-sigma limits instead of 2-sigma limits?

**4-8.** Select three service companies or organizations you are familiar with and indicate how process control charts could be used in each.

**4-9.** Visit a local fast-food restaurant, retail store, grocery store, or bank, and identify the different processes that control charts could be used to monitor.

**4-10.** Explain the different information provided by the process capability ratio and the process capability index.

**4-11.** For the Goliath Tool Company in Example 4.4, if the design tolerances are $\pm 0.07$ cm, is the process capable of meeting tolerances of $\pm 0.08$ cm for the slip-ring bearings?

## PROBLEMS

**4-1.** The Great North Woods Clothing Company sells specialty outdoor clothing through its catalogue. A quality problem that generates customer complaints occurs when a warehouse employee fills an order with the wrong items. The company has decided to implement a process control plan by inspecting the ordered items after they have been obtained from the warehouse and before they have been packaged. The company has taken 30 samples (during a 30-day period), each for 100 orders, and recorded the number of "defective" orders in each sample, as follows:

| Sample | Number of Defectives | Sample | Number of Defectives |
|---|---|---|---|
| 1 | 12 | 16 | 6 |
| 2 | 14 | 17 | 3 |
| 3 | 10 | 18 | 7 |
| 4 | 16 | 19 | 10 |
| 5 | 18 | 20 | 14 |
| 6 | 19 | 21 | 18 |
| 7 | 14 | 22 | 22 |
| 8 | 20 | 23 | 26 |
| 9 | 18 | 24 | 20 |
| 10 | 17 | 25 | 24 |
| 11 | 9 | 26 | 18 |
| 12 | 11 | 27 | 19 |
| 13 | 14 | 28 | 20 |
| 14 | 12 | 29 | 17 |
| 15 | 7 | 30 | 18 |

Construct a $p$-chart for the company that describes 99.74% ($3\sigma$) of the random variation in the process, and indicate if the process seems to be out of control at any time.

**4-2.** The Road King Tire Company in Birmingham wants to monitor the quality of the tires it manufactures. Each day the company quality-control manager takes a sample of 100 tires, tests them, and determines the number of defective tires. The results of 20 samples have been recorded as follows:

| Sample | Number of Defectives | Sample | Number of Defectives |
|---|---|---|---|
| 1 | 14 | 11 | 18 |
| 2 | 12 | 12 | 10 |
| 3 | 9 | 13 | 19 |
| 4 | 10 | 14 | 20 |
| 5 | 11 | 15 | 17 |
| 6 | 7 | 16 | 18 |
| 7 | 8 | 17 | 18 |
| 8 | 14 | 18 | 22 |
| 9 | 16 | 19 | 24 |
| 10 | 17 | 20 | 23 |

Construct a $p$-chart for this process using $2\sigma$ limits and describe the variation in the process.

**4-3.** The Commonwealth Banking Corporation issues a national credit card through its various bank branches in five southeastern states. The bank credit card business is highly competitive and interest rates do not vary substantially, so the company decided to attempt to retain its customers by improving customer service through a reduction in billing errors. The credit card division monitored its billing department process by taking daily samples of 200 customer bills for 30 days and checking their accuracy. The sample results are as follows:

| Sample | Number of Defectives | Sample | Number of Defectives |
|---|---|---|---|
| 1 | 7 | 10 | 10 |
| 2 | 12 | 11 | 9 |
| 3 | 9 | 12 | 6 |
| 4 | 6 | 13 | 3 |
| 5 | 5 | 14 | 2 |
| 6 | 8 | 15 | 8 |
| 7 | 10 | 16 | 10 |
| 8 | 11 | 17 | 12 |
| 9 | 14 | 18 | 14 |

*(Continued)*

| Sample | Number of Defectives | Sample | Number of Defectives |
|---|---|---|---|
| 19 | 16 | 25 | 15 |
| 20 | 15 | 26 | 14 |
| 21 | 13 | 27 | 16 |
| 22 | 9 | 28 | 12 |
| 23 | 10 | 29 | 15 |
| 24 | 12 | 30 | 14 |

Develop a *p*-chart for the billing process using 3$\sigma$ control limits and indicate if the process is out of control.

**4-4.** In the assembly process for automobile engines, at one stage in the process a gasket is placed between the two sections of the engine block before they are joined. If the gasket is damaged (e.g., bent, crimped), oil can leak from the cylinder chambers and foul the spark plugs, in which case the entire engine has to be disassembled and a new gasket inserted. The company wants to develop a *p*-chart with 2$\sigma$ limits to monitor the quality of the gaskets prior to the assembly stage. Historically, 2% of the gaskets have been defective, and management does not want the upper control limit to exceed 3% defective. What sample size will be required to achieve this control chart?

**4-5.** The Great North Woods Clothing Company is a mail-order company that processes thousands of mail and telephone orders each week. They have a customer service number to handle customer order problems, inquiries, and complaints. The company wants to monitor the number of customer calls that can be classified as complaints. The total number of complaint calls the customer service department has received for each of the last 30 weekdays are shown as follows:

| Day | Complaint Calls | Day | Complaint Calls |
|---|---|---|---|
| 1 | 27 | 16 | 19 |
| 2 | 15 | 17 | 12 |
| 3 | 38 | 18 | 17 |
| 4 | 41 | 19 | 18 |
| 5 | 19 | 20 | 26 |
| 6 | 23 | 21 | 31 |
| 7 | 21 | 22 | 14 |
| 8 | 16 | 23 | 18 |
| 9 | 33 | 24 | 26 |
| 10 | 35 | 25 | 27 |
| 11 | 26 | 26 | 35 |
| 12 | 42 | 27 | 20 |
| 13 | 40 | 28 | 12 |
| 14 | 35 | 29 | 16 |
| 15 | 25 | 30 | 15 |

a. Construct a *c*-chart for this process with 3$\sigma$ control limits and indicate if the process was out of control at any time.

b. What nonrandom (i.e., assignable) causes might result in the process being out of control?

**4-6.** One of the stages in the process of making denim cloth at the Southern Mills Company is to spin cotton yarn onto spindles for subsequent use in the weaving process. Occasionally the yarn breaks during the spinning process, and an operator ties it back together. Some number of breaks is considered normal; however, too many breaks may mean that the yarn is of poor quality. In order to monitor this process, the quality-control manager randomly selects a spinning machine each hour and checks the number of breaks during a 15-minute period. Following is a summary of the observations for the past 20 hours:

| Sample | Number of Breaks | Sample | Number of Breaks |
|---|---|---|---|
| 1 | 3 | 11 | 3 |
| 2 | 2 | 12 | 4 |
| 3 | 4 | 13 | 6 |
| 4 | 1 | 14 | 7 |
| 5 | 5 | 15 | 8 |
| 6 | 3 | 16 | 6 |
| 7 | 2 | 17 | 5 |
| 8 | 4 | 18 | 7 |
| 9 | 0 | 19 | 8 |
| 10 | 2 | 20 | 6 |

Construct a *c*-chart using 3$\sigma$ limits for this process and indicate if the process was out of control at any time.

**4-7.** The Xecko Film Company manufactures color photographic film. The film is produced in large rolls of various lengths before it is cut and packaged as the smaller roles purchased in retail stores. The company wants to monitor the quality of these rolls of film using a *c*-chart. Twenty-four rolls have been inspected at random, and the numbers of defects per roll are as follows:

| Roll | Number of Defects | Roll | Number of Defects |
|---|---|---|---|
| 1 | 12 | 13 | 12 |
| 2 | 8 | 14 | 13 |
| 3 | 5 | 15 | 9 |
| 4 | 7 | 16 | 8 |
| 5 | 14 | 17 | 7 |
| 6 | 9 | 18 | 11 |
| 7 | 10 | 19 | 9 |
| 8 | 11 | 20 | 13 |
| 9 | 8 | 21 | 17 |
| 10 | 6 | 22 | 16 |
| 11 | 15 | 23 | 12 |
| 12 | 10 | 24 | 14 |

Construct a *c*-chart with 2$\sigma$ limits for this process and indicate if the process was out of control at any time.

**4-8.** Telecom manufactures electronic components for computers. One measure it uses to monitor the quality of its distribution process is the number of customer invoice errors. The distribution center manager monitored the company's order processing and distribution by recording the number of invoice errors for 30 days. The sample results are as follows:

| Day | Number of Errors | Day | Number of Errors |
|---|---|---|---|
| 1 | 4 | 16 | 6 |
| 2 | 6 | 17 | 9 |
| 3 | 2 | 18 | 12 |
| 4 | 5 | 19 | 10 |
| 5 | 1 | 20 | 11 |
| 6 | 3 | 21 | 8 |
| 7 | 4 | 22 | 8 |
| 8 | 7 | 23 | 7 |
| 9 | 6 | 24 | 3 |
| 10 | 5 | 25 | 4 |
| 11 | 10 | 26 | 7 |
| 12 | 8 | 27 | 10 |
| 13 | 9 | 28 | 12 |
| 14 | 9 | 29 | 12 |
| 15 | 7 | 30 | 14 |

Construct a $c$-chart with $3\sigma$ limits for invoice errors and indicate if the process was out of control at any time.

**4-9.** The National Bread Company daily delivers multiple orders by truck from its regional distribution center to stores in the Wayman's Supermarket chain. One measure of its supply chain performance is the number of late deliveries. The company's goal is to make all deliveries within one day, so a delivery is late if it exceeds one day. The total number of late deliveries for each of the past 20 days are as follows.

| Day | Late Deliveries | Day | Late Deliveries |
|---|---|---|---|
| 1 | 7 | 11 | 6 |
| 2 | 16 | 12 | 12 |
| 3 | 14 | 13 | 15 |
| 4 | 8 | 14 | 10 |
| 5 | 19 | 15 | 17 |
| 6 | 12 | 16 | 16 |
| 7 | 10 | 17 | 14 |
| 8 | 14 | 18 | 12 |
| 9 | 8 | 19 | 18 |
| 10 | 7 | 20 | 20 |

Construct a $c$-chart for late deliveries with $3\sigma$ control limits and indicate if the delivery process was out of control at any time.

**4-10.** BooksCDs.com sells books, videos, DVDs, and CDs through its Internet Web site. The company ships thousands of orders each day from seven national distribution centers. BooksCDs.com wants to establish a $p$-chart to monitor the quality of its distribution process, specifically the number of "problem" orders. A problem order is one that is delivered to a customer late (i.e., after five days), incorrect or incomplete. The company sampled 500 orders every other day for 20 days and tracked them to final customer delivery, the results of which are as follows.

| Sample | Number of Problem Orders | Sample | Number of Problem Orders |
|---|---|---|---|
| 1 | 14 | 11 | 38 |
| 2 | 22 | 12 | 24 |
| 3 | 36 | 13 | 15 |
| 4 | 17 | 14 | 12 |
| 5 | 25 | 15 | 10 |
| 6 | 41 | 16 | 16 |
| 7 | 18 | 17 | 9 |
| 8 | 19 | 18 | 21 |
| 9 | 26 | 19 | 18 |
| 10 | 28 | 20 | 12 |

Construct a $p$-chart for this process using $3\sigma$ limits and indicate if the process was out of control.

**4-11.** Valtec Electronics fills orders for its electronic components and parts by truck to customers through several distribution centers. A measure of its supply chain responsiveness is order fulfillment lead time, which is the number of days from when a company receives an order to when it is delivered to the customer. A distribution center manager has taken 20 samples of 5 orders each during the month and recorded the lead time for each as follows.

| Sample | Lead Time (Days) | | | | |
|---|---|---|---|---|---|
| 1 | 1.3 | 2.4 | 0.7 | 3.0 | 1.8 |
| 2 | 2.1 | 1.2 | 1.0 | 2.5 | 3.6 |
| 3 | 4.2 | 3.3 | 2.6 | 1.5 | 3.0 |
| 4 | 1.6 | 2.1 | 2.8 | 0.9 | 1.5 |
| 5 | 2.6 | 3.0 | 1.4 | 4.6 | 1.9 |
| 6 | 0.8 | 2.7 | 5.8 | 3.7 | 4.5 |
| 7 | 2.6 | 3.5 | 3.1 | 3.6 | 1.4 |
| 8 | 3.4 | 6.1 | 1.5 | 2.5 | 2.8 |
| 9 | 3.1 | 2.5 | 2.2 | 2.9 | 1.8 |
| 10 | 2.4 | 4.8 | 5.9 | 3.2 | 4.4 |
| 11 | 1.9 | 2.7 | 3.4 | 2.2 | 0.4 |
| 12 | 6.1 | 4.9 | 2.1 | 3.6 | 5.2 |
| 13 | 1.2 | 3.4 | 2.8 | 2.3 | 4.5 |
| 14 | 2.4 | 2.9 | 3.4 | 2.3 | 2.5 |
| 15 | 3.7 | 7.0 | 1.4 | 2.4 | 3.3 |
| 16 | 3.6 | 2.7 | 4.8 | 2.0 | 1.7 |
| 17 | 0.4 | 1.8 | 6.5 | 3.2 | 4.8 |
| 18 | 5.3 | 2.9 | 3.4 | 4.8 | 4.4 |
| 19 | 2.7 | 3.6 | 2.9 | 4.1 | 5.2 |
| 20 | 4.7 | 2.0 | 2.0 | 3.1 | 1.8 |

Construct an $\bar{x}$-chart to be used in conjunction with an $R$-chart using $3\sigma$ limits for this data and indicate if the process is in control.

**4-12.** The Stryker Baseball Bat Company manufactures wooden and aluminum baseball bats at its plant in New England. Wooden bats produced for the mass market are turned on a lathe, where a piece of wood is shaped into a bat with a handle and barrel. The bat is cut to its specified length and then finished in subsequent processes. Once bats are cut to length, it is difficult to rework them into a different style, so it is important to catch defects before this step. As such, bats are inspected at this stage of the process. A specific style of wooden bat has a mean barrel circumference of 9 inches at its thickest point with a standard deviation of 0.6 inch. (The process variability is assumed to be normally distributed.)

a. Construct a mean control chart for this process for 3$\sigma$ limits and a sample size of 10 bats.
b. Three samples are taken, and they have average bat diameters of 9.05 inches, 9.10 inches, and 9.08 inches. Is the process in control?
c. What effect will increasing the sample size to 20 bats have on the control charts? Will the conclusions reached in part (b) change for this sample size?

**4-13.** A machine at the Pacific Fruit Company fills boxes with raisins. The labeled weight of the boxes is 9 ounces. The company wants to construct an $R$-chart to monitor the filling process and make sure the box weights are in control. The quality-control department for the company sampled five boxes every two hours for three consecutive working days. The sample observations are as follows:

| Sample | Box Weights (oz) | | | | |
|---|---|---|---|---|---|
| 1 | 9.06 | 9.13 | 8.97 | 8.85 | 8.46 |
| 2 | 8.52 | 8.61 | 9.09 | 9.21 | 8.95 |
| 3 | 9.35 | 8.95 | 9.20 | 9.03 | 8.42 |
| 4 | 9.17 | 9.21 | 9.05 | 9.01 | 9.53 |
| 5 | 9.21 | 8.87 | 8.71 | 9.05 | 9.35 |
| 6 | 8.74 | 8.35 | 8.50 | 9.06 | 8.89 |
| 7 | 9.00 | 9.21 | 9.05 | 9.23 | 8.78 |
| 8 | 9.15 | 9.20 | 9.23 | 9.15 | 9.06 |
| 9 | 8.98 | 8.90 | 8.81 | 9.05 | 9.13 |
| 10 | 9.03 | 9.10 | 9.26 | 9.46 | 8.47 |
| 11 | 9.53 | 9.02 | 9.11 | 8.88 | 8.92 |
| 12 | 8.95 | 9.10 | 9.00 | 9.06 | 8.95 |

Construct an $R$-chart from these data with 3$\sigma$ control limits, plot the sample range values, and comment on process control.

**4-14.** The City Square Grocery and Meat Market has a large meat locker in which a constant temperature of approximately 40°F should be maintained. The market manager has decided to construct an $R$-chart to monitor the temperature inside the locker. The manager had one of the market employees take sample temperature readings randomly five times each day for 20 days in order to gather data for the control chart. Following are the temperature sample observations:

| Sample | Temperature (°F) | | | | |
|---|---|---|---|---|---|
| 1 | 46.3 | 48.1 | 42.5 | 43.1 | 39.6 |
| 2 | 41.2 | 40.5 | 37.8 | 36.5 | 42.3 |
| 3 | 40.1 | 41.3 | 34.5 | 33.2 | 36.7 |
| 4 | 42.3 | 44.1 | 39.5 | 37.7 | 38.6 |
| 5 | 35.2 | 38.1 | 40.5 | 39.1 | 42.3 |
| 6 | 40.6 | 41.7 | 38.6 | 43.5 | 44.6 |
| 7 | 33.2 | 38.6 | 41.5 | 40.7 | 43.1 |
| 8 | 41.8 | 40.0 | 41.6 | 40.7 | 39.3 |
| 9 | 42.4 | 41.6 | 40.8 | 40.9 | 42.3 |
| 10 | 44.7 | 36.5 | 37.3 | 35.3 | 41.1 |
| 11 | 42.6 | 43.5 | 35.4 | 36.1 | 38.2 |
| 12 | 40.5 | 40.4 | 39.1 | 37.2 | 41.6 |
| 13 | 45.3 | 42.0 | 43.1 | 44.7 | 39.5 |
| 14 | 36.4 | 37.5 | 36.2 | 38.9 | 40.1 |
| 15 | 40.5 | 34.3 | 36.2 | 35.1 | 36.8 |
| 16 | 39.5 | 38.2 | 37.6 | 34.1 | 38.7 |
| 17 | 37.6 | 40.6 | 40.3 | 39.7 | 41.2 |
| 18 | 41.0 | 34.3 | 39.1 | 45.2 | 43.7 |
| 19 | 40.9 | 42.3 | 37.6 | 35.4 | 34.8 |
| 20 | 37.6 | 39.2 | 39.3 | 41.2 | 37.6 |

a. Construct an $R$-chart based on these data using 3$\sigma$ limits, and plot the 20 sample range values.
a. Does it appear that the temperature is in control according to the criteria established by management?

**4-15.** The Oceanside Apparel Company manufactures expensive, polo-style men's and women's short-sleeve knit shirts at its plant in Jamaica. The production process requires that material be cut into large patterned squares by operators, which are then sewn together at another stage of the process. If the squares are not of a correct length, the final shirt will be either too large or too small. In order to monitor the cutting process, management takes a sample of four squares of cloth every other hour and measures the length. The length of a cloth square should be 36 inches, and historically, the company has found the length to vary across an acceptable average of 2 inches.

a. Construct an $R$-chart for the cutting process using 3$\sigma$ limits.
b. The company has taken 10 additional samples with the following results:

| Sample | Measurements (in.) | | | |
|---|---|---|---|---|
| 1 | 37.3 | 36.5 | 38.2 | 36.1 |
| 2 | 33.4 | 35.8 | 37.9 | 36.2 |
| 3 | 32.1 | 34.8 | 39.1 | 35.3 |
| 4 | 36.1 | 37.2 | 36.7 | 34.2 |
| 5 | 35.1 | 38.6 | 37.2 | 33.6 |
| 6 | 33.4 | 34.5 | 36.7 | 32.4 |
| 7 | 38.1 | 39.2 | 35.3 | 32.7 |
| 8 | 35.4 | 36.2 | 36.3 | 34.3 |
| 9 | 37.1 | 39.4 | 38.1 | 36.2 |
| 10 | 32.1 | 34.0 | 35.6 | 36.1 |

Plot the new sample data on the control chart constructed in part (a) and comment on the process variability.

**4-16.** For the sample data provided in Problem 4-13, construct an $\bar{x}$-chart in conjunction with the $R$-chart, plot the sample observations, and, using both $\bar{x}$- and $R$-charts, comment on the process control.

**4-17.** For the sample data provided in Problem 4-14, construct an $\bar{x}$-chart in conjunction with the $R$-chart, plot the sample observations, and, using both $\bar{x}$- and $R$-charts, comment on the process control.

**4-18.** Using the process information provided in Problem 4-15, construct an $\bar{x}$-chart in conjunction with the $R$-chart, plot the sample observations provided in part (b), and, using both $\bar{x}$- and $R$-charts, comment on the process control.

**4-19.** Use pattern tests to determine if the sample observations used in the $\bar{x}$-chart in Problem 4-16 reflect any nonrandom patterns.

**4-20.** Use pattern tests to determine if the sample observations in Problem 4-5 reflect any nonrandom patterns.

**4-21.** Use pattern tests to determine if the sample observations in Problem 4-14 reflect any nonrandom patterns.

**4-22.** Use pattern tests to determine if the sample observations used in the $\bar{x}$-chart in Problem 4-17 reflect any nonrandom patterns.

**4-23.** Use pattern tests to determine if the sample observations used in the $p$-chart in Problem 4-1 reflect any nonrandom patterns.

**4-24.** Dave's Restaurant is a chain that employs independent evaluators to visit its restaurants as customers and assess the quality of the service by filling out a questionnaire. The company evaluates restaurants in two categories, products (the food) and service (e.g., promptness, order accuracy, courtesy, friendliness). The evaluator considers not only his or her order experiences but also observations throughout the restaurant. Following are the results of an evaluator's 20 visits to one particular restaurant during a month showing the number of "defects" noted in the service category:

| Sample | Number of Defects | Sample | Number of Defects |
|---|---|---|---|
| 1 | 4 | 11 | 9 |
| 2 | 6 | 12 | 4 |
| 3 | 10 | 13 | 3 |
| 4 | 3 | 14 | 4 |
| 5 | 6 | 15 | 13 |
| 6 | 7 | 16 | 9 |
| 7 | 8 | 17 | 10 |
| 8 | 5 | 18 | 11 |
| 9 | 2 | 19 | 15 |
| 10 | 5 | 20 | 12 |

Construct a control chart for this restaurant using $3\sigma$ limits to monitor quality service and indicate if the process is in control.

**4-25.** The National Bank of Warwick is concerned with complaints from customers about its drive-through window operation. Customers complain that it sometimes takes too long to be served and since there are often cars in front and back of a customer, they cannot leave if the service is taking a long time. To correct this problem the bank installed an intercom system so the drive-through window teller can call for assistance if the line backs up or a customer has an unusually long transaction. The bank's objective is an average customer's waiting and service time of approximately 3 minutes. The bank's operations manager wants to monitor the new drive-through window system with SPC. The manager has timed five customers' waiting and service times at random for 12 days as follows:

| | Observation Times (min) | | | | |
|---|---|---|---|---|---|
| Sample | 1 | 2 | 3 | 4 | 5 |
| 1 | 3.05 | 6.27 | 1.35 | 2.56 | 1.05 |
| 2 | 7.21 | 1.50 | 2.66 | 3.45 | 3.78 |
| 3 | 3.12 | 5.11 | 1.37 | 5.20 | 2.65 |
| 4 | 2.96 | 3.81 | 4.15 | 5.01 | 2.15 |
| 5 | 3.25 | 3.11 | 1.63 | 1.29 | 3.74 |
| 6 | 2.47 | 2.98 | 2.15 | 1.88 | 4.95 |
| 7 | 6.05 | 2.03 | 3.17 | 3.18 | 2.34 |
| 8 | 1.87 | 2.65 | 1.98 | 2.74 | 3.63 |
| 9 | 3.33 | 4.15 | 8.06 | 2.98 | 3.05 |
| 10 | 2.61 | 2.15 | 3.80 | 3.05 | 3.16 |
| 11 | 3.52 | 5.66 | 1.18 | 3.45 | 2.07 |
| 12 | 3.18 | 7.73 | 2.06 | 1.15 | 3.11 |

Develop an $\bar{x}$-chart to be used in conjunction with an $R$-chart to monitor this drive-through window process and indicate if the process is in control using this chart.

**4-26.** The Great Outdoors Clothing Company is a mail-order catalogue operation. Whenever a customer returns an item for a refund, credit, or exchange, he or she is asked to complete a return form. For each item returned the customer is asked to insert a code indicating the reason for the return. The company does not consider the returns related to style, size, or "feel" of the material to be a defect. However, it does consider returns because the item "was not as described in the catalogue," "didn't look like what was in the catalogue," or "the color was different than shown in the catalogue," to be defects in the catalogue. The company has randomly checked 100 customer return forms for 20 days and collected the following data for catalogue defects:

| Sample | Number of Catalogue Defects | Sample | Number of Catalogue Defects |
|---|---|---|---|
| 1 | 18 | 11 | 54 |
| 2 | 26 | 12 | 37 |
| 3 | 43 | 13 | 26 |
| 4 | 27 | 14 | 29 |
| 5 | 14 | 15 | 37 |
| 6 | 36 | 16 | 65 |
| 7 | 42 | 17 | 54 |
| 8 | 28 | 18 | 31 |
| 9 | 61 | 19 | 28 |
| 10 | 37 | 20 | 25 |

Construct a control chart using $3\sigma$ limits to monitor catalogue defects and indicate if the process is in control. Use pattern tests to verify an in-control situation.

**4-27.** The dean of the College of Business at State University wants to monitor the quality of the work performed by the college's secretarial staff. Each completed assignment is returned to the faculty with a check sheet on which the faculty member is asked to list the errors made on the assignment. The assistant dean has randomly collected the following set of observations from 20 three-day work periods:

| Sample | Number of Errors | Sample | Number of Errors |
|---|---|---|---|
| 1 | 17 | 11 | 12 |
| 2 | 9 | 12 | 17 |
| 3 | 12 | 13 | 16 |
| 4 | 15 | 14 | 23 |
| 5 | 26 | 15 | 24 |
| 6 | 11 | 16 | 18 |
| 7 | 18 | 17 | 14 |
| 8 | 15 | 18 | 12 |
| 9 | 21 | 19 | 20 |
| 10 | 10 | 20 | 16 |

Construct a process control chart for secretarial work quality using $3\sigma$ limits and determine if the process was out of control at any point. Use pattern tests to determine if any nonrandom patterns exist.

**4-28.** Martha's Wonderful Cookie Company makes a special super chocolate-chip peanut butter cookie. The company would like the cookies to average approximately eight chocolate chips apiece. Too few or too many chips distort the desired cookie taste. Twenty samples of five cookies each during a week have been taken and the chocolate chips counted. The sample observations are as follows:

| Sample | Chips per Cookie | | | | |
|---|---|---|---|---|---|
| 1 | 7 | 6 | 9 | 8 | 5 |
| 2 | 7 | 7 | 8 | 8 | 10 |
| 3 | 5 | 5 | 7 | 6 | 8 |
| 4 | 4 | 5 | 9 | 9 | 7 |
| 5 | 8 | 8 | 5 | 10 | 8 |
| 6 | 7 | 6 | 9 | 8 | 4 |
| 7 | 9 | 8 | 10 | 8 | 8 |
| 8 | 7 | 6 | 5 | 4 | 5 |
| 9 | 9 | 10 | 8 | 9 | 7 |
| 10 | 11 | 9 | 9 | 10 | 6 |
| 11 | 5 | 5 | 9 | 8 | 8 |
| 12 | 6 | 8 | 8 | 5 | 9 |
| 13 | 7 | 3 | 7 | 8 | 8 |
| 14 | 6 | 9 | 9 | 8 | 8 |
| 15 | 10 | 8 | 7 | 8 | 6 |
| 16 | 5 | 6 | 9 | 9 | 7 |
| 17 | 6 | 10 | 10 | 7 | 3 |
| 18 | 11 | 4 | 6 | 8 | 8 |
| 19 | 9 | 5 | 5 | 7 | 7 |
| 20 | 8 | 8 | 6 | 7 | 3 |

Construct an $\bar{x}$-chart in conjunction with an $R$-chart using $3\sigma$ limits for this data and comment on the cookie-production process.

**4-29.** Thirty patients who check out of the Rock Creek County Regional Hospital each week are asked to complete a questionnaire about hospital service. Since patients do not feel well when they are in the hospital, they typically are very critical of the service. The number of patients who indicated dissatisfaction of any kind with the service for each 30-patient sample for a 16-week period is as follows:

| Sample | Number of Dissatisfied Patients | Sample | Number of Dissatisfied Patients |
|---|---|---|---|
| 1 | 6 | 9 | 6 |
| 2 | 3 | 10 | 6 |
| 3 | 10 | 11 | 5 |
| 4 | 7 | 12 | 3 |
| 5 | 2 | 13 | 2 |
| 6 | 9 | 14 | 8 |
| 7 | 11 | 15 | 12 |
| 8 | 7 | 16 | 8 |

Construct a control chart to monitor customer satisfaction at the hospital using $3\sigma$ limits and determine if the process is in control.

**4-30.** An important aspect of customer service and satisfaction at the Big Country theme park is the maintenance of the restrooms throughout the park. Customers expect the restrooms to be clean; odorless; well stocked with soap, paper towels, and toilet paper; and to have a comfortable temperature. In order to maintain quality, park quality-control inspectors randomly inspect restrooms daily (during the day and evening) and record the number of defects (incidences of poor maintenance). The goal of park management is approximately 10 defects per inspection period. Following is a summary of the observations taken by these inspectors for 20 consecutive inspection periods:

| Sample | Number of Defects | Sample | Number of Defects |
|---|---|---|---|
| 1 | 7 | 11 | 14 |
| 2 | 14 | 12 | 10 |
| 3 | 6 | 13 | 11 |
| 4 | 9 | 14 | 12 |
| 5 | 12 | 15 | 9 |
| 6 | 3 | 16 | 13 |
| 7 | 11 | 17 | 7 |
| 8 | 7 | 18 | 15 |
| 9 | 7 | 19 | 11 |
| 10 | 8 | 20 | 16 |

Construct the appropriate control chart for this maintenance process using $3\sigma$ limits and indicate if the process was out of control at any time. If the process is in control, use pattern tests to determine if any nonrandom patterns exist.

**4-31.** The Great Outdoors Clothing Company, a mail-order catalogue operation, contracts with the Federal Parcel Service to deliver all of its orders to customers. As such, Great Outdoors considers Federal Parcel to be part of its TQM program. Great Outdoors processes orders rapidly and requires Federal Parcel to pick them up and deliver them rapidly. Great Outdoors has tracked the delivery time for five randomly selected orders for 12 samples during a two-week period as follows:

| Sample | Delivery Time (days) | | | | |
|---|---|---|---|---|---|
| 1 | 2 | 3 | 3 | 4 | 3 |
| 2 | 5 | 3 | 6 | 2 | 1 |
| 3 | 4 | 3 | 3 | 2 | 2 |
| 4 | 6 | 1 | 5 | 3 | 3 |
| 5 | 2 | 4 | 1 | 4 | 4 |
| 6 | 5 | 1 | 3 | 3 | 3 |
| 7 | 2 | 3 | 3 | 2 | 1 |
| 8 | 1 | 1 | 3 | 1 | 2 |
| 9 | 6 | 3 | 3 | 3 | 3 |
| 10 | 6 | 7 | 5 | 5 | 6 |
| 11 | 6 | 1 | 1 | 3 | 2 |
| 12 | 5 | 5 | 3 | 1 | 3 |

Construct an $\bar{x}$-chart in conjunction with an $R$-chart using $3\sigma$ limits for the delivery process.

**4-32.** The Great Outdoors Clothing Company in Problem 4-31 has designed its packaging and delivery process to deliver orders to a customer within 3 business days ±1 day, which it tells customers. Using the process mean and control limits developed in 4-31 compute the process capability ratio and index, and comment on the capability of the process to meet the company's delivery commitment.

**4-33.** Martha's Wonderful Cookie Company in Problem 4-28 has designed its special super chocolate-chip peanut butter cookies to have 8 chocolate chips with tolerances of ±2 chips. Using the process mean and control limits developed in 4-28, determine the process capability ratio and index, and comment on the capability of the cookie production process.

**4-34.** The Pacific Fruit Company in Problem 4-13 has designed its packaging process for boxes to hold a net weight (nominal value) of 9.0 oz of raisins with tolerances of ±0.5 oz. Using the process mean and control limits developed in 4-13, compute the process capability ratio and index, and comment on the capability of the process to meet the company's box weight specifications.

**4-35.** Sam's Long Life 75-watt light bulbs are designed to have a life of 1125 hours with tolerances of ±210 hours. The process that makes light bulbs has a mean of 1050 hours, with a standard deviation of 55 hours. Compute the process capability ratio and the process capability index, and comment on the overall capability of the process.

**4-36.** Elon Corporation manufactures parts for an aircraft company. It uses a computerized numerical controlled (CNC) machining center to produce a specific part that has a design (nominal) target of 1.275 inches with tolerances of ±0.024 inch. The CNC process that manufactures these parts has a mean of 1.281 inches and a standard deviation of 0.008 inch. Compute the process capability ratio and process capability index, and comment on the overall capability of the process to meet the design specifications.

**4-37.** Explain to what extent the process for producing Sam's Long Life bulbs in Problem 4-35 would have to be improved in order to achieve 6-sigma quality.

**4-38.** The Elon Company manufactures parts for an aircraft company using three computerized numerical controlled (CNC) turning centers. The company wants to decide which machines are capable of producing a specific part with design specifications of 0.0970 inch ±0.015 inch. The machines have the following process parameters—machine 1 ($\bar{\bar{x}}$ = 0.0995, $\sigma$ = 0.004); machine 2 ($\bar{\bar{x}}$ = 0.1002, $\sigma$ = 0.009); machine 3 ($\bar{\bar{x}}$ = 0.095, $\sigma$ = 0.005). Determine which machines (if any) are capable of producing the products within the design specifications.

**4-39.** The Rollins Sporting Goods Company manufactures baseballs for the professional minor and major leagues at its plants in Costa Rica. According to the rules of major league baseball, a baseball must weigh between 142 and 149 grams. The company has taken 20 samples of five baseballs each and weighed the baseballs as follows:

| Sample | Weight (gm) | | | | |
|---|---|---|---|---|---|
| 1 | 143.1 | 142.5 | 148.1 | 149.4 | 146.3 |
| 2 | 145.8 | 144.0 | 149.8 | 141.2 | 143.5 |
| 3 | 140.3 | 144.5 | 146.2 | 140.4 | 149.7 |
| 4 | 143.4 | 145.2 | 147.8 | 144.1 | 148.6 |
| 5 | 142.5 | 141.7 | 139.6 | 145.4 | 146.3 |
| 6 | 147.4 | 145.2 | 145.0 | 150.3 | 151.2 |
| 7 | 144.7 | 145.0 | 145.2 | 140.6 | 139.7 |
| 8 | 141.4 | 138.5 | 140.3 | 142.6 | 144.4 |
| 9 | 151.3 | 149.7 | 145.4 | 148.2 | 149.0 |
| 10 | 137.3 | 144.6 | 145.8 | 141.9 | 144.5 |
| 11 | 142.3 | 144.7 | 141.6 | 145.8 | 148.3 |
| 12 | 143.6 | 145.4 | 145.0 | 144.3 | 149.1 |
| 13 | 148.4 | 147.3 | 149.1 | 140.6 | 140.9 |
| 14 | 151.3 | 150.6 | 147.2 | 148.3 | 146.5 |
| 15 | 145.2 | 146.3 | 141.2 | 142.5 | 142.7 |
| 16 | 146.3 | 147.4 | 148.2 | 145.4 | 145.1 |
| 17 | 143.9 | 144.6 | 145.2 | 146.1 | 146.3 |
| 18 | 145.6 | 145.3 | 142.1 | 146.7 | 144.3 |
| 19 | 142.8 | 141.7 | 140.9 | 145.6 | 146.3 |
| 20 | 145.4 | 142.3 | 147.5 | 145.0 | 149.4 |

Construct an $\bar{x}$-chart in conjunction with an $R$-chart to monitor the baseball-making process, and comment on the capability of the process.

**4-40.** Explain to what extent the process for manufacturing baseballs in Problem 4-39 must be improved in order to achieve $6\sigma$ quality.

**4-41.** At Samantha's Super Store the customer service area processes customer returns, answers customer questions and provides information, addresses customer complaints, and sells gift certificates. The manager believes that if customers must wait longer than 8 minutes to see a customer service representative they get very irritated. The customer service process has been designed to achieve a customer wait time of between 6 and 12 minutes. The store manager has conducted 10 samples of five observations each of customer waiting time over a two-week period as follows:

| Sample | Wait Time (min) | | | | |
|---|---|---|---|---|---|
| 1 | 8.3 | 9.6 | 10.2 | 7.4 | 3.1 |
| 2 | 2.8 | 5.9 | 6.7 | 8.3 | 9.2 |
| 3 | 11.3 | 7.4 | 16.2 | 20.1 | 9.5 |
| 4 | 10.7 | 7.5 | 9.8 | 11.3 | 4.5 |
| 5 | 4.3 | 12.4 | 10.6 | 16.7 | 11.3 |
| 6 | 5.3 | 9.7 | 10.8 | 11.3 | 7.4 |
| 7 | 18.2 | 12.1 | 3.6 | 9.5 | 14.2 |
| 8 | 8.1 | 10.3 | 8.9 | 7.2 | 5.6 |
| 9 | 9.3 | 12.4 | 13.7 | 7.3 | 5.2 |
| 10 | 6.7 | 8.5 | 8.0 | 10.1 | 12.3 |

Construct an $\bar{x}$-chart in conjunction with an $R$-chart to monitor customer service wait time, and comment on the capability of the service area to meet its designated goal.

**4-42.** Metropolitan General Hospital is a city-owned and -operated public hospital. Its emergency room is the largest and most prominent in the city. Approximately 70% of emergency cases in the city come or are sent to Metro General's emergency room. As a result, the emergency room is often crowded and the staff is overworked, causing concern among hospital administrators and city officials about the quality of service and health care the emergency room is able to provide. One of the key quality attributes administrators focus on is patient waiting time—that is, the time between when a patient checks in and registers and when the patient first sees an appropriate medical staff member. Hospital administration wants to monitor patient waiting time using statistical process control charts. At different times of the day over a period of several days, patient waiting times were recorded at random with the following results:

| | Waiting Times (min) | | | | |
|---|---|---|---|---|---|
| Sample | 1 | 2 | 3 | 4 | 5 |
| 1 | 27 | 18 | 20 | 23 | 19 |
| 2 | 22 | 25 | 31 | 40 | 17 |
| 3 | 16 | 15 | 22 | 19 | 23 |
| 4 | 35 | 27 | 16 | 20 | 24 |
| 5 | 21 | 33 | 45 | 12 | 22 |
| 6 | 17 | 15 | 22 | 20 | 30 |
| 7 | 25 | 21 | 26 | 33 | 19 |
| 8 | 15 | 38 | 23 | 25 | 31 |
| 9 | 31 | 26 | 24 | 35 | 32 |
| 10 | 28 | 23 | 29 | 20 | 27 |

a. Develop an $\bar{x}$-chart to be used in conjunction with an $R$-chart to monitor patient waiting time and indicate if the process appears to be in control.

b. The city has established a requirement that emergency room patients have a waiting time of 25 minutes ±5 minutes. Based on the results in part (a) is the emergency room capable of meeting this requirement with its current process?

**4-43.** The three most important quality attributes at Mike's Super Service fast-food restaurant are considered to be good food, fast service, and a clean environment. The restaurant manager uses a combination of customer surveys and statistical measurement tools to monitor these quality attributes. A national marketing and research firm has developed data showing that when customers are in line up to five minutes their perception of that waiting time is only a few minutes; however, after five minutes customer perception of their waiting time increases exponentially. Furthermore, a five-minute average waiting time results in only 2% of customers leaving. The manager wants to monitor speed of service using a statistical process control chart. At different times during the day over a period of several days the manager had an employee time customers' waiting times (from the time they entered an order line to the time they received their order) at random, with the following results:

| | Waiting Time (min) | | | | | |
|---|---|---|---|---|---|---|
| Sample | 1 | 2 | 3 | 4 | 5 | 6 |
| 1 | 6.3 | 2.7 | 4.5 | 3.9 | 5.7 | 5.9 |
| 2 | 3.8 | 6.2 | 7.1 | 5.4 | 5.1 | 4.7 |
| 3 | 5.3 | 5.6 | 6.2 | 5.0 | 5.3 | 4.9 |
| 4 | 3.9 | 7.2 | 6.4 | 5.7 | 4.2 | 7.1 |
| 5 | 4.6 | 3.9 | 5.1 | 4.8 | 5.6 | 6.0 |
| 6 | 5.5 | 6.3 | 5.2 | 7.4 | 8.1 | 5.9 |
| 7 | 6.1 | 7.3 | 6.5 | 5.9 | 5.7 | 8.4 |
| 8 | 2.2 | 3.6 | 5.7 | 5.3 | 5.6 | 5.0 |
| 9 | 6.5 | 4.7 | 5.1 | 9.3 | 6.2 | 5.3 |
| 10 | 4.7 | 5.8 | 5.4 | 5.1 | 5.0 | 5.9 |
| 11 | 3.4 | 2.9 | 1.6 | 4.8 | 6.1 | 5.3 |
| 12 | 4.5 | 6.3 | 5.4 | 5.7 | 2.1 | 3.4 |
| 13 | 7.4 | 3.9 | 4.2 | 4.9 | 5.6 | 3.7 |
| 14 | 5.7 | 5.3 | 4.1 | 3.7 | 5.8 | 5.7 |
| 15 | 6.0 | 3.6 | 2.4 | 5.4 | 5.5 | 3.9 |

a. Develop an $\bar{x}$-chart to be used in conjunction with an $R$-chart to monitor speed of service and indicate if the process is in control using this chart.

b. Management at Mike's Super Service Drive-In restaurant wants customers to receive their orders within 5 minutes ±1 minute, and it has designed its ordering and food preparation process to meet that goal. Using the process mean and control limits developed in (a), compute the process capability ratio and index, and indicate if the process appears to be capable of meeting the restaurant's goal for speed of service.

## CASE PROBLEM 4.1

### *Quality Control at Rainwater Brewery*

Bob Raines and Megan Waters own and operate the Rainwater Brewery, a micro-brewery that grew out of their shared hobby of making home-brew. The brewery is located in Whitesville, the home of State University where Bob and Megan went to college.

Whitesville has a number of bars and restaurants that are patronized by students at State and the local resident population. In fact, Whitesville has the highest per capita beer consumption in the state. In setting up their small brewery, Bob and Megan decided that they would target their sales toward individuals who would pick up their orders directly from the brewery and toward restaurants and bars, where they would deliver orders on a daily or weekly basis.

The brewery process essentially occurs in three stages. First, the mixture is cooked in a vat according to a recipe; then it is placed in a stainless-steel container, where it is fermented for several weeks. During the fermentation process the specific gravity, temperature, and pH need to be monitored on a daily basis. The specific gravity starts out at about 1.006 to 1.008 and decreases to around 1.002, and the temperature must be between 50 and 60°F. After the brew ferments, it is filtered into another stainless-steel pressurized container, where it is carbonated and the beer ages for about a week (with the temperature monitored), after which it is bottled and is ready for distribution. Megan and Bob brew a batch of beer each day, which will result in about 1000 bottles for distribution after the approximately three-week fermentation and aging process.

In the process of setting up their brewery, Megan and Bob agreed they had already developed a proven product with a taste that was appealing, so the most important factor in the success of their new venture would be maintaining high quality. Thus, they spent a lot of time discussing what kind of quality-control techniques they should employ. They agreed that the chance of brewing a "bad," or "spoiled," batch of beer was extremely remote, plus they could not financially afford to reject a whole batch of 1000 bottles of beer if the taste or color was a little "off" the norm. So they felt as if they needed to focus more on process control methods to identify quality problems that would enable them to adjust their equipment, recipe, or process parameters rather than to use some type of acceptance sampling plan.

Describe the different quality-control methods that Rainwater Brewery might use to ensure good-quality beer and how these methods might fit into an overall TQM program.

## CASE PROBLEM 4.2

### *Quality Control at Grass, Unlimited*

Mark Sumansky owns and manages the Grass, Unlimited, lawn-care service in Middleton. His customers include individual homeowners and businesses that subscribe to his service during the winter months for lawn care beginning in the spring and ending in the fall with leaf raking and disposal. Thus, when he begins his service in April he generally has a full list of customers and does not take on additional customers unless he has an opening. However, if he loses a customer any time after the first of June, it is difficult to find new customers, since most people make lawn-service arrangements for the entire summer.

Mark employs five crews, with three to five workers each, to cut grass during the spring and summer months. A crew normally works 10-hour days and can average cutting about 25 normal-size lawns of less than a half-acre each day. A crew will normally have one heavy-duty, wide-cut riding mower, a regular power mower, and trimming equipment. When a crew descends on a lawn, the normal procedure is for one person to mow the main part of the lawn with the riding mower, one or two people to trim, and one person to use the smaller mower to cut areas the riding mower cannot reach. Crews move very fast, and they can often cut a lawn in 15 minutes.

Unfortunately, although speed is an essential component in the profitability of Grass, Unlimited, it can also contribute to quality problems. In his or her haste, a mower might cut flowers, shrubs, or border plants, nick and scrape trees, "skin" spots on the lawn creating bare spots, trim too close, scrape house paint, cut or disfigure house trim, and destroy toys and lawn furniture, among other things. When these problems occur on a too-frequent basis, a customer cancels service, and Mark has a difficult time getting a replacement customer. In addition, he gets most of his subscriptions based on word-of-mouth recommendations and retention of previous customers who are satisfied with his service. As such, quality is a very important factor in his business.

In order to improve the quality of his lawn-care service, Mark has decided to use a process control chart to monitor defects. He has hired Lisa Anderson to follow the teams and check lawns for defects after the mowers have left. A defect is any abnormal or abusive condition created by the crew, including those items just mentioned. It is not possible for Lisa to inspect the more than 100 lawns the service cuts daily, so she randomly picks a sample of 20 lawns each day and counts the number of defects she sees at each lawn. She also makes a note of each defect, so that if there is a problem, the cause can easily be determined. In most cases the defects are caused by haste, but some defects can be caused by faulty equipment or by a crew member using a poor technique or not being attentive.

Over a three-day period Lisa accumulated the following data on defects:

| DAY 1 | | DAY 2 | | DAY 3 | |
|---|---|---|---|---|---|
| Sample | Number of Defects | Sample | Number of Defects | Sample | Number of Defects |
| 1 | 6 | 1 | 2 | 1 | 5 |
| 2 | 4 | 2 | 5 | 2 | 5 |
| 3 | 5 | 3 | 1 | 3 | 3 |
| 4 | 9 | 4 | 4 | 4 | 2 |
| 5 | 3 | 5 | 5 | 5 | 6 |
| 6 | 8 | 6 | 3 | 6 | 5 |
| 7 | 6 | 7 | 2 | 7 | 4 |
| 8 | 1 | 8 | 2 | 8 | 3 |
| 9 | 5 | 9 | 2 | 9 | 2 |
| 10 | 6 | 10 | 6 | 10 | 2 |
| 11 | 4 | 11 | 4 | 11 | 2 |
| 12 | 7 | 12 | 3 | 12 | 4 |
| 13 | 6 | 13 | 8 | 13 | 1 |
| 14 | 5 | 14 | 5 | 14 | 5 |
| 15 | 8 | 15 | 6 | 15 | 9 |
| 16 | 3 | 16 | 3 | 16 | 4 |
| 17 | 5 | 17 | 4 | 17 | 4 |
| 18 | 4 | 18 | 3 | 18 | 4 |
| 19 | 3 | 19 | 3 | 19 | 1 |
| 20 | 2 | 20 | 4 | 20 | 3 |

Develop a process control chart for Grass, Unlimited, to monitor the quality of its lawn service using 2-sigma limits. Describe any other quality-control or quality-management procedures you think Grass, Unlimited, might employ to improve the quality of its service.

## CASE PROBLEM 4.3

### *Improving Service Time at Dave's Burgers*

Dave's Burgers is a fast-food restaurant franchise in Georgia, South Carolina, and North Carolina. Recently, Dave's Burgers has followed the lead of larger franchise restaurants like Burger King, McDonald's, and Wendy's and constructed drive-through windows at all its locations. However, instead of making Dave's Burgers more competitive, the drive-through windows have been a source of continual problems, and it has lost market share to its larger competitors in almost all locations. To identify and correct the problems, top management has selected three of its restaurants (one in each state) as test sites and has implemented a TQM program at each of them. A quality team made up of employees, managers, and quality specialists from company headquarters, at the Charlotte, North Carolina, test restaurant using traditional TQM methods like Pareto charts, check sheets, fishbone diagrams, and process flowcharts, have determined that the primary problem is slow, erratic service at the drive-through window. Studies show that from the time a customer arrives at the window to the time the order is received averages 2.6 minutes. To be competitive, management believes service time should be reduced to at least 2.0 minutes and ideally 1.5 minutes.

The Charlotte Dave's Burgers franchise implemented a number of production process changes to improve service time at the drive-through window. It provided all employees with more training across all restaurant functions, improved the headset system, improved the equipment layout, developed clearer signs for customers, streamlined the menu, and initiated even-dollar (tax-inclusive) pricing to speed the payment process. Most importantly the restaurant installed large, visible electronic timers that showed how long a customer was at the window. This not only allowed the quality team to measure service speed but also provided employees with a constant reminder that a customer was waiting.

These quality improvements were implemented over several months, and their effect was immediate. Service speed was obviously improved, and market share at the Charlotte restaurant increased by 5%. To maintain quality service, make sure the service time remained fast, and continue to improve service, the quality team decided to use a statistical process control chart on a continuing basis. They collected six service time observations daily over a 15-day period, as follows:

| Sample | OBSERVATIONS OF SERVICE TIME (MIN) 1 | 2 | 3 | 4 | 5 | 6 |
|---|---|---|---|---|---|---|
| 1 | 1.62 | 1.54 | 1.38 | 1.75 | 2.50 | 1.32 |
| 2 | 1.25 | 1.96 | 1.55 | 1.66 | 1.38 | 2.01 |
| 3 | 1.85 | 1.01 | 0.95 | 1.79 | 1.66 | 1.94 |
| 4 | 3.10 | 1.18 | 1.25 | 1.45 | 1.09 | 2.11 |
| 5 | 1.95 | 0.76 | 1.34 | 2.12 | 1.45 | 1.03 |
| 6 | 0.88 | 2.50 | 1.07 | 1.50 | 1.33 | 1.62 |
| 7 | 1.55 | 1.41 | 1.95 | 1.14 | 1.86 | 1.02 |
| 8 | 2.78 | 1.56 | 1.87 | 2.03 | 0.79 | 1.14 |
| 9 | 1.31 | 1.05 | 0.94 | 1.53 | 1.71 | 1.15 |
| 10 | 1.67 | 1.85 | 2.03 | 1.12 | 1.50 | 1.36 |
| 11 | 0.95 | 1.73 | 1.12 | 1.67 | 2.05 | 1.42 |
| 12 | 3.21 | 4.16 | 1.67 | 1.75 | 2.87 | 3.76 |
| 13 | 1.65 | 1.78 | 2.63 | 1.05 | 1.21 | 2.09 |
| 14 | 2.36 | 3.55 | 1.92 | 1.45 | 3.64 | 2.30 |
| 15 | 1.07 | 0.96 | 1.13 | 2.05 | 0.91 | 1.66 |

Construct a control chart to monitor the service at the drive-through window. Determine if your control chart can be implemented on a continuing basis or if additional observations need to be collected. Explain why the chart you developed can or cannot be used. Also discuss what other statistical process control charts Dave's Burgers might use in its overall quality-management program.

## REFERENCES


Charbonneau, H. C., and G. L. Webster. *Industrial Quality Control*. Englewood Cliffs, NJ: Prentice Hall, 1978.

Dodge, H. F., and H. G. Romig. *Sampling Inspection Tables—Single and Double Sampling*. 2nd ed. New York: Wiley.

Duncan, A. J. *Quality Control and Industrial Statistics*. 4th ed. Homewood, IL: Irwin, 1974.

Evans, James R., and William M. Lindsay. *The Management and Control of Quality*. 3rd ed. St. Paul, MN: West, 1993.

Fetter, R. B. *The Quality Control System*. Homewood, IL: Irwin, 1967.

Grant, E. L., and R. S. Leavenworth. *Statistical Quality Control*. 5th ed. New York: McGraw-Hill, 1980.

Montgomery, D. C. *Introduction to Statistical Quality Control*. 2nd ed. New York: Wiley, 1991.

# Operational Decision-Making Tools: Acceptance Sampling

SUPPLEMENT 4

## CHAPTER OUTLINE

In this supplement, you will learn about . . .

- Single-Sample Attribute Plan
- The Operating Characteristic Curve
- Developing a Sampling Plan with Excel
- Average Outgoing Quality
- Double- and Multiple-Sampling Plans

**Acceptance sampling:** accepting or rejecting a production lot based on the number of defects in a sample.

In **acceptance sampling**, a random sample of the units produced is inspected, and the quality of this sample is assumed to reflect the overall quality of all items or a particular group of items, called a *lot*. Acceptance sampling is a statistical method, so if a sample is random, it ensures that each item has an equal chance of being selected and inspected. This enables statistical inferences to be made about the population—the lot—as a whole. If a sample has an acceptable number or percentage of defective items, the lot is accepted, but if it has an unacceptable number of defects, it is rejected.

Acceptance sampling is not consistent with the philosophy of TQM and zero defects.

Acceptance sampling is a historical approach to quality control based on the premise that some acceptable number of defective items will result from the production process. The producer and customer agree on the number of acceptable defects, normally measured as a percentage. However, the notion of a producer or customer agreeing to any defects at all is anathema to the adherents of TQM. The goal of companies that have adopted TQM is to achieve zero defects. Acceptance sampling identifies defective items after the product is already finished, whereas TQM preaches the prevention of defects altogether. To disciples of TQM, acceptance sampling is simply a means of identifying products to throw away or rework. It does nothing to prevent poor quality and to ensure good quality in the future.

TQM companies measure defects as PPM, not percentages.

TQM companies do not even report the number of defective parts in terms of a percentage because the fraction of defective items they expect to produce is so small that a percentage is meaningless. The international measure for reporting defects has become defective parts per million, or PPM. For example, a defect rate of 2%, used in acceptance sampling, was once considered a high-quality standard: 20,000 defective parts per million! This is a totally unacceptable level of quality for TQM companies continuously trying to achieve zero defects. Three or four defects per million would be a more acceptable level of quality for these companies.

Nevertheless, acceptance sampling is still used as a statistical quality control method by many companies that either have not yet adopted TQM or are required by customer demands or government regulations to use acceptance sampling. Since this method still has wide application, it is necessary for it to be studied.

**Sampling plan:** provides the guidelines for accepting a lot.

When a sample is taken and inspected for quality, the items in the sample are being checked to see if they conform to some predetermined specification. A **sampling plan** establishes the guidelines for taking a sample and the criteria for making a decision regarding the quality of the lot from which the sample was taken. The simplest form of sampling plan is a single-sample attribute plan.

## SINGLE-SAMPLE ATTRIBUTE PLAN

Elements of a sampling plan—$N, n, c, d$

A single-sample attribute plan has as its basis an attribute that can be evaluated with a simple, discrete decision, such as defective or not defective or good or bad. The plan includes the following elements:

$N$ = the lot size
$n$ = the sample size (selected randomly)
$c$ = the acceptable number of defective items in a sample
$d$ = the actual number of defective items in a sample

A single sample of size $n$ is selected randomly from a larger lot, and each of the $n$ items is inspected. If the sample contains $d \leq c$ defective items, the entire lot is accepted; if $d > c$, the lot is rejected.

Management must decide the values of these components that will result in the most effective sampling plan, as well as determine what constitutes an effective plan. These are design considerations. The design of a sampling plan includes both the structural components ($n$, the decision criteria, and so on) and performance measures. These performance measures include the *producer's* and *consumer's risks*, the *acceptable quality level*, and the *lot tolerance percent defective*.

## PRODUCER'S AND CONSUMER'S RISKS

When a sample is drawn from a production lot and the items in the sample are inspected, management hopes that if the actual number of defective items exceeds the predetermined acceptable number of defective items ($d > c$) and the entire lot is rejected, then the sample results have accurately portrayed the quality of the entire lot. Management would hate to think that the sample results were not indicative of the overall quality of the lot and a lot that was actually acceptable was erroneously rejected and wasted. Conversely, management hopes that an actual bad lot of items is not erroneously accepted if $d \leq c$. An effective sampling plan attempts to minimize the possibility of wrongly rejecting good items or wrongly accepting bad items.

When an acceptance-sampling plan is designed, management specifies a quality standard commonly referred to as the **acceptable quality level**, or **AQL**. The AQL reflects the consumer's willingness to accept lots with a small proportion of defective items. The AQL is the fraction of defective items in a lot that is deemed acceptable. For example, the AQL might be two defective items in a lot of 500, or 0.004. The AQL may be determined by management to be the level that is generally acceptable in the marketplace and will not result in a loss of customers. Or, it may be dictated by an individual customer as the quality level it will accept. In other words, the AQL is negotiated.

**AQL:** an acceptable proportion of defects in a lot to the consumer.

The probability of rejecting a production lot that has an acceptable quality level is referred to as the **producer's risk**, commonly designated by the Greek symbol $\alpha$. In statistical jargon, $\alpha$ is the probability of committing a type I error.

**Producer's risk:** the probability of rejecting a lot that has an AQL.

There will be instances in which the sample will not accurately reflect the quality of a lot and a lot that does not meet the AQL will pass on to the customer. Although the customer expects to receive some of these lots, there is a limit to the number of defective items the customer will accept. This upper limit is known as the **lot tolerance percent defective**, or **LTPD** (LTPD is also generally negotiated between the producer and consumer). The probability of accepting a lot in which the fraction of defective items exceeds the LTPD is referred to as the **consumer's risk**, designated by the Greek symbol $\beta$. In statistical jargon, $\beta$ is the probability of committing a type II error.

**LTPD:** the maximum number of defective items a consumer will accept in a lot.

**Consumer's risk:** the probability of accepting a lot in which the fraction of defective items exceeds LTPD.

In general, the customer would like the quality of a lot to be as good or better than the AQL but is willing to accept some lots with quality levels no worse than the LTPD. Frequently, sampling plans are designed with the producer's risk ($\alpha$) about 5% and the consumer's risk ($\beta$) around 10%. Be careful not to confuse $\alpha$ with the AQL or $\beta$ with the LTPD. If $\alpha$ equals 5% and $\beta$ equals 10%, then management expects to reject lots that are as good as or better than the AQL about 5% of the time, whereas the customer expects to accept lots that exceed the LTPD about 10% of the time.

**$\alpha$—producer's risk and $\beta$—consumer's risk.**

## THE OPERATING CHARACTERISTIC CURVE

The performance measures we described in the previous section for a sampling plan can be represented graphically with an **operating characteristic (OC) curve**. The OC curve measures the probability of accepting a lot for different quality (proportion defective) levels given a specific sample size ($n$) and acceptance level ($c$). Management can use such a graph to determine if their sampling plan meets the performance measures they have established for AQL, LTPD, $\alpha$, and $\beta$. Thus, the OC curve indicates to management how effective the sampling plan is in distinguishing (more commonly known as *discriminating*) between good and bad lots. The shape of a typical OC curve for a single-sample plan is shown in Figure S4.1 on the next page.

**OC curve:** a graph that shows the probability of accepting a lot for different quality levels with a specific sampling plan.

In Figure S4.1 the percentage defective in a lot is shown along the horizontal axis, whereas the probability of accepting a lot is measured along the vertical axis. The exact shape and location of the curve is defined by the sample size ($n$) and acceptance level ($c$) for the sampling plan.

In Figure S4.1, if a lot has 3% defective items, the probability of accepting the lot (based on the sampling plan defined by the OC curve) is 0.95. If management defines the AQL as 3%, then the probability that an acceptable lot will be rejected ($\alpha$) is 1 minus the probability of accepting a lot or $1 - 0.95 = 0.05$. If management is willing to accept lots

**Figure S4.1**
**An Operating Characteristic Curve**

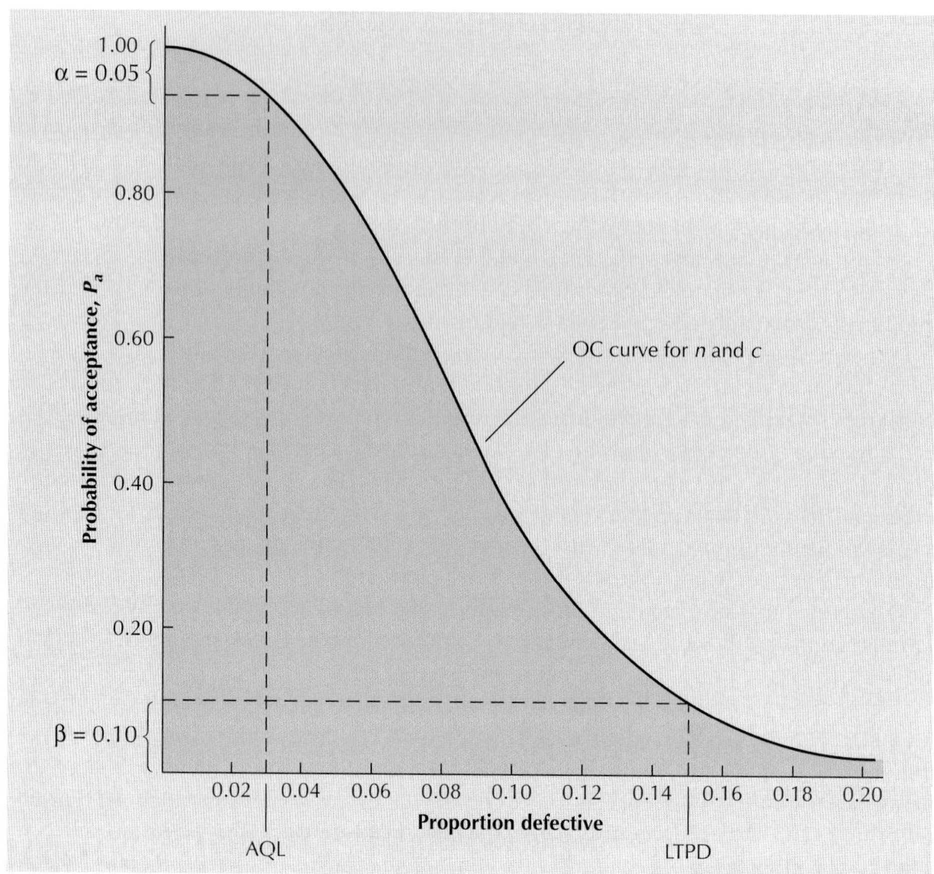


with a percentage defective up to 15% (i.e., the LTPD), this corresponds to a probability that the lot will be accepted ($\beta$) of 0.10. A frequently used set of performance measures is $\alpha = 0.05$ and $\beta = 0.10$.

## DEVELOPING A SAMPLING PLAN WITH EXCEL

Developing a sampling plan manually requires a tedious trial-and-error approach using statistical analysis. $n$ and $c$ are progressively changed until an approximate sampling plan is obtained that meets the specified performance measures. A more practical alternative is to use Excel. Example S4.1 demonstrates the use of Excel to develop a sampling plan.

**Example S4.1**
**Developing a Sampling Plan and Operating Characteristic Curve**

The Anderson Bottle and China (ABC) Company produces a style of solid-colored blue china exclusively for a large department store chain. The china includes a number of different items that are sold in open stock in the stores, including coffee mugs. Mugs are produced in lots of 10,000. Performance measures for the quality of mugs sent to the stores call for a producer's risk ($\alpha$) of 0.05 with an AQL of 1% defective and a consumer's risk ($\beta$) of 0.10 with a LTPD of 5% defective. The ABC Company wants to know what size sample, $n$, to take and what the acceptance number, $c$, should be to achieve the performance measures called for in the sampling plan.

*Solution*

The Excel spreadsheet shown in Exhibit S4.1 is set up to determine an estimated sampling plan, $n$ and $c$, based on the AQL and LTPD values initially input into cells C11 and C12, respectively. The Excel formulas necessary to estimate $n$ and $c$ are embedded in cells C7 and C8. Thus, when the value of "0.01" is entered into cell C11 and "0.05" is typed into cell C12, the value for $n$ = "137" and the value for $c$ = "3" are computed, as shown in cells C7 and C8. At this point cells C13 and C14 and cells C17 and C18 have no values, and the accompanying OC curve does not exist.

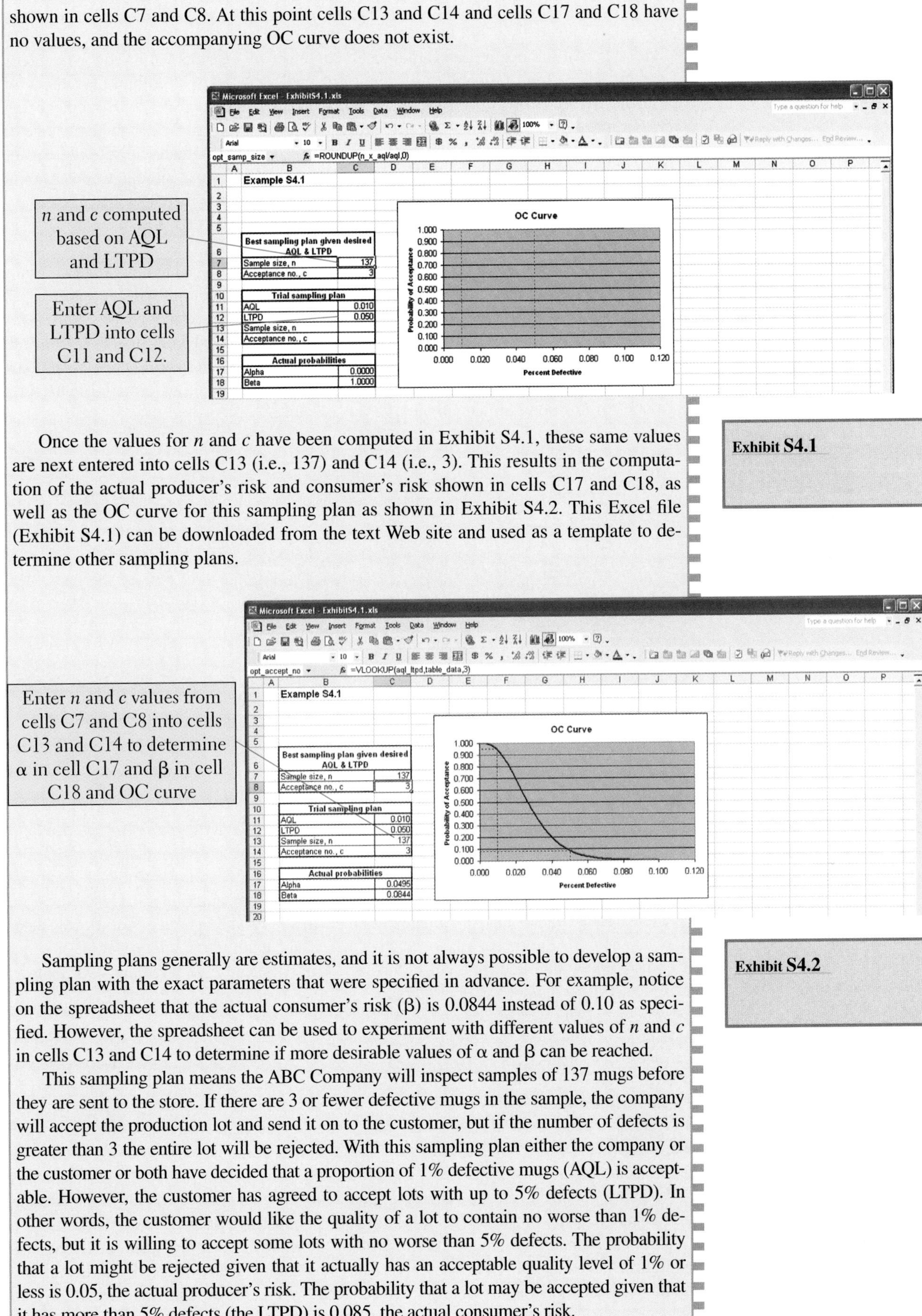


Exhibit S4.1

Once the values for $n$ and $c$ have been computed in Exhibit S4.1, these same values are next entered into cells C13 (i.e., 137) and C14 (i.e., 3). This results in the computation of the actual producer's risk and consumer's risk shown in cells C17 and C18, as well as the OC curve for this sampling plan as shown in Exhibit S4.2. This Excel file (Exhibit S4.1) can be downloaded from the text Web site and used as a template to determine other sampling plans.

Exhibit S4.2

Sampling plans generally are estimates, and it is not always possible to develop a sampling plan with the exact parameters that were specified in advance. For example, notice on the spreadsheet that the actual consumer's risk ($\beta$) is 0.0844 instead of 0.10 as specified. However, the spreadsheet can be used to experiment with different values of $n$ and $c$ in cells C13 and C14 to determine if more desirable values of $\alpha$ and $\beta$ can be reached.

This sampling plan means the ABC Company will inspect samples of 137 mugs before they are sent to the store. If there are 3 or fewer defective mugs in the sample, the company will accept the production lot and send it on to the customer, but if the number of defects is greater than 3 the entire lot will be rejected. With this sampling plan either the company or the customer or both have decided that a proportion of 1% defective mugs (AQL) is acceptable. However, the customer has agreed to accept lots with up to 5% defects (LTPD). In other words, the customer would like the quality of a lot to contain no worse than 1% defects, but it is willing to accept some lots with no worse than 5% defects. The probability that a lot might be rejected given that it actually has an acceptable quality level of 1% or less is 0.05, the actual producer's risk. The probability that a lot may be accepted given that it has more than 5% defects (the LTPD) is 0.085, the actual consumer's risk.

## AVERAGE OUTGOING QUALITY

**Average outgoing quality (AOQ):** the expected number of defective items that will pass on to the customer with a sampling plan.

The shape of the operating characteristic curve shows that lots with a low percentage of defects have a high probability of being accepted, and lots with a high percentage of defects have a low probability of being accepted, as one would expect. For example, using the OC curve for the sampling plan in Example S4.1 ($n = 137$, $c \leq 3$) for a percentage of defects = 0.01, the probability the lot will be accepted is approximately 0.95, whereas for 0.05, the probability of accepting a lot is relatively small. However, all lots, whether or not they are accepted, will pass on some defective items to the customer. The **average outgoing quality (AOQ)** is a measure of the expected number of defective items that will pass on to the customer with the sampling plan selected.

When a lot is rejected as a result of the sampling plan, it is assumed that it will be subjected to a complete inspection, and all defective items will be replaced with good ones. Also, even when a lot is accepted, the defective items found in the sample will be replaced. Thus, some portion of all the defective items contained in all the lots produced will be replaced before they are passed on to the customer. The remaining defective items that make their way to the customer are contained in lots that are accepted. Figure S4.2 shows the average outgoing quality curve for Example S4.1

Figure S4.2
**An Average Outgoing Quality Curve**

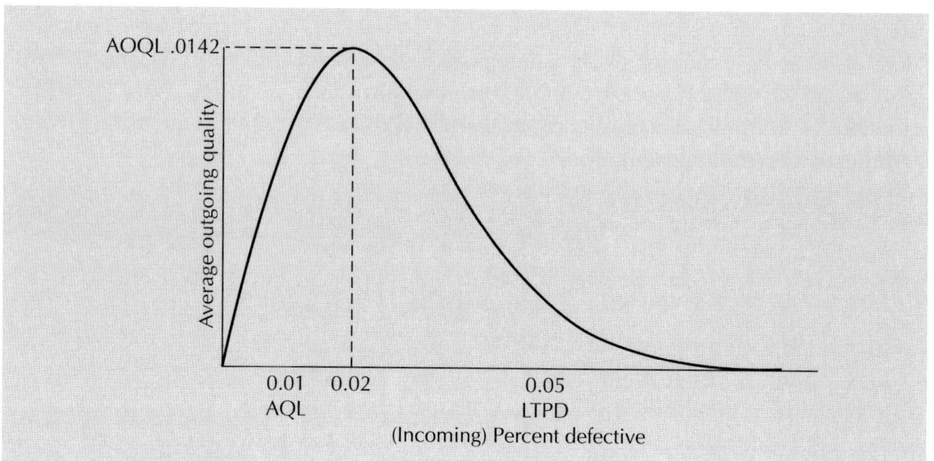


The maximum point on the curve is referred to as the *average outgoing quality limit* (AOQL). For our example, the AOQL is 1.42% defective when the actual proportion defective of the lot is 2%. This is the worst level of outgoing quality that management can expect on average, and if this level is acceptable, then the sampling plan is deemed acceptable. Notice that as the percentage of defects increases and the quality of the lots deteriorates, the AOQ improves. This occurs because as the quality of the lots becomes poorer, it is more likely that bad lots will be identified and rejected, and any defective items in these lots will be replaced with good ones.

## DOUBLE- AND MULTIPLE-SAMPLING PLANS

*Double-sampling plans* are less costly than single-sampling plans.

In a *double-sampling plan*, a small sample is taken first; if the quality is very good, the lot is accepted, and if the sample is very poor, the lot is rejected. However, if the initial sample is inconclusive, a second sample is taken and the lot is either accepted or rejected based on the combined results of the two samples. The objective of such a sampling procedure is to save costs relative to a single-sampling plan. For very good or very bad lots, the smaller, less expensive sample will suffice and a larger, more expensive sample is avoided.

A *multiple-sampling plan* uses the smallest sample size of any sampling plan.

A *multiple-sampling plan*, also referred to as a sequential-sampling plan, generally employs the smallest sample size of any of the sampling plans we have discussed. In its most extreme form, individual items are inspected sequentially, and the decision to accept or reject a lot is based on the cumulative number of defective items. A multiple-sampling plan can result in small samples and, consequently, can be the least expensive of the sampling plans.

The steps of a multiple-sampling plan are similar to those for a double-sampling plan. An initial sample (which can be as small as one unit) is taken. If the number of defective items is less than or equal to a lower limit, the lot is accepted, whereas if it exceeds a specified upper limit, the lot is rejected. If the number of defective items falls between the two limits, a second sample is obtained. The cumulative number of defects is then compared with an increased set of upper and lower limits, and the decision rule used in the first sample is applied. If the lot is neither accepted nor rejected with the second sample, a third sample is taken, with the acceptance/rejection limits revised upward. These steps are repeated for subsequent samples until the lot is either accepted or rejected.

Choosing among single-, double-, or multiple-sampling plans is an economic decision. When the cost of obtaining a sample is very high compared with the inspection cost, a single-sampling plan is preferred. For example, if a petroleum company is analyzing soil samples from various locales around the globe, it is probably more economical to take a single, large sample in Brazil than to return for additional samples if the initial sample is inconclusive. Alternatively, if the cost of sampling is low relative to inspection costs, a double- or multiple-sampling plan may be preferred. For example, if a winery is sampling bottles of wine, it may be more economical to use a sequential sampling plan, tasting individual bottles, than to test a large single sample containing a number of bottles, since each bottle sampled is, in effect, destroyed. In most cases in which quality control requires destructive testing, the inspection costs are high compared with sampling costs.

## SUMMARY

Four decades ago acceptance sampling constituted the primary means of quality control in many U.S. companies. However, it is the exception now, as most quality-conscious firms in the United States and abroad have either adopted or moved toward a quality-management program such as TQM or six sigma. The cost of inspection, the cost of sending lots back, and the cost of scrap and waste are costs that most companies cannot tolerate and remain competitive in today's global market. Still, acceptance sampling is used by some companies and government agencies, and thus it is a relevant topic for study.

## SUMMARY OF KEY TERMS

**acceptable quality level (AQL)** the fraction of defective items deemed acceptable in a lot.

**acceptance sampling** a statistical procedure for taking a random sample in order to determine whether or not a lot should be accepted or rejected.

**average outgoing quality (AOQ)** the expected number of defective items that will pass on to the customer with a sampling plan.

**consumer's risk** ($\beta$) the profitability of accepting a lot in which the fraction of defective items exceeds the most (LTPD) the consumer is willing to accept.

**lot tolerance percent defective (LTPD)** the maximum percentage defective items in a lot that the consumer will knowingly accept.

**operating characteristic (OC) curve** a graph that measures the probability of accepting a lot for different proportions of defective items.

**producer's risk** ($\alpha$) the probability of rejecting a lot that has an acceptable quality level (AQL).

**sampling plan** a plan that provides guidelines for accepting a lot.

## SOLVED PROBLEM

### SINGLE-SAMPLE, ATTRIBUTE PLAN

#### PROBLEM STATEMENT

A product lot of 2000 items is inspected at a station at the end of the production process. Management and the product's customer have agreed to a quality-control program whereby lots that contain no more than 2% defectives are deemed acceptable, whereas lots with 6% or more defectives are not acceptable. Furthermore, management desires to limit the probability that a good lot will be rejected to 5%, and the customer wants to limit the probability that a bad lot will be accepted to 10%. Using Excel, develop a sampling plan that will achieve the quality-performance criteria.

#### SOLUTION

Note that the following Excel spreadsheet was solved using the downloaded file for Exhibit S4.1 (from the text Web site) as a template.

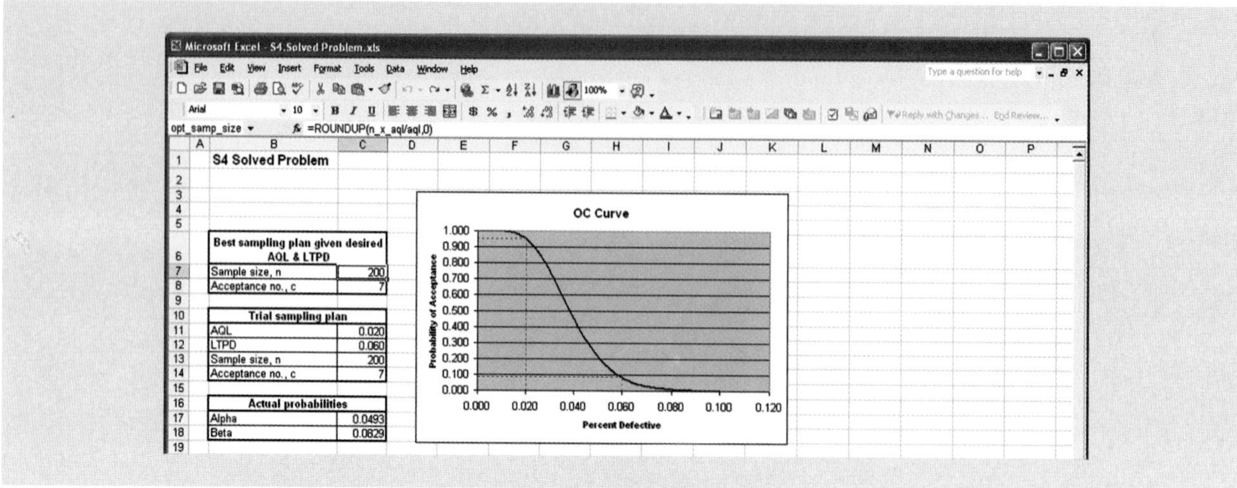


## QUESTIONS

**S4-1.** What is the difference between acceptance sampling and process control?

**S4-2.** Why are sample sizes for attributes necessarily larger than sample sizes for variables?

**S4-3.** How is the sample size determined in a single-sample attribute plan?

**S4-4.** How does the AQL relate to producer's risk ($\alpha$) and the LTPD relate to consumer's risk ($\beta$)?

**S4-5.** Explain the difference between single-, double-, and multiple-sampling plans.

**S4-6.** Why is the traditional view of quality control reflected in the use of acceptance sampling unacceptable to adherents of TQM?

**S4-7.** Under what circumstances is the total inspection of final products necessary?

## PROBLEMS

**S4-1.** The Great Lakes Company, a grocery store chain, purchases apples from a produce distributor in Virginia. The grocery company has an agreement with the distributor that it desires shipments of 10,000 apples with no more than 2% defectives (i.e., severely blemished apples), although it will accept shipments with up to a maximum of 8% defective. The probability of rejecting a good lot is set at 0.05, whereas the probability of accepting a bad-quality lot is 0.10. Determine a sampling plan that will approximately achieve these quality performance criteria, and the operating characteristic curve.

**S4-2.** The Academic House Publishing Company sends out the textbooks it publishes to an independent book binder. When the bound books come back, they are inspected for defective bindings (e.g., warped boards, ripples, cuts, poor adhesion). The publishing company has an acceptable quality level of 4% defectives but will tolerate lots of up to 10% defective. What (approximate) sample size and acceptance level would result in a probability of 0.05 that a good lot will be rejected and a probability of 0.10 that a bad lot will be accepted?

**S4-3.** The Metro Packaging Company in Richmond produces clear plastic bottles for the Kooler Cola Company, a soft-drink manufacturer. Metro inspects each lot of 5000 bottles before they are shipped to the Kooler Company. The soft-drink company has specified an acceptable quality level of 0.06 and a lot tolerance percent defective of 0.12. Metro currently has a sampling plan with $n = 150$ and $c \leq 4$. The two companies have recently agreed that the sampling plan should have a producer's risk of 0.05 and a consumer's risk of 0.10. Will the current sampling plan used by Metro achieve these levels of $\alpha$ and $\beta$?

**S4-4.** The Fast Break Computer Company assembles personal computers and sells them to retail outlets. It purchases keyboards for its PCs from a manufacturer in the Orient. The keyboards are shipped in lots of 1000 units, and when they arrive at the Fast Break Company samples are inspected. Fast Break's contract with the overseas manufacturer specifies that the quality level that they will accept is 4% defective. The personal computer company wants to avoid sending a shipment back because the distance involved would delay and disrupt the assembly process; thus, they want only a 1% probability of sending a good lot back. The worst level of quality the Fast Break Company will accept is 10% defective items. Using Excel develop a sampling plan that will achieve these quality-performance criteria.

**S4-5.** A department store in Beijing, China, has arranged to purchase specially designed sweatshirts with the Olympic logo from a clothing manufacturer in Hong Kong. When the sweatshirts arrive in Beijing in lots of 2000 units, they are inspected. The store's management and manufacturer have agreed on quality criteria of AQL = 2% defective and LTPD = 8% defective. Because sending poor-quality shipments back to Hong Kong would disrupt sales at the stores, management has specified a low producer's risk of 0.01 and will accept a relatively high consumer's risk of 0.10. Using Excel, develop a sampling plan that will achieve these quality-performance criteria.

# Products and Services

CHAPTER 5

Web resources for this chapter include

- Internet Exercises
- Online Practice Quizzes
- Virtual Tours
- Excel Worksheets
- Company and Resource Weblinks
- Animated Demo Problems
- Microsoft Project Exhibits

www.wiley.com/college/russell

## CHAPTER OUTLINE

In this chapter you will learn about . . .

- The Design Process
- Reducing Time-to-Market
- Improving the Quality of Design
- Special Considerations in Service Design

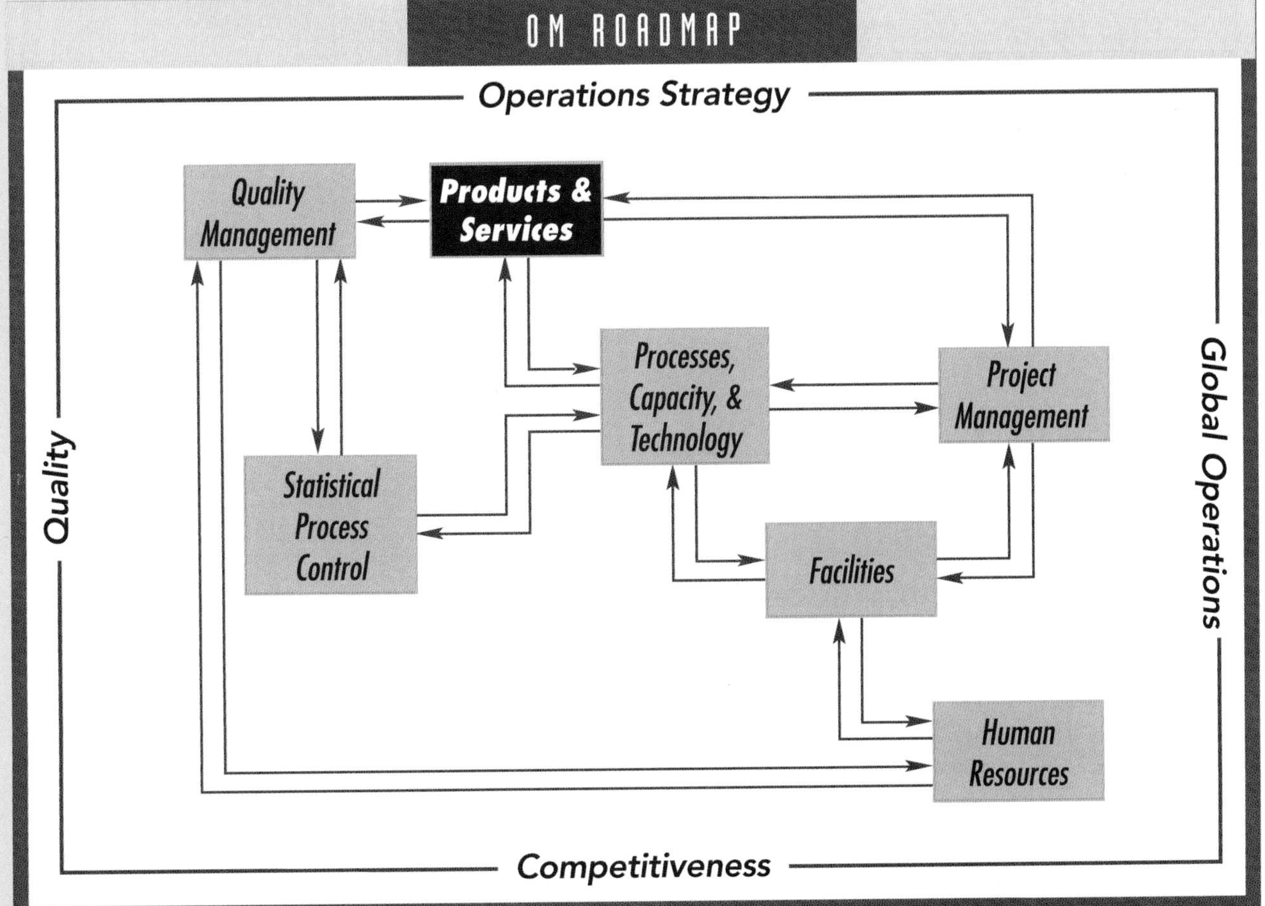

## GM CREATES BETTER DESIGNS FASTER

In the old days, General Motors had trouble predicting what customers wanted, so its decisions were always one step behind the latest trends. Now with a product-design cycle slashed from 4 years to 18 months, GM can design models with a better sense of what will be popular. That allows it to take more chances, as witnessed by a record 29 new models released this year, many of them based on head-turning designs. And with cars designed and built more quickly, few opportunities for error exist. GM now ranks third in quality behind No. 1 Toyota and No. 2 Honda, and is steadily improving.

One of GM's innovations is the two-way OnStar communications system. Wireless sensors, global-positioning technology, and telematics allow OnStar to collect performance data from cars on the road and notify owners right away if their vehicle needs repair. The technology has helped reduce GM's warranty expense and provides useful data for improving future designs, such as an adaptive cruise control that automatically reduces a car's speed when a sensor detects a slower vehicle ahead.

In 1990, GM cars were controlled by about 100,000 lines of software code; by 2010, that number is expected to rise to 100 million. Technology is used in the design process, too, with designers from across the world meeting in virtual-reality-simulated environments to *experience* a new design. GM's fuel cell AUTOnomy project is another example of out-of-the-box design. Look for photos of this modular whiz car later in the chapter.

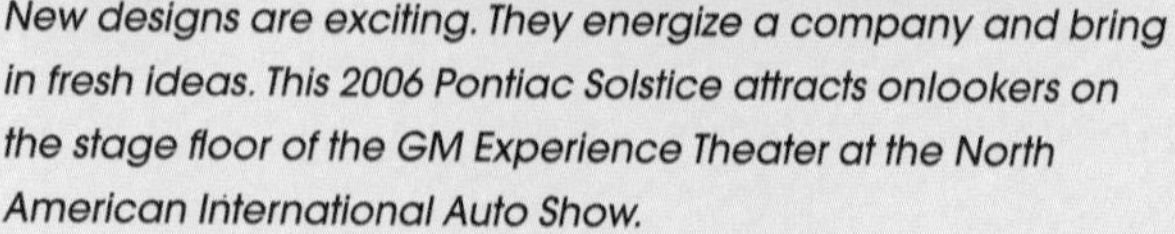
*New designs are exciting. They energize a company and bring in fresh ideas. This 2006 Pontiac Solstice attracts onlookers on the stage floor of the GM Experience Theater at the North American International Auto Show.*

*In the early days of the automotive industry, designers used full-sized chalkboards to sketch a vehicle. From these, engineers developed wooden sections and used clay to define surfaces. Today, at the GM Design Center, creative designers use the latest CAD software to sketch vehicle concepts, record and manipulate them digitally, and display them on room-size screens or in virtual reality environments.*

*Source:* Steve Rosenbush, "At GM, Tech Is Steering," *Business Week* (May 27, 2004); "Being There: Virtual Reality in Automotive Design Engineering," *Industry Search* (December 18, 2000); Company Web site, www.gm.com (accessed June 30, 2004).

New products and services are the lifeblood or an organization. Designs can provide a competitive edge by bringing new ideas to the market quickly, doing a better job of satisfying customer needs, or being easier to manufacture, use, and repair.

Design can provide a competitive edge.

Design is a critical process for a firm. Strategically, it defines a firm's customers, as well as its competitors. It capitalizes on a firm's core competencies and determines what new competencies need to be developed. It is also the most obvious driver of change—new products and services can rejuvenate an organization, define new markets, and inspire new technologies.

The design process itself is beneficial because it encourages companies to look outside their boundaries, bring in new ideas, challenge conventional thinking, and experiment. Product and service design provide a natural venue for learning, breaking down barriers, working in teams, and integrating across functions.

In this chapter we examine the design process with an eye toward innovation, quality, and time-to-market. The impact of technology on design and the differences between product and service design are also discussed.

## THE DESIGN PROCESS

Design has a tremendous impact on the quality of a product or service. Poor designs may not meet customer needs or may be so difficult to make that quality suffers. Costly designs can result in overpriced products that lose market share. If the design process is too lengthy, a competitor may capture the market by being the first to introduce new products, services, or features. However, rushing to be first to the market can result in design flaws and poor performance, which totally negate first-mover advantages. Design may be an art, but the design process must be managed effectively.

An effective design process:

- Matches product or service characteristics with customer requirements,
- Ensures that customer requirements are met in the simplest and least costly manner,
- Reduces the time required to design a new product or service, and
- Minimizes the revisions necessary to make a design workable.

*Product design* defines the appearance of the product, sets standards for performance, specifies which materials are to be used, and determines dimensions and tolerances. *Service design* specifies what physical items, sensual benefits, and psychological benefits the customer is to receive from the service, and defines the environment in which the service will take place. Figure 5.1 outlines the design process from idea generation to product launch. Let's examine each step in detail.

## IDEA GENERATION

The design process begins with understanding the customer and actively identifying customer needs. Ideas for new products or improvements to existing products can be generated from many sources, including a company's own R&D department, customer complaints or suggestions, marketing research, suppliers, salespersons in the field, factory workers, and new technological developments. Competitors are also a source of ideas for new products or services. Perceptual maps, benchmarking, and reverse engineering can help companies learn from their competitors.

**Perceptual map:** visual method of comparing customer perceptions of different products or services.

**Perceptual maps** compare customer perceptions of a company's products with competitors' products. Consider the perceptual map of breakfast cereals in terms of taste and nutrition shown in Figure 5.2. The lack of an entry in the good-taste, high-nutrition category suggests there are opportunities for this kind of cereal in the market. This is why Cheerios introduced honey-nut and apple-cinnamon versions while promoting its "oat" base. Fruit bits and nuts were added to wheat flakes to make them more tasty and nutritious. Shredded Wheat opted for more taste by reducing its size and adding a sugar

**Figure 5.1**
**The Design Process**

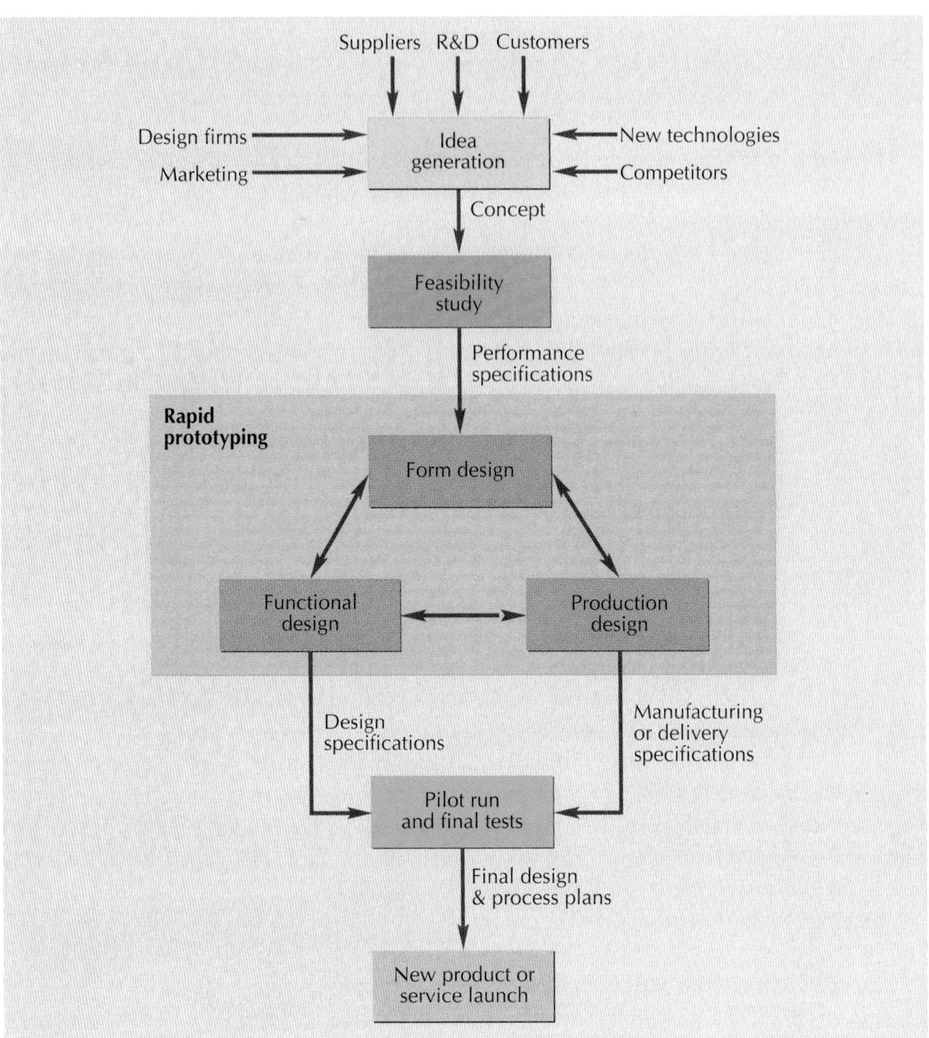


**Benchmarking:** comparing a product or process against the best-in-class product.

frosting or berry filling. Rice Krispies, on the other hand, sought to challenge Cocoa Puffs in the "more tasty" market quadrant with marshmallow and fruit-flavored versions.

**Benchmarking** refers to finding the best-in-class product or process, measuring the performance of your product or process against it, and making recommendations for improvement based on the results. The benchmarked company may be in an entirely differ-

**Figure 5.2**
**A Perceptual Map of Breakfast Cereals**

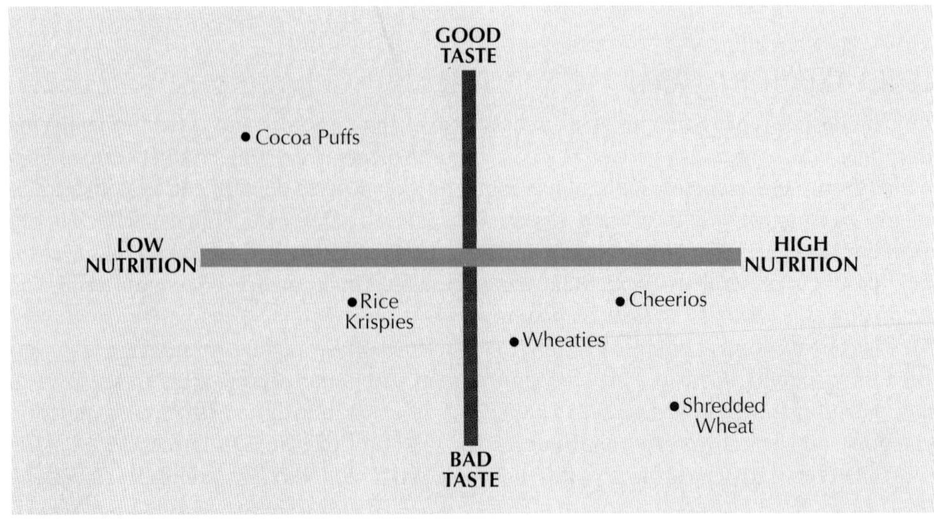

ent line of business. For example, American Express is well known for its ability to get customers to pay up quickly; Disney World, for its employee commitment; Federal Express, for its speed; McDonald's, for its consistency; and Xerox, for its benchmarking techniques.

**Reverse engineering** refers to carefully dismantling and inspecting a competitor's product to look for design features that can be incorporated into your own product. Ford used this approach successfully in its design of the Taurus automobile, assessing 400 features of competitors' products and copying, adapting, or enhancing more than 300 of them, including Audi's accelerator pedal, Toyota's fuel-gauge accuracy, and BMW's tire and jack storage.

**Reverse engineering:** carefully dismantling a competitor's product to improve your own product.

For many products and services, following consumer or competitors' leads is not enough; customers are attracted by superior technology and creative ideas. In these industries, research and development is the primary source of new product ideas. Expenditures for R&D can be enormous ($2 million a day at Kodak!) and investment risky. (Only 1 in 20 ideas ever becomes a product and only 1 in 10 new products is successful.) In addition, ideas generated by R&D may follow a long path to commercialization.

The design process can also be outsourced to a design firm, as shown in the following "Competitive Edge" box.

## THE COMPETITIVE EDGE

### Great Ideas From IDEO

IDEO is a 350-person design firm located in Palo Alto, California, with offices in San Francisco, Chicago, Boston, London, and Munich. Renowned for its innovative approach to design, the firm designs customer "experiences" rather than products or services. You've seen IDEO designs—the Palm V, Polaroid's I-Zone camera, Steelcase's Leap Chair, Zinio interactive magazines, Crest's standup toothpaste tube, AT&T's mMode, and more. IDEO is thorough and fast. Its famous five-step process consists of:

1. ***Observation*** Understand the consumer experience by shadowing customers, photographing customers within a space, tracking consumer interactions, and keeping visual diaries. User interviews are diverse, extreme (those who know nothing about a product and those who know everything), and personal (users tell stories about their experiences).
2. ***Brainstorming*** Generate ideas based on the data gathered through observation. The session lasts no more than an hour and is governed by specific rules that deter judgment, prevent interruptions, and keep the group focused. Participants are encouraged to build on the ideas of others, generate large quantities of ideas, think visually, and say anything that comes to mind, no matter how outlandish.
3. ***Rapid Prototyping*** Mockup models to help visualize proposals and speed up decision making. Build mockups quickly and cheaply. Create scenarios, use videos, and act out customer roles. Don't sweat the details, just get the concept down.
4. ***Refining*** Weed out the prototypes and refine the remaining options. Engage the client in narrowing down the choices. Focus on the outcome of the process. Be disciplined. Get agreement from stakeholders.
5. ***Implementation*** Use a diverse workforce to carry out the plans. IDEO employs engineers of all types, as well as sociologists, psychologists, artists, computer scientists, manufacturers, linguists, and more.

One of IDEO's most unique designs is the interactive dressing room in Prada's upscale retail store. The dressing room is a simple eight-foot-square booth with glass walls that switch from transparent to translucent when a room is occupied. Once inside, the customer can switch the doors back to transparent at the touch of a switch to show off a garment to someone outside the booth. There are two interactive closets in the dressing room, one for hanging clothes and one with shelves. As garments are hung in the closet or placed on the shelves, their RFID (radio frequency ID) tags are automatically scanned and information about alternative sizes, colors, fabrics, and styles is displayed on an interactive touch screen.

The dressing room also contains a video-based *Magic Mirror*. As the customer begins to turn in front of the mirror, the image becomes delayed, allowing the customer to view him- or herself in slow motion from all angles. Different lighting conditions can be selected from a warm evening glow to cool blue daylight. A recording of the session can be saved to the customer's Prada card or e-mailed to a friend.

Sales associates are equipped with a handheld "staff device" for scanning merchandise, checking inventory availability, communicating with the customer in the dressing room, and controlling the video display. This enables the sales associate to spend more time attending personally to a customer and less time chasing to the stock room to check for available items.

At Prada, IDEO combined technology with personal attention for the ultimate shopping experience.

*Sources:* Bruce Nussbaum, "The Power of Design," *Business Week* (May 17, 2004), pp. 86–94; Jeannette Brown, "Prada Gets Personal," *Business Week E-Biz* (March 18, 2002); www.ideo.com/case-studies/prada (accessed June 30, 2004).

## FEASIBILITY STUDY

A feasibility study consists of a *market analysis*, an *economic analysis*, and a *technical/strategic analysis*.

Marketing takes the ideas that are generated and the customer needs that are identified from the first stage of the design process and formulates alternative product and service concepts. The promising concepts undergo a feasibility study that includes several types of analyses, beginning with a *market analysis*. Most companies have staffs of market researchers who can design and evaluate customer surveys, interviews, focus groups, or market tests. The market analysis assesses whether there's enough demand for the proposed product to invest in developing it further.

If the demand potential exists, then there's an *economic analysis* that looks at estimates of production and development costs and compares them to estimated sales volume. A price range for the product that is compatible with the market segment and image of the new product is discussed. Quantitative techniques such as cost/benefit analysis, decision theory, net present value, or internal rate of return are commonly used to evaluate the profit potential of the project. The data used in the analysis are far from certain. Estimates of risk in the new product venture and the company's attitude toward risk are also considered.

Finally, there are *technical* and *strategic analyses* that answer such questions as: Does the new product require new technology? Is the risk or capital investment excessive? Does the company have sufficient labor and management skills to support the required technology? Is sufficient capacity available for production? Does the new product provide a competitive advantage for the company? Does it draw on corporate strengths? Is it compatible with the core business of the firm?

*Performance specifications* are written for product concepts that pass the feasibility study and are approved for development. They describe the function of the product—that is, what the product should do to satisfy customer needs.

## RAPID PROTOTYPING

Designers take general performance specifications and transform them into a physical product or service with technical design specifications. The process involves building a prototype, testing the prototype, revising the design, retesting, and so on, until a viable design is determined.

**Rapid protyping:** testing and revising a preliminary design model.

**Rapid prototyping** as the name implies, creates preliminary design models that are quickly tested and either discarded (as fast failures) or further refined. The models can be physical or electronic, rough facsimiles or full-scale working models. The iterative process involves *form* and *functional design*, as well as *production design*.

## FORM DESIGN

**Form design:** how the product will look.

**Form design** refers to the physical appearance of a product—its shape, color, size, and style. Aesthetics such as image, market appeal, and personal identification are also part of form design. In many cases, functional design must be adjusted to make the product look or feel right. For example, the form design of Mazda's Miata sports car went further than looks—the exhaust had to have a certain "sound," the gearshift lever a certain "feel," and the seat and window arrangement the proper dimensions to encourage passengers to ride with their elbows out.

## FUNCTIONAL DESIGN

**Functional design:** how the product will perform.

**Reliability:** the probability that a product will perform its intended function for a specified period of time.

**Functional design** is concerned with how the product performs. It seeks to meet the performance specifications of fitness for use by the customer. Three performance characteristics considered during this phase of design are *reliability*, *maintainability* and *usability*.

### Reliability

**Reliability** is the probability that a given part or product will perform its intended function for a specified length of time under normal conditions of use. You may be familiar with reliability information from product warranties. A hair dryer might be guaranteed to function (i.e., blow air with a certain force at a certain temperature) for one year under normal conditions of use (defined to be 300 hours of operation). A car warranty might extend for three years or 50,000 miles. Normal conditions of use would include regularly scheduled oil changes and other minor maintenance activities. A missed oil change or mileage in excess of 50,000 miles in a three-year period would not be considered "normal" and would nullify the warranty.

A product or system's reliability is a function of the reliabilities of its component parts and how the parts are arranged. If all parts must function for the product or system to operate, then the system reliability is the *product* of the component part reliabilities.

$$R_s = (R_1)(R_2)\dots(R_n), \text{ where } R_n \text{ is the reliability of the } n\text{th component.}$$

For example, if two component parts are required and each has a reliability of 0.90, the reliability of the system is $0.90 \times 0.90 = 0.81$, or 81%. The system can be visualized as a *series* of components as follows:

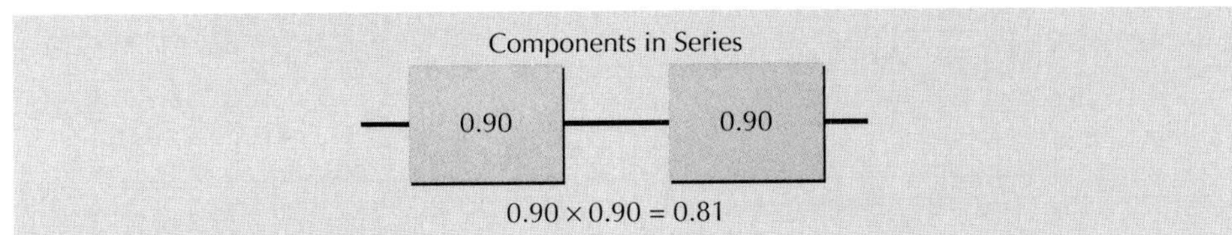


Note that the system reliability of 0.81 is considerably less than the component reliabilities of 0.90. As the number of serial components increases, system reliability will continue to deteriorate. This makes a good argument for simple designs with fewer components!

Failure of some components in a system is more critical than others—the brakes on a car, for instance. To increase the reliability of individual parts (and thus the system as a whole), *redundant* parts can be built in to back up a failure. Providing emergency brakes for a car is an example. Consider the following redundant design with $R_1$ representing the reliability of the original component and $R_2$ the reliability of the backup component.

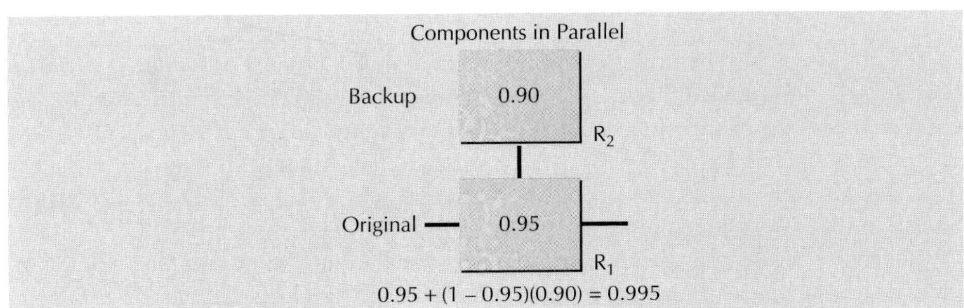


These components are said to operate in *parallel*. If the original component fails (a 5% chance), the backup component will automatically kick in to take its place—but only 90% of the time. Thus, the reliability of the system is[1]

$$\begin{aligned} R_s &= R_1 + (1 - R_1)(R_2) \\ &= 0.95 + (1 - 0.95)(0.90) = 0.995 \end{aligned}$$

Example 5.1

**Reliability**

Determine the reliability of the system of components shown below.

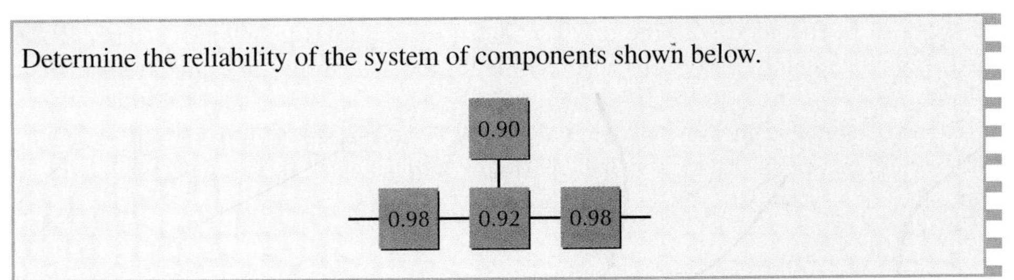


[1]The reliability of parallel components can also be calculated as $R_s = 1 - [(1 - R_1)(1 - R_2)\dots]$.

*Solution*

First, reduce the system to a *series* of three components,

0.98 — 0.92 + (1 − 0.92)(0.90) = 0.99 — 0.98

Then calculate the reliability of the series.

$$0.98 \times 0.99 \times 0.98 = 0.951$$

The Excel solution to this problem is shown in Exhibit 5.1.

Exhibit 5.1

**Using Excel for Calculating Reliability**

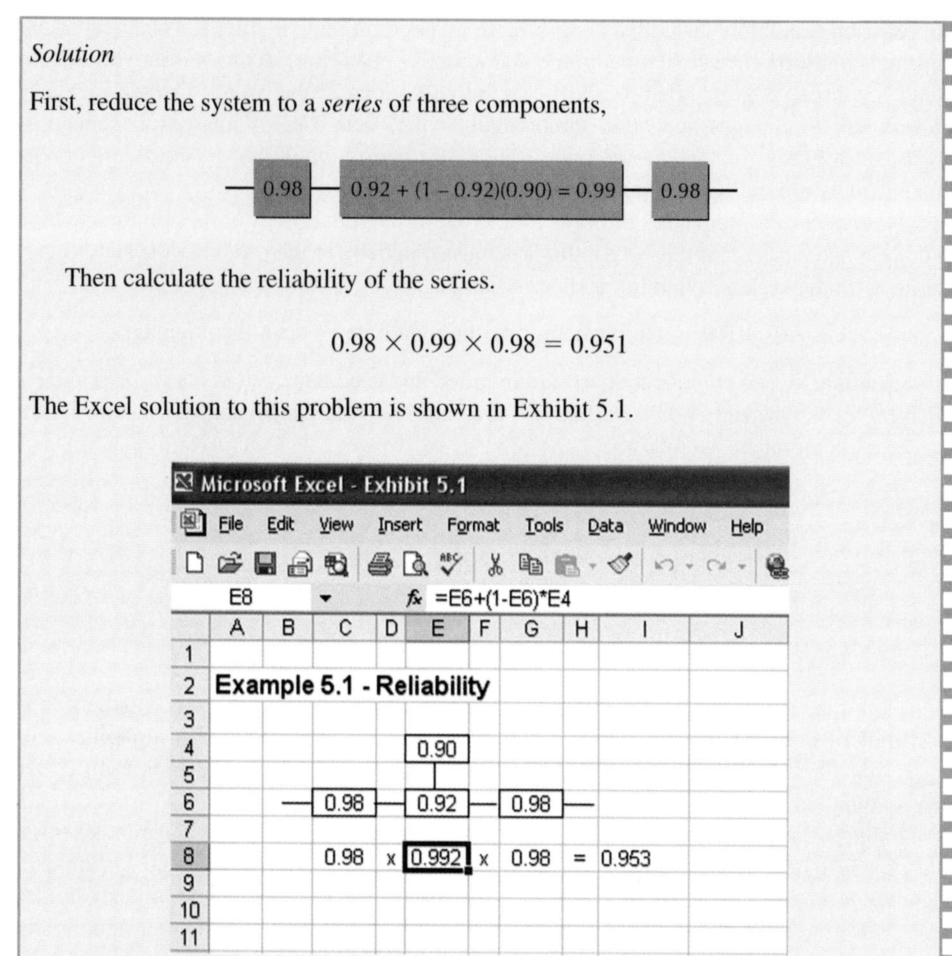


Reliability can also be expressed as the length of time a product or service is in operation before it fails, called the *mean time between failures* (MTBF). In this case, we are concerned with the distribution of failures over time, or the *failure rate*. The MTBF is the reciprocal of the failure rate (MTBF = 1/failure rate). For example, if your laptop battery fails four times in 20 hours of operation, its failure rate would be 4/20 = 0.20, and its MTBF = 1/0.20 = 5 hours.

Reliability can be improved by simplifying product design, improving the reliability of individual components, or adding redundant components. Products that are easier to manufacture or assemble, are well maintained, and have users who are trained in proper use have higher reliability.

**Maintainability:** the ease with which a product is maintained or repaired.

**Maintainability** (also called *serviceability*) refers to the ease and/or cost with which a product or service is maintained or repaired. Products can be made easier to maintain by assembling them in modules, like computers, so that entire control panels, cards, or disk drives can be replaced when they malfunction. The location of critical parts or parts subject to failure affects the ease of disassembly and, thus, repair. Instructions that teach consumers how to anticipate malfunctions and correct them themselves can be included with the product. Specifying regular maintenance schedules is part of maintainability, as is proper planning for the availability of critical replacement parts.

One quantitative measure of maintainability is mean time to repair (MTTR). Combined with the reliability measure of MTBF, we can calculate the average availability or "uptime" of a system as

$$\text{System Availability, SA} = \frac{\text{MTBF}}{\text{MTBF} + \text{MTTR}}$$

**Example 5.2**
**System Availability**

Amy Russell must choose a service provider for her company's e-commerce site. Other factors being equal, she will base her decision on server availability. Given the following server performance data, which provider should she choose?

| Provider | MTBF (hr) | MTTR (hr) |
|---|---|---|
| A | 60 | 4.0 |
| B | 36 | 2.0 |
| C | 24 | 1.0 |

*Solution*

$$SA = \frac{MTBF}{MTBF + MTTR}$$

$$SA_A = 60/(60 + 4) = 0.9375 \text{ or } 94\%$$

$$SA_B = 36/(36 + 2) = 0.9473 \text{ or } 95\%$$

$$SA_C = 24/(24 + 1) = 0.96 \text{ or } 96\%$$

Amy should choose Provider C.

The Excel solution to this problem is shown in Exhibit 5.2 below.

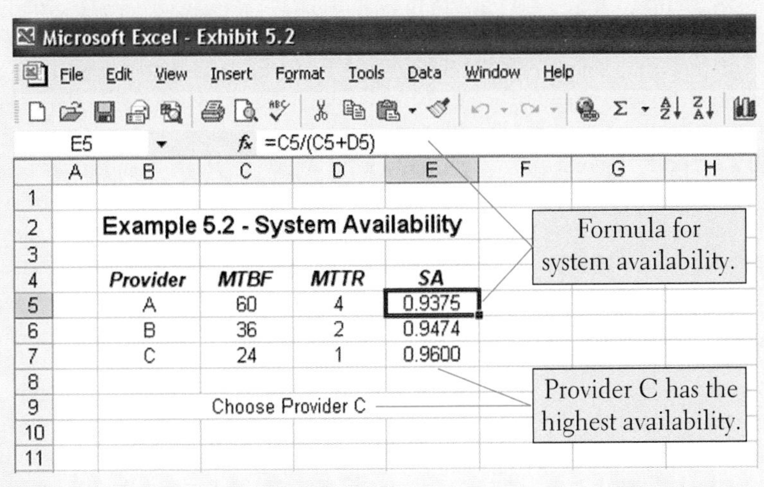

**Exhibit 5.2**
**Using Excel for System Availability**

## Usability

All of us have encountered products or services that are difficult or cumbersome to use. Consider

- Cup holders in cars that, when occupied, hide the radio buttons or interfere with the stick shift.
- Salt shakers that must be turned upside down to fill (thereby losing their contents).
- Speakers in laptop computers that are covered by your wrists as you type.
- Doors that you can't tell whether to pull or push.
- Remote controls with more and more buttons of smaller and smaller size for TV, cable, stereo, VCR, DVD, and more.
- Levers for popping the trunk of a car and unlocking the gas cap located too close together.

These are usability issues in design. **Usability** is what makes a product or service easy to use and a good fit for its targeted customer. It is a combination of factors that affect the user's experience with a product, including ease of learning, ease of use, and ease of

**Usability:** ease of use of a product or service.

*One aspect of usability is assessing how many functions to assign to a product.*

*"Can you hang on a sec? I think I just took another picture of my ear."*

remembering how to use, frequency and severity of errors, and user satisfaction with the experience.[2]

Although usability engineers have long been a part of the design process, their use has skyrocketed with computer, software, and Web site design. Forrester Research estimates that 50% of potential sales from Web sites are lost from customers who cannot locate what they need. Researchers have found that Internet users have a particularly low tolerance for poorly designed sites and cumbersome navigation.

Apple Computer revolutionized the computer industry with its intuitive, easy-to-use designs. Today, Microsoft employs over 140 usability engineers. Before a design is deemed functional, it must go through usability testing. Simpler, more standardized designs are usually easier to use. They are also easier to produce, as we'll see in the next section.

## PRODUCTION DESIGN

**Production design:** how the product will be made.

**Production design** is concerned with how the product will be made. Designs that are difficult to make often result in poor-quality products. Engineers tend to overdesign products, with too many features, options, and parts. Lack of knowledge of manufacturing capabilities can result in designs that are impossible to make or require skills and resources not currently available. Many times, production personnel find themselves redesigning products on the factory floor. Late changes in design are both costly and disruptive. An adjustment in one part may necessitate an adjustment in other parts, "unraveling" the entire product design. That's why production design is considered in the preliminary design phase. Recommended approaches to production design include *simplification, standardization*, and *modularity*.

**Simplification:** reduces the number of parts, assemblies, or options in a product.

Design **simplification** attempts to reduce the number of parts, subassemblies, and options in a product. It also means avoiding tools, separate fasteners, and adjustments. We'll illustrate simplification with an example. Consider the case of the toolbox shown in Figure 5.3. The company wants to increase productivity by using automated assembly. The initial design in Figure 5.3*a* contains 24 common parts (mostly nuts and bolts fasteners) and requires 84 seconds to assemble. The design does not appear to be complex for manual assembly, but can be quite complicated for a robot to assemble.

As shown in Figure 5.3*b*, the team assigned to revise the design simplified the toolbox by molding the base as one piece and eliminating the fasteners. Plastic inserts snap over the spindle to hold it in place. The number of parts was reduced to four, and the assembly time cut to 12 seconds. This represents a significant gain in productivity, from 43 assemblies per hour to 300 assemblies per hour.

[2]These are described on http://www.usability.gov.

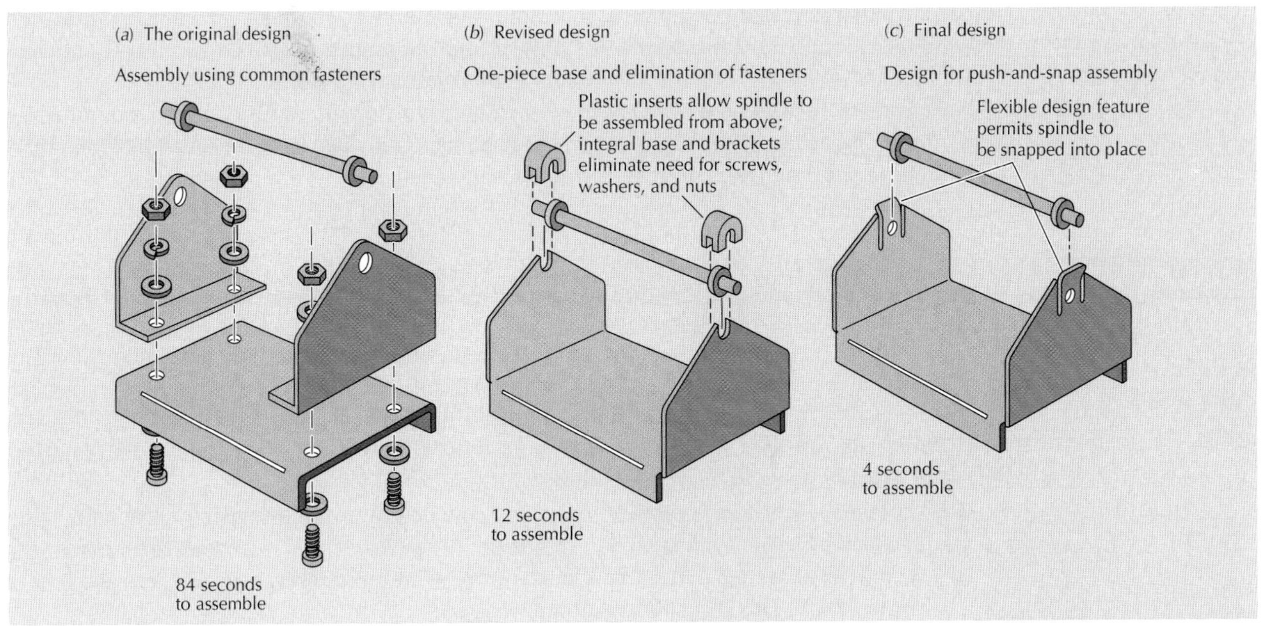


**Figure 5.3**

**Design Simplification**

*Source:* Adapted from G. Boothroyd and P. Dewhurst, "Product Design . . . Key to Successful Robotic Assembly," *Assembly Engineering* (September 1986), pp. 90–93.

Figure 5.3*c* shows an even simpler design, consisting of only two parts, a base and spindle. The spindle is made of flexible material, allowing it to be snapped downward into place in a quick, one-motion assembly. Assembly time is reduced to 4 seconds, increasing production to 900 assemblies an hour. With this final design, the team agreed that the assembly task was too simple for a robot. Indeed, many manufacturers have followed this process in rediscovering the virtues of simplification—in redesigning a product for automation, they found that automation isn't necessary!

Using standard parts in a product or throughout many products saves design time, tooling costs, and production worries. **Standardization** makes possible the interchangeability of parts among products, resulting in higher-volume production and purchasing, lower investment in inventory, easier purchasing and material handling, fewer quality inspections, and fewer difficulties in production. Some products, such as light bulbs, batteries, and DVDs, benefit from being totally standardized. For others, being different is a competitive advantage. The question becomes how to gain the cost benefits of standardization without losing the market advantage of variety and uniqueness.

**Standardization:** when commonly available and interchangeable parts are used.

One solution is **modular design**. Modular design consists of combining standardized building blocks, or *modules*, in a variety of ways to create unique finished products. Modular design is common in the electronics industry and the automobile industry. Dell and Gateway customers build their own PCs from a variety of standard modules. Toyota's Camry, Corolla, and Lexus share the same body chassis. Even Campbell's Soup Company practices modular design by producing large volumes of four basic broths (beef, chicken, tomato, and seafood bisque) and then adding special ingredients to produce 125 varieties of final soup products.

**Modular design:** combines standardized building blocks, or modules, to create unique finished products.

## FINAL DESIGN AND PROCESS PLANS

In the preliminary design stage, prototypes are built and tested. After several iterations, a pilot run of the process is conducted. Adjustments are made as needed before the final design is agreed on. In this way, the *design specifications* for the new product have considered how the product is to be produced, and the *manufacturing* or *delivery specifications* more closely reflect the intent of the design. This should mean fewer revisions in the design as the product is manufactured and service provided. Design changes, known as engineering change orders (ECOs), are a major source of delay and cost overruns in the product development process.

The *final design* consists of detailed drawings and specifications for the new product or service. The accompanying *process plans* are workable instructions for manufacture, including necessary equipment and tooling, component sourcing recommendations, job descriptions and procedures for workers, and computer programs for automated machines. We discuss process planning in more detail in Chapter 6.

Launching the new product or service involves ramping up production, coordinating the supply chain, and rolling out marketing plans. This is one of the areas in which marketing and production must work very closely together.

## REDUCING TIME-TO-MARKET

Many companies known for creativity and innovation in product design are slow and ineffective in getting new products to the market. Problems in converting ideas to finished products may be caused by poor manufacturing practices, but more than likely they are the result of poor design. Design decisions affect sales strategies, efficiency of manufacture, speed of repair, and product cost.

Reducing the time-to-market involves completely restructuring the decision-making process and the participants in that process. The series of *walls* between functional areas portrayed in Figure 5.4, must be broken down and replaced with new alliances and modes of interaction. This feat can be accomplished by:

1. Establishing multifunctional *design teams.*
2. Making design decisions *concurrently* rather than sequentially.
3. Designing for *manufacture* and *assembly*.
4. Using technology in the design process.
5. Engaging in *collaborative design*.

### DESIGN TEAMS

A team approach to design has proved to be successful worldwide. Full-time participants from marketing, manufacturing, and engineering are essential to effective product design. Customers, dealers, suppliers, lawyers, accountants, and others are also useful

**Figure 5.4**
**Breaking Down the Barriers to Effective Design**

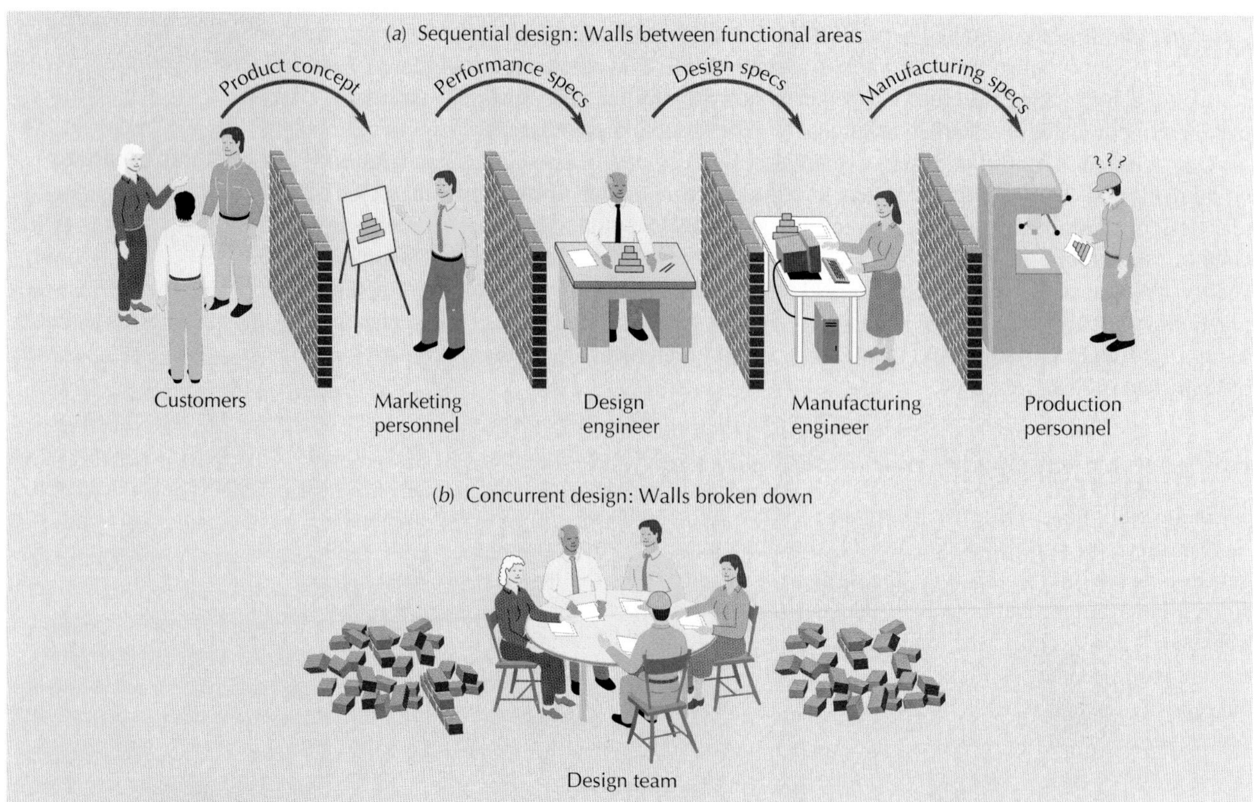

*GM's AUTOnomy design packs all functional elements of a fuel cell powertrain into a flat skateboard-like chassis. The chassis can be detached from the car body so that owners can have new customized bodies with various seating and storage options plugged into their original chassis.*

team members. A study of new product launchings in high-technology firms concluded that the critical factor between success and failure was the involvement and interaction of the "create, make, and market" functions from the beginning of the design project.

Design teams allowed DaimlerChrysler to bring the Viper sports car from concept to full production in less than three years and $2 million under budget. Working in a team was a cultural change for DaimlerChrysler engineers. The team (ranging from 20 to 85 members) met in one large room of a refurbished warehouse. Walls were literally torn down to encourage team members to communicate and work together. The same team approach was later instrumental in the design of the innovative PT Cruiser, a car that combines both "the emotional and rational needs of the customer." The development team used the virtual reality to "step into" a computer-generated three-dimensional interior of the car. Suppliers participated in building pilot models of the car at the Auburn Hills design center and at preproduction planning at the Toluca plant in Mexico where the car is being built. Assembly-line workers were trained at each manufacturing station of the mock assembly line set up in the design facility. By field-testing each work station as it was developed, the workers were able to point out potential assembly problems to the engineers before they committed to a design. When the testing was complete, each worker had received more than 600 hours of training and could assemble the car from scratch. The design team was not dismantled when the design was finished. Although smaller in size, it exists to this day and will remain intact for the life of the product to continually work on design improvements.

Involve production workers in the design.

*By-wire technology replaces the steering column and pedals with a driving control unit. The driver twists the hand-grips to accelerate and squeezes them to brake.*

Team members co-locate.

Design teams at Lands' End consist of a merchandiser, an inventory manager, a quality assurance specialist, a copywriter, an artist, and a support person. Each team is assigned a major product category, such as adult sleepwear. Team members co-locate, sharing a workspace where team meetings, vendor appointments, and product-fit sessions are held. Since the teams have been operational, the average time to bring new products to market has decreased significantly, and fewer design changes are necessary. Teams help people do their jobs better, improve communications, spark creativity, and are "just more fun."

The idea of teamwork in software design has changed, too. Instead of letting individuals "own" large portions of code that are later combined and tested for bugs, new design practices call for pairs of programmers to work on small, well-defined tasks. As the tasks are finished, the programmers move on to test and refine programs written by other programming pairs. Even the office layout reflects the change, with two programmers per workstation and workstations located about a foot apart. This radically different approach to teamwork is called *extreme programming* (XP).[3]

## CONCURRENT DESIGN

**Concurrent design:** a new approach to design that involves the simultaneous design of products and processes by design teams.

**Concurrent design** helps improve the quality of early design decisions and thereby reduces the length and cost of the design process. Design decisions overlap; therefore, one stage of design is not completely finished before another stage begins.

One example of concurrent design is suppliers who complete the detailed design for the parts they will supply. In the traditional design process, manufacturers determine component design in detail, down to the fraction of an inch, including the specific material to be used. Detailed engineering drawings are made, and only then are suppliers called in to submit their bids. Many of today's successful manufacturers, on the other hand, provide general performance specifications to their component suppliers, such as:

> *Design a set of brakes that can stop a 2,200-pound car from 60 miles per hour in 200 feet ten times in succession without fading. The brakes should fit into a space 6 inches × 8 inches × 10 inches at the end of each axle and be delivered to the assembly plant for $40 a set.*[4]

The supplier is asked to prepare a prototype for testing. Detailed decisions are left up to the supplier, as a member of the design team who is the expert in that area. This approach saves considerable development time and resources.

Involve suppliers and manufacturing in the design process.

Concurrent design also involves incorporating the production process into design decisions. In many cases, design engineers do not have a good understanding of the capabilities or limitations of their company's manufacturing facilities; increased contact with manufacturing can sensitize them to the realities of making a product. Simply consulting manufacturing personnel early in the design process about critical factors or constraints can improve the quality of product design. This is where most companies begin their efforts in changing the corporate culture from a separate design function to one that is integrated with operations.

One more difference between sequential design and concurrent design is the manner in which prices are set and costs are determined. In the traditional process, the feasibility study includes some estimate of the price to be charged to the customer. However, that selling price is not firmed up until the end of the design process, when all the product costs are accumulated and a profit margin is attached, and it is determined whether the original price estimate and the resulting figure are close. This is a *cost-plus* approach. If there are discrepancies, either the product is sold at the new price, a new feasibility study is made, or the designers go back and try to cut costs. Remember that design decisions are interrelated; the further back in the process you go, the more expensive are the changes.

Use price-minus costing.

Concurrent design uses a *price-minus* system. A selling price (that will give some advantage in the marketplace) is determined before design details are developed. Then a *target*

[3]Julie Pitta, "Get Smart," *Forbes* (July 9, 2001), p. 142. For more information, see Kent Beck's *Extreme Programming Explained* (Reading, MA: Addison-Wesley, 1999).

[4]J. P. Womack, D. T. Jones, and D. Roos, *The Machine that Changed the World* (New World: Macmillan, 1990), pp. 157, 160.

*cost* of production is set and evaluated at every stage of product and process design. Techniques such as value analysis (which we discuss later) are used to keep costs in line.

Because concurrent design requires that more tasks be performed in parallel, the scheduling of those tasks is more complex than ever. Project-scheduling techniques, such as PERT/CPM (discussed in Chapter 9), are used to coordinate the myriad interconnected decisions that constitute concurrent design.

## DESIGN FOR MANUFACTURE AND ASSEMBLY

**Design for manufacture and assembly (DFMA)** is the process of designing a product so that it can be produced easily and economically. The term was coined in an effort to emphasize the importance of incorporating production design early in the design process. When successful, DFMA not only improves the quality of product design but also reduces both the time and cost of product design and manufacture.

**DFMA:** designing a product so that it can be produced easily and economically.

Specific *design for manufacture* (DFM) software can recommend materials and processes appropriate for a design and provide manufacturing cost estimates throughout the design process. More generally, DFM guidelines promote good design practice, such as:

1. Minimize the number of parts and subassemblies.
2. Avoid tools, separate fasteners, and adjustments.
3. Use standard parts when possible and repeatable, well-understood processes.
4. Design parts for many uses, and modules that can be combined in different ways.
5. Design for ease of assembly, minimal handling, and proper presentation.
6. Allow for efficient and adequate testing and replacement of parts.

**Design for assembly (DFA)** is a set of procedures for reducing the number of parts in an assembly, evaluating methods for assembly, and determining an assembly sequence.[5] The best sequence of assembly differs considerably for manual versus automated assembly. Manual assembly is concerned with maintaining a balance between operations on the assembly line, whereas automated assembly is concerned with minimizing the reorientation of parts for assembly. Common assembly mistakes include hiding parts that later need to be inspected, dissembling already assembled parts to fit new parts in, and making it difficult to access parts that need maintenance or repair.

**DFA:** a set of procedures for reducing the number of parts in an assembly, evaluating methods of assembly, and determining an assembly sequence.

## TECHNOLOGY IN DESIGN

New products for more segmented markets have proliferated over the past decade. Changes in product design are more frequent, and product life cycles are shorter. IBM estimates the average life of its new product offerings is about six months. Sony has introduced more than 160 different models of its Walkman over the past 10 years. The ability to get new products to the market quickly has revolutionized the competitive environment and changed the nature of manufacturing. Read about retailer H&M's remarkable design-to-hanger time in the "Competitive Edge" box that follows.

Part of the impetus for the deluge of new products is the advancement of technology available for designing products. It begins with computer-aided design (CAD) and includes related technologies such as computer-aided engineering (CAE) and computer-aided manufacturing (CAM).

**Computer-aided design (CAD)** is a software system that uses computer graphics to assist in the creation, modification, and analysis of a design. CAD can be used for geometric modeling, automated drafting and documentation, engineering analysis, and design analysis. *Geometric modeling* uses basic lines, curves, and shapes to generate the geometry and topology of a part. The part may appear as a wire mesh image or as a shaded, solid model. Once an object has been input into the system, it can be displayed and manipulated in a variety of ways. The design can be rotated for a front, side, or top view, separated into different parts, enlarged for closer inspection, or shrunk back so that another feature can be highlighted. The

**CAD:** assists in the creation, modification, and analysis of a design.

[5] DFA, developed by Professors Boothroyd and Dewhurst, has been incorporated into a software product called DFMA (design for manufacture and assembly). See www.dfma.com for more information.

## THE COMPETITIVE EDGE

### H&M's Lightning Fast Design-to-Market Time

Design in the fashion industry is paramount, and for 15- to 30-year-olds, Swedish retailer Hennes and Mauritz (H&M) is hot. H&M treats fashion as if it were perishable produce. Its motto is: *keep it fresh, keep it moving*. Faster turnaround means higher sales, which help H&M charge lower prices and earn higher profits. But providing low-cost merchandise fast is not a good combination unless the designs are fashionable.

H&M's 90 designers, all located in the Stockholm office, create design concepts for an international customer base. The concept stage starts with trips around the world observing and studying the way people live and work. Art, music, film, theatre, television, sports, and street fashions are important references. Themes, colors, fabric, and silhouettes start to emerge as a basis for the year's fashions. For example, 2002 featured "simple unconventional fashions with ethnic elements," while 2003 emphasized "individuality in a seventies-inspired mix of styles."

After the theme has been established, the actual design process begins with consultations with pattern designers, buyers, and controllers. The buyer takes care of contacting the production offices, which select and manage the suppliers. The sales merchandiser for each country provides information on sales patterns and trends. The controller establishes a budget and manages the project. "Our employees need to have the right instincts and a great interest in fashion, and they must be sensitive to trends," says CEO Rolf Eriksen.

And sensitive they are—H&M is the fastest source of trends for the fashion market. They accomplish this by constantly putting new merchandise into their stores to test buyer reactions. What sets H&M apart from its competitors is its lightning fast design-to-market time. It can move a garment from design to hanger in just 20 days. Gap's minimum is three months but only for unusual circumstances. Its average turnaround is nine months. H&M's speed allows it to churn out more hot sellers during a season and pull back on those items that aren't selling so well. If it makes a mistake with a design, the damage doesn't last long. And because the merchandise does not stay in the store long, there are no sales and price reductions that cut into profit margins.

H&M stores are restocked daily, except during peak seasons when they are restocked hourly if necessary. Working closely with suppliers, H&M's 21 local production offices have squeezed the slack out of lead times, with reductions of 15 to 20% over the past three years. Ten of the production offices are located in Europe, ten in Asia, and one in Africa. They employ nearly 600 workers who are responsible for working with 900 suppliers that produce over half a billion items for H&M each year. They monitor quality and working conditions, and they also ensure that orders are placed with the appropriate supplier. Where an order is placed depends on many factors, including price, transit times, import regulations, currency exchange rates, and quality. Fabrics are purchased in bulk in advance; dyeing and cutting wait until later. Inspection of sample garments and final decisions on acceptance are made at the local production offices.

*H&M Runway Model. Fashion changes rapidly. Suppliers must be able to react to changing trends and reduced lead times. H&M can turn a garment from design to hanger in 20 days. Courtesy of H&M.*

Over 3000 people work in H&M's logistics function. Fast and efficient flows of material are critical to the company's strategy. Getting the right goods in the right volume to the right country, city, and store at the right time demands a well-functioning distribution system. H&M acts as importer, wholesaler, and retailer, thereby keeping the number of links and stops in the supply chain to a minimum.

H&M wins with great designs. And those great designs are made possible by a fine-tuned operations system that can react to changing trends and nuances in demand.

*Sources:* Sarah Raper Larenaudie, "Inside the H&M Fashion Machine," *Time* (Spring 2004), p. 48; Kerry Capell and Gerry Khermouch, "Hip H&M The Swedish Retailer Reinvents the World of Affordable Fashion," *Business Week* (November 11, 2002), p. 106; Cecilie Rohwedder, "Style & Substance: Making Fashion Faster; As Knockoffs Beat Originals to Market, Designers Speed the Trip from Sketch to Store," *Wall Street Journal* (February 24, 2004), p. B1; Hennes and Mauritz company Web site http://www.hm.com.

*Computer-aided design (CAD) is used to design everything from pencils to submarines. Some of our everyday products are more difficult to design than you may think. Potato chips with ridges, the top of a soda can, a two-liter bottle of soft drink, a car door, and golf balls are examples of simple products that require the sophistication of CAD for effective design and testing. Shown here are two examples of dimple design on Titleist golf balls. The number, size, and patterns of dimples on a golf ball can affect the distance, trajectory, and accuracy of play. The advent of CAD has allowed many more designs to be tested. Today, more than 200 different dimple patterns are used by golf-ball manufacturers. Golf clubs and golf courses are also designed using CAD.*

CAD file created from the geometric design includes not only the dimensions of the product but also tolerance information and material specifications. The ability to sort, classify, and retrieve similar designs from a CAD database facilitates standardization of parts, prompts ideas, and eliminates building a design from scratch. The result is a better design 12 times faster.

CAD-generated products can also be tested more quickly. Engineering analysis, performed with a CAD system, is called **computer-aided engineering (CAE)**. CAE retrieves the description and geometry of a part from a CAD database and subjects it to testing and analysis on the computer screen without physically building a prototype. CAE can maximize the storage space in a car trunk, detect whether plastic parts are cooling evenly, and determine how much stress will cause a bridge to crack. With CAE, design teams can watch a car bump along a rough road, the pistons of an engine move up and down, or a golf ball soar through the air. In the field of chemistry, reactions of chemicals can be analyzed on a computer screen. And, in medicine, the effects of new drugs can be tested on computer-generated DNA molecules. *Cyberman*, a computer mannequin, tests the ergonomics of a design by examining arm reach, pedal position, and steering-column angle for automobiles. Testing by computer significantly reduces the time-to-market for new products, and ensures better fit and performance of product components.

**CAE:**
a software system that tests and analyzes designs on the computer screen.

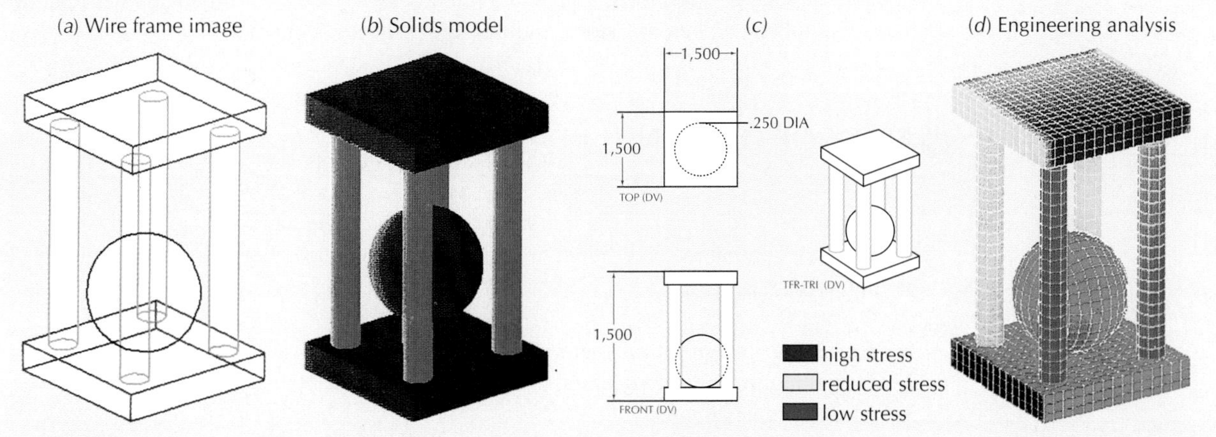


*CAD systems can display a product as a wire mesh image, a solids model, or a blueprint. Coupled with CAE, they can also perform sophisticated engineering analyses.*

**CAD/CAM:** the ultimate design-to-manufacture connection.

The ultimate design-to-manufacture connection is a **CAD/CAM** system. CAM is the acronym for *computer-aided manufacturing*. CAD/CAM involves the automatic conversion of CAD design data into processing instructions for computer-controlled equipment and the subsequent manufacture of the part as it was designed. This integration of design and manufacture can save enormous amounts of time, ensure that parts and products are produced *precisely* as intended, and facilitate revisions in design or customized production.

CAD and its related technologies produce better designs faster.

Besides the time savings, CAD and its related technologies have also improved the *quality* of designs and the products manufactured from them. The communications capabilities of CAD may be more important than its processing capabilities in terms of design quality. CAD systems enhance communication and promote innovation in multifunctional design teams by providing a visual, interactive focus for discussion. Watching a vehicle strain its wheels over mud and ice prompts ideas on product design and customer use better than stacks of consumer surveys or engineering reports. New ideas can be suggested and tested immediately, allowing more alternatives to be evaluated. To facilitate discussion or clarify a design, CAD data can be sent electronically between designer and supplier or viewed simultaneously on computer screens by different designers in physically separate locations. Rapid prototypes can be tested more thoroughly with CAD/CAE. More prototypes can be tested as well. CAD improves every stage of product design and is especially useful as a means of integrating design and manufacture.

### COLLABORATIVE PRODUCT COMMERCE

The benefits of CAD-designed products are magnified when combined with the Internet. The ability to share product-design files and work on them in real time from physically separate locations is invaluable to the development process. Collaborative design can take place between designers in the same company, between manufacturers and suppliers, or between manufacturers and customers. Manufacturers can send out product designs electronically with request for quotes (RFQ) from potential component suppliers. Or performance specs can be posted to a Web site from which suppliers can create and transmit their own designs. Designs can receive final approval from customers before expensive processing takes place. A complex design can involve hundreds of suppliers. The Web allows them to work together throughout the design and manufacturing processes, not just at the beginning and the end.

**CPC:** a software system for collaborative design and development among trading partners; it follows the life cycle of the product.

Software systems for collaborative design are loosely referred to as **collaborative product commerce (CPC)**. These systems provide the interconnectivity and translation capabilities necessary for collaborative work across platforms, departments, and companies. They also manage product data, set up project workspaces, and follow product development through the entire product life cycle from inception through manufacture, service, and retirement.

Collaborative design accelerates product development, helps to resolve product launch issues, and improves the quality of the design. Designers can conduct virtual review sessions, test "what if" scenarios, assign and track design issues, communicate with multiple tiers of suppliers, and create, store, and manage project documents.

## IMPROVING THE QUALITY OF DESIGN

As competitive pressures push more new designs to the market more quickly, it is imperative that companies be diligent about the *quality* of those designs. Design quality can be improved by:

1. Reviewing designs to prevent *failures* and ensure *value*.
2. Designing for the *environment*.
3. Measuring *design quality*.
4. Using *quality function deployment*.
5. Designing for *robustness*.

**Table 5.1**
**Failure Mode and Effects Analysis for Potato Chips**

| Failure Mode | Cause of Failure | Effect of Failure | Corrective Action |
|---|---|---|---|
| Stale | Low moisture content, expired shelf life, poor packaging | Tastes bad, won't crunch, thrown out, lost sales | Add moisture, cure longer, better package seal, shorter shelf life |
| Broken | Too thin, too brittle, rough handling, rough use, poor packaging | Can't dip, poor display, injures mouth, choking, perceived as old, lost sales | Change recipe, change process, change packaging |
| Too salty | Outdated recipe, process not in control, uneven distribution of salt | Eat less, drink more, health hazard, lost sales | Experiment with recipe, experiment with process, introduce low-salt version |

## DESIGN REVIEW

Before finalizing a design, formal procedures for analyzing possible failures and rigorously assessing the value of every part and component should be followed. Three such techniques are failure mode and effects analysis (FMEA), fault tree analysis (FTA), and value analysis (VA).

**Failure mode and effects analysis (FMEA)** is a systematic approach to analyzing the causes and effects of product failures. It begins with listing the functions of the product and each of its parts. Failure modes are then defined and ranked in order of their seriousness and likelihood of failure. Failures are addressed one by one (beginning with the most catastrophic), causes are hypothesized, and design changes are made to reduce the chance of failure. The objective of FMEA is to anticipate failures and prevent them from occurring. Table 5.1 shows a partial FMEA for potato chips.

**Failure mode and effects analysis:** a systematic method of analyzing product failures.

**Fault tree analysis (FTA)** is a visual method of analyzing the *interrelationship* among failures. FTA lists failures and their causes in a tree format using two hatlike symbols, one with a straight line on the bottom representing *and* and one with a curved line on the bottom for *or* Figure 5.5 shows a partial FTA for a food manufacturer who has a problem with potato chip breakage. In this analysis, potato chips break because they are too thin *or* because they are too brittle. The options for fixing the problem of too-thin chips—increasing thickness or reducing size—are undesirable, as indicated by the Xs. The problem of too-brittle chips can be alleviated by adding more moisture *or* having fewer ridges *or*

**Fault tree analysis:** a visual method for analyzing the interrelationships among failures.

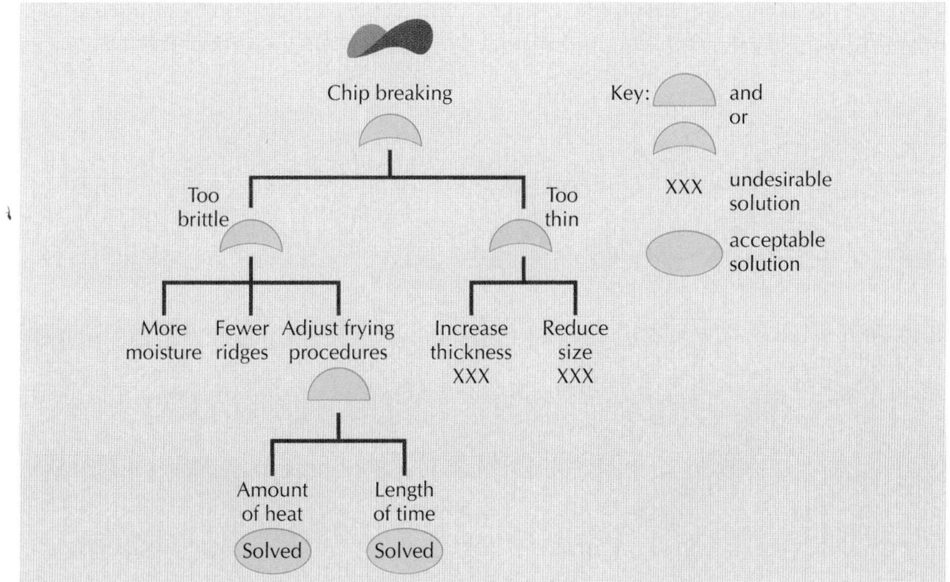


**Figure 5.5**
**Fault Tree Analysis for Potato Chips**

adjusting the frying procedure. We choose to adjust the frying procedure, which leads to the question of how hot the oil should be *and* how long to fry the chips. Once these values are determined, the issue of too-brittle chips (and thus chip breakage) is solved, as indicated.

**Value analysis:** a procedure for eliminating unnecessary features and functions.

**Value analysis (VA)**, also known as value engineering) was developed by General Electric in 1947 to eliminate unnecessary features and functions in product designs. It has reemerged as a technique for use by multifunctional design teams. The design team defines the essential functions of a component, assembly, or product using a verb and a noun. For example, the function of a container might be described as *holds fluid*. Then the team assigns a value to each function and determines the cost of providing the function. With that information, a ratio of value to cost can be calculated for each item. The team attempts to improve the ratio by either reducing the cost of the item or increasing its worth. Every material, every part, and every operation is subjected to such questions as:

1. Can we do without it?
2. Does it do more than is required?
3. Does it cost more than it is worth?
4. Can something else do a better job?
5. Can it be made by a less costly method? with less costly tooling? with less costly material?
6. Can it be made cheaper, better, or faster by someone else?

## DESIGN FOR ENVIRONMENT

Each year Americans dispose of 350 million home and office appliances (50 million of them hair dryers) and more than 10 million PCs. At the current rate of discard, it's not hard to visualize city dumps filled with old refrigerators and computers. These types of images have prompted government and industry to consider the environmental impact of product and service design.

**Design for environment:** designing a product from material that can be recycled or easily repaired rather than discarded.

**Extended producer responsibility:** when companies are held responsible for their product even after its useful life.

**Design for environment (DFE)** involves designing products from recycled material, using materials or components that can be recycled, designing a product so that it is easier to repair than discard, and minimizing unnecessary packaging. As shown in Figure 5.6, it also includes minimizing material and energy use during manufacture, consumption, and disposal.

**Extended producer responsibility (EPR)** is a concept that holds companies responsible for their product even after its useful life. Governments worldwide are enacting regulations, economics incentives, and information requirements for environmentally friendly products and services. German law mandates the collection, recycling, and safe disposal of personal computers and household appliances, including stereos and video appliances, television sets, washing machines, dishwashers, and refrigerators. Some manufacturers pay a tax for recycling; others include the cost of disposal in a product's price.

**Figure 5.6**
**Design for Environment**

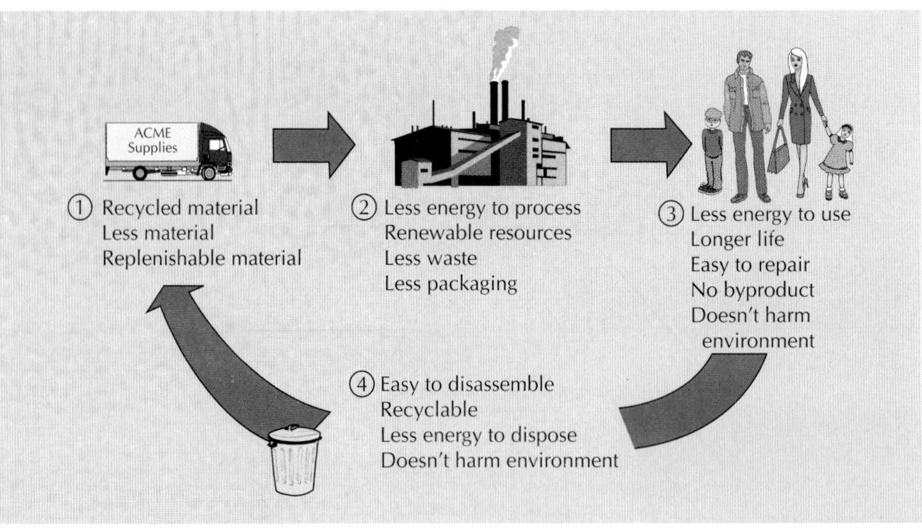

The Netherlands considers television sets chemical waste and requires companies to dispose of them accordingly. Norwegian law requires producers and importers of electronic equipment to recycle or reuse 80% of the product. Nine U.S. states now have "takeback" laws that require the return and recycling of batteries. Brazil considers all packaging that cannot be recycled hazardous waste. The sale of mercury thermometers is banned in the United States, and disposal of them is billed to the producers. Minnesota has an agreement with Sony to take back and recycle Sony electronic products. The European Union requires auto makers to pay for the recycling of old cars. In addition, 80% of the weight of discarded cars must be reused or recycled.

Environmental labeling, such as Germany's Green Dot program, gives the seal of approval to environmentally safe products. International standards for environmental stewardship, called ISO 14000, may soon be required as a condition to do business in certain countries and companies, and to qualify for foreign aid, business loans, and reduced insurance premiums. These types of laws, regulations, and incentives make design for environment an imperative.

Factors such as product life, recoverable value, ease of service, and disposal cost affect decisions on disposal, continued use, and recycling. Many products are discarded because they are difficult or expensive to repair. Materials from discarded products may not be recycled if the product is difficult to disassemble. That's why Hewlett Packard designs its products for disassembly. As a result, HP has been able to disassemble and refurbish 12,000 tons of equipment annually with less than 1% waste. HP also requires its suppliers to meet its own environmental standards such as using specified levels of recycled plastic content.

Recycling programs save money.

Xerox's program to recycle copier parts (cartridges, power supplies, motors, paper-transport systems, printed wiring boards, and metal rollers), called *design for reassembly*, saves the company more than $200 million annually. The process involves disassembling a machine, replacing worn-out parts with new, remanufactured, or used components, cleaning the machine, and then testing it to make sure it meets the same quality and reliability standards as a newly manufactured machine. To achieve its goal of zero waste, recyclability has become an important factor in product design.

The Dell Recycle Program collects redundant equipment from customers, regardless of brand, to be resold, refurbished, recycled, or disposed of in an environmentally friendly fashion. In addition, customers can receive discount coupons if they trade-in, donate to charity, or auction old and unwanted PCs.

## METRICS FOR DESIGN QUALITY

The *quality* of a design depends in large part on how easy or difficult it is to produce. Traditionally, product design is evaluated in terms of the cost of materials and the adherence to performance specifications provided by marketing. After a design is released to manufacturing, the responsibility of producing the product to design specifications is assigned to manufacturing. Clearly, this approach impedes any real improvements in the design process and fails to consider the strategic impact of product development. A more comprehensive and useful evaluation of design quality includes the following metrics:[6]

Sales revenue is not the only measure of a successful design.

1. ***Percent of revenue from new products or services:*** a measure of the extent of new product versus incremental product development. For traditional companies, this number hovers around 15%. For leading-edge companies, it's greater than 30%.
2. ***Percent of products capturing 50% or more of the market:*** the so-called killer products, the home-runs; also measured as capturing twice as much market share as the next largest competitor.
3. ***Percent of process initiatives yielding a 50% or more improvement in effectiveness:*** changes in the product development process, such as utilizing new technology. An improvement in *effectiveness* compares the achieved state to "the way things need to be" rather than an improvement in *efficiency*, which compares the achieved state to "the way things were."

[6]Adapted from D. Burdick, "Metrics for Success for C-Commerce Product Development," *Gartner Group Research Note* (November 2, 1999).

4. ***Percent of suppliers engaged in collaborative design:*** a metric showing a company's ability to leverage the knowledge of suppliers in designing better products. It requires access to technology, discussed earlier in this chapter.
5. ***Percent of parts that can be recycled:*** a measure of the *greenness* of product design, which can also be measured by the average cost of product disassembly and disposal, and the percent of parts that can be used again in a remanufactured product.

Use multiple measures of design quality.

6. ***Percent of parts used in multiple products:*** a measure of standardization and modularity. Standardization means lower costs, fewer errors, better quality, and more flexibility in meeting customer orders.
7. ***Average number of components per product:*** a measure of design simplicity. Products with fewer parts are more reliable and easier to make well.
8. ***Percent of parts with no engineering change orders (ECOs):*** a measure of how realistic the initial design is—that is, how well the design matches production capabilities. At the conclusion of the first production run, a design is certified to be "producible," but changes in the design can still be requested by manufacturing that would make the product easier or cheaper to produce. Fewer ECOs indicate a more thorough and better quality design. Industry leaders strive for an 80% or better *first-pass yield*. The industry average is less than 50%.
9. ***Things gone wrong (TGW):*** a measure of design quality that originates from the customer. It takes into consideration both the frequency and severity of product failure, product recalls, warranty requests, and product liability. A traditional measure of quality for the automotive industry, TGW is measured per 100 vehicles for the first six months of operation. Similar measurements are appearing in other industries in weighted form.

## QUALITY FUNCTION DEPLOYMENT

Coordinating design decisions can be difficult.

Imagine that two engineers are working on two different components of a car sunroof simultaneously but separately.[7] The "insulation and sealing" engineer develops a new seal that will keep out rain, even during a blinding rainstorm. The "handles, knobs, and levers" engineer is working on a simpler lever that will make the roof easier to open. The new lever is tested and works well with the old seal. Neither engineer is aware of the activities of the other. As it turns out, the combination of heavier roof (due to the increased insulation) and lighter lever means that the driver can no longer open the sunroof with one hand! Hopefully, the problem will be detected in prototype testing before the car is put into production. At that point, one or both components will need to be redesigned. Otherwise, cars already produced will need to be reworked and cars already sold will have to be recalled. None of these alternatives is pleasant, and they all involve considerable cost.

Could such problems be avoided if engineers worked in teams and shared information? Not entirely. Even in design teams, there is no guarantee that all decisions will be coordinated. Ford and Firestone have worked together for over 75 years. But teamwork did not prevent Firestone tires designed to fit the Ford Explorer from failing when inflated to Ford specifications. A formal method is needed for making sure that everyone working on a design project knows the design objectives and is aware of the interrelationships of the various parts of the design. Similar communications are needed between the customer and marketing, between marketing and engineering, between engineering and production, and between production and the worker. In broader terms, then, a structured process is needed that will translate the *voice of the customer* to technical requirements at every stage of design and manufacture. Such a process is called **quality function deployment (QFD)**.

**Quality function deployment (QFD):** translates the voice of the customer into technical design requirements.

QFD uses a series of matrix diagrams that resemble connected houses. The first matrix, dubbed the *house of quality*, converts customer requirements into product-design characteristics. As shown in Figure 5.7, the house of quality has six sections: a customer requirements section, a competitive assessment section, a design characteristics section, a relationship matrix, a tradeoff matrix, and a target values section. Let's see how these sections interrelate by building a house of quality for a steam iron.

[7]Adapted from Bob King, *Better Designs in Half the Time* (Methuen, MA: GOAL/QPC, 1989), pp. 1.1–1.3.

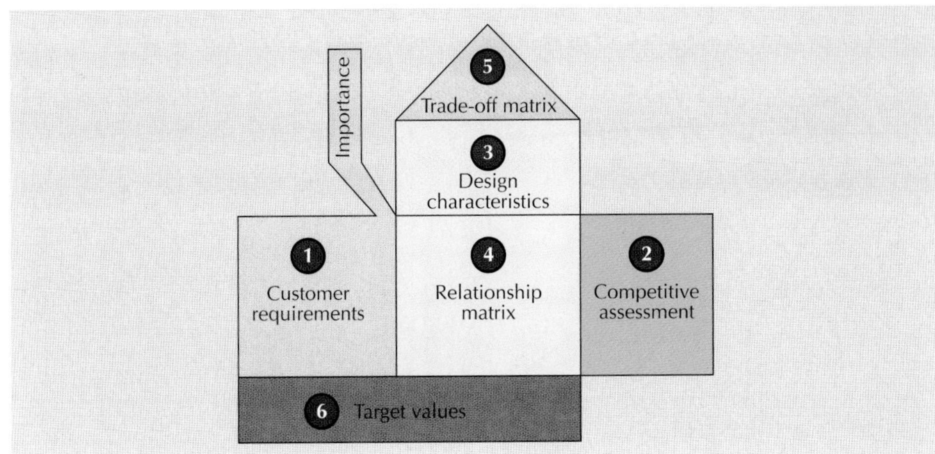


**Figure 5.7**

**Outline of the House of Quality**

Customer requirements

Our customers tell us they want an iron that presses quickly, removes wrinkles, doesn't stick to fabric, provides enough steam, doesn't spot fabric, and doesn't scorch fabric (see Figure 5.8). We enter those attributes into the *customer requirements* section of the house. For easier reference, we can group them into a category called "Irons well." Next we ask our customers to rate the list of requirements on a scale of 1 to 10, with 10 being the most important. Our customers rate presses quickly and doesn't scorch fabric as the most important attributes, with a score of 9. A second group of attributes, called "Easy and safe to use" is constructed in a similar manner.

Competitive assessment

Next, we conduct a *competitive assessment.* On a scale of 1 to 5 (with 5 being the highest), customers evaluate our iron (we'll call it "X") against competitor irons, A and B. We see that our iron excels on the customer attributes of presses quickly, removes wrinkles, provides enough steam, automatic shutoff, and doesn't break when dropped. So there is no critical need to improve those factors. However, we are rated poorly on doesn't stick, doesn't spot, heats quickly, quick cool-down, and not too heavy. These are order qualifiers. We need to improve these factors just to be considered for purchase by customers. None of the irons perform well on doesn't scorch fabric, or doesn't burn when touched. Perhaps we could win some orders if we satisfied these requirements.

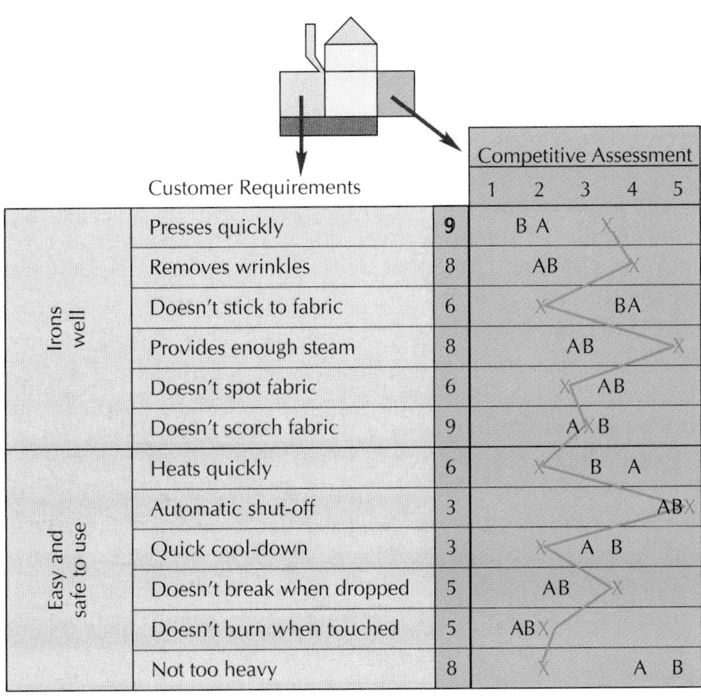


**Figure 5.8**

**A Competitive Assessment of Customer Requirements**

**Figure 5.9**
**Converting Customer Requirements to Design Characteristics**

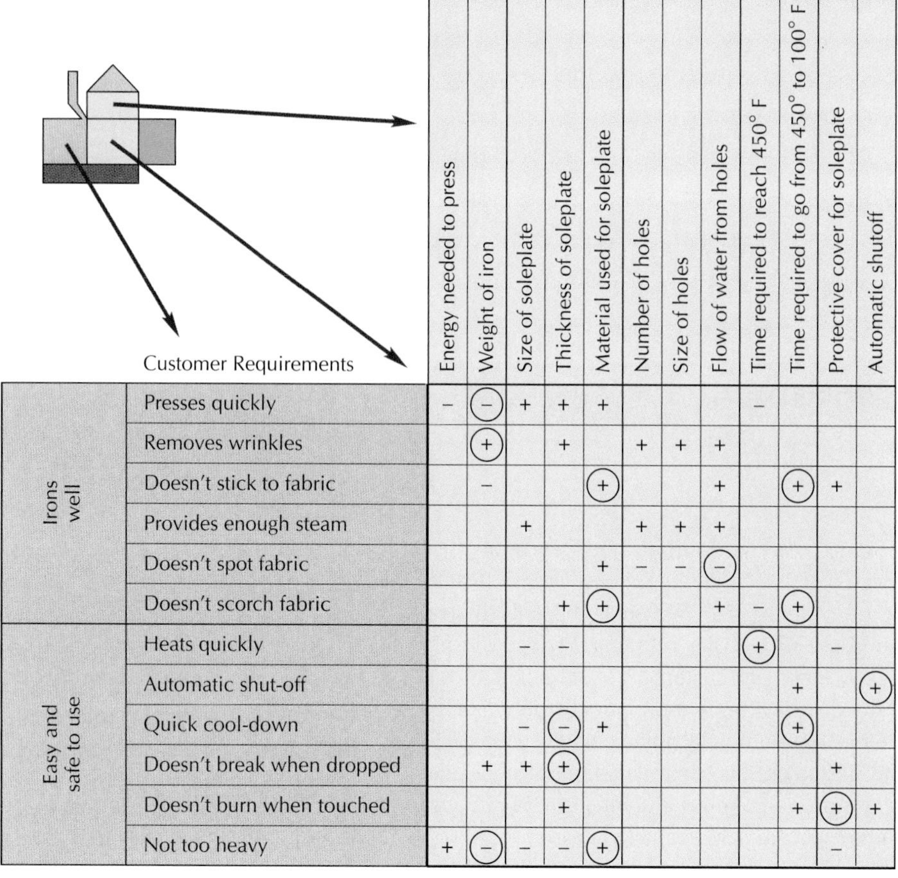

| | Customer Requirements | Energy needed to press | Weight of iron | Size of soleplate | Thickness of soleplate | Material used for soleplate | Number of holes | Size of holes | Flow of water from holes | Time required to reach 450° F | Time required to go from 450° to 100° F | Protective cover for soleplate | Automatic shutoff |
|---|---|---|---|---|---|---|---|---|---|---|---|---|---|
| Irons well | Presses quickly | – | ⊖ | + | + | + | | | | – | | | |
| | Removes wrinkles | | ⊕ | | + | | + | + | + | | | | |
| | Doesn't stick to fabric | | – | | | ⊕ | | | + | | ⊕ | + | |
| | Provides enough steam | | | + | | | + | + | + | | | | |
| | Doesn't spot fabric | | | | | + | – | – | ⊖ | | | | |
| | Doesn't scorch fabric | | | | + | ⊕ | | | + | – | ⊕ | | |
| Easy and safe to use | Heats quickly | | | – | – | | | | | ⊕ | | – | |
| | Automatic shut-off | | | | | | | | | | + | | ⊕ |
| | Quick cool-down | | | – | ⊖ | + | | | | | ⊕ | | |
| | Doesn't break when dropped | | + | + | ⊕ | | | | | | | + | |
| | Doesn't burn when touched | | | | + | | | | | | + | ⊕ | + |
| | Not too heavy | + | ⊖ | – | – | ⊕ | | | | | | – | |

Design characteristics

In order to change the product design to better satisfy customer requirements, we need to translate those requirements to measurable *design characteristics*. We list such characteristics (energy needed to press, weight of iron, size of the soleplate, etc.) across the top of the matrix shown in Figure 5.9. In the body of the matrix, we identify *how* the design characteristics relate to customer requirements. Relationships can be positive, + or minus, –. Strong relationships are designated with a circled plus, ⊕ or minus, ⊖. Examine the plusses and minuses in the row, *Doesn't break when dropped*. We can ensure that the iron doesn't break when dropped by increasing the weight of the iron, increasing the size of the soleplate, increasing the thickness of the soleplate, or adding a protective cover. Of those options, making the soleplate thicker has the strongest impact.

Tradeoff matrix

Product design characteristics are interrelated also, as shown in the roof of the house in Figure 5.10. For example, increasing the thickness of the soleplate would increase the weight of the iron but decrease the energy needed to press. Also, a thicker soleplate would decrease the flow of water through the holes, and increase the time it takes for the iron to heat up or cool down. Designers must take all these factors into account when determining a final design.

Target values

The last section of the house, shown in Figure 5.11, adds quantitative measures to our design characteristics. Measuring our iron X against competitors A and B, we find that our iron is heavier, larger, and has a thicker soleplate. Also, it takes longer to heat up and cool down, but requires less energy to press and provides more steam than other irons. To decide which design characteristics to change, we compare the estimated impact of the change with the estimated cost. We rate these factors on a common scale, from 1 to 5, with 5 being the most. As long as the estimated impact exceeds the estimated cost, we should make a change. Thus, we need to change several product characteristics in our new design, such as weight of the iron, size of the soleplate, thickness of the soleplate, material used for the soleplate, number of holes, time required to heat up, and time required to cool down.

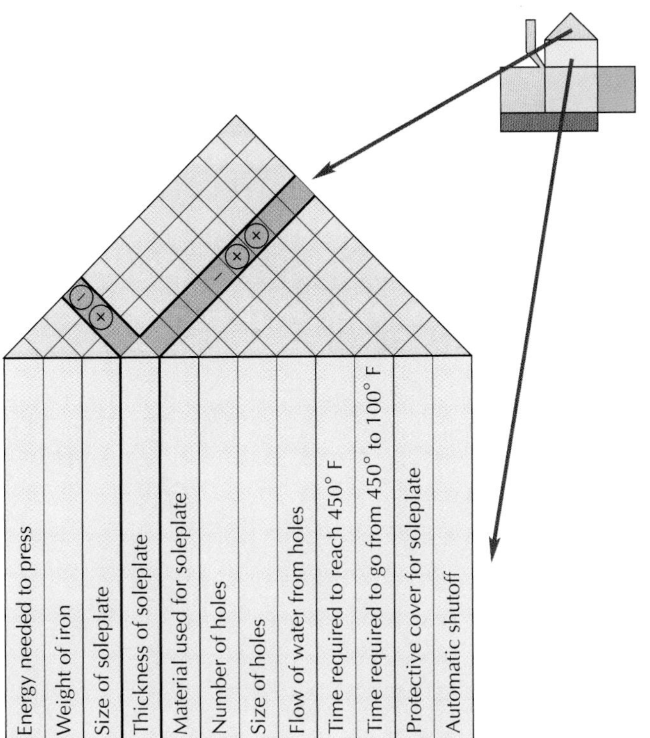


**Figure 5.10**

**The Tradeoff Matrix: Effects of Increasing Soleplate Thickness**

Now visualize a design team discussing target values for these product characteristics using the data provided in the house of quality as a focal point. The house does not tell the team how to change the design, only what characteristics to change. The team decides that the weight of the iron should be reduced to 1.2 lb, the size of the soleplate to 8 in. by 5 in., the thickness of the soleplate to 3 cm, the material used for soleplate to silverstone, the number of holes to 30, time to heat up to 30 seconds, and time to cool down to 500 seconds. Figure 5.12 shows the completed house of quality for the steam iron.

Other houses

The house of quality is the most popular QFD matrix. However, to understand the full power of QFD, we need to consider three other houses that can be linked to the house of

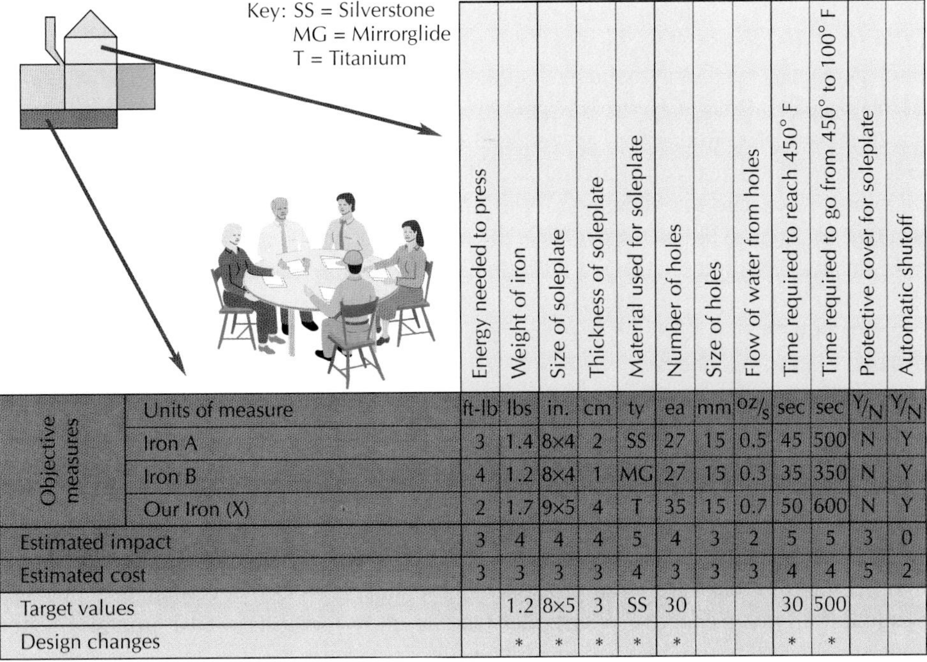


| | | Energy needed to press | Weight of iron | Size of soleplate | Thickness of soleplate | Material used for soleplate | Number of holes | Size of holes | Flow of water from holes | Time required to reach 450° F | Time required to go from 450° to 100° F | Protective cover for soleplate | Automatic shutoff |
|---|---|---|---|---|---|---|---|---|---|---|---|---|---|
| Objective measures | Units of measure | ft-lb | lbs | in. | cm | ty | ea | mm | oz/s | sec | sec | Y/N | Y/N |
| | Iron A | 3 | 1.4 | 8×4 | 2 | SS | 27 | 15 | 0.5 | 45 | 500 | N | Y |
| | Iron B | 4 | 1.2 | 8×4 | 1 | MG | 27 | 15 | 0.3 | 35 | 350 | N | Y |
| | Our Iron (X) | 2 | 1.7 | 9×5 | 4 | T | 35 | 15 | 0.7 | 50 | 600 | N | Y |
| Estimated impact | | 3 | 4 | 4 | 4 | 5 | 4 | 3 | 2 | 5 | 5 | 3 | 0 |
| Estimated cost | | 3 | 3 | 3 | 3 | 4 | 3 | 3 | 3 | 4 | 4 | 5 | 2 |
| Target values | | | 1.2 | 8×5 | 3 | SS | 30 | | | 30 | 500 | | |
| Design changes | | | * | * | * | * | * | | | * | * | | |

**Figure 5.11**

**Targeted Changes in Design**

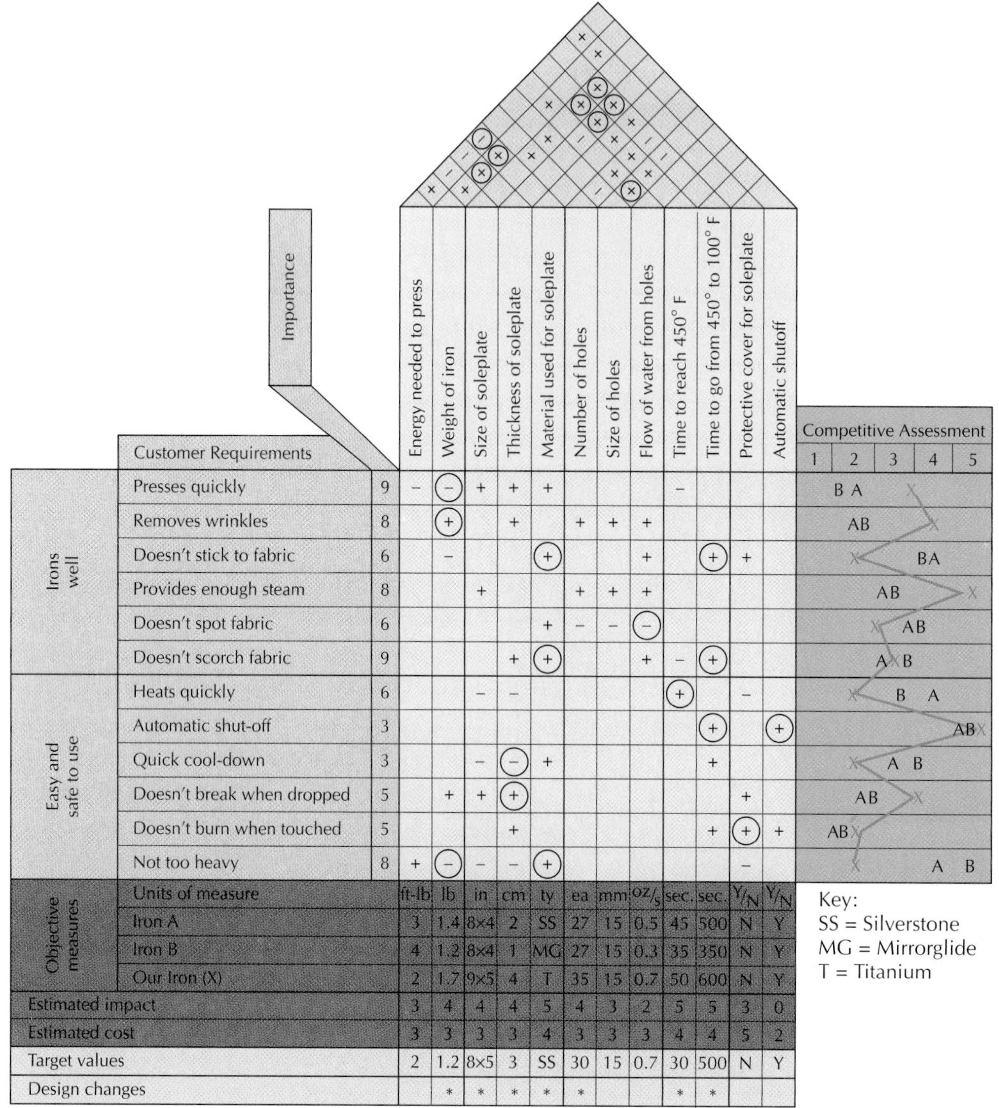


**Figure 5.12**

**The Completed House of Quality for a Steam Iron**

quality (Figure 5.13). In our example, suppose we decide to meet the customer requirement of "heats quickly" by reducing the thickness of the soleplate. The second house, *parts deployment*, examines which component parts are affected by reducing the thickness of the soleplate. Obviously, the soleplate itself is affected, but so are the fasteners used to attach the soleplate to the iron, as well as the depth of the holes and connectors that provide steam. These new part characteristics then become inputs to the third house, *process planning*. To change the thickness of the soleplate, the dies used by the metal-stamping machine to produce the plates will have to change, and the stamping machine will require adjustments. Given these changes, a fourth house, *operating requirements*, prescribes how the fixtures and gauges for the stamping machine will be set, what additional training the operator of the machine needs, and how process control and preventive maintenance procedures need to be adjusted. Nothing is left to chance—all bases are covered from customer to design to manufacturing.

Benefits of QFD

In comparison with traditional design approaches, QFD forces management to spend more time defining the new product changes and examining the ramifications of those changes. More time spent in the early stages of design means less time is required later to revise the design and make it work. This reallocation of time shortens the design process considerably. Some experts suggest that QFD can produce better product designs in *half* the time of conventional design processes. In summary, QFD is a communications and planning tool that promotes better understanding of customer demands, promotes better understanding of design interactions, involves manufacturing in the design process, and provides documentation of the design process.

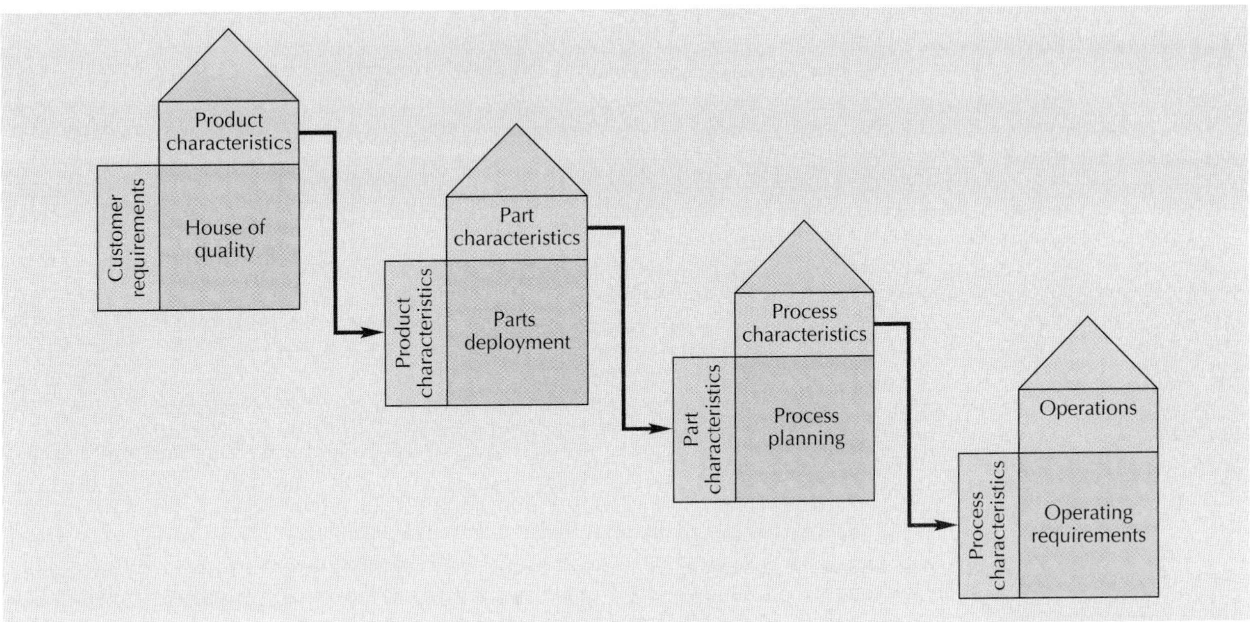


**Figure 5.13**
**A Series of Connected QFD Houses**

## DESIGN FOR ROBUSTNESS

A product can fail because it was manufactured wrong in the factory—*quality of conformance*—or because it was designed incorrectly—*quality of design*. Quality-control techniques, such as statistical process control (SPC) discussed in Chapter 4, concentrate on quality of conformance. Genichi Taguchi, a Japanese industrialist and statistician, suggests that product failure is primarily a function of design quality.

Consumers subject products to an extreme range of operating conditions and still expect them to function normally. The steering and brakes of a car, for example, should continue to perform their function even on wet, winding roads or when the tires are not inflated properly. A product designed to withstand variations in environmental and operating conditions is said to be *robust* or to possess *robust quality*. Taguchi believes that superior quality is derived from products that are more robust and that robust products come from **robust design**.

**Robust design:** yields a product or service designed to withstand variations.

The conditions that cause a product to operate poorly (called *noise*) can be separated into controllable and uncontrollable factors. From a designer's point of view, the *controllable factors* are design parameters such as material used, dimensions, and form of processing. *Uncontrollable factors* are under the user's control (length of use, maintenance, settings, and so on). The designer's job is to choose values for the controllable variables that react in a robust fashion to the possible occurrences of uncontrollable factors.

As part of the design process, design engineers must also specify certain *tolerances*, or allowable ranges of variation in the dimension of a part. It is assumed that producing parts within those tolerance limits will result in a quality product. Taguchi, however, suggests that *consistency* is more important to quality than being within tolerances. He supports this view with the following observations.

- Consistent errors can be more easily corrected than random errors,
- *Parts* within tolerance limits may produce *assemblies* that are not within limits, and
- Consumers have a strong preference for product characteristics near their ideal values.

Let's examine each of these observations.

Consistency is important to quality.

Consistent mistakes are easier to correct. Consider the professor who always starts class 5 minutes late. Students can adjust their arrival patterns to coincide with the professor's, or the professor's clock can be set ahead by 5 minutes. But if the professor sometimes starts class a few minutes early, sometimes on time, and other times 10 minutes late, the students are more apt to be frustrated, and the professor's behavior will be more difficult to change.

**Figure 5.14**
**Taguchi's Quality Loss Function**

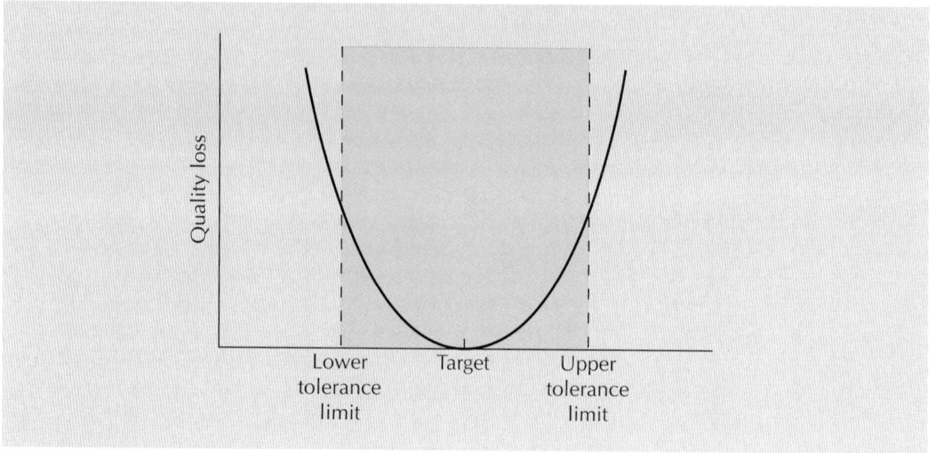


Consistency is especially important for assembled products. The assembly of two parts that are near opposite tolerance limits may result in *tolerance stack-ups* and poor quality. For example, a button diameter that is small (near to the lower tolerance limit) combined with a buttonhole that is large (near to its upper tolerance limit) results in a button that won't stay fastened. Although it is beyond the scope of this book, Taguchi advises how to set tolerance limits so that tolerance stack-up can be avoided.

Manufacturing tolerances define what is acceptable or unacceptable quality. Parts or products measured outside tolerance limits are considered defective and are either reworked or discarded. Parts or products within the limits are considered "good." Taguchi asserts that although all the parts or products within tolerances may be acceptable, they are not all of the same quality. Consider a student who earns an average grade of 60 in a course. He or she will pass, whereas a student who earns an average grade of 59 will fail. A student with a 95 average will also pass the course. Taguchi would claim that there is negligible difference between the quality of the students with averages of 59 and 60, even though one was "rejected" and the other was not. There is, however, a great deal of difference in the quality of the student with an average of 60 and the student with an average of 95. Furthermore, a professor in a subsequent class or a prospective employer will be able to detect the difference in quality and will overwhelmingly prefer the student who passed the course with a 95 average. Quality near the target value is preferable to quality that simply conforms to specifications.

The quality loss function quantifies customer preferences toward quality.

Taguchi quantified customer preferences toward on-target quality in the *quality loss function* (QLF). The quadratic function, graphed in Figure 5.14 implies that a customer's dissatisfaction (or quality loss) increases geometrically as the actual value deviates from the target value. The quality loss function is used to emphasize that customer preferences are strongly oriented toward *consistently* meeting quality expectations. *Design for Six Sigma* (DFSS) uses the Taguchi method to reduce variability in design.

## SPECIAL CONSIDERATIONS IN SERVICE DESIGN

Services that are allowed to just happen rarely meet customer needs. World-class services that come to mind—McDonald's, Nordstrom, Federal Express, Disney World—are all characterized by impeccable design. McDonald's plans every action of its employees (including 49 steps to making perfect french fries); Nordstrom creates a pleasurable shopping environment with well-stocked shelves, live music, fresh flowers in the dressing rooms, and legendary salespersons; Federal Express designs every stage of the delivery process for efficiency and speed; and Disney World in Japan was so well designed that it impressed even the zero-defect Japanese.

Can services be designed in the same manner as products? Yes and no. The design process *looks* much the same, but there are some important differences. Let's examine them.

## CHARACTERISTICS OF SERVICES

Services can be distinguished from manufacturing by the following eight characteristics. Although not all services possess each of these characteristics, they do exhibit at least some of them to some degree.

1. ***Services are intangible.*** It is difficult to design something you cannot see, touch, store on a shelf, or try on for size. Services are *experienced*, and that experience may be different for each individual customer. Designing a service involves describing what the customer is supposed to "experience," which can be a difficult task. Designers begin by compiling information on the way people think, feel, and behave (called *psychographics*).

   Because of its intangibility, consumers perceive a service to be more risky to purchase than a product. Cues (such as physical surroundings, server's demeanor, and service guarantees) need to be included in service design to help form or reinforce accurate perceptions of the service experience and reduce the consumer's risk.

   The quality of a service experience depends largely on the customer's service *expectations*. Expectations can differ according to a customer's knowledge, experience, and self-confidence.

   Customers also have different expectations of different types of service providers. You probably expect more from a department store than from a discount store, or from a car dealer's service center than from an independent repair shop. Understanding the customer and his or her expectations is essential in designing good service.
2. ***Service output is variable.*** This is true because of the various service providers employed and the variety of customers they serve, each with his or her own special needs. Even though customer demands vary, the service experience is expected to remain consistent. According to a recent survey, the most important measures of service quality to the customer are reliability and consistency. Service design, then, must strive for predictability or robustness. Examples of services known for their consistency include McDonald's, Holiday Inn, and ServiceMaster. Extensive employee training, set operating procedures, and standardized materials, equipment, and physical environments are used by these companies to increase consistency.
3. ***Services have higher customer contact.*** The service "encounter" between service provider and customer *is* the service in many cases. Making sure the encounter is a positive one is part of service design. This involves giving the service provider the skills and authority necessary to complete a customer transaction successfully. Studies show a direct link between service provider motivation and customer satisfaction. Moreover, service providers are not motivated primarily by compensation but rather by concurrence with the firm's "service concept" and being able to perform their job competently.

   High customer contact can interfere with the efficiency of a service and make it difficult to control its quality (i.e., there is no opportunity for testing and rework). However, direct contact with customers can also be an advantage for services. Observing customers experiencing a service generates new service ideas and facilitates feedback for improvements to existing services.
4. ***Services are perishable.*** Because services can't be inventoried, the timing and location of delivery are important. Service design should define not only *what* is to be delivered but also *where* and *when*.
5. ***The service and the service delivery are inseparable.*** That means service design and process design must occur concurrently. (This is one area in which services have an advantage over manufacturing—it has taken manufacturing a number of years to realize the benefits of concurrent design.) In addition to deciding what, where, and when, service design also specifies *how* the service should be provided. "How" decisions include the degree of customer participation in the service process, which tasks should be done in the presence of the customer (called front-room activities) and which should be done out of the customer's sight (back-room activities), the role and authority of the service provider in delivering the service, and the balance of "touch" versus "tech" (i.e., how automated the service should be).

6. ***Services tend to be decentralized and geographically dispersed.*** Many service employees are on their own to make decisions. Although this can present problems, careful service design will help employees deal successfully with contingencies. Multiple service outlets can be a plus in terms of rapid prototyping. New ideas can be field-tested with a minimum disturbance to operations. McDonald's considers each of its outlets a "laboratory" for new ideas.
7. ***Services are consumed more often than products,*** so there are more opportunities to succeed or fail with the customer. Jan Carlzon, former president of SAS Airlines, calls these opportunities "moments of truth." Services are confronted with thousands of moments of truth each day. Careful design and redesign of the service encounter can help make each moment of truth a positive experience. In a sense, the service environment lends itself more readily to continuous improvement than does the manufacturing environment.
8. ***Services can be easily emulated.*** Competitors can copy new or improved services quickly. New ideas are constantly needed to stay ahead of the competition. As a result, new service introductions and service improvements occur even more rapidly than new product introductions.

## THE SERVICE DESIGN PROCESS

From the service characteristics given above, it is apparent that service design is more comprehensive and occurs more often than product design. The inherent variability of service processes requires that the service system be carefully designed. Figure 5.15 (an adapted version of Figure 5.1) shows service design beginning with a service concept and ending with service delivery.

**Service concept:** the purpose of a service; it defines the target market and the customer experience.

The **service concept** defines the target customer and the desired customer experience. It also defines how our service is different from others and how it will compete in the marketplace. Sometimes services are successful because their service concept fills a previously unoccupied niche or differs from the generally accepted mode of operation. For example, Citicorp offers 15-minute mortgage approvals through online computer net-

Figure 5.15
**The Service Design Process**

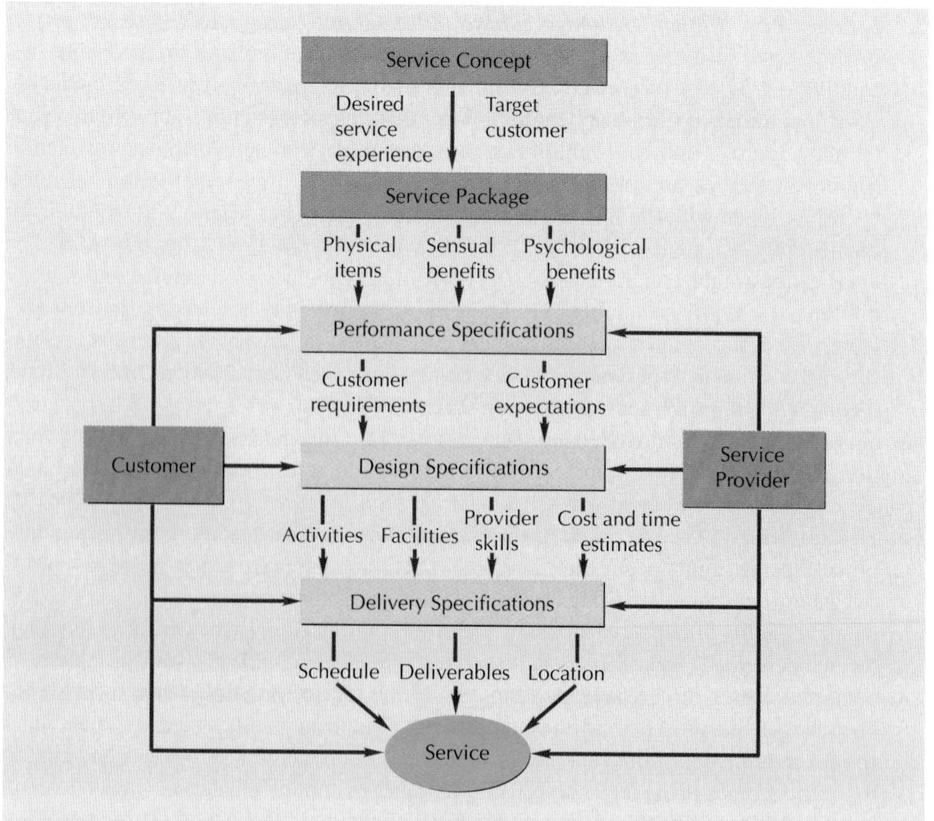

## THE COMPETITIVE EDGE

### Bank of America's Innovation Experiments

Product design follows well-established scientific methods for developing and testing prototypes in a laboratory-type setting. For service design, it is difficult to replicate unique customer-provider interactions in a laboratory. Only live experiments with *real* customers and *real* transactions can provide the type of data needed for truly innovative services. But live tests are difficult to control and risky to both customer relations and firm credibility, so most services are designed by brainstorming and trial-and-error, with limited success. A notable exception is Bank of America's innovation experiments.

Bank of America created an Innovation & Development (I&D) team to pioneer new services and service delivery techniques. The I&D team chose 20 branch banks in the Atlanta region to serve as a test bed for new service ideas. The branch banks agreed to help with the research effort and even funded the experiments out of their own budget (in order to be the first to benefit from the new ideas). Ideas were gleaned from team members, branch office staff, market research, and customer satisfaction surveys. Each potential experiment was entered into an Idea Portfolio spreadsheet that included a description of the idea, the problem addressed, targeted customer segment, priority, and status. In some cases, focus groups were created to test out the feasibility of an idea. Out of 200 ideas, 40 were launched as formal experiments. The experiments were carefully (but quickly) designed and tested in a "prototype branch" set up at Charlotte headquarters. Team members rehearsed the process and ironed out problems before live testing.

Live testing created its own problems. In order to control the "noise" generated in a live experiment, the same experiment was repeated several times at the same branch as well as at different branches. A wash-out period of one to two weeks between the start of the experiment and data collection helped alleviate the Hawthorne effect. Every experiment ran 90 days to ensure a fair assessment of its results. Performance was then compared to that in similar control branches.

It soon became apparent that many of the proposed changes in practices and processes could not be implemented within the confines of traditional branch banking. As a result, 10 out of the 20 branches were redesigned, five as *express centers* and five as *financial centers*. The remaining centers tested incremental changes in processes and technology. They also served as controls for the other experiments.

The express centers provide fast, convenient access for routine transactions via teller services and self-directed options. The financial centers provide access to more personalized service in a spacious relaxed atmosphere. A host (à la Wal-Mart) greets customers at the door. Comfortable couches, free coffee, and financial magazines are available to the customer. An investment bar offers personal computers for surfing the Internet and banking online. Freestanding kiosks with associates nearby help customers open accounts, set up loans, and buy and sell stock. At the traditional branches, customers waiting for tellers can watch television news and electronic stock tickers.

Experiments were evaluated on both their performance (e.g., increased customer satisfaction, productivity, revenue enhancement) and their cost/benefit ratio. Of the 40 initial experiments, 38 were considered a success and 20 were selected for companywide rollout. That's a remarkable 50% success rate.

Through systematic experimentation, Bank of America has shown that service design can undergo the same high-quality standards and rigor of product design. Look for more services to try these kinds of experiments.

*Source:* Adapted from Stephen Thomke, "R&D Comes to Services: Bank of America's Pathbreaking Experiments," *Harvard Business Review* (April 2003), pp. 70–79.

works with real estate offices, credit bureaus, and builder's offices, and an expert system loan-application advisor. Amazon excels at customer service for online orders, and eBay's worldwide reach creates more lively auctions with a huge community of buyers and sellers. Shouldice Hospital performs only inguinal hernia operations, for which its doctors are very experienced and its facilities carefully designed. Local anesthesia is used; patients walk into and out of the operating room under their own power; and telephones, televisions, and dining facilities are located in a communal area some distance from patient rooms. As a result, patients quickly become ambulatory, are discharged within hours (compared to normal week-long stays), and pay one-third less for their operations.

From the service concept, a **service package** is created to meet customer needs. The package consists of a mixture of physical items, sensual benefits, and psychological benefits.[8] For a restaurant the physical items consist of the facility, food, drinks, tableware, napkins, and other touchable commodities. The sensual benefits include the taste and aroma of the food and the sights and sounds of the people. Psychological benefits are rest and relaxation, comfort, status, and a sense of well-being.

**Service package:** the mixture of physical items, sensual benefits, and psychological benefits.

[8]The concept of a service package and its contents comes from W. E. Sasser, R. P. Olsen, and D. Wyckoff, *Management of Service Operations* (Boston: Allyn and Bacon, 1978), pp. 8–10.

Effective service design recognizes and defines *all* the components of a service package. Finding the appropriate mix of physical items and sensual and psychological benefits and designing them to be consistent with each other and the service concept is also important. A fast-food restaurant promises nourishment with speed. The customer is served quickly and is expected to consume the food quickly. Thus, the tables, chairs, and booths are not designed to be comfortable, nor does their arrangement encourage lengthy or personal conversations. The service package is consistent. This is not the case for an upscale restaurant located in a renovated train station. The food is excellent, but it is difficult to enjoy a full-course meal sitting on wooden benches in a drafty facility, where conversations echo and tables shake when the trains pass by. In the hospitality industry, Marriott Corporation is known for its careful design of specialty hotels. From its Courtyard Marriott to Fairfield Inn to residential centers, each facility "fits" its clientele with a well-researched service package.

**Performance specifications**

From the service package, service specifications are developed for performance, design, and delivery. *Performance specifications* outline expectations and requirements for general and specific customers. Performance specifications are converted into design specifications and, finally, delivery specifications (in lieu of manufacturing specifications).

**Design delivery specifications**

*Design specifications* must describe the service in sufficient detail for the desired service experience to be replicated for different individuals at numerous locations. The specifications typically consist of activities to be performed, skill requirements and guidelines for service providers, and cost and time estimates. Facility size, location, and layout, as well as equipment needs, are also included. *Delivery specifications* outline the steps required in the work process, including the work schedule, deliverables, and the locations at which the work is to be performed.

Notice in Figure 5.15 that both customers and service providers may be involved in determining performance, design, and delivery specifications. Recall that Figure 2.4 classified service processes according to degree of customization (involvement of the customer in service design and delivery) and labor intensity (involvement of the service provider in service design and delivery). The degree of customer and provider involve-

Table 5.2
**Differences in Design for High-Contact Services**

| Design Decision | High-Contact Service | Low-Contact Service |
|---|---|---|
| Facility location | Convenient to customer | Near labor or transportation source |
| Facility layout | Must look presentable, accommodate customer needs, and facilitate interaction with customer | Designed for efficiency |
| Quality control | More variable since customer is involved in process; customer expectations and perceptions of quality may differ; customer present when defects occur | Measured against established standards; testing and rework possible to correct defects |
| Capacity | Excess capacity required to handle peaks in demand | Planned for average demand |
| Worker skills | Must be able to interact well with customers and use judgment in decision making | Technical skills |
| Scheduling | Must accommodate customer schedule | Customer concerned only with completion date |
| Service process | Mostly front-room activities; service may change during delivery in response to customer | Mostly back-room activities; planned and executed with minimal interference |
| Service package | Varies with customer; includes environment as well as actual service | Fixed, less extensive |

*Source:* Adapted from R. Chase, N. Aquilano, and R. Jacobs, *Operations Management for Competitive Advantage* (New York: McGraw-Hill, 2001), p. 210.

ment varies by type of service. For example, a charter airline flight entails more customer and provider participation than a commercial flight. A class taught in a large lecture format involves less "customer" interaction than a senior-level seminar. Commissioning a work of art or custom-building a home allows the customer to participate directly in the design process. As shown in Table 5.2, degree of customer contact has an impact on how individual services are designed and delivered. Note that the decisions listed in the table are covered in more detail in subsequent chapters.

## SUMMARY

New products and services enhance a company's image, invigorate employees, and help a firm to grow and prosper. The design process begins with ideas formulated into a product concept. Once a product concept passes a feasibility study, performance specs are given to designers who develop and test prototype designs. For selected prototypes, design and manufacturing specs are taken through a pilot run where the design is finalized and the planning for product launch begins.

Time-to-market can be accelerated by using design teams, concurrent design, design for manufacture concepts, and CAD/CAM systems. The quality of design can be improved through design reviews, design for environment, metrics on design quality, quality function deployment, and Taguchi methods for robust design.

Service design is more comprehensive than product design because the customer considers service delivery as part of the service itself. Thus, service design includes such factors as physical surroundings and the role of the service provider. Taking the time to design a service carefully (often with direct customer participation) helps to prevent disagreements between customer and service provider and results in higher levels of customer satisfaction.

Designs define what goods or services are to be provided to the customer. We must now decide *how* to provide them. The next chapter describes the decisions involved in planning processes and making decisions about technology and capacity.

## SUMMARY OF KEY TERMS

**benchmarking** finding the best-in-class product or process, measuring one's performance against it, and making recommendations for improvements based on the results.

**CAD/CAM** the ultimate design-to-manufacture connection.

**collaborative product commerce (CPC)** software system for collaborative design and development among trading partners; it follows the life cycle of the product.

**computer-aided design (CAD)** a software system that uses computer graphics to assist in the creation, modification, and analysis of a design.

**computer-aided engineering (CAE)** engineering analysis performed at a computer terminal with information from a CAD database.

**concurrent design** a new approach to design that involves the simultaneous design of products and processes by design teams.

**design for assembly (DFA)** a set of procedures for reducing the number of parts in an assembly, evaluating methods of assembly, and determining an assembly sequence.

**design for environment (DFE)** designing a product from material that can be recycled or easily repaired rather than discarded.

**design for manufacture and assembly (DFMA)** designing a product so that it can be produced easily and economically.

**extended producer responsibility** holding a company responsible for its product even after its useful life.

**failure mode and effects analysis (FMEA)** a systematic approach to analyzing the causes and effects of product failures.

**fault tree analysis (FTA)** a visual method for analyzing the interrelationships among failures.

**form design** the phase of product design concerned with how the product looks.

**functional design** the phase of a product design concerned with how the product performs.

**maintainability** the ease with which a product is maintained or repaired.

**modular design** combining standardized building blocks, or modules, in a variety of ways to create unique finished products.

**perceptual map** a visual method for comparing customer perceptions of different products or services.

**production design** the phase of product design concerned with how the product will be produced.

**quality function deployment (QFD)** a structured process that translates the voice of the customer into technical design requirements.

**rapid prototyping** quickly testing and revising a preliminary design model.

**reliability** the probability that a given part or product will perform its intended function for a specified period of time under normal conditions of use.

**reverse engineering** carefully dismantling and inspecting a competitor's product to look for design features that can be incorporated into your own product.

**robust design** the design of a product or a service that can withstand variations in environmental and operating conditions.

**service concept** the purpose of a service; it defines the target market and the customer experience.

**service package** the mixture of physical items, sensual benefits, and psychological benefits provided to the customer.

**simplification** reducing the number of parts, subassemblies, or options in a product.

**standardization** using commonly available parts that are interchangeable among products.

**time-to-market** the length of time from idea conception to product launch.

**usability** ease of use of a product or service.

**value analysis (VA)** an analytical approach for eliminating unnecessary design features and functions.

## SUMMARY OF KEY FORMULAS

Reliability in series

$$R_s = (R_1)(R_2)\ldots(R_n)$$

Reliability in parallel

$$R_s = R_1 + (1 - R_1)R_2$$

or

$$R_s = 1 - [(1 - R_1)(1 - R_2)\ldots(1 - R_n)]$$

Mean time between failures

$$\text{MTBF} = \frac{\text{time}}{\text{\# failures}}$$

System Availability

$$\text{SA} = \frac{\text{MTBF}}{\text{MTBF} + \text{MTTR}}$$

## SOLVED PROBLEMS

### 1. RELIABILITY

Jack McPhee, a production supervisor for McCormick, Inc., is committed to the company's new quality efforts. Part of the program encourages making product components in-house to ensure higher quality levels and instill worker pride. The system seems to be working well. One assembly, which requires a reliability of 0.95, is normally purchased from a local supplier. Now it is being assembled in-house from three components that each boast a reliability of 0.96.

a. Customer complaints have risen in the three months since McCormick started doing its own assembly work. Can you explain why?
b. What level of component reliability is necessary to restore the product to its former level of quality?
c. Jack can't increase the reliability of the individual components; however, he can add a backup with a reliability of 0.90 to each component. If the backups have a reliability of 0.90, how many will be needed to achieve a 0.95 reliability for the assembly?

### SOLUTION

a.

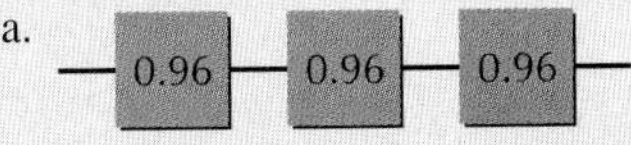


$$0.96 \times 0.96 \times 0.96 = 0.885$$

Complaints are valid

b.

$$\sqrt[3]{0.95} = 0.983$$

Each component would need a reliability of 0.983 to guarantee an assembly reliability of 0.95

c.

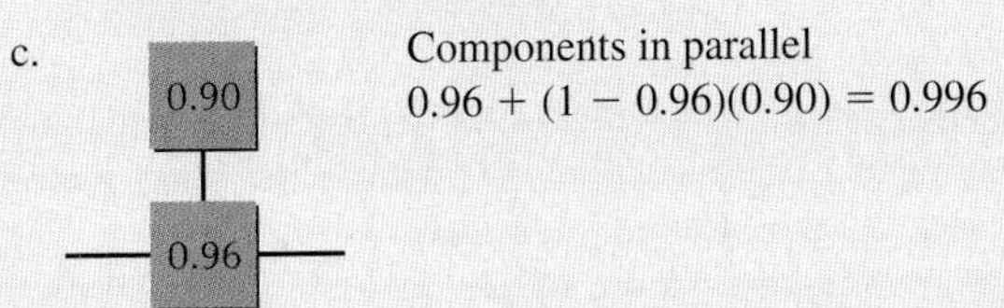


Components in parallel
$0.96 + (1 - 0.96)(0.90) = 0.996$

*One backup*

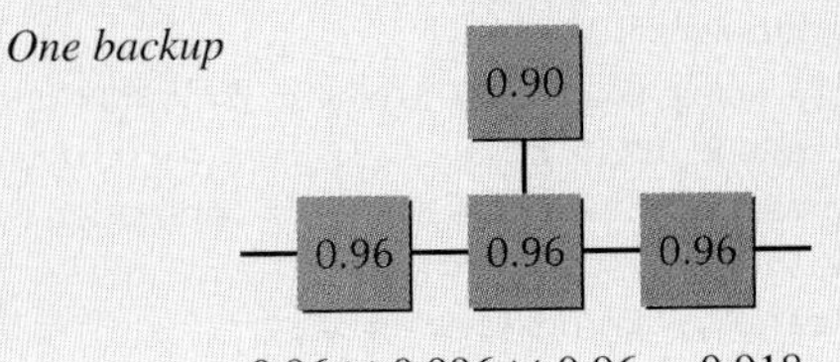


$$0.96 \times 0.996 \times 0.96 = 0.918$$

*Two backups*

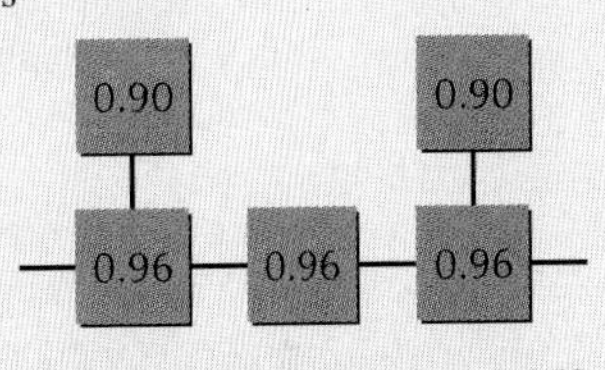


$$0.996 \times 0.96 \times 0.996 = 0.952$$

*Three backups*

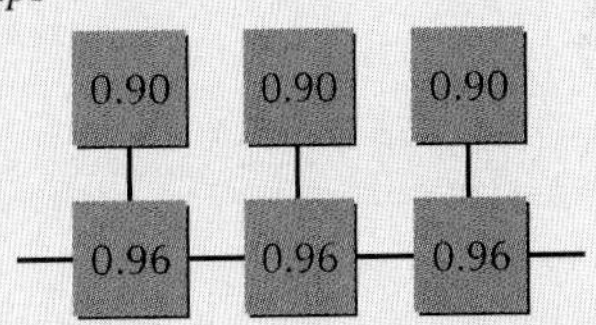


$$0.996 \times 0.996 \times 0.996 = 0.988$$

For a system reliability of 0.95, choose two backups.

### 2. SYSTEM AVAILABILITY

Amanda is trying to decide which Internet service provider to use. Her friends are always complaining about service interruptions and how long it takes to get the service up and running again. Amanda is a conscientious student and wants reliable access to the Internet. With that goal in mind, she has collected data on mean time between failures (MTBF) and mean time to repair (MTTR) for three Internet service providers. Given that cost and speed are comparable among the three options, which provider would you recommend?

| PROVIDER | MTBF | MTTR |
|---|---|---|
| MostTel | 20 | 1 |
| Star | 40 | 4 |
| CableX | 80 | 6 |

### SOLUTION

| PROVIDER | MTBF | MTTR | SYSTEM AVAILABILITY |
|---|---|---|---|
| MostTel | 20 | 1 | 20/(20 + 1) = 0.952 |
| Star | 40 | 4 | 40/(40 + 1) = 0.909 |
| CableX | 80 | 6 | 80/(80 + 6) = 0.930 |

Choose MostTel

## QUESTIONS

**5-1.** Describe the strategic significance of design. How can organizations gain a competitive edge with product or service design?

**5-2.** Look around your classroom and make a list of items that impede your ability to learn. Classify them as problems in *quality of design* or *quality of conformance*.

**5-3.** Give an example of a product or service you have encountered that was poorly designed. Read about more bad designs at the bad designs Web site http://www.baddesigns.com. Make a list of the factors that make a design unworkable.

**5-4.** Sometimes failures provide the best opportunities for new products and services. Read the Post-It Note story at http://www.3m.com. Search the Net for at least one other failure-to-success story.

**5-5.** *Business Week* sponsors a best design competition each year. Read about this year's winners and write a brief summary about what makes these designs special.

**5-6.** Automakers often post concept cars on their Web sites. Find out how the design process for these cars differs. Which cars do you think will be commercially successful? Why?

**5-7.** Construct a perceptual map for the following products or services: (a) business schools in your state or region, (b) software packages, and (c) video rental stores. Label the axes with the dimensions you feel are most relevant. Explain how perceptual maps are used.

**5-8.** Read about benchmarking at the American Productivity and Quality Center http://www.apqc.org and the Benchmarking Exchange http://www.benchnet.com. What is benchmarking? What types of things do these organizations benchmark? How are the studies conducted? If possible, access one of the free benchmarking reports and summarize its findings.

**5-9.** Find out if your university benchmarks itself against other universities. If so, write a summary of the characteristics that are considered, the measures that are used, and the results. Do the data support your views as a customer?

**5-10.** What kinds of analyses are conducted in a feasibility study for new products?

**5-11.** Differentiate between performance specifications, design specifications, and manufacturing specifications. Write sample specifications for a product or service of your choosing.

**5-12.** How are reliability and maintainability related? Give an example for a product or service you have experienced.

**5-13.** Explain how simplification and standardization can improve designs. How does modular design differ from standardization?

**5-14.** How can design teams improve the quality of design? Relate your experiences in working in teams. What were the advantages and disadvantages?

**5-15.** Discuss the concept of concurrent design. What are the advantages of this approach? How would you apply concurrent design to a group project?

**5-16.** What does design for manufacture entail? List several techniques that can facilitate the DFM process.

**5-17.** Describe the objectives of failure mode and effect analysis, fault tree analysis, and value analysis. Apply one of the techniques to a project, computer assignment, or writing assignment you have recently completed.

**5-18.** Access the Environmental Protection Agency http://www.epa.gov/ to read about the U.S. government's commitment to environmental product design. Compare the U.S. approach to that of other countries.

**5-19.** Search the Internet for two or more companies that design for environment. What are the main components of each company's green design initiative? How do their approaches differ?

**5-20.** Link to the International Standards Organization http://www.iso.org and explore ISO 14000. What do these standards entail? How were they developed? How does a company attain ISO 14001 certification? Why would they want to?

**5-21.** What is the purpose of QFD? Find out if companies really use QFD by visiting the QFD Institute http://www.qfdi.org and summarizing one of their case studies.

**5-22.** Discuss the concept of robust design. Give an example of a robust product or service.

**5-23.** How does CAD relate to CAE and CAM? How do CAD and the Internet promote collaborative design?

**5-24.** List eight characteristics of services and explain what impact each characteristic has on the design process.

**5-25.** Describe the service package for (a) a bank, (b) an airline, and (c) a lawn service.

**5-26.** Generate as many ideas as you can for additional services or improvements in service delivery for (a) banking, (b) higher education, and (c) health care.

## PROBLEMS

**5-1.** Use the following instructions to construct and test a prototype paper airplane. Are the instructions clear? How would you improve the design of the airplane or the manner in which the design is communicated?

- Begin with an 8 1/2 in. by 11 in. sheet of paper.
- Fold the paper together lengthwise to make a center line.
- Open the paper and fold the top corners to the center line.
- Fold the two top sides to the center line.
- Fold the airplane in half.
- Fold back the wings to meet the center line.
- Hold the plane by the center line and let it fly.

**5-2.** An alternative airplane design is given here. Follow the assembly instructions and test the airplane. Are the instructions clear? Compare the performance of this airplane design with the one described in Problem 5.1. Which plane was easier to construct? How would you improve the design of this plane or the manner in which the design is communicated?

- Begin with an 8 1/2 in. by 11 in. sheet of paper.
- Fold it lengthwise in alternating directions. The folds should be about 1 in. wide.
- Hold the top of the folded paper in one hand and fan out the back portion with the other hand.
- Make a small fold in the nose of the plane to hold it together, and let it fly.

**5-3.** Calculate the reliability of the following system.

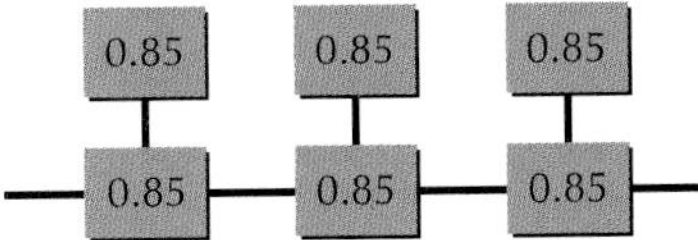


**5-4.** A broadcasting station has five major subsystems that must all be operational before a show can go on the air. If each subsystem has the same reliability, what reliability would be required to be 95% certain of broadcast success? 98% certain? 99% certain?

**5-5.** Competition for a new generation of computers is so intense that MicroTech has funded three separate design teams to create the new systems. Due to varying capabilities of the team members, it is estimated that team A has a 90% probability of coming up with an acceptable design before the competition, team B has an 80% chance, and team C has a 70% chance. What is the probability that MicroTech will beat the competition with its new computers?

**5-6.** MagTech assembles tape players from four major components arranged as follows:

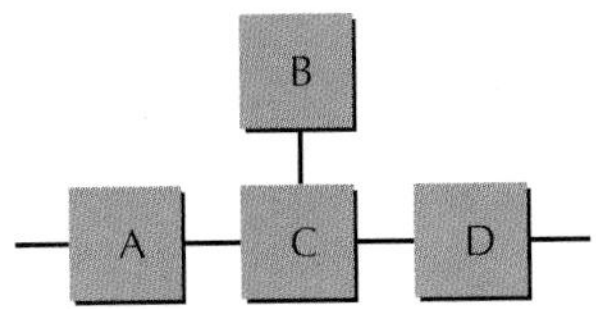


The components can be purchased from three different vendors, who have supplied the following reliability data:

| Component | Vendor 1 | Vendor 2 | Vendor 3 |
|---|---|---|---|
| A | 0.94 | 0.85 | 0.92 |
| B | 0.86 | 0.88 | 0.90 |
| C | 0.90 | 0.93 | 0.95 |
| D | 0.93 | 0.95 | 0.90 |

a. If MagTech has decided to use only one vendor to supply all four components, which vendor should be selected?

b. Would your decision change if all the components were assembled in series?

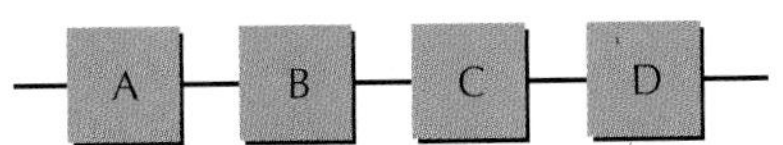


**5-7.** Glen Evans is an emergency medical technician for a local rescue team and is routinely called on to render emergency care to citizens facing crisis situations. Although Glen has received extensive training, he also relies heavily on his equipment for support. During a normal call, Glen uses five essential pieces of equipment, whose individual reliabilities are 0.98, 0.97, 0.95, 0.96, and 0.99, respectively.

a. Glen claims his equipment has maximum probability of failure of 5%. Is he correct?

b. What individual equipment reliabilities would guarantee an overall reliability of 96%?

**5-8.** Examine the systems given below. Which system is more reliable, a or b? c or d? Now calculate the reliability of each system. Were your perceptions correct?

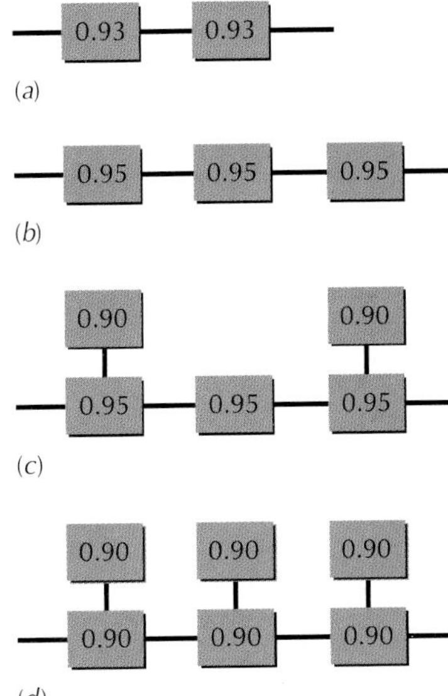


If it costs $1000 for each 90% reliable component, $1500 for each 93% component, $2000 for each 95% reliable component, and $10,000 to replace a failed system, which system would you choose, a or b? c or d?

**5-9.** Omar Marquez is the audio engineer for Summer Musical Enterprises. The group is considering the purchase of a new sound system consisting of five separate components. The components are arranged in series with identical reliabilities. The Basic system with component reliabilities of 80% costs $1000, the Standard system with component reliabilities of 90% costs $2000, and the Professional system with component reliabilities of 99% costs $5000. The cost of a failure during a performance is $50,000.

a. Calculate the reliability of each system. Which system would you recommend?

b. Omar has learned that each system described above can also be purchased in a Plus configuration, where each component has an identical backup, for double the original cost. Which system would you recommend now?

**5-10.** La Pied manufactures high-quality orthopedic shoes. Over the past five years, the general public has "found" La Pied products, and sales have skyrocketed. One unanticipated result has been a sharp increase in factory returns for repair, since local shoe repair shops do not have the materials or expertise to fix La Pied products. The popular walking sandal has been targeted for redesign. Currently, the leather pieces are glued together, then stitched. There is a 70% chance that the glue will last for the life of the sandal, and a 50% chance that the stitching will remain intact. Determine the sandal's reliability. How would the reliability of the sandal increase if the company adds two more rows of stitching?

**5-11.** The Management Department recently purchased a small copier for faculty use. Although the workload of the office

staff has improved somewhat, the secretaries are still making too many trips to the Dean's office when the departmental copier is out of service. Sylvia, the departmental secretary, has been keeping track of failure rates and service times. With a mean time between failures of 100 hours and a mean time to repair of 24 hours, how much of the time is the new copier available for faculty use?

**5-12.** Karen Perez runs an office supply store that also performs simple office services, such as copying. It is time to purchase a new high-speed copier and Karen has learned that machine uptime is a critical factor in selection. She has gathered the following data on reliability and maintainability for the three copiers she is considering. Given that all other factors are equal, which machine should Karen purchase?

| Copier | Mean Time Between Failures (Hours) | Mean Time to Repair (Hours) |
|---|---|---|
| Able Copy | 40 | 1 |
| Business Mate | 80 | 4 |
| Copy Whiz | 240 | 8 |

**5-13.** As a regional sales manager, Nora Burke travels frequently and relies on her cell phone to keep up to date with clients. She has tried three different service providers, Airway, Bellular, and CyCom, with varying degrees of success. The number of failures in a typical eight-hour day and the average time to regain service are shown below. Nora's contract is up for renewal. Which cellular service should she use?

| Cellular Co. | No. of Failures | Time to Regain Service |
|---|---|---|
| Airway | 10 | 2 minutes |
| Bellular | 8 | 4 minutes |
| CyCom | 3 | 10 minutes |

**5-14.** Nadia Algar is the overworked IT resource person for her department. In the next round of computer purchases, she is determined to recommend a vendor who does a better job of documenting possible errors in the system and whose customer service line is more responsive to the needs of her colleagues. Nadia compiled the following data over an eight-week observation period. Assuming 40 hours per week, which computer vendor should Nadia pursue?

| Computer Vendor | Number of Problems | Mean Time to Reach Customer Service (Hours) | Mean Time to Fix Problem (Hours) |
|---|---|---|---|
| JCN | 50 | 3.0 | 2.0 |
| Bell | 100 | 2.0 | 1.0 |
| Comtron | 250 | 1.0 | 0.5 |

**5-15.** The PlayBetter Golf Company has experienced a steady decline in sales of golf bags over the past five years. The basic golf bag design has not changed over that period, and PlayBetter's CEO, Jack Palmer, has decided that the time has come for a customer-focused overhaul of the product. Jack read about a new design method called QFD in one of his professional magazines (it was used to design golf balls), and he commissioned a customer survey to provide data for the design process. Customers considered the following requirements essential for any golf bag they would purchase and rated PlayBetter's bag (X) against two competitor bags (A and B) on those requirements.

| Customer Requirements | Competitive Assessment 1 | 2 | 3 | 4 | 5 |
|---|---|---|---|---|---|
| Lightweight | | B | A | | X |
| Comfortable carrying strap | | | | XBA | |
| Stands upright | | | | | XBA |
| Sturdy handle | | XBA | | | |
| Easy to remove/replace clubs | | X | | B | A |
| Easy to identify clubs | | X | | | BA |
| Protects clubs | | B | X | A | |
| Plenty of compartments | | B | X | | A |
| Place for towel | | | BAX | | |
| Place for scorecard/pencil | | XBA | | | |
| Easy to clean | | X | B | | A |
| Attractive | X | | A | B | |

Construct a house of quality for golf bags. Then write a brief report to Mr. Palmer recommending revisions to the current golf bag design and explaining how those recommendations were determined.

**5-16.** Students often complain that the requirements of assignments or projects are unclear. From the student's perspective, whoever can guess what the professor wants wins the highest grade. Thus, grades appear to be assigned somewhat arbitrarily. If you have ever felt that way, here is your chance to clarify that next project or assignment.

Construct a house of quality for a paper or project. View the professor as the customer. For the perceptual map, have your professor compare one of your papers with typical A, B, or C papers. When you have completed the exercise, give your opinion on the usefulness of QFD for this application.

**5-17.** Create a house of quality for a computer. Develop customer requirements related to ease of use, cost, capabilities, and connectivity. Make sure the customer requirements are a "wish list" stated in nontechnical terms.

**5-18.** Create a QFD example from your own experience. Describe the product or service to be designed and then complete a house of quality using representative data. Explain the entries in the house and how target values were reached. Also, describe how other houses might flow from the initial house you built. Finally, relate how QFD improves the design process for the example you chose.

## CASE PROBLEM 5.1

### *Lean and Mean*

Megan McNeil, product manager for Lean and Mean (L&M) weight reduction company, is considering offering its own brand of prepared dinners to its clients. Clients would order the dinners, usually a month's supply at a time, from L&M's Web site and have them delivered to their home address. The dinners would, of course, encourage weight loss, but would also be more nutritious, tastier, and easier to prepare than current grocery store offerings. The price would most likely be on the high end of the scale.

The product design team has constructed the framework for a house of quality from initial customer interviews. Now the team is set to perform a competitive assessment by selecting three popular grocery store brands and measuring the design characteristics. As the team works on the house, it is anticipated that additional design characteristics may emerge. The target row of the house would represent L&M's new brand.

Complete the following house of quality, and write a report to Megan containing your recommendations for the new product development. Be sure to explain how you arrived at your conclusions.

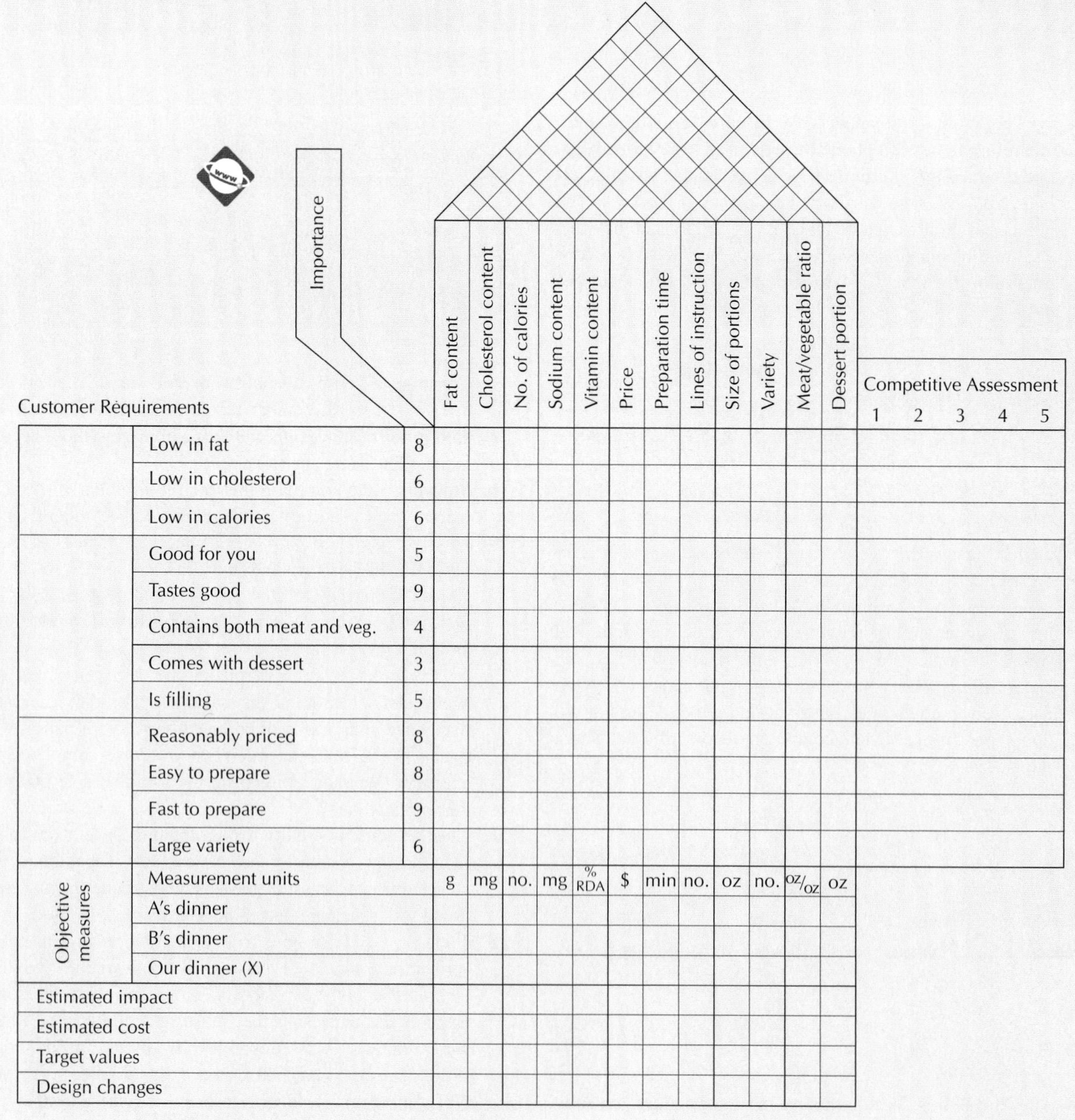

## REFERENCES

Baldwin, C., and K. Clark. *Design Rules: The Power of Modularity*. Boston: MIT Press, 2000.

Blackburn, J. (ed.). *Time-Based Competition: The Next Battleground*. Homewood, IL: Irwin, 1991.

Bowen, H. K., K. Clark, and C. Holloway. *The Perpetual Enterprise Machine*. New York: Oxford University Press, 1994.

Collier, D. A. *The Service/Quality Solution*. New York: Irwin, 1994.

Ealey, L. *Quality by Design: Taguchi Methods and U.S. Industry*. Dearborn, MI: ASI Press, 1988.

Garvin, D. *Managing Quality*. New York: Macmillan, 1988.

Haksever, C., R. Murdick, B. Render, and R. Russell. *Service Management and Operations*. Upper Saddle River, NJ: Prentice Hall, 2000.

Halpern, M. "CPC: Exploiting E-Business for Product Realization." *Gartner Advisory Strategic Analysis Report* February 28, 2001.

Hauser, J. R., and D. Clausing. "The House of Quality." *Harvard Business Review* (May–June 1988), pp. 63–73.

Heskett, J. L., W. E. Sasser, and C. Hart. *Service Breakthroughs: Changing the Rules of the Game*. New York: Macmillan, 1990.

Kelley, T., Jonathan Littman, and Tom Peters, *The Art of Innovation: Lessons in Creativity from IDEO*. New York: Currency/Doubleday, 2001.

King, B. *Better Designs in Half the Time*. Methuen, MA: GOAL/QPC, 1989.

Leonard-Barton, D. *Wellsprings of Knowledge: Building and Sustaining the Sources of Innovation*. Boston: Harvard Business School Press, 1995.

Lovelock, C. H. *Managing Services: Marketing, Operations, and Human Resources*. Englewood Cliffs, NJ: Prentice Hall, 1992.

Prahalad, C. K. and Venkat Ramaswamy. *The Future of Competition: Co-Creating Unique Value with Customers*. Boston: Harvard Business School Press, 2004.

Sampson, S. E. *Understanding Service Businesses* Salt Lake City, UT: Brigham Young University, 1999.

Shostack, G. L. "Designing Services That Deliver." *Harvard Business Review* (January–February 1984), pp. 133–139.

Stoll, H. "Design for Manufacture." *Manufacturing Engineering* (January 1988), pp. 67–73.

Sullivan, L. P. "Quality Function Deployment." *Quality Progress* 19 (6; 1986):39.

Taguchi, G., and D. Clausing. "Robust Quality." *Harvard Business Review* (January–February 1990), pp. 65–75.

Whitney, D. "Manufacturing by Design." *Harvard Business Review* (July–August 1988), pp. 83–91.

Womack, J. P., D. T. Jones, and D. Roos. *The Machine that Changed the World*. New York: Macmillan, 1990.

# Processes, Technology, and Capacity

CHAPTER 6

Web resources for this chapter include

- Internet Exercises
- Online Practice Quizzes
- Virtual Tours
- Excel Worksheets
- Company and Resource Weblinks
- Animated Demo Problems
- Microsoft Project Exhibits

www.wiley.com/college/russell

## CHAPTER OUTLINE

In this chapter you will learn about . . .

- Process Planning
- Process Analysis
- Process Innovation
- Technology Decisions
- Capacity Decisions

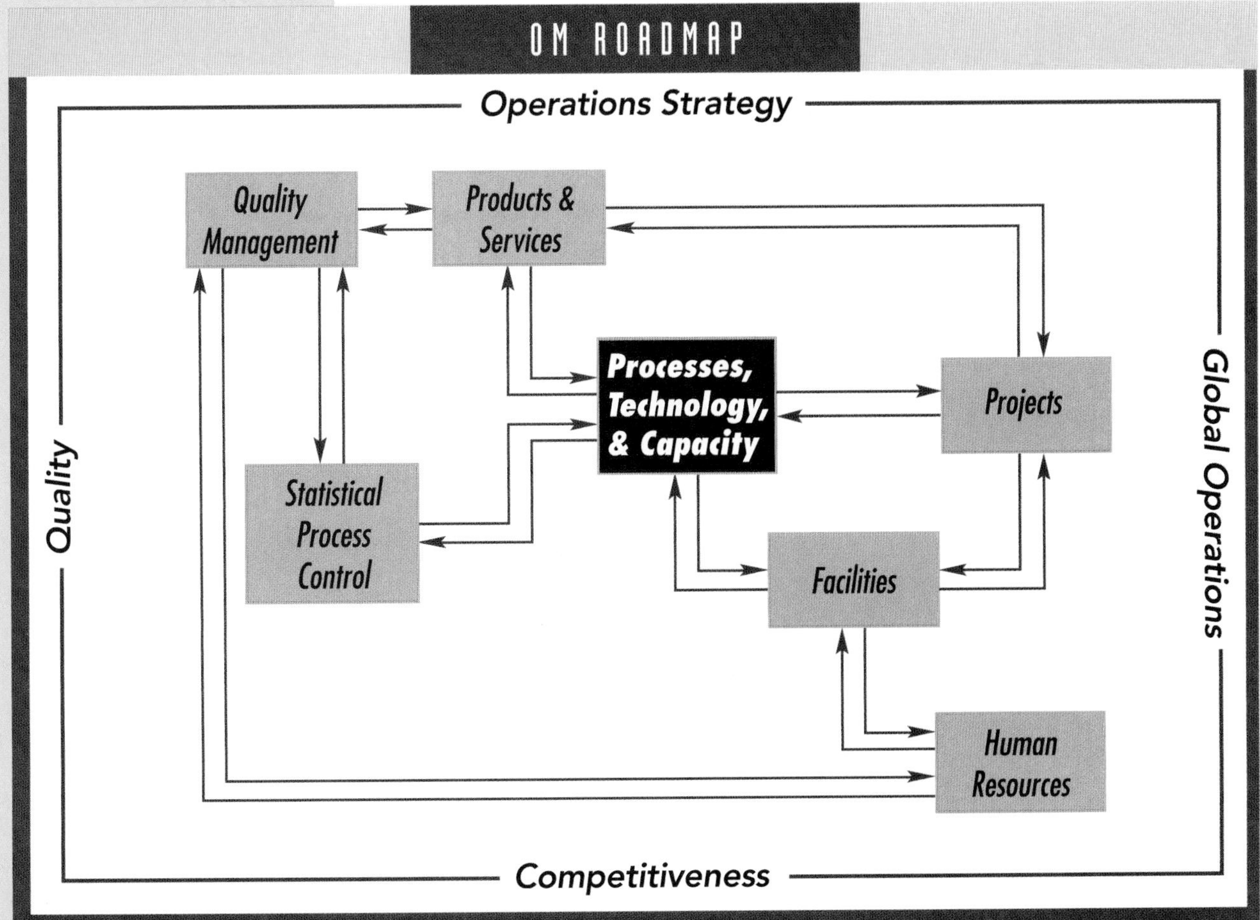

## HOW DELL EXCELS

*Direct from Dell.* Michael Dell reshaped the computer industry with build-to-order computers sold directly to consumers. His business model positioned the company for emerging Internet sales, last year topping $16 billion. But Dell has done more than streamline the selling and distribution process: he's streamlined the manufacturing process as well.

Dell can deliver the latest technology exactly how the customer wants it with blinding speed—eight customized fully loaded PowerEdge servers delivered to NASDAQ within 36 hours; 2000 PCs and 4000 servers loaded with proprietary and multimedia software delivered to 2000 different Wal-Mart stores in six weeks. How does Dell do it? Through close customer contact and carefully orchestrated manufacturing.

Dell manufactures its computer systems in six locations—Texas, Tennessee, Brazil, Ireland, Malaysia, and China. Dell's state-of-the-art OptiPlex plant is a showcase for networked manufacturing. Located in Round Rock, Texas, the plant covers 200,000 square feet (that's 23 football fields), but allocates only 100 square feet (the size of an average bedroom) for incoming parts. That's enough for two hours worth of component inventory. Finished product inventory corporatewide is just five days worth (with a goal of 2 1/2 days), compared to an industry average of 50 to 90 days.

The OptiPlex plant produces in excess of 20,000 custom-ordered machines a day. In the command center, 100 servers send electronic instructions to double-decker conveyors speeding components to assembly stations. Computer screens at the assembly stations tell two-member teams which PC or server to build. Drives, chips, and boards are added according to customer order by workers who respond to red and green signal lights on component drawers. Snap together assembly takes three to four minutes; then products sail along to finishing areas where they are customized, boxed, and sent to delivery trucks waiting at loading dock doors.

i2 Technologies provides the software that runs Dell factories. Online orders are downloaded every hour to *Factory Planner*, which generates a new production schedule every two hours. The system notifies suppliers of Dell's exact material needs, and prioritizes orders based on the availability of those materials. As machines are built, the parts needed for the next two-hour set of orders are being shipped from supplier hubs. Dell suppliers maintain hubs (mini-warehouses) with two weeks' worth of inventory near each Dell factory. The hub has 15 minutes to confirm that it has the needed parts and 1 hour 15 minutes to deliver them to the plant.

WebMethods handles e-procurement for Dell. Major business customers can access *Dell Premier Page*, where an electronic catalogue is posted containing approved product configurations, options, and negotiated prices specific to that customer's account. An online order triggers an internal purchase requisition at the customer's site. If approval of the requisition is not received within 24 hours, it is routed to that person's manager for imme-

*At 21, Michael Dell founded the company that bears his name. Twenty-five years later, Dell Inc. continues to innovate the process of making and selling computers.*

diate response. After two approvals, Dell processes the order and starts building the machines. Delivery averages two days after the order is placed.

When unexpected events delay supplier deliveries, Dell is ready. Consider this scenario:

*A convoy of trucks full of 17-in. monitors overturns on its way from Mexico to Austin, Texas. The trucker notifies Dell electronically of the loss. Dell's computer system accesses its suppliers' inventory to see how many 17-in. monitors are available and where they are. The system also projects when Dell will run out of monitors, and proposes a solution—Dell has another supplier with a 20% surplus of 19-in. monitors. Dell updates its Web site and sends e-mail announcements to customers of a special deal—for only $25, instead of the normal $100, Dell will upgrade 17-in. monitors to 19-in. monitors. Customers are happy and the problem is solved.*

Making processes smoother and seamless between manufacturer, supplier, and customer is all part of Michael Dell's pursuit of *frictionless trade*. That's how Dell excels.

Sources: Stacy Perman, "Automate or Die," *eCompany Now* (July 2001); Betsy Morris and Matthew Boyle, "Can Michael Dell Escape the Box?" *Fortune* (October 2000); Jennifer Merritt, "How Dell Keeps from Stumbling," *Business Week* (May 14, 2001); Michael Kanellos, "Dell's Success in the Details," *CNET News.com* (March 4, 2004).

A **process** is a group of related tasks with specific inputs and outputs. Processes exist to create value for the customer, the shareholder, or society. *Process design* defines what tasks need to be done and how they are to be coordinated among functions, people, and organizations. Planning, analyzing, and improving processes is the essence of operations management.

**Process:** a group of related tasks with specific inputs and outputs.

**Process strategy** is an organization's overall approach for physically producing goods and providing services. Process decisions should reflect how the firm has chosen to compete in the marketplace, reinforce product decisions, and facilitate the achievement of corporate goals. A firm's process strategy defines its:

**Process strategy:** an organization's overall approach for physically producing goods and services.

- ***Capital intensity:*** The mix of capital (i.e., equipment, automation) and labor resources used in the production process.
- ***Process flexibility:*** The ease with which resources can be adjusted in response to changes in demand, technology, products or services, and resource availability.
- ***Vertical integration:*** The extent to which the firm will produce the inputs and control the outputs of each stage of the production process.
- ***Customer involvement:*** The role of the customer in the production process.

Process strategy and capacity strategy are closely linked. In this chapter we examine the planning, analysis, and innovation of processes, as well as the technology and capacity decisions related to those processes.

## PROCESS PLANNING

**Process planning** determines *how* a product will be produced or a service provided. It decides which components will be made in-house and which will be purchased from a supplier, selects processes and develops and documents the specifications for manufacture and delivery. In this section, we discuss make-or-buy decisions, process selection, and process plans.

**Process planning:** converts designs into workable instructions for manufacture or delivery.

### MAKE-OR-BUY DECISIONS

Companies that control the production of virtually all of their component parts, including the source of raw materials, are said to be *vertically integrated*. This strategy was popular for many years when companies did not want to be dependent on others for their livelihood. Today, *outsourcing* is more common, as companies partner with a network of suppliers to provide goods and services to their customers. Chapter 10 discusses the topics of supplier partnerships and supply chain management. For process planning, we need to decide which items will be purchased from an outside supplier and which items will be produced in our own factories. This first-cut sourcing decision is called *make-or-buy*.

The make-or-buy decision rests on an evaluation of the following factors:

Make-or-buy decisions are influenced by many factors.

1. ***Cost.*** Would it be cheaper to make the item or buy it? to perform the service in-house or subcontract it out? This is the primary consideration in most make-or-buy decisions. The cost of *buying* the item includes the purchase price, transportation costs, and various tariffs, taxes, and fees. The cost of coordinating production over long distances and increased inventory levels should also be considered. The cost of *making* the item includes labor, material, and overhead.

   In some situations a company may decide to buy an item rather than make it (or vice versa) when, from a cost standpoint, it would be cheaper to do otherwise. The remaining factors in this list represent noneconomic factors that can influence or dominate the economic considerations.
2. ***Capacity.*** Companies that are operating at less than full capacity may elect to make components rather than buy them, especially if maintaining a level workforce is important. Sometimes the available capacity is not sufficient to make all the components, so choices have to be made. The stability of demand is also important. Typically, it is better to produce in-house those parts or products with steady demand that consume a set capacity, whereas those whose demand patterns are uncertain or volatile are usually subcontracted.
3. ***Quality.*** The capability to provide quality parts consistently is an important consideration in the make-or-buy decision. In general, it is easier to control the quality of items produced in your own factory. However, standardization of parts, supplier certification, and supplier involvement in design can improve the quality of supplied parts.
4. ***Speed.*** The savings from purchasing an item from a far-off vendor can be eaten up by the lengthy transit time of offshore shipments. At other times a supplier can provide goods sooner than the manufacturer. The smaller supplier is often more flexible, too, and can adapt quickly to design and technology changes. Of course, speed is useful only if it is reliable.
5. ***Reliability.*** Suppliers need to be reliable in both the quality and the timing of what they supply. Unexpected delays in shipments or partially filled orders because of quality rejects can wreak havoc with the manufacturing system. Many companies today are requiring that their suppliers meet certain quality and delivery standards to be certified as an approved supplier. As discussed in Chapter 3, the most common quality certification is ISO 9000. Other companies assess huge penalties for unreliable supply. DaimlerChrysler, for example, fines its suppliers $30,000 for each *hour* an order is late.
6. ***Expertise.*** Companies that are especially good at making or designing certain items may want to keep control over their production. Coca-Cola would not want to release its formula to a supplier, even if there were guarantees of secrecy. Although automakers might outsource many of their component parts, they need proprietary control over major components such as engines, transmissions, and electronic guidance systems. Japanese, Taiwanese, and Korean firms are currently learning American expertise in aircraft design and manufacture by serving as suppliers of component parts. Chinese markets are often flooded with cheap knockoffs of goods manufactured by suppliers in that country. The protection of intellectual property is a major concern in expanded supply chains. Thus, the decision of whether to share your expertise with a supplier for economic gains is a difficult one.

The make-or-buy decision is not as simple as the name implies. Rather, choices can be made along a continuum from vertical integration to a single purchasing decision. Figure 6.1 illustrates the sourcing continuum.

## PROCESS SELECTION

The next step in process planning is to select a production process for those items we will produce in-house. We introduced the product-process matrix and four types of production processes in Chapter 2—*projects, batch production, mass production*, and *contin-*

| Vertical Integration (100% ownership) | Joint Venture (equity partner) | Strategic Alliance (long-term supplier contract; collaborative relationship) | Arms-Length Relationship (short-term contract or single purchasing decision) |
|---|---|---|---|

Figure 6.1
**The Sourcing Continuum**

*Source:* Adapted from Robert Hayes, Gary Pisano, David Upton, and Steven Wheelwright, *Operations Strategy and Technology: Pursuing the Competitive Edge* (Hoboken, NJ: 2005), p. 120.

*uous production*. Let's look at them more closely here and explore the implications of process choice for a firm.

## PROJECTS

**Project:** the one-of-a-kind production of a product to customer order.

**Projects** represent one-of-a-kind production for an individual customer. They tend to involve large sums of money and last a considerable length of time. For those reasons, customers are few and customer involvement intense. Customers are heavily involved in the design of the product and may also specify how certain processes are to be carried out. In some cases, the customer will have representatives on site to observe the production process, or send in inspectors to certify quality at critical stages of project development.

Most companies do not have the resources (or time) to complete all the work on a project themselves, so subcontracting is common. The production process, as well as the final product, are basically designed anew for each customer order. Thus, the process is very flexible. And given the lengthy duration of a project, changes in customer preferences, technology, and costs cause frequent adjustments in product and process design. Managing these *engineering change orders* (ECOs) is a major concern in project management.

## THE COMPETITIVE EDGE

### Factories for Hire

Solectron, Flextronics, SCI, Jabil—what do they make? Any type of electronics imaginable, but not for the consumer—for companies like Motorola, Ericsson, Philips, Compaq, Cisco, and Sony. Never heard of Solectron or Flextronics? These companies are contract manufacturers—factories for hire—and they are huge. Flextronics employs 4000 workers at its 125-acre industrial park in Guadalajara, Mexico. Solectron, with 44 factories in 20 countries, expects to reach $20 billion in sales next year.

Electronics firms, like most other industries, have always subcontracted out some of their manufacturing, mostly to assemblers of circuit boards, and mostly when labor was tight. IBM pioneered the outsourcing of entire products in the 1980s when it contracted with SCI to build its PCs. The exception years ago has become the rule today. Today's contractors, called *electronic manufacturing services providers* (EMS), are full-fledged supply chain partners. They help design products to make them easy to manufacture, buy components, and organize distribution and repair. The parties work together building prototypes and smoothing out problems in the production process.

With the Internet, customers and suppliers can integrate technical, production, and financial data. HP can check on the Web in real time whether its printers are being made properly, and act immediately if they aren't. Solectron has real-time access to its customers' sales data to plan its production, and the customer can send design changes directly to automated equipment in Solectron plants. This type of transfer would be impossible in labor-intensive industries, but with most of the work performed by surface-mount technology robots, design and manufacture can be effectively split. Because these robots are expensive and complex, they are best handled by specialists—experts who, through high-volume production of a variety of products, have mastered their use. Contractors also get huge volume discounts from component suppliers.

But flexibility, not cost, is the primary reason for electronics outsourcing. Subcontracting manufacturing is less risky than building new factories. Solectron and Flextronics each have two dozen factories around the world. Firms can ramp up production within weeks, anywhere, and spend more time on core strengths, such as innovation. Start-ups no longer need factories to compete with established firms. Similar trends are emerging in other industries, such as clothing, toys, and pharmaceuticals; and in services as well—banks, education, and health care.

*Sources:* Pete Engaro, "The Barons of Outsourcing," *Business Week* (August 28, 2000); Steven Baker, "Outsourcing Alone Won't Save Nokia's Rivals," *Business Week* (February 12, 2001); "Have Factory, Will Travel," *The Economist* (February 12, 2000); "IBM Outsourcing to Solectron," *Business* (January 7, 2003).

Another concern is keeping track of all the activities that are taking place and making sure they are completed correctly and on time, so as not to delay other activities.

Cutting-edge technology, project teams, and close customer contact make project work exciting. But projects can also be risky, with their large investment in resources, huge swings in resource requirements (as new projects begin and old ones end), limited learning curve, and dependence on a small customer base.

Examples of projects include constructing a building, airplane, or ship; planning a rock concert; and developing a new product. Projects are managed very differently from other types of processes. We discuss project management in detail in Chapter 9.

## Batch Production

Making products one at a time and treating their production as a project can be time consuming and cost-prohibitive. Most products can be made more quickly and more efficiently in volume. A production system that processes items in small groups or *batches* is called batch production. **Batch production** is characterized by fluctuating demand, short production runs of a wide variety of products, customization, and highly skilled workers.

**Batch production:** processing many different jobs through a system in groups (or batches).

Most of the operations in batch production involve fabrication (e.g., cutting, machining, finishing) rather than assembly. Jobs are sent through the system based on their processing requirements, so that jobs requiring lathe work are sent to one location, those requiring painting to another, and so forth. A job may be routed through many different machine centers before it is completed. If you were to track the flow of a particular customer order through the system, you would see a lot of stopping and starting as jobs queue at different machines, waiting to be processed. Work on a particular product is not continuous; it is *discrete* or intermittent.

Batch production is also common in services. In education, for example, a group of students in a classroom are taught by a skilled professor. At the end of class, students disperse following different schedules throughout the day perhaps to rejoin in another class later on.

*The construction of an aircraft carrier is an enormous project. A carrier accommodates a crew of more than 6000 people and a full-load displacement of 91,000 tons. The carrier also houses two nuclear reactors, enabling it to operate for 13 years without refueling. Modular construction, in which a ship is built in huge subassemblies or modules, has cut the production time of carriers and other ships in half. This is accomplished by outfitting several modules at one time and then adding them to the hull. Extensive use of CAD/CAM, precise tolerances, and careful quality control ensure that the modules fit together perfectly.*

*In batch production, items are processed in groups or batches, usually to customer order. Here, skilled workers are preparing various types of cakes in batches for their customers.*

The most flexible systems of batch production, capable of producing an infinite variety of customized products, are called *job shops*. Printers and copy centers, such as Kinko's, are job shops, as are machine tool manufacturers and custom frame shops.

Furniture, musical instruments, and bakery products are produced with batch production. Advantages of this type of system are its flexibility, the customization of output, and the reputation for quality that customization implies. Disadvantages include high per-unit costs, frequent changes in product mix, complex scheduling problems, variations in capacity requirements, and lengthy job completion times.

## Mass Production

**Mass production:** producing large volumes of a standard product for a mass market.

**Mass production**, also known as *repetitive* production, is used by producers who need to create more standardized products in larger quantities than batch production can economically handle. Products are made-to-stock for a mass market, demand is stable, and volume is high. Because of the stability and size of demand, the production system can afford to dedicate equipment to the production of a particular product. Thus, this type of system tends to be capital-intensive and highly repetitive, with specialized equipment and limited labor skills.

Mass production is usually associated with *flow lines* or *assembly lines*. *Flow* describes how a product moves through the system from one workstation to the next in order of the processing requirements for that particular product. (Batch production cannot be set up in this way because the processing requirements are different for each customer order.) *Assembly line* describes the way mass production is typically arranged—most of the operations are assembly-oriented and are performed in a line. Goods that are mass-produced include automobiles, televisions, personal computers, fast food, and most consumer goods.

Advantages of mass production are its efficiency, low per-unit cost, ease of manufacture and control, and speed. Disadvantages include the high cost of equipment, underutilization of human capabilities, the difficulties of adapting to changes in demand, technology, or product design, and the lack of responsiveness to individual customer requests.

## Continuous Production

**Continuous production:** producing very-high-volume commodity products.

**Continuous production** is used for very-high-volume commodity products that are very standardized. The system is highly automated (the worker's role is to monitor the equipment) and is typically in operation continuously 24 hours a day. The output is also

*Automobiles are mass produced on assembly lines worldwide, as shown in this Skoda assembly plant in Mlada Boleslav, Czech Republic.*

continuous, not discrete—meaning individual units are measured rather than counted. Steel, paper, paints, chemicals, and foodstuffs are produced by continuous production. Companies that operate in this fashion are referred to as *process industries*.

The advantages of this type of system are its efficiency, ease of control, and enormous capacity. Disadvantages include the large investment in plant and equipment, the limited variety of items that can be processed, the inability to adapt to volume changes, the cost of correcting errors in production, and the difficulties of keeping pace with new technology.

*Workers stand on a movable cart, called a skillet, to install a car engine on Ford's assembly line in Wayne, Michigan. The car chassis arrives at the workstation on an overhead monorail conveyor. The engine is "pumped up" to the correct height and placed in position. Material-handling equipment such as this helps workers perform their jobs safely and easily.*

| | Project | Batch Production | Mass Production | Continuous Production |
|---|---|---|---|---|
| ***Type of product*** | Unique | Made-to-order (customized) | Made-to-stock (standardized) | Commodity |
| ***Type of customer*** | One-at-a-time | Few individual customers | Mass market | Mass market |
| ***Product demand*** | Infrequent | Fluctuates | Stable | Very stable |
| ***Demand volume*** | Very low | Low to medium | High | Very high |
| ***No. of different products*** | Infinite variety | Many, varied | Few | Very few |
| ***Production system*** | Long-term project | Discrete, job shops | Repetitive, assembly lines | Continuous, process industries |
| ***Equipment*** | Varied | General-purpose | Special-purpose | Highly automated |
| ***Primary type of work*** | Specialized contracts | Fabrication | Assembly | Mixing, treating, refining |
| ***Worker skills*** | Experts, craftspersons | Wide range of skills | Limited range of skills | Equipment monitors |
| ***Advantages*** | Custom work, latest technology | Flexibility, quality | Efficiency, speed, low cost | Highly efficient, large capacity, ease of control |
| ***Disadvantages*** | Nonrepetitive, small customer base, expensive | Costly, slow, difficult to manage | Capital investment; lack of responsiveness | Difficult to change, far-reaching errors, limited variety |
| ***Examples*** | Construction, shipbuilding, spacecraft | Machine shops, print shops, bakeries, education | Automobiles, televisions, computers, fast food | Paint, chemicals, foodstuffs |

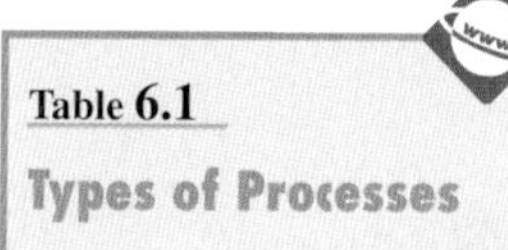
Table 6.1
Types of Processes

Table 6.1 summarizes our discussion of types of processes. As we move from projects to continuous production, demand volume increases; products become more standardized; systems become more capital-intensive, more automated, and less flexible; and customers become less involved.

## PROCESS SELECTION WITH BREAKEVEN ANALYSIS

Several quantitative techniques are available for selecting a process. One that bases its decision on the cost tradeoffs associated with demand volume is **breakeven analysis**. The components of breakeven analysis are volume, cost, revenue, and profit.

**Breakeven analysis:** examines the cost tradeoffs associated with demand volume.

*Volume* is the level of production, usually expressed as the number of units produced and sold. We assume that the number of units produced can be sold.

*Continuous processes are used for very-high-volume, commodity products whose output is measured rather than counted. The production system is capital-intensive and highly automated (with workers who monitor the equipment rather than perform the work) and is typically operated 24 hours a day.*

*Cost* is divided into two categories: fixed and variable. *Fixed costs* remain constant regardless of the number of units produced, such as plant and equipment and other elements of overhead. *Variable costs* vary with the volume of units produced, such as labor and material. The total cost of a process is the sum of its fixed cost and its total variable cost (defined as volume times per unit variable cost).

*Revenue* on a per-unit basis is simply the price at which an item is sold. *Total revenue* is price times volume sold. *Profit* is the difference between total revenue and total cost. These components can be expressed mathematically as follows:

$$\begin{aligned}
\text{Total cost} &= \text{fixed cost} + \text{total variable cost} \\
\text{TC} &= c_f + vc_v \\
\text{Total revenue} &= \text{volume} \times \text{price} \\
\text{TR} &= vp \\
\text{Profit} &= \text{total revenue} - \text{total cost} \\
Z &= \text{TR} - \text{TC} \\
&= vp - (c_f + vc_v)
\end{aligned}$$

where

$c_f$ = fixed cost

$v$ = volume (i.e., number of units produced and sold)

$c_v$ = variable cost per unit

$p$ = price per unit

In selecting a process, it is useful to know at what volume of sales and production we can expect to earn a profit. We want to make sure that the cost of producing a product does not exceed the revenue we will receive from the sale of the product. By equating total revenue with total cost and solving for $v$, we can find the volume at which profit is zero. This is called the *breakeven point*. At any volume above the breakeven point, we will make a profit. A mathematical formula for the breakeven point can be determined as follows:

$$\begin{aligned}
\text{TR} &= \text{TC} \\
vp &= c_f + vc_v \\
vp - vc_v &= c_f \\
v(p - c_v) &= c_f \\
v &= \frac{c_f}{p - c_v}
\end{aligned}$$

**Example 6.1**

**BreakEven Analysis**

Travis and Jeff own an adventure company called Whitewater Rafting. Because of quality and availability problems, the two entrepreneurs have decided to produce their own rubber rafts. The initial investment in equipment is estimated to be \$2000. Labor and material cost is approximately \$5 per raft. If the rafts can be sold at a price of \$10 each, what volume of demand will be necessary to break even?

*Solution*

$$\begin{aligned}
\text{Fixed cost} &= c_f = \$2{,}000 \\
\text{Variable cost} &= c_v = \$5 \text{ per raft} \\
\text{Price} &= p = \$10 \text{ per raft} \\
v &= \frac{c_f}{p - c_v} = \frac{2000}{10 - 5} = 400 \text{ rafts}
\end{aligned}$$

The solution is shown graphically in the following figure. The $x$-axis represents production or demand volume, and the $y$-axis represents dollars of revenue, cost, or profit. The total revenue line extends from the origin, with a slope equal to the unit price of a raft. The total cost line intersects the $y$-axis at a level corresponding to the fixed cost of the process and has a slope equal to the per-unit variable cost. The intersection of these two lines is the breakeven point. If demand is less than the breakeven point, the company will operate at a loss. But if demand exceeds the breakeven point, the company will be profitable. The company needs to sell more than 400 rafts to make a profit.

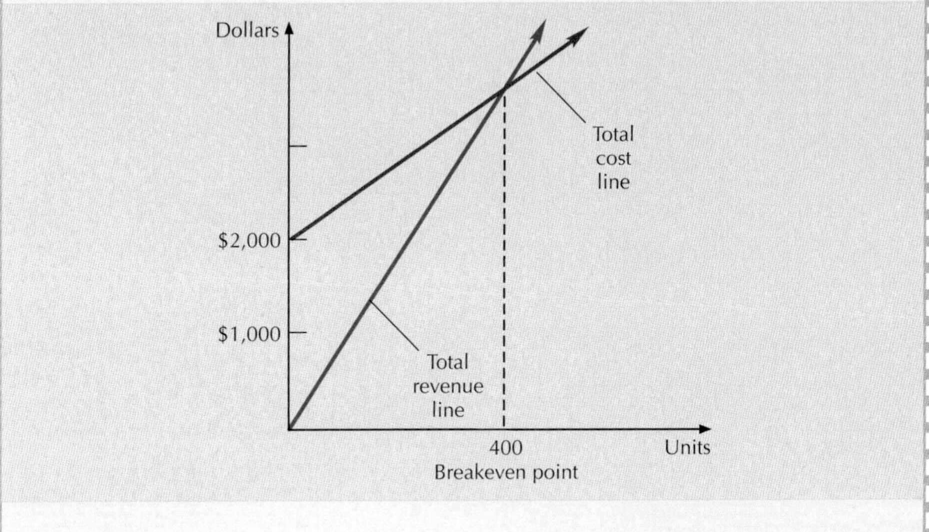


Breakeven analysis is especially useful when evaluating different degrees of automation. More automated processes have higher fixed costs but lower variable costs. The "best" process depends on the anticipated volume of demand for the product and the tradeoffs between fixed and variable costs. Let's see how breakeven analysis can guide the selection of a process among several alternatives.

Example 6.2

**Process Selection**

The owners of Whitewater Rafting believe demand for their product will far exceed the breakeven point in Example 6.1. They are now contemplating a larger initial investment of $10,000 for more automated equipment that would reduce the variable cost of manufacture to $2 per raft.

Compare the old manufacturing process described in Example 6.1 with the new process proposed here. For what volume of demand should each process be chosen?

*Solution*

If we call the old process, A, and the new process, B, the point of indifference between A and B is:

$$\begin{aligned} &\textit{Process A} \qquad\qquad \textit{Process B} \\ \$2{,}000 + \$5v &= \$10{,}000 + \$2v \\ \$3v &= \$8{,}000 \\ v &= 2667 \text{ rafts} \end{aligned}$$

If demand is less than or equal to 2667 rafts, the alternative with the lowest fixed cost, *process A*, should be chosen. If demand is greater than or equal to 2667 rafts, the alternative with the lowest variable cost, *process B*, is preferred. Our decision can be confirmed by examining the next graph. (Because the rafts will be sold for $10 apiece regardless of which process is used to manufacture them, no revenue line is needed.)

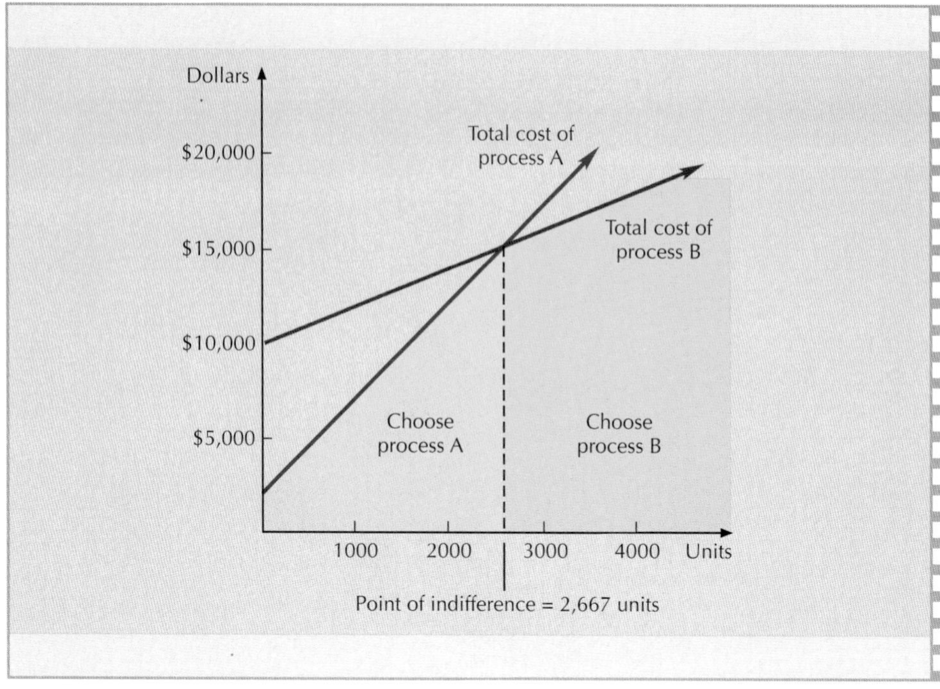


## PROCESS PLANS

**Process plans:** a set of documents that detail manufacturing and service delivery specifications.

**Process plans** are a set of documents that detail manufacturing and service delivery specifications. They begin with detailed drawings of product design (usually from a CAD system) and include *assembly charts* or bills of material (showing the parts and materials needed and how they are to be assembled together), *operations sheets* or routing sheets (listing the operations to be performed with details on equipment, tools, skills, etc.), and *quality-control checksheets* (specifying quality standards and quality data to be recorded).

Process plans are used in both manufacturing and service settings. A hospital, for example, has a set of process plans (often called protocols) for different types of medical procedures and service plans for each particular patient. Similarly, in manufacturing, some process plans are standard, and others are created for each customer order. Figure 6.2 shows an assembly chart for a Big Mac. Figure 6.3 shows an operations sheet for a plastic molded vacuum cleaner attachment.

# PROCESS ANALYSIS

*Process analysis* is the systematic examination of all aspects of a process to improve its operation—to make it faster, more efficient, less costly, or more responsive to the customer. The basic tools of process analysis are process flowcharts, diagrams, and maps.

**Process flowcharts:** highlight nonproductive activities.

**Process flowcharts** look at the manufacture of a product or delivery of a service from a broad perspective. The chart uses five standard symbols, shown in Figure 6.4, to describe a process: ○ for operations, □ for inspections, ⇒ for transportation, D for delay, and ▽ for storage. The details of each process are not necessary for this chart; however, the time required to perform each process and the distance between processes are often included. By incorporating nonproductive activities (*inspection, transportation, delay, storage*), as well as productive activities (*operations*), process flowcharts may be used to analyze the efficiency of a series of processes and to suggest improvements. They also provide a standardized method for documenting the steps in a process and can be used as a training tool. Automated versions of these charts are available that will superimpose the charts on floor plans of facilities. In this fashion, bottlenecks can be identified and layouts

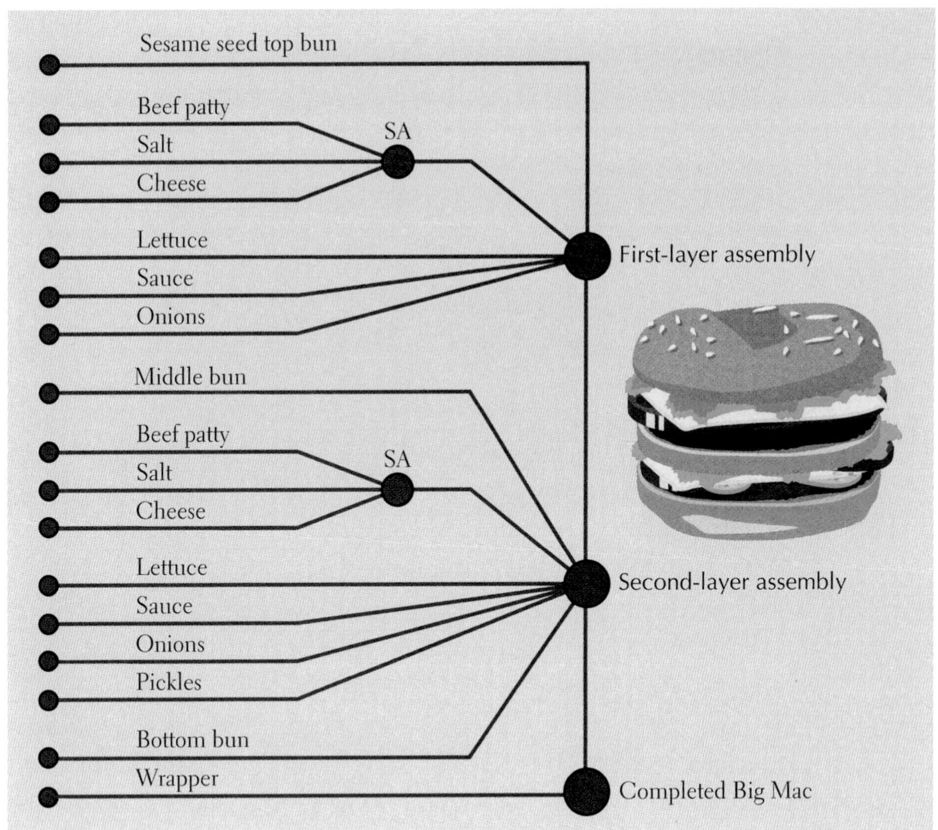


**Figure 6.2**
**An Assembly Chart for a Big Mac**

can be adjusted. Process flowcharts are used in both manufacturing and service operations. They are a basic tool for process innovation, as well as for job design.

Process improvement teams are likely to make a first pass at diagramming a process, with adhesive notes plastered on large sheets of paper connected with hand-drawn arrows. As documentation of the process becomes more complete, departments or companies may prefer particular symbols to represent inputs, outputs, decisions, activities, and resources.

Part name: Crevice Tool
Part No.: 52074
Usage: Hand-Vac
Assembly No.: 520

| *Oper. No.* | *Description* | *Dept.* | *Machine/Tools* | *Time* |
|---|---|---|---|---|
| 10 | Pour in plastic bits | 041 | Injection molding | 1 min |
| 20 | Insert mold | 041 | #076 | 2 min |
| 30 | Check settings & start machine | 041 | 113, 67, 650 | 20 min |
| 40 | Collect parts & lay flat | 051 | Plastics finishing | 10 min |
| 50 | Remove & clean mold | 042 | Parts washer | 15 min |
| 60 | Break off rough edges | 051 | Plastics finishing | 10 min |

**Figure 6.3**
**An Operations Sheet for a Plastic Part**

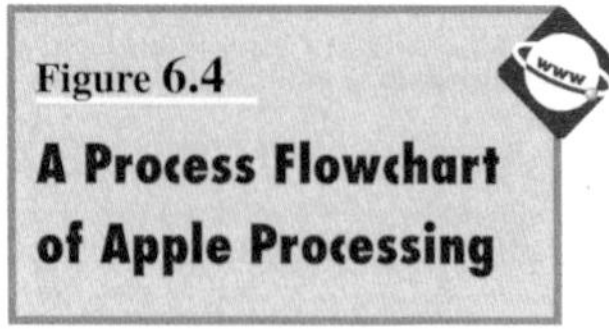

Figure 6.4
**A Process Flowchart of Apple Processing**

| Date: 9-30-06 | | | | | | Location: Graves Mountain | | |
|---|---|---|---|---|---|---|---|---|
| Analyst: TLR | | | | | | Process: Applesauce | | |
| Step | Operation | Transport | Inspect | Delay | Storage | Description of process | Time (min) | Distance (feet) |
| 1 | ● | ⇨ | □ | D | ∇ | Unload apples from truck | 20 | |
| 2 | O | ➡ | □ | D | ∇ | Move to inspection station | | 100 ft |
| 3 | O | ⇨ | ■ | D | ∇ | Weigh, inspect, sort | 30 | |
| 4 | O | ➡ | □ | D | ∇ | Move to storage | | 50 ft |
| 5 | O | ⇨ | □ | D | ▼ | Wait until needed | 360 | |
| 6 | O | ➡ | □ | D | ∇ | Move to peeler | | 20 ft |
| 7 | ● | ⇨ | □ | D | ∇ | Peel and core apples | 15 | |
| 8 | O | ⇨ | □ | D | ▼ | Soak in water until needed | 20 | |
| 9 | ● | ⇨ | □ | D | ∇ | Place on conveyor | 5 | |
| 10 | O | ➡ | □ | D | ∇ | Move to mixing area | | 20 ft |
| | Page 1 of 3 | | | | | Total | 450 | 190 ft |

Flowcharts can take many forms, from freehand drawings to animated simulations. Exhibit 6.1 shows a simple flowchart created in Excel. More sophisticated flowcharting tools are available from SmartDraw (www.smartdraw.com), RFFLow (www.rfflow.com), iGrafx (www.igrafx.com), and others. You may be able to download free trial copies of the software for limited periods of time.

**Service blueprint:** a type of process flowchart that emphasizes customer interaction and service-related terms such as *failure points* and *lines of visibility.*

Figure 6.5 shows a *process map*, so called because it maps out the activities performed by various people in the process. Often process maps will include a time scale as well. Figure 6.6 is a **service blueprint** of an installment lending process. Notice the *line of visibility* behind which "backroom" operations are performed. Potential failure points Ⓕ and time estimates are also included. The term *blueprint* is used to reinforce the idea that service delivery needs to be as carefully designed as a physical product and documented with a blueprint of its own.

*These workers at a Union Carbide chemical plant are displaying a process map they developed to analyze an existing process. The flowchart is not neat and tidy, but it does offer some obvious candidates for improvement. U.S. workers and managers in both industry and government are examining their processes in an attempt to reengineer work for high quality, less waste, and speedier operation.*

Exhibit 6.1

**Flowcharts in Excel**

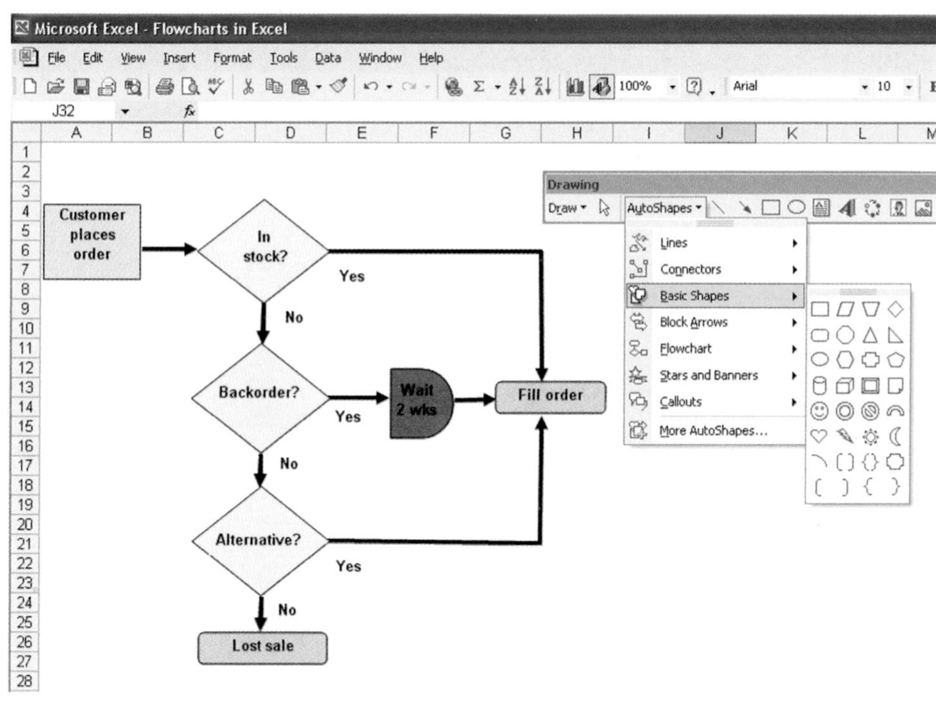


## Flowcharts in Excel

1. Open the *Drawing* toolbar (from the *View* menu, click on *Toolbars*, then *Drawing*)

2. From the *Drawing* toolbar, click on *AutoShapes*, then *Basic Shapes*. Select a shape by clicking on i A crosshair will appear.

3. Move the crosshair to the spreadsheet. Click and hold until the shape is the size you want it. Use the grid to align the shape and adjust to a standard size.

4. Place another shape on the spreadsheet. Connect the two shapes with an arrow by clicking on the arrow icon from the *Drawing* toolbar. Use the grid to keep the arrow straight.

5. Change the thickness of the arrow, the type of line, or the direction of the arrow by clicking on the line style, dash style, or arrow style icons.

6. For more sophisticated shapes, click on *AutoShapes*, then *Flowchart*.

7. Add labels or numbers to your flowchart by typing into a spreadsheet cell or a shape, or using the textbox.

8. After you've completed the flowchart, erase the background grid. From the *Tools* menu, click on *Options*, then uncheck the *Gridlines* box.

9. To copy the flowchart to a *Word* document, click-hold and move the cursor to encompass the entire flowchart. Then copy and *Paste Special* as a *Picture* or *Microsoft Excel Worksheet Object*.

10. Practice for best results.

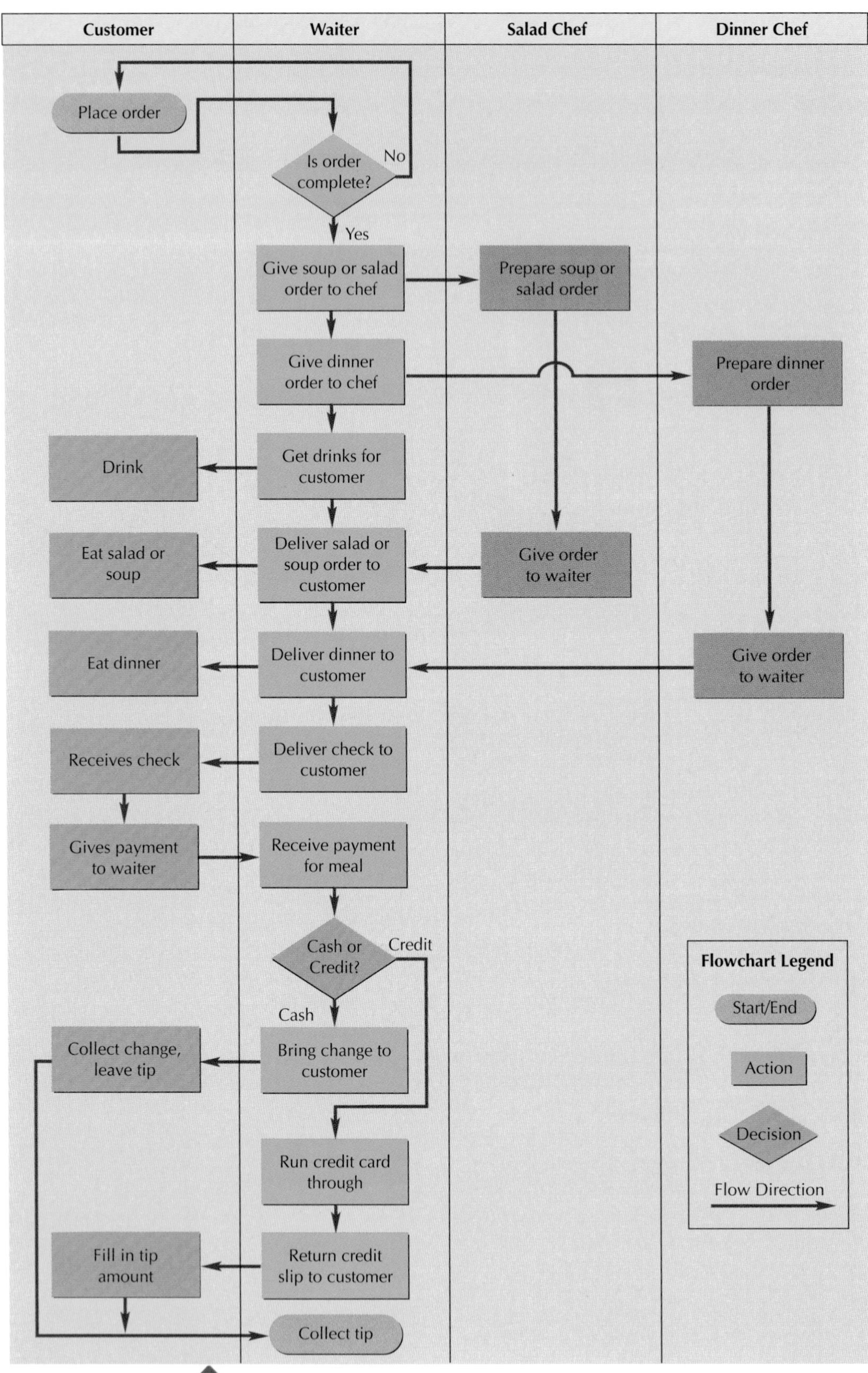


Figure 6.5

**A Process Map of Restaurant Service**

*Source:* www.SmartDraw.com

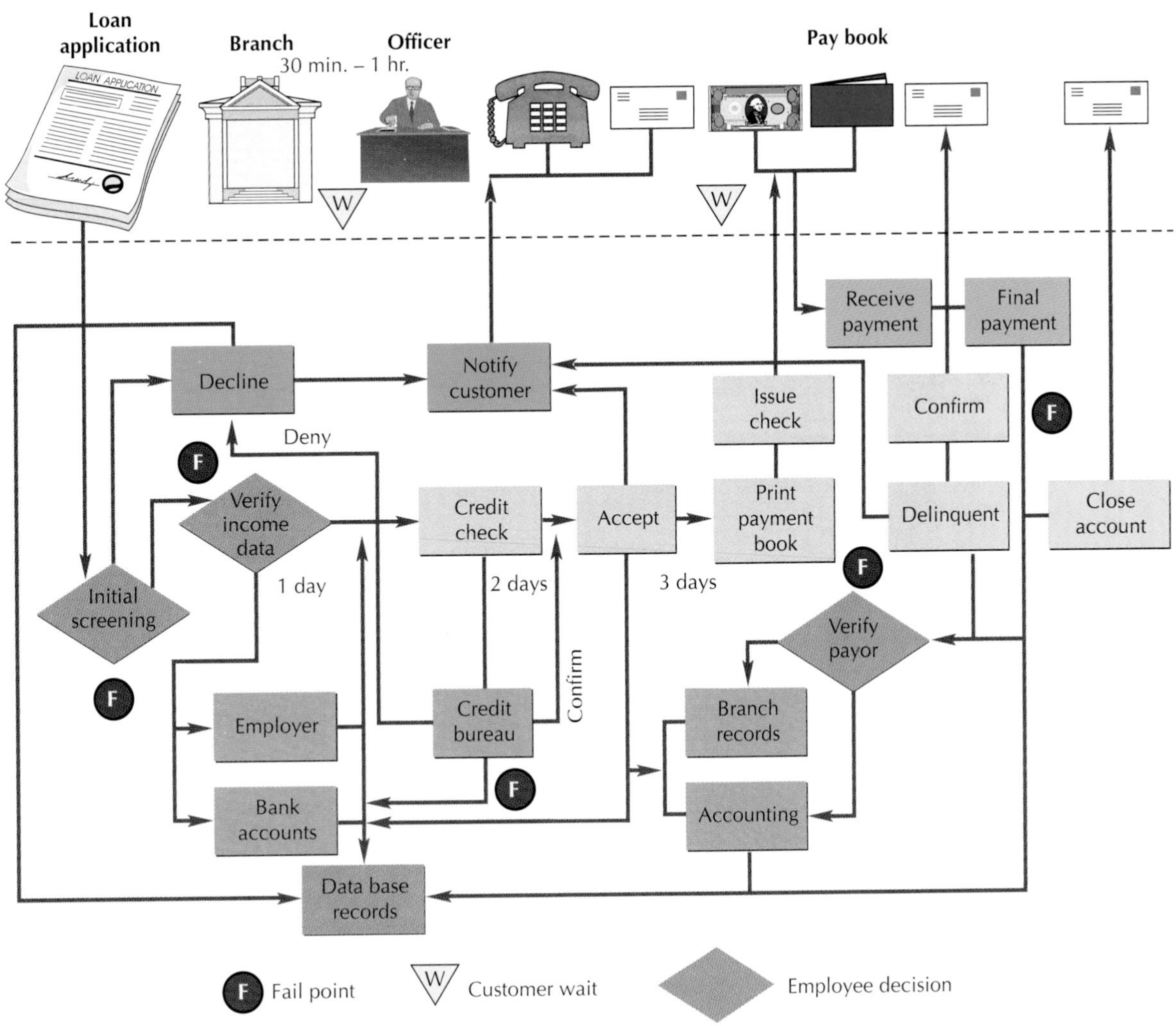


**Figure 6.6**

**Service Blueprint for an Installment Lending Operation**

*Source:* Lynn Shostack, "Service Positioning through Structural Change," *Journal of Marketing* 51 (January 1987), p. 36. Reprinted with permission by the American Marketing Association.

## PROCESS INNOVATION

Processes are *planned* in response to new facilities, new products, new technologies, new markets, or new customer expectations. Processes should be *analyzed* for improvement on a continuous basis. When continual improvement efforts have been exhausted and performance expectations still cannot be reached with an existing process, it is time to completely redesign or innovate the process.

**Process innovation**[1] projects are typically chartered in response to a *breakthrough* goal for rapid, dramatic improvement in process performance. Performance improvement of 50 to 100% within 12 months is common. In order to achieve such spectacular results, an innovation team is encouraged to start with a clean sheet of paper and rethink all aspects of a process, from its purpose to its outputs, structure, tasks, and technology. Figure 6.7 shows the relationship between continuous improvement, breakthrough improvement, and process innovation.

**Process innovation:** the total redesign of a process for breakthrough improvements.

Process innovation is most successful in organizations that can view their system as a set of processes providing value to the customer, instead of functional areas vying for limited resources. Figure 6.8 shows this change from a functional to a process orientation. In an environment of rapid change, the ability to learn faster, reconfigure processes faster, and execute processes faster is a competitive advantage.

[1] Process innovation is also known as business process reengineering (BPR), process redesign, restructuring, and many other company-specific terms.

Figure 6.7
**Continuous Improvements and Breakthroughs**

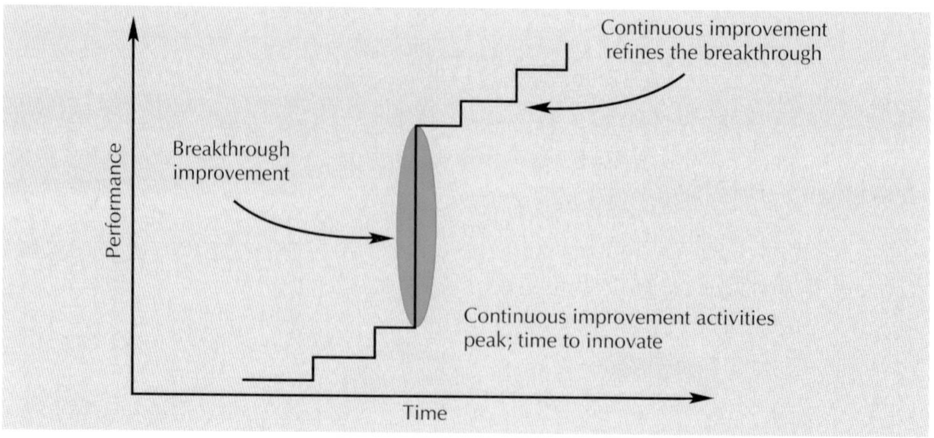


Figure 6.8
**From Function to Process**

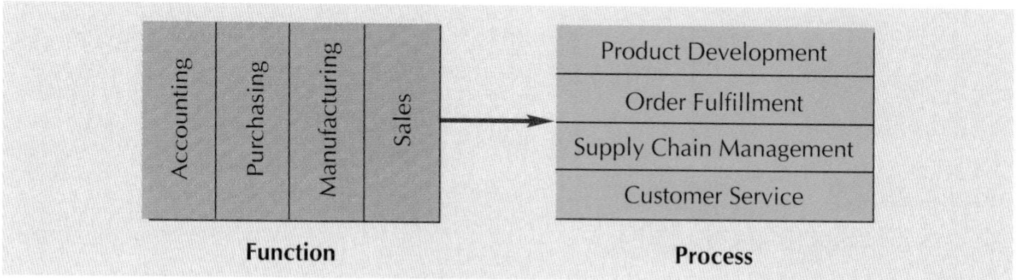


### *Anastasia Thatcher,*

***Senior Business Process Manager for a Public Sector Health-Care Company***

I'm a process manager for the public sector division of one of the largest and best performing health-care corporations in the United States. My region is the Northeast where the processes I oversee are responsible for the health care of over 400,000 lives.

I began my work auditing claims processing, and then became interested in how a claim works its way through the system. I noticed all sorts of inefficiencies. For example, high dollar claims were manually handled with 10 different touch points. The *Claims Processor* would identify high dollar claims and then forward it to the *Special Matters Expert*, who would work with the *Claims Liaison*, who would need approval from the *Executive Director* of the plan, who would consult the *Claims Analyst*, who would ask *Contracting* to get back to them so that they could inform the *Executive Director*, who would make a decision and send it to the *Liaison*, who would notify the *Special Matters Expert*, who would lastly pass along the decision to the *Claims Processor*, who would pay the claim. After redesign, the approval goes from *Claims Processor* to *Special Matters Expert* to *Executive Director*, period. The process flows more efficiently using fewer resources, and the providers are happier because they receive their payments more quickly, which ultimately ensures that members get access to the best care possible.

Like a lot of manufacturing firms, we have more data than we can process efficiently, and it seems that people are always looking for the same information. I remember one situation in particular with case management of high-risk pregnancies. There was a two-month backlog, which meant that by the time the case manager got around to contacting the patient, the pregnancy was too far along for treatment to make much of a difference. I analyzed the process and found that if we developed a shared database between the applicants, the case managers, and the nurses, we could eliminate the manual data entry of cases. That one change reduced the backlog to zero, saved the company millions, and most importantly reduced the number of detained babies (those that need to stay in the hospital after the mother had been released) by 50%. In this job, you can make a real difference. You can save lives.

I was amazed when I took the operations class at Stern in New York City that there's a field of study for what I do. I live by flowcharts and Pareto analysis. We're always configuring and reconfiguring systems. If it doesn't work, we try something else. It's important to take a step back and look at the broader picture. Then you have to take risks and make decisions, and always look for ways of improving the process.

## STEPS IN PROCESS INNOVATION

Figure 6.9 outlines the innovation process. Let's review the process step by step.

The initial step establishes the goals for process performance. Data from the existing process are used as a baseline to which benchmarking data on best industry practices, customer requirements data, and strategic directives are compared.[2] Analyzing the gap between current and desired performance helps to determine whether the process needs to be redesigned. If redesign is necessary, a project team is chartered and provided with the preliminary analysis and resulting goals and specifications for process performance. Although the goals for a process may be specific, the specifications are not (or else the creativity of the group is hampered). It is important that the project team be convinced that total redesign of the process is absolutely necessary to achieve the performance objectives.

Establish goals and specifications.

A useful tool in beginning the redesign of a process is a *high-level process map*. Pared to its simplest form, a high-level map contains only the essential building blocks of a process. As shown in Figure 6.10, it is prepared by focusing on the performance goal—stated in customer terms—and working backward through the desired output, subprocesses, and initial input requirements. Design principles, such as performing subprocesses in parallel whenever possible, help to structure the map efficiently. Table 6.2 lists several additional design principles recommended for process innovation. Innovative ideas can challenge the conventional ordering of subprocesses, or the need for a subprocess. Table 6.3 presents various techniques to prompt innovative thinking.

Process maps work backwards from a performance goal.

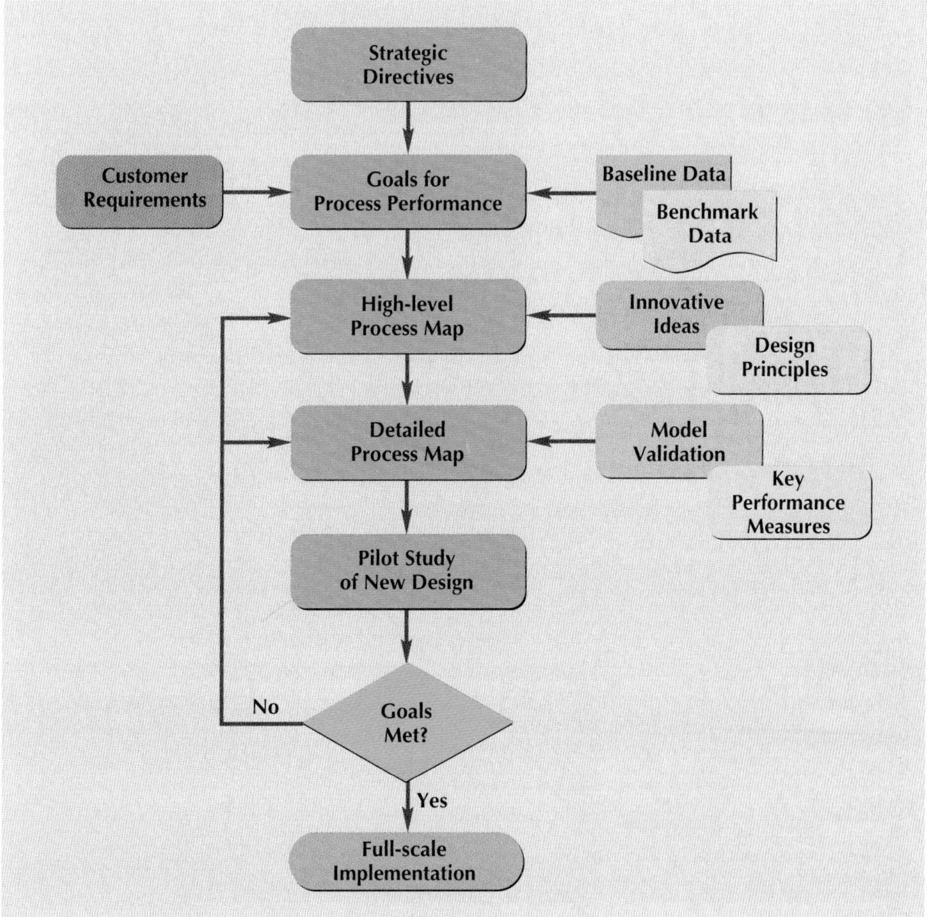


Figure 6.9
**Process Innovation**

[2]Although process innovation means redesigning the process from scratch, it does not mean that the existing process should be ignored. The existing process should be studied long enough to understand "what" the process is and "why" it is performed. Exactly "how" it is performed is less relevant because the how will change dramatically during the course of the project.

Figure 6.10
**A High-Level Process Map**

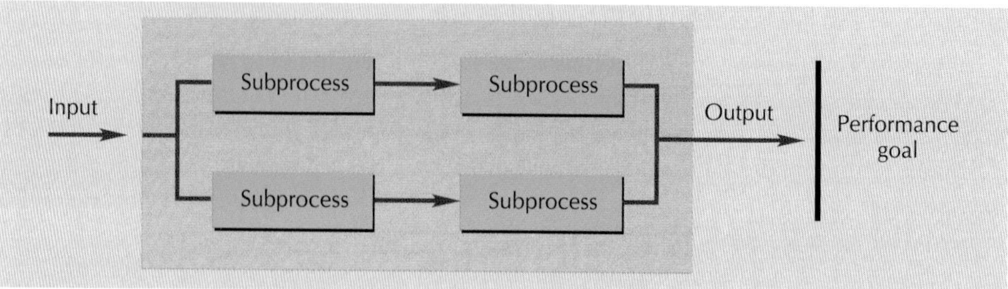


After the general concept of redesign is agreed on, a detailed map is prepared for each subprocess or block in the high-level map. Blocks are added only if an activity can contribute to the output goal. The existence of each block or activity is challenged: Does it add value for the customer? Does it have to be done? Could it be done more quickly, more easily, or sooner? Could someone else do it better?

A detailed map guides decisions on allocation of resources and work methods. To guarantee that the detailed map will produce the desired results, key performance measures are determined and set in place. The model is also validated through simulation, interviewing, and partial testing. When the team is satisfied that the performance objective can be reached with the new design, a pilot study is conducted.

Use pilot studies for rapid prototyping.

Process innovation is not like other projects, which can be carefully planned and flawlessly executed. Innovation is by definition something new and untested. Milestones, costs, and benefits are guesses at best. A pilot study allows the team to try something, see if it works, modify it, and try again.

Table 6.2
**Principles for Redesigning Processes**

1. Remove waste, simplify, and consolidate similar activities.
2. Link processes to create value.
3. Let the swiftest and most capable enterprise execute the process.
4. Flex the process for any time, any place, any way.
5. Capture information digitally at the source and propagate it through the process.
6. Provide visibility through fresher and richer information about process status.
7. Fit the process with sensors and feedback loops that can prompt action.
8. Add analytic capabilities to the process.
9. Connect, collect, and create knowledge around the process through all who touch it.
10. Personalize the process with the preferences and habits of participants.

*Source:* Omar El Sawy, *Redesigning Enterprise Processes for e-Business* (New York: McGraw-Hill, 2001), pp. 57–75.

Table 6.3
**Techniques for Generating Innovative Ideas**

- Vary the entry point to a problem. (In trying to untangle fishing lines, it's best to start from the fish, not the poles!)
- Draw analogies. (A previous solution to an old problem might work.)
- Change your perspective. (Think like a customer; bring in persons who have no knowledge of the process.)
- Try inverse brainstorming. (What would *increase* cost? *displease* the customer?)
- Chain forward as far as possible. (If I solve this problem, what is the next problem?)
- Use attribute brainstorming. (How would this process operate if . . . our workers were mobile and flexible? there were no monetary constraints? we had perfect knowledge?)

*Source:* Adapted from AT&T Quality Steering Committee, *Reengineering Handbook* (Indianapolis: AT&T Technical Publications Center, 1991).

## THE COMPETITIVE EDGE

### Progressive Innovates Processes

Process improvements are great. Excellence in operations is better. But innovation is the best of all. Process innovation can yield a true competitive advantage. Consider Progressive Insurance Company, an automobile insurer that increased its sales from $1.3 billion in 1991 to $9.5 billion in 2002. This sevenfold increase in sales in a little more than a decade was achieved in a mature industry, without diversification, acquisitions, or globalization. No dramatic new products were introduced, and there were no give-aways or big marketing campaigns. Neither did the growth in sales come at the expense of profits. Progressive's processes simply outperformed those of its competitors.

Need proof? The measure of financial performance in the insurance industry is a combined ratio of (expenses + claims payouts)/premiums. The industry average is 102%, that's a 2% loss on underwriting processes. Progressive's combined ratio is 96%.

How do firms decide to use operations as a way to compete? It usually starts with a grassroots employee campaigning against the inadequacies of existing operations, and finally it gets the attention of a key executive. Once top managers are convinced that process innovation is worth pursuing, they can help focus the organization's efforts and be supportive during the disruptive effects of change.

Progressive realized that the key to profits and growth was retaining its customers, and that customers are retained through pleasant interactions with the company. So Progressive set about to streamline its claims process—to make it more pleasant for the customer (not necessarily more cost effective for the company). Most auto insurers view claims as a nuisance and give it low priority in terms of process improvement (much less innovation). Progressive can turn around a claim in nine hours. Now that's impressive.

Michael Hammer says that "at its heart, every process innovation defies an assumption about how work should be done." He suggests that companies that wish to innovate their processes should look outside their industry for the role models, identify a constraining assumption and break it, make special cases the norm, and rethink the critical dimensions of work.

*Source:* Michael Hammer, "Deep Change: How Operational Innovation Can Transform Your Company," *Harvard Business Review* (April 2004), pp. 84–93.

**Manage the change process.**

After a successful pilot study, full-scale implementation can begin. Since process innovation involves radical change, the transition period between introducing the changed process and the incorporation of the new process into day-to-day operations can be difficult. The redesigned process may involve changing the way executives manage, the way employees think about their work, or how workers interact. The transition needs to be managed with a special concern for the "people" aspects of change. The innovation process is complete when the transition has been weathered and the new process consistently reaches its objective.

The concept of process innovation emerged in response to rapid changes in technology that rendered existing processes obsolete. In the next section, we discuss the impact of technology decisions and provide resources for a more in-depth study of technology.

## TECHNOLOGY DECISIONS

Technology decisions involve large sums of money and can have a tremendous impact on the cost, speed, quality, and flexibility of operations. More importantly, they define the future capabilities of a firm and set the stage for competitive interactions. Thus, it is dangerous to delegate technology decisions to technical experts or financial analysts. A manager's ability to ask questions and understand the basic thrust of proposed technology is invaluable in making wise technology choices.

In this section we discuss the financial justification of new technology, followed by a brief technology primer.

## FINANCIAL JUSTIFICATION OF TECHNOLOGY

After it is decided that a part will be produced or service provided in-house, specific technology decisions can be made. Alternatives include using, replacing, or upgrading existing equipment, adding additional capacity, or purchasing new equipment. Any alternative that involves an outlay of funds is considered a *capital investment.* Capital investments involve the commitment of funds in the present with an expectation of returns over some future time period. The expenditures are usually large and can have a significant effect on the future profitability of a firm. These decisions are analyzed carefully and typically require top management approval.

The most effective quantitative techniques for capital investment consider the time value of money as well as the risks associated with benefits that will not accrue until the future. These techniques, known collectively as *capital budgeting* techniques, include payback period, net present value, and internal rate of return. Detailed descriptions can be found in any basic finance text. Although capital budgeting techniques are beyond the scope of this text, we do need to comment on several factors that are often overlooked in the financial analysis of technology.

Capital budgeting techniques are used to evaluate new technology.

### Purchase Cost

Purchasing cost includes the add-ons necessary to make the technology work.

The initial investment in equipment consists of more than its basic purchase price. The cost of special tools and fixtures, installation, training, maintenance, and engineering or programming adjustments can represent a significant additional investment. Operating costs are often underestimated as well.

### Operating Costs

Visualize how the technology will be used.

To assess more accurately the requirements of the new technology, it is useful to consider, step by step, how the equipment will be operated, started, stopped, loaded, unloaded, changed over, upgraded, networked, maintained, repaired, cleaned up, speeded up, and slowed down.

### Annual Savings

New technology can save money through better quality and more efficient operation.

Most new technology is justified based on direct labor savings. However, other savings can actually be more important. For example, a more efficient process may be able to use less material and require less machine time or fewer repairs, so that downtime is reduced. A process that produces a better-quality product can result in fewer inspections and less scrap and rework. New processes (especially those that are automated) may significantly reduce safety costs, in terms of compliance with required regulations, as well as fines or compensation for safety violations.

### Revenue Enhancement

New technology can enhance revenue.

Increases in revenue due to technology upgrades or new-equipment purchases are often ignored in financial analysis because they are difficult to predict. Improvements in product quality, price reductions due to decreased costs, and more rapid or dependable delivery can increase market share and, thus, revenue. Flexibility of equipment can also be important in adapting to the changing needs of the customer.

### Replacement Analysis

Deciding when to upgrade to a new technology often depends on the competitive environment.

As existing equipment ages, it may become slower, less reliable, and obsolete. The decision to replace old equipment with state-of-the-art equipment depends in large measure on the competitive environment. If a major competitor upgrades to a newer technology that improves quality, cost, or flexibility and you do not, your ability to compete will be severely damaged. In some industries, technology changes so rapidly that a replacement decision also involves determining whether this generation of equipment should be purchased or if it would be better to wait for the next generation. Replacement analysis maps out different schedules for equipment purchases over a five- to ten-year period and selects a replacement cycle that will minimize cost.

### Risk and Uncertainty

It is risky to invest in new technology, and it's risky not to.

Investment in new technology can be risky. Estimates of equipment capabilities, length of life, and operating cost may be uncertain. Because of the risk involved, financial analysts tend to assign higher hurdle rates (i.e., required rates of return) to technology investments, making it difficult to gain approval for them.

## Piecemeal Analysis

Investment in equipment and new technology is also expensive. Rarely can a company afford to automate an entire facility all at once. This has led to the proposal and evaluation of equipment purchases in a piecemeal fashion, resulting in pieces of technology that don't fit into the existing system and fail to deliver the expected returns.

Make sure new and existing technology are compatible.

# A TECHNOLOGY PRIMER

Technology is important in both manufacturing and service operations. Cars now have hundreds of embedded systems performing thousands of computerized functions. Pacemakers, vending machines, Xerox copiers, and store shelves notify the manufacturer when repairs or restocking are needed. Coming soon are clothes that measure the wearer's vital statistics and notify a physician or change medication regimes when necessary, and refrigerators that pre-order ingredients to match weekly menus or order milk when the supply is low. We discuss many of the information technology advances that support these systems in more detail in Chapter 9. In this section, we present a brief overview of technology advances in manufacturing systems.

Technology in manufacturing includes computer aided design, robots, automated guided vehicles, computer numerical control machines, automated storage and retrieval systems, and flexible manufacturing systems. Automated manufacturing systems integrated through computer technology are aptly called *computer-integrated manufacturing* (CIM). With the advent of the Internet and the increased globalization of both markets and production, CIM has evolved into a Web-centric collaborative venture known as *e-manufacturing* (eM).

E-manufacturing involves sharing real-time data with trading partners and customers and making collaborative decisions about production based on that data. In order to collaborate, information must be converted into electronic form, protocols for communication must be established, and infrastructure must be in place for connectivity with customers, suppliers, and partners. Rather than making huge volumes of standard products in anticipation of demand, e-manufacturing uses real-time information on customer orders and productive capacity across the supply chain to speed customized products directly to the customer. Figure 6.11 shows the components of e-manufacturing categorized by product, process, manufacturing, and information technologies. Table 6.4 serves as a technology primer, briefly defining the terms listed in the figure.

Figure 6.11
**Components of e-Manufacturing**

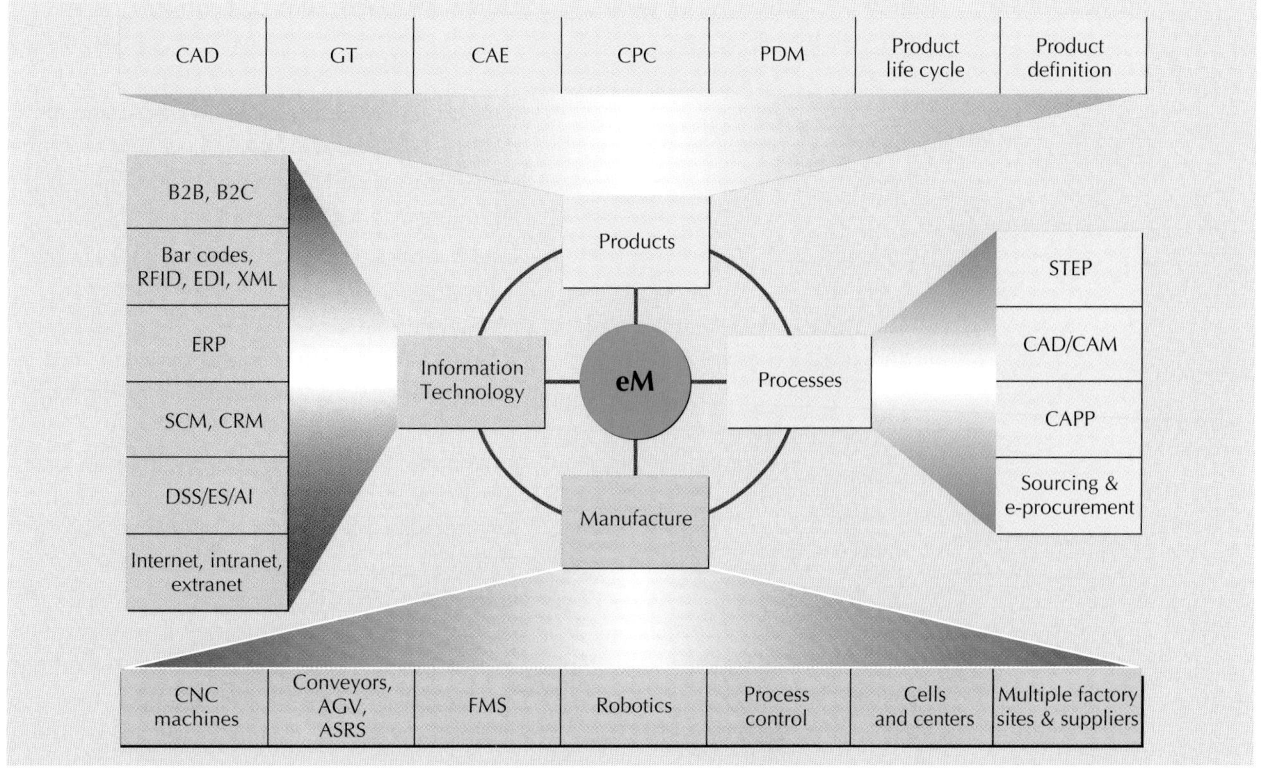

**Table 6.4**
**A Technology Primer**

| Product Technology | | |
|---|---|---|
| **CAD** | Computer-aided design | Creates and communicates designs electronically |
| **GT** | Group technology | Classifies designs into families for easy retrieval and modification |
| **CAE** | Computer-aided engineering | Tests the functionality of CAD designs electronically |
| **CPC** | Collaborative product commerce | Facilitates electronic communication and exchange of information among designers and suppliers |
| **PDM** | Product data management | Keeps track of design specs and revisions for the life of the product |
| **PLC** | Product life cycle management | Integrates the decisions of those involved in product development, manufacturing, sales, customer service, recycling, and disposal |
| **Product definition** | | Defines products "built" by customers who have selected among various options, usually from a Web site |
| **Process Technology** | | |
| **STEP** | Standard for exchange of product model data | Set standards for communication among different CAD vendors; translates CAD data into requirements for automated inspection and manufacture |
| **CAD/CAM** | Computer-aided design and manufacture | The electronic link between automated design (CAD) and automated manufacture (CAM) |
| **CAPP** | Computer aided process planning | Generates process plans based on a database of similar requirements |
| **E-procurement** | | Electronic purchasing of items from e-marketplaces, auctions, or company Web sites |
| **Manufacturing Technology** | | |
| **CNC** | Computer numerically control | Machines controlled by software code to perform a variety of operations with the help of automated tool changers; also collects processing information and quality data |
| **FMS** | Flexible manufacturing system | A collection of CNC machines connected by an automated material handling system to produce a wide variety of parts |
| **Robots** | | Manipulators that can be programmed to perform repetitive tasks; more consistent than workers but less flexible |
| **Conveyors** | | Fixed-path material handling; moves items along a belt or overhead chain; "reads" packages and diverts them to different directions; can be very fast |
| **AGV** | Automatic guided vehicle | A driverless truck that moves material along a specified path; directed by wire or tape embedded in the floor or by radio frequencies; very flexible |
| **ASRS** | Automated storage and retrieval system | An automated warehouse—some 26 stores high—in which items are placed in a carousel-type storage system and retrieved by fast-moving stacker cranes; controlled by computer |
| **Process Control** | | Continuous monitoring of automated equipment; makes real-time decisions on ongoing operation, maintenance, and quality |
| **CIM** | Computer-integrated manufacturing | Automated manufacturing systems integrated through computer technology; also called e-manufacturing |

| Information Technology | | |
|---|---|---|
| **B2B** | Business-to-business | Electronic transactions between businesses usually over the Internet |
| **B2C** | Business-to-consumer | Electronic transactions between businesses and their customers usually over the Internet |
| **Internet** | | A global information system of computer networks that facilitates communication and data transfer |
| **Intranet** | | Communication networks internal to an organization; can be password (i.e., firewall) protected sites on the Internet |
| **Extranet** | | Intranets connected to the Internet for shared access with select suppliers, customers, and trading partners |
| **Bar codes** | | A series of vertical lines printed on most packages that identifies the item and other information when read by a scanner |
| **RFID** | Radio frequency identification tags | An integrated circuit embedded in a tag that can send and receive information; a twenty-first century bar code with read/write capabilities |
| **EDI** | Electronic data interchange | A computer-to-computer exchange of business documents over a proprietary network; very expensive and inflexible |
| **XML** | Extensible markup language | A programming language that enables computer-to-computer communication over the Internet by tagging data before its is sent |
| **ERP** | Enterprise resource planning | Software for managing the basic requirements of an enterprise, including sales & marketing, finance & accounting, production & materials management, and human resources |
| **SCM** | Supply chain management | Software for managing the flow of goods and information among a network of suppliers, manufacturers, and distributors |
| **CRM** | Customer relationship management | Software for managing interactions with customers and compiling and analyzing customer data |
| **DSS** | Decision support systems | An information system that helps managers make decisions; includes a quantitative modeling component and an interactive component for what-if? analysis |
| **ES** | Expert systems | A computer system that uses an expert knowledge base to diagnose or solve a problem |
| **AI** | Artificial intelligence | A field of study that attempts to replicate elements of human thought in computer processes; includes expert systems, genetic algorithms, neural networks, and fuzzy logic (see Chapter 16) |

## CAPACITY DECISIONS

Process and technology decisions lead directly to decisions on capacity and facilities. **Capacity** is the maximum capability to produce. It can be measured as units of output, dollars of output, hours of work, or number of customers processed over a specified period of time. Capacity is affected by the mix of products and services, the choice of technology, the size of a facility, and the resources allocated.

**Capacity:** the maximum capability to produce

**Rated capacity** is the theoretical output that could be attained if a process were operating at full speed without interruption, exceptions, or downtime. **Effective capacity** takes into account the efficiency with which a particular product or customer can be processed, and the utilization of the scheduled hours or work. Effective capacity expressed in hours per day is calculated as:

$$\text{Effective daily capacity} = (\text{no. of machines or workers}) \times (\text{hours per shift}) \times (\text{no. of shifts}) \times (\text{utilization}) \times (\text{efficiency})$$

**Utilization:** the percent of available time spent working.

**Efficiency:** how well a machine or worker performs compared to a standard output level.

**Load:** the standard hours of work assigned to a facility.

**Load percent:** the ratio of load to capacity.

**Utilization** refers to the percentage of available working time that a worker actually works or a machine actually runs. Scheduled maintenance, lunch breaks, and setup time are examples of activities that reduce actual working time. **Efficiency** refers to how well a machine or worker performs compared to a standard output level. Standards can be based on past records of performance or can be developed from the work-measurement techniques discussed in Chapter 8. An efficiency of 100% is considered normal or standard performance, 125% is above normal, and 90% is below normal. Efficiency is also dependent on product mix. Some orders obviously will take longer than others to process, and some machines or workers may be better at processing certain types of orders.

**Load** is the standard hours of work (or equivalent units of production) assigned to a production facility. After load and capacity have been determined, a **load percent** can be calculated as

$$\text{Load percent} = \frac{\text{load}}{\text{capacity}} \times 100\%$$

Centers loaded above 100% will not be able to complete the scheduled work without some adjustment in capacity or reduction in load.

Example 6.3

**Determining Loads and Capacities**

Copy Courier (CC) is a fledgling copy center in downtown Richmond run by two college students. Currently, the equipment consists of two high-speed copiers that can be operated by one operator. If the students work alone, it is conceivable that two shifts per day can be staffed. The students each work 8 hours a day, 5 days a week. They do not take breaks during the day, but they do allow themselves 30 minutes for lunch or dinner. In addition, they service the machines for about 30 minutes at the beginning of each shift. The time required to set up for each order varies by the type of paper, use of color, number of copies, and so on. Estimates of setup time are kept with each order. Since the machines are new, their efficiency is estimated at 90%.

Due to extensive advertising and new customer incentives, orders have been pouring in. The students need help determining the capacity of their operation and the current load on their facility. Use the following information to calculate the normal daily capacity of Copy Courier and to project next Monday's load and load percent.

| Job No. | No. of Copies | Setup Time (min) | Run Time (min/unit) |
|---|---|---|---|
| 10 | 500 | 5.2 | 0.08 |
| 20 | 1000 | 10.6 | 0.10 |
| 30 | 5000 | 3.4 | 0.12 |
| 40 | 4500 | 11.2 | 0.14 |
| 50 | 2000 | 15.3 | 0.10 |

*Solution*

The machines and operators at Copy Courier are out of service for 1 hour each shift for maintenance and lunch. Utilization is thus 7/8, or 87.5%. Daily copy shop capacity is:

$$2 \text{ machines} \times 2 \text{ shifts} \times 8 \text{ hours/shift} \times 90\% \text{ efficiency} \times 87.5\% \text{ utilization} = 25.2 \text{ hours or } 1512 \text{ minutes}$$

The projected load for Monday of next week is as follows:

| Job No. | Total Time |
|---|---|
| 10 | $5.2 + (500 \times 0.08) = 45.20$ |
| 20 | $10.6 + (1000 \times 0.10) = 110.60$ |
| 30 | $3.4 + (5000 \times 0.12) = 603.40$ |
| 40 | $11.2 + (4500 \times 0.14) = 641.20$ |
| 50 | $15.3 + (2000 \times 0.10) = 215.30$ |
| | 1615.70 minutes |

$$\text{Load percent} = \frac{1615.70}{1512} = 1.068 \times 100\% = 106.8\%$$

Copy Courier is overloaded 6.8%. Several options are available to alleviate the overload. If each worker extends his or her working day by approximately 36 minutes, the load percent will reduce to 99%. The same effect can be achieved by increasing efficiency to 97%. This may involve limiting the orders accepted to those that can be processed more efficiently, or grouping jobs by similar processing requirements so that setup time is reduced.

Copy Courier is an example of a short-term capacity problem. Over the medium range, the company could expand capacity by hiring more people or purchasing more machines. Over the long range, a new facility may be necessary. The next section discusses alternatives for such strategic long-term capacity decisions, called capacity planning.

## CAPACITY PLANNING

**Capacity planning** is the long-term strategic decision that establishes a firm's overall level of resources. It extends over a time horizon long enough to obtain those resources—usually a year or more for building new facilities or acquiring new businesses. Capacity decisions affect product lead times, customer responsiveness, operating costs, and a firm's ability to compete. Inadequate capacity can lose customers and limit growth. Excess capacity can drain a company's resources and prevent investments in more lucrative ventures. *When* to increase capacity and *how much* to increase it are critical decisions.

**Capacity planning:** establishes the overall level of productive resources for a firm.

Figure 6.12 *a*, *b*, and *c* show three basic strategies for the timing of capacity expansion in relation to a steady growth in demand.

- ***Capacity lead strategy***. Capacity is expanded in anticipation of demand growth. This aggressive strategy is used to lure customers from competitors who are capacity constrained or to gain a foothold in a rapidly expanding market. It also allows companies to respond to unexpected surges in demand and to provide superior levels of service during peak demand periods.
- ***Average capacity strategy***. Capacity is expanded to coincide with average expected demand. This is a moderate strategy in which managers are certain they will be able to sell at least some portion of expanded output, and endure some periods of unmet demand. Approximately half of the time capacity leads demand, and half of the time capacity lags demand.
- ***Capacity lag strategy***. Capacity is increased after an increase in demand has been documented. This conservative strategy produces a higher return on investment but may lose customers in the process. It is used in industries with standard products and cost-based or weak competition. The strategy assumes that lost customers will return from competitors after capacity has expanded.

As demand grows, a *lead*, *lag*, or *average* capacity strategy can be applied.

Consider higher education's strategy in preparing for a tripling of the state's college-bound population in the next decade. An established university, guaranteed applicants even in lean years, may follow a capacity lag strategy. A young university might lead

Figure 6.12

**Capacity Expansion Strategies**

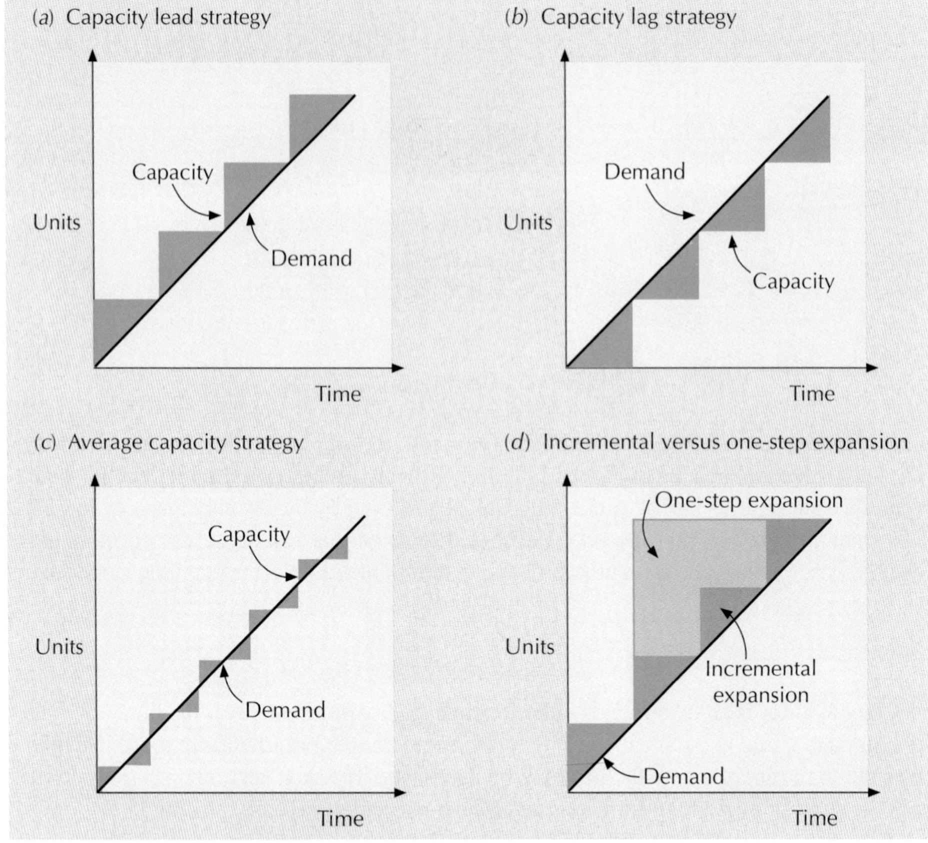


capacity expansion in hopes of capturing students not admitted to the more established universities. A community college may choose the average capacity strategy to fulfill its mission of educating the state's youth but with little risk.

Capacity can be increased incrementally or in large steps.

How much to increase capacity depends on (1) the volume and certainty of anticipated *demand*; (2) *strategic objectives* in terms of growth, customer service, and competition; and (3) the *costs* of expansion and operation.

Capacity can be increased incrementally or in one large step as shown in Figure 6.12*d*. Incremental expansion is less risky but more costly. An attractive alternative to expanding capacity is *outsourcing*, in which suppliers absorb the risk of demand uncertainty.

**Best operating level:** is the percent of capacity utilization that minimizes unit costs.

**Capacity cushion:** is the percent of capacity held in reserve for unexpected occurrences.

The **best operating level** for a facility is the percent of capacity utilization that minimizes average unit cost. Rarely is the best operating level at 100% of capacity—at higher levels of utilization, productivity slows and things start to go wrong. Average capacity utilization differs by industry. An industry with an 80% average utilization would have a 20% **capacity cushion** for unexpected surges in demand or temporary work stoppages. Large-capacity cushions are common in industries in which demand is highly variable, resource flexibility is low, and customer service is important. Utilities, for example, maintain a 20% capacity cushion. Capital-intensive industries with less flexibility and higher costs maintain cushions under 10%. Airlines maintain a negative cushion by overbooking flights. Best operating level can also refer to the most economic size of a facility.

Figure 6.13 shows the best operating level—in this case, the number of rooms for a hotel—as the point at which the *economies of scale* have reached their peak and the *diseconomies of scale* have not yet begun.

**Economies of scale:** when it costs less per unit to produce high levels of output.

**Economies of scale** occur when it costs less per unit to produce or operate at high levels of output. This holds true when:

- Fixed costs can be spread over a larger number of units,
- Production or operating costs do not increase linearly with output levels,
- Quantity discounts are available for material purchases, and
- Operating efficiency increases as workers gain experience.

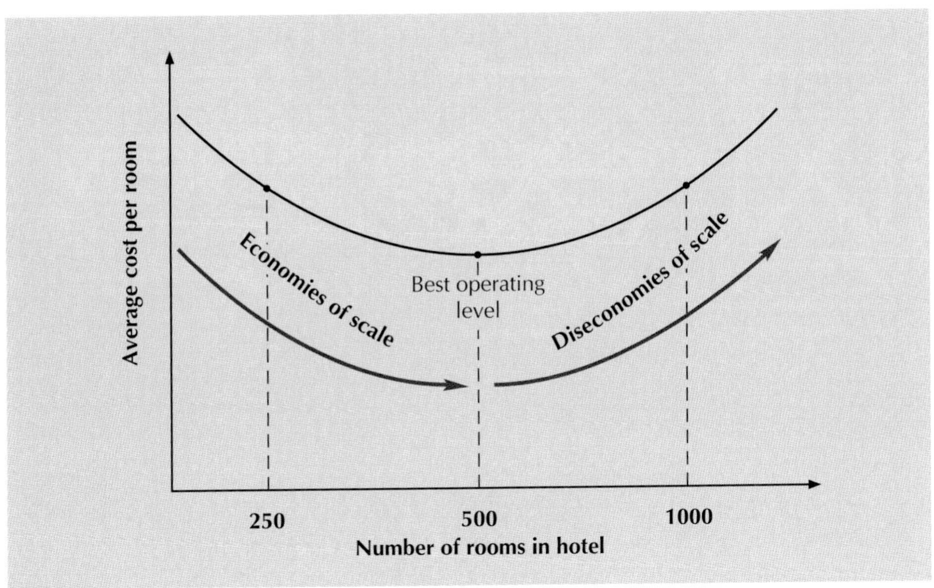


Figure 6.13
**Best Operating Level for a Hotel**

The electronics industry provides a good case example of economies of scale. The average cost per chip placement for printed circuit-board assembly is 32 cents in factories with a volume of 25 million placements, 15 cents in factories with 200 million placements, and only 10 cents in factories with 800 million placements.[3]

## DISECONOMIES OF SCALE

Economies of scale do not continue indefinitely. Above a certain level of output, **diseconomies of scale** can occur. Overtaxed machines and material-handling equipment break down, service time slows, quality suffers requiring more rework, labor costs increase with overtime, and coordination and management activities become difficult. In addition, if customer preferences suddenly change, high-volume production can leave a firm with unusable inventory and excess capacity.

**Diseconomies of scale:** when higher levels of output cost more per unit to produce.

Diseconomies of scale can be divided into four categories:[4]

1. ***Diseconomies of distribution*** Larger stores, distribution centers, or manufacturing facilities tend to serve expanded geographical areas. The cost to supply a larger area may increase faster than the sales volume from the larger customer base. The savings in operating costs that do occur may be negated by customers dissatisfied with longer delivery times or less convenient locations.
2. ***Diseconomies of bureaucracy*** Larger facilities require more staff. A larger staff needs more supervisors and managers, who in turn need more secretaries and assistants. Workers and managers feel less committed to larger organizations and may view their activities as invisible to management. Large facilities invite more government and community scrutiny, and create an increased likelihood of labor disputes. To avoid dominating a community, some companies will set policies on the size of a facility, for example, to a certain percentage of the working population in a community or service area.
3. ***Diseconomies of confusion*** As facilities grow in size, the number of different products, processes, and technologies for which they are responsible tends to grow as well, thus requiring more coordination and integration. Complexity increases with the number of *linkages* between departments or activities, rather than the number of departments themselves, as illustrated in Figure 6.14.

[3]"High Volumes Yield Greater Profits for High-Tech Factories," *IIE Solutions* (April 1996), p. 8.
[4]This section is adapted from Robert Hayes, Gary Pisano, David Upton, and Steven Wheelwright, *Pursuing the Competitive Edge* (Hoboken, NJ: Wiley, 2005), p. 98–101.

Figure 6.14
**Diseconomies of Confusion**

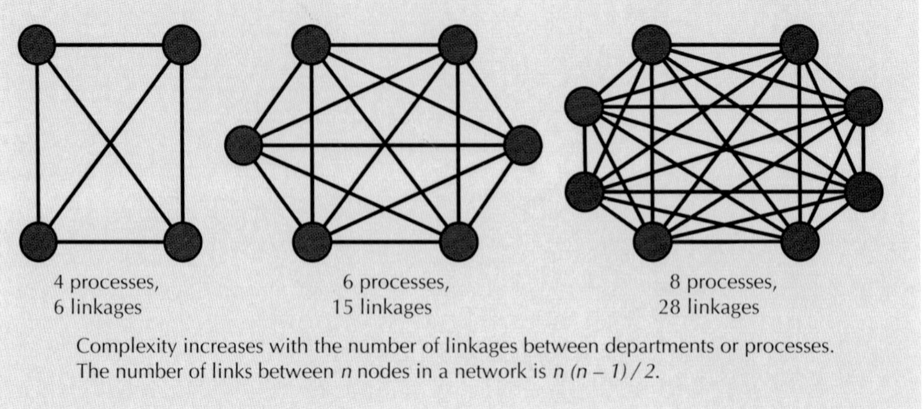


Complexity increases with the number of linkages between departments or processes. The number of links between $n$ nodes in a network is $n(n-1)/2$.

4. ***Diseconomies of Vulnerability*** One larger facility rather than several small ones is a risky proposition. Natural disasters, changing demand patterns, management failures, and economic and political changes at one location can wipe out a business if there are no backup facilities to serve customers. Many firms will purposely divide the production of critical components among suppliers or assign them to different locations for that reason.

Capacity decisions provide a framework for further facility decisions, such as where to locate a new facility and how to arrange the flow of work in the facility. These topics are discussed next in Chapter 7 and in the supplement to Chapter 7.

## SUMMARY

Important issues in process design are types of processes, process planning, analysis, and innovation, and technology decisions. The type of production process selected depends primarily on demand volume and degree of product standardization. *Projects* are produced one at a time to customer order. *Batch production* is used to process a variety of low-volume jobs. *Mass production* produces large volumes of a standard product for a mass market. *Continuous production* is used for very-high-volume commodity products.

Process planning consists of converting product designs into workable instructions for manufacture. They often appear in the form of assembly charts, process flowcharts, operations sheets, and manufacturing or delivery specifications. On a broader scale, process planning involves process selection, technology decisions, and decisions on outsourcing. Process analysis drives the continuous improvement of operations; process innovation drives breakthrough improvements.

*Capacity planning* is the process of establishing the overall level of productive resources for a firm. It involves long-term strategic activities, such as the acquisition of new facilities, technologies, or businesses, that take a year or more to complete.

Capacity expansion can *lead* demand, *lag* behind demand, or meet *average* demand. The *best operating level* for a facility often includes a *capacity cushion* for unexpected occurrences. The tendency of high levels of output to cost less per unit is known as *economies of scale*. This normally holds true up to a certain level of output, at which point *diseconomies of scale* can take over.

## SUMMARY OF KEY TERMS

**assembly chart** a schematic diagram of a product that shows the relationship of component parts to parent assemblies, the groupings of parts that make up a subassembly, and the overall sequence of assembly.

**batch production** the low-volume production of customized products.

**best operating level** the percent of capacity utilization at which unit costs are lowest.

**breakeven analysis** a technique that determines the volume of demand needed to be profitable; it takes into account the trade-off between fixed and variable costs.

**capacity** the maximum capability to produce.

**capacity cushion** a percent of capacity held in reserve for unexpected occurrences.

**capacity planning** a long-term strategic decision that establishes the overall level of productive resources for a firm.

**continuous process** the production of a very-high-volume commodity product with highly automated equipment.

**diseconomies of scale** when higher levels of output cost more per unit to produce.

**economies of scale** when it costs less per unit to produce higher levels of output.

**efficiency** how well a machine or worker performs compared to a standard output level.
**load** the standard hours of work assigned to a facility.
**load percent** the ratio of load to capacity.
**mass production** the high-volume production of a standard product for a mass market.
**operations sheet** a document that shows the series of operations necessary to make each item listed on the assembly chart.
**process** a group of related tasks with specific inputs and outputs.
**process flowchart** a document that uses standardized symbols to chart the productive and nonproductive flow of activities involved in a process; it may be used to document current processes or as a vehicle for process improvement.
**process innovation** the total redesign of a process.
**process planning** the conversion of designs into workable instructions for manufacture, along with associated decisions on component purchase or fabrication and process and equipment selection.
**process plans** a set of documents that detail manufacturing or service delivery specifications.
**process strategy** an organization's overall approach for physically producing goods and services.
**project** the one-of-a-kind production of a product to customer order that requires a long time to complete and a large investment of funds and resources.
**service blueprint** a type of process flowchart that emphasizes customer interaction and service-related terms.
**utilization** the percentage of available working time that a worker spends working or a machine operating.

## SUMMARY OF KEY FORMULAS

*Breakeven point*

$$v = \frac{c_f}{p - c_v}$$

*Point of indifference*

$$\left|\frac{c_{f1} - c_{f2}}{c_{v1} - c_{v2}}\right|$$

*Effective capacity*

$$= (\text{no. of machines or workers}) \times (\text{no. of shifts}) \times (\text{no. of hours per shift}) \times (\text{utilization}) \times (\text{efficiency})$$

*Utilization*

$$\text{Utilization} = \frac{\text{time working}}{\text{total time available}}$$

*Load percent*

$$\text{Load percent} = \frac{\text{load}}{\text{capacity}} \times 100\%$$

## SOLVED PROBLEM—TEXLOY MANUFACTURING

Texloy Manufacturing Company must select a process for its new product, TX2, from among three different alternatives. The following cost data have been gathered:

| | PROCESS A | PROCESS B | PROCESS C |
|---|---|---|---|
| Fixed cost | \$10,000 | \$40,000 | \$70,000 |
| Variable cost | \$5/unit | \$2/unit | \$1/unit |

For what volume of demand would each process be desirable?

### SOLUTION

If $v$ represents the number of TX2s demanded (and, we assume, produced), then

$$\text{Total cost for process A} = \$10,000 + \$5v$$
$$\text{Total cost for process B} = \$40,000 + \$2v$$
$$\text{Total cost for process C} = \$70,000 + \$1v$$

Next, we calculate the points of indifference between each pair of processes by equating their total costs and solving for demand volume, $v$. Always begin with the process that has the lowest fixed cost and compare it to the process with the next lowest fixed cost, and so on. For this example, we'll compare process A to process B and process B to process C.

*Comparison 1: Process A versus Process B*

*Process A*     *Process B*

$$\$10,000 + \$5v = \$40,000 + \$2v$$
$$v = 10,000 \text{ units}$$

If demand is less than or equal to 10,000, we should choose the alternative with the lowest fixed cost, process A. Conversely, if demand is greater than 10,000, we should choose the aternative with the lowest variable cost, process B. At 10,000 units we can actually choose either A or B.

*Comparison 2: Process B versus Process C*

*Process B*     *Process C*

$$\$40,000 + \$2v = \$70,000 + \$1v$$
$$v = 30,000 \text{ units}$$

If demand is greater than 30,000 units, we should choose process C. If demand is less than 30,000 but greater than 10,000 (see comparison 1), we should choose process B. At 30,000, we can choose either B or C.

The Excel solution to this problem is shown in Exhibit 6.2.

To summarize, from the graph in Exhibit 6.2 and our decision rules, we can recommend the following process selection:

- Below 10,000 units, choose process A.
- Between 10,000 and 13,000 units, choose process B.
- Above 30,000 units, choose process C.

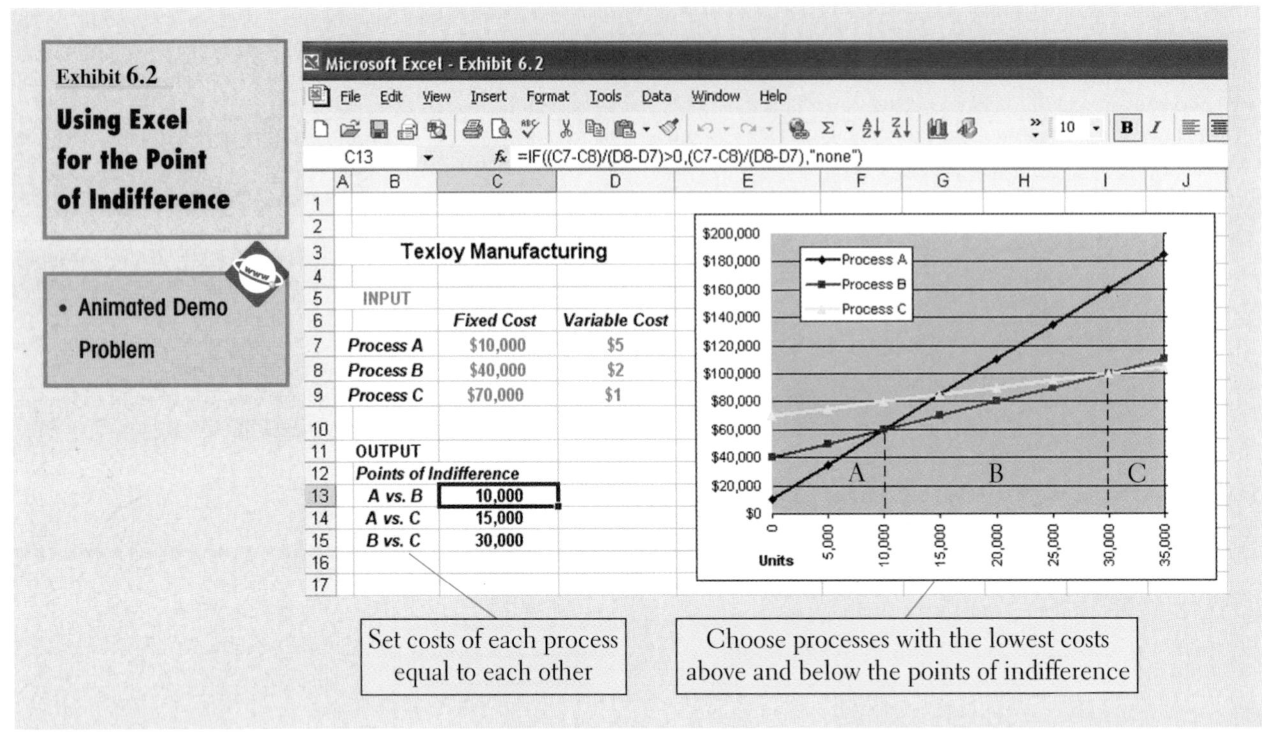


## QUESTIONS

**6-1.** Discuss the types of decisions that are involved in creating a process strategy. Apply the four elements of process strategy to the process of completing a project or paper for one of your classes. Does the process differ from class to class?

**6-2.** List and explain six factors that affect the make-or-buy decision. Explain the sourcing continuum.

**6-3.** Describe the four basic types of production processes. What are the advantages and disadvantages of each? When should each be used?

**6-4.** What are the major cost factors considered in process selection? How is breakeven analysis used for process selection?

**6-5.** What kind of information do the following documents communicate?

a. Assembly chart
b. Operations sheet
c. Process flowchart

**6-6.** What does process planning entail? How would process planning differ for batch and continuous processes?

**6-7.** Explain the basic steps involved in process innovation.

**6-8.** Our thinking process, limited by the paradigms under which we operate, can become very rigid. Try these out-of-box thinking exercises:

a. Where does the letter Z belong in this pattern, above or below the line? Why?

```
 BCD  G  J       OPQRS  U
A   EF HI KLMN         T VWXY
```

b. What letter comes next in the following pattern? Why?

OTTFF

c. Connect the nine dots below with four straight lines. Do not lift your pencil.

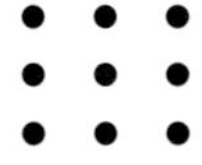

d. Circle the three errors in the following sentence:
There is three misstakes in this sentence.

**6-9.** Describe the factors often overlooked in the financial justification of new technology.

**6-10.** Briefly discuss the components of e-manufacturing. In what ways can companies collaborate in producing goods and services? Report on at least one Web source on collaborative manufacturing or e-manufacturing.

**6-11.** Why is capacity planning strategically important?

**6-12.** Describe three strategies for expanding capacity. What are the advantages and disadvantages of incremental versus one-step expansion?

**6-13.** Explain economies and diseconomies of scale. Give an example of each.

**6-14.** Explore capacity planning at your university or place of business. How is capacity measured? What factors influence the acquisition and allocation of resources?

## PROBLEMS

**6-1.** Construct a process flowchart of a process with which you are familiar. Identify bottlenecks, potential failure points, and opportunities for improvement.

**6-2.** Create an operations chart for making pancakes.

**6-3.** Mikey W. Smitty, an emerging rapper, is getting ready to cut his first CD, called "Western Rap." The cost of recording the CD is $5000 but copies are $5 apiece. If the CDs can be sold for $15 each, how many CDs must be sold to break even? What is the breakeven point in dollars?

**6-4.** Mikey W. Smitty is confident that demand for his "Western Rap" CD will substantially exceed the break-even point computed in Problem 6-3. So, Mikey is contemplating having his CD cut at a classier (and pricier) studio. The cost to record the CD would rise to $9000. However, since this new studio works with very high volume, production costs would fall to $2 per CD.

a. What is the breakeven point for this new process?

b. Compare this process to the process proposed in the previous problem. For what volume of demand should Mikey choose the classier studio?

**6-5.** Patricia Zell, a dollmaker from Olney, Maryland, is interested in the mass marketing and production of a ceramic doll of her own design called Tiny Trisha. The initial investment required for plant and equipment is estimated at $25,000. Labor and material costs are approximately $10 per doll. If the dolls can be sold for $50 each, what volume of demand is necessary for the Tiny Trisha doll to break even?

**6-6.** Although it will fulfill her lifelong dream, Patricia is not confident that demand for her Tiny Trisha doll will exceed the breakeven point computed in Problem 6-5. If she chooses a less appealing site and does more of the work by hand, her initial investment cost can be reduced to $5000, but her per-unit cost of manufacture will rise to $15 per doll.

a. What is the breakeven point for this new process?

b. Compare this process to the process proposed in the previous problem. For what volume of demand should Patricia choose this process?

**6-7.** David Austin recently purchased a chain of dry cleaners in northern Wisconsin. Although the business is making a modest profit now, David suspects that if he invests in a new press, he could recognize a substantial increase in profits. The new press costs $15,400 to purchase and install and can press 40 shirts an hour (or 320 per day). David estimates that with the new press, it will cost $0.25 to launder and press each shirt. Customers are charged $1.10 per shirt.

a. How many shirts will David have to press to break even?

b. So far, David's workload has varied from 50 to 200 shirts a day. How long would it take to break even on the new press at the low-demand estimate? at the high-demand estimate?

c. If David cuts his price to $0.99 a shirt, he expects to be able to stabilize his customer base at 250 shirts per day. How long would it take to break even at the reduced price of $0.99? Should David cut his price and buy the new press?

**6-8.** The school cafeteria can make pizza for approximately $0.30 a slice. The cost of kitchen use and cafeteria staff runs about $200 per day. The Pizza Den nearby will deliver whole pizzas for $9.00 each. The cafeteria staff cuts the pizza into eight pieces and serves them in the usual cafeteria line. With no cooking duties, the staff can be reduced by half, for a fixed cost of $75 per day. Should the school cafeteria make or buy its pizzas?

**6-9.** Soft Key is trying to determine how best to produce its newest product, DVORK keyboards. The keyboards could be produced in-house using either Process A or Process B, or purchased from a supplier. Cost data are given below. For what levels of demand should each process be chosen?

| | Fixed Cost | Variable Cost |
|---|---|---|
| *Process A* | $ 8,000 | $10 |
| *Process B* | $20,000 | $ 4 |
| *Supplier* | $ 0 | $20 |

**6-10.** NanoTech is ready to begin production of its exciting new technology. The company is evaluating three methods of production: (A) a small production facility with older equipment, (B) a larger production facility that is more automated, and (C) subcontracting to an electronics manufacturer in Singapore. The costs of each alternative are shown below. Determine for what level of demand each production process should be chosen.

| Process | Fixed Cost | Variable Cost |
|---|---|---|
| A | $200,000 | $40 |
| B | $600,000 | $20 |
| C | $ 0 | $60 |

**6-11.** Alma McCoy has decided to purchase a cellular phone for her car, but she is confused about which rate plan to choose. The "occasional-user" plan is $0.50/minute, regardless of how many minutes of air time are used. The "frequent-user" plan charges a flat rate of $55/month for 70 minutes of air time plus $0.33/minute for any time over 70 minutes. The "executive" plan charges a flat fee of $75 per month for 100 minutes of air time plus $0.25/minute over 100 minutes. In the interest of simplicity, Alma has decided to go with the occasional-user plan to start with and then upgrade as she sees fit at a later date.

a. How much air time per month would Alma need to use before she upgrades from the occasional-user plan to the frequent-user plan?

b. At what usage rate should she switch from the frequent-user plan to the executive plan?

**6-12.** Merrimac Manufacturing Company has always purchased a certain component part from a supplier on the East Coast for $50 per part. The supplier is reliable and has maintained the same price structure for years. Recently, improvements in operations and reduced product demand have cleared up some capacity in Merrimac's own plant for producing component parts. The particular part in question could be produced at $40 per part, with an annual fixed investment of $25,000. Currently, Merrimac needs 300 of these parts per year.

a. Should Merrimac make or buy the component part?
b. As another alternative, a new supplier located nearby is offering volume discounts for new customers of $50 per part for the first 100 parts ordered and $45 per part for each additional unit ordered. Should Merrimac make the component in-house, buy it from the new supplier, or stick with the old supplier?
c. Would your decision change if Merrimac's annual demand increased to 2000 parts? increased to 5000 parts?
d. Develop a set of rules that Merrimac can use to decide when to make this component, when to buy it from the old supplier, or when to buy it from the new supplier.

**6-13.** Prydain Pharmaceuticals is reviewing its employee health-care program. Currently, the company pays a fixed fee of $300 per month for each employee, regardless of the number or dollar amount of medical claims filed. Another health-care provider has offered to charge the company $100 per month per employee and $30 per claim filed. A third insurer charges $200 per month per employee and $10 per claim filed. Which health-care program should Prydain join? How would the average number of claims filed per employee per month affect your decision?

**6-14.** Gemstone Quarry is trying to decide whether to invest in a new material-handling system. The current system (which is old and completely paid for) has an annual maintenance cost of $10,000 and costs approximately $25 to transport each load of material. The two new systems that are being considered vary both in sophistication and cost. System 1 has a fixed cost of $40,000 and a cost per load estimated at $10. System 2 has a fixed cost of $100,000 but a per-load cost of $5. At what volume of demand (i.e., number of loads) should Gemstone purchase System 1? System 2?

**6-15.** Tribal Systems, Inc., is opening a new plant and has yet to decide on the type of process to employ. A labor-intensive process would cost $10,000 for tools and equipment and $14 for labor and materials per item produced. A more automated process costs $50,000 in plant and equipment but has a labor/material cost of $8 per item produced. A fully automated process costs $300,000 for plant and equipment and $2 per item produced. If process selection were based solely on lowest cost, for what range of production would each process be chosen?

**6-16.** Lydia and Jon order their holiday gifts through the mail. They have spent many evenings at home comparison-shopping through gift catalogues and have found all the things they need from three mail-order houses, B.B. Lean, Spoogle's, and Sea's End. The purchase price for their selections from each catalogue is given here. The shipping and handling charge per item is also given. If Lydia and Jon want to order all their gifts from the same source, which catalogue should they choose? How does the number of items ordered affect your recommendation?

| | B.B. Lean | Spoogle's | Sea's End |
|---|---|---|---|
| Purchase price | $400 | $500 | $460 |
| Shipping/handling per item | $6 | $3 | $4 |

**6-17.** Sandra Saunders and her design team are analyzing the production costs for three alternative monitor designs. Given the cost information below, and assuming form and function are similar for each design, which monitor design would you recommend?

| Monitor | Fixed Cost | Variable Cost |
|---|---|---|
| A | $700,000 | $250 |
| B | $1,000,000 | $125 |
| C | $1,500,000 | $100 |

**6-18.** Three Bags Full is a small grocery store chain in the Lehigh Valley. The company is trying to decide whether to include a bakery section in its stores. You have been asked to run the numbers using pies as an example. Baking the pies in-house would cost $80 per day and $1 per pie. Pies can be purchased for $4 each from a local bakery, or $3 each from a large regional bakery. The regional bakery requires a minimum purchase of 25 pies per day. Which alternative would you recommend? (Hint: graph the problem.)

**6-19.** Keisha has been inundated with product-of-the-month offers from various marketing companies. She is considering joining a club that allows DVDs to be downloaded from a members-only Web site, but can't decide which membership offers the best deal. Given the cost information below, which club would you recommend for Keisha?

| Club | Membership fee | Cost per DVD |
|---|---|---|
| Almost Free Flicks | $40 | $5 |
| Best Movies | $65 | $4 |
| Choice Cinema | $100 | $3 |

**6-20.** Pizza Express offers large pepperoni pizzas for $5 on Tuesdays from 5:00 to 9:00 in the evening. Three cooks are on duty during that time. The fixed cost for the four-hour period is $100. The variable cost is $2 per pizza.

a. If it takes 10 minutes to prepare each pizza, worker efficiency is approximately 95% and employees get a 10-minute break each hour, how many pepperoni pizzas can Pizza Express produce during its four-hour special?
b. Assuming all pizzas produced can be sold, is the promotion worth the effort?

**6-21.** Amy gets home from classes around 5 P.M. each day and can only reasonably work on her studies until midnight. She usually watches an hour of television to relax, works out for 30 minutes, and takes 30 minutes to eat dinner. She has found that if she takes a 5-minute break each hour, she can remain more focused. Today she feels 80% on task. Homework for the evening includes two critical analyses for Government, one thesis for American Lit, and three Spanish translations. Estimated processing times are shown below. Setup time includes time spent online gathering resources and finding reference books around the apartment.

a. What is Amy's effective capacity to do work this evening?
b. What is her load percent?
c. How would you suggest she adjust her capacity to complete her tasks on time?

| Tasks | Setup Time | Processing Time per Task |
|---|---|---|
| Government | 15 minutes | 40 minutes |
| American Lit | 30 minutes | 120 minutes |
| Spanish | 10 minutes | 30 minutes |

**6-22.** The Best Wheels Bicycle Company has scheduled the production of the following bicycles this month.

| | | Week | | | |
|---|---|---|---|---|---|
| | Model | 1 | 2 | 3 | 4 |
| (B2610) | 26-inch 10-speed | 50 | 100 | 195 | 150 |
| (B2003) | 20-inch 3-speed | 15 | 30 | 65 | 45 |
| (B2001) | 20-inch 1-speed | 20 | 40 | 80 | 60 |

The two critical work centers for producing these bikes are welding and assembly. Welding has an efficiency of 95% and a utilization of 90%. Assembly has an efficiency of 90% and a utilization of 92%. The time required (in hours) by each bike in the two work centers is as follows:

| | Welding | Assembly |
|---|---|---|
| B2610 | 0.20 | 0.18 |
| B2003 | 0.15 | 0.15 |
| B2001 | 0.07 | 0.10 |

Assume 40 hours is available per week for each work center. Calculate the capacity and load percent per work center per week.

**6-23.** Bryan is Professor Russell's graduate assistant. He would like to leave for Spring Break tomorrow, but first he has to grade the midterm exams from four classes. These classes are new for Bryan, so he estimates his grading efficiency to be 80%. Professor Russell has estimated the time required to create the key and the time to grade each paper as shown below. Bryan anticipates that he'll need five hours of sleep, an hour to pack, an hour to get to the airport, an hour to post the grades, and three twenty minute breaks during the day for meals. Can Bryan finish his work and make it to the airport on time in a 24 hour day?

| Class | Time to Create Key | Time to Grade Each Paper | # Papers |
|---|---|---|---|
| 1 | 10 | 2 | 35 |
| 2 | 15 | 5 | 50 |
| 3 | 5 | 1 | 60 |
| 4 | 20 | 10 | 25 |

## CASE PROBLEM 6.1

### *A Manager's Woes*

Kyle Peschken has been a manager for the discount store, Zelmart, for the past two years. It's time for his annual performance review, and Kyle would like to make a big impression on the corporate staff. Walking through the store, he makes a mental note of which departments need to be straightened, which ones need to be reorganized, and which employees he'd like to schedule during the week of his review. And then he sees it—blocking the aisles, creating commotion, and looking very unprofessional—the long line in the electronics department. It's time to confront Chris, the sales clerk.

"Chris what's the holdup here?"

"I'm waiting for a manager to approve this $120 check. And then I have to show this lady a digital camera from the display cabinet. She's been waiting half an hour, and then. . . ."

"Alright Chris. . . . I can help out for a little while . . ."

Two hours later, Kyle exited the electronics department disheartened.That's no way for a store manager to spend his afternoon. There's got to be a logical way to solve this, thought Kyle. He walked back to his office and wrote down the facts as he knew them.

1. Customer service managers (CSMs) must approve all checks over $100, and over 50% of purchases in electronics exceed $100.
2. It's more efficient to stage CSMs at the front of the store by the 12 checkout lines.
3. It takes an average of 10 minutes for the CSM to reach electronics after being paged.
4. Because of cost controls, the number of CSMs is limited to two per shift, and there is no room in the budget for additional hires of any type.
5. Electronics must be purchased in the electronics department (to prevent theft).
6. Store policy allows customers to check out other items at the electronics counter if they are making purchases in that department. (This makes sense especially if the customer wants to write a check for the entire purchase.)
7. Store clerks must monitor the locked cabinets and stay with a customer who wants to view an item from the cabinet.
8. Because of the size of the enclosed department, only two checkout counters will fit in electronics.

9. Moving the electronics department to the front of the store would not be wise because shoppers tend to pick up impulse items on their way to the center of the store where electronics are located.
10. The average time a customer spends in electronics during peak periods is an unacceptable 40 minutes.

Help Kyle come up with a solution to his inefficient department. Draw a flowchart of the current process from the customer's point of view and try to identify areas for improvement. If small improvements will not fix the problem, try a more innovative approach. Chart out your suggestions and bring them to class. (It may help to visit a similar store and watch their checkout process.)

## CASE PROBLEM 6.2

### *Herding the Patient*

Bayside General Hospital is trying to streamline its operations. A problem-solving group consisting of a nurse, a technician, a doctor, an administrator, and a patient is examining outpatient procedures in an effort to speed up the process and make it more cost-effective. Listed here are the steps that a typical patient follows for diagnostic imaging:

- Patient enters main hospital entrance.
- Patient takes a number and waits to be called to registration desk.
- Patient registers.
- Patient is taken to diagnostic imaging department.
- Patient registers at diagnostic imaging reception.
- Patient sits in department waiting area until dressing area clears.
- Patient changes in dressing area.
- Patient waits in dressing area.
- Patient is taken to exam room.
- Exam is performed.
- Patient is taken to dressing area.
- Patient dresses.
- Patient leaves.

Create a process flowchart of the procedure and identify opportunities for improvement.

## CASE PROBLEM 6.3

### *Streamlining the Refinancing Process*

First National Bank has been swamped with refinancing requests this year. To handle the increased volume, it divided the process into five distinct stages and created departments for each stage.

The process begins with a customer completing a loan application for a *loan agent.* The loan agent discusses the refinancing options with the customer and performs quick calculations based on customer-reported data to see if the customer qualifies for loan approval. If the numbers work, the customer signs a few papers to allow a credit check and goes home to wait for notification of the loan's approval.

The customer's file is then passed on to a *loan processor*, who requests a credit check, verification of loans or mortgages from other financial institutions, an appraisal of the property, and employment verification. If any problems are encountered, the loan processor goes to the loan agent for advice. If items appear on the credit report that are not on the application or if other agencies have requested the credit report, the customer is required to explain the discrepancies in writing. If the explanation is acceptable, the letter is placed in the customer's file and the file is sent to the loan agent (and sometimes the bank's board) for final approval.

The customer receives a letter of loan approval and is asked to call the *closing agent* to schedule a closing date and to lock in a loan rate if the customer has not already done so.

The closing agent requests the name of the customer's attorney to forward the loan packet. The attorney is responsible for arranging a termite inspection, a survey, a title search, and insurance and for preparing the closing papers. The attorney and the closing agent correspond back and forth to verify fees, payment schedules, and payoff amounts.

The *loan-servicing specialist* makes sure the previous loan is paid off and the new loan is set up properly. After the closing takes place, the bank's *loan-payment specialist* takes care of issuing payment books or setting up the automatic drafting of mortgage fees and calculating the exact monthly payments, including escrow amounts. The loan-payment specialist also monitors late payment of mortgages.

It is difficult to evaluate the success or failure of the process, since the volume of refinancing requests is so much greater than it has ever been before. However, customer comments solicited by the loan-servicing specialist have been disturbing to management.

*Customer Comments:*

- I refinanced with the same bank that held my original loan, thinking erroneously that I could save time and money. You took two months longer processing my loan than the other bank would have, and the money I saved on closing costs was more than eaten up by the extra month's higher mortgage payments.
- I just got a call from someone at your bank claiming my mortgage payment was overdue. How can it be overdue when you draft it automatically from my checking account?
- How come you do everything in writing and through the mail? If you would just call and ask me these questions instead of sending forms for me to fill out, things would go much more quickly.
- If I haven't made any additions to my house or property in the past year, you appraised it last year, and you have access to my tax assessment, why bother with another appraisal? You guys just like to pass around the business.
- I never know who to call for what. You have so many people working on my file. I know I've repeated the same thing to a dozen different people.
- It took so long to get my loan approved that my credit report, appraisal report, and termite inspection ran out. You should pay for the new reports, not me.
- I drove down to your office in person today to deliver the attorney's papers, and I hoped to return them with your signature and whatever else you add to the closing packet. The loan specialist said that the closing agent wouldn't get to my file until the morning of the scheduled closing and that if she hit a snag, the closing could be postponed! I'm taking off half a day from work to attend the closing and "rescheduling" is not convenient. I know you have lots of business, but I don't like being treated this way.
- I received a letter from one of your loan-payment specialists today, along with a stack of forms to complete specifying how I want to set up my mortgage payments. I signed all these at closing—don't you read your own work? I'm worried that if I fill them out again you'll withdraw the payment twice from my account!

**1.** Create a process flowchart of the refinancing process. Why do you think the bank organized its process this way? What problems have ensued?

**2.** Examine the process carefully. Which steps create value for the customer? Which steps can be eliminated? Construct a new map showing how the overall process can be improved.

## REFERENCES


Bedworth, D., M. Henderson, and P. Wolfe. *Computer-Integrated Design and Manufacturing*. New York: McGraw-Hill, 1991.

Bylinsky, Gene. "Hot New Technologies for American Factories." *Fortune Now* (June 26, 2000).

Curan, Thomas, Gerhard Keller, and Andrew Ladd. *SAP R/3 Business Blueprint*. Upper Saddle River, NJ: Prentice Hall, 1998.

El Sawy, Omar. *Redesigning Enterprise Processes for e-Business*. New York: McGraw-Hill, 2001.

Foston, L. *Fundamentals of Computer Integrated Manufacturing*. Upper Saddle River, NJ: Prentice Hall, 1991.

Hammer, Michael, and James Champy. *Reengineering the Corporation*. New York: HarperCollins, 1993.

Hammer, Michael, and Steven Stanton. *The Reengineering Revolution*. New York: HarperCollins, 1995.

Hayes, Robert, Gary Pisano, David Upton, and Steven Wheelwright. *Operations Strategy and Technology: Pursuing the Competitive Edge*. Hoboken, NJ: Wiley, 2005.

Hunt, V. Daniel. *Process Mapping*. New York: Wiley, 1996.

Keen, Peter. *The Process Edge*. Boston: Harvard Business School Press, 1997.

Nevens, J., D. Whitney, T. DeFazio, A. Edsall, R. Gustavson, R. Metzinger, and W. Dvorak. *Concurrent Design of Products and Process: A Strategy for the Next Generation in Manufacturing*. New York: McGraw-Hill, 1989.

Noori, H. *Managing the Dynamics of New Technology*. Upper Saddle River, NJ: Prentice Hall, 1990.

Reinhardt, Andy. "Log On, Link Up, Save Big." *Business Week* (June 22, 1998), pp. 132–138.

Richards, Bill. "Superplant." *eCompany Now* (November 2000).

Skinner, W. *Manufacturing: The Formidable Competitive Weapon*. (New York: Wiley, 1985).

Teresko, John. "The Dawn of e-Manufacturing." *Industry Week* (October 2, 2000).

Valery, N. "Factory of the Future." *The Economist* (May 30, 1987), pp. 3–18.

*Worldwide Robotics Survey and Directory*. Pittsburgh: The Robotic Institute of America, 1999.

Zurawski, Laura, and Mark Hoske. "E-manufacturing: A Catchy Name for What You Should be Doing Anyway." *Control Engineering* (February 13, 2001).

# Facilities

CHAPTER **7**

Web resources for this chapter include

- Internet Exercises
- Online Practice Quizzes
- Virtual Tours
- Excel Worksheets
- Company and Resource Weblinks
- Animated Demo Problems
- Microsoft Project Exhibits

www.wiley.com/college/russell

## CHAPTER OUTLINE

In this chapter you will learn about . . .

- Basic Layouts
- Designing Process Layouts
- Designing Service Layouts
- Designing Product Layouts
- Hybrid Layouts

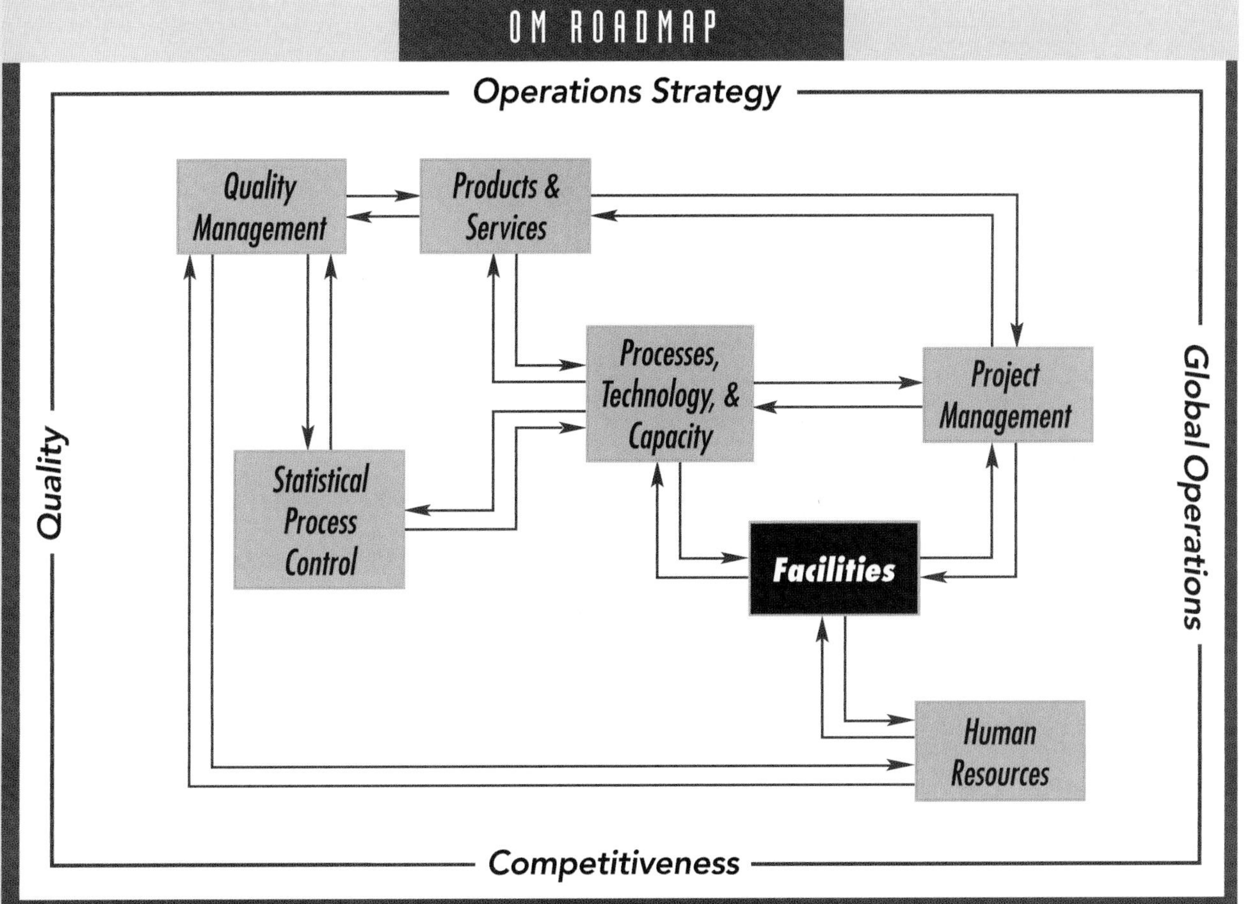

## THE ROUGE REVISITED

There has never been anything like the Rouge, Ford's most famous car-making facility. Located on 1100 acres along the Rouge River in Michigan, the complex at its heyday consisted of 29 factories, 50 miles of railroad tracks, and its own power plant and steel mill. The Rouge employed more than 100,000 people and produced a new car every 49 seconds. Iron ore, coal, and other raw materials went in one end and came out the other as a completed automobile. Today, the Rouge employs about 7000 people and assembles the Ford F-150. Outside suppliers provide most of the components and subassemblies. But great things are happening at this famous facility.

Bill Ford has built a new assembly plant on the site, designed for flexibility and *sustainable manufacturing*. With flexible equipment and new processes, Ford's able to ship 90% of vehicle orders the same day. By manufacturing three vehicle platforms and nine different models on a single assembly line, the line has 40% fewer workstations and teams of workers controlling "their own piece of the world." The flexible manufacturing body shop consists of 16 work cells producing 300 standard parts. Web connections on the plant floor enable workers to share information directly with suppliers, product engineers, and customers. A team leader, for example, can take a digital photo of a poorly fitting part, send it over the Web to a supplier, and get an engineering fix in minutes. Parts delivered directly to the assembly area cut inventory in half, to just 2 hours' worth and 10 hours offline. Adjustable wooden palettes at workstations can be raised and lowered to facilitate assembly tasks.

Advanced environmental concepts are also incorporated into the new Rouge. Its 10.4 acre "living roof" made of grass and other ground cover vegetation can hold an hour's worth of rainwater and will insulate the factory in both winter and summer. Instead of hauling contaminated soil to landfills, mustard seed and other plants will remove toxins from the soil. Shallow green ditches replace giant underground culverts to siphon off storm water, and porous pavement lets rainwater seep through. Ford hopes to restore the natural balance to the marshy land as well, with meadows, mulberry bushes, and other indigenous plants. Skylights and common areas make the facility a more pleasant place to work. The new Rouge is a showcase for flexibility and a new era of environmental consciousness in manufacturing.

*A $2 billion overhaul of Ford's River Rouge factory includes a living roof that consists of a 10.4-acre blanket of sedum and native grasses to capture rainwater and cool the building. Large roof monitors and skylights flood the plant's assembly area with natural light.*

*Sources:* Frank Gibney, "The Rebel Driving." *Time* (May 14, 2001), pp. 43–48; Joann Muller, "A Ford Redesign." *Business Week* (November 13, 2000), pp. 79–83; Emily Burch, "Lean and Green." *Plants, Sites and Parks Magazine* (April/May 2001, Joann Muller, "Lean Green Machine," *Forbes* (February 3, 2003); "Dearborn Truck Plant to Showcase Lean, Flexible Manufacturing in Best-in-Class Facility," June 13, 2003, www.ford-trucks.com.

Facilities make a difference. They can provide a competitive edge by enabling and leveraging the latest process concepts. For example, factories that once positioned shipping and receiving departments at one end of the building, now construct *t*-shaped buildings so that deliveries can be made directly to points of use within the factory. Stores sport portable kiosks for customer inquiry and checkout at various locations throughout the facility. Classrooms incorporate desks on wheels to be repositioned for different teaching styles and student interaction. Where work is performed has an impact on both quality and productivity. Facility decisions affect how efficiently workers can do their jobs, how much and how fast goods can be produced, how difficult it is to automate a system, and how responsive the system can be to changes in product or service design, product mix, or demand volume. Facilities must be planned, located, and laid out. In this chapter we discuss various types of facility layouts. In the chapter supplement we present several methods for determining facility location.

**Facility layout** refers to the arrangement of machines, processes, departments, workstations, storage areas, aisles, and common areas within an existing or proposed facility. The basic objective of the layout decision is to ensure a smooth flow of work, material, people, and information through the system. Effective layouts also:

**Facility layout:** the arrangement of areas within a facility.

Facility layout decisions involve multiple objectives.

- Minimize material handling costs;
- Utilize space efficiently;
- Utilize labor efficiently;
- Eliminate bottlenecks;
- Facilitate communication and interaction between workers, between workers and their supervisors, and between workers and customers;
- Reduce manufacturing cycle time and customer service time;
- Eliminate wasted or redundant movement;
- Facilitate the entry, exit, and placement of material, products, and people;
- Incorporate safety and security measures;
- Promote product and service quality;
- Encourage proper maintenance activities;
- Provide a visual control of activities;
- Provide flexibility to adapt to changing conditions;
- Increase capacity.

Layout decisions affect quality and competitiveness.

## BASIC LAYOUTS

There are three basic types of layouts: process, product, and fixed-position; and three hybrid layouts: cellular layouts, flexible manufacturing systems, and mixed-model assembly lines. We discuss basic layouts in this section and hybrid layouts later in the chapter.

## PROCESS LAYOUTS

**Process layouts**, also known as *functional layouts*, group similar activities together in departments or work centers according to the process or function they perform. For example, in a machine shop, all drills would be located in one work center, lathes in another work center, and milling machines in still another work center. In a department store, women's clothes, men's clothes, children's clothes, cosmetics, and shoes are located in separate departments. A process layout is characteristic of intermittent operations, service shops, job shops, or batch production, which serve different customers with different needs. The volume of each customer's order is low, and the sequence of operations required to complete a customer's order can vary considerably.

**Process layouts:** group similar activities together according to the process or function they perform.

The equipment in a process layout is general purpose, and the workers are skilled at operating the equipment in their particular department. The advantage of this layout is flexibility. The disadvantage is inefficiency. Jobs or customers do not flow through the system in an orderly manner, backtracking is common, movement from department to department can take a considerable amount of time, and queues tend to develop. In addition,

**Figure 7.1**
**A process layout in services**

| Women's lingerie | Shoes | Housewares |
|---|---|---|
| Women's dresses | Cosmetics and jewelry | Children's department |
| Women's sportswear | Entry and display area | Men's department |

each new arrival may require that an operation be set up differently for its particular processing requirements. Although workers can operate a number of machines or perform a number of different tasks in a single department, their workload often fluctuates—from queues of jobs or customers waiting to be processed to idle time between jobs or customers. Figures 7.1 and 7.2 show schematic diagrams of process layouts in services and manufacturing.

Material storage and movement are directly affected by the type of layout. Storage space in a process layout is large to accommodate the large amount of in-process inventory. The factory may look like a warehouse, with work centers strewn between storage aisles. In-process inventory is high because material moves from work center to work center in batches waiting to be processed. Finished goods inventory, on the other hand, is low because the goods are being made for a particular customer and are shipped out to that customer on completion.

Process layouts in manufacturing firms require flexible material handling equipment (such as forklifts) that can follow multiple paths, move in any direction, and carry large loads of in-process goods. A *forklift* moving pallets of material from work center to work center needs wide aisles to accommodate heavy loads and two-way movement. Scheduling of forklifts is typically controlled by radio dispatch and varies from day to day and hour to hour. Routes have to be determined and priorities given to different loads competing for pickup.

Process layouts in service firms require large aisles for customers to move back and forth and ample display space to accommodate different customer preferences.

The major layout concern for a process layout is where to locate the departments or machine centers in relation to each other. Although each job or customer potentially has a different route through the facility, some paths will be more common than others. Past information on customer orders and projections of customer orders can be used to develop patterns of flow through the shop.

**Figure 7.2**
**A process layout in manufacturing**

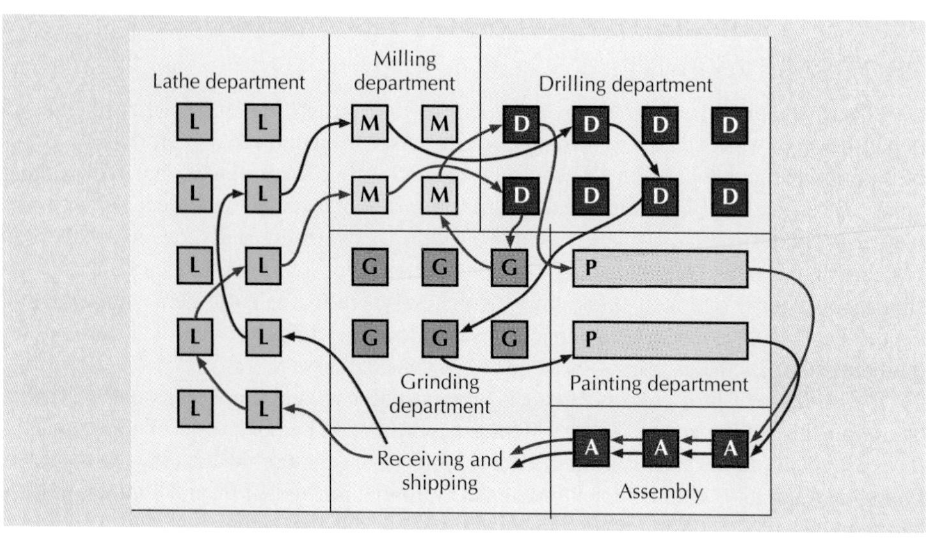

*Good layouts can increase revenues, as well as save operating expenses. Pittsburgh International Airport's innovative X-design allows planes to approach the airport from any direction, significantly increasing the airspace capacity of the airport.*

## PRODUCT LAYOUTS

**Product layouts:** arrange activities in a line according to the sequence of operations for a particular product or service.

**Product layouts**, better known as *assembly lines*, arrange activities in a line according to the sequence of operations that need to be performed to assemble a particular product. Each product has its own "line" specifically designed to meet its requirements. The flow of work is orderly and efficient, moving from one workstation to another down the assembly line until a finished product comes off the end of the line. Since the line is set up for one type of product or service, special machines can be purchased to match a product's specific processing requirements. Product layouts are suitable for mass production or repetitive operations in which demand is stable and volume is high. The product or service

*The photo on the left shows a process layout: a forklift moves pallets of material from department to department. The photo on the right shows a product layout: Krispy Kreme doughnuts move down the conveyor under the glazing waterfall. The production line continues until the doughnuts are cooled enough to be packaged.*

Figure 7.3
**A Product Layout**

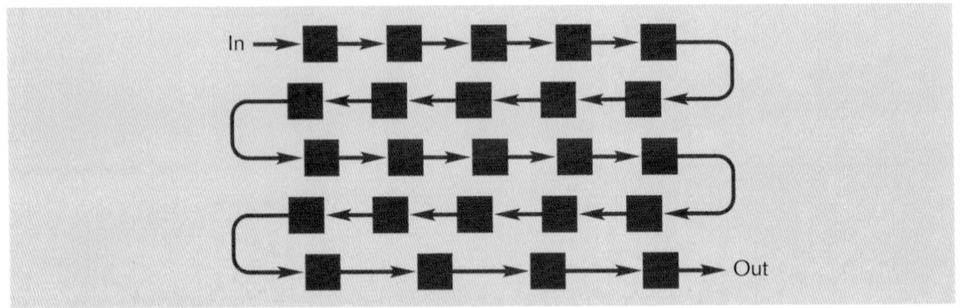


is a standard one made for a general market, not for a particular customer. Because of the high level of demand, product layouts are more automated than process layouts, and the role of the worker is different. Workers perform narrowly defined assembly tasks that do not demand as high a wage rate as those of the more versatile workers in a process layout.

Process layouts are flexible; product layouts are efficient.

The advantage of the product layout is its efficiency and ease of use. The disadvantage is its inflexibility. Significant changes in product design may require that a new assembly line be built and new equipment be purchased. This is what happened to U.S. automakers when demand shifted to smaller cars. The factories that could efficiently produce six-cylinder engines could not be adapted to produce four-cylinder engines. A similar inflexibility occurs when demand volume slows. The fixed cost of a product layout (mostly for equipment) allocated over fewer units can send the price of a product soaring.

The major concern in a product layout is balancing the assembly line so that no one workstation becomes a bottleneck and holds up the flow of work through the line. Figure 7.3 shows the product flow in a product layout. Contrast this with the flow of products through the process layout shown in Figure 7.2.

A product layout needs material moved in one direction along the assembly line and always in the same pattern. Conveyors are the most common material handling equipment for product layouts. Conveyors can be *paced* (automatically set to control the speed of work) or *unpaced* (stopped and started by the workers according to their pace). Assembly work can be performed *online* (i.e., on the conveyor) or *offline* (at a workstation serviced by the conveyor).

Table 7.1
**A Comparison of Product and Process Layouts**

| | Product Layout | Process Layout |
|---|---|---|
| 1. Description | Sequential arrangement of activities | Functional grouping of activities |
| 2. Type of process | Continuous, mass production, mainly assembly | Intermittent, job shop, batch production, mainly fabrication |
| 3. Product | Standardized, made to stock | Varied, made to order |
| 4. Demand | Stable | Fluctuating |
| 5. Volume | High | Low |
| 6. Equipment | Special purpose | General purpose |
| 7. Workers | Limited skills | Varied skills |
| 8. Inventory | Low in-process, high finished goods | High in-process, low finished goods |
| 9. Storage space | Small | Large |
| 10. Material handling | Fixed path (conveyor) | Variable path (forklift) |
| 11. Aisles | Narrow | Wide |
| 12. Scheduling | Part of balancing | Dynamic |
| 13. Layout decision | Line balancing | Machine location |
| 14. Goal | Equalize work at each station | Minimize material handling cost |
| 15. Advantage | Efficiency | Flexibility |

Aisles are narrow because material is moved only one way, it is not moved very far, and the conveyor is an integral part of the assembly process, usually with workstations on either side. Scheduling of the conveyors, once they are installed, is simple—the only variable is how fast they should operate.

Storage space along an assembly line is quite small because in-process inventory is consumed in the assembly of the product as it moves down the assembly line. Finished goods, however, may require a separate warehouse for storage before they are shipped to dealers or stores to be sold.

Product and process layouts look different, use different material handling methods, and have different layout concerns. Table 7.1 summarizes the differences between product and process layouts.

**Fixed-position layouts:** are used for projects in which the product cannot be moved.

## FIXED-POSITION LAYOUTS

**Fixed-position layouts** are typical of projects in which the product produced is too fragile, bulky, or heavy to move. Ships, houses, and aircraft are examples. In this layout, the product remains stationary for the entire manufacturing cycle. Equipment, workers,

***John Snead,***

***Senior Manager of Financial Planning and Analysis for Air Products***

I began working at Air Products as a business analyst assessing the profitability of capital projects. Air Products spends between $700 and $800 million a year on capital projects, 25% of which support existing operations. The remaining 75% is invested in growth opportunities, predominantly building new or expanded production facilities. Our company was founded on the strength of a simple, yet revolutionary, idea—producing and selling industrial gases "on-site." That means building gas-generating facilities adjacent to customer sites to reduce distribution costs.

Air Products has since broadened its scope to include specialty gases and chemicals, but "on-sites," as we call them, remain a core business. Because we are investing a great deal of money in new plant and equipment to supply each customer, we negotiate 15-year contracts with minimum-volume commitments and cost pass-through provisions. Capital project analysis is more than "running the numbers." As a business analyst, I worked with operations, engineering, marketing, and sales to put together a thorough analysis of each investment opportunity.

My current job involves setting policies for financial analysis (such as worldwide hurdle rates and risk assessment) and developing the financial plan for the company using multiyear cash flow projections to make decisions on capital and acquisition spending, dividend policy, and debt restructuring. A portion of my time is spent monitoring working capital. By lowering inventories, purchasing costs, and receivables, we have more capital to invest in growth. Two fairly recent corporate initiatives that are significantly reducing costs are e-procurement and ERP (enterprise resource planning.)

We are about halfway through a five-year implementation of SAP's ERP system. The system automates transactions, streamlines processes, and provides us with more useful information with which to make decisions. For example, we're getting a better handle on our costs through newly designed cost centers. SAP also helps us rationalize our facilities and make better sourcing decisions. Implementation has been going well. It's been more of a cultural and process change than a technical one. We can standardize processes, but getting people to consistently follow them is another matter.

We use APDirect, an Ariba product, for various e-procurement initiatives. For B2B, we are members of industry exchanges such as Elemica for the chemical industry and Rosetta Net for electronics. Many of our transactions take place over established EDI (electronic data interchange) systems. For strategic sourcing, we've joined a consortium called LSN (Leveraged Sourcing Network) consisting of 20 to 25 companies from a variety of industries who, when combined, represent the purchasing power of a *Fortune* 10 company. We also have a direct sourcing application that allows closed bids, forward and reverse auctions, and project workspaces for collaboration. We probably save $10 million annually in costs with our e-procurement initiatives.

In our company, like many others, most of our capital projects and cost savings opportunities involve operations. By streamlining our processes, automating and standardizing our systems, and working collaboratively across functional lines, we can increase our efficiency and profitability—not to mention "face time" with our customers. Air Products is successful today not only because of its operational excellence, but also because of the ability of its people to create lasting relationships built on understanding our customers' needs.

materials, and other resources are brought to the production site. Equipment utilization is low because it is often less costly to leave equipment idle at a location where it will be needed again in a few days, than to move it back and forth. Frequently, the equipment is leased or subcontracted because it is used for limited periods of time. The workers called to the work site are highly skilled at performing the special tasks they are requested to do. For instance, pipefitters may be needed at one stage of production, and electricians or plumbers at another. The wage rate for these workers is much higher than minimum wage. Thus, if we were to look at the cost breakdown for fixed-position layouts, the fixed cost would be relatively low (equipment may not be owned by the company), whereas the variable costs would be high (due to high labor rates and the cost of leasing and moving equipment).

Fixed-position layouts are specialized to individual projects and thus are beyond the scope of this book. Projects are covered in more detail in the next chapter. In the sections that follow, we examine some quantitative approaches for designing product and process layouts.

## DESIGNING PROCESS LAYOUTS

Process layout objective: Minimize material handling costs.

In designing a process layout, we want to minimize movement or material handling cost, which is a function of the amount of material moved times the distance it is moved. This implies that departments that incur the most interdepartment movement should be located closest to each other, and those that do not interact should be located further away. Two techniques used to design process layouts, block diagramming and relationship diagramming, are based on logic and the visual representation of data.

### BLOCK DIAGRAMMING

**Unit load:** the quantity in which material is normally moved.

We begin with data on historical or predicted movement of material between departments in the existing or proposed facility. This information is typically provided in the form of a from/to chart, or *load summary chart*. The chart gives the average number of **unit loads** transported between the departments over a given period of time. A unit load can be a single unit, a pallet of material, a bin of material, or a crate of material—however material is normally moved from location to location. In automobile manufacturing, a single

*Aircraft production generally takes place in a fixed position layout due to the size and complexity of assembly. Boeing, however, is experimenting with a s-l-o-w-l-y moving assembly line for its smaller aircraft, the 100-seat Boeing 717, shown here at the Long Beach, California production facility.*

car represents a unit load. For a ball-bearing producer, a unit load might consist of a bin of 100 or 1000 ball bearings, depending on their size.

The next step in designing the layout is to calculate the *composite movements* between departments and rank them from most movement to least movement. Composite movement, represented by a two-headed arrow, refers to the back-and-forth movement between each pair of departments.

Finally, trial layouts are placed on a grid that graphically represents the relative distances between departments in the form of uniform blocks. The objective is to assign each department to a block on the grid so that *nonadjacent loads* are minimized. The term *nonadjacent* is defined as a distance farther than the next block, either horizontally, vertically, or diagonally. The trial layouts are scored on the basis of the number of nonadjacent loads. Ideally, the optimal layout would have zero nonadjacent loads. In practice, this is rarely possible, and the process of trying different layout configurations to reduce the number of nonadjacent loads continues until an acceptable layout is found.

Block diagramming tries to minimize nonadjacent loads.

**Example 7.1**

**Process Layout**

Barko, Inc. makes *bark scalpers*, processing equipment that strips the bark off trees and turns it into nuggets or mulch for gardens. The facility that makes bark scalpers is a small-job shop that employs 50 workers and is arranged into five departments: (1) bar stock cutting, (2) sheet metal, (3) machining, (4) painting, and (5) assembly. The average number of loads transported between the five departments per month is given in the accompanying load summary chart. The current layout of the facility is shown schematically on the 2 × 3 grid. Notice that there is quite a bit of flexibility in the facility, as indicated by the six possible locations (i.e., intersections) available for five departments. In addition, the forklift used in the facility is very flexible, allowing horizontal, vertical, and diagonal movement of material.

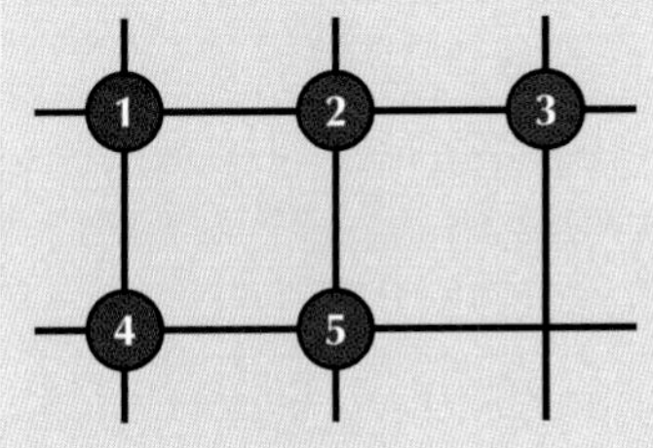


**Load Summary Chart**

| from/to | Department | | | | |
|---|---|---|---|---|---|
| Department | 1 | 2 | 3 | 4 | 5 |
| 1 | — | 100 | 50 | | |
| 2 | | — | 200 | 50 | |
| 3 | 60 | | — | 40 | 50 |
| 4 | | 100 | | — | 60 |
| 5 | | 50 | | | — |

Barko management anticipates that a new bark scalper plant will soon be necessary and would like to know if a similar layout should be used or if a better layout can be designed. You are asked to evaluate the current layout in terms of nonadjacent loads, and if needed, propose a new layout on a 2 × 3 grid that will minimize the number of nonadjacent loads.

*Solution*

In order to evaluate the current layout, we need to calculate the composite, or back-and-forth, movements between departments. For example, the composite movement between department 1 and department 3 is the sum of 50 loads moved from 1 to 3, plus 60 loads moved from 3 to 1, or 110 loads of material. If we continue to calculate composite movements and rank them from highest to lowest, the following list results:

| *Composite Movements* | | *Composite Movements* | |
|---|---|---|---|
| 2 ↔ 3 | 200 loads | 3 ↔ 5 | 50 loads |
| 2 ↔ 4 | 150 loads | 2 ↔ 5 | 50 loads |
| 1 ↔ 3 | 110 loads | 3 ↔ 4 | 40 loads |
| 1 ↔ 2 | 100 loads | 1 ↔ 4 | 0 loads |
| 4 ↔ 5 | 60 loads | 1 ↔ 5 | 0 loads |

Next, we evaluate the "goodness" of the layout by scoring it in terms of nonadjacent loads. The results are shown visually in Grid 1.

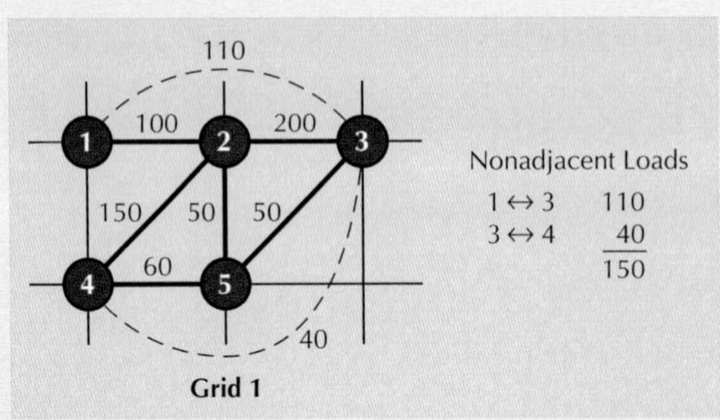


The adjacent moves are marked with a solid line and the nonadjacent moves are shown with a curved dashed line to highlight the fact that material is moved farther than we would like, that is, across more than one square. Following our composite movement list, 2 ↔ 3 and 2 ↔ 4 are adjacent moves, but 1 ↔ 3 is not. Our nonadjacent score starts with 110 loads of material from 1 ↔ 3. Continuing down our list, all moves are adjacent and are marked with solid lines until 3 ↔ 4. Movement 3 ↔ 4 is nonadjacent, so we designate it as such and add 40 loads to our nonadjacent score. The remaining movements have zero loads. Thus, our score for this layout is 110 + 40 = 150 nonadjacent loads.

To improve the layout, we note that departments 3 and 4 should be located adjacent to department 2, and that departments 4 and 5 may be located away from department 1 without adding to the score of nonadjacent loads. Let's put departments 4 and 5 on one end of the grid and department 1 on the other and then fill in departments 2 and 3 in the middle. The revised solution is shown in Grid 2. The only nonadjacent moves are between departments 1 and 4, and 1 and 5. Since no loads of material are moved along those paths, the score for this layout is zero.

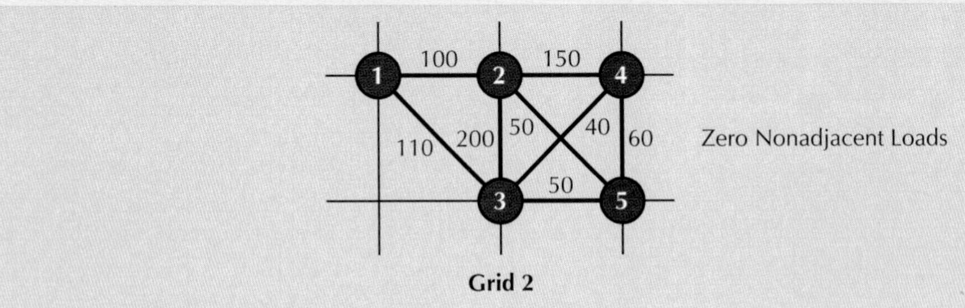


The Excel setup for this problem is shown in Exhibit 7.1.

**Block diagram:** a type of schematic layout diagram that includes space requirements.

The layout solution in Grid 2 represents the relative position of each department. The next step in the layout design is to add information about the space required for each department. Recommendations for workspace around machines can be requested from equipment vendors or found in safety regulations or operating manuals. In some cases, vendors provide templates of equipment layouts, with work areas included. Workspace allocations for workers can be specified as part of job design, recommended by professional groups, or agreed on through union negotiations. A **block diagram** can be created by "blocking in" the work areas around the departments on the grid. The *final block diagram* adjusts the block diagram for the desired or proposed shape of the building. Standard building shapes include rectangles, L shapes, T shapes, and U shapes.

Figure 7.4*a* shows an initial block diagram for Example 7.1, and Figure 7.4*b* shows a final block diagram. Notice that the space requirements vary considerably from department to department, but the relative location of departments has been retained from the grid.

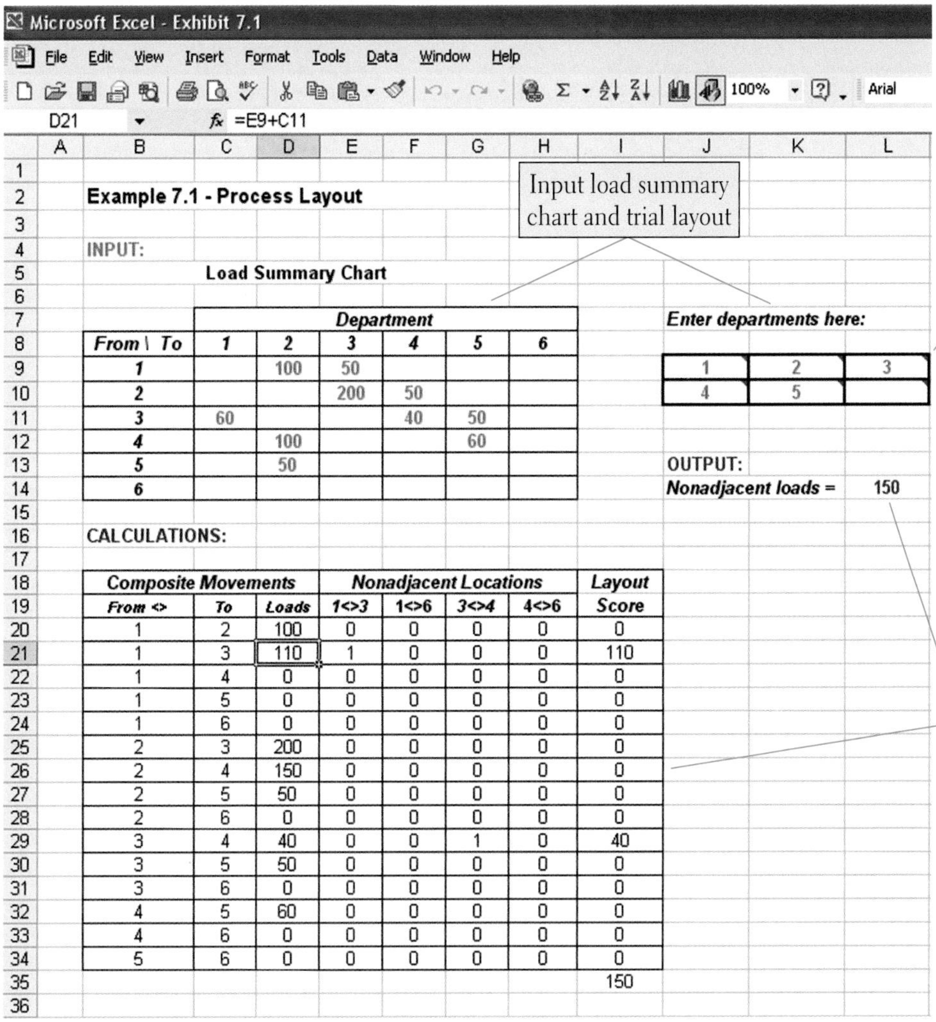

Exhibit 7.1
**Using Excel for Process Layouts**

Microsoft Excel - Exhibit 7.1

D21 $f_x$ =E9+C11

**Example 7.1 - Process Layout**

INPUT:

Load Summary Chart

| From \ To | 1 | 2 | 3 | 4 | 5 | 6 |
|---|---|---|---|---|---|---|
| | Department | | | | | |
| 1 | | 100 | 50 | | | |
| 2 | | | 200 | 50 | | |
| 3 | 60 | | | 40 | 50 | |
| 4 | | 100 | | | 60 | |
| 5 | | 50 | | | | |
| 6 | | | | | | |

Input load summary chart and trial layout

Enter departments here:

| 1 | 2 | 3 |
|---|---|---|
| 4 | 5 | |

Try different layout configurations

OUTPUT:
Nonadjacent loads = 150

CALCULATIONS:

| Composite Movements | | | Nonadjacent Locations | | | | Layout |
|---|---|---|---|---|---|---|---|
| From <> | To | Loads | 1<>3 | 1<>6 | 3<>4 | 4<>6 | Score |
| 1 | 2 | 100 | 0 | 0 | 0 | 0 | 0 |
| 1 | 3 | 110 | 1 | 0 | 0 | 0 | 110 |
| 1 | 4 | 0 | 0 | 0 | 0 | 0 | 0 |
| 1 | 5 | 0 | 0 | 0 | 0 | 0 | 0 |
| 1 | 6 | 0 | 0 | 0 | 0 | 0 | 0 |
| 2 | 3 | 200 | 0 | 0 | 0 | 0 | 0 |
| 2 | 4 | 150 | 0 | 0 | 0 | 0 | 0 |
| 2 | 5 | 50 | 0 | 0 | 0 | 0 | 0 |
| 2 | 6 | 0 | 0 | 0 | 0 | 0 | 0 |
| 3 | 4 | 40 | 0 | 0 | 1 | 0 | 40 |
| 3 | 5 | 50 | 0 | 0 | 0 | 0 | 0 |
| 3 | 6 | 0 | 0 | 0 | 0 | 0 | 0 |
| 4 | 5 | 60 | 0 | 0 | 0 | 0 | 0 |
| 4 | 6 | 0 | 0 | 0 | 0 | 0 | 0 |
| 5 | 6 | 0 | 0 | 0 | 0 | 0 | 0 |
| | | | | | | | 150 |

Excel will calculate composite movements and nonadjacent loads

## RELATIONSHIP DIAGRAMMING

The preceding solution procedure is appropriate for designing process layouts when quantitative data are available. However, in situations for which quantitative data are difficult to obtain or do not adequately address the layout problem, the load summary chart can be replaced with subjective input from analysts or managers. Richard Muther developed a format for displaying manager preferences for departmental locations, known as **Muther's grid.**[1]

**Muther's grid:** a format for displaying manager preferences for department locations.

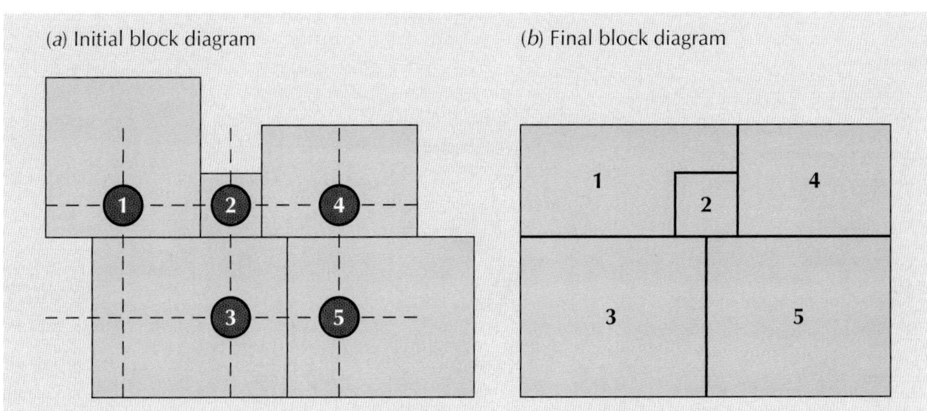


Figure 7.4
**Block Diagrams**

[1]R. Muther, *Systematic Layout Planning* (Boston: Industrial Education Institute, 1961).

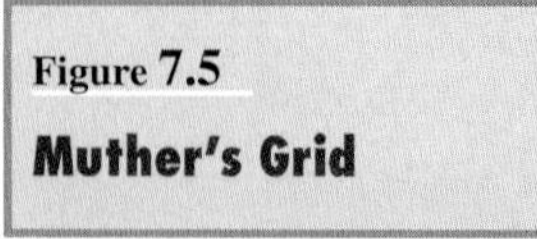
Figure 7.5
**Muther's Grid**

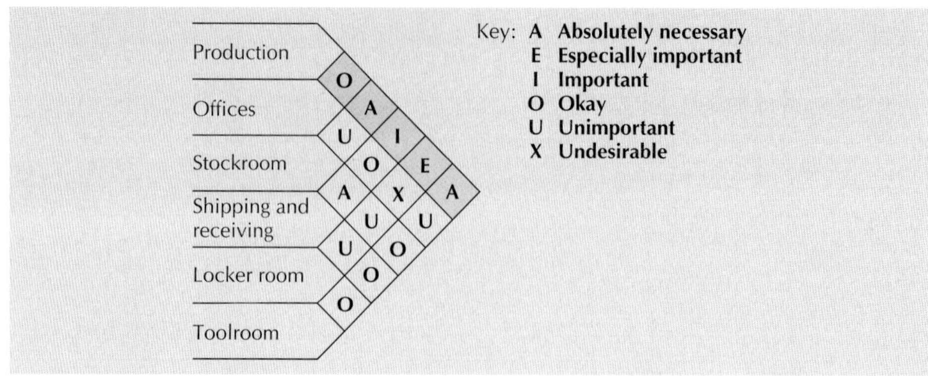


Manager preferences for department locations are displayed as A, E, I, O, U, or X.

The preference information is coded into six categories associated with the five vowels, *A, E, I, O,* and *U*, plus the letter *X*. As shown in Figure 7.5, the vowels match the first letter of the closeness rating for locating two departments next to each other. The diamond-shaped grid is read similarly to mileage charts on a road map. For example, reading down the highlighted row in Figure 7.5, it is *okay* if the offices are located next to production, *absolutely necessary* that the stockroom be located next to production, *important* that shipping and receiving be located next to production, *especially important* that the locker room be located next to production, and *absolutely necessary* that the toolroom be located next to production.

**Relationship diagram:** a schematic diagram that uses weighted lines to denote location preference.

The information from Muther's grid can be used to construct a **relationship diagram** that evaluates existing or proposed layouts. Consider the relationship diagram shown in Figure 7.6*a*. A schematic diagram of the six departments from Figure 7.5 is given in a 2 × 3 grid. Lines of different thicknesses are drawn from department to department. The thickest lines (three, four, or five strands) identify the closeness ratings with the highest priority—that is, for which departments it is *important, especially important,* or *absolutely necessary* that they be located next to each other. The priority diminishes with line thickness. *Undesirable* closeness ratings are marked with a zigzagged line. Visually, the best solution would show short heavy lines and no zigzagged lines (undesirable locations are noted only if they are adjacent). Thin lines (one or two strands, representing *unimportant* or *okay* ) can be of any length and for that reason are sometimes eliminated from the analysis. An alternative form of relationship diagramming uses colors instead of line thickness to visualize closeness ratings.

From Figure 7.6*a*, it is obvious that production and shipping and receiving are located too far from the stockroom and that the offices and locker room are located too close to one another. Figure 7.6*b* shows a revised layout and evaluates the layout with a relationship diagram. The revised layout appears to satisfy the preferences expressed in Muther's

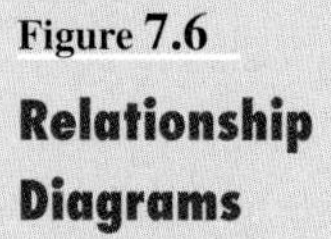
Figure 7.6
**Relationship Diagrams**

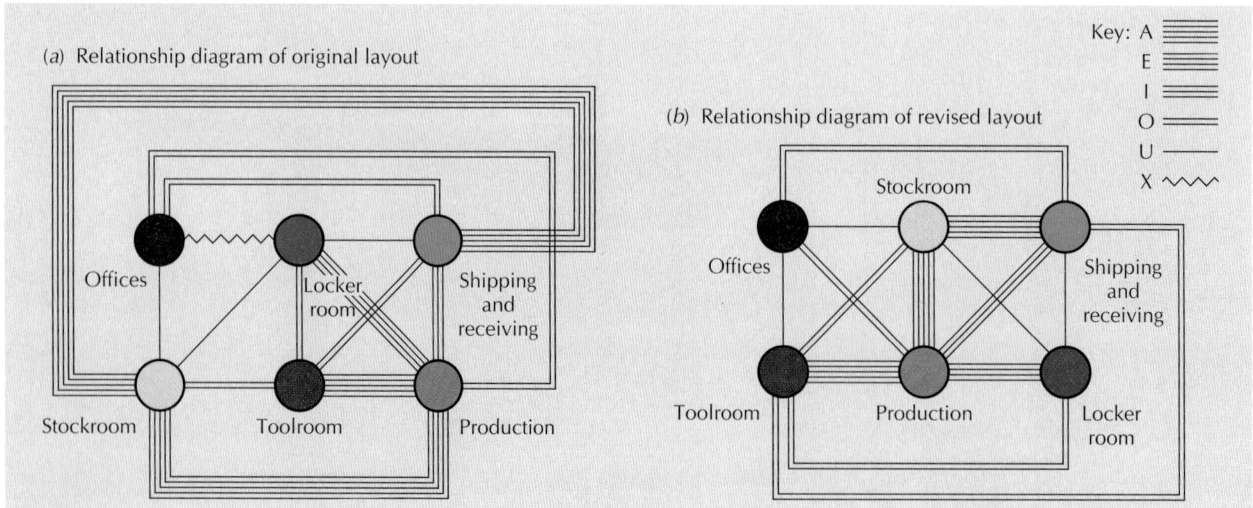

grid. The heavy lines are short and within the perimeter of the grid. The lengthy lines are thin, and there are no zigzagged lines (X's are shown only if the departments are adjacent).

## COMPUTERIZED LAYOUT SOLUTIONS

The diagrams just discussed help formulate ideas for the arrangement of departments in a process layout, but they can be cumbersome for large problems. Fortunately, several computer packages are available for designing process layouts. The best known are CRAFT (Computerized Relative Allocation of Facilities Technique) and CORELAP (Computerized Relationship Layout Planning). CRAFT takes a load summary chart and block diagram as input and then makes pairwise exchanges of departments until no improvements in cost or nonadjacency score can be found. The output is a revised block diagram after each iteration for a rectangular-shaped building, which may or may not be optimal. CRAFT is sensitive to the initial block diagram used; that is, different block diagrams as input will result in different layouts as outputs. For this reason, CRAFT is often used to improve on existing layouts or to enhance the best manual attempts at designing a layout.

CORELAP uses nonquantitative input and relationship diagramming to produce a feasible layout for up to 45 departments and different building shapes. It attempts to create an acceptable layout from the beginning by locating department pairs with A ratings first, then those with E ratings, and so on.

Simulation software for layout analysis, such as PROMODEL and EXTEND provide visual feedback and allow the user to quickly test a variety of scenarios. Three-D modeling and CAD-integrated layout analysis are available in VisFactory and similar software.

## DESIGNING SERVICE LAYOUTS

Service layouts may have different objectives than manufacturing layouts.

Most service organizations use process layouts. This makes sense because of the variability in customer requests for service. Service layouts are designed in much the same way as process layouts in manufacturing firms, but the objectives may differ. For example, instead of minimizing the flow of materials through the system, services may seek to minimize the flow of paperwork or to maximize customer exposure, to as many goods as possible. Grocery stores take this approach when they locate milk on one end of the store and bread on the other, forcing the customer to travel through aisles of merchandise that might prompt additional purchases.

In addition to the location of departments, service layout is concerned with the circulation of customer traffic through the facility. There are a variety of ways to prompt the flow of customers through various processes or departments. You may have experienced a free-flow layout in The Disney Store, a grid layout in your grocery store, a spine layout in Barnes and Noble, or a circular layout in Kohl's department store. These layouts are

*Service layouts must be attractive as well as functional. In this photo, modular office units without permanent walls allow maximum flexibility, save space, and encourage communication.*

Figure 7.7
**Types of Store Layouts**

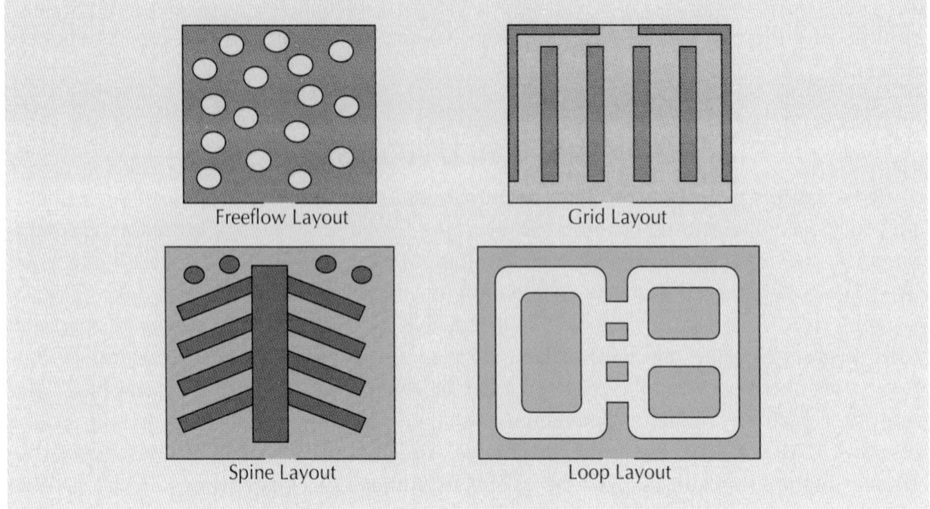


## THE COMPETITIVE EDGE

### Shared Spaces

Facility design is an important factor in encouraging collaborative activities. Here are two examples.

Valeo, an automotive equipment supplier, designed its new technical center in Auburn Hills, Michigan, to support collaborative work in cross-functional teams of designers, manufacturing engineers, and testing staff. As shown in the photo above, glass is used extensively throughout the building to open up and connect offices and keep people in touch. The laboratory and testing areas are divided by soundproof glass, so that employees are in constant visual contact throughout the work process. Dropped lighting armatures contain data and power supplies for easy connection and reconfiguration. This permits Valeo to adjust the size and mix of teams to the tasks at hand. The cafeteria opens onto a shaded outdoor space for more informal interaction.

Sticks, Inc. designs and manufactures contemporary art objects from fallen timber. Its new building, located in a grove of mature oak trees, integrates artist studios with manufacturing and shipping. Output is up 20% since it opened, while time for handling and transportation is down.

*Source:* Bruce Nussbaum, "Super Structures." *Business Week* (November 6, 2000), p. 122.

shown in Figure 7.7. *Free flow layouts* encourage browsing, increase impulse purchasing, and are flexible and visually appealing. *Grid layouts* encourage customer familiarity, are low cost, easy to clean and secure, and good for repeat customers. *Loop layouts* and *spine layouts* fall between the extremes of free flow and grids. They both increase customer sightlines and exposure to products, while encouraging the customer to circulate through the entire store.[2]

**Service layouts encourage a customer to circulate through a facility in a *free flow, grid, loop,* or *spine* pattern.**

Service layouts are also concerned with the allocation of space to departments, the location of special displays, the efficiency of checkout procedures, and protection from pilferage. Space allocation is determined by evaluating the sales per square foot of a product or product line versus the willingness of a vendor to pay for product placement. Queuing analysis, discussed in Chapter 17, is a quantitative technique for improving waiting lines that often form at checkouts.

Industry-specific recommendations are available for layout and display decisions. Computerized versions, such as SLIM (Store Labor and Inventory Management) and COSMOS (Computerized Optimization and Simulation Modeling for Operating Supermarkets), consider shelf space, demand rates, profitability, and stockout probabilities in layout design.

Finally, services may have both a *back office* (invisible to the customer) and a *front office* (in full view of the customer) component. Back offices can be organized for efficiency and functionality, while front office layouts must be aesthetically pleasing as well as functional. For that reason, service layouts are often considered part of the service design process.

## DESIGNING PRODUCT LAYOUTS

A product layout arranges machines or workers in a line according to the operations that need to be performed to assemble a particular product. From this description, it would seem the layout could be determined simply by following the order of assembly as contained in the bill of material for the product. To some extent, this is true. Precedence requirements specifying which operations must precede others, which can be done concurrently and which must wait until later are an important input to the product layout decision. But there are other factors that make the decision more complicated.

**Product layout objective: Balance the assembly line.**

Product layouts or assembly lines are used for high-volume production. To attain the required output rate as efficiently as possible, jobs are broken down into their smallest indivisible portions, called *work elements*. Work elements are so small that they cannot be performed by more than one worker or at more than one workstation. But it is common for one worker to perform several work elements as the product passes through his or her workstation. Part of the layout decision is concerned with grouping these work elements into workstations so products flow through the assembly line smoothly. A *workstation* is any area along the assembly line that requires at least one worker or one machine. If each workstation on the assembly line takes the same amount of time to perform the work elements that have been assigned, then products will move successively from workstation to workstation with no need for a product to wait or a worker to be idle. The process of equalizing the amount of work at each workstation is called **line balancing**.

**Line balancing:** tries to equalize the amount of work at each workstation.

### LINE BALANCING

Assembly-line balancing operates under two constraints: precedence requirements and cycle time restrictions.

**Precedence requirements:** physical restrictions on the order in which operations are performed.

**Precedence requirements** are physical restrictions on the *order* in which operations are performed on the assembly line. For example, we would not ask a worker to package a product before all the components were attached, even if he or she had the time to do so before passing the product to the next worker on the line. To facilitate line balancing, precedence requirements are often expressed in the form of a precedence diagram. The

[2]The material in this section is adapted from Patrick Dunne, Robert Lusch, and David Griffith, *Retailing*, 4th ed. (Southwestern College Publishing, 2001).

*precedence diagram* is a network, with work elements represented by circles or nodes and precedence relationships represented by directed line segments connecting the nodes. We will construct a precedence diagram later in Example 7.2.

**Cycle time:** the maximum amount of time a product is allowed to spend at each workstation.

**Cycle time**, the other restriction on line balancing, refers to the maximum amount of time the product is allowed to spend at each workstation if the targeted production rate is to be reached. *Desired cycle time* is calculated by dividing the time available for production by the number of units scheduled to be produced:

$$C_d = \frac{\text{production time available}}{\text{desired units of output}}$$

Suppose a company wanted to produce 120 units in an 8-hour day. The cycle time necessary to achieve the production quota is

$$C_d = \frac{(8 \text{ hours} \times 60 \text{ minutes/hour})}{(120 \text{ units})}$$
$$= \frac{480}{120} = 4 \text{ minutes}$$

Cycle time can also be viewed as the time between completed items rolling off the assembly line. Consider the three-station assembly line shown here.

1 → 2 → 3 →

4 minutes 4 minutes 4 minutes

Flow time = 4 + 4 + 4 = 12 minutes

Cycle time = max {4, 4, 4} = 4 minutes

Cycle time is different from flow time.

It takes 12 minutes (i.e., 4 + 4 + 4) for each item to pass completely through all three stations of the assembly line. The time required to complete an item is referred to as its *flow time*. However, the assembly line does not work on only one item at a time. When fully operational, the line will be processing three items at a time, one at each workstation, in various stages of assembly. Every 4 minutes a new item enters the line at workstation 1, an item is passed from workstation 1 to workstation 2, another item is passed from workstation 2 to workstation 3, and a completed item leaves the assembly line. Thus, a completed item rolls off the assembly line every 4 minutes. This 4-minute interval is the actual cycle time of the line.

Actual cycle time is the result from the balancing procedure.

The *actual cycle time*, $C_a$, is the maximum workstation time on the line. It differs from the desired cycle time when the production quota does not match the maximum output attainable by the system. Sometimes the production quota cannot be achieved because the time required for one work element is too large. To correct the situation, the quota can be revised downward or parallel stations can be set up for the bottleneck element.

Calculate line *efficiency* and the *theoretical minimum number of workstations.*

Line balancing is basically a trial-and-error process. We group elements into workstations recognizing time and precedence constraints. For simple problems, we can evaluate all feasible groupings of elements. For more complicated problems, we need to know when to stop trying different workstation configurations. The *efficiency* of the line can provide one type of guideline; the *theoretical minimum number of workstations* provides another. The formulas for efficiency, $E$, and minimum number of workstations, $N$, are

$$E = \frac{\sum_{i=1}^{j} t_i}{nC_a}; \qquad N = \frac{\sum_{i=1}^{j} t_i}{C_d}$$

where

$t_i$ = completion time for element $i$

$j$ = number of work elements

$n$ = actual number of workstations

$C_a$ = actual cycle time

$C_d$ = desired cycle time

The total idle time of the line, called **balance delay**, is calculated as (1 − efficiency). Efficiency and balance delay are usually expressed as percentages. In practice, it may be difficult to attain the theoretical number of workstations or 100% efficiency.

**Balance delay:** the total idle time of the line.

The line balancing process can be summarized as follows:

Line balancing groups elements into workstations.

1. Draw and label a precedence diagram.
2. Calculate the desired cycle time required for the line.
3. Calculate the theoretical minimum number of workstations.
4. Group elements into workstations, recognizing cycle time and precedence constraints.
5. Calculate the efficiency of the line.
6. Determine if the theoretical minimum number of workstations or an acceptable efficiency level has been reached. If not, go back to step 4.

**Example 7.2**
**Line Balancing**

Real Fruit Snack Strips are made from a mixture of dried fruit, food coloring, preservatives, and glucose. The mixture is pressed out into a thin sheet, imprinted with various shapes, rolled, and packaged. The precedence and time requirements for each step in the assembly process are given below. To meet demand, Real Fruit needs to produce 6000 fruit strips every 40-hour week. Design an assembly line with the fewest number of workstations that will achieve the production quota without violating precedence constraints.

| | Work Element | Precedence | Time (min) |
|---|---|---|---|
| A | Press out sheet of fruit | — | 0.1 |
| B | Cut into strips | A | 0.2 |
| C | Outline fun shapes | A | 0.4 |
| D | Roll up and package | B, C | 0.3 |

*Solution*

First, we draw the precedence diagram as follows.

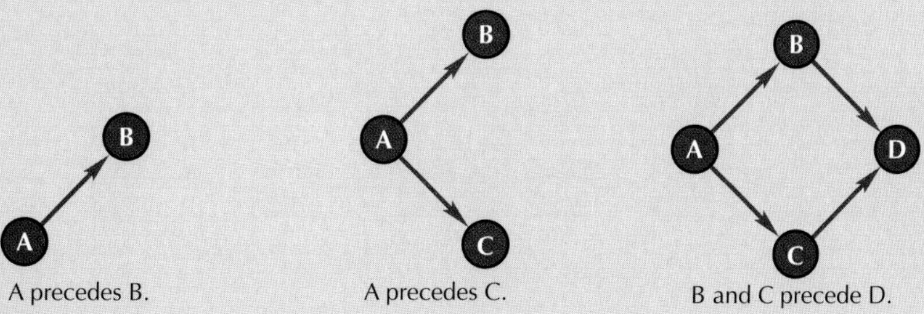


The precedence diagram is completed by adding the time requirements beside each node. Next, we calculate the desired cycle time and the theoretical minimum number of workstations:

$$C_d = \frac{40 \text{ hours} \times 60 \text{ minutes/hour}}{6000 \text{ units}} = \frac{2400}{6000} = 0.4 \text{ minutes}$$

$$N = \frac{0.1 + 0.2 + 0.3 + 0.4}{0.4} = \frac{1.0}{0.4} = 2.5 \approx 3 \text{ workstations (round up)}$$

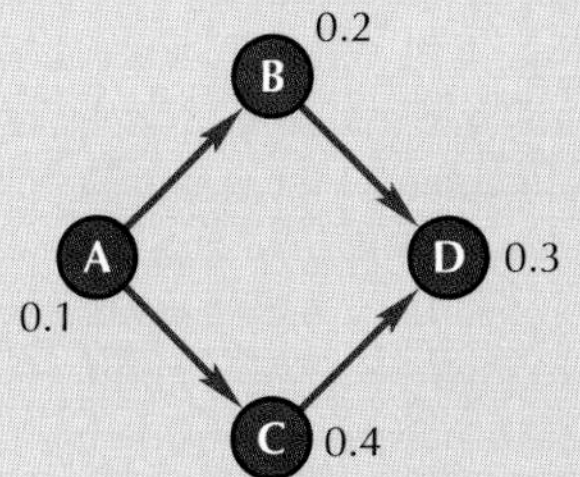

To balance the line, we must group elements into workstations so that the sum of the element times at each workstation is less than or equal to the desired cycle time of 0.4 minute. Examining the precedence diagram, we begin with A since it is the only element that does not have a precedence. We assign A to workstation 1. B and C are now available for assignment. Cycle time is exceeded with A and C in the same workstation, so we assign B to workstation 1 and place C in a second workstation. No other element can be added to workstation 2, due to cycle time constraints. That leaves D for assignment to a third workstation. Elements grouped into workstations are circled on the precedence diagram and placed into workstations shown on the assembly line diagram.

| Workstation | Element | Remaining Time | Remaining Elements |
|---|---|---|---|
| 1 | A | 0.3 | B, C |
| | B | 0.1 | C, D |
| 2 | C | 0.0 | D |
| 3 | D | 0.1 | none |

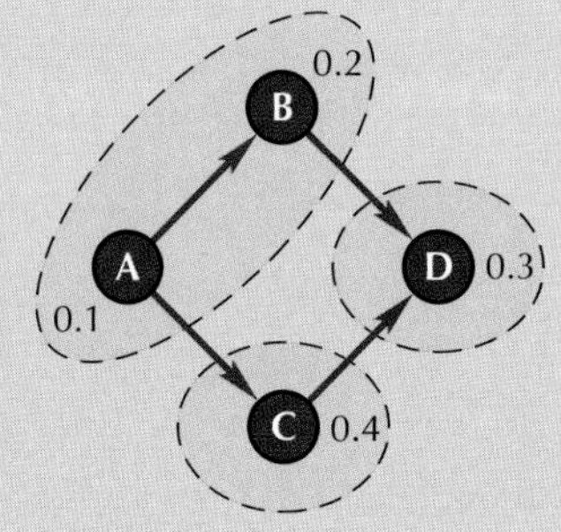


Assembly-line diagram:

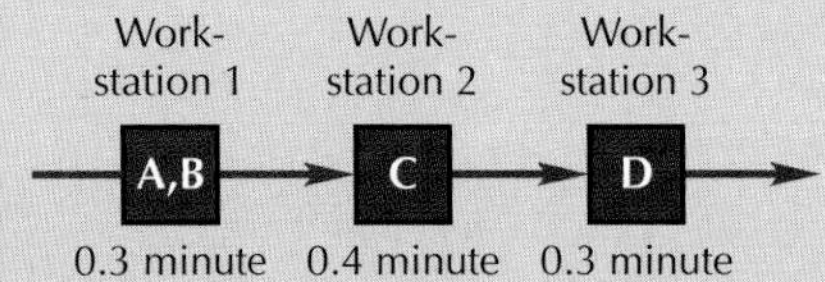


Since the theoretical minimum number of workstations was three, we know we have balanced the line as efficiently as possible. The assembly line has an efficiency of

$$E = \frac{0.1 + 0.2 + 0.3 + 0.4}{3(0.4)} = \frac{1.0}{1.2} = 0.833 = 83.3\%$$

The Excel solution to this problem is shown in Exhibit 7.2.

## COMPUTERIZED LINE BALANCING

Line-balancing heuristics specify the order in which work elements are allocated to workstations.

Line balancing by hand becomes unwieldy as the problems grow in size. Fortunately, there are software packages that will balance large lines quickly. IBM's COMSOAL (Computer Method for Sequencing Operations for Assembly Lines) and GE's ASYBL (Assembly Line Configuration Program) can assign hundreds of work elements to workstations on an assembly line. These programs, and most that are commercially available, do not guarantee optimal solutions. They use various *heuristics*, or rules, to balance the line at an acceptable level of efficiency. Five common heuristics are: longest operation time, shortest operation time, most number of following tasks, least number of following tasks, and ranked positional weight. Positional weights are calculated by summing the processing times of those tasks that follow an element. These heuristics specify the *order*

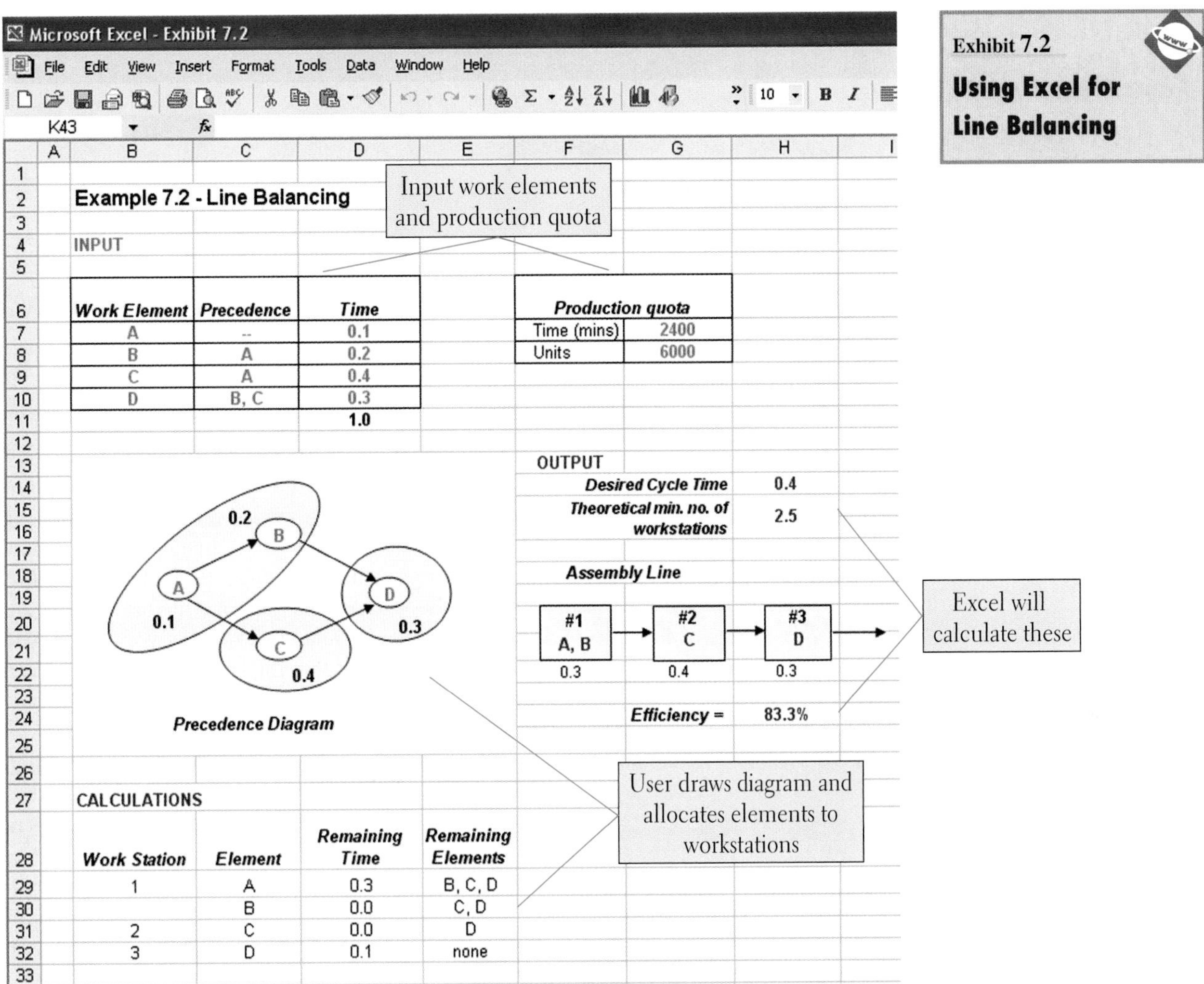


**Exhibit 7.2**

**Using Excel for Line Balancing**

in which work elements are considered for allocation to workstations. Elements are assigned to workstations in the order given until the cycle time is reached or until all tasks have been assigned.

## HYBRID LAYOUTS

Hybrid layouts modify and/or combine some aspects of product and process layouts. We discuss three hybrid layouts: cellular layouts, flexible manufacturing systems, and mixed-model assembly lines.

## CELLULAR LAYOUTS

**Cellular layouts** attempt to combine the flexibility of a process layout with the efficiency of a product layout. Based on the concept of group technology (GT), dissimilar machines or activities are grouped into work centers, called *cells,* to process families of parts or customers with similar requirements. (Figure 7.8 shows a family of parts with similar shapes, and a family of related grocery items.) The cells are arranged in relation to each other so that material movement is minimized. Large machines that cannot be split among cells are located near to the cells that use them, that is, at their *point of use.*

**Cellular layouts** group dissimilar machines into work centers (called cells) that process families of parts with similar shapes or processing requirements.

The layout of machines *within* each cell resembles a small assembly line. Thus, line-balancing procedures, with some adjustment, can be used to arrange the machines within the cell. The layout *between* cells is a process layout. Therefore, computer programs such as CRAFT can be used to locate cells and any leftover equipment in the facility.

**Figure 7.8**

**Group Technology (*a*) A family of similar parts. (*b*) A family of related grocery items.**

*Source:* Adapted from Mikell P. Groover, *Automation, Production Systems, and Computer Integrated Manufacturing* © 1987. Adapted by permission of Pearson Education, Inc., Upper Saddle River, NJ.

Consider the process layout in Figure 7.9. Machines are grouped by function into four distinct departments. Component parts manufactured in the process layout section of the factory are later assembled into a finished product on the assembly line. The parts follow different flow paths through the shop. Three representative routings, for parts A, B, and C, are shown in the figure. Notice the distance that each part must travel before completion and the irregularity of the part routings. A considerable amount of "paperwork" is needed to direct the flow of each individual part and to confirm that the right operation has been performed. Workers are skilled at operating the types of machines within a single department and typically can operate more than one machine at a time.

**Production flow analysis:** reorders part routing matrices to identify families of parts with similar processing requirements.

Figure 7.9 gives the complete part routing matrix for the eight parts processed through the facility. In its current form, there is no apparent pattern to the routings. **Production flow analysis (PFA)** is a group technology technique that reorders part routing matrices to identify families of parts with similar processing requirements. The reordering process can be as simple as using the "Data Sort" command in Excel for the most common machines, or as sophisticated as pattern-recognition algorithms from the field of artificial intelligence. Figure 7.10 shows the results of reordering. Now the part families and cell formations are clear. Cell 1, consisting of machines 1, 2, 4, 8, and 10, will process parts A, D, and F; Cell 2, consisting of machines 3, 6, and 9, will process products C and G; and Cell 3, consisting of machines 5, 7, 11, and 12, will process parts B, H, and E. A complete cellular layout showing the three cells feeding a final assembly line is also given in Figure 7.10. The representative part flows for parts A, B, and C are much more direct than those in the process layout. There is no backtracking or crisscrossing of routes, and the parts travel a shorter distance to be processed. Notice that parts G and E cannot be completely processed within cells 2 and 3, to which they have been assigned. However, the two cells are located in such a fashion that the transfer of parts between the cells does not involve much extra movement.

The U shape of cells 1 and 3 is a popular arrangement for manufacturing cells because it facilitates the rotation of workers among several machines. Workers in a cellular layout

**Figure 7.9**

**Original Process Layout with Routing Matrix**

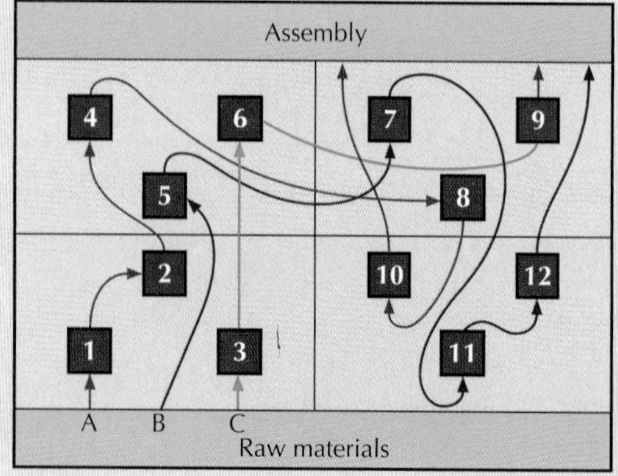


| Parts | Machines 1 | 2 | 3 | 4 | 5 | 6 | 7 | 8 | 9 | 10 | 11 | 12 |
|---|---|---|---|---|---|---|---|---|---|---|---|---|
| A | × | × | | × | | | | × | | × | | |
| B | | | | | × | | × | | | | × | × |
| C | | | × | | | × | | | × | | | |
| D | × | × | | × | | | | × | | × | | |
| E | | | | | × | × | | | | | | × |
| F | × | | | × | | | | × | | | | |
| G | | | × | | | × | | | × | | | × |
| H | | | | | | | × | | | | × | × |

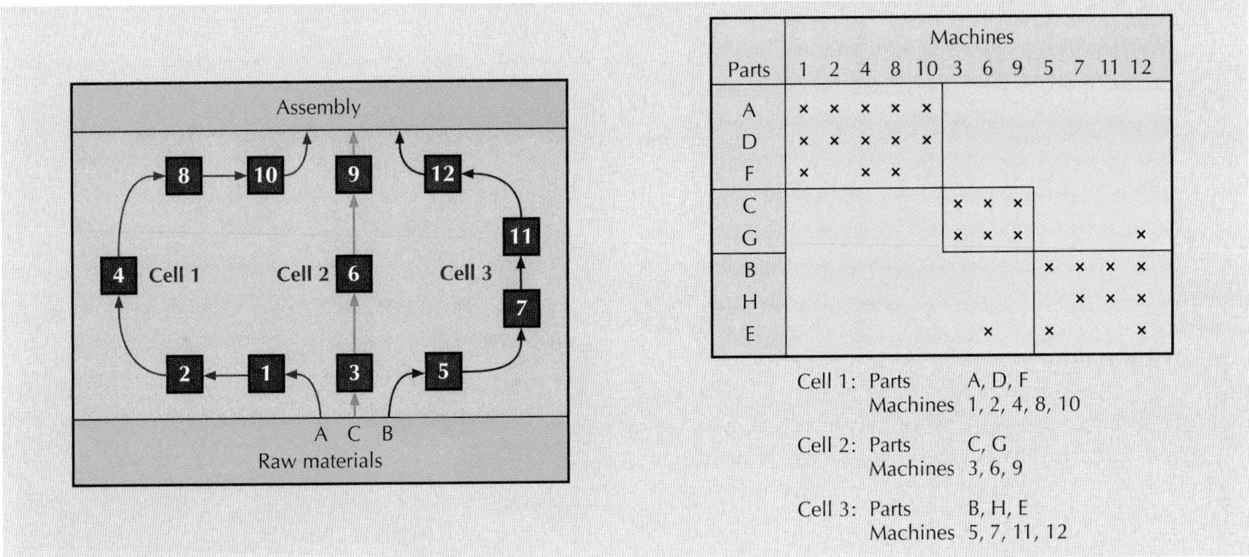


| Parts | 1 | 2 | 4 | 8 | 10 | 3 | 6 | 9 | 5 | 7 | 11 | 12 |
|---|---|---|---|---|---|---|---|---|---|---|---|---|
| | Machines | | | | | | | | | | | |
| A | × | × | × | × | × | | | | | | | |
| D | × | × | × | × | × | | | | | | | |
| F | × | | × | × | | | | | | | | |
| C | | | | | | × | × | × | | | | |
| G | | | | | | × | × | × | | | | × |
| B | | | | | | | | | × | × | × | × |
| H | | | | | | | | | | × | × | × |
| E | | | | | | | × | | × | | | × |

Cell 1: Parts A, D, F
Machines 1, 2, 4, 8, 10

Cell 2: Parts C, G
Machines 3, 6, 9

Cell 3: Parts B, H, E
Machines 5, 7, 11, 12

**Figure 7.10**

**Revised Cellular Layout with Reordered Routing Matrix**

typically operate more than one machine, as was true of the process layout. However, workers who are assigned to each cell must now be multifunctional—that is, skilled at operating many different kinds of machines, not just one type, as in the process layout. In addition, workers are assigned a *path* to follow among the machines that they operate, which may or may not coincide with the path the product follows through the cell. Figure 7.11 shows a U-shaped manufacturing cell including worker paths.

## Advantages of Cellular Layouts

Cellular layouts have become popular in the past decade as the backbone of modern factories. Cells can differ considerably in size, in automation, and in the variety of parts

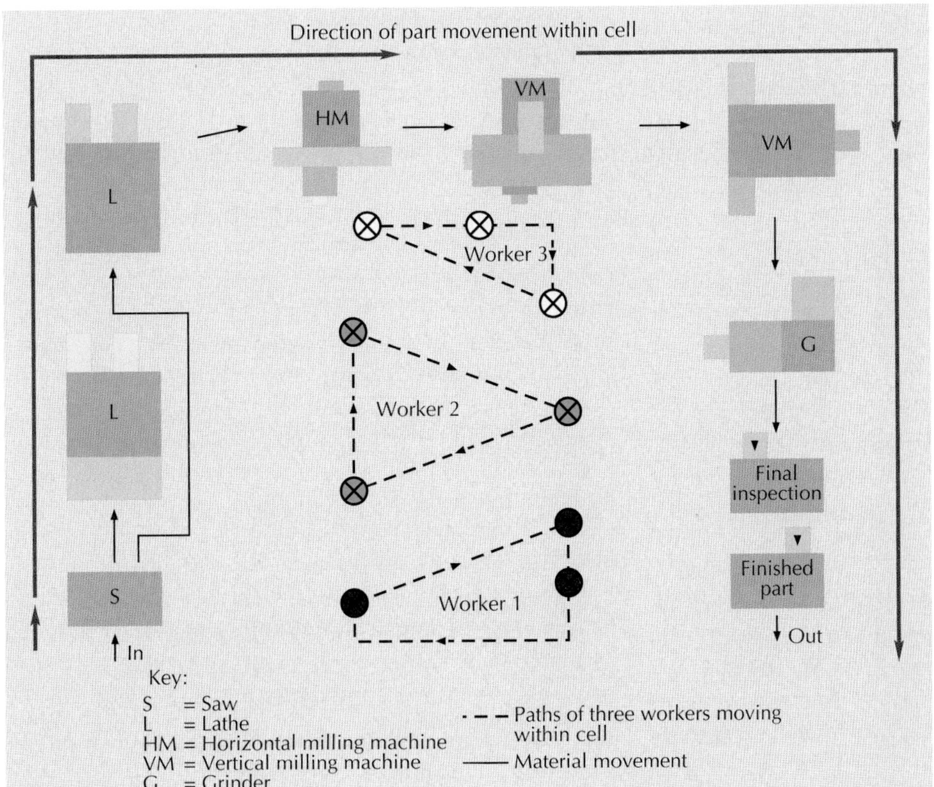


**Figure 7.11**

**A Manufacturing Cell with Worker Paths**

*Source:* J.T. Black, "Cellular Manufacturing Systems Reduce Setup Time, Make Small Lot Production Economical." *Industrial Engineering* (November 1983). Reprinted with the permission of the Institute of Industrial Engineers, 3577 Parkway Lane, Suite 200, Norcross, GA 30092, 770-449-0461 © 1983.

## THE COMPETITIVE EDGE

### Rowe's Cells Make Sofas Fly

How do you manufacture at home and stay competitive with those who outsource overseas? Bruce Birnbach, President and COO of Rowe Furniture, does it by promising the impossible—a 10-day sofa, upholstered in the fabric of your choice. Rowe Furniture provides sofas, chairs, and ottomans in over 600 fabrics to 1500 retailers across the country. If you've ever ordered furniture, you know it can take from one to six months to get that chair looking just like you wanted it. Rowe's 10-day goal is quite a stretch, one that requires completely new ways of thinking about how work is done.

Rowe' factories, like most furniture manufacturing, are based on batch production. Cutting sewing, framing, and upholstering take place in separate departments dispersed throughout the plant. There's very little interaction between the departments, and as a result each department is furiously working to produce output that may or may not be needed by the next process. Some orders are held up to be batched together with similar items, increasing the confusion and delaying completion. Huge piles of cut fabric, cushions, and frames overflow aisles and work areas as workers search for their next job. Orders get lost, materials get damaged, and foremen spend hours looking for missing items. Cushion covers that take 10 minutes to stitch take 27.5 hours to get through to the next process, stuffing.

To fight through these inefficiencies, Rowe turned to lean manufacturing principles and improving workflow. They set up one area of the plant as a U-shaped flow line, or cell, to produce a set of similar products. Cutters, sewers, framers, and upholsterers sit together, roughly in production sequence, close enough to hand pieces to one another and discuss quality issues. Most are cross-trained to help each other out if needed. Work does not pile up because it is used right away at the next process. Since every process needed to complete a product is contained in the cell, it becomes a virtual "factory within a factory." Academicians call this *cellular manufacturing* or a *focused factory*.

Rowe has several manufacturing cells now, each one a little different from before. The company sets the basic outlines of the cell, but the team members work with plant engineers to decide what goes where and how work is to be structured. Once the line is up and running, the workers are responsible for continually improving the process as well. Supervisor Fred Stanley gives a different team member a legal pad each week and asks them to write down "five things we're doing right and five things we're doing wrong." Giving feedback is a new experience for Rowe workers, and they like it.

Results from the first cell are not just encouraging, they're astounding. The cell produces 100 more pieces of furniture a day with 10% fewer workers. The 95% reduction in inventory has cleared 80,000 square feet of space in the plant and freed up thousands of dollars in working capital. Because work gets inspected and repaired immediately, the defect rate is 0.1% compared to 3% plant wide. Quality is better in other ways, too. For example, since workers who sew arm pieces can see at firsthand how upholsterers attach them to frames, they recognize the need for precision in their half-inch seams.

*Rowe's new factory layout creates small assembly lines (called cells) for groups of products. All activities from cutting fabric to stuffing cushions to framing are performed in or around the cell. Here completed sofas leave line 1.*
*Photo Credit: Courtesy Rowe Furniture*

Overall, the atmosphere is less stressful in the focused factory, absenteeism is half what it is elsewhere in the plant, and employees report a greater sense of job satisfaction. Employees sign a pledge when they join the unit, promising to stay committed to team goals and to helping colleagues achieve those goals. To keep morale and productivity up, several new incentives have been initiated. Each morning, the cell is assigned a set number of pieces a day. When the work is done, everyone goes home early, but they still get paid for a full day's work. In the future, portions of the savings accrued from worker suggestions and increased productivity will be passed on to team members.

So far Rowe is using cellular manufacturing for 10% of its total output. Within a year, it expects to have 12 cells in operation. By then, Rowe will be able to handle a 50% increase in business and the 10-day sofa will fly out the door!

*Source:* Chuck Salter, "When Couches Fly," *FastCompany*, 84 (July 2004), p. 80.

processed. As small interconnected layout units, cells are common in services, as well as manufacturing.

The advantages of cellular layouts are as follows:

Cellular layouts reduce transit time, setup time, and in-process inventory.

- ***Reduced material handling and transit time.*** Material movement is more direct. Less distance is traveled between operations. Material does not accumulate or wait long periods of time to be moved. Within a cell, the worker is more likely to carry a partially finished item from machine to machine than wait for material-handling equipment, as is characteristic of process layouts where larger loads must be moved farther distances.
- ***Reduced setup time.*** Since similar parts are processed together, the adjustments required to set up a machine should not be that different from item to item. If it does not take that long to change over from one item to another, then the changeover can occur more frequently, and items can be produced and transferred in very small batches or lot sizes.
- ***Reduced work-in-process inventory.*** In a work cell, as with assembly lines, the flow of work is balanced so that no bottleneck or significant buildup of material occurs between stations or machines. Less space is required for storage of in-process inventory between machines, and machines can be moved closer together, thereby saving transit time and increasing communication.
- ***Better use of human resources.*** Typically, a cell contains a small number of workers responsible for producing a completed part or product. The workers act as a self-managed team, in most cases more satisfied with the work that they do and more particular about the quality of their work. Labor in cellular manufacturing is a flexible resource. Workers in each cell are multifunctional and can be assigned to different routes within a cell or between cells as demand volume changes.
- ***Easier to control.*** Items in the same part family are processed in a similar manner through the work cell. There is a significant reduction in the paperwork necessary to document material travel, such as where an item should be routed next, if the right operation has been performed, and the current status of a job. With fewer jobs processed through a cell, smaller batch sizes, and less distance to travel between operations, the progress of a job can be verified *visually* rather than by mounds of paperwork.
- ***Easier to automate.*** Automation is expensive. Rarely can a company afford to automate an entire factory all at once. Cellular layouts can be automated one cell at a time. Figure 7.12 shows an automated cell with one robot in the center to load and unload material from several CNC machines and an incoming and outgoing conveyor. Automating a few workstations on an assembly line will make it difficult to balance the line and achieve the increases in productivity expected. Introducing automated equipment in a job shop has similar results, because the "islands of automation" speed up only certain processes and are not integrated into the complete processing of a part or product.

## Disadvantages of Cellular Layouts

In spite of their many advantages, cellular layouts are not appropriate for all types of businesses. The following disadvantages of cellular layouts must be considered:

- ***Inadequate part families.*** There must be enough similarity in the types of items processed to form distinct part families. Cellular manufacturing is appropriate for medium levels of product variety and volume. The formation of part families and the allocation of machines to cells is not always an easy task. Part families identified for design purposes may not be appropriate for manufacturing purposes.
- ***Poorly balanced cells.*** Balancing the flow of work through a cell is more difficult than assembly-line balancing because items may follow different sequences through the cell that require different machines or processing times. The sequence in which parts are processed can thus affect the length of time a worker spends at a certain stage of processing and thus delay his arrival to a subsequent stage in his worker path. Poorly balanced cells can be very inefficient. It is also important to balance the workload among cells in the system, so that one cell is not overloaded while others are idle. This

Cellular layouts require distinct part families, careful balancing, expanded worker training, and increased capital investment.

Figure 7.12
**An Automated Manufacturing Cell**

*Source:* J. T. Black, "Cellular Manufacturing Systems Reduce Setup Time, Make Small Lot Production Economical." *Industrial Engineering* (November 1983). Reprinted with the permission of the Institute of Industrial Engineers, 3577 Parkway Lane, Suite 200, Norcross, GA 30092, 770-449-0461, © 1983.

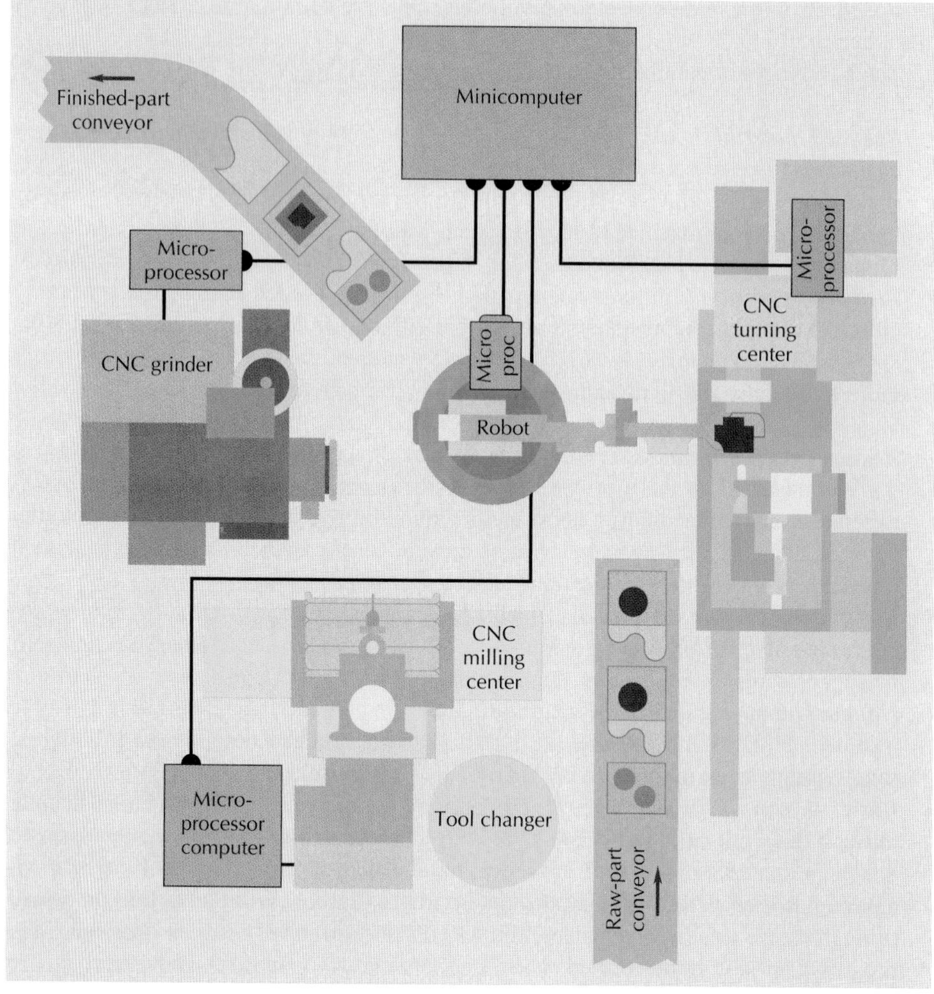


may be taken care of in the initial cellular layout, only to become a problem as changes occur in product designs or product mix. Severe imbalances may require the reformation of cells around different part families, and the cost and disruption that implies.

- ***Expanded training and scheduling of workers.*** Training workers to do different tasks is expensive and time-consuming and requires the workers' cooperation. Some tasks are too different for certain workers to master. Although flexibility in worker assignment is one of the advantages of cellular layouts, the task of determining and adjusting worker paths within or between cells can be quite complex.
- ***Increased capital investment.*** In cellular manufacturing, multiple smaller machines are preferable to single large machines. Implementing a cellular layout can be economical if new machines are being purchased for a new facility, but it can be quite expensive and disruptive in existing production facilities where new layouts are required. Existing equipment may be too large to fit into cells or may be underutilized when placed in a single cell. Additional machines of the same type may have to be purchased for different cells. The cost and downtime required to move machines can also be high.

## FLEXIBLE MANUFACTURING SYSTEMS

**Flexible manufacturing system:** can produce an enormous variety of items.

A **flexible manufacturing system (FMS)** consists of numerous programmable machine tools connected by an automated material handling system and controlled by a common computer network. It is different from traditional automation, which is fixed or "hard wired" for a specific task. *Fixed automation* is very efficient and can produce in very high volumes, but is not flexible. Only one type or model of product can be produced on most automated production lines, and a change in product design would require extensive changes in the line and its equipment.

An FMS combines flexibility with efficiency. Tools change automatically from large storage carousels at each machine, which hold hundreds of tools. The material-handling system (usually conveyors or automated guided vehicles) carries workpieces on pallets, which can be locked into a machine for processing. Pallets are transferred between the conveyor and machine automatically. Computer software keeps track of the routing and processing requirements for each pallet. Pallets communicate with the computer controller by way of bar codes or radio signals. Parts can be transferred between any two machines in any routing sequence. With a variety of programmable machine tools and large tool banks, an FMS can theoretically produce thousands of different items as efficiently as a thousand of the same item.

The efficiency of an FMS is derived from reductions in setup and queue times. Setup activities take place *before* the part reaches the machine. A machine is presented only with parts and tools ready for immediate processing. Queuing areas at each machine hold pallets ready to move in the moment the machine finishes with the previous piece. The pallet also serves as a work platform, so no time is lost transferring the workpiece from pallet to machine or positioning and fixturing the part. The machines in an advanced FMS, such as five-axis CNC *machining centers*, simultaneously perform up to five operations on a workpiece that would normally require a series of operations on individual machines.

FMS layouts differ based on the variety of parts that the system can process, the size of the parts processed, and the average processing time required for part completion. Figure 7.13 shows a simple FMS where parts rotate on a conveyor until a machine is available for processing.

## MIXED-MODEL ASSEMBLY LINES

Traditional assembly lines, designed to process a single model or type of product, can be used to process more than one type of product but not efficiently. Models of the same type are produced in long production runs, sometimes lasting for months, and then the line is shut down and changed over for the next model. The next model is also run for an extended time, producing perhaps half a year to a year's supply; then the line is shut down again and changed over for yet another model; and so on. The problem with this arrangement is the difficulty in responding to changes in customer demand. If a certain model is selling well and customers want more of it, they have to wait until the next batch of

Figure 7.13
**A Flexible Manufacturing System**

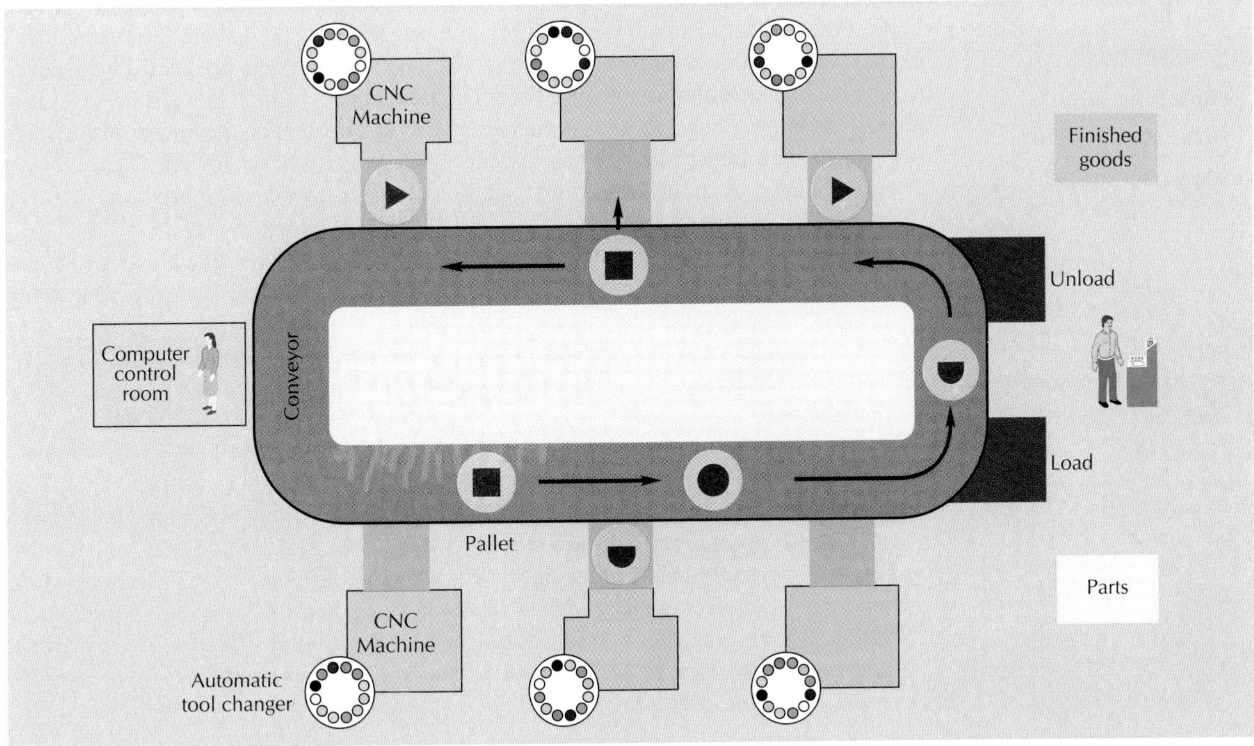

*The only manual operations in this FMS are performed at the load/unload stations in the center of the photograph. Blank stock to be machined is shown in the foreground. The items rotating on the carousel are different fixturing devices that the workers build up and tear down to hold the various blanks in place for machining. Automated guided vehicles transport items to and from machining centers and the load/unload stations. Notice the computers at each machining center and the main control room in the rear. Nearly 1200 CNC part programs and 900 verification programs for part geometry are contained in the system.*

that model is scheduled to be produced. On the other hand, if demand is disappointing for models that have already been produced, the manufacturer is stuck with unwanted inventory.

Recognizing that this mismatch of production and demand is a problem, some manufacturers concentrated on devising more sophisticated forecasting techniques. Others changed the manner in which the assembly line was laid out and operated so that it really became a **mixed-model assembly line**. First, they reduced the time needed to change over the line to produce different models. Then they trained their workers to perform a variety of tasks and allowed them to work at more than one workstation on the line, as needed. Finally, they changed the way in which the line was arranged and scheduled. The following factors are important in the design and operation of mixed-model assembly lines.

**Mixed-model assembly line:** processes more than one product model.

- ***Line balancing.*** In a mixed-model line, the time to complete a task can vary from model to model. Instead of using the completion times from one model to balance the line, a distribution of possible completion times from the array of models must be considered. In most cases, the expected value, or average, times are used in the balancing procedure. Otherwise, mixed-model lines are balanced in much the same way as single-model lines.

Single-model and mixed-model assembly lines differ in layout and operation.

- ***U-shaped lines.*** To compensate for the different work requirements of assembling different models, it is necessary to have a flexible workforce and to arrange the line so that workers can assist one another as needed. Figure 7.14 shows how the efficiency of an assembly line can be improved when a U-shaped line is used.
- ***Flexible workforce.*** Although worker paths are predetermined to fit within a set cycle time, the use of average time values in mixed-model lines will produce variations in worker performance. Hence, the flexibility of workers helping other workers makes a tremendous difference in the ability of the line to adapt to the varied length of tasks inherent in a mixed-model line.

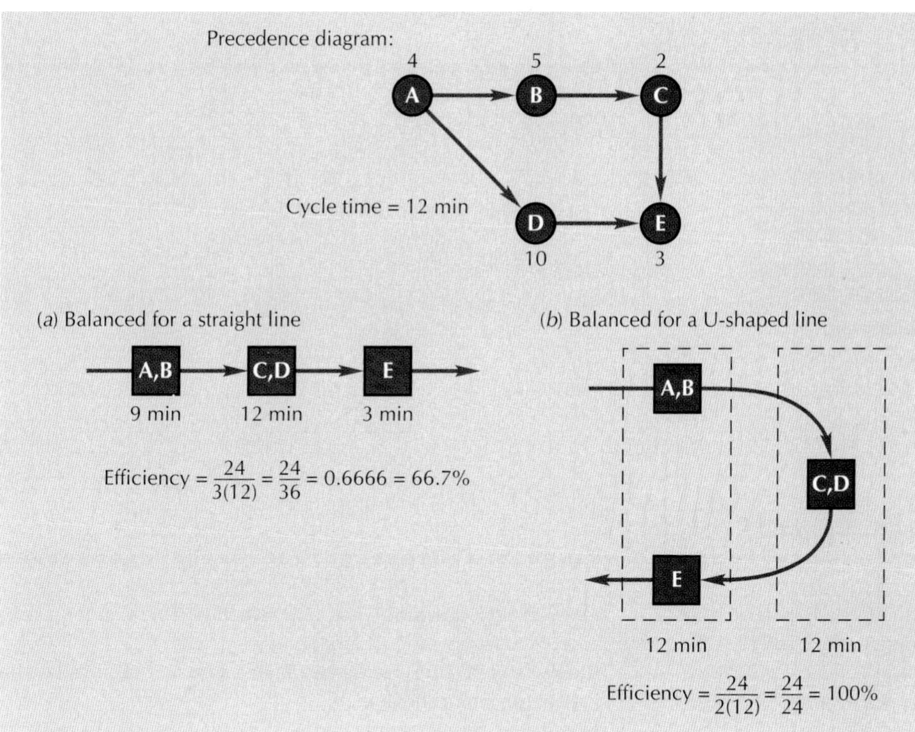


**Figure 7.14**
**Balancing U-Shaped Lines**

- ***Model sequencing.*** Since different models are produced on the same line, mixed-model scheduling involves an additional decision—the order, or sequence, of models to be run through the line. From a logical standpoint, it would be unwise to sequence two models back to back that require extra long processing times. It would make more sense to mix the assembling of models so that a short model (requiring less than the average time) followed a long one (requiring more than the average time). With this pattern, workers could "catch up" from one model to the next.

  Another objective in model sequencing is to spread out the production of different models as evenly as possible throughout the time period scheduled. This concept of *uniform production* will be discussed in Chapter 15, "Lean Production."

## SUMMARY

Facility decisions are an important part of operations strategy. An effective layout reflects a firm's competitive priorities and enables the firm to reach its strategic objectives. Batch production, which emphasizes flexibility, is most often organized into a *process layout*, whereas mass production uses a *product layout* for maximum efficiency. Because of their size and scope, projects tend to use *fixed-position layouts*. *Service layouts* may try to process customers through the system as quickly as possible or maximize customer exposure to products and services.

In the current manufacturing environment of new product introductions, rapidly changing technologies, and intense competition, the ability of a manufacturing system to adapt is essential. Thus, several hybrid layouts have emerged that combine flexibility and efficiency. Reductions in setup times have made *mixed-model assembly lines* feasible. The newest *flexible manufacturing systems (FMSs)* can process any item that fits the dimensions of the pallet on which it is transported. *Manufacturing cells* that resemble small assembly lines are designed to process families of items. Some companies are placing wheels and casters on their machines so that the cells can be adjusted as needed. Others are experimenting with modular conveyor systems that allow assembly lines to be rearranged while workers are on their lunch break.

As important as flexibility is, the cost of moving material is still a primary consideration in layout design. Today, as in the past, layout decisions are concerned with minimizing material flow. However, with reduced inventory levels, the emphasis has shifted from minimizing the *number* of loads moved to minimizing the *distance* they are moved. Instead of accumulating larger loads of material and moving them less often, machines are located closer together to allow the frequent movement of smaller loads. Planners who used to devote a considerable amount of time to designing the location of storage areas and the movement of material into and out of storage areas are now concerned with the rapid movement of material to and from the facility itself. The logistics of material transportation is discussed in Chapter 10, "Supply Chain Management." Facility location is the topic of the supplement to this chapter.

## SUMMARY OF KEY FORMULAS

*Desired Cycle Time*

$$C_d = \frac{\text{production time available}}{\text{desired units of output}}$$

*Actual Cycle Time*

$$C_a = \text{maximum workstation time}$$

*Theoretical Minimum Number of Workstations*

$$N = \frac{\sum_{i=1}^{j} t_i}{C_d}$$

*Efficiency*

$$E = \frac{\sum_{i=1}^{j} t_i}{nC_a}$$

*Balance Delay*

$$1 - \text{efficiency}$$

## SUMMARY OF KEY TERMS

**balance delay** the total idle time of an assembly line.

**block diagram** a schematic layout diagram that includes the size of each work area.

**cellular layout** a layout that creates individual cells to process parts or customers with similar requirements.

**cycle time** the maximum amount of time an item is allowed to spend at each workstation if the targeted production rate is to be achieved; also, the time between successive product completions.

**facility layout** the arrangement of machines, departments, workstations, and other areas within a facility.

**fixed-position layout** a layout in which the product remains at a stationary site for the entire manufacturing cycle.

**flexible manufacturing system (FMS)** programmable equipment connected by an automated material-handling system and controlled by a central computer.

**line balancing** a layout technique that attempts to equalize the amount of work assigned to each workstation on an assembly line.

**mixed-model assembly line** an assembly line that processes more than one product model.

**Muther's grid** a format for displaying manager preferences for department locations.

**precedence requirements** physical restrictions on the order in which operations are performed.

**process layout** a layout that groups similar activities together into work centers according to the process or function they perform.

**product layout** a layout that arranges activities in a line according to the sequence of operations that are needed to assemble a particular product.

**production flow analysis (PFA)** a group technology technique that reorders part routing matrices to identify families of parts with similar processing requirements.

**relationship diagram** a schematic diagram that denotes location preference with different line thicknesses.

**unit load** the quantity in which material is normally moved, such as a unit at a time, a pallet, or a bin of material.

## SOLVED PROBLEMS

### 1. PROCESS LAYOUT

Mohawk Valley Furniture Warehouse has purchased a retail outlet with six departments, as shown below. The anticipated number of customers that move between the departments each week is given in the load summary chart.

a. Calculate the nonadjacent loads for the layout shown below.
b. Revise Mohawk's layout such that nonadjacent loads are minimized.

| DEPARTMENT | A | B | C | D | E | F |
|---|---|---|---|---|---|---|
| A | — | 70 | | | | 50 |
| B | | — | | | 100 | |
| C | | 70 | — | | | |
| D | | | 80 | — | | |
| E | 40 | | | | — | 30 |
| F | | 60 | | | 100 | — |

#### SOLUTION

Composite movements ranked from highest to lowest are as follows:

| | | | |
|---|---|---|---|
| E↔F | 130 | B↔C | 70 |
| B↔E | 100 | B↔F | 60 |
| C↔D | 80 | A↔F | 50 |
| A↔B | 70 | A↔E | 40 |

a.

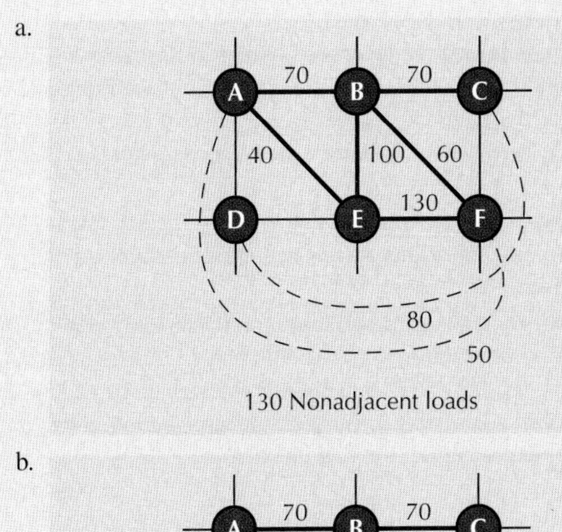

130 Nonadjacent loads

b.

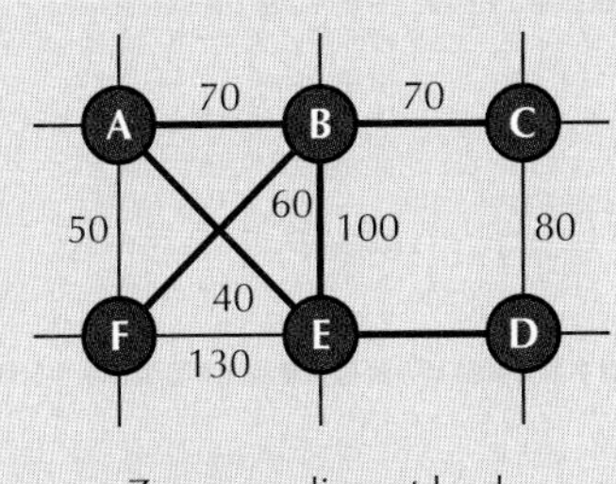

Zero nonadjacent loads

### 2. PRODUCT LAYOUT

The Basic Block Company needs to produce 4000 boxes of blocks per 40-hour week to meet upcoming holiday demand. The process of making blocks can be broken down into six work elements. The precedence and time requirements for each element are as follows. Draw and label a precedence diagram for the production process. Set up a balanced assembly line and calculate the efficiency of the line.

| WORK ELEMENT | PRECEDENCE | PERFORMANCE TIME (MIN) |
|---|---|---|
| A | — | 0.10 |
| B | A | 0.40 |
| C | A | 0.50 |
| D | — | 0.20 |
| E | C, D | 0.60 |
| F | B, E | 0.40 |

**SOLUTION**

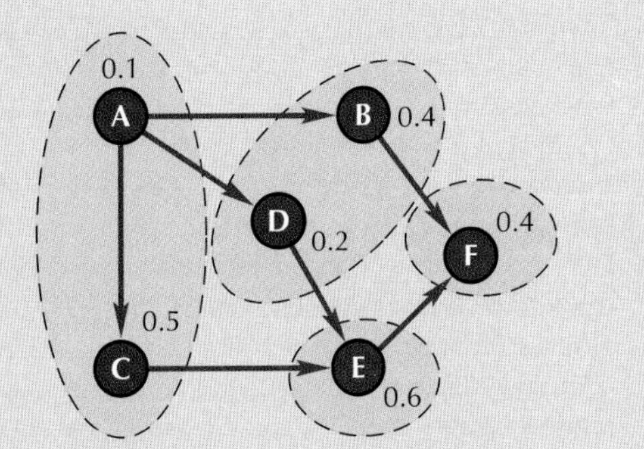


Start at the beginning of the network and group elements into workstations until cycle time has been reached. Do not violate precedence requirements.

$$C_d = \frac{\text{time}}{\text{units}} = \frac{40 \times 60}{4000} = \frac{2400}{4000} = 0.60$$

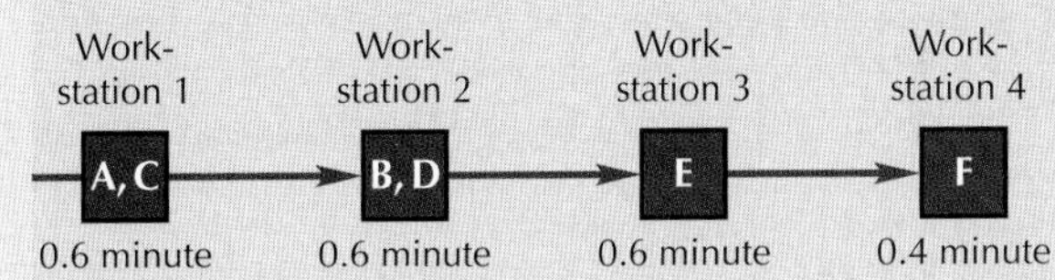


$$\text{Efficiency} = \frac{\sum t}{nC_a} = \frac{0.60 + 0.60 + 0.60 + 0.40}{4(0.60)}$$

$$= \frac{2.2}{2.4} = 91.67\%$$

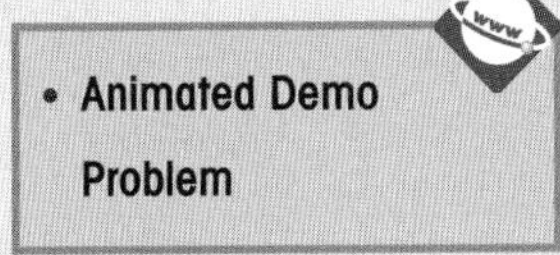


## QUESTIONS

**7-1.** Look around your classroom. Which layout characteristics help the learning process, and which ones hinder it? How does layout affect the manner in which the class is taught?

**7-2.** Visit a local McDonald's, Burger King, and Taco Bell (or similar establishments). How do their layouts differ? Which appears to be most efficient? Why?

**7-3.** Does layout make a difference? Think of a time when the layout of a facility impeded a process with which you were involved. Think of a time when a layout made it easier for a process to be completed.

**7-4.** List five goals of facility layout. Give an example of a facility you know that emphasizes each goal.

**7-5.** Distinguish between a process and product layout. Give an example of each.

**7-6.** Give an example of a fixed-position layout for producing a product and providing a service.

**7-7.** What type of layout(s) would be appropriate for:
a. A grocery store?
b. Home construction?
c. Electronics assembly?
d. A university?

**7-8.** What are the fixed and variable cost tradeoffs among product, process, and fixed-position layouts? Draw a cost/volume graph to illustrate your answer.

**7-9.** What is the difference between block diagramming and relationship diagramming? When might each be used?

**7-10.** How do service layouts differ from manufacturing layouts? Give an example of a well-designed service layout and an example of a poorly designed layout.

**7-11.** What are the objectives of line balancing? Describe several heuristic approaches to line balancing.

**7-12.** How are manufacturing cells formed? How does the role of the worker differ in cellular manufacturing?

**7-13.** Discuss the advantages and disadvantages of cellular layouts. How does a cellular layout combine a product and process layout?

**7-14.** Describe a flexible manufacturing system. How does it differ from a cellular layout?

**7-15.** How do mixed-model assembly lines differ from traditional assembly lines? What additional decisions are required?

**7-16.** Look for layout software packages on the Internet. What do systems like VisFactory do? Can you find any of the layout approaches discussed in the text?

**7-17.** Virtual tours are a great way to study facility layout. Tour links and questions to answer are contained on the text website.

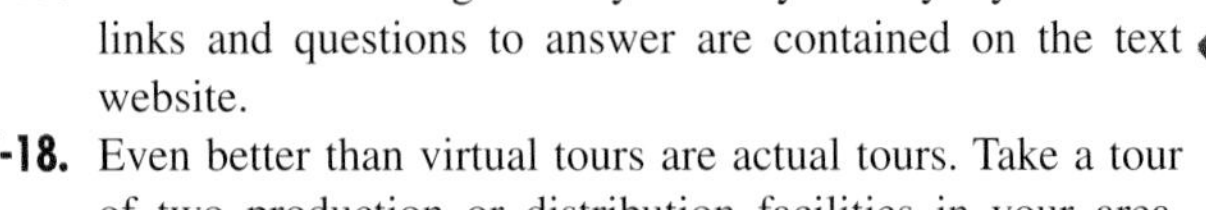

**7-18.** Even better than virtual tours are actual tours. Take a tour of two production or distribution facilities in your area. Look for the basic and hybrid layouts discussed in this chapter. Also, look for bottlenecks and smooth flow. Write a paper comparing the two layouts.

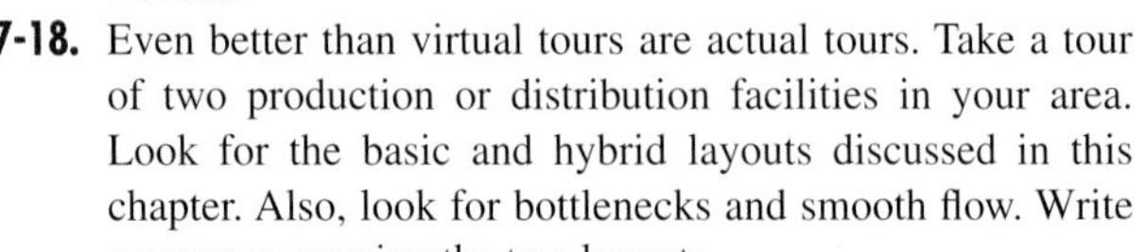

## PROBLEMS

**7-1.** Maureen Marcy is designing the layout for a new business in town, *The Collegiate Spa*. From visiting spas in neighboring towns, she has compiled the following data on movement between spa activities. Help Maureen determine where to locate each activity on a 2 × 3 grid so that nonadjacent moves are minimized.

| | 1 | 2 | 3 | 4 | 5 | 6 |
|---|---|---|---|---|---|---|
| 1 - Relaxation Lounge | | 50 | 25 | | 75 | |
| 2 - Facial | 10 | | | | | 75 |
| 3 - Massage | 30 | | | 50 | | 50 |
| 4 - Power Shower | | | | | | 25 |
| 5 - Mineral Bath | | | 50 | | | 50 |
| 6 - Sauna | | | | | | |

**7-2.** Spiffy Dry Cleaners has recently changed management, and the new owners want to revise the current layout. The store performs six main services: (1) laundry, (2) dry cleaning, (3) pressing, (4) alterations, (5) delivery, and (6) tuxedo rental. Each is located in a separate department, as shown here. The load summary chart gives the current level of interaction between the departments. Calculate the number of nonadjacent loads for the current layout. Design an alternative layout to minimize the number of nonadjacent loads.

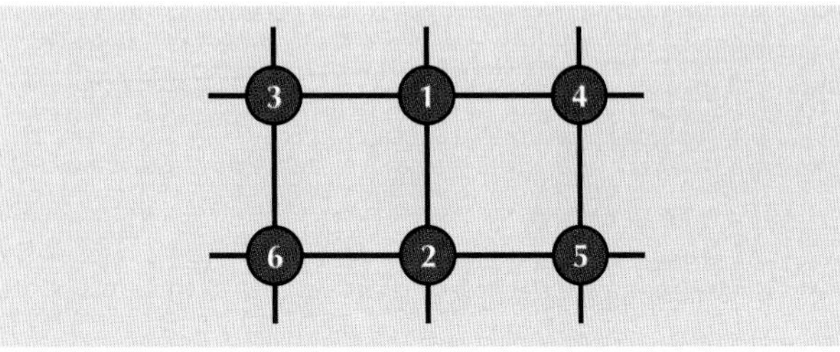


| | Load Summary Chart | | | | | |
|---|---|---|---|---|---|---|
| | 1 | 2 | 3 | 4 | 5 | 6 |
| 1 | — | | 125 | 40 | | |
| 2 | | — | 45 | 75 | | |
| 3 | | | — | 20 | 235 | 200 |
| 4 | 60 | 30 | 10 | — | 85 | 50 |
| 5 | | | | | — | 10 |
| 6 | | | 40 | 30 | 150 | — |

**7-3.** Given the following load summary chart, design a layout on a 2 × 3 grid that will minimize nonadjacent loads.

| | Load Summary Chart | | | | |
|---|---|---|---|---|---|
| From/To | 1 | 2 | 3 | 4 | 5 |
| 1 | — | | 50 | | 25 |
| 2 | | — | 20 | 100 | |
| 3 | 30 | 10 | — | | 75 |
| 4 | | | 40 | — | |
| 5 | | 60 | | | — |

**7-4.** Pratt's Department Store is opening a new store in The Center's Mall. Customer movement tracked in its existing stores is shown below. Design a layout for Pratt's new store on a 2 × 3 grid that will minimize nonadjacent customer movement.

| | Number of Customers | | | | | |
|---|---|---|---|---|---|---|
| From/To | Women's | Men's | Boys' | Girls' | Infants | Housewares |
| Women's | — | 20 | 50 | 50 | 50 | 70 |
| Men's | | — | 20 | 10 | | 20 |
| Boys' | | 20 | — | 20 | | |
| Girls' | 30 | | 50 | — | 30 | |
| Infants | 30 | | | | — | |
| Housewares | 40 | | | | | — |

**7-5.** Rent With Us Management Inc. has purchased a large housing complex and must decide where to locate its offices and service facilities. The company has learned that locating each service in a different apartment building helps control the behavior of tenants, but it would also like to keep unnecessary transit time to a minimum. Data collected on movements between facilities during a six month period from a similar apartment complex are shown below. Construct a layout diagram on a 2 × 3 grid that minimizes nonadjacent movement.

**Site to Site Travel**

| From/To | Management | Rent Collection | Sales | Grounds | Maintenance |
|---|---|---|---|---|---|
| 1. Management | — | 20 | 35 | 25 | 20 |
| 2. Rent collection | 50 | — | | | 35 |
| 3. Sales | 40 | | — | | 10 |
| 4. Grounds | 20 | | | — | 40 |
| 5. Maintenance | 20 | 10 | | 50 | — |

**7-6.** Avalanche, Inc. is a manufacturer of premium snow skis. The work is a combination of precision machining and skilled craftsmanship. Before completion, skis are processed back and forth between six different departments: (1) molding, (2) cutting, (3) fiberglass weaving, (4) gluing, (5) finishing, and (6) waxing. Avalanche is opening a new production facility and wants to lay it out as efficiently as possible. The number of loads of material moved from department to department at existing operations in other plants is shown below. Arrange the department for Avalanche's new plant in a 2 × 3 grid so that nonadjacent loads are minimized.

**Load Summary Chart**

| From \ To | 1 | 2 | 3 | 4 | 5 | 6 |
|---|---|---|---|---|---|---|
| 1 | — | 100 | 75 | | 100 | 60 |
| 2 | 10 | — | | 45 | 60 | |
| 3 | 30 | | — | | 85 | |
| 4 | 100 | 50 | | — | 70 | |
| 5 | 25 | 70 | 30 | 40 | — | 65 |
| 6 | 65 | | | | 35 | — |

**7-7.** Marillion Hospital is building a satellite clinic in the Cold Harbor area of Richmond. The design committee has collected data on patient movement from similar facilities in hopes of making the new facility more efficient and customer-friendly.

**Patient Movements**

| From \ To | 1 | 2 | 3 | 4 | 5 | 6 |
|---|---|---|---|---|---|---|
| 1 Intake | — | 50 | 10 | 25 | 10 | 100 |
| 2 Exam room | | — | 30 | 40 | 20 | 20 |
| 3 Radiology | | 40 | — | 20 | 60 | 40 |
| 4 Laboratory | | 10 | 10 | — | 10 | 40 |
| 5 Orthopedics | | 30 | 20 | 10 | — | 30 |
| 6 Waiting room | 40 | 60 | 50 | 20 | 50 | — |

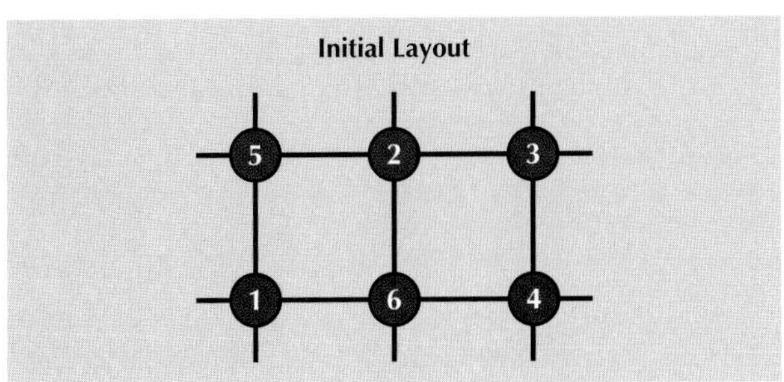


a. Calculate the nonadjacent loads for the initial layout.

b. Which pairwise exchange of departments would most improve the layout?

**7-8.** Social Services is moving into a new facility. Historical data on client visitation per month among its six departments is shown below. Design a layout for the new facility on a 2 × 3 grid that minimizes the distance clients must travel to receive services.

| From \ To | 1 | 2 | 3 | 4 | 5 | 6 |
|---|---|---|---|---|---|---|
| 1 | — | 140 | | | | 100 |
| 2 | | — | | | 200 | |
| 3 | | 100 | — | | | |
| 4 | | | 80 | — | | |
| 5 | 70 | | | | — | 60 |
| 6 | | 60 | | | 100 | — |

**7-9.** Tech Express provides technical assistance to customers through six separate departments. While much of the communication is electronic, it is helpful for departments working together on a customer's request to be physically located near to each other. Given the following data on customer "flow" between departments, design a layout on a 2 × 3 grid that will facilitate the maximum collaboration among departments. How much customer flow is nonadjacent?

**Customer Flow**

| From \ To | 1 | 2 | 3 | 4 | 5 | 6 |
|---|---|---|---|---|---|---|
| 1 | — | 50 | 100 | 25 | 60 | |
| 2 | 40 | — | 80 | | 150 | |
| 3 | 10 | 70 | — | 55 | | |
| 4 | 10 | | 80 | — | | |
| 5 | 40 | | | 80 | — | 30 |
| 6 | | 60 | 50 | | | — |

**7-10.** Flying Flags is opening a new theme park in southern Indiana. The park will have six main attractions: (a) animal kingdom, (b) Broadway shows, (c) carousel and other kiddie rides, (d) daredevil roller coasters, (e) eating places, (f) flying machines, and (g) games. Data on customer flow patterns from similar parks is shown here, along with the layout for a similar park in Virginia. Calculate the nonadjacent loads for the Virginia park; then improve the design for the new Indiana location.

| From/To | 1 | 2 | 3 | 4 | 5 | 6 |
|---|---|---|---|---|---|---|
| 1 | — | 20 | 100 | 10 | 10 | 20 |
| 2 | | — | 30 | | 50 | |
| 3 | | 20 | — | | | |
| 4 | 50 | | | — | 50 | 300 |
| 5 | 30 | 50 | 60 | 40 | — | 50 |
| 6 | 10 | | | 200 | 60 | — |

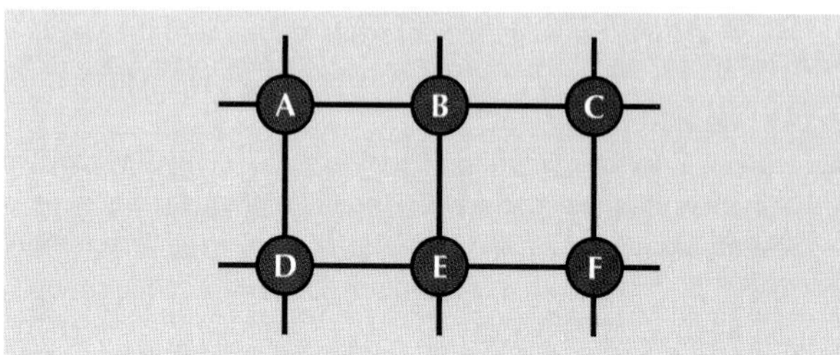


**7-11.** Design a layout on a 2 × 3 grid that satisfies the preferences listed here.

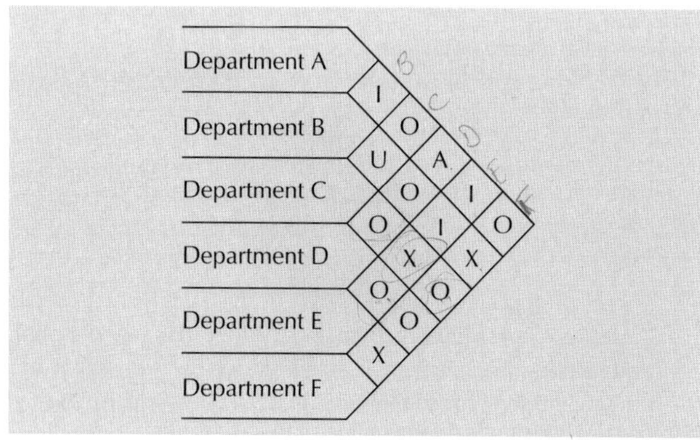


**7-12.** Design a layout on a 2 × 3 grid that satisfies these preferences.

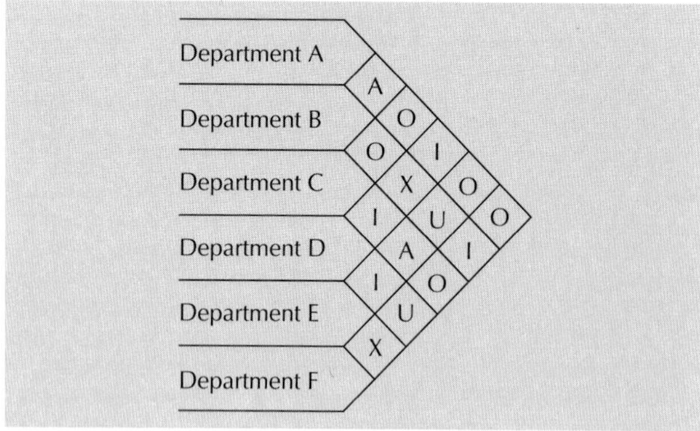


**7-13.** Amber Ale use a simple five-step process to prepare its products for shipment. Because of recent increases in demand, the company is setting up an assembly line to do the work. How should the line be constructed if Amber needs a new product off the line every 10 minutes? Draw a precedence diagram, group the tasks into workstations, determine the efficiency of the line, and calculate the expected output for an eight-hour day. (*There are multiple solutions to this problem.*)

| Task | Precedence | Time (mins) |
|---|---|---|
| A | None | 5 |
| B | A | 2 |
| C | A | 4 |
| D | A | 7 |
| E | B, C, D | 5 |

**7-14.** The Henry Street Mission uses volunteers to assemble care packages for needy families during the holiday season. The mission would like to organize the work as efficiently as possible. A list of tasks, task times, and precedence requirements follows:

| Task | Precedence | Time (mins) |
|---|---|---|
| A | — | 6 |
| B | A | 3 |
| C | B | 7 |
| D | B | 5 |
| E | C, D | 4 |
| F | E | 5 |

a. If the mission wants to complete a care package every 10 minutes, how many volunteers should be called in? Balance the line and calculate the efficiency. How many packages can be assembled in a four-hour period?

b. Suppose that volunteers are plentiful. Balance the line to maximize output. What is the efficiency of the line? How many care packages can be assembled in a four-hour period?

**7-15.** Best Vision is revamping its assembly lines to improve efficiency. As shown below, there are 10 steps to assembling a television set. (a) If Best needs to produce 120 televisions in a 40-hour work week, how should the line be balanced? Given that one worker is assigned to each workstation, how many workers are required to operate the line? What is the efficiency of the line? (b) If demand for televisions is reduced to 100 sets per 40-hour week, how many workers will be needed to man the line? Re-balance the line and recalculate its efficiency.

| Task | Precedence | Time (min) |
|---|---|---|
| A | None | 8 |
| B | A | 4 |
| C | A | 7 |
| D | A | 3 |
| E | B | 7 |
| F | C, E | 11 |
| G | D | 2 |
| H | G | 8 |
| I | F, H | 5 |
| J | I | 7 |

**7-16.** Professional Image Briefcases is an exclusive producer of handcrafted, stylish cases. The company assembles each case with care and attention to detail. This laborious process requires the completion of the six primary work elements listed here.

| Work Element | | Precedence | Time (min) |
|---|---|---|---|
| A | Tan leather | — | 30 |
| B | Dye leather | A | 15 |
| C | Shape case | B | 10 |
| D | Mold hinges and fixtures | — | 5 |
| E | Install hinges and fixtures | C, D | 10 |
| F | Assemble case | E | 10 |

a. Construct a precedence diagram for the manufacturing of briefcases.
b. Compute the flow time required for assembling one briefcase and the cycle time necessary to assemble 50 cases in a 40-hour week.
c. Balance the line and compute its efficiency.
d. How would you change the line to produce 80 cases per week?

**7-17.** The TLB Yogurt Company must be able to make 600 party cakes in a 40-hour week. Use the following information to draw and label a precedence diagram, compute cycle time, compute the theoretical minimum number of workstations, balance the assembly line, and calculate its efficiency.

| Work Element | Precedence | Performance Time (min) |
|---|---|---|
| A | — | 1 |
| B | A | 2 |
| C | B | 2 |
| D | A, E | 4 |
| E | — | 3 |
| F | C, D | 4 |

**7-18.** The Speedy Pizza Palace is revamping its order-processing and pizza-making procedures. In order to deliver fresh pizza fast, six elements must be completed.

| Work Element | | Precedence | Time (min) |
|---|---|---|---|
| A | Receive order | — | 2 |
| B | Shape dough | A | 1 |
| C | Prepare toppings | A | 2 |
| D | Assemble pizza | B, C | 3 |
| E | Bake pizza | D | 3 |
| F | Deliver pizza | E | 3 |

a. Construct a precedence diagram and compute the lead time for the process.
b. If the demand for pizzas is 120 per night (5:00 P.M. to 1:00 A.M.), what is the cycle time?
c. Balance the line and calculate its efficiency.
d. How would the line change to produce 160 pizzas per night?

**7-19.** Professor Garcia has assigned 15 cases in his POM Seminar class to be completed in a 15-week semester. The students, of course, are moaning and groaning that the caseload cannot possibly be completed in the time allotted. Professor Garcia sympathetically suggests that the students work in groups and learn to organize their work efficiently. Knowing when a situation is hopeless, the students make a list of the tasks that have to be completed in preparing a case. These tasks are listed here, along with precedence requirements and estimated time in days. Assuming students will work five days a week on this assignment, how many students should be assigned to each group, and what is the most efficient allocation of tasks? Can 15 cases be completed in a semester? Explain your answer.

| Element | Description | Precedence | Time (days) |
|---|---|---|---|
| a | Read case | — | 1 |
| b | Gather data | a | 4 |
| c | Search literature | a | 3 |
| d | Load in data | b | 1 |
| e | Run computer analysis | d | 4 |
| f | Write/type case | c, e | 4 |

**7-20.** The precedence diagram and task times (in minutes) for assembling McCauley's Mystifier are shown here. Set up an assembly line to produce 125 mystifiers in a 40-hour week. Balance the line and calculate its efficiency.

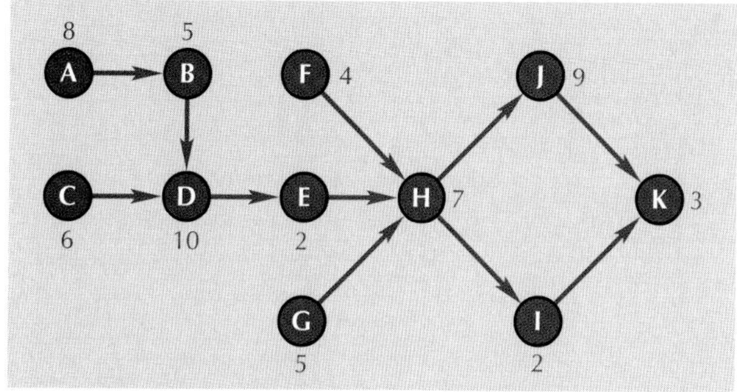


**7-21.** The precedence diagram and task times (in minutes) for assembling modular furniture are shown below. Set up an assembly line to assemble 1000 sets of modular furniture in a 40-hour week. Balance the line and calculate its efficiency.

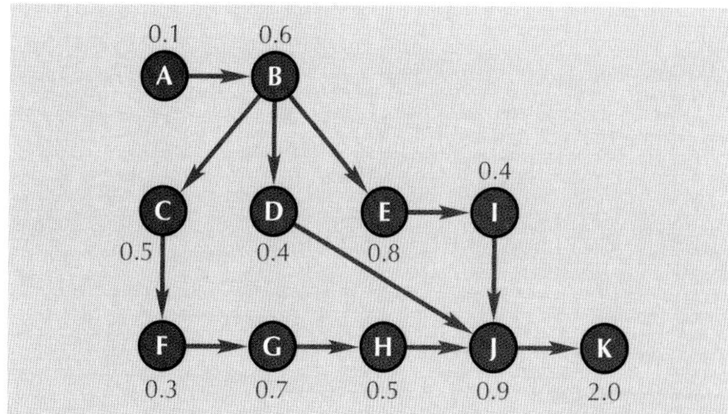


**7-22.** The Costplus Corporation has set a processing quota of 80 insurance claims per 8-hour day. The claims process consists of five elements, which are detailed in the following table. Costplus has decided to use an assembly-line arrangement to process the forms and would like to make sure they have set up the line in the most efficient fashion. Construct a precedence diagram for the claims process and calculate the cycle time required to meet the processing quota. Balance the assembly line and show your arrangement of workstations. Calculate the line's efficiency. How many claims can actually be processed on your line?

| Element | Precedence | Performance Time (min) |
|---|---|---|
| A | — | 4 |
| B | A | 5 |
| C | B | 2 |
| D | A | 1 |
| E | C, D | 3 |

**7-23.** Given in the following table are the tasks necessary for final assembly of a hospital bed, the length of time needed to perform each task, and the operations that must be completed prior to subsequent operations. Construct a precedence diagram and balance the assembly line for a desired cycle time of 14 minutes. Draw a schematic diagram of the balanced line. How many beds can actually be assembled in an 8-hour period?

| Element | Precedence | Time (min) |
|---|---|---|
| A | None | 4 |
| B | None | 5 |
| C | None | 8 |
| D | A | 4 |
| E | A, B | 3 |
| F | B | 3 |
| G | D, E | 5 |
| H | F | 7 |
| I | G, H | 1 |
| J | I | 7 |
| K | C, J | 4 |

**7-24.** Given in the following table are the tasks necessary for the assembly of Fine Cedar Chests, the length of time needed to perform each task, and the operations that must be completed prior to subsequent operations.

| Element | Precedence | Time (min) |
|---|---|---|
| A | None | 2 |
| B | A | 4 |
| C | B | 5 |
| D | None | 5 |
| E | D | 3 |
| F | None | 1 |
| G | F | 2 |
| H | C, E, G | 4 |

a. Calculate the cycle time necessary to complete 300 cedar chests in a 35-hour week.

b. What is the minimum number of workstations that can be used on the assembly line and still reach the production quota? Balance the line and calculate the line's efficiency.

c. Rebalance the line with a cycle time of 9 minutes. How do the number of workstations, output, and line efficiency change?

**7-25.** Quick Start Technologies (QST) helps companies design facility layouts. One of its clients is building five new assembly plants across the continental United States. QST will design the assembly-line layout and ship the layout instructions, along with the appropriate machinery to each new locale. Use the precedence and time requirements given below to design an assembly line that will produce a new product every 12 minutes. Construct a precedence diagram, group the tasks into workstations, determine the efficiency of the line, and calculate the expected output for an eight hour day.

| Task | Precedence | Time (mins) |
|---|---|---|
| A | None | 6 |
| B | A | 2 |
| C | B | 2 |
| D | A | 1 |
| E | A | 7 |
| F | A | 5 |
| G | C | 6 |
| H | D, E, F | 5 |
| I | H | 3 |
| J | G | 5 |
| K | I, J | 4 |

**7-26.** ALR Consulting has been hired to arrange Martin Electronics' new production facility. The firm manufactures six basic products that are routed through the 12 production processes as shown below. Although demand volume does not justify setting up assembly lines for each product, Martin hopes that a more efficient arrangement than a traditional job shop can be designed. ALR uses the term *flow shop* to refer to low-volume production systems with limited product variety and one-directional flow. The layout diagram below shows 12 possible locations (i.e., circles) for the departments. Arrange the departments so that the production process has a smooth flow and nonadjacent movements are minimized. Departments at the beginning or end of a production sequence should be located adjacent to a loading or unloading dock.

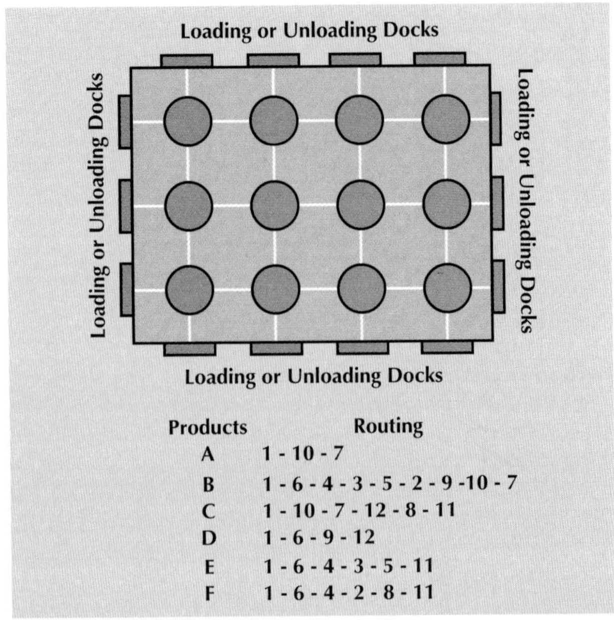


| Products | Routing |
|---|---|
| A | 1 - 10 - 7 |
| B | 1 - 6 - 4 - 3 - 5 - 2 - 9 -10 - 7 |
| C | 1 - 10 - 7 - 12 - 8 - 11 |
| D | 1 - 6 - 9 - 12 |
| E | 1 - 6 - 4 - 3 - 5 - 11 |
| F | 1 - 6 - 4 - 2 - 8 - 11 |

**7-27.** Electronics is a dynamic industry. Six months after ALR had arranged the layout for Martin's production facility (see Problem 7-21), four new products with different routings replaced the previous six. Using the facility diagram from Problem 7-21, arrange the 12 machines to process the following four jobs so that nonadjacent movement is minimized. Diagonal moves are permitted, but no backtracking is allowed.

| Products | Routing |
|---|---|
| W | 1–2–3–4–5–6–7 |
| X | 1–2–3–6–7–8–9 |
| Y | 1–2–6–10–11–12 |
| Z | 1–6–8–9–10–11–12 |

**7-28.** Print-for-All is a family-owned print shop that has grown from a three-press two-color operation to a full-service facility capable of performing a range of jobs from simple copying to four-color printing, scanning, binding, and more. The company is moving into a new facility and would like some help arranging its 16 processes into an efficient, yet flexible, layout. A list of the most popular jobs is shown with processing information. How would you arrange the processes to ensure an efficient *and* flexible operation?

| | Processes | | | | | | | | | | | | | | | |
|---|---|---|---|---|---|---|---|---|---|---|---|---|---|---|---|---|
| Jobs | 1 | 2 | 3 | 4 | 5 | 6 | 7 | 8 | 9 | 10 | 11 | 12 | 13 | 14 | 15 | 16 |
| A | X | X | | | | | | | | | | X | | | | |
| B | | | | | | X | | X | | | | | | | | |
| C | X | | | | | | X | | | | | | | X | | |
| D | X | X | | | | | X | | | | | | | X | | |
| E | | | | X | | X | | | | | | | | | | |
| F | | | | | | X | | X | | | X | | | | | |
| G | X | X | | | | | | | | | | X | | | | |
| H | | | | | X | | | | | X | | | | | X | |
| I | X | X | X | | | | | | | | | | | X | | |
| J | | | | | | X | | | | | X | | | | | |
| K | | | | | | | | | | X | | | | | X | X |
| L | | | | X | | X | | | | | X | | X | | | |
| M | | X | | | | | | | X | | | X | | | | |
| N | | | | | | | | | | X | | | | | X | X |
| O | | | | | X | | | | | X | | | | | X | X |
| P | | | | X | | X | | | | | X | | | | | |
| Q | | | | | | | | X | | | | | | | | |

## CASE PROBLEM 7.1

### *Workout Plus*

Workout Plus is a health club that offers a full range of services to its clients. Recently, two other fitness clubs have opened up in town, threatening Workout's solvency. While Workout is tops among serious fitness buffs, it has not attracted a wide spectrum of members. Shannon Hiller, owner and manager, has decided it's time for a face lift. She started the process by sponsoring a week-long "ideathon" among club members. Nonmembers who frequented an adjacent grocery store were also canvassed for suggestions. Their comments are provided below, along with the current facility layout.

*Current layout:*

| Free Weights | Circuit Training |
|---|---|
| Aerobics Room | Cardio Machines |

*Member comments:*

- The cardio machines fill up too fast on rainy days. Then everything else gets backed up.
- I don't feel like strutting through the gym from one end to the other just to finish my workout.
- How about a quick 30-minute workout routine for busy folks?
- I like working out with my friends, but aerobics is not for me. What other group activities are good for cardio?
- Separate the people who want to gab from the people who want to pump.
- It's so confusing with all those machines and weights. You need a novice section that's not so intimidating.
- It's hard to work yourself in when you come from across the gym. I'd like to see the machines I'll be using to gauge my time.
- Circuit training is for wimps. The next thing you know you'll be stopping and starting the music to tell us when to change machines.
- We all seem to arrive at the popular machines at once. Can you space us out?
- I'd like for my kids to get some exercise too while I'm working out. But I don't want them wandering all over the place trying to find me.
- This place is too crowded and disorganized. It's not fun anymore.

- You have classes only at busy times. During the day the gym is empty, but you don't provide many services. I think you're missing a great opportunity to connect with the not-so-fit at off-peak times.

**1.** How can Workout update its facility to attract new customers? What additional equipment or services would you suggest? How could something as simple as revising the layout help?

**2.** It is your job to design a new layout for Workout Plus. Visit a nearby gym to get ideas. Watch the customer flow, unused space, and bottlenecks. What aspects of a process layout do you see? a product layout? cells? Draw a simple diagram of your proposed layout. (You'll want to be more detailed than the original layout.) How does your layout respond to the comments collected by Shannon?

## CASE PROBLEM 7.2

### *Photo Op—Please Line Up*

Tech is modernizing its college ID system. Beginning this term, all faculty, staff, and students will be required to carry a "smart" identification card, called a student *passport.* What makes it smart is a magnetic strip with information on club memberships, library usage, class schedules (for taking exams), restrictions (such as no alcohol), medical insurance, emergency contacts, and medical conditions. If desired, it can also be set up as a debit card to pay fines or purchase items from the bookstore, vending machines, cash machines, copy machines, and several local retailers.

University administrators are excited about the revenue potential and increased control of the passport, but they are not looking forward to the process of issuing approximately 60,000 new cards. If applicants could be processed at the rate of 60 an hour, the entire university could be issued passports in a month's time (with a little overtime).

The steps in the process and approximate times follow. Steps 1 and 2 must be completed before step 3 can begin. Steps 3 and 4 must precede step 5, and step 5 must be completed before step 6.

| *Steps in Process* | *Approximate Time* |
|---|---|
| 1. Review application for correctness | 10 seconds |
| 2. Verify information and check for outstanding debt | 60 seconds |
| 3. Process and record payment | 30 seconds |
| 4. Take photo | 20 seconds |
| 5. Attach photo and laminate | 10 seconds |
| 6. Magnetize and issue passport | 10 seconds |

**a.** Is it possible to process one applicant every minute? Explain.

**b.** How would you assign tasks to workers in order to process 60 applicants an hour?

**c.** How many workers are required? How efficient is your line?

## CASE PROBLEM 7.3

### *Jetaway Industries*

Jetaway, a small manufacturer of replacement parts for the aircraft industry, had always maintained a simple layout—all like machines were located together. That way the firm could be as flexible as possible in producing small amounts of the variety of parts its customers required. No one questioned the production arrangement until Chris Munnelly started to work for the company. Chris was actually hired to upgrade Jetaway's computer system. In the process of creating a database of part routings, Chris began to see similarities in the parts produced. A part routing matrix for nine of the most popular parts is shown on the facing page, along with a schematic of the factory layout.

Chris, who was already tired of being a programmer, decided to reorder the matrix and see what he could find. If he could identify distinct part families, he could reorganize the placement of machines into the cells he had been reading about in his business magazines. Maybe then someone would notice his management potential.

Help Chris gain status in Jetaway by creating a cellular layout for the company. Show your results in a schematic diagram. Be sure to include the reordered routing matrix.

*Part Routing Matrix*

| Parts | Machines 1 | 2 | 3 | 4 | 5 | 6 | 7 | 8 | 9 | 10 | 11 | 12 |
|---|---|---|---|---|---|---|---|---|---|---|---|---|
| A | × | | | × | × | | | | | | | |
| B | | × | × | | | × | | | | | | |
| C | | | | | | | | × | | | × | |
| D | × | | | × | × | | × | | | | | |
| E | | × | × | | | × | | | × | | | × |
| F | | | | | | | | × | | × | × | |
| G | × | | | | × | | × | | | | | |
| H | | × | × | | | × | | | × | | | |
| I | | | | | | | | × | | × | | |

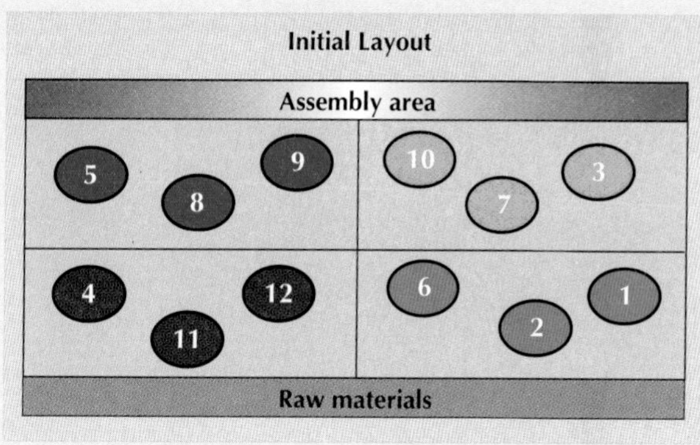


## REFERENCES

Benjaafar, Saif, Sunderesh Heragu, and Shahrukh Irani. "Next Generation Factory Layouts: Research Challenges and Recent Progress. "*Interfaces* (November/December 2002), p. 58–78.

Black, J. T. *The Design of the Factory with a Future*. New York: McGraw-Hill, 1991.

Flanders, R. E. "Design, Manufacture and Production Control of a Standard Machine." *Transactions of ASME* 46 (1925).

Goetsch, D. *Advanced Manufacturing Technology*. Albany, NY: Delmar, 1990.

Hyer, Nancy, and Urban Wemmerlov. *Reorganizing the Factory: Competing Through Cellular Manufacturing*. Portland, OR: Productivity Press, 2002.

Jablonowski, J. "Reexamining FMSs." *American Machinist*, Special Report 774 (March 1985).

Luggen, W. *Flexible Manufacturing Cells and Systems*. Upper Saddle River, NJ: Prentice Hall, 1991.

Monden, Y. *Toyota Production System*, 3rd ed. Atlanta: IIE Press, 1993.

Muther, R. *Systematic Layout Planning*. Boston: Industrial Education Institute, 1961.

Russell, R. S., P. Y. Huang, and Y. Y. Leu. "A Study of Labor Allocation in Cellular Manufacturing." *Decision Sciences* 22 (3; 1991), pp. 594–611.

Sumichrast, R. T., R. S. Russell, and B. W. Taylor. "A Comparative Analysis of Sequencing Procedures for Mixed-Model Assembly Lines in a Just-In-Time Production System." *International Journal of Production Research* 30 (1; 1992), pp. 199–214.

*Towards a New Era in Manufacturing Studies Board*. Washington, DC: National Academy Press, 1986.

# Operational Decision-Making Tools: Facility Location Models

SUPPLEMENT 7

## CHAPTER OUTLINE

In this supplement, you will learn about . . .

- Types of Facilities
- Site Selection: Where to Locate
- Location Analysis Techniques

The physical location of business facilities can have a significant impact on the success of a company. In this supplement we will briefly discuss some of the factors that are important in locating facilities. We will focus on several quantitative methods for facility location, including location factor ratings, the center-of-gravity technique, and the load-distance technique.

## TYPES OF FACILITIES

The type of facility is a major determinant of its location. The factors important in determining the location of a manufacturing plant are usually different from those important in locating a service facility or a warehouse. In this section we discuss the major categories of facilities and the different factors that are important in the location desired.

*Heavy-manufacturing facilities* are large, require a lot of space, and are expensive.

*Heavy manufacturing facilities* are plants that are large, require a lot of space, and are expensive to construct, such as automobile plants, steel mills, and oil refineries.

Factors in the location decision for plants include construction costs, land costs, modes of transportation for shipping heavy manufactured items and receiving bulk shipments of raw materials, proximity to raw materials, utilities, means of waste disposal, and labor availability. Sites for manufacturing plants are normally selected where construction and land costs can be kept at a minimum and raw material sources are nearby in order to reduce transportation costs. Access to railroads is frequently a factor in locating a plant. Environmental issues have increasingly become a factor in plant location decisions.

*Light-industry facilities* are smaller, cleaner plants and are usually less costly.

*Light-industry facilities* are perceived as cleaner plants that produce electronic equipment and components, computer products, or assembled products like TVs; breweries; or pharmaceutical firms.

Distribution centers for The Gap in Gallatin, Tennessee, Target in Augusta City, Virginia, and Home Depot in Savannah, Georgia, each encompass more than 1.4 million square feet of space—about 30 times bigger than the area of a football field! The UPS Worldwide Logistics warehouse in Louisville, Kentucky, includes 1.3 million square feet of floor space. Because of their role as intermediate points in the supply chain, transportation costs are often an important factor in the location decision for warehouses. The proximity to markets is also a consideration, depending on the delivery requirements, including frequency of delivery required by the customer.

*Retail and service facilities* are the smallest and least costly.

*Retail and service facilities* are usually the smallest and least costly. Examples include retail facilities such as groceries and department stores, among many others, and such service facilities as restaurants, banks, hotels, cleaners, clinics, and law offices. However, there are always exceptions, and some service facilities, such as a hospital, a company headquarters, a resort hotel, or a university academic building can be large and expensive. One of the most important factors for locating a service or retail facility is proximity to customers. It is often critical that a service facility be near the customers it serves, and a retail facility must be near the customers who buy from it. Construction costs tend to be less important, although land or leasing costs can be high. For retail operations, for which the saying "location is everything" is meaningful, site costs can be very high. Factors like zoning, utilities, transportation, environmental constraints, and labor tend to be less important for service operations, and closeness to suppliers is not usually as important as it is to manufacturing firms, which must be close to materials and parts suppliers.

## SITE SELECTION: WHERE TO LOCATE

When we see in the news that a company has selected a site for a new plant, or a new store is opening, the announcement can appear trivial. Usually it is reported that a particular site was selected from among two or three alternatives, and a few reasons are provided, such as good community, heavy customer traffic, or available land. However, such media reports do not reveal the long, detailed process for selecting a site for a business facility. It is usually the culmination of a selection process that can take several years and the evaluation of dozens or hundreds of potential sites.

Decisions regarding where to locate a business facility or plant are not made frequently, but they tend to be crucial in terms of a firm's profitability and long-term survival. A mistake in location is not easily overcome. Business success often is being "in the right place at the right time." For a service operation such as a restaurant, hotel, or retail store, being in the right place usually means in a location that is convenient and easily accessible to customers.

Location decisions for services tend to be an important part of the overall market strategy for the delivery of their products or services to customers. However, a business cannot simply survey the demographic characteristics of a geographic area and build a facility at the location with the greatest potential for customer traffic; other factors, particularly financial considerations, must be part of the location decision. Obviously, a site on Fifth Avenue in New York City would be attractive for a McDonald's restaurant, but can enough hamburgers and french fries be sold to pay the rent? In this case, the answer is yes.

Location decisions are usually made more frequently for service operations than manufacturing facilities. Facilities for service-related businesses tend to be smaller and less costly, although a hospital, or hotel can require a huge investment and be very large. Services depend on a certain degree of market saturation; the location is actually part of their product. Where to locate a manufacturing facility is also important, but for different reasons, not the least of which is the very high expense of building a plant or factory. Although the primary location criteria for a service-related business is usually access to customers, a different set of criteria is important for a manufacturing facility. These include the nature of the labor force, and labor costs, proximity to suppliers and markets, distribution and transportation costs, energy availability and cost, the community infrastructure of roads, sewers, and utilities, quality of life in a community, and government regulations and taxes.

When the site selection process is initiated, the pool of potential locations for a manufacturing or service facility is, literally, global. In today's international marketplace, countries around the world become potential sites. The site selection process is one of gradually and methodically narrowing down the pool of alternatives until the final location is determined. In the following discussion, we identify some of the factors that companies consider when determining the country, region, community, and site at which to locate a facility.

## GLOBAL LOCATION FACTORS

In recent years U.S. companies have begun to locate in foreign countries to be closer to newly emerging markets and to take advantage of lower labor costs. New trade agreements between countries have knocked down trade barriers around the world and created new markets like the European Community (EC). The fall of communism has opened up new markets in Eastern Europe and Asia.

Foreign firms have also begun to locate in the United States to be closer to their customers. For both U.S. and foreign companies, the motivation is the same—to reduce supply chain costs and better serve their customers. Relatively slow overseas transportation requires multinational companies to maintain large, costly inventories to serve their foreign customers in a timely manner. This drives up supply chain costs and makes it economical for companies to relocate closer to their markets.

While foreign markets offer great opportunities, the problems with locating in a foreign country can be substantial, making site location a very important part of supply chain design. For example, although China offers an extremely attractive potential market because of its huge population, growing economy, and cheap labor force, it has probably the most inefficient transportation and distribution system in Asia, and a morass of government regulations. Emerging markets in Russia and the former Soviet states are attractive; however they can also be risky since the free market economy is new to these states. Lack of familiarity with standard business practices and corruption can threaten success for foreign companies.

Some of the factors that multinational firms must consider when locating in a foreign country include the following:

- Government stability
- Government regulations
- Political and economic systems
- Economic stability and growth
- Exchange rates
- Culture
- Climate
- Export and import regulations, duties, and tariffs
- Raw material availability
- Number and proximity of suppliers
- Transportation and distribution systems
- Labor force cost and education
- Available technology
- Commercial travel
- Technical expertise
- Cross-border trade regulations
- Group trade agreements

## REGIONAL AND COMMUNITY LOCATION FACTORS IN THE UNITED STATES

Manufacturing facilities in the United States were historically located in the Midwest, especially in the Great Lakes region. Industry migrated to the sunbelt areas, the Southeast and Southwest, during the 1960s and 1970s, where labor was cheaper (and not unionized), the climate was better, and the economy was growing. However, in the late 1990s, there was a perceptible shift in new plants and plant expansion back to the nation's agricultural heartland. The North Central region, consisting of Illinois, Michigan, and Ohio, attracted more new and expanded facilities than any other region in the country. The South Atlantic region was second during this period. Ohio was the top state for new and expanded business facilities; Texas was second. Ohio was also the top state in attracting foreign firms.

The most growth in manufacturing facilities is in the Midwest.

Certain states are successful in attracting new manufacturing facilities for a variety of reasons. Ohio, for example, is well located to serve the auto industry along the Interstate-75 corridor, and it is within 1-day truck delivery of 60% of the U.S. population and two-thirds of its purchasing power. It has a good base of skilled and educated labor, a large mass of industry that spawns other businesses, and it has established good incentive programs to attract new businesses. Ohio also benefits from a number of towns and cities with populations less than 50,000 that have a rich agricultural heritage. The residents of these communities have a strong work ethic and are self-reliant and neighborly. These communities typically have quality health services; low crime rates; solid infrastructures of roads, water and sewer systems; open spaces to expand; and quality education.

Ohio attracts manufacturing facilities because of good transportation, skilled labor with a strong work ethic, incentive programs, and quality social services.

Labor is one of the most important factors in a location decision, including the cost of labor, availability, work ethic, the presence of organized labor and labor conflict, and skill and educational level. Traditionally, labor costs have been lower and organized labor has been less visible across the South and Southwest. While labor conflict is anathema to many companies, in some cases labor unions have assisted in attracting new plants or in keeping existing plants from relocating by making attractive concessions.

Labor—cost, availability, work ethic, conflict, and skill—is important in a company's location decision.

The proximity of suppliers and markets are important location factors. Manufacturing companies need to be close to materials, and service companies like fast-food restaurants, retail stores, groceries, and service stations need to be close to customers and distribution centers. Transportation costs can be significant if frequent deliveries over long distances are required. The closeness of suppliers can determine the amount of inventory a company must keep on hand and how quickly it can serve its own customers. Uncertainty in delivery schedules from suppliers can require excessive inventories.

Closeness to customers can be a factor in providing quality service.

It is important for service-related businesses to be located near their customers. Many businesses simply look for a high volume of customer traffic as the main determinant of location, regardless of the competition. An interstate highway exit onto a major thoroughfare always has a number of competing service stations and fast-food restaurants. Shopping malls are an example of a location in which a critical mass of customer traffic is sought to support a variety of similar and dissimilar businesses.

Service facilities generally require high customer-traffic volume.

Another important factor, **infrastructure**, is the collection of physical support systems of a location, including the roads, water and sewer, and utilities. If a community does not

**Infrastructure:** the roads, water and sewer, and utilities at a location.

have a good infrastructure, it must make improvements if it hopes to attract new business facilities. From a company's perspective, an inadequate infrastructure will add to its supply chain costs and inhibit its customer service.

Factors that are considered when selecting the part of the country and community for a facility are summarized as follows:

- Labor (availability, education, cost, and unions)
- Proximity of customers
- Number of customers
- Construction/leasing costs
- Land cost
- Modes and quality of transportation
- Transportation costs
- Community government
- Local business regulations
- Government services (e.g., Chamber of Commerce)
- Business climate
- Community services
- Incentive packages
- Government regulations
- Environmental regulations
- Raw material availability
- Commercial travel
- Climate
- Infrastructure (e.g., roads, water, sewers)
- Quality of life
- Taxes
- Availability of sites
- Financial services
- Community inducements
- Proximity of suppliers
- Education system

## LOCATION INCENTIVES

Besides physical and societal characteristics, local incentives have increasingly become a major important factor in attracting companies to specific locations. Incentive packages typically include job tax credits, relaxed government regulations, job training, road and sewage infrastructure improvements, and sometimes just plain cash. These incentives plus the advantages of a superior location can significantly reduce a company's supply chain costs while helping it achieve its strategic goal for customer service.

*Location incentives* **include tax credits, relaxed government regulations, job training, infrastructure improvements, and money.**

North Carolina has an attractive incentive program administered through its Industrial Recruitment Competitive Fund. Inducements available to companies include cash incentives and a strong worker training program through the statewide community college system. Its tax credit program provides new or expanding businesses tax credits per new job created, and an industrial development fund provides direct funds for each new job created. Also available are industrial development bonds. Locally, communities will prepare sites, make infrastructure improvements, and extend rails and utilities to plant sites.

States and communities cannot afford to overlook incentives if they hope to attract new companies and jobs. However, they must make sure that the amount of their investment in incentive packages and the costs they incur for infrastructure improvements are balanced against the number of new jobs developed and the expansion of the economy the new plant will provide. Incentives are a good public investment unless they bankrupt the locality. While some small communities are successful in attracting new businesses, they are left with little remaining tax base to pay for the infrastructure improvements needed to support the increased population drawn by job demand. Thus, states and communities, much like businesses, need a strategy for economic development that weighs the costs versus the benefits of attracting companies.

## LOCATION ANALYSIS TECHNIQUES

We will discuss three techniques to help make a location decision—the location rating factor, the center-of-gravity technique, and the load-distance technique. The location factor rating mathematically evaluates location factors, such as those identified in the previous section. The center-of-gravity and load-distance techniques are quantitative models that centrally locate a proposed facility among existing facilities.

## LOCATION FACTOR RATING

The decision where to locate is based on many different types of information and inputs. There is no single model or technique that will select the "best" site from a group. However, techniques are available that help to organize site information and that can be used as a starting point for comparing different locations.

**Location factor rating:** a method for identifying and weighting important location factors.

In the **location factor rating** system, factors that are important in the location decision are identified. Each factor is weighted from 0 to 1.00 to prioritize the factor and reflect its importance. A subjective score is assigned (usually between 0 and 100) to each factor based on its attractiveness compared with other locations, and the weighted scores are summed. Decisions typically will not be made based solely on these ratings, but they provide a good way to organize and rank factors.

**Example S7.1**

**Location Factor Rating**

The Dynaco Manufacturing Company is going to build a new plant to manufacture ring bearings (used in automobiles and trucks). The site selection team is evaluating three sites, and they have scored the important factors for each as follows. They want to use these ratings to compare the locations.

| | | Scores (0 to 100) | | |
|---|---|---|---|---|
| **Location Factor** | **Weight** | ***Site 1*** | ***Site 2*** | ***Site 3*** |
| Labor pool and climate | 0.30 | 80 | 65 | 90 |
| Proximity to suppliers | 0.20 | 100 | 91 | 75 |
| Wage rates | 0.15 | 60 | 95 | 72 |
| Community environment | 0.15 | 75 | 80 | 80 |
| Proximity to customers | 0.10 | 65 | 90 | 95 |
| Shipping modes | 0.05 | 85 | 92 | 65 |
| Air service | 0.05 | 50 | 65 | 90 |

*Solution*

The weighted scores for each site are computed by multiplying the factor weights by the score for that factor. For example, the weighted score for "labor pool and climate" for site 1 is

$$(0.30)(80) = 24 \text{ points}$$

The weighted scores for each factor for each site and the total scores are summarized as follows:

| | Weighted Scores | | |
|---|---|---|---|
| **Location Factor** | ***Site 1*** | ***Site 2*** | ***Site 3*** |
| Labor pool and climate | 24.00 | 19.50 | 27.00 |
| Proximity to suppliers | 20.00 | 18.20 | 15.00 |
| Wage rates | 9.00 | 14.25 | 10.80 |
| Community environment | 11.25 | 12.00 | 12.00 |
| Proximity to customers | 6.50 | 9.00 | 9.50 |
| Shipping modes | 4.25 | 4.60 | 3.25 |
| Air service | 2.50 | 3.25 | 4.50 |
| Total score | 77.50 | 80.80 | 82.05 |

Site 3 has the highest factor rating compared with the other locations; however, this evaluation would have to be used with other information, particularly a cost analysis, before making a decision.

## LOCATION FACTOR RATING WITH EXCEL

Exhibit S7.1 shows the Excel spreadsheet for Example S7.1. Notice that the location score for Site 1 is shown in cell E12 and the formula for the computation of the site 1 score (embedded in E12) is shown on the formula bar at the top of the spreadsheet.

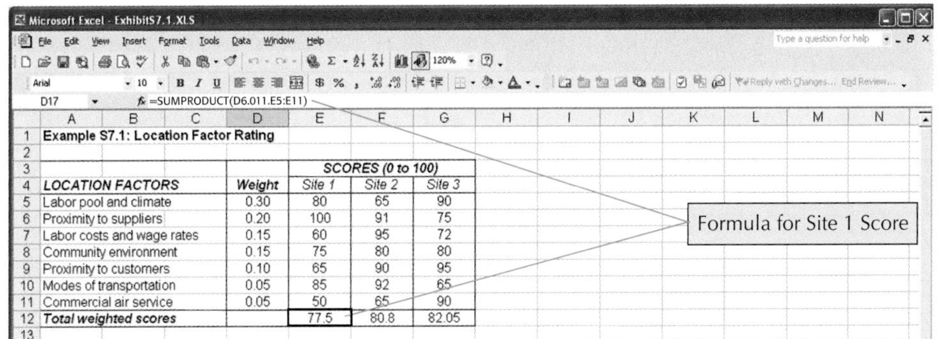


**Example S7.1: Location Factor Rating**

| LOCATION FACTORS | Weight | SCORES (0 to 100) Site 1 | Site 2 | Site 3 |
|---|---|---|---|---|
| Labor pool and climate | 0.30 | 80 | 65 | 90 |
| Proximity to suppliers | 0.20 | 100 | 91 | 75 |
| Labor costs and wage rates | 0.15 | 60 | 95 | 72 |
| Community environment | 0.15 | 75 | 80 | 80 |
| Proximity to customers | 0.10 | 65 | 90 | 95 |
| Modes of transportation | 0.05 | 85 | 92 | 65 |
| Commercial air service | 0.05 | 50 | 65 | 90 |
| *Total weighted scores* | | 77.5 | 80.8 | 82.05 |

Exhibit S7.1

## CENTER-OF-GRAVITY TECHNIQUE

In general, transportation costs are a function of distance, weight, and time. The **center-of-gravity**, or *weight center*, **technique** is a quantitative method for locating a facility such as a warehouse at the center of movement in a geographic area based on weight and distance. This method identifies a set of coordinates designating a central location on a map relative to all other locations.

**Center of gravity technique:** the center of movement in a geographic area based on transport weight and distance.

The starting point for this method is a grid map set up on a Cartesian plane, as shown in Figure S7.1. There are three locations, 1, 2, and 3, each at a set of coordinates $(x_i, y_i)$ identifying its location in the grid. The value $W_i$ is the annual weight shipped from that location. The objective is to determine a central location for a new facility.

The coordinates for the location of the new facility are computed using the following formulas:

$$x = \frac{\sum_{i=1}^{n} x_i W_i}{\sum_{i=1}^{n} W_i}, \qquad y = \frac{\sum_{i=1}^{n} y_i W_i}{\sum_{i=1}^{n} W_i}$$

where

$x, y$ = coordinates of the new facility at center of gravity

$x_i, y_i$ = coordinates of existing facility $i$

$W_i$ = annual weight shipped from facility $i$

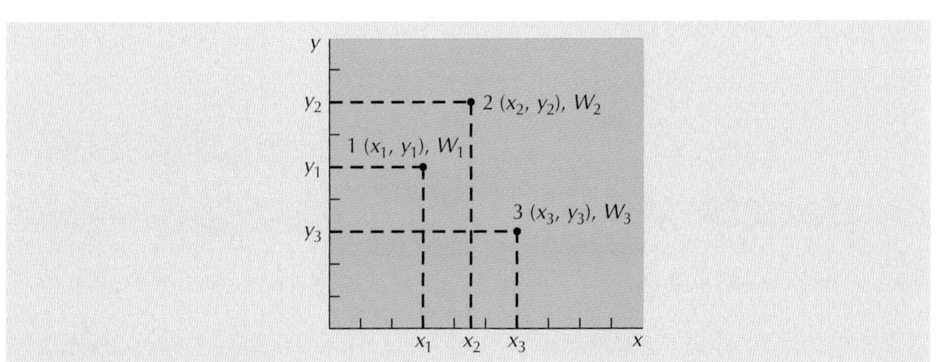


Figure S7.1 **Grid Map Coordinates**

**Example S7.2**

**The Center-of-Gravity Technique**

The Burger Doodle restaurant chain purchases ingredients from four different food suppliers. The company wants to construct a new central distribution center to process and package the ingredients before shipping them to their various restaurants. The suppliers transport ingredient items in 40-foot truck trailers, each with a capacity of 38,000 lbs. The locations of the four suppliers, A, B, C, and D, and the annual number of trailer loads that will be transported to the distribution center are shown in the following figure:

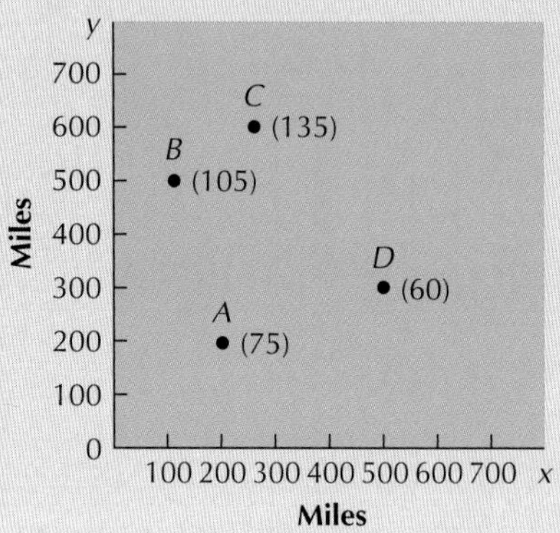


Using the center-of-gravity method, determine a possible location for the distribution center.

*Solution*

| A | B | C | D |
|---|---|---|---|
| $x_A = 200$ | $x_B = 100$ | $x_C = 250$ | $x_D = 500$ |
| $y_A = 200$ | $y_B = 500$ | $y_C = 600$ | $y_D = 300$ |
| $W_A = 75$ | $W_B = 105$ | $W_C = 135$ | $W_D = 60$ |

$$x = \frac{\sum_{i=A}^{D} x_i W_i}{\sum_{i=A}^{D} W_i}$$

$$= \frac{(200)(75) + (100)(105) + (250)(135) + (500)(60)}{75 + 105 + 135 + 60}$$

$$= 238$$

$$y = \frac{\sum_{i=A}^{D} y_i W_i}{\sum_{i=A}^{D} W_i}$$

$$= \frac{(200)(75) + (500)(105) + (600)(135) + (300)(60)}{75 + 105 + 135 + 60}$$

$$= 444$$

Thus, the suggested coordinates for the new distribution center location are $x = 238$ and $y = 444$. However, it should be kept in mind that these coordinates are based on straight-line distances, and in a real situation actual roads might follow more circuitous routes.

## CENTER-OF-GRAVITY TECHNIQUE WITH EXCEL

Exhibit S7.2 shows the Excel spreadsheet for Example S7.2. The formula for computing the *x*-coordinate in cell C13 is shown on the formula bar at the top of the spreadsheet.

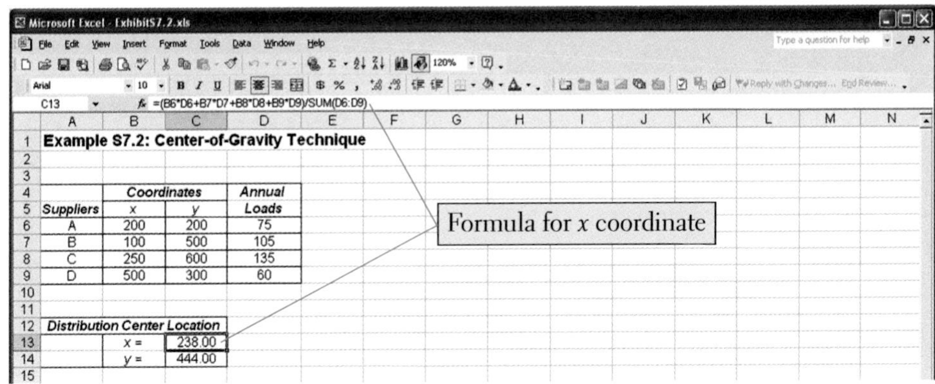


Exhibit S7.2

## LOAD-DISTANCE TECHNIQUE

A variation of the center-of-gravity method for determining the coordinates of a facility location is the **load-distance technique**. In this method, a single set of location coordinates is not identified. Instead, various locations are evaluated using a load-distance value that is a measure of weight and distance. For a single potential location, a load-distance value is computed as follows:

**Load-distance technique:** a method of evaluating different locations based on the load being transported and the distance.

$$LD = \sum_{i=1}^{n} l_i d_i$$

where

$LD$ = the load-distance value

$l_i$ = the load expressed as a weight, number of trips, or units being shipped from the proposed site to location $i$

$d_i$ = the distance between the proposed site and location $i$

The distance $d_i$ in this formula can be the travel distance, if that value is known, or can be determined from a map. It can also be computed using the following formula for the straight-line distance between two points, which is also the hypotenuse of a right triangle:

$$d_i = \sqrt{(x_i - x)^2 + (y_i - y)^2}$$

where

$(x, y)$ = coordinates of proposed site

$(x_i, y_i)$ = coordinates of existing facility

The load-distance technique is applied by computing a load-distance value for each potential facility location. The implication is that the location with the lowest value would result in the minimum transportation cost and thus would be preferable.

**Example S7.3**

**The Load-Distance Technique**

Burger Doodle wants to evaluate three different sites it has identified for its new distribution center relative to the four suppliers identified in Example S7.2. The coordinates of the three sites under consideration are as follows:

Site 1: $x_1 = 360, y_1 = 180$
Site 2: $x_2 = 420, y_2 = 450$
Site 3: $x_3 = 250, y_3 = 400$

*Solution*

First, the distances between the proposed sites (1, 2, and 3) and each existing facility (A, B, C, and D), are computed using the straight-line formula for $d_i$:

$$\text{Site 1: } d_A = \sqrt{(x_A - x_1)^2 + (y_A - y_1)^2}$$
$$= \sqrt{(200 - 360)^2 + (200 - 180)^2}$$
$$= 161.2$$
$$d_B = \sqrt{(x_B - x_1)^2 + (y_B - y_1)^2}$$
$$= \sqrt{(100 - 360)^2 + (500 - 180)^2}$$
$$= 412.3$$
$$d_C = \sqrt{(x_C - x_1)^2 + (y_C - y_1)^2}$$
$$= \sqrt{(250 - 360)^2 + (600 - 180)^2}$$
$$= 434.2$$
$$d_D = \sqrt{(x_D - x_1)^2 + (y_D - y_1)^2}$$
$$= \sqrt{(500 - 360)^2 + (300 - 180)^2}$$
$$= 184.4$$
$$\text{Site 2: } d_A = 333,\ d_B = 323.9,\ d_C = 226.7,\ d_D = 170$$
$$\text{Site 3: } d_A = 206.2,\ d_B = 180.3,\ d_C = 200,\ d_D = 269.3$$

Next, the formula for load distance is computed for each proposed site:

$$\text{LD (site 1)} = \sum_{i=A}^{D} l_i d_i$$
$$= (75)(161.2) + (105)(412.3) + (135)(434.2) + (60)(184.4)$$
$$= 125,063$$
$$\text{LD (site 2)} = (75)(333) + (105)(323.9) + (135)(226.7) + (60)(170)$$
$$= 99,789$$
$$\text{LD (site 3)} = (75)(206.2) + (105)(180.3) + (135)(200) + (60)(269.3)$$
$$= 77,555$$

Since site 3 has the lowest load-distance value, it would be assumed that this location would also minimize transportation costs. Notice that site 3 is very close to the location determined using the center-of-gravity method in Example S7.2.

## LOAD-DISTANCE TECHNIQUE WITH EXCEL

Exhibit S7.3 shows the Excel spreadsheet for Example S7.3. The formula for computing the distance from supplier location A to site 1 is embedded in C11 and is shown on the formula bar at the top of the spreadsheet. The formula for computing the location-distance formula for site 1 is shown in the call out box attached to cell C17.

**Exhibit S7.3**

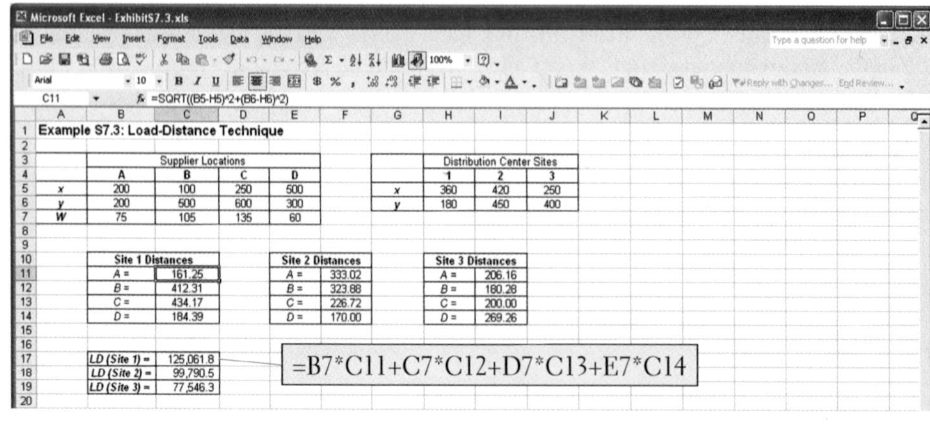

## SUMMARY

Facility location is an often overlooked but important aspect of a company's strategic plan. What kind of facility to build and where to locate it are expensive decisions. A location decision is not easily reversed if it is a bad one. For a service operation, the wrong location can result in too few customers to be profitable, whereas for a manufacturing operation, a wrong location can result in excessive costs, especially for transportation and distribution, and high inventories. The quantitative tools presented in this supplement are not usually sufficient for making an actual location decision, but they do provide means for helping in the location analysis and decision process.

## SUMMARY OF KEY FORMULAS

*Center-of-Gravity Coordinates*

$$x = \frac{\sum_{i=1}^{n} x_i W_i}{\sum_{i=1}^{n} W_i}, \qquad y = \frac{\sum_{i=1}^{n} y_i W_i}{\sum_{i=1}^{n} 1\ W_i}$$

*Load-Distance Technique*

$$\text{LD} = \sum_{i=1}^{n} l_i d_i$$

$$d_i = \sqrt{(x_i - x)^2 + (y_i - y)^2}$$

## SUMMARY OF KEY TERMS

**center-of-gravity technique** a quantitative method for locating a facility at the center of movement in a geographic area based on weight and distance.

**infrastructure** the physical support structures in a community, including roads, water and sewage systems, and utilities.

**load-distance technique** a quantitative method for evaluating various facility locations using a value that is a measure of weight and distance.

**location factor rating** a system for weighting the importance of different factors in the location decision, scoring the individual factors, and then developing an overall location score that enables a comparison of different location sites.

## SOLVED PROBLEM

### 1. CENTER-OF-GRAVITY TECHNIQUE

A company is going to construct a new warehouse served by suppliers A, B, and C. The locations of the three suppliers and the annual number of truck carriers that will serve the warehouse are shown in the following figure:

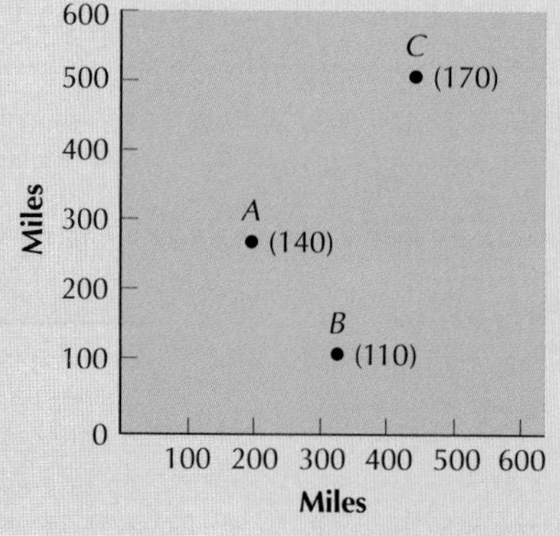

| A | B | C |
|---|---|---|
| $x_A = 150$ | $x_B = 300$ | $x_C = 400$ |
| $y_A = 250$ | $y_B = 100$ | $y_C = 500$ |
| $W_A = 140$ | $W_B = 110$ | $W_C = 170$ |

Determine the best site for the warehouse using the center of gravity technique.

**SOLUTION**

$$x = \frac{\sum_{i=A}^{C} x_i W_i}{\sum_{i=A}^{C} W_i} = \frac{(150)(140) + (300)(110) + (400)(170)}{140 + 110 + 170}$$
$$= 290.5$$

$$y = \frac{\sum_{i=A}^{C} y_i W_i}{\sum_{i=A}^{C} W_i} = \frac{(250)(140) + (100)(110) + (500)(170)}{140 + 110 + 170}$$
$$= 311.9$$

The suggested coordinates for the new warehouse are $x = 290.5$ and $y = 311.9$.

## QUESTIONS

**S7-1.** How are the location decisions for service operations and manufacturing operations similar, and how are they different?

**S7-2.** Indicate what you perceive to be general location trends for service operations and manufacturing operations.

**S7-3.** What factors make the southern region of the United States an attractive location for service and manufacturing businesses?

**S7-4.** Describe the positive and negative factors for a company contemplating locating in a foreign country.

**S7-5.** What would be the important location factors that McDonald's might consider before opening a new restaurant?

**S7-6.** The following businesses are considering locating in your community:
a. A pizza delivery service
b. A sporting goods store
c. A small brewery
d. A plant making aluminum cans
Describe the positive and negative location factors for each of these businesses.

**S7-7.** What location factors make small cities and towns in the Midwest attractive to companies?

**S7-8.** Select a major (light or heavy) manufacturing facility in your community or immediate geographic area (within a radius of 100 miles), and identify the factors that make it a good or poor site, in your opinion.

**S7-9.** Assume that you are going to open a fast-food restaurant in your community. Select three sites. Perform a location factor analysis for each and select the best site.

**S7-10.** Suppose your college or university was planning to develop a new student center and athletic complex with a bookstore, theaters, meeting areas, pool, gymnasium, and weight and exercise rooms. Identify three potential sites on your campus for this facility and rank them according to location factors you can identify.

**S7-11.** Select four fast-food restaurants (e.g., McDonald's, Burger King, Wendy's, Domino's, etc.) in your town, and develop a scoring model including decision criteria, weights, and grades to rank the restaurants from the best to worst.

## PROBLEMS

**S7-1.** Sweats and Sweaters is a small chain of stores specializing in casual cotton clothing. The company currently has five stores in Georgia, South Carolina, and North Carolina, and it wants to open a new store in one of four new mall locations in the Southeast. A consulting firm has been hired to help the company decide where to locate its new store. The company has indicated five factors that are important to its decision, including proximity of a college, community median income, mall vehicle traffic flow and parking, quality and number of stores in the mall, and proximity of other malls or shopping areas. The consulting firm had the company weight the importance of each factor. The consultants visited each potential location and rated them according to each factor, as follows:

| Location Factor | Weight | Scores (0 to 100) | | | |
|---|---|---|---|---|---|
| | | *Mall 1* | *Mall 2* | *Mall 3* | *Mall 4* |
| College proximity | 0.30 | 40 | 60 | 90 | 50 |
| Median income | 0.25 | 75 | 80 | 75 | 70 |
| Vehicle traffic | 0.25 | 60 | 90 | 79 | 74 |
| Mall quality and size | 0.10 | 90 | 100 | 80 | 90 |
| Proximity of other shopping | 0.10 | 80 | 30 | 60 | 70 |

Given that all sites have basically the same leasing costs and labor and operating costs, recommend a location based on the rating factors.

**S7-2.** Exotech Computers manufactures computer components such as chips, circuit boards, motherboards, keyboards, LCD panels, and the like and sells them around the world. It wants to construct a new warehouse/distribution center in Asia to serve emerging Asian markets. It has identified sites in Shanghai, Hong Kong, and Singapore and has rated the important location factors for each site as follows:

| Location Factors | Weight | Scores (0 to 100) | | |
|---|---|---|---|---|
| | | *Shanghai* | *Hong Kong* | *Singapore* |
| Political stability | 0.25 | 50 | 80 | 90 |
| Economic growth | 0.18 | 90 | 80 | 75 |
| Port facilities | 0.15 | 60 | 95 | 90 |
| Container support | 0.10 | 50 | 80 | 90 |
| Land and construction cost | 0.08 | 90 | 50 | 30 |
| Transportation/distribution | 0.08 | 50 | 80 | 70 |
| Duties and tariffs | 0.07 | 70 | 90 | 90 |
| Trade regulations | 0.05 | 70 | 95 | 95 |
| Airline service | 0.02 | 60 | 80 | 70 |
| Area roads | 0.02 | 60 | 70 | 80 |

Recommend a site based on these location factors and ratings.

**S7-3.** State University is going to construct a new student center and athletic complex that will include a bookstore, post office, theaters, market, mini-mall, meeting rooms, swimming pool, and weight and exercise rooms. The university administration has hired a site selection specialist to identify the best potential sites on campus for the new facility. The site specialist has identified four sites on campus and has rated the important location factors for each site as follows:

| Location Factors | Weight | Scores (0 to 100) | | | |
|---|---|---|---|---|---|
| | | *South* | *West A* | *West B* | *East* |
| Proximity to housing | 0.23 | 70 | 90 | 65 | 80 |
| Student traffic | 0.22 | 75 | 80 | 60 | 85 |
| Parking availability | 0.16 | 90 | 60 | 80 | 70 |
| Plot size, terrain | 0.12 | 80 | 70 | 90 | 65 |
| Infrastructure | 0.10 | 50 | 60 | 40 | 60 |
| Off-campus accessibility | 0.06 | 90 | 70 | 70 | 70 |
| Proximity to dining facilities | 0.05 | 60 | 80 | 70 | 80 |
| Visitor traffic | 0.04 | 70 | 80 | 65 | 55 |
| Landscape/aesthetics | 0.02 | 50 | 40 | 60 | 70 |

Recommend a site based on these location factors and ratings.

**S7-4.** Arsenal Electronics is going to construct a new $1.2 billion semiconductor plant and has selected four towns in the Midwest as potential sites. The important location factors and ratings for each town are as follows:

| Location Factors | Weight | Scores (0 to 100) | | | |
|---|---|---|---|---|---|
| | | *Abbeton* | *Bayside* | *Cane Creek* | *Dunnville* |
| Work ethic | 0.18 | 80 | 90 | 70 | 75 |
| Quality of life | 0.16 | 75 | 85 | 95 | 90 |
| Labor laws/unionization | 0.12 | 90 | 60 | 60 | 70 |
| Infrastructure | 0.10 | 60 | 50 | 60 | 70 |
| Education | 0.08 | 80 | 90 | 85 | 95 |
| Labor skill and education | 0.07 | 75 | 65 | 70 | 80 |
| Cost of living | 0.06 | 70 | 80 | 85 | 75 |
| Taxes | 0.05 | 65 | 70 | 55 | 60 |
| Incentive package | 0.05 | 90 | 95 | 70 | 80 |
| Government regulations | 0.03 | 40 | 50 | 65 | 55 |
| Environmental regulations | 0.03 | 65 | 60 | 70 | 80 |
| Transportation | 0.03 | 90 | 80 | 95 | 80 |
| Space for expansion | 0.02 | 90 | 95 | 90 | 90 |
| Urban proximity | 0.02 | 60 | 90 | 70 | 80 |

Recommend a site based on these location factors and ratings.

**S7-5.** Herriott Hotels, Inc. wants to develop a new beachfront resort along the coast of South Carolina. A number of sites are available, and the hotel chain has narrowed the choice to five locations. They have graded their choices according to the weighted criteria shown as follows:

| Location Factors | Weight | Resort Location Scores (0 to 100) | | | | |
|---|---|---|---|---|---|---|
| | | *Albermarle* | *Oceanfront* | *Calypso* | *Dafuskie* | *Edenisle* |
| Annual tourist population | 0.40 | 80 | 70 | 70 | 90 | 60 |
| Cost | 0.20 | 50 | 70 | 90 | 60 | 90 |
| Road proximity to beach | 0.15 | 70 | 60 | 70 | 50 | 80 |
| Quality of beach | 0.05 | 90 | 80 | 90 | 60 | 80 |
| Infrastructure | 0.05 | 40 | 60 | 70 | 80 | 100 |
| Shopping and restaurants | 0.05 | 70 | 90 | 90 | 80 | 90 |
| Crowdedness of beach | 0.05 | 30 | 80 | 50 | 70 | 60 |
| Other attractions | 0.05 | 100 | 70 | 90 | 80 | 90 |

Recommend a resort site based on these location factors and ratings.

**S7-6.** Robin Dillon has recently accepted a new job in the Washington, D.C., area and has been hunting for a condominium to purchase. From friends and co-workers she has compiled a list of five possible condominium complexes that she might move into. The following table indicates the weighted criteria that Robin intends to use in her decision-making process and a grade indicating how well each complex satisfies each criterion.

| | | Condominium Complexes | | | | |
|---|---|---|---|---|---|---|
| **Decision Criteria** | **Weights** | *Fairfax Forrest* | *Dupont Gardens* | *Tysons Terrace* | *Alexandria Commons* | *Manassas Farms* |
| Purchase price | 0.30 | 92 | 85 | 75 | 62 | 79 |
| Neighborhood location | 0.18 | 76 | 63 | 95 | 90 | 80 |
| Proximity to Metro train | 0.12 | 78 | 75 | 76 | 85 | 60 |
| Shopping | 0.10 | 65 | 80 | 98 | 92 | 75 |
| Security | 0.10 | 75 | 78 | 90 | 95 | 83 |
| Recreational facilities | 0.05 | 96 | 90 | 82 | 81 | 93 |
| Distance to job | 0.05 | 85 | 67 | 95 | 75 | 65 |
| Condo floor plan | 0.05 | 80 | 78 | 86 | 92 | 90 |
| Complex size | 0.05 | 65 | 60 | 92 | 89 | 70 |

Recommend a condominium for Robin based on these location factors and ratings.

**S7-6.** The Federal Parcel Service wants to build a new distribution center in Charlotte, North Carolina. The center needs to be in the vicinity of uncongested Interstate-77 and Interstate-85 interchanges, and the Charlotte-Douglas International Airport. The coordinates of these three sites and the number of weekly packages that flow to each are as follows:

| I-77 | I-85 | Airport |
|---|---|---|
| $x = 14$ | $x = 20$ | $x = 30$ |
| $y = 30$ | $y = 8$ | $y = 14$ |
| $w = 17{,}000$ | $w = 12{,}000$ | $w = 9000$ |

Determine the best site location using the center-of-gravity technique.

**S7-8.** The Burger Doodle restaurant chain uses a distribution center to prepare the food ingredients it provides its individual restaurants. The company is attempting to determine the location for a new distribution center that will service five restaurants. The grid-map coordinates of the five restaurants and the annual number of 40-foot trailer trucks transported to each restaurant are as follows:

| | Coordinates | | Annual |
|---|---|---|---|
| **Restaurant** | $x$ | $y$ | **Truck Shipments** |
| 1 | 100 | 300 | 35 |
| 2 | 210 | 180 | 24 |
| 3 | 250 | 400 | 15 |
| 4 | 300 | 150 | 19 |
| 5 | 400 | 200 | 38 |

a. Determine the least-cost location using the center-of-gravity method.

b. Plot the five restaurants and the proposed new distribution center on a grid map.

**S7-9.** The Burger Doodle restaurant chain in Problem S7-8 is considering three potential sites, with the following grid-map coordinates, for its new distribution center: A(350, 300), B(150, 250), and C(250, 300). Determine the best location using the load-distance formula, and plot this location on a grid map with the five restaurants. How does this location compare with the location determined in Problem S7-8?

**S7-10.** A development company is attempting to determine the location for a new outlet mall. The region where the outlet mall will be constructed includes four towns, which together have a sizable population base. The grid-map coordinates of the four towns and the population of each are as follows:

| | Coordinates | | |
|---|---|---|---|
| **Town** | $x$ | $y$ | **Population (10,000s)** |
| Four Corners | 30 | 60 | 8.5 |
| Whitesburg | 50 | 40 | 6.1 |
| Russellville | 10 | 70 | 7.3 |
| Whistle Stop | 40 | 30 | 5.9 |

a. Determine the best location for the outlet mall using the center-of-gravity method.

b. Plot the four towns and the location of the new mall on a grid map.

**S7-11.** State University in Problem S7-3 is attempting to locate the best site for a new student center and athletic complex. The university administration would like to know what the best location is relative to the four main concentrations of student housing and classroom activity on campus. These coordinates of these housing and classroom areas (in yards) and daily student populations are as follows:

| Campus Student Concentrations | | | |
|---|---|---|---|
| *Anderson Dorm Complex* | *Ball Housing Complex* | *Carter Classroom Complex* | *Derring Classroom Complex* |
| $x_A = 1000$ | $x_B = 1500$ | $x_C = 2000$ | $x_D = 2200$ |
| $y_A = 1250$ | $y_B = 2700$ | $y_C = 700$ | $y_D = 2000$ |
| $w_A = 7000$ | $w_B = 9000$ | $w_C = 11{,}500$ | $w_D = 4300$ |

Determine the best site using the center-of-gravity method.

**S7-12.** Mega-Mart, a discount store chain, wants to build a new superstore in an area in southwest Virginia near four small towns with populations between 8000 and 42,000. The coordinates (in miles) of these four towns and the market population in each are as follows:

| Whitesburg | Altonville | Campburg | Milligan |
|---|---|---|---|
| $x = 12$ | $x = 18$ | $x = 30$ | $x = 32$ |
| $y = 20$ | $y = 15$ | $y = 7$ | $y = 25$ |
| $w = 26{,}000$ | $w = 12{,}000$ | $w = 18{,}300$ | $w = 9700$ |

Determine the best site using the center-of-gravity technique.

**S7-13.** Home-Base, a home improvement/building supply chain, is going to build a new warehouse facility to serve its stores in six North Carolina cities—Charlotte, Winston-Salem, Greensboro, Durham, Raleigh, and Wilmington. The coordinates of these cities (in miles), using Columbia, South Carolina, as the origin (0,0) of a set of coordinates, and the annual truckloads that supply each city are shown as follows:

a. Determine the best site using the center-of-gravity technique.

b. Look at a map of North Carolina, and identify the closest town to the grid coordinates developed in Part (a). Looking at the map, can you suggest a better location in the vicinity? Explain your answer.

| Charlotte | Winston-Salem | Greensboro |
|---|---|---|
| $x = 15$ | $x = 42$ | $x = 88$ |
| $y = 85$ | $y = 145$ | $y = 145$ |
| $w = 160$ | $w = 90$ | $w = 105$ |

| Durham | Raleigh | Wilmington |
|---|---|---|
| $x = 125$ | $x = 135$ | $x = 180$ |
| $y = 140$ | $y = 125$ | $y = 18$ |
| $w = 35$ | $w = 60$ | $w = 75$ |

**S7-14.** In Problem S7-13, Home-Base has two parcels of land in Fayetteville and Statesville, North Carolina. Use the load-distance technique (and a map of North Carolina) to determine which would be better.

**S7-15.** An army division in Iraq has five troop encampments in the desert, and the division leaders want to determine the best location for a supply depot to serve the camps. The $(x, y)$ coordinates (in miles) of the camps, A, B, C, D, and E, and the daily amount of supplies (in tons) required at each camp are as follows:

| Camp | Coordinates | | Daily Tonnage (1000s) |
|---|---|---|---|
| | x | y | |
| A | 110 | 120 | 85 |
| B | 70 | 300 | 110 |
| C | 520 | 350 | 75 |
| D | 300 | 450 | 60 |
| E | 400 | 600 | 100 |

Determine the best site for the supply depot using the center-of-gravity technique.

**S7-16.** In Problem S7-15, suppose the division commanders are limited to three possible sites for the supply depot because of airfield locations and enemy troop concentrations. The coordinates (in miles) of these three potential sites are site 1 (400, 250), site 2 (100, 200), and site 3 (200, 500). Using the load-distance technique, determine the best site for the supply depot.

## CASE PROBLEM S7.1

### *Selecting a European Distribution Center Site for American International Automotive Industries*

American International Automotive Industries (AIAI) manufactures auto and truck engine, transmission, and chassis parts for manufacturers and repair companies in the United States, South America, Canada, Mexico, Asia and Europe. The company transports to its foreign markets by container ships. To serve its customers in South America and Asia, AIAI has large warehouse/distribution centers. In Europe it ships into Hamburg and Gdansk, where it has contracted with independent distribution companies to deliver its products to customers throughout Europe. However, AIAI has been displeased with a recent history of late deliveries and rough handling of its products. For a time AIAI was not overly concerned since its European market wasn't too big and its European customers didn't complain. In addition, it had more pressing supply chain problems elsewhere. In the past five years, since trade barriers have fallen in Europe and Eastern European markets have opened up, its European business has expanded, as has new competition, and its customers have become more demanding and quality conscious. As a result, AIAI has initiated the process to select a site for a new European warehouse/distribution center. Although it provides parts to a number of smaller truck and auto maintenance and service centers in Europe, it has seven major customers—auto and truck manufacturers in Vienna, Leipzig, Budapest, Prague, Krakow, Munich, and Frankfurt. Its customers in Vienna and Budapest have adopted manufacturing processes requiring continuous replenishment of parts and materials.

AIAI's European headquarters is in Hamburg. The vice-president for construction and development in Dayton, Ohio, has asked the Hamburg office to do a preliminary site search based on location, geography, transportation, proximity to customers, and costs. The Hamburg office has identified five potential sites in Dresden, Lodz, Hamburg, Gdansk, and Frankfurt. The Hamburg office has forwarded information about each of these sites to corporate headquarters, including forecasts of the number of containers shipped annually to each customer as follows: Vienna, 160; Leipzig, 100; Budapest, 180; Prague, 210; Krakow, 90; Munich, 120; and Frankfurt, 50. When the vice-president of construction in Dayton received this information, he pulled out his map of Europe and began to study the sites.

Assist AIAI with its site selection process in Europe. Recommend a site from the five possibilities, and indicate what other location factors you might consider in the selection process.

## REFERENCES


Bowersox, D. J. *Logistics Management*, 2nd ed. New York: Macmillan, 1978.

Francis, R. L., and J. A. White. *Facilities Layout and Location: An Analytical Approach*. Upper Saddle River, NJ: Prentice Hall, 1987.

Fulton, M. "New Factors in Plant Location." *Harvard Business Review* (May–June 1971), pp. 4–17, 166–168.

Johnson, J. C., and D. F. Wood. *Contemporary Logistics*, 6th ed. Upper Saddle River, NJ: Prentice Hall, 1996.

Schmenner, R. W. *Making Business Location Decisions*. Upper Saddle River, NJ: Prentice Hall, 1982.

# Human Resources

CHAPTER **8**

Web resources for this chapter include

- Internet Exercises
- Online Practice Quizzes
- Virtual Tours
- Excel Worksheets
- Company and Resource Weblinks
- Animated Demo Problems
- Microsoft Project Exhibits

www.wiley.com/college/russell

## CHAPTER OUTLINE

In this chapter, you will learn about . . .

- Human Resources and Quality Management
- The Changing Nature of Human Resources Management
- Contemporary Trends in Human Resources Management
- Employee Compensation
- Managing Diversity in the Workplace
- Job Analysis
- Learning Curves

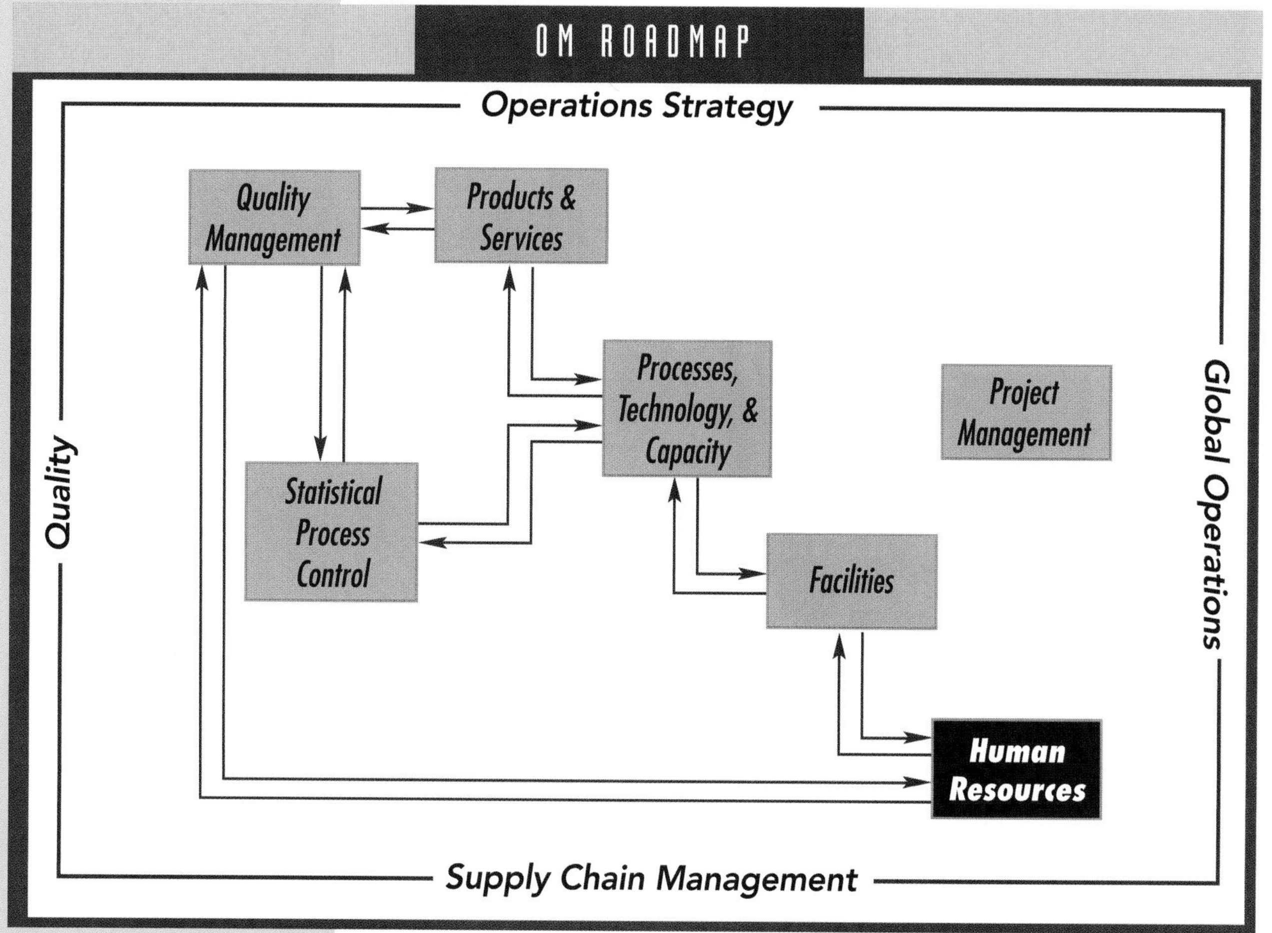

## HUMAN RESOURCES MANAGEMENT AT BALDRIGE NATIONAL QUALITY AWARD-WINNING COMPANIES

The National Institute of Standards and Technology, the administering body for the Malcolm Baldrige National Quality Award, in an effort to define quality performance developed a set of basic principles for quality management; prominent among them is *employee satisfaction.* These principles form the basis of the seven categories of criteria that are used to assess a Baldrige Award applicant's performance. Included among these categories is the "human resource focus" of a company. The European Quality Award for companies in 16 European countries has as one of its four primary award criteria, "people management." The Deming Prize for quality in Japan includes among its award criteria, "human resources." The President's Quality Award for government organizations and agencies includes "employee participation and development" as one of the core values on which its award criteria are based. The consistent inclusion of human resources among the criteria for these various awards attests to the importance placed on employees in any successful quality-management program. A company's success in improving quality and performance depends increasingly on the skills and motivation of its workforce. And employee success is more and more dependent on job training and responsibility.

A common attribute among Baldrige Quality Award winners is their commitment to their employees and the resulting high level of employee satisfaction, which these companies monitor on a regular and continuing basis with surveys. Baldrige Award winner, the Spicer Driveshaft Division of Dana Corporation, America's largest manufacturer of driveshafts, has a workforce of 3400 employees. According to surveys, their employees' perception of productivity and job satisfaction is 91%, and for opportunity and growth development 71%, both better than the company's best competitor. Employee turnover rate is below 1% and the attendance rate has been above 98% for 6 years.

At Los Alamos (New Mexico) National Bank, another Baldrige Award winner, 60% of employees receive leadership training, as compared with only 8% of bank employ-

*Over 800 applications have been submitted for the Baldrige Award since its inception in 1987, and more than 40 companies have received the award. However, thousands of companies have also used the award criteria to establish their own quality-improvement programs.*

ees nationally, and 60% receive external training, including college courses, as compared with 21% nationally.

At two-time Baldrige Award winner, Ritz-Carlton Hotel, 85% of the company's 17,000 employees are front-line hotel workers. First-year managers and employees receive from 250 to 310 hours of training. Their "Pride and Joy" program gives employees a role in job design, and turnover rates have steadily declined over a 10-year period, as employee satisfaction ratings have increased.

At another Baldrige Award winner, Sunny Fresh Foods, a manufacturer of egg-based food products with 380 employees, production employees rotate workstations every 20 minutes to prevent boredom and repetitive stress injuries and to reinforce quality processes. Their employees' rising level of job satisfaction as measured by annual surveys correlated directly with increased customer satisfaction, which resulted in a 25% increase in sales over a five-year period.

These Baldrige Award-winning companies provide a benchmark for human resources management among companies committed to quality improvement and total quality management. They exhibit common human resource characteristics, including extensive job training, employee empowerment, incentive plans, teamwork, job flexibility, and close monitoring of employee satisfaction via annual surveys.[1]

[1]Malcolm Baldrige National Quality Award Web site, http://www.quality.nist.gov.

Employees—the people who work in an organization—are "resources," as important as other company resources, such as natural resources and technology. In fact, it is the one resource that all companies have available to them. A company in Taiwan, Japan, or Denmark may have different and few natural resources, certainly fewer than U.S. companies have, but they all have people. With the same or superior technologies as their competitors, and with good people, foreign companies can compete and thrive. Increasingly, *skilled* human resources are the difference between successfully competing or failing.

The traditional view of employees or labor was not so much as a valuable resource, but as a replaceable part of the productive process that must be closely directed and controlled. The trend toward quality management, more than anything else, changed this perspective. W. E. Deming, the international quality expert, emphasized that good employees who are always improving are the key to successful quality management and a company's ultimate survival. More than half of Deming's 14 points for quality improvement relate to employees. His point is that if a company is to attain its goals for quality improvement and customer service, its employees must be involved and committed. However, to get employees "with the program," the company must regard them and manage them as a valuable resource. Moreover, the company must have a commitment to its employees.

Another thing that has changed the way companies regard employees and work is the shift in the U.S. economy toward the service sector and away from manufacturing. Since services tend to be more people-intensive than capital-intensive, human resources are becoming a more important competitive factor for service companies. Advances in information technologies have also changed the working environment, especially in service companies. Because they rely heavily on information technology and communication, services need employees who are technically skilled and can communicate effectively with customers. They also need flexible employees who can apply these skills to a variety of tasks and who are continuously trained to keep up with rapid advances in information technology.

Increasing technological advances in equipment and machinery have also resulted in manufacturing work that is more technically sophisticated. Employees are required to be better educated, have greater skill levels, and have greater technical expertise, and are expected to take on greater responsibility. This work environment is a result of changing technologies and international market conditions, global competition that emphasizes diverse products, and an emphasis on product and service quality.

In this chapter we first discuss employees' role in a company's TQM program. Next we provide a perspective on how work has developed and changed in the United States and then look at some of the current trends in human resources. We will also discuss some of the traditional aspects of work and job design.

## HUMAN RESOURCES AND QUALITY MANAGEMENT

Most successful quality-oriented firms today recognize the importance of their employees when developing a competitive strategy. Quality management is an integral part of most companies' strategic design, and the role of employees is an important aspect of quality management. To change management's traditional control-oriented relationship with employees to one of cooperation, mutual trust, teamwork, and goal orientation necessary in a quality-focused company generally requires a long-term commitment as a key part of a company's strategic plan.

In the traditional management–employee relationship, employees are given precise directions to achieve narrowly defined individual objectives. They are rewarded with merit pay based on individual performance in competition with their co-workers. Often individual excellence is rewarded while other employees look on in envy. In a successful TQM program, employees are given broad latitude in their jobs, they are encouraged to improvise, and they have the power to use their own initiative to correct and prevent problems. Strategic goals are for quality and customer service instead of maximizing profit or minimizing cost, and rewards are based on group achievement. Instead of limited training for specific, narrowly defined jobs, employees are trained in a broad range of skills so they know more about the entire productive process, making them flexible in where they can work.

To manage human resources from this perspective, a company must focus on employees as a key, even central, component in their strategic design. All of the Malcolm

### THE COMPETITIVE EDGE

### Employee-Driven Success at Sears

In 1992 Sears had a net loss of $3.9 billion on sales of $52.3 billion. This was the worst year in Sears' history, and it capped a negative trend that was directly related to Sears' widespread diversification into nonretail businesses in the 1980s. Sears responded by selling off its nonretail businesses and refocusing on merchandising, its historical roots. Its merchandising initiatives in 1993 included focusing its service and marketing strategy on women and their families, putting more of its best employees in stores during evenings and weekends when the best customers were shopping, emphasizing employee training and incentives, eliminating the 101-year-old Sears catalogue (which was losing more than $100 million annually), closing 113 mall-based stores, and renovating the remaining 800 stores at a cost of $4 billion, and accepting all major credit cards instead of just its own Discover and Sears cards. Sears experienced an immediate turnaround, recording one of its most profitable years ever in 1993 with a 9% increase in sales and net income of $752 million. However, Sears did not want this quick recovery, as remarkable and satisfying as it was, to be a short-term peak, and to relax or fall back into old trends and habits; it wanted to develop a long-term plan for sustained excellence. The result was the evolution of Sears' "employee–customer–profit" model.

Sears' "formula" for business success, "employee–customer–profit," was not just a slogan, but also a mathematical formula that would indicate causation and results. The driving force (the first term in the formula) was employees. For example, if money was spent to increase employees' knowledge of the products they sell, would this lead to higher customer retention, higher revenues, and greater market share?

The first, "employee," component of the model is defined by the two most important dimensions of employee satisfaction indicated by employee survey data and focus groups—"attitude about the job" and "attitude about the company." These dimensions have the greatest impact on employee loyalty and behavior toward customers. The resulting model shows, for example, that a 5-point improvement in employee attitudes will result in a 1.3-point improvement in customer satisfaction, which in turn will generate a 0.5% increase in revenue growth. The quantitative results of the model are referred to as Sears Total Performance Indicators (TPI).

Deployment of the employee–customer–profit/TPI model in mid-1995 required an educational process to change perceptions and attitudes of the 300,000 Sears' employees, providing them with a better understanding of how the business worked, and focusing on their interaction with customers. Independent surveys showed that although national retail customer satisfaction declined between 1996 and 1998, in 1997 employee satisfaction at Sears as measured by the TPI model rose 4%, and customer satisfaction increased by the same amount. According to the TPI model, that translated into a $200 million increase in revenue.

*Source:* Based on A. J. Rucci, S. Kirn, and R. Quinn, "The Employee–Customer–Profit Chain at Sears," *Harvard Business Review* 76(1; January–February 1998), pp. 83–97.

Baldrige National Quality Award winners have a pervasive human resource focus. Sears's "employee–customer–profit chain" model for long-term company success has "employees" as the model's driving force. Federal Express's strategic philosophy, "People, Service, Profit," starts with people, reflecting its belief that its employees are its most important resource.

Companies that successfully integrate this kind of "employees first" philosophy into their strategic design share several common characteristics. Employee training and education are recognized as necessary long-term investments. Strategic planning for product and technological innovation is tied to the development of employees' skills, not only to help in the product development process but also to carry out innovations as they come to fruition. Motorola provides employees with 160 hours of training annually to keep up with technological changes and to learn how to understand and compete in newly emerging global markets.

Another characteristic of companies with a strategic design that focuses on quality is that employees have the power to make decisions that will improve quality and customer service. At AT&T employees can stop a production line if they detect a quality problem, and an employee at Ritz-Carlton can spend up to $2000 to satisfy a guest, on his or her own initiative.

To make sure their strategic design for human resources is working, companies regularly monitor employee satisfaction using surveys and make changes when problems are identified. All Baldrige Quality Award–winning companies conduct annual employee surveys, to assess employee satisfaction and make improvements. For example, 2002 Baldrige award winner, Branch-Smith Printing, conducts an annual employment survey to gauge employee satisfaction and determine areas of employee concern and focus.

A safe, healthy working environment is a basic necessity to keep employees satisfied. Successful companies provide special services like recreational activities, day care, flexible work hours, cultural events, picnics, and fitness centers. Notice that these are services that treat employees like customers, an acknowledgment that there is a direct and powerful link between employee satisfaction and customer satisfaction.

Strategic goals for quality and customer satisfaction require teamwork and group participation. Texas Instruments has as a goal that all employees be a member of at least one team to locate and solve quality-related problems. Team members and individuals are encouraged to make suggestions to improve group performance. The motivation for such suggestions is viewed as that of a concerned family member, not as a complainant or as "sticking one's nose in." Cadillac shows its respect for employees' ideas by responding to all employee suggestions within 24 hours.

It is important that employees understand what the strategic goals of the company are and that they feel like they can participate in achieving these goals. Employees need to believe they make a difference to be committed to goals and have pride in their work. Employee commitment and participation in the strategic plan can be enhanced if employees are involved in the planning process, especially at the local level. As the strategic plan passes down through the organization to the employee level, employees can participate in the development of local plans to achieve overall corporate goals.

## THE CHANGING NATURE OF HUMAN RESOURCES MANAGEMENT

The principles of *scientific management* developed by F. W. Taylor in the 1880s and 1890s dominated operations management during the first part of the twentieth century. Taylor's approach was to break jobs down into their most elemental activities and to simplify job designs so that only limited skills were required to learn a job, thus minimizing the time required for learning. This approach divided the jobs requiring less skill from the work required to set up machinery and maintain it, which required greater skill. In Taylor's system, a **job** is the set of all the tasks performed by a worker, **tasks** are individual activities consisting of *elements*, which encompass several **job motions**, or basic physical movements.

***Scientific management*** **involves breaking down jobs into elemental activities and simplifying job design.**

**Jobs:** comprise a set of **tasks**, *elements*, and **job motions** (*basic physical movements*).

Scientific management broke down a job into its simplest elements and motions, eliminated unnecessary motions, and then divided the tasks among several workers so that each would require only minimal skill. This system enabled companies to hire large numbers of cheap, unskilled laborers, who were basically interchangeable and easily replaced. If a worker was fired or quit, another could easily be placed on the job with virtually no training expense. In this system, the timing of job elements (by stopwatch) enabled management to develop *standard times* for producing one unit of output. Workers were paid according to their total output in a *piece-rate system*. A worker was paid "extra" wages according to the amount he or she exceeded the "standard" daily output. Such a wage system is based on the premise that the single motivating factor for a worker to increase output is monetary reward.

Traditionally, time has been a measure of job efficiency.

In a *piece-rate wage system*, pay is based on output.

F. W. Taylor's work was not immediately accepted or implemented. This system required high volumes of output to make the large number of workers needed for the expanded number of jobs cost effective. The principles of scientific management and mass production were brought together by Henry Ford and the assembly-line production of automobiles.

## THE ASSEMBLY LINE

The adoption of scientific management at Ford was the catalyst for its subsequent widespread acceptance.

Between 1908 and 1929, Ford Motor Company created and maintained a mass market for the Model-T automobile, more than 15 million of which were eventually produced. During this period, Ford expanded production output by combining standardized parts and product design, continuous-flow production, and Taylor's scientific management. These elements were encompassed in the assembly-line production process.

Assembly-line production meshed with the principles of scientific management.

On an assembly line, workers no longer moved from place to place to perform tasks, as they had in the factory/shop. Instead they remained at a single workplace, and the work was conveyed to them along the assembly line. Technology had advanced from the general-purpose machinery available at the turn of the century, which required the abilities of a skilled machinist, to highly specialized, semiautomatic machine tools, which required less skill to feed parts into or perform repetitive tasks. Fifteen thousand of these machines were installed at Ford's Highland Park plant. The pace of work was established mechanically by the line and not by the worker or management. The jobs along the line were broken down into highly repetitive, simple tasks.

The assembly line at Ford was enormously successful. The amount of labor time required to assemble a Model-T chassis was reduced from more than 12 hours in 1908 to a little less than 3 hours by 1913. By 1914 the average time for some tasks was as low as $1\frac{1}{2}$ minutes. The basic assembly-line structure and many job designs that existed in 1914 remained virtually unchanged for the next 50 years.

## LIMITATIONS OF SCIENTIFIC MANAGEMENT

Advantages of task specialization include high output, low costs, and minimal training.

Scientific management had obvious advantages. It resulted in increased output and lower labor costs. Workers could easily be replaced and trained at low cost, taking advantage of a large pool of cheap unskilled labor shifting from farms to industry. Because of low-cost mass production, the U.S. standard of living was increased enormously and became the envy of the rest of the world. It also allowed unskilled, uneducated workers to gain employment based almost solely on their willingness to work hard physically at jobs that were mentally undemanding.

Disadvantages of task specialization include boredom, lack of motivation, and physical and mental fatigue.

Scientific management also proved to have serious disadvantages. Workers frequently became bored and dissatisfied with the numbing repetition of simple job tasks that required little thought, ingenuity, or responsibility. The skill level required in repetitive, specialized tasks is so low that workers do not have the opportunity to prove their worth or abilities for advancement. Repetitive tasks requiring the same monotonous physical motions can result in unnatural physical and mental fatigue.

## EMPLOYEE MOTIVATION

Modern psychologists and behaviorists in the 1950s and 1960s eschewed the principles of scientific management, and they developed theories (as summarized in Table 8.1), that proposed that in order to get employees to work productively and efficiently they must be

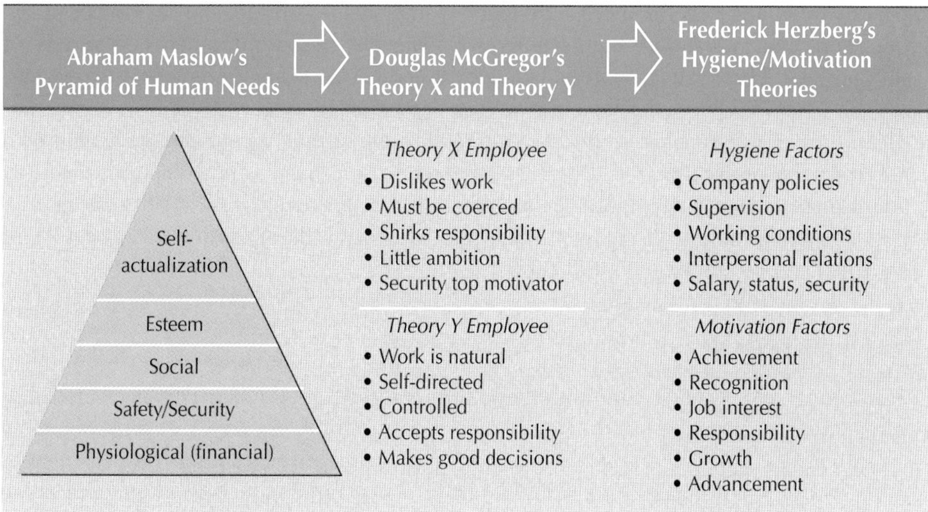


**Table 8.1**
**Evolution of Theories of Employee Motivation**

motivated. **Motivation** is a willingness by an employee to work hard to achieve the company's goals because that effort satisfies some employees need or objective. Thus, employee motivation is a key factor in achieving company goals such as product quality and creating a quality workplace. However, different things motivate employees. Obviously, financial compensation is a major motivating factor, but it is not the only one and may not be the most important. Other factors that motivate employees include self-actualization (such as integrity, responsibility, and naturalness), achievement and accomplishment, recognition, relationships with co-workers and supervisors, the type and degree of work supervision, job interest, trust and responsibility, and the opportunity for growth and advancement.

**Motivation:** a willingness to work hard because that effort satisfies an employee need.

In general, job performance is a function of motivation combined with ability. Ability depends on education, experience, and training, and its improvement can follow a slow but clearly defined process. On the other hand, motivation can be improved more quickly, but there is no clear-cut process for motivating people. However, certain basic elements in job design and management have been shown to improve motivation, including

- positive reinforcement and feedback
- effective organization and discipline
- fair treatment of people
- satisfaction of employee needs
- setting of work-related goals
- design of jobs to fit the employee
- work responsibility
- empowerment
- restructuring of jobs when necessary
- rewards based on company as well as individual performance
- achievement of company goals

## CONTEMPORARY TRENDS IN HUMAN RESOURCES MANAGEMENT

During the last two decades of the twentieth century the competitive advantage gained by many Japanese companies in international markets, and especially in the automobile industry, caused U.S. firms to reevaluate their management practices vis-à-vis those of the Japanese. Human resources management is one area where there was a striking difference between Japanese and U.S. approaches and results. For example, in the 1980s one Japanese automobile company was able to assemble a car with half the blue-collar labor of a comparable U.S. auto company—about 14 hours in Japan, compared with 25 hours in the United States. Japan had not adopted the traditional Western approaches to work. Instead

Japanese work allowed for more individual worker responsibility and less supervision, group work and interaction, higher worker skill levels, and training across a variety of tasks and jobs. There was initially a tendency among Americans to think that these characteristics were unique to the Japanese culture. However, the successes of U.S. companies such as Ford and Motorola in implementing quality-management programs as well as successful Japanese companies operating in America, such as Nissan and Honda, showed that cultural factors were less important than management practices. As a result certain contemporary trends in human resource management became the norm for successful TQM companies in the United States and abroad.

Japanese successes are due less to cultural factors than to management practices.

## JOB TRAINING

In companies with a commitment to quality, job training is extensive and varied. Expectations for performance and advancement from both the employee and management tend to be high. Typically, numerous courses are available for training in different jobs and functions. Job training is considered part of a structured career-development system that includes cross training and job rotation. This system of training and job rotation enhances the flexibility of the production process we mentioned earlier. It creates talent reserves that can be used as the need arises when products or processes change or the workforce is reduced.

Two of Deming's 14 points refer to employee education and training.

Training is a major feature of all companies with TQM programs. Two of W. E. Deming's 14 points refer to employee education and training. Most large TQM companies have extensive training staffs with state-of-the-art facilities. Federal Express has a television network that broadcasts more than 2000 different training course titles to employees. Many UPS employees are part-time college students, but each receives more training than most skilled factory workers in the United States. Employees at STMicroelectronics, a Texas-based manufacturer of semiconductor integrated circuits, and a Baldrige Award winner, averages 50% more annual training than its competitors.

At Ritz-Carlton Hotels, the only two-time Baldrige Quality Award winner in the service category, first-year managers and employees receive 250 to 310 hours of training. Xerox Business Services, a division of Xerox Corporation and a Baldrige Award winner, is continually searching for innovative approaches to training and learning; examples include mini-camps to help employees contemplate and prepare for future changes in their work, and personal learning plans that are regularly reviewed by "coaches." Ames Rubber, another Baldrige Award recipient, worked with a community college to develop a training program that resulted in high school equivalency diplomas for 20% of its workforce. Ames credits this training combined with its employee teamwork for reducing the number of defective parts it supplied to its largest customer, Xerox, from 30,000 per million to 11 per million.

## CROSS TRAINING

**Cross Training:** an employee learns more than one job.

In **cross training** an employee learns more than one job in the company. Cross training has a number of attractive features that make it beneficial to the company and the employee. For the company it provides a safety measure with more job coverage in the event of employee resignations and absenteeism, and sudden increases in a particular job activity. Employees are given more knowledge and variety so that they won't get as easily bored, they will find more value in what they do, and their interest level in the company will increase. Because of their increased knowledge, they will have the opportunity to move to other jobs within the company without leaving. Employees will respect each other because they will be more familiar with each other's jobs. However, cross training requires a significant investment in time and money, so the company should be committed to its implementation and sure of the benefits it hopes to realize from cross training.

Pal's Sudden Service, a drive-through restaurant chain with 17 locations in the Kingsport, Tennessee, area was the recipient of the 2001 Malcolm Baldrige Award in the Small Business category. Cross training is required of all its store-level staff to ensure their complete understanding of all production and service processes as well as quality standards.

**Job rotation** is not exactly the same as cross training. Cross training gives an employee the ability to move between jobs if needed. Job rotation requires cross training, but it also includes the horizontal movement between two or more jobs according to a plan or schedule. This not only creates a flexible employee, but it also reduces boredom and increases employee interest.

**Job rotation:** the horizontal movement between two or more jobs according to a plan.

## JOB ENRICHMENT

The objective of job enrichment is to create more opportunities for individual achievement and recognition by adding variety, responsibility, and accountability to the job. This can also lead to greater worker autonomy, increased task identity, and greater direct contact with other workers. Frederick Herzberg (Table 8.1) developed the following set of principles for job enrichment:

- Allow employees control over their own work and some of the supervisory responsibilities for the job, while retaining accountability, also called **vertical job enlargement**.
- Assign each worker a complete unit of work that includes all the tasks necessary to complete a process or product with clearly defined start and end points so that the employee feels a sense of closure and achievement. This is also called **horizontal job enlargement**.
- Provide additional authority and freedom for employees.
- Make periodic reports available to workers instead of just supervisors.
- Introduce new and more difficult tasks into the job.
- Encourage development of expertise by assigning individuals to specialized tasks.

**Vertical job enlargement:** allows employees control over their work.

**Horizontal job enlargement:** an employee is assigned a complete unit of work with defined start and end.

## EMPOWERMENT

**Empowerment** is giving employees responsibility and authority to make decisions. For TQM programs to work, it is generally conceded that employees must be empowered so that they are willing to innovate and act on their own in an atmosphere of trust and respect. Five of W. E. Deming's 14 points for quality improvement (see page 85) relate to employee empowerment. Empowerment requires employee education and training, and participation in goal setting. The advantages of empowerment include more attention to product quality and the ability to fix quality problems quickly, increased respect and trust among employees, lower absenteeism and higher productivity, more satisfying work, less conflict with management, and fewer middle managers. However, empowerment can also have some negative aspects. Employees may abuse the power given to them; empowerment may provide too much responsibility for some employees; it may create conflicts with middle management; it will require additional training for employees and managers which can be costly; group work, which often is an integral part of empowerment, can be time-consuming and some employees may not make good decisions.

**Empowerment:** giving employees authority to make decisions.

The motto of Baldrige Award winner, Operations Management International, a Colorado-based wastewater and water treatment company, is "Exceed our customer's expectations, empower our employees, enhance the environment." A Motorola sales representative is empowered to replace a customer's defective product up to six years after its purchase. GM plant employees can call in suppliers to help them solve problems. Federal Express employees are empowered to do whatever it takes to ensure 100% customer satisfaction. The authority of TQM company workers to halt an entire production operation or line on their own initiative if they discover a quality problem is well documented at companies like AT&T.

## TEAMS

Empowerment and employee involvement are often realized through work groups or teams. Quality circles, discussed in Chapter 3 ("Quality Management"), in which a group of 8 to 10 employees plus their supervisor work on problems in their immediate work area, is a well-known example of a team approach. Teams can differ according to their purpose, level of responsibility, and longevity. Some teams are established to work on a specific problem and then disband; others are more long-term, formed to monitor a work area or process for continual improvement. Most teams are not totally democratic and have some supervisory oversight, although some have more authority than others. Quality circles typically have a supervisor in charge. In general, for teams to be effective, they must know what their purpose and roles are relative to the company's goal's, as well as the extent of their empowerment, have the skills and training necessary to achieve their goals, and possess the ability to work together as a team.

*Self-directed* teams, though not totally independent, are usually empowered to make decisions and changes relative to the processes in their own work area. This degree of responsibility is based on trust and management's belief that the people who are closest to a work process know how to make it work best. Team members tend to feel more responsibility to make their solutions work, and companies typically reward teams for performance improvement.

Self-directed teams generally require more training to work together as a team; however, benefits include less managerial control (and fewer managers), quicker identification and solution of problems, more job satisfaction, positive peer pressure, and a feeling of "not wanting to let the team down," common to sports teams and military groups. Alternatively, such teams can have some negative aspects. Supervisors and managers may have difficulty adjusting to their changed role in which they monitor and oversee rather than direct work. Also, conflict between team members can hinder a team's effectiveness.

At Baldrige Award winner, Texas-based STMicroelectronics, one of the world's top manufacturers of semiconductor integrated circuits, teams determine workflow, job assignments, and break and vacation schedules. They also set up and monitor their training plans and conduct peer reviews that are included in formal company performance reviews and merit pay increases. A variable incentive plan provides monthly bonuses to teams that meet production goals. Another Baldrige Award winner, Clarke American Checks, Inc., a San Antonio-based producer of personalized checks and banking accessories, makes extensive use of teams for operational improvements. Cross-functional project teams address "change the business" initiatives. Knowledge is shared between teams through a systematic approach to communication and a highly competitive team excellence award process.

## FLEXIBLE WORK SCHEDULES

**Flextime:** part of a daily work schedule in which employees can choose time of arrival and departure.

Flexible work schedules or **flextime** is becoming an increasingly important workplace format. It refers to a variety of arrangements in which fixed times of arrival and departure are replaced by a combination of "core" or fixed time and flexible time. Core time is the designated period during which all employees are present, say 9:00 A.M. to 2:30 P.M. Flexible time is part of the daily work schedule where employees can choose their time of arrival and departure. In some cases, an employee may bank or credit hours—that is, work more hours one day and bank those hours in order to take a shorter work day in the future. In other cases, an employee may vary work days during the week, for example, work four 10-hour days followed by a three-day weekend. While flextime helps the company attract and retain employees and promotes job satisfaction, it can make it difficult to compensate for sudden changes in the workload or problems that can arise that require quick reactions.

## ALTERNATIVE WORKPLACES AND TELECOMMUTING

**Alternative workplace:** a nontraditional work location.

An **alternative workplace** is a combination of nontraditional work locations, settings, and practices that supplements or replaces the traditional office. An alternative workplace can be a home office, a satellite office, a shared office, or even a shared desk. Another form of alternative workplace is telecommuting, performing work electronically wherever the worker chooses.

The motivation for companies to create alternative workplaces is primarily financial. Eliminating physical office space—that is, real estate—and reducing related overhead costs can result in significant cost reductions. In one five-year period, IBM realized $1 billion in real estate savings alone by equipping and training 17% of its worldwide workforce to work in alternative workplaces. Alternative workplaces can increase productivity by relieving employees of typical time-consuming office routines, allowing them more time to devote to customers. They can also help companies recruit and retain talented, motivated employees who find the flexibility of telecommuting or a home office very attractive. Eliminating commuting time to a remote office can save employees substantial work time. Customer satisfaction can also increase as customers find it easier to contact employees and receive more personalized attention.

In general, companies that use alternative workplaces employ a mix of different formats and tailor the workplace to fit specific company needs. There are also costs associated with establishing alternative workplace formats, including training, hardware and software, networks, phone charges, technical support, and equipment, although these costs are usually less than real estate costs, which are ever-increasing. Of course, alternative workplaces are not feasible for some companies, such as manufacturing companies, which require employees to be located at specific workstations, facilities, or stationary equipment or which require direct management supervision. Employees who work on an assembly line or in a hotel are not candidates for an alternative workplace. Alternative workplaces are more appropriate for companies that are informational—that is, they operate through voice and data communication between their employees and their customers.

One of the more increasingly common new alternative workplace formats is **telecommuting**, also referred to as "telework," in which employees work electronically from whatever location they choose, either exclusively or some of the time. It is estimated that about 40% of U.S. companies offer some form of telecommuting to employees. Companies that use telecommuting sites experience such benefits as lower real estate costs, reduced turnover, decreased absenteeism and leave usage, increased productivity, and increased ability to comply with federal workplace laws such as the Americans with Disabilities Act. At PeopleSoft, telecommuting is the predominant form of work for the whole company, and at IBM telecommuters make up whole units.

**Telecommuting:** employees work electronically from a location they choose.

It has been estimated that through telecommuting absenteeism can be reduced by as much as 25%. Texas has reported a 25% increase in the productivity of its state employees since introducing telecommuting, and California has reported up to a 30% increase in the productivity of its employees with telecommuting. For employees, telecommuting eliminates commuting time and travel costs, allows for a more flexible work schedule, and allows them to blend work with family and personal responsibilities.

Telecommuting also has negative aspects. Its biggest disadvantage is that it may negatively affect the relationship between employees and their immediate supervisors. Supervisors and middle managers may feel uncomfortable not having employees under direct visual surveillance. Furthermore, they may feel that they do not have control and authority over their employees if they are not physically present. In fact, some employees may not be well suited for telecommuting; they may not be self-motivated and may require more direct supervision and external motivation.

## THE COMPETITIVE EDGE

### Telecommuting at Merrill Lynch

Merrill Lynch implemented a formal telecommuting program in 1996 with about 100 telecommuters, and today it has over 3500 employees who work from home between one and four days per week. As preparation for its program, Merrill Lynch developed a 21-page manager's guide for telecommuting that includes a workshop where the employee and manager work out potentially harmful issues in advance. Employees and managers agree on ways to measure performance and time management, determine how to best communicate with fellow employees, and discuss how career advancement will be considered since they will be physically absent much of the time. The final preparation step is a two-week, on-site telecommuting lab (i.e., school) where employees communicate by phone, e-mail, or instant messenger just as they would from home. They also learn how to troubleshoot with their computers, software, and other equipment they will use at home. Merrill Lynch reports that telecommuting resulted in a 15 to 20% increase in productivity, 3.5 fewer sick days per year, and a 6% decrease in employee turnover during the first year of the program. In addition, the company was able to retain 40 to 60 employees it would have otherwise lost due to the closing and movement of one of its offices.

*Source:* Susan J. Wells, "Making Telecommuting Work," *HR Magazine* 46(10; October 2001), pp. 34–45.

## THE COMPETITIVE EDGE

### Part-Time Employees at UPS

UPS hires more than 95,000 part-time, seasonal employees to help it deliver more than 325 million packages, as many as 19 million on its busiest day, during the period from Thanksgiving to Christmas. These part-time employees will work four to five hours per day, and include 30,000 driver helpers, 60,000 package handlers and sorters, and 3500 extra delivery drivers. Although these peak season hires are not guaranteed employment beyond December 31, part-time employees still represent a large segment of the workforce at UPS during the rest of the year. *Your Money* magazine has cited UPS for "providing the best part-time job in America." The company offers good wages and benefits to permanent part-time employees including full health benefits for employees and their families, a 401k plan, life insurance, paid holidays, and tuition assistance.

UPS's "Earn and Learn" program provides part-time college student employees up to $1500 per semester and $3000 per calendar year up to a lifetime maximum of $15,000 for tuition, approved fees, and books. For part-time management employees, these benefits increase to a maximum of $4000 per year and a lifetime maximum of $20,000. In 2000 almost 7500 UPS employees were enrolled in this program. The UPS "School-to-Work" program builds a bridge to help students go from high school to college and to consider a college education. High school students work 15 to 20 hours per week as package handlers and scanners on a "student" shift from 5:30 P.M. to 9:30 P.M. They receive the same benefits as all UPS part-time employees. These students learn the basic elements of employment such as punctuality, integrity, teamwork, and time management, and are also "mentored" by members of management and the supervisory staff to encourage them in their academic studies and to make sure they are able to balance their high school studies with their responsibilities as a UPS employee. Since 1997, UPS has hired over 25,000 welfare recipients as part-time employees through its "Welfare-to-Work" program. UPS has formed partnerships with government, social services, and community organizations to facilitate this program, including the recruitment of qualified welfare recipients, and to provide transportation to and from the workplace. These programs serve to provide UPS with an educated and committed pool of employees.

*Source:* UPS Web site, http://www.ups.com.

### TEMPORARY AND PART-TIME EMPLOYEES

A trend among service companies in particular is the use of temporary, or *contingent*, employees. Part-time employees accounted for over 40% of job growth in the retail industry during the 1990s. Fast-food and restaurant chains, retail companies, package delivery services, and financial firms tend to use a large number of temporary employees. Companies that have seasonal demand make extensive use of temporary employees. L.L.Bean needs a lot more telephone service operators, and UPS needs many more package sorters in the weeks before Christmas. Sometimes a company will undertake a project requiring technical expertise its permanent employees do not have. Instead of reassigning or retraining its employees, the company will bring in temporary employees having the necessary expertise. There has been a growing market for firms that *lease* people for jobs, especially for computer services. As companies downsize to cut costs, they turn to temporary employees to fill temporary needs without adding to their long-term cost base. People with computer skills able to work from home have also increased the pool of available temporary workers.

Unfortunately, temporary employees do not always have the commitment to goals for quality and service that a company might want. Companies dependent on temporary employees may suffer not only the inconsistent levels of their work ethic and skills, they may also sacrifice productivity for lower costs. To offset this possible inconsistency and to protect product and service quality, firms sometimes try to hire temporary employees only into isolated work areas away from their core businesses that most directly affect quality.

## EMPLOYEE COMPENSATION

Good human resource management practices or motivation factors cannot compensate for insufficient monetary rewards. If the reward is perceived as good, other things will motivate employees to give their best performance. Self-motivation can go only so far—it must be reinforced by financial rewards. Merit must be measured and rewarded regularly; otherwise performance levels will not be sustained.

## TYPES OF PAY

The two traditional forms of employee payment are the hourly wage and the individual incentive, or piece-rate, wage, both of which are tied to time. The hourly wage is self-explanatory; the longer someone works, the more he or she is paid. In a piece-rate system, employees are paid for the number of units they produce during the workday. The faster the employee performs, the more output generated and the greater the pay. These two forms of payment are also frequently combined with a guaranteed base hourly wage and additional incentive piece-rate payments based on the number of units produced above a standard hourly rate of output. Other basic forms of compensation include straight salary, the most common form of payment for management, and commissions, a payment system usually applied to sales and salespeople.

An individual piece-rate system provides incentive to increase output, but it does not ensure high quality. It can do just the opposite! In an effort to produce as much as possible, the worker will become sloppy, take shortcuts, and pay less attention to detail. As a result, TQM companies have tried to move away from individual wage incentive systems based on output and time. There has been a trend toward other measures of performance, such as quality, productivity, cost reduction, and the achievement of organizational goals. These systems usually combine an hourly base payment or even a salary with some form of incentive payment. However, incentives are not always individual but are tied to group, team, or company performance.

## GAINSHARING AND PROFIT SHARING

**Gainsharing** is an incentive plan that includes employees in a common effort to achieve a company's objectives in which they share in the gains. Although gainsharing systems vary broadly, they all generally include some type of financial measurement and frequent feedback system to monitor company performance and distribute gains periodically in the form of bonuses. **Profit sharing** sets aside some portion of company profits and distributes it among employees usually at the end of the fiscal year. The objective behind both incentive programs is to create a sense among employees that it is in their self-interest for the company to do well; the company wants employees to buy into the company's financial goals.

**Gainsharing:** an incentive plan joins employees in a common effort to achieve company goals, who share in gain.

**Profit sharing:** sets aside a portion of profits for employees at year's end.

Both programs have been shown to result in an increase in employee productivity; however, gainsharing is different from profit sharing in several ways. Gainsharing programs provide frequent payouts or bonuses, sometimes weekly or monthly, while profit-sharing bonuses are awarded once a year. Thus, gainsharing provides a more frequent reinforcement of good performance for the average employee. It is also generally easier for average employees to see results of gainsharing than profit sharing. Gainsharing focuses more on performance measures that are directly linked to the performance of employees or groups of employees than does profit sharing. Gainsharing spells out clearly what employees need to do to achieve a short-term goal and what will happen when they do achieve it. Profit sharing does not have the same emphasis on specifically what needs to happen to achieve short-term (weekly or monthly) goals. For these reasons, profit sharing is typically an incentive program that is more applicable to higher level employees and executives.

Los Alamos (New Mexico) National Bank, a Baldrige Award winner, has an Employee Stock Ownership Plan and an employee profit-sharing plan. Contributions to these plans are equal to about 21% of an employee's base salary. Incentive payouts for performance at Solar Turbines, another Baldrige Award winner, averaged 10.4% of salary. Employees at BI, a Minneapolis-based company with 1400 employees that offers full-service business improvement and incentive programs to other companies, and a Baldrige Award winner, work on a profit-sharing plan based on BI's financial performance. They are also eligible for performance bonuses, which in some years were given to more than 80% of the workforce.

## MANAGING DIVERSITY IN THE WORKPLACE

Diversity in U.S. companies has been a critical management issue for several decades. However, as more and more companies move into the global marketplace, diversity has become an even more pervasive factor in human resource management around the world. The spread of global business combined with the geographic mobility of employees has resulted in companies with a more diverse workforce than ever before. U.S. companies outsource business activities and operate facilities and businesses overseas with a mix of foreign and U.S. management teams and employees, and foreign companies operate plants and businesses in the United States with similar mixes. According to the U.S. Bureau of Labor Statistics, 4 out of every 10 people entering the workforce during the decade from 1998 to 2008 will be members of minority groups. In addition, the 2000 U.S. Census showed that some minorities, primarily Hispanic and Asian, are becoming majorities.

In order to be successful with a diverse workforce, companies must provide a climate in which all employees feel comfortable, can do their job, feel like they are valued by the organization, and perceive that they are treated fairly. However, inequalities too often exist for employees because of race, gender, religion, cultural origin, age, and physical or mental limitations. The elimination of racism, sexism, cultural indifference, and religious intolerance cannot be mandated by higher management or managed by financial incentives. Companies as a whole, starting with top management, must develop a strategic approach to managing diversity in order to meet the challenges posed by a diverse workforce.

### AFFIRMATIVE ACTION AND EQUAL OPPORTUNITY

In the United States affirmative action and equal opportunity are sometimes confused with managing diversity, but they are not the same thing. Affirmative action is an outgrowth of laws and regulations and is government initiated and mandated. It contains goals and timetables designed to increase the level of participation by women and minorities to attain parity levels in a company's workforce. Affirmative action is not directly concerned with increasing company success or increasing profits. Alternatively, managing diversity is the process of creating a work environment in which all employees can contribute to their full potential in order to achieve a company's goals. It is voluntary in nature, not mandated. It seeks to improve internal communications and interpersonal relationships, resolve conflict, and in doing so increase product quality, productivity, and efficiency. Managing diversity is creating an environment where everyone works in concert to do the best job possible. Whereas affirmative action has a short-term result, managing diversity is a long-term process. The objective of managing diversity is to find a way to let everyone do their best so that the company can gain a competitive edge.

Although affirmative action and diversity management are not the same thing, they are not independent of each other. A company that successfully manages diversity and implements successful programs that eliminate diversity issues and discrimination will also eliminate costly affirmative action liability and government mandates. A 1999 racial bias lawsuit against Coca-Cola has cost that company almost $270 million in settlements. An independent diversity task force was established in the settlement process to monitor how Coke planned to manage diversity. This panel was authorized to make recommendations that the company must carry out regarding hiring, promotions, compensation, and evaluation processes related to women and minorities. In effect, the courts mandated diversity management.

**Managing diversity:** includes education, awareness, communication, fairness, and commitment.

### DIVERSITY MANAGEMENT PROGRAMS

Although there is no magic formula for successfully **managing diversity**, education, awareness, communication, fairness, and commitment are critical elements in the process. We have explained on several occasions that employee training is an essential element in achieving product quality; the same holds true for creating a quality work environment for a diverse workforce. Prejudice feeds on ignorance. Employees must be educated about racial, gender, religious, and ethnic differences; they must be made aware of what it is like to be someone who is different from themselves. This also requires that lines of communication be open between different groups, and between employees and management. Most importantly, successful diversity management requires a commitment from top management. Although top management cannot mandate that the workplace be diversity friendly, strong leadership can successfully influence it.

A recent survey of *Fortune* 1000 companies conducted by the Society for Human Resource Management and *Fortune* magazine showed that diversity initiatives and programs can have a beneficial effect on company profits and success. Nearly all of the survey respondents (91%) indicated that their company's diversity initiatives helped them to maintain a competitive advantage by improving corporate culture (83%), improving employee morale (79%), decreasing interpersonal conflict among employees (58%), and increasing creativity (59%) and productivity (52%). Seventy-seven percent of the respondents indicated that their diversity initiatives improved employee recruitment, and 52% claimed they improved customer relations. The most common diversity initiatives and programs identified in the survey were recruiting efforts designed to increase diversity; diversity training; education and awareness programs; and community outreach. However, the survey also noted that the initiatives were time consuming, costly, and sometimes generate false hopes.

One approach being used by a number of companies is to create groups or networks that enable employees with diverse backgrounds to interact with each other. Kodak has a number of diversity groups, including a Women's Forum and a gay-employees network, which collaborate on different workplace issues. Many employees belong to multiple groups and learn about each others' issues and concerns, which helps develop sensitivity and mutual respect. Unisys and AT&T have resource groups for disabled employees which allow them to provide suggestions for designing products to make them more accessible to people with disabilities. Other diversity initiatives that have shown success within companies include internships, mentoring programs, career management programs, and skill enhancement programs.

## GLOBAL DIVERSITY ISSUES

Trends toward the globalization of companies, the use of global teams within and across companies, and global outsourcing have resulted in unique diversity issues. Cultural and language differences and geography are significant barriers to managing a globally diverse workforce. E-mails, faxes, the Internet, phones, and air travel make managing a global workforce possible but not necessarily effective.

In the case of culturally diverse groups, differences may be more subtle, and defined diversity programs may be less effective in dealing with them. Some nationalities and cultures have a more relaxed view of time than, say, Americans or Europeans; deadlines are less important. In some cultures, religious and national holidays have more significance than in others. Americans will frequently work at home in the evening, stay late at work, or work over the weekend or on vacations, and on the average take less vacation time than employees in most European countries; in many foreign countries such behavior is unheard of. Some cultures seem to have their own rules of communication. An employee in a foreign country, for example, may politely nod yes in response to a question from a U.S. manager as a polite face-saving gesture, when in fact it's not an indication of agreement at all.

Such cultural differences require unique forms of diversity management. Managers cannot interpret their employees' behavior through their own cultural background. It is important to identify critical cultural elements such as important holidays and a culturally acceptable work schedule, and to learn the informal rules of communication that may exist in a foreign culture among a diverse group of employees. It is often helpful to use a third party who is better able to bridge the cultural gap as a go-between. A manager who is culturally aware, and most importantly, speaks the language, is less likely to incorrectly interpret the behavior of diverse employees. Similarly, it is beneficial to teach employees the cultural norm for the organization so that they understand all the rules.

## JOB DESIGN

In the preceding sections we have discussed how to motivate employees to perform well in their jobs. A key element in employee motivation and job performance is to make sure the employee is well suited for a job and vice versa. If a job is not designed properly and it is not a good fit for the employee, then it will not be performed well. Frederick Herzberg identified several attributes of good job design, as follows:

- An appropriate degree of repetitiveness
- An appropriate degree of attention and mental absorption
- Some employee responsibility for decisions and discretion
- Employee control over their own job
- Goals and achievement feedback
- A perceived contribution to a useful product or service
- Opportunities for personal relationships and friendships
- Some influence over the way work is carried out in groups
- Use of skills

In this section we will focus on the factors that must be considered in job design—the things that must be considered to create jobs with the attributes listed above.

### THE ELEMENTS OF JOB DESIGN

The elements of job design fall into three categories: an analysis of the tasks included in the job, employee requirements, and the environment in which the job takes place. These categories address the questions of how the job is performed, who does it, and where it is done. Table 8.2 summarizes a selection of individual elements that would generally be considered in the job design process.

### TASK ANALYSIS

*Task analysis*: how tasks fit together to form a job.

*Task analysis* determines how to do each task and how all the tasks fit together to form a job. It includes defining the individual tasks and determining their most efficient sequence, their duration, their relationship with other tasks, and their frequency. Task analy-

**Table 8.2 Elements of Job Design**

| Task Analysis | Worker Analysis | Environmental Analysis |
|---|---|---|
| • Description of tasks to be performed | • Capability requirements | • Workplace location |
| • Task sequence | • Performance requirements | • Process location |
| • Function of tasks | • Evaluation | • Temperature and humidity |
| • Frequency of tasks | • Skill level | • Lighting |
| • Criticality of tasks | • Job training | • Ventilation |
| • Relationship with other jobs/tasks | • Physical requirements | • Safety |
| • Performance requirements | • Mental stress | • Logistics |
| • Information requirements | • Boredom | • Space requirements |
| • Control requirements | • Motivation | • Noise |
| • Error possibilities | • Number of workers | • Vibration |
| • Task duration(s) | • Level of responsibility | |
| • Equipment requirements | • Monitoring level | |
| | • Quality responsibility | |
| | • Empowerment level | |

sis should be sufficiently detailed so that it results in a step-by-step procedure for the job. The sequence of tasks in some jobs is a logical ordering; for example, the wedges of material used in making a baseball cap must be cut before they can be sewn together, and they must all be sewn together before the cap bill can be attached. The *performance requirements of a task* can be the time required to complete the task, the accuracy in performing the task to specifications, the output level or productivity yield, or quality performance. The performance of some tasks requires information such as a measurement (cutting furniture pieces), temperature (food processing), weight (filling bags of fertilizer), or a litmus test (for a chemical process).

*Performance requirements of a task*: time, accuracy, productivity, quality.

## WORKER ANALYSIS

Worker analysis determines the characteristics the worker must possess to meet the job requirements, the responsibilities the worker will have in the job, and how the worker will be rewarded. Some jobs require manual labor and physical strength, whereas others require none. Physical requirements are assessed not only to make sure the right worker is placed in a job but also to determine if the physical requirements are excessive, necessitating redesign. The same type of design questions must be addressed for mental stress.

Determining worker capabilities and responsibilities for a job.

## ENVIRONMENTAL ANALYSIS

Environmental analysis refers to the physical location of the job in the production or service facility and the environmental conditions that must exist. These conditions include things such as proper temperature, lighting, ventilation, and noise. The production of microchips requires an extremely clean, climatically controlled, enclosed environment. Detail work, such as engraving or sewing, requires proper lighting; some jobs that create dust levels, such as lint in textile operations, require proper ventilation. Some jobs require a large amount of space around the immediate job area.

*Job environment*: the physical characteristics and location of a job.

## ERGONOMICS

Put simply, **ergonomics** as it is applied to work is fitting the task to the person. It deals with the interaction of work, technology, and humans. Ergonomics applies human sciences like anatomy, physiology, and psychology to the design of the work environment and jobs, and objects and equipment used in work. The objective of ergonomics is to make the best use of employees' capabilities while maintaining the employees' health and well-being. The job should never limit the employee or compromise an employee's capabilities or physical and mental health because of poor job design. Good ergonomics shortens learning times; makes the job easier with less fatigue; improves equipment maintenance; reduces absenteeism, labor turnover, and job stress and injury; and meets legislative requirements for health and safety. In order to achieve these objectives, the job activity must be carefully analyzed, and the demands placed on the employee must be understood.

**Ergonomics:** fitting the task to the person in a work environment.

The contribution of anatomy in ergonomics is the improvement of the physical aspect of the job: achieving a good physical fit between the employee and the things the employee uses on the job whether it's a hand tool, a computer, a video camera, a forklift, or a lathe. Physiology is concerned with how the body functions. It addresses the energy required from the employee to do the job as well as the acceptable workload and work rate, and the physical working conditions—heat, cold, light, noise, vibration, and space. Psychology is concerned with the human mind. Its objective is to create a good psychological fit between the employee and the job.

## TECHNOLOGY AND AUTOMATION

The worker–machine interface is possibly the most crucial aspect of job design, both in manufacturing industries and in service companies where workers interface with computers. New technologies have increased the educational requirements and need for employee training. The development of computer technology and systems has heightened the need for workers with better skills and more job training.

Technology has broadened the scope of job design in the United States and overseas.

*Robots do not necessarily perform a job faster than humans, but they can tolerate hostile environments, work longer hours, and do a job more consistently. Robots are used for a wide range of manufacturing jobs, including material handling, machining, assembly, and inspection.*

During the 1990s, there was a substantial investment in new plants and equipment in the United States to compete globally. Companies developed and installed a new generation of automated equipment and robotics that enhanced their abilities to achieve higher output and lower costs. This new equipment also reduced the manual labor necessary to perform jobs and improve safety. Computer systems provided workers with an expanded array of information that increased their ability to identify and locate problems in the production process and monitor product quality. New job designs and redesigns of existing jobs were required that reflected these new technologies.

## JOB ANALYSIS

*Work methods*: studying how a job is done.

Part of job design is to study the *methods* used in the work included in the job to see how it should be done. This has traditionally been referred to as *methods analysis*, or simply *work methods*.

Methods analysis is used to redesign or improve existing jobs. An analyst will study an existing job to determine if the work is being done in the most efficient manner possible; if all the present tasks are necessary; or if new tasks should be added. The analyst might also want to see how the job fits in with other jobs—that is, how well a job is integrated into the overall production process or a sequence of jobs. The development and installation of new machinery or equipment, new products or product changes, and changes in quality standards can all require that a job be analyzed for redesign.

Methods analysis is also used to develop new jobs. In this case, the analyst must work with a description or outline of a proposed job and attempt to develop a mental picture of how the job will be performed.

The primary tools of methods analysis are a variety of charts that illustrate in different ways how a job or a work process is done. These charts allow supervisors, managers, and workers to see how a job is accomplished and to get their input and feedback on the design or redesign process. Two of the more popular charts are the *process flowchart* and the *worker–machine chart*.

### PROCESS FLOWCHART

**Process flowchart:** a graph of the steps of a job.

A **process flowchart** is used to analyze how the steps of a job or how a set of jobs fit together into the overall flow of the production process. Examples might include the flow of a product through a manufacturing assembly process, the making of a pizza, the activities of a surgical team in an operating room, or the processing of a catalogue mail or telephone order.

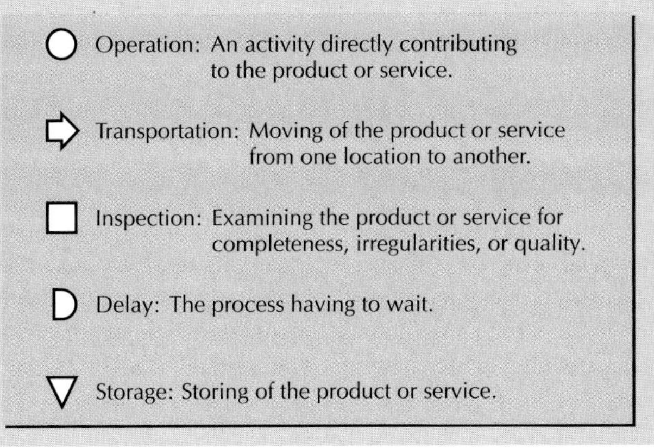

Figure 8.1
**Symbols for a Process Flowchart**

○ Operation: An activity directly contributing to the product or service.

⇨ Transportation: Moving of the product or service from one location to another.

□ Inspection: Examining the product or service for completeness, irregularities, or quality.

D Delay: The process having to wait.

▽ Storage: Storing of the product or service.

A process flowchart uses some basic symbols shown in Figure 8.1 to describe the tasks or steps in a job or a series of jobs. The symbols are connected by lines on the chart to show the flow of the process.

Example 8.1
**Developing a Job Process Flowchart**

The QuikCopy Store does copying jobs for walk-in customers. When a customer comes in with a copy job, a desk operator fills out a work order (name, number of copies, quality of paper, and so on) and places it in a box. An operator subsequently picks up the job, makes the copies, and returns the completed job to the cashier, where the job transaction is completed. The store would like a job process flowchart that describes this sequence of tasks.

*Solution*

The process flowchart for the steps in this copying job are shown in Figure 8.2. Although the process encompasses several operators and jobs, it focuses primarily on the tasks of the copy machine operator, who actually makes the copies.

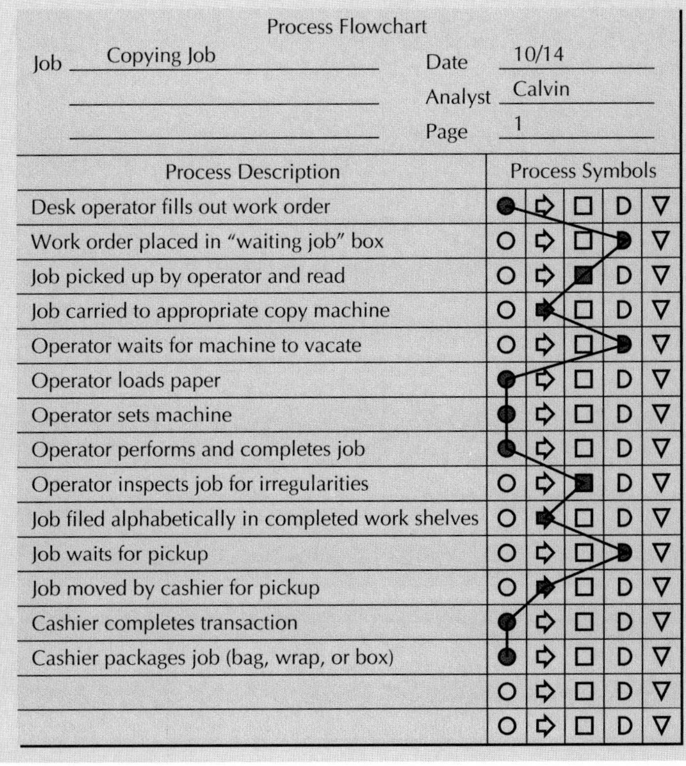

Figure 8.2
**Process Flowchart of Copying Job**

Process Flowchart

Job: Copying Job    Date: 10/14
Analyst: Calvin
Page: 1

| Process Description | Process Symbols | | | | |
|---|---|---|---|---|---|
| Desk operator fills out work order | **●** | ⇨ | □ | D | ▽ |
| Work order placed in "waiting job" box | ○ | ⇨ | □ | **D** | ▽ |
| Job picked up by operator and read | ○ | ⇨ | **■** | D | ▽ |
| Job carried to appropriate copy machine | ○ | **➡** | □ | D | ▽ |
| Operator waits for machine to vacate | ○ | ⇨ | □ | **D** | ▽ |
| Operator loads paper | **●** | ⇨ | □ | D | ▽ |
| Operator sets machine | **●** | ⇨ | □ | D | ▽ |
| Operator performs and completes job | **●** | ⇨ | □ | D | ▽ |
| Operator inspects job for irregularities | ○ | ⇨ | **■** | D | ▽ |
| Job filed alphabetically in completed work shelves | ○ | **➡** | □ | D | ▽ |
| Job waits for pickup | ○ | ⇨ | □ | **D** | ▽ |
| Job moved by cashier for pickup | ○ | **➡** | □ | D | ▽ |
| Cashier completes transaction | **●** | ⇨ | □ | D | ▽ |
| Cashier packages job (bag, wrap, or box) | **●** | ⇨ | □ | D | ▽ |
| | ○ | ⇨ | □ | D | ▽ |
| | ○ | ⇨ | □ | D | ▽ |

Often a process flowchart is used in combination with other types of methods analysis charts and a written job description to form a comprehensive and detailed picture of a job. Essentially, the methods analyst is a "job detective," who wants to get as much evidence as possible about a job from as many perspectives as possible in order to improve the job.

## WORKER–MACHINE CHART

**Worker–machine chart:** determines if worker and machine time are used efficiently.

A **worker–machine chart** illustrates the amount of time a worker and a machine are working or idle in a job. This type of chart is occasionally used in conjunction with a process flowchart when the job process includes equipment or machinery. The worker–machine chart shows if the worker's time and the machine time are being used efficiently—that is, if the worker or machine is idle an excessive amount of time.

**Example 8.2**
**Developing a Worker–Machine Chart**

The QuikCopy Store described in Example 8.1 also makes photo ID cards. An operator types in data about the customer on a card, submits this to the photo machine, positions the customer for the photo, and takes the photograph. The machine processes the photo ID card. The store would like to develop a worker–machine chart for this job.

*Solution*

Figure 8.3 shows the worker–machine chart for the job of making photo ID cards.

The time scale along the left side of the chart provides a visual perspective of the amount of work and idle time in the job process. For this job, the summary at the bottom of Figure 8.3 indicates that the operator and machine were both working and idle approximately the same amount of time.

**Figure 8.3**
**Worker–Machine Chart**

Worker–Machine Chart

Job Photo-ID Cards Date 10/14

| Time (min) | Operator | Time (min) | Photo Machine |
|---|---|---|---|
| 1, 2 | *Key in customer data on card* | *2.6* | *Idle* |
| 3 | *Feed data card in* | *0.4* | *Accept card* |
| | *Position customer for photo* | *1.0* | *Idle* |
| 4 | *Take picture* | *0.6* | *Begin photo process* |
| 5, 6, 7 | *Idle* | *3.4* | *Photo/card processed* |
| 8, 9 | *Inspect card and trim edges* | *1.2* | *Idle* |
| 10 | | | |

Summary

| | Operator Time | % | Photo Machine Time | % |
|---|---|---|---|---|
| Work | *5.8* | *63* | *4.8* | *52* |
| Idle | *3.4* | *37* | *4.4* | *48* |
| Total | *9.2 min* | *100%* | *9.2 min* | *100%* |

Another type of worker–machine chart is the *gang process chart*, which illustrates a job in which a team of workers are interacting with a piece of equipment or a machine. Examples include workers at a coal furnace in a steel mill or a military gunnery team on a battleship. A gang chart is constructed the same way as the chart in Figure 8.3, except there are columns for each of the different operators. The purpose of a gang process chart is to determine if the interaction between the workers is efficient and coordinated.

## MOTION STUDY

The most detailed form of job analysis is **motion study**, the study of the individual human motions used in a task. The purpose of motion study is to make sure that a job task does not include any unnecessary motion by the worker and to select the sequence of motions that ensure that the task is being performed in the most efficient way.

**Motion study:** used to ensure efficiency of motion in a job.

Motion study originated with Frank Gilbreth, a colleague of F. W. Taylor's at the beginning of the twentieth century. F.W. Taylor's approach to the study of work methods was to select the best worker among a group of workers and use that worker's methods as the standard by which other workers were trained. Alternatively, Gilbreth studied many workers and from among them picked the best way to perform each activity. Then he combined these elements to form the "one best way" to perform a task.

Frank and Lillian Gilbreth developed motion study.

Gilbreth and his wife Lillian used movies to study individual work motions in slow motion and frame by frame, called *micromotion analysis*. Using motion pictures, the Gilbreths carefully categorized the basic physical elements of motion used in work.

The Gilbreths' research eventually evolved into a set of widely adopted *principles of motion study*, which companies have used as guidelines for the efficient design of work. These principles are categorized according to the efficient use of the *human body*, the efficient arrangement of the *workplace*, and the efficient use of *equipment and machinery*. The principles of motion study include about 25 rules for conserving motion. These rules can be grouped in the three categories shown in Table 8.3.

*Principles of motion study*: guidelines for work design.

Motion study and scientific management complemented each other. Motion study was effective for designing the repetitive, simplified, assembly-line-type jobs characteristic of

Table 8.3 **Summary of General Guidelines for Motion Study**

| Efficient Use of the Human Body |
|---|
| • Work should be simplified, rhythmic, and symmetric. |
| • Hand/arm motions should be coordinated and simultaneous. |
| • The full extent of physical capabilities should be employed; all parts of the body should perform; the hand should never be idle. |
| • Energy should be conserved by letting machines perform tasks when possible, minimizing the distance of movements, and physical momentum should be in favor of the worker. |
| • Tasks should be simple, requiring minimal eye contact and minimal muscular effort, with no unnecessary motions, delays, or idleness. |
| **Efficient Arrangement of the Workplace** |
| • All tools, materials, and equipment should have a designated, easily accessible location that minimizes the motions required to get them. |
| • Seating and the general work environment should be comfortable and healthy. |
| **Efficient Use of Equipment** |
| • Equipment and mechanized tools enhance worker abilities. |
| • The use of foot-operated mechanized equipment that relieves the hand/arms of work should be maximized. |
| • Equipment should be constructed and arranged to fit worker use. |

manufacturing operations. Frank Gilbreth's first subject was a bricklayer; through his study of this worker's motions, he was able to improve the bricklayer's productivity threefold. However, in Gilbreth's day, bricklayers were paid on the basis of how many bricks they could lay in an hour in a piece-rate wage system. Who would be able to find a bricklayer today paid according to such a system!

There has been a movement away from task specialization and simple, repetitive jobs in lieu of greater job responsibility and a broader range of tasks, which has reduced the use of motion study. Nevertheless, motion study is still employed for repetitive jobs, especially in service industries, such as postal workers in mailrooms, who process and route thousands of pieces of mail.

Pioneers in the field of operations management.

The Gilbreths, together with F. W. Taylor and Henry Gantt, are considered pioneers in operations management. The Gilbreths' use of motion pictures is still popular today. Computer-generated images are used to analyze an athlete's movements to enhance performance, and video cameras are widely used to study everything from surgical procedures in the operating room to telephone operators.

## LEARNING CURVES

**Learning curve:** illustrates the improvement rate of workers as a job is repeated.

A **learning curve**, or *improvement curve*, is a graph that reflects the fact that as workers repeat their tasks, they will improve performance. The learning curve effect was introduced in 1936 in an article in the *Journal of Aeronautical Sciences* by T. P. Wright, who described how the direct labor cost for producing airplanes decreased as the number of planes produced increased. This observation and the rate of improvement were found to be strikingly consistent across a number of airplane manufacturers. The premise of the learning curve is that improvement occurs because workers learn how to do a job better as they produce more and more units. However, it is generally recognized that other production-related factors also improve performance over time, such as methods analysis and improvement, job redesign, retooling, and worker motivation.

As workers produce more items, they become better at their jobs.

Figure 8.4 illustrates the general relationship defined by the learning curve; as the number of cumulative units produced increases, the labor time per unit decreases. Specifically, the learning curve reflects the fact that each time the number of units produced doubles, the processing time per unit decreases by a constant percentage.

The processing time per unit decreases by a constant percentage each time output doubles.

The decrease in processing time per unit as production doubles will normally range from 10 to 20%. The convention is to describe a learning curve in terms of 1, or 100%, minus the percentage rate of improvement. For example, an 80% learning curve describes an improvement rate of 20% each time production doubles, a 90% learning curve indicates a 10% improvement rate, and so forth.

**Figure 8.4**
**Learning Curve**

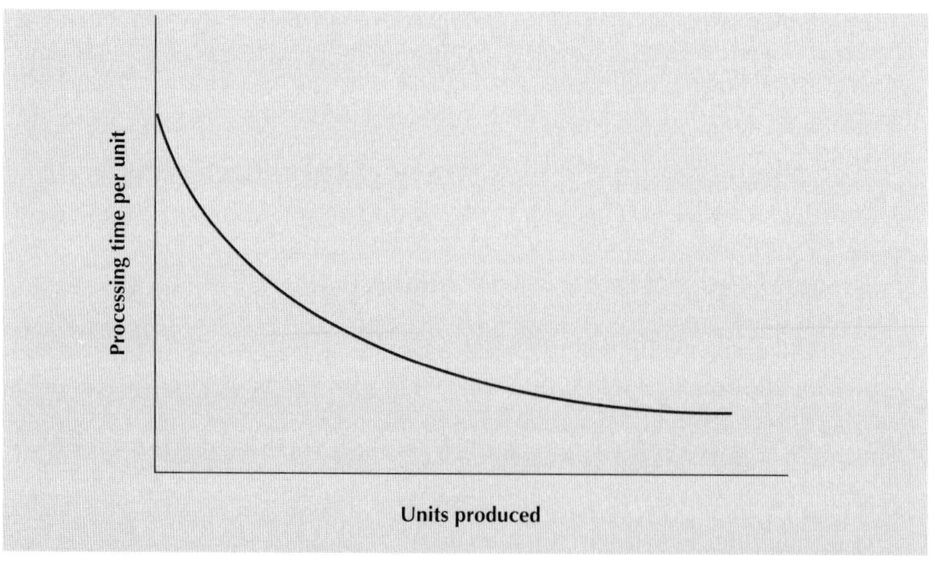

The learning curve in Figure 8.4 is similar to an exponential distribution. The corresponding learning curve formula for computing the time required for the $n$th unit produced is

$$t_n = t_1 n^b$$

where

$t_n$ = the time required for the $n$th unit produced

$t_1$ = time required for the first unit produced

$n$ = the cumulative number of units produced

$b$ = ln $r$/ln 2, where $r$ is the learning curve percentage (decimal coefficient)

**Example 8.3**

**Determining the Learning Curve Effect**

Paulette Taylor and Maureen Becker, two undergraduates at State University, produce customized personal computer systems at night in their apartment (hence the name of their enterprise, PM Computer Services). They shop around and purchase cheap components and then put together generic personal computers, which have various special features, for faculty, students, and local businesses. Each time they get an order, it takes them a while to assemble the first unit, but they learn as they go, and they reduce the assembly time as they produce more units. They have recently received their biggest order to date from the statistics department at State for 36 customized personal computers. It is near the end of the university's fiscal year, and the computers are needed quickly to charge them on this year's budget. Paulette and Maureen assembled the first unit as a trial and found that it took them 18 hours of direct labor. To determine if they can fill the order in the time allotted, they want to apply the learning curve effect to determine how much time the 9th, 18th, and 36th units will require to assemble. Based on past experience, they believe their learning curve is 80%.

*Solution*

The time required for the 9th unit is computed using the learning curve formula:

$$\begin{aligned} t_n &= t_1 n^b \\ t_9 &= (18)(9)^{\ln(0.8)/\ln 2} \\ &= (18)(9)^{-0.322} = 18/(9)^{0.322} \\ &= (18)(0.493) \\ &= 8.874 \text{ hours} \end{aligned}$$

The times required for the 18th and 36th units are computed similarly:

$$\begin{aligned} t_{18} &= (18)(18)^{\ln(0.8)/\ln 2} \\ &= (18)(0.394) \\ &= 7.092 \text{ hours} \end{aligned}$$

and

$$\begin{aligned} t_{36} &= (18)(36)^{\ln(0.8)/\ln 2} \\ &= (18)(0.315) \\ &= 5.67 \text{ hours} \end{aligned}$$

Learning curves are not effective for mass production jobs.

Learning curves are useful for measuring work improvement for nonrepetitive, complex jobs requiring a long time to complete, such as building airplanes. For short, repetitive, and routine jobs, there may be little relative improvement, and it may occur in a brief time span during the first (of many) job repetitions. For that reason, learning curves can have limited use for mass production and assembly-line-type jobs. A learning curve for this type of operation sometimes achieves any improvement early in the process and then flattens out and shows virtually no improvement, as reflected in Figure 8.5.

Figure 8.5
**Learning Curve for Mass Production Job**

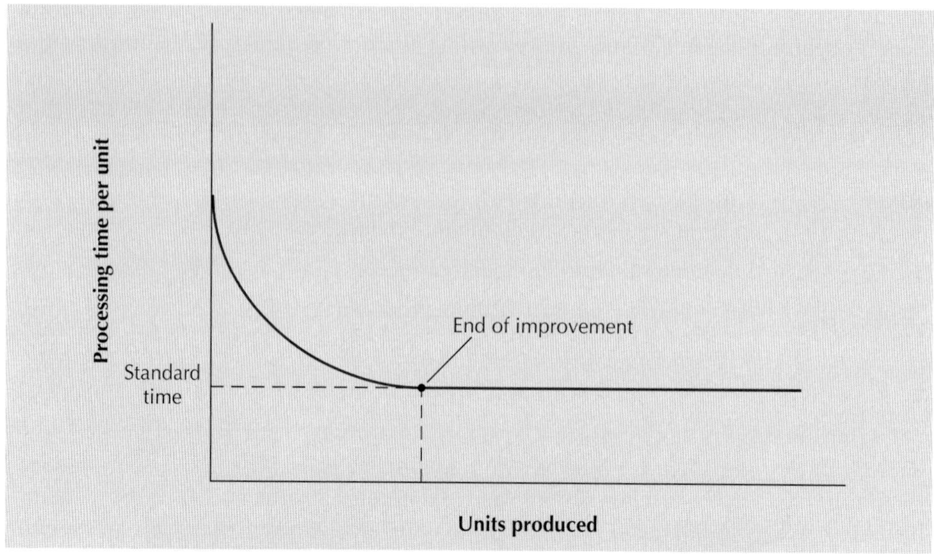

*Worker assembling P3C Orion Airframe. Aircraft manufacturers have long relied on learning curves for production planning. Learning curves were first recognized in the aircraft industry in 1936 by T. P. Wright. Aircraft production at that time required a large amount of direct labor for assembly work; thus any marked increases in productivity were clearly recognizable. Based on empirical analysis, Wright discovered that on average when output doubled in the aircraft industry, labor requirements decreased by approximately 20%; that is, an 80% learning curve. During World War II when aircraft manufacturing proliferated, the learning curve became a tool for planning and an integral part of military aircraft contracts. Studies during these years demonstrated the existence of the learning curve in other industries as well. For example, studies of historical production figures at Ford Motor Company from 1909 to 1926 showed productivity improved for the Model T according to an 86% learning curve. The learning curve effect was subsequently shown to exist not only in labor-intensive manufacturing but also in capital-intensive manufacturing industries such as petroleum refining, steel, paper, construction, electronics and apparel, as well as in clerical operations.*

Learning curves help managers project labor and budgeting requirements in order to develop production scheduling plans. Knowing how many production labor hours will be required over time can enable managers to determine the number of workers to hire. Also, knowing how many labor hours will eventually be required for a product can help managers make overall product cost estimates to use in bidding for jobs and later for determining the product selling price. However, product or other changes during the production process can negate the learning curve effect.

*Advantages of learning curves*: planning labor, budget, and scheduling requirements.

Although learning curves can be applied to many different businesses, its impact is most pronounced in businesses and industries that include complex, repetitive operations where the work pace is determined mostly by people, not machines. Examples of industries where the learning curve is used extensively include aerospace, electronics, shipbuilding, construction, and defense. The learning curve in the aerospace and shipbuilding industries is estimated to be 85%, while it is estimated to be 90% to 95% in the electronics industry. NASA, for example, uses the learning curve to estimate costs of space shuttle production and the times to complete tasks in space.

*Limitations of learning curves*: product modifications negate *lc* effect, improvement can derive from sources besides learning, industry-derived *lc* rates may be inappropriate.

## DETERMINING LEARNING CURVES WITH EXCEL

The Excel spreadsheet for Example 8.3 is shown in Exhibit 8.1. Notice that cell C8 is highlighted and the learning curve formula for computing the time required for the 9th unit is shown on the toolbar at the top of the screen. This formula includes the learning curve coefficient in cell D4, the time required for the first unit produced in cell D3, and the target unit in B8.

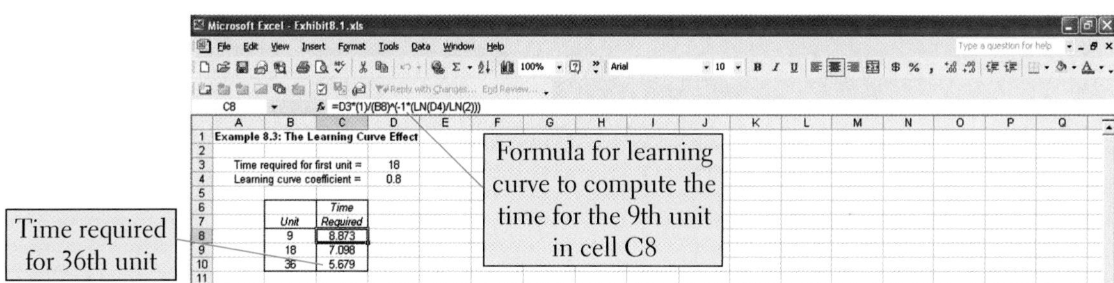


**Exhibit 8.1**

## SUMMARY

As with many other areas in production and operations management, the quality movement and increased international competition have had a dramatic impact on human resources. Traditional approaches to work in the United States that once focused on task specialization, simplification, and repetition are being supplanted by approaches that promote higher job skill levels, broader task responsibility, more worker involvement, and, most importantly, worker responsibility for quality. A number of U.S. manufacturing and service firms have attempted to adopt new approaches to human resources management.

## SUMMARY OF KEY FORMULAS

*Learning Curve Formula*

$$t_n = t_1 n^{\ln r/\ln 2}$$

## SUMMARY OF KEY TERMS

**alternative workplace** a combination of nontraditional work locations, settings and practices that supplements or replaces the traditional office.

**cross training** an employee learns more than one job in the organization.

**empowerment** the authority and responsibility of the workers to alert management about job-related problems.

**ergonomics** the application of human sciences like anatomy, physiology, and psychology to the design of the work environment and jobs, and objects and equipment used in work; fitting the task to the person.

**flextime** a work schedule in which fixed times of arrival and departure are replaced by a combination of fixed and variable times.

**gainsharing** an incentive plan that includes employees in a common effort to achieve a company's objectives in which they share in the gains.

**horizontal job enlargement** the scope of a job that includes all tasks necessary to complete a product or process.

**job** a defined set of tasks that comprise the work performed by employees that contributes to the production of a product or delivery of a service.

**job rotation** the horizontal movement between two or more jobs according to a plan or schedule.

**learning curve** a graph that reflects the improvement rate of workers as a job is repeated and more units are produced.

**motion study** the study of the individual human motions used in a task.

**process flowchart** a flowchart that illustrates, with symbols, the steps for a job or how several jobs fit together within the flow of the production process.

**profit sharing** the company sets aside a portion of profits and distributes it among employees usually at the end of the fiscal year.

**tasks** individual, defined job activities that consist of one or more elements.

**telecommuting** employees work electronically from whatever location they choose, either exclusively or some of the time.

**vertical job enlargement** the degree of self-determination and control allowed workers over their own work; also referred to as job enrichment.

**worker–machine chart** a chart that illustrates on a time scale the amount of time an operator and a machine are working or are idle in a job.

## SOLVED PROBLEM

### 1. LEARNING CURVE

A military contractor is manufacturing an electronic component for a weapons system. It is estimated from the production of a prototype unit that 176 hours of direct labor will be required to produce the first unit. The industrial standard learning curve for this type of component is 90%. The contractor wants to know the labor hours that will be required for the 144th (and last) unit produced.

### SOLUTION

Determine the time for the 144th unit.

$$t_n = t_1 n^b$$

$$t_{144} = (176)(144)^{\ln(0.9)/\ln 2}$$

$$= (176)(0.4698)$$

$$= 82.69 \text{ hours}$$

## QUESTIONS

**8-1.** Discuss how human resources affect a company's strategic planning process.

**8-2.** Why has "human resources" become popular in recent years?

**8-3.** Describe the characteristics of job design according to the scientific management approach.

**8-4.** Describe the contributions of F. W. Taylor and the Gilbreths to job design and analysis, and work measurement.

**8-5.** Explain the difference between horizontal and vertical job enlargement.

**8-6.** What is the difference between tasks, elements, and motions in a basic job structure?

**8-7.** How did the development of the assembly-line production process at Ford Motor Company popularize the scientific management approach to job design?

**8-8.** The principles of scientific management were not adopted in Japan during the first half of the twentieth century as they were in the United States and other Western nations. Speculate as to why this occurred.

**8-9.** Contrast the traditional U.S. approaches to job design with current trends.

**8-10.** What are the advantages of the scientific management approach to job design (specifically, task specialization, simplicity, and repetition) to both management and the worker?

**8-11.** Describe the primary characteristics of the behavioral approach to job design.

**8-12.** How has the increased emphasis on quality improvement affected human resources management in the United States?

**8-13.** How successful have companies in the United States been in adapting new trends in job design that mostly have originated in Japan?

**8-14.** Describe the three major categories of the elements of job design.

**8-15.** Describe the differences between a process flowchart and a worker–machine chart and what they are designed to achieve.

**8-16.** Pick an activity you are familiar with in your daily life such as washing a car, cutting grass, or taking a shower and develop a process flowchart for it.

**8-17.** Describe some of the advantages and disadvantages of telecommuting from both the employee and manager's perspective.

**8-18.** Why is empowerment a critical element in total quality management? What are the disadvantages of empowerment?

**8-19.** Select an article (or articles) from *HR Magazine* and write a report on a human resource management application in a company similar to the Competitive Edge boxes in this chapter.

**8-20.** Go to the Malcolm Baldrige Web site at http://www.quality.nist.gov and write a brief report on the role of human resource management at a Baldrige award-winning company or organization.

**8-21.** Select a workplace at your university such as an academic department office, the athletic department, the bookstore, and the cafeteria, and describe the compensation program for rank-and-file employees and any additional programs used to create job satisfaction and motivate employees. Also indicate the amount and type of job training and the involvement of employees in quality management. Identify any problems you see in the workplace environment and how it might be approved.

**8-22.** Describe a job you have had in the past or a job you are very familiar with and indicate the negative aspects of the job and how it could be improved with human resource management techniques.

**8-23.** For what type of jobs are learning curves most useful?

**8-24.** What does a learning curve specifically measure?

**8-25.** Discuss some of the uses and limitations of learning curves.

## PROBLEMS

**8-1.** The United Mutual and Accident Insurance Company has a large pool of clerical employees who process insurance application forms on networked computers. When the company hires a new clerical employee, it takes that person about 48 minutes to process a form. The learning curve for this job is 88%, but no additional learning will take place after about the 100th form is processed. United Mutual has recently acquired a smaller competitor that will add 800 new forms per week to its clerical pool. If an employee works six hours per day (excluding breaks, meals, and so on) per five-day week, how many employees would be hired to absorb the extra workload?

**8-2.** Professor Cook teaches operations management at State University. She is scheduled to give her class of 35 students a final exam on the last day of exam week, and she is leaving town the same day. She is concerned about her ability to finish grading her exams. She estimates that with everything else she has to do she has only five hours to grade the exams. From past experience she knows the first exam will take her about 12 minutes to grade. She estimates her learning curve to be about 90%, and it will be fully realized after about 10 exams. Will she get the exams graded on time?

**8-3.** Nite-Site, Inc., manufactures image intensification devices used in products such as night-vision goggles and aviator's night-vision imaging systems. The primary customer for these products is the U.S. military. The military requires that learning curves be employed in the bid process for awarding military contracts. The company is planning to make a bid for 120 image intensifiers to be used in a military vehicle. The company estimates the first unit will require 80 hours of direct labor to produce. The industry learning curve for this particular type of product is 92%. Determine how many hours will be required to produce the 60th and 120th units.

**8-4.** Jericho Vehicles manufactures special-purpose all-terrain vehicles primarily for the military and government agencies in the United States and for foreign governments. The company is planning to bid on a new all-terrain vehicle specially equipped for desert military action. The company has experienced an 87% learning curve in the past for producing similar vehicles. Based on a prototype model, it estimates the first vehicle produced will require 1600 hours of direct labor. The order is for 60 all-terrain vehicles. Determine the time that will be required for the 30th and 60th units.

**8-5.** Jericho Vehicles is considering making a bid for a mobile rocket-launching system for the U.S. military. However, the company has almost no experience in producing this type of vehicle. In an effort to develop a learning curve for the production of this new mobile weapon system, management has called contacts from several former competitors who went bankrupt. Although management could not obtain direct learning curve rates, they did learn from one contact that for a system with similar features, the first unit required 2400 hours of direct labor to produce and the 30th and final unit required 1450 hours to produce. Determine the learning curve rate for this vehicle.

**8-6.** PM Computer Services (described in Example 8.3) has received an order for 120 custom configured personal computers for a local business. Paulette and Maureen have so many orders that they can no longer perform the work themselves, and they must hire extra labor to assemble the units for this new order. They have hired eight students from the university to work part-time, 20 hours per week, to assemble the computers. Paulette and Maureen assembled a prototype unit and it required 26 hours of direct labor; from experience they know their computer assembly operation has an 84% learning curve. Approximately when will PM Computer Services be able to deliver the completed order?

**8-7.** Hanna's Super Service Burgers and Fries fast-food restaurant trains its new employees (all of which are part-time) for three days to assemble its different burgers. The most time-consuming item to assemble is the Super Mega-Burger because it includes a lot of ingredients. After three days of training, an employee can assemble his or her first Mega-Burger as a regular employee in an average of 126 seconds. The learning curve for this assembly operation is estimated to be 85%, and no additional learning will take place after assembly of the eightieth Mega-Burger. Determine how many seconds will be required for an employee to assemble his or her eightieth Mega-Burger.

**8-8.** The housekeeping staff at the five-star Ritz Hotel has a specific, detailed list of activities for cleaning an occupied room. Each activity is completed whether or not it looks like it is necessary. When the hotel hires a new housekeeper, it takes that employee about 55 minutes to clean a room the first time. The learning curve for this job is 92%, and the average minimum time for an experienced housekeeper to clean a room is 32 minutes. How many rooms will a newly hired housekeeper have to clean before it can be done in 32 minutes? If a housekeeper has an eight-hour work day with 1.5 hours off for lunch and breaks, how many work days will be required before the housekeeper is fully proficient and able to clean a room in the minimum average time?

**8-9.** Prior to the invention of the printing press in the mid-1400s, the process of producing fine books, called illuminated manuscripts, was strictly manual and performed by skilled craftsmen. A scribe would copy the manuscript in ornate handwriting (or calligraphy) from an original text called an exemplar, and artists decorated (or illuminated) the books with pictures. It is estimated that an apprentice scribe could initially copy approximately 50 lines per day. This roughly translates to about 15 minutes per line for a scribe just starting out. A scribe was generally thought to have completed his apprenticeship and was considered a craftsman after completing eight books where each book consisted of about 17,000 lines. (After eight books a scribe would show little additional improvement in accurate copying speed.) Assuming a learning curve of 91%, how long would it take for an experienced scribe to copy a line, and how many lines could he copy in a day?

## CASE PROBLEM 8.1

### *Maury Mills*

The Maury Mills Company is a producer and distributor of food products and handmade crafts located in southwest Virginia. Anne Maury and Dana Mills were roommates in college when they started selling homemade cookies, candy, apple butter, and breads at craft fairs in the region. As they attended craft fairs, they made acquaintances with a number of craftspeople, artisans, and vendors who also had booths. After Anne and Dana graduated from college with degrees in English and Theater Arts, respectively, they decided to start their own business selling crafts they would buy from the artisans they knew from craft fairs and food items they would make themselves or contract with locals to make. They leased a building previously occupied by an auto parts store to use as an office warehouse, and distribution center. Their plan was to sell their products to grocery stores, specialty food stores, and gift shops in the region.

Initially, Anne and Dana ran the business themselves. Anne did all the buying and bookkeeping while Dana handled sales. Both of them did a lot of telephoning and traveled around the region visiting their suppliers and potential customers, picking up purchased goods and making deliveries. In the evening and on weekends they made their own brand of cookies, candy, apple butter, breads, and cakes and packaged them. Their products sold well primarily because of their high quality and uniqueness, and both suppliers and customers liked the two hard-working ladies. They were able to purchase the crafts they sold at modest prices from local artisans, and because they had relatively low overhead and expenses and no employees, their profit margin was high. However, their business soon exceeded their capacity, and they began to hire additional employees. Initially, they hired high school students part time to help with strictly physical work like packaging, picking up purchased items, and making deliveries. However, they soon realized they needed more skilled, reliable, full-time employees, including people to handle phone orders and customer service. They moved their business out of the old building they were using into a new office and warehouse facility that included an on-site bakery and food processing plant.

Anne and Dana moved more into a managerial role and spent less direct hands-on time with operations, which was a new experience for them and one for which they did not feel totally prepared. Managing employees was a particularly daunting task, and they were forced to learn as they went along. They used basic common sense and a commitment to treating their employees fairly and nicely, which proved to be successful. They could not help feeling responsible for their employees' well-being, and they soon considered themselves a large family of friends who were all working together for a common goal.

Maury Mills's sales continued to grow at a rapid pace, profits were high, and the employee base expanded. With the help of an E-Business consultant, Maury Mills developed a Web site and a print catalogue and began selling to individuals, stores, and shops around the country through their catalogue and online. The two friends turned over more of the daily operation of the company to managers and stepped back to relax and take some time for their own lives. They enrolled in an executive MBA program in the Northeast. They also began to travel for business and pleasure, exploring new markets and suppliers overseas, and sometimes attending business seminars and workshops in Europe, Hong Kong, and the Caribbean to fill in some of the gaps in their business expertise.

Within a few years, the crafts and specialty products business became more competitive, and online Web sites and catalogues for craft items and food products began to proliferate. At Maury Mills this caused the cost of purchasing their products to increase, and profit margins began to decline. At the same time the economy went into recession, and sales decreased. Anne and Dana became concerned that the financial health of the business they worked so hard to establish and that had been so successful was in peril. They quickly re-immersed themselves in the daily operations of Maury Mills, but the problems seemed overwhelming. They felt that their employees had become complacent and spoiled and weren't as committed to the business as they had been when they were smaller and more of a family. Walking around their facilities, they felt they hardly knew anyone who worked for them. Despite the seminars and business courses they had attended, they decided to hire a management consulting firm to come in and advise them how to turn things around.

The consulting firm spent a month at Maury Mills analyzing the company's financial data and operations, and looking closely at its markets and customer base. Their report offered several sweeping recommendations. The consulting firm found that the market for craft and specialty products had become saturated while the market for their food products, especially in the region, was still strong. They therefore recommended Maury Mills cut back on their craft products business while expanding their food products business. Thus, their first recommendation was that the company workforce be cut by 20% in all areas except food products processing. Anne and Dana had earlier expressed their concern about employee malaise to the consulting team, and this group picked up on that. The consultants felt that the food products business could be increased without capital expansion by increasing productivity through adopting various incentive measures and compensation programs to motivate employees. They also suggested that employees in packaging and distribution be paid according to an incentive plan based on the number of packages they processed daily. Another recommendation was that all orders arriving in the distribution center by 3:00 P.M. should be processed and shipped that same day. These changes would not only increase productivity but also speed order fulfillment, which would appeal to customers. They recommended a group bonus plan tied to the percentage of incoming orders shipped the same day. The consultants also thought that phone operators currently spent too much time talking with customers and suppliers and that their calls should be cut from an average of 7 minutes to less than 4 minutes. It was recommended that employees in the food products area should also increase their productivity. A group incentive plan was suggested for the food products area that would provide monthly bonuses for increased productivity and for process improvements that would save food processing time and result in higher production levels. The report recommended that the sales force be placed on a partial commission plan based on dollar sales and that salespeople be empowered to offer discounts to customers to gain orders especially at food stores. It was also recommended that buyers be empowered to shop for lower cost goods and be paid a percentage of cost savings as bonuses. Anne and Dana adopted the consultants' recommendations across the board and instructed their managers to implement the changes.

Within a few months, productivity increased throughout the company; the volume of phone orders increased by over 50%; and despite cutbacks, the distribution center increased the number of packages it was processing on a daily basis by 40%, and the number of orders shipped the same day as received rose to 95%. The food products area showed an increase in its production rate of 30%. Sales were up and purchasing costs had decreased.

Anne and Dana felt a great sense of relief, but this feeling was short-lived. Six months later over the course of a few days, several events stunned them. First, Anne was grocery shopping at the local Kroger's when she eavesdropped on the following conversation between two shoppers:

"I hear things aren't going so well over at M 'n Ms"

"No, everybody seems to be at each other's throat and the whole place seems to be falling apart"

"What happened? It seemed to be such a great place to work when my sister was there back when they first started."

"Well, I don't know what it was like back then, but things aren't so nice now. We have a lot of irate customers and they're returning stuff right and left, and our supervisors are leaning on everyone to do more. Most of us are exhausted and fed up."

Anne couldn't believe what she had heard; she immediately told Dana, and they decided to investigate. Sure enough, they discovered that returns had increased substantially and were clogging the warehouse. When they asked the manager in charge why customers were returning items, he told them there were complaints of poor quality. The next day they received another jolt. Dana's secretary told her that a group of black and Hispanic employees from the warehouse and distribution center had asked for an appointment to see Anne and Dana. Upon asking what the purpose of the meeting was, Dana was told that there was a lot of built-up resentment over earlier cutbacks in the distribution center, which was made up mostly of minority employees, while at the same time there weren't any cutbacks in the food products area which was made up mostly of Caucasian employees. Dana's secretary also said that she had heard some complaining about inequities in the incentive plan that had been set up. Later that same day Anne received a phone call from Jim Barnett, the regional manager for the Market Place grocery chain. He told Anne that as a courtesy he wanted to personally let her know that they were not going to continue to carry Maury Mill's food products in their specialty foods sections at his stores. He said he regretted it, especially since they had enjoyed a long-standing positive relationship with Maury Mills and they had been providing such low prices in recent months, but they had received a lot of customer complaints about poor quality items. They had also received a lot of incomplete, late, and messed up orders; when they would call to try and resolve problems, the people they talked to were abrupt and seemed to be in a hurry to get off the phone. Immediately after this conversation ended, Anne went down to the sales office and discovered that there were a number of other old, established customers who were no longer placing orders. They also tracked several recent shipments and found that while orders were being processed on time, they often sat at the loading dock or were a long time in transit.

Anne and Dana were dazed. They were in worse shape than they had been before the changes!

Why do you think Maury Mills got in the shape it is? What are some of the mistakes you think they may have made in managing their human resources? What would you recommend that Dana and Anne do to resolve their problems? Are their problems solvable?

## REFERENCES


Barnes, R. M. *Motion and Time Study: Design and Measurement of Work*, 8th ed. New York: Wiley, 1980.

Belkaoui, A. *The Learning Curve*. Westport, CT: Quorum Books, 1986.

Emerson, H. P., and D. C. E. Maehring. *Origins of Industrial Engineering*. Atlanta: Institute of Industrial Engineers, 1988.

Evans, J. R., and W. M. Lindsay. *The Management and Control of Quality*, 3rd ed. St. Paul, MN: West, 1996.

Gilbreth, F. *Motion Study*. New York: Van Nostrand, 1911.

Herzberg, F. "One More Time: How Do You Motivate Employees?" *Harvard Business Review* 81 (1; January 2003), pp. 87–96.

Knights, D., H. Willmott, and D. Collinson, eds. *Job Redesign: Critical Perspectives on the Labor Process*. Hants, England: Gower, 1985.

Taylor, F. W. *The Principles of Scientific Management*. New York: Harper, 1911.

Wood, S., ed. *The Transformation of Work*. London: Unwin Hyman, 1989.

# Operational Decision-Making Tools: Work Measurement

SUPPLEMENT 8

## CHAPTER OUTLINE

**In this supplement, you will learn about . . .**

- **Time Studies**
- **Work Sampling**

*Work measurement* is determining how long it takes to do a job. Managing human resources requires managers to know how much work employees can do during a specific period. Otherwise they cannot plan production schedules or output. Without a good idea of how long it takes to do a job, a company will not know if it can meet customer expectations for delivery or service time. Despite the unpopularity of wage-incentive systems among some TQM proponents, they are still widely used in the United States, and work measurement is required to set the output standards on which incentive rates are based. These wage rates determine the cost of a product or service.

Work measurement has also seen a revival within the ever-growing service sector. Services tend to be labor-intensive, and service jobs, especially clerical ones, are often repetitive. For example, sorting mail in a postal service, processing income tax returns in the IRS, making hamburgers at McDonald's, and inputting data from insurance forms in a computer at Prudential are all repetitive service jobs that can be measured, and standards can be set for output and wages. As a result, work measurement is still an important aspect of operations management for many companies.

## TIME STUDIES

The traditional means for determining an estimate of the time to do a job has been the time study, in which a stopwatch is used to time the individual elements of a job. These elemental times are summed to get a time estimate for a job and then adjusted by a performance rating of the worker and an allowance factor for unavoidable delays, resulting in a **standard time**. The standard time is the time required by an "average" worker to perform a job once under normal circumstances and conditions.

**Standard time:** the time required by an average worker to perform a job once.

Incentive piece-rate wage system based on time study

Work measurement and time study were introduced by Frederick W. Taylor in the late 1880s and 1890s. One of his objectives was to determine a "fair" method of job performance evaluation and payment, which at that time was frequently a matter of contention between management and labor. The basic form of wage payment was an incentive piece-rate system, in which workers were paid a wage rate per unit of output instead of an hourly wage rate; the more workers produced, the more they earned. The problem with this system at the time was that there was no way to determine a "normal," or "fair," rate of output. Management wanted the normal rate high, labor wanted it low. Since management made pay decisions, the piece rate was usually "tight," making it hard for the worker to make the expected, or fair, output rate. Thus, workers earned less. This was the scenario in which Taylor introduced his time study approach to develop an equitable piece-rate wage system based on fair standard job times.

Stopwatch time study used for work measurement

The stopwatch time study approach for work measurement was popular and widespread into the 1970s. Many union contracts in the automotive, textile, and other manufacturing industries for virtually every production job in a company were based almost entirely on standard times developed from time studies. However, the basic principle underlying an incentive wage system is that pay is the sole motivation for work. We pointed out in chapter 8 that this principle has been disproved. In fact, in recent years incentive wage systems have been shown to inhibit quality improvement.

However, performance evaluation represents only one use for time study and work measurement. It is still widely used for planning purposes in order to predict the level of output a company might achieve in the future.

### STOPWATCH TIME STUDY

The result of a time study is a *standard time* for performing a repetitious job once. Time study is a statistical technique that is accurate for jobs that are highly repetitive.

The basic steps in a time study are:

Steps of a stopwatch time study

1. ***Establish the standard job method.*** The job should be analyzed using methods analysis to make sure the best method is being used.

*This person is performing a time study of an employee doing a manual task at a Hewlett-Packard plant. Although time studies are no longer as popular for establishing performance-based wage rates as they once were, they are still an effective means for studying jobs in order to improve them. Many jobs in manufacturing and especially in service businesses include simple, repetitive tasks, such as making a hamburger and wrapping it at McDonald's, checking in a rental car at Avis, or making a bed at a Ritz-Carlton. Reducing the time required to perform these tasks, while still making sure that they are done conscientiously and correctly by the employee, can result in quicker and more efficient customer service and improved quality. However, speed and quickness only translates to good quality if they result in customer satisfaction.*

2. ***Break down the job into elements.*** The job is broken down into short, elemental tasks with obvious "break points" between them. The more detailed the elements, the easier it is to eliminate elemental times that are not normally included in each job cycle and might abnormally affect the standard time.
3. ***Study the job.*** Times studies have traditionally been conducted using a stopwatch attached to a clipboard, although handheld electronic time-study machines (similar to an electronic calculator) are now available that store elemental times in a memory that can be transferred to a computer for processing. To conduct a time study with a stopwatch, the industrial engineer or technician takes a position near the worker and records each elemental time on an observation sheet. In recent years, video cameras have been used to videotape jobs, with the time study conducted outside the workplace at a later time.
4. ***Rate the worker's performance.*** As the time study is being conducted, the worker's performance is also rated by the person doing the study. The objective of the study is to determine a "normal," or average, time for the job, so the engineer/technician must adjust the elemental times up or down with a rating factor. A performance rating factor

**Determining the average time for a job**

of 100% reflects normal work performance, below 100% represents a below-average performance, and above 100% indicates performance better than normal. Rating factors usually range between 80% and 120%.

Judging job performance

The observer conducting the study must, in effect, "judge" the difficulty of the job and mentally assess what normal performance is, primarily in terms of *speed*. Effort, or physical exertion, can also be a characteristic of performance; however, it must be viewed with caution, since a poor worker might exhibit a lot of exertion, whereas a good worker might exhibit little exertion in doing the same job.

The performance rating factor is a crucial component of the time study, but it is also subjective. The person conducting the study must be very familiar with the job in order to rate the worker's performance accurately. Films and videos are available that show different levels of performance, effort, and speed for a variety of motions, tasks, and jobs. Even then it is often difficult to evaluate performance during an actual study.

Workers are not always cooperative, and they sometimes resent time studies, especially if they know they are being used to set wages. They will purposely slow or speed up their normal work rate, make frequent mistakes, or alter the normal work methods, all designed to disrupt the work study.

It is easy to understand why quality consultants and teachers perceive incentive wage systems and work measurement to be detrimental to quality improvement.

5. ***Compute the average time.*** Once a sufficient number of job cycles have been observed, an average time for each work element is calculated. We talk more about the appropriate number of cycles to include in the study a little later.

**Normal time:** the elemental average time multiplied by a performance rating.

6. ***Compute the normal time.*** The **normal time** is calculated by multiplying the elemental average time by the performance rating factor:

$$\text{Normal time} = (\text{elemental average time})(\text{rating factor})$$

or

Allowing for abnormal factors

$$\text{N}t = (\bar{t})(RF)$$

The normal cycle time (NT) is computed by summing the elemental normal times,

$$\text{NT} = \Sigma \text{N}t$$

7. ***Compute the standard time.*** The standard time is computed by adjusting the normal cycle time by an allowance factor for unavoidable work delays (such as a machine breakdown), personal delays (such as using the rest room), and normal mental or physical fatigue. The allowance factor is a percentage increase in the normal cycle time. The standard time is calculated as follows:

$$\text{Standard time} = (\text{normal cycle time})(1 + \text{allowance factor})$$

or

$$\text{ST} = (\text{NT})(1 + \text{AF})$$

Example S8.1

**Performing a Time Study and Developing a Standard Time**

The Metro Food Services Company delivers fresh sandwiches each morning to vending machines throughout the city. Workers work through the night to prepare the sandwiches for morning delivery. A worker normally makes several kinds of sandwiches. A time study for a worker making ham and cheese sandwiches is shown in Figure S8.1. Notice that each element has two readings. Row $t$ includes the individual elemental times, whereas the $R$ row contains a cumulative (running) clock reading recorded going down the column. In this case the individual elemental times are determined by subtracting the cumulative times between sequential readings.

*Solution*

In Figure S8.1 the average element times are first computed as

$$\bar{t} = \frac{\Sigma t}{10}$$

Time Study Observation Sheet

| Identification of operation | Sandwich Assembly | | Date 5/17 |
|---|---|---|---|
| | Operator Smith | Approval Jones | Observer Russell |

| | | | Cycles | | | | | | | | | | Summary | | | |
|---|---|---|---|---|---|---|---|---|---|---|---|---|---|---|---|---|
| | | | 1 | 2 | 3 | 4 | 5 | 6 | 7 | 8 | 9 | 10 | $\Sigma t$ | $\bar{t}$ | RF | Nt |
| 1 | Grasp and lay out bread slices | t | 0.04 | 0.05 | 0.05 | 0.04 | 0.06 | 0.05 | 0.06 | 0.06 | 0.07 | 0.05 | 0.53 | 0.053 | 1.05 | 0.056 |
| | | R | 0.04 | 0.38 | 0.72 | 1.05 | 1.40 | 1.76 | 2.13 | 2.50 | 2.89 | 3.29 | | | | |
| 2 | Spread mayonnaise on both slices | t | 0.07 | 0.06 | 0.07 | 0.08 | 0.07 | 0.07 | 0.08 | 0.10 | 0.09 | 0.08 | 0.77 | 0.077 | 1.00 | 0.077 |
| | | R | 0.11 | 0.44 | 0.79 | 1.13 | 1.47 | 1.83 | 2.21 | 2.60 | 2.98 | 3.37 | | | | |
| 3 | Place ham, cheese, and lettuce on bread | t | 0.12 | 0.11 | 0.14 | 0.12 | 0.13 | 0.13 | 0.13 | 0.12 | 0.14 | 0.14 | 1.28 | 0.128 | 1.10 | 0.141 |
| | | R | 0.23 | 0.55 | 0.93 | 1.25 | 1.60 | 1.96 | 2.34 | 2.72 | 3.12 | 3.51 | | | | |
| 4 | Place top on sandwich, slice, and stack | t | 0.10 | 0.12 | 0.08 | 0.09 | 0.11 | 0.11 | 0.10 | 0.10 | 0.12 | 0.10 | 1.03 | 0.103 | 1.10 | 0.113 |
| | | R | 0.33 | 0.67 | 1.01 | 1.34 | 1.71 | 2.07 | 2.44 | 2.82 | 3.24 | 3.61 | | | | |
| 5 | | t | | | | | | | | | | | | | | |
| | | R | | | | | | | | | | | | | | |
| 6 | | t | | | | | | | | | | | | | | |
| | | R | | | | | | | | | | | | | | |
| 7 | | t | | | | | | | | | | | | | | |
| | | R | | | | | | | | | | | | | | |
| 8 | | t | | | | | | | | | | | | | | |
| | | R | | | | | | | | | | | | | | |
| 9 | | t | | | | | | | | | | | | | | |
| | | R | | | | | | | | | | | | | | |
| 10 | | t | | | | | | | | | | | | | | |
| | | R | | | | | | | | | | | | | | |

Normal cycle time 0.387 + Allowance 15% = Std. time 0.445 min.

**Figure S8.1**

**Time Study Observation Sheet**

For element 1 the average time is

$$\bar{t} = \frac{0.53}{10} = 0.053$$

The normal elemental times are computed by adjusting the average time, $\bar{t}$, by the performance rating factor, RF. For element 1 the normal time is

$$\begin{aligned} \mathrm{N}t &= (\bar{t})(RF) \\ &= (0.053)(1.05) \\ &= 0.056 \end{aligned}$$

The normal cycle time, NT, is computed by summing the normal times for all elements, which for this example is 0.387. The standard time is computed by adjusting the normal cycle time by an allowance factor,

$$\begin{aligned} \mathrm{ST} &= (\mathrm{NT})(1 + \mathrm{AF}) \\ &= (0.387)(1 + 0.15) \\ &= 0.445 \text{ min} \end{aligned}$$

If, for example, the company wants to know how many ham and cheese sandwiches can be produced in a two-hour period, they could simply divide the standard time into 120 minutes:

$$\frac{120 \text{ min}}{0.445 \text{ min/sandwich}} = 269.7 \text{ or } 270 \text{ sandwiches}$$

**Example S8.2**

**An Incentive Piece-Rate System**

If the Metro Food Services Company pays workers a piece-rate of \$0.04 per sandwich, what would an average worker be paid per hour, and what would the subject of the time study in Example S8.1 expect to be paid?

*Solution*

The average worker would produce the following number of sandwiches in an hour:

$$\frac{60 \text{ min}}{0.445 \text{ min/sandwich}} = 134.8 \text{ or } 135 \text{ sandwiches}$$

The hourly wage rate would thus average

$$(135)(0.04) = \$5.40$$

Alternatively, the worker from Example S8.3 would produce at the average cycle time not adjusted by the rating factor, or 0.361 minute. Adjusting this time by the allowance time results in a time of

$$(0.361)(1 + 0.15) = 0.415 \text{ min}$$

This worker could be expected to produce the following number of sandwiches per hour:

$$\frac{60 \text{ min}}{0.415 \text{ min/sandwich}} = 144.6 \text{ or } 145 \text{ sandwiches}$$

The average hourly wage rate for this worker would be

$$(145)(0.04) = \$5.80$$

or \$0.40 more per hour.

An Excel spreadsheet of the time study observation sheet shown in Figure S8.1 is shown in Exhibit S8.1.

**Exhibit S8.1**

Microsoft Excel - ExhibitS8.1.XLS

**Example S8.2. Performing a Time Study**

Time Study Observation Sheet

Identification of Operation: *Sandwich Assembly* | Date *5/17*

Operator: *Smith* | Approval: *Jones* | Observer: *Tillar*

| | | Cycles | | | | | | | | | | Summary | | | |
|---|---|---|---|---|---|---|---|---|---|---|---|---|---|---|---|
| | | 1 | 2 | 3 | 4 | 5 | 6 | 7 | 8 | 9 | 10 | *Sum t* | *t* | *RF* | *Nt* |
| 1. Grasp and lay out | *t* | 0.04 | 0.05 | 0.05 | 0.04 | 0.06 | 0.05 | 0.06 | 0.06 | 0.07 | 0.05 | 0.53 | 0.053 | 1.05 | 0.056 |
| bread slices | *R* | 0.04 | 0.38 | 0.72 | 1.05 | 1.40 | 1.76 | 2.13 | 2.50 | 2.89 | 3.29 | | | | |
| 2. Spread mayonaise | *t* | 0.07 | 0.06 | 0.07 | 0.08 | 0.07 | 0.07 | 0.08 | 0.10 | 0.09 | 0.08 | 0.77 | 0.077 | 1.00 | 0.077 |
| on both slices | *R* | 0.11 | 0.44 | 0.79 | 1.13 | 1.47 | 1.83 | 2.21 | 2.60 | 2.98 | 3.37 | | | | |
| 3. Place ham,cheese | *t* | 0.12 | 0.11 | 0.14 | 0.12 | 0.13 | 0.13 | 0.13 | 0.12 | 0.14 | 0.14 | 1.28 | 0.128 | 1.10 | 0.141 |
| and lettuce on bread | *R* | 0.23 | 0.55 | 0.93 | 1.25 | 1.60 | 1.96 | 2.34 | 2.72 | 3.12 | 3.51 | | | | |
| 4. Place top, slice | *t* | 0.10 | 0.12 | 0.08 | 0.09 | 0.11 | 0.11 | 0.10 | 0.10 | 0.12 | 0.10 | 1.03 | 0.103 | 1.10 | 0.113 |
| and stack | R | 0.33 | 0.67 | 1.01 | 1.34 | 1.71 | 2.07 | 2.44 | 2.82 | 3.24 | 3.61 | | | | |

Normal cycle time = *0.387* + Allowance *15%* = Standard time *0.445 min.*

## NUMBER OF CYCLES

Determining the statistically appropriate number of job cycles to study

In Example S8.1 the time study was conducted for 10 cycles. However, was this sufficient for us to have confidence that the standard time was accurate? The time study is actually a statistical sample distribution, where the number of cycles is the sample size.

Assuming that this distribution of sample times is normally distributed (a traditional assumption for time study), we can use the following formula to determine the sample size, $n$, for a time study:

$$n = \left(\frac{zs}{eT}\right)^2$$

where

$z$ = the number of standard deviations from the mean in a normal distribution reflecting a level of statistical confidence

$s = \sqrt{\dfrac{\Sigma(x_i - \bar{x})^2}{n-1}}$ = sample standard deviation from the sample time study

$\bar{T}$ = the average job cycle time from the sample time study

$e$ = the degree of error from the true mean of the distribution

**Example S8.3**

**Determining the Number of Cycles for a Time Study**

In Example S8.1 the Metro Food Services Company conducted a time study for 10 cycles of a job assembling ham and cheese sandwiches, which we will consider to be a sample. The average cycle time, $\bar{T}$, for the job was 0.361 minute, computed by dividing the total time for 10 cycles of the job, 3.61, by the number of cycles, 10. The standard deviation of the sample was 0.03 minute. The company wants to determine the number of cycles for a time study such that it can be 95% confident that the average time computed from the time study is within 5% of the true average cycle time.

*Solution*

The sample size is computed using $z = 1.96$ for a probability of 0.95, as follows:

$$n = \left(\frac{zs}{e\bar{T}}\right)^2 = \left[\frac{(1.96)(0.03)}{(0.05)(0.361)}\right]^2 = 10.61, \text{ or } 11$$

The time study should include 11 cycles to be 95% confident that the time-study average job cycle time is within 5% of the true average job cycle time. The 10 cycles that were used in our time study were just about right.

## ELEMENTAL TIME FILES

Workers often do not like to be the subject of a time study and will not cooperate, and rating workers can be a difficult, subjective task. Time studies can also be time-consuming and costly. As an alternative, many companies have accumulated large files of time-study data over time for elements common to many jobs throughout their organization. Instead of conducting an actual time study, these **elemental standard time files** can be accessed to derive the standard time, or the elemental times in the files can be used in conjunction with current time-study data, reducing the time and cost required for the study.

**Elemental standard time files:** predetermined job element times.

It can be difficult, however, to put together a standard time without the benefit of a time study. The engineer/technician is left wondering if anything was left out or if the environment or job conditions have changed enough since the data were collected to alter the original elemental times. Also, the individuals who develop the current standard time must have a great deal of confidence in their predecessor's abilities and competence.

## PREDETERMINED MOTION TIMES

The use of elemental standard times from company files is one way to construct a standard time without a time study, or before a task or job is even in effect yet. Another approach for developing time standards without a time study is to use a system of **predetermined motion times**. A predetermined motion time system provides normal times for basic, generic micromotions, such as reach, grasp, move, position, and release, that are common to many jobs. These basic motion times have been developed in a laboratory-type environment from studies of workers across a variety of industries and, in some cases, from motion pictures of workers.

**Predetermined motion times:** predetermined times for basic micromotions.

To develop a standard time using predetermined motion times, a job must be broken down into its basic micromotions. Then the appropriate motion time is selected from a set of tables (or a computerized database), taking into account job conditions such as the weight of an object moved and the distance it might be moved. The standard time is determined by summing all the motion times. As might be suspected, even a very short job can have many motions; a job of only 1 minute can have more than 100 basic motions.

*Advantages of predetermined motion times*: worker cooperation unnecessary, workplace uninterrupted, performance ratings unnecessary, consistent.

Several systems of predetermined motion times exist, the two most well known being methods time measurement (MTM) and basic motion time study (BMT). Table S8.1 provides an example of an MTM table for the motion *move*. The motion times are measured in *time measurement units*, or *TMUs*, where one TMU equals 0.0006 minute and 100,000 TMUs equal 1 hour.

There are several advantages of using a predetermined motion time system. It enables a standard time to be developed for a new job before the job is even part of the production process. Worker cooperation and compliance are not required, and the workplace is not disrupted. Performance ratings are included in the motion times, eliminating this subjective part of developing standard times.

*Disdvantages of predetermined motion times*: ignores job context, may not reflect skills and abilities of local workers.

There are also disadvantages with a predetermined motion time system. It ignores the job context within which a single motion takes place—that is, where each motion is considered independently of all others. What the hand comes from doing when it reaches for an object may affect the motion time as well as the overall sequence of motion. Also, although predetermined motion times are generally determined from a broad sample of workers across several industries, they may not reflect the skill level, training, or abilities of workers in a specific company.

Table S8.1
**MTM Table For *Move***

| | Time (TMU) | | | | Weight Allowance | | | |
|---|---|---|---|---|---|---|---|---|
| Distance Moved (inches) | A | B | C | Hand In Motion B | Weight (lb) up to: | Dynamic Factor | Static Constant TMU | Case and Description |
| ¾ or less | 2.0 | 2.0 | 2.0 | 1.7 | | | | |
| 1 | 2.5 | 2.9 | 3.4 | 2.3 | 2.5 | 1.00 | 0 | |
| 2 | 3.6 | 4.6 | 5.2 | 2.9 | | | | A. Move object to other hand or against stop. |
| 3 | 4.9 | 5.7 | 6.7 | 3.6 | 7.5 | 1.06 | 2.2 | |
| 4 | 6.1 | 6.9 | 8.0 | 4.3 | | | | |
| 5 | 7.3 | 8.0 | 9.2 | 5.0 | 12.5 | 1.11 | 3.9 | |
| 6 | 8.1 | 8.9 | 10.3 | 5.7 | | | | |
| 7 | 8.9 | 9.7 | 11.1 | 6.5 | 17.5 | 1.17 | 5.6 | |
| 8 | 9.7 | 10.6 | 11.8 | 7.2 | | | | |
| 9 | 10.5 | 11.5 | 12.7 | 7.9 | 22.5 | 1.22 | 7.4 | B. Move object to approximate or indefinite location. |
| 10 | 11.3 | 12.2 | 13.5 | 8.6 | | | | |
| 12 | 12.9 | 13.4 | 15.2 | 10.0 | 27.5 | 1.28 | 9.1 | |
| 14 | 14.4 | 14.6 | 16.9 | 11.4 | | | | |
| 16 | 16.0 | 15.8 | 18.7 | 12.8 | 32.5 | 1.33 | 10.8 | |
| 18 | 17.6 | 17.0 | 20.4 | 14.2 | | | | |
| 20 | 19.2 | 18.2 | 22.1 | 15.6 | 37.5 | 1.39 | 12.5 | |
| 22 | 20.8 | 19.4 | 23.8 | 17.0 | | | | |
| 24 | 22.4 | 20.6 | 25.5 | 18.4 | 42.5 | 1.44 | 14.3 | C. Move object to exact location. |
| 26 | 24.0 | 21.8 | 27.3 | 19.8 | | | | |
| 28 | 25.5 | 23.1 | 29.0 | 21.2 | 47.5 | 1.50 | 16.0 | |
| 30 | 27.1 | 24.3 | 30.7 | 22.7 | | | | |
| Additional | 0.8 | 0.6 | 0.85 | | | TMU per inch over 30 in. | | |

*Source:* MTM Association for Standards and Research.

## WORK SAMPLING

**Work sampling** is a technique for determining the proportion of time a worker or machine spends on various activities. The procedure for work sampling is to make brief, random observations of a worker or machine over a period of time and record the activity in which they are involved. An estimate of the proportion of time that is being spent on an activity is determined by dividing the number of observations recorded for that activity by the total number of observations. A work sample can indicate the proportion of time a worker is busy or idle or performing a task or how frequently a machine is idle or in use. A secretary's work can be sampled to determine what portion of the day is spent word processing, answering the telephone, filing, and so on. It also can be used to determine the allowance factor that was used to calculate the standard time for a time study. (Recall that the allowance factor was a percentage of time reflecting worker delays and idle time for machine breakdowns, personal needs, and so on.)

**Work sampling:** determines the proportion of time a worker spends on activities.

At Lands' End, the catalogue retailer, phone sales representatives should be busy about 85% of the time and idle about 15%. If phone occupancy increases to 89%, the company knows it cannot meet its service goal.

The primary uses of work sampling are to determine *ratio delay*, which is the percentage of time a worker or machine is delayed or idle, and to analyze jobs that have *nonrepetitive tasks*—for example, a secretary, a nurse, or a police officer. The information from a work sample in the form of the percentage of time spent on each job activity or task can be useful in designing or redesigning jobs, developing job descriptions, and determining the level of work output that can be expected from a worker for use in planning.

The steps in work sampling are summarized as follows:

Steps of work sampling

1. ***Define the job activities.*** The activities that are to be observed must be exhaustive so that any time an observation is made, an activity is clearly indicated. For example, if the activities of interest are "worker idle" and "worker not idle," this clearly defines all possible activities for the work sample.
2. ***Determine the number of observations in the work sample.*** The purpose of the work sample is to calculate a proportion of time that a worker is performing a specific job activity. The degree of accuracy of the work sample depends on the number of observations, or sample size. The larger the sample size, the more accurate the proportion estimate will be. The accuracy of the proportion, $p$, is usually expressed in terms of an allowable degree of error, $e$ (for example, 3 or 4%), with a degree of confidence of, for example, 95 to 98%. Using these parameters and assuming the sample is approximately normally distributed, we can determine the sample size using the following formula:

$$n = \left(\frac{z}{e}\right)^2 p(1 - p)$$

where

$n$ = the sample size (number of sample observations)

$z$ = the number of standard deviations from the mean for the desired level of confidence

$e$ = the degree of allowable error in the sample estimate

$p$ = the proportion of time spent on a work activity estimated prior to calculating the work sample

3. ***Determine the length of the sampling period.*** The length of the work sampling study must be sufficient to record the number of observations for the work activity determined in step 2. The schedule of observations must be random. (If workers knew an observation would be taken every half hour, they might alter their normal work activity.) The most direct way to achieve randomness is to tie the observation schedule to a table or computer program of random numbers. For example, if a table of three-digit random numbers is used, the first one or two random numbers in the digit could specify the time in minutes between observations.
4. ***Conduct the work sampling study and record the observations.*** In the final step the observations are tallied, and the proportion, $p$, is computed by dividing the number of activity observations by the total number of observations.

5. ***Periodically recompute the number of observations.*** Recall from step 2 that $p$ is an estimate of the proportion of time spent on a work activity made prior to the sample. As the work sample is conducted, it may be discovered that the actual proportion is different from what was originally estimated. Therefore, it is beneficial periodically to recompute the sample size, $n$, based on preliminary values of $p$ to see if more or fewer observations are needed than first determined.

Example S8.4

**Conducting a Work Sampling Study**

The Northern Lights Company is a retail catalogue operation specializing in outdoor clothing. The company has a pool of 28 telephone operators to take catalogue orders during the business hours of 9 A.M. to 5:00 P.M. (The company uses a smaller pool of operators for the remaining 16 off-peak hours.) The company has recently been experiencing a larger number of lost calls because operators are busy and suspects it is because the operators are spending around 30% of their time describing products to customers. The company believes that if operators knew more about the products instead of having to pull up a description screen on the computer each time a customer asked a question about a product, they could save a lot of operator time, so it is thinking about instituting a product awareness training program. However, first the company wants to perform a work sampling study to determine the proportion of time operators are answering product-related questions. The company wants the proportion of this activity to be accurate within ±2%, with a 95% degree of confidence.

*Solution*

First determine the number of observations to take, as follows:

$$\begin{aligned} n &= \left(\frac{z}{e}\right)^2 p(1-p) \\ &= \left(\frac{1.96}{0.02}\right)^2 (0.3)(0.7) \\ &= 2016.84, \text{ or } 2017 \end{aligned}$$

This is a large number of observations; however, since there are 28 operators, only 2017/28, or 72, visits to observe the operators need to be taken. Actually, the observations could be made by picking up a one-way phone line to listen in on the operator–customer conversation. The "conversation" schedule was set up using a two-digit random number table (similar to Table S12.3). The random numbers are the minutes between each observation, and since the random numbers ranged from 00 to 99, the average time between observations is about 50 minutes. The study was expected to take about 8 days (with slightly more than 9 observations per day).

In fact, after 10 observation trips and a total of 280 observations, the portion of time the operators spent answering the customers' product-related questions was 38%, so the random sample size was recomputed:

$$\begin{aligned} n &= \left(\frac{1.96}{0.02}\right)^2 (0.38)(0.62) \\ &= 2263 \end{aligned}$$

This number of observations is 246 more than originally computed, or almost 9 additional observation trips, resulting in a total of 81. (As noted previously, it is beneficial periodically to recompute the sample size based on preliminary results in order to ensure that the final result will reflect the degree of accuracy and confidence originally specified.)

Work sampling is a cheaper, easier approach to work measurement.

Work sampling is an easier, cheaper, and quicker approach to work measurement than time study. It tends to be less disruptive of the workplace and less annoying to workers, because it requires much less time to sample than time study. Also, the "symbolic" stopwatch is absent. A disadvantage is the large number of observations needed to obtain an accurate sample estimate, sometimes requiring the study to span several days or weeks.

## SUMMARY

As the nature of work changes, the techniques and approaches to methods analysis and work measurement also change. Time study has historically been used to establish piece-rate incentive wage systems; however, as such systems are increasingly being perceived as counter to quality-improvement efforts, work measurement and time study are being used less and less for that purpose. However, work-measurement techniques are still useful and widely used, especially in service companies, for production planning, scheduling, and cost control.

## SUMMARY OF KEY FORMULAS

*Normal Elemental Time*

$$Nt = (\bar{t})(RF)$$

*Normal Cycle Time*

$$NT = \Sigma\, Nt$$

*Standard Job Time*

$$ST = (NT)(1 + AF)$$

*Time-Study Sample Size*

$$n = \left(\frac{zs}{e\bar{T}}\right)^2$$

*Work Sampling Sample Size*

$$n = \left(\frac{z}{e}\right)^2 p(1 - p)$$

## SUMMARY OF KEY TERMS

**elemental standard time files** company files containing historical data of elemental time studies that can be used to develop a standard time.

**job motions** basic physical movements that comprise a job element.

**normal time** in a time study, the elemental average time multiplied by a performance rating.

**predetermined motion times** normal times for basic, generic micromotions developed by an outside organization in a laboratory-type environment.

**standard time** the time required by an "average" worker to perform a job once under normal circumstances and conditions.

**work sampling** a technique for determining the proportion of time a worker or machine spends on job activities.

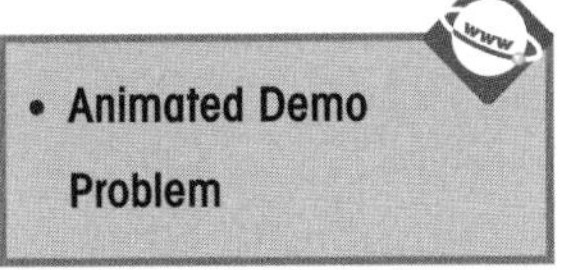


## SOLVED PROBLEMS

### 1. STANDARD JOB TIME

A manufacturing company has conducted a time study for 10 cycles of a job. The job has five elements, and the total elemental times (minutes) for each element and performance rating factors are as follows:

| ELEMENT | $\Sigma t$ (MIN) | *RF* |
|---|---|---|
| 1 | 3.61 | 1.05 |
| 2 | 4.84 | 0.90 |
| 3 | 2.93 | 1.00 |
| 4 | 4.91 | 1.10 |
| 5 | 1.78 | 0.95 |

Compute the standard time using an allowance factor of 18%.

### SOLUTION

*Step 1.* Determine the normal elemental times by multiplying the average elemental times by the rating factors.

| ELEMENT | $\Sigma t$ | $\bar{t}$ | *RF* | $N\bar{t}$ |
|---|---|---|---|---|
| 1 | 3.61 | 0.361 | 1.05 | 0.379 |
| 2 | 4.84 | 0.484 | 0.90 | 0.436 |
| 3 | 2.93 | 0.293 | 1.00 | 0.293 |
| 4 | 4.91 | 0.491 | 1.10 | 0.542 |
| 5 | 1.78 | 0.178 | 0.95 | 0.169 |

*Step 2.* Compute the normal cycle time.

$$NT = \Sigma\, Nt = 1.819 \text{ min}$$

*Step 3.* Compute the standard time.

$$ST = NT(1 + AF) = 1.819(1 + 0.18) = 2.146 \text{ min}$$

**2. TIME-STUDY SAMPLE SIZE**

For the previous problem, determine the sample size, $n$, for a time study so there is 98% confidence that the average time computed from the time study is within 4% of the actual average cycle time. The sample standard deviation is 0.23.

**SOLUTION**

*Step 1.* Determine the value of $z$ for a probability of 0.98 from the normal table in Appendix A and $\bar{t}$.

$$\bar{T} = \Sigma \bar{t} = 1.807 \text{ min}$$

$$z = 2.33$$

*Step 2.* Compute the sample size.

$$n = \left(\frac{zs}{e\bar{T}}\right)^2$$

$$= \left[\frac{(2.33)(0.23)}{(0.04)(1.807)}\right]^2$$

$$= 54.97, \text{ or } 55 \text{ cycles}$$

**3. WORK SAMPLING**

A technician is conducting a work sampling study of a machine maintenance worker to determine the portion of the time the worker spends in one particular department. Management has indicated that they believe that repairs in this department consume 50% of the maintenance worker's time, and they want the estimate to be within ±5 percent of the true proportion, with 95% confidence.

**SOLUTION**

Determine the number of observations in the sample.

$$n = \left(\frac{z}{e}\right)^2 p(1 - p)$$

$$= \left(\frac{1.96}{0.05}\right)^2 (0.5)(0.5)$$

$$= 384.16, \text{ or } 385 \text{ observations}$$

## QUESTIONS

**S8-1.** Compare the use of predetermined motion times for developing time standards instead of using time-study methods, and discuss the advantages and disadvantages.

**S8-2.** Describe the steps involved in conducting a time study, and discuss any difficulties you might envision at various steps.

**S8-3.** What are some of the criticisms of work measurement, in general, and time study, specifically, that have caused its popularity to wane in recent years?

**S8-4.** A traditional performance rating benchmark (or guideline) for "normal" effort, or speed, is dealing 52 cards into four piles, forming a square with each pile 1 foot apart, in 0.50 minute. Conduct an experiment with one or more fellow students in which one deals the cards and the others rate the dealer's performance, and then compare these subjective ratings with the actual time of the dealer.

**S8-5.** When conducting a work sampling study, how can the number of observations required by the study be reduced?

**S8-6.** When is work sampling a more appropriate work-measurement technique than time study?

**S8-7.** Describe the steps involved in conducting a work sample.

**S8-8.** Select a job that you are conveniently able to observe, such as a secretary, store clerk, or custodian, and design a work sampling study for a specific job activity. Indicate how the initial estimate of the proportion of time for the activity would be determined and how the observation schedule would be developed. (However, do not conduct the actual study.)

## PROBLEMS

**S8-1.** A time-study technician at the Southern Textile Company has conducted a time study of a spinning machine operator that spins rough cotton yarn into a finer yarn on bobbins for use in a weaving operation. The time study was requested as the result of a union grievance. The average cycle time for the operator to replace all the full bobbins on the machine with empty bobbins was 3.62 minutes. The technician assigned an overall performance rating for the job of 100%, and the allowance factor specified by the union contract is 15%. Compute the standard time for this job.

**S8-2.** A sewing operator at the Gameday Sportswear Company assembles baseball-style caps with a team logo from precut wedges of material that form the crown, a precut bill, and additional precut pieces of material for the headband and reinforcing. The job encompasses seven basic elements. A time technician for the company has conducted a time study of the job for 20 cycles and accumulated for the following elemental times and assigned performance ratings:

| Element | $\Sigma t$ | *RF* |
|---|---|---|
| 1 | 3.15 | 1.10 |
| 2 | 8.67 | 1.05 |
| 3 | 14.25 | 1.10 |
| 4 | 11.53 | 1.00 |
| 5 | 6.91 | 0.95 |
| 6 | 5.72 | 1.05 |
| 7 | 5.38 | 1.05 |

Determine the standard time for this job using an allowance factor of 12%.

**S8-3.** The Braykup China Company makes an assortment of gift and commemorative items with team and college logos, such as plates, bowls, and mugs. One popular item is a commemorative stein. The steins are all physically identical, with the only style change being the team colors, name, and logo. The stein parts include a porcelain mug, a hinged pewter top that is opened up when someone drinks from the mug, and a bracket that attaches the top to the mug handle. The bracket is soldered together from two matching parts; on one end, the bracket encircles the handle and the other end attaches to the lid mechanism. The stein is assembled from these parts in one job. A time-study chart for this job with the elements of the job and the time observations obtained from a stopwatch time study are shown below.

a. Using an allowance factor of 15%, determine the standard time for this job.

b. If the company pays workers a piece rate of $0.18 per stein, what wage would an average worker make per hour and what would the subject of this time study make per hour?

**S8-4.** Puff 'n' Stuff Services is a small company that assembles mailings for clients in the Atlanta area. Different-size envelopes are stuffed with various items such as coupons, advertisements, political messages, and so on, by a staff of workers, who are paid on a piece-rate basis. A time study of a job has been conducted by an engineering consulting firm using a subject stuffing manila envelopes. The observations from the time study for 10 cycles of the five-element job and the performance rating for each element are as follows.

| Element | Elemental Times (min) 1 | 2 | 3 | 4 | 5 | 6 | 7 | 8 | 9 | 10 | RF |
|---|---|---|---|---|---|---|---|---|---|---|---|
| 1 | 0.09 | 0.10 | 0.12 | 0.09 | 0.08 | 0.07 | 0.09 | 0.06 | 0.10 | 0.09 | 1.10 |
| 2 | 0.08 | 0.09 | 0.08 | 0.07 | 0.10 | 0.10 | 0.08 | 0.06 | 0.11 | 0.09 | 0.95 |
| 3 | 0.15 | 0.13 | 0.14 | 0.16 | 0.12 | 0.15 | 0.16 | 0.15 | 0.15 | 0.14 | 0.90 |
| 4 | 0.10 | 0.09 | 0.09 | 0.08 | 0.11 | 0.08 | 0.09 | 0.10 | 0.10 | 0.09 | 1.00 |
| 5 | 0.06 | 0.05 | 0.09 | 0.06 | 0.07 | 0.05 | 0.08 | 0.05 | 0.09 | 0.07 | 0.95 |

a. Using an allowance factor of 10%, compute the standard time for this job.

b. If the firm pays workers a piece rate of $0.03 per envelope for this job, what would the average worker make per hour, and what would the subject of the study make per hour?

**S8-5.** The Konishi Electronics Company manufactures computer microchips. A particular job that has been under analysis as part of a quality-improvement program was the subject of a time study. The time study encompassed 20 job cycles, and the results include the following cumulative times and performance rating factors for each element:

| Element | $\Sigma$ *T* (min) | RF |
|---|---|---|
| 1 | 10.52 | 1.15 |
| 2 | 18.61 | 1.10 |
| 3 | 26.20 | 1.10 |
| 4 | 16.46 | 1.05 |

a. Compute the standard time for this job using an allowance factor of 15%.

Time-Study Observation Sheet

Identification of operation: *Stein assembly* — Date: *7/15*

Operator: *Smith* — Approval: *Jones* — Observer: *Russell*

| | | | Cycles 1 | 2 | 3 | 4 | 5 | 6 | 7 | 8 | 9 | 10 | Summary $\Sigma t$ | $\bar{t}$ | RF | Nt |
|---|---|---|---|---|---|---|---|---|---|---|---|---|---|---|---|---|
| 1 | *Place mug in vise/ holder upside down* | *t* | | | | | | | | | | | | | | |
| | | *R* | 0.12 | 2.05 | 4.04 | 5.92 | 7.86 | 9.80 | 11.73 | 13.65 | 15.64 | 17.59 | | | 1.05 | |
| 2 | *Press both bracket sides around handle* | *t* | | | | | | | | | | | | | | |
| | | *R* | 0.19 | 2.12 | 4.09 | 6.01 | 7.94 | 9.88 | 11.81 | 13.72 | 15.7 | 17.66 | | | 1.00 | |
| 3 | *Solder bracket seam on inside of handle* | *t* | | | | | | | | | | | | | | |
| | | *R* | 1.05 | 3.01 | 4.91 | 6.87 | 8.81 | 10.71 | 12.66 | 14.56 | 16.52 | 18.50 | | | 1.10 | |
| 4 | *Turn stein right side up* | *t* | | | | | | | | | | | | | | |
| | | *R* | 1.13 | 3.08 | 4.98 | 6.93 | 8.90 | 10.79 | 12.74 | 14.66 | 16.63 | 18.59 | | | 1.10 | |
| 5 | *Solder lid top to bracket* | *t* | | | | | | | | | | | | | | |
| | | *R* | 1.75 | 3.76 | 5.65 | 7.60 | 9.56 | 11.45 | 13.36 | 15.34 | 17.31 | 19.28 | | | 1.05 | |
| 6 | *Remove stein from holder and place in box* | *t* | | | | | | | | | | | | | | |
| | | *R* | 1.91 | 3.90 | 5.79 | 7.75 | 9.70 | 11.61 | 13.53 | 15.49 | 17.46 | 19.44 | | | 1.00 | |
| | | *t* | | | | | | | | | | | | | | |

b. Using a sample standard deviation of 0.51 minutes, determine the number of cycles for this time study such that the company would be 95% confident that the average time from the time study is within 5% of the true average cycle time.

**S8-6.** Data Products, Inc., packages and distributes a variety of personal computer-related products. A time study has been conducted for a job packaging 3.5-inch personal computer diskettes for shipment to customers. The job requires a packager to place 20 diskettes in a rectangular plastic bag, close the bag with a twist tie, and place the filled bag into a bin, which is replaced by another worker when it is filled. The job can be broken into four basic elements. The elemental times (in minutes) were obtained from the time study for 10 job cycles shown in the following table.

| | Elemental Times | | | | | | | | | | |
|---|---|---|---|---|---|---|---|---|---|---|---|
| **Element** | *1* | *2* | *3* | *4* | *5* | *6* | *7* | *8* | *9* | *10* | *RF* |
| 1 | 0.36 | 0.31 | 0.42 | 0.35 | 0.38 | 0.30 | 0.41 | 0.42 | 0.35 | 0.35 | 1.05 |
| 2 | 0.81 | 0.95 | 0.76 | 0.85 | 1.01 | 1.02 | 0.95 | 0.90 | 0.87 | 0.88 | 0.90 |
| 3 | 0.56 | 0.38 | 0.42 | 0.45 | 0.51 | 0.48 | 0.50 | 0.52 | 0.39 | 0.46 | 1.00 |
| 4 | 0.19 | 0.12 | 0.16 | 0.21 | 0.15 | 0.16 | 0.18 | 0.19 | 0.19 | 0.15 | 1.05 |

a. Using an allowance factor of 16%, determine the standard time for this job.

b. Determine the number of cycles for this time study such that the company would be 95% confident that the average time from the time study is within ±4% of the true average cycle time.

**S8-7.** In Problem S8-2, a time study was conducted for the job of sewing baseball-style caps. Using a sample standard deviation of 0.25, determine the number of cycles for the time study such that the company would be 98% confident that the average cycle time for the job is within 6% of the actual average cycle time.

**S8-8.** Determine the sample size for the time study of the stein assembly operation described in Problem S8-3. The Braykup China Company wants to be 95% confident that the average cycle time from the study is within 2% of the true average.

**S8-9.** Sonichi Electronics manufactures small electronic consumer items such as portable clocks, calculators, and radios. The company is concerned about the high cost of its product-inspection operation. As a result, it had its industrial engineering department conduct a time study of an inspector who inspects portable radios. The operation consists of seven elements, as follows: (1) The package is opened and the radio is removed; (2) the battery casing cover is removed; (3) two AA batteries are inserted; (4) the radio is turned on, and the inspector tunes to a station and listens briefly to at least two stations; (5) the radio is turned off and the batteries are removed; (6) the battery cover is replaced; and (7) the radio is repackaged. The time-study observations (in minutes) for 10 cycles are shown in the following table.

| | Elemental Times | | | | | | | | | | |
|---|---|---|---|---|---|---|---|---|---|---|---|
| **Element** | *1* | *2* | *3* | *4* | *5* | *6* | *7* | *8* | *9* | *10* | *RF* |
| 1 | 0.23 | 0.20 | 0.19 | 0.20 | 0.18 | 0.18 | 0.24 | 0.25 | 0.17 | 0.20 | 1.05 |
| 2 | 0.12 | 0.10 | 0.08 | 0.09 | 0.10 | 0.10 | 0.13 | 0.14 | 0.10 | 0.11 | 1.00 |
| 3 | 0.16 | 0.18 | 0.17 | 0.17 | 0.17 | 0.20 | 0.16 | 0.15 | 0.18 | 0.18 | 1.05 |
| 4 | 0.26 | 0.28 | 0.32 | 0.19 | 0.35 | 0.33 | 0.22 | 0.28 | 0.28 | 0.27 | 0.95 |
| 5 | 0.10 | 0.08 | 0.09 | 0.10 | 0.11 | 0.11 | 0.09 | 0.12 | 0.12 | 0.12 | 1.00 |
| 6 | 0.06 | 0.08 | 0.08 | 0.08 | 0.07 | 0.06 | 0.10 | 0.08 | 0.09 | 0.11 | 1.05 |
| 7 | 0.20 | 0.28 | 0.25 | 0.36 | 0.17 | 0.22 | 0.33 | 0.19 | 0.20 | 0.16 | 1.05 |

a. The allowance factor for this job is 15%. Determine the standard time.

b. If management wants the estimate of the average cycle time to be within ±0.03 minute with a 95% level of confidence, how many job cycles should be observed?

c. Management is considering putting inspectors on a piece-rate wage system in order to provide them with greater incentive to inspect more items. What effect might this have on the quality-inspection function?

**S8-10.** Baker Street Stereo is a catalogue ordering operation. The company maintains an ordering staff of 30 telephone operators, who take orders from customers. Management wants to determine the proportion of time that operators are idle. A work sampling study was conducted at random over a four-day period, and the following random observations were recorded:

| Observation | | Operators Idle |
|---|---|---|
| 10/15: | 1 | 6 |
| | 2 | 5 |
| | 3 | 4 |
| | 4 | 7 |
| | 5 | 5 |
| | 6 | 2 |
| 10/16: | 7 | 4 |
| | 8 | 3 |
| | 9 | 5 |
| | 10 | 6 |
| | 11 | 4 |
| 10/17: | 12 | 7 |
| | 13 | 3 |
| | 14 | 3 |
| | 15 | 6 |
| | 16 | 5 |
| | 17 | 7 |
| | 18 | 4 |
| 10/19: | 19 | 5 |
| | 20 | 6 |

If management wants the proportion of time from the work sampling study to be ±2% accurate with a confidence level of 98%, how many additional sample observations should be taken?

**S8-11.** The associate dean of the college of business at Tech has succumbed to faculty pressure to purchase a new fax machine, although she has always contended that the machine would have minimal use. She has estimated that the machine will be used only 20% of the time. Now that the machine has been installed, she has asked the students in the introductory OM course to conduct a work sampling study to see what proportion of time the new fax machine is used. She wants the estimate to be within 3% of the actual proportion, with a confidence level of 95%. Determine the sample size for the work sample.

**S8-12.** The Rowntown Cab Company has 26 cabs. The local manager wants to conduct a work sampling study to determine what proportion of the time a cab driver is sitting idle, which he estimates is about 30%. The cabs were observed at random during a five-day period by the dispatcher, who simply called each cab and checked on its status. The manager wants the estimate to be within ±3% of the proportion, with a 95% level of confidence.

a. Determine the sample size for this work sampling study.
b. The results of the first 20 observations of the work sampling study are shown as follows.

| Observation | Idle Cabs | Observation | Idle Cabs |
|---|---|---|---|
| 1 | 4 | 11 | 6 |
| 2 | 3 | 12 | 4 |
| 3 | 5 | 13 | 3 |
| 4 | 8 | 14 | 5 |
| 5 | 7 | 15 | 2 |
| 6 | 5 | 16 | 0 |
| 7 | 3 | 17 | 3 |
| 8 | 6 | 18 | 4 |
| 9 | 4 | 19 | 5 |
| 10 | 3 | 20 | 4 |

What is the revised estimate of the sample size based on these initial results?

**S8-13.** The head of the department of management at State University has noticed that the four secretaries in the departmental office seem to spend a lot of time answering questions from students that could better be answered by the college advising office, by faculty advisors, or simply from the available literature; that is, course schedules, catalogues, the student handbook, and so on. As a result, the department head is considering remodeling the office with cubicles so students do not have easy access to the secretaries. However, before investing in this project the head has decided to conduct a work sampling study to determine the proportion of time the secretaries spend assisting students. The head arranged for a graduate assistant to make observations for the work sample, but the graduate student's schedule enabled her to make only 300 random observations in the time allotted for the study. The results of the work sampling study showed that the secretaries assisted students 12% of the time, somewhat less than the head anticipated.

a. Given the number of observations that were included in the work sampling study, how confident can the department head be that the sample result is within 3% of the actual proportion?
b. How many fewer or additional observations would be required for the department head to be 95% confident in the work sampling results?

**S8-14.** In Problem S8-11, the OM students have completed 100 observations of the work sampling study and have a preliminary result showing the fax machine is in use 31% of the time. How many additional observations are required based on this result?

**S8-15.** Northwoods Backpackers is a mail-order operation specializing in outdoor camping and hiking equipment and clothing. In addition to its normal pool of telephone operators to take customer orders, the company has a group of customer service operators to respond to customer complaints and product-related inquiries. The time required for customer service operators to handle customer calls differs, based on an operator's ability to think fast and quickly recall from memory product information (without using product description screens on the computer). The company wants to determine the standard time required for a customer service operator to complete a call without having to resort to a time study. Instead, management had a work sampling study of an operator conducted during an eight-hour workday that included 160 observations. The study showed the operator was talking to customers only 78% of the time, and call records indicated that the operator handled 120 customer calls during the day. The customer service manager has indicated that the particular operator that was studied performs at about 110% compared with a normal operator. Company policy allows 15% personal time on the job for lunch, breaks, and so on. Determine the standard time per customer call.

**S8-16.** In Problem S8-15 how confident can Northwoods Backpackers be in the standard time it computed if it assumed that the proportion of time that an operator is busy determined from the work sampling study is accurate within ±4%? How many additional observations might be needed for Northwoods to be 95% confident in the standard time per customer call?

**S8-17.** The manager of the order-distribution center for Northwoods Backpackers has a company directive to downsize his operation. He has decided to conduct work sampling studies of employees in the order-processing department, the warehouse area, and the packaging area. In the warehouse area he has 17 employees who locate items, pull them, and put them on conveyors to the packaging area. A work sampling study was conducted over a five-day period to determine the proportion of time warehouse employees were idle, and out of the 50 random observations, 400 employees were idle.

a. How many observations should be taken if the manager wants to be 90% confident the estimate is within ±5% of the actual proportion of time a warehouse employee is idle?
b. The manager also conducted a work sampling study of the packaging area and discovered that the 28 employees were idle approximately 37% of the time. How might the manager redesign his operation to downsize and be more efficient?

**S8-18.** The manager of the Burger Doodle restaurant believes the time to fill orders at the drive-through window is too long. She suspects that the window cashier spends too much time making change, and she is considering using even pricing for most menu items to reduce the window time. She has decided to conduct a work sampling study to determine the proportion of time the cashier is making change. During a three-day period the manager checked the cashier 150 times and recorded 84 observations in which the cashier was making change.

a. How many more observations should be taken if the manager wants to be 99% confident that her estimate is within $\pm 1\%$ of the actual proportion of time the cashier is making change?

b. Based on the time required to take the first 150 observations, how many days will be required to conduct this study?

c. How could the manager reduce the number of days required to conduct in part (b)?

**S8-19.** The National Bank of Hamilton has opened up two new drive-through teller windows outside its main office building in downtown Hamilton. The bank is not sure that it needs both windows open all day so it has decided to conduct a work sampling study to determine the proportion of time the two tellers are idle between the hours of 10:00 A.M. to 11:30 A.M. and 1:00 P.M. to 3:00 P.M. The work sampling study was conducted at random over a five-day period, and the following observations were recorded:

| Observation | Tellers Idle | Observation | Tellers Idle |
|---|---|---|---|
| 1 | 1 | 11 | 1 |
| 2 | 1 | 12 | 1 |
| 3 | 0 | 13 | 2 |
| 4 | 0 | 14 | 2 |
| 5 | 0 | 15 | 0 |
| 6 | 2 | 16 | 1 |
| 7 | 1 | 17 | 2 |
| 8 | 2 | 18 | 2 |
| 9 | 2 | 19 | 0 |
| 10 | 1 | 20 | 1 |
| 21 | 2 | 26 | 1 |
| 22 | 2 | 27 | 0 |
| 23 | 2 | 28 | 2 |
| 24 | 0 | 29 | 0 |
| 25 | 1 | 30 | 2 |

a. Bank management wants the study to be $\pm 5\%$ accurate with a 95% confidence level. How many additional sample observations should be taken?

b. If the bank does not want to conduct a study of more than 100 observations, what level of confidence could it expect?

## CASE PROBLEM S8.1

### *Measuring Faculty Work Activity at State University*

At several recent meetings of the faculty senate at State University there has been discussion of media reports that college faculty are more concerned about their research than about teaching and, specifically, that faculty don't spend enough time working with students, which should be their main task. These media reports imply that faculty work only during the time they are in class, which for most faculty is between 6 and 12 hours per week. The faculty believes this information is misleading and dangerous to higher education in general. The faculty representatives on the senate claim that the time they spend in class is only a small portion of their actual workload, and although they spend some time on their research, they also dedicate a large portion of their time outside of class to class preparation and meeting with students. Unfortunately, few people outside of the faculty appear to believe this, including the students, parents, certain legislators, and, recently, several highly placed university administrators.

In an attempt to educate the students more about what faculty actually do with their time, the senate invited several student leaders to one of its meetings, where they discussed the issue. Among the students invited to this meeting was Mary Shipley, editor of *The Daily State*, the student newspaper. Subsequently, Mary wrote an editorial in the paper about how faculty members spent their time.

Mary was a student in the college of business at State; coincidentally, the topic currently under discussion in her operations management class was "Job Design and Work Measurement." The day after her editorial appeared, she was asked the following question in her class by a fellow student, Art Cohen:

"Mary, it looks like to me that all you did in your editorial was repeat what you had been told by the faculty at the faculty senate meeting. I don't really believe you have any idea about what faculty do, any more than the rest of us!"

Before Mary could respond, another student, Angela Watts, broke in, "Well, it shouldn't be too hard to check out. That's what we're studying in class right now—how to measure work. Why don't we check out how much time the faculty work at different tasks?"

At this point their teacher, Dr. Larry Moore, broke in. "That's a good idea, Angela, it sounds to me as if you just resolved our problem of a class project for this term. I'm going to break you all into teams and let each team monitor a specific faculty member, using work sampling to determine the amount of time the faculty member spends with students outside the classroom."

"That's not really going to provide any relevant information," interrupted Bobby Jenkins. "That will just provide us with a percentage of time faculty work with students. If professors spend 90% of their time working with students, that sounds great, but if they are only in their offices 2 hours a day, 90% of 2 hours is not very much."

"I see what you mean," Dr. Moore replied. "That's a good point. Somehow we need to determine how many hours a day a faculty member devotes to his or her job to have a frame of reference."

"The way it looks to me, a professor works only about 3 or 4 hours a day," said Rodney Jefferson. This drew laughter from the class and Dr. Moore.

"I don't think that's really true," responded Mary Shipley. "One of the things the faculty pointed out to me and I indicated in my editorial was that even though faculty members may not be in their offices all the time, they may still be working, either at home or in the library. And a lot of times they have committee work at various locations around campus." A lot of the class seemed to be in general agreement with this. "Anyway," Mary continued, "I don't think the issue is how much a professor works. I believe we all agree they put in a full 7- or 8-hour day like almost anyone else. The point as I see it is, what do they do with that time? Do they spend it all on their own research and writing or are they working with students?"

"Okay then," said Dr. Moore. "If we can all agree that the number of hours of work is a moot point, then let's set up our work sampling experiment. We'll break down the activities outside of classroom teaching as 'working with students,' or 'not working with students,' which could include anything else the faculty member is working on, such as research, making out tests, preparing for class, and so on. That should be all-inclusive. What proportion of time do you think a faculty member spends with students outside the classroom, to use a starting point? 10%? 20%?"

The class seemed to mull this over for a few minutes and someone shouted, "20%." Someone else said 30%, and after a few seconds people were simply talking back and forth.

"Okay, okay," said Dr. Moore, "everyone calm down. Let's say 20%. That sounds like a reasonable number to me, and you can always adjust it in the course of your experiment. Let's allow for an error of 3% and use a confidence level of 95%. Does this sound okay to everybody?" He waited a few moments for any negative reaction, but there seemed to be general agreement. "Good, I'll post teams on my office door by tomorrow, and I'll let each team select the faculty member they want to study. Let me know by the end of the week and I'll alert the faculty members so they will know what to expect. Also, it's possible someone might not want to participate, and I'll let you know that too so you can select someone else. Please be as unobtrusive as possible and try not to bother anybody. Okay, if there are no other questions, that's it. Get busy."

Describe how you would set up this work sampling experiment at your school, and, if your teacher is agreeable, carry out this project. Also, describe how you might alter the work sample to analyze other faculty work activities.

## REFERENCES

Barnes, R. M. *Motion and Time Study: Design and Measurement of Work*, 8th ed. New York: Wiley, 1980.

Emerson, H. P., and D. C. E. Maehring. *Origins of Industrial Engineering*. Atlanta: Institute of Industrial Engineers, 1988.

Gilbreth, F. *Motion Study*. New York: Van Nostrand, 1911.

Mundel, M. E. *Motion and Time Study: Improving Productivity*, 6th ed. Upper Saddle River, NJ: Prentice Hall, 1985.

Smith, G. L., Jr. *Work Measurement: A Systems Approach*. Columbus, OH: Grid Publishing, 1978.

Taylor, F. W. *The Principles of Scientific Management*. New York: Harper, 1911.

Wood, S., ed. *The Transformation of Work* (London: Unwin Hyman, 1989).

# Project Management

CHAPTER 9

Web resources for this chapter include

- Internet Exercises
- Online Practice Quizzes
- Virtual Tours
- Excel Worksheets
- Company and Resource Weblinks
- Animated Demo Problems
- Microsoft Project Exhibits

www.wiley.com/college/russell

## CHAPTER OUTLINE

In this chapter, you will learn about . . .

- Project Planning
- Project Scheduling
- Project Control
- CPM/PERT
- Probabilistic Activity Times
- *Microsoft Project*
- Project Crashing and Time–Cost Trade-off

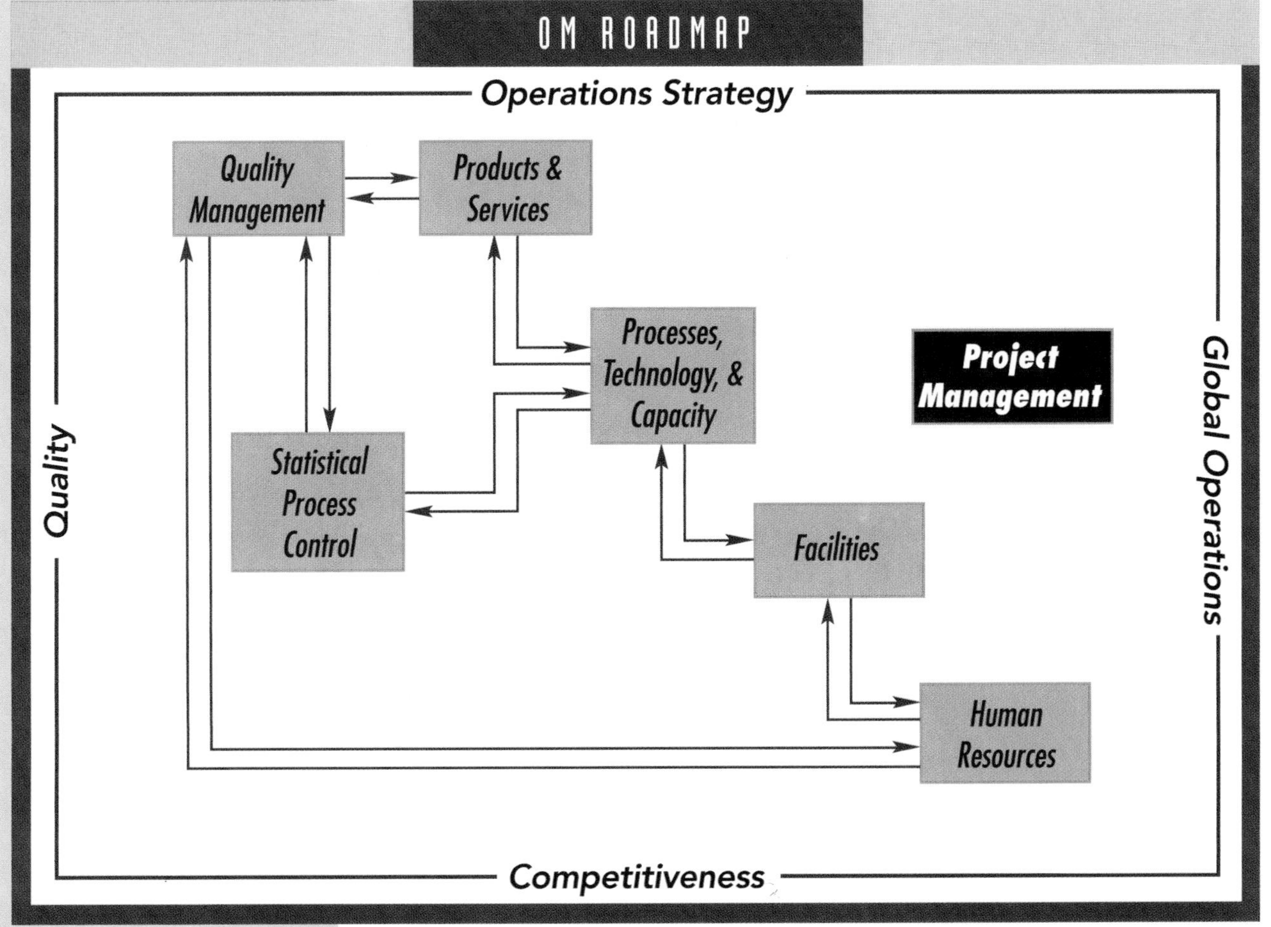

## PROJECT "MAGIC" AT WALT DISNEY IMAGINEERING

Projects for the development of new attractions and rides at the Disney theme parks are unique and challenging, like all operations at Disney. Budgets are tight, schedules are aggressive, and Disney standards for design quality and guest experience are high. It takes more than "pixie dust" to manage a project to completion successfully. Consider a project for an automobile manufacturer to design and build a new high-performance car that looks great, exceeds all current safety standards, is less expensive than last year's model, must be delivered one year early with an 800,000 mile warranty, and every customer who drives it must like it. This is equivalent to the challenge faced in the project management process at Disney with a new show or attraction that requires new technology, has a schedule driven by an opening day requirement, needs a high guest satisfaction ranking, and the show's components and attraction need to last 20 to 30 years and operate up to 20 hours per day, 7 days a week.

Walt Disney Imagineering (WDI) is the group at Disney that manages and delivers the magic required in its projects. An Imagineering project team is organized to support the special demands of a Disney theme park project. It includes a project manager and show producer, as well as core team members and project control specialists. Over 100 specialized work groups must all be coordinated so that they are engaged at the appropriate time and deliver their assigned tasks on time to keep the project on schedule to meet the opening day deadline. The Disney core team usually consists of an architecture and engineering manager, a ride project engineer, a show program manager, and a construction manager.

Each new project evolves through a multi-phase process that establishes the project life cycle and the project schedule. The first phase, Concept, is the evolutionary phase that is used to ensure that an attraction can be designed to integrate a Disney story line into three dimensions using feasible technology—that is, the time required to develop an unproven concept into a feasible concept within budget constraints. The next phase, Design, involves the complete schematic design for the attraction, including the building and show/attraction layouts, and the selection of show/attraction systems. In the Implementation phase the show and attraction design requirements are completed so that bids can be solicited, show and attraction production is started, the facilities are constructed, and the shows and attractions are installed, tested, and adjusted. In the final phase, Close out, operations training is completed. A fully integrated project master schedule is developed by the project team to successfully deliver the project, based on Critical Path Method (CPM) logic.

The key individual in the project management process is the project manager (PM), who must lead the team to success. The project manager has full accountability for project results. The PM assigns work to divisions and

*Main Street, Disneyworld. Each year Walt Disney Imagineering considers dozens of projects for new attractions, rides and shows at its theme parks.*

groups, is the project facilitator, must resolve conflicts between team members, and must deal with problems and obstacles from a single, coordinated viewpoint. No one will ever explain how to do this to a project manager, nor will it ever be put down in any type of manual. Above all, the project manager must be a leader. How to be an effective leader was best said by one of Disney's best project managers in history.

*Courage is the main quality of leadership, in my opinion, no matter where it is exercised. Usually it implies some risk—especially in new undertakings. Courage to initiate something and to keep it going.*

*Walt Disney*[1]

[1] Frank Addeman, "Managing the Magic," *PM Network* 13(7; July 1999), pp. 31–36.

In other chapters we discuss the scheduling of repetitive operations and activities, such as work scheduling and job scheduling, as an important aspect of managing an operation. Operational schedules are established to keep the flow of products or services through the supply chain on time. However, not all operational activities are repetitive; some are unique, occurring only once within a specified time frame. Such unique, one-time activities are referred to as **projects**.

**Project:** a unique, one-time operational activity or effort.

Project management is the management of the work to develop and implement an innovation or change in an existing operation. It encompasses planning the project and controlling the project activities, subject to resource and budget constraints, to keep the project on schedule. Examples of projects include constructing facilities and buildings, such as houses, factories, a shopping mall, an athletic stadium, or an arena; developing a military weapons system, new aircraft, or new ship; launching a satellite system; constructing an oil pipeline, developing and implementing a new computer system; planning a rock concert, football bowl game, or basketball tournament; and introducing new products into the market.

Projects have become increasingly pervasive in companies in recent years. The nature of the global business environment is such that new machinery and equipment, as well as new production processes and computer support systems, are constantly evolving. This provides the capability of developing new products and services, which generates consumer demand for even greater product diversity. As a result, a larger proportion of total organizational effort now goes toward project-oriented activities than in the past. Thus, the planning and management of projects has taken on a more crucial role in operations management.

In this chapter we focus on project management using CPM and PERT network scheduling techniques that are popular because they provide a graph or visual representation of the interrelationship and sequence of individual project activities. However, prior to our presentation of the CPM/PERT technique, we will discuss the primary elements of the project management process—planning, scheduling, and control.

## PROJECT PLANNING

The general management process is concerned with the planning, organization, and control of an ongoing process or activity such as the production of a product or delivery of a service. Project management is different in that it requires a commitment of resources and people to an important undertaking that is not repetitive and involves a relatively short period of time, after which the management effort is dissolved. A project has a unique purpose, it is temporary, and it draws resources from various areas in the organization; as a result, it is subject to more uncertainty than the normal management process. Thus, the features and characteristics of the project management process tend to be unique.

Figure 9.1 provides an overview of the project management process, which encompasses three other major processes—planning, scheduling, and control. It also includes a number of the more prominent elements of these processes. In the remainder of this section, we will discuss some features of the project planning process, and in the following few sections we will discuss the scheduling and control processes.

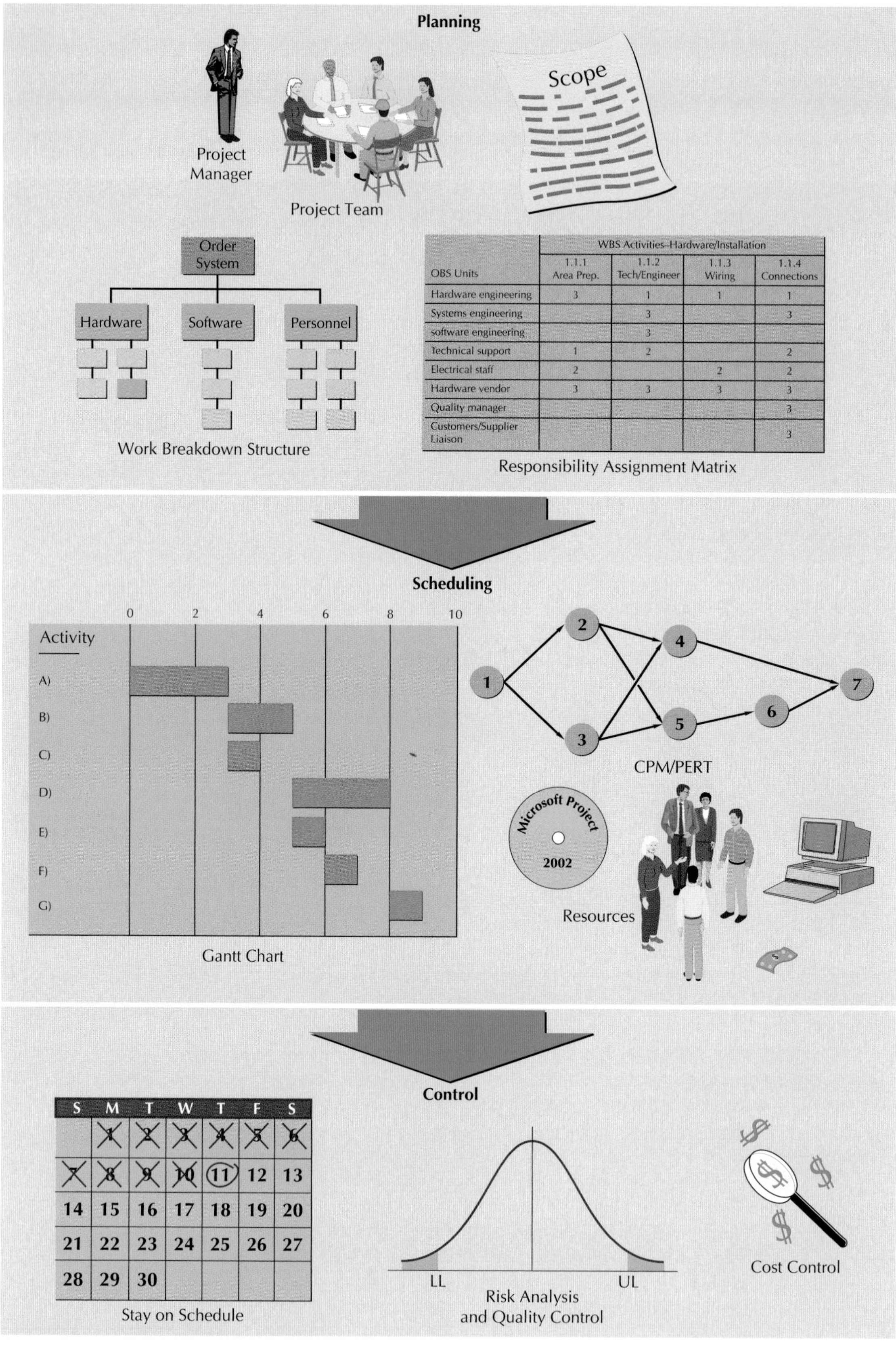


**Figure 9.1**

**The Project Management Process**

## ELEMENT OF A PROJECT PLAN

Project plans generally include the following basic elements.

- *Objectives*—a detailed statement of what the project is to accomplish and how it will achieve the company's goals and meet the strategic plan; and an estimate of when it needs to be completed, the cost and the return.
- *Project scope*—a discussion of how to approach the project, the technological and resource feasibility, the major tasks involved, and a preliminary schedule; includes a justification of the project and what constitutes project success.
- *Contract requirements*—a general structure of managerial, reporting, and performance responsibilities, including a detailed list of staff, suppliers, subcontractors, managerial requirements and agreements, reporting requirements, and a projected organizational structure.
- *Schedules*—a list of all major events, tasks, and subschedules, from which a master schedule is developed.
- *Resources*—the overall project budget for all resource requirements and procedures for budgetry control.
- *Personnel*—identification and recruitment of personnel required for the project team, including special skills and training.
- *Control*—procedures for monitoring and evaluating progress and performance including schedules and cost.
- *Risk and problem analysis*—anticipating and assessing uncertainties, problems and potential difficulties that might increase the risk of project delays and/or failure and threaten project success.

## THE PROJECT TEAM

The project team is typically cross-functional, consisting of a group of individuals selected from other areas in the organization or from outside the organization because of their special skills, expertise, and experience related to the project activities. Members of the engineering staff are often assigned to project work because of their technical skills, especially if the project is related to production processes or equipment. The project team may also include managers and staff personnel from specific areas related to the project. Workers can also be involved on the project team if their job is a function of the project activity. For example, a project team for the construction of a new loading dock facility might include truck drivers, forklift operators, dock workers, and staff personnel and managers from purchasing, shipping, receiving, and packaging, as well as engineers to assess vehicle flow, routes, and space considerations.

Project teams are made up of individuals from various areas and departments within a company.

The term **matrix organization** refers to a team approach to special projects. The team is developed from members of different functional areas or departments in the company. For example, team members might come from engineering, production, marketing, or human resources, depending on the specialized skills required by the project. The team members are, in effect, on loan from their home departments to work on a project. The term *matrix* is derived from the two-dimensional characteristics of this type of organizational structure. On one dimension, the vertical, is the company's normal organizational structure for performing jobs, whereas the horizontal dimension is the special functional structure (i.e., the functional team members) required by the project.

**Matrix organization:** a team structure with members from functional areas, depending on the skills required.

Assignment to a project team is usually temporary, which can have both positive and negative repercussions. The temporary loss of workers and staff from their permanent jobs can be disruptive for both the employee and the work area. The employee must sometimes "serve two masters," reporting to both the project manager and a regular supervisor. Since projects are usually exciting, they provide an opportunity to do work that is new and innovative, making the employee reluctant to report back to a more mundane, regular job after the project is completed.

## THE PROJECT MANAGER

The project manager is often under greater pressure.

The most important member of the project team is the *project manager*. Managing a project is subject to lots of uncertainty and the distinct possibility of failure. Since a project is unique and usually has not been attempted previously, the outcome is not as certain as the outcome of an ongoing process would be. A degree of security is attained in the supervision of a continuing process that is not present in project management. The project team members are often from diverse areas of the organization and possess different skills, which must be coordinated into a single, focused effort to complete the project successfully. The project is subject to time and budgetary constraints that are not the same as normal work schedules and resource consumption in an ongoing process. There is usually more perceived and real pressure associated with project management than in a normal management position. However, there are potential opportunities, including demonstrating management abilities in a difficult situation, the challenge of working on a unique project, and the excitement of doing something new.

## SCOPE STATEMENT

**Scope statement:** a document that provides an understanding, justification, and expected result of a project.

**Statement of work:** a written description of the objectives of a project.

The **scope statement** is a document that provides a common understanding of a project. It includes a justification for the project that describes which factors created a need within the company for the project. It also includes an indication of what the expected results of the project will be and what will constitute project success. The scope statement might also include a list of the types of planning reports and documents that are part of the project management process.

A similar planning document is the **statement of work (SOW)**. In a large project, the statement of work is often prepared for individual team members, groups, departments, subcontractors, and suppliers. This statement describes the work in sufficient detail so that the team members responsible for it know what is required and if they have sufficient resources to accomplish the work successfully and on time. For suppliers and subcontractors it is often the basis for determining whether they can perform the work and for bidding on it. Some companies require that a statement of work be part of an official contract with a supplier or subcontractor.

## WORK BREAKDOWN STRUCTURE

**Work breakdown structure (WBS):** breaks down a project into components, subcomponents, activities, and tasks.

The **work breakdown structure (WBS)** is a tool used for project planning. The WBS organizes the work to be done on a project. In a WBS, a project is broken down into its major components, referred to as modules. These components are then subdivided into detailed subcomponents, which are further broken down into activities and, finally, individual tasks. The end result is a project hierarchical organizational structure made up of different levels, with the overall project at the top of the structure and the individual tasks for each activity at the bottom level. The WBS format is a good way to identify activities and to determine the individual task, module, and project workloads and resources required. It also helps to identify relationships between modules and activities as well as unnecessary duplication of activities. Finally, it provides the basis for developing and managing the project schedule, resources, and modifications.

There is no specific model to follow for the development of a WBS. It can be in the form of a chart or a table. It can be organized around project groups, project phases, or project tasks and events. However, experience has shown that there are two good ways for a project team to develop a WBS. One way is to start at the top and work one's way down asking, "What components constitute this level?" until the WBS is developed in sufficient detail. The other way is simply to brainstorm the entire project, writing down each item on a sticky note and then organizing them together into the branches of a WBS. The upper levels of the WBS hierarchy tend to indicate the summary activities, major components, or functional areas involved in the project. They are typically described by nouns that indicate "what" is to be done. The lower levels of the WBS tend to describe the detailed work activities of the project required under the major components or areas. They are typically described by verbs that indicate "how" things are done.

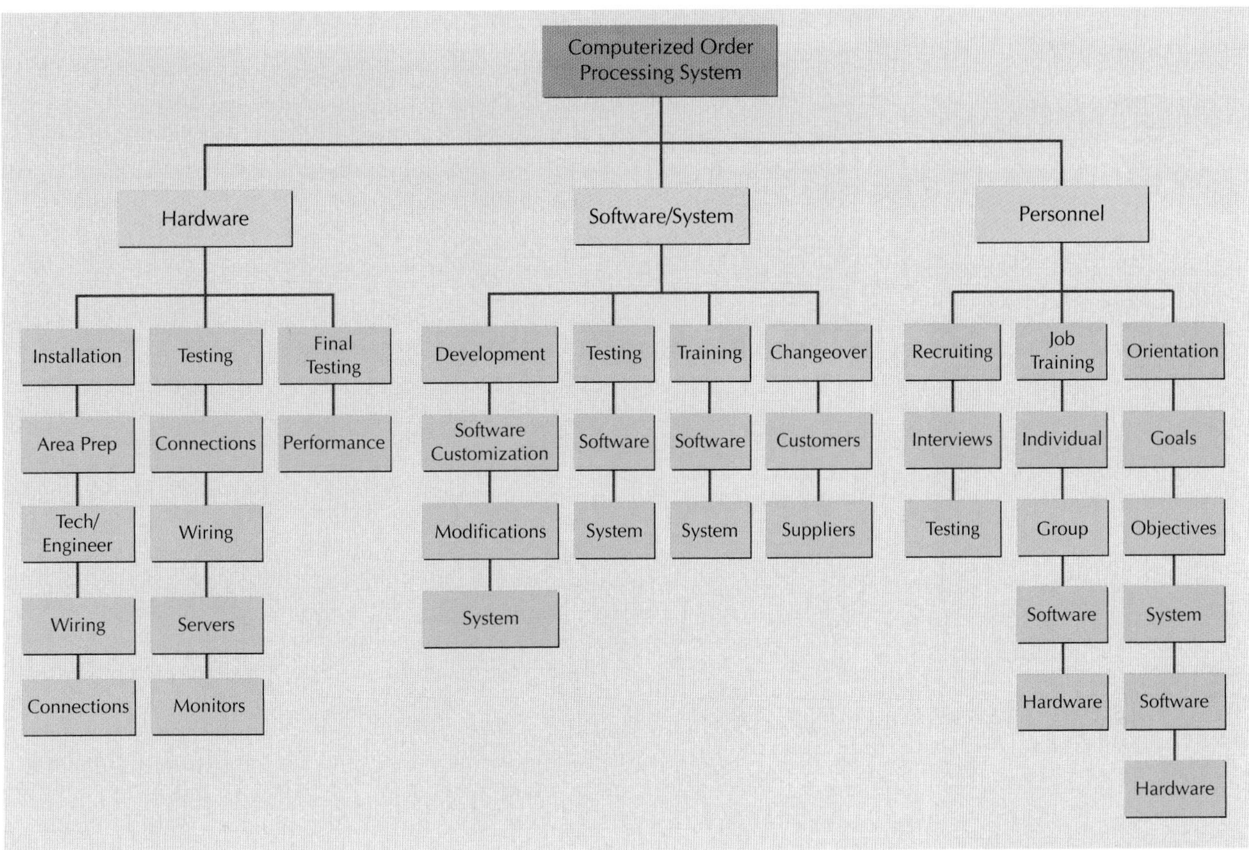


**Figure 9.2**
**Work Breakdown Structure for Computer Order Processing System Project**

Figure 9.2 shows a WBS for a project for installing a new computerized order processing system for a textile manufacturer that links customers, the manufacturer, and suppliers (see Example 9.1). The WBS is organized according to the three major project categories for development of the system—hardware, software/system, and personnel. Within each of these categories the major tasks and activities under those tasks are detailed. For example, under hardware, a major task is "installation," and activities required in installation include area preparation, technical/engineering layouts and configurations, and wiring and electrical connections.

## RESPONSIBILITY ASSIGNMENT MATRIX

After the work breakdown structure is developed, which organizes the project work into smaller, manageable elements, the project manager assigns the work elements to organizational units—departments, groups, individuals, or subcontractors—using an **organizational breakdown structure (OBS)**. The OBS is an organizational chart that shows which organizational units are responsible for work items. After the OBS is developed, the project manager can then develop a **responsibility assignment matrix (RAM)**. The RAM shows who in the organization is responsible for doing the work in the project. Figure 9.3 on the next page shows a RAM for the "Hardware/Installation" category from the work breakdown structure for the computerized order processing project shown in Figure 9.2. Notice that there are three levels of work assignment in the matrix reflecting who is responsible for the work, who actually performs the work, and those who perform support activities. As with the WBS, both the OBS and RAM can take many different forms depending on the needs and preferences of the company, project team, and project manager.

**Organizational breakdown structure (OBS):**
a chart that shows which organizational units are responsible for work items.

**Responsibility assignment matrix (RAM):**
shows who is responsible for the work in a project.

## GLOBAL ISSUES IN PROJECT PLANNING

Global projects that involve companies and team members from different countries have expanded dramatically in recent years as a result of increased information and communication technology. Teamwork is a critical element in achieving project success, and

**Figure 9.3**
**A Responsibility Assignment Matrix**

| OBS Units | WBS Activities–Hardware/Installation 1.1.1 Area Prep | 1.1.2 Tech/Engineer | 1.1.3 Wiring | 1.1.4 Connections |
|---|---|---|---|---|
| Hardware engineering | 3 | 1 | 1 | 1 |
| Systems engineering | | 3 | | 3 |
| Software engineering | | 3 | | |
| Technical support | 1 | 2 | | 2 |
| Electrical staff | 2 | | 2 | 2 |
| Hardware vendor | 3 | 3 | 3 | 3 |
| Quality manager | | | | 3 |
| Customer/supplier liaison | | | | 3 |

Level of responsibility: 1 = overall responsibility
2 = performance responsibility
3 = support

in global projects diversity among international team members can add an extra dimension to project planning. For projects to be successful, cultural differences, idiosyncrasies, and issues must be considered as important parts of the planning process. The basics of project management tend to be universal, but cultural differences in priorities, nuances, and terminology can result in communication failures. Since English is used widely around the world, language is not necessarily an overriding problem. However, often it is not what people say that matters but what they mean.

An example of one cultural difference that can play havoc with developing project schedules is the difference in work days and holidays in different countries. Southern Europeans take a lot of holidays, which can mess up a project schedule if they are not planned for. In the United States you can ask people to move their vacations or work while on vacation (via phone or Internet), but in countries like France or Italy, don't ask. In India the work ethic is closer to the European than the U.S. model: when the day ends it's over, and weekends are inviolate. In some cultures, certain days are auspicious for starting a new venture or ending a task.

Some cultures tend to be less aggressive than others, and team members will avoid confrontation so that when problems on a project occur (such as cost overruns or missed due dates) they will not be as aggressively addressed as they might be in the United States or in Germany, for example. Some team members in underdeveloped countries may bow to the perceived superiority of those from developed countries and not aggressively press their points even though they may be correct. Some people may simply have trouble working with others with cultural differences. Team members may think they do not understand team members from a foreign country, when it's actually their culture they don't understand.

As a result, the project manager must address the issue of cultural diversity up front in the planning process. Project managers have to approach diversity differently from country to country. The project manager should never assume that something that works at home will work abroad or that what will work in country A will work in country B. This makes cultural research and communication important elements in the planning process. The manager must determine what cultural faux pas must be avoided—the things you don't do. It's important to discover at the start what holidays and cultural celebrations exist and the work ethic of team members.

The project manager must often find team members who are particularly adept at bridging cultural differences. It may be helpful to identify a team associate who can keep the project manager and other team members informed of important cultural differences. Although long-distance communication via phone or e-mail is very easy, the face-to-face meeting is often better with someone with cultural differences, even with the added expense of travel. The "Competitive Edge" box on page 390 notes that one project team leader for the Kodak Advantix project logged over a million flying miles between New York and Japan in a five-year period.

## PROJECT SCHEDULING

The project schedule evolves from the planning documents we discussed in the previous section. It is typically the most critical element in the project management process, especially during the implementation phase (i.e., the actual project work), and it is the source of most conflict and problems. One reason is that frequently the single most important criterion for the success of a project is that it be finished on time. If a stadium is supposed to be finished in time for the first game of the season and it's not, there will be a lot of angry ticket holders; if a school building is not completed by the time the school year starts, there will be a lot of angry parents; if a shopping mall is not completed on time, there will be a lot of angry tenants; if a new product is not completed by the scheduled launch date, millions of dollars can be lost; and if a new military weapon is not completed on time, it could affect national security. Time is also a measure of progress that is very visible. It is an absolute with little flexibility; you can spend less money or use fewer people, but you cannot slow down or stop the passage of time.

Developing a schedule encompasses the following basic steps. First, *define the activities* that must be performed to complete the project; second, *sequence the activities* in the order in which they must be completed; next, *estimate the time* required to complete each activity; and finally, *develop the schedule* based on this sequencing and time estimates of the activities.

Because scheduling involves a quantifiable measure, time, several quantitative techniques, including the Gantt chart and CPM/PERT networks, are available that can be used to develop a project schedule. There are also various computer software packages that can be used to schedule projects, including the popular Microsoft Project. Later in this chapter we are going to discuss CPM/PERT and Microsoft Project in greater detail. For now, we are going to describe one of the oldest and most widely used scheduling techniques, the Gantt chart.

### THE GANTT CHART

A **Gantt chart** (also called a *bar chart*) was developed by Henry Gantt, a pioneer in the field of industrial engineering at the artillery ammunition shops of the Frankford Arsenal in 1914. The Gantt chart has been a popular project scheduling tool since its inception and is still widely used today. It is the direct precursor of the CPM/PERT technique, which we will discuss later.

**Gantt chart:** a graph or bar chart with a bar for each project activity that shows the passage of time.

The Gantt chart is a graph with a bar representing time for each activity in the project being analyzed. Figure 9.4 on the next page illustrates a Gantt chart of a simplified project description for building a house. The project contains only seven primary activities, such as designing the house, laying the foundation, ordering materials, and so forth. The first activity is "design house and obtain financing," and it requires three months to complete, shown by the bar from left to right across the chart. After the first activity is finished, the next two activities, "lay foundation" and "order and receive materials," can start simultaneously. This set of activities demonstrates how a precedence relationship works; the design of the house and the financing must precede the next two activities.

The activity "lay foundation" requires two months to complete, so it will be finished, at the earliest, at the end of month 5. "Order and receive materials" requires one month to complete, and it could be finished after month 4. However, observe that it is possible to delay the start of this activity one month until month 4. This delay would still enable the activity to be completed by the end of month 5, when the next activity, "build house," is scheduled to start. This extra time for the activity "order materials" is called *slack*. **Slack** is the amount by which an activity can be delayed without delaying any of the activities

**Slack:** the amount of time an activity can be delayed without delaying the project.

Figure 9.4
**A Gantt Chart**

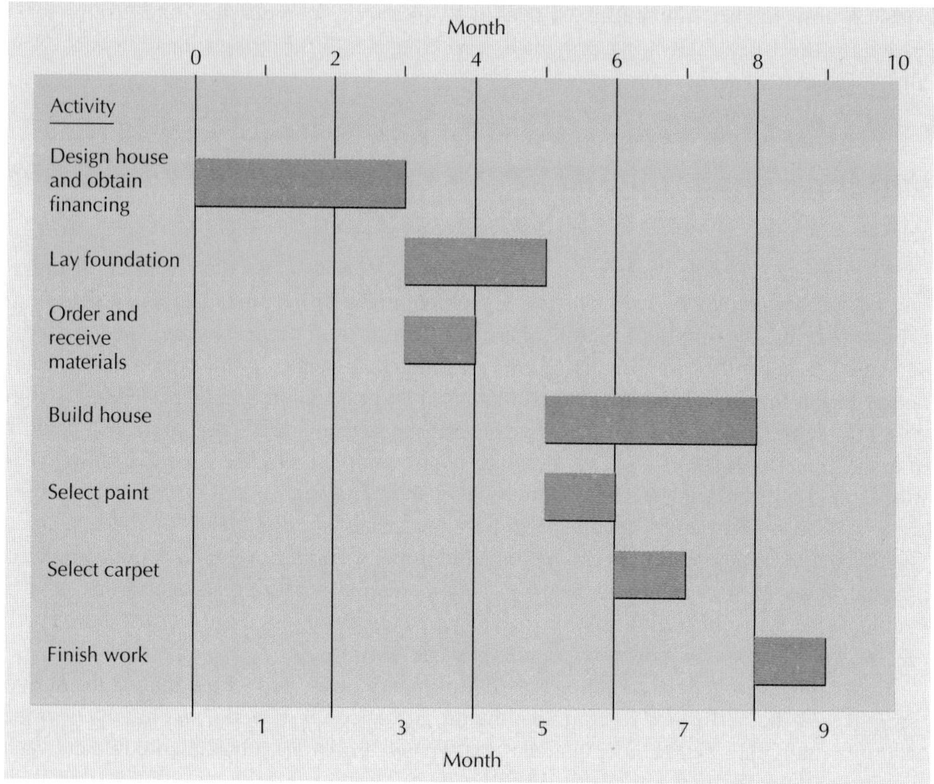


that follow it or the project as a whole. The remainder of the Gantt chart is constructed in a similar manner, and the project is scheduled to be completed at the end of month 9.

The Gantt chart provides a visual display of the project schedule, indicating when activities are scheduled to start, when they will be finished, and where extra time is available and activities can be delayed. The project manager can use the chart to monitor the progress of the activities and see which ones are ahead of schedule and which ones are behind schedule. The Gantt chart also indicates the precedence relationships between activities; however, these relationships are not always easily discernible. This problem is one of the disadvantages of the Gantt chart method, and it sometimes limits the chart's use to smaller projects with relatively few activities. The CPM/PERT network technique does not suffer this disadvantage.

## PROJECT CONTROL

Project control is the process of making sure the project progresses toward a successful completion. It requires that the project be monitored and progress be measured so that any deviations from the project plan, and particularly the project schedule, are minimized. If the project is found to be deviating from the plan—that is, it is not on schedule, cost overruns are occurring, activity results are not as expected, and so on—then corrective action must be taken. In the rest of this section we will describe several key elements of project control, including time management, quality control, performance monitoring, and communication.

### TIME MANAGEMENT

Time management is the process of making sure the project schedule does not slip and it is on time. This requires the monitoring of individual activity schedules and frequent updates. If the schedule is being delayed to an extent that jeopardizes the project success, then the project manager may have to shift resources to accelerate critical activities. Some activities may have slack time, and resources can be shifted from them to activities that are not on schedule. This is referred to as *time–cost tradeoff*. However, this can also push the project cost above budget. In some cases, the work may need to be corrected or made more efficient. In other cases, original activity time estimates upon implementation may prove to be unrealistic, with the result that the schedule must be changed and the repercussions of such changes on project success evaluated.

## COST MANAGEMENT

Cost management is often closely tied to time management because of the time–cost tradeoff occurrences that we mentioned previously. If the schedule is delayed, costs tend to increase in order to get the project back on schedule. Also, as the project progresses, some cost estimates may prove to be unrealistic or erroneous. As such, it will be necessary to revise cost estimates and develop budget updates. If cost overruns are excessive, then corrective actions must be taken.

## QUALITY MANAGEMENT

Quality management and control are an integral part of the project management process. The process requires that project work be monitored for quality and that improvements be made as the project progresses just the same as in a normal production or manufacturing operation. Tasks and activities must be monitored to make sure that work is done correctly and that activities are completed correctly according to plan. If the work on an activity or task is flawed, subsequent activities may be affected, requiring rework, delaying the project, and threatening project success. Poor-quality work increases the risk of project failure, just as a defective part can result in a defective final product if not corrected. As such, the same principles of total quality management (TQM) and many of the same techniques for statistical analysis and statistical process control discussed in earlier chapters for traditional production processes can also be applied to the project management process.

## PERFORMANCE MANAGEMENT

Performance management is the process of monitoring a project and developing timed (i.e., daily, weekly, monthly) status reports to make sure that goals are being met and the plan is being followed. It compares planned target dates for events, milestones, and work completion with dates actually achieved to determine whether the project is on schedule or behind schedule. Key measures of performance include deviation from the schedule, resource usage, and cost overruns. These reports are developed by the project manager and by individuals and organizational units with performance responsibility.

**Earned value analysis (EVA)** is a specific system for performance management. Activities "earn value" as they are completed. EVA is a recognized standard procedure for numerically measuring a project's progress, forecasting its completion date and final cost, and providing measures of schedule and budget variation as activities are completed. For example, an EVA metric such as "schedule variance" compares the work performed during a time period with the work that was scheduled to be performed. A negative variance means the project is behind schedule. "Cost variance" is the budgeted cost of work performed minus the actual cost of the work. A negative variance means the project is over budget. EVA works best when it is used in conjunction with a work breakdown structure (WBS) that compartmentalizes project work into small packages that are easier to measure. The drawbacks of EVA are that it's sometimes difficult to measure work progress and the time required for data measurement can be considerable.

**Earned value analysis:** a standard procedure for numerically measuring a project's progress, forecasting its completion date and cost and measuring schedule and budget variation.

## COMMUNICATION

Communication needs for project and program management control in today's global business environment tend to be substantial and complex. The distribution of design documents, budget and cost documents, plans, status reports, schedules, and schedule changes in a timely manner is often critical to project success. As a result, more and more companies are using the Internet to communicate project information, and are using company intranet project Web sites to provide a single location for team members to access project information. Internet communication and software combined with faxing, videoconferencing systems, phones, handheld computers, and jet travel are enabling transnational companies to engage in global project management.

## ENTERPRISE PROJECT MANAGEMENT

In many companies, project control takes place within the larger context of a multiple project environment. *Enterprise project management* refers to the management and control of a companywide portfolio of projects. In the enterprise approach to managing projects, a company's goals are achieved through the coordination of simultaneous projects. The company grows, changes, and adds value by systematically implementing projects of all types across the enterprise. The aggregate result of an organization's portfolio of projects becomes the company's bottom line. As such, program management is a managerial approach that sits above project management. Whereas project management concentrates on delivering a clearly defined, tangible outcome with its own scope and goals within a specified time frame, in a program management environment the company's goals and changes are achieved through a carefully planned and coordinated set of projects. Programs tend to cut across and affect all business areas and thus require a higher degree of cross-business functional coordination than individual projects.

## THE COMPETITIVE EDGE

### The Mars Pathfinder Project

Since the early days of U.S. space exploration, project management has played a crucial role in its success. Engineers, scientists, and managers at NASA and related agencies and organizations have used project management techniques to develop, manage, and control sophisticated projects that have not only brought back valuable information about space, but also resulted in technological advances on Earth. One of the most significant and widely publicized of these projects was the Mars Pathfinder Project.

On July 4, 1997, the Mars Pathfinder spacecraft successfully landed on the surface of Mars. The following day the Sojourner Rover rolled down its deployment ramp and began to traverse the surface. During its three months of operation on Mars, the Sojourner and Sagan Memorial Station transmitted nearly 2.6 gigabits of science and engineering data, including 16,000 camera images from the lander and 550 images from the rover; 8.5 million temperature, pressure, and wind measurements; 16 separate chemical measurements of rocks and soil; and the results of 10 technology experiments on the rover.

In November 1993, NASA selected the Jet Propulsion Laboratory, a division of the California Institute of Technology, to manage the project. The mission was conceived as an engineering demonstration of a reliable, low-cost system for delivering payloads to the surface of Mars, and focused primarily on scientific objectives. NASA initiated the project with the desire for "better, faster, cheaper" missions with a maximum three-year development period and a cost cap of $150 million. The mission faced several significant technical challenges, including the assembly, integration, and test of the Pathfinder flight system; the demonstration and test of the entry, descent, and landing system; and the development and operation of the surface rover with an autonomous navigation capability.

Maintaining the launch schedule was an extremely critical aspect of the project due to the orbital relationship between Earth and Mars. The 30-day launch window necessary for a successful trajectory to Mars occurs only once every 26 months, so a schedule slip of more than 30 days would mean a 26-month delay in the launch. The flight system manager and the project scheduler maintained the project schedule, carefully tracking critical project events and milestones. The actual launch took place on December 4, 1996, the third day of the targeted launch window. Another significant challenge was the management of costs and resources. The baseline budget for project development of $131 million with $40 million held in reserve was based on a product-oriented WBS and was formalized in July 1993. The actual development cost was approximately $400,000 less than the NASA cost cap of $150 million. By contrast, the two Viking missions, which landed on Mars in 1976, had a six-year development period and cost $915 million (equivalent to $3 billion in 1992 dollars). The Mars Pathfinder project met all of its technical challenges, was completed on schedule and under the NASA cost cap, and proved that planetary missions could succeed in a "better, faster, cheaper" environment.

*Source:* C. Sholes and N. Chalfin, "Mars Pathfinder Project: 1998 International Project of the Year," *PM Network* 13(1; January 1999), pp. 30–35.

## CPM/PERT

In 1956, a research team at E. I. du Pont de Nemours & Company, Inc., led by a du Pont engineer, Morgan R. Walker, and a Remington-Rand computer specialist, James E. Kelley, Jr., initiated a project to develop a computerized system to improve the planning, scheduling, and reporting of the company's engineering programs (including plant maintenance and construction projects). The resulting network approach is known as the *critical path method (CPM)*. At the same time, the U.S. Navy established a research team composed of members of the Navy Special Projects Office, Lockheed, and the consulting firm of Booz, Allen, and Hamilton, led by D. G. Malcolm. They developed a similar network approach for the design of a management control system for the development of the Polaris Missile Project (a ballistic missile-firing nuclear submarine). This network scheduling technique was named the *program evaluation and review technique*, or *PERT*. The Polaris project eventually included 23 PERT networks encompassing 3000 activities.

Both CPM and PERT are derivatives of the Gantt chart and, as a result, are very similar. There were originally two primary differences between CPM and PERT. With CPM a single estimate for activity time was used that did not allow for any variation in activity times—activity times were treated as if they were known for certain, or "deterministic." With PERT, multiple time estimates were used for each activity that allowed for variation in activity times—activity times were treated as "probabilistic." The other difference was related to the mechanics of drawing the project network. In PERT, activities were represented as arcs, or arrowed lines, between two nodes, or circles, whereas in CPM activities were represented as the nodes or circles. However, over time CPM and PERT have been effectively merged into a single technique conventionally referred to as CPM/PERT.

The advantage of CPM/PERT over the Gantt chart is in the use of a network to depict the precedence relationships between activities. The Gantt chart does not clearly show precedence relationships, which is a disadvantage that limited its use to small projects. The CPM/PERT network is a more efficient and direct means of displaying precedence relationships. In other words, in a network it is visually easier to see the precedence relationships, which makes CPM/PERT popular with managers and other users, especially for large projects with many activities.

CPM/PERT uses a network to depict the precedence relationships among activities.

## THE PROJECT NETWORK

A CPM/PERT network consists of *branches* and *nodes*, as shown in Figure 9.5. When CPM and PERT were first developed, they employed different conventions for constructing a network. With CPM the nodes, or circles in Figure 9.5, represented the project activities. The arrows in between the nodes indicated the precedence relationships between activities. For the network in Figure 9.5, activity 1, represented by node 1, precedes activity 2, and 2 precedes 3. This approach to network construction is called **activity-on-node (AON)**. With PERT the opposite convention was taken. The branches represented the activities, and the nodes in between them reflected events, or points in time such as the end of one activity and the beginning of another. In this approach, referred to as **activity-on-arrow (AOA)**, the activities are normally identified by the node numbers at the start and end of an activity; for example, activity 1–2 precedes activity 2–3 in Figure 9.5. In this book, we will focus on the AON convention, but we will also provide an overview of AOA networks.

**Activity-on-node (AON):** nodes represent activities, and arrows show precedence relationships.

**Activity-on-arrow (AOA):** arrows represent activities and nodes are events for points in time.

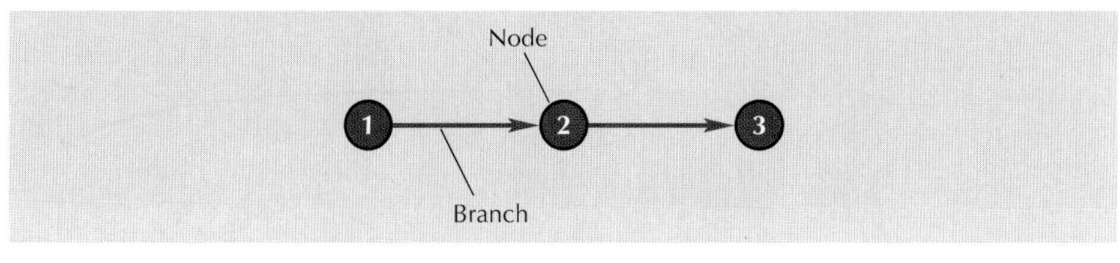


**Figure 9.5**
**Network Components**

Figure 9.6
**The AOA Project Network for Building a House**

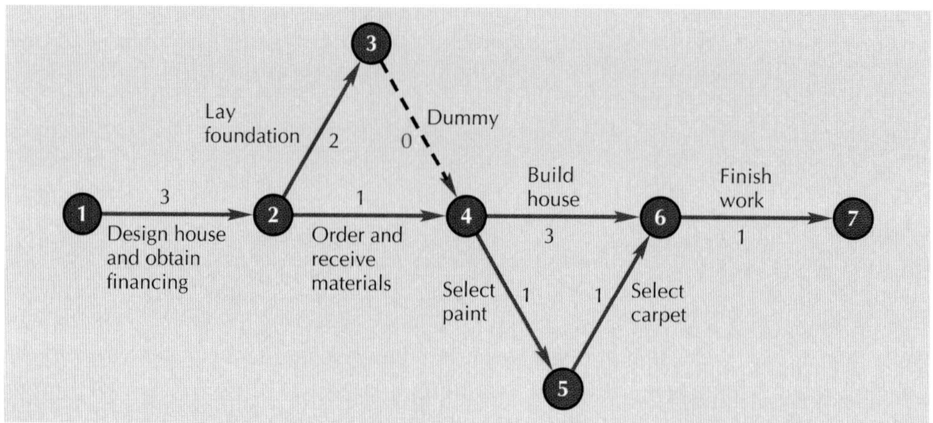


## AOA NETWORK

To demonstrate how these components are used to construct the two types of network, we will use our example project of building a house used in the Gantt chart in Figure 9.4. The comparable AOA CPM/PERT network for this project is shown in Figure 9.6. The precedence relationships are reflected in this network by the arrangement of the arrowed (or directed) branches in Figure 9.6. The first activity (1–2) in the project is to design the house and obtain financing. This activity must be completed before any subsequent activities can begin. Thus, activities 2–3, laying the foundation, and 2–4, ordering and receiving materials, can start only when node 2 is *realized*, indicating the event that activity 1–2 is finished. (Notice in Figure 9.6 that a time estimate of three months has been assigned for the completion of this activity). Activity 2–3 and activity 2–4 can occur concurrently; neither depends on the other, and both depend only on the completion of activity 1–2.

When the activities of laying the foundation (2–3) and ordering and receiving materials (2–4) are completed, then activities 4–5 and 4–6 can begin simultaneously. However, before discussing these activities further, notice activity 3–4, referred to in the network as a dummy.

*The Lafayette, the nuclear-powered ballistic missile submarine shown here, is a direct descendent of the USS George Washington, the first nuclear submarine of this type. In the late 1950s the Polaris Fleet Ballistic Missile Project included more than 250 prime contractors and 9000 subcontractors. The Navy Department credited PERT with bringing the Polaris missile submarine to combat readiness approximately two years ahead of the originally scheduled completion date.*

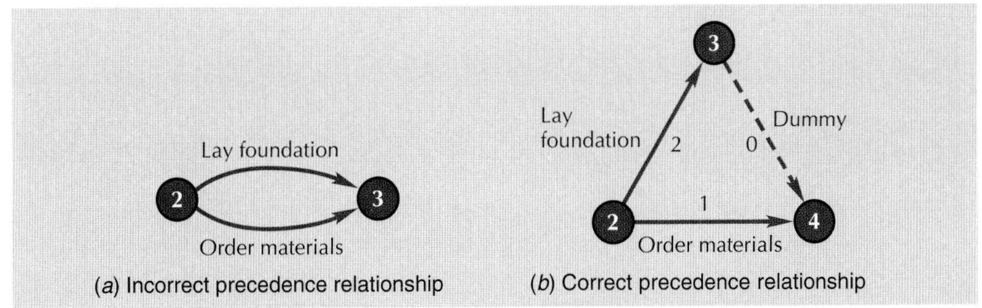


Figure 9.7
**Concurrent Activities**

A **dummy** activity is inserted into the network to show a precedence relationship, but it does not represent any actual passage of time. Activities 2–3 and 2–4 have the precedence relationship shown in Figure 9.7*a*. However, in an AOA network, two or more activities are not allowed to share the same starting and ending nodes. Instead, activity 3–4 is inserted to give two activities separate end nodes and, thus, two separate identities as shown in Figure 9.7*b*. Notice, however, that a time of zero months has been assigned to activity 3–4. The dummy activity shows that activity 2–3 must be completed prior to any activities beginning at node 4, but it does not represent the passage of time.

**Dummy:** two or more activities cannot share the same start and end nodes.

Returning to the network in Figure 9.6, we see that two activities start at node 4. Activity 4–6 is the actual building of the house, and activity 4–5 is the search for and selection of the paint for the exterior and interior of the house. Activity 4–6 and activity 4–5 can begin simultaneously and take place concurrently. Following the selection of the paint (activity 4–5) and the realization of node 5, the carpet can be selected (since the carpet color depends on the paint color). This activity can also occur concurrently with the building of the house (activity 4–6). When the building is completed and the paint and carpet are selected, the house can be finished (activity 6–7).

## AON NETWORK

Figure 9.8 shows the comparable AON network to the AOA network in Figure 9.6 for our house building project. Notice that the activities and activity times are on the nodes and not on the activities as they were previously with the AOA network. The branches or arrows simply show the precedence relationships between the activities. Also, notice that there is no dummy activity; dummy activities are not required in an AON network since two activities will never be confused because they have the same start and end nodes. This is one advantage of the AON convention, although each has minor advantages and disadvantages. In general, both of the two methods accomplish the same thing, and the one that is used is usually a matter of individual preference. However, for our purposes the AON network has one distinct advantage—it is the convention used in the popular *Microsoft Project* software package, and because we want to demonstrate how to use this software, we will use the AON convention in this chapter.

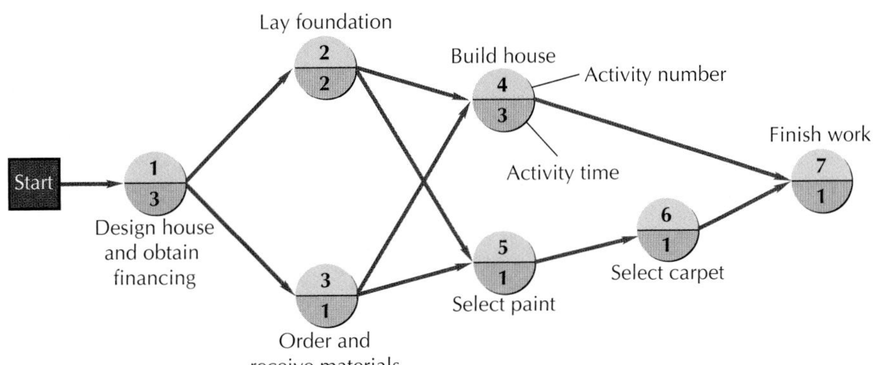


Figure 9.8
**AON Network for House Building Project**

## THE CRITICAL PATH

A network path is a sequence of connected activities that runs from the start to the end of the network. The network in Figure 9.8 has several paths through it. In fact, close observations of this network show four paths, identified as A, B, C, and D:

A: 1–2–4–7
B: 1–2–5–6–7
C: 1–3–4–7
D: 1–3–5–6–7

**Critical path:** the longest path through a network; it is the minimum project completion time.

The project cannot be completed (i.e., the house cannot be built) sooner than the time required by the longest path in the network, in terms of time. The path with the longest duration of time is referred to as the **critical path**.

By summing the activity times (shown in Figure 9.8) along each of the four paths, we can compute the length of each path, as follows:

Path A: 1–2–4–7
$3 + 2 + 3 + 1 = 9$ months
Path B: 1–2–5–6–7
$3 + 2 + 1 + 1 + 1 = 8$ months
Path C: 1–3–4–7
$3 + 1 + 3 + 1 = 8$ months
Path D: 1–3–5–6-7
$3 + 1 + 1 + 1 + 1 = 7$ months

Because path A is the longest, it is the critical path; thus, the minimum completion time for the project is nine months. Now let us analyze the critical path more closely. From Figure 9.9 we can see that activity 3 cannot start until 3 months have passed. It is also easy to see that activity 4 will not start until five months have passed. The start of activity 4 is dependent on two activities leading into node 4. Activity 2 is completed after 5 months, but activity 3 is completed at the end of four months. Thus, we have two possible start times for activity 4, five months and four months. However, since the activity at node 4 cannot start until all preceding activities have been finished, the soonest node 4 can be realized is five months.

Now consider the activity following node 4. Using the same logic as before, activity 7 cannot start until after eight months (five months at node 4 plus the three months required by activity 4) or after seven months. Because all activities preceding node 7 must be completed before activity 7 can start, the soonest this can occur is eight months. Adding one month for activity 7 to the start time at node 7 gives a project duration of nine months. This is the time of the longest path in the network—the critical path.

This brief analysis demonstrates the concept of a critical path and the determination of the minimum completion time of a project. However, this was a cumbersome method for determining a critical path. Next, we discuss a mathematical approach to scheduling the project activities and determining the critical path.

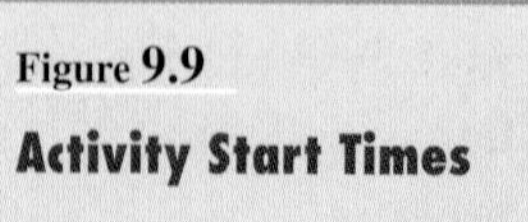

Figure 9.9
**Activity Start Times**

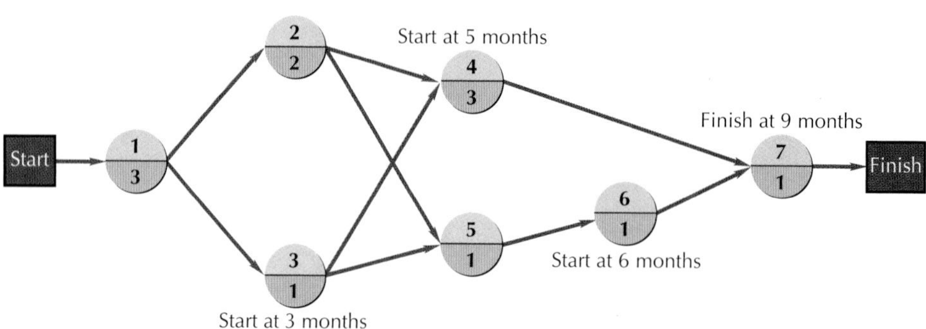

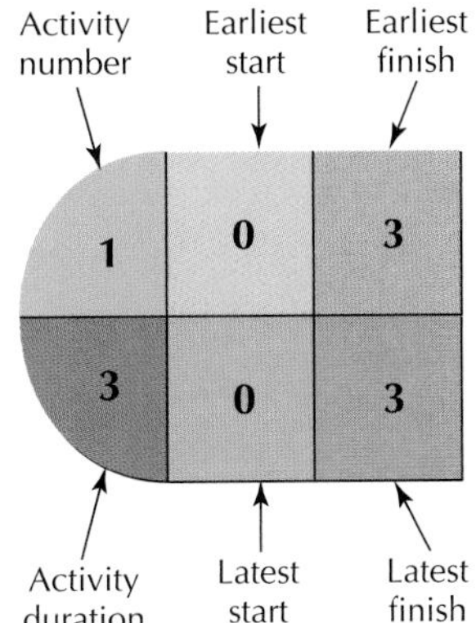


Figure 9.10
**Node Configuration**

## ACTIVITY SCHEDULING

In our analysis of the critical path, we determined the earliest time that each activity could be finished. For example, we found that the earliest time activity 4 could start was five months. This time is referred to as the **earliest start time**, and it is expressed symbolically as **ES**. In order to show the earliest start time on the network as well as some other activity times we will develop in the scheduling process, we will alter our node structure a little. Figure 9.10 shows the structure for node 1, the first activity in our example network for designing the house and obtaining financing.

**Earliest start time (ES):** the earliest time an activity can start.

To determine the earliest start time for every activity, we make a **forward pass** through the network. That is, we start at the first node and move forward through the network. The earliest start time for an activity is the maximum time in which all preceding activities have been completed—the time when the activity start node is realized.

**Forward pass:** starts at the beginning of a CPM/PERT network to determine the earliest activity times.

The **earliest finish time (EF)**, for an activity is simply the earliest start time plus the activity time estimate. For example, if the earliest start time for activity 1 is at time 0, then the earliest finish time is three months. In general, the earliest start and finish times for an activity are computed according to the following mathematical relationship.

**Earliest finish time (EF):** is the earliest start time plus the activity time.

$$\text{ES} = \text{maximum (EF) of immediate predecessors}$$
$$\text{EF} = \text{ES} + t$$

The earliest start and earliest finish times for all the activities in our project network are shown in Figure 9.11.

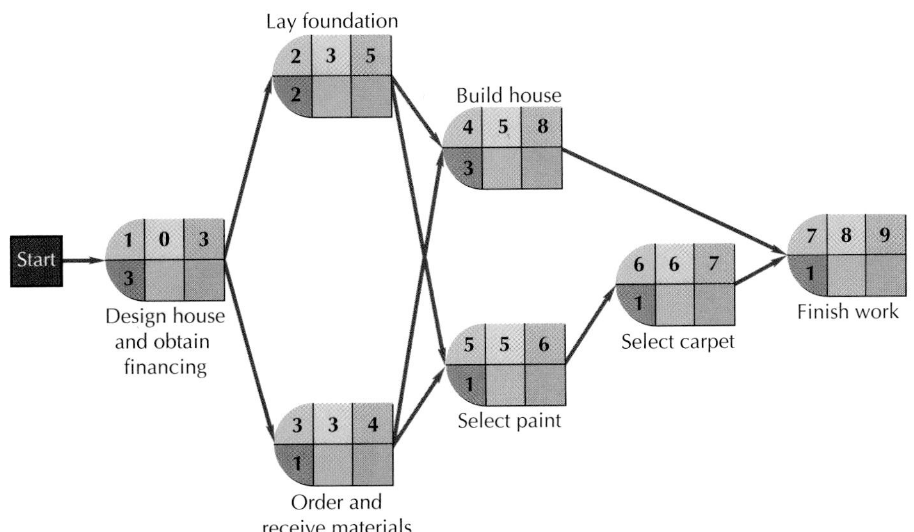


Figure 9.11
**Earliest Activity Start and Finish Times**

The earliest start time for the first activity in the network (for which there are no predecessor activities) is always 0, or, ES = 0. This enables us to compute the earliest finish time for activity 1 as

$$\begin{aligned} \text{EF} &= \text{ES} + t \\ &= 0 + 3 \\ &= 3 \text{ months} \end{aligned}$$

The earliest start for activity 2 is

$$\begin{aligned} \text{ES} &= \max \text{ (EF immediate predecessors)} \\ &= 3 \text{ months} \end{aligned}$$

and the corresponding earliest finish time is

$$\begin{aligned} \text{EF} &= \text{ES} + t \\ &= 3 + 2 \\ &= 5 \text{ months} \end{aligned}$$

For activity 3 the earliest start time (ES) is three months, and the earliest finish time (EF) is four months.

Now consider activity 4, which has two predecessor activities. The earliest start time is

$$\begin{aligned} \text{ES} &= \max \text{ (EF immediate predecessors)} \\ &= \max (5, 4) \\ &= 5 \text{ months} \end{aligned}$$

and the earliest finish time is

$$\begin{aligned} \text{EF} &= \text{ES} + t \\ &= 5 + 3 \\ &= 8 \text{ months} \end{aligned}$$

All the remaining earliest start and finish times are computed similarly. Notice in Figure 9.11 that the earliest finish time for activity 7, the last activity in the network, is nine months, which is the total project duration, or critical path time.

**Latest start time (LS):** the latest time an activity can start without delaying critical path time.

**Latest finish time (LF):** the latest time an activity can be completed and still maintain the project critical path time.

Companions to the earliest start and finish are the **latest start** and **latest finish times, LS** and **LF**. The latest start time is the latest time an activity can start without delaying the completion of the project beyond the project critical path time. For our example, the project completion time (and earliest finish time) at node 7 is nine months. Thus, the objective of determining latest times is to see how long each activity can be delayed without the project exceeding nine months.

In general, the latest start and finish times for an activity are computed according to the following formulas:

$$\begin{aligned} \text{LS} &= \text{LF} - t \\ \text{LF} &= \min \text{ (LS immediate following activities)} \end{aligned}$$

**Backward pass:** determines latest activity times by starting at the end of a CPM/PERT network and working forward.

Whereas a forward pass through the network is made to determine the earliest times, the latest times are computed using a **backward pass**. We start at the end of the network at node 7 and work backward, computing the latest times for each activity. Since we want to determine how long each activity in the network can be delayed without extending the project time, the latest finish time at node 7 cannot exceed the earliest finish time. Therefore, the latest finish time at node 7 is nine months. This and all other latest times are shown in Figure 9.12.

Starting at the end of the network, the critical path time, which is also equal to the earliest finish time of activity 7, is nine months. This automatically becomes the latest finish time for activity 7, or

$$\text{LF} = 9 \text{ months}$$

Using this value, the latest start time for activity 7 is

$$\begin{aligned} \text{LS} &= \text{LF} - t \\ &= 9 - 1 \\ &= 8 \text{ months} \end{aligned}$$

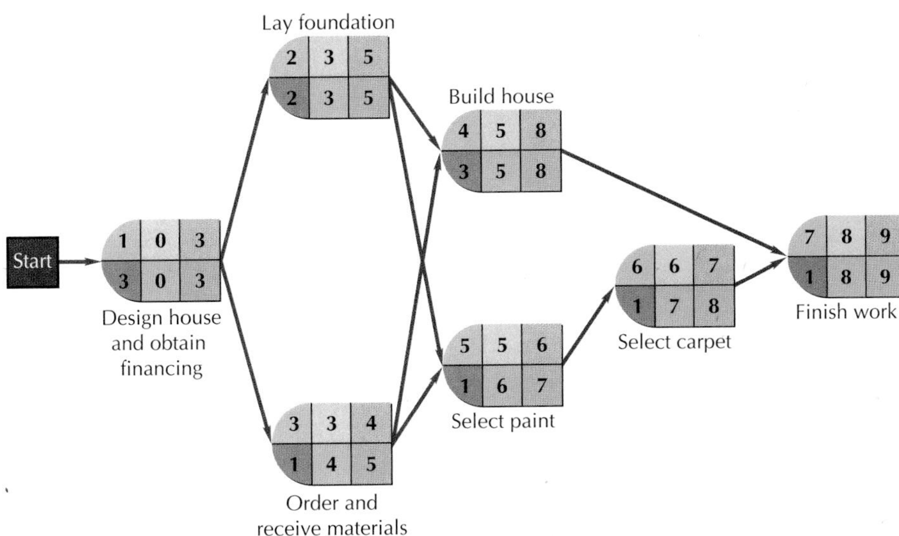


Figure 9.12
**Latest Activity Start and Finish Times**

The latest finish time for activity 6 is the minimum of the latest start times for the activities following node 6. Since activity 7 follows node 6, the latest finish time is

$$\begin{aligned} LF_6 &= \min \text{ (LS following activities)} \\ &= 8 \text{ months} \end{aligned}$$

The latest start time for activity 6 is

$$\begin{aligned} LS &= LF - t \\ &= 8 - 1 \\ &= 7 \text{ months} \end{aligned}$$

For activity 4, the latest finish time (LF) is 8 months, and the latest start time (LS) is 5 months; for activity 5, the latest finish time (LF) is seven months, and the latest start time (LS) is six months.

Now consider activity 3, which has two activities, 4 and 5, following it. The latest finish time is computed as

$$\begin{aligned} LF &= \min \text{ (LS following activities)} \\ &= \min (5, 6) \\ &= 5 \text{ months} \end{aligned}$$

The latest start time is

$$\begin{aligned} LS &= LF - t \\ &= 5 - 1 \\ &= 4 \text{ months} \end{aligned}$$

All the remaining latest start and latest finish times are computed similarly. Figure 9.12 includes the earliest and latest start times, and earliest and latest finish times for all activities.

## ACTIVITY SLACK

The project network in Figure 9.12, with all activity start and finish times, highlights the critical path (1–2–4–7) we determined earlier by inspection. Notice that for the activities on the critical path, the earliest start times and latest start times are equal. This means that these activities on the critical path must start exactly on time and cannot be delayed at all. If the start of any activity on the critical path is delayed, then the overall project time will be increased. We now have an alternative way to determine the critical path besides simply inspecting the network. The activities on the critical path can be determined by seeing for which activities ES = LS or EF = LF. In Figure 9.12 the activities 1, 2, 4, and 7 all have earliest start times and latest start times that are equal (and EF = LF); thus, they are on the critical path.

**Table 9.1**
**Activity Slack**

| Activity | LS | ES | LF | EF | Slack S |
|---|---|---|---|---|---|
| *1 | 0 | 0 | 3 | 3 | 0 |
| *2 | 3 | 3 | 5 | 5 | 0 |
| 3 | 4 | 3 | 5 | 4 | 1 |
| *4 | 5 | 5 | 8 | 8 | 0 |
| 5 | 6 | 5 | 7 | 6 | 1 |
| 6 | 7 | 6 | 8 | 7 | 1 |
| *7 | 8 | 8 | 9 | 9 | 0 |

* = critical path.

For activities not on the critical path for which the earliest and latest start times (or earliest and latest finish times) are not equal, *slack* time exists. We introduced slack with our discussion of the Gantt chart in Figure 9.4. Slack is the amount of time an activity can be delayed without affecting the overall project duration. In effect, it is extra time available for completing an activity.

Slack, *S*, is computed using either of the following formulas:

$$S = LS - ES$$

or

$$S = LF - EF$$

For example, the slack for activity 3 is

$$\begin{aligned} S &= LS - ES \\ &= 4 - 3 \\ &= 1 \text{ month} \end{aligned}$$

If the start of activity 3 were delayed for one month, the activity could still be completed by month 5 without delaying the project completion time. The slack for each activity in our example project network is shown in Table 9.1. Table 9.1 shows there is no slack for the activities on the critical path (marked with an asterisk); activities not on the critical path have slack.

*A primary use of CPM/PERT is to plan, manage and control construction projects of all types, such as the velodrome venue shown here under construction at the 2004 Athens Olympic Games.*

## THE COMPETITIVE EDGE

### Disposing of the Trojan Nuclear Reactor

The conventional method for decommissioning a nuclear reactor is to dismantle the reactor and its internal components into as many as 90 separate shipments for burial. The project involving the decommissioning of Portland (Oregon) General Electric's Trojan Nuclear Power Plant was unique in that the complete nuclear reactor was removed, transported, and disposed of in one piece. When packaged for shipment, it weighed over 1000 tons. This was the first time such an approach to decommissioning a reactor had been attempted.

Disposing of the reactor vessel was an ambitious project since it was laden with radioactivity after 19 years of service. However, removing and transporting it as a whole unit exposed workers and the public to a fraction of the potential radiation that would have resulted from separating and dismantling it. It also resulted in less than half the radioactive waste and significant cost savings. The project cost of $21.9 million was $19 million less than the estimated cost of the conventional disposal method and $4.2 million under budget.

The entire project spanned three and a half years. The reactor vessel was more than 42 feet long, with a diameter of 17 feet and carbon steel walls 5 to 10 inches thick. It was drained and filled with 200 tons of concrete and provided with steel shielding to reduce radiation levels. To remove it, a large section of the containment building was cut away. Heavy lift systems had to be designed and built to lift the reactor from the containment building and onto a rail system from which it was loaded onto a specially customized transporter. A special tie-down system was developed to mount the reactor on the transporter, both of which were then moved by a prime mover a quarter mile to a ship on the Columbia River, where they were loaded onto a custom-built barge. The barge, accompanied by two tugboats and a U.S. Coast Guard escort, transported the transporter and reactor 270 miles up the Columbia River to the Port of Benton, Washington. The transporter and reactor were moved off the barge and then transported 22 miles by road to the disposal site at the U.S. Ecology Low-Level Radioactive Waste Facility at the Hanford Nuclear Reservation. A few days after arrival it was placed in a 45-foot-deep trench and covered with earth.

*Source:* J. Holtzman, "PMI 2000 International Project of the Year: The Trojan Reactor Vessel and Internals Removal Project," *PM Network* 15(1; January 2001), pp. 28–32.

Notice in Figure 9.12 that activity 3 can be delayed one month and activity 5 that follows it can be delayed one more month, but then activity 6 cannot be delayed at all even though it has one month of slack. If activity 3 starts late at month 4 instead of month 3, then it will be completed at month 5, which will not allow activity 5 to start until month 5. If the start of activity 5 is delayed one month, then it will be completed at month 7, and activity 6 cannot be delayed at all without exceeding the critical path time. The slack on these three activities is called *shared slack*. This means that the sequence of activities 3–5–6 can be delayed two months jointly without delaying the project, but not three months.

Slack is beneficial to the project manager because it enables resources to be temporarily diverted from activities with slack and used for other activities that might be delayed for various reasons or for which the time estimate has proved to be inaccurate.

The times for the network activities are simply estimates, for which there is usually not a lot of historical basis (since projects tend to be unique undertakings). As such, activity time estimates are subject to quite a bit of uncertainty. However, the uncertainty inherent in activity time estimates can be reflected to a certain extent by using probabilistic time estimates instead of the single, deterministic estimates we have used so far.

## PROBABILISTIC ACTIVITY TIMES

In the project network for building a house in the previous section, all activity time estimates were single values. By using only a single activity time estimate, we are, in effect, assuming that activity times are known with certainty (i.e., they are deterministic). For example, in Figure 9.8, the time estimate for activity 2 (laying the foundation) is two months. Since only this one value is given, we must assume that the activity time does not vary (or varies very little) from two months. It is rare that activity time estimates can be made with certainty. Project activities are likely to be unique with little historical evidence that can be used as a basis to predict activity times. Recall that one of the primary differences between CPM and PERT is that PERT uses probabilistic activity times.

**Probabilistic time estimates reflect uncertainty of activity times.**

## PROBABILISTIC TIME ESTIMATES

**Beta distribution:** a probability distribution traditionally used in CPM/PERT.

In the PERT-type approach to estimating activity times, three time estimates for each activity are determined, which enables us to estimate the mean and variance of a **beta distribution** of the activity times.

We assume that the activity times can be described by a beta distribution for several reasons. The beta distribution mean and variance can be approximated with three time estimates. Also, the beta distribution is continuous, but it has no predetermined shape (such as the bell shape of the normal curve). It will take on the shape indicated—that is, be skewed—by the time estimates given. This is beneficial, since typically we have no prior knowledge of the shapes of the distributions of activity times in a unique project network. Although other types of distributions have been shown to be no more or less accurate than the beta, it has become traditional to use the beta distribution to estimate probabilistic activity times.

**Optimistic ($a$), most likely ($m$), and pessimistic ($b$):** time estimates for an activity.

The three time estimates for each activity are the **most likely time ($m$)**, the **optimistic time ($a$)**, and the **pessimistic time ($b$)**. The most likely time is a subjective estimate of the activity time that would most frequently occur if the activity were repeated many times. The optimistic time is the shortest possible time to complete the activity if everything went right. The pessimistic time is the longest possible time to complete the activity assuming everything went wrong. The person most familiar with an activity or the project manager makes these "subjective" estimates to the best of his or her knowledge and ability.

These three time estimates are used to estimate the mean and variance of a beta distribution, as follows:

$$\text{Mean (expected time): } t = \frac{a + 4m + b}{6}$$

$$\text{Variance: } \sigma^2 = \left(\frac{b - a}{6}\right)^2$$

where

$a$ = optimistic time estimate
$m$ = most likely time estimate
$b$ = pessimistic time estimate

These formulas provide a reasonable estimate of the mean and variance of the beta distribution, a distribution that is continuous and can take on various shapes, or exhibit skewness.

Figure 9.13 illustrates the general form of beta distributions for different relative values of $a$, $m$, and $b$.

Figure 9.13
**Examples of the Beta Distribution**

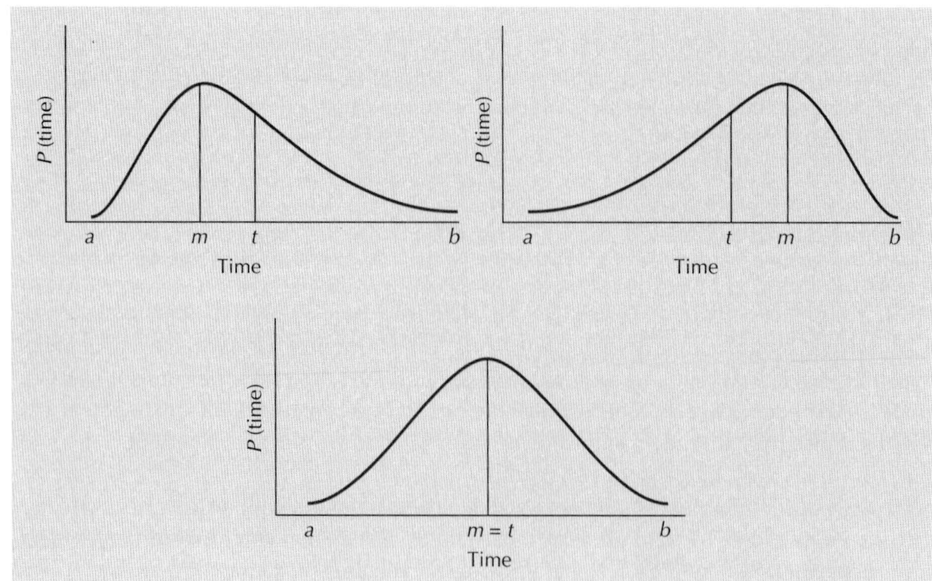

Example 9.1

**A Project Network with Probabilistic Time Estimates**

The Southern Textile Company has decided to install a new computerized order processing system that will link the company with customers and suppliers. In the past, orders were processed manually, which contributed to delays in delivery orders and resulted in lost sales. The new system will improve the quality of the service the company provides. The company wants to develop a project network for the installation of the new system. The network for the installation of the new order processing system is shown in the following figure.

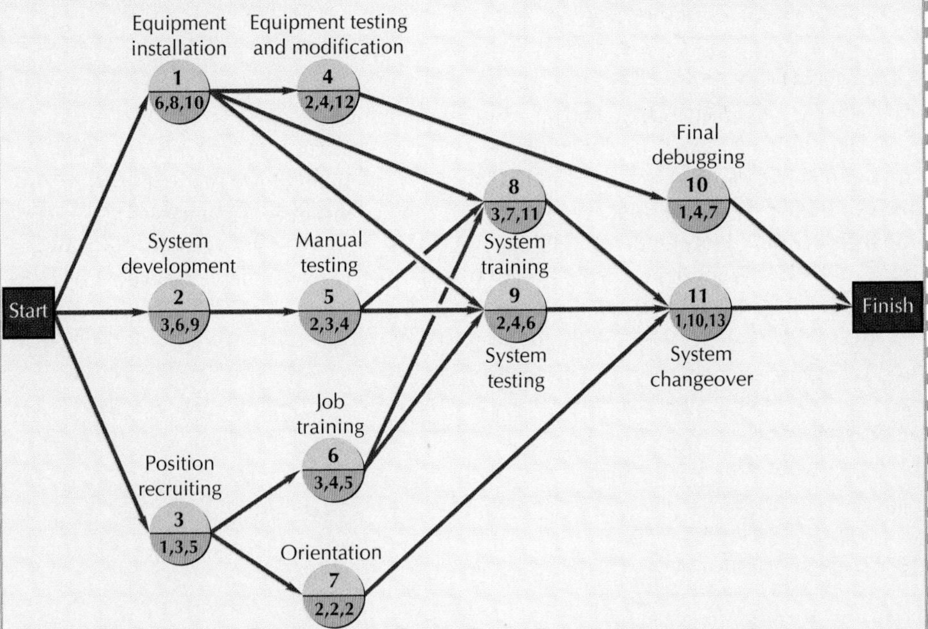


The network begins with three concurrent activities: The new computer equipment is installed (activity 1); the computerized order processing system is developed (activity 2); and people are recruited to operate the system (activity 3). Once people are hired, they are trained for the job (activity 6), and other personnel in the company, such as marketing, accounting, and production personnel, are introduced to the new system (activity 7). Once the system is developed (activity 2) it is tested manually to make sure that it is logical (activity 5). Following activity 1, the new equipment is tested, any necessary modifications are made (activity 4), and the newly trained personnel begin training on the computerized system (activity 8). Also, node 9 begins the testing of the system on the computer to check for errors (activity 9). The final activities include a trial run and changeover to the system (activity 11), and final debugging of the computer system (activity 10).

The three time estimates, the mean, and the variance for all the activities in the network as shown in the figure are provided in the following table:

**Activity Time Estimates for Example 9.1**

| | Time Estimates (weeks) | | | Mean Time | Variance |
|---|---|---|---|---|---|
| **Activity** | $a$ | $m$ | $b$ | $t$ | $\sigma^2$ |
| 1 | 6 | 8 | 10 | 8 | 0.44 |
| 2 | 3 | 6 | 9 | 6 | 1.00 |
| 3 | 1 | 3 | 5 | 3 | 0.44 |
| 4 | 2 | 4 | 12 | 5 | 2.78 |
| 5 | 2 | 3 | 4 | 3 | 0.11 |
| 6 | 3 | 4 | 5 | 4 | 0.11 |
| 7 | 2 | 2 | 2 | 2 | 0.00 |
| 8 | 3 | 7 | 11 | 7 | 1.78 |
| 9 | 2 | 4 | 6 | 4 | 0.44 |
| 10 | 1 | 4 | 7 | 4 | 1.00 |
| 11 | 1 | 10 | 13 | 9 | 4.00 |

*Solution*

As an example of the computation of the individual activity mean times and variance, consider activity 1. The three time estimates ($a = 6$, $m = 8$, $b = 10$) are substituted in the formulas as follows:

$$t = \frac{a + 4m + b}{6} = \frac{6 + 4(8) + 10}{6} = 8 \text{ weeks}$$

$$\sigma^2 = \left(\frac{b - a}{6}\right)^2 = \left(\frac{10 - 6}{6}\right)^2 = \frac{4}{9} \text{ week}$$

The other values for the mean and variance are computed similarly.

Once the mean times have been computed for each activity, we can determine the critical path the same way we did in the deterministic time network, except that we use the expected activity times, $t$. Recall that in the home building project network, we identified the critical path as the one containing those activities with zero slack. This requires the determination of earliest and latest start and finish times for each activity, as shown in the following table and figure:

**Activity Earliest and Latest Times and Slack**

| Activity | $t$ | $\sigma^2$ | ES | EF | LS | LF | S |
|---|---|---|---|---|---|---|---|
| 1 | 8 | 0.44 | 0 | 8 | 1 | 9 | 1 |
| 2 | 6 | 1.00 | 0 | 6 | 0 | 6 | 0 |
| 3 | 3 | 0.44 | 0 | 3 | 2 | 5 | 2 |
| 4 | 5 | 2.78 | 8 | 13 | 16 | 21 | 8 |
| 5 | 3 | 0.11 | 6 | 9 | 6 | 9 | 0 |
| 6 | 4 | 0.11 | 3 | 7 | 5 | 9 | 2 |
| 7 | 2 | 0.00 | 3 | 5 | 14 | 16 | 11 |
| 8 | 7 | 1.78 | 9 | 16 | 9 | 16 | 0 |
| 9 | 4 | 0.44 | 9 | 13 | 12 | 16 | 3 |
| 10 | 4 | 1.00 | 13 | 17 | 21 | 25 | 8 |
| 11 | 9 | 4.00 | 16 | 25 | 16 | 25 | 0 |

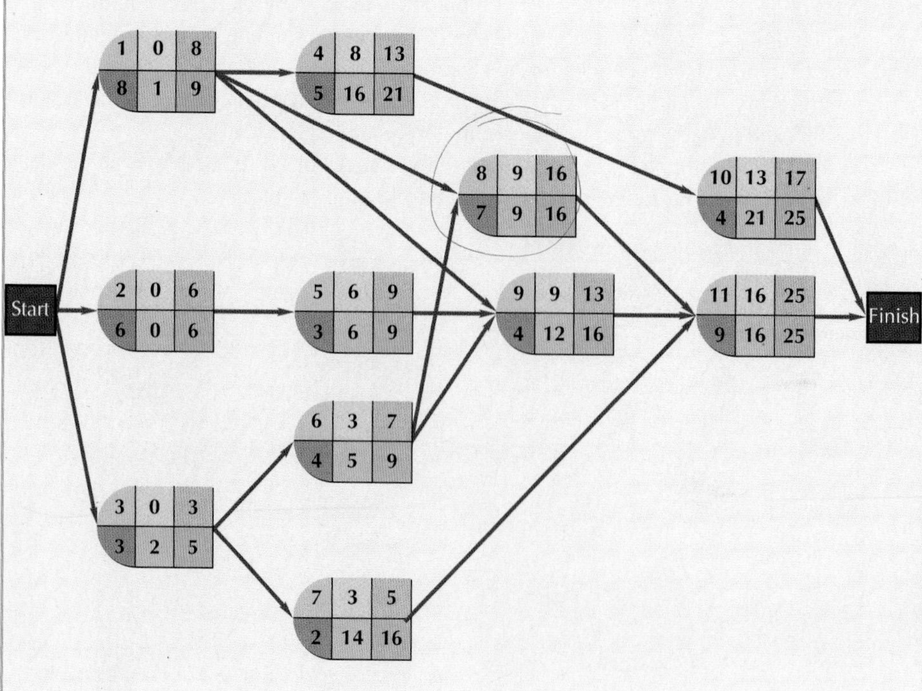

From the table, we can see that the critical path encompasses activities 2–5–8–11, since these activities have no available slack. We can also see that the expected project completion time ($t_p$) is the same as the earliest or latest finish for activity 11, or $t_p = 25$ weeks. To determine the project variance, we *sum the variances for the activities on the critical path.* Using the variances shown in the table for the critical path activities, we can compute the total project variance as follows:

$$\begin{aligned}\sigma^2 &= \sigma_2^2 + \sigma_5^2 + \sigma_8^2 + \sigma_{11}^2 \\ &= 1.00 + 0.11 + 1.78 + 4.00 \\ &= 6.89 \text{ weeks}\end{aligned}$$

Project variance is the sum of variances on the critical path.

## PROBABILISTIC NETWORK ANALYSIS

The CPM/PERT method assumes that the activity times are statistically independent, which allows us to sum the individual expected activity times and variances to get an expected project time and variance. It is further assumed that the network mean and variance are normally distributed. This assumption is based on the central limit theorem of probability, which for CPM/PERT analysis and our purposes states that if the number of activities is large enough and the activities are statistically independent, then the sum of the means of the activities along the critical path will approach the mean of a normal distribution. For the small examples in this chapter, it is questionable whether there are sufficient activities to guarantee that the mean project completion time and variance are normally distributed. Although it has become conventional in CPM/PERT analysis to employ probability analysis using the normal distribution regardless of the network size, the prudent user should bear this limitation in mind.

Probabilistic analysis of a CPM/PERT network is the determination of the probability that the project will be completed within a certain time period given the mean and variance of a normally distributed project completion time. This is illustrated in Figure 9.14. The value $Z$ is computed using the following formula:

$$Z = \frac{x - \mu}{\sigma}$$

where

$\mu = t_p$ = project mean time

$x$ = the proposed project time

$Z$ = number of standard devisions $x$ is from the mean

This value of $Z$ is then used to find the corresponding probability in Table A.1 (Appendix A).

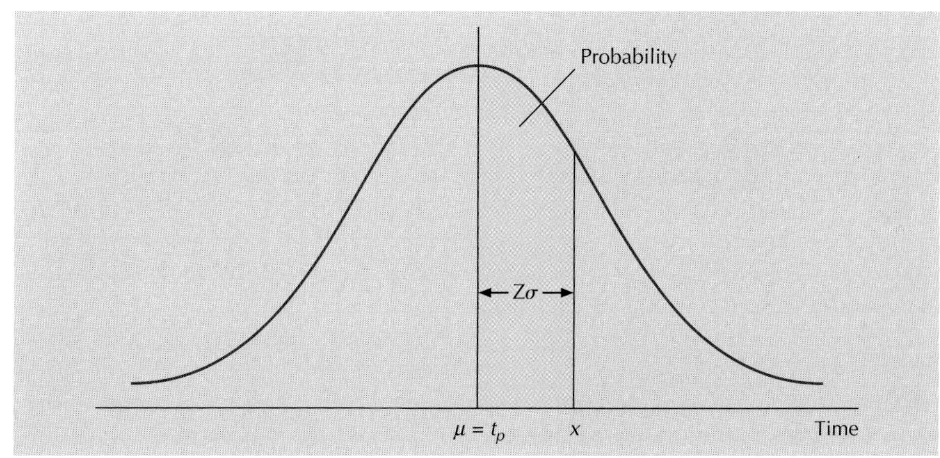


Figure 9.14
**Normal Distribution of Project Time**

**Example 9.2**

**Probabilistic Analysis of the Project Network**

The Southern Textile Company in Example 9.1 has told its customers that the new order processing system will be operational in 30 weeks. What is the probability that the system will be ready by that time?

*Solution*

The probability that the project will be completed within 30 weeks is shown as the shaded area in the accompanying figure. To compute the $Z$ value for a time of 30 weeks, we must first compute the standard deviation ($\sigma$) from the variance ($\sigma^2$).

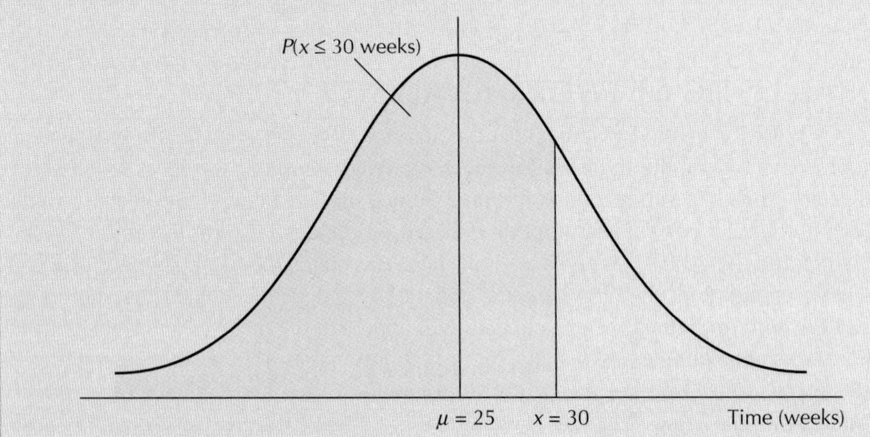


$$\sigma^2 = 6.89 \text{ weeks}$$
$$\sigma = \sqrt{6.89}$$
$$= 2.62 \text{ weeks}$$

Next we substitute this value for the standard deviation along with the value for the mean, 25 weeks, and our proposed project completion time, 30 weeks, into the following formula:

$$Z = \frac{x - \mu}{\sigma}$$
$$= \frac{30 - 25}{2.62}$$
$$= 1.91$$

A $Z$ value of 1.91 corresponds to a probability of 0.4719 in Table A.1 in Appendix A. This means that there is a 0.9719 probability of completing the project in 30 weeks or less (adding the probability of the area to the left of $\mu = 25$, or 0.5000 to 0.4719).

**Example 9.3**

**Probabilistic Analysis of the Project Network**

A customer of the Southern Textile Company has become frustrated with delayed orders and told the company that if the new ordering system is not working within 22 weeks, it will not do any more business with the textile company. What is the probability the order processing system will be operational within 22 weeks?

*Solution*

The probability that the project will be completed within 22 weeks is shown as the shaded area in the accompanying figure.

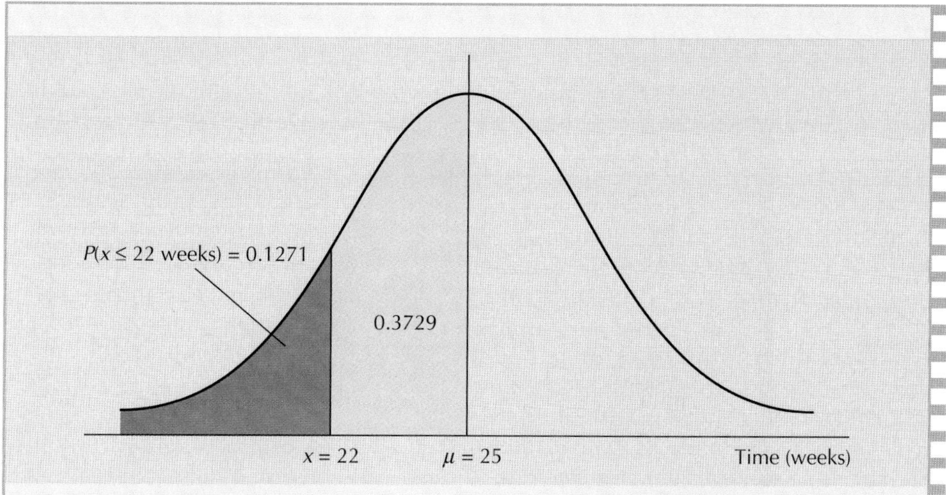


The probability of the project's being completed within 22 weeks is computed as follows:

$$\begin{aligned} Z &= \frac{22 - 25}{2.62} \\ &= \frac{-3}{2.62} \\ &= -1.14 \end{aligned}$$

A $Z$ value of $-1.14$ corresponds to a probability of 0.3729 in the normal table in Appendix A. Thus, there is only a 0.1271 (i.e., $0.5000 - 0.3729$) probability that the system will be operational in 22 weeks.

## MICROSOFT PROJECT

*Microsoft Project* is a very popular and widely used software package for project management and CPM/PERT analysis. It is also relatively easy to use. We will demonstrate how to use *Microsoft Project 2002* using our project network for building a house in Exhibit 9.8. Note that the *Microsoft Project* file for this example beginning with Exhibit 9.1 can be downloaded from the text Web site.

When you open *Microsoft Project*, a screen comes up for a new project. Click on the "Tasks" button and the screen like the one shown in Exhibit 9.1 will appear. Notice the set of steps on the left side of the screen starting with "Define project." If you click on "Define project," it enables you to set a start date and in step 3 name the project and save it. We set the start date for our house building project as September 18, 2004, and named the project "House Building Project."

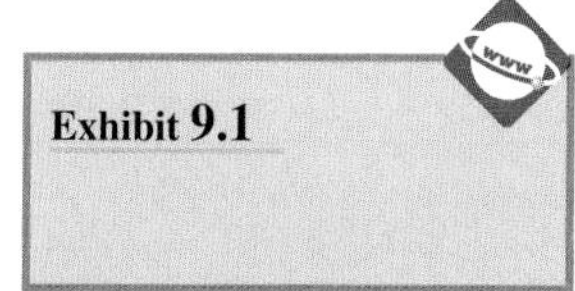


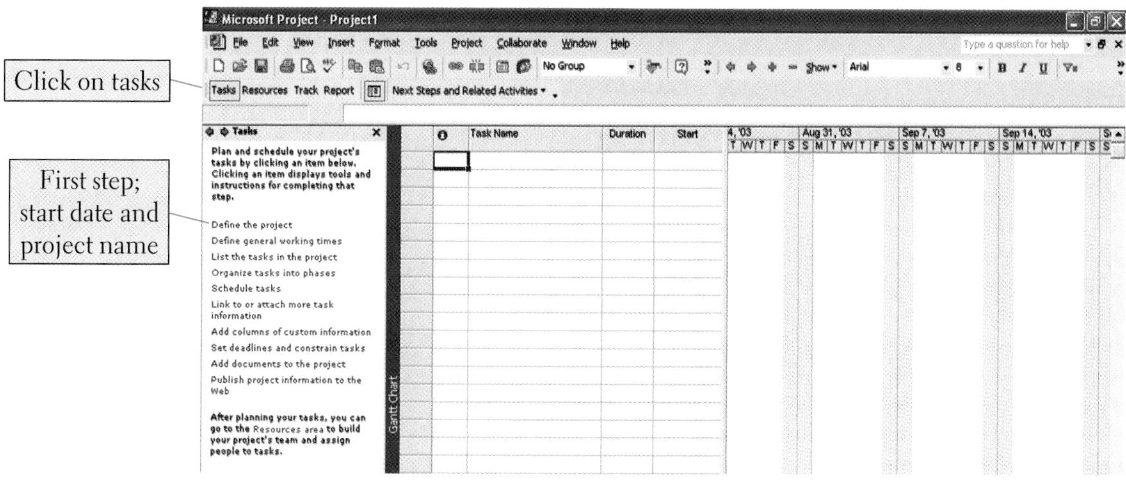

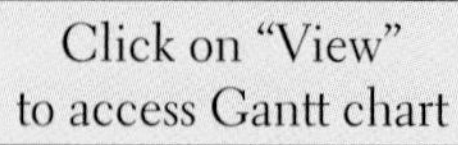


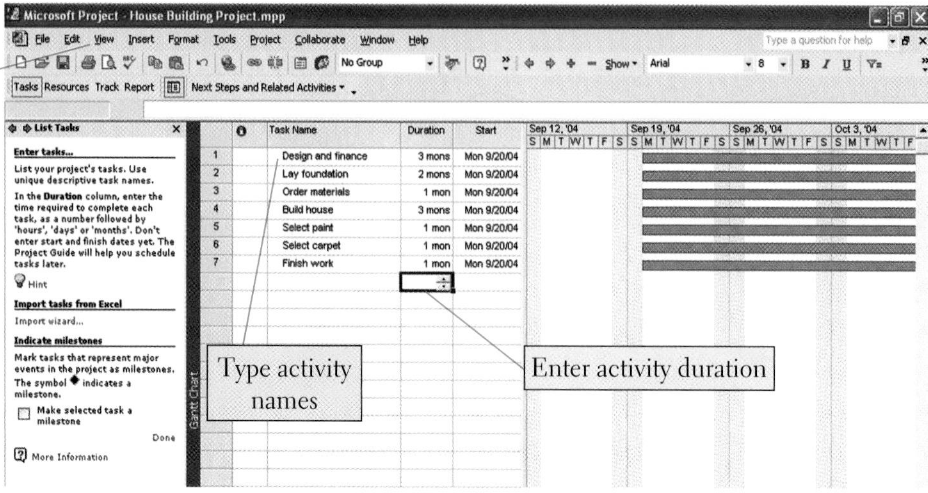


**Exhibit 9.2**

The second step in the "Tasks" menu, "Define general working times," allows the user to specify general work rules and a work calendar including such things as working hours per day, holidays, and weekend days off. In the third step in the "Tasks" menu, we can "List the tasks in the project." The tasks for our house building project are shown in Exhibit 9.2. Notice that we also indicated the duration of each task in the "Duration" column. For example, to enter the duration of the first activity, you would type in "3 months" in the duration column. Notice that the first task is shown to start on September 20—and not September 18, our previously indicated start date. This is because September 18 occurs on a Saturday and we specified that there would be no weekend work. The bars on the far right are for a Gantt chart, but since we haven't established the task sequencing yet the chart shows nothing but bars.

The next thing we will do is "Schedule tasks" by specifying the predecessor and successor activities in our network. This is done by using the buttons under the "Link dependent tasks" in Exhibit 9.3. For example, to show that activity 1 precedes activity 2, we put the cursor on activity 1 and then hold down the "Ctrl" key while clicking on activity 2. This makes a "finish to start" link between two activities, which means that activity 2 cannot start until activity 1 is finished. This creates the precedence relationship between these two activities, which is shown under the "Predecessor" column in Exhibit 9.3.

Exhibit 9.3 also shows the completed Gantt chart for our network. The Gantt chart is accessed by clicking on the "View" button on the toolbar at the top of the screen and then clicking on the "Gantt Chart." You may also need to alter the time frame to get all of the

**Exhibit 9.3**

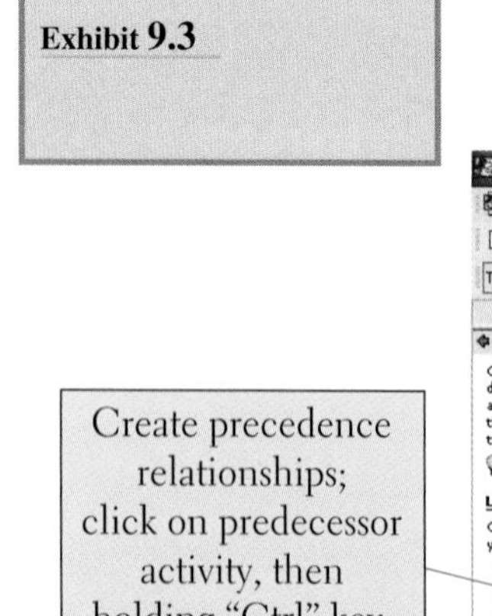


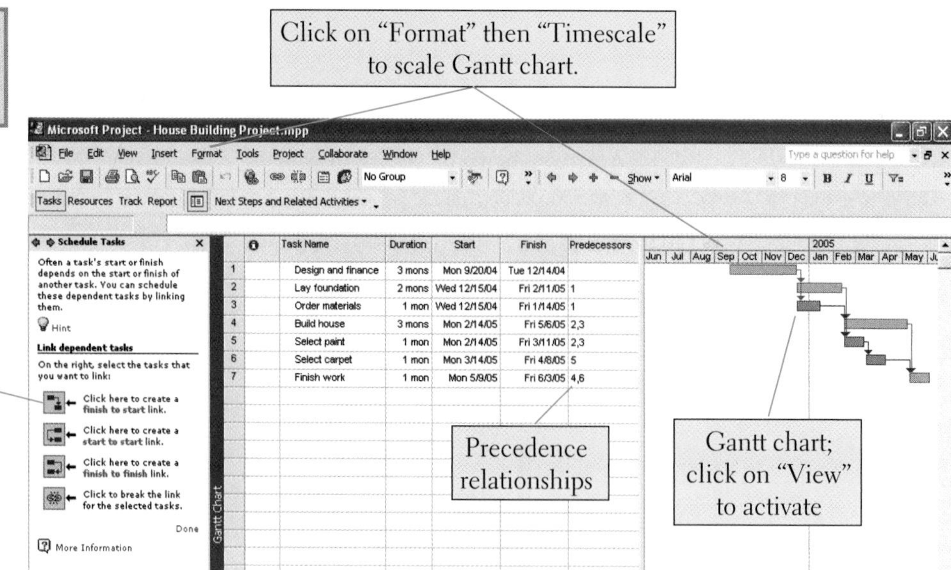

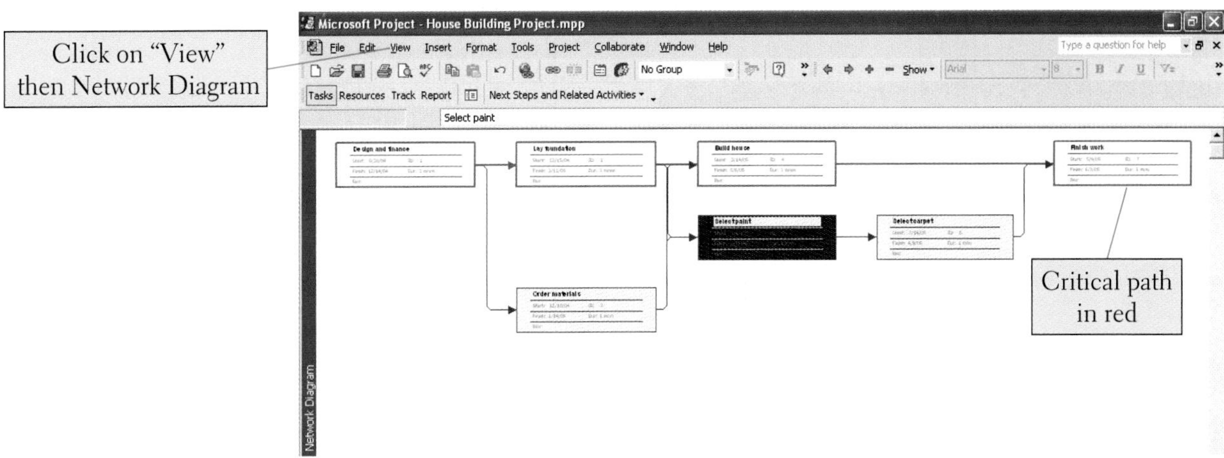


Exhibit 9.4

Gantt chart on your screen as shown in Exhibit 9.3. This can be accomplished by clicking on the "Format" button on the toolbar and then clicking on the "Timescale" option. This results in a window from which you can adjust the timescale from "days" as shown in Exhibit 9.2 to "months" as shown in Exhibit 9.3. Notice in Exhibit 9.3 that the critical path is highlighted in red. You can show the critical path by again clicking on "Format" on the toolbar and then activating the "Gantt Chart Wizard," which allows you to highlight the critical path, among other options.

To see the project network, click on the "View" button again on the toolbar and then click on "Network Diagram." Exhibit 9.4 shows the project network with the critical path highlighted in red. We used the "Zoom" option under the "View" menu to get the entire network on the screen. (We also removed the "Tasks" menu on the left side of the screen for the moment to show the complete network; it can be restored by clicking on the "Tasks" button again.) Exhibit 9.5 shows the project network without using the "Zoom" feature to reduce the network size. Notice that each node includes the start and finish dates and the activity number.

*Microsoft Project* has many additional tools and features for project updating and resource management. As an example, we will demonstrate one feature that updates the project schedule. First we double click on the first task, "Design and finance," resulting in the window labeled "Task Information" shown in Exhibit 9.6. On the "General" tab screen we have entered 100% in the "Percent complete" window, meaning this activity has been completed. We will also indicate that activities 2 and 3 have been completed while activity 4 is 60% complete and activity 5 is 20% complete. The resulting screen is shown in Exhibit 9.7. Notice that the dark lines through the Gantt chart bars indicates the degree of completion.

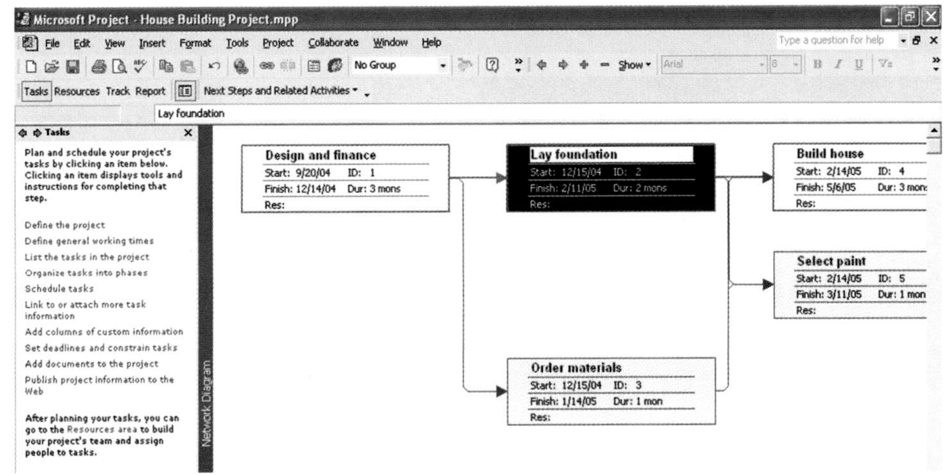


Exhibit 9.5

Exhibit 9.6

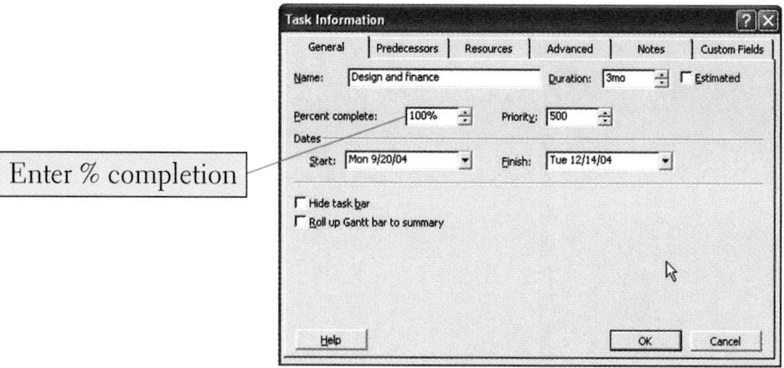


Exhibit 9.7

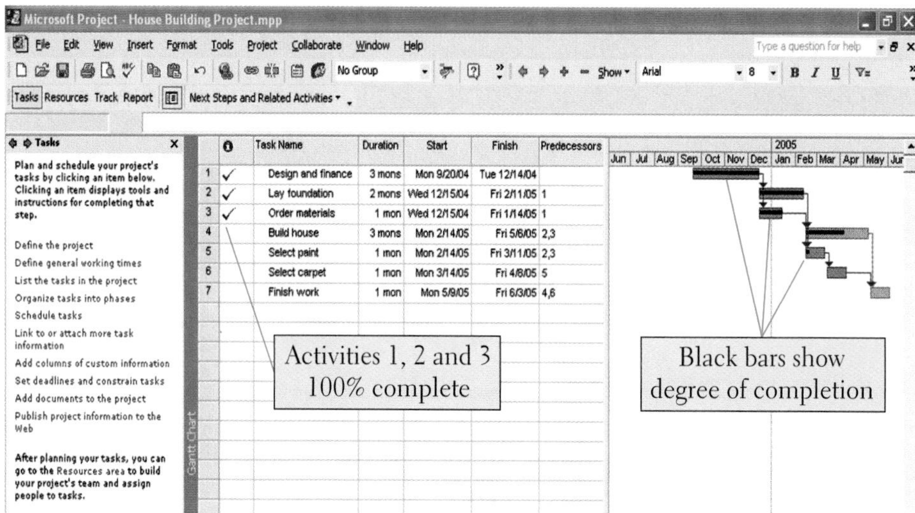


## PERT ANALYSIS WITH MICROSOFT PROJECT

A PERT network with three time estimates can also be developed using *Microsoft Project*. We will demonstrate this capability using our "Order Processing System" project from Example 9.1. After all of the project tasks are listed, then the three activity time estimates are entered by clicking on the "PERT Entry Sheet" button on the toolbar. If this button is not on your toolbar, you must add it in by clicking on "View" and then from the Toolbars options select "PERT Analysis." (If PERT Analysis is still not available to you, it must be added in through "COM Add-ins." Exhibit 9.8 shows the PERT time estimate entries for the activities in our order processing system project example. Exhibit 9.9 shows the estimated activity durations based on the three time estimates for each activity, the precedence relationships, and the project Gantt chart. Exhibit 9.10 shows the project network.

Exhibit 9.8

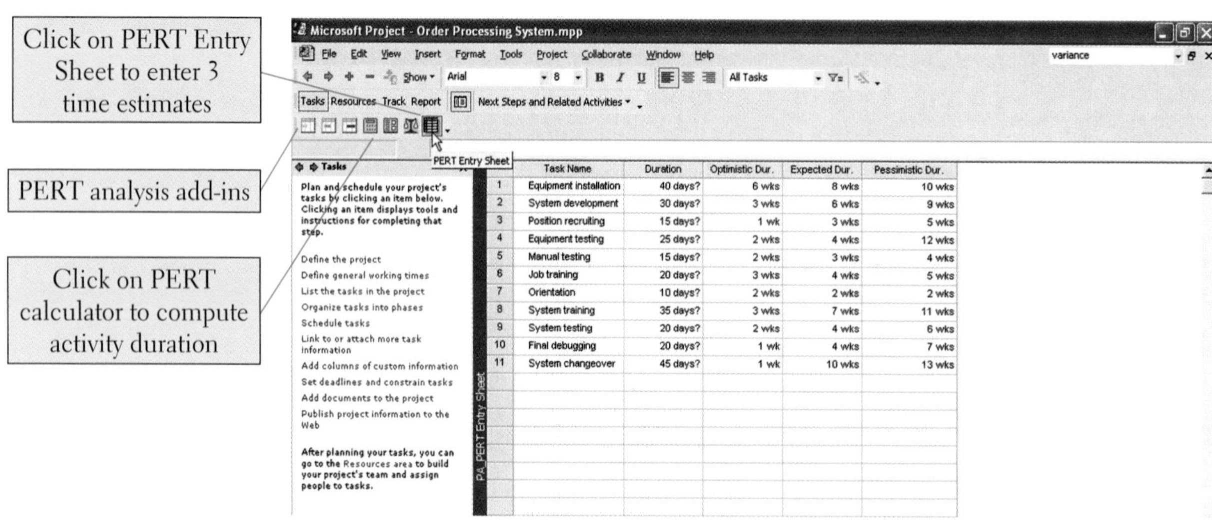

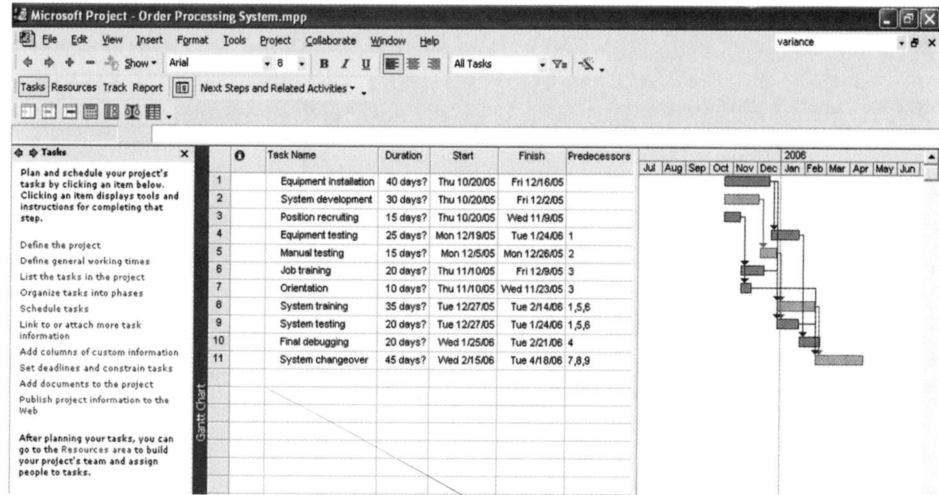


Exhibit 9.9

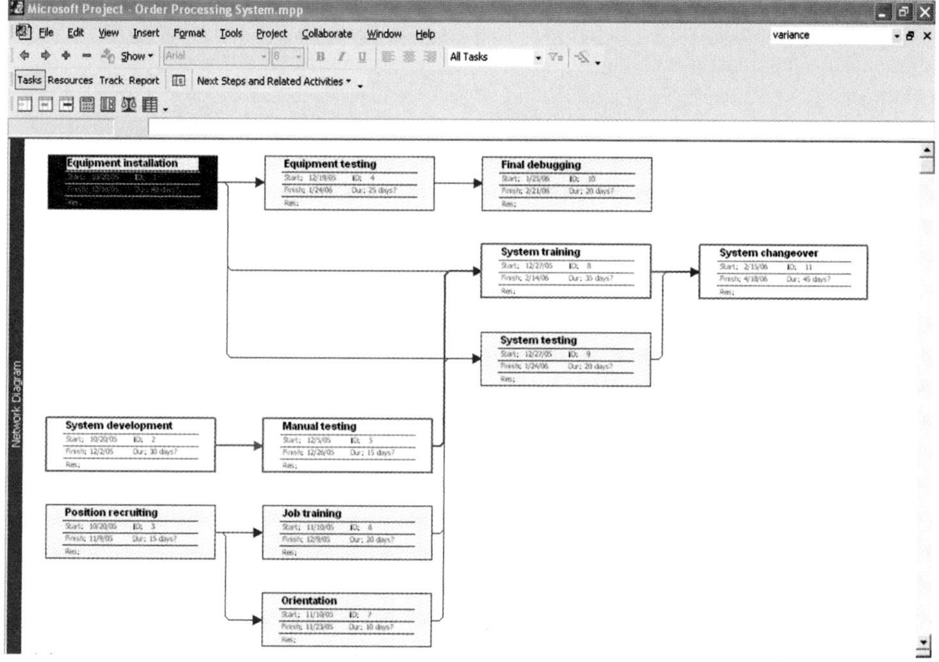


Exhibit 9.10

## PROJECT CRASHING AND TIME–COST TRADEOFF

The project manager is frequently confronted with having to reduce the scheduled completion time of a project to meet a deadline. In other words, the manager must finish the project sooner than indicated by the CPM/PERT network analysis. Project duration can often be reduced by assigning more labor to project activities, in the form of overtime, and by assigning more resources (material, equipment, and so on). However, additional labor and resources increase the project cost. Thus, the decision to reduce the project duration must be based on an analysis of the tradeoff between time and cost. *Project crashing* is a method for shortening the project duration by reducing the time of one (or more) of the critical project activities to less than its normal activity time. This reduction in the normal activity time is referred to as **crashing**. Crashing is achieved by devoting more resources, usually measured in terms of dollars, to the activities to be crashed.

**Crashing:** reducing project time by expending additional resources.

## THE COMPETITIVE EDGE

### Kodak's *Advantix* Advanced Photo System (APS) Project

On April 22, 1996, consumers around the world were able to purchase products and services from an entirely new photographic system developed by Kodak: the Advantix Advanced Photo System (APS). This new system included a film cassette that could be easily loaded into a camera without the need to thread the film, and a film format 60% of the size of traditional 35-mm film negative, allowing for smaller, more portable cameras. It also enabled a user to select from any of three print sizes when taking a photo, it returned processed negatives in their original cassette, and it included an index print with a miniature image of each picture in the set. This photographic system project was the most complicated ever undertaken by Kodak.

Kodak wanted to develop one worldwide industry standard, and it wanted to minimize the risk of competing standards that would only confuse the industry and consumers, so it began searching for project partners. In November 1991 Eastman Kodak reached an agreement with three leading camera companies, Canon, Minolta, and Nikon, as well as its top film competitor, Fuji, to initiate the project. (Licenses were subsequently offered to other photographic companies so they could also make products or offer services for the APS.)

Kodak was the only non-Japanese company among the five partners, which resulted in cultural, language, and geographic barriers. While there was a shared vision for a new photographic system, each company worked to protect its own interests. Project deadlines were established but could not be enforced. However, the shared vision among the partners and strong internal support from senior management allowed Kodak to overcome several major setbacks in technology and in reaching consensus on how the new system would look. The five partnered companies created a series of interlocking global teams, including a steering committee to set overall strategy, a working committee to evaluate and recommend key features and technologies, a specifications subcommittee to define the detailed key dimensions and protocols, and a licensing committee to transfer knowledge about the system to the industry through licensing agreements. Faxes and e-mails were essential in daily communication among the companies, as well as an in-person meeting every six weeks. In five years one team leader logged over 1 million flying miles between Rochester, New York, and Japan.

Kodak established its own formal project management team in early 1992. It included approximately 1000 employees dedicated full-time to the project, and another 7000 employees received security clearance to work on the project at various times. Special attention was given to project security, and no information was given to other Kodak employees until the new system was introduced. The project team managed the project via 300 key project milestones established using project software, primarily *Microsoft Project*. Progress against milestones in each area was reported monthly at scheduled meetings. Each area filed a one- to two-page report that included accomplishments, concerns, and plans.

When the new system was formally announced to the public in February 1996, Kodak had invested $500 million in the project and expected to spend another $500 million before the success of the system could be fully measured. New technologies included the leaderless film cassette that "thrusts" the film out of the cassette and across the inside of the camera and a magnetic layer on the film that allowed reliable machine reading and writing of information without creating undesirable print effects. Also, new high-speed photo-finishing environments had to be created.

Cameras using the APS system have become some of the most popular products among the companies licensed to use the system, including the three original camera company partners.

*Source:* C. Adams, "A Kodak Moment: *Advantix* Project Named 1997 International Project of the Year," *PM Network* 12(1; January 1998), pp. 21–27.

## PROJECT CRASHING

To demonstrate how project crashing works, we will employ the CPM/PERT network for constructing a house in Figure 9.8. This network is repeated in Figure 9.15, except that the activity times previously shown as months have been converted to weeks. Although this sample network encompasses only single-activity time estimates, the project crashing procedure can be applied in the same manner to PERT networks with probabilistic activity time estimates.

We will assume that the times (in weeks) shown on the network activities are the normal activity times. For example, 12 weeks are normally required to complete activity 1. Furthermore, we will assume that the cost required to complete this activity in the time indicated is $3000. This cost is referred to as the *normal activity cost*. Next, we will assume

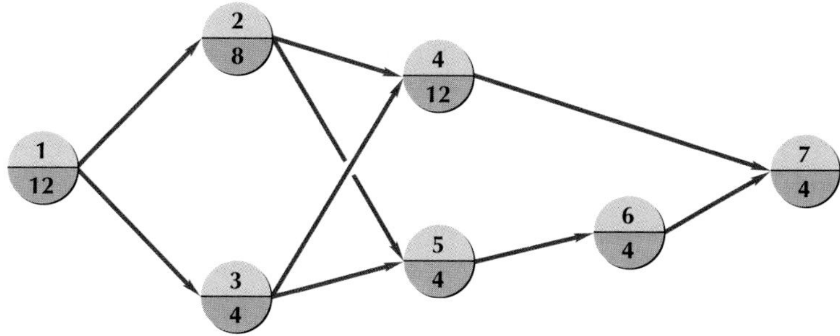


Figure 9.15
**The Project Network for Building a House**

that the building contractor has estimated that activity 1 can be completed in seven weeks, but it will cost $5000 instead of $3000 to complete the activity. This new estimated activity time is known as the **crash time**, and the cost to achieve the crash time is referred to as the **crash cost**.

**Crash time:** an amount of time an activity is reduced.

**Crash cost:** is the cost of reducing activity time.

Activity 1 can be crashed a total of five weeks (normal time − crash time = 12 − 7 = 5 weeks) at a total crash cost of $2000 (crash cost − normal cost = $5000 − 3000 = $2000). Dividing the total crash cost by the total allowable crash time yields the crash cost per week:

$$\frac{\text{Total crash cost}}{\text{Total crash time}} = \frac{\$2000}{5} = \$400 \text{ per week}$$

If we assume that the relationship between crash cost and crash time is linear, then activity 1 can be crashed by any amount of time (not exceeding the maximum allowable crash time) at a rate of $400 per week. For example, if the contractor decided to crash activity 1–2 by only two weeks (reducing activity time to 10 weeks), the crash cost would be $800 ($400 per week × 2 weeks). The linear relationships between crash cost and crash time and between normal cost and normal time are illustrated in Figure 9.16.

The goal of crashing is to reduce project duration at minimum cost.

The objective of project crashing is to reduce project duration while minimizing the cost of crashing. Since the project completion time can be shortened only by crashing activities on the critical path, it may turn out that not all activities have to be crashed. However, as activities are crashed, the critical path may change, requiring crashing of previously noncritical activities to reduce the project completion time even further.

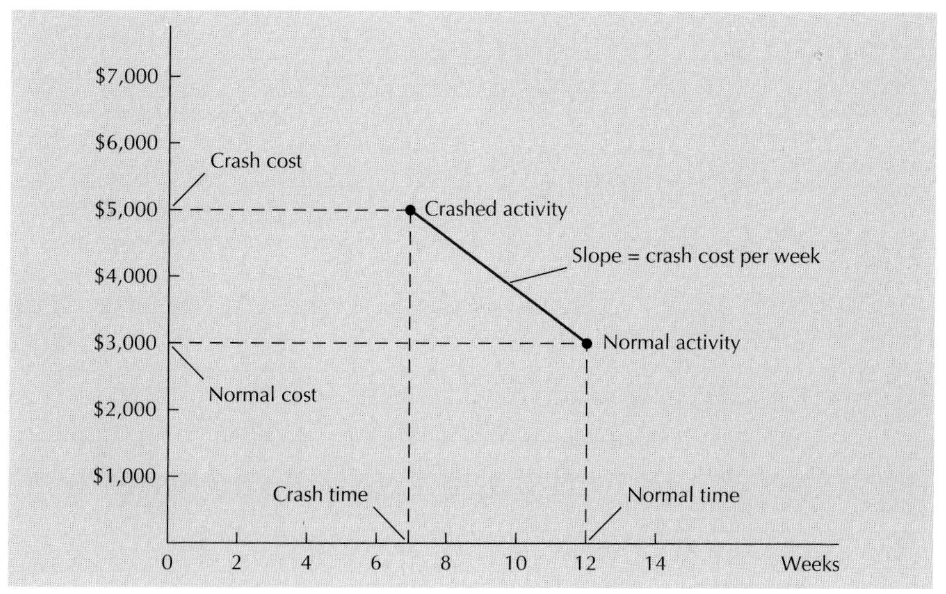


Figure 9.16
**The Relationship Between Normal Time and Cost, and Crash Time and Cost**

**Example 9.4**
**Project Crashing**

Recall that the critical path for the house building network in Figure 9.15 encompassed activities 1–2–7 and the project duration was nine months, or 36 weeks. Suppose the home builder needed the house in 30 weeks and wanted to know how much extra cost would be incurred to complete the house by this time.

The normal times and costs, the crash times and costs, the total allowable crash times, and the crash cost per week for each activity in the network in Figure 9.15 are summarized in the following table:

**Normal Activity and Crash Data**

| Activity | Normal Time (weeks) | Crash Time (weeks) | Normal Cost | Crash Cost | Total Allowable Crash Time (weeks) | Crash Cost per Week |
|---|---|---|---|---|---|---|
| 1 | 12 | 7 | $3,000 | $5,000 | 5 | $400 |
| 2 | 8 | 5 | 2,000 | 3,500 | 3 | 500 |
| 3 | 4 | 3 | 4,000 | 7,000 | 1 | 3,000 |
| 4 | 12 | 9 | 50,000 | 71,000 | 3 | 7,000 |
| 5 | 4 | 1 | 500 | 1,100 | 3 | 200 |
| 6 | 4 | 1 | 500 | 1,100 | 3 | 200 |
| 7 | 4 | 3 | 15,000 | 22,000 | 1 | 7,000 |
| | | | $75,000 | $110,700 | | |

*Solution*

We start by looking at the critical path and seeing which activity has the minimum crash cost per week. Observing the preceding table and the figure below, we see activity 1 has the minimum crash cost of $400. Activity 1 will be reduced as much as possible. The table shows that the maximum allowable reduction for activity 1 is five weeks, but we can reduce activity 1 only to the point at which another path becomes critical. When two paths simultaneously become critical, activities on both must be reduced by the same amount. If we reduce the activity time beyond the point at which another path becomes critical, we may be incurring an unnecessary cost. This last stipulation means that we must keep up with all the network paths as we reduce individual activities, a condition that makes manual crashing very cumbersome. For that reason the computer is geneally required for project crashing; however, we will solve this example manually in order to demonstrate the logic of project crashing.

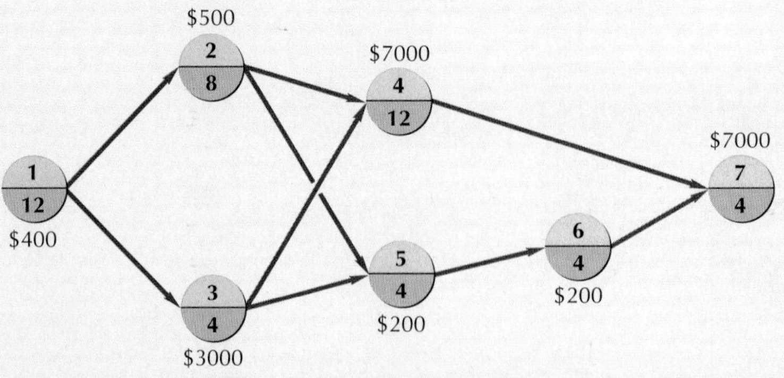


It turns out that activity 1 can be crashed by the total amount of five weeks without another path becoming critical, since activity 1 is included in all four paths in the network. Crashing this activity results in a revised project duration of 31 weeks at a crashing cost of $2000. The revised network is shown in the following figure.

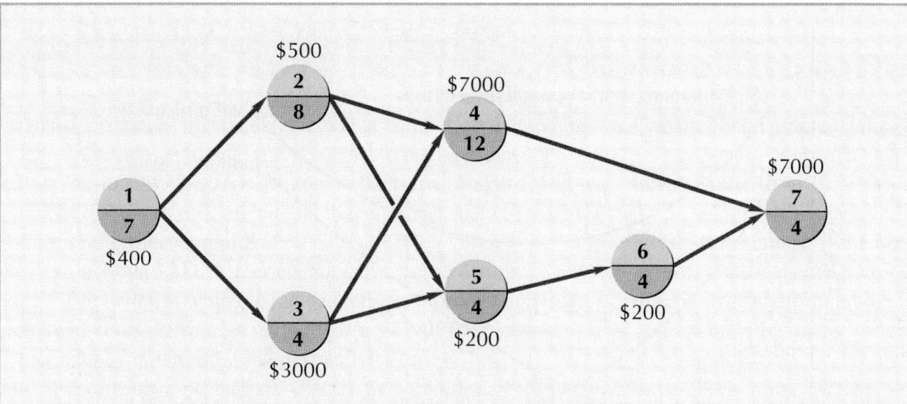


Since we have not reached our crashing goal of 30 weeks, we must continue, and the process is repeated. The critical path in the preceding figure remains the same, and the minimum activity crash cost on the critical path is $500 for activity 2. Activity 2 can be crashed a total of three weeks, but since the contractor desires to crash the network only to 30 weeks, we need to crash activity 2 by only one week. Crashing activity 2 by one week does not result in any other path becoming critical, so we can safely make this reduction. Crashing activity 2 to seven weeks (i.e., a 1-week reduction) costs $500 and reduces the project duration to 30 weeks.

The total cost of crashing the project to 30 weeks is $2500. The contractor could inform the customer that an additional cost of only $2500 would be incurred to finish the house in 30 weeks.

Suppose we wanted to continue to crash this network, reducing the project duration down to the minimum time possible—that is, crashing the network the maximum amount possible. We can determine how much the network can be crashed by crashing each activity the maximum amount possible and then determining the critical path of this completely crashed network. For example, activity 1 is seven weeks, activity 2 is five weeks, 3 is three weeks, and so on. The critical path of this totally crashed network is 1–2–4–6–7, with a project duration of 24 weeks. This is the least amount of time in which the project can be completed. If we crashed all the activities by their maximum amount, the total crashing cost would be $35,700, computed by subtracting the total normal cost of $75,000 from the total crash cost of $110,700 in the preceding table. However, if we followed the crashing procedure outlined in this example, the network could be crashed to 24 weeks at a cost of $31,500, a savings of $4000.

## THE GENERAL RELATIONSHIP OF TIME AND COST

In our discussion of project crashing, we demonstrated how the project critical path time could be reduced by increasing expenditures for labor and other direct resources. The objective of crashing was to reduce the scheduled completion time to reap the results of the project sooner. However, there may be other reasons for reducing project time. As projects continue over time, they consume *indirect costs*, including the cost of facilities, equipment, and machinery, interest on investment, utilities, labor, personnel costs, and the loss of skills and labor from members of the project team who are not working at their regular jobs. There also may be direct financial penalties for not completing a project on time. For example, many construction contracts and government contracts have penalty clauses for exceeding the project completion date.

Crashing costs increase as project time decreases; indirect costs increase as project time increases.

In general, project crashing costs and indirect costs have an inverse relationship; crashing costs are highest when the project is shortened, whereas indirect costs increase as the project duration increases. This time–cost relationship is illustrated in Figure 9.17. The best, or optimal, project time is at the minimum point on the total cost curve.

## SOLUTION

*Step 1.* Compute the expected activity times and variances:

$$t = \frac{a + 4m + b}{6}$$

$$\sigma^2 = \left(\frac{b - a}{6}\right)^2$$

For example, the expected time and variance for activity 1 are

$$t = \frac{5 + 4(8) + 17}{6} = 9 \text{ days}$$

$$\sigma^2 = \left(\frac{17 - 5}{6}\right)^2 = 4 \text{ days}$$

These values and the remaining expected times and variances for each activity are shown in the following table:

| ACTIVITY | $t$ | $\sigma^2$ |
|---|---|---|
| 1 | 9 | 4 |
| 2 | 10 | 1 |
| 3 | 5 | 4/9 |
| 4 | 3 | 4/9 |
| 5 | 6 | 4/9 |
| 6 | 3 | 0 |
| 7 | 4 | 1/9 |

*Step 2.* Determine the earliest and latest activity times and activity slack:

| ACTIVITY | $t$ | ES | EF | LS | LF | S |
|---|---|---|---|---|---|---|
| 1 | 9 | 0 | 9 | 0 | 9 | 0 |
| 2 | 10 | 0 | 10 | 4 | 14 | 4 |
| 3 | 5 | 9 | 14 | 9 | 14 | 0 |
| 4 | 3 | 9 | 12 | 17 | 20 | 8 |
| 5 | 6 | 14 | 20 | 14 | 20 | 0 |
| 6 | 3 | 14 | 17 | 21 | 24 | 7 |
| 7 | 4 | 20 | 24 | 20 | 24 | 0 |

As an example, the earliest start and finish times for activity 1 are

$$\begin{aligned} \text{ES} &= \max(\text{EF immediate predecessors}) \\ &= 0 \\ \text{EF} &= \text{ES} + t \\ &= 0 + 9 \\ &= 9 \end{aligned}$$

The latest start and finish times for activity 7 are

$$\begin{aligned} \text{LF} &= \min(\text{LS following activities}) \\ &= 24 \\ \text{LS} &= \text{LF} - t \\ &= 24 - 4 \\ &= 20 \end{aligned}$$

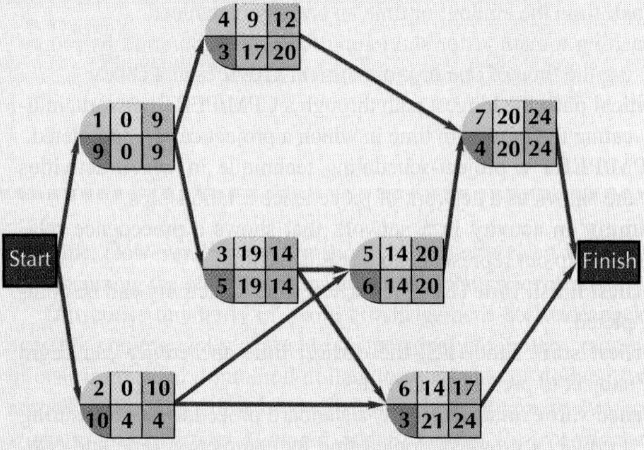


*Step 3.* Identify the critical path and compute expected project completion time and variance. Observing the preceding table and those activities with no slack (i.e., $s = 0$), we can identify the critical path as 1–3–5–7. The expected project completion time ($t_p$) is 24 days. The variance is computed by summing the variances for the activities in the critical path:

$$\begin{aligned} \sigma^2 &= 4 + \frac{4}{9} + \frac{4}{9} + \frac{1}{9} \\ &= 5 \text{ days} \end{aligned}$$

*Step 4.* Determine the probability that the project will be completed in 28 days or less. The following normal probability distribution describes the probability analysis.

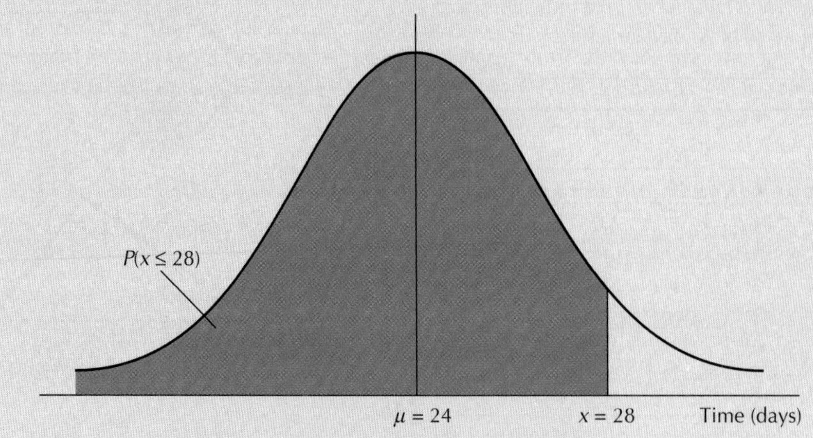

Compute $Z$ using the following formula:

$$Z = \frac{x - \mu}{\sigma} = \frac{28 - 24}{\sqrt{5}} = 1.79$$

The corresponding probability from the normal table in Appendix A is 0.4633; thus,

$$P(x \leq 28) = 0.9633$$

## QUESTIONS

**9-1.** Why is CPM/PERT a popular and widely applied project scheduling technique?

**9-2.** What is the purpose of a CPM/PERT network?

**9-3.** Why are dummy activities used in a CPM/PERT network?

**9-4.** What is the critical path, and what is its importance in project planning?

**9-5.** What is slack, and how is it computed?

**9-6.** How are the mean activity times and activity variances computed in probabilistic CPM/PERT analysis?

**9-7.** How is total project variance determined in CPM/PERT analysis?

**9-8.** What is the purpose of project crashing analysis?

**9-9.** Describe the process of manually crashing a project network.

**9-10.** Which method for determining activity time estimates, deterministic or probabilistic, do you perceive to be preferable? Explain.

**9-11.** Explain how a Gantt chart differs from a CPM/PERT network, and indicate the advantage of the latter.

**9-12.** Discuss the relationship of direct and indirect costs in project management.

**9-13.** Describe the limitations and disadvantages of CPM/PERT.

**9-14.** Describe the difference between activity-on-node and activity-on-arrow project networks.

**9-15.** Identify and briefly describe the major elements of project management.

**9-16.** Select an everyday "project" you are familiar with such as a class project, preparing a meal, making a pizza, repairing your car, and develop a work breakdown schedule for it.

**9-17.** Prepare a WBS for a spaghetti with meatballs dinner that includes a Caesar salad, a loaf of Italian bread, and wine. (Include the different components of the dinner at the upper level and the various detailed work activities required by each component at the lower level.)

## PROBLEMS

**9–1.** Construct a Gantt chart for the project described by the following set of activities, and indicate the project completion time:

| Activity | Activity Predecessor | Time (weeks) |
|---|---|---|
| 1 | — | 5 |
| 2 | — | 4 |
| 3 | 1 | 3 |
| 4 | 2 | 6 |

**9-2.** Construct a Gantt chart for the project described by the following set of activities, and indicate the project completion time and the available slack for each activity:

| Activity | Activity Predecessor | Time (weeks) |
|---|---|---|
| 1 | — | 3 |
| 2 | — | 7 |
| 3 | 1 | 2 |
| 4 | 2 | 5 |
| 5 | 2 | 6 |
| 6 | 4 | 1 |
| 7 | 5 | 4 |

**9-3.** Use the project activities that follow to determine the following:

a. Construct a Gantt chart; indicate the project completion time and slack for each activity.

b. Construct the CPM/PERT network, compute the length of each path in the network, and indicate the critical path.

| Activity | Activity Predecessor | Time (weeks) |
|---|---|---|
| 1 | — | 4 |
| 2 | — | 7 |
| 3 | 1 | 8 |
| 4 | 1 | 3 |
| 5 | 2 | 9 |
| 6 | 3 | 5 |
| 7 | 3 | 2 |
| 8 | 4, 5, 6 | 6 |
| 9 | 2 | 5 |

**9-4.** Construct a network from the information in the following table and identify all the paths in the network, compute the length of each, and indicate the critical path.

| Activity | Activity Predecessor | Time (weeks) |
|---|---|---|
| 1 | — | 7 |
| 2 | — | 10 |
| 3 | 1 | 6 |
| 4 | 2 | 5 |
| 5 | 2 | 4 |
| 6 | 3, 4 | 3 |
| 7 | 5, 6 | 2 |

**9-5.** For the network in Problem 9-4, determine the earliest start and finish times, latest start and finish times, and slack for each activity. Indicate how the critical path would be determined from this information.

**9-6.** Given the following network with activity times in months, determine the earliest start and finish times, latest start and finish times, and slack for each activity. Indicate the critical path and the project duration.

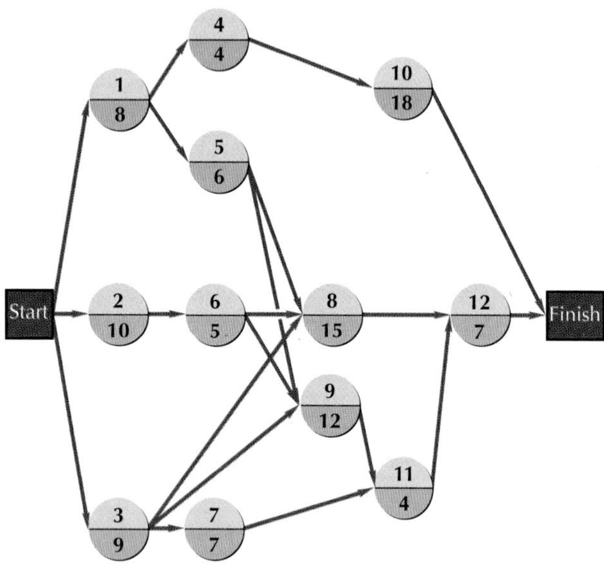


**9-7.** Given the following network with activity times in weeks, determine the earliest start and finish times, latest start and finish times, and slack for each activity. Indicate the critical path and the project duration.

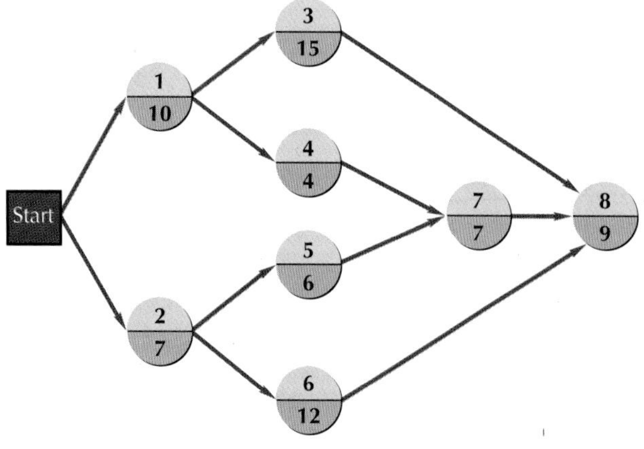


**9-8.** A marketing firm is planning to conduct a survey of a segment of the potential product audience for one of its customers. The planning process for preparing to conduct the survey consists of six activities with procedure relationships and activity time estimates as follows:

| Activity | Description | Activity Predecessor | Time Estimates (days) |
|---|---|---|---|
| a | Determine survey objectives | — | 3 |
| b | Select and hire personnel | a | 3 |
| c | Design questionnaire | a | 5 |
| d | Train personnel | b, c | 4 |
| e | Select target audience | c | 3 |
| f | Make personnel assignments | d, e | 2 |

a. Determine all paths through the network from node a to node f and the duration of each, and indicate the critical path.
b. Determine the earliest and latest activity start and finish times.
c. Determine the slack for each activity.

**9-9.** In one of the little-known battles of the Civil War, General Tecumseh Beauregard lost the Third Battle of Bull Run because his preparations were not complete when the enemy attacked. If the critical path method had been available, the general could have planned better. Suppose that the following project network below with activity times in days had been available. Determine the earliest start and finish times, latest start and finish times, and activity slack for the network. Indicate the critical path and the time between the general's receipt of battle orders and the onset of battle.

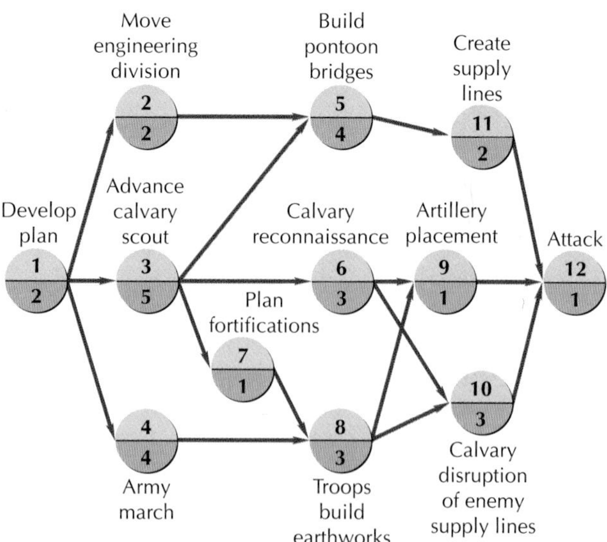


**9-10.** A group of developers is building a new shopping center. A consultant for the developers has constructed the CPM/PERT network at the top of the next page and assigned activity times in weeks. Determine the earliest start and finish times, latest start and finish times, activity slack, critical path, and duration for the project.

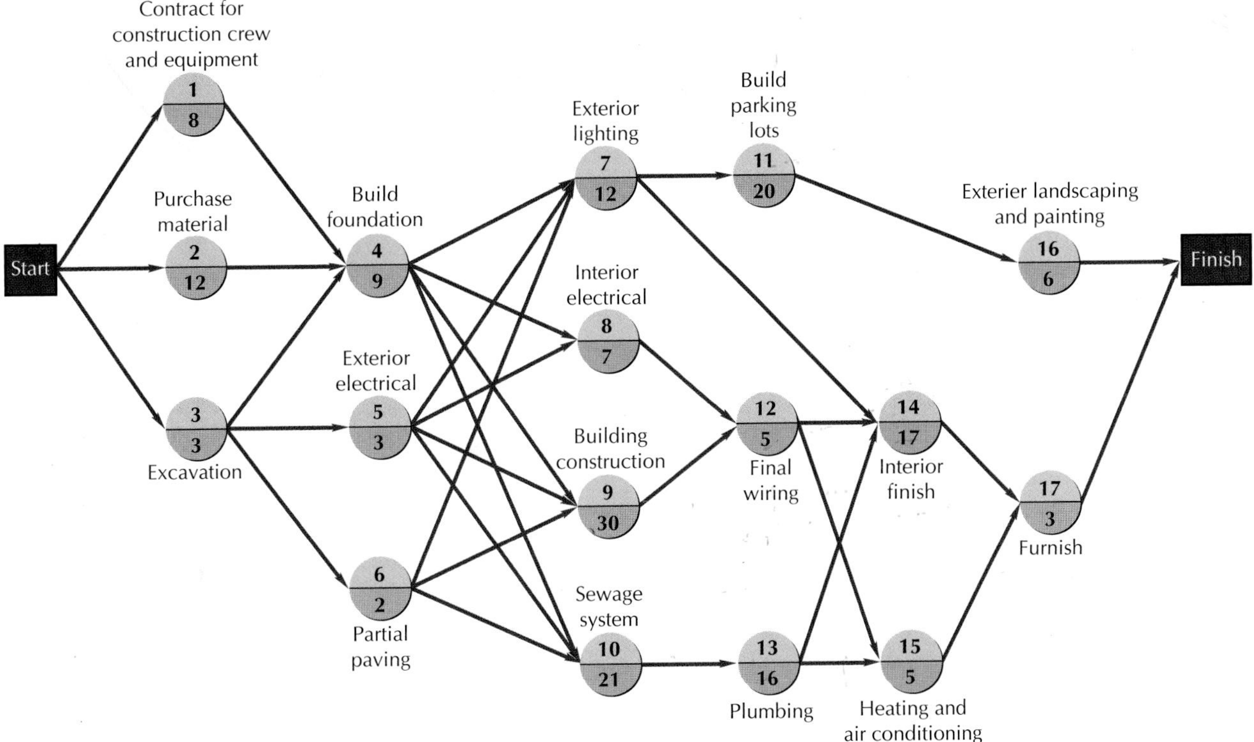


**9-11.** The management of a factory is going to erect a maintenance building with a connecting electrical generator and water tank. The activities, activity descriptions, and estimated durations are given in the following table:

| Activity | Description | Activity Predecessor | Activity Duration (weeks) |
|---|---|---|---|
| a | Excavate | — | 2 |
| b | Erect building | a | 6 |
| c | Intstall generator | a | 4 |
| d | Install tank | a | 2 |
| e | Install maintenance equipment | b | 4 |
| f | Connect generator and tank to building | b, c, d | 5 |
| g | Paint on a finish | b | 3 |
| h | Check out facility | e,f | 2 |

Construct the network for this project, identify the critical path, and determine the project duration time.

**9-12.** Given the following network and probabilistic activity time estimates, determine the expected time and variance for each activity and indicate the critical path:

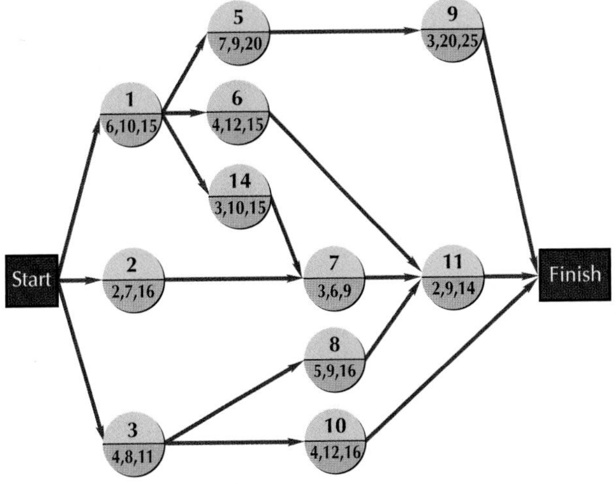


| Activity | Time Estimates (weeks) *a* | *m* | *b* |
|---|---|---|---|
| 1 | 6 | 10 | 15 |
| 2 | 2 | 7 | 16 |
| 3 | 4 | 8 | 11 |
| 4 | 3 | 10 | 15 |
| 5 | 7 | 9 | 20 |
| 6 | 4 | 12 | 15 |
| 7 | 3 | 6 | 9 |
| 8 | 5 | 9 | 16 |
| 9 | 3 | 20 | 35 |
| 10 | 4 | 12 | 16 |
| 11 | 2 | 9 | 14 |

**9-13.** The Farmer's American Bank of Leesburg is planning to install a new computerized accounts system. Bank management has determined the activities required to complete the project, the precedence relationships of the activities, and activity time estimates as follows:

| Activity | Description | Activity Predecessor | Time Estimates (weeks) a | m | b |
|---|---|---|---|---|---|
| a | Position recruiting | — | 5 | 8 | 17 |
| b | System development | — | 3 | 12 | 15 |
| c | System training | a | 4 | 7 | 10 |
| d | Equipment training | a | 5 | 8 | 23 |
| e | Manual system test | b, c | 1 | 1 | 1 |
| f | Preliminary system changeover | b, c | 1 | 4 | 13 |
| g | Computer–personnel interface | d, e | 3 | 6 | 9 |
| h | Equipment modification | d, e | 1 | 2.5 | 7 |
| i | Equipment testing | h | 1 | 1 | 1 |
| j | System debugging and installation | f, g | 2 | 2 | 2 |
| k | Equipment changeover | g, i | 5 | 8 | 11 |

Determine the earliest and latest activity times, the expected completion time and standard deviation, and the probability that the project will be completed in 40 weeks or less.

**9-14.** The following probabilistic activity time estimates are for the network in Problem 9-6:

| Activity | Time Estimates (months) a | m | b |
|---|---|---|---|
| 1 | 4 | 8 | 12 |
| 2 | 6 | 10 | 15 |
| 3 | 2 | 10 | 14 |
| 4 | 1 | 4 | 13 |
| 5 | 3 | 6 | 9 |
| 6 | 3 | 6 | 18 |
| 7 | 2 | 8 | 12 |
| 8 | 9 | 15 | 22 |
| 9 | 5 | 12 | 21 |
| 10 | 7 | 20 | 25 |
| 11 | 5 | 6 | 12 |
| 12 | 3 | 8 | 20 |

Determine the following:

a. Expected activity times
b. Earliest start and finish times
c. Latest start and finish times
d. Activity slack
e. Critical path
f. Expected project duration and standard deviation

**9-15.** The following probabilistic activity time estimates are for the CPM/PERT network in Problem 9-9:

| Activity | Time Estimates (days) a | m | b | Activity | Time Estimates (days) a | m | b |
|---|---|---|---|---|---|---|---|
| 1 | 1 | 2 | 6 | 7 | 1 | 1.5 | 2 |
| 2 | 1 | 3 | 5 | 8 | 1 | 3 | 5 |
| 3 | 3 | 5 | 10 | 9 | 1 | 1 | 5 |
| 4 | 3 | 6 | 14 | 10 | 2 | 4 | 9 |
| 5 | 2 | 4 | 9 | 11 | 1 | 2 | 3 |
| 6 | 2 | 3 | 7 | 12 | 1 | 1 | 1 |

Determine the following:

a. Expected activity times
b. Earliest start and finish times
c. Latest start and finish times
d. Activity slack
e. Critical path
f. Expected project duration and standard deviation

**9-16.** For the CPM/PERT network in Problem 9-14, determine the probability that the network duration will exceed 50 months.

**9-17.** The Stone River Textile Mill was inspected by OSHA and found to be in violation of a number of safety regulations. The OSHA inspectors ordered the mill to alter some existing machinery to make it safer (e.g., add safety guards); purchase some new machinery to replace older, dangerous machinery; and relocate some machinery to make safer passages and unobstructed entrances and exits. OSHA gave the mill only 35 weeks to make the changes; if the changes were not made by then, the mill would be fined $300,000. The mill determined the activities in a PERT network that would have to be completed and then estimated the indicated activity times, as shown in the table below. Construct the PERT network for this project and determine the following:

a. Expected activity times
b. Earliest and latest activity times and activity slack
c. Critical path
d. Expected project duration and variance
e. The probability that the mill will be fined $300,000

| Activity | Description | Activity Predecessor | Time Estimates (weeks) a | m | b |
|---|---|---|---|---|---|
| a | Order new machinery | — | 1 | 2 | 3 |
| b | Plan new physical layout | — | 2 | 5 | 8 |
| c | Determine safety changes in existing machinery | — | 1 | 3 | 5 |
| d | Receive equipment | a | 4 | 10 | 25 |
| e | Hire new employees | a | 3 | 7 | 12 |
| f | Make plant alterations | b | 10 | 15 | 25 |
| g | Make changes in existing machinery | c | 5 | 9 | 14 |
| h | Train new employees | d, e | 2 | 3 | 7 |
| i | Install new machinery | d, e, f | 1 | 4 | 6 |
| j | Relocate old machinery | d, e, f, g | 2 | 5 | 10 |
| k | Conduct employee safety orientation | h, i, j | 2 | 2 | 2 |

**9-18.** In the Third Battle of Bull Run, for which a CPM/PERT network was developed in Problem 9-15, General Beauregard would have won if his preparations had been completed in 15 days. What would the probability of General Beauregard's winning the battle have been?

**9-19.** On May 21, 1927, Charles Lindbergh landed at Le Bourget Field in Paris, completing his famous transatlantic solo flight. The preparation period prior to his flight was quite hectic and time was critical, since several other famous pilots of the day were also planning transatlantic flights. Once Ryan Aircraft was contracted to build the *Spirit of St. Louis*, it took only a little over 2½ months to construct the plane and fly it to New York for the takeoff. If CPM/PERT had been available to Charles Lindbergh, it no doubt would have been useful in helping him plan this project. Use your imagination and assume that a CPM/PERT network, as shown in the figure below, with the following estimated activity times, was developed for the flight.

| Activity | Time Estimates (days) *a* | *m* | *b* |
|---|---|---|---|
| 1 | 1 | 3 | 5 |
| 2 | 4 | 6 | 10 |
| 3 | 20 | 35 | 50 |
| 4 | 4 | 7 | 12 |
| 5 | 2 | 3 | 5 |
| 6 | 8 | 12 | 25 |
| 7 | 10 | 16 | 21 |
| 8 | 5 | 9 | 15 |
| 9 | 1 | 2 | 2 |
| 10 | 6 | 8 | 14 |
| 11 | 5 | 8 | 12 |
| 12 | 5 | 10 | 15 |
| 13 | 4 | 7 | 10 |
| 14 | 5 | 7 | 12 |
| 15 | 5 | 9 | 20 |
| 16 | 1 | 3 | 7 |

Determine the expected project duration and variance and the probability of completing the project in 67 days.

**9-20.** RusTech Tooling, Inc., is a large job shop operation that builds machine tools and dies to manufacture parts for specialized items. The company bids primarily on contracts for government-related activities to produce parts for things such as military aircraft, weapons systems, and the space program. The company is bidding on a contract to produce a component part for the fuselage assembly in a new space shuttle. A major criterion for selecting the winning bid besides low cost is the time required to produce the part. However, if the company is awarded the contract it will be held strictly to the completion date specified in the bid, and any delays will result in severe financial penalties. In order to determine the project completion time to put in its bid, the company has identified the project activities, precedence relationships, and activity times shown in the following table:

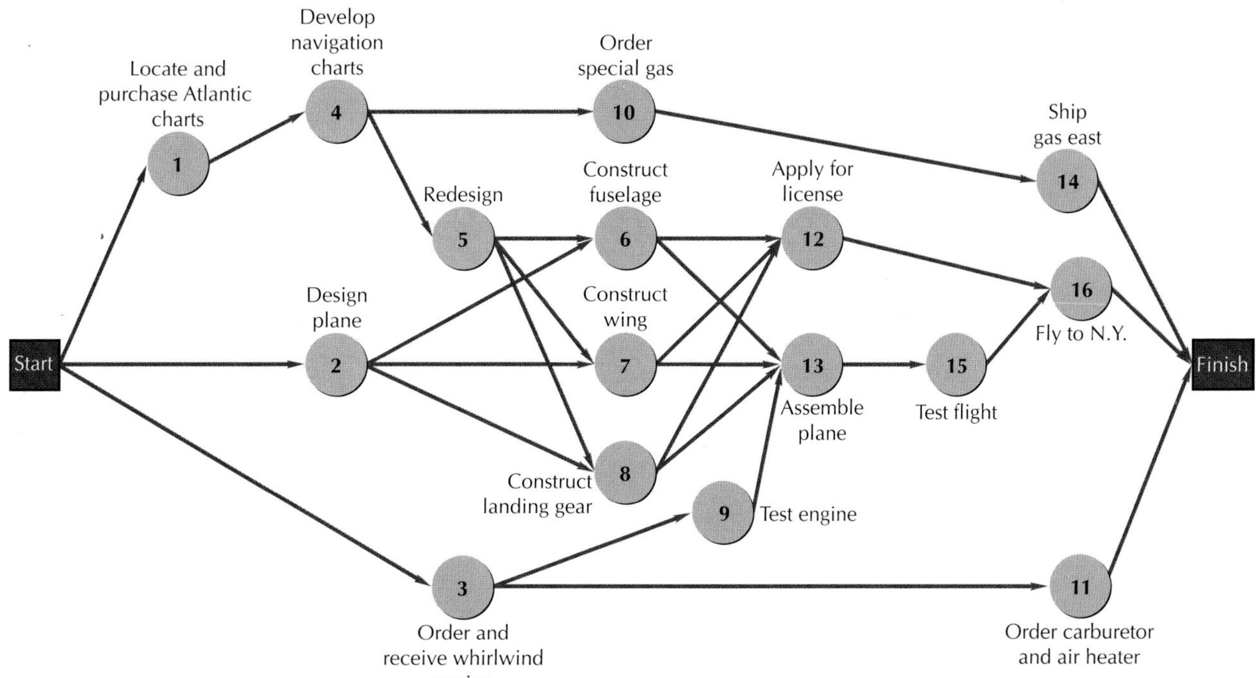

| Activity | Activity Predecessors | Time Estimates (weeks) | | |
|---|---|---|---|---|
| | | *a* | *m* | *b* |
| a | — | 3 | 5 | 9 |
| b | a | 2 | 5 | 8 |
| c | a | 1 | 4 | 6 |
| d | a | 4 | 6 | 10 |
| e | b | 2 | 8 | 11 |
| f | b | 5 | 9 | 16 |
| g | c | 4 | 12 | 20 |
| h | c | 6 | 9 | 13 |
| i | d | 3 | 7 | 14 |
| j | d | 8 | 14 | 22 |
| k | f, g | 9 | 12 | 20 |
| l | h, i | 6 | 11 | 15 |
| m | e | 4 | 7 | 12 |
| n | j | 3 | 8 | 16 |
| o | n | 5 | 8 | 10 |

If RusTech, Inc., wants to be 90% certain that it can deliver the part without incurring a penalty, what time frame should it specify in the bid?

**9-21.** PM Computers is an international manufacturer of computer equipment and software. It is going to introduce a number of new products in the coming year, and it wants to develop marketing programs to accompany the product introductions. The marketing program includes the preparation of printed materials distributed directly by the company and used by the company's marketing personnel, vendors, and representatives; print advertising in regular magazines, trade journals, and newspapers; and television commercials. The program also includes extensive training programs for marketing personnel, vendors, and representatives about the new products. A project management team with members from the marketing department and manufacturing areas has developed the following list of activities for the development of the marketing program:

| Activity | Description | Activity Predecessors | Time Estimates (days) | | |
|---|---|---|---|---|---|
| | | | *a* | *m* | *b* |
| a | Preliminary budget and plan approval | — | 10 | 15 | 20 |
| b | Select marketing personnel for training | — | 5 | 9 | 12 |
| c | Develop overall media plan | a | 15 | 25 | 30 |
| d | Prepare separate media plans | c | 12 | 20 | 25 |
| e | Develop training plan | c | 5 | 8 | 12 |
| f | Design training course | e | 6 | 14 | 20 |
| g | Train marketing personnel | b, f | 16 | 20 | 25 |
| h | Plan TV commercials with agency | d | 15 | 25 | 35 |
| i | Draft in-house print materials | d | 8 | 15 | 20 |
| j | Develop print advertising layouts with agency | d | 16 | 23 | 30 |
| k | Review print advertising layouts | j | 4 | 9 | 12 |
| l | Review TV commercials | h | 3 | 7 | 12 |
| m | Review and print in-house materials | i | 3 | 5 | 7 |
| n | Release advertising to print media | g, i, k | 2 | 4 | 8 |
| o | Release TV commercials to networks | l | 4 | 7 | 10 |
| p | Final marketing personnel review | g, i, k | 4 | 5 | 9 |
| q | Run media advertising, mailings | m, n, o | 15 | 20 | 30 |

Construct the network for this project and determine the activity schedule. Identify the critical path and determine the expected project duration time and variance. What is the probability the program can be completed within four months?

**9-22.** The following table provides the information necessary to construct a project network and project crash data:

| Activity | Activity Predecessor | Activity Time (weeks) | | Activity Cost ($) | |
|---|---|---|---|---|---|
| | | *Normal* | *Crash* | *Normal* | *Crash* |
| 1 | — | 20 | 8 | 1,000 | 1,480 |
| 2 | — | 24 | 20 | 1,200 | 1,400 |
| 3 | — | 14 | 7 | 700 | 1,190 |
| 4 | 1 | 10 | 6 | 500 | 820 |
| 5 | 3 | 11 | 5 | 550 | 730 |

a. Construct the project network.
b. Determine the maximum possible crash time for the network, and crash the network the maximum amount possible.
c. Compute the normal project cost and the cost of the crashed project.

**9-23.** The following table provides the information necessary to construct a project network and project crash data:

| Activity | Predecessor | Activity Time (weeks) | | Activity Cost ($) | |
|---|---|---|---|---|---|
| | | *Normal* | *Crash* | *Normal* | *Crash* |
| a | — | 16 | 8 | 2,000 | 4,400 |
| b | — | 14 | 9 | 1,000 | 1,800 |
| c | a | 8 | 6 | 500 | 700 |
| d | a | 5 | 4 | 600 | 1,300 |
| e | b | 4 | 2 | 1,500 | 3,000 |
| f | b | 6 | 4 | 800 | 1,600 |
| g | c | 10 | 7 | 3,000 | 4,500 |
| h | d, e | 15 | 10 | 5,000 | 8,000 |

Construct the project network, and crash the network the maximum amount possible.

**9-24.** For the Solved Problem at the end of this chapter, assume that the most likely times ($m$) are the normal activity times and the optimistic times ($a$) are the activity crash times. Further assume that the activities have the following normal and crash costs:

| Activity | Costs (Normal Cost, Crash Cost) |
|---|---|
| 1 | ($100, 400) |
| 2 | ($250, 400) |
| 3 | ($400, 800) |
| 4 | ($200, 400) |
| 5 | ($150, 300) |
| 6 | ($100, 100) |
| 7 | ($300, 500) |

Crash the network the maximum amount possible and indicate the total crash cost.

**9-25.** The following table provides the crash data for the project network in Problem 9-13. The normal activity times are considered to be deterministic and not probabilistic.

| | Activity Time (weeks) | | Activity Cost ($) | |
|---|---|---|---|---|
| Activity | *Normal* | *Crash* | *Normal* | *Crash* |
| a | 9 | 7 | 4,800 | 6,300 |
| b | 11 | 9 | 9,100 | 15,500 |
| c | 7 | 5 | 3,000 | 4,000 |
| d | 10 | 8 | 3,600 | 5,000 |
| e | 1 | 1 | 0 | 0 |
| f | 5 | 3 | 1,500 | 2,000 |
| g | 6 | 5 | 1,800 | 2,000 |
| h | 3 | 3 | 0 | 0 |
| i | 1 | 1 | 0 | 0 |
| j | 2 | 2 | 0 | 0 |
| k | 8 | 6 | 5,000 | 7,000 |

Crash the network the maximum amount, indicate how much it would cost the bank, and identify the new critical path(s).

**9-26.** The Center for Information Technology at State University has outgrown its office in Bates (B) Hall and is moving to Allen (A) Hall, which has more space. The move will take place during the three-week break between the end of summer semester and the beginning of fall semester. Movers will be hired from the university's physical plant to move the furniture, boxes of books, and files that the faculty will pack. The center has hired a local retail computer firm to move its office computers so they will not be damaged. Following is a list of activities, their precedence relationships, and probabilistic time estimates for this project:

| | | | Time Estimates (days) | | |
|---|---|---|---|---|---|
| Activity | Description | Activity Predecessor | *a* | *m* | *b* |
| a | Pack "A" offices | — | 1 | 3 | 5 |
| b | Network "A" offices | — | 2 | 3 | 5 |
| c | Pack "B" offices | — | 2 | 4 | 7 |
| d | Movers move "A" offices | a | 1 | 3 | 4 |
| e | Paint and clean "A" offices | d | 2 | 5 | 8 |
| f | Move computers | b, e | 1 | 2 | 2 |
| g | Movers move "B" offices | b, c, e | 3 | 6 | 8 |
| h | Computer installation | f | 2 | 4 | 5 |
| i | Faculty move and unpack | g | 3 | 4 | 6 |
| j | Faculty set up computers and offices | h, i | 1 | 2 | 4 |

Determine the earliest and latest start and finish times, the critical path, and the expected project duration. What is the probability the center will complete its move before the start of the fall semester?

**9-27.** The Valley United Soccer Club is planning a soccer tournament for the weekend of April 29–30. The club's officers know that by March 30 they must send out acceptances to teams that have applied to enter and by April 15 they must send out the tournament game schedule to teams that have been selected to play. Their tentative plan is to begin the initial activities for tournament preparation including sending out the application forms to prospective teams, on January 20. Following is a list of tournament activities, their precedence relationships, and estimates of their duration in days. Develop a project network for the club's tournament preparation process and determine the likelihood that they will meet their schedule milestones and complete the process according to the scheduled tournament start date of April 29.

| | | | Time Estimates (days) | | |
|---|---|---|---|---|---|
| Activity | Activity Description | Activity Predecessor | *a* | *m* | *b* |
| a | Send application forms | — | 5 | 7 | 10 |
| b | Get volunteer workers | — | 10 | 18 | 26 |
| c | Line up referees | — | 7 | 10 | 14 |
| d | Reserve fields | — | 14 | 21 | 35 |
| e | Receive and process forms | a | 30 | 30 | 30 |
| f | Determine age divisions | b, c, d, e | 4 | 9 | 12 |
| g | Assign fields to divisions | f | 4 | 7 | 10 |
| h | Sell program ads | b | 14 | 21 | 30 |
| i | Acquire donated items for team gift bags | b | 15 | 20 | 26 |
| j | Schedule games | g | 6 | 14 | 18 |
| k | Design ads | h | 5 | 8 | 10 |
| l | Fill gift bags | i | 9 | 12 | 17 |
| m | Process team t-shirt orders | e | 7 | 10 | 14 |
| n | Send acceptance letters | f | 4 | 7 | 12 |
| o | Design and print programs | j, k, l, n | 14 | 18 | 24 |
| p | Put together registration boxes (programs, gifts, etc.) | o | 5 | 7 | 10 |
| q | Send out game schedules | j, k, l, n | 5 | 8 | 12 |
| r | Assign referees to games | j, k, l, n | 4 | 7 | 10 |
| s | Get trophies | f | 20 | 28 | 35 |
| t | Silk-screen t-shirts | m | 12 | 17 | 25 |
| u | Package team t-shirt orders | t | 5 | 8 | 12 |

**9-28.** During a violent thunderstorm with very high wind gusts in the third week of March, the broadcast tower for the public radio station, WVPR, atop Poor Mountain in Roanoke, Virginia, collapsed. This greatly reduced the strength of the station's signal in the area. The station management immediately began plans to construct a new tower. Following is a list of the required activities for building the new tower with most likely ($m$), optimistic ($a$), and pessimistic ($b$) time estimates (in days). However, the sequence of the activities has not been designated.

| | | Time Estimates (days) | | |
|---|---|---|---|---|
| | **Activity** | *a* | *m* | *b* |
| a | Removal of debris | 5 | 8 | 12 |
| b | Survey new tower site | 3 | 6 | 8 |
| c | Procure structural steel | 15 | 21 | 30 |
| d | Procure electrical/broadcasting equipment | 18 | 32 | 40 |
| e | Grade tower site | 4 | 7 | 10 |
| f | Pour concrete footings and anchors | 10 | 18 | 22 |
| g | Deliver and unload steel | 3 | 5 | 9 |
| h | Deliver and unload electrical/broadcast equipment | 1 | 2 | 4 |
| i | Erect tower | 25 | 35 | 50 |
| j | Connect electrical cables between tower and building | 4 | 6 | 10 |
| k | Construct storm drains and tiles | 10 | 15 | 21 |
| l | Backfill and grade tower site | 4 | 7 | 9 |
| m | Clean up | 3 | 6 | 10 |
| n | Obtain inspection approval | 1 | 4 | 7 |

Using your best judgment, develop a CPM/PERT network for this project and determine the expected project completion time. Also determine the probability that the station signal will be back at full strength within three months.

**9-29.** The following table contains the activities for planning a wedding and the activity time estimates. However, the precedence relationships between activities are not included.

| | | Time (days) | | |
|---|---|---|---|---|
| | **Activity** | *a* | *m* | *b* |
| a | Determine date | 1 | 10 | 15 |
| b | Obtain marriage license | 1 | 5 | 8 |
| c | Select bridal attendants | 3 | 5 | 7 |
| d | Order dresses | 10 | 14 | 21 |
| e | Fit dresses | 5 | 10 | 12 |
| f | Select groomsmen | 1 | 2 | 4 |
| g | Order tuxedos | 3 | 5 | 7 |
| h | Find and rent church | 6 | 14 | 20 |
| i | Hire florist | 3 | 6 | 10 |
| j | Develop/print programs | 15 | 22 | 30 |
| k | Hire photographer | 3 | 10 | 15 |
| l | Develop guest list | 14 | 25 | 40 |
| m | Order invitations | 7 | 12 | 20 |
| n | Address and mail invitations | 10 | 15 | 25 |
| o | Compile RSVP list | 30 | 45 | 60 |
| p | Reserve reception hall | 3 | 7 | 10 |
| q | Hire caterer | 2 | 5 | 8 |
| r | Determine reception menu | 10 | 12 | 16 |
| s | Make final order | 2 | 4 | 7 |
| t | Hire band | 10 | 18 | 21 |
| u | Decorate reception hall | 1 | 2 | 3 |
| v | Wedding ceremony | .5 | .5 | .5 |
| w | Wedding reception | .5 | .5 | .5 |

Using your best judgment, determine the project network, critical path, and expected project duration. If it is the first of January and a couple is planning a June 1 wedding, what is the probability that it can be done on time?

## CASE PROBLEM 9.1

### *The Bloodless Coup Concert*

John Aaron had just called the meeting of the Programs and Arts Committee of the Student Government Association to order.

"Okay, okay, everybody, quiet down. I have an important announcement to make," he shouted above the noise. The room got quiet and John started again. "Well, you guys, we can have the Coup."

His audience looked puzzled and Randy Jones asked, "What coup have we scored this time, John?"

"The Coup, the Coup! You know, the rock group, the Bloodless Coup!"

Everyone in the room cheered and started talking excitedly. John stood up, waved his arms, and shouted, "Hey, calm down, everybody, and listen up." The room quieted again and everyone focused on John. "The good news is that they can come." He paused a moment. "The bad news is that they will be here in 18 days."

The students groaned and seemed to share Jim Hasting's feelings, "No way, man. It can't be done. Why can't we put it off for a couple of weeks?"

John answered, "They're just starting their new tour and are looking for some warm-up concerts. They will be traveling near here for their first concert date in D.C. and saw they had a letter from us, so they said they could come now—but that's it, now or never." He looked around the room at the solemn faces. "Look you guys, we can handle this. Let's think of what we have to do. Come on, perk up. Let's make a list of everything we have to do to get ready and figure out how long it will take. So somebody tell me what we have to do first!"

Anna Mendoza shouted from the back of the room, "We have to find a place; you know, get an auditorium somewhere. I've done that before, and it should take anywhere from 2 days up to 7 days, most likely about 4 days."

"Okay, that's great," John said as he wrote down the activity "secure auditorium" on the blackboard with the times out to the side. "What's next?"

"We need to print tickets and quick," Tracey Shea blurted. "It could only take a day if the printer isn't busy, but it could take up to 4 days if it is. It should probably take about 2 days."

"But we can't print tickets until we know where the concert will be because of the security arrangement," Andy Taylor noted.

"Right," said John. "Get the auditorium first then print the tickets. What else?"

"We need to make hotel and transportation arrangements for the Coup and their entourage while they are here," Jim Hastings said. "But we better not do that until we get the auditorium. If we can't find a place for the concert, everything falls through."

"How long do you think it will take to make the arrangements?" John asked.

"Oh, between 3 and 10 days, probably about 5, most likely," Jim answered.

"We also have to negotiate with the local union for concert employees, stagehands, and whomever else we need to hire," said Reggie Wilkes. "That could take a day or up to 8 days, but 3 days would be my best guess."

"We should probably also hold off on talking to the union until we get the auditorium," John added. "That will probably be a factor in the negotiations."

"After we work things out with the union we can hire some stagehands," Reggie continued. "That could take as few as 2 days but as long as 7. I imagine it'll take about 4 days. We should also be able to get some student ushers at the same time once we get union approval. That could take only a day, but it has taken 5 days in the past; 3 days is probably the most likely."

"We need to arrange a press conference," said Art Cohen, leaning against a wall. "This is a heavy group, big-time."

"But doesn't a press conference usually take place at the hotel?" John asked.

"Yeah, that's right," said Art. "We can't make arrangements for the press conference until we work things out with the hotel. When we do that it should take about 3 days to set up a press conference, 2 days if we're lucky and 4 at the most."

The room got quiet as everyone thought.

"What else?" John said.

"Hey, I know," said Annie Roark. "Once we hire the stagehands they have to set up the stage. I think that could be done in a couple of days, but it could take up to 6 days, with 3 most likely." She paused for a moment before adding, "And we can assign the ushers to their jobs once we hire them. That shouldn't take long, maybe only a day, 3 days worst. Probably 2 days would be a good time to put down."

"We also have to do some advertising and promotion if we want anyone to show for this thing," said Art nonchalantly. "I guess we need to wait until we print the tickets first so we'll have something to sell. That depends on the media, the paper, and radio stations. I've worked with this before. It could get done really quick, like 2 days, if we can make the right contacts, but it could take a lot longer, like 12 days if we hit any snags. We probably ought to count on 6 days as our best estimate."

"Hey, if we're going to promote this, shouldn't we also have a preliminary act, some other group?" said Annie.

"Wow, I forgot all about that," said John. "Hiring another act will take me between 4 and 8 days; I can probably do it in 5. I can start on that right away at the same time you guys are arranging for an auditorium." He thought for a moment. "But we really can't begin to work on the promotion until I get the lead-in group. So what's left?"

"Sell the tickets," shouted several people at once.

"Right," said John, "we have to wait until they are printed; but I don't think we have to wait for the advertising and promotion to start do we?"

"No," said Jim, "but we should hire the preliminary act first so people will know what they're buying a ticket for."

"Agreed," said John. "The tickets could go quick; I suppose in the first day."

"Or," interrupted Mike Eggleston, "it could take longer. I remember two years ago it took 12 days to sell out for the Cosmic Modem."

"Okay, so it's between 1 and 12 days to sell the tickets," said John, "but I think about 5 days is more likely. Everybody agree?"

The group nodded in unison and they all turned at once to the list of activities and times John had written on the blackboard.

Use PERT analysis to determine the probability the concert preparations will be completed in time.

## CASE PROBLEM 9.2

### *Moore Housing Contractors*

Moore Housing Contractors is negotiating a deal with Countryside Realtors to build six houses in a new development. Countryside wants Moore Contractors to start in late winter or early spring when the weather begins to moderate and build through the summer into the fall. The summer months are a busy time for the realty company, and it believes it can sell the houses almost as soon as they are ready—sometimes before. The houses all have similar floor plans and are of approximately equal size; only the exteriors are noticeably different. The completion time is so critical for Countryside Realtors that it is insisting a project management network accompany the contractor's bid for the job with an estimate of the completion time for a house. The realtor also needs to be able to plan its offerings and marketing for the summer. The realtor wants each house to be completed within 45 days after it is started. If a house is not completed within this time frame, the realtor wants to be able to charge the contractor a penalty. Mary and Sandy Moore, the president and vice president of Moore Housing Contractors, are concerned about the prospect of a penalty. They want to be confident they can meet the deadline for a house before entering into any agreement with a penalty involved. (If there is a reasonable likelihood they cannot finish a house within 45 days, they want to increase their bid to cover potential penalty charges.)

The Moores are experienced home builders, so it was not difficult for them to list the activities involved in building a house or to estimate activity times. However, they made their estimates conservatively and tended to increase their pessimistic estimates to compensate for the possibility of bad weather and variations in their workforce. Following is a list of the activities for building a house and the activity time estimates:

| Activity | Description | Predecessors | TIME (DAYS) | | |
|---|---|---|---|---|---|
| | | | *a* | *m* | *b* |
| a | Excavation, pour footers | — | 3 | 4 | 6 |
| b | Lay foundation | a | 2 | 3 | 5 |
| c | Frame and roof | b | 2 | 4 | 5 |
| d | Lay drain tiles | b | 1 | 2 | 4 |
| e | Sewer (floor) drains | b | 1 | 2 | 3 |
| f | Install insulation | c | 2 | 4 | 5 |
| g | Pour basement floor | e | 2 | 3 | 5 |
| h | Rough plumbing, pipes | e | 2 | 4 | 7 |
| i | Install windows | f | 1 | 3 | 4 |
| j | Rough electrical wiring | f | 1 | 2 | 4 |
| k | Install furnace, air conditioner | c, g | 3 | 5 | 8 |
| l | Exterior brickwork | i | 5 | 6 | 10 |
| m | Install plasterboard, mud, plaster | j, h, k | 6 | 8 | 12 |
| n | Roof shingles, flashing | l | 2 | 3 | 6 |
| o | Attach gutter, downspouts | n | 1 | 2 | 5 |
| p | Grading | d, o | 2 | 3 | 7 |
| q | Lay subflooring | m | 3 | 4 | 6 |
| r | Lay driveway, walks, landscape | p | 4 | 6 | 10 |
| s | Finish carpentry | q | 3 | 5 | 12 |
| t | Kitchen cabinetry, sink, and appliances | q | 2 | 4 | 8 |
| u | Bathroom cabinetry, fixtures | q | 2 | 3 | 6 |
| v | Painting (interior and exterior) | t, u | 4 | 6 | 10 |
| w | Finish wood floors, lay carpet | v, s | 2 | 5 | 8 |
| x | Final electrical, light fixtures | v | 1 | 3 | 4 |

**1.** Develop a CPM/PERT network for Moore House Contractors and determine the probability that the contractors can complete a house within 45 days. Does it appear that the Moores might need to increase their bid to compensate for potential penalties?

**2.** Indicate which project activities Moore Contractors should be particularly diligent to keep on schedule by making sure workers and materials are always available. Also indicate which activities the company might shift workers from as the need arises.

## REFERENCES


Burman, P. J. *Precedence Networks for Project Planning and Control*. New York: McGraw-Hill, 1972.

Cleland, D. I., and W. R. King. *Project Management Handbook*. New York: Van Nostrand Reinhold, 1983.

Levy, F., G. Thompson, and J. Wiest. "The ABC's of the Critical Path Method." *Harvard Business Review* 41(5; October 1963).

Moder, J., C. R. Phillips, and E. W. Davis. *Project Management with CPM and PERT and Precedence Diagramming*, 3rd ed. New York: Van Nostrand Reinhold, 1983.

O'Brian, J. *CPM in Construction Management* New York: McGraw-Hill, 1965.

Wiest, J. D., and F. K. Levy. *A Management Guide to PERT/CPM*, 2nd ed. Upper Saddle River, NJ: Prentice Hall, 1977.

# Supply Chain Management

CHAPTER 10

Web resources for this chapter include

- Internet Exercises
- Online Practice Quizzes
- Virtual Tours
- Excel Worksheets
- Company and Resource Weblinks
- Animated Demo Problems
- Microsoft Project Exhibits

www.wiley.com/college/russell

## CHAPTER OUTLINE

In this chapter, you will learn about . . .

- The Management of Supply Chains
- Information Technology: A Supply Chain Enabler
- Supply Chain Integration
- Suppliers
- E-Procurement
- Distribution
- Supply Chain Management (SCM) Software
- Measuring Supply Chain Performance
- The Global Supply Chain

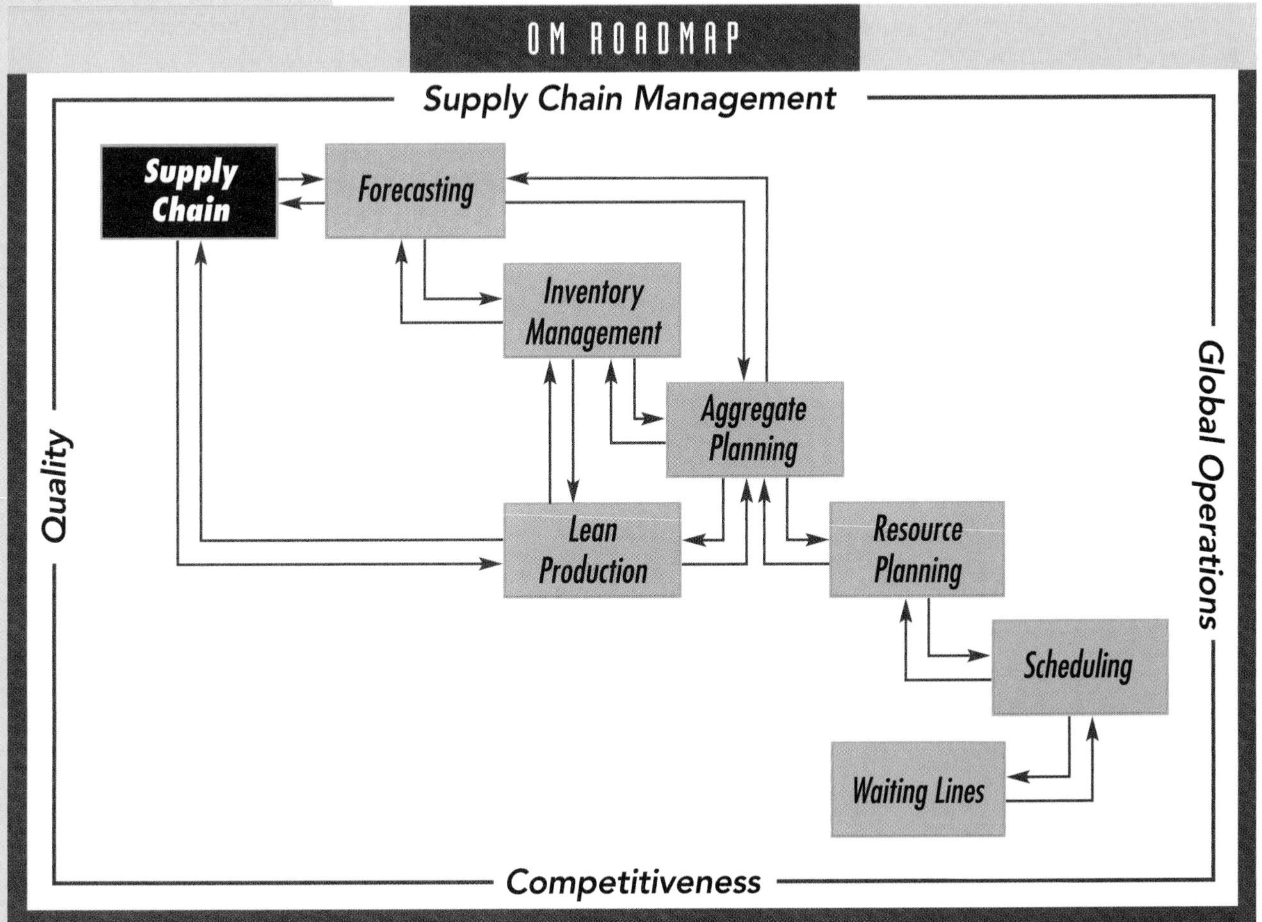

## SUPPLY CHAIN SUCCESS AT HARLEY-DAVIDSON

In the early 1980s Wisconsin-based Harley-Davidson Motor Company, the country's largest manufacturer of motorcycles, was struggling to survive. Faced with an onslaught of severe competition from Japan, failing new products, and strategic errors that allowed their engineering capabilities to atrophy, Harley-Davidson was challenged to remain profitable. However, not only did Harley-Davidson survive, it became a huge success story. A significant factor in its turnaround was the strategic changes it made in managing its supply chain during the next decade.

It was once a company that did not take a thoughtful approach to selecting suppliers, making purchasing decisions, and evaluating delivery and inventory costs. As a result components, parts, and materials were often delivered late with less than desirable quality, which drove up production and inventory costs. However, in the mid-1990s Harley-Davidson initiated sophisticated supply chain strategies to reduce inventory and purchasing costs while improving product quality and delivery times from suppliers.

Harley-Davidson now expects suppliers to focus strategically on cost, delivery, and quality improvement and to hit established cost and quality targets. Suppliers are expected to meet "twice the level of quality" and to develop a written strategic plan to achieve goals for quality improvement. Suppliers are graded according to defective "parts-per-million" and it has a target goal of 48 defective parts-per-million that suppliers are expected to achieve. Harley-Davidson sends suppliers a monthly report showing their quality and delivery performance, and if the supplier receives a bad report Harley-Davidson sends their people to the supplier to determine the problems and help them resolve them. If the supplier does not improve its performance, it is replaced. In 1995 defective parts-per-million for suppliers were generally around 10,000; however, by 2000 approximately 60% of Harley-Davidson's supplier base was performing at 48 defective parts-per-million or better, and 36 suppliers were performing at zero defective parts-per-million. Harley-Davidson also expects its suppliers to develop and deliver new products in "half the time," and they are expected to develop tools for faster product development and plans that are supportive of Harley-Davidson's design and development efforts. On-site suppliers take part in new product design, creating an interface between the company and its suppliers that helps Harley-Davidson improve quality and cut costs.

These objectives have consciously eliminated half of Harley-Davidson's supplier base that could not meet expectations for cost, quality, and delivery. In some cases Harley-Davidson has moved toward single-source relationships with suppliers. In these instances, the company partners with one supplier for a part, system, or component—for example, lighting systems, instrumentation gauges, or ignition systems—and works closely with the supplier to develop technology that the company needs to remain competitive. In return, Harley-Davidson remains loyal to the supplier and reduces supplier uncertainty, provided of course that the supplier continues to meet the company's objectives for improvement. In order for Harley-Davidson suppliers to remain competitive they must enforce similar exacting goals and standards on their own suppliers, thus creating efficiency and cost effectiveness along the entire length of the supply chain from Harley-Davidson's suppliers to its suppliers' suppliers, and so on.

Harley-Davidson is using the Internet to further improve its supply chain performance. In 2000 the company launched an interactive Internet-based supply chain management strategy that was expected to place a large portion of the company's supply chain management onto the Internet. It provided all suppliers with information they need to conduct online financial transactions and reduce

*Assembly-line workers at Harley-Davidson. This 100-year-old motorcycle manufacturer was named "Company of the Year" by* **Forbes** *Magazine in 2002.*

the time spent chasing invoices. Suppliers are linked by a window—or electronic portal—to critical business transaction information, including data on delivery and quality performance and the status of financial transactions. They can look at production schedules and delivery requirements and assess their ability to meet those schedules. Documents and information previously sent using an EDI format are now sent more cheaply through the Internet, which is also more universally available to supply companies, particularly smaller ones.

What has been the effect of these changes in supply chain management at Harley-Davidson? They reduced supply chain costs (i.e., goods and services) by $37 million; the company now manages its inventory according to a just-in-time (JIT) system, and it runs on 6.5 to 10 days' worth of inventory compared to 8 to 15 days of inventory in 1995; its logistics and distribution center costs as a percentage of sales decreased by 59%. By any measure Harley-Davidson's supply chain management strategy has been a success.

*Source:* B. Milligan, "Harley-Davidson Wins by Getting Suppliers on Board," *Purchasing* 129 (5; September 21, 2000), pp. 51–65.

Since the 1970s, quality management has been a preeminent strategic focus of companies. In the 1980s, topics like lean and flexible manufacturing, and just-in-time (JIT) became the means for companies to gain a competitive advantage in a quality-management environment. Now globalization and the evolution of information technology have provided the catalysts for supply chain management to become the strategic means for companies to manage quality, satisfy customers, and remain competitive.

**Supply chain:** the facilities, functions, and activities involved in producing and delivering a product or service from suppliers (and their suppliers) to customers (and their customers).

A **supply chain** encompasses all activities associated with the flow and transformation of goods and services from the raw materials stage through to the end user (customer), as well as the associated information flows. In essence, it is all the assets, information, and processes that provide "supply." It is made up of many interrelated members, starting with raw material suppliers, and including parts and components suppliers, subassembly suppliers, the product or service producer, and distributors and ending with the end-use customer.

Figure 10.1 illustrates the stages, facilities, and physical movement of products and services in a supply chain. The supply chain begins with suppliers, which can be as basic as raw

Figure 10.1 **The Supply Chain**

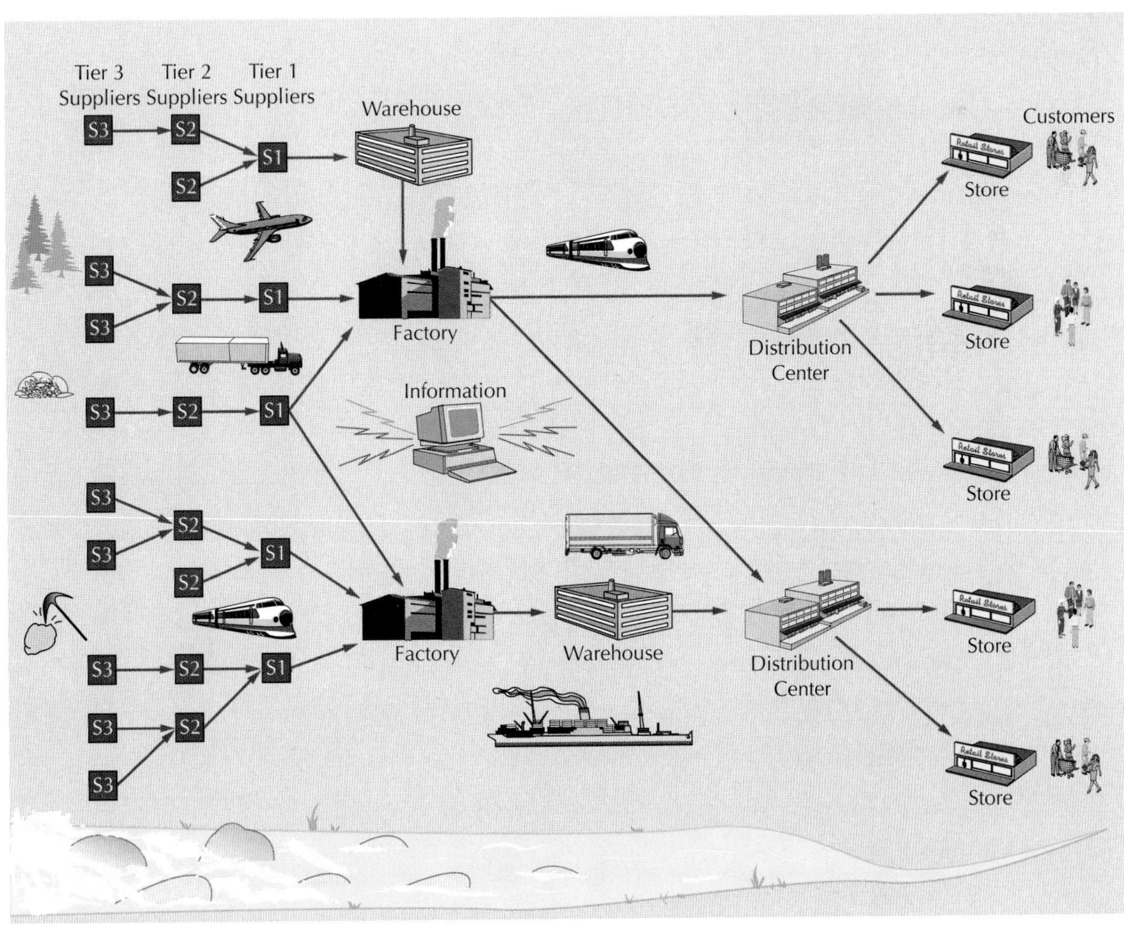

material providers. These suppliers are referred to as *upstream* supply chain members, while the distributors, warehouses, and eventual end-use customers are referred to as *downstream* supply chain members. The stream at the bottom of the figure denotes the flow of goods and services (i.e., demand) as the supply chain moves downstream. Notice that the stream is very rough at the upstream end and gets smoother as it moves downstream, a characteristic we will discuss in greater detail later. Also note that "information" is at the center of Figure 10.1; it is the "heart and brains" of the supply chain, another characteristic we will talk more about later.

The supply chain in Figure 10.1 can represent a single producer directly linked to one level of suppliers and one set of end-use customers. A grocery store that gets food products like milk, eggs, or vegetables directly from a farmer (and not through a broker or middle man), and sells them directly to the customer who consumes them reflects this basic level of supply chain. However, supply chains are more typically a series of linked suppliers and customers; every customer is in turn a supplier to the next, up to the final end user of the product or service. For example, Figure 10.2 shows the supply chain for denim jeans, a straightforward manufacturing process with a distinct set of suppliers. Notice that the jeans manufacturer has suppliers that produce denim who in turn have suppliers who produce cotton and dye.

As Figures 10.1 and 10.2 show, the delivery of a product or service to a customer is a complex process, encompassing many different interrelated processes and activities. First,

**Figure 10.2**
**The Supply Chain for Denim Jeans**

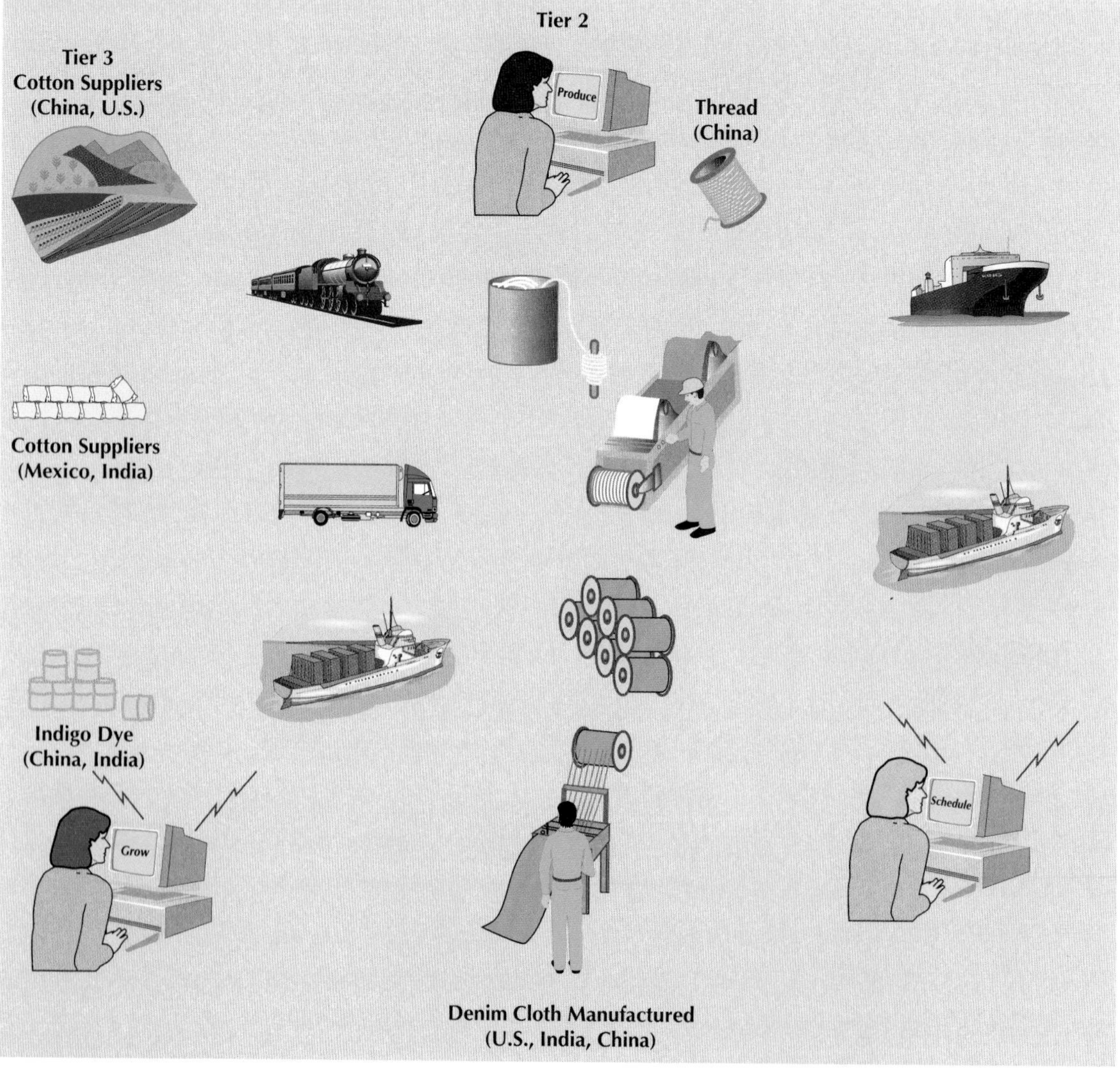

demand for a product or service is forecast, and plans and schedules are made to meet demand within a time frame. The product or service can require multiple suppliers (who have their own suppliers) who prepare and then ship parts and materials to manufacturing or service sites. One of the largest producers, General Motors, has more than 2500 suppliers that serve its 120 parts plants and 30 auto and truck assembly plants, including first-tier suppliers that supply it directly, second-tier suppliers that supply those suppliers, third-tier suppliers that supply second-tier suppliers, and so on. Parts and materials are transformed into final products or services. These products may then be stored at a distribution center or warehouse. Finally, these products are transported by carriers to external or internal customers. However, this may not be the final step at all, as these customers may transform the product or service further and ship it on to their customers. All of this is part of the supply chain—that is, the flow of goods and services from the materials stage to the end user.

The **supply chain** is also an integrated group of business processes and activities with the same goal—providing customer satisfaction. As shown in Figure 10.3, these processes include the *procurement* of services, materials, and components from suppliers; *production* of the products and services; and *distribution* of products to the customer including taking and filling orders. Information and information technology tie these processes together; it is what "integrates" them into a supply chain.

**Supply chain:** also an integrated group of processes to "source," "make," and "deliver" products.

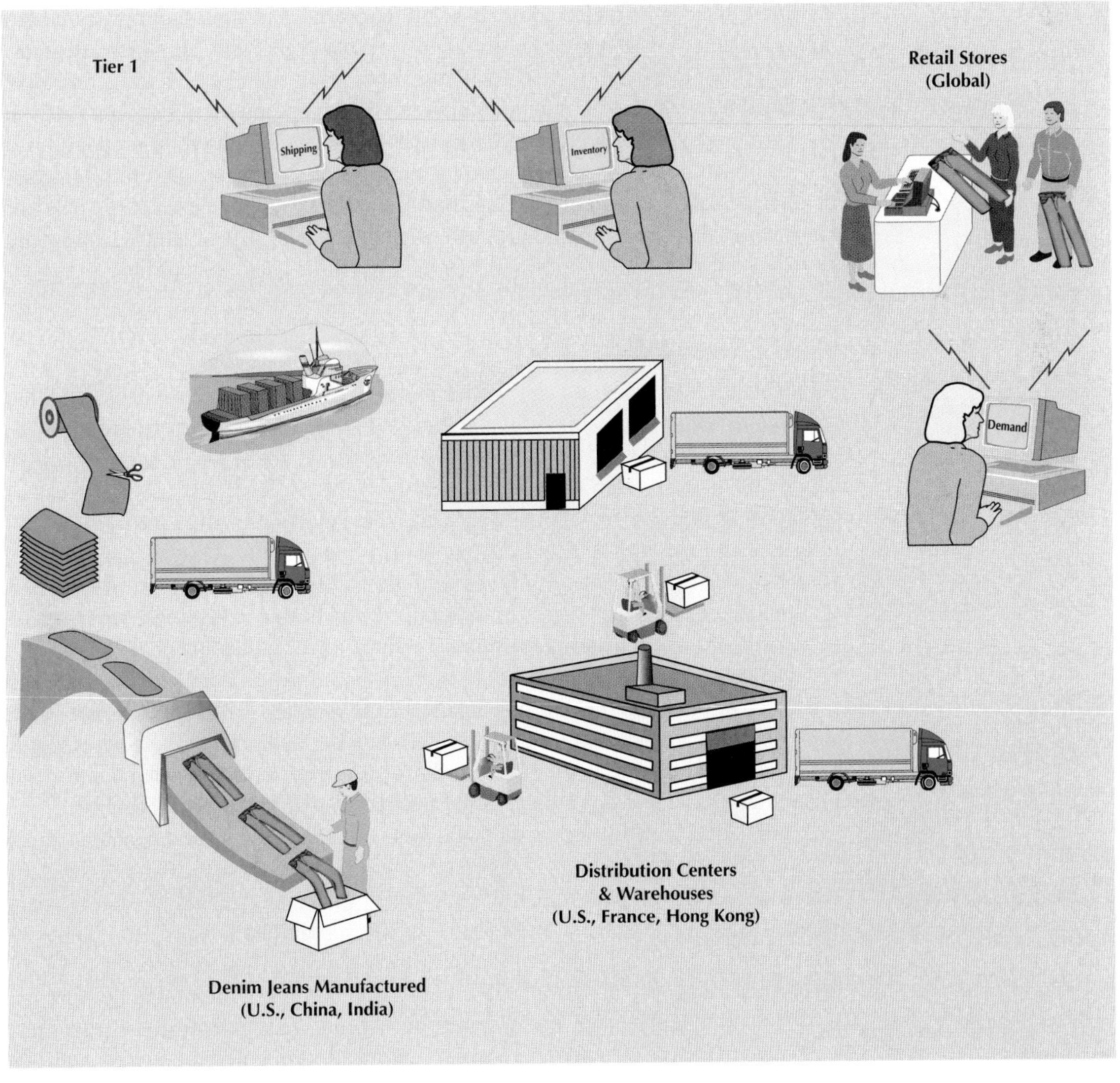

Figure 10.3
**Supply Chain Processes**

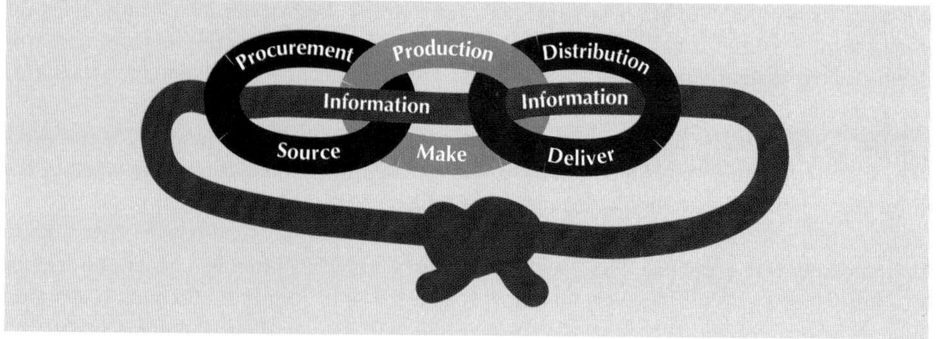


## SUPPLY CHAINS FOR SERVICE PROVIDERS

Supply chains for services are sometimes not as easily defined as supply chains for manufacturing operations. Since the supply chain of a service provider does not always provide the customer with a physical good, its supply chain does not focus as much on the flow of physical items (material, parts, and subassemblies) through the supply chain. It instead may focus more on the human resources and support services necessary to provide its own service. The supply chain of a service provider also tends to be more compact and less extended than a manufacturing supply chain. It generally does not have as many tiers of suppliers, and its distribution network is smaller or nonexistent. However, supply chains of service companies are definable and can be effectively managed using many of the same principles. Service companies and organizations have suppliers (who have suppliers), and they distribute their products to customers (who may have their own customers). Although a hospital and HMO do not provide actual goods to its customers, they nevertheless purchase equipment, computers, drugs, and medical supplies from suppliers (who have suppliers). They also contract for services (such as food preparation or laundry); hire doctors, nurses, accountants, administrators, and staff; and provide health care. They have quality-management issues throughout their supply chain. They also encounter the same problems and inefficiencies as a manufacturing-based supply chain. Other service companies, like McDonald's, do, in fact, provide a physical product.

## VALUE CHAINS

In recent years, terms such as *value* chain and *demand* chain have been used instead of, or interchangeably with, supply chain. Are there any differences between the two terms? Originally, a value chain was thought to have a broader focus than a supply chain. A value chain included every step from raw materials to the eventual end user, whereas a supply chain focused more narrowly on the activities that get raw materials and subassemblies into the manufacturing operation, that is, supply. In this context, the ultimate goal of a value chain is the delivery of maximum value to the end user. However, we have already indicated that the general perception of a supply chain is that it also encompasses this same broad focus, from raw material to end user. Alternatively, a demand chain has been referred to as a network of trading partners that extends from manufacturers to end-use consumers. The objective of demand chain management is to increase value for any part or all of the chain. This perhaps is a somewhat more narrowly defined perspective then a supply chain or value chain. However, in reality all of these terms have come to mean approximately the same thing to most people, and the terms are frequently used interchangeably.

**Value:** the creation of *value* for the customer is an important aspect of supply chain management.

A common thread among these perceptions of supply, value, and demand chains is that of **value**. Value to the customer is good quality, a fair price, and fast and accurate delivery. To achieve value for the customer, the members of the supply chain must act as partners to systematically create value at every stage of the supply chain. Thus, companies not only look for ways to create value internally in their own production processes, but they also look to their supply chain partners to create value by improving product design and quality, enhancing supply chain performance and speed, and lowering costs. To accomplish these value enhancers, supply chain members must often collaborate with each other and integrate their processes, topics that we will continually return to in this chapter.

## THE MANAGEMENT OF SUPPLY CHAINS

**Supply chain management (SCM)** focuses on integrating and managing the flow of goods and services and information through the supply chain in order to make it responsive to customer needs while lowering total costs. Traditionally, each segment of the supply chain was managed as a separate (stand-alone) entity focused on its own goals. However, the ability of a company to compete in today's global marketplace is determined by the combined effort of all members of the supply chain.

**Supply chain management (SCM):** requires managing the flow of information through the supply chain in order to attain the level of synchronization that will make it more responsive to customer needs while lowering costs.

Supply chains require close collaboration, cooperation, and communication among members to be effective. Suppliers, and their customers must share information. It is the rapid flow of information among customers, suppliers, distributors, and producers that characterizes today's supply chain management. Suppliers and customers must also have the same goals. They need to be able to trust each other: Customers need to be able to count on the quality and timeliness of the products and services of their suppliers. Furthermore, suppliers and customers must participate together in the design of the supply chain to achieve their shared goals and to facilitate communication and the flow of information.

*Keys to effective supply chain management* are information, communication, cooperation, and trust.

## SUPPLY CHAIN UNCERTAINTY AND INVENTORY

One of a company's main objectives in managing its supply chain is to synchronize the upstream flow of incoming materials, parts, subassemblies, and services with production and distribution downstream so that it can respond to uncertainty in customer demand without creating costly excess inventory. Examples of factors that contribute to uncertainty, and hence variability, in the supply chain are inaccurate demand forecasting, long variable lead times, late deliveries, incomplete shipments, product changes, batch ordering, price fluctuations and discounts, and inflated orders. The primary negative effects of supply chain uncertainty and variability are lateness and incomplete orders. If deliveries from suppliers are late or incomplete, they slow down the flow of goods and services through the supply chain, ultimately resulting in poor-quality customer service. Companies cope with this uncertainty and try to avoid delays with their own form of "insurance," **inventory**.

**Inventory:** insurance against supply chain uncertainty.

Supply chain members carry buffer (or extra) inventory at various stages of the supply chain to minimize the negative effects of uncertainty and to keep goods and services flowing smoothly from suppliers to customers. For example, if a parts order arrives late (or does not arrive at all) from a supplier, the producer is able to continue production and maintain its delivery schedule to its customers by using parts it has stored in inventory for just such an occurrence.

Companies also accumulate inventory because they may order in large batches in order to keep down order and transportation costs or to receive a discount or special price from a supplier. However, inventory is very costly. Products sitting on a shelf or in a warehouse are just like money sitting there not being used when it could be used for something else. It is estimated that the cost of carrying a retail product in inventory for one year is over 25% of what the item cost. Inventory-carrying costs were over $300 billion in the United States in 2000. As such, suppliers and customers would like to minimize or eliminate it.

## THE BULLWHIP EFFECT

Distorted information or the lack of information, such as inaccurate demand data or forecasts, from the customer end can ripple back upstream through the supply chain and magnify demand variability at each stage. This can result in high buffer inventories, poor customer service, missed production schedules, wrong capacity plans, inefficient shipping, and high costs. This phenomenon, which has been observed across different industries, is known as the **bullwhip effect**. It occurs when slight to moderate demand variability becomes magnified as demand information is transmitted back upstream in the supply chain. In Figure 10.1 the stream at the bottom of the figure reflects this occurrence;

**Bullwhip effect:** occurs when slight demand variability is magnified as information moves back upstream.

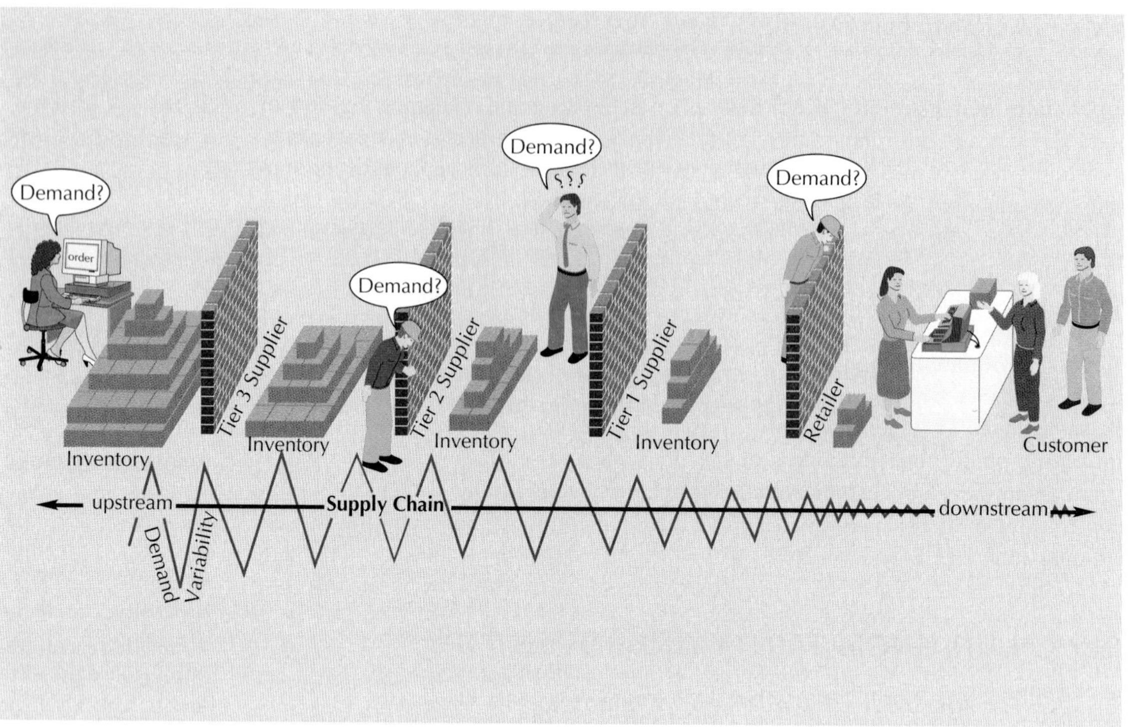


**Figure 10.4**
**The Bullwhip Effect**

the flow is greater (and the waters more turbulent) further upstream. Figure 10.4 presents a more detailed perspective of the bullwhip effect.

The bullwhip effect is created when supply chain members make ordering decisions with an eye to their own self-interest and/or they do not have accurate demand information from the adjacent supply chain members. If each supply chain member is uncertain and not confident about what the actual demand is for the succeeding member it supplies and is making its own demand forecast, then it will stockpile extra inventory to compensate for the uncertainty. In other words, they create a security blanket of inventory. As shown in Figure 10.4, demand for the end user is relatively stable. However, if slight changes in demand occur, and the distributor does not know why this change occurred, then the distributor will tend to overreact and increase its own demand, or conversely reduce its own demand too much if demand from its customer unexpectedly drops. This creates an even greater overreaction by the manufacturer who supplies the distributor and the suppliers who supply the manufacturer. One way to cope with the bullwhip effect is for supply chain members to share information, especially demand forecasts. If the supply chain exhibits *transparency*, then members can have access to each other's information, which reduces or eliminates uncertainty.

Procter & Gamble experienced the bullwhip effect when it noticed erratic shifts in ordering for Pampers production up and down its supply chain. Retail sales of Pampers were relatively uniform, and there was no particular day or month in which demand was significantly higher or lower than any other. Orders should have been stable and inventories low. Since Pampers end users (i.e., infants and toddlers) were not creating these extreme demand swings, P&G began to work back through the supply chain to look for the cause. It discovered that distributors' orders placed to the factory fluctuated more than retail sales. Their orders were more variable than the variability in demand at the retail stores warranted. Searching further back upstream through the supply chain, P&G found its orders to its main supplier, 3M, fluctuated even more; they reflected the greatest variability of all. Variability was being magnified at each upstream link as demand worked its way back through the supply chain as an overreaction to variability in the downstream stage, resulting in larger than necessary inventory stocks at each stage. Demand uncertainty at the extreme user-end of the supply chain had been "bullwhipped" back through the supply chain and magnified at each stage.

THE COMPETITIVE EDGE

### Supply Chain Management at 3M

Minnesota Mining and Manufacturing (3M) Company manufactures over 60,000 products for diverse markets ranging from Post-It notes to fiber-optic connectors. Since its beginnings in 1904, it has been known for its innovative products based on adhesives, substrates, and coatings that it currently markets to consumer, industrial, professional, and commercial customers in over 50 countries. However, despite its history of innovation and success, in the mid-1990s 3M became concerned about several disturbing trends, including a slowdown in the introduction of new products, the loss of market share in several key markets, and a decline in customer service, with corresponding customer complaints about late deliveries, inventory stock-outs, and poor product quality. These trends prompted 3M to introduce a companywide initiative, "Supply Chain Excellence," as a challenge to each of its units and its support organizations to understand and improve their business processes.

The 3M supply chain consists of four basic processes, including acquiring customer orders, procuring raw materials and components, manufacturing products, and filling customer orders. At the corporate level, 3M established oversight committees consisting of corporate-level executives and a supply chain team of corporate-level technical staff to review and support supply chain initiatives for its 40 business units (product divisions). All business-unit heads were responsible for developing their own supply chain excellence initiatives and plans. These initiatives included current performance and improvement projects that would lead to their unit's meeting companywide goals for commitments to customers for on-time and in-full deliveries, improving customer satisfaction (as measured by a survey-based customer satisfaction and loyalty index), increasing the speed of business processes (measured by the number of days from 3M's purchase of raw materials to the receipt of payment from its customers), and reducing supply chain costs (the sum of factory, logistics, and inventory-carrying costs).

As a result of its supply chain initiatives, one 3M business unit was able to double its sales, and it was selected for a vendor-of-the-year award. Another business unit reduced its work-in-process inventory to less than a day's worth, improved the accuracy of promised delivery times to within one day, and reduced new product introductions from 80 days to less than 30 days. Initiatives by another business unit resulted in on-time delivery improvement from 50% to 99.5%, a reduction in finished goods inventory to a two-week supply, and a $500,000 reduction in air freight costs. In another business unit order lead time was reduced from 30 days to 3 days, customer inventory was reduced by 70%, and raw material inventories were reduced by 26 days' worth. The initiatives implemented by another business unit cut inventory by 25%, reduced the order-expediting process from 8 steps to only 3, and increased on-time shipments from 85% to 95%. These are only some of the examples of the tangible benefits 3M achieved throughout the company and all of its business units from projects and innovative approaches initiated through its very successful Supply Chain Excellence program.

*Source:* A. Lockamy III, R. M. Beal and W. Smith, "Supply-Chain Excellence for Accelerated Improvement," *Interfaces* 30 (4; July–August 2000), pp. 22–31.

## INFORMATION TECHNOLOGY: A SUPPLY CHAIN ENABLER

Information links all aspects of the supply chain.

Information is the essential link between all supply chain processes and members. Computer and information technology allows real-time, online communications throughout the supply chain. Technologies that enable the efficient flow of products and services through the supply chain are referred to as "enablers," and information technology has become the most important enabler of effective supply chain management.

Supply chain experts and consultants like to use the phrase "in modern supply chain management, information replaces inventory." Although this statement is not literally true—companies need inventory at some point, not just information—information does change the way supply chains are managed, and these changes can lead to lower inventories. Without information technology it is likely that supply chain management would not be possible at the level it is currently being accomplished. Some of the more important IT supply chain enablers are shown in Figure 10.5.

### ELECTRONIC BUSINESS

**E-business:** the replacement of physical business processes with electronic ones.

**E-business** replaces physical processes with electronic ones. In e-business, supply chain transactions are conducted via a variety of electronic media, including EDI, e-mail, electronic funds transfer (EFT), electronic publishing, image processing, electronic bulletin boards,

**Figure 10.5**
**Supply Chain Enablers**

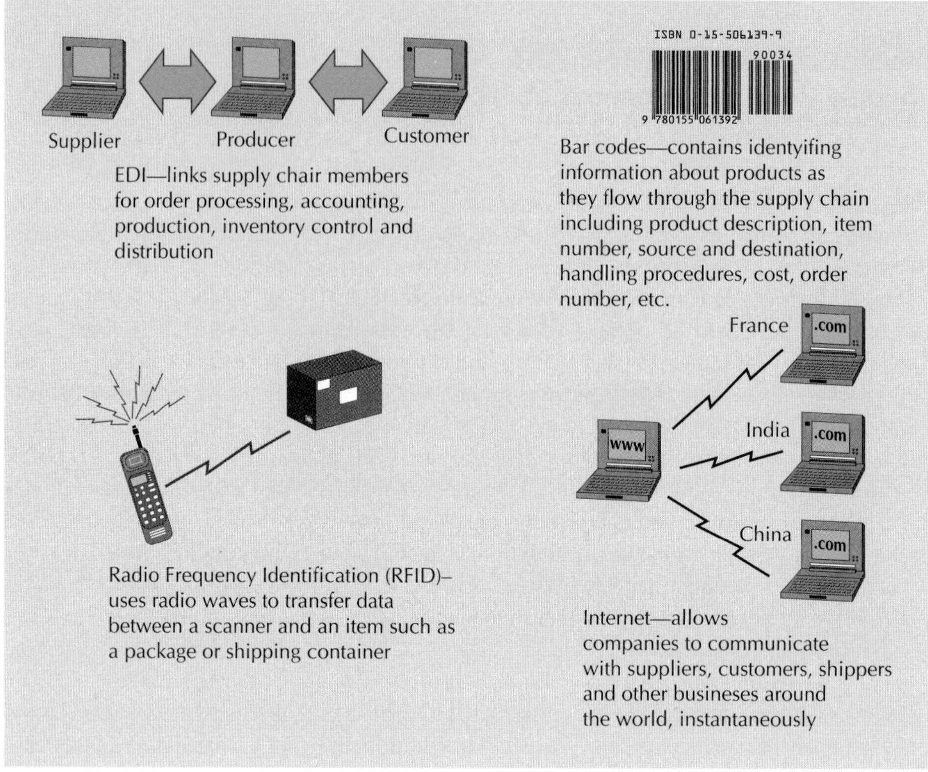


shared databases, bar coding, fax, automated voice mail, CD-ROM catalogues, the Internet, Web sites, and so on. Companies are able to automate the process of moving information electronically between suppliers and customers. This saves both labor costs and time.

Some of the features that e-business brings to supply chain management include:

- Cost savings and price reductions derived from lower transaction costs (including labor and document savings)
- Reduction or elimination of the role of intermediaries and even retailers and service providers, thus reducing costs
- Shortening supply chain response and transaction times for ordering and delivery
- Gaining a wider presence and increased visibility for companies
- Greater choices and more information for customers
- Improved service as a result of instant accessibility to services
- Collection and analysis of voluminous amounts of customer data and preferences
- The creation of virtual companies like Amazon.com that distribute only through the Web, which can afford to sell at lower prices because they do not need to maintain retail space
- Leveling the playing field for small companies, which lack resources to invest in infrastructure (plant and facilities) and marketing
- Gaining global access to markets, suppliers, and distribution channels

Table 10.1 illustrates the evolution of supply chain management at Nabisco that has taken place as a result of e-business capabilities. The table compares the flow of one example product, cashews used in its Planters brand, through both its "old" and "new" supply chains, from the process of ordering raw cashews from Nabisco's Brazilian suppliers to its final customer, a supermarket chain in New York.

## ELECTRONIC DATA INTERCHANGE

**Electronic data interchange (EDI):** a computer-to-computer exchange of business documents.

**Electronic data interchange (EDI)** is a computer-to-computer exchange of business documents in a standard format, which has been established by the American National Standards Institute (ANSI) and the International Standards Organization (ISO). It creates

**Table 10.1**
**Supply Chain @volution at Nabisco**

**Forecasting/Ordering**

**Then:** Nabisco determines the amount of Planters cashews a customer in New York might sell in a quarter, without consulting the customer.

**Now:** Nabisco and its customer share sales forecasts based on current point-of-sale data, past demand patterns, and upcoming promotions via the Web, and agree on an amount to supply.

**Procurement**

**Then:** Nabisco phones its Brazilian office and employees deliver the orders in person to local farmers, who put the raw cashews on trucks, which take them to the port.

**Now:** Nabisco contacts its Brazilian office by e-mail, but employees still must contact local farmers personally.

**Transportation**

**Then:** The shipping company notifies Nabisco when the cashews have sailed. When the cashews arrive in Jacksonville, Florida, a freight forwarder processes the paperwork to clear the shipment through customs, and scurries to locate a truck to deliver them to Nabisco plants. The truck takes the cashews to Nabisco's manufacturing plant, although it may be only half-full and return empty, costing Nabisco money.

**Now:** Shippers and truckers share up-to-date data online via a collaborative global logistics system that connects multiple manufacturers and transportation companies and handles the customs process. The system matches orders with carriers to make certain trucks travel with full loads.

**Distribution**

**Then:** The nuts are roasted and packed, and trucks take them to Nabisco's 12 warehouses across the country, where they are ready to be shipped to stores. However, they may not be near the store where the customer needs them because regional demand has not been discussed.

**Now:** After the nuts are roasted and packed at the plant, Nabisco sends the cashews to a third-party distributor, which relieves Nabisco of a supply chain activity not among its core competencies. The distributor consolidates the nuts on trucks with other products from Nabisco's competitors going to a customer resulting in full loads.

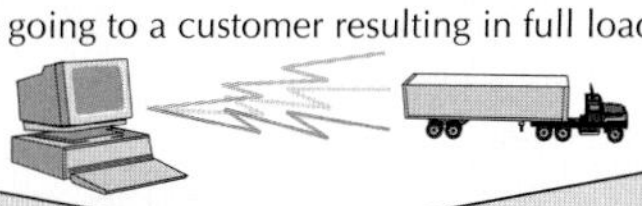

**Customer**

**Then:** If Nabisco ordered too many cashews they will turn soft in the warehouses, and if they ordered too few the customer will buy cashews elsewhere.

**Now:** Nabisco correctly knows the customer's needs so there is neither a shortage nor an oversupply of cashews. Transportation, distribution, warehousing, and inventory costs drop, and product and service quality improve.

*Source:* F. Keenan, "Logistics Gets a Little Respect," *Business Week* (November 20, 2000), pp. 112–115.

a data exchange that allows trading partners to use Internet transactions instead of paper when performing purchasing, shipping, and other business. EDI links supply chain members together for order processing, accounting, production, and distribution. It provides quick access to information, allows better customer service, reduces paperwork, allows better communication, increases productivity, improves tracking and expediting, and improves billing and cost efficiency.

EDI can be effective in reducing or eliminating the bullwhip effect discussed earlier in this chapter. With EDI, supply chain members are able to share demand information in real time, and thus are able to develop more accurate demand forecasts and reduce the uncertainty that tends to be magnified at each upstream stage of the supply chain.

## BAR CODES

In bar coding, computer-readable codes are attached to items flowing through the supply chain, including products, containers, packages and even vehicles. The bar code contains identifying information about the item. It might include such things as a product description, item number, its source and destination, special handling procedures, cost, and order number. A food product can be identified down to the farmer who grew it and the field it was grown in. When the bar code information is scanned into a company's computer by an electronic scanner, it provides supply chain members with critical information about the item's location in the supply chain.

Bar code technology has had a huge influence on supply chain management, and it is used by thousands of companies in different situations. Package delivery companies like FedEx and UPS use bar codes to provide themselves and customers with instantaneous detailed tracking information. Supermarkets use scanners at cash registers to read prices, products, and manufacturers from Universal Product Codes (UPCs). Airlines use bar codes to route luggage between terminals and "theoretically" to track lost luggage (although the high incidence of luggage sent to wrong destinations makes one wonder if airlines are using this technology effectively).

**Point-of-sale data:** creates an instantaneous computer record of a sale.

When bar codes are scanned at checkout counters, it also creates **point-of-sale data**—an instantaneous computer record of the sale of a product. This piece of information can be instantly transmitted throughout the supply chain to update inventory records. Point-of-sale data enable supply chain members—suppliers, producers, and distributors—to quickly identify trends, order parts and materials, schedule orders and production, and plan for deliveries.

## RADIO FREQUENCY IDENTIFICATION

**Radio frequency identification (RFID):** can send product data from an item to a reader via radio waves.

A recent innovation that's seen as a likely bar code partner is **radio frequency identification (RFID)**. RFID technology uses radio waves to transfer data between a reader, that is, scanner, and an item such as a shipping container or a carton. RFID consists of a tiny microchip and computer, often a small, thin ribbon, which can be put in almost any form—for example between layers of cardboard in a box, or on a piece of tape or a label. An RFID "tag" stores a unique identification number. RFID scanners transmit a radio signal via an antenna to turn on the tag, which then responds with its number. In the future, the tag could be an Electronic Product Code (EPC), and this proposed EPC could be linked to databases with detailed information about a product item. Unlike bar codes, RFID tags do not need line of sight to read, and many tags can be read simultaneously over a long distance.

The RFID tags would make it possible for a supplier or retailer to know automatically what goods they have and where they are. For example, a retailer could distinguish between three cartons of the same product and know that one was in the warehouse, one was in the store, and one was in transit, which would speed up product location, delivery, and replenishment. Figure 10.6 shows some of the advantages RFID provides. RFID technology also has obvious security benefits by being able to identify all items being shipped into the United States on an airplane or a ship. Wal-Mart has asked that its 100 top suppliers put RFID tags carrying EPCs on pallets and cases by 2005, which they estimate will result in savings of $8 billion the following year. However, it's unlikely that RFID technology will totally replace bar codes, because RFID will always be more costly.

## THE INTERNET

It is doubtful that any recent technological innovation has had a bigger impact on supply chain management, and business in general, than the Internet. Through the Internet a business can communicate with customers and other businesses within its supply chain anywhere in the world in real time.

The Internet has torn down geographic barriers, enabling companies to access markets and suppliers around the world that were previously inaccessible. By doing so, the Internet has shifted the advantage in the transaction process from the seller to the buyer, because the Internet makes it easier for companies to deal with many more suppliers around the world in order to get lower prices and better service.

The Internet adds speed and accessibility to the supply chain. Companies are able to reduce or eliminate traditional time-consuming activities associated with ordering and

**Figure 10.6**
**RFID Capabilities**

purchasing transactions by using the Internet to link directly to suppliers, factories, distributors, and customers. It enables companies to speed up ordering and delivery, track orders and delivery in real time, instantaneously update inventory information, and get instantaneous feedback from customers. This combination of accurate information and speed allows companies to reduce uncertainty and inventory. Internet commerce is expected to exceed $6 trillion some time in this decade.

General Electric, the world's largest diversified manufacturer, has made the Web the focus of its business activities with both suppliers and customers. GE gives the Internet credit for much of its recent financial success. It currently does more business on the Internet than any other noncomputer manufacturer.

*With RFID technology, small individual electronic "tags" like these are attached to cartons, packages, or containers, which allows companies and organizations to track their every move around the world.*

## BUILD-TO-ORDER (BTO)

Dell was the first computer company to move to a direct-sell-to-customers model over the Internet. Its popular build-to-order (BTO) models were initially based on telephone orders by customers. Dell created an efficient supply chain using a huge number of weekly purchase orders faxed to suppliers. However, Dell now sends out orders to suppliers over the Internet every few hours or less. Dell's suppliers are able to access the company's inventories and production plans, and they receive constant feedback on how well they are meeting shipping schedules.

Dell's Web site allows the customer to configure a PC with the desired features; to order and track the order status, allowing the customer to follow their purchase in real time from order to delivery; and to be notified by e-mail as soon as the order is shipped. Also, Dell created secure private sites for corporate and public sector customers to provide access to service and support information customized to the customer's products. In addition, Dell provides online access to technical reference materials and self-diagnostic tools that include symptom-specific troubleshooting modules that walk customers interactively through common systems problems.

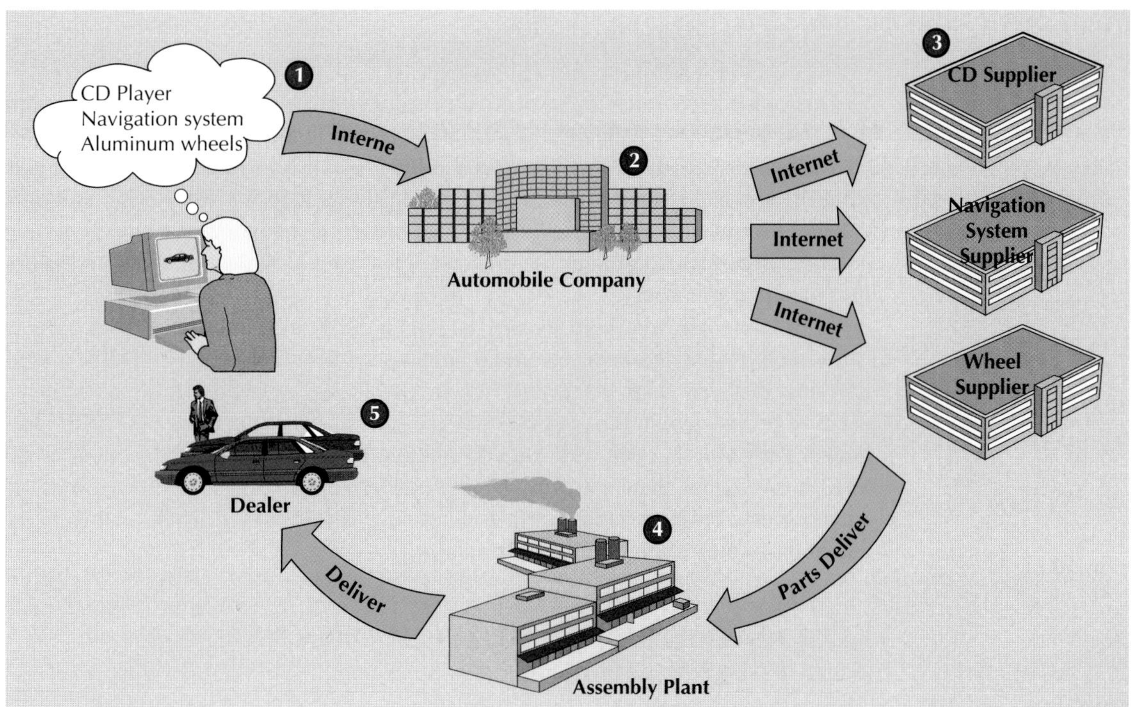


**Figure 10.7**
**Build-to-Order Cars over the Internet**

Now most major automotive manufacturers including Ford Motor Co., General Motors Corp., DaimlerChrysler, Volkswagen AG, and Toyota Motor Corp. have launched Web-based initiatives to build vehicles to individual customer specifications (i.e., BTO) provided over the Internet. Figure 10.7 shows the proposed Internet-based supply chain model for build-to-order cars. However, the supply chains for automobile companies are significantly more complex than the supply chain for a computer manufacturer like Dell. Most car models come in thousands of possible option configurations, automobile parts come from a complex multitiered web of thousands of suppliers, and finished cars are distributed through a network of independent dealers. Thus, to make Internet-based BTO cars a reality will require massive investments in new systems, and automobile manufacturers and suppliers will have to reengineer their traditional supply chain processes. Table 10.2 describes the changes in supply chain processes that must occur for the Internet-based BTO model to work.

**Table 10.2**
**The E-Automotive Supply Chain**

| Supply Chain Processes | Automotive Past | E-Automotive |
|---|---|---|
| Customer sales | Push—sell from inventory stock | Pull—build-to-order |
| Production | Goal of even and stable production | Focus on customer demand, respond with supply chain flexibility |
| Distribution | Mass approach | Fast, reliable, and customized to get cars to specific customer location |
| Customer relationship | Dealer-owned | Shared by dealers and manufacturers |
| Managing uncertainty | Large car inventory at dealers | Small inventories with shared information and strategically placed parts inventories |
| Procurement | Batch-oriented; dealers order based on allocations | Orders made in real time based on available-to-promise information |
| Product design | Complex products don't match customer needs | Simplified products based on better information about what customers want |

## SUPPLY CHAIN INTEGRATION

One of the keys to having a successful, efficient supply chain is to get the various supply chain members to collaborate and work together, that is, to get "in-sync." This level of coordination is referred to as *supply chain integration*. Information technology is the key element in achieving supply chain integration through four areas—information sharing, collaborative planning, workflow coordination, and the adoption of new models and technologies. Table 10.3 describes the positive effect each of these elements can have on supply chain performance.

Information sharing includes any data that are useful to other members of the supply chain such as demand data, inventory stocks, and production and shipping schedules—anything that can help the supply chain members improve performance. Information needs to be transparent (i.e., not hidden) and easily accessible, online. Collaborative planning defines *what* is done with the information that is shared. Workflow coordination defines *how* supply chain partners work together to coordinate their activities. Finally, adopting new business models and technologies is how supply chain members redesign and improve their supply chain performance.

### COLLABORATIVE PLANNING, FORECASTING, AND REPLENISHMENT

**CPFR:** a process for two or more companies in a supply chain to synchronize their demand forecasts into a single plan to meet customer demand.

**Collaborative planning, forecasting, and replenishment (CPFR)** is a process for two or more companies in a supply chain to synchronize their individual demand forecasts in order to develop a single plan for meeting customer demand. With CPFR, parties electronically exchange a series of written comments and supporting data, which includes past sales trends, point-of-sale data, on-hand inventory, scheduled promotions, and forecasts. This allows participants to coordinate joint forecasts by concentrating on differences in forecast numbers. They review the data together, compare calculations, and collaborate on what is causing discrepancies. If there are no exceptions they can develop a purchase order and ship. CPFR does not require EDI; data can be sent via spreadsheets or over the Internet. CPFR is actual collaboration because both parties do the work and both parties

**Table 10.3 Supply Chain Integration**

| Supply Chain Integration |
|---|
| *Information sharing among supply chain members*<br>• Reduced bullwhip effect<br>• Early problem detection<br>• Faster response<br>• Builds trust and confidence |
| *Collaborative planning, forecasting, replenishment, and design*<br>• Reduced bullwhip effect<br>• Lower costs (material, logistics, operating, etc.)<br>• Higher capacity utilization<br>• Improved customer service levels |
| *Coordinated workflow, production and operations, procurement*<br>• Production efficiencies<br>• Fast response<br>• Improved service<br>• Quicker to market |
| *Adopt new business models and technologies*<br>• Penetration of new markets<br>• Creation of new products<br>• Improved efficiency<br>• Mass customization |

share in fixing the problems. Sharing forecasts in this type of collaborative system can result in a significant decrease in inventory levels for both the manufacturer and distributor since it tends to reduce the "bullwhip effect," and thus lower costs.

## SUPPLIERS

Supply chains begin with supply at the farthest upstream point in the supply chain, inevitably from raw materials, as was shown in Figure 10.1. Purchased materials have historically accounted for about half of U.S. manufacturing costs, and many manufacturers purchase over half of their parts. Companies want the materials, parts, and services necessary to produce their products to be delivered on time, to be of high quality, and to be low cost, which are the responsibility of their suppliers. If deliveries are late from suppliers, a company will be forced to keep large, costly inventories to keep their own products from being late to their customers. Thus, purchasing goods and services from suppliers, or **procurement**, plays a crucial role in supply chain management.

**Procurement:** the purchase of goods and services from suppliers.

### SUPPLIER TEAMWORK

A key element in the development of a successful partnership between a company and a supplier is the establishment of linkages. The most important linkage is information flow; companies and suppliers must communicate—about product demand, about costs, about quality, and so on—in order to coordinate their activities. To facilitate communication and the sharing of information many companies use teams. *Cross-enterprise teams* coordinate processes between a company and its supplier. For example, suppliers may join a company in its product-design process as on-site suppliers do at Harley-Davidson. Instead of a company designing a product and then asking a supplier if it can provide the required part or a company trying to design a product around an existing part, the supplier works with the company in the design process to ensure the most effective design possible. This form of cooperation makes use of the expertise and talents of both parties. It also ensures that quality features will be designed into the product.

Cross-enterprise teams coordinate processes between a company and supplier.

In an attempt to minimize inventory levels, companies frequently require that their suppliers provide **on-demand**, also referred to as **direct-response**, delivery to support a just-in-time (JIT) or comparable inventory system. In **continuous replenishment**, a company shares real-time demand and inventory data with its suppliers, and goods and services are provided as they are needed. For the supplier, these forms of delivery often mean making more frequent, partial deliveries, instead of the large-batch orders suppliers have traditionally been used to filling. While large-batch orders are easier for the supplier to manage, and less costly, they increase the customer's inventory. They also reduce the customer's flexibility to deal with sudden market changes because of their large investment in inventory. Every part used at Honda's Marysville, Ohio, plant is delivered on a daily basis. Sometimes parts deliveries are required several times a day. This often requires that suppliers move their location to be close to their customer. For example, over 75% of the U.S. suppliers for Honda are within a 150-mile radius of their Marysville, Ohio, assembly plant. Each day grocers send Campbell's Soup Company demand and inventory data at their distribution centers via EDI, which Campbell's uses to replenish inventory of its products on a daily basis.

**On-demand (direct-response) delivery:** requires the supplier to deliver goods when demanded by the customer.

**Continuous replenishment:** supplying orders in a short period of time according to a predetermined schedule.

In addition to meeting their customers' demands for quality, lower inventory, and prompt delivery, suppliers are also expected to help their customers lower product cost by lowering the price of its goods and services. These customer demands on its suppliers—high quality, prompt delivery, and lower prices—are potentially very costly to suppliers. Prompt delivery of products and services as they are demanded from its customers may require the supplier to maintain excessive inventories itself. These demands require the supplier to improve its own processes and make its own supply chain more efficient. Suppliers require of their own suppliers what has been required of them—high quality, lower prices, process improvement, and better delivery performance.

## OUTSOURCING

**Sourcing:** the selection of suppliers.

**Outsourcing:** the purchase of goods and services from an outside supplier.

**Core competencies:** what a company does best.

Traditionally, the relationship between suppliers and customers was limited to the purchasing transaction. Companies purchased goods and services from suppliers based mostly on price and promised delivery date. However, the relationship between suppliers and customers has evolved to a more collaborative relationship, in which the selection of suppliers is called **sourcing**. Suppliers are literally the "source" of supply.

**Outsourcing** is the act of purchasing goods and services that were originally produced in-house from an outside supplier. Outsourcing is nothing new; for decades companies have outsourced as a short-term solution to problems such as an unexpected increase in demand, breakdowns in plants and equipment, testing products, or a temporary lack of plant capacity. However, outsourcing has become a long-term strategic decision instead of simply a short-term tactical one. Companies, especially large, multinational companies, are moving more production, service, and inventory functions into the hands of suppliers. Figure 10.8 shows the three major categories of goods and services that companies tend to outsource.

Many companies are outsourcing as a strategic move so that they can focus more on their **core competencies**, that is, what they do best. They let a supplier do what the company is not very good at and what the supplier is most competent to do. Traditionally, many companies, especially large ones, attempted to own and operate all of their sources

**Figure 10.8**
**Categories of Goods and Services that Companies Outsource**

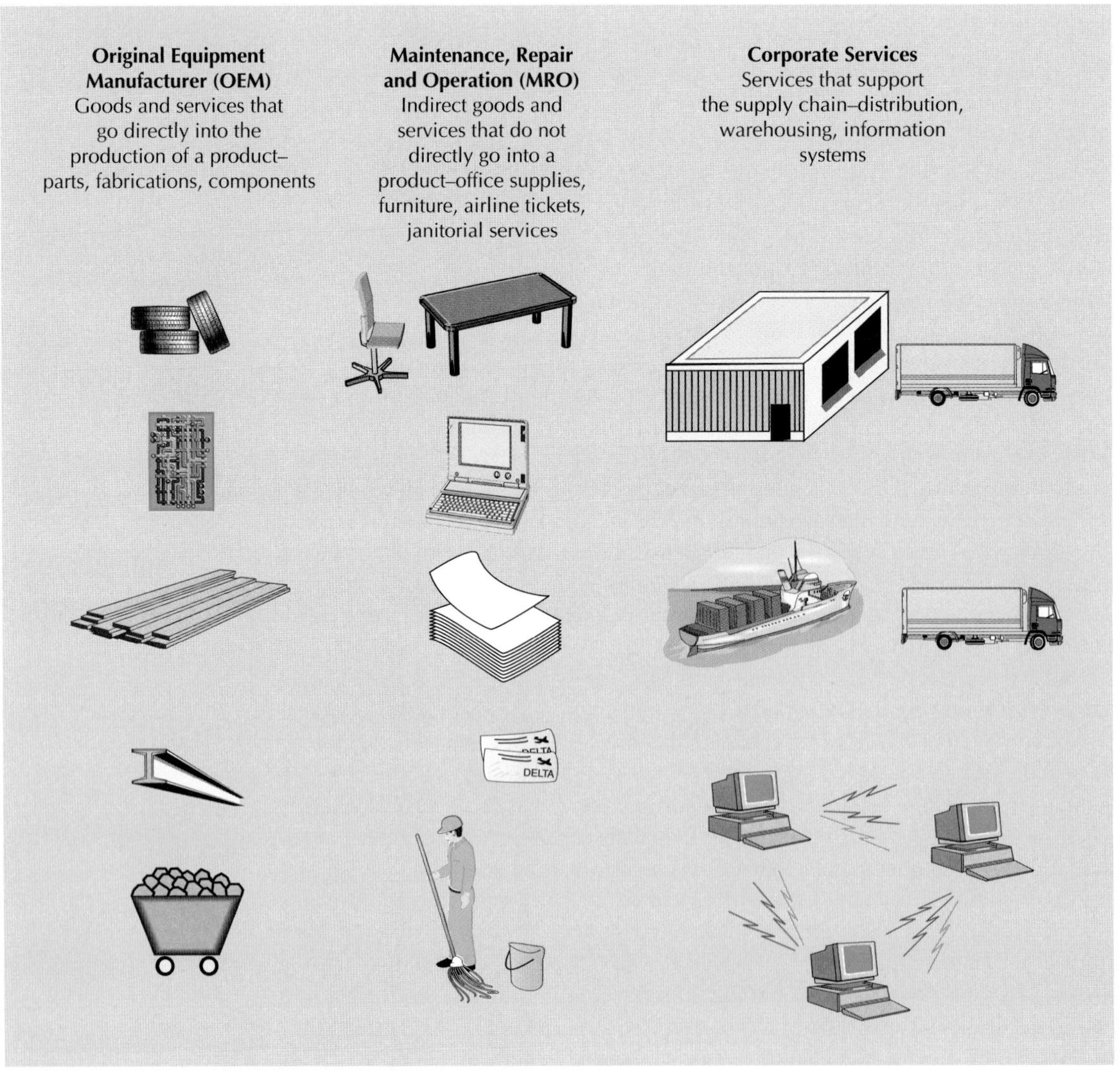

of supply and distribution along the supply chain so that they would have direct managerial control and reduce their dependence on potentially unreliable suppliers. They also thought it was more cost effective. However, this stretched these companies' resources thin, and they discovered they did not have the expertise to do everything well. In addition, management of unwieldy, complex supply chains was often difficult. Large inventories were kept throughout the supply chain to buffer against uncertainties and poor management practices. The recent trend toward outsourcing provides companies with greater flexibility and resources to focus on their own core competencies, and partnering relationships with suppliers provides them with control.

## SINGLE-SOURCING

**Single-sourcing:** a company purchases goods and services from only a few (or one) suppliers.

With single-sourcing, a company purchases goods and services from very few suppliers, sometimes only one. In the past, many companies purposefully purchased parts or materials from many different suppliers. It was not unusual for a company to limit its purchase of a part from any single supplier to a maximum percentage (for example, 10 or 15%) so the company would not be dependent on any one supplier. If a supplier was unable to meet delivery schedules, delivered a poor-quality product, or even went out of business, the effect on the customer would be dampened by the other suppliers.

With single-sourcing, however, a company has more direct influence and control over the quality, cost, and delivery performance of a supplier if the company has a major portion of that supplier's volume of business. The company and supplier enter into a partnership in which the supplier agrees to meet the customer's quality standards for products and services and helps lower the customer's costs. The company can also stipulate delivery schedules from the supplier that enables them to reduce inventory. In return, the company enters into a long-term relationship with the supplier, providing the supplier with security and stability. It may seem that all the benefits of such an arrangement are with the customer, and that is basically true. The customer dictates cost, quality, and performance to the supplier. However, the supplier passes similar demands on to its own suppliers, and in this manner the entire supply chain becomes more efficient and cost effective.

## THE COMPETITIVE EDGE

### Supplier Awards at Intel

Many companies have instituted supplier certification and/or award programs to recognize their best suppliers. For example, Intel uses two supplier awards—the Preferred Quality Supplier (PQS) award and the Supplier Continuous Quality Improvement (SCQI) award—to recognize its suppliers who consistently meet or exceed its exacting performance standards. Winning these awards requires the supplier to take significant risks in terms of investment and operational changes, but it can have significant beneficial results for the supplier in terms of a long-term commitment from Intel. Intel determines award recipients through the following process. Commodity managers and teams nominate critical suppliers who have previously shown a willingness to invest, be innovative, and improve. Intel business leaders meet annually to decide which nominated suppliers will be considered for their awards. For suppliers who are targeted for possible awards, breakthrough performance goals are established; then Intel offers training, assistance and other resources to help suppliers. Next Intel tracks and measures performance scores. To determine award winners, Intel's business leaders look for examples of "breakthrough" performance—activities that go beyond the company's wildest hopes and dreams for the supplier. Intel recognizes award winners with ads in the *Wall Street Journal* and *Purchasing* magazine, and allows award winners to publicize their award-winning relationship with Intel. In 1998 Intel awarded the PQS and SCQI awards to 15 suppliers, and in 2002 it made 40 supplier awards. This represented a 170 percent increase in the number of suppliers who were able to meet or exceed Intel's high performance standards. The payoff for Intel has been a significant increase in material quality, lower costs, and greater customer satisfaction.

*Source:* A. Porter, "Intel's SCQI Lifts ALL Boats," *Purchasing* 131 (November 21, 2002), pp. 38–42.

## E-PROCUREMENT

**E-procurement:** direct purchase from suppliers over the Internet.

**E-procurement** is part of the business-to-business (B2B) commerce being conducted on the Internet, in which buyers make purchases directly from suppliers through their Web sites, by using software packages or through e-marketplaces, e-hubs, and trading exchanges. In one year alone IBM spent $40 billion in e-procurement from 32,000 suppliers and 280 Web-based catalogues, saving an estimated $400 million. Prior to e-procurement it took 30 days to process an order at IBM, whereas it now takes 1 day. The Internet has the potential to streamline and speed up the purchase order and transaction process from companies. Benefits include lower transaction costs associated with purchasing, lower prices for goods and services, reduced labor (clerical) costs, and faster ordering and delivery times.

Direct products go directly into the production process of a product; indirect products do not.

What do companies buy over the Internet? Purchases can be classified according to two broad categories: manufacturing inputs (direct products) and operating inputs (indirect products). Direct products are the raw materials and components that go directly into the production process of a product. Because they tend to be unique to a particular industry, they are usually purchased from industry-specific suppliers and distributors. They also tend to require specialized delivery; UPS does not typically deliver engine blocks. Indirect products do not go directly into the production of finished goods. They are the maintenance, repair, and operation (MRO) goods and services we mentioned previously (Figure 10.8). They tend not to be industry-specific; they include things like office supplies, computers, furniture, janitorial services, and airline tickets. As a result they can often be purchased from vendors like Staples or Gateway, and they can be delivered by services like UPS.

More companies tend to purchase indirect goods and services over the Internet than direct goods. One reason is that a company does not have to be as careful about indirect goods since they typically cost less than direct products and they do not directly affect the quality of the company's own final product. Companies that purchase direct goods over the Internet tend to do so through suppliers with whom they already have an established relationship.

## E-MARKETPLACES

E-marketplaces or e-hubs, consolidate suppliers' goods and services at one Internet site like a catalogue. For example, e-hubs for MROs include consolidated catalogues from a wide array of suppliers that enable buyers to purchase low-value goods and services with relatively high transaction costs more cheaply and efficiently over the Internet. E-hubs for direct goods and services are similar in that they bring together groups of suppliers at a few easy-to-use Web sites.

**E-marketplaces:** Web sites where companies and suppliers conduct business-to-business activities.

In 1998 Weirton Steel Corporation initiated the formation of a Pittsburgh-based metals industry e-marketplace called MetalSite, which is now partly owned by five top U.S. steel producers. This and other new **e-marketplaces** like Freemarkets provide a neutral ground on the Internet where companies can streamline supply chains and find new business partners. An e-marketplace also offers services such as online auctions where suppliers bid on order contracts, online product catalogues with multiple supplier listings that generate online purchase orders, and request-for-quote (RFQ) service through which buyers can submit an RFQ for their needs and users can respond. E-marketplaces are projected to account for as much as 35% of B2B Internet trade by 2005 according to some industry experts.

## REVERSE AUCTIONS

**Reverse auction:** a company posts orders on the Internet for suppliers to bid on.

One increasingly popular process used by e-marketplaces for buyers to purchase items is the **reverse auction**. In a reverse auction, a company posts contracts for items it wants to purchase that suppliers can bid on. The auction is usually open for a specified time frame, and vendors can bid as often as they want in order to provide the lowest purchase price. When the auction is closed, the company can compare bids on the basis of purchase price, delivery time, and supplier reputation for quality. Some e-marketplaces restrict participation to vendors who have been previously screened or certified for reliability and

## THE COMPETITIVE EDGE

### Virtual Manufacturing at Palm Inc.

Palm Inc., maker of the Palm Pilot, is the world leader in handheld computing, with annual revenues of approximately $1 billion. In 2003 Palm shipped 4.2 million handheld computing devices. Palm is a so-called virtual manufacturer—it designs and markets its products but outsources manufacturing to electronics contract manufacturers and distribution to a logistics company. It also uses original design manufacturers (ODMs) to help design and make some of its products. As such, there is no Palm factory or distribution center. However, while it outsources two of the links in its supply chain, manufacturing and distribution, it closely manages sourcing of the critical components (microprocessors, semiconductors, displays, plastics, mechanicals, etc.) it uses in its handheld devices. Although contract manufacturers do a good job of manufacturing in low-cost areas such as Brazil and China, they do less well in sourcing. In Palm's Strategic Sourcing organization, commodity managers negotiate contracts, look for new suppliers, evaluate supplier performance, and work with marketing, engineering, and new product introduction teams. They also scout out new advanced technologies and are involved in product design. The commodity manager makes sure suppliers can deliver components in the volume and price that Palm will require in the future, and can adapt to rapid technological changes. With strategic sourcing Palm has strong relationships, referred to as alliances, with only a few leading-edge suppliers, who have the technology and capability to respond to its needs in the future. For example, Texas Instruments is a major supplier of microprocessors. Working closely with suppliers, Palm uses a "should-cost" model wherein Palm forecasts what it expects its products to be and what they will cost in the future. For example, strategic sourcing enabled Palm to introduce its Zire PDA (personal digital assistant) in 2002 for a price of $99, whereas most comparable PDAs were selling for $400 to $500, and it became the fastest selling PDA in its category.

*Source:* J. Carbone, "Strategic Sourcing Is Palm's Pilot," *Purchasing* 132 (7; April 17, 2003), pp. 32–36.

product quality. Reverse auctions are not only used to purchase manufacturing items; they are also being used to purchase services. For example, transportation exchanges hold reverse auctions for carriers to bid on shipping contracts.

Although some companies like General Electric make extensive use of reverse auctions, other companies like IBM rarely use them. Sometimes companies use reverse auctions to create price competition among the suppliers it does business with; other times companies simply go through a reverse auction only to determine the lowest price without any intention of awarding a contract. It only wants to determine a baseline price to use in negotiations with its regular supplier. Companies that award contracts to low bidders in auctions can later discover their purchases are delivered late or not at all, and are of poor quality.

Figure 10.9 on the next page illustrates the sourcing and procurement process using reverse auctions at a typical online B2B supplier exchange. Traditionally, each of these steps in this figure were (and still are in many cases) conducted manually, one-to-one, using face-to-face meetings, courier, telephone, Fax, regular mail, and e-mail. An online supplier exchange streamlines and accelerates the procurement process.

## THE WAL-MART SUPPLY CHAIN

Wal-Mart is widely known as a supply chain innovator that has established unique relationships with its suppliers. Through state-of-the-art information technology, Wal-Mart shares real-time, point-of-sale information from its many retail stores directly with its major suppliers. It established a well-known alliance with Procter & Gamble. P&G has a customer account team at the Wal-Mart corporate headquarters in Bentonville, Arkansas, to facilitate the sharing of point of sale data on transactions and customer demand, and information on distribution and inventory. P&G maintains and replensihes product inventory at Wal-Mart stores, and Wal-Mart gives control to P&G for replenishment timing and quantities, with on-site inventory limits. This frees Wal-Mart from having to manage P&G's products and inventory at its stores. This innovative relationship fostered between these two companies is referred to as *vendor managed inventory (VMI)*.

**Figure 10.9**
**Online Sourcing/ Procurement Process**

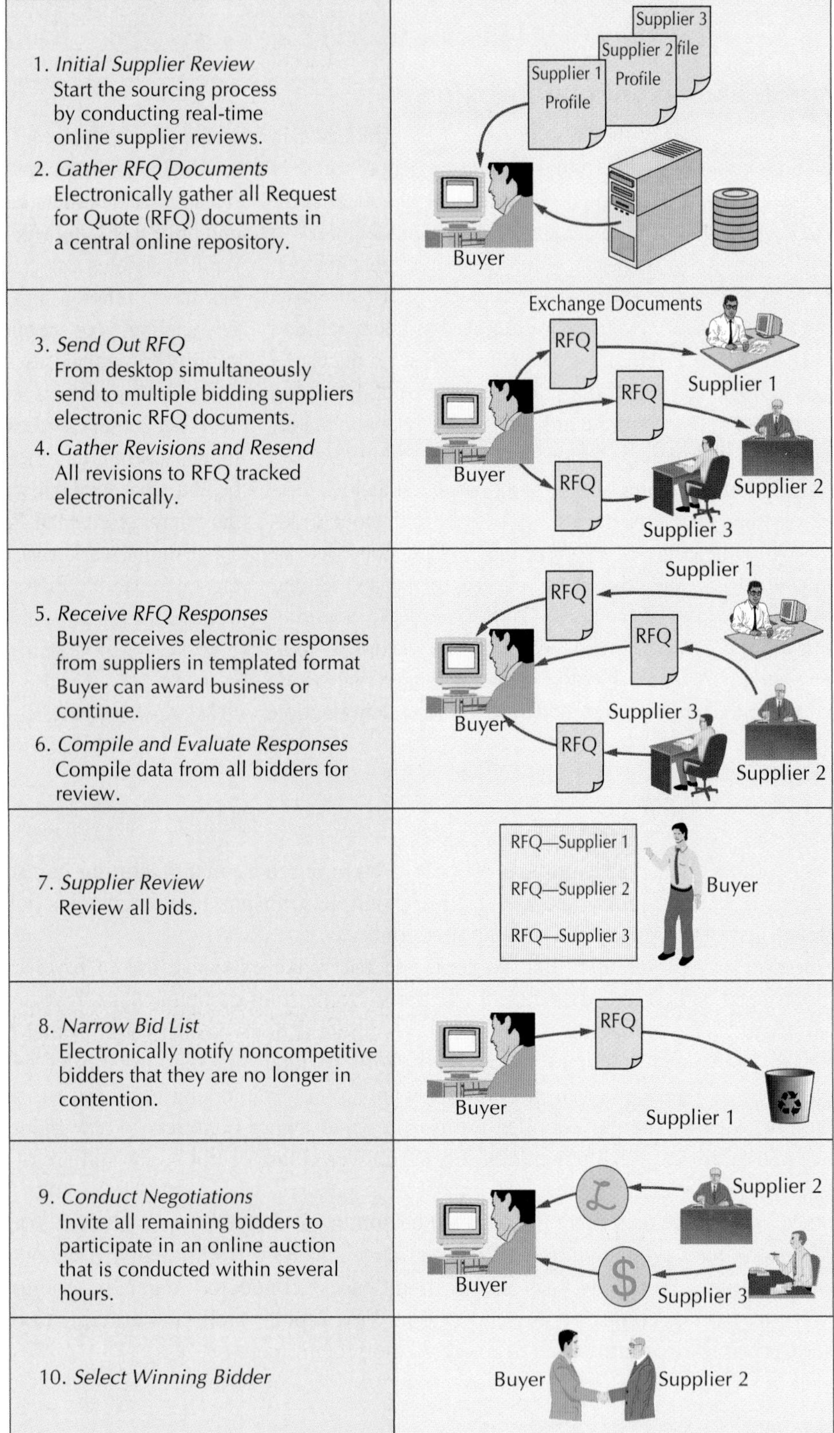


For example, Wal-Mart used to hold large inventories of a P&G product, Pampers diapers, in its warehouse before shipping them to stores. However, looking closely at its supply chain costs, Wal-Mart realized that Pampers took up so much space and had such a low-profit margin that the company was losing about 20 cents per case just handling the inventory. Working together, P&G and Wal-Mart discovered it was less costly and more profitable to have diapers shipped directly from the supplier to the store more frequently even though the cost of transportation and store labor would both be higher. It was more cost-effective to bypass traditional distribution centers and warehouses altogether. In other relationships with suppliers, Wal-Mart has found it to be more effective to let them take over warehousing and distribution. For example, Johnson Wax forecasts demand for its products (such as shaving gel and air freshener) in Wal-Mart stores using the point-of-sales data it receives from Wal-Mart and places its own products on the store shelves.

Another innovation at Wal-Mart was **cross-docking**. In its cross-docking system, products are delivered to Wal-Mart's warehouses on a continual basis, where they are sorted, repackaged, and distributed to stores without sitting in inventory. Goods "cross" from one loading dock to another in 48 hours or less. This system allows Wal-Mart to purchase full truckloads of goods while avoiding the inventory and handling costs, in the process reducing its costs of sales to 2 to 3% less than the industry average. Wal-Mart then passes these cost savings on to its customers as lower prices. Low prices enable them to forgo frequent discount promotions, which stabilizes prices and in turn makes sales forecasting more reliable, thus reducing stockouts and the need for excess inventory.

**Cross-docking:** goods "cross" from one loading dock to another in 48 hours or less.

Not all retailers use cross-docking because it is difficult to coordinate and manage. To make it work, Wal-Mart has invested heavily in an integrated information system that provides continuous contact between all of Wal-Mart's suppliers, distribution centers, and even *point-of-sale* in every store via its own satellite communication system and the Internet. This information system sends out point-of-sale (bar code) data directly to Wal-Mart's suppliers. In addition, Wal-Mart uses its own trucks to service its distribution centers; this allows the company to ship goods from warehouses to stores within 48 hours and restock store shelves an average of twice a week, compared to the industry average of once every two weeks. Cross-docking also requires close management cooperation at all levels. Store managers are connected to each other and to corporate headquarters via a video link that allows for frequent information exchanges about products, pricing, sales, and promotions. Figure 10.10 illustrates the relationship between facilities and processes along the Wal-Mart supply chain.

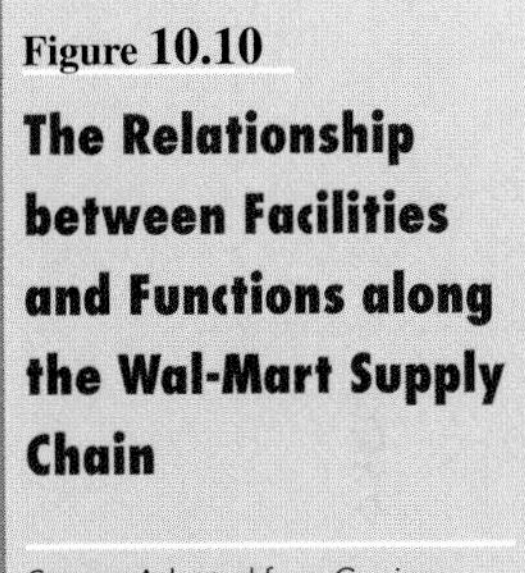


**Figure 10.10**
**The Relationship between Facilities and Functions along the Wal-Mart Supply Chain**

*Source:* Adapted from Garrison Wieland for "Wal-Mart's Supply Chain," *Harvard Business Review* 70(2; March–April 1992), pp. 60–71.

## DISTRIBUTION

**Order fulfillment:** the process of ensuring on-time delivery of an order.

**Logistics:** the transportation and distribution of goods and services.

Distribution encompasses all of the channels, processes, and functions, including warehousing and transportation, that a product passes through on its way to the final customer (end user). It is the actual movement of products and materials between locations. Distribution management involves managing the handling of materials and products at receiving docks, storing products and materials, packaging, and the shipment of orders. The focus of distribution, what it accomplishes, is referred to as **order fulfillment**. It is the process of ensuring on-time delivery of the customer's order.

Distribution and transportation are also often referred to as **logistics**. Logistics management in its broadest interpretation is similar to supply chain management. However, it is frequently more narrowly defined as being concerned with just transportation and distribution, in which case logistics is a subset of supply chain management. In 2001 the total U.S. business logistics cost was $970 billion.

## SPEED AND QUALITY

The most important factor in transportation and distribution is speed.

Distribution is not simply a matter of moving products from point A to point B. The driving force behind distribution and transportation in today's highly competitive business environment is *speed*. One of the primary quality attributes on which companies compete is speed of service. Customers have gotten used to instant access to information, rapid Internet-based order transactions, and quick delivery of goods and services. As a result, walking next door to check on what's in the warehouse is not nearly fast enough when customers want to buy a product now and a company has to let them know if it's in stock. That demands real-time inventory information. Calling a trucking firm and asking it when it will have a truck in the vicinity to pick up a delivery is not nearly fast enough when a customer has come to expect delivery in a few days or overnight. That also requires real-time information about carrier location, schedules, and capacity. Thus, the key to distribution speed is information, as it has been in our discussion of other parts of the supply chain.

## AMAZON.COM

Distribution is a particularly important supply chain component for Internet dot.coms, that is, virtual companies like Amazon.com, whose supply chains consist almost entirely of supply and distribution. These companies have no production process; they simply sell and distribute products that they acquire from suppliers. Dot.coms are not driven from the front end of the supply chain—the Web site—they are driven by distribution at the back end. Their success ultimately depends on the capability to ship each order when the customer needs or wants it. This was discovered with a shock by many dot.com companies like Amazon.com and Toysrus.com during the Christmas seasons of 1999 and 2000, when they took in a huge volume of Internet orders but their distribution systems were not able to get the orders delivered to customers in a timely manner.

Figure 10.11 illustrates the order fulfillment process at Amazon.com when one of its millions of customers places an order via the Internet (or by phone).[1] The order is transmitted to the closest distribution center that has the product. Items are stored in a warehouse in shelved bins each with a red light. When the light comes on, it signals that the product has been ordered; workers move from light to light, retrieving items from the shelves and pushing a button to reset the lights. Workers are told where to go by computers. The worker places each item in a crate with other orders, and when the crate is full it moves by conveyor through the plant to a central point. At this central sorting area bar codes are matched with order numbers to determine which items go with which order, and the items that fulfill an order are sorted into one of over 2000 3-foot-wide chutes. The items that make up an order are placed in a box as they come off the chute with a new bar code that identifies the order. The boxes are then packed, taped, weighed, and shipped by

[1] J. Zeff, "From Your Mouse to Your House," *Time* 154(26; December 27, 1999), pp. 72–73.

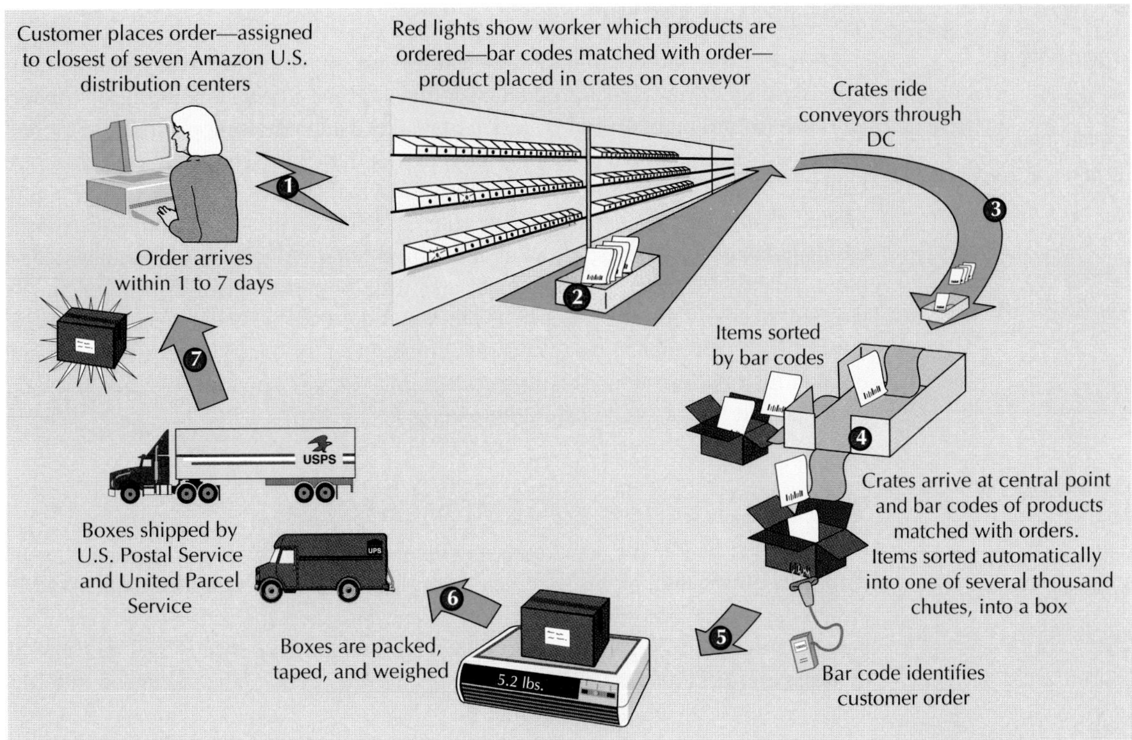


**Figure 10.11**
**Order Fulfillment at Amazon.com**

a carrier, for example, the U.S. Postal Service or UPS. On its busiest days during the Christmas season a warehouse is able to pack and ship over 200,000 items. Orders arrive between one and seven days after being placed. The key to Amazon.com's success has been not so much its ability to get customers to order online as it has been to develop the capacity and capability to fulfill orders reliably and quickly.

## DISTRIBUTION CENTERS AND WAREHOUSING

Distribution centers (DCs), which typically incorporate warehousing and storage, are buildings that are used to receive, handle, store, package, and then ship products. Some of the largest business facilities in the United States are distribution centers. The UPS Worldwide Logistics warehouse in Louisville, Kentucky, includes 1.3 million square feet of floor space. Distribution centers for The Gap in Gallatin, Tennessee, Target in Augusta City, Virginia, and Home Depot in Savannah, Georgia, each encompass more than 1.4 million square feet of space—about 30 times bigger than the area of a football field, and about three-fourths the floor space of the Empire State Building.

As in other areas of supply chain management, information technology is having a significant impact on distribution management. The Internet has altered how companies distribute goods by adding more frequent orders in smaller amounts and higher customer service expectations to the already difficult task of rapid response fulfillment. To fill Internet orders successfully, warehouses and distribution centers must be set up as "flow-through" facilities, using automated material-handling equipment to speed up the processing and delivery of orders.

Retailers have shifted from buying goods in bulk and storing them to pushing inventory and storage and final configuration back up the supply chain (upstream). They expect suppliers (and/or distributors) to make frequent deliveries of merchandise that includes a mix of different product items in small quantities (referred to as "mixed-pallet"), properly labeled, packed, and shipped in store-ready configurations. For example, some clothing retailers may want sweaters delivered already folded, ready for the store shelf, while others may want them to be on their own hangers. To adequately handle retailer requirements, distribution centers must be able to handle cross docking, automated high-volume sorting, custom labeling, custom packing, and returns processing.

## POSTPONEMENT

**Postponement:** moves some manufacturing steps into the distribution center.

A recent trend in distribution, **postponement**, moves some final manufacturing steps like assembly or individual product customization into the warehouse or distribution center. Generic products or component parts (like computer components) are stored at the warehouse, and then final products are built-to-order (BTO), or personalized, to meet individual customer demand. It is a response to the adage that whoever can get the desired product to the customer first gets the sale. Postponement actually pulls distribution into the manufacturing process, allowing lead times to be reduced so that demand can be met more quickly. However, postponement also usually means that a distributor must stock a large number of inventory items at the warehouse to meet the final assembly or customization requirements; this can create higher inventory-carrying costs. The manufacturing and distribution supply chain members must therefore work together to synchronize their demand forecasts and carefully manage inventory.

## WAREHOUSE MANAGEMENT SYSTEMS

**WMS:** an automated system that runs the day-to-day operations of a distribution center.

In order to handle the new trends and demands of distribution management, companies employ sophisticated, highly automated **warehouse management systems (WMS)** to run day-to-day operations of a distribution center and keep track of inventories. The WMS places an item in storage at a specific location (a *putaway*), locates and takes an item out of storage (a *pick*), packs the item, and ships it via a *carrier*. The WMS acknowledges that

### THE COMPETITIVE EDGE

#### Distribution and Warehouse Management at Timberland

Timberland's Ontario, Canada, distribution center stocks and distributes 80% of the company's footwear line, which amounts to between 10,000 and 20,000 SKUs (i.e., stock-keeping units, indicating a specific style and size pair of shoes) at any one time. Developing an inventory management system that would process and keep track of that many units was a challenge, especially given Timberland's goal of a 24-hour turnaround from the time a retailer places an order to the time it is shipped from the distribution center. Timberland purchased a computer-based warehouse management system (WMS) to handle its problem.

All of Timberland's footwear is manufactured in the Far East and shipped in containers through the Port of Los Angeles and then on to Ontario. The WMS begins as soon as the shipments arrive on the loading dock in Ontario. Boxes are labeled with a bar code from the overseas manufacturing plant, which indicates shipping number, purchase order number, style, and size. Using handheld radio frequency (RF) readers, Timberland's receiving personnel scan the bar code into the WMS. The WMS software then prints out a large purple proprietary bar code that contains all the original information about the box's contents and more. The WMS assigns each box a unique identity that includes its content and its status in the warehouse. Any time a box is moved from one place to another the purple bar code is scanned to update its location.

Storing items (i.e., SKUs), at locations in the distribution center, called the "putaway process," is difficult because of the huge range of styles, sizes, and colors of the footwear and demand, which will vary depending on consumer preferences, time of year, and so on. As a result, storage locations cannot be permanently assigned to specific SKUs. New deliveries are taken to a general putaway region determined by SKU and then placed in an available location; the bar code of that location is scanned, and the box's bar code is also scanned, fixing the location of that box in the WMS.

Sorting and shipping orders is also managed by the WMS. Most orders from retailers consist of a variety of styles, sizes, and quantities. During the peak season from July through September, an average of 65,000 to 70,000 boxes will be sorted for shipment each day, with highs of 100,000 on some days. When an order is complete, a shipping label and packing slips are printed, the cases are sealed, and a conveyor takes the complete order to shipping, where they are placed on pallets. When a pallet is full, it triggers a complete order and the WMS creates a manifest with content information to the customer. It also creates a bill of lading with the number of cartons being shipped and a load sheet that details the customer's ID number and name. When the bill of lading is entered in the WMS, it indicates the exact pallet location and loading door where the order has been staged for shipment.

The WMS achieves 99.9% inventory accuracy.

*Source:* B. Schwartz, "Technology Safeguards the Timberland Tradition," *Transportation and Distribution* 41(4; April 2000), pp. 35–40.

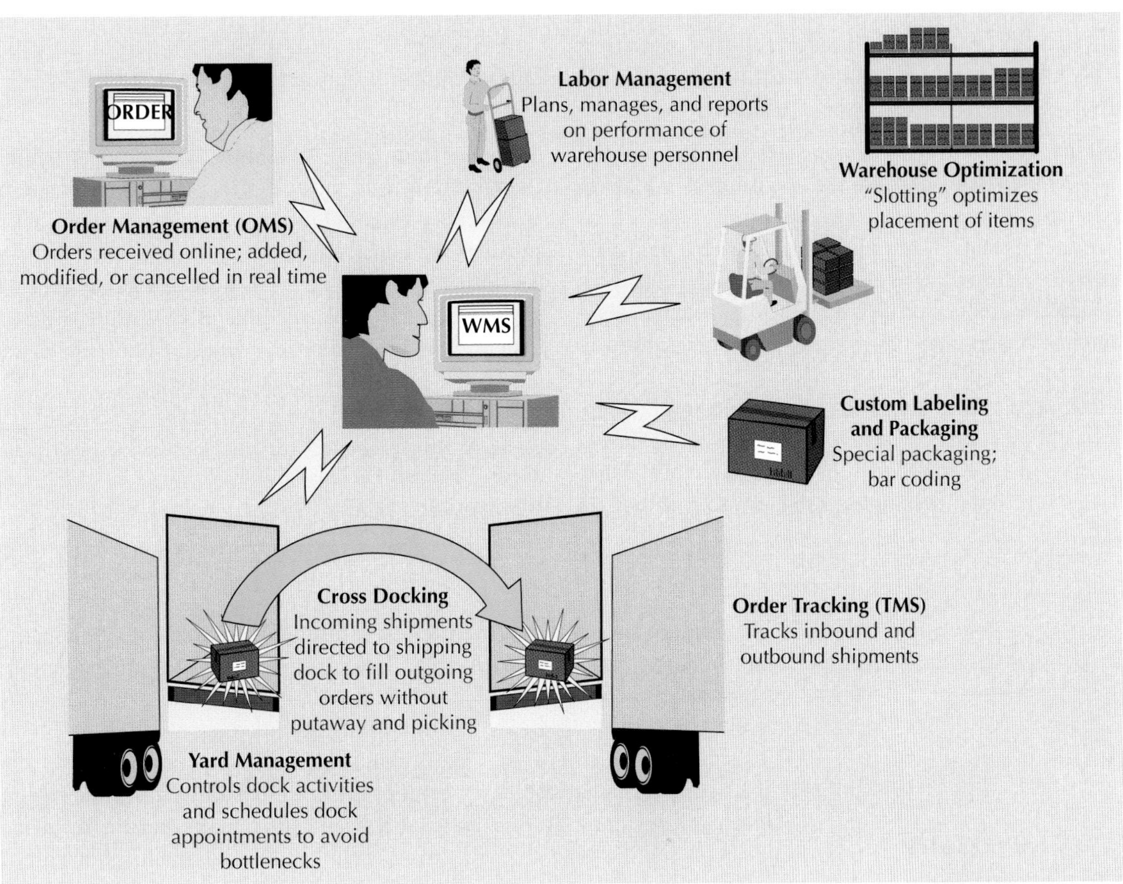


Figure **10.12**
**A Warehouse Management System (WMS)**

a product is available to ship, and, if it is not available, the system will determine from suppliers in real time when it will be available.

Figure 10.12 illustrates the features of a WMS. Orders flow into a WMS through an *order management system* (OMS). The OMS enables the distribution center to add, modify, or cancel orders in real time. When the OMS receives customer order information online, it provides a snapshot of product availability from the WMS and from suppliers via EDI. If an item is not in stock, the OMS looks into the supplier's production schedule to see when it will be available. The OMS then allocates inventory from the warehouse site to fill an order, establishes a delivery date, and passes these orders onto the transportation management system for delivery.

The *transportation management system (TMS)* allows the DC to track inbound and outbound shipments, to consolidate and build economical loads, and to select the best carrier based on cost and service. *Yard management* controls activities at the facility's dock and schedules dock appointments to reduce bottlenecks. *Labor management* plans, manages, and reports the performance level of warehouse personnel. *Warehouse optimization* optimizes the warehouse placement of items, called "slotting," based on demand, product groupings, and the physical characteristics of the item. A WMS also creates custom labeling and packaging. A WMS facilitates cross-docking, the system that Wal-Mart originated which allows a DC to direct incoming shipments straight to a shipping dock to fill outgoing orders, eliminating costly putaway and picking operations.

A WMS may include the following features: transportation management, order management, yard management, labor management, and warehouse optimization.

## VENDOR-MANAGED INVENTORY

As we noted in our previous description of the Wal-Mart supply chain, in **vendor-managed inventory (VMI)** manufacturers, instead of distributors or retailers, generate orders. Under VMI, manufacturers receive data electronically via EDI or the Internet about distributors' sales and stock levels. Manufacturers can see which items distributors carry, as well as several years of point-of-sale data, expected growth, promotions, new and

**VMI:** manufacturers rather than vendors generate orders.

## THE COMPETITIVE EDGE

### Vendor-Managed Inventory (VMI) at Dell

Dell Inc., the world's largest computer systems company, bypasses retailers and sells directly to customers via phone or the Internet. Once an order is processed, it is sent to one of its assembly plants in Austin, Texas, where the product is built tested, and packaged within eight hours. Many of Dell's suppliers are located in Southeast Asia, and their shipping times to Austin range from 7 days for air transport to 30 days for water and ground transport. To compensate for these long lead times, Dell's suppliers keep inventory in small warehouses called "revolvers" (for revolving inventory), which are a few miles from Dell's assembly plants. Dell keeps very little inventory at its plants, so it withdraws inventory from the revolvers every few hours while most suppliers deliver to their revolvers three times a week. Dell has a vendor-managed inventory (VMI) arrangement with its suppliers who decide how much to order and when to send their orders to the revolvers. Dell sets target inventory levels for its suppliers—typically 10 days of inventory—and keeps track of how much suppliers deviate from these targets and reports this information back to suppliers.

*Source:* R. Kapuscinski, R. Zhang, P. Carbonneau, R. Moore, and B. Reeves, "Inventory Decisions in Dell's Supply Chain," *Interfaces* 34(3; May–June 2004), pp. 191–205.

lost business, and inventory goals, and use this information to create and maintain a forecast and an inventory plan. VMI is a form of "role reversal"—usually the buyer completes the administrative tasks of ordering; with VMI the responsibility for planning shifts to the manufacturer.

VMI is usually an integral part of supply chain collaboration. The vendor has more control over the supply chain and the buyer is relieved of administrative tasks, thereby increasing supply chain efficiency. Both manufacturers and distributors benefit from increased processing speed, and fewer data entry errors occur because communications are through computer-to-computer EDI or the Internet. Distributors have fewer stockouts; planning and ordering costs go down because responsibility is shifted to manufacturers; and service is improved because distributors have the right product at the right time. Manufacturers benefit by receiving distributors' point-of-sale data, which makes forecasting easier.

## COLLABORATIVE LOGISTICS

Rival companies are also finding ways to collaborate in distribution. They have found that by pooling their distribution resources, which can create greater economies of scale, they can reduce their costs.

For example, Nabisco discovered it was paying for too many half-empty trucks so they moved to collaborative logistics. Using the Web as a central coordination tool between producers, carriers, and retailers, Nabisco can share trucks and warehouse space with other companies, even competitors, like Dole and Lea & Perrins, that are shipping to the same retail locations. Nabisco and 10 other companies, including General Mills and Pillsbury, started using a collaborative logistics network from Nistevo Corporation. At Nistevo.com companies post the warehouse space they need or have available and share space, trucks, and expenses. The goal is that everyone, from suppliers to truckers to retailers, shares in the savings. General Mills also worked out a collaborative arrangement with Fort James Corporation, the maker of paper towels and Dixie Cups, sharing a truck route that saved General Mills $800,000 in its first year.

## DISTRIBUTION OUTSOURCING

Distribution outsourcing allows a company to focus on its core competencies and can lower inventory and reduce costs.

Another recent trend in distribution is outsourcing. Just as companies outsource to suppliers activities that they once performed themselves, producers and manufacturers are increasingly outsourcing distribution activities. The reason is basically the same for producers as it is for suppliers; outsourcing allows the company to focus on its core competencies. It also takes advantage of the expertise that distribution companies have developed. Outsourcing distribution activities tends to lower inventory levels and reduce costs for the outsourcing company.

Nabisco Inc., with annual sales of $9 billion, delivers 500 types of cookies, more than 10,000 candies, and hundreds of other food items to 80,000 buyers and has incoming shipments of countless raw ingredients. It outsources many distribution and transportation activities to third-party logistics (3PL) companies. Outsourcing is more cost-effective and allows Nabisco to focus on core competencies. Even Wal-Mart, with its sophisticated distribution system, supplants its own distribution centers with third-party services for seasonal overflows and forward buys.

## TRANSPORTATION

In a supply chain, *transportation* is the movement of a product from one location to another as it makes its way to the end-use customer. Although supply chain experts agree that transportation tends to fall through the supply chain management cracks, receiving less attention than it should, it can be a significant supply chain cost. For some manufacturing companies, transportation costs can be as much as 20% of total production costs and run as high as 6% of revenue. Transportation costs in the United States are over $600 billion per year, which is about 6% of the gross domestic product. Domestic freight by all modes increased 65% from the 1970s to the 1990s. For some retail companies primarily involved in the distribution of goods, like L.L. Bean and Amazon.com, transportation is not only a major cost of doing business, it is also a major determinant of prompt delivery service. L.L. Bean ships over 12 million packages in a year—125,000 on its busiest day—mostly by UPS.

The principal modes of transportation within the United States are railroads, air, truck, intermodal, water, package carriers, and pipeline. In the United States the greatest volume of freight is shipped by railroad (approximately one-third of the total), followed by trucking, pipeline, and inland waterways. The different transport modes and some of their advantages and disadvantages are shown in Figure 10.13.

*Railroads* are cost-effective for transporting low-value, high-density, bulk products such as raw materials, coal, minerals, and ores over long distances. Railroads operate on less flexible and slower schedules than trucks, and they usually cannot go directly from one business location to another as trucks can. Rail freight service has the worst record of quality performance of all modes of freight transport, with a higher incidence of product damage and almost 10 times more late deliveries than trucking.

*Trucking* is the main mode of freight transportation in the United States, generating over 75% of the nation's total freight cost each year. U.S. motor freight costs at the start of the twenty-first century were almost $500 billion. Trucks provide flexible point-to-point service, delivering small loads over short and long distances over widely dispersed geographic areas. Trucking service is typically more reliable and less damage-prone then railroads.

Figure 10.13 **Transportation Modes**

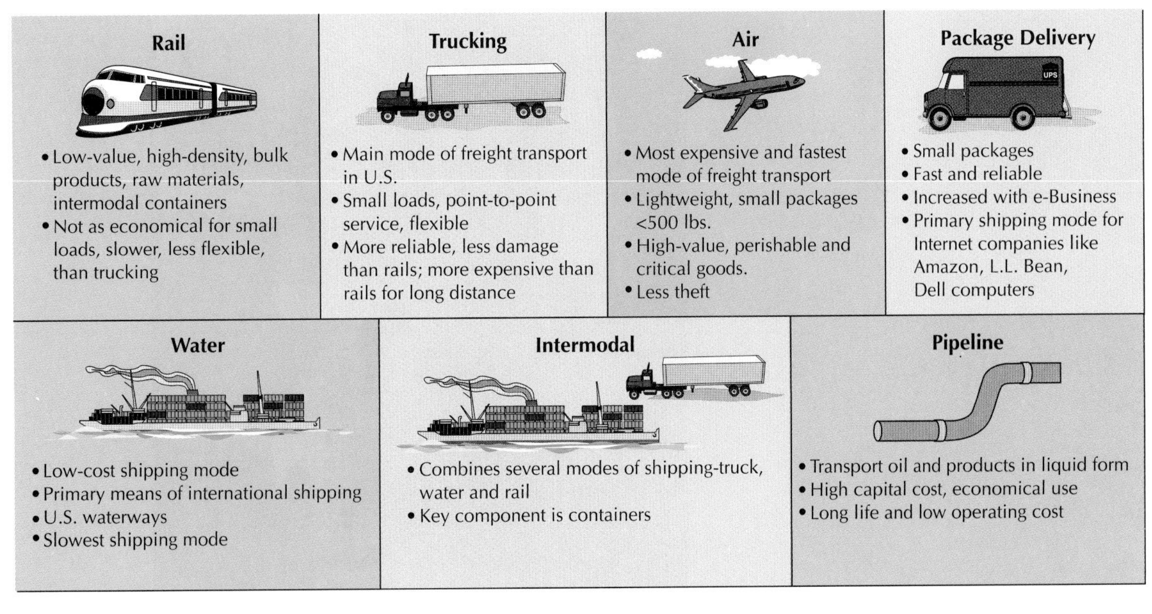

*Air freight* is the most expensive and fastest mode of freight transportation; it is also the fastest segment of the airline industry. For companies that use air freight, service is more important than price. Production stoppages because of missing parts or components, are much more expensive than the increased cost of air freight. For high-value goods such as pharmaceuticals, high technology, and consumer electronics, speed to market is important, and in addition, shorter shipping times reduce the chances for theft and other losses. The general rule for international air freight is that anything that's physically or economically perishable has to move by air instead of by ship. The major product groups that are shipped by international air freight, from largest to smallest, are perishables, construction and engineering equipment, textiles and wearing apparel, documents and small package shipments, and computers, peripherals, and spare parts.

*Package carriers* such as UPS, FedEx, and the U.S. Postal Service transport small packages, up to about 150 pounds. The growth of e-business has significantly increased the use of package carriers. Package carriers combine various modes of transportation, mostly air and truck, to ship small packages rapidly. They are not economical for large-volume shipments; however, they are fast and reliable, and they provide unique services that some companies must have. Package carriers have been innovative in the use of bar codes and the Internet to arrange and track shipments. The FedEx Web site attracts more than 1 million hits per day, and it receives 70% of its customer orders electronically. FedEx delivers 5 million packages daily in 210 countries.

*Water* transport over inland waterways, canals, the Great Lakes, and along coastlines is a slow but very low-cost form of shipping. It is limited to heavy, bulk items such as raw materials, minerals, ores, grains, chemicals, and petroleum products. If delivery speed is not a factor, water transport is cost competitive with railroads for shipping these kinds of bulk products. Water transport is the primary means of international shipping between countries separated by oceans for most products.

*Intermodal transportation* combines several modes of transportation to move shipments. The most common intermodal combination in the United States is truck–rail–truck, and the truck–water–rail/truck combination is the primary means of global transport. Intermodal transportation carries over 35% of all freight shipments over 500 miles in the United

*The Federal Express Superhub in Memphis, Tennessee, is the headquarters of Federal Express. Federal Express is the industry leader in overnight package delivery service.*

*One of the most popular forms of intermodal transportation uses containers that are transported via rail or truck to ports where they are loaded onto container ships for shipment overseas.*

States. Intermodal truck–rail shipping can be as much as 40% cheaper than long-haul trucking.

The key component in intermodal transportation is the *container*. Within the United States containers are hauled as trailers attached to trucks to rail terminals, where they are double- or triple-stacked on railroad flatcars or specially designed "well cars," which feature a well-like lower section in which the trailer or container rides. The containers are then transported to another rail terminal, where they are reattached to trucks for direct delivery to the customer. For overseas shipments, container ships transport containers to ports where they are off-loaded to trucks or rail for transport. Over 6 million cargo containers enter the United States from overseas each year.

*Pipelines* in the United States are used primarily for transporting oil and petroleum products. Pipelines called slurry lines carry other products such as coal and kaolin that have been pulverized and transformed into liquid form. Once the product arrives at its destination, the water is removed, leaving the solid material. Although pipelines require a high initial capital investment to construct, they are economical because they can carry materials over terrain that would be difficult for trucks or trains to travel across, for example, the Trans-Alaska pipeline. Once in place, pipelines have a long life and are low cost in terms of operation, maintenance, and labor.

## INTERNET TRANSPORTATION EXCHANGES

Internet transportation exchanges bring together shippers who post loads and carriers who post their available capacity in order to arrange shipments. In some exchanges once the parties have matched up at a Web site, all the negotiation is done offline. In others the online service manages the load matches automatically; the services match up shipments and carriers based on shipment characteristics, trailer availability, and the like. For example, shippers tender load characteristics, and the online service returns with recommendations on carrier price and service levels. Some services also provide an online international exchange structured as a reverse auction. The shippers will tender their loads, and carriers will bid on the shipment. Shipments remain up for bid until a shipper-specified auction closing time (like on e-bay). However, the lowest price, or lowest bid, is not always conducive to quality service. At some sites the low bid does not necessarily win; the service takes into account quality issues such as transit time, the carrier, and availability in addition to price.

Two of the more successful Internet exchange services are www.nte.com (National Transportation Exchange), and www.freightquote.com. At these sites (and others like it) shippers and carriers identify their available shipment or capacity needs and their business requirements. The exchanges automatically match compatible shippers with carriers based on price and service. Automated processes make the trade within a few hours with no phone calls, invoices, and so on.

## SUPPLY CHAIN MANAGEMENT (SCM) SOFTWARE

**ERP:** software that integrates the components of a company by sharing and organizing information and data.

**Enterprise resource planning (ERP)** is software that helps integrate the components of a company, including most of the supply chain processes, by sharing and organizing information and data among supply chain members. It transforms transactional data like sales into useful information that supports business decisions in other parts of the company. For example, when data such as a sale becomes available in one part of the business, it is transmitted through ERP software, which automatically determines the effects of the transaction on other areas, such as manufacturing, inventory, procurement, invoicing, distribution, and accounting, and on suppliers. Through these information flows ERP organizes and manages a company's supply chain. Most ERP vendors systems handle external, Web-based interactions, and have software specifically for supply chain management called "SCM."

SAP was the first ERP software provider and is the largest, which has made it almost synonymous with ERP applications software. mySAP.com is the umbrella brand name for the SAP software. mySAP.com is a suite of Web-enabled SAP modules that allow a company to collaborate with its customers and business partners along its supply chain. When a customer submits an order, that transaction ripples throughout the company's supply chain, adjusting inventory, part supplies, accounting entries, production schedules and shipping schedules, and balance sheets. Different nations' laws, currencies, and business practices are embedded in the software, which enables it to translate sales transactions smoothly between business partners in different countries—for example, a company in Taiwan and its customer in Brazil.

Figure 10.14 provides an example of how SCM software works. In this example a Japanese retailer of cellular phones places an order with the sales representative of a manufacturer in the United States for 1000 model A cell phones.

## MEASURING SUPPLY CHAIN PERFORMANCE

**Key performance indicators:** metrics used to measure supply chain performance.

As we indicated in previous sections, inventory is a key element in supply chain management. On one hand, it enables a company to cope with uncertainty by serving as a buffer between stages in the supply chain. Inventory allows items to flow smoothly through the system to meet customer demand when stages are not in sync. On the other hand, inventory can be very costly. As such, it is important for a company to maintain an efficient supply chain by lowering inventory levels (and costs) as much as possible. In order to accomplish this objective, several numerical measures, also called **key performance indicators (KPIs)** or metrics, are often used to measure supply chain performance. Three of the more widely used key performance indicators are *inventory turnover*, *inventory days of supply*, and *fill rate*.

### KEY PERFORMANCE INDICATORS

**Inventory turnover (or turns)** is computed by dividing the cost of goods sold (i.e., the cost of annual sales) by the average aggregate inventory value:

$$\text{Inventory turns} = \frac{\text{Cost of goods sold}}{\text{Average aggregate value of inventory}}$$

1. The customer, a Japanese cellular phone retailer, places an order with the manufacturer's rep for 1000 model A phones.
2. A sales rep for the manufacturer takes the order for 1000 model A phones and from his laptop checks the price, possible discounts, and customer credit history.
3. The stock of model A cell phones is checked and the rep sees that half can be filled from their Hong Kong warehouse and the other 500 can be delivered in 1 week from their factory in Mexico.
4. Production of 500 cell phones at the factory in Mexico is scheduled while the warehouse manager in Hong Kong is instructed to ship the other 500 phones to the customer.
5. The shipment of phones from the warehouse is arranged with the company's distributor in Hong Kong, and transport is scheduled.
6. Available labor at the factory to produce this order is checked.
7. The purchasing manager orders cell phone components from suppliers in Brazil and Taiwan.
8. The customer logs on to the manufacturer's system through the Internet, and sees that in Mexico the phones are ready to be placed in their housing. The customer also observes there are 200 red model B phones in stock and places a follow-up order on the Internet.
9. Forecasting and financial models indicate high demand and profits from their colored phone models, and they develop plans with their business partners to expand their model lines.

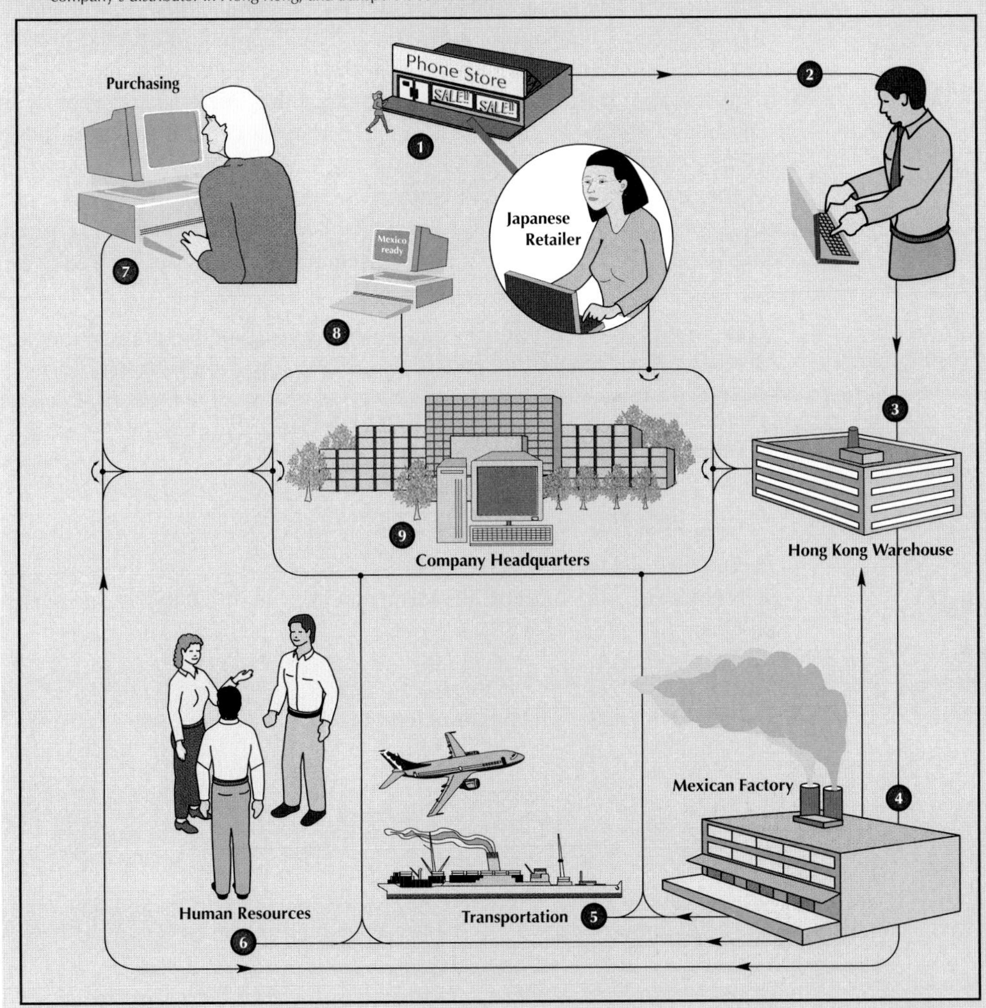


Figure 10.14
**Linking the Supply Chain with SAP**

The average aggregate value of inventory is the total value (at cost) of all items being held in inventory, including such things as raw materials, work-in-process (WIP), and finished goods. It is computed by summing for all individual inventory items, the product of the average number of units on hand in inventory at any one time multiplied by the unit value:

$$\text{Average aggregate value of Inventory} = \Sigma(\text{average inventory for item } i) \times (\text{unit value item } i)$$

The cost of goods sold is only for finished goods, valued at cost, not the final sale price (which might include discounts or markups).

A poor, or comparatively low, inventory turnover value indicates that a large amount of inventory is required to satisfy demand. In general, a good (or poor) number of inventory turns is relative to what is being achieved at various stages across a company and what the norm is for the industry. In the early 1980s, inventory turns for many manufacturing companies were less than 5; however, the advent of lean production (see Chapter 14) and the increased emphasis on quality management and supply chain management have increased inventory turns in much of the manufacturing sector.

In recent years, Ford and General Motors have experienced inventory turns in the high teens. Toyota had inventory turns in the 60s in the 1980s when its supply chain was mostly in Japan, but this has fallen to the low teens in recent years as it has expanded globally and the complexities of its supply chain have increased accordingly. High-tech companies typically have around 6 turns per year, but Dell has achieved inventory turns greater than 50, belying its success. Palm has inventory turns of around 26. In one year Palm increased its number of turns from 12 to 26, which decreased inventory from $55 million to $23 million. Alternatively, pharmaceutical giant Pfizer has had recent inventory turns as low as 1.5. However, this does not mean that Pfizer is doing poorly financially—it has been very profitable. It does mean that perhaps it could manage its supply chain more efficiently.

Another commonly used KPI is **days (or weeks) of supply**. This is a measure of how many days (or weeks) of inventory is available at any point in time. It is computed by dividing the aggregate average value of inventory by the daily (or weekly) cost of goods sold,

$$\text{Days of supply} = \frac{\text{Average aggregate value of inventory}}{\text{(Cost of goods sold)/(365 days)}}$$

Automotive companies like Ford and GM typically carry about 60 days of finished goods supply.

**Example 10.1**

**Computing Key Performance Indicators**

The Tomahawk Motorcycle Company manufactures motorcycles. Last year the cost of goods sold was $425 million. The company had the following average value of production materials and parts, work-in-process, and finished goods inventory:

| | |
|---|---|
| Production materials and parts | $ 4,629,000 |
| Work-in-process | 17,465,000 |
| Finished goods | 12,322,000 |
| Total average aggregate value of inventory | $34,416,000 |

The company wants to know the number of inventory turns and days of supply being held in inventory.

*Solution*

$$\text{Inventory turns} = \frac{\text{Cost of goods sold}}{\text{Average aggregate value of inventory}}$$

$$= \frac{\$425{,}000{,}000}{34{,}416{,}000}$$

$$\text{Inventory turns} = 12.3$$

$$\text{Days of supply} = \frac{\text{Average aggregate value of inventory}}{\text{(Cost of goods sold)/(365 days)}}$$

$$= \frac{\$34{,}416{,}000}{(425{,}000{,}000)/(365)}$$

$$\text{Days of supply} = 29.6$$

Another frequently used KPI is **fill rate**. Fill rates are the fraction of orders placed by a customer with a supplier distribution center or warehouse which are filled within a specific period of time, typically one day. High fill rates indicate that inventory is moving from the supplier to the customer at a faster rate, which thereby reduces inventory at the distribution center. For example, Nabisco's fill rate for its Planter's peanuts at Wegman's grocery store chain is 97% meaning that when the store places an order with the Nabisco distribution center 97% of the time it is filled within one day.

**Fill rate:** the fraction of orders filled by a distribution center within a specific time period.

## PROCESS CONTROL

In Chapter 3 on Quality Management, we talked about various techniques that could be employed to monitor product and service quality. One of the more powerful techniques we presented was statistical process control, the subject of Chapter 4. Although we tend to think that process control is used to monitor and control quality for manufacturing operations, it can also be used to monitor and control any of the processes in the supply chain. If products are defective, then the effects are obvious. However, other problems along the supply chain that create uncertainty and variability are most often caused by errors. If deliveries are missed or are late, if orders are lost, if errors are made in filling out forms, if items with high obsolescence rates (like PCs) or perishable items are allowed to stay too long in inventory, if demand forecast errors are made, if plant and equipment are not properly maintained, then the supply chain can be disrupted, thereby reducing supply chain performance. Thus, at any stage in the process, statistical process control charts can be used to monitor process performance.

## SCOR

The Supply Chain Operations Reference (**SCOR**) model is a supply chain diagnostic tool that provides a cross-industry standard for supply chain management. It was developed and is maintained by the Supply Chain Council, a global not-for-profit trade association organized in 1996 with membership open to companies interested in improving supply chain efficiency primarily through the use of SCOR. The Supply Chain Council (SCC) has over 750 corporate members around the world, including many *Fortune* 500 companies.

**SCOR:** a cross-industry supply chain diagnostic tool maintained by the Supply Chain Council.

The purpose of the SCOR model is to define a company's current supply chain processes, quantify the performance of similar companies to establish targets to achieve "best-in-class" performance, and identify the practices and software solutions that will yield "best in class" performance. It is organized around a set of five primary management processes—plan, source, make, deliver, and return, as shown in Figure 10.15. These

Figure 10.15 **SCOR Model Processes**

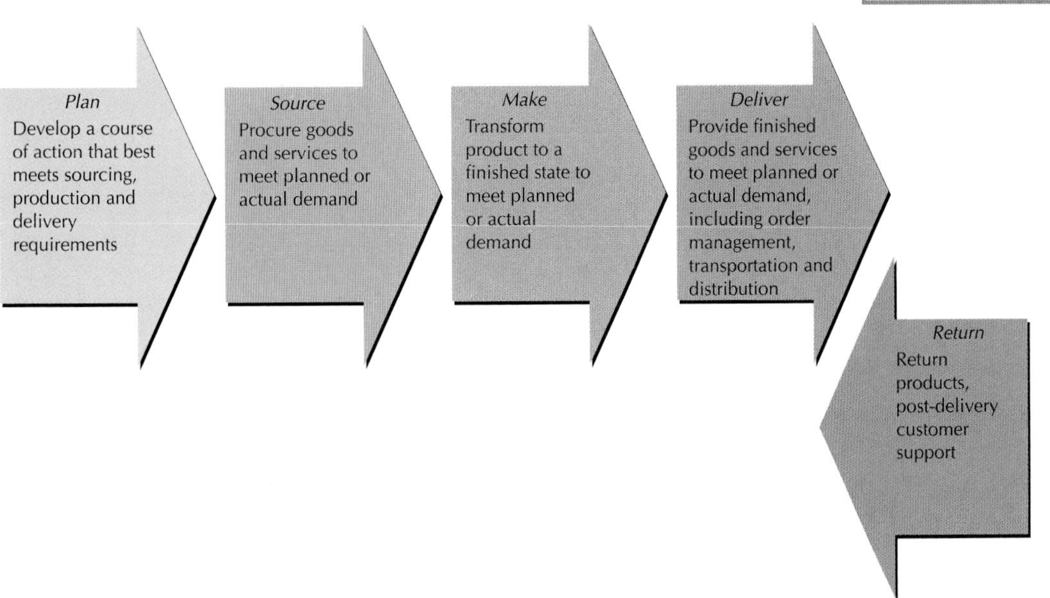

processes provide a common set of definitions, or building blocks, that SCOR uses to describe any supply chain, from simple to complex. This allows supply chains for different companies to be linked and compared.

A primary feature of the SCOR model is the use of a set of performance indicators or "metrics" to measure supply chain performance. These metrics are categorized as "customer-facing" or "internal-facing" as shown in Table 10.4. Customer-facing metrics measure supply chain delivery reliability, responsiveness, and flexibility with respect to customers and suppliers. Internal-facing metrics measure supply chain cost and asset management efficiency. The metrics may be used for multiple supply chain processes.

These metrics are used to develop a "SCORcard" that measures both a company's current supply chain performance for different processes and its competitor's metrics. The company then projects the level of metrics it needs to be on a par with its competitors, to have an advantage over its competitors, or to be superior. The value associated with these measured improvements in performance is then projected for the different performance attributes. For example, a company may know that the industry "median fill rate" is 90% and the industry best-in-class performance is 99%. The company has determined that its current fill rate is 65%, and that a fill rate of 90% will give it parity with its competitors, a 95% fill rate will give it an advantage, and a 99% fill rate will make it superior to most of

**Table 10.4**
**SCOR Performance Metrics**

| | Performance Attribute | Performance Metric | Definition |
|---|---|---|---|
| Customer Facing | Supply chain delivery reliability | Delivery performance | Percentage of orders delivered on time and in full to the customer |
| | | Fill rate | Percentage of orders shipped within 24 hours of order receipt |
| | | Perfect order fulfillment | Percentage of orders delivered on time and in full, perfectly matched with order with no errors |
| | Supply chain responsiveness | Order fulfillment lead time | Number of days from order receipt to customer delivery |
| | Supply chain flexibility | Supply chain response time | Number of days for the supply chain to respond to an unplanned significant change in demand without a cost penalty |
| | | Production flexibility | Number of days to achieve an unplanned 20% change in orders without a cost penalty |
| Internal Facing | Supply chain cost | Supply chain management cost | The direct and indirect cost to plan, source and deliver products and services |
| | | Cost of goods sold | The direct cost of material and labor to produce a product or service |
| | | Value-added productivity | Direct material cost subtracted from revenue and divided by the number of employees, similar to sales per employee |
| | | Warranty/returns processing cost | Direct and indirect costs associated with returns including defective, planned maintenance and excess inventory |
| | Supply Chain Asset Management Efficiency | Cash-to-cash cycle time | The number of days that cash is tied up as working capital |
| | | Inventory days of supply | The number of days that cash is tied up as inventory |
| | | Asset turns | Revenue divided by total assets including working capital and fixed assets |

THE COMPETITIVE EDGE

### Supply Chain Management at Kraft Foods

Kraft Foods North America had over $25 billion in revenues in 2002. At Kraft the supply chain includes all the logistics activities that go into delivering products to customers, from bringing raw materials, ingredients, and packaging into the manufacturing plants, planning capacity and scheduling production at the plants, and managing the inventory flow of products though the distribution networks. Over 5000 employees including warehouse handlers and drivers work directly in logistics activities. Kraft believes that an efficient integrated supply chain encompassing all company activities can reduce internal costs while enhancing customer value.

Kraft knows that its customers will pick the manufacturer that offers the best product availability, delivers orders on time and damage free, invoices accurately, and is generally easier to do business with. These performance characteristics are known in the supply chain world as the "perfect order." As such, Kraft constantly measures its performance in on-time delivery, order fulfillment, invoice accuracy, and damage-free shipments. By achieving high levels of performance in these areas, its customers can reduce their inventory stock, for example, from three to two weeks. This is real *value* for the customer because it frees up cash for other purposes such as store remodeling and expansion. Kraft also works with its customers to offer intelligent discounts, such as shipping directly from plant to store for high-volume customers. Such relationships require trust and confidence between Kraft and its customers and within Kraft among its supply chain areas.

*Source:* David Drickhamer, "Looking for Value," *Industrial Week's* The Value Chain, Industryweek.com, December 1, 2002.

its competitors. The company may then project that the improvement in its fill rate plus improvements in the other supply chain reliability attributes (i.e., delivery performance and perfect order fulfillment) will increase supply chain value by $10 million in revenue. This process wherein a company measures its current supply chain performance, compares it to its competition, and then projects the performance levels it needs to compete is referred to as "gap analysis." SCOR then provides a framework not only for measuring performance but for diagnosing problems and identifying practices and solutions that will enable a company to achieve its competitive performance objectives.

## THE GLOBAL SUPPLY CHAIN

A number of factors have combined to create a global marketplace. International trade barriers have fallen, and new trade agreements between countries and nations have been established. The dissolution of communism opened up new markets in Russia and Middle and Eastern Europe, and the creation of the European Community resulted in the world's largest economic market—400 million people. Europe, with a total population of 850 million is the largest, best-educated economic group in the world. Emerging markets in China, growing Asian export-driven economies, burgeoning global trading centers in Hong Kong and Singapore, and a newly robust economy in India have linked with the rest of the world to form a vigorous global economic community. Global trade now exceeds $25 trillion per year.

Globalization is no longer restricted to giant companies. Technology advances have made it possible for middle-tier companies to establish a global presence. Companies previously regional in scope are using the Internet to become global overnight. Information technology is the "enabler" that lets companies gain global visibility and link disparate locations, suppliers, and customers. However, many companies are learning that it takes more than a glitzy Web site to be a global player. As with the domestic U.S. market, it takes a well-planned and coordinated supply chain to be competitive and successful.

**To compete globally requires an effective supply chain.**

## OBSTACLES TO GLOBAL SUPPLY CHAIN MANAGEMENT

Moving products across international borders is like negotiating an intricate maze, riddled with potential pitfalls. For U.S. companies eager to enter new and growing markets, trading in foreign countries is not "business as usual." Global supply chain management, though global in nature, must still take into account national and regional differences. Customs, business practices, and regulations can vary widely from country to country and even within a country. Foreign markets are not homogeneous and often require customized service in terms of packaging and labeling. Quality can be a major challenge when dealing with Third World markets in countries with different languages and customers.

Some of the other major differences between domestic and global supply chain transactions include:

- Increased documentation for invoices, cargo insurance, letters of credit, ocean bills of lading or air waybills, and inspections
- Ever changing regulations that vary from country to country that govern the import and export of goods
- Trade groups, tariffs, duties, and landing costs
- Limited shipping modes
- Differences in communication technology and availability
- Different business practices as well as language barriers
- Government codes and reporting requirements that vary from country to country
- Numerous players, including forwarding agents, custom house brokers, financial institutions, insurance providers, multiple transportation carriers, and government agencies
- Since 9/11, numerous security regulations and requirements

**Nation groups:** nations joined together into trading groups.

**Tariffs (duties):** taxes on imported goods.

## DUTIES, TARIFFS, AND GLOBAL TRADING GROUPS

The proliferation of trade agreements has changed global markets and has accelerated global trade activity. Nations have joined together to form trading groups, also called **nation groups**, and customs unions, and within these groups products move freely with no import tax, called **tariffs** or **duties**, charged on member products. The members of a group charge uniform import duties to nations outside their group, thus removing tariff trade barriers within the group and raising barriers for outsiders. The group adopts rules and regulations for freely transporting goods across borders that, combined with reduced tariffs, give member nations a competitive advantage over nonmembers. These trade advantages among member nations lower supply chain costs and reduce cycle time—that is, the time required for products to move through the supply chain.

Figure 10.16 shows the international trade groups, or customs unions, that trade with the United States. NAFTA is the North American Free Trade Agreement, and EU is the European Community trade group, which includes many of the countries of Western Europe.

Figure 10.16 **Global Trading Groups (customs unions)**

(See footnote on page 20 for an explanation of these trade group abbreviations.)

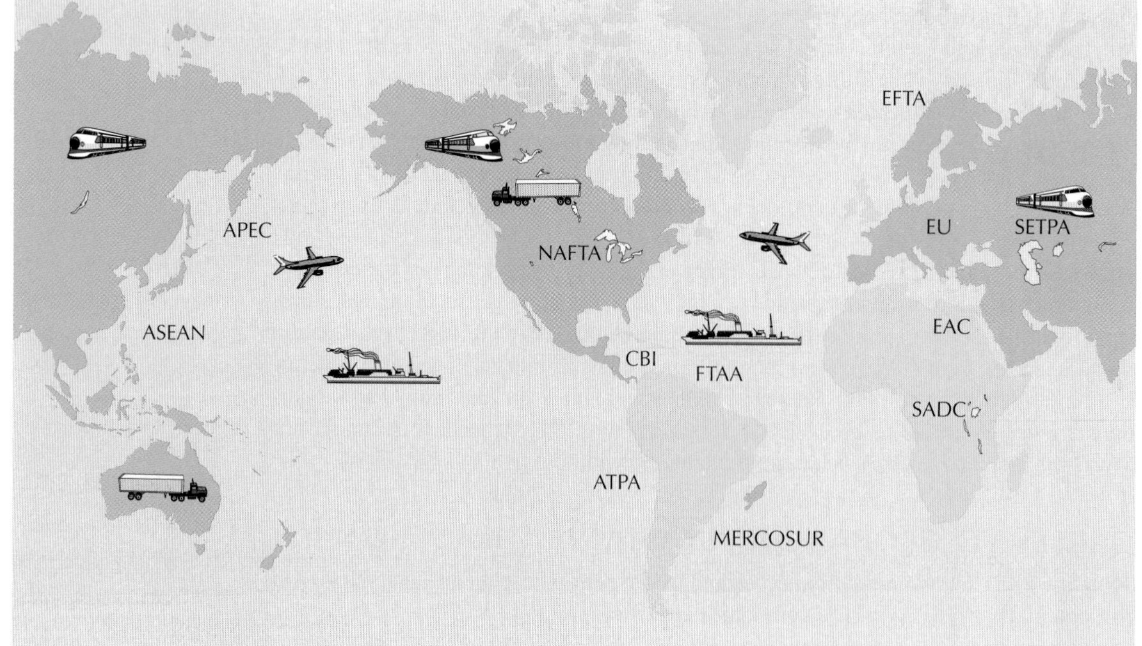

## THE COMPETITIVE EDGE

### Hong Kong–Based Global Supply Chain Management at Li & Fung

Li & Fung is Hong Kong's largest export trading company, with 35 offices in 20 countries. Originally, a broker putting buyers and sellers together when it was founded in Canton in 1906, the company became a manager, manufacturer, and deliverer of production programs. For example, the clothing store chain, The Limited, might tell Li & Fung that for the coming season they are thinking about a type of look in certain colors and in certain quantities and ask them to develop a complete production program. Using the designers' sketches, Li & Fung would search the market for the right yarn and dye swatches to match the colors, develop prototypes for the buyers to look at, and then based on the buyers' preferences they would create an entire program for the season with a product mix and schedule. They would contract for all the resources and work with factories in Hong Kong to plan and monitor production to ensure quality and on-time delivery. Li & Fung does not own any factories itself. However, as competition increased from Korea and Taiwan and other Asian countries, Hong Kong became an increasingly expensive and uncompetitive place for manufacturing.

In response, Li & Fung developed the concept of "dispersed manufacturing." As China became more open, Li & Fung began moving the labor-intensive portion of production into southern China. They packaged the necessary components for production and shipped them to southern China; then the finished goods would be shipped back to Hong Kong for final inspection and testing. This concept spread to other industries in Hong Kong. As a result, between 1979 and 1997 Hong Kong's position as a trading center rose from 21st to 8th in the world. Hong Kong was transformed into a service economy, with 84% of its gross domestic product coming from services.

Li & Fung next developed a model of borderless manufacturing with networks of hubs that do the sophisticated planning for regional manufacturing, moving raw materials and semifinished parts around Asia to produce products to meet customer demand in North America and Western Europe. Overall, Li & Fung works with approximately 7500 suppliers in more than 26 countries, with over a million factory workers engaged on behalf of its customers. For example, if a European retailer orders 10,000 garments, Li & Fung might buy yarn from a Korean producer and ship it to Taiwan to have it woven and dyed. The Japanese have the best zippers and buttons, which they manufacture in China, so Li & Fung would order zippers from the Chinese plants. Then because of quotas and labor conditions, they might decide the best place to make the garments is Thailand. So everything would be shipped there, and if the customer needs quick delivery, production may be divided across five Thai factories. Five weeks after Li & Fung receives the order, the 10,000 garments are on the shelves in Europe, all with a label saying "Made in Thailand" and looking like they came from the same factory. However, they truly are a global product.

This model of dispersed manufacturing makes managing the global supply chain a complex challenge for Li & Fung. They must manage suppliers and the flow of materials and parts around the world. Consumer-driven, fast-moving markets, in which customers' tastes change rapidly, has shortened product life cycles and increased the problem of obsolete inventories. A Li & Fung retail-clothing customer like The Limited now has six or seven fashion seasons each year instead of two or three. Supply chain management means buying the right things and shortening delivery cycles, which requires Li & Fung to "reach into their suppliers" to make sure things are done at the right quality level and on time.

*Source:* J. Magtetta, "Fast, Global, and Entrepreneurial: Supply Chain Management, Hong Kong Style, An Interview with Victor Fung," *Harvard Business Review* 76(5; September–October 1998), pp. 102–114.

The World Trade Organization (WTO) is an international organization dealing with the global rules of trade. It ensures that trade flows as smoothly and freely as possible among its 146 members. The trade agreements and rules are negotiated and signed by governments, and their purpose is to help exporters and importers conduct business. Most-favored-nation trade status (MFN) is an arrangement in which WTO member countries must extend to other members the most favorable treatment given to any trading partner. For example, MFN status for China translates into lower duties on goods entering the United States.

To overcome the obstacles and problems of global supply chain management, many companies hire one or more **international trade specialists**. Figure 10.17 summarizes the activities of the different types of trade specialists.

**Trade specialists:** include freight forwarders, customs house brokers, export packers, and export management and trading companies.

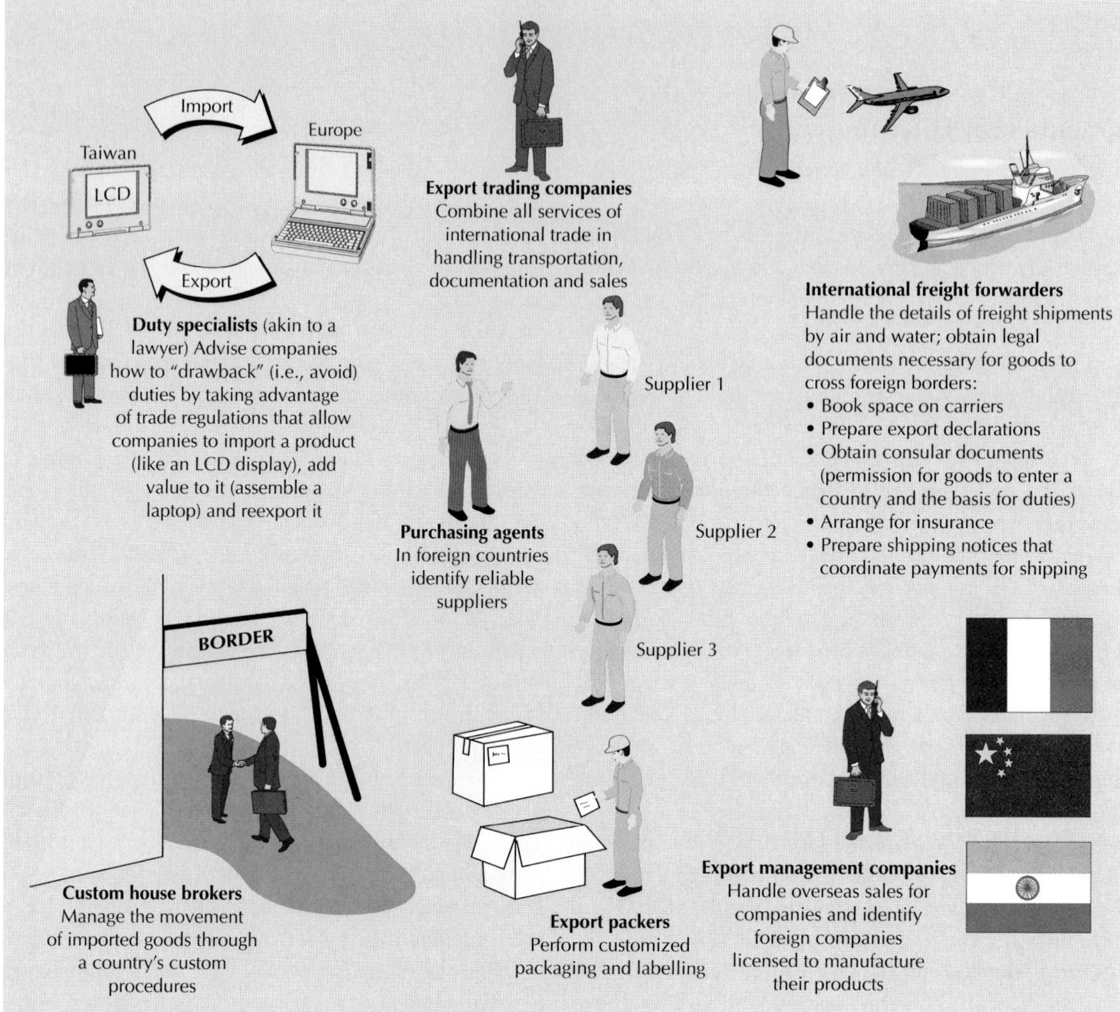


**Figure 10.17**
**International Trade Specialists**

■ **Landed cost:** the total cost of producing, storing, and transporting a product to its destination or port.

■ **Value-added tax (VAT):** an indirect tax assessed on the increase in value of a good at any stage of the production process from raw material to final product.

## LANDED COST

In global trade **landed cost** is the total cost of producing, storing, and transporting a product to the site of consumption or another port. As many as 80 components can be included in landed cost; however, 85% of these components fall into two broad categories: (1) transportation cost and duty, and (2) governmental charges such as **value added tax (VAT)** and excise tax. Landed costs are important because the duty assessed by different governments incorporates varying portions of landed costs. For example, for U.S. imports, duty is charged FOB (e.g., free on board) the factory. This means that transportation costs from the point of entry into the United States to the factory destination are not calculated as part of the import duty charge. However, in other countries the duty assessed can include the cost of transportation from beginning to end.

By knowing the landed cost of a product before it is purchased, a company can make more informed decisions, while poorly projected landed costs can balloon the price of a product move. Accurately estimating true landed costs helps avoid "clicker shock." Clicker shock occurs when an overseas customer places an order with a company that does not have the capability of calculating landed cost. Then the order gets shipped, and along the way tariffs get added on top—in some cases it can double the original purchase price.

## WEB-BASED INTERNATIONAL TRADE LOGISTICS SYSTEMS

As we have indicated global supply chain management involves a stunningly complex matrix of language barriers, currency conversions, international trade agreements, taxes, tariffs, embargoes, duties, quotas, document requirements, local rules, and new trading

*The Port of Singapore handles over 10 million TEUs (20-foot container equivalent units) annually at three container terminals. The Brani terminal shown here has 9 berths, 31 Quay cranes, and a capacity of 5.5 million TEUs. The Port of Singapore has been the world's busiest port in terms of shipping tonnage since 1986.*

## THE COMPETITIVE EDGE

### Global Supply Chains in France

Two foreign-based companies, Toyota and Columbia Sportswear, recently started initiatives in France that have expanded their global supply chains.

Columbia Sportswear Company, based in Portland, Oregon, one of the world's largest outerwear brands and the leading seller of ski clothing in the United States, sells products in over 30 countries to over 10,000 retailers. In 2002 it opened a new high-tech, 269,000 sq. ft. distribution center (DC) in Cambrai, France, about 90 miles north of Paris. The DC includes the latest material-handling equipment plus a state-of-the-art warehouse management system (WMS). This new DC reflects the growth in Columbia's European market that saw sales revenue go from 1% of annual revenues to 10% in the last decade. The company had previously been using a third-party logistics (3PL) company in Holland to manage its European distribution, but it decided to build its own DC in order to provide the level of customer service it wanted. It selected the Cambrai location because France is Columbia's largest European customer, labor was readily available, and work rules were flexible, which accommodates Columbia's seasonal business. Also, in Holland Columbia could use only trucks for shipping, whereas in France barge, rail, and truck transport were all available at reasonable costs. According to CEO Tim Boyle, the new DC was designed to deliver superior quality products, superior execution, and superior service.

In 1999 Toyota, the third largest automaker in the world, introduced the Yaris, an economy car for Japanese and European markets. However, exporting the Yaris to Europe from Japan was not viable, so the company constructed a new 1.4 million sq. ft. assembly plant in Onnaing, France, near the Belgian border. The plant originally produced 184,000 cars per year, with demand expected to grow to 800,000 by 2005. Although the plant's manufacturing process is state of the art with high-tech assembly lines, robots, and a gigantic stamping machine, it is its supply chain management, particularly of the inflow of parts and material, which is the key to the plant's success. Parts arrive from Japan twice per week in either Rotterdam or Antwerp, and six containers per day of parts are transported from these ports to the plant by barge and then truck, while 60 trucks per day arrive from 177 suppliers in Europe, including France, UK, Italy, Germany, Spain, and Portugal. Toyota also uses five 3PL regional cross-docking distribution centers throughout Europe where they pick up small-lot containers as often as eight times a day. There is no actual inventory management at the plant; it is all handled by the suppliers. Toyota has just two hours of inventory on hand at the plant. Parts and material flow into the plant as ordered, trucks are unloaded at the exact times, and special tote trains refill and deliver parts to the production line at strict 30-minute intervals in order to maintain a constant level of inventory.

*Sources:* L. H. Harrington, "Columbia Goes Its Own Way," *Transportation and Distribution* 44(2; February 2003), pp. 43–44; and "Toyota's Supply Chain Delivers the Yaris," *Transportation and Distribution* 44(2; February 2003), pp. 45–48.

International trade logistics software systems reduce obstacles to global trade.

partners. These factors require an automated, information technology solution for any company with any real volume of international shipments. International trade logistics (ITL) companies use Web-based software products that link directly to customers' Web sites to eliminate or reduce the obstacles to global trade. They convert language and currency from the U.S. system into those used by many of the United States' trading partners, giving potential buyers in other nations easy access to product and price information. ITL systems also provide information on tariffs, duties, and customs processes and some link with financial institutions to facilitate letters of credit and payment. Through the use of extensive databases these systems can attach the appropriate weights, measurements, and unit prices to individual products ordered over the Web. These systems can also incorporate transportation costs and conversion rates so that purchasers can electronically see the landed cost of ordering a product and having it delivered. Some ITL systems use a landed cost search engine that calculates shipping costs online while a company enters an order so it will know exactly what the costs will be in U.S. funds. They also track global shipments.

Through their Web sites and software products, ITL companies do many of the things international trade specialists do (Figure 10.17). They let their customers know which international companies they can do business with and which companies can do business with them. They identify export and import restrictions between buyers and vendors. They provide the documents required to export and import products, and they determine the duties, taxes, and landed costs and other government charges associated with importing a product.

Vastera, a Dulles, Virginia, global trade management company, enables customers through its web-based software products to calculate landed costs, screen for restricted parties, generate shipment documentation, and manage duties, and it also handles repairs and returns. It has an online library of trade regulations for different countries, and it has over 200 customers including Ford, Gateway, Motorola, and Nortel.

## THE COMPETITIVE EDGE

### Global Supply Chain Management at Hyundai Motor Company

Hyundai Motor Company of Korea began its passenger car production in 1968 by assembling imported parts and subassemblies from Ford Motor Company. By 1975 Hyundai was the first Korean auto company with integrated manufacturing facilities. By 2000 it had production facilities in 13 countries in addition to Korea, with a total annual production capacity of 1.8 million cars, making it one of the top 10 automobile companies in the world in volume. As is typical of the auto industry, Hyundai's supply chain is very complex, with thousands of (mostly) domestic and foreign suppliers. Hyundai's distribution within Korea is handled by 700 of its own sales offices and 200 independent dealers. These sales offices and dealers have demonstration models but do not hold any inventory. Customer orders are filled by delivery from inventory at plants or distribution centers or directly from production, which enables Hyundai to respond quickly to specific customer demands with low overall costs. Hyundai's goal for domestic customer delivery is 7 days or less if the ordered model has popular colors and option packages and 15 days otherwise. The company exports its autos to over 80 countries, which accounts for approximately 45% of total sales. Export autos are shipped through regularly scheduled shipping lines, with a delivery lead time of 45 days. A goal of Hyundai's sales and distribution system is to minimize inventory of finished autos while having competitive delivery times. It tries to keep no more than 7 days' worth of inventory on hand, which is a very aggressive goal even when compared with Japanese companies. This requires very careful coordination and synchronization of its delivery commitments to customers, production schedules, and supplier deliveries.

In order to manage the conflicting supply chain goals of increasing product variety, reducing delivery lead times, and reducing costs, Hyundai developed a centralized production-and-sales-control (P/SC) department to create an interface between purchasing, production, and sales and to mediate conflicts between manufacturing, the domestic and export sales departments, and the domestic and foreign purchasing department. The P/SC department synchronizes production planning across facilities and functional areas. It has final responsibility for master (six-month), weekly, and daily production schedules for all of Hyundai's domestic manufacturing facilities. Implementation of this centralized approach to supply chain management improved communication between supply chain members and promoted mutual understanding and coordination among functional areas.

*Source:* C. Hahn, E. Duplaga, and J. Hartley, "Supply-Chain Synchronization: Lessons from Hyundai Motor Company," *Interfaces 30* (4; July–August 2000), pp. 32–45.

Another ITL firm, TradeBeam, located in San Mateo, California, solves global supply chain problems through its Web-based software, which includes three business process modules called "order," "ship," and "settle." The "order" module creates purchase and sales orders and then performs a compliance check to make sure the transaction is within the bounds of customs rules and regulations. It then secures cargo insurance coverage and also settles trade-related claims. The "ship" module books carriers and coordinates carriers with ports. It processes all the information required for a shipment to clear customs, and it prepares all shipping documentation, including the bill of lading and customs invoice. It tracks the shipment and provides proof of delivery when the goods reach the final destination. The "settle" module completes the global trade process through the final payment. It manages letters of credit electronically, it handles disputes and reconciliations, and it manages actual payments from banks or buyers. TradeBeam customers include Mitsubishi Chemical, Horizon Scientific, and Parker Hannifin.

Nistevo, an Eden Prairie, Minnesota, ITL company, operates a collaborative Web-based logistics network and transportation exchange for shippers and customers, including General Mills/Pillsbury, Georgia-Pacific, International paper, Kellogg's, and Land O'Lakes. The company helps its customers plan and execute over 4000 shipments per day with more then 300 carriers.

## RECENT TRENDS IN GLOBALIZATION FOR U.S. COMPANIES: MEXICO AND CHINA

Two significant changes that prompted many U.S. companies to expand globally were the passage of NAFTA almost a decade ago and the admission of China into the World Trade Organization in 2001. NAFTA opened up business opportunities with Mexico, which in 2002 replaced Japan as the United States' second leading trading partner, with cross-border trade exceeding $240 billion. Approximately 700 of the *Fortune* 1000 companies have a portion of their operations, production components, or affiliates in Mexico. Besides cheap labor, Mexico is also close to the United States, and thus Mexican companies can meet the just-in time requirements of many U.S. companies. However, Mexico's economic gains also lead to more jobs and increased worker skills, and as a result, higher wages, which in turn has led U.S. and foreign companies away from Mexico to China with its even lower wage rates. The wage rate for unskilled labor in China was around $0.60 per hour in 2002 compared to approximately $2.50 per hour in Mexico, $5 per hour in Singapore, and $25 per hour in Japan. As companies have moved their manufacturing into China because of lower labor costs, new Chinese suppliers have also emerged, and U.S., Japanese, Taiwanese, and Korean suppliers have set up operations in China as well. This is basically the same pattern followed previously in Japan in the 1960s and 1970s and later in Korea, Taiwan, and Singapore before Mexico became a global hot spot. In 2003 China replaced Mexico as the number two exporter of goods to the United States.

An example of how globalization has evolved in this type of environment is the electronics industry. Electronics firms have been leaders in global sourcing and manufacturing for many years because about 70% of the cost of electronics equipment is in components and manufacturing services. This has been especially prevalent in the last three decades since the development of personal computers and microelectronics. Major electronics and computer manufacturers have moved their supply chains into China, not solely because it is a potentially good market (which it is), but because China has low-cost labor, as well as hard-working and reliable employees, who are improving their skill levels. The Microsoft X-Box game system was first built in Mexico and Hungary, but production has been shifted to China. Palm Pilots used to be built in the United States and Europe but are now mostly manufactured in China. Laptop computer manufacturing in Taiwan is moving to China.

Both Mexico and China have positive and negative aspects in terms of supply chain development for U.S. companies. You can ship from Mexico to the United States in about eight hours; however, it takes 21 to 23 days to ship from China. Many people speak English in Mexico, and many Americans speak Spanish; the same situation does not exist in China. Government regulations, especially in terms of business ownership, are sometimes restrictive in China, but in China a company can work 24 hours a day, 7 days a week compared to an average workweek in Mexico of approximately 44 hours. Trade regulations and tariffs are increasingly being lowered in Mexico. China has a good physical infrastructure in manufacturing areas and a good water supply, whereas water availability is a problem in Mexico. Alternatively, China has a weak information technology infrastructure, and companies lack the capability to keep track of orders and to make sure items are shipped on time. EDI is not common in China, and most orders are faxed or e-mailed. Chinese companies rarely use ERP software; more likely their e-commerce capability is limited to a few shared personal computers. Quality is a problem in both Mexico and China where it can vary dramatically between companies. Chinese and Mexican suppliers generally lack quality-management systems and do not often use statistical process control or have ISO certification.

Another critical problem somewhat unique to China is the proliferation of counterfeit parts. Individuals and companies in China steal intellectual properties from a U.S. or Japanese-based company, set up their company and sell an identical, generic product, often with the brand labels of legitimate companies. Sometimes parts will be stolen from legitimate companies for use in counterfeit products. These bogus products may be functional, but the quality will generally be poor. In other cases, the products may not be functional at all. When China joined the World Trade Organization, it pledged to crack down on counterfeiting.

## EFFECTS OF 9/11 ON GLOBAL SUPPLY CHAINS

The events of 9/11 have affected global supply chains as they have much of everything else in our lives. The two primary modes of transport in global supply chains are airfreight and ocean carriers, both of which enter the United States through portals from the outside world and thus are obvious security risks. Since 9/11, the U.S. government in concert with countries around the world has adopted security measures, which besides increasing security, has added time to supply chain schedules and increased supply chain costs. Air and ocean carriers must file an advance manifest with the U.S. government 24 hours before loading the containers on a U.S.-bound ship or airplane so the government can conduct "risk screening." This 24-hour rule requires extensive documentation at the airport or seaport of origin, which can extend supply chain time by three to four days. Even if shipments reach the U.S. port on time, stricter customs inspections can leave the shipment tied up for hours or days. For example, food imports can be diverted for inspections for possible bioterrorism alterations. For airfreight, a delay of three or four days would negate the benefit of shipping by air at all. As a result of new security measures since 9/11, inventory levels have increased almost 5% requiring more than $75 billion in extra working capital, as companies coped with delays with buffer inventory. The cost of insuring U.S. imports increased from $36 billion to over $40 billion in 2001 to 2002. The Brookings Institute has estimated that the cost of slowing the delivery of imported goods by one day because of additional security checks is approximately $7 billion per year. These costs do not even include the costs of new people, technologies, equipment, surveillance, communication, and security systems, and training necessary for screening at airports and seaports around the world.

## SUMMARY

Supply chain management is one of the most important, strategic aspects of operations management because it encompasses so many related functions. Whom to buy materials from, how to transport goods and services, and how to distribute them in the most cost-effective, timely manner constitutes much of an organization's strategic planning. Contracting with the wrong supplier can result in poor-quality materials and late deliveries. Selecting the wrong mode of transportation or carrier can mean late deliveries to customers that will require high, costly inventories to offset. All of these critical functional supply chain decisions are complicated by the fact that they often occur in a global environment within cultures and markets at a distance and much different from those in the United States.

## SUMMARY OF KEY TERMS

**bullwhip effect** occurs when demand variability is magnified at various upstream points in the supply chain.

**collaborative planning, forecasting, and replenishment (CPFR)** a process for two or more companies in a supply chain to synchronize their demand forecasts into a single plan to meet customer demand.

**continuous replenishment** supplying orders in a short period of time according to a predetermined schedule.

**core competencies** the activities that a company does best.

**cross-docking** crossing of goods from one loading dock to another without being placed in storage.

**e-business** the replacement of physical business processes with electronic ones.

**e-marketplaces** Web sites where companies and suppliers conduct business-to-business activities.

**e-procurement** business-to-business commerce in which purchases are made directly through a supplier's Web site.

**electronic data interchange (EDI)** a computer-to-computer exchange of business documents.

**enterprise resource planning (ERP)** software that connects the components of a company by sharing and organizing information and data.

**fill rate** the fraction of orders placed by a customer with a supplier distribution center or warehouse which are filled within 24 hours.

**intermodal transportation** combines several modes of transportation.

**inventory** insurance against supply chain uncertainty held between supply chain stages.

**inventory turns** a supply chain performance metric computed by dividing the cost of goods sold by the average aggregate value of inventory.

**key performance indicator (KPI)** a metric used to measure supply chain performance.

**landed cost** total cost of producing, storing, and transporting a product to the site of consumption.

**logistics** the transportation and distribution of goods and services.

**nation groups** nations joined together to form trading groups or partners.

**order fulfillment** the process of ensuring on-time delivery of a customer's order.

**on-demand (direct-response) delivery** requires the supplier to deliver goods when demanded by the customer.

**outsourcing** purchasing goods and services that were originally produced in-house from an outside supplier.

**point-of-sale data** computer records of sales at retail sites.

**postponement** moving some final manufacturing steps like final assembly or product customization into the warehouse or distribution center.

**procurement** purchasing goods and services from suppliers.

**radio frequency identification (RFID)** radio waves used to transfer data, like an electronic product code, between an item with an embedded microchip and a reader.

**reverse auction** a company posts items it wants to purchase on an Internet e-marketplace for suppliers to bid on.

**SCOR** the supply chain operations reference model; a diagnostic tool that provides a cross-industry standard for supply chain management.

**single-sourcing** limiting suppliers or transportation carriers for a company to a relative few.

**sourcing** the selection of suppliers.

**supply chain** the facilities, functions, and activities involved in producing and delivering a product or service from suppliers (and their suppliers) to customers (and their customers).

**supply chain management (SCM)** managing the flow of information through the supply chain in order to attain the level of synchronization that will make it more responsive to customer needs while lowering costs.

**tariffs (duties)** taxes on imported goods.

**trade specialists** specialists who help manage transportation and distribution operations in foreign countries.

**value added tax (VAT)** an indirect tax on the increase in value of a good at any stage in the supply chain from raw material to final product.

**vendor-managed inventory (VMI)** a system in which manufacturers instead of distributors generate orders.

**warehouse management system (WMS)** an automated system that runs the day-to-day operations of a warehouse or distribution center and keeps track of inventory.

## SUMMARY OF KEY FORMULAS

$$\text{Inventory turns} = \frac{\text{Cost of goods sold}}{\text{Average aggregate value of inventory}}$$

$$\text{Days of supply} = \frac{\text{Average aggregate value of inventory}}{(\text{Cost of goods sold})/(365 \text{ days})}$$

## SOLVED PROBLEM

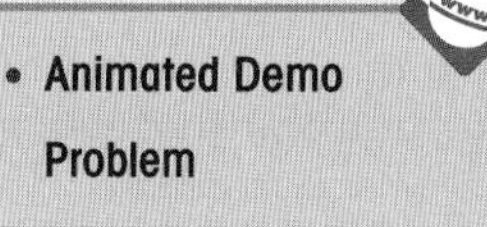


### INVENTORY TURNS AND DAYS OF SUPPLY

A manufacturing company had the following average raw materials, work-in-process, and finished goods inventory on hand at any one time during the past year.

| RAW MATERIALS | AVERAGE INVENTORY | UNIT COST |
|---|---|---|
| 1 | 135 | $26.50 |
| 2 | 67 | 18.20 |
| 3 | 210 | 9.75 |
| 4 | 97 | 31.25 |

| | | |
|---|---|---|
| WORK-IN-PROCESS | | |
| 5 | 40 | $165.00 |
| 6 | 65 | 230.00 |
| FINISHED GOODS | | |
| 7 | 25 | $ 670.00 |
| 8 | 18 | 1050.00 |
| 9 | 35 | 520.00 |

The company's cost of goods sold last year was $2.73 million, and it operates 365 days per year.

Determine the company's inventory turns and days of supply.

**SOLUTION**

*Step 1.* Compute the average aggregate value of inventory.

Raw materials: (135)($26.50) = $3,577.50
(67)(18.20) = 1,219.40
(210)(9.75) = 2,047.50
(97)(31.25) = 3,031.25
Work-in-process: (40)(165) = 6,600.00
(65)(230) = 14,950.00
Finished goods: (25)(670) = 16,750.00
(18)(1050) = 18,900.00
(35)(520) = 18,200.00
Total $85,275.65

*Step 2.* Compute inventory turns.

$$\text{Inventory turns} = \frac{\text{Cost of goods sold}}{\text{Average aggregate value of inventory}} = \frac{2{,}730{,}000}{85{,}275.65} = 32$$

*Step 3.* Compute days of supply.

$$\text{Days of supply} = \frac{\text{Average aggregate value of inventory}}{(\text{cost of goods sold})/(365)} = \frac{85{,}275.65}{(2{,}730{,}000)/(365)} = 11.4 \text{ days}$$

## QUESTIONS

**10-1.** Describe the supply chain, in general terms, for McDonald's and for Ford.

**10-2.** Discuss why single-sourcing has become attractive to companies.

**10-3.** Define the strategic goals of supply chain management, and indicate how each element of a supply chain (purchasing, production, inventory, and transportation and distribution) has an impact on these goals.

**10-4.** Identify five businesses in your community and determine what mode of transportation is used to supply them.

**10-5.** Describe an example of a business you are familiar with and describe its primary transportation model and determine transport routes.

**10-6.** Select a company and determine the type of suppliers it has, then indicate the criteria that you think the company might use to evaluate and select suppliers.

**10-7.** Select a company that has a global supply chain and describe it, including purchasing, production, distribution, and transportation.

**10-8.** Locate an e-marketplace site on the Internet and describe it and the type of producers and suppliers it connects.

**10-9.** Locate a transportation exchange on the Internet, describe the services it provides to its users, and indicate some of the customers that use it.

**10-10.** Explore the Web site of an ERP provider and describe the services it indicates it provides.

**10-11.** Locate an international logistics provider on the Internet; describe the services it provides and identify some of its customers.

**10-12.** *Purchasing* is a trade magazine with the subtitle, "The Magazine of Total Supply Chain Management and e-Procurement." Its articles include many examples of supply chain management at various companies. Research an article from *Purchasing* and write a brief paper on a company reporting on its supply chain activities similar to "The Competitive Edge" boxes in this chapter.

**10-13.** *Transportation & Distribution* is a trade magazine that focuses on supply chain management, especially logistics. In fact, its Web site is www.totalsupplychain.com. The magazine includes numerous articles reporting on companies' experiences with supply chain management. Select an article from *Transportation & Distribution* and write a brief paper similar to "The Competitive Edge" boxes in this chapter about a specific company's distribution or logistics activities.

**10-14.** Several automobile manufacturers are beginning to implement programs for "build-to-order" cars. Identify an auto company that has initiated a BTO program and describe what it entails. Contrast the BTO program of this auto manufacturer with a company experienced in BTO production like Dell Computers. Discuss the differences in the supply chains between these companies that makes BTO production more difficult for an auto manufacturer.

**10-15.** As Amazon.com grew rapidly after it first went "online" with Internet sales in 1995, it experienced several supply chain problems that other retail companies like LL. Bean, Sears, and J.C. Penney were able to avoid. What are some of these problems, and why did Amazon and other new dot.com companies experience them?

**10-16.** Explain why radio frequency identification (RFID) offers enhanced opportunities for security in global transportation and distribution, and how this in turn could improve supply chain efficiency.

**10-17.** Wal-Mart is one of the leaders in promoting the development and use of RFID and electronic product codes. Explain how Wal-Mart plans to use RFID, why Wal-Mart wants its suppliers to adopt RFID, and what obstacles you think may exist for this new technology.

**10-18.** It has been suggested that SCOR might serve as an international supply chain certification tool much like ISO certification for quality. Explain how you think SCOR might be used as a certification tool.

**10-19.** Describe the differences and/or similarities between VMI and postponement, and explain how the two might complement each other.

**10-20.** Explain how Wal-Mart uses cross-docking to improve its supply chain efficiency.

**10-21.** Describe the supply chain for your university or college. Who are the suppliers, producers, and distributors in this supply chain? Are there different supplier tiers? How would you evaluate this supply chain? Does inventory even exist, and if it does, what form does it take?

**10-22.** One of the key elements in supply chain management is forecasted demand. Customer demand is obviously an important, if not the most important, factor in determining production and distribution plans and inventory levels all along the supply chain. If more product is produced than demanded, the company and its suppliers are left with crippling inventories; if less product is produced than demanded, current and future lost sales can be devastating. Thus, it is critical that companies know what customer demand will be as closely as possible.

It is also generally assumed that a company cannot control demand; customers determine demand, and customers don't control their customers. As such, demand is often perceived to be strictly an input to supply chain management. This is not always the case, however, as is demonstrated by the unfortunate experiences of many companies. Following are a few examples of companies that treated demand as an independent factor in their supply chain management decision, to their chagrin.[2]

1. At midyear Volvo found itself with a surplus of green cars in inventory. In order to get rid of this inventory, the sales and marketing group offered discounts and rebates to distributors on green cars. The marketing plan was successful, and the demand for green cars increased. However, supply chain planners, unaware of the marketing plan, perceived that a new customer demand pattern had developed for green cars so they produced more green cars. As a result, Volvo had a huge inventory of green cars at the end of the year.
2. When Hewlett-Packard introduced a new PC, demand faltered when Compaq and Packard Bell cut prices. In reaction, supply chain planners at HP cut production back without realizing sales and marketing had decided to match their competitors' price cuts. The resulting stockouts HP experienced resulted in a less than merry Christmas season.
3. Campbell Soup heavily promoted its chicken noodle soup during the winter when demand peaked, which resulted in even greater than normal demand. In order to meet this spike in demand, it had to prepare large amounts of ingredients like chicken in advance and store it. Also, in order to meet the demand, production facilities had to operate in overtime during the winter, which in turn required them to prepare other products in advance and to store them too. The huge inventories and production costs exceeded the revenues from the increased customer demand of chicken noodle soup.
4. Italian pasta maker, Barilla, offered discounts to customers who ordered full truckloads. This created such erratic demand patterns, however, that supply costs overwhelmed the revenue benefits.

In each of these brief examples, the company was successfully able to influence customer demand with price discounts and effective marketing, demonstrating that demand is not a completely independent factor. In addition, in each case an increase in sales did not result in increased revenues because they were overwhelmed by increased supply chain costs. This presents a complex problem in supply chain management. Effective marketing is generally a good thing because it does increase sales; however, it also makes forecasting demand more difficult because it creates erratic demand patterns tied to price changes. So what should companies do? Should they forego price discounts and promotions to render demand more stable in order to create a more consistent supply chain that can be effectively managed? One company we mentioned in this chapter has, in effect, done this. Identify this company and explain how it manages its supply chain. Also, discuss the complexities associated with managing a supply chain in which price changes from promotions and discounts are used and discuss strategies for overcoming these complexities.

[2]H. L. Lee, "Ultimate Enterprise Value Creation Using Demand-Based Management," *Stanford Global Supply Chain Management Forum*, http://www.stanford.edu/group/scforum/, September 2001.

## PROBLEMS

**10-1.** The Fizer Drug Company manufactures over-the-counter and prescription drugs. Last year the company's cost of goods sold was $470 million. It carried average raw material inventory of $17.5 million, average work-in-process of $9.3 million, and average finished goods inventory of $6.4 million. The company operates 365 days per year. Compute the company's inventory turns and days of supply for last year.

**10-2.** The Ashton Furniture Company manufactures coffee tables and chest of drawers. Last year the company's cost of goods sold was $3,700,000, and it carried inventory of oak, pine, stains, joiners, and brass fixtures, work-in-process of furniture frames, drawers and wood panels, and finished chests and coffee tables. Its average inventory levels for a 52-week business year were as follows.

| Raw Materials | Average Inventory | Unit Cost |
|---|---|---|
| oak | 8000 | $6.00 |
| pine | 4500 | 4.00 |
| brass fixtures | 1200 | 8.00 |
| stains | 3000 | 2.00 |
| joiners | 900 | 1.00 |
| **Work-in-Process** | | |
| frames | 200 | $30 |
| drawers | 400 | 10 |
| panels | 600 | 50 |
| chests | 120 | 110 |
| tables | 90 | 90 |
| **Finished Goods** | | |
| chests | 300 | $500 |
| coffee tables | 200 | 350 |

Determine the number of inventory turns and the days of supply for the furniture company.

**10-3.** Barington Mills manufactures denim cloth from two primary raw materials, cotton and dye. Work-in-process includes lapped cotton, spun yarn, and undyed cloth, while finished goods includes three grades of dyed cloth. The average inventory amounts on hand at any one time last year and the unit costs are as follows.

| Raw Materials | Average Inventory | Unit Cost |
|---|---|---|
| cotton | 70,000 lb. | $2.75 |
| dye | 125,000 gal. | 5.00 |
| **Work-in-Process** | | |
| lapped cotton | 2000 rolls | $10.50 |
| spun yarn | 5000 spools | 6.75 |
| undyed cloth | 500 rolls | 26.10 |
| **Finished Goods** | | |
| Grade 1 cloth | 250 rolls | $65.00 |
| Grade 2 cloth | 190 rolls | 80.00 |
| Grade 3 cloth | 310 rolls | 105.00 |

The company operates 50 weeks per year, and its cost of goods sold for the past year was $17.5 million.

Determine the company's inventory turns and weeks of supply.

**10-4.** House Max Builders constructs modular homes, and last year their cost of goods sold was $18,500,000. It operates 50 weeks per year. The company has the following inventory of raw materials, work-in-process, and finished goods.

| Raw Materials | Average Inventory | Unit Cost |
|---|---|---|
| 1 | 7200 | $8.50 |
| 2 | 4500 | 7.20 |
| 3 | 3200 | 15.40 |
| 4 | 4800 | 13.70 |
| 5 | 6900 | 10.50 |
| **Work-in-Process** | | |
| A | 100 | $16,200 |
| B | 70 | 13,500 |
| C | 60 | 6,100 |
| D | 35 | 14,400 |
| **Finished Goods** | | |
| Model X | 20 | $78,700 |
| Model Y | 10 | 65,300 |
| Model Z | 10 | 86,000 |

Determine the number of inventory turns and the days of supply for House Max.

**10-5.** The PM Computer Company makes build-to-order (BTO) computers at its distribution center year round. The following table shows the average value (in $ millions) of component parts, work-in-process, and finished computers at the DC for the past four years.

| | Year | | | |
|---|---|---|---|---|
| | 1 | 2 | 3 | 4 |
| Component parts | $20.5 | 27.8 | 30.8 | 37.3 |
| Work-in-process | 4.2 | 6.7 | 7.1 | 9.5 |
| Finished computers | 3.6 | 7.2 | 8.6 | 10.1 |
| Cost of goods sold | 226.0 | 345.0 | 517.0 | 680.0 |

a. Determine the number of inventory turns and the days of supply for each year.
b. As the company has grown, does it appear that the company's supply chain performance has improved? Explain your answer.
c. If the company wants to improve its supply chain performance, what items should it focus on? Why?

**10-6.** Delph Manufacturing Company is going to purchase an auto parts component from one of two competing suppliers. Delph is going to base its decision, in part, on the supply chain performance of the two suppliers. The company has obtained the following data for average raw materials, work-in-process, and finished goods inventory value, as well as cost of goods sold for the suppliers.

| | Supplier 1 | Supplier 2 |
|---|---|---|
| Cost of goods sold | $8,360,000 | $14,800,000 |
| Raw materials | 275,000 | 870,000 |
| Work-in-process | 62,000 | 550,000 |
| Finished goods | 33,000 | 180,000 |

Each company operates 52 weeks per year.

Determine which supplier has the best supply chain performance according to inventory turns and weeks of supply. What other factors would the company likely take into account in selecting a supplier?

**10-7.** Solve Problem 4-8 in Chapter 4 to construct a *c*-chart for monitoring invoice errors at Telcom Manufacturing Company.

**10-8.** Solve Problem 4-9 in Chapter 4 to construct a *c*-chart to monitor late order deliveries at the National Bread Company.

**10-9.** Solve Problem 4-10 in Chapter 4 to construct a *p*-chart to monitor order problems at BooksCDs.com

**10-10.** Solve Problem 4-11 in Chapter 4 to construct an $\bar{x}$-chart in conjunction with an $R$-chart for order fulfillment lead time at Valtec Electronics.

**10-11.** Solve Problem 4-31 in Chapter 4 to construct an $\bar{x}$-bar chart in conjunction with an $R$-chart for delivery time at the Great Outdoors Clothing Company.

## CASE PROBLEM 10.1

### *Somerset Furniture Company's Global Supply Chain*

The Somerset Furniture Company was founded in 1957 in Randolph County, Virginina. It traditionally has manufactured large, medium-priced, ornate residential home wood furniture such as bedroom cabinets and chests of draws, and dining and living room cabinets, tables, and chairs, at its primary manufacturing facility in Randolph County. It employed a marketing strategy of rapidly introducing new product lines every few years. Over time it developed a reputation for high-quality, affordable furniture for a growing U.S. market of homeowners during the last half of the twentieth century. The company was generally considered to be an innovator in furniture manufacturing processes and in applying TQM principles to furniture manufacturing. However, in the mid-1990s, faced with increasing foreign competition, high labor rates, and diminishing profits, the Somerset Company contracted to outsource several of its furniture product lines to manufacturers in China, simultaneously reducing the size of its own domestic manufacturing facility and labor force. This initially proved to be very successful in reducing costs and increasing profits, and by 2000 Somerset had decided to close its entire manufacturing facility in the United States and outsource all of its manufacturing to suppliers in China. The company set up a global supply chain in which it arranges for shipments of wood from the United States and South America to manufacturing plants in China where the furniture products are produced by hand by Chinese laborers. The Chinese manufacturers are very good at copying the Somerset ornate furniture designs by hand without expensive machinery. The average labor rate for furniture manufacturing in the United States is between \$9 and \$20 per hour, whereas the average labor rate for furniture manufacturers in China is \$2 per day. Finished furniture products are shipped by container ship from Hong Kong or Shanghai to Norfolk, Virginia, where the containers are then transported by truck to Somerset warehouses in Randolph County. Somerset supplies retail furniture stores from this location. All hardware is installed on the furniture at the retail stores in order to reduce the possibility of damage during transport.

The order processing and fulfillment system for Somerset includes a great deal of variability, as does all aspects of the company's global supply chain. The company processes orders weekly and biweekly. In the United States it takes between 12 and 25 days for the company to develop a purchase order and release it to their Chinese suppliers. This process includes developing a demand forecast, which may take from one to two weeks; converting the forecast to an order fulfillment schedule; and then developing a purchase order. Once the purchase order is processed overseas by the Chinese manufacturer, which may take 10 to 20 days depending on the number of changes made, the manufacturing process requires approximately 60 days. The foreign logistics process requires finished furniture items to be transported from the manufacturing plants to the Chinese ports, which can take up to several weeks depending on trucking availability and schedules. An additional 5 to 10 days is required to arrange for shipping containers and prepare the paperwork for shipping. However, shipments can then wait from one day to a week for enough available containers. There are often too few containers at the ports because large U.S. importers, like "Big W" discount stores in the United States, reserve all the available containers for their continual stream of overseas shipments. Once enough containers are secured, it requires from three to six days to optimally load the containers. The furniture pieces often have odd dimensions that result in partially filled containers. Since 9/11, random security checks of containers can delay shipment another one to three weeks, and smaller companies like Somerset are more likely to be extensively checked than larger shippers like Big W, who the port authorities don't want upset with delays. The trip overseas to Norfolk requires 28 days. Once in port, one to two weeks are required for a shipment to clear customs and to be loaded onto trucks for transport to Somerset's warehouse in Randolph County, which takes from one to three days. When a shipment arrives, it can take from one day up to a month to unload a trailer, depending on the urgency to fill store orders from the shipment.

Because of supply chain variability, shipments can be off schedule (i.e., delayed) by as much as 40%. The company prides itself on customer service and fears that late deliveries to its customers would harm its credibility and result in cancelled orders and lost customers. At the same time, keeping excess inventories on hand in its warehouses is very costly, and since Somerset redesigns its product lines so frequently a real problem of product obsolescence arises if products remain in inventory very long. Somerset has also been experiencing quality problems. The Chinese suppliers employ quality auditors who rotate among plants every few weeks to perform quality control tests and monitor the manufacturing process for several days before visiting another plant. However, store and individual customer complaints have forced Somerset to inspect virtually every piece of furniture it receives from overseas before forwarding it to stores. In some instances, customers have complained that tables and chairs creak noisily during use. Somerset subsequently discovered that the creaking was caused by humidity differences between the locations of the Chinese plants and the geographic areas in the United States where their furniture is sold. Replacement parts (like cabinet doors or table legs) are difficult to secure because the Chinese suppliers will only agree to provide replacement parts for the product lines currently in production. However, Somerset provides a one-year warranty on its furniture, which means that they often need parts for a product no longer being produced. Even when replacement parts were available, it took too long to get them from the supplier in order to provide timely customer service.

Although Somerset was initially successful at outsourcing its manufacturing process on a limited basis, it has since discovered, as many companies do, that outsourcing can result in a host of supply chain problems, as indicated above. Discuss Somerset's global supply chain and possible remedies for its supply chain problems, including strategic and tactical changes that might improve the company's supply chain performance, reduce system variability, and improve quality and customer service. As part of your discussion, determine the product lead time by developing a timeline from the initiation of a purchase order to product delivery.

## REFERENCES


Chopra, S. and P. Meindl. *Supply Chain Management*, 2nd ed. Upper Saddle River, N.J.: Prentice Hall, 2004.

Christopher, M. *Logistics and Supply Chain Management*, 2nd ed. Upper Saddle River, N.J.: Prentice Hall, 1998.

Dornier, P., R. Ernst, M. Fender and P. Kouvelis. *Global Operations and Logistics*. New York: John Wiley & Sons, 1998.

Schecter, D. and Gordon S. *Delivering the Goods: The Art of Managing Your Supply Chain.* New York: John Wiley & Sons, 2002.

# Operational Decision-Making Tools: Transportation and Transshipment Models SUPPLEMENT 10

## CHAPTER OUTLINE

**In this supplement, you will learn about . . .**

- **The Transportation Model**
- **The Transshipment Model**

**Transportation model:**
involves transporting items from sources with fixed supply to destinations with fixed demand at the lowest cost.

An important factor in supply chain management is determining the lowest-cost transportation provider from among several alternatives. In most cases, items are transported from a plant or warehouse to a producer, a retail outlet, or distributor via truck, rail, or air. Sometimes the modes of transportation may be the same, but the company must decide among different transportation carriers—for example, different trucking firms. Two quantitative techniques that are used for determining the least cost means of transporting goods or services are the *transportation method* and the *transshipment method.*

## THE TRANSPORTATION MODEL

A **transportation model** is formulated for a class of problems with the following characteristics: (1) a product is *transported* from a number of sources to a number of destinations at the minimum possible cost, and (2) each source is able to supply a fixed number of units of the product and each destination has a fixed demand for the product. The following example demonstrates the formulation of the transportation model.

**Example S10.1**
**A Transportation Problem**

Potatoes are grown and harvested on farms in the Midwest and then shipped to distribution centers in Kansas City, Omaha, and Des Moines where they are cleaned and sorted. These distribution centers supply three manufacturing plants operated by the Frodo-Lane Foods Company, located in Chicago, St. Louis, and Cincinnati, where they make potato chips. Potatoes are shipped to the manufacturing plants by railroad or truck. Each distribution center is able to supply the following tons of potatoes to the plants on a monthly basis:

| Distribution Center | Supply |
|---|---|
| 1. Kansas City | 150 |
| 2. Omaha | 175 |
| 3. Des Moines | 275 |
| | 600 tons |

Each plant demands the following tons of potatoes per month:

| Plant | Demand |
|---|---|
| A. Chicago | 200 |
| B. St. Louis | 100 |
| C. Cincinnati | 300 |
| | 600 tons |

The cost of transporting 1 ton of potatoes from each distribution center (source) to each plant (destination) differs according to the distance and method of transport. These costs are shown next. For example, the cost of shipping 1 ton of potatoes from the distribution center at Omaha to the plant at Chicago is $7.

| Distribution | Plant | | |
|---|---|---|---|
| Center | *Chicago* | *St. Louis* | *Cincinnati* |
| Kansas City | $6 | $ 8 | $10 |
| Omaha | 7 | 11 | 11 |
| Des Moines | 4 | 5 | 12 |

The problem is to determine how many tons of potatoes to transport from each distribution center to each plant on a monthly basis to minimize the total cost of transportation. A diagram of the different transportation routes with supply, demand, and cost figures is given in Figure S10.1.

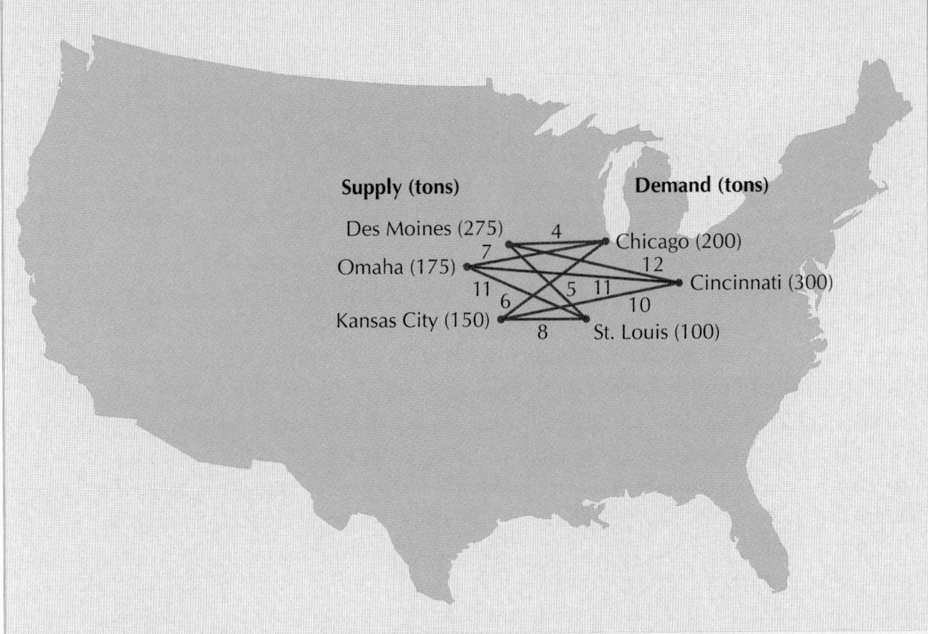


Figure S10.1
**Network of Transportation Routes**

Transportation models are solved within the context of a transportation table, which for our example is shown as follows. Each cell in the table represents the amount transported from one source to one destination. The smaller box within each cell contains the unit transportation cost for that route. For example, in the cell in the upper left-hand corner, the value $6 is the cost of transporting 1 ton of potatoes from Kansas City to Chicago. Along the outer rim of the tableau are the supply and demand constraint quantity values, referred to as *rim requirements*.

**The Transportation Table**

| **from** \ **to** | *Chicago* | *St. Louis* | *Cincinnati* | **Supply** |
|---|---|---|---|---|
| *Kansas City* | 6 | 8 | 10 | 150 |
| *Omaha* | 7 | 11 | 11 | 175 |
| *Des Moines* | 4 | 5 | 12 | 275 |
| **Demand** | 200 | 100 | 300 | 600 |

There are several quantitative methods for solving transportation models manually, including the *stepping-stone method* and the *modified distribution method*. These methods require a number of computational steps and are very time consuming if done by hand. We will not present the detailed solution procedure for these methods here. We will focus on a computer solution of the transportation model using Excel.

## SOLUTION OF THE TRANSPORTATION MODEL WITH EXCEL

Transportation models can be solved using spreadsheets like Microsoft Excel. Exhibit S10.1 shows the initial Excel screen for Example S10.1 (which can be downloaded from the text website).

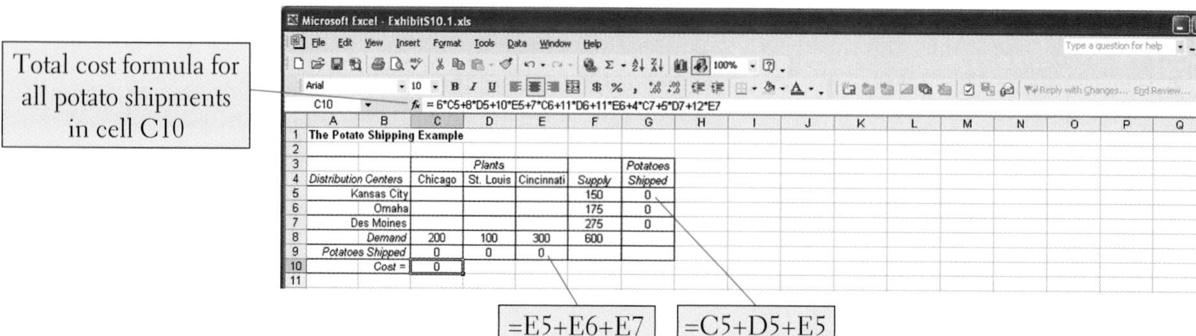

Exhibit **S10.1**

Notice in this screen that the formula for the total transportation cost is embedded in cell C10 shown on the formula bar across the top of the screen. Total cost is computed by multiplying each cell cost by each value in cells **C5:E7** inclusive that represent the shipments (currently 0) and summing these products.

Formulas must also be developed for the supply and demand rim requirements. Each distribution center can supply only the amount it has available, and the amount shipped to each plant must not exceed what it demands. For example, the amount shipped from Kansas City is the sum of the shipments to Chicago, St. Louis, and Cincinnati.

Similar summation formulas for the other distribution centers and each plant are also developed. If you click on cells G5, G6, G7, C9, D9, and E9, you will see these formulas on the formula bar. Since this is a balanced transportation problem, where total supply equals total demand (i.e., 600 tons), then each amount shipped from each distributor equals the available supply, and each amount shipped to each plant equals the amount demanded. These mathematical relationships are included in the "Solver" screen (shown in Exhibit S10.2) accessed from the "Tools" menu on the toolbar.

The "target" cell containing total cost is C10, and it is set equal to "min" since our objective is to minimize cost. The "variables" in our problem representing individual shipments from each distributor to each plant are cells C5 to E7 inclusive. This is designated as "**C5:E7**." (Excel adds the $s.) The constraints mathematically specify that the amount shipped equals the amount available or demanded. For example, "**C9 = C8**" means that the sum of all shipments to Chicago from all three distributors, which is embedded in C9, equals the demand contained in C8. There are six constraints, one for each distributor and plant. There are two more requirements. First, "C5:E7≥0." This specifies that all the amounts shipped must be zero or positive. This can be accomplished by adding this as a constraint, or (as is the case here), clicking on "Options" and then activating the "Assume non-negative" button. Also on the "Options" window activate the "Assume linear models" button. Once all the model parameters have been entered into the solver, click on "Solve." The solution is shown on the Excel screen in Exhibit S10.3.

Exhibit **S10.2**

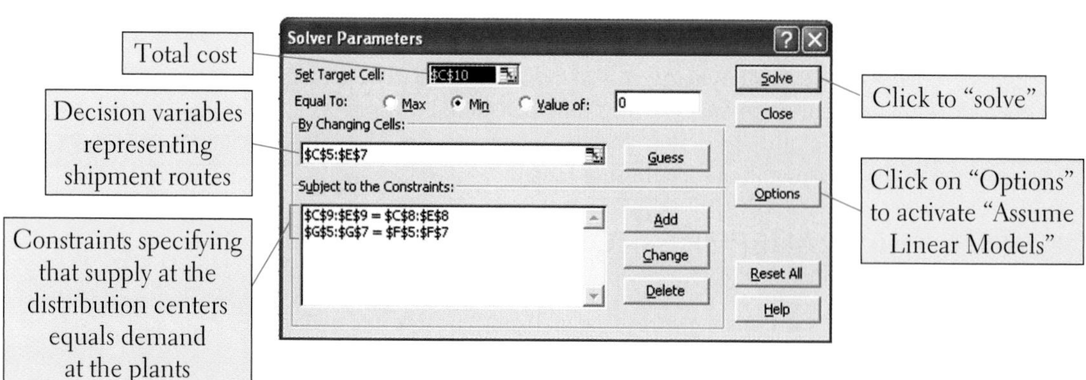

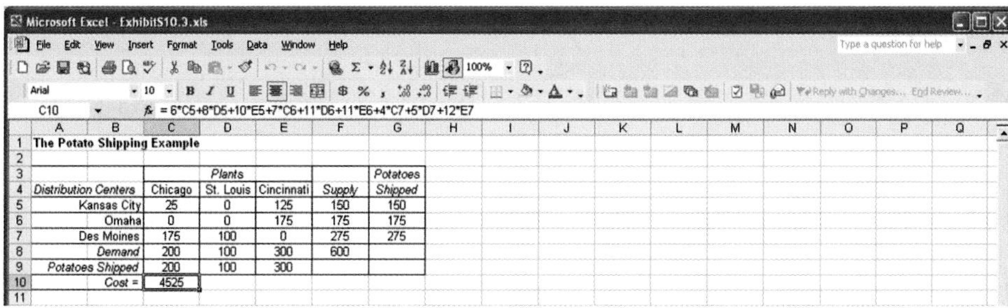

Microsoft Excel - ExhibitS10.3.xls

C10 = 6*C5+8*D5+10*E5+7*C6+11*D6+11*E6+4*C7+5*D7+12*E7

**The Potato Shipping Example**

| | Plants | | | | Potatoes |
|---|---|---|---|---|---|
| *Distribution Centers* | Chicago | St. Louis | Cincinnati | *Supply* | *Shipped* |
| Kansas City | 25 | 0 | 125 | 150 | 150 |
| Omaha | 0 | 0 | 175 | 175 | 175 |
| Des Moines | 175 | 100 | 0 | 275 | 275 |
| *Demand* | 200 | 100 | 300 | 600 | |
| *Potatoes Shipped* | 200 | 100 | 300 | | |
| *Cost =* | 4525 | | | | |

**Exhibit S10.3**

Interpreting this solution, we find that 125 tons are shipped from Kansas City to Cincinnati, 175 tons are shipped from Omaha to the plant at Cincinnati, and so on. The total shipping cost is $4525. The company could use these results to make decisions about how to ship potatoes and to negotiate new rate agreements with railway and trucking shippers.

In this computer solution there is an alternative optimal solution, meaning there is a second solution reflecting a different shipping distribution but with the same total cost of $4525. Manual solution is required to identify this alternative; however, it could provide a different shipping pattern that the company might view as advantageous.

In Example S10.1 the unique condition occurred in which there were the same number of sources as destinations, three, and the supply at all three sources equaled the demand at all three destinations, 600 tons. This is the simplest form of transportation model; however, solution is not restricted to these conditions. Sources and destinations can be unequal, and total supply does not have to equal total demand, which is called an *unbalanced* problem. In addition, routes can be **prohibited**. If a route is prohibited, units cannot be transported from a particular source to a particular destination.

In an *unbalanced transportation problem*, supply exceeds demand or vice versa.

**Prohibited route:** transportation route over which goods cannot be transported.

Exhibit S10.4 shows the solution for a modified version of our potato shipment example in which supply at Des Moines has been increased to 375 tons and the shipping route from Kansas City to Chicago is prohibited because of a railway track being repaired. An extra column (H) has been added to show the sources that now have excess supply. The cost for cell C5 has been changed from $6 to $100 to prohibit the route from Kansas City to Chicago. The value of $100 is arbitrary; any value can be used that is much larger relative to the other route shipping costs. (Alternatively, this variable, CS, could be eliminated.) Exhibit S10.5 shows the solver for this problem. The only change in the solver is that the constraints for the potatoes shipped in column "G" are ≤ the supply values in column "F."

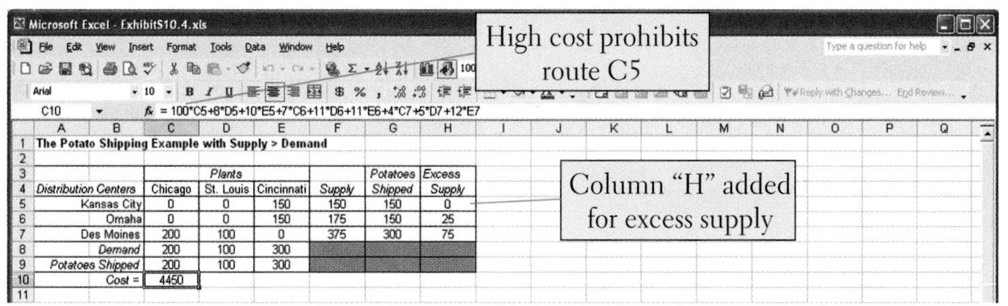


Microsoft Excel - ExhibitS10.4.xls

C10 = 100*C5+8*D5+10*E5+7*C6+11*D6+11*E6+4*C7+5*D7+12*E7

**The Potato Shipping Example with Supply > Demand**

| | Plants | | | | Potatoes | Excess |
|---|---|---|---|---|---|---|
| *Distribution Centers* | Chicago | St. Louis | Cincinnati | *Supply* | *Shipped* | *Supply* |
| Kansas City | 0 | 0 | 150 | 150 | 150 | 0 |
| Omaha | 0 | 0 | 150 | 175 | 150 | 25 |
| Des Moines | 200 | 100 | 0 | 375 | 300 | 75 |
| *Demand* | 200 | 100 | 300 | | | |
| *Potatoes Shipped* | 200 | 100 | 300 | | | |
| *Cost =* | 4450 | | | | | |

**Exhibit S10.4**

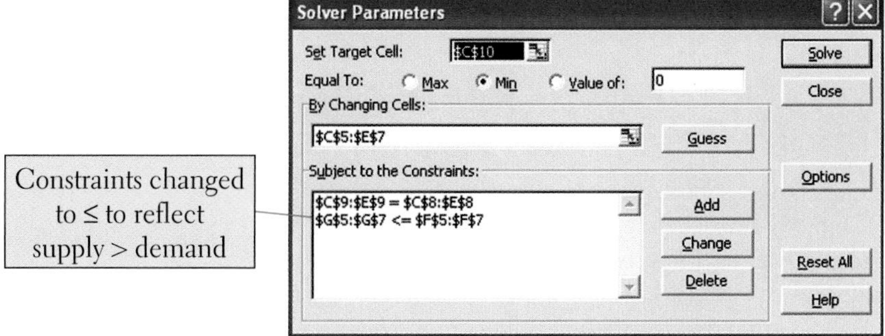


**Exhibit S10.5**

## THE TRANSSHIPMENT MODEL

**Transshipment model:** a variation of the transportation model with intermediate points between sources and destinations.

The **transshipment model** is an extension of the transportation model in which intermediate transshipment points are added between the sources and destinations. An example of a transshipment point is a distribution center or warehouse located between plants and stores. In a transshipment problem, items may be transported from sources through transshipment points on to destinations, from one source to another, from one transshipment point to another, from one destination to another, or directly from sources to destinations, or some combination of these alternatives.

**Example S10.2**
**A Transshipment Problem**

We will expand our potato shipping example to demonstrate the formulation of a transshipment model. Potatoes are harvested at farms in Nebraska and Colorado before being shipped to the three distribution centers in Kansas City, Omaha, and Des Moines, which are now transshipment points. The amount of potatoes harvested at each farm is 300 tons. The potatoes are then shipped to the plants in Chicago, St. Louis, and Cincinnati. The shipping costs from the distributors to the plants remain the same, and the shipping costs from the farms to the distributors are as follows.

| | Distribution Centers | | |
|---|---|---|---|
| Farm | 3. Kansas City | 4. Omaha | 5. Des Moines |
| 1. Nebraska | $16 | 10 | 12 |
| 2. Colorado | 15 | 14 | 17 |

The basic structure of this model is shown in the following graphical network.

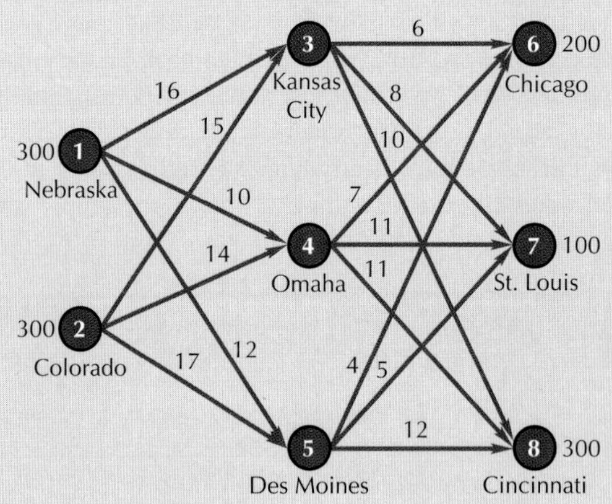


As with the transportation problem, this model includes supply constraints at the farms in Nebraska and Colorado, and demand constraints at the plants in Chicago, St. Louis, and Cincinnati. However, there are several additional mathematical relationships that express the condition that whatever amount is shipped into a distribution center must also be shipped out; that is, the amount shipped into a transshipment point must equal the amount shipped out.

## SOLUTION OF THE TRANSSHIPMENT PROBLEM WITH EXCEL

Exhibit S10.6 shows the spreadsheet solution and Exhibit S10.7 the Solver for our potato shipping transshipment example. The spreadsheet is similar to the original spreadsheet for the regular transportation problem in Exhibit S10.1, except there are two tables of variables—one for shipping from the farms to the distribution centers and one for shipping potatoes from the distribution centers to the plants. Thus, the decision variables (i.e.,

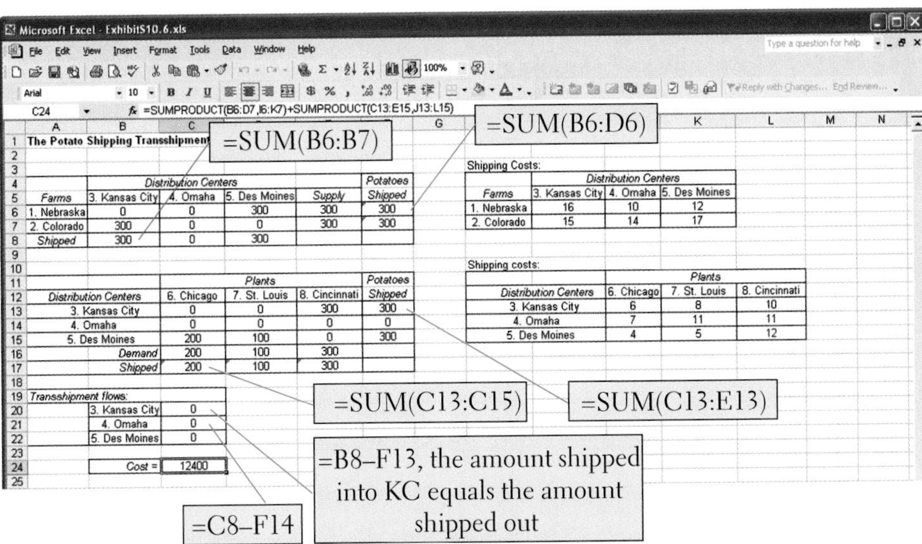


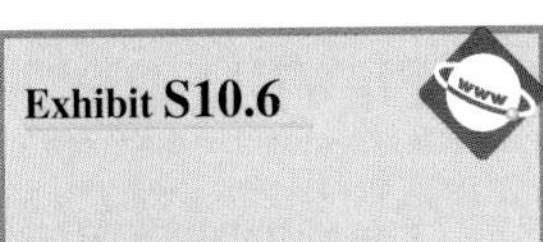


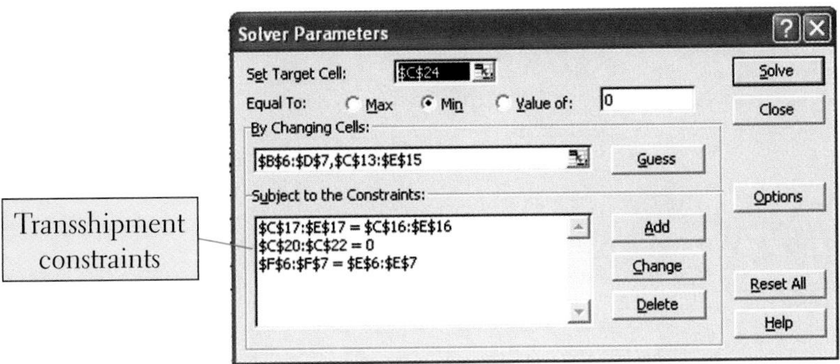


Exhibit S10.7

the amounts shipped from sources to destinations) are in cells **B6:D7** and **C13:E15**. The constraint for the amount of potatoes shipped from the farm in Nebraska to the three distributors (i.e., the supply constraint for Nebraska) in cell F6 is "**=SUM(B6:D6)**," which sums cells "**B6+C6+D6**." The amount of potatoes shipped to Kansas City from the farms in cell B8 is "**=SUM(B6:B7)**." Similar constraints are developed for the shipments from the distributors to the plants.

The objective function in Exhibit S10.6 is also constructed a bit differently than it was in Exhibit S10.1. Instead of typing in a single objective function in cell C24, two cost arrays have been developed for the shipping costs in cells **I6:K7** and cells **J13:L15,** which are then multiplied times the variables in cells **B6:D7** and **C13:E15,** and added together. This objective function, "**=SUMPRODUCT(B6:D7,I6:K7)+SUMPRODUCT(C13:E15, J13:L15),**" is shown on the toolbar at the top of Exhibit S10.6. Constructing the objective function with cost arrays like this is a little easier than typing in all the variables and costs in a single objective function when there are a lot of variables and costs.

## SUMMARY

Transportation and transshipment models are quantitative techniques that are used to analyze logistical supply chain problems, specifically the distribution of items from sources to destinations. The objective is frequently to minimize transportation costs. Both models can be solved using Excel spreadsheets which were demonstrated in this chapter.

## SUMMARY OF KEY TERMS

**prohibited route** a transportation route over which items cannot be transported.

**transportation model** transporting items from sources with fixed supplies to destinations with fixed demands at the minimum cost, time, etc.

**transshipment model** a special case of the transportation problem in which intermediate shipping points exist between the sources and final destinations.

## SOLVED PROBLEM

### TRANSPORTATION MODEL

A manufacturing firm ships its finished products from three plants to three distribution warehouses. The supply capacities of the plants, the demand requirements at the warehouses, and the transportation costs per ton are shown as follows:

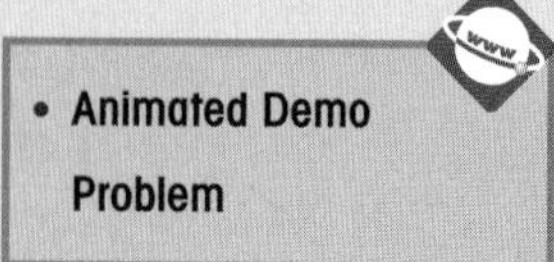


| PLANT | Warehouses *A* | *B* | *C* | Supply (*units*) |
|---|---|---|---|---|
| 1 | $ 8 | 5 | 6 | 120 |
| 2 | 15 | 10 | 12 | 80 |
| 3 | 3 | 9 | 10 | 80 |
| Demand (*units*) | 150 | 70 | 60 | 280 |

Solve this problem using Excel.

**SOLUTION**

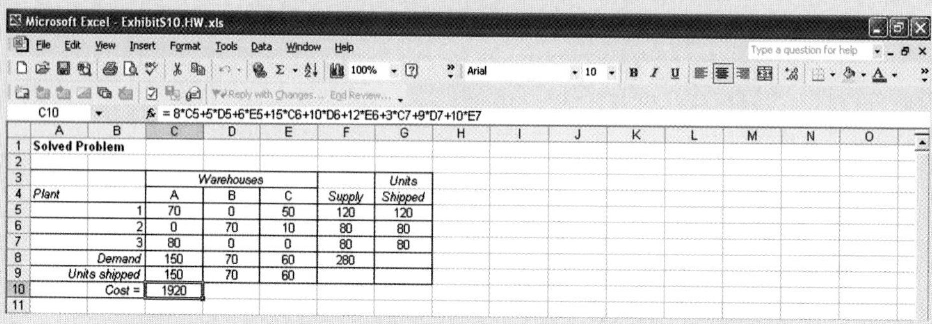


| | A | B | C | D | E | F | G |
|---|---|---|---|---|---|---|---|
| 1 | Solved Problem | | | | | | |
| 2 | | | | | | | |
| 3 | | | Warehouses | | | | Units |
| 4 | Plant | | A | B | C | Supply | Shipped |
| 5 | | 1 | 70 | 0 | 50 | 120 | 120 |
| 6 | | 2 | 0 | 70 | 10 | 80 | 80 |
| 7 | | 3 | 80 | 0 | 0 | 80 | 80 |
| 8 | | Demand | 150 | 70 | 60 | 280 | |
| 9 | | Units shipped | 150 | 70 | 60 | | |
| 10 | | Cost = | 1920 | | | | |
| 11 | | | | | | | |

## PROBLEMS

**S10-1.** Steel mills in three cities produce the following amounts of steel:

| Location | Weekly Production (tons) |
|---|---|
| A. Bethlehem | 180 |
| B. Birmingham | 250 |
| C. Gary | 310 |
| | 740 |

These mills supply steel to four cities, where manufacturing plants have the following demand:

| Location | Weekly Demand (tons) |
|---|---|
| 1. Detroit | 160 |
| 2. St. Louis | 120 |
| 3. Chicago | 170 |
| 4. Norfolk | 220 |
| | 670 |

Shipping costs per ton of steel are as follows:

| from | to 1 | 2 | 3 | 4 |
|---|---|---|---|---|
| A | $130 | $ 90 | $140 | $170 |
| B | 120 | 110 | 70 | 150 |
| C | 180 | 130 | 100 | 210 |

Because of a truckers' strike, shipments are prohibited from Birmingham to Chicago. Solve this problem.

**S10-2.** In Problem S10-1, what would be the effect of a reduction in production capacity at the Gary location from 310 tons to 260 tons per week?

**S10-3.** Oranges are grown, picked, and then processed and packaged at distribution centers in Tampa, Miami, and Fresno. These centers supply oranges to markets in New York, Philadelphia, Chicago, and Boston. The following table shows the shipping costs per truckload ($100s), supply, and demand:

| | to | | | | |
|---|---|---|---|---|---|
| from | New York | Philadelphia | Chicago | Boston | Supply |
| Tampa | $ 9 | $14 | $12 | $17 | 300 |
| Miami | 11 | 10 | 6 | 10 | 200 |
| Fresno | 12 | 8 | 15 | 7 | 250 |
| Demand | 160 | 210 | 130 | 180 | |

Because of an agreement between distributors, shipments are prohibited from Miami to Chicago. Solve this problem.

**S10-4.** In Exhibit S10.4, shipments are prohibited from Kansas City to Chicago because of railroad construction. Once the rail construction is completed, what will be the effect on the optimal shipping routes?

**S10-5.** A manufacturing firm produces diesel engines in four cities—Phoenix, Seattle, St. Louis, and Detroit. The company is able to produce the following numbers of engines per month:

| Plant | Production |
|---|---|
| 1. Phoenix | 10 |
| 2. Seattle | 20 |
| 3. St. Louis | 15 |
| 4. Detroit | 25 |

Three trucking firms purchase the following numbers of engines for their plants in three cities:

| Firm | Demand |
|---|---|
| A. Greensboro | 10 |
| B. Charlotte | 20 |
| C. Louisville | 15 |

The transportation costs per engine ($100s) from sources to destinations are as shown:

| | to | | |
|---|---|---|---|
| from | A | B | C |
| 1 | $7 | $8 | $5 |
| 2 | 6 | 10 | 6 |
| 3 | 10 | 4 | 5 |
| 4 | 3 | 9 | 11 |

However, the Charlotte firm will not accept engines made in Seattle, and the Louisville firm will not accept engines from Detroit; therefore, these routes are prohibited. Solve this problem.

**S10-6.** The US-Haul Truck Rental firm has accumulated extra trucks at three of its truck leasing outlets, as shown:

| Leasing Outlet | Extra Trucks |
|---|---|
| 1. Atlanta | 70 |
| 2. St. Louis | 115 |
| 3. Charlotte | 60 |
| | 245 |

The firm also has four outlets with shortages of rental trucks, as follows:

| Leasing Outlet | Truck Shortage |
|---|---|
| A. New Orleans | 80 |
| B. Buffalo | 50 |
| C. Dallas | 90 |
| D. Pittsburgh | 25 |
| | 245 |

The firm wants to transfer trucks from the outlets with extras to those with shortages at the minimum total cost. The following costs of transporting these trucks from city to city have been determined:

| | to | | | |
|---|---|---|---|---|
| from | A | B | C | D |
| 1 | $70 | $100 | $90 | $60 |
| 2 | 120 | 80 | 50 | 40 |
| 3 | 110 | 140 | 120 | 70 |

Solve this problem.

**S10-7.** In Problem S10-6, what would be the effect on the optimal solution if there were no shortage of rental trucks at the New Orleans outlet?

**S10-8.** The John Adams Brewing Company has breweries in three cities; the breweries can supply the following numbers of barrels of draft beer to the company's distributors each month:

| Brewery | Monthly Supply (barrels) |
|---|---|
| A. Tampa | 4,000 |
| B. St. Louis | 5,000 |
| C. Milwaukee | 3,500 |
| | 12,500 |

The distributors, spread throughout six states, have the following total monthly demand:

| Distributor | Monthly Demand (barrels) |
|---|---|
| 1. Tennessee | 1800 |
| 2. Georgia | 2100 |
| 3. North Carolina | 1700 |
| 4. South Carolina | 1050 |
| 5. Kentucky | 2350 |
| 6. Virginia | 1400 |
| | 10,400 |

The company must pay the following shipping costs per barrel:

| | to | | | | | |
|---|---|---|---|---|---|---|
| from | 1 | 2 | 3 | 4 | 5 | 6 |
| A | $0.50 | $0.35 | $0.60 | $0.45 | $0.80 | $0.75 |
| B | 0.25 | 0.65 | 0.40 | 0.55 | 0.20 | 0.65 |
| C | 0.40 | 0.70 | 0.55 | 0.50 | 0.35 | 0.50 |

Determine the minimum cost shipping routes for the company.

**S10-9.** In Problem S10-8, the Adams Brewing Company management has negotiated a new shipping contract with a trucking firm between its Tampa brewery and its distributor in Kentucky that reduces the shipping cost per barrel from \$0.80 per barrel to \$0.55 per barrel. How will this cost change affect the optimal solution?

**S10-10.** Systems Unlimited sells personal computers to universities and colleges on the East Coast and ships them from three distribution warehouses. The firm is able to supply the following numbers of computers to the universities by the beginning of the academic year:

| Distribution Warehouse | Supply (computers) |
|---|---|
| 1. Richmond | 420 |
| 2. Atlanta | 610 |
| 3. Washington, DC | 340 |
| | 1370 |

Four universities have ordered computers that must be delivered and installed by the beginning of the academic year:

| University | Demand (computers) |
|---|---|
| A. Tech | 560 |
| B. A & M | 280 |
| C. State | 410 |
| D. Central | 340 |
| | 1590 |

The shipping and installation costs per computer from each distributor to each university are as follows:

| | to | | | |
|---|---|---|---|---|
| from | A | B | C | D |
| 1 | \$22 | 17 | 30 | 18 |
| 2 | 15 | 35 | 20 | 25 |
| 3 | 28 | 21 | 16 | 14 |

Determine the shipments that will minimize total costs.

**S10-11.** In Problem S10-10, Systems Unlimited wants to meet demand more effectively at the four universities it supplies. It is considering two alternatives: (1) expand its warehouse at Richmond to a capacity of 600 at a cost equivalent to an additional \$6 in handling and shipping per unit; or (2) purchase a new warehouse in Charlotte that can supply 300 units with shipping costs of \$19 to Tech, \$26 to A&M, \$22 to State, and \$16 to Central. Which alternative should management select based solely on transportation costs (i.e., no capital costs)?

**S10-12.** A manufacturing company is closing three of its existing plants and intends to transfer some of its more skilled employees to three plants that will remain open. The number of employees available for transfer from each closing plant is as follows:

| Closing Plant | Transferable Employees |
|---|---|
| 1 | 60 |
| 2 | 105 |
| 3 | 70 |
| | 235 |

The following number of employees can be accommodated at the three plants remaining open:

| Open Plants | Employees Demanded |
|---|---|
| A | 55 |
| B | 80 |
| C | 40 |
| | 175 |

Each transferred employee will increase product output (units) per day at each plant as follows:

| | to | | |
|---|---|---|---|
| from | A | B | C |
| 1 | 5 | 8 | 6 |
| 2 | 10 | 9 | 12 |
| 3 | 7 | 6 | 8 |

Determine the best way to transfer employees in order to ensure the maximum increase in product output.

**S10-13.** The Sunshine Rental Car Agency has six lots in Orlando, and it wants to have a certain number of cars available at each lot at the beginning of each day for local rental. The agency would like a model it could quickly solve at the end of each day that would tell how to redistribute the cars among the six lots at the minimum total mileage. The distances between the six lots are as follows:

| | to (miles) | | | | | |
|---|---|---|---|---|---|---|
| from | 1 | 2 | 3 | 4 | 5 | 6 |
| 1 | — | 12 | 17 | 18 | 10 | 20 |
| 2 | 14 | — | 10 | 19 | 16 | 15 |
| 3 | 14 | 10 | — | 12 | 8 | 9 |
| 4 | 8 | 16 | 14 | — | 12 | 15 |
| 5 | 11 | 21 | 16 | 18 | — | 10 |
| 6 | 24 | 12 | 9 | 17 | 15 | — |

The agency would like the following number of cars at each lot at the end of the day. Also shown is the number of available cars at each lot at the end of a particular day. Determine the optimal reallocation of rental cars that will minimize the total mileage.

| Lot | 1 | 2 | 3 | 4 | 5 | 6 |
|---|---|---|---|---|---|---|
| Available | 42 | 21 | 18 | 23 | 35 | 27 |
| Desire | 27 | 26 | 22 | 44 | 31 | 16 |

**S10-14.** The Roadnet Shipping Company has expanded its shipping capacity by purchasing 90 trailer trucks from a competitor that went bankrupt. The company subsequently located 30 of the purchased trucks at each of its shipping warehouses in Charlotte, Memphis, and Louisville. The company makes shipments from each of these warehouses to terminals in St. Louis, Atlanta, and New York. Each truck is capable of making one shipment per week. The terminal managers have each indicated their capacity for extra shipments. The manager at St. Louis can accommodate 30 additional trucks per week, the manager at Atlanta can accommodate 50 additional trucks, and the manager at New York can accommodate

40 additional trucks. The company makes the following profit per truckload shipment from each warehouse to each terminal. The profits differ as a result of differences in products shipped, shipping costs, and transport rates.

| | Terminal | | |
|---|---|---|---|
| **Warehouse** | ***St. Louis*** | ***Atlanta*** | ***New York*** |
| Charlotte | $1800 | $2100 | $1600 |
| Memphis | 1000 | 700 | 900 |
| Louisville | 1400 | 800 | 2200 |

Determine how many trucks to assign to each route (i.e., warehouse to terminal) to maximize profit.

**S10-15.** The Beacon Publishing Company hires eight college students as salespeople to sell children's books during the summer. The company desires to distribute them to three sales territories. Territory 1 requires three salespeople, and territories 2 and 3 require two salespeople each. It is estimated that each salesperson will be able to generate the following amounts of dollar sales per day in each of the three territories:

| | Territory | | |
|---|---|---|---|
| **Salesperson** | ***1*** | ***2*** | ***3*** |
| A | $110 | $150 | $130 |
| B | 90 | 120 | 80 |
| C | 205 | 160 | 175 |
| D | 125 | 100 | 115 |
| E | 140 | 105 | 150 |
| F | 100 | 140 | 120 |
| G | 180 | 210 | 160 |
| H | 110 | 120 | 70 |

Determine which salespeople to allocate to the three territories so that sales will be maximized.

**S10-16.** The Big Ten Athletic Conference has nine basketball officials who must be assigned to three conference games, three to each game. The conference office wants to assign the officials so that the time they travel the total distances will be minimized. The hours each official would have to travel to each game is given in the following table:

| | Game | | |
|---|---|---|---|
| **Official** | *Columbus* | *Madison* | *Bloomington* |
| 1 | 2.3 | 4.5 | 1.6 |
| 2 | 4.1 | 8.7 | 7.2 |
| 3 | 6.5 | 7.0 | 2.9 |
| 4 | 3.4 | 6.3 | 4.5 |
| 5 | 8.1 | 1.9 | 5.2 |
| 6 | 6.4 | 2.6 | 3.5 |
| 7 | 3.9 | 4.8 | 7.4 |
| 8 | 5.2 | 4.2 | 6.5 |
| 9 | 4.6 | 5.6 | 3.9 |

Determine the optimal game assignments that will minimize the total time traveled by the officials.

**S10-17.** Maryville has built a new elementary school so that the town now has a total of four schools—Addison, Beeks, Canfield, and Daley. Each has a capacity of 400 students. The school wants to assign children to schools so that their travel time by bus is as short as possible. The school has partitioned the town into five districts conforming to population density—north, south, east, west, and central. The average bus travel time from each district to each school is shown as follows:

| | Travel Time (min) | | | | Student |
|---|---|---|---|---|---|
| **District** | *Addison* | *Beeks* | *Canfield* | *Daley* | **Population** |
| North | 12 | 23 | 35 | 17 | 270 |
| South | 26 | 15 | 21 | 27 | 310 |
| East | 18 | 20 | 22 | 31 | 320 |
| West | 29 | 24 | 35 | 10 | 220 |
| Central | 15 | 10 | 23 | 16 | 280 |

Determine the number of children that should be assigned from each district to each school in order to minimize total student travel time.

**S10-18.** In Problem S10-17, the school board has determined that it does not want any of the schools to be overly crowded compared with the other schools. It would like to assign students from each district to each school so that enrollments are evenly balanced between the four schools. However, the school board is concerned that this might significantly increase travel time. Determine the number of students to be assigned from each district to each school such that school enrollments are evenly balanced. Does this new solution appear to significantly increase travel time per student?

**S10-19.** The Atlantic Grocery chain operates in major metropolitan areas on the eastern seaboard. The stores have a "no-frills" approach, with low overhead and high volume. They generally buy their stock in volume at low prices. However, in some cases they actually buy stock at stores in other areas and ship it in. They can do this because of high prices in the cities they operate in compared with costs in other locations. One example is baby food. Atlantic purchases baby food at stores in Albany, Binghamton, Claremont, Dover, and Edison, and then trucks it to six stores in and around New York City. The stores in the outlying areas know what Atlantic is up to, so they limit the number of cases of baby food Atlantic can purchase. The following table shows the profit Altantic makes per case of baby food based on where the chain purchases it and which store it is sold at, plus the available baby food per week at purchase locations and the shelf space available at each Atlantic store per week:

| | Atlantic Store | | | | | | |
|---|---|---|---|---|---|---|---|
| **Purchase Location** | *1* | *2* | *3* | *4* | *5* | *6* | **Supply** |
| Albany | 9 | 8 | 11 | 12 | 7 | 8 | 26 |
| Binghamton | 10 | 10 | 8 | 6 | 9 | 7 | 40 |
| Claremont | 8 | 6 | 6 | 5 | 7 | 4 | 20 |
| Dover | 4 | 6 | 9 | 5 | 8 | 10 | 40 |
| Edison | 12 | 10 | 8 | 9 | 6 | 7 | 45 |
| Demand | 25 | 15 | 30 | 18 | 27 | 35 | |

Determine where Atlantic should purchase baby food and how the food should be distributed in order to maximize profit.

**S10-20.** Suppose that in Problem S10-19 Atlantic could purchase all the baby food it needs from a New York City distributor at a price that would result in a profit of $9 per case at stores 1, 3, and 4, $8 per case at stores 2 and 6, and $7 per case at store 5. Should Atlantic purchase all, none, or some of its baby food from the distributor rather than purchasing it at other stores and trucking it in?

**S10-21.** During the war in Iraq large amounts of military matériél and supplies had to be shipped daily from supply depots in the United Sates to bases in the Middle East. The critical factor in the movement of these supplies was speed. The following table shows the number of planeloads of supplies available each day from each of six supply depots and the number of daily loads demanded at each of five bases. (Each planeload is approximately equal in tonnage.) Also included in the table are the transport hours per plane (where transport hours include loading and fueling time, actual flight time, and unloading and refueling times).

| | Military Base | | | | | |
|---|---|---|---|---|---|---|
| **Supply Depot** | *A* | *B* | *C* | *D* | *E* | **Supply** |
| 1 | 36 | 40 | 32 | 43 | 29 | 8 |
| 2 | 28 | 27 | 29 | 40 | 38 | 12 |
| 3 | 34 | 35 | 41 | 29 | 31 | 7 |
| 4 | 41 | 42 | 35 | 27 | 36 | 10 |
| 5 | 25 | 28 | 40 | 34 | 38 | 9 |
| 6 | 31 | 30 | 43 | 38 | 40 | 6 |
| Demand | 9 | 6 | 12 | 8 | 10 | |

Determine the optimal daily flight schedule that will minimize total transport time.

**S10-22.** A severe winter ice storm has swept across North Carolina and Virginia followed by more than a foot of snow and frigid, single-digit temperatures. These weather conditions have resulted in numerous downed power lines and power outages in the region, causing dangerous conditions for much of the population. Local utility companies have been overwhelmed and have requested assistance from unaffected utility companies across the Southeast. The following table shows the number of utility trucks with crews available from five different companies in Georgia, South Carolina, and Florida; the demand for crews in seven different areas that local companies cannot get to; and the weekly cost ($1000s) of a crew going to a specific area (based on the visiting company's normal charges, the distance the crew has to come, and living expenses in an area). Determine the number of crews that should be sent from each utility to each affected area that will minimize total costs.

| | Area (Cost = $1000s) | | | | | | | Crews |
|---|---|---|---|---|---|---|---|---|
| **Crew** | *NC-E* | *NC-SW* | *NC-P* | *NC-W* | *VA-SW* | *VA-C* | *VA-T* | **Available** |
| GA-1 | 15.2 | 14.3 | 13.9 | 13.5 | 14.7 | 16.5 | 18.7 | 14 |
| GA-2 | 12.8 | 11.3 | 10.6 | 12.0 | 12.7 | 13.2 | 15.6 | 12 |
| SC-1 | 12.4 | 10.8 | 9.4 | 11.3 | 13.1 | 12.8 | 14.5 | 15 |
| FL-1 | 18.2 | 19.4 | 18.2 | 17.9 | 20.5 | 20.7 | 22.7 | 16 |
| FL-2 | 19.3 | 20.2 | 19.5 | 20.2 | 21.2 | 21.3 | 23.5 | 11 |
| Crews Needed | 9 | 7 | 5 | 8 | 10 | 9 | 7 | |

**S10-23.** TransAm Foods Company has five plants where it processes and packages fruits and vegetables. It has suppliers in six cities in California, Texas, Alabama, and Florida. The company has owned and operated its own trucking system in the past for transporting fruits and vegetables from its suppliers to its plants. However, it is now considering transferring all of its shipping to outside trucking firms and getting rid of its own trucks. It currently spends $245,000 per month to operate its own trucking system. It has determined monthly shipping costs (in $1000s per ton) using outside shippers from each of its suppliers to each of its plants, as shown in the following table.

| | Processing Plants ($1000s per ton) | | | | | Supply |
|---|---|---|---|---|---|---|
| **Suppliers** | *Denver* | *St. Paul* | *Louisville* | *Akron* | *Topeka* | **(tons)** |
| Sacramento | 3.7 | 4.6 | 4.9 | 5.5 | 4.3 | 19 |
| Bakersfield | 3.4 | 5.1 | 4.4 | 5.9 | 5.2 | 14 |
| San Antonio | 3.3 | 4.1 | 3.7 | 2.9 | 2.6 | 12 |
| Montgomery | 1.9 | 4.2 | 2.7 | 5.4 | 3.9 | 10 |
| Jacksonville | 6.1 | 5.1 | 3.8 | 2.5 | 4.1 | 22 |
| Ocala | 6.6 | 4.8 | 3.5 | 3.6 | 4.5 | 17 |
| Demand (tons) | 20 | 15 | 15 | 15 | 20 | |

Should National Foods continue to operate its own shipping network or sell its trucks and outsource its shipping to independent trucking firms?

**S10-24.** In Problem S10-23, TransAm Foods would like to know what the effect would be on the optimal solution and the company's decision regarding its shipping if it negotiates with its suppliers in Sacramento, Jacksonville, and Ocala to increase their capacity to 25 tons per month? What would be the effect of negotiating instead with its suppliers at San Antonio and Montgomery to increase their capacity to 25 tons each?

**S10-25.** Orient Transport Express (OTE) is a global distribution company that transports its clients' products to customers in Hong Kong, Singapore, and Taipei. All of the products OTE ships are stored at three distribution centers—one in Los Angeles, one in Savannah, and one in Galveston. For the coming month the company has 450 containers of computer components available at the Los Angeles center, 600 containers available at Savannah, and 350 containers available in Galveston. The company has orders for 600 containers from Hong Kong, 500 containers from Singapore, and 500 containers from Taipei. The shipping costs per container from each U.S. port to each of the overseas ports are shown in the following table:

| **U.S. Distribution Center** | Overseas Port | | |
|---|---|---|---|
| | *Hong Kong* | *Singapore* | *Taipei* |
| Los Angeles | $300 | 210 | 340 |
| Savannah | 490 | 520 | 610 |
| Galveston | 360 | 320 | 500 |

OTE, as the overseas broker for its U.S. customers, is responsible for unfulfilled orders, and it incurs stiff penalty costs from overseas customers if it does not meet an order. The Hong Kong customers charge a penalty cost of $800 per container for unfulfilled demand, Singapore customers charge a penalty cost of $920 per container, and Taipei customers charge $1100 per container. Formulate and solve a transportation model to determine the shipments from each U.S. distribution center to each overseas port that will minimize shipping costs. Indicate what portion of the total cost is a result of penalties.

**S10-26.** Globalnet Foods, Inc., imports food products such as meats, cheeses, and pastries to the United States from warehouses at ports in Hamburg, Marseilles, and Liverpool. Ships from these ports deliver the products to Norfolk, New York, and Savannah, where they are stored in company warehouses before being shipped to distribution centers in Dallas, St. Louis, and Chicago. The products are then distributed to specialty food stores and sold through catalogues. The shipping costs ($/1000 lb) from the European ports to the U.S. cities and the available supply (1000 lb) at the European ports are provided in the following table.

| | U.S. Cities | | | |
|---|---|---|---|---|
| **European Port** | *4. Norfolk* | *5. New York* | *6. Savannah* | **Supply** |
| 1. Hamburg | $420 | $390 | $610 | 55 |
| 2. Marseilles | 510 | 590 | 470 | 78 |
| 3. Liverpool | 450 | 360 | 480 | 37 |

The transportation costs ($/1000 lb) from each U.S. warehouse to the three distribution centers and the demand (1000 lb) at the distribution centers are as follows.

| | Distribution Center | | |
|---|---|---|---|
| **Warehouse** | *7. Dallas* | *8. St. Louis* | *9. Chicago* |
| 4. Norfolk | $75 | $63 | $81 |
| 5. New York | 125 | 110 | 95 |
| 6. Savannah | 68 | 82 | 95 |
| | 60 | 45 | 50 |

Determine the optimal shipments between the European ports and the warehouses and the distribution centers that will minimize total transportation costs.

**S10-27.** A sports apparel company has received an order for a college basketball team's national championship T-shirt. The company can purchase the T-shirts from textile factories in Mexico, Puerto Rico, and Haiti. The shirts are shipped from the factories to companies in the United States that silk-screen the shirts before they are shipped to distribution centers. Following are the production and transportation costs ($/shirt) from the T-shirt factories to the silk-screen companies to the distribution centers, plus the supply of T-shirts at the factories and demand for the shirts at the distribution centers.

| | Silk-screen Companies | | | |
|---|---|---|---|---|
| **T-shirt Factory** | *4. Miami* | *5. Atlanta* | *6. Houston* | **Supply (1000s)** |
| 1. Mexico | $4 | $6 | $3 | 18 |
| 2. Puerto Rico | 3 | 5 | 5 | 15 |
| 3. Haiti | 2 | 4 | 4 | 23 |

| | Distribution Centers | | |
|---|---|---|---|
| **Silk-screen Company** | *7. New York* | *8. St. Louis* | *9. Los Angeles* |
| 4. Miami | $5 | $7 | $9 |
| 5. Atlanta | 7 | 6 | 10 |
| 6. Houston | 8 | 6 | 8 |
| Demand (1000s) | 20 | 12 | 20 |

Determine the optimal shipments that will minimize total production and transportation costs for the apparel company.

**S10-28.** Walsh's Fruit Company contracts with growers in Ohio, Pennsylvania, and New York to purchase grapes. The grapes are processed into juice at the farms and stored in refrigerated vats. Then the juice is shipped to two plants, where it is processed into bottled grape juice and frozen concentrate. The juice and concentrate are then transported to four food warehouses/distribution centers. The transportation costs per ton from the farms to the plants and from the plants to the distributors, and the supply at the farms and demand at the distribution centers are summarized in the following tables.

| | Plant | | |
|---|---|---|---|
| **Farm** | *4. Indiana* | *5. Georgia* | **Supply (1000 tons)** |
| 1. Ohio | $16 | $21 | 72 |
| 2. Pennsylvania | 18 | 16 | 105 |
| 3. New York | 22 | 25 | 83 |

| | Distribution Centers | | |
|---|---|---|---|
| **Plant** | *6. Virginia* | *7. Kentucky* | *8. Louisiana* |
| 4. Indiana | $23 | $15 | $29 |
| 5. Georgia | 20 | 17 | 24 |
| Demand (1000 tons) | 90 | 80 | 120 |

a. Determine the optimal shipments from farms to plants to distribution centers that will minimize total transportation costs.

b. What would be the effect on the solution if the capacity at each plant was 140,000 tons?

**S10-29.** A national catalogue and Internet retailer has three warehouses and three major distribution centers located around the country. Normally, items are shipped directly from the warehouses to the distribution centers; however, each of the distribution centers can also be used as an intermediate transshipment point. The transportation costs ($/unit) between warehouses and distribution centers, the supply at the warehouses (100 units), and the demand at the distribution centers (100 units) for a specific week are shown in the following table.

| | Distribution Center | | | |
|---|---|---|---|---|
| **Warehouse** | *A* | *B* | *C* | **Supply** |
| 1 | $12 | $11 | $7 | 70 |
| 2 | 8 | 6 | 14 | 80 |
| 3 | 9 | 10 | 12 | 50 |
| Demand | 60 | 100 | 40 | |

The transportation costs ($/unit) between the distribution centers are

| Distribution Center | Distribution Center A | B | C |
|---|---|---|---|
| A | — | 8 | 3 |
| B | 1 | — | 2 |
| C | 7 | 2 | — |

Determine the optimal shipments between warehouses and distribution centers that will minimize total transportation costs.

**S10-30.** Horizon Computers manufactures laptops in Germany, Belgium, and Italy. Because of high tariffs between international trade groups, it is sometimes cheaper to ship partially completed laptops to factories in Puerto Rico, Mexico, and Panama and have them completed before final shipment to U.S. distributors in Texas, Virginia, and Ohio. The cost ($/unit) of the completed laptops plus tariffs and shipment costs from the European plants directly to the United States and supply and demand are shown as follows.

| European Plants | U.S. Distributors 7. Texas | 8. Virginia | 9. Ohio | Supply (1000s) |
|---|---|---|---|---|
| 1. Germany | $2600 | $1900 | $2300 | 5.2 |
| 2. Belgium | 2200 | 2100 | 2600 | 6.3 |
| 3. Italy | 1800 | 2200 | 2500 | 4.5 |
| Demand (1000s) | 2.1 | 3.7 | 7.8 | |

Alternatively, the unit costs of shipping partially completed laptops to plants for finishing before sending them to the United States are as follows.

| European Plants | Factories 4. Puerto Rico | 5. Mexico | 6. Panama |
|---|---|---|---|
| 1. Germany | $1400 | $1200 | $1100 |
| 2. Belgium | 1600 | 1100 | 900 |
| 3. Italy | 1500 | 1400 | 1200 |

| Factories | U.S. Distributors 7. Texas | 8. Virginia | 9. Ohio |
|---|---|---|---|
| 4. Puerto Rico | $800 | $700 | $900 |
| 5. Mexico | 600 | 800 | 1100 |
| 6. Panama | 900 | 700 | 1200 |

Determine the optimal shipments of laptops that will meet demand at the U.S. distributors at the minimum total cost.

## CASE PROBLEM S10.1

### *Stateline Shipping and Transport Company*

Rachel Sundusky is the manager of the South-Atlantic office of the Stateline Shipping and Transport Company. She is in the process of negotiating a new shipping contract with Polychem, a company that manufactures chemicals for industrial use. Polychem wants Stateline to pick up and transport waste products from its six plants to four waste disposal sites. Rachel is very concerned about this proposed arrangement. The chemical wastes that will be hauled can be hazardous to humans and the environment if they leak. In addition, a number of towns and communities in the region where the plants are located prohibit hazardous materials from being shipped through their municipal limits. Thus, not only will the shipments have to be handled carefully and transported at reduced speeds, they will also have to traverse circuitous routes in many cases.

Rachel has estimated the cost of shipping a barrel of waste from each of the six plants to each of the three waste disposal sites as shown in the following table:

| Plants | Waste Disposal Sites Whitewater | Los Canos | Duras |
|---|---|---|---|
| Kingsport | $12 | $15 | $17 |
| Danville | 14 | 9 | 10 |
| Macon | 13 | 20 | 11 |
| Selma | 17 | 16 | 19 |
| Columbus | 7 | 14 | 12 |
| Allentown | 22 | 16 | 18 |

Each week the plants generate amounts of waste as shown in the following table:

| Plant | Waste per Week (BBL) |
|---|---|
| Kingsport | 35 |
| Danville | 26 |
| Macon | 42 |
| Selma | 53 |
| Columbus | 29 |
| Allentown | 38 |

The three waste disposal sites at Whitewater, Los Canos, and Duras can accommodate a maximum of 65, 80, and 105 barrels per week, respectively.

The estimated shipping cost per barrel between each of the three waste disposal sites is shown in the following table:

| Waste Disposal Site | Whitewater | Los Canos | Duras |
|---|---|---|---|
| Whitewater | $— | $12 | $10 |
| Los Canos | 12 | — | 15 |
| Duras | 10 | 15 | — |

In addition to shipping directly from each of the six plants to one of the three waste disposal sites, Rachel is also considering using each of the plants and waste disposal sites as intermediate shipping points. Trucks would be able to drop a load at a plant or disposal site to be picked up and carried on to the final destination by another truck, and vice versa. Stateline would not incur any handling costs since Polychem has agreed to take care of all local handling of the waste materials at the plants and the waste disposal sites. In other words, the only cost Stateline incurs is the actual transportation cost. So Rachel wants to be able to consider the possibility that it may be cheaper to drop and pick up loads at intermediate points rather than shipping them directly.

The following table shows how much Rachel estimates the shipping costs per barrel between each of the six plants to be.

| Plants | Kingsport | Danville | Macon | Selma | Columbus | Allentown |
|---|---|---|---|---|---|---|
| Kingsport | $— | $6 | $4 | $9 | $7 | $8 |
| Danville | 6 | — | 11 | 10 | 12 | 7 |
| Macon | 5 | 11 | — | 3 | 7 | 15 |
| Selma | 9 | 10 | 3 | — | 3 | 16 |
| Columbus | 7 | 12 | 7 | 3 | — | 14 |
| Allentown | 8 | 7 | 15 | 16 | 14 | — |

Rachel wants to determine the shipping routes that will minimize Stateline's total cost in order to develop a contract proposal to submit to Polychem for waste disposal. She particularly wants to know if it is cheaper to ship directly from the plants to the waste sites or if she should drop and pick up some loads at the various plants and waste sites. Develop a model to assist Rachel and solve the model to determine the optimal routes.

## CASE PROBLEM S10.2

### *Global Supply Chain Management at Cantrex Apparel International*

Cantrex Apparel International manufactures clothing items around the world. It has currently contracted with a U.S. retail clothing wholesale distributor for men's goatskin and lambskin leather jackets for the next Christmas season. The distributor has distribution centers in Ohio, Tennessee, and New York. The distributor supplies the leather jackets to a discount retail chain, a chain of mall boutique stores, and a department store chain. The jackets arrive at the distribution centers unfinished, and at the centers the distributor adds a unique lining and label specific to each of its customers. The distributor has contracted with Cantrex to deliver the following number of leather jackets to its distribution centers in late fall:

| Distribution Center | Goatskin Jackets | Lambskin Jackets |
|---|---|---|
| Ohio | 1000 | 780 |
| Tennessee | 1400 | 950 |
| New York | 1600 | 1150 |

Cantrex has tanning factories and clothing manufacturing plants to produce leather jackets in Spain, France, Italy, Venezuela, and Brazil. Its tanning facilities are in Mende in France, Foggia in Italy, Saragosa in Spain, Feira in Brazil, and El Tigre in Venezuela. Its manufacturing plants are in Limoges, Naples, Madrid in Europe, and São Paulo and Caracas in South America. Following are the supplies of available leather from each tanning facility and the processing capacity at each plant (in lb) for this particular order of leather jackets.

| Tanning Factory | Goatskin Supply (lb) | Lambskin Supply (lb) |
|---|---|---|
| Mende | 4000 | 4400 |
| Foggia | 3700 | 5300 |
| Saragosa | 6500 | 4650 |
| Feira | 5100 | 6850 |
| El Tigre | 3600 | 5700 |

| Plant | Production Capacity (lb) |
|---|---|
| Madrid | 7800 |
| Naples | 5700 |
| Limoges | 8200 |
| São Paulo | 7600 |
| Caracas | 6800 |

In the production of jackets at the plants 37.5% of the goatskin leather and 50% of the lambskin leather are waste (i.e., it is discarded during the production process and sold for other byproducts). After production, a goatskin jacket weighs approximately 3 lb and a lambskin jacket weighs approximately 2.5 lb (neither with linings which are added in the United States).

Following are the costs/lb (in U.S.$) for tanning the uncut leather, shipping it, and producing the leather jackets at each plant.

| Tanning Factory | Plants ($/lb) | | | | |
|---|---|---|---|---|---|
| | *Madrid* | *Naples* | *Limoges* | *São Paulo* | *Caracas* |
| Mende | 24 | 22 | 16 | 21 | 23 |
| Foggia | 31 | 17 | 22 | 19 | 22 |
| Saragosa | 18 | 25 | 28 | 23 | 25 |
| Feira | XX | XX | XX | 16 | 18 |
| El Tigre | XX | XX | XX | 14 | 15 |

Note that the cost of jacket production is the same for goatskin and lambskin. Also, leather can be tanned in France, Spain, and Italy and shipped directly to the South American plants for jacket production, but the opposite is not possible (due to high tariff restrictions); that is, tanned leather is not shipped to Europe for production.

Once the leather jackets are produced at the plants in Europe and South America, Cantrex uses load match sites and international trade logistics (ITL) systems on the Internet to contract for available rail, truck, and ship transport from the plants to ports in Lisbon, Marseilles, and Caracas, and for shipping from these ports to U.S. ports in New Orleans, Jacksonville, and Savannah. Cantrex has arrangements with trade specialists in these port cities to handle the legal import and export regulations and documentations. The available shipping capacity at each port and transportation costs from the plants to the ports are as follows:

| Plants | Ports ($/lb) | | |
|---|---|---|---|
| | *Lisbon* | *Marseilles* | *Caracas* |
| Madrid | 0.75 | 1.05 | XX |
| Naples | 3.45 | 1.35 | XX |
| Limoges | 2.25 | 0.60 | XX |
| São Paulo | XX | XX | 1.15 |
| Caracas | XX | XX | 0.20 |
| Capacity (lb) | 8000 | 5500 | 9000 |

The shipping costs ($/lb) from each port in Europe and South America to the U.S. ports, and the available truck and rail capacity for transport at the U.S. ports are as follows.

| Ports | U.S. Ports ($/lb) | | |
|---|---|---|---|
| | *New Orleans* | *Jacksonville* | *Savannah* |
| Lisbon | 2.35 | 1.90 | 1.80 |
| Marseilles | 3.10 | 2.40 | 2.00 |
| Caracas | 1.95 | 2.15 | 2.40 |
| Capacity (lb) | 8000 | 5200 | 7500 |

Once in the United States, Cantrex outsources transportation to third-party logistics companies it has used previously, and it makes use of load match sites on the Internet. The transportation costs ($/lb) from the U.S. ports to the three distribution centers are as follows.

| U.S. Ports | Distribution Centers ($/lb) | | |
|---|---|---|---|
| | *Ohio* | *Tennessee* | *New York* |
| New Orleans | 0.65 | 0.52 | 0.87 |
| Jacksonville | 0.43 | 0.41 | 0.65 |
| Savannah | 0.38 | 0.34 | 0.50 |

Cantrex wants to determine the least costly flow of materials and goods along this supply chain that will meet the demand at the U.S. distribution centers. Develop a transshipment supply chain model for Cantrex that will result in a minimum cost solution.

## REFERENCES

Hitchcock, F. L. "The Distribution of a Product from Several Sources to Numerous Localities." *Journal of Mathematics and Physics* 20 (1941), pp. 224, 230.

Taylor, B. W. *Introduction to Management Science*, 8th ed. Upper Saddle River, NJ: Prentice Hall, 2004.

# Forecasting

CHAPTER **11**

Web resources for this chapter include

- Internet Exercises
- Online Practice Quizzes
- Virtual Tours
- Excel Worksheets
- Company and Resource Weblinks
- Animated Demo Problems
- Microsoft Project Exhibits

www.wiley.com/college/russell

## CHAPTER OUTLINE

In this chapter, you will learn about . . .

- The Strategic Role of Forecasting in Supply Chain Management and TQM
- Components of Forecasting Demand
- Time Series Methods
- Forecast Accuracy
- Time Series Forecasting Using Excel
- Regression Methods

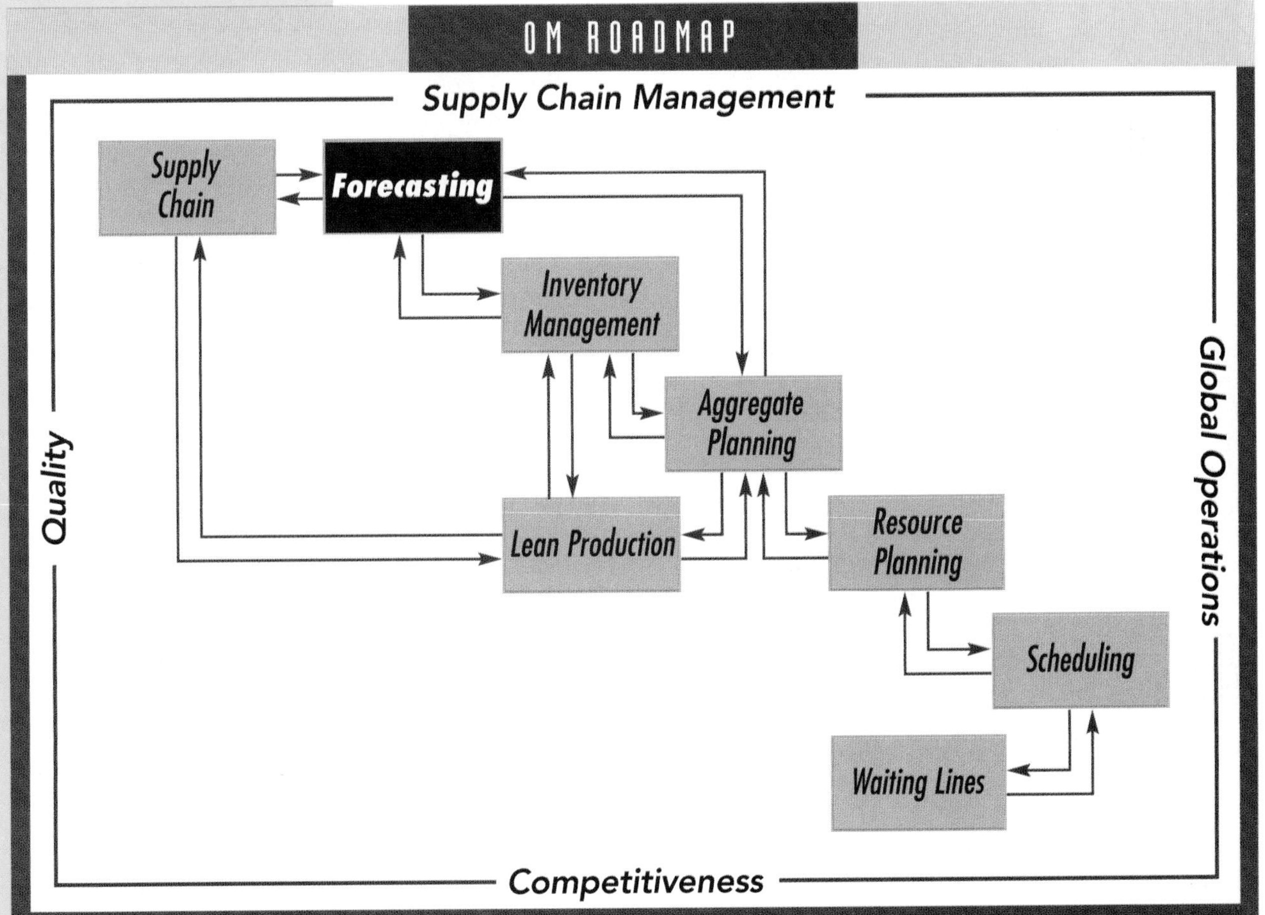

## PRODUCT FORECASTING AT NABISCO

In recent years, probably no business function within companies has grown as rapidly as forecasting, in large part due to the emphasis on supply chain management. Accurate forecasts are critical for managing and planning within a total supply chain environment, with its emphasis on quality customer service, efficiency, timing and decreased inventories. A decade ago only a few companies had full-time forecasting departments, but now most major corporations including Coca-Cola, Eastman Kodak, Hewlett-Packard, Johnson & Johnson, Pfizer, Federal Express, and Nabisco have full-time forecasting staffs. Levi Strauss, which started a separate forecasting department in 1995, had a full-time forecasting staff of 30 people and a corporate vice president of forecasting four years later. At Nabisco the Centralized Forecasting Group does sales forecasting.

Nabisco Biscuit Company is the largest domestic operating company within Nabisco, a *Fortune* 500 company. Nabisco Biscuit Company is the largest cookie and cracker manufacturing company in the United States, with annual sales of $3.5 billion. Over 30 company-owned and contract bakeries produce hundreds of different cookie, cracker, and snack products, including Oreo, Chips Ahoy!, Ritz, and SnackWell's. These products are shipped from the bakeries to over 100 distribution warehouses throughout the United States, and then from these distribution centers Nabisco delivers orders to over 100,000 final destinations, mostly retail grocery and convenience stores. Orders placed with a distribution center are delivered to a store within a short time, typically 24 to 48 hours. An accurate weekly forecast of product demand from the distribution centers is particularly critical to Nabisco because of the short lead time for orders, the wide geographic dispersion of the distribution centers, the large number of Nabisco products, and the limited product shelf life of bakery products. The forecasting process is complicated by product promotional events at the stores and the continual introduction of new products.

*A worker at a Nabisco cracker production process.*

Nabisco uses what is referred to as a "top-down" approach to forecasting. It starts with a national production forecast for each product for a four-week sales period. This national forecast considers information from finance and marketing and from a national product promotional schedule. It is provided to the distribution centers on a weekly basis to help create weekly forecasts of product demand using statistical forecasting methods based on sales history. (One of the forecast techniques it uses is a moving average, which is presented in this chapter.) This demand forecast is combined with a statistical forecast based on individual accounts (e.g., store), promotional events, and activities. Nabisco then uses this combined set of forecasts to determine the appropriate shipments from the bakeries to the distribution centers.

Forecasts for new products present Nabisco with a different challenge. Most of the forecasting techniques used for existing products are developed using several years of historical data, which is not available for new products. At Nabisco a planning forecast is used to develop initial production planning and scheduling and to establish initial inventory levels for a new product. However, when the product is introduced, which is generally a gradual process across different geographic regions, actual sales can be different than planned, depending on consumer acceptance of the product. If consumer acceptance is greater than planned, then the company can expect shortages and lost sales. If consumer demand is lower than planned and the new product fails, then the company can be stuck with excess inventory that must be destroyed. Thus, it is important that Nabisco be able to adjust its forecasts quickly during the product introductory period so that they will be as accurate as possible. Nabisco uses a forecast model for new products developed using the exponential smoothing technique with adjustments for trend and seasonality (a forecast technique presented in this chapter).

*Source:* S. Amrute, "Forecasting New Products with Limited History: Nabisco's Experience," *Journal of Business Forecasting* 17(3; Fall 1998), pp. 7–11; M. Barash and D. Mitchell, "Account Based Forecasting at Nabisco Biscuit Company," *Journal of Business Forecasting* 17(2; Summer 1998), pp. 3–6.

A forecast is a prediction of what will occur in the future. Meteorologists forecast the weather, sportscasters and gamblers predict the winners of football games, and companies attempt to predict how much of their product will be sold in the future. A forecast of product demand is the basis for most important planning decisions. Planning decisions regarding scheduling, inventory, production, facility layout and design, workforce, distribution, purchasing, and so on, are functions of customer demand. Long-range, strategic plans by top management are based on forecasts of the type of products consumers will demand in the future and the size and location of product markets.

Forecasting is an uncertain process depicted as in Figure 11.1. It is not possible to predict consistently what the future will be, even with the help of a crystal ball and a deck of tarot cards. Management generally hopes to forecast demand with as much accuracy as possible, which is becoming increasingly difficult to do. In the current international business environment, consumers have more product choices and more information on which to base choices. They also demand and receive greater product diversity, made possible by rapid technological advances. This makes forecasting products and product demand more difficult. Consumers and markets have never been stationary targets, but they are moving more rapidly now than they ever have before.

Companies sometimes use **qualitative** methods based on judgment, opinion, past experience, or best guesses, to make forecasts. A number of **quantitative** forecasting methods are also available to aid management in making planning decisions. In this chapter we discuss two of the traditional types of mathematical forecasting methods, time series analysis and regression, as well as several nonmathematical, qualitative approaches to forecasting. Although no technique will result in a totally accurate forecast, these methods can provide reliable guidelines in making decisions.

**Qualitative forecast methods:** subjective methods.

**Quantitative forecast methods:** are based on mathematical formulas.

## THE STRATEGIC ROLE OF FORECASTING IN SUPPLY CHAIN MANAGEMENT AND TQM

In today's global business environment, strategic planning and design tend to focus on supply chain management and total quality management (TQM).

Figure 11.1
**Forecasting—Predicting the Future**

## SUPPLY CHAIN MANAGEMENT

A company's supply chain encompasses all of the facilities, functions, and activities involved in producing a product or service from suppliers (and their suppliers) to customers (and their customers). Supply chain functions include purchasing, inventory, production, scheduling, facility location, transportation, and distribution. All these functions are affected in the short run by product demand and in the long run by new products and processes, technology advances, and changing markets.

Accurate forecasting determines how much inventory a company must keep at various points along its supply chain.

Forecasts of product demand determine how much inventory is needed, how much product to make, and how much material to purchase from suppliers to meet forecasted customer needs. This in turn determines the kind of transportation that will be needed and where plants, warehouses, and distribution centers will be located so that products and services can be delivered on time. Without accurate forecasts, large stocks of costly inventory must be kept at each stage of the supply chain to compensate for the uncertainties of customer demand. If there are insufficient inventories, customer service suffers because of late deliveries and stockouts. This is especially hurtful in today's competitive global business environment, where customer service and on-time delivery are critical factors.

While accurate forecasts are necessary, completely accurate forecasts are never possible. Hopefully, the forecast will reduce uncertainty about the future as much as possible, but it will never eliminate uncertainty. As such, all of the supply chain processes need to be flexible to respond to some degree of uncertainty.

In Chapter 10 on supply chain management, we talked about the "bullwhip effect" and its negative impact on the supply chain. The bullwhip effect is the distortion of information about product demand (including forecasts) as it is transmitted up the supply chain back toward suppliers. As demand moves further away from the ultimate end-use consumer, the variation in demand becomes greater and demand forecasts become less reliable. This increased variation can result in excessive, costly safety stock inventories at each stage in the supply chain and poorer customer service.

The bullwhip effect is caused when slight demand variability is magnified as information moves back upstream in the supply chain (see Figure 10.4). It is created when supply chain members make ordering decisions with an eye to their own self-interest and/or they do not have accurate demand forecasts from adjacent supply chain members. If each supply chain member is uncertain and not confident about what the actual demand is for the succeeding member it supplies, and it's making its own demand forecast, then it will stockpile extra inventory to compensate for the uncertainty; that is, the member creates a security blanket of inventory. One way to cope with the bullwhip effect is to develop demand forecasts that will reduce uncertainty and for supply chain members to share these forecasts with each other. Ideally, a single forecast of demand for the final customer in the supply chain would drive the development of subsequent forecasts for each supply chain member back up through the supply chain.

In *continuous replenishment*, the supplier and customer share continuously updated data.

One trend in supply chain design is *continuous replenishment*, wherein continuous updating of data is shared between suppliers and customers. In this system, customers are continuously being replenished, daily or even more often, by their suppliers based on actual sales. Continuous replenishment, typically managed by the supplier, reduces inventory for the company and speeds customer delivery. Variations of continuous replenishment include quick response, JIT, VMI (vendor-managed inventory), and stockless inventory. Such systems rely heavily on accurate short-term forecasts, usually on a weekly basis, of end-use sales to the ultimate customer. The supplier at one end of a company's supply chain must forecast the company's customer demand at the other end of the supply chain in order to maintain continuous replenishment. The forecast also has to be able to respond to sudden, quick changes in demand. Longer forecasts based on historical sales data for 6 to 12 months into the future are also generally required to help make weekly forecasts and suggest trend changes.

## TOTAL QUALITY MANAGEMENT

Forecasting customer demand is a key to providing good-quality service.

Forecasting is crucial in a total quality management (TQM) environment. More and more, customers perceive good-quality service to mean having a product when they demand it. This holds true for manufacturing and service companies. When customers walk into a McDonald's to order a meal, they do not expect to wait long to place orders. They expect McDonald's to have the item they want, and they expect to receive their orders within a short period of time. A good forecast of customer traffic flow and product demand enables McDonald's to schedule enough servers, to stock enough food, and to schedule food production to provide high-quality service. An inaccurate forecast causes service to break down, resulting in poor quality. For manufacturing operations, especially for suppliers, customers expect parts to be provided when demanded. Accurately forecasting customer demand is a crucial part of providing the high-quality service.

Continuous replenishment and JIT complement TQM. JIT is an inventory system wherein parts or materials are not provided at a stage in the production process until they are needed. This eliminates the need for buffer inventory, which, in turn, reduces both waste and inventory costs, a primary goal of TQM. For JIT to work, there must be a smooth, uninterrupted process flow with no defective items. Traditionally inventory was held at in-process stages to compensate for defects, but with TQM the goal is to eliminate defects, thus obviating the need for inventory. Good forecasting is critical for a company that adopts both JIT and TQM. It is especially important for suppliers, who are expected to provide materials as needed. Failure to meet expectations violates the principles of TQM and is perceived as poor-quality service. TQM requires a finely tuned, efficient production process, with no defects, minimal inventory, and no waste. In this way costs are reduced. Accurate forecasting is essential for maintaining this type of process.

JIT requires accurate forecasting to be successful.

## STRATEGIC PLANNING

There can be no strategic planning without forecasting. The ultimate objective of strategic planning is to determine what the company should be in the future—what markets to compete in, with what products, to be successful and grow. To answer these questions, the company needs to know what new products its customers will want, how much of these products customers will want, and the level of quality and other features that will be expected in these products. Forecasting answers these questions and is a key to a company's long-term competitiveness and success. The determination of future new products and their design subsequently determines process design, the kinds of new equipment and technologies that will be needed, and the design of the supply chain, including the facilities, transportation, and distribution systems that will be required. These elements are ultimately based on the company's forecast of the long-run future.

Successful strategic planning requires accurate forecasts of future products and markets.

The type of forecasting method depends on time frame, demand behavior, and causes of behavior.

# COMPONENTS OF FORECASTING DEMAND

The type of forecasting method to use depends on several factors, including the **time frame** of the forecast (i.e., how far in the future is being forecasted), the *behavior* of demand, and the possible existence of patterns (trends, seasonality, and so on), and the *causes* of demand behavior.

**Time frame:** indicates how far into the future is forecast.

## TIME FRAME

Forecasts are either short- to mid-range, or long-range. **Short-range (to mid-range) forecasts** are typically for daily, weekly, or monthly sales demand for up to approximately two years into the future, depending on the company and the type of industry. They are primarily used to determine production and delivery schedules and to establish inventory levels. At Unisys Corporation, an $8 billion producer of computer systems, monthly demand forecasts are prepared going out one year into the future. At Hewlett-Packard monthly forecasts for ink-jet printers are constructed from 12 to 18 months into the future, while at Levi Strauss weekly forecasts are prepared for five years into the future.

**Short- to mid-range forecast:** typically encompasses the immediate future—daily up to two years.

A **long-range forecast** is usually for a period longer than two years into the future. A long-range forecast is normally used for strategic planning—to establish long-term goals, plan new products for changing markets, enter new markets, develop new facilities, develop technology, design the supply chain, and implement strategic programs such as

**Long-range forecast:** usually encompasses a period of time longer than two years.

TQM. At Unisys, long-range strategic forecasts project three years into the future; Hewlett-Packard's long-term forecasts are developed for years 2 through 6; and at Fiat, the Italian automaker, strategic plans for new and continuing products go 10 years into the future.

These classifications are generalizations. The line between short- and long-range forecasts is not always distinct. For some companies a short-range forecast can be several years, and for other firms a long-range forecast can be in terms of months. The length of a forecast depends a lot on how rapidly the product market changes and how susceptible the market is to technological changes.

## DEMAND BEHAVIOR

**Trend:** a gradual, long-term up or down movement of demand.

**Random variations:** movements in demand that do not follow a pattern.

**Cycle:** an up-and-down repetitive movement in demand.

**Seasonal pattern:** an up-and-down repetitive movement in demand occurring periodically.

Demand sometimes behaves in a random, irregular way. At other times it exhibits predictable behavior, with trends or repetitive patterns, which the forecast may reflect. The three types of demand behavior are *trends*, *cycles*, and *seasonal patterns*.

A **trend** is a gradual, long-term up or down movement of demand. For example, the demand for houses has followed an upward trend during the past few decades, without any sustained downward movement in the market. Trends are often the starting points for developing forecasts. Figure 11.2 (*a*) illustrates a demand trend in which there is a general upward movement, or increase. Notice that Figure 11.2(*a*) also includes several random movements up and down. **Random variations** are movements that are not predictable and follow no pattern (and thus are virtually unpredictable). They are routine variations that have no "assignable" cause.

A **cycle** is an up-and-down movement in demand that repeats itself over a lengthy time span (i.e., more than a year). For example, new housing starts and, thus, construction-related products tend to follow cycles in the economy. Automobile sales also tend to follow cycles. The demand for winter sports equipment increases every four years before and after the Winter Olympics. Figure 11.2(*b*) shows the behavior of a demand cycle.

A **seasonal pattern** is an oscillating movement in demand that occurs periodically (in the short run) and is repetitive. Seasonality is often weather-related. For example, every winter the demand for snowblowers and skis increases, and retail sales in general increase during the holiday season. However, a seasonal pattern can occur on a daily or weekly

Figure 11.2
**Forms of Forecast Movement**

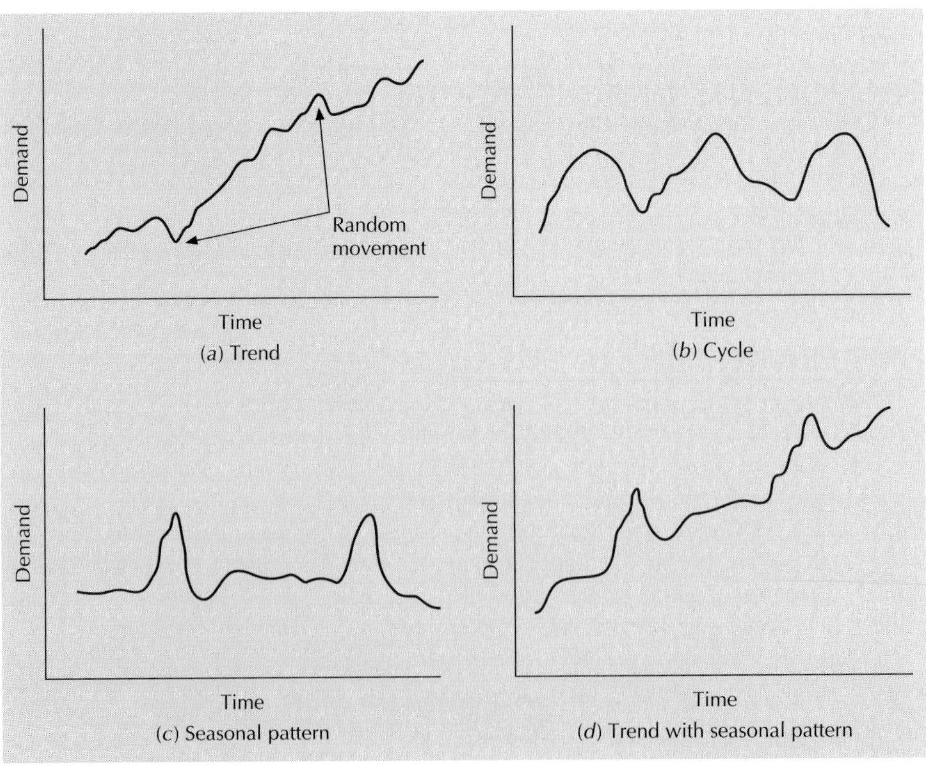

## THE COMPETITIVE EDGE

### Forecasting Service Calls at Federal Express

Federal Express is the world's largest express delivery company, with annual revenues of $14 billion. With a workforce of 145,000 employees, 600 planes, and 42,000 ground vehicles, it delivers more than 3 million packages per day to 210 countries. To support their global delivery network, FedEx has 51 customer service call centers, including 16 in the United States and 35 overseas. The customer service centers in the United States handle about 500,000 calls daily for requests for pickup, dropoff locations, package tracking, package rating, and the like. FedEx's service level goal is to answer 90 percent of all calls within 20 seconds, and it has some of the highest customer satisfaction levels in the industry.

FedEx has three major service call networks: domestic for calls related to packages sent and delivered within the United States; international for packages sent overseas from the United States; and freight for calls related to packages over 150 lb. For each of these call networks, FedEx uses four different forecasts encompassing different forecasting horizons: strategic plan, business plan, tactical forecast, and operational forecast. The strategic plan is for a five-year horizon and includes forecasts for the number of calls to service representatives, average call handling time, staffing requirements, and technology calls. This plan is revised and updated once a year. The business plan includes the same forecasts as the strategic plan except it is for a one-year horizon, with updates and revisions as management requires. The tactical forecast is a daily forecast of the number of calls offered to service representatives provided once per month and rolled over for six months. The goal for the tactical forecast is to be within a 2% error per month and within a 4 percent error on a daily basis. The operational forecast is a daily forecast of number of calls offered to service representatives and average call handle time per half-hour. It is prepared on a weekly basis and forecasted one month in advance.

The forecasting models used include exponential smoothing, linear regression, and time series, with adjustments for trend and seasonality. For example, the tactical forecast employs a time series model based on eight years of historical data with adjustments for seasonalities—that is, month, week day, and day of month. Trend adjustments are also used.

*Source:* W. Xu, "Long Range Planning for Call Centers at FedEx," *Journal of Business Forecasting* 18(4; Winter 1999–2000), pp. 7–11.

basis. For example, some restaurants are busier at lunch than at dinner, and shopping mall stores and theaters tend to have higher demand on weekends. At FedEx seasonalities include the month of the year, day of the week, and day of the month, as well as various holidays. Figure 11.2*c* illustrates a seasonal pattern in which the same demand behavior is repeated each year at the same time.

Demand behavior frequently displays several of these characteristics simultaneously. Although housing starts display cyclical behavior, there has been an upward trend in new house construction over the years. Demand for skis is seasonal; however, there has been an upward trend in the demand for winter sports equipment during the past two decades. Figure 11.2*d* displays the combination of two demand patterns, a trend with a seasonal pattern.

Instances when demand behavior exhibits no pattern are referred to as *irregular movements*, or variations. For example, a local flood might cause a momentary increase in carpet demand, or a competitor's promotional campaign might cause a company's product demand to drop for a time. Although this behavior has a cause and, thus, is not totally random, it still does not follow a pattern that can be reflected in a forecast.

## FORECASTING METHODS

Types of methods: time series, causal, and qualitative.

The factors discussed previously in this section determine to a certain extent the type of forecasting method that can or should be used. In this chapter we are going to discuss three basic types of forecasting: *time series methods, regression methods*, and *qualitative methods*.

**Regression forecasting methods:** relate demand to other factors that cause demand behavior.

*Time series* methods are statistical techniques that use historical demand data to predict future demand. **Regression** (or **causal**) **forecasting methods** attempt to develop a mathematical relationship (in the form of a regression model) between demand and factors that cause it to behave the way it does. Most of the remainder of this chapter will be about time series and regression forecasting methods. In this section we will focus our discussion on qualitative forecasting.

Management, marketing and purchasing, and engineering are sources for internal qualitative forecasts.

*Qualitative* (or judgmental) methods use management judgment, expertise, and opinion to make forecasts. Often called "the jury of executive opinion," they are the most common type of forecasting method for the long-term strategic planning process. There are normally individuals or groups within an organization whose judgments and opinions regarding the future are as valid or more valid than those of outside experts or other structured approaches. Top managers are the key group involved in the development of forecasts for strategic plans. They are generally most familiar with their firms' own capabilities and resources and the markets for their products.

The sales force of a company represents a direct point of contact with the consumer. This contact provides an awareness of consumer expectations in the future that others may not possess. Engineering personnel have an innate understanding of the technological aspects of the type of products that might be feasible and likely in the future.

Consumer, or market, research is an organized approach using surveys and other research techniques to determine what products and services customers want and will purchase, and to identify new markets and sources of customers. Consumer and market research is normally conducted by the marketing department within an organization, by industry organizations and groups, and by private marketing or consulting firms. Although market research can provide accurate and useful forecasts of product demand, it must be skillfully and correctly conducted, and it can be expensive.

**Delphi method:** involves soliciting forecasts about technological advances from experts.

The **Delphi method** is a procedure for acquiring informed judgments and opinions from knowledgeable individuals using a series of questionnaires to develop a consensus forecast about what will occur in the future. It was developed at the Rand Corporation shortly after World War II to forecast the impact of a hypothetical nuclear attack on the United States. Although the Delphi method has been used for a variety of applications, forecasting has been one of its primary uses. It has been especially useful for forecasting technological change and advances.

Technological forecasting has become increasingly crucial to compete in the modern international business environment. New enhanced computer technology, new production methods, and advanced machinery and equipment are constantly being made available to companies. These advances enable them to introduce more new products into the marketplace faster than ever before. The companies that succeed manage to get a "technological" jump on their competitors by accurately predicting what technology will be available in the future and how it can be exploited. What new products and services will be technologically feasible, when they can be introduced, and what their demand will be are questions about the future for which answers cannot be predicted from historical data. Instead, the informed opinion and judgment of experts are necessary to make these types of single, long-term forecasts.

## FORECASTING PROCESS

Forecasting is a continuous process.

Forecasting is not simply identifying and using a method to compute a numerical estimate of what demand will be in the future. It is a continuing process that requires constant monitoring and adjustment illustrated by the steps in Figure 11.3.

In the next few sections, we present several different forecasting methods applicable for different patterns of demand behavior. Thus, one of the first steps in the forecasting process is to plot the available historical demand data and, by visually looking at them, to attempt to determine the forecasting method that best seems to fit the patterns the data exhibit. Historical demand is usually past sales or orders data. There are several measures for comparing historical demand with the forecast to see how accurate the forecast is. Following our discussion of the forecasting methods, we present several measures of forecast accuracy. If the forecast does not seem to be accurate, another method can be tried until an accurate forecast method is identified. After the forecast is made over the desired planning horizon, it may be possible to use judgment, experience, knowledge of the market, or even intuition to adjust the forecast to enhance its accuracy. Finally, as demand actually occurs over the planning period, it must be monitored and compared with the forecast in order to assess the performance of the forecast method. If the forecast is accurate, then it is appropriate to continue using the forecast method. If it is not accurate, a new model or adjusting the existing one should be considered.

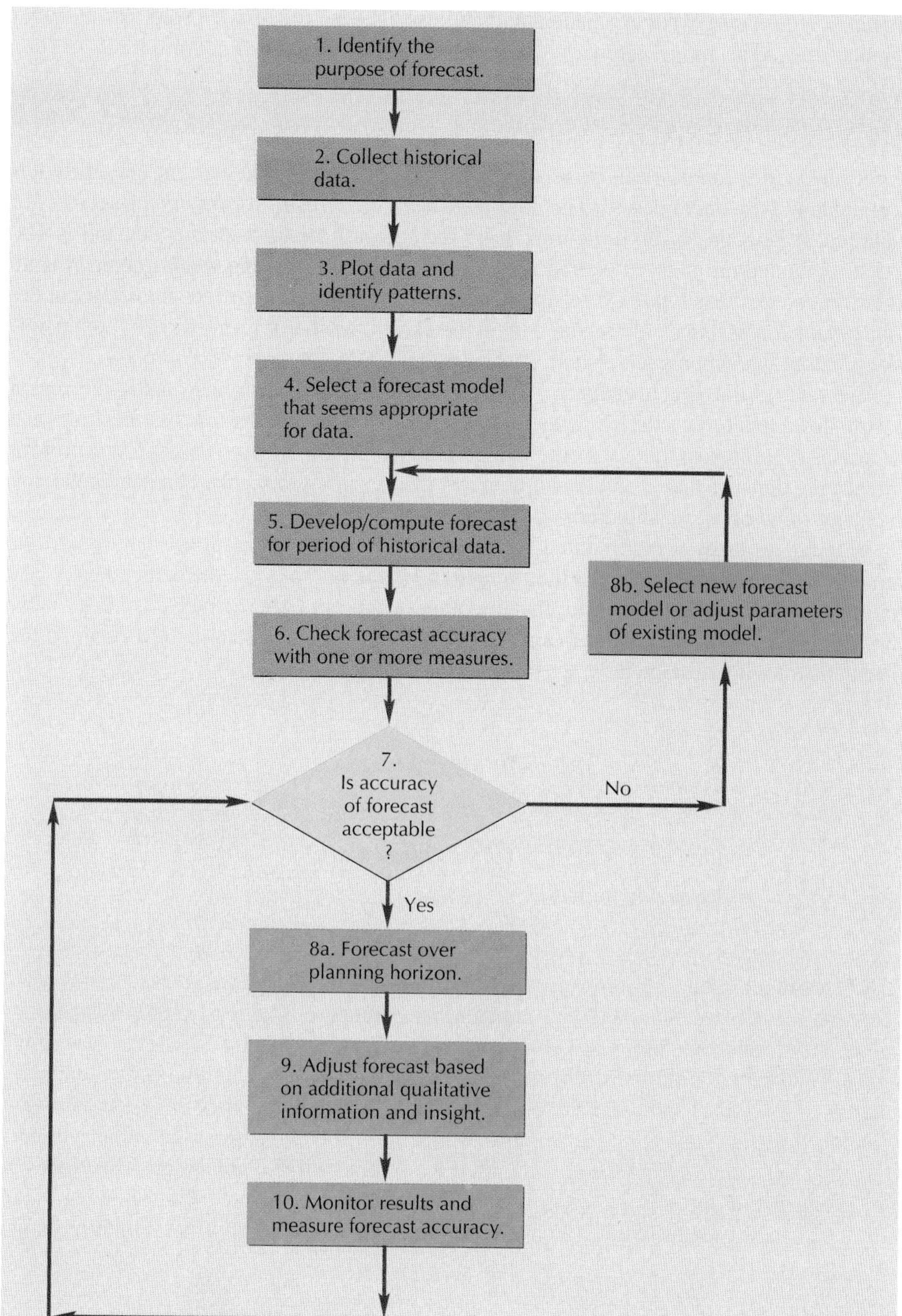


Figure 11.3
**Steps of the Forecasting Process**

## TIME SERIES METHODS

**Time series methods** are statistical techniques that make use of historical data accumulated over a period of time. Time series methods assume that what has occurred in the past will continue to occur in the future. As the name *time series* suggests, these methods relate the forecast to only one factor—time. These methods assume that identifiable historical patterns or trends for demand over time will repeat themselves. They include the moving average, exponential smoothing, and linear trend line; and they are among the most popular methods for short-range forecasting among service and manufacturing companies. In a 2002 survey of firms across different industries conducted by the Institute of Business Forecasting, over 60% of the firms used time series models, making it the most popular forecasting method by far. One of the reasons time series models are so popular is

**Time series methods:** use historical demand data over a period of time to predict future demand.

that they are relatively easy to understand and use. The survey also showed that the most popular time series models are moving averages and exponential smoothing.[1]

## MOVING AVERAGE

In a *naive* forecast demand in the current period is used as the next period's forecast.

A time series forecast can be as simple as using demand in the current period to predict demand in the next period. This is sometimes called a *naive* or *intuitive* forecast. For example, if demand is 100 units this week, the forecast for next week's demand is 100 units; if demand turns out to be 90 units instead, then the following week's demand is 90 units, and so on. This type of forecasting method does not take into account historical demand *behavior*; it relies only on demand in the current period. It reacts directly to the normal, random movements in demand.

**Moving average:** method uses average demand for a fixed sequence of periods.

Moving average is good for stable demand with no pronounced behavioral patterns.

The simple **moving average** method uses several demand values during the recent past to develop a forecast. This tends to *dampen*, or *smooth out*, the random increases and decreases of a forecast that uses only one period. The simple moving average is useful for forecasting demand that is stable and does not display any pronounced demand behavior, such as a trend or seasonal pattern.

Moving averages are computed for specific periods, such as three months or five months, depending on how much the forecaster desires to "smooth" the demand data. The longer the moving average period, the smoother it will be. (Alternatively, a shorter moving average is more susceptible to simple random variation.) The formula for computing the simple moving average is

$$MA_n = \frac{\sum_{i=1}^{n} D_i}{n}$$

where

$n$ = number of periods in the moving average

$D_i$ = demand in period $i$

Example 11.1

**Computing a Simple Moving Average**

The Heartland Produce Company sells and delivers food produce to restaurants and catering services within a 100-mile radius of its warehouse. The food supply business is competitive, and the ability to deliver orders promptly is a factor in getting new customers and keeping old ones. The manager of the company wants to be certain enough drivers and vehicles are available to deliver orders promptly and they have adequate inventory in stock. Therefore, the manager wants to be able to forecast the number of orders that will occur during the next month (i.e., to forecast the demand for deliveries).

From records of delivery orders, management has accumulated the following data for the past 10 months, from which it wants to compute three- and five-month moving averages.

| Month | Orders |
|---|---|
| January | 120 |
| February | 90 |
| March | 100 |
| April | 75 |
| May | 110 |
| June | 50 |
| July | 75 |
| August | 130 |
| September | 110 |
| October | 90 |

[1] C. L. Jain, "Benchmarking Forecasting Models," *Journal of Business Forecasting* 21(3; Fall 2002), pp. 18–20.

*Solution*

Let us assume that it is the end of October. The forecast resulting from either the three- or the five-month moving average is typically for the next month in the sequence, which in this case is November. The moving average is computed from the demand for orders for the prior three months in the sequence according to the following formula:

$$MA_3 = \frac{\sum_{i=1}^{3} D_i}{3} = \frac{90 + 110 + 130}{3} = 110 \text{ orders for November}$$

The five-month moving average is computed from the prior five months of demand data as follows:

$$MA_5 = \frac{\sum_{i=1}^{5} D_i}{5} = \frac{90 + 110 + 130 + 75 + 50}{5} = 91 \text{ orders for November}$$

The three- and five-month moving average forecasts for all the months of demand data are shown in the following table. Actually, the manager would use only the forecast for November based on the most recent monthly demand. However, the earlier forecasts for prior months allow us to compare the forecast with actual demand to see how accurate the forecasting method is—that is, how well it does.

**Three- and Five-Month Averages**

| Month | Orders per Month | Three-Month Moving Average | Five-Month Moving Average |
|---|---|---|---|
| January | 120 | — | — |
| February | 90 | — | — |
| March | 100 | — | — |
| April | 75 | 103.3 | — |
| May | 110 | 88.3 | — |
| June | 50 | 95.0 | 99.0 |
| July | 75 | 78.3 | 85.0 |
| August | 130 | 78.3 | 82.0 |
| September | 110 | 85.0 | 88.0 |
| October | 90 | 105.0 | 95.0 |
| November | — | 110.0 | 91.0 |

Both moving average forecasts in the preceding table tend to smooth out the variability occurring in the actual data. This smoothing effect can be observed in the following figure in which the three-month and five-month averages have been superimposed on a graph of the original data:

are easy to understand by management. Virtually all forecasting computer software packages include modules for exponential smoothing. Most importantly, exponential smoothing has a good track record of success. It has been employed over the years by many companies that have found it to be an accurate method of forecasting.

The exponential smoothing forecast is computed using the formula

$$F_{t+1} = \alpha D_t + (1 - \alpha)F_t$$

where

$F_{t+1}$ = the forecast for the next period

$D_t$ = actual demand in the present period

$F_t$ = the previously determined forecast for the present period

$\alpha$ = a weighting factor referred to as the **smoothing constant**

**Smoothing constant:** the weighting factor given to the most recent data in exponential smoothing forecasts.

The smoothing constant, $\alpha$, is between 0.0 and 1.0. It reflects the weight given to the most recent demand data. For example, if $\alpha = 0.20$,

$$F_{t+1} = 0.20D_t + 0.80F_t$$

which means that our forecast for the next period is based on 20% of recent demand ($D_t$) and 80% of past demand (in the form of forecast $F_t$, since $F_t$ is derived from previous demands and forecasts). If we go to one extreme and let $\alpha = 0.0$, then

$$\begin{aligned} F_{t+1} &= 0D_t + 1F_t \\ &= F_t \end{aligned}$$

and the forecast for the next period is the same as the forecast for this period. In other words, *the forecast does not reflect the most recent demand at all.*

On the other hand, if $\alpha = 1.0$, then

$$\begin{aligned} F_{t+1} &= 1D_t + 0F_t \\ &= 1D_t \end{aligned}$$

The closer $\alpha$ is to 1.0, the greater the reaction to the most recent demand.

and we have considered only the most recent data (demand in the present period) and nothing else. Thus, the higher $\alpha$ is, the more sensitive the forecast will be to changes in recent demand, and the smoothing will be less. The closer $\alpha$ is to zero, the greater will be the dampening, or smoothing, effect. As $\alpha$ approaches zero, the forecast will react and adjust more slowly to differences between the actual demand and the forecasted demand.

*At many service-oriented businesses like fast food restaurants quality service often equates with fast service. Taco Bell, like this one at UCLA, needs an accurate forecast of customer demand at different times during the day in order to provide fast, good quality service during peak demand periods around lunch and dinner and between classes.*

The most commonly used values of $\alpha$ are in the range of 0.01 to 0.50. However, the determination of $\alpha$ is usually judgmental and subjective and is often based on trial-and-error experimentation. An inaccurate estimate of $\alpha$ can limit the usefulness of this forecasting technique.

Example 11.3

**Computing an Exponentially Smoothed Forecast**

HiTek Computer Services repairs and services personal computers at its store, and it makes local service calls. It primarily uses part-time State University students as technicians. The company has had steady growth since it started. It purchases generic computer parts in volume at a discount from a variety of sources whenever they see a good deal. Thus, they need a good forecast of demand for repairs so that they will know how many computer component parts to purchase and stock, and how many technicians to hire.

The company has accumulated the demand data shown in the accompanying table for repair and service calls for the past 12 months, from which it wants to consider exponential smoothing forecasts using smoothing constants ($\alpha$) equal to 0.30 and 0.50.

**Demand for Repair and Service Calls**

| Period | Month | Demand | Period | Month | Demand |
|---|---|---|---|---|---|
| 1 | January | 37 | 7 | July | 43 |
| 2 | February | 40 | 8 | August | 47 |
| 3 | March | 41 | 9 | September | 56 |
| 4 | April | 37 | 10 | October | 52 |
| 5 | May | 45 | 11 | November | 55 |
| 6 | June | 50 | 12 | December | 54 |

*Solution*

To develop the series of forecasts for the data in this table, we will start with period 1 (January) and compute the forecast for period 2 (February) using $\alpha = 0.30$. The formula for exponential smoothing also requires a forecast for period 1, which we do not have, so we will use the demand for period 1 as both *demand* and *forecast* for period 1. (Other ways to determine a starting forecast include averaging the first three or four periods or making a subjective estimate.) Thus, the forecast for February is

$$\begin{aligned} F_2 &= \alpha D_1 + (1 - \alpha)F_1 \\ &= (0.30)(37) + (0.70)(37) \\ &= 37 \text{ service calls} \end{aligned}$$

The forecast for period 3 is computed similarly:

$$\begin{aligned} F_3 &= \alpha D_2 + (1 - \alpha)F_2 \\ &= (0.30)(40) + (0.70)(37) \\ &= 37.9 \text{ service calls} \end{aligned}$$

The remainder of the monthly forecasts are shown in the following table. The final forecast is for period 13, January, and is the forecast of interest to HiTek:

$$\begin{aligned} F_{13} &= \alpha D_{12} + (1 - \alpha)F_{12} \\ &= (0.30)(54) + (0.70)(50.84) \\ &= 51.79 \text{ service calls} \end{aligned}$$

**Exponential Smoothing Forecasts, α = 0.30 and α = 0.50**

| | | | Forecast, $F_{t+1}$ | |
|---|---|---|---|---|
| **Period** | **Month** | **Demand** | **α = 0.30** | **α = 0.50** |
| 1 | January | 37 | — | — |
| 2 | February | 40 | 37.00 | 37.00 |
| 3 | March | 41 | 37.90 | 38.50 |
| 4 | April | 37 | 38.83 | 39.75 |
| 5 | May | 45 | 38.28 | 38.37 |
| 6 | June | 50 | 40.29 | 41.68 |
| 7 | July | 43 | 43.20 | 45.84 |
| 8 | August | 47 | 43.14 | 44.42 |
| 9 | September | 56 | 44.30 | 45.71 |
| 10 | October | 52 | 47.81 | 50.85 |
| 11 | November | 55 | 49.06 | 51.42 |
| 12 | December | 54 | 50.84 | 53.21 |
| 13 | January | — | 51.79 | 53.61 |

This table also includes the forecast values using α = 0.50. Both exponential smoothing forecasts are shown in the following figure together with the actual data.

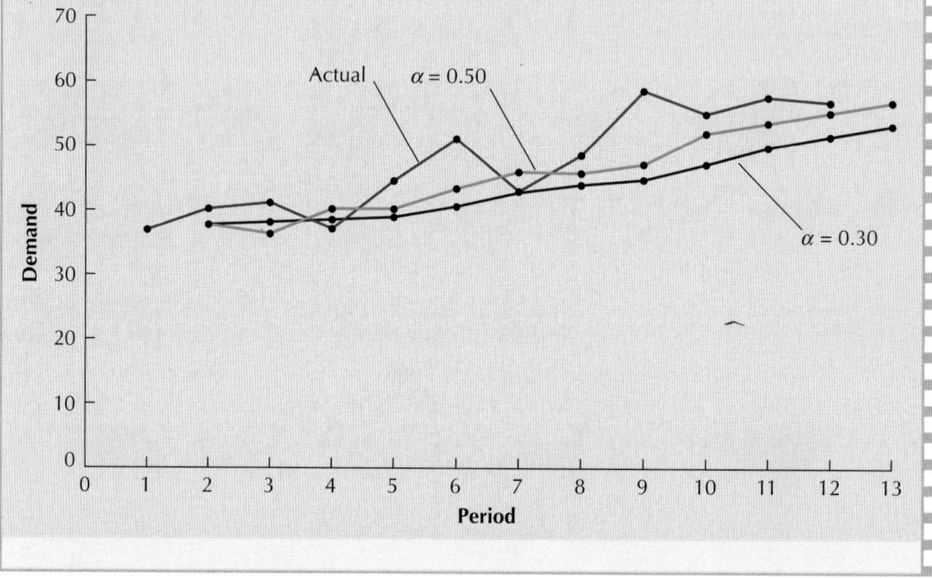


In Example 11.3, the forecast using the higher smoothing constant, α = 0.50, seems to react more strongly to changes in demand than does the forecast with α = 0.30, although both smooth out the random fluctuations in the forecast. Notice that both forecasts lag behind the actual demand. For example, a pronounced downward change in demand in July is not reflected in the forecast until August. If these changes mark a change in trend (i.e., a long-term upward or downward movement) rather than just a random fluctuation, then the forecast will always lag behind this trend. We can see a general upward trend in service calls throughout the year. Both forecasts tend to be consistently lower than the actual demand; that is, the forecasts lag the trend.

Based on simple observation of the two forecasts in Example 11.3, α = 0.50 seems to be the more accurate of the two in the sense that it seems to follow the actual data more closely. (Later in this chapter we discuss several quantitative methods for determining forecast accuracy.) When demand is relatively stable without any trend, a small value for α is more appropriate to simply smooth out the forecast. When actual demand displays an increasing (or decreasing) trend, as is the case in the figure, a larger value of α is better. It will react more quickly to more recent upward or downward movements in the actual data. In some approaches to exponential smoothing, the accuracy of the forecast is monitored in terms of the difference between the actual values and the forecasted values. If these differences become larger, then $\alpha$ is changed (higher or lower) in an attempt to adapt the forecast to the actual data. However, the exponential smoothing forecast can also be adjusted for the effects of a trend.

In Example 11.3, the final forecast computed was for one month, January. A forecast for two or three months could have been computed by grouping the demand data into the required number of periods and then using these values in the exponential smoothing computations. For example, if a three-month forecast were needed, demand for January, February, and March could be summed and used to compute the average forecast for the next three-month period, and so on, until a final three-month forecast results. Alternatively, if a trend is present, the final period forecast can be used for an extended forecast by adjusting it by a trend factor.

## ADJUSTED EXPONENTIAL SMOOTHING

The **adjusted exponential smoothing forecast** consists of the exponential smoothing forecast with a trend adjustment factor added to it:

**Adjusted exponential smoothing forecast:** an exponential smoothing forecast with an adjustment for a trend added to it.

$$AF_{t+1} = F_{t+1} + T_{t+1}$$

where

$T$ = an exponentially smoothed trend factor

The trend factor is computed much the same as the exponentially smoothed forecast. It is, in effect, a forecast model for trend:

$$T_{t+1} = \beta(F_{t+1} - F_t) + (1 - \beta)T_t$$

where

$T_t$ = the last period's trend factor

$\beta$ = a smoothing constant for trend

$\beta$ is a value between 0.0 and 1.0. It reflects the weight given to the most recent trend data. $\beta$ is usually determined subjectively based on the judgment of the forecaster. A high $\beta$ reflects trend changes more than a low $\beta$. It is not uncommon for $\beta$ to equal $\alpha$ in this method.

The closer $\beta$ is to 1.0 the stronger the trend is reflected.

Notice that this formula for the trend factor reflects a weighted measure of the increase (or decrease) between the next period forecast, $F_{t+1}$, and the current forecast, $F_t$.

Example 11.4

**Computing an Adjusted Exponentially Smoothed Forecast**

HiTek Computer Services now wants to develop an adjusted exponentially smoothed forecast using the same 12 months of demand shown in the table for Example 11.3. It will use the exponentially smoothed forecast with $\alpha = 0.5$ computed in Example 11.3 with a smoothing constant for trend, $\beta$, of 0.30.

*Solution*

The formula for the adjusted exponential smoothing forecast requires an initial value for $T_t$ to start the computational process. This initial trend factor is often an estimate determined subjectively or based on past data by the forecaster. In this case, since we have a long sequence of demand data (i.e., 12 months) we will start with the trend $T_t$ equal to zero. By the time the forecast value of interest $F_{13}$ is computed, we should have a relatively good value for the trend factor.

The adjusted forecast for February, $AF_2$, is the same as the exponentially smoothed forecast, since the trend computing factor will be zero (i.e., $F_1$ and $F_2$ are the same and $T_2 = 0$). Thus, we compute the adjusted forecast for March, $AF_3$, as follows, starting with the determination of the trend factor, $T_3$:

$$\begin{aligned} T_3 &= \beta(F_3 - F_2) + (1 - \beta)T_2 \\ &= (0.30)(38.5 - 37.0) + (0.70)(0) \\ &= 0.45 \end{aligned}$$

and

$$\begin{aligned} AF_3 &= F_3 + T_3 \\ &= 38.5 + 0.45 \\ &= 38.95 \text{ service cells} \end{aligned}$$

This adjusted forecast value for period 3 is shown in the accompanying table, with all other adjusted forecast values for the 12-month period plus the forecast for period 13, computed as follows:

$$\begin{aligned} T_{13} &= \beta(F_{13} - F_{12}) + (1 - \beta)T_{12} \\ &= (0.30)(53.61 - 53.21) + (0.70)(1.77) \\ &= 1.36 \end{aligned}$$

and

$$\begin{aligned} AF_{13} &= F_{13} + T_{13} \\ &= 53.61 + 1.36 \\ &= 54.97 \text{ service calls} \end{aligned}$$

**Adjusted Exponential Smoothing Forecast Values**

| Period | Month | Demand | Forecast $F_{t+1}$ | Trend $T_{t+1}$ | Adjusted Forecast $AF_{t+1}$ |
|---|---|---|---|---|---|
| 1 | January | 37 | 37.00 | — | — |
| 2 | February | 40 | 37.00 | 0.00 | 37.00 |
| 3 | March | 41 | 38.50 | 0.45 | 38.95 |
| 4 | April | 37 | 39.75 | 0.69 | 40.44 |
| 5 | May | 45 | 38.37 | 0.07 | 38.44 |
| 6 | June | 50 | 41.68 | 1.04 | 42.73 |
| 7 | July | 43 | 45.84 | 1.97 | 47.82 |
| 8 | August | 47 | 44.42 | 0.95 | 45.37 |
| 9 | September | 56 | 45.71 | 1.05 | 46.76 |
| 10 | October | 52 | 50.85 | 2.28 | 53.13 |
| 11 | November | 55 | 51.42 | 1.76 | 53.19 |
| 12 | December | 54 | 53.21 | 1.77 | 54.98 |
| 13 | January | — | 53.61 | 1.36 | 54.96 |

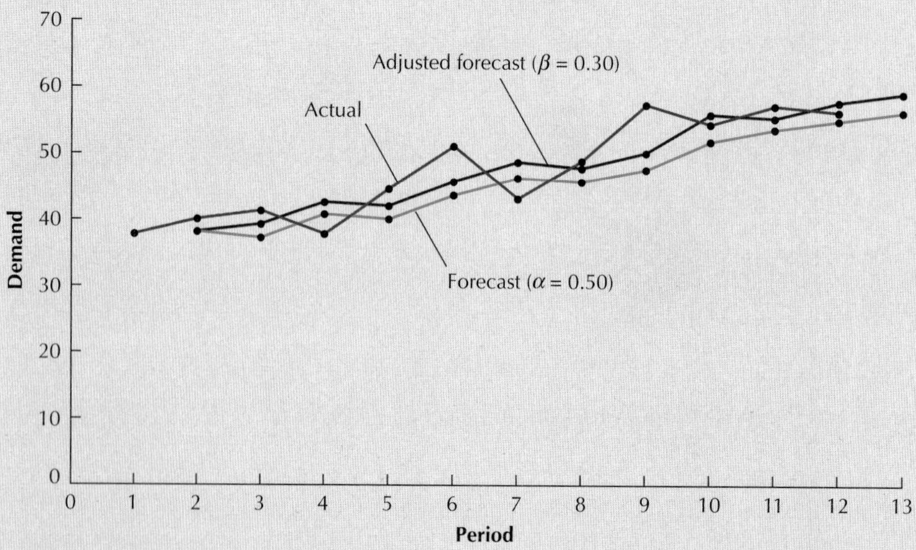


The adjusted exponentially smoothed forecast values shown in the table are compared with the exponentially smoothed forecast values and the actual data in the figure. Notice that the adjusted forecast is consistently higher than the exponentially smoothed forecast and is thus more reflective of the generally increasing trend of the actual data. However, in general, the pattern, or degree of smoothing, is very similar for both forecasts.

## LINEAR TREND LINE

Linear regression is a causal method of forecasting in which a mathematical relationship is developed between demand and some other factor that causes demand behavior. However, when demand displays an obvious trend over time, a least squares regression line, or **linear trend line**, that relates demand to time, can be used to forecast demand.

**Linear trend line:** a linear regression model relating demand to time.

A linear trend line relates a dependent variable, which for our purposes is demand, to one independent variable, time, in the form of a linear equation:

$$y = a + bx$$

where

$a$ = intercept (at period 0)

$b$ = slope of the line

$x$ = the time period

$y$ = forecast for demand for period $x$

These parameters of the linear trend line can be calculated using the least squares formulas for linear regression:

$$b = \frac{\sum xy - n\overline{x}\overline{y}}{\sum x^2 - n\overline{x}^2}$$

$$a = \overline{y} - b\overline{x}$$

where

$n$ = number of periods

$\overline{x} = \frac{\sum x}{n}$ = the mean of the $x$ values

$\overline{y} = \frac{\sum y}{n}$ = the mean of the $y$ values

Example 11.5

**Computing a Linear Trend Line**

The data for HiTek Computer Services (shown in the table for Example 11.3) appears to follow an increasing linear trend. The company wants to compute a linear trend line to see if it is more accurate than the exponential smoothing and adjusted exponential smoothing forecasts developed in Examples 11.3 and 11.4.

*Solution*

The values required for the least squares calculations are as follows:

**Least Squares Calculations**

| *x* (period) | *y* (demand) | *xy* | $x^2$ |
|---|---|---|---|
| 1 | 37 | 37 | 1 |
| 2 | 40 | 80 | 4 |
| 3 | 41 | 123 | 9 |
| 4 | 37 | 148 | 16 |
| 5 | 45 | 225 | 25 |
| 6 | 50 | 300 | 36 |
| 7 | 43 | 301 | 49 |
| 8 | 47 | 376 | 64 |
| 9 | 56 | 504 | 81 |
| 10 | 52 | 520 | 100 |
| 11 | 55 | 605 | 121 |
| 12 | 54 | 648 | 144 |
| 78 | 557 | 3867 | 650 |

Using these values, we can compute the parameters for the linear trend line as follows:

$$\bar{x} = \frac{78}{12} = 6.5$$

$$\bar{y} = \frac{557}{12} = 46.42$$

$$b = \frac{\sum xy - n\bar{x}\bar{y}}{\sum x^2 - n\bar{x}^2}$$

$$= \frac{3867 - (12)(6.5)(46.42)}{650 - 12(6.5)^2}$$

$$= 1.72$$

$$a = \bar{y} - b\bar{x}$$

$$= 46.42 - (1.72)(6.5)$$

$$= 35.2$$

Therefore, the linear trend line equation is

$$y = 35.2 + 1.72x$$

To calculate a forecast for period 13, let $x = 13$ in the linear trend line:

$$y = 35.2 + 1.72(13)$$

$$= 57.56 \text{ service cells}$$

The following graph shows the linear trend line compared with the actual data. The trend line appears to reflect closely the actual data—that is, to be a good fit—and would thus be a good forecast model for this problem. However, a disadvantage of the linear trend line is that it will not adjust to a change in the trend, as the exponential smoothing forecast methods will; that is, it is assumed that all future forecasts will follow a straight line. This limits the use of this method to a shorter time frame in which you can be relatively certain that the trend will not change.

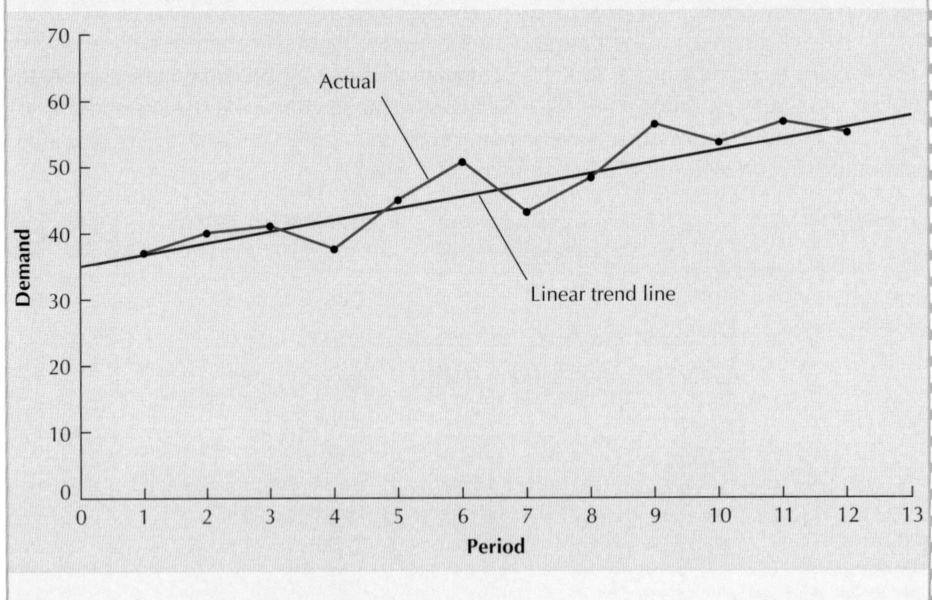


## SEASONAL ADJUSTMENTS

A seasonal pattern is a repetitive increase and decrease in demand. Many demand items exhibit seasonal behavior. Clothing sales follow annual seasonal patterns, with demand for warm clothes increasing in the fall and winter and declining in the spring and summer as the demand for cooler clothing increases. Demand for many retail items, including toys, sports equipment, clothing, electronic appliances, hams, turkeys, wine, and fruit, increase during the holiday season. Greeting card demand increases in conjunction

*Snow skiing is an industry that exhibits several different patterns of demand behavior. It is primarily a seasonal (i.e., winter) industry and over a long period of time the snow skiing industry has exhibited a generally increasing growth trend. Random factors can cause variations, or abrupt peaks and valleys, in demand. For example, demand for skiing products showed a pronounced increase after the 2002 Winter Olympics in Salt Lake City. Conversely, warm weather and a lack of snow in some regions of the United States during several winters in the 1990s depressed the skiing industry, resulting in decreased demand.*

with special days such as Valentine's Day and Mother's Day. Seasonal patterns can also occur on a monthly, weekly, or even daily basis. Some restaurants have higher demand in the evening than at lunch or on weekends as opposed to weekdays. Traffic—hence sales—at shopping malls picks up on Friday and Saturday.

There are several methods for reflecting seasonal patterns in a time series forecast. We will describe one of the simpler methods using a *seasonal factor*. A **seasonal factor** is a numerical value that is multiplied by the normal forecast to get a seasonally adjusted forecast.

**Seasonal factor:** adjust for seasonality by multiplying the normal forecast by a seasonal factor.

One method for developing a demand for seasonal factors is to divide the demand for each seasonal period by total annual demand, according to the following formula:

$$S_i = \frac{D_i}{\Sigma D}$$

The resulting seasonal factors between 0 and 1.0 are, in effect, the portion of total annual demand assigned to each season. These seasonal factors are multiplied by the annual forecasted demand to yield adjusted forecasts for each season.

**Example 11.6**

**Computing a Forecast with Seasonal Adjustments**

Wishbone Farms grows turkeys to sell to a meat-processing company throughout the year. However, its peak season is obviously during the fourth quarter of the year, from October to December. Wishbone Farms has experienced the demand for turkeys for the past three years shown in the following table:

**Demand for Turkeys at Wishbone Farms**

| | Demand (1000s) per Quarter | | | | |
|---|---|---|---|---|---|
| **Year** | *1* | *2* | *3* | *4* | **Total** |
| 2002 | 12.6 | 8.6 | 6.3 | 17.5 | 45.0 |
| 2003 | 14.1 | 10.3 | 7.5 | 18.2 | 50.1 |
| 2004 | 15.3 | 10.6 | 8.1 | 19.6 | 53.6 |
| Total | 42.0 | 29.5 | 21.9 | 55.3 | 148.7 |

*Solution*

Because we have three years of demand data, we can compute the seasonal factors by dividing total quarterly demand for the three years by total demand across all three years:

$$S_1 = \frac{D_1}{\Sigma D} = \frac{42.0}{148.7} = 0.28$$

$$S_2 = \frac{D_2}{\Sigma D} = \frac{29.5}{148.7} = 0.20$$

$$S_3 = \frac{D_3}{\Sigma D} = \frac{21.9}{148.7} = 0.15$$

$$S_4 = \frac{D_4}{\Sigma D} = \frac{55.3}{148.7} = 0.37$$

Next, we want to multiply the forecasted demand for the next year, 2005, by each of the seasonal factors to get the forecasted demand for each quarter. To accomplish this, we need a demand forecast for 2005. In this case, since the demand data in the table seem to exhibit a generally increasing trend, we compute a linear trend line for the three years of data in the table to get a rough forecast estimate:

$$\begin{aligned} y &= 40.97 + 4.30x \\ &= 40.97 + 4.30(4) \\ &= 58.17 \end{aligned}$$

Thus, the forecast for 2005 is 58.17, or 58,170 turkeys.

Using this annual forecast of demand, we find that the seasonally adjusted forecasts, $\text{SF}_i$, for 2005 are

$$\begin{aligned} \text{SF}_1 &= (S_1)(F_5) = (0.28)(58.17) = 16.28 \\ \text{SF}_2 &= (S_2)(F_5) = (0.20)(58.17) = 11.63 \\ \text{SF}_3 &= (S_3)(F_5) = (0.15)(58.17) = 8.73 \\ \text{SF}_4 &= (\text{S}_4)(\text{F}_5) = (0.37)(58.17) = 21.53 \end{aligned}$$

Comparing these quarterly forecasts with the actual demand values in the table, we see that they would seem to be relatively good forecast estimates, reflecting both the seasonal variations in the data and the general upward trend.

## THE COMPETITIVE EDGE

### Seasonal Forecasting at Dell

Dell Inc. sells computer systems directly to customers via phone or Internet orders. Once an order is received and processed, it is sent to an assembly plant in Austin, Texas, where it builds, tests, and packages a product within eight hours. Dell's direct-sales model is dependent on its arrangement with its suppliers, many of which are located in Southeast Asia with shipping times to Austin from 7 to 30 days. To compensate for these long lead times, Dell requires its suppliers to keep specified (i.e., target) inventory levels—typically 10 days of inventory—on hand at small warehouses called revolvers (short for revolving inventory). In a vendor-managed inventory (VMI) arrangement (see Chapter 10), Dell's suppliers determine how much inventory to order and when to order to meet Dell's target inventory levels at the revolvers. To help its suppliers make good ordering decisions Dell shares its demand forecast with them on a monthly basis. Dell uses a six-month rolling forecast developed by its marketing department that is updated weekly. Buyers receive weekly forecasts from commodity teams that break the forecasts down for specific parts and components. These forecasts reflect product-specific trends and seasonality. For home computer systems, Christmas is the major sales period of the year. Other high-demand periods include back-to-school season and the end of the year when the government makes big purchases.

*Source:* R. Kapuscinski, R. Zhang, P. Carbonneau, R. Moore, and B. Reeves, "Inventory Decisions in Dell's Supply Chain," *Interfaces* 34(3; May–June 2004), pp. 191–205.

*Turkeys are an example of a product with a long-term trend for increasing demand with a seasonal pattern. Turkey sales show a distinct seasonal pattern by increasing markedly during the Thanksgiving holiday season. For example, turkey sales are lowest from January to May, they begin to rise in June and July and peak in August when distributors begin to build up their inventory of frozen turkeys for increased sales in November. Sales remain high for September, October, and November and then begin to decline in December and January.*

## FORECAST ACCURACY

A forecast is never completely accurate; forecasts will always deviate from the actual demand. This difference between the forecast and the actual is the **forecast error**. Although forecast error is inevitable, the objective of forecasting is that it be as slight as possible. A large degree of error may indicate that either the forecasting technique is the wrong one or it needs to be adjusted by changing its parameters (for example, $\alpha$ in the exponential smoothing forecast).

**Forecast error:** the difference between the forecast and actual demand.

There are different measures of forecast error. We will discuss several of the more popular ones: mean absolute deviation (MAD), mean absolute percent deviation (MAPD), cumulative error, and average error or bias ($\bar{E}$).

## MEAN ABSOLUTE DEVIATION

The **mean absolute deviation**, or **MAD**, is one of the most popular and simplest to use measures of forecast error. MAD is an average of the difference between the forecast and actual demand, as computed by the following formula:

**MAD:** the average, absolute difference between the forecast and demand.

$$\text{MAD} = \frac{\Sigma|D_t - F_t|}{n}$$

where

$t$ = the period number

$D_t$ = demand in period $t$

$F_t$ = the forecast for period $t$

$n$ = the total number of periods

$| \,|$ = absolute value

Example 11.7

**Measuring Forecasting Accuracy with MAD**

In Examples 11.3, 11.4, and 11.5, forecasts were developed using exponential smoothing, ($\alpha = 0.30$ and $\alpha = 0.50$), adjusted exponential smoothing ($\alpha = 0.50$, $\beta = 0.30$), and a linear trend line, respectively, for the demand data for HiTek Computer Services. The company wants to compare the accuracy of these different forecasts using MAD.

*Solution*

We will compute MAD for all four forecasts; however, we will present the computational detail for the exponential smoothing forecast with $\alpha = 0.30$ only. The following table shows the values necessary to compute MAD for the exponential smoothing forecast:

**Computational Values for MAD**

| Period | Demand, $D_t$ | Forecast $F_t(\alpha = 0.30)$ | Error ($e_t$) $(D_t - F_t)$ | $\lvert D_t - F_t \rvert$ |
|---|---|---|---|---|
| 1 | 37 | 37.00 | — | — |
| 2 | 40 | 37.00 | 3.00 | 3.00 |
| 3 | 41 | 37.90 | 3.10 | 3.10 |
| 4 | 37 | 38.83 | −1.83 | 1.83 |
| 5 | 45 | 38.28 | 6.72 | 6.72 |
| 6 | 50 | 40.29 | 9.69 | 9.69 |
| 7 | 43 | 43.20 | −0.20 | 0.20 |
| 8 | 47 | 43.14 | 3.86 | 3.86 |
| 9 | 56 | 44.30 | 11.70 | 11.70 |
| 10 | 52 | 47.81 | 4.19 | 4.19 |
| 11 | 55 | 49.06 | 5.94 | 5.94 |
| 12 | 54 | 50.84 | 3.15 | 3.15 |
| | 557 | | 49.32 | 53.38[a] |

[a]The computation of MAD will be based on 11 periods, periods 2 through 12, excluding the initial demand and forecast values for period 1 since they both equal 37.

Using the data in the table, MAD is computed as

$$\text{MAD} = \frac{\Sigma \lvert D_t - F_t \rvert}{n}$$

$$= \frac{53.39}{11}$$

$$= 4.85$$

The lower the value of MAD, relative to the magnitude of the data, the more accurate the forecast.

The smaller the value of MAD, the more accurate the forecast, although viewed alone, MAD is difficult to assess. In this example, the data values were relatively small, and the MAD value of 4.85 should be judged accordingly. Overall, it would seem to be a "low" value; that is, the forecast appears to be relatively accurate. However, if the magnitude of the data values were in the thousands or millions, then a MAD value of a similar magnitude might not be bad either. The point is, you cannot compare a MAD value of 4.85 with a MAD value of 485 and say the former is good and the latter is bad; they depend to a certain extent on the relative magnitude of the data.

One benefit of MAD is to compare the accuracy of several different forecasting techniques, as we are doing in this example. The MAD values for the remaining forecasts are as follows:

Exponential smoothing($\alpha = 0.50$): MAD = 4.04

Adjusted exponential smoothing ($\alpha = 0.50$, $\beta = 0.30$): MAD = 3.81

Linear trend line: MAD = 2.29

Since the linear trend line has the lowest MAD value of 2.29, it would seem to be the most accurate, although it does not appear to be significantly better than the adjusted exponential smoothing forecast. Furthermore, we can deduce from these MAD values that increasing $\alpha$ from 0.30 to 0.50 enhanced the accuracy of the exponentially smoothed forecast. The adjusted forecast is even more accurate.

The **mean absolute percent deviation (MAPD)** measures the absolute error as a percentage of demand rather than per period. As a result, it eliminates the problem of interpreting the measure of accuracy relative to the magnitude of the demand and forecast values, as MAD does. The mean absolute percent deviation is computed according to the following formula:

**MAPD:** the absolute error as a percentage of demand.

$$\text{MAPD} = \frac{\Sigma |D_t - F_t|}{\Sigma D_t}$$

Using the data from the table in Example 11.7 for the exponential smoothing forecast ($\alpha = 0.30$) for HiTek Computer Services,

$$\begin{aligned}\text{MAPD} &= \frac{53.39}{557} \\ &= 0.096 \text{ or } 9.6\%\end{aligned}$$

A lower % deviation implies a more accurate forecast. The MAPD values for our other three forecasts are

$$\begin{aligned}\text{Exponential smoothing } (\alpha = 0.50)\text{:} \quad & \text{MAPD} = 7.9\% \\ \text{Adjusted exponential smoothing } (\alpha = 0.50, \beta = 0.30)\text{:} \quad & \text{MAPD} = 7.5\% \\ \text{Linear trend line:} \quad & \text{MAPD} = 4.9\%\end{aligned}$$

## CUMULATIVE ERROR

**Cumulative error** is computed simply by summing the forecast errors, as shown in the following formula.

**Cumulative error:** the sum of the forecast errors.

$$E = \Sigma e_t$$

A large positive value indicates that the forecast is probably consistently lower than the actual demand, or is biased low. A large negative value implies that the forecast is consistently higher than actual demand, or is biased high. Also, when the errors for each period are scrutinized, a preponderance of positive values shows the forecast is consistently less than the actual value and vice versa.

Large $+E$ indicates forecast is biased low; large $-E$, forecast is biased high.

The cumulative error for the exponential smoothing forecast ($\alpha = 0.30$) for HiTek Computer Services can be read directly from the table in Example 11.7; it is simply the sum of the values in the "Error" column:

$$\begin{aligned}E &= \Sigma e_t \\ &= 49.31\end{aligned}$$

This large positive error for cumulative error, plus the fact that the individual errors for all but two of the periods in the table are positive, indicates that this forecast is consistently below the actual demand. A quick glance back at the plot of the exponential smoothing ($\alpha = 0.30$) forecast in Example 11.3 visually verifies this result.

The cumulative error for the other forecasts are

$$\begin{aligned}\text{Exponential smoothing } (\alpha = 0.50)\text{:} \quad & E = 33.21 \\ \text{Adjusted exponential smoothing } (\alpha = 0.50, \beta = 0.30)\text{:} \quad & E = 21.14\end{aligned}$$

We did not show the cumulative error for the linear trend line. $E$ will always be near zero for the linear trend line.

A measure closely related to cumulative error is the **average error**, or *bias*. It is computed by averaging the cumulative error over the number of time periods:

**Average error:** the per-period average of cumulative error.

$$\bar{E} = \frac{\Sigma e_t}{n}$$

**Table 11.1**
**Comparison of Forecasts for HiTek Computer Services**

| Forecast | MAD | MAPD | $E$ | $\bar{E}$ |
|---|---|---|---|---|
| Exponential smoothing ($\alpha = 0.30$) | 4.85 | 9.6% | 49.31 | 4.48 |
| Exponential smoothing ($\alpha = 0.50$) | 4.04 | 8.5% | 33.21 | 3.02 |
| Adjusted exponential smoothing ($\alpha = 0.50$, $\beta = 0.30$) | 3.81 | 7.5% | 21.14 | 1.92 |
| Linear trend line | 2.29 | 4.9% | — | — |

For example, the average error for the exponential smoothing forecast ($\alpha = 0.30$) is computed as follows. (Notice a value of 11 was used for $n$, since we used actual demand for the first-period forecast, resulting in no error, that is, $D_1 = F_1 = 37$.)

$$\bar{E} = \frac{49.32}{11} = 4.48$$

The average error is interpreted similarly to the cumulative error. A positive value indicates low bias, and a negative value indicates high bias. A value close to zero implies a lack of bias.

Table 11.1 summarizes the measures of forecast accuracy we have discussed in this section for the four example forecasts we developed in Examples 11.3, 11.4, and 11.5 for HiTek Computer Services. The results are consistent for all four forecasts, indicating that for the HiTek Computer Services example data, a larger value of $\alpha$ is preferable for the exponential smoothing forecast. The adjusted forecast is more accurate than the exponential smoothing forecasts, and the linear trend is more accurate than all the others. Although these results are for specific examples, they indicate how the different forecast measures for accuracy can be used to adjust a forecasting method or select the best method.

## FORECAST CONTROL

There are several ways to monitor forecast error over time to make sure that the forecast is performing correctly—that is, the forecast is in control. Forecasts can go "out of control" and start providing inaccurate forecasts for several reasons, including a change in trend, the unanticipated appearance of a cycle, or an irregular variation such as unseasonable weather, a promotional campaign, new competition, or a political event that distracts consumers.

**Tracking signal:** monitors the forecast to see if it is biased high or low.

A **tracking signal** indicates if the forecast is consistently biased high or low. It is computed by dividing the cumulative error by MAD, according to the formula

$$\text{Tracking signal} = \frac{\Sigma(D_t - F_t)}{\text{MAD}} = \frac{E}{\text{MAD}}$$

The tracking signal is recomputed each period, with updated, "running" values of cumulative error and MAD. The movement of the tracking signal is compared to *control limits*; as long as the tracking signal is within these limits, the forecast is in control.

Typically, forecast errors are normally distributed, which results in the following relationship between MAD and the standard deviation of the distribution of error, $\sigma$:

$$1 \text{ MAD} \cong 0.8\sigma$$

This enables us to establish statistical control limits for the tracking signal that corresponds to the more familiar normal distribution. For example, statistical control limits of $\pm 3$ standard deviations, corresponding to 99.7% of the errors, would translate to $\pm 3.75$ MADs; that is, $3\sigma \div 0.8 = 3.75$ MADs. Control limits of $\pm 2$ to $\pm 5$ MADs are used most frequently.

**Example 11.8**
**Developing a Tracking Signal**

In Example 11.7, the mean absolute deviation was computed for the exponential smoothing forecast ($\alpha = 0.30$) for HiTek Computer Services. Using a tracking signal, monitor the forecast accuracy using control limits of $\pm 3$ MADs.

*Solution*

To use the tracking signal, we must recompute MAD each period as the cumulative error is computed.

Using MAD = 3.00, we find that the tracking signal for period 2 is

$$TS_2 = \frac{E}{MAD} = \frac{3.00}{3.00} = 1.00$$

The tracking signal for period 3 is

$$TS_3 = \frac{6.10}{3.05} = 2.00$$

The remaining tracking signal values are shown in the following table:

**Tracking Signal Values**

| Period | Demand, $D_t$ | Forecast, $F_t$ | Error, $D_t - F_t$ | $E = \Sigma(D_t - F_t)$ | MAD | Tracking Signal |
|---|---|---|---|---|---|---|
| 1 | 37 | 37.00 | — | — | — | — |
| 2 | 40 | 37.00 | 3.00 | 3.00 | 3.00 | 1.00 |
| 3 | 41 | 37.90 | 3.10 | 6.10 | 3.05 | 2.00 |
| 4 | 37 | 38.83 | −1.83 | 4.27 | 2.64 | 1.62 |
| 5 | 45 | 38.28 | 6.72 | 10.99 | 3.66 | 3.00 |
| 6 | 50 | 40.29 | 9.69 | 20.68 | 4.87 | 4.25 |
| 7 | 43 | 43.20 | −0.20 | 20.48 | 4.09 | 5.01 |
| 8 | 47 | 43.14 | 3.86 | 24.34 | 4.06 | 6.00 |
| 9 | 56 | 44.30 | 11.70 | 36.04 | 5.01 | 7.19 |
| 10 | 52 | 47.81 | 4.19 | 40.23 | 4.92 | 8.18 |
| 11 | 55 | 49.06 | 5.94 | 46.17 | 5.02 | 9.20 |
| 12 | 54 | 50.84 | 3.15 | 49.32 | 4.85 | 10.17 |

The tracking signal values in the table above move outside ±3 MAD control limits (i.e., ±3.00) in period 5 *and* continue increasing. This suggests that the forecast is not performing accurately or, more precisely, is consistently biased low (i.e., actual demand consistently exceeds the forecast). This is illustrated in the following graph. Notice that the tracking signal moves beyond the upper limit of 3 following period 5 and continues to rise. For the sake of comparison, the tracking signal for the linear trend line forecast computed in Example 11.5 is also plotted on this graph. Notice that it remains within the limits (touching the upper limit in period 3), indicating a lack of consistent bias.

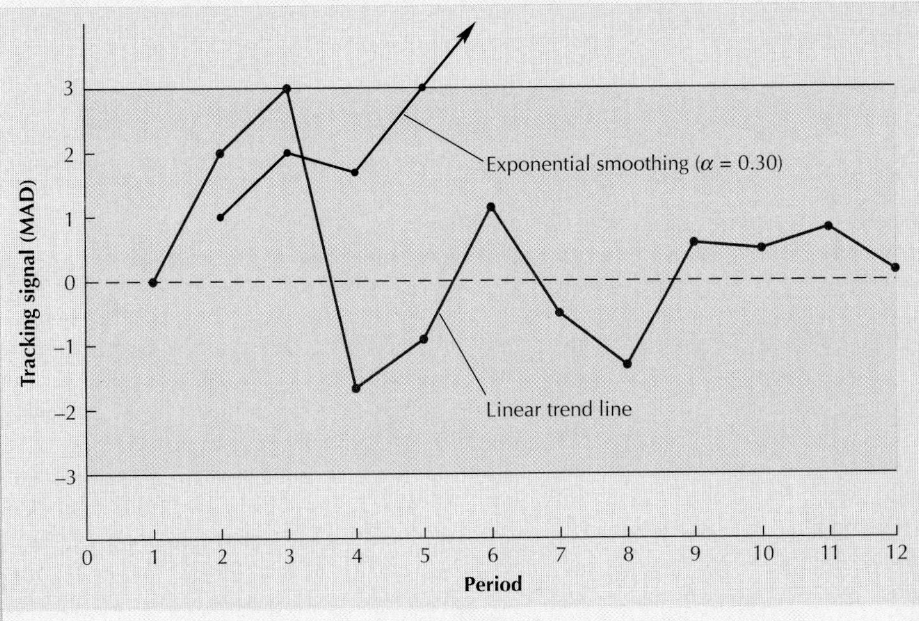

Another method for monitoring forecast error is statistical control charts. For example, $\pm 3\sigma$ control limits would reflect 99.7% of the forecast errors (assuming they are normally distributed). The sample standard deviation, $\sigma$, is computed as

$$\sigma = \sqrt{\frac{\Sigma(D_t - F_t)^2}{n - 1}}$$

**MSE:** the average of the squared forecast errors.

This formula without the square root is known as the **mean squared error (MSE)**, and it is sometimes used as a measure of forecast error. It reacts to forecast error much like MAD does. (For our Example 11.8, MSE = 37.57.)

**Example 11.9**

**Forecast Error with Statistical Control Charts**

Using the same example for the exponential smoothing forecast ($\alpha = 0.30$) for HiTek Computer Services, as in Example 11.8, we compute the standard deviation as

$$\sigma = \sqrt{\frac{375.61}{10}} = 6.13$$

Using this value of $\sigma$ we can compute statistical control limits for forecast errors for our exponential smoothing forecast ($\alpha = 0.30$) example for HiTek Computer Services. Plus or minus $3\sigma$ control limits, reflecting 99.7% of the forecast errors, gives $\pm 3(6.13)$, or $\pm 18.39$. Although it can be observed from the table in Example 11.8 that all the error values are within the control limits, we can still detect that most of the errors are positive, indicating a low bias in the forecast estimates. This is illustrated in the following graph of the control chart with the errors plotted on it.

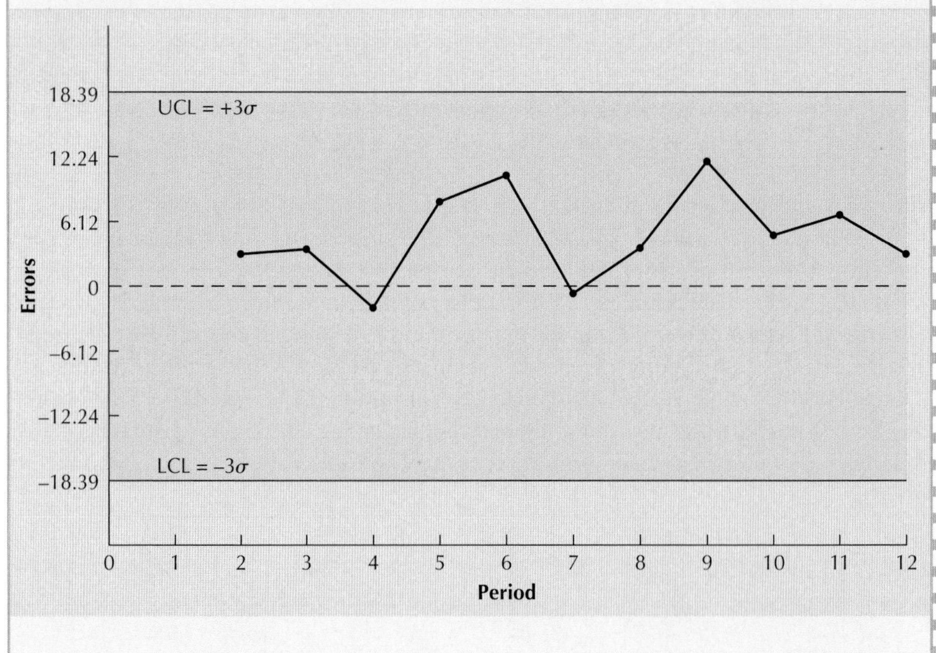


## TIME SERIES FORECASTING USING EXCEL

Excel can be used to develop forecasts using the moving average, exponential smoothing, adjusted exponential smoothing, and linear trend line techniques. In a recent survey of companies across different industries that use forecasting, almost half use Excel spreadsheets for forecasting, while the rest use a variety of different forecasting software packages.[2]

First we will demonstrate how to determine exponentially smoothed and adjusted exponentially smoothed forecasts using Excel, as shown in Exhibit 11.1. We will demonstrate Excel using Examples 11.3 and 11.4 for forecasting demand at HiTek Computer Services, including the Excel spreadsheets showing the exponentially smoothed forecast

[2] C. L. Jain, "Benchmarking Forecasting Software and Systems," *The Journal of Business Forecasting* 21(3; Fall 2002), pp. 24–25.

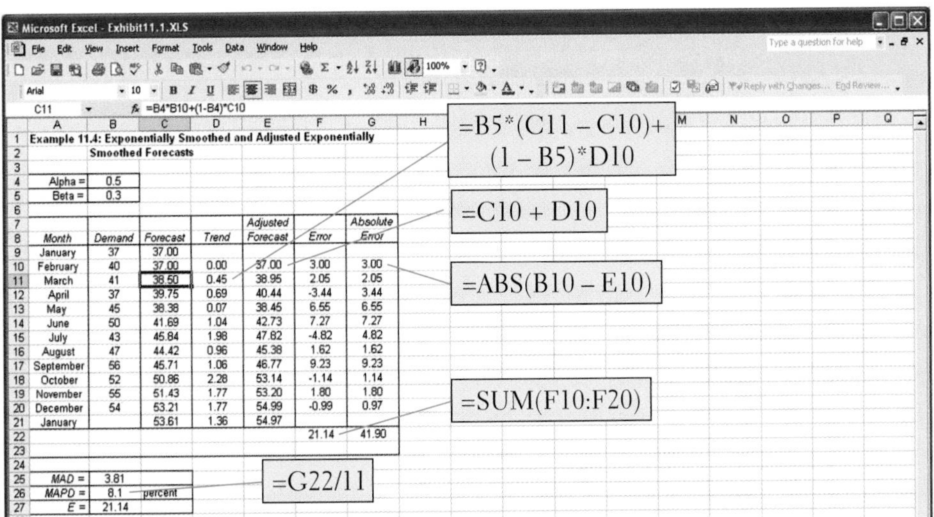

Microsoft Excel - Exhibit11.1.XLS

C11 =B4*B10+(1-B4)*C10

Example 11.4: Exponentially Smoothed and Adjusted Exponentially Smoothed Forecasts

| | |
|---|---|
| Alpha = | 0.5 |
| Beta = | 0.3 |

| Month | Demand | Forecast | Trend | Adjusted Forecast | Error | Absolute Error |
|---|---|---|---|---|---|---|
| January | 37 | 37.00 | | | | |
| February | 40 | 37.00 | 0.00 | 37.00 | 3.00 | 3.00 |
| March | 41 | 38.50 | 0.45 | 38.95 | 2.05 | 2.05 |
| April | 37 | 39.75 | 0.69 | 40.44 | -3.44 | 3.44 |
| May | 45 | 38.38 | 0.07 | 38.45 | 6.55 | 6.55 |
| June | 50 | 41.69 | 1.04 | 42.73 | 7.27 | 7.27 |
| July | 43 | 45.84 | 1.98 | 47.82 | -4.82 | 4.82 |
| August | 47 | 44.42 | 0.96 | 45.38 | 1.62 | 1.62 |
| September | 56 | 45.71 | 1.06 | 46.77 | 9.23 | 9.23 |
| October | 52 | 50.86 | 2.28 | 53.14 | -1.14 | 1.14 |
| November | 55 | 51.43 | 1.77 | 53.20 | 1.80 | 1.80 |
| December | 54 | 53.21 | 1.77 | 54.99 | -0.99 | 0.97 |
| January | | 53.61 | 1.36 | 54.97 | | |
| | | | | | 21.14 | 41.90 |

| | | |
|---|---|---|
| MAD = | 3.81 | |
| MAPD = | 8.1 | percent |
| E = | 21.14 | |

Exhibit 11.1

with $\alpha = 0.5$ and the adjusted exponentially smoothed forecast with $\beta = 0.3$. We have also computed the values for MAD, MAPD, and *E*.

Notice that the formula in Exhibit 11.1 for computing the exponentially smoothed forecast for March is embedded in cell C11 and shown on the formula bar at the top of the screen. The same formula is used to compute all the other forecast values in column C. The formula for computing the trend value for March is = B5∗(C11 − C10) + (1 − B5)∗D10. The formula for the adjusted forecast in column *E* is computed by typing the formula = C10 + D10 in cell E10 and copying it to cells E11:E21 (using the copy and paste options from the right mouse key). The error is computed for the adjusted forecast, and the formula for computing the error for March is = B11 − E11, while the formula for absolute error for March is = ABS (F11).

A graph of the forecast can also be developed with Excel. To plot the exponentially smoothed forecast in column C and demand in column B, cover all cells from A8 to C21 with the mouse and click on "Insert" on the toolbar at the top of the worksheet. Next click on "Chart," which will invoke a window for constructing a chart. After verifying that the range of cells to include is correct, click on "Next." This will provide a menu of different chart types. Select a line chart and go to the next window where you can select a chart format that connects the data points with a line. Go to the next window that shows a chart. The next window allows you to label the axes, and then clicking on "Finish" brings up a full-screen version of the graph. To clean it up you can double click on the lines and data points. The resulting graph for demand and the exponentially smoothed forecast for our example is shown in Exhibit 11.2.

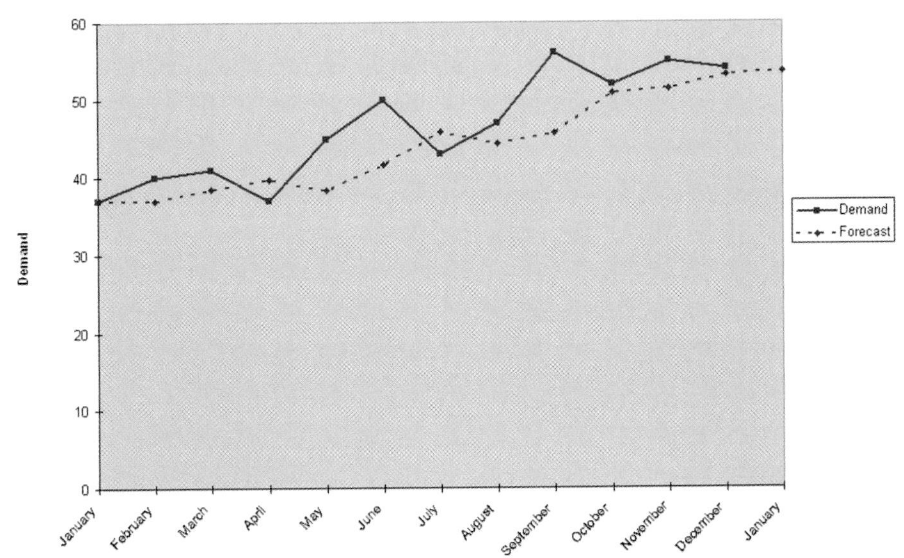



Exhibit 11.2

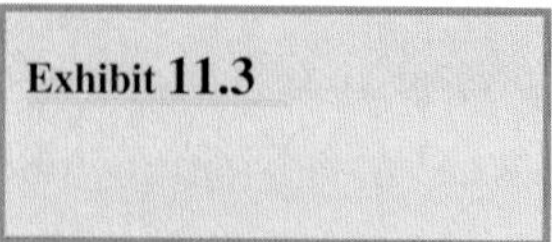
Exhibit 11.3

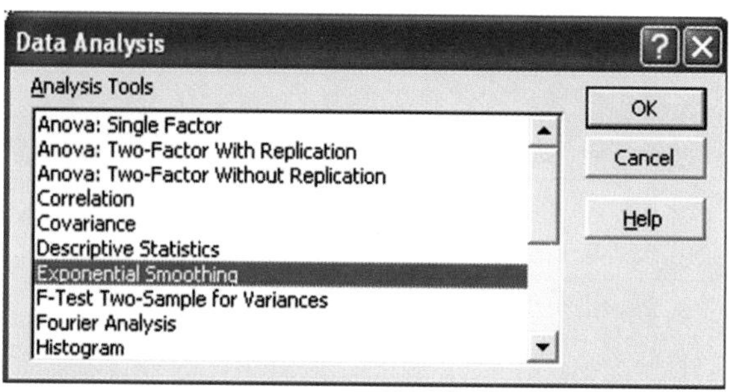

Exhibit 11.4

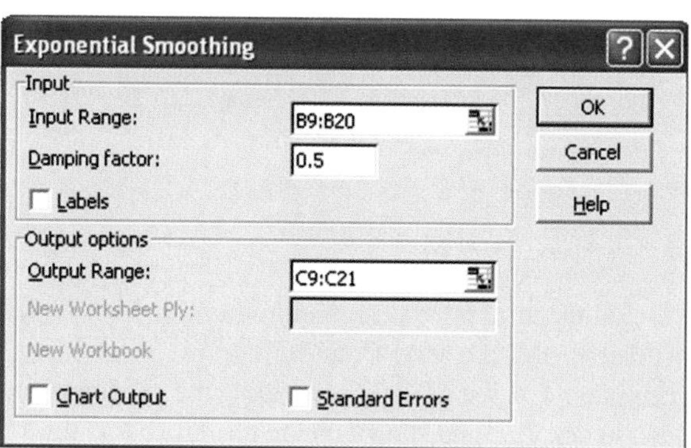


The exponential smoothing forecast can also be developed directly from Excel without "customizing" a spreadsheet and entering formulas as we did in Exhibit 11.1. From the Tools menu at the top of the spreadsheet select the "Data Analysis" option. (If your Tools menu does not include this menu item, you should add it by accessing the add-ins option from the Tools menu.) Exhibit 11.3 shows the "Data Analysis" window and the "Exponential Smoothing" menu item, which should be selected by clicking on "OK." The resulting "Exponential Smoothing" window is shown in Exhibit 11.4. The "input range" includes the demand values in column B in Exhibit 11.1, the damping factor is α, which in this case is 0.5, and the output should be placed in column C in Exhibit 11.1. Clicking on "OK" will result in the same forecast values in column C of Exhibit 11.1 as we computed using our own exponential smoothing formula. Note that the Data Analysis group of analysis tools does not have an adjusted exponential smoothing selection; that is one reason we developed our own customized spreadsheet in Exhibit 11.1. The "Data Analysis" tools also have a moving average menu item that you can use to compute a moving average forecast.

Excel can also be used to develop more customized forecast models, like seasonal forecasts. Exhibit 11.5 shows an Excel screen for the seasonal forecast model developed in Example 11.6. Notice that the computation of the seasonal forecast for the first quarter (SF1) in cell B12 is computed using the formula shown on the formula bar at the top of the screen. The forecast value for SF1 is slightly different than the value in Example 11.6 because of rounding.

Exhibit 11.5

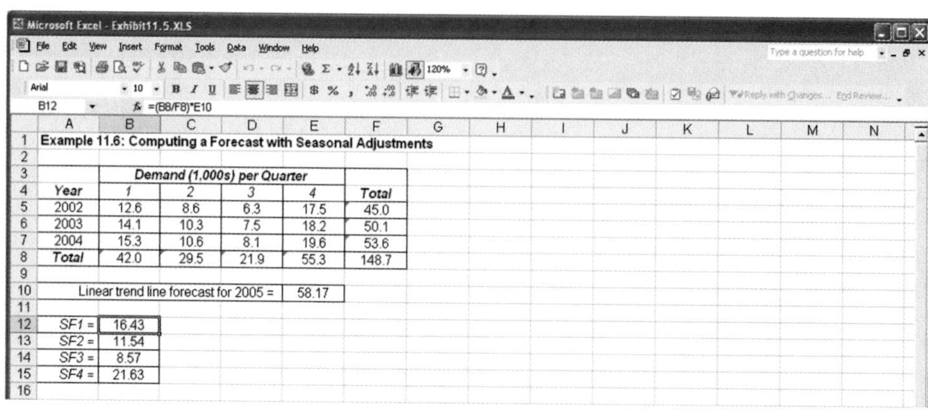


| Year | 1 | 2 | 3 | 4 | Total |
|---|---|---|---|---|---|
| | Demand (1,000s) per Quarter | | | | |
| 2002 | 12.6 | 8.6 | 6.3 | 17.5 | 45.0 |
| 2003 | 14.1 | 10.3 | 7.5 | 18.2 | 50.1 |
| 2004 | 15.3 | 10.6 | 8.1 | 19.6 | 53.6 |
| Total | 42.0 | 29.5 | 21.9 | 55.3 | 148.7 |

Linear trend line forecast for 2005 = 58.17

| | |
|---|---|
| SF1 = | 16.43 |
| SF2 = | 11.54 |
| SF3 = | 8.57 |
| SF4 = | 21.63 |

## REGRESSION METHODS

In the Institute of Business Forecasting survey we referred to previously in the section on time series models, the second most popular forecasting technique among various industrial firms was regression. Regression is used for forecasting by establishing a mathematical relationship between two or more variables. We are interested in identifying relationships between variables and demand. If we know that something has caused demand to behave in a certain way in the past, we would like to identify that relationship so if the same thing happens again in the future, we can predict what demand will be. For example, there is a relationship between increased demand in new housing and lower interest rates. Correspondingly, a whole myriad of building products and services display increased demand if new housing starts increase. The rapid increase in sales of DVDs has resulted in an increase in demand for DVD movies.

The simplest form of regression is linear regression, which we used previously to develop a linear trend line for forecasting. Now we will show how to develop a regression model for variables related to demand other than time.

### LINEAR REGRESSION

**Linear regression** is a mathematical technique that relates one variable, called an *independent variable*, to another, the *dependent variable*, in the form of an equation for a straight line. A linear equation has the following general form:

**Linear regression:** a mathematical technique that relates a dependent variable to an independent variable in the form of a linear equation.

$$y = a + bx$$

where

$y$ = the dependent variable

$a$ = the intercept

$b$ = the slope of the line

$x$ = the independent variable

Because we want to use linear regression as a forecasting model for demand, the dependent variable, $y$, represents demand, and $x$ is an independent variable that causes demand to behave in a linear manner.

Linear regression relates demand (dependent variable) to an independent variable.

To develop the linear equation, the slope, $b$, and the intercept, $a$, must first be computed using the following least squares formulas:

$$a = \bar{y} - b\bar{x}$$

$$b = \frac{\Sigma xy - n\bar{x}\bar{y}}{\Sigma x^2 - n\bar{x}^2}$$

where

$$\bar{x} = \frac{\Sigma x}{n} = \text{mean of the } x \text{ data}$$

$$\bar{y} = \frac{\Sigma y}{n} = \text{mean of the } y \text{ data}$$

Example 11.10

**Developing a Linear Regression Forecast**

The State University athletic department wants to develop its budget for the coming year using a forecast for football attendance. Football attendance accounts for the largest portion of its revenues, and the athletic director believes attendance is directly related to the number of wins by the team. The business manager has accumulated total annual attendance figures for the past eight years.

| Wins | Attendance | Wins | Attendance |
|---|---|---|---|
| 4 | 36,300 | 6 | 44,000 |
| 6 | 40,100 | 7 | 45,600 |
| 6 | 41,200 | 5 | 39,000 |
| 8 | 53,000 | 7 | 47,500 |

Given the number of returning starters and the strength of the schedule, the athletic director believes the team will win at least seven games next year. Develop a simple regression equation for this data to forecast attendance for this level of success.

*Solution*

The computations necessary to compute $a$ and $b$ using the least squares formulas are summarized in the accompanying table. (Note that $y$ is given in 1000s to make manual computation easier.)

**Least Squares Computations**

| $x$ (Wins) | $y$ (Attendance, 1000s) | $xy$ | $x^2$ |
|---|---|---|---|
| 4 | 36.3 | 145.2 | 16 |
| 6 | 40.1 | 240.6 | 36 |
| 6 | 41.2 | 247.2 | 36 |
| 8 | 53.0 | 424.0 | 64 |
| 6 | 44.0 | 264.0 | 36 |
| 7 | 45.6 | 319.2 | 49 |
| 5 | 39.0 | 195.0 | 25 |
| 7 | 47.5 | 332.5 | 49 |
| 49 | 346.9 | 2167.7 | 311 |

$$\bar{x} = \frac{49}{8} = 6.125$$

$$\bar{y} = \frac{346.9}{8} = 43.36$$

$$\begin{aligned} b &= \frac{\Sigma xy - n\bar{x}\bar{y}}{\Sigma x^2 - n\bar{x}^2} \\ &= \frac{(2167.7) - (8)(6.125)(43.36)}{(311) - (8)(6.125)^2} \\ &= 4.06 \\ a &= \bar{y} - b\bar{x} \\ &= 43.36 - (4.06)(6.125) \\ &= 18.46 \end{aligned}$$

Substituting these values for $a$ and $b$ into the linear equation line, we have

$$y = 18.46 + 4.06x$$

Thus, for $x = 7$ (wins), the forecast for attendance is

$$\begin{aligned} y &= 18.46 + 4.06(7) \\ &= 46.88, \text{ or } 46{,}880 \end{aligned}$$

The data points with the regression line are shown in the following figure at the top of page 507. Observing the regression line relative to the data points, it would appear that the data follow a distinct upward linear trend, which would indicate that the forecast should be relatively accurate. In fact, the MAD value for this forecasting model is 1.41, which suggests an accurate forecast.

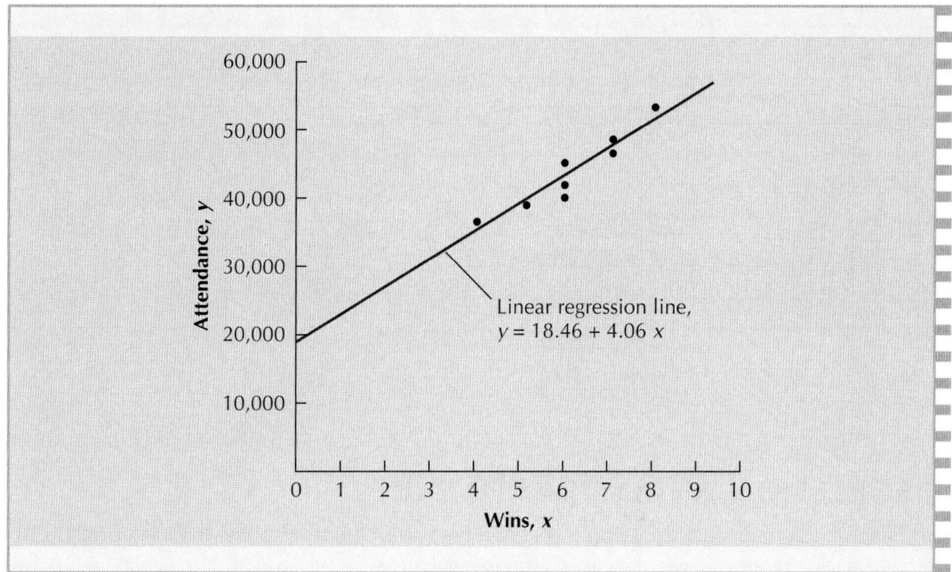


## CORRELATION

**Correlation:** a measure of the strength of the relationship between independent and dependent variables.

**Correlation** in a linear regression equation is a measure of the strength of the relationship between the independent and dependent variables. The formula for the correlation coefficient is

$$r = \frac{n \sum xy - \sum x \sum y}{\sqrt{[n \sum x^2 - (\sum x)^2][n \sum y^2 - (\sum y)^2]}}$$

The value of $r$ varies between $-1.00$ and $+1.00$, with a value of $+1.00$ indicating a strong linear relationship between the variables. If $r = 1.00$, then an increase in the independent variable will result in a corresponding linear increase in the dependent variable. If $r = -1.00$, an increase in the dependent variable will result in a linear decrease in the dependent variable. A value of $r$ near zero implies that there is little or no linear relationship between variables.

We can determine the correlation coefficient for the linear regression equation determined in Example 11.9 by substituting most of the terms calculated for the least squares formula (except for $\sum y^2$) into the formula for $r$:

$$r = \frac{(8)(2167.7) - (49)(346.9)}{\sqrt{[(8)(311) - (49)^2][(8)(15{,}224.7) - (346.9)^2]}}$$

$$= 0.947$$

This value for the correlation coefficient is very close to 1.00, indicating a strong linear relationship between the number of wins and home attendance.

**Coefficient of determination:** the percentage of the variation in the dependent variable that results from the independent variable.

Another measure of the strength of the relationship between the variables in a linear regression equation is the **coefficient of determination**. It is computed by squaring the value of $r$. It indicates the percentage of the variation in the dependent variable that is a result of the behavior of the independent variable. For our example, $r = 0.947$; thus, the coefficient of determination is

$$r^2 = (0.947)^2$$
$$= 0.897$$

This value for the coefficient of determination means that 89.7% of the amount of variation in attendance can be attributed to the number of wins by the team (with the remaining 10.3% due to other unexplained factors, such as weather, a good or poor start, or publicity). A value of 1.00 (or 100%) would indicate that attendance depends totally on wins. However, since 10.3% of the variation is a result of other factors, some amount of forecast error can be expected.

Exhibit 11.6

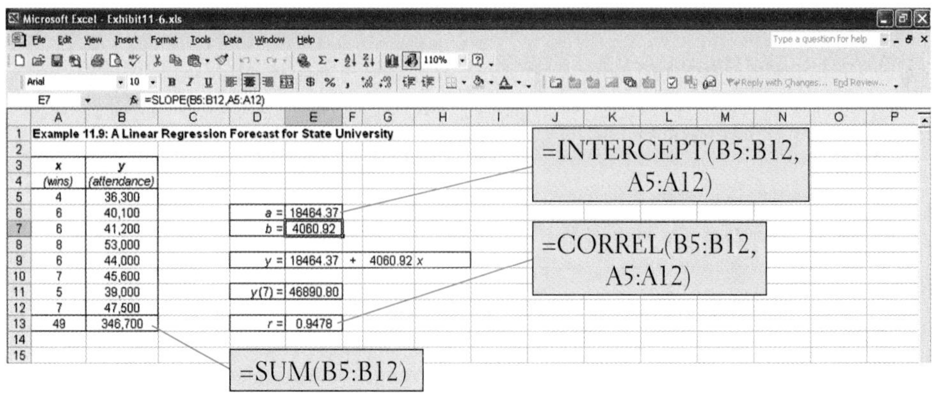


## REGRESSION ANALYSIS WITH EXCEL

The development of the simple linear regression equation and the correlation coefficient for our example was not too difficult because the amount of data was relatively small. However, manual computation of the components of simple linear regression equations can become very time-consuming and cumbersome as the amount of data increases. Excel has the capability of performing linear regression.

Exhibit 11.6 shows a spreadsheet set up to develop the linear regression forecast for Example 11.10 for the State University Athletic Department. Notice that Excel computes the slope directly with the formula "=SLOPE(B5:B12,A5:A12)" entered in cell D7 and shown on the formula bar at the top of the spreadsheet. The formula for the intercept in cell D6 is "=INTERCEPT(B5:B12,A5:A12)." The values for the slope and intercept are subsequently entered into cells D9 and F9 to form the linear regression equation. The correlation coefficient in cell E13 is computed using the formula "=CORREL(B5:B12, A5:A12)." Although it is not shown on the spreadsheet, the coefficient of determination ($r^2$) could be computed using the formula "=RSQ(B5:B12,A5:A12)."

A linear regression forecast can also be developed directly with Excel using the "Data Analysis" option from the Tools menu we accessed previously to develop an exponentially smoothed forecast. Exhibit 11.7 shows the selection of "Regression" from the Data Analysis menu, and Exhibit 11.8 shows the Regression window. We first enter the cells from Exhibit 11.6 that include the $y$ values (for attendance), B5:B12. Next enter the $x$ value cells, A5:A12. The output range is the location on the spreadsheet where you want to put the output results. This range needs to be large (18 cells by 9 cells) and not overlap with anything else on the spreadsheet. Clicking on "OK" will result in the spreadsheet shown in Exhibit 11.9. (Note that the "Summary Output" has been slightly moved around so that all the results could be included on the screen in Exhibit 11.9).

The "Summary Output" in Exhibit 11.9 provides a large amount of statistical information, the explanation and use of which are beyond the scope of this book. The essential items that we are interested in are the intercept and slope (labeled "X Variable 1") in the "Coefficients" column at the bottom of the spreadsheet, and the "Multiple R" (or correlation coefficient) value shown under "Regression Statistics."

Exhibit 11.7

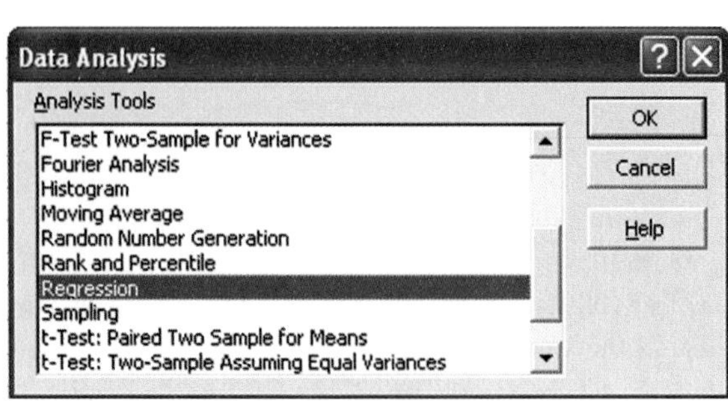

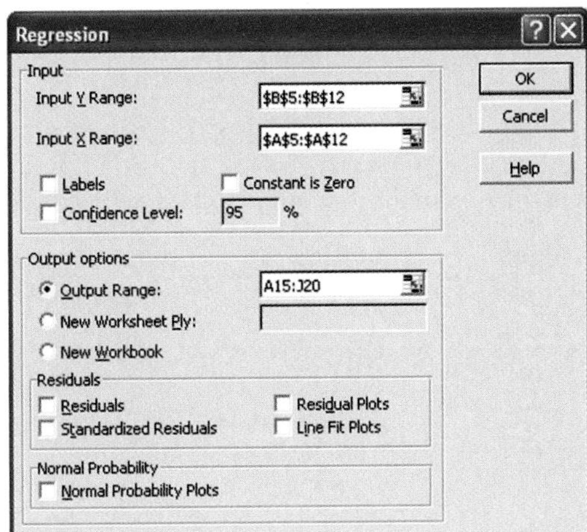

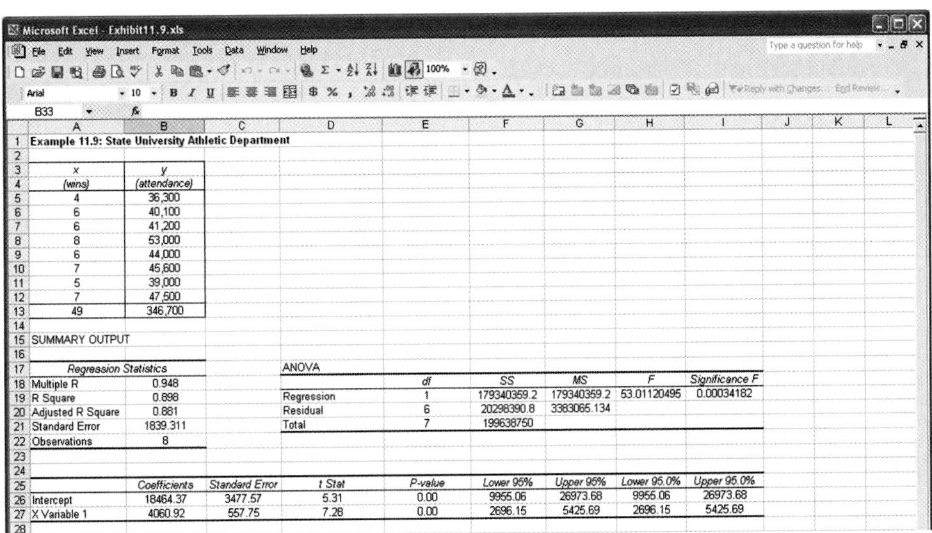
Microsoft Excel - Exhibit11.9.xls

Example 11.9: State University Athletic Department

| x (wins) | y (attendance) |
|---|---|
| 4 | 36,300 |
| 6 | 40,100 |
| 6 | 41,200 |
| 8 | 53,000 |
| 6 | 44,000 |
| 7 | 45,600 |
| 5 | 39,000 |
| 7 | 47,500 |
| 49 | 346,700 |

SUMMARY OUTPUT

| *Regression Statistics* | |
|---|---|
| Multiple R | 0.948 |
| R Square | 0.898 |
| Adjusted R Square | 0.881 |
| Standard Error | 1839.311 |
| Observations | 8 |

ANOVA

| | *df* | *SS* | *MS* | *F* | *Significance F* |
|---|---|---|---|---|---|
| Regression | 1 | 179340359.2 | 179340359.2 | 53.01120495 | 0.00034182 |
| Residual | 6 | 20298390.8 | 3383065.134 | | |
| Total | 7 | 199638750 | | | |

| | *Coefficients* | *Standard Error* | *t Stat* | *P-value* | *Lower 95%* | *Upper 95%* | *Lower 95.0%* | *Upper 95.0%* |
|---|---|---|---|---|---|---|---|---|
| Intercept | 18464.37 | 3477.57 | 5.31 | 0.00 | 9955.06 | 26973.68 | 9955.06 | 26973.68 |
| X Variable 1 | 4060.92 | 557.75 | 7.28 | 0.00 | 2696.15 | 5425.69 | 2696.15 | 5425.69 |

## MULTIPLE REGRESSION WITH EXCEL

Another causal method of forecasting is **multiple regression**, a more powerful extension of linear regression. Linear regression relates demand to one other independent variable, whereas multiple regression reflects the relationship between a dependent variable and two or more independent variables. A multiple regression model has the following general form:

**Multiple regression:** a relationship of demand to two or more independent variables.

$$y = \beta_0 + \beta_1 x_1 + \beta_2 x_2 + \ldots + \beta_k x_k$$

where

$\beta_0$ = the intercept

$\beta_1, \ldots, \beta_k$ = parameters representing the contribution of the independent variables

$x_1, \ldots, x_k$ = independent variables

For example, the demand for new housing ($y$) in a region might be a function of several independent variables, including interest rates, population, housing prices, and personal income. Development and computation of the multiple regression equation, including the compilation of data, is more complex than linear regression. The only means for forecasting using multiple regression is with a computer.

**Example 11.11**

## Developing a Multiple Regression Forecast with Excel

To demonstrate the capability to solve multiple regression problems with Excel spreadsheets, we will expand our State University athletic department Example 11.10 for forecasting attendance at football games that we used to demonstrate linear regression. Instead of attempting to predict attendance based on only one variable, wins, we will include a second variable for advertising and promotional expenditures as follows:

| Wins | Promotion ($) | Attendance |
|---|---|---|
| 4 | 29,500 | 36,300 |
| 6 | 55,700 | 40,100 |
| 6 | 71,300 | 41,200 |
| 8 | 87,000 | 53,000 |
| 6 | 75,000 | 44,000 |
| 7 | 72,000 | 45,600 |
| 5 | 55,300 | 39,000 |
| 7 | 81,600 | 47,500 |

We will use the "Data Analysis" option (add-in) from the Tools menu at the top of the spreadsheet that we used in the previous section to develop our linear regression equation, and then the "Regression" option from the "Data Analysis" menu. The resulting spreadsheet with the multiple regression statistics is shown in Exhibit 11.10.

*Solution*

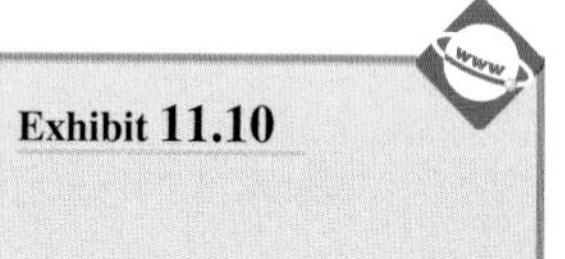

**Exhibit 11.10**

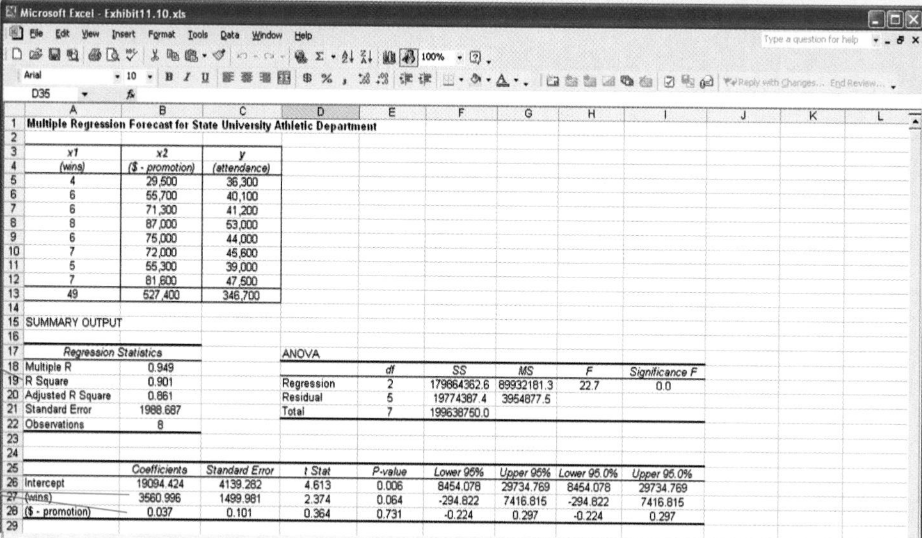

Microsoft Excel - Exhibit11.10.xls

Multiple Regression Forecast for State University Athletic Department

| x1 (wins) | x2 ($ - promotion) | y (attendance) |
|---|---|---|
| 4 | 29,500 | 36,300 |
| 6 | 55,700 | 40,100 |
| 6 | 71,300 | 41,200 |
| 8 | 87,000 | 53,000 |
| 6 | 75,000 | 44,000 |
| 7 | 72,000 | 45,600 |
| 5 | 55,300 | 39,000 |
| 7 | 81,600 | 47,500 |
| 49 | 527,400 | 346,700 |

SUMMARY OUTPUT

| Regression Statistics | |
|---|---|
| Multiple R | 0.949 |
| R Square | 0.901 |
| Adjusted R Square | 0.861 |
| Standard Error | 1988.687 |
| Observations | 8 |

ANOVA

| | df | SS | MS | F | Significance F |
|---|---|---|---|---|---|
| Regression | 2 | 179864362.6 | 89932181.3 | 22.7 | 0.0 |
| Residual | 5 | 19774387.4 | 3954877.5 | | |
| Total | 7 | 199638750.0 | | | |

| | Coefficients | Standard Error | t Stat | P-value | Lower 95% | Upper 95% | Lower 95.0% | Upper 95.0% |
|---|---|---|---|---|---|---|---|---|
| Intercept | 19094.424 | 4139.282 | 4.613 | 0.006 | 8454.078 | 29734.769 | 8454.078 | 29734.769 |
| (wins) | 3560.996 | 1499.981 | 2.374 | 0.064 | -294.822 | 7416.815 | -294.822 | 7416.815 |
| ($ - promotion) | 0.037 | 0.101 | 0.364 | 0.731 | -0.224 | 0.297 | -0.224 | 0.297 |

$r^2$, the coefficient of determination

Regression equation coefficients for $x_1$ and $x_2$

Note that the data must be set up on the spreadsheet so that the two $x$ variables are in adjacent columns (in this case A and B). Then we enter the "Input X Range" as A4:B12 as shown in Exhibit 11.11.

**Exhibit 11.11**

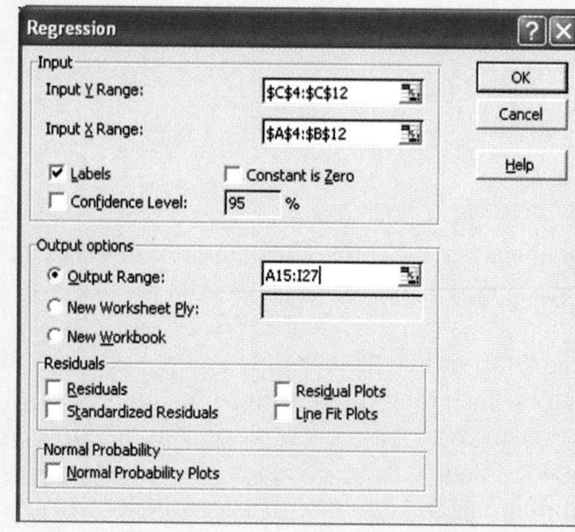

The regression coefficients for our $x$ variables, wins and promotion, are shown in cells B27 and B28. Thus, the multiple regression equation is formulated as

$$y = 19{,}094.42 + 3560.99x_1 + 0.0368x_2$$

This equation can now be used to forecast attendance based on both projected football wins and promotional expenditure. For example, if the athletic department expects the team to win seven games and plans to spend $60,000 on promotion and advertising, the forecasted attendance is

$$\begin{aligned} y &= 19{,}094.42 + 3560.99(7) + 0.0368(60{,}000) \\ &= 46{,}229.35 \end{aligned}$$

If the promotional expenditure is held constant, every win will increase attendance by 3560.99, whereas if the wins are held constant, every $1000 of advertising spent will increase attendance by 36.8 fans. This would seem to suggest that the number of wins has a more significant impact on attendance than promotional expenditures.

$r^2$, the coefficient of determination, shown in cell B19 is 0.900, which suggests that 90% of the amount of variation in attendance can be attributed to the number of wins and the promotional expenditures. However, as we have already noted, the number of wins would appear to probably account for a larger part of the variation in attendance.

## THE COMPETITIVE EDGE

### Forecasting Daily Demand in the Gas Industry

Vermont Gas Systems is a natural gas utility serving approximately 26,000 business, industrial, and residential customers in 13 towns and cities in northwestern Vermont. Demand forecasts are a critical part of Vermont Gas Systems' supply chain that stretches across Canada from suppliers in western Canada to storage facilities along the Trans-Canada pipeline to Vermont Gas Systems' pipeline. Gas orders must be specified to suppliers at least 24 hours in advance. Vermont Gas Systems has storage capacity available for a buffer inventory of only one hour of gas use, so an accurate daily forecast of gas demand is essential.

Vermont Gas Systems uses regression to forecast daily gas demand. In its forecast models, gas demand is the dependent variable, and factors such as weather information and industrial customer demand are independent variables. During the winter customers use more gas for heat, making an accurate weather forecast a very important factor. Detailed three-day weather forecasts are provided to Vermont Gas Systems five times per day from a weather forecasting service. Individual regression forecasts are developed for 24 large-use industrial and municipal customers such as factories, hospitals, and schools. End-use demand is the total potential capacity of all natural gas appliances in the system. It changes daily as new customers move into a new house, apartment, or business adding new appliances or equipment to the system. The utility uses only the most recent 30 days of demand data in developing its forecast models and updates the models on a weekly basis. The results of the forecast model are interpreted by Vermont Gas Systems and supplemented with its individual knowledge of the supply chain distribution system and customer usage to develop an overall, accurate daily forecast of gas demand.

Columbia Gas Company of Ohio, a subsidiary of Virginia-based Columbia Energy Group, is the largest natural gas utility in Ohio, with nearly 1.3 million customers in over 1000 communities. Columbia employs two types of daily forecast: the design day forecast and the daily operational forecast. The design day forecast is used to determine the amount of gas supply, transportation capacity, and storage capacity that Columbia requires to meet its customer needs. It is very important that the design day forecast be accurate; if it is not, Columbia may not contract for enough gas from its suppliers, which could create shortages and put their customers at risk. The daily operational forecast is used to ensure that scheduled supplies are balanced with forecasted demands over the next five-day period. It is used to balance supply and demand on a daily basis. The forecasting process is similar for both types of forecast. Columbia uses multiple regression analysis based on daily demand for two years and several weather-related independent variables to develop the parameters of a time series forecast model for the design day forecast and the daily operational forecast.

*Source:* M. Flock, "Forecasting Winter Daily Gas Demand at Vermont Gas Systems," *Journal of Business Forecasting* 13(1; Spring 1994), p. 2; and H. Catron, "Daily Demand Forecasting at Columbia Gas," *Journal of Business Forecasting* 19(2; Summer 2000), pp. 10–15.

A problem often encountered in multiple regression is *multicollinearity*, or the amount of "overlapping" information about the dependent variable that is provided by several independent variables. This problem usually occurs when the independent variables are highly correlated, as in this example, in which wins and promotional expenditures are both positively correlated (i.e., more wins coincide with higher promotional expenditures and vice versa). (Possibly the athletic department increased promotional expenditures when it thought it would have a better team that would achieve more wins.) The topic of multicollinearity and how to cope with it is beyond the scope of this book and this brief section on multiple regression; however, most statistics textbooks discuss this topic in detail.

## SUMMARY

Forecasts of product demand are a necessity for almost all aspects of operational planning. Short-range demand forecasts determine the daily resource requirements needed for production, including labor and material, as well as for developing work schedules and shipping dates and controlling inventory levels. Long-range forecasts are needed to plan new products for development and changes in existing products and to acquire the plant, equipment, personnel, resources, and supply chain necessary for future operations.

We have presented several methods of forecasting useful for different time frames. These quantitative forecasting techniques are easy to understand, simple to use, and not especially costly unless the data requirements are substantial. They also have exhibited a good track record of performance for many companies that have used them. For these reasons, regression methods, and especially times series, are popular.

When managers and students are first introduced to forecasting methods, they are sometimes surprised and disappointed at the lack of exactness of the forecasts. However, they soon learn that forecasting is not easy, and exactness is not possible. Nonetheless, companies that have the skill and experience to obtain more accurate forecasts than their competitors' will gain a competitive edge.

## SUMMARY OF KEY FORMULAS

*Moving Average*

$$\text{MA}_n = \frac{\sum_{i=1}^{n} D_i}{n}$$

*Weighted Moving Average*

$$\text{WMA}_n = \sum_{i=1}^{n} W_i D_i$$

*Exponential Smoothing*

$$F_{t+1} = \alpha D_t + (1 - \alpha)F_t$$

*Adjusted Exponential Smoothing*

$$AF_{t+1} = F_{t+1} + T_{t+1}$$

*Trend Factor*

$$T_{t+1} = \beta(F_{t+1} - F_t) + (1 - \beta)T_t$$

*Linear Trend Line*

$$y = a + bx$$

*Least Squares*

$$b = \frac{\sum xy - n\overline{x}\overline{y}}{\sum x^2 - n\overline{x}^2}$$

$$a = \overline{y} - b\overline{x}$$

*Seasonal Factor*

$$S_i = \frac{D_i}{\sum D}$$

*Seasonally Adjusted Forecast*

$$\text{SF}_i = (S_i)(F_t)$$

*Mean Absolute Deviation*

$$\text{MAD} = \frac{\sum|D_t - F_t|}{n}$$

*Mean Absolute Percent Deviation*

$$\text{MAPD} = \frac{\sum|D_t - F_t|}{\sum D_t}$$

*Cumulative Error*

$$E = \sum e_t$$

*Average Error (Bias)*

$$\overline{E} = \frac{\sum e_t}{n}$$

*Tracking Signal*

$$\text{TS} = \frac{\sum(D_t - F_t)}{\text{MAD}} = \frac{E}{\text{MAD}}$$

*Mean Squared Error*

$$\text{MSE} = \frac{\sum(D_t - F_t)^2}{n - 1}$$

*Linear Regression Equation*

$$y = a + bx$$

*Correlation Coefficient*

$$r = \frac{n\sum xy - \sum x \sum y}{\sqrt{[n\sum x^2 - (\sum x)^2][n\sum y^2 - (\sum y)^2]}}$$

*Coefficient of Determination*

$$\text{Coefficient of determination} = r^2$$

## SUMMARY OF KEY TERMS

**adjusted exponential smoothing** an exponential smoothing forecast adjusted for trend.

**average error** the cumulative error averaged over the number of time periods.

**coefficient of determination** the correlation coefficient squared; it measures the portion of the variation in the dependent variable that can be attributed to the independent variable.

**correlation** a measure of the strength of the causal relationship between the independent and dependent variables in a linear regression equation.

**cumulative error** a sum of the forecast errors; also known as bias.

**cycle** an up-and-down movement in demand over time.

**Delphi method** a procedure for acquiring informed judgments and opinions from knowledgeable individuals to use as a subjective forecast.

**exponential smoothing** an averaging method that weights the most recent data more strongly than more distant data.

**forecast error** the difference between actual and forecasted demand.

**linear regression** a mathematical technique that relates a dependent variable to an independent variable in the form of a linear equation.

**linear trend line** a forecast using the linear regression equation to relate demand to time.

**long-range forecast** a forecast encompassing a period longer than two years into the future.

**mean absolute deviation (MAD)** the per-period average of the absolute difference between actual and forecasted demand.

**mean absolute percent deviation (MAPD)** the absolute forecast error measured as a percentage of demand.

**mean squared error (MSE)** the average of the squared forecast errors.

**moving average** average demand for a fixed sequence of periods including the most recent period.

**multiple regression** a mathematical relationship that relates a dependent variable to two or more independent variables.

**qualitative forecast methods** nonquantitative, subjective forecasts based on judgment, opinion, experience, and expert opinion.

**quantitative forecast methods** forecasts derived from a mathematical formula.

**random variations** movements in demand that are not predictable and follow no pattern.

**regression forecasting methods** a class of mathematical techniques that relate demand to factors that cause demand behavior.

**seasonal factor** a numerical value that is multiplied by the normal forecast to get a seasonally adjusted forecast.

**seasonal pattern** an oscillating movement in demand that occurs periodically in the short run and is repetitive.

**short- (to mid-range) forecast** a forecast encompassing the immediate future, usually days or weeks, but up to two years.

**smoothing constant** the weighting factor given to the most recent data in exponential smoothing forecasts.

**time frame** how far into the future something is forecasted.

**time series methods** a class of statistical methods that uses historical demand data over a period of time to predict future demand.

**tracking signal** a measure computed by dividing the cumulative error by MAD; used for monitoring bias in a forecast.

**trend** a gradual, long-term up or down movement of demand.

**weighted moving average** a moving average with more recent demand values adjusted with weights.

## SOLVED PROBLEMS

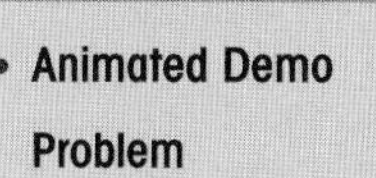


• Animated Demo Problem

### 1. MOVING AVERAGE

A manufacturing company has monthly demand for one of its products as follows:

| MONTH | DEMAND |
|---|---|
| February | 520 |
| March | 490 |
| April | 550 |
| May | 580 |
| June | 600 |
| July | 420 |
| August | 510 |
| September | 610 |

Develop a three-period moving average forecast and a three-period weighted moving average forecast with weights of 0.50, 0.30, and 0.20 for the most recent demand values, in that order. Calculate MAD for each forecast, and indicate which would seem to be most accurate.

### SOLUTION

*Step 1.* Compute the three-month moving average using the formula

$$MA_3 = \sum_{i=1}^{3} \frac{D_i}{3}$$

For May, the moving average forecast is

$$MA_3 = \frac{520 + 490 + 550}{3} = 520$$

*Step 2.* Compute the three-month weighted moving average using the formula

$$WMA_3 = \Sigma W_i D_i$$

For May, the weighted average forecast is

$$\begin{aligned} WMA_3 &= (0.50)(550) + (0.30)(490) + (0.20)(520) \\ &= 526.00 \end{aligned}$$

The values for both moving average forecasts are shown in the following table:

| MONTH | DEMAND | $MA_3$ | $WMA_3$ |
|---|---|---|---|
| February | 520 | — | — |
| March | 490 | — | — |
| April | 550 | — | — |
| May | 580 | 520.00 | 526.00 |
| June | 600 | 540.00 | 553.00 |
| July | 420 | 576.67 | 584.00 |
| August | 510 | 533.33 | 506.00 |
| September | 610 | 510.00 | 501.00 |
| October | — | 513.33 | 542.00 |

*Step 3.* Compute the MAD value for both forecasts:

$$\text{MAD} = \frac{\Sigma|D_t - F_t|}{n}$$

The MAD value for the three-month moving average is 80.0, and the MAD value for the three-month weighted moving average is 75.6, indicating there is not much difference in accuracy between the two forecasts, although the weighted moving average is slightly better.

## 2. EXPONENTIAL SMOOTHING

A computer software firm has experienced the following demand for its "Personal Finance" software package:

| PERIOD | UNITS |
|---|---|
| 1 | 56 |
| 2 | 61 |
| 3 | 55 |
| 4 | 70 |
| 5 | 66 |
| 6 | 65 |
| 7 | 72 |
| 8 | 75 |

Develop an exponential smoothing forecast using $\alpha = 0.40$ and an adjusted exponential smoothing forecast using $\alpha = 0.40$ and $\beta = 0.20$. Compare the accuracy of the two forecasts using MAD and cumulative error.

## SOLUTION

*Step 1.* Compute the exponential smoothing forecast with $\alpha = 0.40$ using the following formula:

$$F_{t+1} = \alpha D_t + (1 - \alpha)F_t$$

For period 2, the forecast (assuming $F_1 = 56$) is

$$\begin{aligned} F_2 &= \alpha D_t + (1 - \alpha)F_1 \\ &= (0.40)(56) + (0.60)(56) \\ &= 56 \end{aligned}$$

For period 3, the forecast is

$$\begin{aligned} F_3 &= (0.40)(61) + (0.60)(56) \\ &= 58 \end{aligned}$$

The remaining forecasts are computed similarly and are shown in the accompanying table.

*Step 2.* Compute the adjusted exponential smoothing forecast with $\alpha = 0.40$ and $\beta = 0.20$ using the formula

$$\text{AF}_{t+1} = F_{t+1} + T_{t+1}$$
$$T_{t+1} = \beta(F_{t+1} - F_t) + (1 - \beta)T_t$$

Starting with the forecast for period 3 (since $F_1 = F_2$, and we will assume $T_2 = 0$),

$$\begin{aligned} T_3 &= \beta(F_3 - F_2) + (1 - \beta)T_2 \\ &= (0.20)(58 - 56) + (0.80)(0) \\ &= 0.40 \\ \text{AF}_3 &= F_3 + T_3 \\ &= 58 + 0.40 \\ &= 58.40 \end{aligned}$$

The remaining adjusted forecasts are computed similarly and are shown in the following table:

| PERIOD | $D_t$ | $F_t$ | $AF_t$ | $D_t - F_t$ | $D_t - AF_t$ |
|---|---|---|---|---|---|
| 1 | 56 | — | — | — | — |
| 2 | 61 | 56.00 | 56.00 | 5.00 | 5.00 |
| 3 | 55 | 58.00 | 58.40 | −3.00 | −3.40 |
| 4 | 70 | 56.80 | 56.88 | 13.20 | 13.12 |
| 5 | 66 | 62.08 | 63.20 | 3.92 | 2.80 |
| 6 | 65 | 63.65 | 64.86 | 1.35 | 0.14 |
| 7 | 72 | 64.18 | 65.26 | 7.81 | 6.73 |
| 8 | 75 | 67.31 | 68.80 | 7.68 | 6.20 |
| 9 | — | 70.39 | 72.19 | — | — |
| | | | | 35.97 | 30.60 |

*Step 3.* Compute the MAD value for each forecast:

$$\begin{aligned} \text{MAD}(F_t) &= \frac{\Sigma|D_t - F_t|}{n} \\ &= \frac{41.97}{7} \\ &= 5.99 \\ \text{MAD}(\text{AF}_t) &= \frac{37.39}{7} \\ &= 5.34 \end{aligned}$$

*Step 4.* Compute the cumulative error for each forecast:

$$E(F_t) = 35.97$$
$$E(\text{AF}_t) = 30.60$$

Because both MAD and the cumulative error are less for the adjusted forecast, it would appear to be the most accurate.

## 3. LINEAR REGRESSION

A local building products store has accumulated sales data for 2 × 4 lumber (in board feet) and the number of building permits in its area for the past 10 quarters:

| QUARTER | BUILDING PERMITS $x$ | LUMBER SALES (1000S OF BOARD FEET) $y$ |
|---|---|---|
| 1 | 8 | 12.6 |
| 2 | 12 | 16.3 |
| 3 | 7 | 9.3 |
| 4 | 9 | 11.5 |
| 5 | 15 | 18.1 |
| 6 | 6 | 7.6 |
| 7 | 5 | 6.2 |
| 8 | 8 | 14.2 |
| 9 | 101 | 15.0 |
| 10 | 12 | 17.8 |

Develop a linear regression model for these data and determine the strength of the linear relationship using correlation. If the model appears to be relatively strong, determine the forecast for lumber given ten building permits in the next quarter.

**SOLUTION**

*Step 1.* Compute the components of the linear regression equation, $y = a + bx$, using the least squares formulas

$$\bar{x} = \frac{92}{10} = 9.2$$

$$\bar{y} = \frac{128.6}{10} = 12.86$$

$$b = \frac{\sum xy - n\bar{x}\bar{y}}{\sum x^2 - n\bar{x}^2}$$

$$= \frac{(1290.3) - (10)(9.2)(12.86)}{(932) - (10)(9.2)^2}$$

$$b = 1.25$$

$$a = \bar{y} - b\bar{x}$$

$$= 12.86 - (1.25)(9.2)$$

$$a = 1.36$$

*Step 2.* Develop the linear regression equations:

$$y = a + bx$$

$$y = 1.36 + 1.25x$$

*Step 3.* Compute the correlation coefficient:

$$r = \frac{n\sum xy - \sum x \sum y}{\sqrt{[(n\sum x^2 - (\sum x)^2][(n\sum y^2 - (\sum y)^2]}}$$

$$= \frac{(10)(1290.3) - (92)(128.6)}{\sqrt{[(10)(932) - (92)^2][(10)(1810.48) - (128.6)^2]}}$$

$$= 0.925$$

Thus, there appears to be a strong linear relationship.

*Step 4.* Calculate the forecast for $x = 10$ permits.

$$y = a + bx$$

$$= 1.36 + 1.25(10)$$

$$= 13.86 \text{ or } 13{,}860 \text{ board feet}$$

## QUESTIONS

**11-1.** List some of the operations and functions in a company that are dependent on a forecast for product demand.

**11-2.** What is the difference between quantitative forecast methods and qualitative forecast methods?

**11-3.** Describe the difference between short- and long-range forecasts.

**11-4.** Discuss the role of forecasting in supply chain management.

**11-5.** Why is accurate forecasting so important to companies that use a continuous replenishment inventory system?

**11-6.** Discuss the relationship between forecasting and TQM.

**11-7.** What kinds of forecasting methods are used for long-range strategic planning?

**11-8.** Describe the Delphi method for forecasting.

**11-9.** What is the difference between a trend and a cycle and a seasonal pattern?

**11-10.** How is the moving average method similar to exponential smoothing?

**11-11.** In the chapter examples for time series methods, the starting forecast was always assumed to be the same as actual demand in the first period. Suggest other ways that the starting forecast might be derived in actual use.

**11-12.** What effect on the exponential smoothing model will increasing the smoothing constant have?

**11-13.** How does adjusted exponential smoothing differ from exponential smoothing?

**11-14.** What determines the choice of the smoothing constant for trend in an adjusted exponential smoothing model?

**11-15.** How does the linear trend line forecasting model differ from a linear regression model for forecasting?

**11-16.** Of the time series models presented in this chapter, including the moving average and weighted moving average, exponential smoothing and adjusted exponential smoothing, and linear trend line, which one do you consider the best? Why?

**11-17.** What advantages does adjusted exponential smoothing have over a linear trend line for forecasted demand that exhibits a trend?

**11-18.** Describe how a forecast is monitored to detect bias.

**11-19.** Explain the relationship between the use of a tracking signal and statistical control limits for forecast control.

**11-20.** Selecting from MAD, MAPD, MSE, $E$, and $\bar{E}$, which measure of forecast accuracy do you consider superior? Why?

**11-21.** What is the difference between linear and multiple regression?

**11-22.** Define the different components ($y$, $x$, $a$, and $b$) of a linear regression equation.

**11-23.** A company that produces video equipment, including VCRs, video cameras, and televisions, is attempting to forecast what new products and product innovations might be technologically feasible and that customers might demand 10 years into the future. Speculate on what type of qualitative methods it might use to develop this type of forecast.

## PROBLEMS

**11-1.** The Hartley-Davis motorcycle dealer in the Minneapolis–St. Paul area wants to be able to forecast accurately the demand for the Roadhog Super motorcycle during the next month. From sales records, the dealer has accumulated the data in the adjacent table for the past year.

a. Compute a three-month moving average forecast of demand for April through January (of the next year).

b. Compute a five-month moving average forecast for June through January.

c. Compare the two forecasts computed in parts (a) and (b) using MAD. Which one should the dealer use for January of the next year?

| Month | Motorcycle Sales |
|---|---|
| January | 9 |
| February | 7 |
| March | 10 |
| April | 8 |
| May | 7 |
| June | 12 |
| July | 10 |
| August | 11 |
| September | 12 |
| October | 10 |
| November | 14 |
| December | 16 |

**11-2.** The manager of the I-85 Carpet outlet needs to be able to forecast accurately the demand for Soft Shag carpet (its biggest seller). If the manager does not order enough carpet from the carpet mill, customers will buy their carpets from one of the outlets many competitors. The manager has collected the following demand data for the past eight months.

| Month | Demand for Soft Shag Carpet (1000 yd) |
|---|---|
| 1 | 5 |
| 2 | 10 |
| 3 | 6 |
| 4 | 8 |
| 5 | 14 |
| 6 | 10 |
| 7 | 9 |
| 8 | 12 |

a. Compute a three-month moving average forecast for months 4 through 9.

b. Compute a weighted three-month moving average forecast for months 4 through 9. Assign weights of 0.55, 0.33, and 0.12 to the months in sequence, starting with the most recent month.

c. Compare the two forecasts using MAD. Which forecast appears to be more accurate?

**11-3.** The LawnPlus Fertilizer Company distributes fertilizer to various lawn and garden shops. The company must base its quarterly production schedule on a forecast of how many tons of fertilizer will be demanded from it. The company has gathered the following data for the past three years from its sales records.

| Year | Quarter | Demand for Fertilizer (ton) |
|---|---|---|
| 1 | 1 | 105 |
| | 2 | 150 |
| | 3 | 93 |
| | 4 | 121 |
| 2 | 5 | 140 |
| | 6 | 170 |
| | 7 | 105 |
| | 8 | 150 |
| 3 | 9 | 150 |
| | 10 | 170 |
| | 11 | 110 |
| | 12 | 130 |

a. Compute a three-quarter moving average forecast for quarters 4 through 13 and compute the forecast error for each quarter.

b. Compute a five-quarter moving average forecast for quarters 6 through 13 and compute the forecast error for each quarter.

c. Compute a weighted three-quarter moving average forecast using weights of 0.50, 0.33, and 0.17 for the most recent, next recent, and most distant data, respectively, and compute the forecast error for each quarter.

d. Compare the forecasts developed in parts (a), (b), and (c) using cumulative error. Which forecast appears to be most accurate? Do any exhibit any bias?

**11-4.** Graph the demand data in Problem 11-3. Can you identify any trends, cycles, and/or seasonal patterns?

**11-5.** The chairperson of the department of management at Tech wants to forecast the number of students who will enroll in operations management next semester in order to determine how many sections to schedule. The chair has accumulated the following enrollment data for the past eight semesters:

| Semester | Students Enrolled in OM |
|---|---|
| 1 | 270 |
| 2 | 310 |
| 3 | 250 |
| 4 | 290 |
| 5 | 370 |
| 6 | 410 |
| 7 | 400 |
| 8 | 450 |

a. Compute a three-semester moving average forecast for semesters 4 through 9.
b. Compute the exponentially smoothed forecast ($\alpha$ = 0.20) for the enrollment data.
c. Compare the two forecasts using MAD and indicate the most accurate.

**11-6.** The manager of the Excom Service Station wants to forecast the demand for unleaded gasoline next month so that the proper number of gallons can be ordered from the distributor. The owner has accumulated the following data on demand for unleaded gasoline from sales during the past 10 months:

| Month | Gasoline Demanded (gal) |
|---|---|
| October | 800 |
| November | 725 |
| December | 630 |
| January | 500 |
| February | 645 |
| March | 690 |
| April | 730 |
| May | 810 |
| June | 1200 |
| July | 980 |

a. Compute an exponentially smoothed forecast using an $\alpha$ value of 0.30.
b. Compute an adjusted exponentially smoothed forecast ($\alpha$ = 0.30 and $\beta$ = 0.20).
c. Compare the two forecasts using MAPD and indicate which seems to be the most accurate.

**11-7.** The Intrepid mutual fund of growth stocks has had the following average monthly price for the past 10 months.

| Month | Fund Price |
|---|---|
| 1 | 62.7 |
| 2 | 63.9 |
| 3 | 68.0 |
| 4 | 66.4 |
| 5 | 67.2 |
| 6 | 65.8 |
| 7 | 68.2 |
| 8 | 69.3 |
| 9 | 67.2 |
| 10 | 70.1 |

Compute the exponentially smoothed forecast with $\alpha$ = 0.40, the adjusted exponentially smoothed forecast with $\alpha$ = 0.40 and $\beta$ = 0.30, and the linear trend line forecast. Compare the accuracy of the three forecasts using cumulative error and MAD, and indicate which forecast appears to be most accurate.

**11-8.** The Oceanside Hotel is adjacent to City Coliseum, a 24,000-seat arena that is home to the city's professional basketball and ice hockey teams and that hosts a variety of concerts, trade shows, and conventions throughout the year. The hotel has experienced the following occupancy rates for the nine years since the coliseum opened:

| Year | Occupancy Rate |
|---|---|
| 1 | 75% |
| 2 | 70 |
| 3 | 72 |
| 4 | 77 |
| 5 | 83 |
| 6 | 81 |
| 7 | 86 |
| 8 | 91 |
| 9 | 87 |

Compute an exponential smoothing forecast with $\alpha$ = 0.20, an adjusted exponential smoothing forecast with $\alpha$ = 0.20 and $\beta$ = 0.20, and a linear trend line forecast. Compare the three forecasts using MAD and average error ($\bar{E}$), and indicate which forecast seems to be most accurate.

**11-9.** Mary Hernandez has invested in a stock mutual fund and she is considering liquidating and investing in a bond fund. She would like to forecast the price of the stock fund for the next month before making a decision. She has collected the following data on the average price of the fund during the past 20 months.

| Month | Fund Price | Month | Fund Price |
|---|---|---|---|
| 1 | 63 1/4 | 11 | 68 1/8 |
| 2 | 60 1/8 | 12 | 63 1/4 |
| 3 | 61 3/4 | 13 | 64 3/8 |
| 4 | 64 1/4 | 14 | 68 5/8 |
| 5 | 59 3/8 | 15 | 70 1/8 |
| 6 | 57 7/8 | 16 | 72 3/4 |
| 7 | 62 1/4 | 17 | 74 1/8 |
| 8 | 65 1/8 | 18 | 71 3/4 |
| 9 | 68 1/4 | 19 | 75 1/2 |
| 10 | 65 1/2 | 20 | 76 3/4 |

a. Using a three-month moving average, forecast the fund price for month 21.
b. Using a three-month weighted average with the most recent month weighted 0.60, the next most recent month weighted 0.30, and the third month weighted 0.10, forecast the fund price for month 21.
c. Compute an exponentially smoothed forecast using $\alpha$ = 0.40 and forecast the fund price for month 21.
d. Compare the forecasts in (a), (b), and (c) using MAD and indicate the most accurate.

**11-10.** Globetron manufactures components for use in small electronic products such as computers, CD players, and radios at plants in Belgium, Germany, and France. The parts are transported by truck to Hamburg, where they are shipped overseas to customers in Mexico, South America, the United States, and the Pacific Rim. The company has to reserve space on ships, months and sometimes years in advance, and as such needs an accurate forecasting model. Following are the number of cubic feet of container space the company has used in each of the past 18 months.

| Month | Space (1000s ft³) | Month | Space (1000s ft³) |
|---|---|---|---|
| 1 | 10.6 | 10 | 19.2 |
| 2 | 12.7 | 11 | 16.3 |
| 3 | 9.8 | 12 | 14.7 |
| 4 | 11.3 | 13 | 18.2 |
| 5 | 13.6 | 14 | 19.6 |
| 6 | 14.4 | 15 | 21.4 |
| 7 | 12.2 | 16 | 22.8 |
| 8 | 16.7 | 17 | 20.6 |
| 9 | 18.1 | 18 | 18.7 |

Develop a forecasting model that you believe would provide the company with relatively accurate forecasts for the next year and indicate the forecasted shipping space required for the next 3 months.

**11-11.** The Bee Line Café is well known for its popular homemade ice cream, which it makes in a small plant in back of the cafe. People drive long distances to buy the ice cream. The two ladies who own the café want to develop a forecasting model so they can plan their ice cream production operation and determine the number of employees they need to sell ice cream in the café. They have accumulated the following sales records for their ice cream for the past 12 quarters:

| Year/Quarter | Ice Cream Sales (gal) |
|---|---|
| 2002: 1 | 350 |
| 2 | 510 |
| 3 | 750 |
| 4 | 420 |
| 2003: 5 | 370 |
| 6 | 480 |
| 7 | 860 |
| 8 | 500 |
| 2004: 9 | 450 |
| 10 | 550 |
| 11 | 820 |
| 12 | 570 |

Develop an adjusted exponential smoothing model with $\alpha = 0.50$ and $\beta = 0.50$ to forecast demand, and assess its accuracy using cumulative error ($E$) and average error ($\bar{E}$). Does there appear to be any bias in the forecast?

**11-12.** For the demand data in Problem 11-11, develop a seasonally adjusted forecast for 2005. (Use a linear trend line model to develop a forecast estimate for 2005.) Which forecast model do you perceive to be the most accurate, the adjusted exponential smoothing model from Problem 11-11 or the seasonally adjusted forecast?

**11-13.** Develop a seasonally adjusted forecast for the demand data for fertilizer in Problem 11-3. Use a linear trend line model to compute a forecast estimate for demand in year 4.

**11-14.** Backstreet's Pizza delivery service has randomly selected eight weekdays during the past month and recorded orders for pizza at four different time periods per day, as follows:

| Time Period | Days 1 | 2 | 3 | 4 | 5 | 6 | 7 | 8 |
|---|---|---|---|---|---|---|---|---|
| 10:00 A.M.–3:00 P.M. | 62 | 49 | 53 | 35 | 43 | 48 | 56 | 43 |
| 3:00 P.M.–7:00 P.M. | 73 | 55 | 81 | 77 | 60 | 66 | 85 | 70 |
| 7:00 P.M.–11:00 P.M. | 42 | 38 | 45 | 50 | 29 | 37 | 35 | 44 |
| 11:00 P.M.–2:00 A.M. | 35 | 40 | 36 | 39 | 26 | 25 | 36 | 31 |

Develop a seasonally adjusted forecasting model for daily pizza demand and forecast demand for each of the time periods for a single upcoming day.

**11-15.** The Willow River Mining Company mines and ships coal. It has experienced the following demand for coal during the past eight years:

| Year | Coal Sales (tons) |
|---|---|
| 1 | 4260 |
| 2 | 4510 |
| 3 | 4050 |
| 4 | 3720 |
| 5 | 3900 |
| 6 | 3470 |
| 7 | 2890 |
| 8 | 3100 |

Develop an adjusted exponential smoothing model ($\alpha = 0.30$, $\beta = 0.20$) and a linear trend line model, and compare the forecast accuracy of the two using MAD. Indicate which forecast seems to be most accurate.

**11-16.** The Great Northwest Outdoor Company is a catalogue sales operation that specializes in outdoor recreational clothing. Demand for its items is very seasonal, peaking during the holiday season and during the spring. It has accumulated the following data for order per "season" (quarter) during the past five years:

| Quarter | Orders (1000s) 2000 | 2001 | 2002 | 2003 | 2004 |
|---|---|---|---|---|---|
| January–March | 18.6 | 18.1 | 22.4 | 23.2 | 24.5 |
| April–June | 23.5 | 24.7 | 28.8 | 27.6 | 31.0 |
| July–September | 20.4 | 19.5 | 21.0 | 24.4 | 23.7 |
| October–December | 41.9 | 46.3 | 45.5 | 47.1 | 52.8 |

a. Develop a seasonally adjusted forecast model for these order data. Forecast demand for each quarter for 2005 (using a linear trend line forecast estimate for orders in 2005).
b. Develop a separate linear trend line forecast for each of the four seasons and forecast each season for 2005.
c. Which of the two approaches used in parts (a) and (b) appear to be the most accurate? Use MAD to verify your selection.

**11-17.** Townside Food Vending operates vending machines in office buildings, the airport, bus stations, colleges, and other businesses and agencies around town and operates vending trucks for building and construction sites. The company believes its sandwich sales follow a seasonal pattern. It has accumulated the following data for sandwich sales per season during the past four years.

| | Sandwich Sales (1000s) | | | |
|---|---|---|---|---|
| **Season** | *2001* | *2002* | *2003* | *2004* |
| Fall | 42.7 | 44.3 | 45.7 | 40.6 |
| Winter | 36.9 | 42.7 | 34.8 | 41.5 |
| Spring | 51.3 | 55.6 | 49.3 | 47.3 |
| Summer | 62.9 | 64.8 | 71.2 | 74.5 |

Develop a seasonally adjusted forecast model for these sandwich sales data. Forecast demand for each season for 2005 using a linear trend line estimate for sales in 2005. Do the data appear to have a seasonal pattern?

**11-18.** During the past 5 months the emergency room at the new County Hospital has observed the number of patients during two parts of every other week—the weekend (Friday through Sunday) and weekdays (Monday through Thursday). They typically experience greater patient traffic on weekends than during the week:

| | Number of Patients | |
|---|---|---|
| **Week** | *Weekend* | *Weekdays* |
| 1 | 105 | 73 |
| 2 | 119 | 85 |
| 3 | 122 | 89 |
| 4 | 128 | 83 |
| 5 | 117 | 96 |
| 6 | 136 | 78 |
| 7 | 141 | 91 |
| 8 | 126 | 100 |
| 9 | 143 | 83 |
| 10 | 140 | 101 |

a. Develop a seasonally adjusted forecasting model for number of patients during each part of the week for week 11.

**11-19.** Temco Industries has developed a forecasting model that was used to forecast during a 10-month period. The forecasts and actual demand are shown as follows:

| Month | Actual Demand | Forecast Demand |
|---|---|---|
| 1 | 160 | 170 |
| 2 | 150 | 165 |
| 3 | 175 | 157 |
| 4 | 200 | 166 |
| 5 | 190 | 183 |
| 6 | 220 | 186 |
| 7 | 205 | 203 |
| 8 | 210 | 204 |
| 9 | 200 | 207 |
| 10 | 220 | 203 |

Measure the accuracy of the forecast using MAD, MAPD, and cumulative error. Does the forecast method appear to be accurate?

**11-20.** Monitor the forecast in Problem 11-19 for bias using a tracking signal and a control chart with $\pm 3$ MAD. Does there appear to be any bias in the forecast?

**11-21.** Develop a statistical control chart for the forecast error in Problem 11-11 using $\pm 3\sigma$ control limits, and indicate if the forecast seems to be biased.

**11-22.** Monitor the adjusted exponential smoothing forecast in Problem 11-15 for bias using a tracking signal and a control chart with $\pm 3$ MAD.

**11-23.** RAP Computers assembles computers from generic parts it purchases at discount and sells the units via phone orders it receives from customers responding to their ads in trade journals. The business has developed an exponential smoothing forecast model to forecast future computer demand. Actual demand for their computers for the past eight months is as follows:

| Month | Demand | Forecast |
|---|---|---|
| March | 120 | — |
| April | 110 | 120.0 |
| May | 150 | 116.0 |
| June | 130 | 129.6 |
| July | 160 | 129.7 |
| August | 165 | 141.8 |
| September | 140 | 151.1 |
| October | 155 | 146.7 |
| November | — | 150.0 |

a. Using the measure of forecast accuracy of your choice, ascertain if the forecast appears to be accurate.
b. Determine if a three-month moving average would provide a better forecast.
c. Use a tracking signal to monitor the forecast in part (a) for bias.

**11-24.** Develop an exponential smoothing forecast with $\alpha = 0.20$ for the demand data in Problem 11-1. Compare this forecast with the three-month moving average computed in 11-1(a) using MAD and indicate which forecast seems to be most accurate.

**11-25.** The Fieldale Dairy produces cheese, which it sells to supermarkets and food processing companies. Because of concerns about cholesterol and fat in cheese, the company has seen demand for its products decline during the past decade. It is now considering introducing some alternative low-fat dairy products and wants to determine how much available plant capacity it will have next year. The company has developed an exponential smoothing forecast with $\alpha = 0.40$ to forecast cheese. The actual demand and the forecasts from its model are shown as follows:

| | Demand | |
|---|---|---|
| **Year** | *(1000s lb)* | *Forecast* |
| 1 | 16.8 | — |
| 2 | 14.1 | 16.8 |
| 3 | 15.3 | 15.7 |
| 4 | 12.7 | 15.5 |
| 5 | 11.9 | 14.4 |
| 6 | 12.3 | 13.4 |
| 7 | 11.5 | 12.9 |
| 8 | 10.8 | 12.4 |

Assess the accuracy of the forecast model using MAD and cumulative error, and determine if the forecast error reflects bias using a tracking signal and ±3 MAD control limits. If the exponential smoothing forecast model is biased, determine if a linear trend model would provide a more accurate forecast.

**11-26.** The manager of the Commander Hotel near City Stadium believes that how well the local Blue Sox professional baseball team is playing has an impact on the occupancy rate at the hotel during the summer months. Following are the number of victories for the Blue Sox (in a 162-game schedule) for the past eight years and the hotel occupancy rates:

| Year | Number of Blue Sox Wins | Occupancy Rate |
|---|---|---|
| 1 | 70 | 81% |
| 2 | 65 | 74 |
| 3 | 81 | 83 |
| 4 | 88 | 84 |
| 5 | 80 | 85 |
| 6 | 92 | 91 |
| 7 | 83 | 88 |
| 8 | 64 | 80 |

Develop a linear regression model for these data, and forecast the occupancy rate for next year if the Blue Sox win 85 games. Does there appear to be a strong relationship between wins and occupancy rate?

**11-27.** The I-85 Carpet Outlet wants to develop a means to forecast its carpet sales. The store manager believes that the store's sales are directly related to the number of new housing starts in town. The manager has gathered data from county records of monthly house construction permits and from store records on monthly sales. These data are as follows:

| Monthly Carpet Sales (1000s yd) | Monthly Construction Permits |
|---|---|
| 5 | 17 |
| 12 | 30 |
| 6 | 12 |
| 5 | 14 |
| 8 | 18 |
| 4 | 10 |
| 14 | 38 |
| 9 | 20 |
| 9 | 16 |
| 16 | 31 |

a. Develop a linear regression model for this data and forecast carpet sales if 25 construction permits for new homes are filed.

b. Determine the strength of the causal relationship between monthly sales and new home construction using correlation.

**11-28.** The manager of Sarah's Ice Cream store needs an accurate forecast of the demand for ice cream. The store orders ice cream from a distributor a week ahead, and if too little is ordered the store loses business. If it orders too much, it must be thrown away. The manager believes that a major determinant of ice cream sales is temperature; that is, the hotter it is, the more ice cream people buy. Using an almanac, the manager has determined the average daytime temperature for 10 weeks selected at random and then, from store records, has determined the ice cream consumption for the same 10 weeks. The data are summarized as follows:

| Week | Temperature | (Gallons Sold) |
|---|---|---|
| 1 | 75° | 95 |
| 2 | 67 | 90 |
| 3 | 83 | 125 |
| 4 | 89 | 150 |
| 5 | 77 | 85 |
| 6 | 80 | 115 |
| 7 | 84 | 110 |
| 8 | 92 | 145 |
| 9 | 89 | 130 |
| 10 | 65 | 100 |

a. Develop a linear regression model for this data and forecast the ice cream consumption if the average weekly daytime temperature is expected to be 80°.

b. Determine the strength of the linear relationship between temperature and ice cream consumption using correlation.

**11-29.** Compute the coefficient of determination for the data in Problem 11-28 and explain its meaning.

**11-30.** The registrar at State University believes that decreases in the number of freshman applications that have been experienced are directly related to tuition increases. They have collected the following enrollment and tuition data for the past decade:

| Year | Freshman Applications | Annual Tuition ($) |
|---|---|---|
| 1 | 6010 | 3600 |
| 2 | 5560 | 3600 |
| 3 | 6100 | 4000 |
| 4 | 5330 | 4400 |
| 5 | 4980 | 4500 |
| 6 | 5870 | 5700 |
| 7 | 5120 | 6000 |
| 8 | 4750 | 6000 |
| 9 | 4615 | 7500 |
| 10 | 4100 | 8000 |

a. Develop a linear regression model for these data and forecast the number of applications for State University if tuition increases to $10,000 per year and if tuition is lowered to $7000 per year.

b. Determine the strength of the linear relationship between freshman applications and tuition using correlation.

c. Describe the various planning decisions for State University that would be affected by the forecast for freshman applications.

**11-31.** Employees at Hubbell Engine Parts Company produce parts using precision machine tools according to exact design specifications. The employees are paid partially according to a piece rate system wherein if they work faster and produce more parts, they are eligible for monthly bonuses. Management suspects that this method of pay may contribute to a high number of defective parts. A specific part requires a normal, standard time of 23 minutes to produce. The quality control manager has checked the actual average times to produce this part for 10 different employees during 20 days selected at random during the past month, and determined the corresponding percentage of defective parts, as follows.

| Average Time (min) | % Defective | Average Time (min) | % Defective |
|---|---|---|---|
| 21.6 | 4.1 | 20.8 | 3.1 |
| 22.5 | 4.6 | 18.9 | 6.1 |
| 23.1 | 1.2 | 21.4 | 3.8 |
| 24.6 | 1.5 | 23.7 | 1.9 |
| 22.8 | 2.6 | 23.8 | 1.7 |
| 23.7 | 1.9 | 24.9 | 0.8 |
| 20.9 | 3.7 | 19.8 | 4.3 |
| 19.7 | 5.3 | 19.7 | 5.1 |
| 24.5 | 1.8 | 21.2 | 3.9 |
| 26.7 | 2.3 | 20.8 | 1.7 |

Develop a linear regression model relating average production time to percentage defects to determine if a relationship exists, and the percentage of defective items that would be expected with the normal production time of 23 minutes.

**11-32.** Apperson and Fitz is a chain of clothing stores that caters to high school and college students. It publishes a quarterly catalogue and operates a Web site that features provocatively attired males and females. The Web site is very expensive to maintain, and company executives are not sure if the number of hits at the site relate to sales; that is, people may be looking at the site for the pictures rather than as potential customers. The Web master has accumulated the following data for hits per month and orders placed at the Web site for the past 20 months.

| Hits (1000s) | Orders (1000s) | Hits (1000s) | Orders (1000s) |
|---|---|---|---|
| 34.2 | 8.2 | 46.7 | 9.1 |
| 28.5 | 5.7 | 43.5 | 7.2 |
| 36.7 | 9.1 | 52.6 | 10.7 |
| 42.3 | 7.5 | 61.8 | 9.3 |
| 25.8 | 6.3 | 37.3 | 3.1 |
| 52.3 | 10.4 | 28.9 | 4.4 |
| 35.2 | 7.5 | 26.4 | 5.2 |
| 27.9 | 6.2 | 39.4 | 6.8 |
| 31.4 | 4.8 | 44.7 | 8.4 |
| 29.4 | 5.3 | 46.3 | 7.9 |

Develop a linear regression model for these data and indicate if there appears to be a strong relationship between Web site hits and orders. What would be the forecast for orders with 60,000 hits per month?

**11-33.** Develop a linear trend line model for the freshman applications data at State University in Problem 11-30.

a. Does this forecast appear to be more or less accurate than the linear regression forecast developed in Problem 11-30? Justify your answer.
b. Compute the correlation coefficient for the linear trend line forecast and explain its meaning.

**11-34.** Explain what the numerical value of the slope of the linear regression equation in Problem 11-28 means.

**11-35.** ITown is a large computer discount store that sells computers and ancillary equipment and software in the town where State University is located. It has collected historical data on computer sales and printer sales for the past 10 years as follows:

| Year | Personal Computer Sales | Printers Sold |
|---|---|---|
| 1 | 1045 | 381 |
| 2 | 1610 | 579 |
| 3 | 860 | 312 |
| 4 | 1211 | 501 |
| 5 | 975 | 296 |
| 6 | 1117 | 415 |
| 7 | 1066 | 535 |
| 8 | 1310 | 592 |
| 9 | 1517 | 607 |
| 10 | 1246 | 473 |

a. Develop a linear trend line forecast to forecast printer demand in year 11.
b. Develop a linear regression model relating printer sales to computer sales to forecast printer demand in year 11 if 1500 computers are sold.
c. Compare the forecasts developed in parts (a) and (b) and indicate which one appears to be the best.

**11-36.** Develop an exponential smoothing model with $\alpha = 0.30$ for the data in Problem 11-35 to forecast printer demand in year 11, and compare its accuracy to the linear regression forecast developed in 11-35(a).

**11-37.** Arrow Air is a regional East Coast airline. It has collected data for the percentage of available seats occupied on its flights for four quarters—(1) January–March, (2) April–June, (3) July–September, and (4) October–December—for the past five years. The company also has collected data for the average percentage fare discount for each of these quarters as follows:

| Year | Quarter | % Seat Occupancy | % Average Fare Discount |
|---|---|---|---|
| 1 | 1 | 63 | 21 |
| | 2 | 75 | 34 |
| | 3 | 76 | 18 |
| | 4 | 58 | 26 |
| 2 | 1 | 59 | 18 |
| | 2 | 62 | 40 |
| | 3 | 81 | 25 |
| | 4 | 76 | 30 |

| Year | Quarter | % Seat Occupancy | % Average Fare Discount |
|---|---|---|---|
| 3 | 1 | 65 | 23 |
| | 2 | 70 | 28 |
| | 3 | 78 | 30 |
| | 4 | 69 | 35 |
| 4 | 1 | 59 | 20 |
| | 2 | 61 | 35 |
| | 3 | 83 | 26 |
| | 4 | 71 | 30 |
| 5 | 1 | 60 | 25 |
| | 2 | 66 | 37 |
| | 3 | 86 | 25 |
| | 4 | 74 | 30 |

a. Develop a seasonally adjusted forecast model for seat occupancy. Forecast seat occupancy for year 6 (using a linear trend line forecast estimate for seat occupancy in year 6).

b. Develop linear regression models relating seat occupancy to discount fares to forecast seat occupancy for each quarter in year 6. Assume a fare discount of 20% for quarter 1, 36% for quarter 2, 25% for quarter 3, and 30% for quarter 4.

c. Compare the forecasts developed in parts (a) and (b) and indicate which one appears to be the best.

**11-38.** Develop an adjusted exponential smoothing forecast model ($\alpha = 0.40$ and $\beta = 0.40$) for the data in Problem 11-37 to forecast seat occupancy, and compare its accuracy with the seasonally adjusted model developed in 11.37(a).

**11-39.** The consumer loan department at National Bank wants to develop a forecasting model to help determine its potential loan application volume for the coming year. Since adjustable-rate home mortgages are based on government long-term Treasury note rates, the bank has collected the following data for three- to five-year Treasury note interest rates for the past 24 years:

| Year | Rate | Year | Rate | Year | Rate |
|---|---|---|---|---|---|
| 1 | 5.77 | 9 | 9.71 | 17 | 7.68 |
| 2 | 5.85 | 10 | 11.55 | 18 | 8.26 |
| 3 | 6.92 | 11 | 14.44 | 19 | 8.55 |
| 4 | 7.82 | 12 | 12.92 | 20 | 8.26 |
| 5 | 7.49 | 13 | 10.45 | 21 | 6.80 |
| 6 | 6.67 | 14 | 11.89 | 22 | 6.12 |
| 7 | 6.69 | 15 | 9.64 | 23 | 5.48 |
| 8 | 8.29 | 16 | 7.06 | 24 | 6.09 |

Develop an appropriate forecast model for the bank to use to forecast Treasury note rates in the future, and indicate how accurate it appears to be compared to historical data.

**11-40.** The Vantage Fund is a balanced mutual fund that includes a mix of stocks and bonds. Following are the year-end share prices of the fund and Dow Jones Industrial Average for a 20-year period.

| Year | Share Price | DJIA | Year | Share Price | DJIA |
|---|---|---|---|---|---|
| 1 | 14.75 | 1046 | 11 | 19.08 | 3301 |
| 2 | 15.06 | 1258 | 12 | 20.40 | 3754 |
| 3 | 14.98 | 1211 | 13 | 19.39 | 3834 |
| 4 | 15.73 | 1546 | 14 | 24.43 | 5117 |
| 5 | 16.11 | 1895 | 15 | 26.46 | 6448 |
| 6 | 16.07 | 1938 | 16 | 29.45 | 7908 |
| 7 | 16.78 | 2168 | 17 | 29.35 | 9181 |
| 8 | 17.69 | 2753 | 18 | 27.96 | 11497 |
| 9 | 16.90 | 2633 | 19 | 28.21 | 10786 |
| 10 | 17.81 | 3168 | 20 | 27.26 | 10150 |

Develop a linear regression model for these data and forecast the fund share price for a DJIA of 12,000. Does there appear to be a strong relationship between the fund's share price and the DJIA?

**11-41.** The admission data for freshmen at Tech during the past 10 years are as follows:

| Year | Applicants | Offers | % Offers | Acceptances | % Acceptances |
|---|---|---|---|---|---|
| 1 | 13,876 | 11,200 | 80.7 | 4112 | 36.7 |
| 2 | 14,993 | 11,622 | 77.8 | 4354 | 37.3 |
| 3 | 14,842 | 11,579 | 78.0 | 4755 | 41.1 |
| 4 | 16,285 | 13,207 | 81.1 | 5068 | 38.0 |
| 5 | 16,922 | 11,382 | 73.2 | 4532 | 39.8 |
| 6 | 16,109 | 11,937 | 74.1 | 4655 | 39.0 |
| 7 | 15,883 | 11,616 | 73.1 | 4659 | 40.1 |
| 8 | 18,407 | 11,539 | 62.7 | 4620 | 40.0 |
| 9 | 18,838 | 13,138 | 69.7 | 5054 | 38.5 |
| 10 | 17,756 | 11,952 | 67.3 | 4822 | 40.3 |

Tech's admission objective is a class of 5000 entering freshmen, and it wants to forecast the percentage of offers it will likely have to make in order to achieve this objective.

a. Develop a linear trend line to forecast next year's applicants and percentage acceptances and use these results to estimate the percentage offers that Tech should expect to make.

b. Develop a linear trend line to forecast the percentage offers that Tech should expect to make and compare this result with the result in part (a). Which forecast do you think is more accurate?

c. Assume Tech receives 18,300 applicants in year 11. How many offers do you think it should make to get 5000 acceptances?

**11-42.** Some members of management of the Fairface Cosmetics Firm believe that demand for its products is related to the promotional activities of local department stores where its cosmetics are sold. However, others in management believe that other factors, such as local demographics, are stronger determinants of demand behavior. The following data for local annual promotional expenditures for all Fairface products and local annual unit sales for Fairface lip gloss have been collected from 20 stores selected at random from different localities:

| Store | Annual Unit Sales ($1000s) | Annual Promotional Expenditures ($1000s) |
|---|---|---|
| 1 | 5.3 | 12.6 |
| 2 | 4.2 | 15.5 |
| 3 | 3.1 | 10.8 |
| 4 | 2.7 | 8.7 |
| 5 | 5.9 | 20.3 |
| 6 | 5.6 | 21.9 |
| 7 | 10.3 | 25.6 |
| 8 | 4.1 | 14.3 |
| 9 | 9.9 | 15.1 |
| 10 | 5.7 | 18.7 |
| 11 | 3.5 | 9.6 |
| 12 | 3.2 | 12.7 |
| 13 | 8.1 | 16.3 |
| 14 | 3.6 | 8.1 |
| 15 | 5.3 | 7.5 |
| 16 | 5.8 | 12.4 |
| 17 | 8.1 | 17.3 |
| 18 | 6.1 | 11.2 |
| 19 | 3.1 | 18.5 |
| 20 | 9.5 | 16.7 |

Based on these data, does it appear that the strength of the relationship between lip gloss sales and promotional expenditures is sufficient to warrant using a linear regression forecasting model? Explain your response.

**11-43.** The Pro Apparel company manufactures baseball-style caps with various team logos. The caps come in an assortment of designs and colors. The company has had monthly sales for the past 24 months as follows:

| Month | Demand (1000s) | Month | Demand (1000s) |
|---|---|---|---|
| 1 | 8.2 | 13 | 10.3 |
| 2 | 7.5 | 14 | 10.5 |
| 3 | 8.1 | 15 | 11.7 |
| 4 | 9.3 | 16 | 9.8 |
| 5 | 9.1 | 17 | 10.8 |
| 6 | 9.5 | 18 | 11.3 |
| 7 | 10.4 | 19 | 12.6 |
| 8 | 9.7 | 20 | 11.5 |
| 9 | 10.2 | 21 | 10.8 |
| 10 | 10.6 | 22 | 11.7 |
| 11 | 8.2 | 23 | 12.5 |
| 12 | 9.9 | 24 | 12.8 |

Develop a forecast model using the method you believe best, and justify your selection using a measure (or measures) of forecast accuracy.

**11-44.** State University administrators believe their freshman applications are influenced by two variables: tuition and the size of the applicant pool of eligible high school seniors in the state. The following data for an eight-year period show the tuition rates (per semester) and the sizes of the applicant pool for each year:

| Tuition ($) | Applicant Pool | Applicants |
|---|---|---|
| 900 | 76,200 | 11,060 |
| 1250 | 78,050 | 10,900 |
| 1375 | 67,420 | 8,670 |
| 1400 | 70,390 | 9,050 |
| 1550 | 62,550 | 7,400 |
| 1625 | 59,230 | 7,100 |
| 1750 | 57,900 | 6,300 |
| 1930 | 60,080 | 6,100 |

a. Using Excel, develop the multiple regression equation for these data.
b. What is the coefficient of determination for this regression equation?
c. Determine the forecast for freshman applicants for a tuition rate of $1500 per semester with a pool of applicants of 60,000.

**11-45.** In Problem 11-35, ITown believes its printer sales are also related to the average price of its printers. It has collected historical data on average printer prices for the past 10 years as follows:

| Year | Average Printer Prices ($) |
|---|---|
| 1 | 475 |
| 2 | 490 |
| 3 | 520 |
| 4 | 420 |
| 5 | 410 |
| 6 | 370 |
| 7 | 350 |
| 8 | 300 |
| 9 | 280 |
| 10 | 250 |

a. Using Excel, develop the multiple regression equation for these data.
b. What is the coefficient of determination for this regression equation?
c. Determine a forecast for printer sales based on personal computer sales of 1500 units and an average printer price of $300.

**11-46.** The manager of the Salem police department motor pool wants to develop a forecast model for annual maintenance on police cars based on mileage in the past year and age of the cars. The following data have been collected for eight different cars:

| Miles Driven | Car Age (years) | Maintenance Cost ($) |
|---|---|---|
| 14,320 | 6 | $1120 |
| 15,100 | 7 | 1610 |
| 17,415 | 8 | 1545 |
| 9,370 | 3 | 900 |
| 7,230 | 3 | 650 |
| 12,045 | 5 | 1500 |
| 8,100 | 2 | 550 |
| 6,300 | 3 | 730 |

a. Using Excel develop a multiple regression equation for these data.
b. What is the coefficient of determination for this regression equation?
c. Forecast the annual maintenance cost for a police car that is four years old and will be driven 10,000 miles in one year.

**11-47.** The busiest time of the day at the Taco Town fast-food restaurant is between 11:00 A.M. and 2:00 P.M. Taco Town's service is very labor-dependent, and a critical factor for providing quick service is the number of employees on hand during this three-hour period. In order to determine the number of employees it needs during each hour of the three-hour lunch period Taco Town requires an accurate forecasting model. Following are the number of customers served at Taco Town during each hour of the lunch period for the past 20 weekdays.

| | Hour | | | | Hour | | |
|---|---|---|---|---|---|---|---|
| **Day** | *11–12* | *12–1* | *1–2* | **Day** | *11–12* | *12–1* | *1–2* |
| 1 | 90 | 125 | 87 | 11 | 57 | 114 | 106 |
| 2 | 76 | 131 | 93 | 12 | 68 | 125 | 95 |
| 3 | 87 | 112 | 99 | 13 | 75 | 206 | 102 |
| 4 | 83 | 149 | 78 | 14 | 94 | 117 | 118 |
| 5 | 71 | 156 | 83 | 15 | 103 | 145 | 122 |
| 6 | 94 | 178 | 89 | 16 | 67 | 121 | 93 |
| 7 | 56 | 101 | 124 | 17 | 94 | 113 | 76 |
| 8 | 63 | 91 | 66 | 18 | 83 | 166 | 94 |
| 9 | 73 | 146 | 119 | 19 | 79 | 124 | 87 |
| 10 | 101 | 104 | 96 | 20 | 81 | 118 | 115 |

Develop a forecast model that you believe will best forecast Taco Town's customer demand for the next day and explain why you selected this model.

**11-48.** The State of Virginia has instituted a series of Standards of Learning (SOL) tests in math, history, English, and science that all high school students must pass with a grade of 70 before that are allowed to graduate and receive their diploma. The school superintendent of Montgomery County believes the tests are unfair because they are closely related to teacher salaries and teacher school tenure (i.e., the years a teacher has been at a school). The superintendent has sampled 12 other county school systems in the state and accumulated the following data for average teacher salaries and average teacher tenure.

| School | Average SOL Score | Average Teacher Salaries ($) | Average Teacher Tenure (yr) |
|---|---|---|---|
| 1 | 81 | $34,300 | 9.3 |
| 2 | 78 | 28,700 | 10.1 |
| 3 | 76 | 26,500 | 7.6 |
| 4 | 77 | 36,200 | 8.2 |
| 5 | 84 | 35,900 | 8.8 |
| 6 | 86 | 32,500 | 12.7 |
| 7 | 79 | 31,800 | 8.4 |
| 8 | 91 | 38,200 | 11.5 |
| 9 | 68 | 27,100 | 8.3 |
| 10 | 73 | 31,500 | 7.3 |
| 11 | 90 | 37,600 | 12.3 |
| 12 | 85 | 40,400 | 14.2 |

a. Using Excel, develop the multiple regression equation for these data.
b. What is the coefficient of determination for this regression equation? Do you think the superintendent is correct in his beliefs?
c. Montgomery County has an average SOL score of 74 with an average teacher's salary of $27,500 and an average teacher tenure of 7.8 years. The superintendent has proposed to the school board a salary increase that would raise the average salary to $30,000 and a benefits program with a goal of increasing the average tenure to nine years. He has suggested that if the board passes his proposals the average SOL score will increase to 80. Is he correct according to the forecasting model?

## CASE PROBLEM 11.1

### *Forecasting at State University*

During the past few years the legislature has severely reduced funding for State University. In reaction, the administration at State has significantly raised tuition each year for the past five years. A bargain five years ago, State is now considered an expensive state-supported university. Some parents and students now question the value of a State education, and applications for admission have declined. Since a portion of state educational funding is based on a formula tied to enrollments, State has maintained its enrollment levels by going deeper into its applicant pool and accepting less qualified students.

On top of these problems, an increase in the college-age population is expected in this decade. Key members of the state legislature have told the university administration that State will be expected to absorb additional students during this decade. However, because of the economic outlook and the budget situation, State should not expect any funding increases for additional facilities, classrooms, dormitory rooms, or faculty. The university already has a classroom deficit in excess of 25%, and class sizes are above the average of their peer institutions.

The president of the university, Tanisha Lindsey, established several task forces consisting of faculty and administrators to address these problems. These groups made a number of recommendations, including the implementation of total quality management (TQM) practices and more in-depth, focused planning.

Discuss in general terms how forecasting might be used for planning to address these specific problems and the role of forecasting in initiating a TQM approach. Include in your discussion the types of forecasting methods that might be used.

## CASE PROBLEM 11.2

### *The University Bookstore Student Computer Purchase Program*

The University Bookstore is owned and operated by State University through an independent corporation with its own board of directors. The bookstore has three locations on or near the State University campus. It stocks a range of items, including textbooks, trade books, logo apparel, drawing and educational supplies, and computers and related products such as printers, modems, and software. The bookstore has a program to sell personal computers to incoming freshmen and other students at a substantial educational discount partly passed on from computer manufacturers. This means that the bookstore just covers computer costs with a very small profit margin remaining.

Each summer all incoming freshmen and their parents come to the State campus for a three-day orientation program. The students come in groups of 100 throughout the summer. During their visit the students and their parents are given details about the bookstore's computer purchase program. Some students place their computer orders for the fall semester at this time, while others wait until later in the summer. The bookstore also receives orders from returning students throughout the summer. This program presents a challenging supply chain management problem for the bookstore.

Orders come in throughout the summer, many only a few weeks before school starts in the fall, and the computer suppliers require at least six weeks for delivery. Thus, the bookstore must forecast computer demand to build up inventory to meet student demand in the fall. The student computer program and the forecast of computer demand have repercussions all along the bookstore supply chain. The bookstore has a warehouse near campus where it must store all computers since it has no storage space at its retail locations. Ordering too many computers not only ties up the bookstore's cash reserves, but also takes up limited storage space and limits inventories for other bookstore products during the bookstore's busiest sales period. Since the bookstore has such a low profit margin on computers, its bottom line depends on these other products. As competition for good students has increased, the university has become very quality-conscious and insists that all university facilities provide exemplary student service, which for the bookstore means meeting all student demands for computers when the fall semester starts. The number of computers ordered also affects the number of temporary warehouse and bookstore workers that must be hired for handling and assisting with PC installations. The number of truck trips from the warehouse to the bookstore each day of fall registration is also affected by computer sales.

The bookstore student computer purchase program has been in place for 14 years. Although the student population has remained stable during this period, computer sales have been somewhat volatile. Following is the historical sales data for computers during the first month of fall registration:

| Year | Computers Sold | Year | Computers Sold |
|---|---|---|---|
| 1 | 518 | 8 | 792 |
| 2 | 651 | 9 | 877 |
| 3 | 708 | 10 | 693 |
| 4 | 921 | 11 | 841 |
| 5 | 775 | 12 | 1009 |
| 6 | 810 | 13 | 902 |
| 7 | 856 | 14 | 1103 |

Develop an appropriate forecast model for bookstore management to use to forecast computer demand for the next fall semester and indicate how accurate it appears to be. What other forecasts might be useful to the bookstore in managing its supply chain?

## CASE PROBLEM 11.3

### *Cascades Swim Club*

The Cascades Swim Club has 300 stockholders, each holding one share of stock in the club. A share of club stock allows the shareholder's family to use the club's heated outdoor pool during the summer upon payment of annual membership dues of $175. The club has not issued any stock in years, and only a few of the existing shares come up for sale each year. The board of directors administers the sale of all stock. When a shareholder wants to sell, he or she turns the stock into the board, which sells it to the person at the top of the waiting list. For the past few years, the length of the waiting list has remained relatively steady at approximately 20 names.

However, during the past winter two events occurred that have suddenly increased the demand for shares in the club. The winter was especially severe, and subzero weather and heavy ice storms caused both the town and the county pools to buckle and crack. The problems were not discovered until maintenance crews began to prepare the pools for the summer, and repairs cannot be completed until the fall. Also during the winter, the manager of the local country club had an argument with her board of directors and one night burned down the clubhouse. Although the pool itself was not damaged, the dressing room facilities, showers, and snack bar were destroyed. As a result of these two events, the Cascades Swim Club was inundated with applications to purchase shares. The waiting list suddenly grew to 250 people as the summer approached.

The board of directors of the swim club had refrained from issuing new shares in the past because there never was a very great demand, and the demand that did exist was usually absorbed within a year by stock turnover. In addition, the board has a real concern about overcrowding. It seemed like the present membership was about right, and there were very few complaints about overcrowding, except on holidays such as Memorial Day and the Fourth of July. However, at a recent board meeting a number of new applicants had attended and asked the board to issue new shares. In addition, a number of current shareholders suggested that this might be an opportunity for the club to raise some capital for needed repairs and to improve some of the existing facilities. This was tempting to the board. Although it had set the share price at $500 in the past, the board could set it at a much higher level now. In addition, an increase in attendance could create a need for more lifeguards.

Before the board of directors could make a decision on whether to sell more shares and, if so, how many, the board members felt they needed more information. Specifically, they would like a forecast of the average number of people (family members, guests, etc.) who might attend the pool each day during the summer with the current number of shares.

The board of directors has the following daily attendance records for June through August from the previous summer; it thinks the figures would provide accurate estimates for the upcoming summer.

| M-139 | W-380 | F-193 | Su-399 | T-177 | Th-238 |
|---|---|---|---|---|---|
| T-273 | Th-367 | Sa-378 | M-197 | W-161 | F-224 |
| W-172 | F-359 | Su-461 | T-273 | Th-308 | Sa-368 |
| Th-275 | Sa-463 | M-242 | W-213 | F-256 | Su-541 |
| F-337 | Su-578 | T-177 | Th-303 | Sa-391 | M-235 |
| Sa-402 | M-287 | W-245 | F-262 | Su-400 | T-218 |
| Su-487 | T-247 | Th-390 | Sa-447 | M-224 | W-271 |
| M-198 | W-356 | F-284 | Su-399 | T-239 | Th-259 |
| T-310 | Th-322 | Sa-417 | M-275 | W-274 | F-232 |
| W-347 | F-419 | Su-474 | T-241 | Th-205 | Sa-317 |
| Th-393 | Sa-516 | M-194 | W-190 | F-361 | Su-369 |
| F-421 | Su-478 | T-207 | Th-243 | Sa-411 | M-361 |
| Sa-595 | M-303 | W-215 | F-277 | Su-419 | |
| Su-497 | T-223 | Th-304 | Sa-241 | M-258 | |
| M-341 | W-315 | F-331 | Su-384 | T-130 | |
| T-291 | Th-258 | Sa-407 | M-246 | W-195 | |

Develop a forecasting model to forecast daily demand during the summer.

## REFERENCES


Box, G. E. P., and G. M. Jenkins. *Time Series Analysis: Forecasting and Control*, 2nd ed. Oakland, CA: Holden-Day, 1976.

Brown, R. G. *Statistical Forecasting for Inventory Control*. New York: McGraw-Hill, 1959.

Chambers, J. C., K. M. Satinder, and D. D. Smith. "How to Choose the Right Forecasting Technique." *Harvard Business Review* (July–August 1971), pp. 45–74.

Gardner, E. S. "Exponential Smoothing: The State of the Art." *Journal of Forecasting* 4(1; 1985).

Gardner, E. S., and D. G. Dannenbring. "Forecasting with Exponential Smoothing: Some Guidelines for Model Selection." *Decision Sciences* 11(2; 1980), pp. 370–383.

Makridakis, S., S. C. Wheelwright, and V. E. McGee. *Forecasting: Methods and Applications*. 2nd ed. New York: John Wiley, 1983.

Tersine, R. J., and W. Riggs. "The Delphi Technique: A Long-Range Planning Tool." *Business Horizons* 19(2; 1976).

# Inventory Management

CHAPTER **12**

Web resources for this chapter include

- Internet Exercises
- Online Practice Quizzes
- Virtual Tours
- Excel Worksheets
- Company and Resource Weblinks
- Animated Demo Problems
- Microsoft Project Exhibits

www.wiley.com/college/russell

## CHAPTER OUTLINE

In this chapter, you will learn about . . .

- The Elements of Inventory Management
- Inventory Control Systems
- Economic Order Quantity Models
- Quantity Discounts
- Reorder Point
- Order Quantity for a Periodic Inventory System

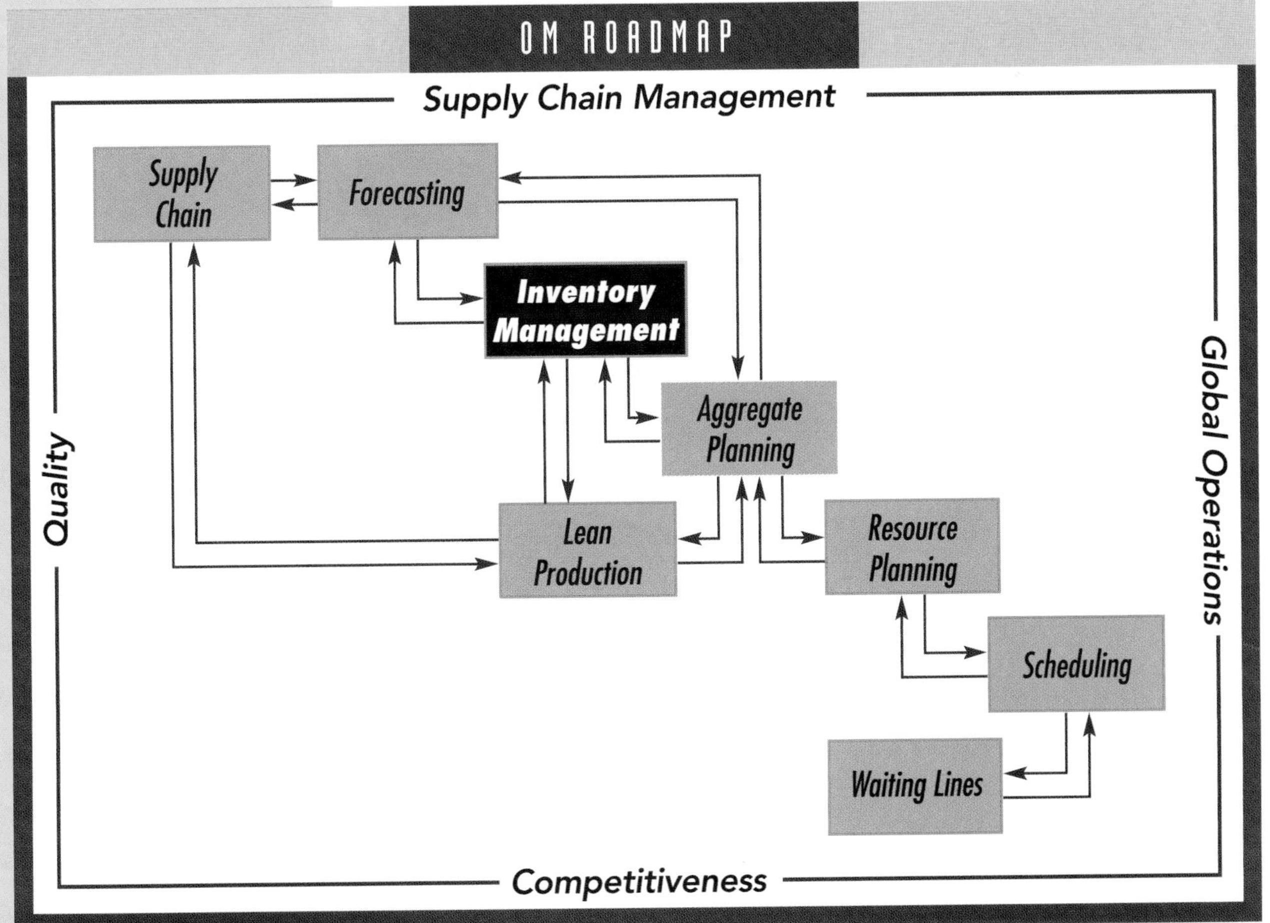

## INVENTORY MANAGEMENT ALONG IBM'S SUPPLY CHAIN

IBM is the largest producer of computer software, hardware, and services in the world. Its supply chain encompasses manufacturing sites linked with tens of thousands of suppliers and distribution channels around the world. A single product line may involve thousands of parts, with varied lead times and costs and dozens to hundreds of manufacturing and distribution sites connected by different modes of transportation. In 1994, faced with increasing competition and rapid technological advances, IBM began a reengineering effort to streamline its global supply chain in order to improve the flow of material and information. The reengineering effort focused on improving customer satisfaction and IBM's competitiveness by increasing the speed, reliability, and efficiency with which it delivers its products to the marketplace. Key objectives related to inventory management were to set strategic inventory and customer-service targets, to optimize inventory allocation and placement, and to reduce inventory while meeting customer service targets.

The IBM Personal Systems Group (PSG) is responsible for the development, manufacture, sale, and service of personal computers. It employs 18,500 workers, with manufacturing plants in the United States, Latin America, Europe, and Asia. Faced with increased competition from PC manufacturers like Dell and Gateway, which sells computers to customers direct and built-to-order, PSG felt it needed to redesign its supply chain. An objective was to determine the inventory safety stock for each product at each location in the supply chain in order to minimize the investment in total inventory. PSG was able to reduce its overall inventory by 50% from 1998 to 1999 without affecting customer service, with savings of over $100 million. IBM was able to reduce the time between parts procurement and actual sales by four to six weeks, which resulted in additional annual cost savings of $650 million. IBM also found that demand forecast accuracy greatly affected inventory and customer services, and, as a result of the system implementation it was able to determine the level of service it should promise customers based on the accuracy of its forecasts.

*Source:* G. Lin, M. EHl, S. Buckley, S. Bagchi, D. Yao, B. Naccarato, R. Allen, K. Kim, and L. Koenig, "Extended-Enterprise Supply Chain Management at IBM Personal Systems Group and Other Divisions," *Interfaces* 30(1; January–February 2000): pp. 7–25.

The objective of inventory management has been to keep enough inventory to meet customer demand and also be cost effective. However, inventory has not always been perceived as an area to control cost. Traditionally, companies maintained "generous" inventory levels to meet long-term customer demand because there were fewer competitors and products in a generally sheltered market environment. In the current global business environment, with more competitors and highly diverse markets in which new products and new product features are rapidly and continually introduced, the cost of inventory has increased due in part to quicker product obsolescence. At the same time, companies are continuously seeking to lower costs so they can provide a better product at a "lower" price.

Inventory is an obvious candidate for cost reduction. The U.S. Department of Commerce estimates that U.S. companies carry $1.1 trillion in inventory spread out along the supply chain with $450 billion at manufacturers, $290 billion at wholesalers and distributors, and $400 billion at retailers. It is estimated that the average holding cost of manufacturing goods inventory in the United States is approximately 30% of the total value of the inventory. That means if a company has $10 million worth of products in inventory, the cost of holding the inventory (including insurance, obsolescence, depreciation, interest, opportunity costs, storage costs, and so on) is approximately $3 million. If inventory could be reduced by half, to $5 million, then $1.5 million would be saved, a significant cost reduction.

The high cost of inventory has motivated companies to focus on efficient supply chain management and quality management. They believe that inventory can be significantly reduced by reducing uncertainty at various points along the supply chain. In many cases, uncertainty is created by poor quality on the part of the company or its suppliers or both. This can be in the form of variations in delivery times, uncertain production schedules caused by late deliveries, or large numbers of defects that require higher levels of production or service than what should be necessary, large fluctuations in customer demand, or poor forecasts of customer demand.

With efficient supply chain management, products or services are moved from one stage in the supply chain to the next according to a system of constant communication between customers and suppliers. Items are replaced as they are diminished without maintaining larger buffer stocks of inventory at each stage to compensate for late deliveries, inefficient service, poor quality, or uncertain demand. An efficient, well-coordinated supply chain reduces or eliminates these types of uncertainty so that this type of system will work.

Some companies maintain in-process, buffer inventories between production stages to offset irregularities and problems and keep production flowing smoothly. Quality-oriented companies consider large buffer inventories to be a costly crutch that masks problems and inefficiency primarily caused by poor quality. Adherents of quality management believe that inventory should be minimized. However, this works primarily for a production or manufacturing process. For the retailer who sells finished goods directly to the consumer or the supplier who sells parts or materials to the manufacturer, inventory is a necessity. Few shoe stores, discount stores, or department stores can stay in business with only one or two items on their shelves or racks. For these operations the traditional inventory decisions of how much to order and when to order continue to be important. In addition, the traditional approaches to inventory management are still widely used by most companies.

Despite TQM goal to minimize inventory, it's still required for retailers and suppliers.

In this chapter we review the basic elements of traditional inventory management and discuss several of the more popular models and techniques for making cost-effective inventory decisions. These decisions are basically *how much to order* and *when to order* to replenish inventory to an optimal level.

## THE ELEMENTS OF INVENTORY MANAGEMENT

**Inventory** is a stock of items kept by an organization to meet internal or external customer demand. Virtually every type of organization maintains some form of inventory. Department stores and grocery stores carry inventories of all the retail products they sell; a nursery has inventories of different plants, trees, and flowers; a rental-car agency has

**Inventory:** a stock of items kept to meet demand.

inventories of cars; and a major league baseball team maintains an inventory of players on its minor league teams. Even a family household maintains inventories of items such as food, clothing, medical supplies, and personal hygiene products.

Most people think of inventory as a final product waiting to be sold to a retail customer—a new car or a can of tomatoes. This is certainly one of its most important uses. However, especially in a manufacturing firm, inventory can take on forms besides finished goods, including:

- Raw materials
- Purchased parts and supplies
- Work-in-process (partially completed) products (WIP)
- Items being transported
- Tools, and equipment

*Inventory management:* how much and when to order.

The purpose of *inventory management* is to determine the amount of inventory to keep in stock—how much to order and when to replenish, or order. In this chapter we describe several different inventory systems and techniques for making these determinations.

## THE ROLE OF INVENTORY IN SUPPLY CHAIN MANAGEMENT

A company employs an inventory strategy for many reasons. The main reason is holding inventories of finished goods to meet customer demand for a product, especially in a retail operation. However, customer demand can also be a secretary going to a storage closet to get a printer cartridge or paper, or a carpenter getting a board or nails from a storage shed.

Since demand is usually not known with certainty, it is not possible to produce exactly the amount demanded. An additional amount of inventory, called safety, or buffer, stocks, is kept on hand to meet variations in product demand. In the *bullwhip effect* (which we have discussed previously in our chapters on supply chain and forecasting), demand information is distorted as it moves away from the end-use customer. This uncertainty about demand back upstream in the supply chain causes distributors, manufacturers, and suppliers to stock increasingly higher safety stock inventories to compensate.

Additional stocks of inventories are sometimes built up to meet demand that is seasonal or cyclical. Companies will continue to produce items when demand is low to meet high seasonal demand for which their production capacity is insufficient. For example, toy manufacturers produce large inventories during the summer and fall to meet anticipated demand during the holiday season. Doing so enables them to maintain a relatively smooth supply chain flow throughout the year. They would not normally have the production capacity or logistical support to produce enough to meet all of the holiday demand during that season. In the same way retailers might find it necessary to keep large stocks of inventory on their shelves to meet peak seasonal demand, or for display purposes to attract buyers.

At the other end of the supply chain from finished goods inventory, a company might keep large stocks of parts and material inventory to meet variations in supplier deliveries. Inventory provides independence from vendors that a company does not have direct control over. Inventories of raw materials and purchased parts are kept on hand so that the production process will not be delayed as a result of missed or late deliveries or shortages from a supplier.

A company will purchase large amounts of inventory to take advantage of price discounts, as a hedge against anticipated price increases in the future, or because it can get a lower price by purchasing in volume. Wal-Mart stores have been known to purchase a manufacturer's entire stock of soap powder or other retail item because they can get a very low price, which they subsequently pass on to their customers. Companies purchase large stocks of low-priced items when a supplier liquidates. In some cases, large orders will be made simply because the cost of ordering may be very high, and it is more cost-effective to have higher inventories than to order frequently.

Many companies find it necessary to maintain buffer inventories at different stages of their production process to provide independence between stages and to avoid work stoppages or delays. Inventories are kept between stages in the manufacturing process so that production can continue smoothly if there are temporary machine breakdowns or other work stoppages. Similarly, a stock of finished parts or products allows customer demand to be met in the event of a work stoppage or problem with transportation or distribution.

Inventory is kept between stages of a production process.

## DEMAND

The starting point for the management of inventory is customer demand. Inventory exists to meet customer demand. Customers can be inside the organization, such as a machine operator waiting for a part or partially completed product to work on. Customers can also be outside the organization—for example, an individual purchasing groceries or a new DVD player. In either case, an essential determinant of effective inventory management is an accurate forecast of demand. For this reason the topics of forecasting (Chapter 11) and inventory management are directly interrelated.

In general, the demand for items in inventory is either dependent or independent. **Dependent demand** items are typically component parts or materials used in the process of producing a final product. If an automobile company plans to produce 1000 new cars, then it will need 5000 wheels and tires (including spares). The demand for wheels is dependent on the production of cars—the demand for one item depends on demand for another item.

**Dependent demand:** items are used internally to produce a final product.

Cars, retail items, grocery products, and office supplies are examples of independent demand items. **Independent demand** items are final or finished products that are not a function of, or dependent on, internal production activity. Independent demand is usually determined by external market conditions and, thus, is beyond the direct control of the organization. In this chapter we focus on the management of inventory for independent demand items.

**Independent demand:** items are final products demanded by external customers.

*Tires like these stored at a Goodyear plant are an example of a dependent demand item. Cars are an example of independent demand, as are appliances, computers, and houses.*

## INVENTORY AND QUALITY MANAGEMENT

Inventory must be sufficient to provide high-quality customer service in TQM.

A company maintains inventory to meet its own demand and its customers' demand for items. The ability to meet effectively internal organizational demand or external customer demand in a timely, efficient manner is referred to as the *level of customer service*. A primary objective of supply chain management is to provide as high a level of customer service in terms of on-time delivery as possible. This is especially important in today's highly competitive business environment, where quality is such an important product characteristic. Customers for finished goods usually perceive quality service as availability of goods they want when they want them. (This is equally true of internal customers, such as company departments or employees.) To provide this level of quality customer service, the tendency is to maintain large stocks of all types of items. However, there is a cost associated with carrying items in inventory, which creates a cost tradeoff between the quality level of customer service and the cost of that service.

As the level of inventory increases to provide better customer service, inventory costs increase, whereas quality-related customer service costs, such as lost sales and loss of customers, decrease. The conventional approach to inventory management is to maintain a level of inventory that reflects a compromise between inventory costs and customer service. However, according to the contemporary "zero defects" philosophy of quality management, the long-term benefits of quality in terms of larger market share outweigh lower short-term production-related costs, such as inventory costs. Attempting to apply this philosophy to inventory management is not simple because one way of competing in today's diverse business environment is to reduce prices through reduced inventory costs.

## INVENTORY COSTS

*Inventory costs:* carrying, ordering, and shortage costs.

Three basic costs are associated with inventory: carrying, or holding, costs; ordering costs; and shortage costs.

**Carrying costs:** the costs of holding an item in inventory.

**Carrying costs** are the costs of holding items in inventory. Annual inventory carrying costs in the United States are estimated to be over $30 billion. These costs vary with the level of inventory in stock and occasionally with the length of time an item is held. That is, the greater the level of inventory over a period of time, the higher the carrying costs. In general, any cost that grows linearly with the number of units in stock is a carrying cost. Carrying costs can include the following items:

- Facility storage (rent, depreciation, power, heat, cooling, lighting, security, refrigeration, taxes, insurance, etc.)
- Material handling (equipment)
- Labor
- Record keeping
- Borrowing to purchase inventory (interest on loans, taxes, insurance)
- Product deterioration, spoilage, breakage, obsolescence, pilferage

Carrying costs can range from 10 to 40% of the value of a manufactured item.

Carrying costs are normally specified in one of two ways. The usual way is to assign total carrying costs, determined by summing all the individual costs just mentioned, on a per-unit basis per time period, such as a month or year. In this form, carrying costs are commonly expressed as a per-unit dollar amount on an annual basis; for example, $10 per unit per year. Alternatively, carrying costs are sometimes expressed as a percentage of the value of an item or as a percentage of average inventory value. It is generally estimated that carrying costs range from 10 to 40% of the value of a manufactured item.

**Ordering costs:** the costs of replenishing inventory.

**Ordering costs** are the costs associated with replenishing the stock of inventory being held. These are normally expressed as a dollar amount per order and are independent of the order size. Annual ordering costs vary with the number of orders made—as the number of orders increases, the ordering cost increases. In general, any cost that increases linearly with the number of orders is an ordering cost. Costs incurred each time an order is made can include requisition and purchase orders, transportation and shipping, receiving, inspection, handling, and accounting and auditing costs.

Ordering costs react inversely to carrying costs. As the size of orders increases, fewer orders are required, reducing ordering costs. However, ordering larger amounts results in higher inventory levels and higher carrying costs. In general, as the order size increases, ordering costs decrease and carrying costs increase.

**Shortage costs**, also referred to as *stockout costs*, occur when customer demand cannot be met because of insufficient inventory. If these shortages result in a permanent loss of sales, shortage costs include the loss of profits. Shortages can also cause customer dissatisfaction and a loss of goodwill that can result in a permanent loss of customers and future sales. Some studies have shown that approximately 8% of shoppers will not find the product they want to purchase in stock, which will ultimately result in total lost sales of about 3%.

**Shortage costs:** temporary or permanent loss of sales when demand cannot be met.

In some instances, the inability to meet customer demand or lateness in meeting demand results in penalties in the form of price discounts or rebates. When demand is internal, a shortage can cause work stoppages in the production process and create delays, resulting in downtime costs and the cost of lost production (including indirect and direct production costs).

Costs resulting from lost sales because demand cannot be met are more difficult to determine than carrying or ordering costs. Therefore, shortage costs are frequently subjective estimates and sometimes an educated guess.

Shortages occur because carrying inventory is costly. As a result, shortage costs have an inverse relationship to carrying costs—as the amount of inventory on hand increases, the carrying cost increases, whereas shortage costs decrease.

The objective of inventory management is to employ an inventory control system that will indicate how much should be ordered and when orders should take place so that the sum of the three inventory costs just described will be minimized.

## INVENTORY CONTROL SYSTEMS

An inventory system controls the level of inventory by determining how much to order (the level of replenishment) and when to order. There are two basic types of inventory systems: a *continuous* (or *fixed-order-quantity*) *system* and a *periodic* (or *fixed-time-period*) *system*. In a continuous system, an order is placed for the same constant amount whenever the inventory on hand decreases to a certain level, whereas in a periodic system, an order is placed for a variable amount after specific regular intervals.

## CONTINUOUS INVENTORY SYSTEMS

In a **continuous inventory system** (also referred to as a *perpetual system* and a *fixed-order-quantity system*), a continual record of the inventory level for every item is maintained. Whenever the inventory on hand decreases to a predetermined level, referred to as the *reorder point*, a new order is placed to replenish the stock of inventory. The order that is placed is for a fixed amount that minimizes the total inventory costs. This amount, called the *economic order quantity*, is discussed in greater detail later.

**Continuous inventory:** a constant amount is ordered when inventory declines to a predetermined level.

A positive feature of a continuous system is that the inventory level is continuously monitored, so management always knows the inventory status. This is advantageous for critical items such as replacement parts or raw materials and supplies. However, maintaining a continual record of the amount of inventory on hand can also be costly.

A simple example of a continuous inventory system is a ledger-style checkbook that many of us use on a daily basis. Our checkbook comes with 300 checks; after the 200th check has been used (and there are 100 left), there is an order form for a new batch of checks. This form, when turned in at the bank, initiates an order for a new batch of 300 checks. Many office inventory systems use *reorder cards* that are placed within stacks of stationery or at the bottom of a case of pens or paper clips to signal when a new order should be placed. If you look behind the items on a hanging rack in a Kmart store, there will be a card indicating it is time to place an order for the item for an amount indicated on the card.

Continuous inventory systems often incorporate information technology tools to improve the speed and accuracy of data entry. A familiar example is the computerized

*To consumers the most familiar type of bar code scanners are used with cash registers at retail stores, where the bar code is a single line with 11 digits, the first 6 identifying a manufacturer and the last 5 assigned to a specific product by the manufacturer. This employee is using a portable hand-held bar code scanner to scan a bar code for inventory control. In addition to identifying the product, it can indicate where a product came from, where it is supposed to go, and how the product should be handled in transit.*

checkout system with a laser scanner used by many supermarkets and retail stores. The laser scanner reads the universal product code (UPC), or bar code, from the product package; the transaction is instantly recorded, and the inventory level updated. Such a system is not only quick and accurate, it also provides management with continuously updated information on the status of inventory levels. Many manufacturing companies' suppliers and distributors also use bar code systems and handheld laser scanners to inventory materials, supplies, equipment, in-process parts, and finished goods.

## PERIODIC INVENTORY SYSTEMS

**Periodic inventory system:** an order is placed for a variable amount after a fixed passage of time.

In a **periodic inventory system** (also referred to as a *fixed-time-period system* or a *periodic review system*), the inventory on hand is counted at specific time intervals—for example, every week or at the end of each month. After the inventory in stock is determined, an order is placed for an amount that will bring inventory back up to a desired level. In this system, the inventory level is not monitored at all during the time interval between orders, so it has the advantage of little or no required record keeping. The disadvantage is less direct control. This typically results in larger inventory levels for a periodic inventory system than in a continuous system to guard against unexpected stockouts early in the fixed period. Such a system also requires that a new order quantity be determined each time a periodic order is made.

An example of a periodic inventory system is a college or university bookstore. Textbooks are normally ordered according to a periodic system, wherein a count of textbooks in stock (for every course) is made after the first few weeks of a semester or quarter. An order for new textbooks for the next semester is then made according to estimated course enrollments for the next term (i.e., demand) and the amount remaining in stock. Smaller retail stores, drugstores, grocery stores, and offices sometimes use periodic systems—the stock level is checked every week or month, often by a vendor, to see how much should be ordered.

## THE ABC CLASSIFICATION SYSTEM

The **ABC system** is a method for classifying inventory according to several criteria, including its dollar value to the firm. Typically, thousands of independent demand items are held in inventory by a company, especially in manufacturing, but a small percentage is of such a high dollar value to warrant close inventory control. In general, about 5 to 15% of all inventory items account for 70 to 80% of the total dollar value of inventory. These are classified as *A*, or *Class A*, items. *B* items represent approximately 30% of total inventory units but only about 15% of total inventory dollar value. *C* items generally account for 50 to 60% of all inventory units but represent only 5 to 10% of total dollar value. For example, a discount store such as Wal-Mart normally stocks a relatively small number of televisions, a somewhat larger number of bicycles or sets of sheets, and hundreds of boxes of soap powder, bottles of shampoo, and AA batteries. Figure 12.1 shows the approximate ABC classes.

**ABC system:** an inventory classification system in which a small percentage of (A) items account for most of the inventory value.

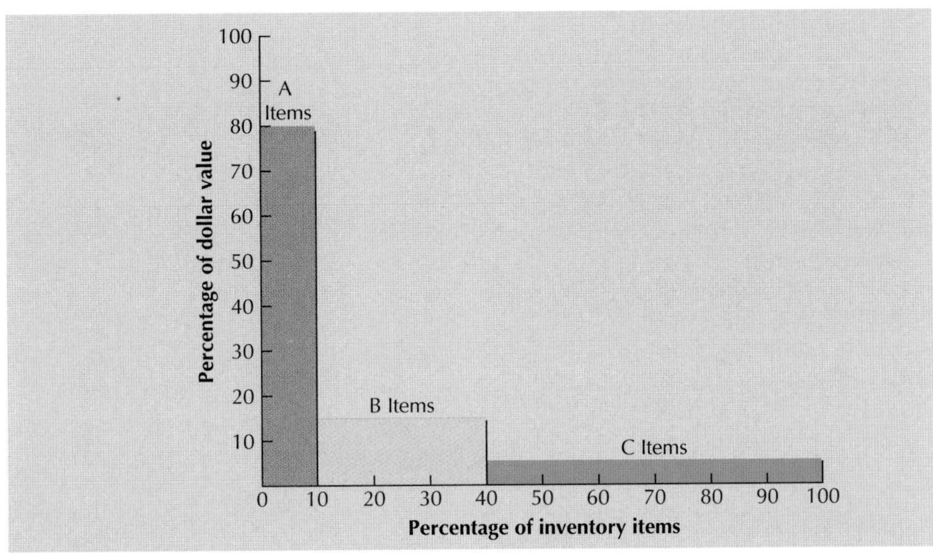


**Figure 12.1**
**ABC Classifications**

In ABC analysis each class of inventory requires different levels of inventory monitoring and control—the higher the value of the inventory, the tighter the control. Class A items should experience tight inventory control; B and C require more relaxed (perhaps minimal) attention. However, the original rationale for ABC analysis was that continuous inventory monitoring was expensive and not justified for many items. The wide use of bar code scanners may have eroded that reasoning. At least for larger companies, bar codes have made continuous monitoring cheap enough to use for all item classes.

The first step in ABC analysis is to classify all inventory items as either A, B, or C. Each item is assigned a dollar value, which is computed by multiplying the dollar cost of one unit by the annual demand for that item. All items are then ranked according to their annual dollar value, with, for example, the top 10% classified as A items, the next 30% as B items, and the last 60% as C items. These classifications will not be exact, but they have been found to be close to the actual occurrence in firms with remarkable frequency.

A items require close inventory control because of their high value; B and C items less control.

The next step is to determine the level of inventory control for each classification. Class A items require tight inventory control because they represent such a large percentage of the total dollar value of inventory. These inventory levels should be as low as possible, and safety stocks minimized. This requires accurate demand forecasts and detailed record keeping. The appropriate inventory control system and inventory modeling procedure to determine order quantity should be applied. In addition, close attention should be given to purchasing policies and procedures if the inventory items are acquired from outside the firm. B and C items require less stringent inventory control. Since carrying costs are usually lower for C items, higher inventory levels can sometimes be maintained with larger safety stocks. It may not be necessary to control C items beyond simple observation.

In general, A items frequently require a continuous control system, where the inventory level is continuously monitored; a periodic review system with less monitoring will suffice for C items.

Although cost is the predominant reason for inventory classification, other factors such as scarcity of parts or difficulty of supply may also be reasons for giving items a higher priority. For example, long lead times for some parts might be a problem for a company in Australia ordering from Europe, thus requiring a higher-priority classification for those parts.

**Example 12.1**

**ABC System Classification**

The maintenance department for a small manufacturing firm has responsibility for maintaining an inventory of spare parts for the machinery it services. The parts inventory, unit cost, and annual usage are as follows:

| Part | Unit Cost | Annual Usage |
|---|---|---|
| 1 | $ 60 | 90 |
| 2 | 350 | 40 |
| 3 | 30 | 130 |
| 4 | 80 | 60 |
| 5 | 30 | 100 |
| 6 | 20 | 180 |
| 7 | 10 | 170 |
| 8 | 320 | 50 |
| 9 | 510 | 60 |
| 10 | 20 | 120 |

The department manager wants to classify the inventory parts according to the ABC system to determine which stocks of parts should most closely be monitored.

*Solution*

First rank the items according to their total value and also compute each item's percentage of total value and quantity.

| Part | Total Value | % of Total Value | % of Total Quantity | % Cumulative |
|---|---|---|---|---|
| 9 | $30,600 | 35.9 | 6.0 | 6.0 |
| 8 | 16,000 | 18.7 | 5.0 | 11.0 |
| 2 | 14,000 | 16.4 | 4.0 | 15.0 |
| 1 | 5,400 | 6.3 | 9.0 | 24.0 |
| 4 | 4,800 | 5.6 | 6.0 | 30.0 |
| 3 | 3,900 | 4.6 | 10.0 | 40.0 |
| 6 | 3,600 | 4.2 | 18.0 | 58.0 |
| 5 | 3,000 | 3.5 | 13.0 | 71.0 |
| 10 | 2,400 | 2.8 | 12.0 | 83.0 |
| 7 | 1,700 | 2.0 | 17.0 | 100.0 |
| | $85,400 | | | |

Based on simple observation, it appears that the first three items form a group with the highest value, the next three items form a second group, and the last four items constitute a group. Thus, the ABC classification for these items is as follows:

| Class | Items | % of Total Value | % of Total Quantity |
|---|---|---|---|
| A | 9, 8, 2 | 71.0 | 15.0 |
| B | 1, 4, 3 | 16.5 | 25.0 |
| C | 6, 5, 10, 7 | 12.5 | 60.0 |

## ECONOMIC ORDER QUANTITY MODELS

In a continuous, or fixed-order-quantity, system when inventory reaches a specific level, referred to as the *reorder point*, a fixed amount is ordered. The most widely used and traditional means for determining how much to order in a continuous system is the **economic order quantity (EOQ)** model, also referred to as the economic lot-size model. The earliest published derivation of the basic EOQ model formula in 1915 is credited to Ford Harris, an employee at Westinghouse.

**EOQ:** the optimal order quantity that will minimize total inventory costs.

The function of the EOQ model is to determine the optimal order size that minimizes total inventory costs. There are several variations of the EOQ model, depending on the assumptions made about the inventory system. We will describe two model versions: the basic EOQ model and the production quantity model.

## THE BASIC EOQ MODEL

The *basic EOQ model* is a formula for determining the optimal order size that minimizes the sum of carrying costs and ordering costs. The model formula is derived under a set of simplifying and restrictive assumptions, as follows:

Assumptions of EOQ model

- Demand is known with certainty and is constant over time.
- No shortages are allowed.
- Lead time for the receipt of orders is constant.
- The order quantity is received all at once.

These basic model assumptions are reflected in Figure 12.2, which describes the continuous-inventory **order cycle** system inherent in the EOQ model. An order quantity, $Q$, is received and is used up over time at a constant rate. When the inventory level decreases to the reorder point, $R$, a new order is placed; a period of time, referred to as the *lead time*, is required for delivery. The order is received all at once just at the moment when demand depletes the entire stock of inventory—the inventory level reaches 0—so there will be no shortages. This cycle is repeated continuously for the same order quantity, reorder point, and lead time.

**Order cycle:** the time between receipt of orders in an inventory cycle.

EOQ is a continuous inventory system.

As we mentioned, the economic order quantity is the order size that minimizes the sum of carrying costs and ordering costs. These two costs react inversely to each other. As the order size increases, fewer orders are required, causing the ordering cost to decline, whereas the average amount of inventory on hand will increase, resulting in an increase in carrying costs. Thus, in effect, the optimal order quantity represents a compromise between these two inversely related costs.

The total annual ordering cost is computed by multiplying the cost per order, designated as $C_o$, times the number of orders per year. Since annual demand, $D$, is assumed

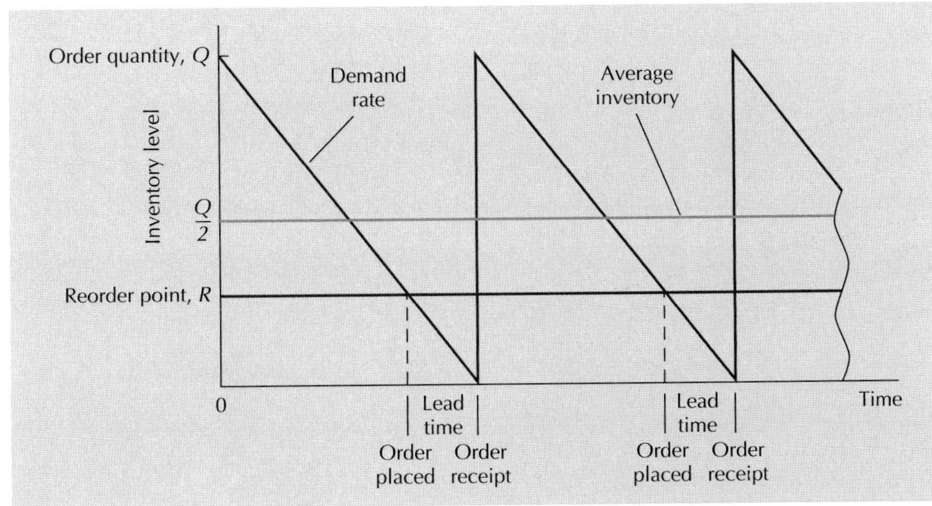


**Figure 12.2 The Inventory Order Cycle**

to be known and to be constant, the number of orders will be $D/Q$, where $Q$ is the order size and

$$\text{Annual ordering cost} = \frac{C_o D}{Q}$$

The only variable in this equation is $Q$; both $C_o$ and $D$ are constant parameters. Thus, the relative magnitude of the ordering cost is dependent on the order size.

Total annual carrying cost is computed by multiplying the annual per-unit carrying cost, designated as $C_c$, multiplied by the average inventory level. The average inventory level is one-half of $Q$ or $Q/2$, as shown in Figure 12.2.

$$\text{Annual carrying cost} = \frac{C_c Q}{2}$$

The total annual inventory cost is the sum of the ordering and carrying costs:

$$\text{TC} = \frac{C_o D}{Q} + \frac{C_c Q}{2}$$

Optimal $Q$ corresponds to the lowest point on the total cost curve.

The graph in Figure 12.3 shows the inverse relationship between ordering cost and carrying cost, resulting in a convex total cost curve.

The optimal order quantity occurs at the point in Figure 12.3 where the total cost curve is at a minimum, which coincides exactly with the point where the carrying cost curve intersects the ordering cost curve. This enables us to determine the optimal value of $Q$ by equating the two cost functions and solving for $Q$:

$$\frac{C_o D}{Q} = \frac{C_c Q}{2}$$

$$Q^2 = \frac{2C_o D}{C_c}$$

$$Q_{\text{opt}} = \sqrt{\frac{2C_o D}{C_c}}$$

Alternatively, the optimal value of $Q$ can be determined by differentiating the total cost curve with respect to $Q$, setting the resulting function equal to zero (the slope at the minimum point on the total cost curve), and solving for $Q$:

$$\text{TC} = \frac{C_o D}{Q} + \frac{C_c Q}{2}$$

$$\frac{\partial \text{TC}}{\partial Q} = -\frac{C_o D}{Q^2} + \frac{C_c}{2}$$

$$0 = -\frac{C_o D}{Q^2} + \frac{C_c}{2}$$

$$Q_{\text{opt}} = \sqrt{\frac{2C_o D}{C_c}}$$

**Figure 12.3**
**The EOQ Cost Model**

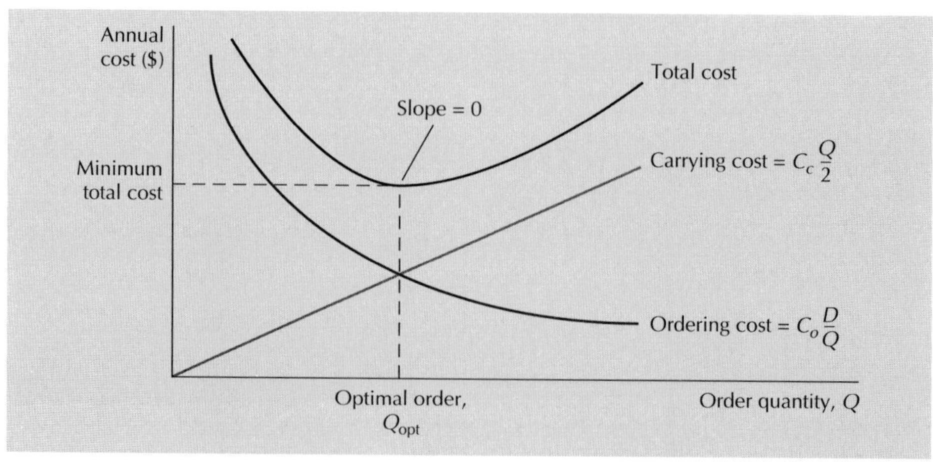

The total minimum cost is determined by substituting the value for the optimal order size, $Q_{opt}$, into the total cost equation:

$$TC_{min} = \frac{C_o D}{Q_{opt}} + \frac{C_c Q_{opt}}{2}$$

**Example 12.2**

**The Economic Order Quantity**

The ePaint Store stocks paint in its warehouse and sells it online on its Internet Web site. The store stocks several brands of paint; however, its biggest seller is Sharman-Wilson Ironcoat paint. The company wants to determine the optimal order size and total inventory cost for Ironcoat paint given an estimated annual demand of 10,000 gallons of paint, an annual carrying cost of \$0.75 per gallon, and an ordering cost of \$150 per order. They would also like to know the number of orders that will be made annually and the time between orders (i.e., the order cycle).

*Solution*

$$C_c = \$0.75 \text{ per gallon}$$
$$C_o = \$150$$
$$D = 10{,}000 \text{ gallons}$$

The optimal order size is

$$Q_{opt} = \sqrt{\frac{2C_o D}{C_c}} = \sqrt{\frac{2(150)(10{,}000)}{(0.75)}} = 2000 \text{ gallons}$$

The total annual inventory cost is determined by substituting $Q_{opt}$ into the total cost formula:

$$TC_{min} = \frac{C_o D}{Q_{opt}} + \frac{C_c Q_{opt}}{2} = \frac{(150)(10{,}000)}{2000} + \frac{(0.75)(2000)}{2} = \$750 + 750 = \$1500$$

The number of orders per year is computed as follows:

$$\text{Number of orders per year} = \frac{D}{Q_{opt}} = \frac{10{,}000}{2000} = 5 \text{ orders per year}$$

Given that the company processes orders 311 days annually (365 days minus 52 Sundays, Thanksgiving, and Christmas), the order cycle is

$$\text{Order cycle time} = \frac{311 \text{ days}}{D/Q_{opt}} = \frac{311}{5} = 62.2 \text{ days}$$

The optimal order quantity, determined in this example, and in general, is an approximate value, since it is based on estimates of carrying and ordering costs as well as uncertain demand (although all of these parameters are treated as known, certain values in the EOQ model). In practice it is desirable to round the $Q$ values off to some nearby pragmatic value. The precision of a decimal place is generally not necessary. In addition,

**The EOQ model is *robust*; because $Q$ is a square root, errors in the estimation of $D$, $C_c$, and $C_o$ are dampened.**

because the optimal order quantity is computed from a square root, errors or variations in the cost parameters and demand tend to be dampened. For instance, in Example 12.2, if the order cost had actually been 30% higher, or $200, the resulting optimal order size would have varied only by a little under 10% (i.e., 2190 gallons instead of 2000 gallons). Variations in both inventory costs will tend to offset each other, since they have an inverse relationship. As a result, the EOQ model is relatively resilient to errors in the cost estimates and demand, or is *robust*, which has tended to enhance its popularity.

## THE PRODUCTION QUANTITY MODEL

**Production quantity model:** an inventory system in which an order is received gradually, as inventory is simultaneously being depleted.

Relaxing the assumption that $Q$ is received all at once.

A variation of the basic EOQ model is the **production quantity model**, also referred to as the *gradual usage* and *non-instantaneous receipt model*. In this EOQ model the assumption that orders are received all at once is relaxed. The order quantity is received gradually over time, and the inventory level is depleted at the same time it is being replenished. This situation is commonly found when the inventory user is also the producer, as in a manufacturing operation where a part is produced to use in a larger assembly. This situation also can occur when orders are delivered continuously over time or when a retailer is also the producer.

The noninstantaneous receipt model is shown graphically in Figure 12.4. The inventory level is gradually replenished as an order is received. In the basic EOQ model, average inventory was half the maximum inventory level, or $Q/2$, but in this model variation, the maximum inventory level is not simply $Q$; it is an amount somewhat lower than $Q$, adjusted for the fact the order quantity is depleted during the order receipt period.

In order to determine the average inventory level, we define the following parameters unique to this model:

$p$ = daily rate at which the order is received over time, also known as the *production rate*
$d$ = the daily rate at which inventory is demanded

The demand rate cannot exceed the production rate, since we are still assuming that no shortages are possible, and, if $d = p$, there is no order size, since items are used as fast as they are produced. For this model the production rate must exceed the demand rate, or $p \geq d$.

Observing Figure 12.4 we see that the time required to finish receiving an order is the order quantity divided by the rate at which the order is received, or $Q/p$. For example, if the order size is 100 units and the production rate, $p$, is 20 units per day, the order will be received over five days. The amount of inventory that will be depleted or used up during this time period is determined by multiplying by the demand rate: $(Q/p)d$. For example, if it takes five days to receive the order and during this time inventory is depleted at the rate of two units per day, then 10 units are used. As a result, the maximum amount of inventory on hand is the order size minus the amount depleted during the receipt period, computed as

$$\text{Maximum inventory level} = Q - \frac{Q}{p}d$$

$$= Q\left(1 - \frac{d}{p}\right)$$

Figure 12.4
**The Production Quantity Model**

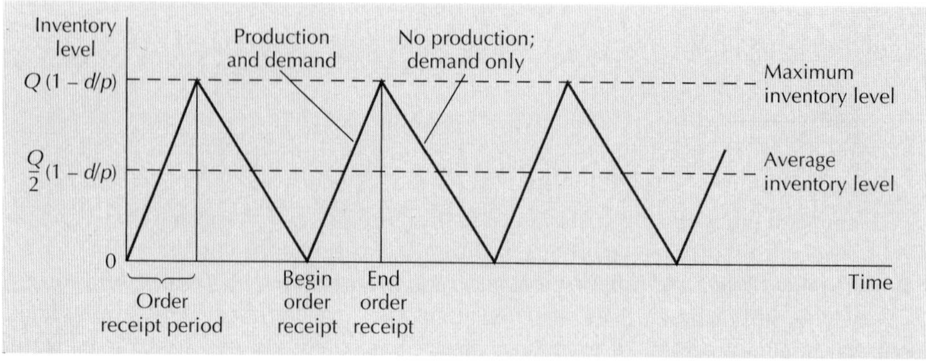

Since this is the maximum inventory level, the average inventory level is determined by dividing this amount by 2:

$$\text{Average inventory level} = \frac{1}{2}\left[Q\left(1 - \frac{d}{p}\right)\right]$$
$$= \frac{Q}{2}\left(1 - \frac{d}{p}\right)$$

The total carrying cost using this function for average inventory is

$$\text{Total carrying cost} = \frac{C_c Q}{2}\left(1 - \frac{d}{p}\right)$$

In this case the ordering cost, $C_o$, is often the **setup cost** for production.

Thus, the total annual inventory cost is determined according to the following formula:

$$\text{TC} = \frac{C_o D}{Q} + \frac{C_c Q}{2}\left(1 - \frac{d}{p}\right)$$

Solving this function for the optimal value $Q$,

$$Q_{\text{opt}} = \sqrt{\frac{2C_o D}{C_c\left(1 - \frac{d}{p}\right)}}$$

**Example 12.3**

**The Production Quantity Model**

Assume that the ePaint Store has its own manufacturing facility in which it produces Ironcoat paint. The ordering cost, $C_o$, is the cost of setting up the production process to make paint. $C_o$ = \$150. Recall that $C_c$ = \$0.75 per gallon and $D$ = 10,000 gallons per year. The manufacturing facility operates the same days the store is open (i.e., 311 days) and produces 150 gallons of paint per day. Determine the optimal order size, total inventory cost, the length of time to receive an order, the number of orders per year, and the maximum inventory level.

*Solution*

$$C_o = \$150$$
$$C_c = \$0.75 \text{ per gallons}$$
$$D = 10{,}000 \text{ gallons}$$
$$d = \frac{10{,}000}{311} = 32.2 \text{ gallons per day}$$
$$p = 150 \text{ gallons per day}$$

The optimal order size is determined as follows:

$$Q_{\text{opt}} = \sqrt{\frac{2C_o D}{C_c\left(1 - \frac{d}{p}\right)}}$$
$$= \sqrt{\frac{2(150)(10{,}000)}{0.75\left(1 - \frac{32.2}{150}\right)}}$$
$$= 2256.8 \text{ gallons}$$

Although an order of 2256.8 gallons should be rounded to 2257, we will use the 2256.8 to compute total cost.

This value is substituted into the following formula to determine total minimum annual inventory cost:

$$\text{TC}_{\min} = \frac{C_o D}{Q} + \frac{C_c Q}{2}\left(1 - \frac{d}{p}\right)$$
$$= \frac{(150)(10{,}000)}{2256.8} + \frac{(0.75)(2256.8)}{2}\left(1 - \frac{32.2}{150}\right)$$
$$= \$1329$$

The length of time to receive an order for this type of manufacturing operation is commonly called the length of the *production run*.

$$\text{Production run} = \frac{Q}{p}$$

$$= \frac{2256.8}{150}$$

$$= 15.05 \text{ days per order}$$

The number of orders per year is actually the number of production runs that will be made:

$$\text{Number of production runs (from orders)} = \frac{D}{Q}$$

$$= \frac{10{,}000}{2256.8}$$

$$= 4.43 \text{ runs per year}$$

Finally, the maximum inventory level is

$$\text{Maximum inventory level} = Q\left(1 - \frac{d}{p}\right)$$

$$= 2256.8\left(1 - \frac{32.2}{150}\right)$$

$$= 1772 \text{ gallons}$$

Thus, ePaint will need to set aside storage space sufficient to accommodate these 1772 gallons of paint.

## COMPUTER SOLUTION OF EOQ MODELS WITH EXCEL

EOQ analysis can be done with Excel. The Excel solution screen for Example 12.2 is shown in Exhibit 12.1. The Excel screen for the production quantity model in Example 12.3 is shown in Exhibit 12.2.

Exhibit 12.1

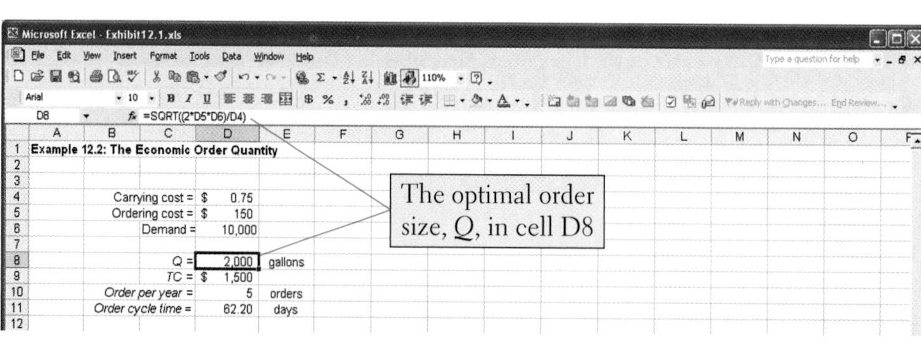


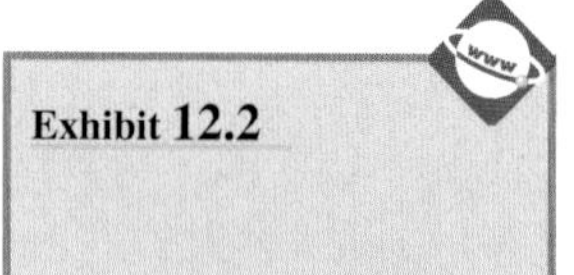

Exhibit 12.2

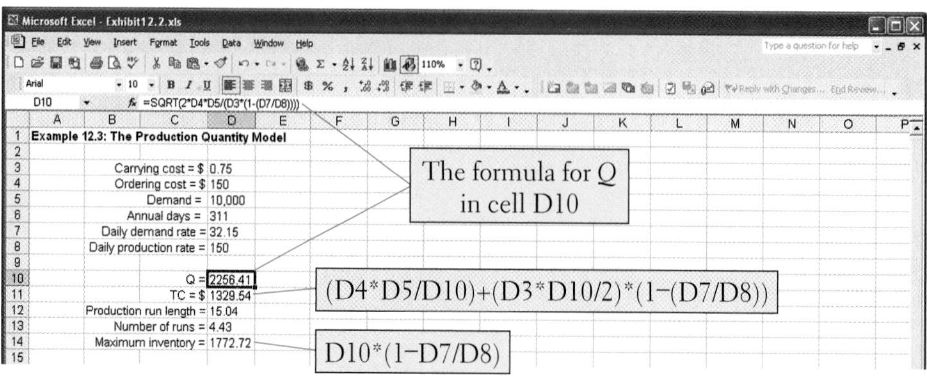

## QUANTITY DISCOUNTS

A **quantity discount** is a price discount on an item if predetermined numbers of units are ordered. In the back of a magazine you might see an advertisement for a firm stating that it will produce a coffee mug (or hat) with a company or organizational logo on it, and the price will be \$5 per mug if you purchase 100, \$4 per mug if you purchase 200, or \$3 per mug if you purchase 500 or more. Many manufacturing companies receive price discounts for ordering materials and supplies in high volume, and retail stores receive price discounts for ordering merchandise in large quantities.

**Quantity discount:** given for specific higher order quantities.

The basic EOQ model can be used to determine the optimal order size with quantity discounts; however, the application of the model is slightly altered. The total inventory cost function must now include the purchase price of the item being ordered:

**Determining if an order size with a discount is more cost effective than optimal $Q$.**

$$\text{TC} = \frac{C_oD}{Q} + \frac{C_cQ}{2} + PD$$

where

$P$ = per-unit price of the item
$D$ = annual demand

### THE COMPETITIVE EDGE

#### Parts Inventory Management at Teradyne

Teradyne is a major manufacturer of electronic testers, which semiconductor and other electronic manufacturers around the world use in their assembly plants. The testers are often bottlenecks in the production lines of companies that use them; thus, it is essential that they be reliable. The testers are complex electronic devices composed of many parts and circuit boards, and although very reliable, they are subject to random failures. It has been estimated that if a tester is down for one hour it can cost a typical semiconductor fabrication plant as much as \$50,000. Thus, when a tester fails, Teradyne customers demand quick and reliable parts service.

Teradyne's Replacement-Parts-Service (RPS) Division provides and repairs over 10,000 parts and distributes them around the world through a multisite logistic network. Many of these parts cost as much as \$10,000 but are used infrequently; thus, RPS's challenge is to make efficient inventory investment allocations at its stocking locations while maintaining a high service level to minimize customer downtime.

There are two categories of parts: consumables and repairables. A defective repairable item must be returned by the customer, which is then fixed at a repair center. A defective consumable item is not returned by the customer, and they usually have higher usage rates and cost less. To provide quick parts service Teradyne has eight worldwide inventory locations—a U.S. central depot and seven local centers in Asia and Europe. The central depot ships parts to all North American customers directly, replenishes the inventory at the global local centers, and operates a repair center for U.S. and global customers. Teradyne replenishes its inventory from outside vendors or its manufacturing facility. The RPS division offers emergency service—which is more expensive but fills orders the same day they arrive—and regular service—which fills parts orders within 12 days for U.S. customers and 20 days for non-U.S. customers, after the defective part is received. Approximately 47% of orders are for emergency service. In 1994 the average customer-service rate was 88% of orders met on time, which Teradyne considered too low; its goal was a customer service rate of 94% without increasing its parts inventory.

Analyzing data related to parts lateness, Teradyne discovered that out of 10,000 parts only 707 were late, and 80% of the lateness occurred in consumables. Although consumables are usually less critical and expensive than repairables, their high rate of lateness can still decrease customer satisfaction; a delay in supplying a \$1 part can cause as much downtime as a delay in supplying a \$10,000 part. However, Teradyne managers tended to focus on maintaining higher inventory levels of the higher cost repairables because they assumed they were more important. Teradyne concluded that it must manage consumables inventory much differently. With a redesigned inventory management system, Teradyne was able to reduce the number of late orders for consumables by 90% with less than a 3% increase in inventory. Furthermore, customer service for repairables could be improved by 4% with a corresponding 37% reduction in inventory investment, by not stocking high-cost parts at the local centers, and stocking them instead at the central depot.

*Source:* M. Cohen, Y.-S. Zheng, and Y. Wang, "Identifying Opportunities for Improving Teradyne's Service-Parts Logistics System," *Interfaces* 29(4; July–August 1999), pp. 1–18.

Purchase price was not considered as part of our basic EOQ formulation earlier because it had no impact on the optimal order size. In the preceding formula $PD$ is a constant value that would not alter the basic shape of the total cost curve; that is, the minimum point on the cost curve would still be at the same location, corresponding to the same value of $Q$. Thus, the optimal order size is the same no matter what the purchase price is. However, when a discount price is available, it is associated with a specific order size, which may be different from the optimal order size, and the customer must evaluate the tradeoff between possibly higher carrying costs with the discount quantity versus EOQ cost. As a result, the purchase price does affect the order-size decision when a discount is available.

## QUANTITY DISCOUNTS WITH CONSTANT CARRYING COST

The EOQ cost model with constant carrying costs for a pricing schedule with two discounts, $d_1$ and $d_2$, is illustrated in Figure 12.5 for the following discounts:

| Order Size | Price |
|---|---|
| 0–99 | $10 |
| 100–199 | 8 ($d_1$) |
| 200+ | 6 ($d_2$) |

Notice in Figure 12.5 that the optimal order size, $Q_{opt}$, is the same regardless of the discount price. Although the total cost curve decreases with each discount in price (i.e., $d_1$ and $d_2$), since ordering and carrying cost are constant, the optimal order size, $Q_{opt}$, does not change.

The graph in Figure 12.5 reflects the composition of the total cost curve resulting from the discounts kicking in at two successively higher order quantities. The first segment of the total cost curve (with no discount) is valid only up to 99 units ordered. Beyond that

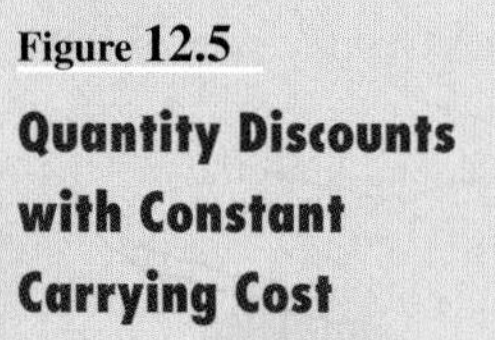

Figure 12.5 **Quantity Discounts with Constant Carrying Cost**

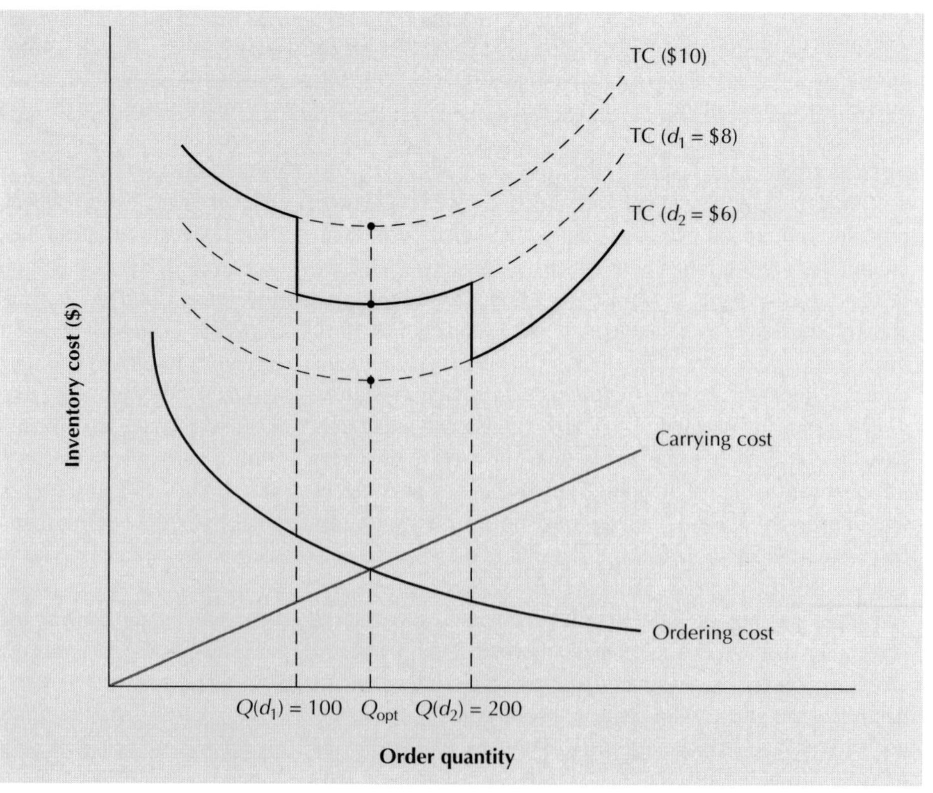

## THE COMPETITIVE EDGE

### Electronic Auctions for Quantity-Discount Orders at Mars, Inc.

Mars, Inc., with $14 billion in sales, is one of the world's largest privately owned companies. Mars has grown from selling buttercream candies door to door to a global business spanning 100 countries that includes food, pet care, drinks vending, and electronic payment systems. It produces such well-known products as Mars candies, M&M's, Snickers, and Uncle Ben's rice. Mars relies on a small number of suppliers for each of the huge number of materials it purchases to use in its products, and it purchases these materials in a number of ways. One increasingly popular means for material procurement at Mars is through electronic auctions, in which Mars buyers negotiate bids for orders with suppliers on line. The most important "strategic" purchases are of high value and large volume in which the suppliers provide quantity discounts that they specify as a supply curve with a quantity range associated with each price level (similar to the figure in Exhibit 12.5). Quantity-discount auctions with supply curves are tailored to industries in which volume discounts are common, such as bulk chemicals and agricultural commodities. The supplier provides its bid as a supply curve (i.e., quantity-discount schedule), and the auction may be for one product or many. A Mars buyer selects the bids that minimize total procurement costs subject to several rules—there must be a minimum and maximum number of suppliers so that Mars is not dependent on too few suppliers nor loses quality control over too many; there must be a maximum amount purchased from each supplier to limit the influence of any one supplier; and a minimum amount must be ordered that avoids economically inefficient orders (i.e., less than a truckload).

*Source:* G. Hohner, J. Rich, E. Ng, A. Davenport, J. Kalagnanam, H. Lee, and C. An, "Combinatorial and Quantity-Discount Procurement Auctions Benefit Mars, Incorporated and Its Suppliers," *Interfaces* 33(1: January–February 2003), pp. 23–35.

quantity, the total cost curve (represented by the topmost dashed line) is meaningless because above 100 units there is a discount ($d_1$). Between 100 and 199 units the total cost drops down to the middle curve. This middle-level cost curve is valid only up to 199 units because at 200 units there is another, lower discount ($d_2$). So the total cost curve has two discrete steps, starting with the original total cost curve, dropping down to the next level cost curve for the first discount, and finally dropping to the third-level cost curve for the final discount.

Notice that the optimal order size, $Q_{opt}$, is feasible only for the middle level of the total cost curve, TC($d_1$)—it does not coincide with the top level of the cost curve, TC, or the lowest level, TC($d_2$). If the optimal EOQ order size had coincided with the lowest level of the total cost curve, TC($d_2$), it would have been optimal order size for the entire discount price schedule. Since it does not coincide with the lowest level of the total cost curve, the total cost with $Q_{opt}$ must be compared to the lower-level total cost using $Q(d_2)$ to see which results in the minimum total cost. In this case the optimal order size is 200.

**Example 12.4**

**A Quantity Discount with Constant Carrying Cost**

Avtek, a distributor of audio and video equipment, wants to reduce a large stock of televisions. It has offered a local chain of stores a quantity discount pricing schedule, as follows:

| Quantity | Price |
|---|---|
| 1–49 | $1400 |
| 50–89 | 1100 |
| 90+ | 900 |

The annual carrying cost for the stores for a TV is $190, the ordering cost is $2,500, and annual demand for this particular model TV is estimated to be 200 units. The chain wants to determine if it should take advantage of this discount or order the basic EOQ order size.

*Solution*

First determine the optimal order size and total cost with the basic EOQ model.

$$C_o = \$2500$$
$$C_c = \$190 \text{ per TV}$$
$$D = 200 \text{ TVs per year}$$
$$Q_{\text{opt}} = \sqrt{\frac{2C_oD}{C_c}}$$
$$= \sqrt{\frac{2(2500)(200)}{190}}$$
$$= 72.5 \text{ TVs}$$

Although we will use $Q_{\text{opt}} = 72.5$ in the subsequent computations, realistically the order size would be 73 televisions. This order size is eligible for the first discount of $1100; therefore, this price is used to compute total cost:

$$\text{TC}_{\min} = \frac{C_0D}{Q_{\text{opt}}} + \frac{C_cQ_{\text{opt}}}{2} + PD$$
$$= \frac{(2500)(200)}{72.5} + \frac{(190)(72.5)}{2} + (1100)(200)$$
$$\text{TC}_{\min} = \$233{,}784$$

Since there is a discount for a larger order size than 50 units (i.e., there is a lower cost curve), this total cost of $233,784 must be compared with total cost with an order size of 90 and a discounted price of $900:

$$\text{TC} = \frac{C_oD}{Q} + \frac{C_cQ}{2} + PD$$
$$= \frac{(2500)(200)}{90} + \frac{(190)(90)}{2} + (900)(200)$$
$$= \$194{,}105$$

Since this total cost is lower ($194,105 < $233,784), the maximum discount price should be taken, and 90 units should be ordered. We know that there is no order size larger than 90 that would result in a lower cost, since the minimum point on this total cost curve has already been determined to be 73.

## QUANTITY-DISCOUNT MODEL SOLUTION WITH EXCEL

It is also possible to use Excel to solve the quantity-discount model with constant carrying cost. Exhibit 12.3 shows the Excel solution screen for Example 12.4. Notice that the selection of the appropriate order size, $Q$, that results in the minimum total cost for each discount range is determined by the formulas embedded in cells, E8, E9, and E10. For example, the formula for the first quantity-discount range, "1–49," is embedded in cell E8 and shown on the formula bar at the top of the screen, "**=IF(D8>=B8,D8,B8)**." This

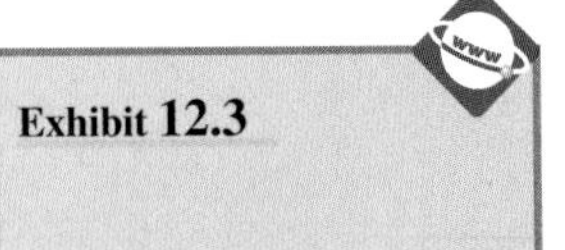


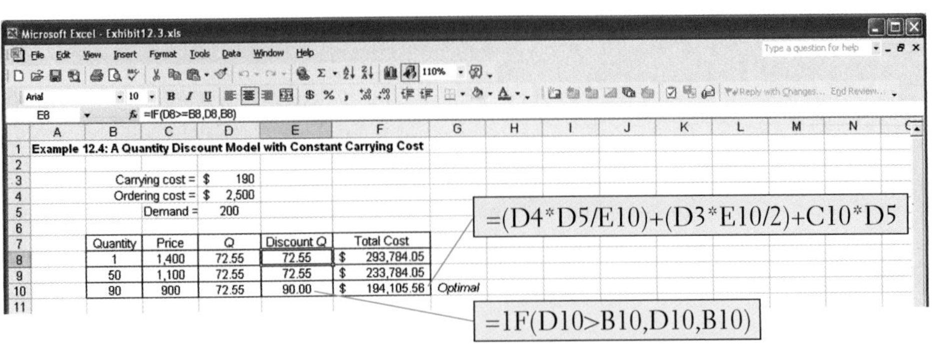

means that if the discount order size in cell D8 (i.e., $Q = 72.55$) is greater than or equal to the quantity in cell B8 (i.e., 1), then the quantity in cell D8 (72.55) is selected; otherwise the amount in cell B8 is selected. The formulas in cells E9 and E10 are constructed similarly. The result is that the order quantity for the final discount range, $Q = 90$, is selected.

## REORDER POINT

In our description of the EOQ models in the previous sections, we addressed how much should be ordered. Now we will discuss the other aspect of inventory management, when to order. The determinant of when to order in a continuous inventory system is the **reorder point**, the inventory level at which a new order is placed.

**Reorder point:** the level of inventory at which a new order should be placed.

The reorder point for our basic EOQ model with constant demand and a constant lead time to receive an order is equal to the amount demanded during the lead time,

$$R = dL$$

where

$d$ = demand rate per period (e.g., daily)
$L$ = lead time

**Example 12.5 Reorder Point for the Basic EOQ Model**

The ePaint Internet Store in Example 12.2 is open 311 days per year. If annual demand is 10,000 gallons of Ironcoat paint and the lead time to receive an order is 10 days, determine the reorder point for paint.

*Solution*

$$\begin{aligned} R &= dL \\ &= \left(\frac{10{,}000}{311}\right)(10) \\ &= 321.54 \text{ gallons} \end{aligned}$$

When the inventory level falls to approximately 321 gallons of paint, a new order is placed. Notice that the reorder point is not related to the optimal order quantity or any of the inventory costs.

## SAFETY STOCKS

In Example 12.5, an order is made when the inventory level reaches the reorder point. During the lead time, the remaining inventory in stock will be depleted at a constant demand rate, such that the new order quantity will arrive at exactly the same moment as the inventory level reaches zero. Realistically, demand—and, to a lesser extent lead time—are uncertain. The inventory level might be depleted at a faster rate during lead time. This is depicted in Figure 12.6 for uncertain demand and a constant lead time.

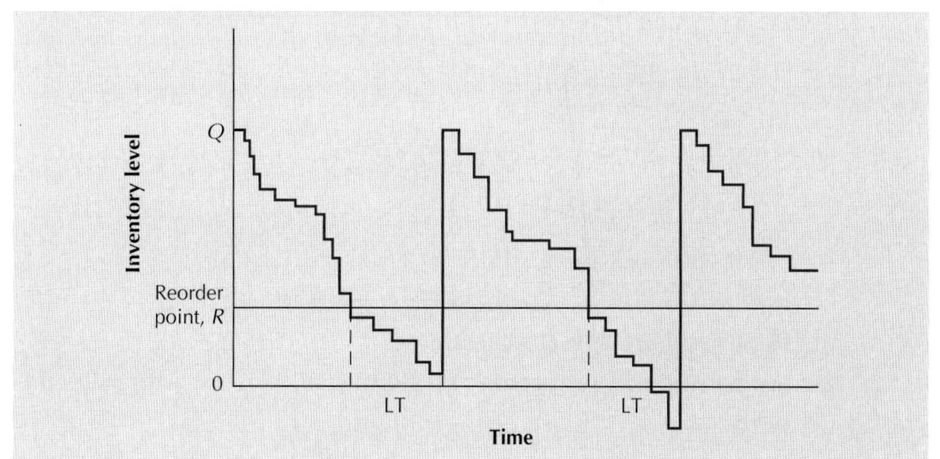


**Figure 12.6 Variable Demand with a Reorder Point**

**Figure 12.7**
**Reorder Point with a Safety Stock**

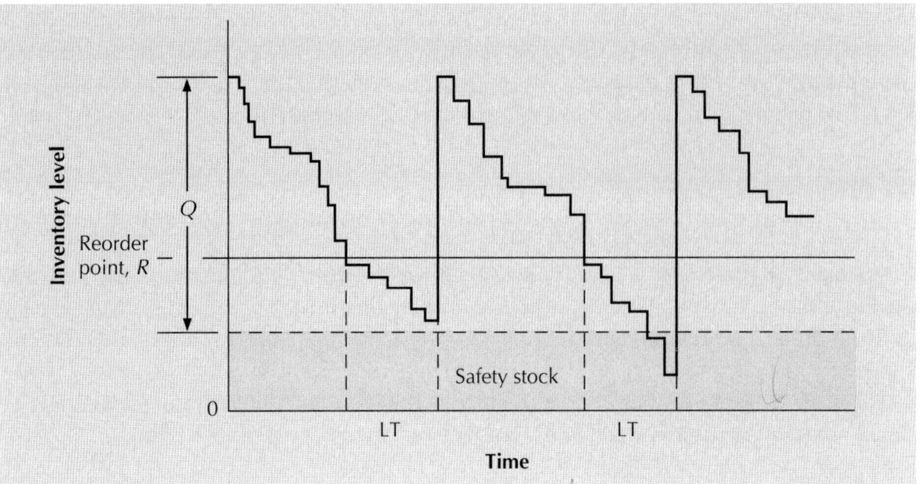


**Stockout:** an inventory shortage.

**Safety stock:** a buffer added to the inventory on hand during lead time.

Notice in the second order cycle that a **stockout** occurs when demand exceeds the available inventory in stock. As a hedge against stockouts when demand is uncertain, a **safety stock** of inventory is frequently added to the expected demand during lead time. The addition of a safety stock to the stockout occurrence shown in Figure 12.6 is displayed in Figure 12.7.

## SERVICE LEVEL

**Service level:** the probability that the inventory available during lead time will meet demand.

There are several ways to determine the amount of the safety stock. One popular method is to establish a safety stock that will meet a specified **service level**. The service level is the probability that the amount of inventory on hand during the lead time is sufficient to meet expected demand—that is, the probability that a stockout will not occur. The term *service* is used, since the higher the probability that inventory will be on hand, the more likely that customer demand will be met—that is, that the customer can be served. A service level of 90% means that there is a 0.90 probability that demand will be met during the lead time, and the probability that a stockout will occur is 10%. The service level is typically a policy decision based on a number of factors, including carrying costs for the extra safety stock and lost sales if customer demand cannot be met.

## REORDER POINT WITH VARIABLE DEMAND

To compute the reorder point with a safety stock that will meet a specific service level, we will assume the demand during each day of lead time is uncertain, independent, and can be described by a normal distribution. The average demand for the lead time is the sum of the average daily demand for the days of the lead time, which is also the product of the average daily demands multiplied by the lead time. Similarly, the variance of the distribution is the sum of the daily variances for the number of days in the lead time. Using these parameters, we can compute the reorder point to meet a specific service level as

$$R = \bar{d}L + z\sigma_d\sqrt{L}$$

where

$\bar{d}$ = average daily demand

$L$ = lead time

$\sigma_d$ = the standard deviation of daily demand

$z$ = number of standard deviations corresponding to the service level probability

$z\sigma_d\sqrt{L}$ = safety stock

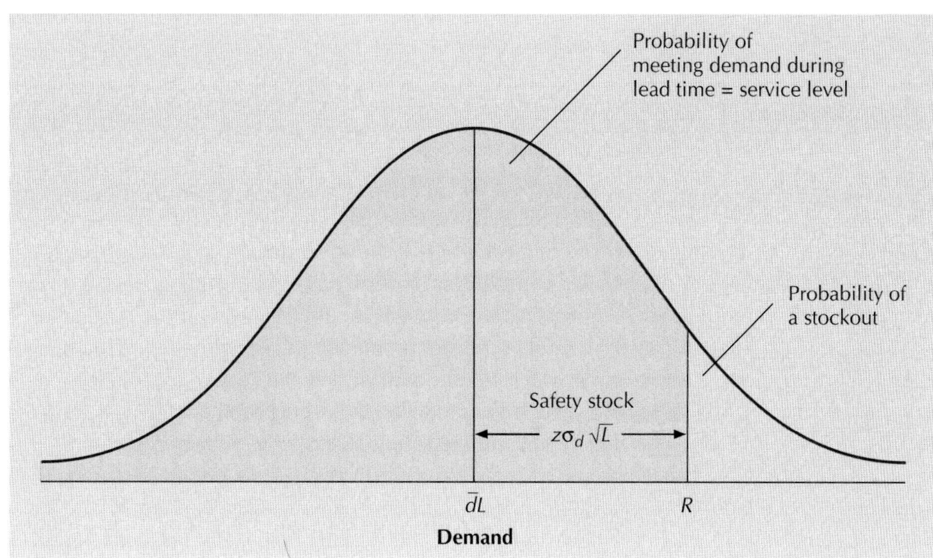


**Figure 12.8**

**Reorder Point for a Service Level**

The term $\sigma_d\sqrt{L}$ in this formula for the reorder point is the square root of the sum of the daily variances during lead time:

$$\begin{aligned}\text{Variance} &= (\text{daily variance}) \times (\text{number of days of lead time}) \\ &= \sigma_d^2 L \\ \text{Standard deviation} &= \sqrt{\sigma_d^2 L} \\ &= \sigma_d\sqrt{L}\end{aligned}$$

The reorder point relative to the service level is shown in Figure 12.8. The service level is the shaded area, or probability, to the left of the reorder point, $R$.

**Example 12.6**

**Reorder Point for Variable Demand**

For the ePaint Internet Store in Example 12.2, we will assume that daily demand for Ironcoat paint is normally distributed with an average daily demand of 30 gallons and a standard deviation of 5 gallons of paint per day. The lead time for receiving a new order of paint is 10 days. Determine the reorder point and safety stock if the store wants a service level of 95%—that is, the probability of a stockout is 5%.

*Solution*

$$\begin{aligned}\bar{d} &= 30 \text{ gallons per day} \\ L &= 10 \text{ days} \\ \sigma_d &= 5 \text{ gallons per day}\end{aligned}$$

For a 95% service level, the value of $z$ (from the Normal table in Appendix A) is 1.65. The safety stock is:

$$\begin{aligned}\text{Safety stock} &= z\sigma_d\sqrt{L} \\ &= (1.65)(5)(\sqrt{10}) \\ &= 26.1 \text{ gallons}\end{aligned}$$

The reorder point is computed as follows:

$$\begin{aligned}R &= \bar{d}L + z\sigma_d\sqrt{L} \\ &= 30(10) + (1.65)(5)(\sqrt{10}) \\ &= 300 + 26.1 \\ &= 326.1 \text{ gallons}\end{aligned}$$

## THE COMPETITIVE EDGE

### Establishing Inventory Safety Stocks at Kellogg's

Kellogg's is the world' largest cereal producer and a leading producer of convenience foods, with worldwide sales in 1999 of almost $7 billion. The company started with a single product, Kellogg's Corn Flakes, in 1906 and over the years developed a product line of other cereals including Rice Krispies and Corn Pops, and convenience foods such as Pop-Tarts and Nutri-Grain cereal bars. Kellogg's operates five plants in the United States and Canada and seven distribution centers, and it contracts with 15 co-packers to produce or pack some of Kellogg's products. Kellogg's must coordinate the production, packaging, inventory, and distribution of roughly 80 cereal products alone at these various facilities.

For more than a decade, Kellogg's has been using a model called the Kellogg Planning System (KPS) to plan its weekly production, inventory, and distribution decisions. The data used in the model is subject to much uncertainty, and the greatest uncertainty is in product demand. Demand in the first few weeks of a planning horizon is based on customer orders and is fairly accurate; however, demand in the third and fourth weeks may be significantly different from marketing forecasts. Kellogg's primary goal is to meet customer demand, and in order to achieve this goal Kellogg's employs safety stocks as a buffer against uncertain demand. The safety stock for a product at a specific production facility in week $t$ is the sum of demands for weeks $t$ and $t + 1$. However, for a product that is being promoted in an advertising campaign, the safety stock is the sum of forecasted demand for a four-week horizon or longer. KPS has saved Kellogg's many millions of dollars since the mid-1990s. The tactical version of KPS recently helped the company consolidate production capacity with estimated projected savings of almost $40 million.

*Source:* G. Brown, J. Keegan, B. Vigus, and K. Wood, "The Kellogg Company Optimizes Production, Inventory, and Distribution," *Interfaces* 31, no. 6 (November–December 2001), pp. 1–15.

## DETERMINING THE REORDER POINT WITH EXCEL

Excel can be used to determine the reorder point for variable demand. Exhibit 12.4 shows the Excel screen for Example 12.6. Notice that the reorder point is computed using the formula in cell E7, which is shown on the formula bar at the top of the screen.

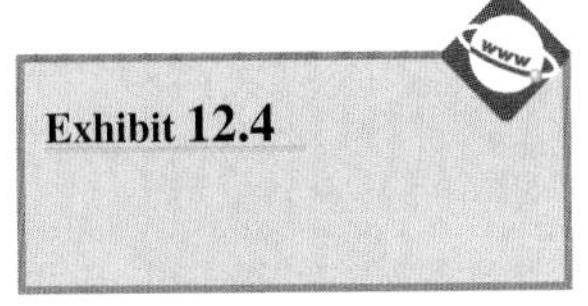


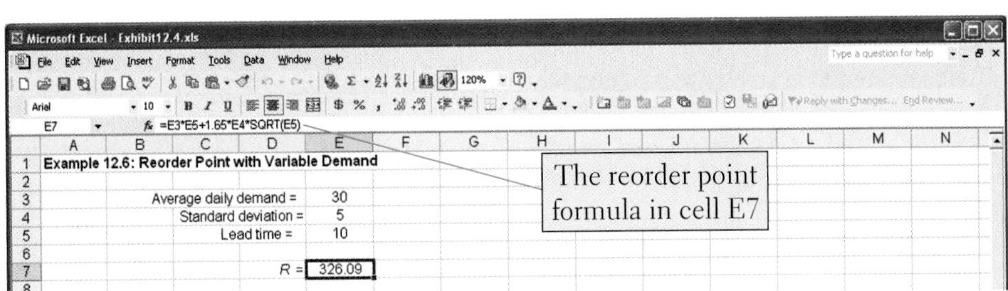


## ORDER QUANTITY FOR A PERIODIC INVENTORY SYSTEM

We defined a continuous, or fixed-order-quantity, inventory system as one in which the order quantity was constant and the time between orders varied. So far this type of inventory system has been the focus of our discussion. The less common *periodic*, or *fixed-time-period, inventory system* is one in which the time between orders is constant and the order size varies. Small retailers often use this sytem. Drugstores are one example of a business that sometimes uses a fixed-period inventory system. Drugstores stock a number of personal hygiene- and health-related products such as shampoo, toothpaste, soap, bandages, cough medicine, and aspirin.

Normally, the vendors who provide these items to the store will make periodic visits—every few weeks or every month—and count the stock of inventory on hand for their product. If the inventory is exhausted or at some predetermined reorder point, a new order will be placed for an amount that will bring the inventory level back up to the desired level.

The drugstore managers will generally not monitor the inventory level between vendor visits but instead will rely on the vendor to take inventory.

Under this system, the vendor would bundle many small, low-cost items into a single order and delivery thereby saving costs. Since the items are generally of low value, larger safety stocks will not pose a significant cost. Also, if the items are noncritical, even if there is a stockout, it is not a big deal. However, inventory might be exhausted early in the time period between visits, resulting in a stockout that will not be remedied until the next scheduled order. As a result, a larger safety stock for more critical items is sometimes required for the fixed-interval system.

A periodic inventory system normally requires a larger safety stock.

## ORDER QUANTITY WITH VARIABLE DEMAND

If the demand rate and lead time are constant, then the fixed-period model will have a fixed-order quantity that will be made at specified time intervals, which is the same as the fixed-quantity (EOQ) model under similar conditions. However, as we have already explained, the fixed-period model reacts differently than the fixed-order model when demand is a variable.

The order size for a fixed-period model given variable daily demand that is normally distributed is determined by

$$Q = \bar{d}(t_b + L) + z\sigma_d\sqrt{t_b + L} - I$$

where

$$\begin{aligned}
\bar{d} &= \text{average demand rate} \\
t_b &= \text{the fixed time between orders} \\
L &= \text{lead time} \\
\sigma_d &= \text{standard deviation of demand} \\
z\sigma_d\sqrt{t_b + L} &= \text{safety stock} \\
I &= \text{inventory in stock}
\end{aligned}$$

The first term in this formula, $\bar{d}(t_b + L)$, is the average demand during the order cycle time plus the lead time. It reflects the amount of inventory that will be needed to protect against the entire time from this order to the next and the lead time until the order is received. The second term, $z\sigma_d\sqrt{t_b + L}$, is the safety stock for a specific service level, determined in much the same way as previously described for a reorder point. These first two terms combined are a "target" level of inventory to maintain. The final term, $I$, is the amount of inventory on hand when the inventory level is checked and an order is made.

Figure 12.9 shows a periodic inventory system in which variable order sizes ($Q$) are placed at fixed time intervals ($t_b$).

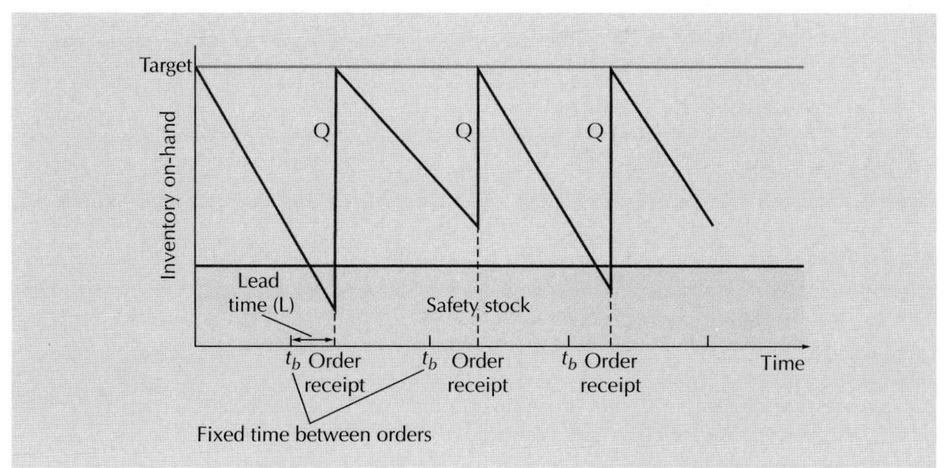


**Figure 12.9**
**Periodic Inventory System**

**Example 12.7**

**Order Size for Fixed-Period Model with Variable Demand**

The KVS Pharmacy stocks a popular brand of over-the-counter flu and cold medicine. The average demand for the medicine is 6 packages per day, with a standard deviation of 1.2 packages. A vendor for the pharmaceutical company checks KVS's stock every 60 days. During one visit the store had 8 packages in stock. The lead time to receive an order is 5 days. Determine the order size for this order period that will enable KVS to maintain a 95% service level.

*Solution*

$$\bar{d} = 6 \text{ packages per day}$$
$$\sigma_d = 1.2 \text{ packages}$$
$$t_b = 60 \text{ days}$$
$$L = 5 \text{ days}$$
$$I = 8 \text{ packages}$$
$$z = 1.65 \text{ (for a 95\% service level)}$$
$$\begin{aligned} Q &= \bar{d}(t_b + L) + z\sigma_d\sqrt{t_b + L} - I \\ &= (6)(60 + 5) + (1.65)(1.2)\sqrt{60 + 5} - 8 \\ &= 397.96 \text{ packages} \end{aligned}$$

This will be rounded to 398 packages, or perhaps 400 if it is shipped in boxes of 100 packages.

## DETERMINING THE ORDER QUANTITY FOR THE FIXED-PERIOD MODEL WITH EXCEL

The order quantity for the fixed-period model with variable demand can be determined using Excel. The Excel screen for Example 12.7 is shown in Exhibit 12.5. Notice that the order quantity in cell D10 is computed with the formula shown on the formula bar at the top of the screen.

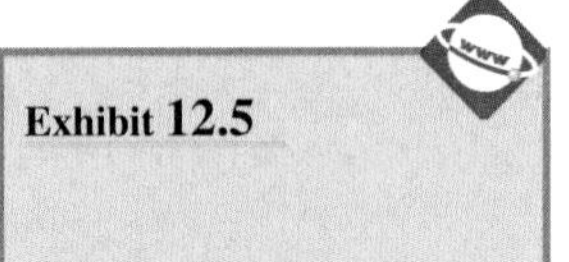

**Exhibit 12.5**

Microsoft Excel - Exhibit12.5.xls

D10 = =D3*(D4+5)+D7-D8

Formula for order size, $Q$, in cell D10

| | C | D | E |
|---|---|---|---|
| 1 | Example 12.7: Fixed Period Model with Variable Demand | | |
| 2 | | | |
| 3 | Average demand rate = | 6 | packages per day |
| 4 | Time between orders = | 60 | days |
| 5 | Lead time = | 5 | days |
| 6 | Standard deviation of demand = | 1.2 | packages |
| 7 | Safety stock = | 15.96 | packages |
| 8 | Inventroy in stock = | 8 | packages |
| 9 | | | |
| 10 | Q = | 397.96 | packages |
| 11 | | | |

## SUMMARY

The two types of systems for managing inventory are continuous and periodic, and we presented several models for determining how much to order and when to order for each system. However, we focused our attention primarily on the more commonly used continuous, fixed-order-quantity systems with EOQ models for determining order size and reorder points for determining when to order.

The objective of these order quantity models is to determine the optimal tradeoff between inventory carrying costs and ordering costs that would minimize total inventory cost. However, a drawback of approaching inventory management in this manner is that it can delude management into thinking that if they determine the minimum cost order quantity, they have achieved all they can in reducing inventory costs, which is not the case. Management should continually strive both to accurately assess and to reduce individual inventory costs. If management has accurately determined carrying and order costs, then they can seek ways to lower them that will reduce overall inventory costs regardless of the order size and reorder point.

## SUMMARY OF KEY FORMULAS

*Basic EOQ Model*

$$\text{TC} = \frac{C_oD}{Q} + \frac{C_cQ}{2}$$

$$Q_{\text{opt}} = \sqrt{\frac{2C_oD}{C_c}}$$

*EOQ Model with Noninstantaneous Receipt*

$$\text{TC} = \frac{C_oD}{Q} + \frac{C_cQ}{2}\left(1 - \frac{d}{p}\right)$$

$$Q_{\text{opt}} = \sqrt{\frac{2C_oD}{C_c\left(1 - \frac{d}{p}\right)}}$$

*Inventory Cost for Quantity Discounts*

$$\text{TC} = \frac{C_oD}{Q} + \frac{C_cQ}{2} + PD$$

*Reorder Point with Constant Demand and Lead Time*

$$R = dL$$

*Reorder Point with Variable Demand*

$$R = \bar{d}L + z\sigma_d\sqrt{L}$$

*Fixed-Time-Period Order Quantity with Variable Demand*

$$Q = \bar{d}(t_b + L) + z\sigma_d\sqrt{t_b + L} - I$$

## SUMMARY OF KEY TERMS

**ABC system** a method for classifying inventory items according to their dollar value to the firm based on the principle that only a few items account for the greatest dollar value of total inventory.

**carrying costs** the cost of holding an item in inventory, including lost opportunity costs, storage, rent, cooling, lighting, interest on loans, and so on.

**continuous inventory system** a system in which the inventory level is continually monitored; when it decreases to a certain level, the reorder point, a fixed amount is ordered.

**dependent demand** typically, component parts or materials used in the process to produce a final product.

**economic order quantity (EOQ)** a fixed-order quantity that minimizes total inventory costs.

**fixed-time-period system** also known as a periodic system; an inventory system in which a variable amount is ordered after a predetermined, constant passage of time.

**independent demand** final or finished products whose demand is not a function of, or dependent on, internal production activity.

**inventory** a stock of items kept by an organization to meet internal or external customer demand.

**in-process inventory** stocks of partially completed items kept between stages of a production process.

**order cycle** the time between the receipt of orders in an inventory system.

**ordering costs** the cost of replenishing the stock of inventory including requisition cost, transportation and shipping, receiving, inspection, handling, and so forth.

**periodic inventory system** a system in which the inventory level is checked after a specific time period and a variable amount is ordered, depending on the inventory in stock.

**production quantity model** also known as the production lot-size model; an inventory system in which an order is received gradually and the inventory level is depleted at the same time it is being replenished.

**quantity discount** a pricing schedule in which lower prices are provided for specific (higher) order quantities.

**reorder point** a level of inventory in stock at which a new order is placed.

**safety stock** an amount added to the expected amount demanded during the lead time (the reorder point level) as a hedge against a stockout.

**service level** the probability that the amount of inventory on hand during the lead time is sufficient to meet expected demand.

**shortage costs** temporary or permanent loss of sales that will result when customer demand cannot be met.

**stockout** an inventory shortage occurring when demand exceeds the inventory in stock.

## SOLVED PROBLEMS

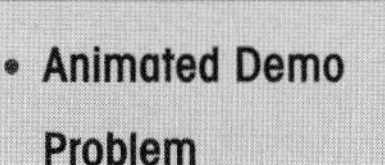


### 1. BASIC EOQ MODEL

Electronic Village stocks and sells a particular brand of personal computer. It costs the store $450 each time it places an order with the manufacturer for the personal computers. The annual cost of carrying the PCs in inventory is $170. The store manager estimates that annual demand for the PCs will be 1200 units. Determine the optimal order quantity and the total minimum inventory cost.

**SOLUTION**

$D = 1200$ personal computers

$C_c = \$170$

$C_o = \$450$

$$Q_{\text{opt}} = \sqrt{\frac{2C_oD}{C_c}} = \sqrt{\frac{2(450)(1200)}{170}}$$

$= 79.7$ personal computers

$$\text{TC} = \frac{C_oD}{Q_{\text{opt}}} + \frac{C_cQ_{\text{opt}}}{2} = 450\left(\frac{1200}{79.7}\right) + 170\left(\frac{79.7}{2}\right)$$

$= \$13{,}549.91$

### 2. PRODUCTION QUANTITY MODEL

I-75 Discount Carpets manufactures Cascade carpet, which it sells in its adjoining showroom store near the interstate. Estimated annual demand is 20,000 yards of carpet with an annual carrying cost of $2.75 per yard. The manufacturing facility operates the same 360 days the store is open and produces 400 yards of carpet per day. The cost of setting up the manufacturing process for a production run is $720. Determine the optimal order size, total inventory cost, length of time to receive an order, and maximum inventory level.

#### SOLUTION

$$C_o = \$720$$

$$C_c = \$2.75 \text{ per yard}$$

$$D = 20{,}000 \text{ yards}$$

$$d = \frac{20{,}000}{360} = 55.56 \text{ yards per day}$$

$$p = 400 \text{ yards per day}$$

$$Q_{\text{opt}} = \sqrt{\frac{2C_oD}{C_c\left(1 - \frac{d}{p}\right)}}$$

$$= \sqrt{\frac{2(720)(20{,}000)}{2.75\left(1 - \frac{55.56}{400}\right)}}$$

$$= 3487.4 \text{ yards}$$

$$\text{TC}_{\min} = \frac{C_oD}{Q} + \frac{C_cQ}{2}\left(1 - \frac{d}{p}\right)$$

$$= \frac{(720)(20{,}000)}{3487.4} + \frac{(2.75)(3487.4)}{2}\left(1 - \frac{55.6}{400}\right)$$

$$= \$8258.33$$

$$\text{Production run} = \frac{Q}{p}$$

$$= \frac{3487.4}{400}$$

$$= 8.72 \text{ days per order}$$

$$\text{Maximum inventory level} = Q\left(1 - \frac{d}{p}\right)$$

$$= 3487.4\left(1 - \frac{55.6}{400}\right)$$

$$= 3003 \text{ yards}$$

### 3. QUANTITY DISCOUNT

A manufacturing firm has been offered a particular component part it uses according to the following discount pricing schedule provided by the supplier.

| | |
|---|---|
| 1–199 | $65 |
| 200–599 | 59 |
| 600+ | 56 |

The manufacturing company uses 700 of the components annually, the annual carrying cost is $14 per unit, and the ordering cost is $275. Determine the amount the firm should order.

#### SOLUTION

First, determine the optimal order size and total cost with the basic EOQ model.

$$C_o = \$275$$

$$C_c = \$14$$

$$D = 700$$

$$Q_{\text{opt}} = \sqrt{\frac{2C_oD}{C_c}}$$

$$= \sqrt{\frac{2(275)(700)}{14}}$$

$$Q_{\text{opt}} = 165.83$$

$$\text{TC} = \frac{C_oD}{Q_{\text{opt}}} + \frac{C_cQ_{\text{opt}}}{2} + PD$$

$$= \frac{(275)(700)}{165.83} + \frac{(14)(165.83)}{2} + (\$65)(700)$$

$$= \$47{,}821$$

Next, compare the order size with the second-level quantity discount with an order size of 200 and a discount price of $59.

$$\text{TC} = \frac{(275)(700)}{200} + \frac{(14)(200)}{2} + (59)(700)$$

$$= \$43{,}662.50$$

This discount results in a lower cost.

Finally, compare the current discounted order size with the fixed-price discount for $Q = 600$.

$$\text{TC} = \frac{(275)(700)}{600} + \frac{(14)(600)}{2} + (56)(700)$$

$$= \$43{,}720.83$$

Since this total cost is higher, the optimal order size is 200 with a total cost of $43,662.50.

### 4. REORDER POINT WITH VARIABLE DEMAND

A computer products store stocks color graphics monitors, and the daily demand is normally distributed with a mean of 1.6 monitors and a standard deviation of 0.4 monitor. The lead time to receive an order from the manufacturer is 15 days. Determine the reorder point that will achieve a 98% service level.

#### SOLUTION

$$\bar{d} = 1.6 \text{ monitors per day}$$

$$L = 15 \text{ days}$$

$$\sigma_d = 0.4 \text{ monitor per day}$$

$$z = 2.05 \text{ (for a 98\% service level)}$$

$$R = \bar{d}L + z\sigma_d\sqrt{L}$$

$$= (1.6)(15) + (2.05)(0.4)\sqrt{15}$$

$$= 24 + 3.18$$

$$= 27.18 = 28 \text{ monitors}$$

## QUESTIONS

**12-1.** Describe the difference between independent and dependent demand and give an example of each for a pizza restaurant such as Domino's or Pizza Hut.

**12-2.** Distinguish between a fixed-order-quantity system and fixed-time-period system and give an example of each.

**12-3.** Discuss customer service level for an inventory system within the context of quality management.

**12-4.** Explain the ABC inventory classification system and indicate its advantages.

**12-5.** Identify the two basic decisions addressed by inventory management and discuss why the responses to these decisions differ for continuous and periodic inventory systems.

**12-6.** Describe the major cost categories used in inventory analysis and their functional relationship to each other.

**12-7.** Explain how the order quantity is determined using the basic EOQ model.

**12-8.** What are the assumptions of the basic EOQ model, and to what extent do they limit the usefulness of the model?

**12-9.** How are the reorder point and lead time related in inventory analysis?

**12-10.** Describe how the production quantity model differs from the basic EOQ model.

**12-11.** How must the application of the basic EOQ model be altered in order to reflect quantity discounts?

**12-12.** Why do the basic EOQ model variations not include the price of an item?

**12-13.** In the production quantity EOQ model, what would be the effect of the production rate becoming increasingly large as the demand rate became increasingly small, until the ratio $d/p$ was negligible?

**12-14.** Explain in general terms how a safety stock level is determined using customer service level.

## PROBLEMS

**12-1.** AV City stocks and sells a particular brand of laptop. It costs the firm $625 each time it places an order with the manufacturer for the laptops. The cost of carrying one laptop in inventory for a year is $130. The store manager estimates that total annual demand for the laptops will be 1500 units, with a constant demand rate throughout the year. Orders are received within minutes after placement from a local warehouse maintained by the manufacturer. The store policy is never to have stockouts of the laptops. The store is open for business every day of the year except Christmas Day. Determine the following:

a. Optimal order quantity per order
b. Minimum total annual inventory costs
c. The number of orders per year
d. The time between orders (in working days)

**12-2.** AV City (Problem 12-1) assumed with certainty that the ordering cost is $625/order and the inventory carrying cost is $130/unit/year. However, the inventory model parameters are frequently only estimates that are subject to some degree of uncertainty. Consider four cases of variation in the model parameters as follows: (a) Both ordering cost and carrying cost are 10% less than originally estimated; (b) both ordering cost and carrying cost are 10% higher than originally estimated; (c) ordering cost is 10% higher and carrying cost is 10% lower than originally estimated; and (d) ordering cost is 10% lower and carrying cost is 10% higher than originally estimated. Determine the optimal order quantity and total inventory cost for each of the four cases. Prepare a table with values from all four cases and compare the sensitivity of the model solution to changes in parameter values.

**12-3.** A firm is faced with the attractive situation in which it can obtain immediate delivery of an item it stocks for retail sale. The firm has therefore not bothered to order the item in any systematic way. However, recently profits have been squeezed due to increasing competitive pressures, and the firm has retained a management consultant to study its inventory management. The consultant has determined that the various costs associated with making an order for the item stocked are approximately $70 per order. She has also determined that the costs of carrying the item in inventory amount to approximately $27 per unit per year (primarily direct storage costs and forgone profit on investment in inventory). Demand for the item is reasonably constant over time, and the forecast is for 16,500 units per year. When an order is placed for the item, the entire order is immediately delivered to the firm by the supplier. The firm operates 6 days a week plus a few Sundays, or approximately 320 days per year. Determine the following:

a. Optimal order quantity per order
b. Total annual inventory costs
c. Optimal number of orders to place per year
d. Number of operating days between orders, based on the optimal ordering

**12-4.** The Sofaworld Company purchases upholstery material from Barrett Textiles. The company uses 45,000 yards of material per year to make sofas. The cost of ordering material from the textile company is $1,500 per order. It costs Sofaworld $0.70 per yard annually to hold a yard of material in inventory. Determine the optimal number of yards of material Sofaworld should order, the minimum total inventory cost, the optimal number of orders per year, and the optimal time between orders.

**12-5.** The Wallace Stationary Company purchases paper from the Seaboard Paper Company. Wallace produces stationary that require 1,415,000 sq. yards of stationary per year. The cost per order for the company is $2,200; the cost of holding 1 yard of paper in inventory is $0.08 per year. Determine the following:

a. Economic order quantity
b. Minimum total annual cost
c. Optimal number of orders per year
d. Optimal time between orders

**12-6.** The Ambrosia Bakery makes cakes for freezing and subsequent sale. The bakery, which operates five days a week, 52 weeks a year, can produce cakes at the rate of 116 cakes per day. The bakery sets up the cake-production operation and produces until a predetermined number ($Q$) have been produced. When not producing cakes, the bakery uses its personnel and facilities for producing other bakery items. The setup cost for a production run of cakes is $700. The cost of holding frozen cakes in storage is $9 per cake per year. The annual demand for frozen cakes, which is constant over time, is 6000 cakes. Determine the following:

a. Optimal production run quantity ($Q$)
b. Total annual inventory costs
c. Optimal number of production runs per year
d. Optimal cycle time (time between run starts)
e. Run length in working days

**12-7.** The EastCoasters Bicycle Shop operates 364 days a year, closing only on Christmas Day. The shop pays $300 for a particular bicycle purchased from the manufacturer. The annual holding cost per bicycle is estimated to be 25% of the dollar value of inventory. The shop sells an average of 18 bikes per week. The ordering cost for each order is $250. Determine the optimal order quantity and the total minimum cost.

**12-8.** The Chemco Company uses a highly toxic chemical in one of its manufacturing processes. It must have the product delivered by special cargo trucks designed for safe shipment of chemicals. As such, ordering (and delivery) costs are relatively high, at $3600 per order. The chemical product is packaged in 1-gallon plastic containers. The cost of holding the chemical in storage is $50 per gallon per year. The annual demand for the chemical, which is constant over time, is 7,000 gallons per year. The lead time from time of order placement until receipt is 10 days. The company operates 310 working days per year. Compute the optimal order quantity, total minimum inventory cost, and the reorder point.

**12-9.** The Food Place Supermarket stocks Munchkin Cookies. Demand for Munchkins is 5000 boxes per year (365 days). It costs the store $80 per order of Munchkins, and it costs $0.50 per box per year to keep the cookies in stock. Once an order for Munchkins is placed, it takes four days to receive the order from a food distributor. Determine the following:

a. Optimal order size
b. Minimum total annual inventory cost
c. Reorder point

**12-10.** Kroft Foods makes cheese to supply to stores in its area. The dairy can make 350 pounds of cheese per day, and the demand at area stores is 205 pounds per day. Each time the dairy makes cheese, it costs $175 to set up the production process. The annual cost of carrying a pound of cheese in a refrigerated storage area is $12. Determine the optimal order size and the minimum total annual inventory cost.

**12-11.** The Shotz Brewery produces an ale, which it stores in barrels in its warehouse and supplies to its distributors on demand. The demand for ale is 1800 barrels per day. The brewery can produce 3000 barrels per day. It costs $7500 to set up a production run for ale. Once it is brewed, the ale is stored in a refrigerated warehouse at an annual cost of $60 per barrel. Determine the economic order quantity and the minimum total annual inventory cost.

**12-12.** The purchasing manager for the Pacific Steel Company must determine a policy for ordering coal to operate 12 converters. Each converter requires exactly 5 tons of coal per day to operate, and the firm operates 360 days per year. The purchasing manager has determined that the ordering cost is $80 per order, and the cost of holding coal is 20% of the average dollar value of inventory held. The purchasing manager has negotiated a contract to obtain the coal for $12 per ton for the coming year.

a. Determine the optimal quantity of coal to receive in each order.
b. Determine the total inventory-related costs associated with the optimal ordering policy (do not include the cost of the coal).
c. If five days' lead time is required to receive an order of coal, how much coal should be on hand when an order is placed?

**12-13.** The TransCanada Lumber Company and Mill processes 10,000 logs annually, operating 250 days per year. Immediately upon receiving an order, the logging company's supplier begins delivery to the lumber mill at the rate of 60 logs per day. The lumber mill has determined that the ordering cost is $1600 per order, and the cost of carrying logs in inventory before they are processed is $15 per log on an annual basis. Determine the following:

a. The optimal order size
b. The total inventory cost associated with the optimal order quantity
c. The number of operating days between orders
d. The number of operating days required to receive an order

**12-14.** The Goodstone Tire Company produces a brand of tire called the Rainpath. The annual demand at its distribution center is 12,400 tires per year. The transport and handling costs are $2600 each time a shipment of tires is ordered at the distribution center. The annual carrying cost is $3.75 per tire.

a. Determine the optimal order quantity and the minimum total annual cost.
b. The company is thinking about relocating its distribution center, which would reduce transport and handling costs to $1900 per order but increase carrying costs to $4.50 per tire per year. Should the company relocate based on inventory costs?

**12-15.** The Deer Valley Farm produces a natural organic fertilizer, which it sells mostly to gardeners and homeowners. The annual demand for fertilizer is 220,000 pounds. The farm is able to produce 305,000 pounds annually. The cost to transport the fertilizer from the plant to the farm is $620 per load. The annual carrying cost is $0.12 per pound.

a. Compute the optimal order size, the maximum inventory level, and the total minimum cost.
b. If the farm can increase production capacity to 360,000 pounds per year, will it reduce total inventory cost?

**12-16.** Tradewinds Imports is an importer of ceramics from overseas. It has arranged to purchase a particular type of ceramic pottery from a Korean artisan. The artisan makes the pottery in 120-unit batches and will ship only that exact amount. The transportation and handling cost of a shipment is $7600 (not including the unit cost). The importer estimates its annual demand to be 1400 units.

What storage and handling cost per unit does it need to achieve in order to minimize its inventory cost?

**12-17.** The KVS Pharmacy is open from 10:00 A.M. to 8:00 P.M., and it receives 200 calls per day for delivery orders. It costs the pharmacy $25 to send out its cars to make deliveries. The pharmacy estimates that each minute a customer spends waiting for their order costs the pharmacy $0.20 in lost sales.

a. How frequently should KVS send out its delivery cars each day? Indicate the total daily cost of deliveries.

b. If a car could only carry six orders how often would deliveries be made and what would be the cost?

**12-18.** The Olde Town Microbrewery makes Townside beer, which it bottles and sells in its adjoining restaurant and by the case. It costs $1700 to set up, brew, and bottle a batch of the beer. The annual cost to store the beer in inventory is $1.25 per bottle. The annual demand for the beer is 21,000 bottles and the brewery has the capacity to produce 30,000 bottles annually.

a. Determine the optimal order quantity, total annual inventory cost, the number of production runs per year, and the maximum inventory level.

b. If the microbrewery has only enough storage space to hold a maximum of 2500 bottles of beer in inventory, how will that affect total inventory costs?

**12-19.** JAL Trading is a Hong Kong manufacturer of electronic components. During the course of a year it requires container cargo space on ships leaving Hong Kong bound for the United States, Mexico, South America, and Canada. The company needs 280,000 cubic feet of cargo space annually. The cost of reserving cargo space is $7000 and the cost of holding cargo space is $0.80/ft$^3$. Determine how much storage space the company should optimally order, the total cost, and how many times per year it should place an order to reserve space.

**12-20.** County Hospital orders syringes from a hospital supply firm. The hospital expects to use 40,000 per year. The cost to order and have the syringes delivered is $800. The annual carrying cost is $1.90 per syringe because of security and theft. The hospital supply firm offers the following quantity discount pricing schedule.

| Quantity | Price |
|---|---|
| 0–9999 | $3.40 |
| 10,000–19,999 | 3.20 |
| 20,000–29,999 | 3.00 |
| 30,000–39,999 | 2.80 |
| 40,000–49,999 | 2.60 |
| 50,000+ | 2.40 |

Determine the order size for the hospital.

**12-21.** The Interstate Carpet Discount Store has annual demand of 10,000 yards of Super Shag carpet. The annual carrying cost for a yard of this carpet is $1.25, and the ordering cost is $300. The carpet manufacturer normally charges the store $8 per yard for the carpet. However, the manufacturer has offered a discount price of $6.50 per yard if the store will order 5000 yards. How much should the store order, and what will be the total annual inventory cost for that order quantity?

**12-22.** Kelly's Tavern buys Shamrock draft beer by the keg from a local distributor. The bar has an annual demand of 900 kegs, which it purchases at a price of $60 per keg. The annual carrying cost is $7.20, and the cost per order is $160. The distributor has offered the bar a reduced price of $52 per barrel if it will order a minimum of 300 barrels. Should the bar take the discount?

**12-23.** The bookstore at Tech purchases jackets emblazoned with the school name and logo from a vendor. The vendor sells the jackets to the store for $38 apiece. The cost to the bookstore for placing an order is $120, and the annual carrying cost is 25% of the cost of a jacket. The bookstore manager estimates that 1700 jackets will be sold during the year. The vendor has offered the bookstore the following volume discount schedule:

| Order Size | Discount |
|---|---|
| 1–299 | 0% |
| 300–499 | 2% |
| 500–799 | 4% |
| 800+ | 5% |

What is the bookstore's optimal order quantity, given this quantity discount information?

**12-24.** Determine the optimal order quantity of jackets and total annual cost in Problem 12-23 if the carrying cost is a constant $8 per jacket per year.

**12-25.** The office manager for the Metro Life Insurance Company orders letterhead stationery from an office products firm in boxes of 500 sheets. The company uses 6500 boxes per year. Annual carrying costs are $3 per box, and ordering costs are $28. The following discount price schedule is provided by the office supply company:

| Order Quantity (boxes) | Price per Box |
|---|---|
| 200–999 | $16 |
| 1000–2999 | 14 |
| 3000–5999 | 13 |
| 6000+ | 12 |

Determine the optimal order quantity and the total annual inventory cost.

**12-26.** Determine the optimal order quantity and total annual inventory cost for boxes of stationery in Problem 12-25 if the carrying cost is 20% of the price of a box of stationery.

**12-27.** The 21,000-seat Air East Arena houses the local professional ice hockey, basketball, indoor soccer, and arena football teams as well as various trade shows, wrestling and boxing matches, tractor pulls, and circuses. Arena vending annually sells large quantities of soft drinks and beer in plastic cups with the name of the arena and the various team logos on them. The local container cup manufacturer that supplies the cups in boxes of 100 has offered arena management the following discount price schedule for cups:

| Order Quantity (boxes) | Price per Box |
|---|---|
| 2000–6999 | $47 |
| 7000–11,999 | 43 |
| 12,000–19,999 | 41 |
| 20,000+ | 38 |

The annual demand for cups is 2.3 million, the annual carrying cost per box of cups is $1.90, and ordering cost is $320. Determine the optimal order quantity and total annual inventory cost.

**12-28.** Determine the optimal order quantity and total annual inventory cost for cups in Problem 12-27 if the carrying cost is 5% of the price of a box of cups.

**12-29.** The amount of denim used daily by the Southwest Apparel Company in its manufacturing process to make jeans is normally distributed with an average of 4000 yards of denim and a standard deviation of 600 yards. The lead time required to receive an order of denim from the textile mill is a constant 7 days. Determine the safety stock and reorder point if the company wants to limit the probability of a stockout and work stoppage to 5%.

**12-30.** In Problem 12-29, what level of service would a safety stock of 2000 yards provide?

**12-31.** The Paramount Paper company produces paper from wood pulp ordered from a lumber products firm. The paper company's daily demand for wood pulp is normally distributed, with a mean of 9000 pounds and a standard deviation of 1900 pounds. Lead time is 8 days. Determine the reorder point if the paper company wants to limit the probability of a stockout and work stoppage to 2%.

**12-32.** Kelly's Tavern serves Shamrock draft beer to its customers. The daily demand for beer is normally distributed, with an average of 20 gallons and a standard deviation of 4 gallons. The lead time required to receive an order of beer from the local distributor is 12 days. Determine the safety stock and reorder point if the restaurant wants to maintain a 90% service level. What would be the increase in the safety stock if a 95% service level were desired?

**12-33.** The daily demand for Ironcoat paint at the Top Value Hardware Store in North Bay is normally distributed, with a mean of 30 gallons and a standard deviation of 10 gallons. The lead time for receiving an order of paint from the paint distributor is 8 days. Since this is the only paint store in North Bay, the manager is interested in maintaining only a 75% service level. What reorder point should be used to meet this service level? The manager subsequently learned that a new paint store would open soon in North Bay, which has prompted her to increase the service level to 95%. What reorder point will maintain this service level?

**12-34.** IM Systems assembles microcomputers from generic components. It purchases its color monitors from a manufacturer in Taiwan; thus, there is a long lead time of 25 days. Daily demand is normally distributed with a mean of 3.5 monitors and a standard deviation of 1.2 monitors. Determine the safety stock and reorder point corresponding to a 90% service level.

**12-35.** IM Systems (Problem 12-34) is considering purchasing monitors from a U.S. manufacturer that would guarantee a lead time of eight days, instead of from the Taiwanese company. Determine the new reorder point given this lead time and identify the factors that would enter into the decision to change manufacturers.

**12-36.** KVS Pharmacy fills prescriptions for a popular children's antibiotic, Amoxycilin. The daily demand for Amoxycilin is normally distributed with a mean of 200 ounces and a standard deviation of 80 ounces. The vendor for the pharmaceutical firm that supplies the drug calls the drugstore's pharmacist every 30 days and checks the inventory of Amoxycilin. During a call the druggist indicated the store had 60 ounces of the antibiotic in stock. The lead time to receive an order is four days. Determine the order size that will enable the drugstore to maintain a 99% service level.

**12-37.** Food Place Market stocks frozen pizzas in a refrigerated display case. The average daily demand for the pizzas is normally distributed, with a mean of 8 pizzas and a standard deviation of 2.5 pizzas. A vendor for a packaged food distributor checks the market's inventory of frozen foods every 10 days; during a particular visit there were no pizzas in stock. The lead time to receive an order is three days. Determine the order size for this order period that will result in a 98% service level. During the vendor's following visit there were 5 frozen pizzas in stock. What is the order size for the next order period?

**12-38.** The Mediterranean Restaurant stocks a red Chilean table wine it purchases from a wine merchant in a nearby city. The daily demand for the wine at the restaurant is normally distributed, with a mean of 18 bottles and a standard deviation of 4 bottles. The wine merchant sends a representative to check the restaurant's wine cellar every 30 days, and during a recent visit there were 25 bottles in stock. The lead time to receive an order is two days. The restaurant manager has requested an order size that will enable him to limit the probability of a stockout to 5%.

**12-39.** The Aztec Company stocks a variety of parts and materials it uses in its manufacturing processes. Recently, as demand for its finished goods has increased, management has had difficulty managing parts inventory; they frequently run out of some crucial parts and seem to have an endless supply of others. In an effort to control inventory more effectively, they would like to classify their inventory of parts according to the ABC approach. Following is a list of selected parts and the annual usage and unit value for each:

| Item Number | Annual Usage | Unit Cost | Item Number | Annual Usage | Unit Cost |
|---|---|---|---|---|---|
| 1 | 36 | $ 350 | 16 | 60 | $ 610 |
| 2 | 510 | 30 | 17 | 120 | 20 |
| 3 | 50 | 23 | 18 | 270 | 15 |
| 4 | 300 | 45 | 19 | 45 | 50 |
| 5 | 18 | $1900 | 20 | 19 | 3200 |
| 6 | 500 | 8 | 21 | 910 | 3 |
| 7 | 710 | 4 | 22 | 12 | 4750 |
| 8 | 80 | 26 | 23 | 30 | 2710 |
| 9 | 344 | 28 | 24 | 24 | 1800 |
| 10 | 67 | 440 | 25 | 870 | 105 |
| 11 | 510 | 2 | 26 | 244 | 30 |
| 12 | 682 | 35 | 27 | 750 | 15 |
| 13 | 95 | 50 | 28 | 45 | 110 |
| 14 | 10 | 3 | 29 | 46 | 160 |
| 15 | 820 | 1 | 30 | 165 | 25 |

Classify the inventory items according to the ABC approach using dollar value of annual demand.

**12-40.** The EastCoasters Bicycle Shop stocks bikes; helmets; clothing; a variety of bike parts including chains, gears, tires, wheels; and biking accessories. The shop is in a storefront location on a busy street and it has very limited storage space for inventory. It often runs out of items and is unable to serye customers. To help manage its inventory the shop would like to classify the stock using the ABC system. Following is a list of items the shop stocks and the annual demand and unit value for each:

| Item Number | Annual Demand | Unit Cost | Item Number | Annual Demand | Unit Cost |
|---|---|---|---|---|---|
| 1 | 10 | $ 8 | 17 | 110 | $ 23 |
| 2 | 18 | 16 | 18 | 74 | 18 |
| 3 | 36 | 30 | 19 | 8 | 610 |
| 4 | 9 | 1230 | 20 | 10 | 935 |
| 5 | 4 | 760 | 21 | 7 | 270 |
| 6 | 3 | 810 | 22 | 5 | 1400 |
| 7 | 19 | 420 | 23 | 5 | 900 |
| 8 | 56 | 35 | 24 | 46 | 67 |
| 9 | 105 | 17 | 25 | 32 | 160 |
| 10 | 27 | 350 | 26 | 101 | 45 |
| 11 | 19 | 36 | 27 | 83 | 12 |
| 12 | 12 | 115 | 28 | 54 | 16 |
| 13 | 7 | 2300 | 29 | 14 | 42 |
| 14 | 10 | 245 | 30 | 9 | 705 |
| 15 | 6 | 665 | 31 | 7 | 37 |
| 16 | 18 | 28 | 32 | 16 | 26 |

Classify the inventory items according to the ABC approach using dollar value of annual demand.

**12-41.** Tara McCoy is the office administrator for the Department of Management at State University. The faculty uses a lot of printer paper and Tara is constantly reordering and frequently runs out. She orders the paper from the university central stores and several faculty have determined that the lead time to receive an order is normally distributed, with a mean of 2 days and a standard deviation of 0.5 day. The faculty have also determined that daily demand for the paper is normally distributed, with a mean of 2.6 packages and a standard deviation of 0.8 packages. What reorder point should Tracy use in order not to run out 99% of the time?

**12-42.** The concession stand at the Shelby High School stadium sells slices of pizza during boys' and girls' soccer games. Concession stand sales are a primary source of revenue for the high school athletic programs, so the athletic director wants to sell as much food as possible; however, any pizza not sold is given away free to the players, coaches, and referees or it is thrown away. As such, the athletic director wants to determine a reorder point that will meet the demand for pizza. Pizza sales are normally distributed with a mean of 6 pizzas per hour and a standard deviation of 2.5 pizzas. The pizzas are ordered from Pizza Beth's restaurant, and the mean delivery time is 30 minutes, with a standard deviation of 8 minutes.

a. Currently the concession stand places an order when they have 1 pizza left. What level of service does this result in?

b. What should the reorder point be to have a 98% service level?

## CASE PROBLEM 12.1

### *The Instant Paper Clip Office Supply Company*

Christie Levine is the manager of the Instant Paper Clip Office Supply Company in Louisville. The company attempts to gain an advantage over its competitors by providing quality customer service, which includes prompt delivery of orders by truck or van and always being able to meet customer demand from its stock. In order to achieve this degree of customer service, it must stock a large volume of items on a daily basis at a central warehouse and at three retail stores in the city and suburbs. Christie maintains these inventory levels by borrowing cash on a daily basis from the First American Bank. She estimates that for the coming fiscal year the company's demand for cash to pay for inventory will be $17,000 per day for 305 working days. Any money she borrows during the year must be repaid with interest by the end of the year. The annual interest rate currently charged by the bank is 9%. Any time Christie takes out a loan to purchase inventory, the bank charges the company a loan origination fee of $1200 plus 2 ¼ points (2.25% of the amount borrowed).

Christie often uses EOQ analysis to determine optimal amounts of inventory to order for different office supplies. Now she is wondering if she can use the same type of analysis to determine an optimal borrowing policy. Determine the amount of the loan Christie should borrow from the bank, the total annual cost of the company's borrowing policy, and the number of loans the company should obtain during the year. Also determine the level of cash on hand at which the company should apply for a new loan given that it takes 15 days for a loan to be processed by the bank.

Suppose the bank offers Christie a discount as follows. On any loan amount equal to or greater than $500,000, the bank will lower the number of points charged on the loan origination fee from 2.25% to 2.00%. What would be the company's optimal amount borrowed?

## CASE PROBLEM 12.2

### *The Texas Gladiators Apparel Store*

The Texas Gladiators won the Super Bowl last year. As a result, sportswear such as hats, sweatshirts, sweatpants, and jackets with the Gladiator's logo are popular. The Gladiators operate an apparel store outside the football stadium. It is near a busy highway, so the store has heavy customer traffic throughout the year, not just on game days. In addition, the stadium has high school or college football and soccer games almost every week in the fall, and baseball games in the spring and summer. The most popular single item the stadium store sells is a red and silver baseball-style cap with the Gladiators' logo on it. The cap has an elastic headband inside it, which conforms to different head sizes. However, the store has had a difficult time keeping the cap in stock, especially during the time between the placement and receipt of an order. Often customers come to the store just for the hat; when it is not in stock, customers are upset, and the store management believes they tend to go to other competing stores to purchase their Gladiators' clothing. To rectify this problem, the store manager, Jessica James, would like to develop an inventory control policy that would ensure that customers would be able to purchase the cap 99% of the time they asked for it. Jessica has accumulated the following demand data for the cap for a 30-week period. (Demand includes actual sales plus a record of the times a cap has been requested but not available and an estimate of the number of times a customer wanted a cap when it was not available but did not ask for it.)

| Week | Demand | Week | Demand | Week | Demand |
|---|---|---|---|---|---|
| 1 | 38 | 11 | 28 | 21 | 52 |
| 2 | 51 | 12 | 41 | 22 | 38 |
| 3 | 25 | 13 | 37 | 23 | 49 |
| 4 | 60 | 14 | 44 | 24 | 46 |
| 5 | 35 | 15 | 45 | 25 | 47 |
| 6 | 42 | 16 | 56 | 26 | 41 |
| 7 | 29 | 17 | 62 | 27 | 39 |
| 8 | 46 | 18 | 53 | 28 | 50 |
| 9 | 55 | 19 | 46 | 29 | 28 |
| 10 | 19 | 20 | 41 | 30 | 34 |

The store purchases the hats from a small manufacturing company in Jamaica. The shipments from Jamaica are erratic, with a lead time of 20 days.

In the past, Ms. James has placed an order whenever the stock got down to 150 caps. What level of service does this reorder point correspond to? What would the reorder point and safety stock need to be to achieve the desired service level? Discuss how Jessica James might determine the order size of caps and what additional, if any, information would be needed to determine the order size.

## CASE PROBLEM 12.3

### *Pharr Foods Company*

Pharr Foods Company produces a variety of food products including a line of candies. One of its most popular candy items is "Far Stars," a bag of a dozen, individually wrapped, star-shaped candies made primarily from a blend of dark and milk chocolates, macadamia nuts, and a blend of heavy cream fillings. The item is relatively expensive, so Pharr Foods only produces it for its eastern market encompassing urban areas such as New York, Atlanta, Philadelphia, and Boston. The item is not sold in grocery or discount stores but mainly in specialty shops and specialty groceries, candy stores, and department stores. Pharr Foods supplies the candy to a single food distributor which has several warehouses on the East Coast. The candy is shipped in cases with 60 bags of the candy per case. Far Stars sell well despite the fact that they are expensive at $9.85 per bag (wholesale). Pharr uses high-quality, fresh ingredients and does not store large stocks of the candy in inventory for very long periods of time.

Pharr's distributor believes that demand for the candy follows a seasonal pattern. It has collected demand data (i.e., cases sold) for Far Stars from its warehouses and the stores it supplies for the past three years, as follows.

| | Demand (cases) | | |
|---|---|---|---|
| **Month** | *Year 1* | *Year 2* | *Year 3* |
| January | 192 | 212 | 228 |
| February | 210 | 223 | 231 |
| March | 205 | 216 | 226 |
| April | 260 | 252 | 293 |
| May | 228 | 235 | 246 |
| June | 172 | 220 | 229 |

| Month | Demand (cases) | | |
|---|---|---|---|
| | *Year 1* | *Year 2* | *Year 3* |
| July | 160 | 209 | 217 |
| August | 147 | 231 | 226 |
| September | 256 | 263 | 302 |
| October | 342 | 370 | 410 |
| November | 261 | 260 | 279 |
| December | 273 | 277 | 293 |

The distributor must hold the candy inventory in climate-controlled warehouses and be careful in handling it. The annual carrying cost is $116 per case. The item must be shipped a long distance from the manufacturer to the distributor. In order to keep the candy as fresh as possible, trucks must be air-conditioned and shipments must be direct, and are often less-than-truckload. As a result, ordering cost is $4700.

Pharr Foods makes Far Stars from three primary ingredients it orders from different suppliers: dark and milk chocolate, macadamia nuts, and, a special heavy cream filling. Except for its unique star shape, a Far Star is almost like a chocolate truffle. Each Far Star weighs 1.2 ounces and requires 0.70 ounce of blended chocolates, 0.50 ounce of macadamia nuts, and 0.40 ounce of filling to produce (including spillage and waste). Pharr Foods orders chocolate, nuts, and filling from its suppliers by the pound. The annual ordering cost is $5700 for chocolate, and the carrying cost is $0.45 per pound. The ordering cost for macadamia nuts is $6300, and the annual carrying cost is $0.63 per pound. The ordering cost for filling is $4500, and the annual average carrying cost is $0.55 per pound.

Each of the suppliers offers the candy manufacturer a quantity-discount price schedule for the ingredients as follows:

| Chocolate | | Macadamia Nuts | | Filling | |
|---|---|---|---|---|---|
| Price | Quantity (lb) | Price | Quantity (lb) | Price | Quantity (lb) |
| $3.05 | 0–50,000 | $6.50 | 0–30,000 | $1.50 | 0–40,000 |
| 2.90 | 50,001–100,000 | 6.25 | 30,001–70,000 | 1.35 | 40,001–80,000 |
| 2.75 | 100,001–150,000 | 5.95 | 70,000+ | 1.25 | 80,000+ |
| 2.60 | 150,000+ | | | | |

Determine the inventory order quantity for Pharr's distributor. Compare the optimal order quantity with a seasonally adjusted forecast for demand. Does the order quantity seem adequate to meet the seasonal demand pattern for Far Stars? That is, is it likely that shortages or excessive inventories will occur? Can you identify the causes of the seasonal demand pattern for Far Stars? Determine the inventory order quantity for each of the three primary ingredients that Pharr Foods orders from its suppliers. Discuss the possible impact of the order policies of the food distributor and Pharr Foods on quality management and supply chain management.

## REFERENCES


Brown, R. G. *Decision Rules for Inventory Management*. New York: Holt, Rinehart and Winston, 1967.

Buchan, J., and E. Koenigsberg. *Scientific Inventory Management*. Upper Saddle River, N.J.: Prentice Hall, 1963.

Buffa, E. S., and Jefferey Miller. *Production-Inventory Systems: Planning and Control*, rev. ed. Homewood, IL: Irwin, 1979.

Churchman, C. W., R. L. Ackoff, and E. L. Arnoff. *Introduction to Operations Research*. New York: Wiley, 1957.

Fetter, R. B., and W. C. Dalleck. *Decision Models for Inventory Management*. Homewood, IL: Irwin, 1961.

Greene, J. H. *Production and Inventory Control*. Homewood, IL: Irwin, 1974.

Hadley, G., and T. M. Whitin. *Analysis of Inventory Systems*. Upper Saddle River, N.J.: Prentice Hall, 1963.

McGee, J. F., and D. M. Boodman. *Production Planning and Inventory Control*, 2nd ed. New York: McGraw-Hill, 1967.

Starr, M. K., and D. W. Miller. *Inventory Control: Theory and Practice*. Upper Saddle River, N.J.: Prentice Hall, 1962.

Wagner, H. M. *Statistical Management of Inventory Systems*. New York: Wiley, 1962.

Whitin, T. M. *The Theory of Inventory Management*. Princeton, N.J.: Princeton University Press, 1957.

# Operational Decision-Making Tools: Simulation

SUPPLEMENT 12

## CHAPTER OUTLINE

**In this supplement you will learn about . . .**

- **Monte Carlo Simulation**
- **Computer Simulation with Excel**
- **Areas of Simulation Application**

**Simulation:** a mathematical and computer modeling technique for replicating real-world problem situations.

**Simulation** is popular because it can be applied to virtually any type of problem. It can frequently be used when there is no other applicable quantitative method; it is the technique of last resort for many problems. It is a modeling approach primarily used to analyze probabilistic problems. It does not normally provide a solution; instead it provides information that is used to make a decision.

Much of the experimentation in space flight was conducted using physical simulation that re-created the conditions of space. Conditions of weightlessness were simulated using rooms filled with water. Other examples include wind tunnels that simulate the conditions of flight and treadmills that simulate automobile tire wear in a laboratory instead of on the road.

This supplement is concerned with another type of simulation, *computerized mathematical simulation*. In this form of simulation, systems are replicated with mathematical models, which are analyzed with a computer. This type of simulation is very popular and has been applied to a wide variety of operational problems.

## MONTE CARLO SIMULATION

Some problems are difficult to solve analytically because they consist of random variables represented by probability distributions. Thus, a large proportion of the applications of simulations are for probabilistic models.

**Monte Carlo technique:** a method for selecting numbers randomly from a probability distribution for use in a simulation.

The term *Monte Carlo* has become synonymous with probabilistic simulation in recent years. However, the **Monte Carlo technique** can be more narrowly defined as a technique for selecting numbers *randomly* from a probability distribution (i.e., sampling) for use in a *trial* (computer) run of a simulation. As such, the Monte Carlo technique is not a type of simulation model but rather a mathematical process used within a simulation.

The name *Monte Carlo* is appropriate, since the basic principle behind the process is the same as in the operation of a gambling casino in Monaco. In Monaco devices like roulette wheels, dice, and playing cards produce numbered results at random from well-defined populations. For example, a 7 resulting from thrown dice is a random value from a population of eleven possible numbers (i.e., 2 through 12). This same process is employed, in principle, in the Monte Carlo process used in simulation models.

The Monte Carlo process of selecting random numbers according to a probability distribution will be demonstrated using the following example. The manager of ComputerWorld, a store that sells computers and related equipment, is attempting to determine how many laptops the store should order each week. A primary consideration in this decision is the average number of laptops that the store will sell each week and the average weekly revenue generated from the sale of laptops. A laptop sells for \$4300. The number of laptops demanded each week is a random variable (which we will define as $x$) that ranges from 0 to 4. From past sales records, the manager has determined the frequency of demand for laptops for the past 100 weeks. From this frequency distribution, a probability distribution of demand can be developed, as shown in Table S12.1.

The purpose of the Monte Carlo process is to generate the random variable, demand, by "sampling" from the probability distribution, $P(x)$. The demand per week could be randomly

**Table S12.1 Probability Distribution of Demand**

| Laptops Demanded per Week, $x$ | Frequency of Demand | Probability of Demand $P(x)$ |
|---|---|---|
| 0 | 20 | 0.20 |
| 1 | 40 | 0.40 |
| 2 | 20 | 0.20 |
| 3 | 10 | 0.10 |
| 4 | 10 | 0.10 |
| | 100 | 1.00 |

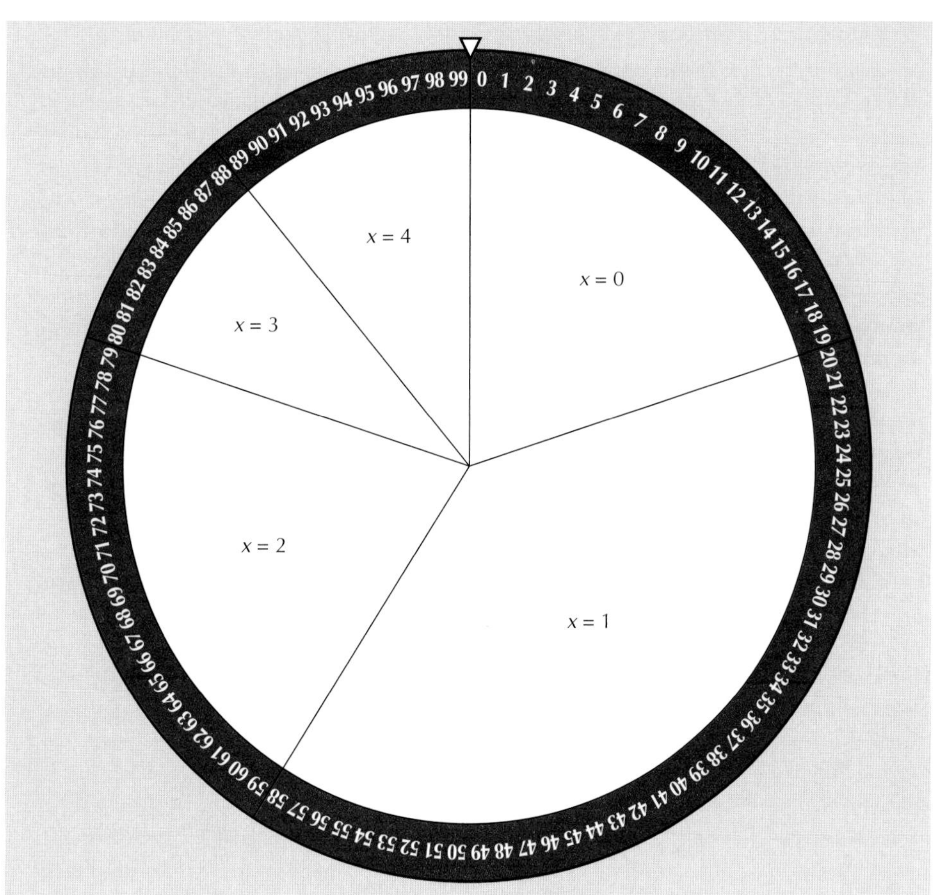


Figure S12.1
**A Roulette Wheel of Demand**

generated according to the probability distribution by spinning a roulette wheel that is partitioned into segments corresponding to the probabilities, as shown in Figure S12.1.

There are 100 numbers from 0 to 99 on the outer rim of the wheel, and they have been partitioned according to the probability of each demand value. For example, 20 numbers from 0 to 19 (i.e., 20% of the total 100 numbers) correspond to a demand of zero laptops. Now we can determine the value of demand by the number the wheel stops at and the segment of the wheel.

When the manager spins this wheel, the demand for laptops will be determined by a number. For example, if the number 71 comes up on a spin, the demand is 2 laptops per week; the number 30 indicates a demand of 1. Since the manager does not know which number will come up prior to the spin and there is an equal chance of any of the 100 numbers occurring, the numbers occur at random. That is, they are **random numbers**.

**Random numbers:** numbers that have an equal likelihood of being selected at random.

It is not generally practical to predict weekly demand for laptops by spinning a wheel. Alternatively, the process of spinning a wheel can be replicated using random numbers alone.

First, we will transfer the ranges of random numbers for each demand value from the roulette wheel to a table, as in Table S12.2. Next, instead of spinning the wheel to get a ran-

Table S12.2
**Generating Demand from Random Numbers**

| Demand, $x$ | | Ranges of Random Numbers, $r$ | | |
|---|---|---|---|---|
| 0 | | 0–19 | | |
| 1 | ← | 20–59 | ← | $r = 39$ |
| 2 | | 60–79 | | |
| 3 | | 80–89 | | |
| 4 | | 90–99 | | |

**Table S12.3**
**Random Number Table**

| | | | | |
|---|---|---|---|---|
| 39 65 76 45 45 | 19 90 69 64 61 | 20 26 36 31 62 | 58 24 97 14 97 | 95 06 70 99 00 |
| 73 71 23 70 90 | 65 97 60 12 11 | 31 56 34 19 19 | 47 83 75 51 33 | 30 62 38 20 46 |
| 72 18 47 33 84 | 51 67 47 97 19 | 98 40 07 17 66 | 23 05 09 51 80 | 59 78 11 52 49 |
| 75 12 25 69 17 | 17 95 21 78 58 | 24 33 45 77 48 | 69 81 84 09 29 | 93 22 70 45 80 |
| 37 17 79 88 74 | 63 52 06 34 30 | 01 31 60 10 27 | 35 07 79 71 53 | 28 99 52 01 41 |
| 02 48 08 16 94 | 85 53 83 29 95 | 56 27 09 24 43 | 21 78 55 09 82 | 72 61 88 73 61 |
| 87 89 15 70 07 | 37 79 49 12 38 | 48 13 93 55 96 | 41 92 45 71 51 | 09 18 25 58 94 |
| 98 18 71 70 15 | 89 09 39 59 24 | 00 06 41 41 20 | 14 36 59 25 47 | 54 45 17 24 89 |
| 10 83 58 07 04 | 76 62 16 48 68 | 58 76 17 14 86 | 59 53 11 52 21 | 66 04 18 72 87 |
| 47 08 56 37 31 | 71 82 13 50 41 | 27 55 10 24 92 | 28 04 67 53 44 | 95 23 00 84 47 |
| 93 90 31 03 07 | 34 18 04 52 35 | 74 13 39 35 22 | 68 95 23 92 35 | 36 63 70 35 33 |
| 21 05 11 47 99 | 11 20 99 45 18 | 76 51 94 84 86 | 13 79 93 37 55 | 98 16 04 41 67 |
| 95 89 94 06 97 | 27 37 83 28 71 | 79 57 95 13 91 | 09 61 87 25 21 | 56 20 11 32 44 |
| 97 18 31 55 73 | 10 65 81 92 59 | 77 31 61 95 46 | 20 44 90 32 64 | 26 99 76 75 63 |
| 69 08 88 86 13 | 59 71 74 17 32 | 48 38 75 93 29 | 73 37 32 04 05 | 60 82 29 20 25 |
| 41 26 10 25 03 | 87 63 93 95 17 | 81 83 83 04 49 | 77 45 85 50 51 | 79 88 01 97 30 |
| 91 47 14 63 62 | 08 61 74 51 69 | 92 79 43 89 79 | 29 18 94 51 23 | 14 85 11 47 23 |
| 80 94 54 18 47 | 08 52 85 08 40 | 48 40 35 94 22 | 72 65 71 08 86 | 50 03 42 99 36 |
| 67 06 77 63 99 | 89 85 84 46 06 | 64 71 06 21 66 | 89 37 20 70 01 | 61 65 70 22 12 |
| 59 72 24 13 75 | 42 29 72 23 19 | 06 94 76 10 08 | 81 30 15 39 14 | 81 33 17 16 33 |
| 63 62 06 34 41 | 79 53 36 02 95 | 94 61 09 43 62 | 20 21 14 68 86 | 84 95 48 46 45 |
| 78 47 23 53 90 | 79 93 96 38 63 | 34 85 52 05 09 | 85 43 01 72 73 | 14 93 87 81 40 |
| 87 68 62 15 43 | 97 48 72 66 48 | 53 16 71 13 81 | 59 97 50 99 52 | 24 62 20 42 31 |
| 47 60 92 10 77 | 26 97 05 73 51 | 88 46 38 03 58 | 72 68 49 29 31 | 75 70 16 08 24 |
| 56 88 87 59 41 | 06 87 37 78 48 | 65 88 69 58 39 | 88 02 84 27 83 | 85 81 56 39 38 |
| 22 17 68 65 84 | 87 02 22 57 51 | 68 69 80 95 44 | 11 29 01 95 80 | 49 34 35 36 47 |
| 19 36 27 59 46 | 39 77 32 77 09 | 79 57 92 36 59 | 89 74 39 82 15 | 08 58 94 34 74 |
| 16 77 23 02 77 | 28 06 24 25 93 | 22 45 44 84 11 | 87 80 61 65 31 | 09 71 91 74 25 |
| 78 43 76 71 61 | 97 67 63 99 61 | 30 45 67 93 82 | 59 73 19 85 23 | 53 33 65 97 21 |
| 03 28 28 26 08 | 69 30 16 09 05 | 53 58 47 70 93 | 66 56 45 65 79 | 45 56 20 19 47 |
| 04 31 17 21 56 | 33 73 99 19 87 | 26 72 39 27 67 | 53 77 57 68 93 | 60 61 97 22 61 |
| 61 06 98 03 91 | 87 14 77 43 96 | 43 00 65 98 50 | 45 60 33 01 07 | 98 99 46 50 47 |
| 23 68 35 26 00 | 99 53 93 61 28 | 52 70 05 48 34 | 56 65 05 61 86 | 90 92 10 70 80 |
| 15 39 25 70 99 | 93 86 52 77 65 | 15 33 59 05 28 | 22 87 26 07 47 | 86 96 98 29 06 |
| 58 71 96 30 24 | 18 46 23 34 27 | 85 13 99 24 44 | 49 18 09 79 49 | 74 16 32 23 02 |
| 93 22 53 64 39 | 07 10 63 76 35 | 87 03 04 79 88 | 08 13 13 85 51 | 55 34 57 72 69 |
| 78 76 58 54 74 | 92 38 70 96 92 | 52 06 79 79 45 | 82 63 18 27 44 | 69 66 92 19 09 |
| 61 81 31 96 82 | 00 57 25 60 59 | 46 72 60 18 77 | 55 66 12 62 11 | 08 99 55 64 57 |
| 42 88 07 10 05 | 24 98 65 63 21 | 47 21 61 88 32 | 27 80 30 21 60 | 10 92 35 36 12 |
| 77 94 30 05 39 | 28 10 99 00 27 | 12 73 73 99 12 | 49 99 57 94 82 | 96 88 57 17 91 |

dom number, we will select a random number from Table S12.3, which is referred to as a *random number table*. (These random numbers have been generated by computer so that they are *equally likely to occur*, just as if we had spun a wheel.) As an example, let us select the number 39 in Table S12.3. Looking again at Table S12.2, we can see that the random number 39 falls in the range 20–59, which corresponds to a weekly demand of 1 laptop.

By repeating this process of selecting random numbers from Table S12.3 (starting anywhere in the table and moving in any direction but not repeating the same sequence) and then determining weekly demand from the random number, we can simulate demand for a period of time. For example, Table S12.4 shows demand simulated for a period of 15 consecutive weeks.

These data can now be used to compute the estimated average weekly demand.

$$\text{Estimated average demand} = \frac{31}{15}$$

$$= 2.07 \text{ laptops per week}$$

Table S12.4
**The Simulation Experiment**

| Week | $r$ | Demand ($x$) | Revenue ($) |
|---|---|---|---|
| 1 | 39 | 1 | 4,300 |
| 2 | 73 | 2 | 8,600 |
| 3 | 72 | 2 | 8,600 |
| 4 | 75 | 2 | 8,600 |
| 5 | 37 | 1 | 4,300 |
| 6 | 02 | 0 | 0 |
| 7 | 87 | 3 | 12,900 |
| 8 | 98 | 4 | 17,200 |
| 9 | 10 | 0 | 0 |
| 10 | 47 | 1 | 4,300 |
| 11 | 93 | 4 | 17,200 |
| 12 | 21 | 1 | 4,300 |
| 13 | 95 | 4 | 17,200 |
| 14 | 97 | 4 | 17,200 |
| 15 | 69 | 2 | 8,600 |
| | | $\Sigma = 31$ | $133,300 |

The manager can then use this information to determine the number of laptops to order each week.

Although this example is convenient for illustrating how simulation works, the average demand could have been more appropriately calculated *analytically* using the formula for expected value. The *expected value*, or average, for weekly demand can be computed analytically from the probability distribution, $P(x)$, as follows:

$$\begin{aligned} E(x) &= (0.20)(0) + (0.40)(1) + (0.20)(2) + (0.10)(3) + (0.10)(4) \\ &= 1.5 \text{ laptops per week} \end{aligned}$$

The analytical result of 1.5 laptops is not very close to the simulated result of 2.07 laptops. The difference (0.57 laptops) between the simulated value and the analytical value is a result of the number of periods over which the simulation was conducted. The results of any simulation study are subject to the number of times the simulation occurred (i.e., the number of *trials*). Thus, the more periods for which the simulation is conducted, the more accurate the result. For example, if demand were simulated for 1000 weeks, in all likelihood an average value exactly equal to the analytical value (1.5 laptops per week) would result.

Once a simulation has been repeated enough times, it reaches an average result that remains constant, called a **steady-state result**. For this example, 1.5 laptops is the long-run average or steady-state result, but we have seen that the simulation would have to be repeated more than 15 times (i.e., weeks) before this result is reached.

**Steady-state result:** an average result that remains constant after enough trials.

## COMPUTER SIMULATION WITH EXCEL

The simulation we performed manually for this example was not too difficult. However, if we had performed the simulation for 1000 weeks, it would have taken several hours. On the other hand, this simulation could be done on the computer in several seconds. Also, our simulation example was not very complex. As simulation models get progressively more complex, it becomes virtually impossible to perform them manually, making the computer a necessity.

Although we will not develop a simulation model in computer language, we will demonstrate how a computerized simulation model is developed using Excel spreadsheets. We will do so by simulating our inventory example for ComputerWorld.

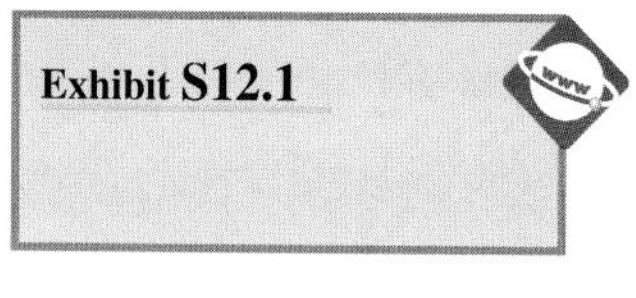

Exhibit S12.1

Microsoft Excel - ExhibitS12.1.xls

A3 = 0.629923723538247

| | A | B | C | D | E | F | G | H | I | J |
|---|---|---|---|---|---|---|---|---|---|---|
| 1 | 100 Random Numbers Generated Using RAND() | | | | | | | | | |
| 2 | | | | | | | | | | |
| 3 | 0.6299 | 0.6922 | 0.4634 | 0.0433 | 0.0755 | 0.0641 | 0.3189 | 0.2599 | 0.2288 | 0.7371 |
| 4 | 0.4191 | 0.7927 | 0.6893 | 0.9192 | 0.8019 | 0.4114 | 0.3443 | 0.5397 | 0.8936 | 0.6944 |
| 5 | 0.7306 | 0.4968 | 0.5271 | 0.2341 | 0.3518 | 0.1129 | 0.7664 | 0.5752 | 0.7673 | 0.7338 |
| 6 | 0.8712 | 0.5170 | 0.8834 | 0.9357 | 0.6817 | 0.6175 | 0.9635 | 0.0216 | 0.9409 | 0.3832 |
| 7 | 0.8718 | 0.2347 | 0.3095 | 0.8006 | 0.7955 | 0.0621 | 0.3317 | 0.4863 | 0.4599 | 0.3011 |
| 8 | 0.0935 | 0.0287 | 0.1110 | 0.6009 | 0.1023 | 0.3886 | 0.3424 | 0.2876 | 0.1904 | 0.1980 |
| 9 | 0.2892 | 0.0149 | 0.5325 | 0.4057 | 0.0385 | 0.4983 | 0.8286 | 0.1043 | 0.3955 | 0.1855 |
| 10 | 0.4016 | 0.8078 | 0.0656 | 0.2995 | 0.5729 | 0.5776 | 0.8871 | 0.4656 | 0.9582 | 0.6215 |
| 11 | 0.4508 | 0.3710 | 0.1533 | 0.9799 | 0.4267 | 0.7611 | 0.2242 | 0.8883 | 0.7665 | 0.5268 |
| 12 | 0.6573 | 0.4849 | 0.6997 | 0.4905 | 0.8855 | 0.9194 | 0.5891 | 0.0643 | 0.2703 | 0.9780 |
| 13 | | | | | | | | | | |

The first step in developing a simulation model is to generate random numbers. Random numbers between 0 and 1 can be generated in Excel by entering the formula, =RAND(), in a cell. Exhibit S12.1 is an Excel spreadsheet with 100 random numbers generated by entering the formula, =RAND(), in cell A3 and copying to the cells in the range A3:J12. We can copy things into a range of cells in two ways. You can first cover cells A3:J12 with the cursor; then type the formula "=RAND()" into cell A3; and finally hit the "Ctrl" and "Enter" keys simultaneously. Alternatively, you can type "=RAND()" into cell A3, "copy" this cell (using the right mouse button), then cover cells A4:J12 with the cursor, and (again with the right mouse button) paste this formula into these cells.

If you attempt to replicate this spreadsheet you will generate random numbers different from those shown in Exhibit S12.1. Every time you generate random numbers they will be different. In fact, any time you recalculate anything on your spreadsheet the random numbers will change. You can see this by hitting the F9 key and observing that all the random numbers change. However, sometimes it is useful in a simulation model to be able to use the same set (or stream) of random numbers over and over. You can freeze the random numbers you are using on your spreadsheet by first covering the cells with random numbers in them with the cursor, for example cells A3:J12 in Exhibit S12.1. Next copy these cells (using the right mouse button); then click on the "Edit" menu at the top of your spreadsheet and select "Paste Special" from this menu. Next select the "Values" option and click on "OK." This procedure pastes a copy of the numbers in these cells over the same cells with (=RAND()) formulas in them, thus freezing the numbers in place.

Notice one more thing from Exhibit S12.1; the random numbers are all between 0 and 1, whereas the random numbers in Table S12.3 are whole numbers between 0 and 100. We used whole random numbers previously for illustrative purposes; however, computer programs like Excel generally provide random numbers between 0 and 1.

Now we are ready to duplicate our example simulation model for the ComputerWorld store using Excel. The spreadsheet in Exhibit S12.2 includes the simulation model originally developed in Table S12.4.

Exhibit S12.2

=AVERAGE (G6:G20)

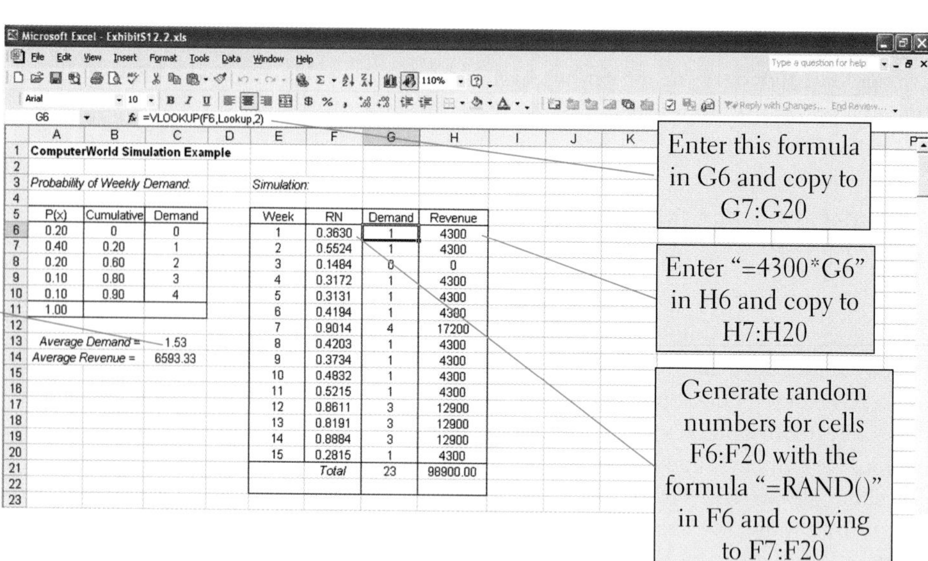



| | A | B | C | D | E | F | G | H |
|---|---|---|---|---|---|---|---|---|
| 1 | ComputerWorld Simulation Example | | | | | | | |
| 2 | | | | | | | | |
| 3 | *Probability of Weekly Demand:* | | | | *Simulation:* | | | |
| 4 | | | | | | | | |
| 5 | P(x) | Cumulative | Demand | | Week | RN | Demand | Revenue |
| 6 | 0.20 | 0 | 0 | | 1 | 0.3630 | 1 | 4300 |
| 7 | 0.40 | 0.20 | 1 | | 2 | 0.5524 | 1 | 4300 |
| 8 | 0.20 | 0.60 | 2 | | 3 | 0.1484 | 0 | 0 |
| 9 | 0.10 | 0.80 | 3 | | 4 | 0.3172 | 1 | 4300 |
| 10 | 0.10 | 0.90 | 4 | | 5 | 0.3131 | 1 | 4300 |
| 11 | 1.00 | | | | 6 | 0.4194 | 1 | 4300 |
| 12 | | | | | 7 | 0.9014 | 4 | 17200 |
| 13 | *Average Demand =* | | 1.53 | | 8 | 0.4203 | 1 | 4300 |
| 14 | *Average Revenue =* | | 6593.33 | | 9 | 0.3734 | 1 | 4300 |
| 15 | | | | | 10 | 0.4832 | 1 | 4300 |
| 16 | | | | | 11 | 0.5215 | 1 | 4300 |
| 17 | | | | | 12 | 0.8611 | 3 | 12900 |
| 18 | | | | | 13 | 0.8191 | 3 | 12900 |
| 19 | | | | | 14 | 0.8884 | 3 | 12900 |
| 20 | | | | | 15 | 0.2815 | 1 | 4300 |
| 21 | | | | | | *Total* | 23 | 98900.00 |
| 22 | | | | | | | | |
| 23 | | | | | | | | |

First note that the probability distribution for the weekly demand for laptops has been entered in cells A5:C11. Also notice that we have entered a set of cumulative probability values in column B. We generated these cumulative probabilities by first entering 0 in cell B6, then entering the formula "=A6+B6" in cell B7, and copying this formula to cells B8:B10. This cumulative probability creates a range of random numbers for each demand value. For example, any random number less than 0.20 will result in a demand value of 0, whereas any random number greater than 0.20 but less than 0.60 will result in a demand value of 1, and so on.

Random numbers are generated in cells F6:F20 by entering the formula "=RAND()" in cell F6 and copying it to the range of cells in F7:F20.

Now we need to be able to generate demand values for each of these random numbers in column F. We accomplish this by first covering the cumulative probabilities and the demand values in cells B6:C10 with the cursor. Then we give this range of cells the name "Lookup." This can be done by typing "Lookup" directly on the formula bar in place of B6 or by clicking on the "Insert" button at the top of the spreadsheet and selecting "Name" and "Define" and then entering the name "Lookup." This has the effect of creating a table called "Lookup" with the ranges of random numbers and associated demand values in it. Next we enter the formula "=VLOOKUP(F6,Lookup,2)" in cell G6 and copy it to the cells in the range G7:G20. This formula will compare the random numbers in column F with the cumulative probabilities in B6:B10 and generate the correct demand value from cells C6:C10.

Once the demand values have been generated in column G we can determine the weekly revenue values by entering the formula "=4300*G6" in H6 and copying it to cells H7:H20.

Average weekly demand is computed in cell C13 by using the formula "=AVERAGE(G6:G20)," and the average weekly revenue is computed by entering a similar formula in cell C14.

Notice that the average weekly demand value of 1.53 in Exhibit S12.2 is different from the simulation result (2.07) we obtained from Table S12.4. This is because we used a different stream of random numbers. As we mentioned previously, to acquire an average closer to the true steady state value the simulation needs to include more repetitions than 15 weeks. As an example, Exhibit S12.3 simulates demand for 100 weeks. The window has been "frozen" at row 16 and scrolled up to show the first 10 weeks and the last 6 on the screen in Exhibit S12.3.

**Exhibit S12.3**

Microsoft Excel - ExhibitS12.3.xls

G6 =VLOOKUP(F6,Lookup,2)

| | A | B | C | D | E | F | G | H |
|---|---|---|---|---|---|---|---|---|
| 1 | **ComputerWorld Simulation Example (100 Weeks)** | | | | | | | |
| 2 | | | | | | | | |
| 3 | *Probability of Weekly Demand:* | | | | *Simulation:* | | | |
| 4 | | | | | | | | |
| 5 | P(x) | Cumulative | Demand | | Week | RN | Demand | Revenue |
| 6 | 0.20 | 0 | 0 | | 1 | 0.3630 | 1 | 4300 |
| 7 | 0.40 | 0.20 | 1 | | 2 | 0.5524 | 1 | 4300 |
| 8 | 0.20 | 0.60 | 2 | | 3 | 0.1484 | 0 | 0 |
| 9 | 0.10 | 0.80 | 3 | | 4 | 0.3172 | 1 | 4300 |
| 10 | 0.10 | 0.90 | 4 | | 5 | 0.3131 | 1 | 4300 |
| 11 | 1.00 | | | | 6 | 0.4194 | 1 | 4300 |
| 12 | | | | | 7 | 0.9014 | 4 | 17200 |
| 13 | | *Average Demand =* | 1.49 | | 8 | 0.4203 | 1 | 4300 |
| 14 | *Average Revenue =* | | 6407.00 | | 9 | 0.3734 | 1 | 4300 |
| 15 | | | | | 10 | 0.4832 | 1 | 4300 |
| 100 | | | | | 95 | 0.2370 | 1 | 4300 |
| 101 | | | | | 96 | 0.1215 | 2 | 8600 |
| 102 | | | | | 97 | 0.0809 | 2 | 8600 |
| 103 | | | | | 98 | 0.8202 | 0 | 0 |
| 104 | | | | | 99 | 0.9290 | 0 | 0 |
| 105 | | | | | 100 | 0.3653 | 2 | 8600 |
| 106 | | | | | | *Total* | 149 | 640700 |
| 107 | | | | | | | | |

Spreadsheet "frozen" at row 16 to show first 10 weeks and last 6

## DECISION MAKING WITH SIMULATION

In our previous example, the manager of the ComputerWorld store acquired some useful information about the weekly demand and revenue for laptops that would be helpful in making a decision about how many laptops would be needed each week to meet demand. However, this example did not lead directly to a decision. Next we will expand our ComputerWorld store example so that a possible decision will result.

From the simulation in Exhibit S12.3 the manager of the store knows that the average weekly demand for laptop PCs will be approximately 1.49; however, the manager cannot order 1.49 laptops each week. Since fractional laptops are not possible, either 1 or 2 must be ordered. Thus, the manager wants to repeat the earlier simulation with two possible order sizes, 1 and 2. The manager also wants to include some additional information in the model that will affect the decision.

If too few laptops are on hand to meet demand during the week, not only will there be a loss of revenue, but there will also be a shortage, or customer goodwill, cost of $500 per unit incurred because the customer will be unhappy. However, each laptop still in stock at the end of each week that has not been sold will incur an inventory or storage cost of $50. Thus, it costs the store money either to have too few or too many laptops on hand each week. Given this scenario the manager wants to order either one or two laptops, depending on which order size will result in the greatest average weekly revenue.

Exhibit S12.4 shows the Excel spreadsheet for this revised example. The simulation is for 100 weeks. The columns labeled "1," "2," and "4" for "Week," "RN," and "Demand" were constructed similarly to the model in Exhibit S12.3. The array of cells B6:C10 were given the name "Lookup," and the formula "=VLOOKUP(F6,Lookup,2)" was entered in cell H6 and copied to cells H7:H105.

The simulation in Exhibit S12.4 is for an order size of one laptop each week. The "Inventory" column (3) keeps track of the amount of inventory available each week—the one laptop that comes in on order plus any laptops carried over from the previous week. The cumulative inventory is computed each week by entering the formula "=1+MAX(G6-H6,0)" in cell G7 and copying it to cells G8:G105. This formula adds the one laptop on order to either the amount left over from the previous week (G6–H6) or 0 if there were not enough laptops on hand to meet demand. It does not allow for negative inventory levels, called backorders. In other words, if a sale cannot be made due to a shortage, it is gone. The inventory values in column 3 are eventually multiplied by the inventory cost of $50 per unit in column 8 using the formula "=G6*50".

If there is a shortage it is recorded in column 5 labeled "Shortage." The shortage is computed by entering the formula "=MIN(G6-H6,0)" in cell I6 and copying it to cells I7:I105. Shortage costs are computed in column 7 by multiplying the shortage values in column 5 by $500, entering the formula "=I6*500" in cell K6, and copying it to cells K7:K105.

Weekly revenues are computed in column 6 by entering the formula "=4300*MIN(H6,G6)" in cell J6 and copying it to cells J7:J105. In other words, the revenue is determined by either the inventory level in column 3 or the demand in column 4, whichever is smaller.

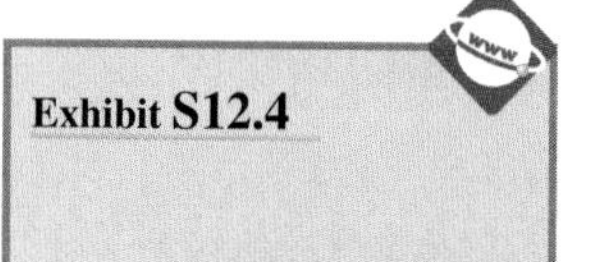

**Exhibit S12.4**

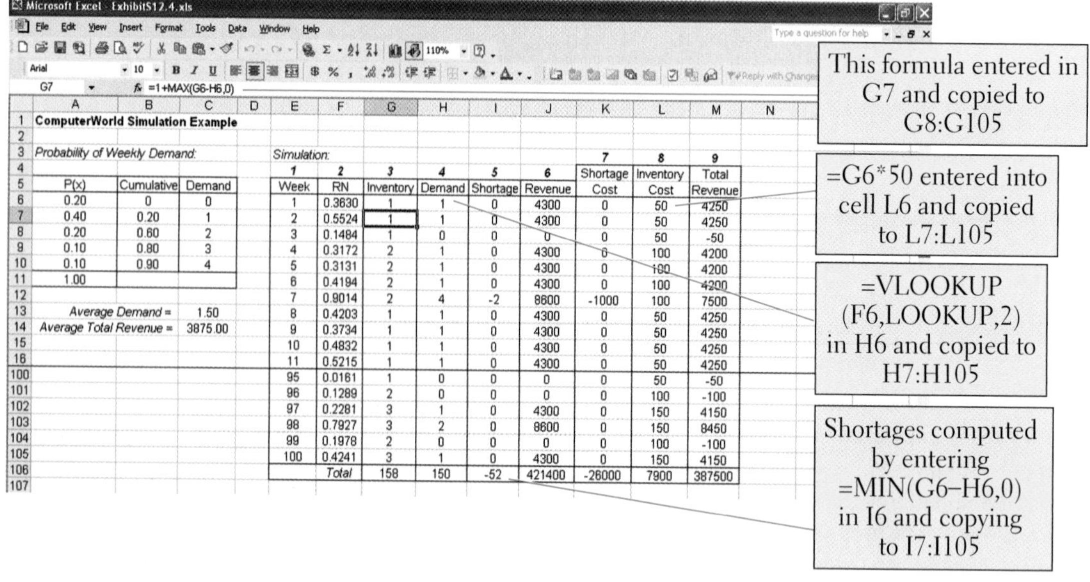


**ComputerWorld Simulation Example**

*Probability of Weekly Demand:*

| P(x) | Cumulative | Demand |
|---|---|---|
| 0.20 | 0 | 0 |
| 0.40 | 0.20 | 1 |
| 0.20 | 0.60 | 2 |
| 0.10 | 0.80 | 3 |
| 0.10 | 0.90 | 4 |
| 1.00 | | |

*Average Demand* = 1.50
*Average Total Revenue* = 3875.00

*Simulation:*

| 1<br>Week | 2<br>RN | 3<br>Inventory | 4<br>Demand | 5<br>Shortage | 6<br>Revenue | 7<br>Shortage Cost | 8<br>Inventory Cost | 9<br>Total Revenue |
|---|---|---|---|---|---|---|---|---|
| 1 | 0.3630 | 1 | 1 | 0 | 4300 | 0 | 50 | 4250 |
| 2 | 0.5524 | 1 | 1 | 0 | 4300 | 0 | 50 | 4250 |
| 3 | 0.1484 | 1 | 0 | 0 | 0 | 0 | 50 | -50 |
| 4 | 0.3172 | 2 | 1 | 0 | 4300 | 0 | 100 | 4200 |
| 5 | 0.3131 | 2 | 1 | 0 | 4300 | 0 | 100 | 4200 |
| 6 | 0.4194 | 2 | 1 | 0 | 4300 | 0 | 100 | 4200 |
| 7 | 0.9014 | 2 | 4 | -2 | 8600 | -1000 | 100 | 7500 |
| 8 | 0.4203 | 1 | 1 | 0 | 4300 | 0 | 50 | 4250 |
| 9 | 0.3734 | 1 | 1 | 0 | 4300 | 0 | 50 | 4250 |
| 10 | 0.4832 | 1 | 1 | 0 | 4300 | 0 | 50 | 4250 |
| 11 | 0.5215 | 1 | 1 | 0 | 4300 | 0 | 50 | 4250 |
| 95 | 0.0161 | 1 | 0 | 0 | 0 | 0 | 50 | -50 |
| 96 | 0.1289 | 2 | 0 | 0 | 0 | 0 | 100 | -100 |
| 97 | 0.2281 | 3 | 1 | 0 | 4300 | 0 | 150 | 4150 |
| 98 | 0.7927 | 3 | 2 | 0 | 8600 | 0 | 150 | 8450 |
| 99 | 0.1978 | 2 | 0 | 0 | 0 | 0 | 100 | -100 |
| 100 | 0.4241 | 3 | 1 | 0 | 4300 | 0 | 150 | 4150 |
| | *Total* | 158 | 150 | -52 | 421400 | -26000 | 7900 | 387500 |

Exhibit S12.5

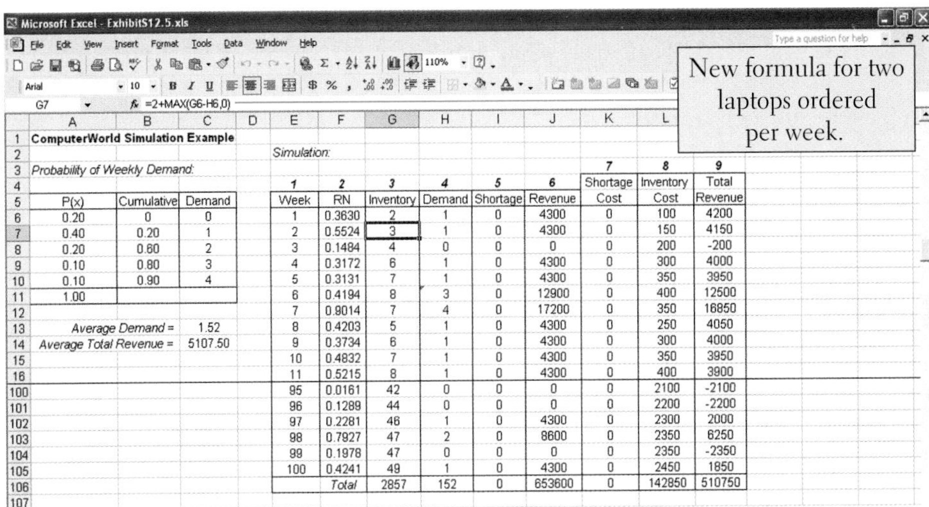


ComputerWorld Simulation Example

Probability of Weekly Demand:

| P(x) | Cumulative | Demand |
|---|---|---|
| 0.20 | 0 | 0 |
| 0.40 | 0.20 | 1 |
| 0.20 | 0.60 | 2 |
| 0.10 | 0.80 | 3 |
| 0.10 | 0.90 | 4 |
| 1.00 | | |

Average Demand = 1.52
Average Total Revenue = 5107.50

Simulation:

| 1 Week | 2 RN | 3 Inventory | 4 Demand | 5 Shortage | 6 Revenue | 7 Shortage Cost | 8 Inventory Cost | 9 Total Revenue |
|---|---|---|---|---|---|---|---|---|
| 1 | 0.3630 | 2 | 1 | 0 | 4300 | 0 | 100 | 4200 |
| 2 | 0.5524 | 3 | 1 | 0 | 4300 | 0 | 150 | 4150 |
| 3 | 0.1484 | 4 | 0 | 0 | 0 | 0 | 200 | -200 |
| 4 | 0.3172 | 6 | 1 | 0 | 4300 | 0 | 300 | 4000 |
| 5 | 0.3131 | 7 | 1 | 0 | 4300 | 0 | 350 | 3950 |
| 6 | 0.4194 | 8 | 3 | 0 | 12900 | 0 | 400 | 12500 |
| 7 | 0.9014 | 7 | 4 | 0 | 17200 | 0 | 350 | 16850 |
| 8 | 0.4203 | 5 | 1 | 0 | 4300 | 0 | 250 | 4050 |
| 9 | 0.3734 | 6 | 1 | 0 | 4300 | 0 | 300 | 4000 |
| 10 | 0.4832 | 7 | 1 | 0 | 4300 | 0 | 350 | 3950 |
| 11 | 0.5215 | 8 | 1 | 0 | 4300 | 0 | 400 | 3900 |
| 95 | 0.0161 | 42 | 0 | 0 | 0 | 0 | 2100 | -2100 |
| 96 | 0.1289 | 44 | 0 | 0 | 0 | 0 | 2200 | -2200 |
| 97 | 0.2281 | 46 | 1 | 0 | 4300 | 0 | 2300 | 2000 |
| 98 | 0.7927 | 47 | 2 | 0 | 8600 | 0 | 2350 | 6250 |
| 99 | 0.1978 | 47 | 0 | 0 | 0 | 0 | 2350 | -2350 |
| 100 | 0.4241 | 49 | 1 | 0 | 4300 | 0 | 2450 | 1850 |
| | Total | 2857 | 152 | 0 | 653600 | 0 | 142850 | 510750 |

Total weekly revenue is computed by summing revenue, shortage costs, and inventory costs in column 9 by entering the formula "=J6+K6−L6" in cell M6 and copying it to cells M7:M105.

The average weekly demand, 1.50, is shown in cell C13. The average weekly revenue, \$3875, is computed in cell C14.

Next we must repeat this same simulation for an order size of two laptops each week. The spreadsheet for an order size of 2 is shown in Exhibit S12.5. Notice that the only actual difference is the use of a new formula to compute the weekly inventory level in column 3. This formula in cell G7 reflecting two laptops ordered each week is shown on the formula bar at the top of the spreadsheet.

This second simulation in Exhibit S12.5 results in average weekly demand of 1.52 laptops and average weekly total revenue of \$5,107.50. This is higher than the total weekly revenue of \$3,875 achieved in the first simulation run in Exhibit S12.4, even though the store would incur significantly higher inventory costs. Thus, the correct decision—based on weekly revenue—would be to order two laptops per week. However, there are probably additional aspects of this problem the manager would want to consider in the decision-making process, such as the increasingly high inventory levels as the simulation progresses. For example, there may not be enough storage space to accommodate this much inventory. Such questions as this and others can also be analyzed with simulation. In fact, that is one of the main attributes of simulation—its usefulness as a model to experiment on, called "what if?" analysis.

This example briefly demonstrates how simulation can be used to make a decision, i.e., to "optimize." In this example we experimented with two order sizes and determined the one that resulted in the greatest revenue. The same basic modeling principles can be used to solve larger problems with hundreds of possible order sizes and a probability distribution for demand with many more values plus variable lead times (i.e., the time it takes to receive an order), the ability to backorder and other complicating factors. These factors make the simulation model larger and more complex, but such models are frequently developed and used in business.

## AREAS OF SIMULATION APPLICATION

Simulation can be used to address many types of operational problems.

Simulation is one of the most popular of all quantitative techniques because it can be applied to operational problems that are too difficult to model and solve analytically. Some analysts feel that complex systems should be studied via simulation whether or not they can be analyzed analytically, because it provides an easy vehicle for experimenting on the system. Surveys indicate that a large majority of major corporations use simulation in such functional areas as production, planning, engineering, financial analysis, research and development, information systems, and personnel. Following are descriptions of some of the more common applications of simulation.

## WAITING LINES/SERVICE

A major application of simulation has been in the analysis of waiting line, or queuing, systems. For complex queuing systems, it is not possible to develop analytical formulas, and simulation is often the only means of analysis. For example, for a busy supermarket with multiple waiting lines, some for express service and some for regular service, simulation may be the only form of analysis to determine how many registers and servers are needed to meet customer demand.

## INVENTORY MANAGEMENT

Product demand is an essential component in determining the amount of inventory a commercial enterprise should keep. Many of the traditional mathematical formulas used to analyze inventory systems make the assumption that this demand is certain (i.e., not a random variable). In practice, however, demand is rarely known with certainty. Simulation is one of the best means for analyzing inventory systems in which demand is a random variable. Simulation has been used to experiment with innovative inventory systems such as just-in-time (JIT). Companies use simulation to see how effective and costly a JIT system would be in their own manufacturing environment without having to implement the system physically.

## PRODUCTION AND MANUFACTURING SYSTEMS

Simulation is often applied to production problems, such as production scheduling, production sequencing, assembly line balancing (of in-process inventory), plant layout, and plant location analysis. Many production processes can be viewed as queuing systems that can be analyzed only by using simulation. Since machine breakdowns typically occur according to some probability distributions, maintenance problems are also frequently analyzed using simulation. In the past few years, several software packages for the personal computer have been developed to simulate all aspects of manufacturing operations.

## CAPITAL INVESTMENT AND BUDGETING

Capital budgeting problems require estimates of cash flows, often resulting from many random variables. Simulation has been used to generate values of the various contributing factors to derive estimates of cash flows. Simulation has also been used to determine the inputs into rate-of-return calculations, where the inputs are random variables such as market size, selling price, growth rate, and market share.

## LOGISTICS

Logistics problems typically include numerous random variables, such as distance, different modes of transport, shipping rates, and schedules. Simulation can be used to analyze different distribution channels to determine the most efficient logistics system.

## SERVICE OPERATIONS

The operations of police departments, fire departments, post offices, hospitals, court systems, airports, and other public service systems have been analyzed using simulation. Typically, such operations are so complex and contain so many random variables that no technique except simulation can be employed for analysis.

## ENVIRONMENTAL AND RESOURCE ANALYSIS

Some of the more recent innovative applications of simulation have been directed at problems in the environment. Simulation models have been developed to ascertain the impact of projects such as manufacturing plants, waste-disposal facilities, and nuclear power plants. In many cases, these models include measures to analyze the financial feasibility of such projects. Other models have been developed to simulate waste and population conditions. In the area of resource analysis, numerous simulation models have been developed in recent years to simulate energy systems and the feasibility of alternative energy sources.

## SUMMARY

Simulation has become an increasingly important quantitative technique for solving problems in operations. Surveys have shown simulation to be one of the techniques most widely applied to real-world problems. Evidence of this popularity is the number of specialized simulation languages that have been developed by the computer industry and academia to deal with complex problem areas.

The popularity of simulation is due in large part to the flexibility it allows in analyzing systems, compared with more confining analytical techniques. In other words, the problem does not have to fit the model (or technique); the simulation model can be constructed to fit the problem. Simulation is popular also because it is an excellent experimental technique, enabling systems and problems to be tested within a laboratory setting.

In spite of its versatility, simulation has limitations and must be used with caution. One limitation is that simulation models are typically unstructured and must be developed for a system or problem that is also unstructured. Unlike some of the structured techniques presented in this book, the models cannot simply be applied to a specific type of problem. As a result, developing simulation models often requires a certain amount of imagination and intuitiveness that is not required by some of the more straightforward solution techniques we have presented. In addition, the validation of simulation models is an area of serious concern. It is often impossible to validate simulation results realistically or to know if they accurately reflect the system under analysis. This problem has become an area of such concern that *output analysis* of simulation results is a field of study in its own right. Another limiting factor in simulation is the cost in terms of money and time of model building. Because simulation models are developed for unstructured systems, they often take large amounts of staff, computer time, and money to develop and run. For many business companies, these costs can be prohibitive.

The computer programming aspects of simulation can also be quite difficult. Fortunately, generalized simulation languages have been developed to perform many of the functions of a simulation study. Each of these languages requires at least some knowledge of a scientific or business-oriented programming language.

## SUMMARY OF KEY TERMS

**Monte Carlo technique** a technique for selecting numbers randomly from a probability distribution for use in a simulation model.

**random numbers** numbers in a table or generated by a computer, each of which has an equal likelihood of being selected at random.

**simulation** an approach to operational problem solving in which a real-world problem situation is replicated within a mathematical model.

**steady-state result** an average model result that approaches constancy after a sufficient passage of time or enough repetitions or trials.

## SOLVED PROBLEM

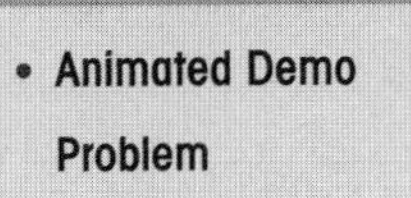


### SIMULATION

Members of the Willow Creek Emergency Rescue Squad know from past experience that they will receive between zero and six emergency calls each night, according to the following discrete probability distribution:

| CALLS | PROBABILITY |
|---|---|
| 0 | 0.05 |
| 1 | 0.12 |
| 2 | 0.15 |
| 3 | 0.25 |
| 4 | 0.22 |
| 5 | 0.15 |
| 6 | 0.06 |
| | 1.00 |

The rescue squad classifies each emergency call into one of three categories: minor, regular, or major emergency. The probability that a particular call will be each type of emergency is as follows:

| EMERGENCY TYPE | PROBABILITY |
|---|---|
| Minor | 0.30 |
| Regular | 0.56 |
| Major | 0.14 |
| | 1.00 |

The type of emergency call determines the size of the crew sent in response. A minor emergency requires a two-person crew, a regular call requires a three-person crew, and a major emergency requires a five-person crew.

The warehouse presently has five stereos in stock. Orders are always received at the beginning of the week. Simulate the Stereo Warehouse's ordering and sales policy for 20 weeks, using the first column of random numbers in Table S12.3. Compute the average weekly cost.

**S12-4.** A baseball game consists of plays that can be described as follows:

| Play | Description |
|---|---|
| No advance | An out where no runners advance. This includes strikeouts, pop ups, short flies, and the like. |
| Groundout | All runners can advance one base. |
| Possible double play | Double play if there is a runner on first base and fewer than two outs. The lead runner can be forced out; runners not out advance one base. If there is no runner on first or there are two outs, this play is treated as a "no advance." |
| Long fly | A runner on third base can score. |
| Very long fly | Runners on second and third base advance one base. |
| Walk | Includes a hit batter. |
| Infield single | All runners advance one base. |
| Outfield single | A runner on first base advances one base, but a runner on second or third base scores. |
| Long single | All runners can advance a maximum of two bases. |
| Double | Runners can advance a maximum of two bases. |
| Long double | All runners score. |
| Triple | |
| Home run | |

*Note:* Singles also include a factor for errors, allowing the batter to reach first base.

Distributions for these plays for two teams, the White Sox (visitors) and the Yankees (home), are as follows:

**Team: White Sox**

| Play | Probability |
|---|---|
| No advance | 0.03 |
| Groundout | 0.39 |
| Possible double play | 0.06 |
| Long fly | 0.09 |
| Very long fly | 0.08 |
| Walk | 0.06 |
| Infield single | 0.02 |
| Outfield single | 0.10 |
| Long single | 0.03 |
| Double | 0.04 |
| Long double | 0.05 |
| Triple | 0.02 |
| Home run | 0.03 |
| | 1.00 |

**Team: Yankees**

| Play | Probability |
|---|---|
| No advance | 0.04 |
| Groundout | 0.38 |
| Possible double play | 0.04 |
| Long fly | 0.10 |
| Very long fly | 0.06 |
| Walk | 0.07 |
| Infield single | 0.04 |
| Outfield single | 0.10 |
| Long single | 0.04 |
| Double | 0.05 |
| Long double | 0.03 |
| Triple | 0.01 |
| Home run | 0.04 |
| | 1.00 |

Simulate a nine-inning baseball game using this information.[1]

**S12-5.** The Saki automobile dealer in the Minneapolis–St. Paul area orders the Saki sport compact, which gets 50 miles per gallon of gasoline, from the manufacturer in Japan. However, the dealer never knows for sure how many months it will take to receive an order once it is placed. It can take one, two, or three months with the following probabilities:

| Months to Receive an Order | Probability |
|---|---|
| 1 | .50 |
| 2 | .30 |
| 3 | .20 |
| | 1.00 |

The demand per month is given by the following distribution:

| Demand per Month (cars) | Probability |
|---|---|
| 1 | .10 |
| 2 | .30 |
| 3 | .40 |
| 4 | .20 |
| | 1.00 |

The dealer orders when the number of cars on the lot gets down to a certain level. In order to determine the appropriate level of cars to use as an indicator of when to order, the dealer needs to know how many cars will be demanded during the time required to receive an order. Simulate the demand for 30 orders, and compute the average number of cars demanded during the time required to receive an order. At what level of cars in stock should the dealer place an order?

[1]This problem was adapted from R. E. Trueman, "A Computer Simulation Model of Baseball: with Particular Application to Strategy Analysis," in R. E. Machol, S. P. Ladany, and D. G. Morrison, eds., *Management Science in Sports* (New York: North Holland Publishing, Co., 1976), pp. 1–14.

**S12-6.** The Paymor Rental Car Agency rents cars in a small town. It wants to determine how many rental cars it should maintain. Based on market projections and historical data, the manager has determined probability distributions for the number of rentals per day and rental duration (in days only) as shown in the following tables:

| Number of Customers/Day | Probability |
|---|---|
| 0 | .20 |
| 1 | .20 |
| 2 | .50 |
| 3 | .10 |

| Rental Duration (days) | Probability |
|---|---|
| 1 | .10 |
| 2 | .30 |
| 3 | .40 |
| 4 | .10 |
| 5 | .10 |

Design a simulation experiment for the car agency and simulate, using a fleet of four rental cars, for 10 days. Compute the probability that the agency will not have a car available on demand. Should the agency expand its fleet? Explain how a simulation experiment could be designed to determine the optimal fleet size for the Paymor Agency.

**S12-7.** The emergency room of the community hospital in Farmburg has a receptionist, one doctor, and one nurse. The emergency room opens at time zero, and patients begin to arrive sometime later. Patients arrive at the emergency room according to the following probability distribution:

| Time Between Arrivals (min) | Probability |
|---|---|
| 5 | .06 |
| 10 | .10 |
| 15 | .23 |
| 20 | .29 |
| 25 | .18 |
| 30 | .14 |

The attention needed by a patient who comes to the emergency room is defined by the following probability distribution:

| Patient Needs to See | Probability |
|---|---|
| Doctor alone | .50 |
| Nurse alone | .20 |
| Both | .30 |

If a patient needs to see both the doctor and the nurse, he or she cannot see one before the other; that is, the patient must wait to see both together. The length of the patient's visit (in minutes) is defined by the following probability distributions:

| Doctor | Probability | Nurse | Probability | Both | Probability |
|---|---|---|---|---|---|
| 10 | .22 | 5 | .08 | 15 | .07 |
| 15 | .31 | 10 | .24 | 20 | .16 |
| 20 | .25 | 15 | .51 | 25 | .21 |
| 25 | .12 | 20 | .17 | 30 | .28 |
| 30 | .10 | | | 35 | .17 |
| | | | | 40 | .11 |

Simulate the arrival of 30 patients to the emergency room and compute the probability that a patient must wait and the average waiting time. Based on this one simulation, does it appear this system provides adequate patient care?

**S12-8.** A robbery has just been committed at the Corner Market in the downtown area of the city. The market owner was able to activate the alarm, and the robber fled on foot. Police officers arrived a few minutes later and asked the owner, "How long ago did the robber leave?" "He left only a few minutes ago," the store owner responded. "He's probably 10 blocks away by now," one of the officers said to the other. "Not likely," said the store owner. "He was so stoned on drugs that I bet even if he has run 10 blocks, he's still only within a few blocks of here! He's probably just running in circles!"

Perform a simulation experiment that will test the store owner's hypothesis. Assume that at each corner of a city block there is an equal chance that the robber will go in any one of the four possible directions, north, south, east, or west. Simulate for five trials and then indicate in how many of the trials the robber is within two blocks of the store.

**S12-9.** Compcomm, Inc., is an international communications and information technology company that has seen the value of its common stock appreciate substantially in recent years. A stock analyst would like to predict the stock prices of Compcomm for an extended period with simulation. Based on historical data, the analyst has developed the following probability distribution for the movement of Compcomm stock prices per day:

| Stock Price Movement | Probability |
|---|---|
| Increase | .45 |
| Same | .30 |
| Decrease | .25 |

The analyst has also developed the following probability distributions for the amount of the increases or decreases in the stock price per day:

| | Probability | |
|---|---|---|
| Stock Price Change | *Increase* | *Decrease* |
| $\frac{1}{8}$ | .40 | .12 |
| $\frac{1}{4}$ | .17 | .15 |
| $\frac{3}{8}$ | .12 | .18 |
| $\frac{1}{2}$ | .10 | .21 |
| $\frac{5}{8}$ | .08 | .14 |
| $\frac{3}{4}$ | .07 | .10 |
| $\frac{7}{8}$ | .04 | .05 |
| 1 | .02 | .05 |

The price of the stock is currently 62.

Develop a Monte Carlo simulation model to track the stock price of Compcomm stock and simulate for 30 days. Indicate the new stock price at the end of the 30 days. How would this model be expanded to conduct a complete simulation of one year's stock price movement?

**S12-10.** The Western Outfitter Store specializes in denim jeans. The variable cost of the jeans varies according to several factors, including the cost of the jeans from the distributor, labor costs, handling, packaging, and so on. Price also is a random variable that varies according to competitors' prices. Sales volume also varies each month. The probability distributions for price, volume, and variable costs each month are as follows:

| Sales Volume | Probability |
|---|---|
| 300 | .12 |
| 400 | .18 |
| 500 | .20 |
| 600 | .23 |
| 700 | .17 |
| 800 | .10 |
| | 1.00 |

| Price | Probability |
|---|---|
| $22 | .07 |
| 23 | .16 |
| 24 | .24 |
| 25 | .25 |
| 26 | .18 |
| 27 | .10 |
| | 1.00 |

| Variable Cost | Probability |
|---|---|
| $ 8 | .17 |
| 9 | .32 |
| 10 | .29 |
| 11 | .14 |
| 12 | .08 |
| | 1.00 |

Fixed costs are $9000 per month for the store.

Simulate 20 months of store sales and compute the probability the store will at least break even.

**S12-11.** Randolph College and Salem College are within 20 miles of each other, and the students at each college frequently date. The students at Randolph College are debating how good their dates are at Salem College. The Randolph students have sampled several hundred of their fellow students and asked them to rate their dates from 1 to 5 (where 1 is excellent and 5 is poor) according to physical attractiveness, intelligence, and personality. Following are the resulting probability distributions for these three traits:

| Physical Attractiveness | Probability |
|---|---|
| 1 | .27 |
| 2 | .35 |
| 3 | .14 |
| 4 | .09 |
| 5 | .15 |
| | 1.00 |

| Intelligence | Probability |
|---|---|
| 1 | .10 |
| 2 | .16 |
| 3 | .45 |
| 4 | .17 |
| 5 | .12 |
| | 1.00 |

| Personality | Probability |
|---|---|
| 1 | .15 |
| 2 | .30 |
| 3 | .33 |
| 4 | .07 |
| 5 | .15 |
| | 1.00 |

Simulate 20 dates and compute an average overall rating of the Salem students.

**S12-12.** In Problem S12-11 discuss how you might assess the accuracy of the average rating for Salem College students based on only 20 simulated dates.

## REFERENCES


Banks, J., and J. S. Carson. *Discrete-Event System Simulation*. Upper Saddle River, NJ: Prentice Hall, 1984.

Christy, D., and H. Watson. "The Applications of Simulation: A Survey of Industry Practice." *Interfaces* 13(5; October 1983), pp. 47–52.

Hammersly, J. M., and D. C. Handscomb. *Monte Carlo Methods*. New York: Wiley, 1984.

Law, A. M., and W. D. Kelton. *Simulation Modeling and Analysis*. New York: McGraw-Hill, 1982.

Meier, R. C., W. T. Newell, and H. L. Pazer. *Simulation in Business and Economics*. Upper Saddle River, NJ: Prentice Hall, 1969.

Naylor, T. H., J. L. Balintfy, D. S. Burdinck, and K. Chu. *Computer Simulation Techniques*. New York: Wiley, 1966.

Payne, J. A. *Introduction to Simulation*. New York: McGraw-Hill, 1982.

Pritsker, A. A. B., C. E. Sigal, and R. D. Hammesfahr. *SLAM II: Network Models for Decision Support*. Upper Saddle River, NJ: Prentice Hall, 1989.

Taha, H. A. *Simulation Modeling and Simen*. New York: McGraw-Hill, 1988.

Taylor, B. W. *Introduction to Management Science*, 5th ed. Upper Saddle River, NJ: Prentice Hall, 1996.

# Aggregate Planning

CHAPTER **13**

Web resources for this chapter include

- Internet Exercises
- Online Practice Quizzes
- Virtual Tours
- Excel Worksheets
- Company and Resource Weblinks
- Animated Demo Problems
- Microsoft Project Exhibits

www.wiley.com/college/russell

## CHAPTER OUTLINE

In this chapter, you will learn about . . .

- The Aggregate Planning Process
- Strategies for Adjusting Capacity
- Strategies for Managing Demand
- Quantitative Techniques for Aggregate Production Planning
- The Hierarchical Nature of Planning
- Aggregate Planning for Services

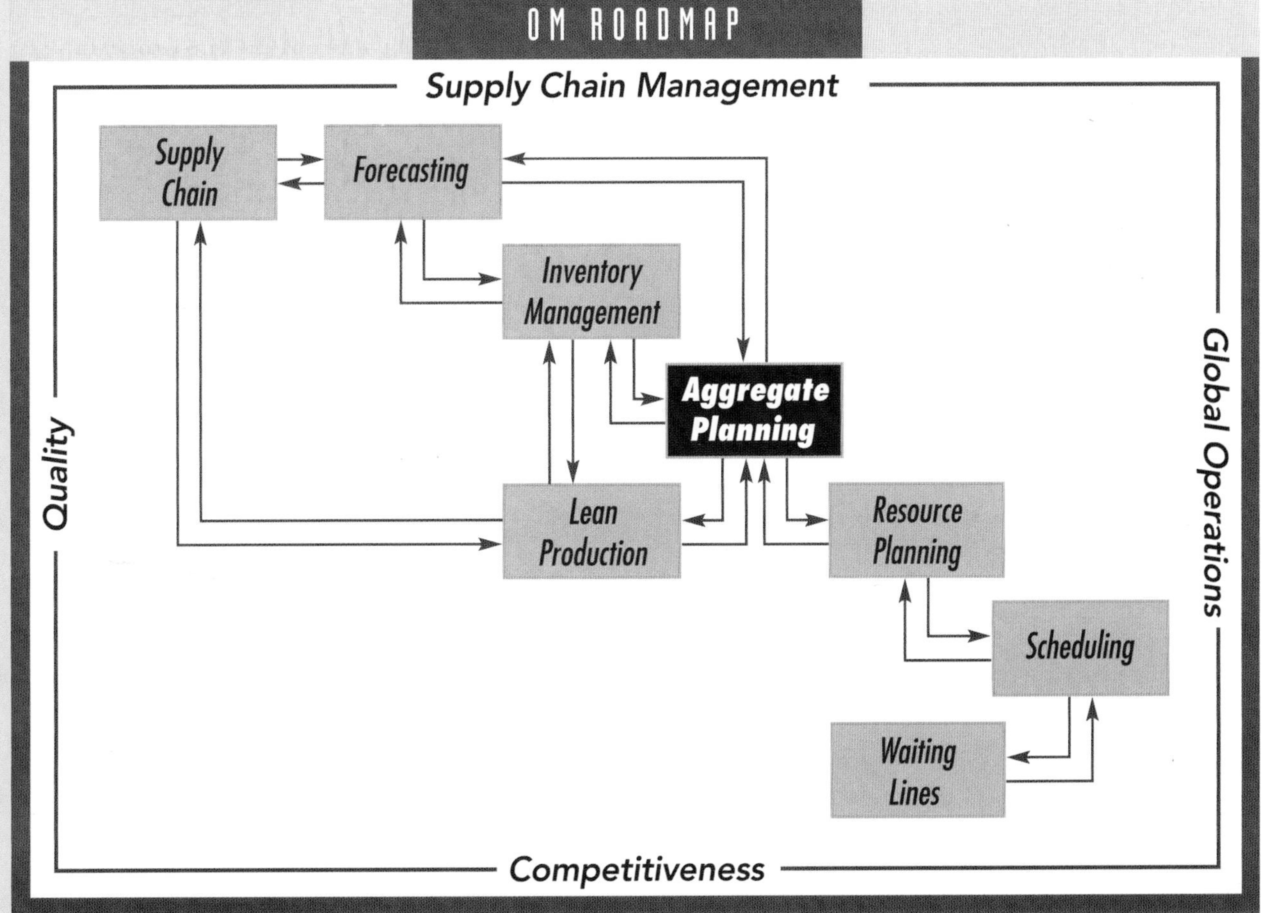

## DISNEY'S MAGIC NUMBERS

Aggregate planning at Disney World is all about people—how many people visit the parks and what they do while there. The Disney property in Florida includes 4 parks, 20 hotels, 27,500 rooms, 160 miles of roads, and 56,000 employees. Forecasting attendance and guest behavior helps plan for more than 1 billion customer interactions per year, and the purchase of 9 million hamburgers, 50 million Cokes, and tons of "tangible memories."

Planning begins with a five-year forecast of attendance based on a combination of econometric models, experience-based models, extensive research, and a magic mirror. The econometric model examines the international economies of seven key countries, their GDP growth, foreign exchange rate, and consumer confidence. The experience-based model looks at demographics, planned product introductions, capacity expansions, and marketing strategies. Extensive research is conducted by 35 analysts and 70 field personnel year round. Over 1 million surveys are administered to key household segments, current guests, cast members, and travel industry personnel. The magic mirror is the patented part of the forecasting procedure that, in part, accounts for the mere 5% error in the five-year attendance forecast and the 0% error in annual forecasts.

Disney's five-year plan is converted to an annual operating plan (AOP) for each park. (*The AOP is what we call the aggregate plan in this chapter.*) Demand is highly seasonal and varies by month and day of the week. Economic conditions affect annual plans, as do history and holidays, school calendars, societal behavior, and sales promotions. The AOP is updated monthly with information from airline specials, hotel bookings, recent forecast accuracies, Web site monitoring, and competitive influences. A daily forecast of attendance is made by tweaking the AOP and adjusting for monthly variations, weather forecasts, and the previous day's crowds. Attendance drives all other decisions.

Disney is a master at adjusting its capacity and managing its demand. Capacity can be increased by lengthening park hours, opening more rides or shows, adding roving food and beverage carts, and deploying more "cast members." Demand is managed by limiting access to the park, shifting crowds to street activities, and taking reservations for attractions (*ever used a fast pass?*). Operating standards strictly regulate when these actions are taken. Obsessive collection of data ensures the response is timely.

Parks generally open at 9:00 A.M. each day, but an unusually high count of 7:30 A.M. breakfast patrons at on-property hotels will prompt early openings at select locations. By 11:00 A.M. the day's attendance forecast is updated based on traffic, the weather, entry patterns, and crowds at key attractions. The daily operating plan is continually updated every 20 minutes throughout the day from data collected by cast members using handheld computers. To maintain flexibility, cast members are scheduled in 15-minute intervals at various jobs throughout the park.

For Disney, pleasing the customer *and* making a profit takes careful planning.

*Disney is a master at forecasting aggregate demand for its theme parks, as well as adjusting capacity in time increments as small as 15 minutes.*

*Source:* Joni Newkirk and Mark Haskell, "Forecasting in the Service Sector," Presented at the Twelfth Annual Meeting of the Production Operations Management Society, Orlando, FL, April 1, 2001.

Few manufacturing firms are as adaptive as Disney to changes in demand, but with demanding customers and short lead times, responsiveness is a competitive must in every industry. In this chapter we'll learn how companies plan their resource levels to match supply and demand. We begin with a discussion of the nature of aggregate planning, then continue with strategies for managing demand and adjusting capacity. Hierarchical planning decisions, collaborative planning with trading partners, and aggregate planning for services are also discussed.

## THE AGGREGATE PLANNING PROCESS

**Aggregate planning** determines the resource capacity a firm will need to meet its demand over an intermediate time horizon—6 to 12 months in the future. Within this time frame, it is usually not feasible to increase capacity by building new facilities or purchasing new equipment; however, it *is* feasible to hire or lay off workers, increase or reduce the workweek, add an extra shift, subcontract out work, use overtime, or build up and deplete inventory levels.

**Aggregate planning:** determines the resource capacity needed to meet demand over an intermediate time horizon.

We use the term *aggregate* because the plans are developed for product lines or product families, rather than individual products. An aggregate production plan (APP) might specify how many bicycles are to be produced but would not identify them by color, size, tires, or type of brakes. Resource capacity is also expressed in aggregate terms, typically as labor or machine hours. Labor hours would not be specified by type of labor, nor machine hours by type of machine. And they may be given only for critical processes.

*Aggregate* refers to product lines or families.

For services, capacity is often limited by *space*—number of airline seats, number of hotel rooms, number of beds in a correctional facility. *Time* can also affect capacity. The number of customers who can be served lunch in a restaurant is limited by the number of seats, as well as the number of hours lunch is served. In some overcrowded schools, lunch begins at 10:00 A.M. so that all students can be served by 2:00 P.M.!

There are two objectives to aggregate planning:

Aggregate planning matches supply and demand.

1. To establish a companywide game plan for allocating resources, and
2. To develop an economic strategy for meeting demand

*Producers of pulp, paper, lumber, and other wood products have an interesting aggregate planning problem—they must plan for the renewable resource of trees. Aggregate planning starts with a mathematical simulation model of tree growth that determines the maximum sustainable flow of wood fiber from each acreage. Decisions are made as to which trees to harvest now; which ones to leave until later; where to plant new trees; and the type, amount, and location of new timberland that should be purchased. The planning horizon is the biological lead time to grow trees—more than 80 years!*

The first objective refers to the long-standing battle between the marketing and production functions within a firm. Personnel who are evaluated solely on sales volume have the tendency to make unrealistic sales commitments (either in terms of quantity or timing) that production is expected to meet, sometimes at an exorbitant price. Production personnel who are evaluated on keeping manufacturing costs down may refuse to accept orders that require additional financial resources (such as overtime wage rates) or hard-to-meet completion dates. The job of production planning is to match forecasted demand with available capacity. If capacity is inadequate, it can usually be expanded, but at a cost. The company needs to determine if the extra cost is worth the increased revenue from the sale, and if the sale is consistent with the strategy of the firm. Thus, the aggregate production plan should not be determined by manufacturing personnel alone; rather, it should be agreed on by top management from all the functional areas of the firm—operations, marketing, and finance. Furthermore, as shown in Figure 13.1, it should reflect company policy (such as avoiding layoffs, limiting inventory levels, or maintaining a specified customer service level) and strategic objectives (such as capturing a certain share of the market or achieving targeted levels of quality or profit). These inputs are reflected in the aggregate planning process shown in Figure 13.1. Other inputs are demand forecasts, capacity constraints, and financial constraints.

The outputs of aggregate planning include output per month or quarter by product or service family, the size of the workforce, and the amount of regular, overtime, and subcontracted production required. Inventory and backlog levels are projected, along with the number of units or dollars to be backordered or lost. For companies that outsource most of their production, the aggregate plan also includes *where* the production will take place. For services, the aggregate plan outlines how much work can be completed (or new work accepted) in a specified time period.

Because of the various factors and viewpoints considered, the aggregate plan is often referred to as the company's *game plan* for the coming year, and deviations from the plan are carefully monitored. Monthly meetings of sales, marketing, production, sourcing and finance staff reconcile differences in supply, demand, and new product plans.[1]

An economic strategy for meeting demand can be attained by either *adjusting capacity* or *managing demand.* We discuss both approaches in the following sections.

**Figure 13.1**

**The Aggregate Planning Process**

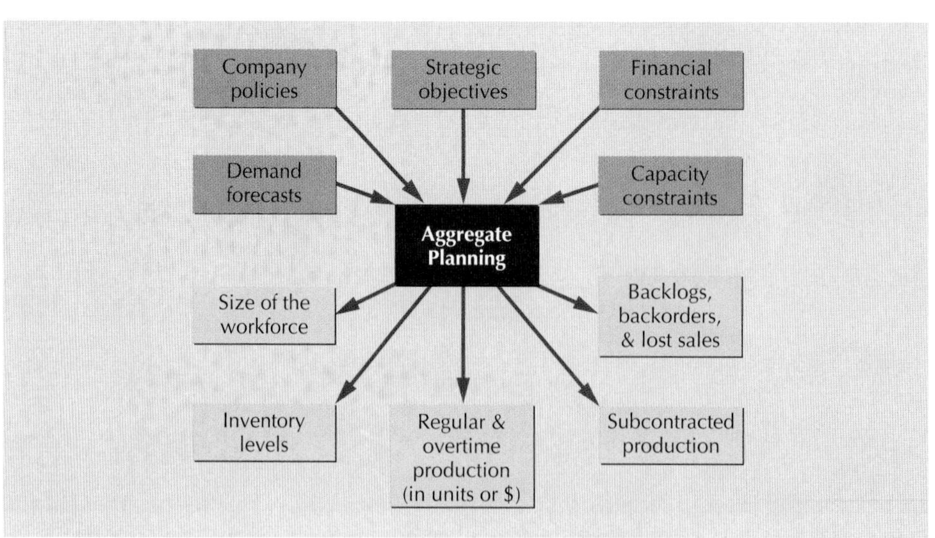


[1]The aggregate planning process is called *sales and operations planning (S&OP)* in many firms to emphasize the iterative and collaborative nature of aligning sales plans with production. Software vendors use the term *sales and operations planning* as well.

## STRATEGIES FOR ADJUSTING CAPACITY

If demand for a company's products or services is stable over time, then the resources necessary to meet demand are acquired and maintained over the time horizon of the plan, and minor variations in demand are handled with overtime or undertime. Aggregate planning becomes more of a challenge when demand fluctuates over the planning horizon. For example, seasonal demand patterns can be met by:

**APP evaluates alternative capacity sources to find an economic strategy for satisfying demand.**

1. Producing at a constant rate and using inventory to absorb fluctuations in demand (*level production*)
2. Hiring and firing workers to match demand (*chase demand*)
3. Maintaining resources for high-demand levels
4. Increasing or decreasing working hours (*overtime* and *undertime*)
5. Subcontracting work to other firms
6. Using part-time workers
7. Providing the service or product at a later time period (*backordering*)

When one of these alternatives is selected, a company is said to have a **pure strategy** for meeting demand. When two or more are selected, a company has a **mixed strategy**.

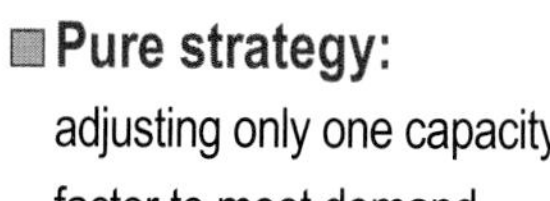

**Pure strategy:** adjusting only one capacity factor to meet demand.

### LEVEL PRODUCTION

The **level production** strategy, shown in Figure 13.2*a*, sets production at a fixed rate (usually to meet average demand) and uses inventory to absorb variations in demand. During periods of low demand, overproduction is stored as inventory, to be depleted in periods of high demand. The cost of this strategy is the cost of holding inventory, including the cost of obsolete or perishable items that may have to be discarded.

**Level production:** producing at a constant rate and using inventory as needed to meet demand.

### CHASE DEMAND

The **chase demand** strategy, shown in Figure 13.2*b*, matches the production plan to the demand pattern and absorbs variations in demand by hiring and firing workers. During periods of low demand, production is cut back and workers are laid off. During periods of high demand, production is increased and additional workers are hired. The cost of this strategy is the cost of hiring and firing workers. This approach would not work for industries in which worker skills are scarce or competition for labor is intense, but it can be quite cost-effective during periods of high unemployment or for industries with low-skilled workers.

**Chase demand:** changing workforce levels so that production matches demand.

A variation of chase demand is *chase supply*. For some industries, the production planning task revolves around the supply of raw materials, not the demand pattern. Consider Motts, the applesauce manufacturer, whose raw material is available only 40 days during a year. The workforce size at its peak is 1500 workers, but it normally consists of around 350 workers. Almost 10% of the company's payroll is made up of unemployment benefits—the price of doing business in that particular industry.

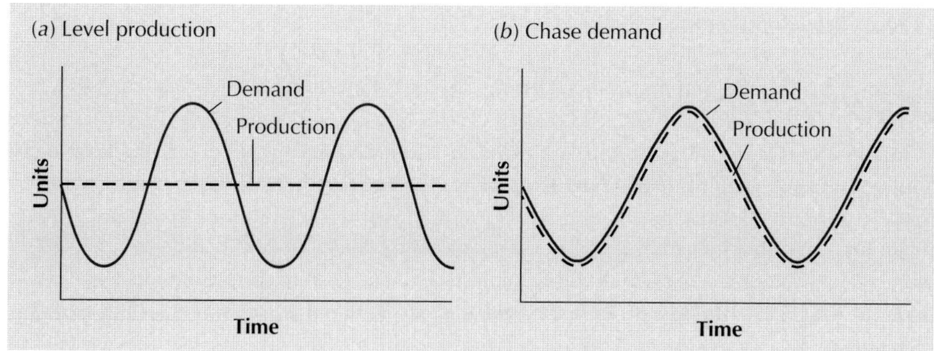


**Figure 13.2 Pure Strategies for Meeting Demand**

## THE COMPETITIVE EDGE

### Following the Harvest

There's nothing more seasonal than fruits and vegetables. Dole's salads are made from fresh vegetables grown in Salinas Valley, California, from April to November, and in Yuma, Arizona, from November through March. State-of-the-art packaging facilities process the lettuce and prepare the salads in each location. The two processing plants are strategically located to process peak-season vegetables within 24 hours of harvest, but each plant operates only during certain months of the year.

So in November of every year, Dole closes down the processing center in Salinas Valley and loads its equipment onto 76 flatbed trucks for the 600-mile ride to Yuma. This unlikely "caravan that follows the lettuce" takes 18 hours, but saves the company a bundle in capital equipment costs.

Dole's salad-making plants convert 360 million pounds of raw vegetables into 190 million pounds of salad each year. Inside the plant, the vegetables are inspected, trimmed by hand, and cleaned. The trimmed lettuce moves down a conveyor belt to the *megacutter*. The cut lettuce then enters a triple-wash system of chilled, chlorinated water, where it is blended with other vegetables to make different salad mixes.

The mixed salad ingredients then travel to high-tech packaging lines, where they are weighed and fed into bags of various sizes. The packaging machine is capable of producing up to 100 packages of salad a minute.

From the plant, salads travel to a huge cold storage and distribution facility. Inside the facility, a computer system automatically retrieves the product and brings it to a dock area. From here, the packaged salads are loaded into refrigerated trucks to begin the journey to local grocery stores, 365 days a year.

Dole chases supply, not demand.

*Source: Salad Factory Virtual Tour.* http://www.dole.com.

## PEAK DEMAND

**Peak demand:** staffing for high levels of customer service.

*Maintaining resources* for **peak demand** levels ensures high levels of customer service but can be very costly in terms of the investment in extra workers and machines that remain idle during low-demand periods. This strategy is used when superior customer service is important (such as Nordstrom's department store) or when customers are willing to pay extra for the availability of critical staff or equipment. Professional services trying to generate more demand may keep staff levels high, defense contractors may be paid to keep extra capacity "available," child-care facilities may elect to maintain staff levels for continuity when attendance is low, and full-service hospitals may invest in specialized equipment that is rarely used but is critical for the care of a small number of patients.

## OVERTIME AND UNDERTIME

Overtime and undertime adjust working hours to meet demand.

*Overtime* and *undertime* are common strategies when demand fluctuations are not extreme. A competent staff is maintained, hiring, and firing costs are avoided, and demand is met temporarily without investing in permanent resources. Disadvantages include the premium paid for overtime work, a tired and potentially less efficient workforce, and the possibility that overtime alone may be insufficient to meet peak demand periods.

Undertime can be achieved by working fewer hours during the day or fewer days per week. In addition, vacation time can be scheduled during months of slow demand. For example, furniture manufacturers typically shut down the entire month of July, while shipbuilding goes dormant in December.

## SUBCONTRACTING

Subcontracting lets outside companies complete the work.

*Subcontracting* or outsourcing is a feasible alternative if a supplier can reliably meet quality and time requirements. This is a common solution for component parts when demand exceeds expectations for the final product. The subcontracting decision requires maintaining strong ties with possible subcontractors and first-hand knowledge of their work. Disadvantages of subcontracting include reduced profits, loss of control over production, long lead times, and the potential that the subcontractor may become a future competitor.

*Retailers do almost 50% of their annual business during the holiday season. Manufacturers of holiday items, such as wrapping paper, have an even more skewed demand pattern. Sixty-eight% of the annual demand for wrapping paper takes place during the months of November and December, 25% in the two weeks prior to Christmas. Producing early in the year and building up inventory is not cost-effective because of the bulkiness of the product and the humidity requirements for storage. Heightened production levels mean hiring more workers and using overtime in late summer and fall.*

## PART-TIME WORKERS

Using *part-time workers* is feasible for unskilled jobs or in areas with large temporary labor pools (such as students, homemakers, or retirees). Part-time workers are less costly than full-time workers—they receive no health-care or retirement benefits—and are more flexible—their hours usually vary considerably. Part-time workers have been the mainstay of retail, fast-food, and other services for some time and are becoming more accepted in manufacturing and government jobs. Japanese manufacturers traditionally use a large percentage of part-time or temporary workers. IBM staffs its entire third shift at Research Triangle Park, North Carolina, with temporary workers (college students). Part-time and temporary workers now account for about one-third of our nation's workforce. The temp agency Manpower Inc. is the largest private employer in the world. Problems with part-time workers include high turnover, accelerated training requirements, less commitment, and scheduling difficulties.

**Backlog:** accumulated customer orders to be completed at a later date.

## BACKLOGS, BACKORDERING, AND LOST SALES

Companies that offer customized products and services accept customer orders and fill them at a later date. The accumulation of these orders creates a **backlog** that grows during periods of high demand and is depleted during periods of low demand. The planned backlog is an important part of the aggregate plan. For make-to-stock companies, customers who request an item that is temporarily out-of-stock may have the option of **backordering** the item. If the customer is unwilling to wait for the backordered item, the sale will be lost. Although in general both backorders and **lost sales** should be avoided, the aggregate plan may include an estimate of both. Backorders are added to the next period's requirements; lost sales are not.

**Backordering:** ordering an item that is temporarily out-of-stock.

**Lost sales:** forfeited sales for out-of-stock items.

## THE COMPETITIVE EDGE

### More Green for Green Mountain Coffee

Green Mountain Coffee Roasters has great products and excellent customer service, but profits have been harder to come by—that is, until the company revamped its forecasting and production planning systems. Improved forecasting and production planning software is making operations better equipped to handle the holiday season, when orders from consumers typically double. Not long ago, if an unexpected order for one of its special Gingerbread or Spicy Eggnog coffees came in, there would be a knee-jerk reaction to schedule a production run without fully assessing the consequences. Inventory goals of no more than a one and a half week's supply were impossible to achieve without soaring production costs.

In the past, if the company expected to sell 100,000 pounds of coffee over a 10-week period, it would set up a level production schedule of 10,000 pounds a week. If orders accelerated to 30,000 pounds of coffee in one week, the company would simply increase the production level to 30,000 a week, assuming erroneously that the increased demand would continue. Now the coffee company relies on much tighter forecasts and monitors sales, promotions, and distribution on a day-to-day basis to determine how much coffee it should be producing.

The tools behind this more scientific process are incorporated in production planning software. CIO Jim Prevo says it has significantly improved the lives of the employees who work on the production floor. "They used to have to do a lot of dive-and-catch expediting," he says. "Now, we schedule a week in advance and [adjust] the schedule each day so we can have higher throughput." With better production planning, the company can respond more quickly to changes in customer demand, which is particularly critical during the holiday season.

The C. F. Sauer Company, a manufacturer of spices, oils, sauces, and spreads, also sees a seasonal spike in demand during the holiday season. With demand planning and production planning software installed at its four manufacturing sites, the company can more efficiently manage its production *and* meet customer demand. For example, when one of C. F. Sauer's customers informed the company that it was going to promote a particular product through mid-November, the increased sales estimate was entered into the forecasting system one evening and a new production plan was generated by the next morning. Effective demand and production planning helps Sauer keep its perishable inventory low, while at the same time increasing its customer service level.

*Source:* Adapted from Beth Bacheldor, "Steady Supply," *InformationWeek*, November 24, 2003.

## STRATEGIES FOR MANAGING DEMAND

Aggregate planning can also involve proactive demand management. Strategies for managing demand include:

- Shifting demand into other time periods with incentives, sales promotions, and advertising campaigns;
- Offering products or services with countercyclical demand patterns; and
- Partnering with suppliers to reduce information distortion along the supply chain.

**Shift demand into other time periods.**

Winter coat specials in July, bathing-suit sales in January, early-bird discounts on dinner, lower long-distance rates in the evenings, and getaway weekends at hotels during the off-season are all attempts to shift demand into different time periods. Electric utilities are especially skilled at off-peak pricing. Promotions can also be used to extend high demand into low-demand seasons. Holiday gift buying is encouraged earlier each year, and beach resorts plan festivals in September and October to extend the season. Successful demand management depends on accurate forecasts of demand and accurate forecasts of the changes in demand brought about by sales, promotions, and special offers.

**Create demand for idle resources.**

For industries with extreme variations in demand, offering products or services with countercyclical demand patterns helps smooth out resource requirements. This approach involves examining the idleness of resources and creating a demand for those resources. McDonald's offers breakfast to keep its kitchens busy during the prelunch hours, pancake restaurants serve lunch and dinner, and heating firms also sell air conditioners.

Amadas Industries, a small U.S. manufacturer of peanut harvesting equipment, does an especially good job of finding countercyclical products to smooth the load on its manufacturing facilities. The company operates a job shop production system with general-purpose equipment, 50 highly skilled workers, and a talented engineering staff. With these flexible resources, the company can make virtually anything its engineers can design. In-

*A carefully planned mix of services can smooth out resource requirements. At this resort, the pristine golf course during the summer months becomes a cross-country skiing path during the winter. The same company that maintains the fairways, grooms the snow for the skiers.*

ventories of finished goods are limited because of the significant investment in funds and the size of the finished product. Demand for the product is highly seasonal. Peanut-harvesting equipment is generally purchased on an as-needed basis from August to October, so during the spring and early summer, the company makes bark-scalping equipment for processing mulch and pine nuggets used by landscaping services. Demand for peanut-harvesting equipment is also affected by the weather each growing season, so during years of extensive drought, the company produces and sells irrigation equipment. The company also decided to market its products internationally with a special eye toward countries whose growing seasons are opposite to that of the United States. Thus, many of its sales are made in China and India during the very months when demand in the United States is low.

**Share information along the supply chain.**

Another approach to managing demand recognizes the information distortion caused by ordering goods in batches along a supply chain. Even though a customer may require daily usage of an item, he or she probably does not purchase that item daily. Neither do retail stores restock their shelves continuously. By the time a replenishment order reaches distributors, wholesalers, manufacturers, and their suppliers, the demand pattern for a product can appear extremely erratic. This *bullwhip effect* was discussed in Chapter 10. To control the situation, manufacturers, their suppliers, and customers form partnerships in which demand information is shared and orders are placed in a more continuous fashion.

## QUANTITATIVE TECHNIQUES FOR AGGREGATE PRODUCTION PLANNING

One aggregate planning strategy is not always preferable to another. The most effective strategy depends on the demand distribution, competitive position, and cost structure of a firm or product line. Several quantitative techniques are available to help with the aggregate planning decision. In the sections that follow, we discuss pure and mixed strategies, linear programming, the *transportation method*, and other quantitative techniques.

### APP USING PURE STRATEGIES

Solving aggregate production planning problems involves formulating strategies for meeting demand, constructing production plans from those strategies, determining the cost and feasibility of each plan, and selecting the lowest cost plan from among the feasible alternatives. The effectiveness of the aggregate planning process is directly related to management's understanding of the cost variables involved and the reasonableness of the scenarios tested. Example 13.1 compares the cost of two pure strategies: *level production* and *chase demand*.

**Example 13.1**

**Aggregate Production Planning Using Pure Strategies**

The Good and Rich Candy Company makes a variety of candies in three factories worldwide. Its line of chocolate candies exhibits a highly seasonal demand pattern, with peaks during the winter months (for the holiday season and Valentine's Day) and valleys during the summer months (when chocolate tends to melt and customers are watching their weight). Given the following costs and quarterly sales forecasts, determine whether (a) level production, or (b) chase demand would more economically meet the demand for chocolate candies:

| Quarter | Sales Forecast (lb) |
|---|---|
| Spring | 80,000 |
| Summer | 50,000 |
| Fall | 120,000 |
| Winter | 150,000 |

Hiring cost = $100 per worker

Firing cost = $500 per worker

Inventory carrying cost = $0.50 per pound per quarter

Regular production cost per pound = $2.00

Production per employee = 1000 pounds per quarter

Beginning workforce = 100 workers

*Solution*

a. For the level production strategy, we first need to calculate average quarterly demand.

$$\frac{(80{,}000 + 50{,}000 + 120{,}000 + 150{,}000)}{4} = \frac{400{,}000}{4} = 100{,}000 \text{ pounds}$$

This becomes our planned production for each quarter. Since each worker can produce 1000 pounds a quarter, 100 workers will be needed each quarter to meet the production requirements of 100,000 pounds. Production in excess of demand is stored in inventory, where it remains until it is used to meet demand in a later period. Demand in excess of production is met by using inventory from the previous quarter. The production plan and resulting inventory costs are as follows:

| Quarter | Demand | Regular Production | Inventory |
|---|---|---|---|
| Spring | 80,000 | 100,000 | 100,000 − 80,000 = 20,000 |
| Summer | 50,000 | 100,000 | 20,000 + 100,000 − 50,000 = 70,000 |
| Fall | 120,000 | 100,000 | 70,000 + 100,000 − 120,000 = 50,000 |
| Winter | 150,000 | 100,000 | 50,000 + 100,000 − 150,000 = 0 |
| ***Total*** | ***400,000*** | ***400,000*** | ***140,000*** |

***Cost of Level Production Strategy*** = (400,000 × $2.00) + (140,000 × $.50) = $870,000

b. For the chase demand strategy, production each quarter matches demand. To accomplish this, workers are hired and fired at a cost of $100 for each one hired and $500 for each one fired. Since each worker can produce 1000 pounds per quarter, we divide the quarterly sales forecast by 1000 to determine the required workforce size each quarter. We begin with 100 workers and hire and fire as needed. The production plan and resulting hiring and firing costs are given here.

| Quarter | Demand | Regular Production | Workers Needed | Workers Hired | Workers Fired |
|---|---|---|---|---|---|
| Spring | 80,000 | 80,000 | 80,000/1000 = 80 | | 100 − 80 = 20 |
| Summer | 50,000 | 50,000 | 50,000/1000 = 50 | | 80 − 50 = 30 |
| Fall | 120,000 | 120,000 | 120,000/1000 = 120 | 120 − 50 = 70 | |
| Winter | 150,000 | 150,000 | 150,000/1000 = 150 | 150 − 120 = 30 | |
| *Total* | *400,000* | *400,000* | | *100* | *50* |

***Cost of Chase Demand Strategy*** $= (400{,}000 \times \$2.00) + (100 \times \$100) + (50 \times \$500) = \$835{,}000$

Comparing the cost of level production with chase demand, we find that chase demand is the best strategy for the Good and Rich line of candies.

The problem can also be solved using Excel. Exhibit 13.1 shows two worksheets from the Excel file, Exhibit 13.1.xls, available on the text Web site.

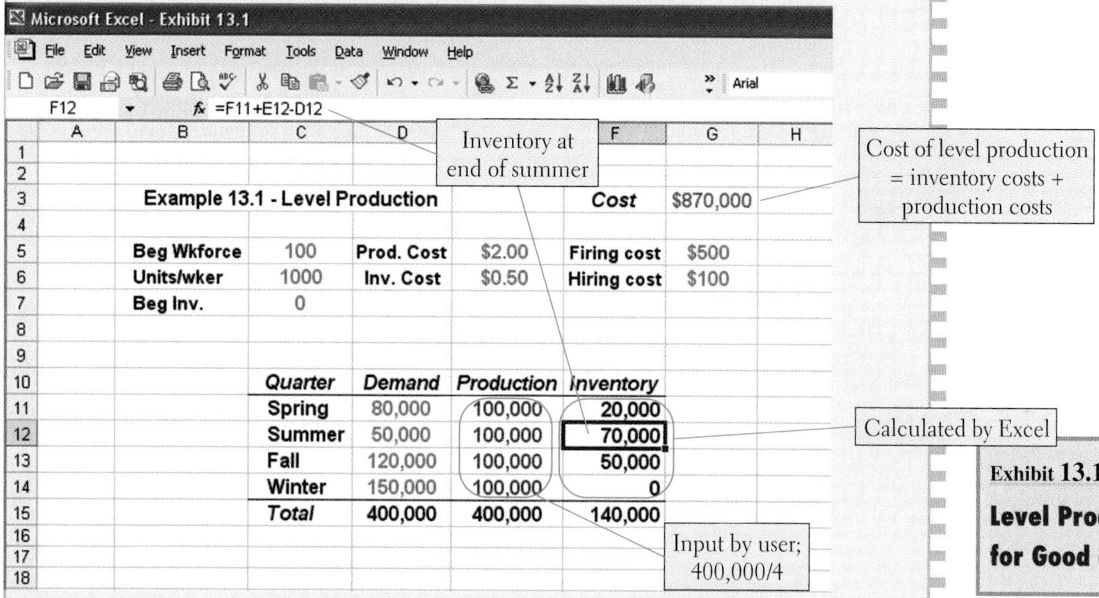

Microsoft Excel - Exhibit 13.1

F12 =F11+E12-D12

**Example 13.1 - Level Production** — *Cost* $870,000

| | | | | | |
|---|---|---|---|---|---|
| Beg Wkforce | 100 | Prod. Cost | $2.00 | Firing cost | $500 |
| Units/wker | 1000 | Inv. Cost | $0.50 | Hiring cost | $100 |
| Beg Inv. | 0 | | | | |

| *Quarter* | *Demand* | *Production* | *Inventory* |
|---|---|---|---|
| Spring | 80,000 | 100,000 | 20,000 |
| Summer | 50,000 | 100,000 | 70,000 |
| Fall | 120,000 | 100,000 | 50,000 |
| Winter | 150,000 | 100,000 | 0 |
| *Total* | 400,000 | 400,000 | 140,000 |

Inventory at end of summer

Cost of level production = inventory costs + production costs

Calculated by Excel

Input by user; 400,000/4

**Exhibit 13.1a**
**Level Production for Good and Rich**

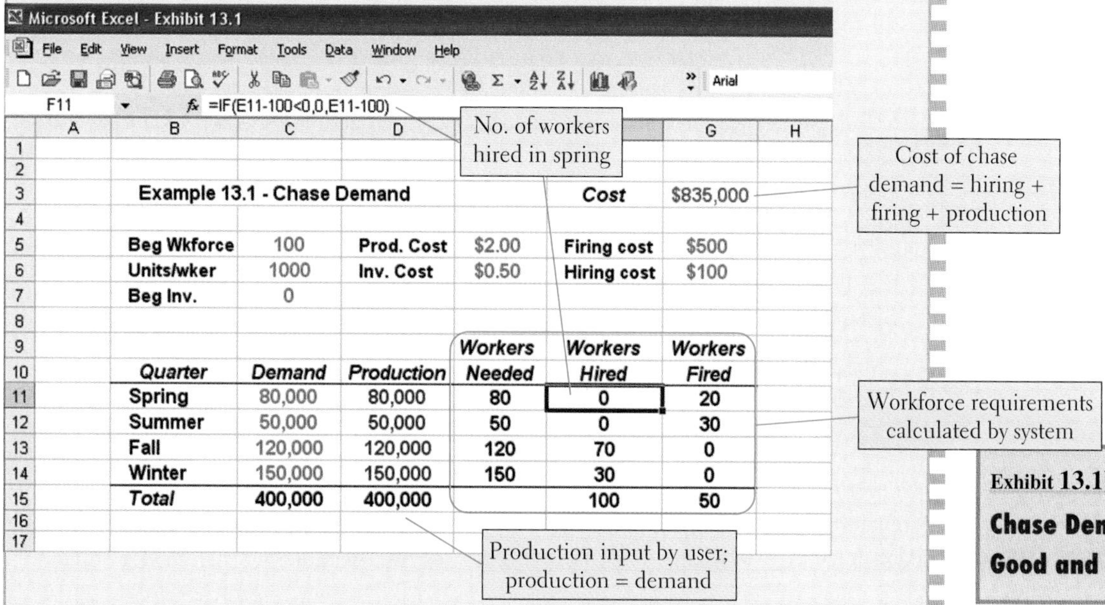

Microsoft Excel - Exhibit 13.1

F11 =IF(E11-100<0,0,E11-100)

**Example 13.1 - Chase Demand** — *Cost* $835,000

| | | | | | |
|---|---|---|---|---|---|
| Beg Wkforce | 100 | Prod. Cost | $2.00 | Firing cost | $500 |
| Units/wker | 1000 | Inv. Cost | $0.50 | Hiring cost | $100 |
| Beg Inv. | 0 | | | | |

| *Quarter* | *Demand* | *Production* | *Workers Needed* | *Workers Hired* | *Workers Fired* |
|---|---|---|---|---|---|
| Spring | 80,000 | 80,000 | 80 | 0 | 20 |
| Summer | 50,000 | 50,000 | 50 | 0 | 30 |
| Fall | 120,000 | 120,000 | 120 | 70 | 0 |
| Winter | 150,000 | 150,000 | 150 | 30 | 0 |
| *Total* | 400,000 | 400,000 | | 100 | 50 |

No. of workers hired in spring

Cost of chase demand = hiring + firing + production

Workforce requirements calculated by system

Production input by user; production = demand

**Exhibit 13.1b**
**Chase Demand for Good and Rich**

Although chase demand is the better strategy for Good and Rich from an economic point of view, it may seem unduly harsh on the company's workforce. An example of a good "fit" between a company's chase demand strategy and the needs of the workforce is Hershey's, located in rural Pennsylvania, with a demand and cost structure much like that of Good and Rich. The location of the manufacturing facility is essential to the effectiveness of the company's production plan. During the winter, when demand for chocolate is high, the company hires farmers from surrounding areas, who are idle at that time of year. The farmers are let go during the spring and summer, when they are anxious to return to their fields and the demand for chocolate falls. The plan is cost-effective, and the extra help is content with the sporadic hiring and firing practices of the company.

## APP USING MIXED STRATEGIES

Most companies use mixed strategies for production planning. Mixed strategies can incorporate management policies, such as "no more than $x\%$ of the workforce can be laid off in one quarter" or "inventory levels cannot exceed $x$ dollars." They can also be adapted to the quirks of a company or industry. For example, many industries that experience a slowdown during part of the year may simply shut down manufacturing during the low-demand season and schedule employee vacations during that time.

Example 13.2 compares pure and mixed strategies in a more extensive aggregate planning problem. Excel spreadsheets are used to make the calculations. The user inputs demand and cost data, as well as values for regular, overtime, and subcontracted production. The spreadsheet calculates resulting inventory levels, workforce levels, hiring/firing and total cost. The Excel file for this example, Exhibit 13.2.xls is available on the textbook Web site. Although this problem can be solved by hand, you may wish to use the spreadsheet as a template for solving other aggregate planning problems.

Example 13.2

**Aggregate Production Planning Using Pure and Mixed Strategies**

Demand for Quantum Corporation's action toy series follows a seasonal pattern—growing through the fall months and culminating in December, with smaller peaks in January (for after-season markdowns, exchanges, and accessory purchases) and July (for Christmas-in-July specials).

| Month | Demand (cases) | Month | Demand (cases) |
|---|---|---|---|
| January | 1000 | July | 500 |
| February | 400 | August | 500 |
| March | 400 | September | 1000 |
| April | 400 | October | 1500 |
| May | 400 | November | 2500 |
| June | 400 | December | 3000 |

Each worker can produce on average 100 cases of action toys each month. Overtime is limited to 300 cases, and subcontracting is unlimited. No action toys are currently in inventory. The wage rate is \$10 per case for regular production, \$15 for overtime production, and \$25 for subcontracting. No stockouts are allowed. Holding cost is \$1 per case per month. Increasing the workforce costs approximately \$1000 per worker; decreasing the workforce costs \$500 per worker.

Management wishes to test the following scenarios for planning production:

a. Level production over the 12 months.
b. Produce to meet demand each month.
c. Increase or decrease regular production in 500 unit increments or steps.

*Solution*

Excel was used to evaluate the three planning scenarios. The solution printouts are shown in Exhibit 13.2. From the scenarios tested (c) step production yields the lowest cost.

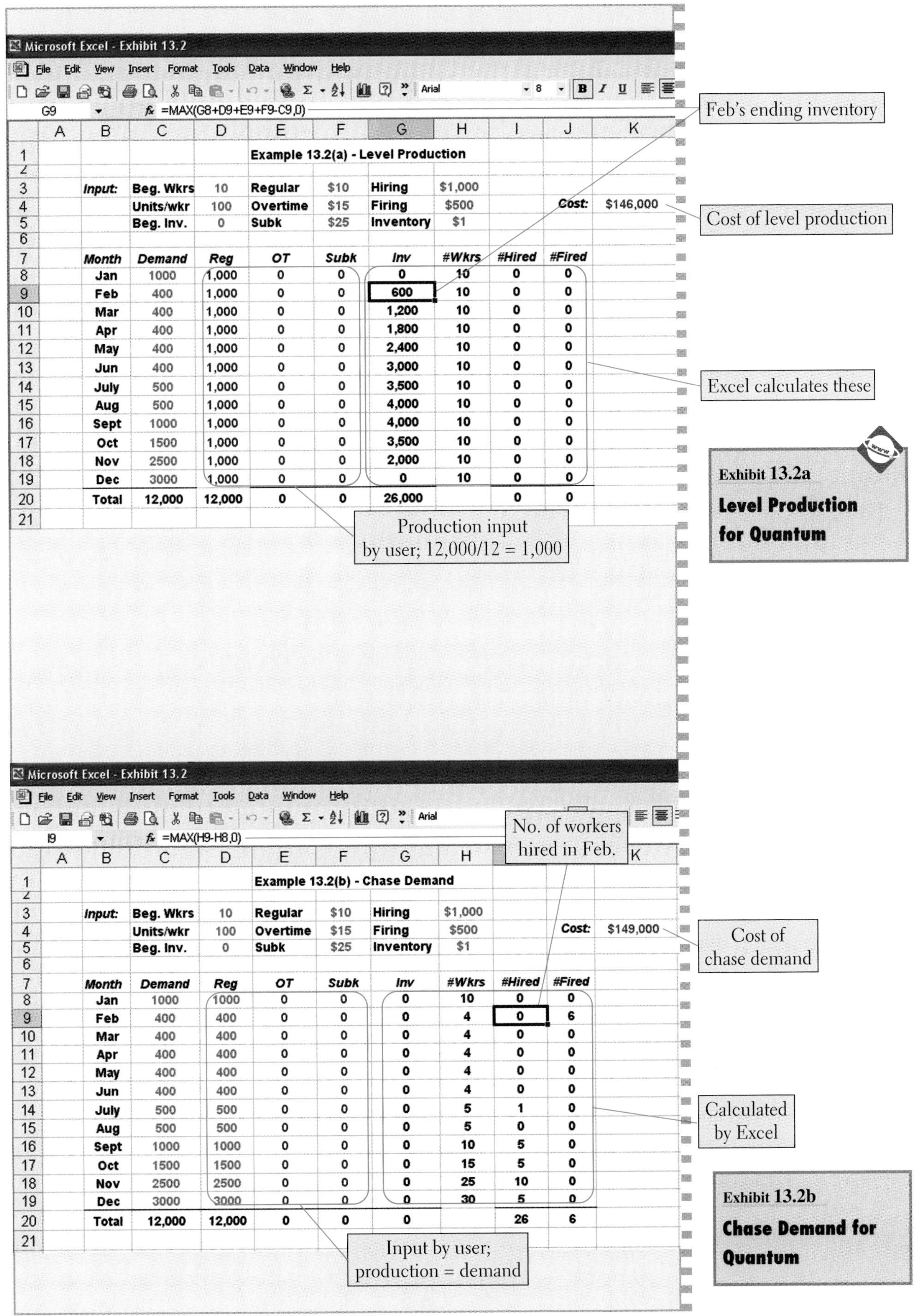

Microsoft Excel - Exhibit 13.2

G9 =MAX(G8+D9+E9+F9-C9,0)

**Example 13.2(a) - Level Production**

| Input: | | | | | | | |
|---|---|---|---|---|---|---|---|
| Beg. Wkrs | 10 | Regular | $10 | Hiring | $1,000 | | |
| Units/wkr | 100 | Overtime | $15 | Firing | $500 | Cost: | $146,000 |
| Beg. Inv. | 0 | Subk | $25 | Inventory | $1 | | |

| Month | Demand | Reg | OT | Subk | Inv | #Wkrs | #Hired | #Fired |
|---|---|---|---|---|---|---|---|---|
| Jan | 1000 | 1,000 | 0 | 0 | 0 | 10 | 0 | 0 |
| Feb | 400 | 1,000 | 0 | 0 | 600 | 10 | 0 | 0 |
| Mar | 400 | 1,000 | 0 | 0 | 1,200 | 10 | 0 | 0 |
| Apr | 400 | 1,000 | 0 | 0 | 1,800 | 10 | 0 | 0 |
| May | 400 | 1,000 | 0 | 0 | 2,400 | 10 | 0 | 0 |
| Jun | 400 | 1,000 | 0 | 0 | 3,000 | 10 | 0 | 0 |
| July | 500 | 1,000 | 0 | 0 | 3,500 | 10 | 0 | 0 |
| Aug | 500 | 1,000 | 0 | 0 | 4,000 | 10 | 0 | 0 |
| Sept | 1000 | 1,000 | 0 | 0 | 4,000 | 10 | 0 | 0 |
| Oct | 1500 | 1,000 | 0 | 0 | 3,500 | 10 | 0 | 0 |
| Nov | 2500 | 1,000 | 0 | 0 | 2,000 | 10 | 0 | 0 |
| Dec | 3000 | 1,000 | 0 | 0 | 0 | 10 | 0 | 0 |
| Total | 12,000 | 12,000 | 0 | 0 | 26,000 | | 0 | 0 |



**Exhibit 13.2a**
**Level Production for Quantum**

Microsoft Excel - Exhibit 13.2

I9 =MAX(H9-H8,0)

**Example 13.2(b) - Chase Demand**

| Input: | | | | | | | |
|---|---|---|---|---|---|---|---|
| Beg. Wkrs | 10 | Regular | $10 | Hiring | $1,000 | | |
| Units/wkr | 100 | Overtime | $15 | Firing | $500 | Cost: | $149,000 |
| Beg. Inv. | 0 | Subk | $25 | Inventory | $1 | | |

| Month | Demand | Reg | OT | Subk | Inv | #Wkrs | #Hired | #Fired |
|---|---|---|---|---|---|---|---|---|
| Jan | 1000 | 1000 | 0 | 0 | 0 | 10 | 0 | 0 |
| Feb | 400 | 400 | 0 | 0 | 0 | 4 | 0 | 6 |
| Mar | 400 | 400 | 0 | 0 | 0 | 4 | 0 | 0 |
| Apr | 400 | 400 | 0 | 0 | 0 | 4 | 0 | 0 |
| May | 400 | 400 | 0 | 0 | 0 | 4 | 0 | 0 |
| Jun | 400 | 400 | 0 | 0 | 0 | 4 | 0 | 0 |
| July | 500 | 500 | 0 | 0 | 0 | 5 | 1 | 0 |
| Aug | 500 | 500 | 0 | 0 | 0 | 5 | 0 | 0 |
| Sept | 1000 | 1000 | 0 | 0 | 0 | 10 | 5 | 0 |
| Oct | 1500 | 1500 | 0 | 0 | 0 | 15 | 5 | 0 |
| Nov | 2500 | 2500 | 0 | 0 | 0 | 25 | 10 | 0 |
| Dec | 3000 | 3000 | 0 | 0 | 0 | 30 | 5 | 0 |
| Total | 12,000 | 12,000 | 0 | 0 | 0 | | 26 | 6 |



**Exhibit 13.2b**
**Chase Demand for Quantum**

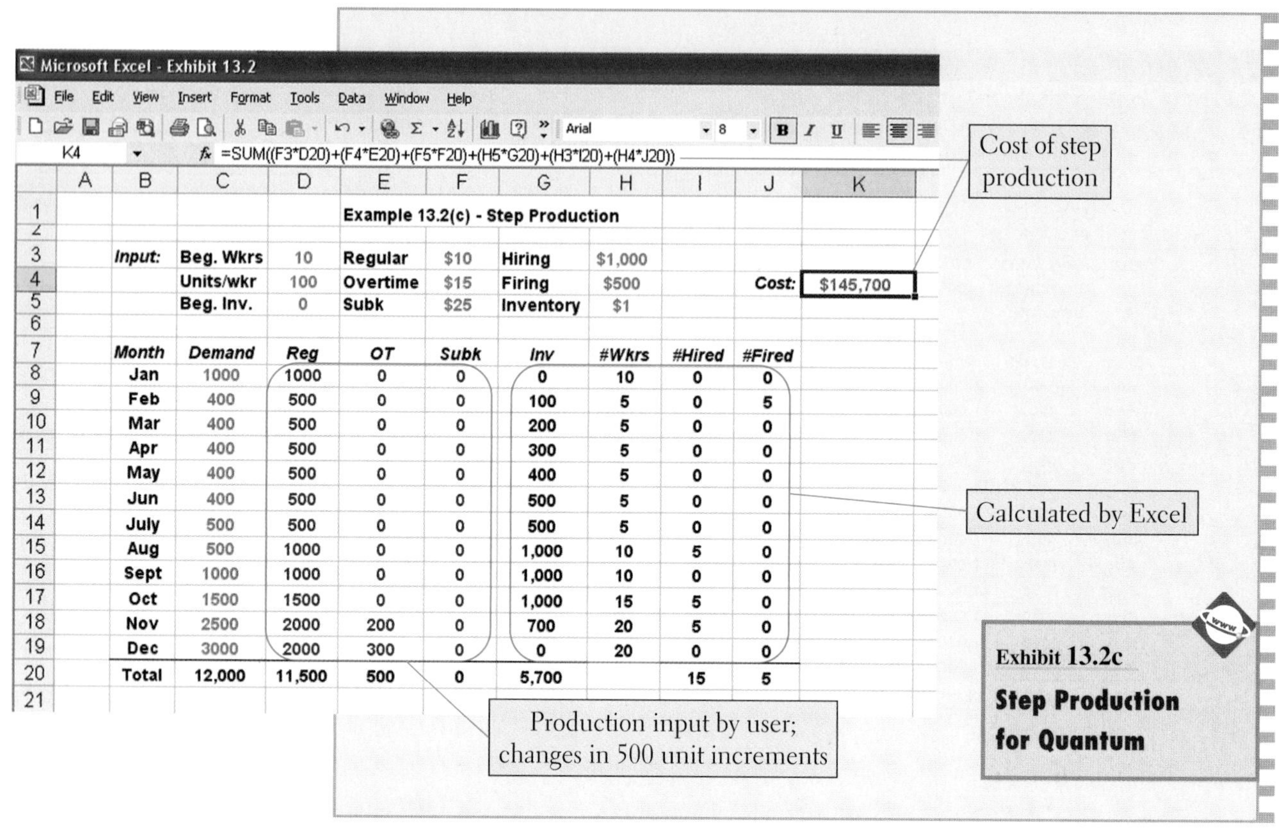


**Example 13.2(c) - Step Production**

| Input: | | | | | | | |
|---|---|---|---|---|---|---|---|
| Beg. Wkrs | 10 | Regular | $10 | Hiring | $1,000 | | |
| Units/wkr | 100 | Overtime | $15 | Firing | $500 | Cost: | $145,700 |
| Beg. Inv. | 0 | Subk | $25 | Inventory | $1 | | |

| Month | Demand | Reg | OT | Subk | Inv | #Wkrs | #Hired | #Fired |
|---|---|---|---|---|---|---|---|---|
| Jan | 1000 | 1000 | 0 | 0 | 0 | 10 | 0 | 0 |
| Feb | 400 | 500 | 0 | 0 | 100 | 5 | 0 | 5 |
| Mar | 400 | 500 | 0 | 0 | 200 | 5 | 0 | 0 |
| Apr | 400 | 500 | 0 | 0 | 300 | 5 | 0 | 0 |
| May | 400 | 500 | 0 | 0 | 400 | 5 | 0 | 0 |
| Jun | 400 | 500 | 0 | 0 | 500 | 5 | 0 | 0 |
| July | 500 | 500 | 0 | 0 | 500 | 5 | 0 | 0 |
| Aug | 500 | 1000 | 0 | 0 | 1,000 | 10 | 5 | 0 |
| Sept | 1000 | 1000 | 0 | 0 | 1,000 | 10 | 0 | 0 |
| Oct | 1500 | 1500 | 0 | 0 | 1,000 | 15 | 5 | 0 |
| Nov | 2500 | 2000 | 200 | 0 | 700 | 20 | 5 | 0 |
| Dec | 3000 | 2000 | 300 | 0 | 0 | 20 | 0 | 0 |
| Total | 12,000 | 11,500 | 500 | 0 | 5,700 | | 15 | 5 |

Exhibit 13.2c
**Step Production for Quantum**

## GENERAL LINEAR PROGRAMMING MODEL

*Linear programming* gives an optimal solution, but demand and costs must be linear.

Pure and mixed strategies for production planning are easy to evaluate, but they do not necessarily provide an optimal solution. Consider the Good and Rich Company of Example 13.1. The *optimal* production plan is probably some combination of inventory and workforce adjustment. We could simply try different combinations and compare the costs (i.e., the trial-and-error approach), or we could find the optimal solution by using *linear programming*. If you are unfamiliar with linear programming, please review the supplement to this chapter. Example 13.3 develops an optimal aggregate production plan for Good and Rich chocolate candies using linear programming.

Example 13.3
**Aggregate Production Planning Using Linear Programming**

Formulate a linear programming model for Example 13.1 that will satisfy demand for Good and Rich chocolate candies at minimum cost. Solve the model with Excel Solver.

*Solution*

*Model Formulation:*

$$\begin{aligned}\text{Minimize } Z = {} & \$100\,(H_1 + H_2 + H_3 + H_4) \\ & + \$500\,(F_1 + F_2 + F_3 + F_4) \\ & + \$0.50\,(I_1 + I_2 + I_3 + I_4) \\ & + \$2\,(P_1 + P_2 + P_3 + P_4)\end{aligned}$$

subject to

Demand constraints

$$\begin{aligned} P_1 - I_1 &= 80{,}000 && (1)\\ I_1 + P_2 - I_2 &= 50{,}000 && (2)\\ I_2 + P_3 - I_3 &= 120{,}000 && (3)\\ I_3 + P_4 - I_4 &= 150{,}000 && (4)\end{aligned}$$

Production constraints

$$1000W_1 = P_1 \quad (5)$$
$$1000W_2 = P_2 \quad (6)$$
$$1000W_3 = P_3 \quad (7)$$
$$1000W_4 = P_4 \quad (8)$$

Workforce constraints

$$100 + H_1 - F_1 = W_1 \quad (9)$$
$$W_1 + H_2 - F_2 = W_2 \quad (10)$$
$$W_2 + H_3 - F_3 = W_3 \quad (11)$$
$$W_3 + H_4 - F_4 = W_4 \quad (12)$$

where

$H_t$ = number of workers hired for period $t$

$F_t$ = number of workers fired for period $t$

$I_t$ = units in inventory at the end of period $t$

$P_t$ = units produced in period $t$

$W_t$ = workforce size for period $t$

- ***Objective function***: The objective function seeks to minimize the cost of hiring workers, firing workers, and holding inventory. Cost values are provided in the problem statement for Example 13.1. The number of workers hired and fired each quarter and the amount of inventory held are variables whose values are determined by solving the linear programming (LP) problem.
- ***Demand constraints***: The first set of constraints ensures that demand is met each quarter. Demand can be met from production in the current period and inventory from the previous period. Units produced in excess of demand remain in inventory at the end of the period. In general form, the demand equations are constructed as

$$I_{t-1} + P_t = D_t + I_t$$

  where $D_t$ is the demand in period $t$, as specified in the problem. Leaving demand on the right-hand side, we have

$$I_{t-1} + P_t - I_t = D_t$$

  There are four demand constraints, one for each quarter. Since there is no beginning inventory, $I_0 = 0$, and it can be dropped from the first demand constraint.
- ***Production constraints***: The four production constraints convert the workforce size to the number of units that can be produced. Each worker can produce 1000 units a quarter, so the production each quarter is 1000 times the number of workers employed, or

$$1000W_t = P_t$$

- ***Workforce constraints***: The workforce constraints limit the workforce size in each period to the previous period's workforce plus the number of workers hired in the current period minus the number of workers fired.

$$W_{t-1} + H_t - F_t = W_t$$

  Notice the first workforce constraint shows a beginning workforce size of 100.
- ***Additional constraints***: Additional constraints can be added to the LP formulation as needed to allow (and limit) such options as subcontracting or overtime. The cost of those options is then added to the objective function.

The LP formulation is solved using Excel Solver as shown in Exhibit 13.3.[2] The Excel file, Exhibit 13.3.xls, is available on the text Web site. The cost of the optimum solution is \$32,000, an improvement of \$3000 over the chase demand strategy and \$38,000 over the level production strategy.

[2]Be careful not to confuse the cell addresses on the Excel spreadsheet with the letter variables used in the LP model formulation.

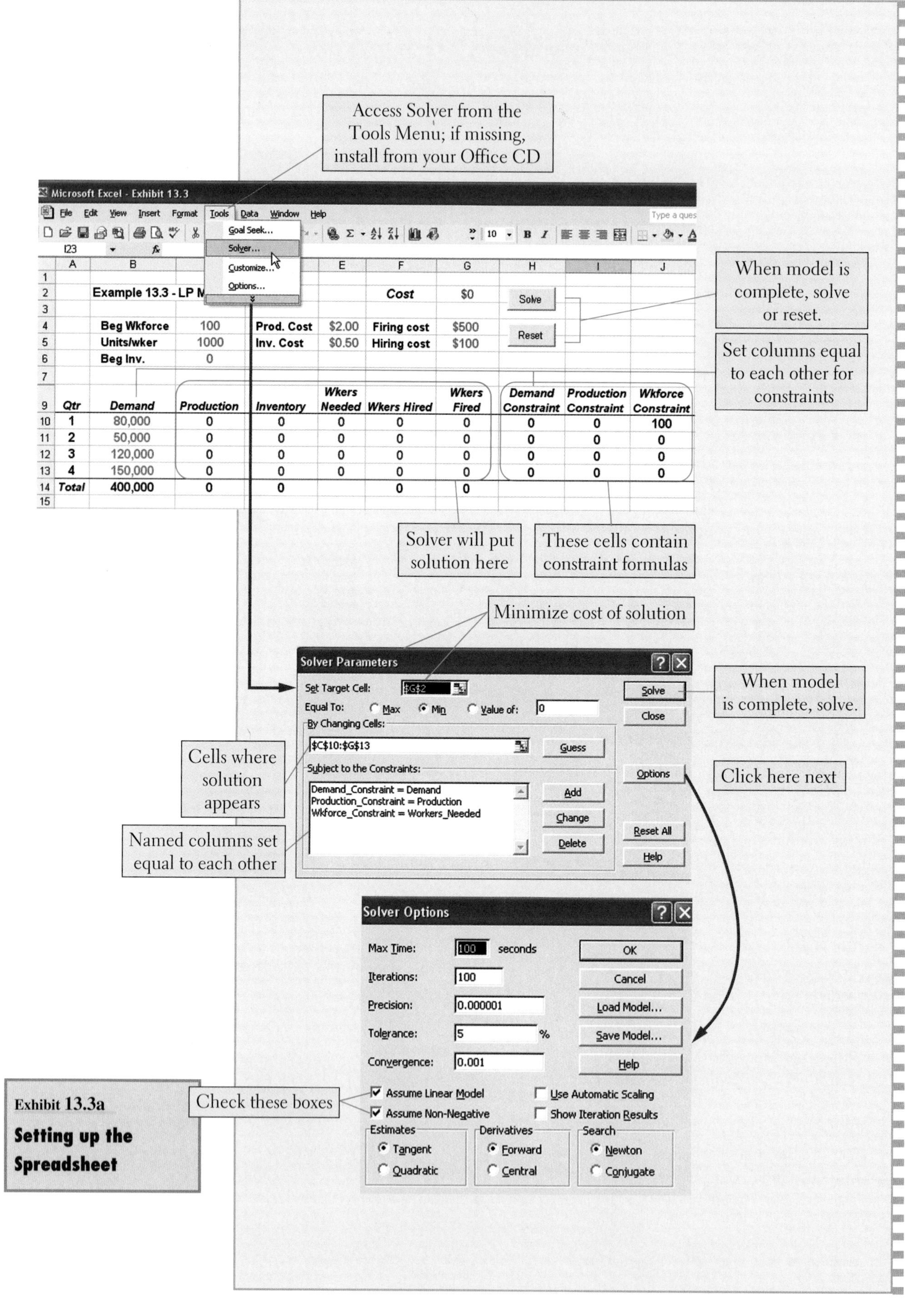


**Exhibit 13.3a**

**Setting up the Spreadsheet**

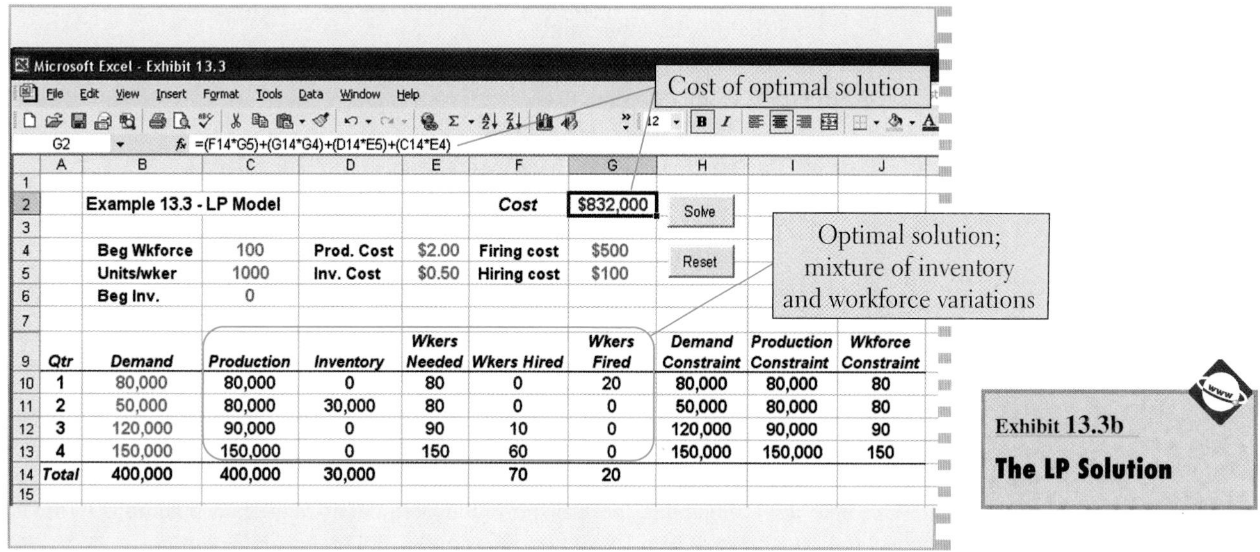


Example 13.3 - LP Model

| | | | | | Cost | $832,000 |
|---|---|---|---|---|---|---|
| Beg Wkforce | 100 | Prod. Cost | $2.00 | Firing cost | $500 | |
| Units/wker | 1000 | Inv. Cost | $0.50 | Hiring cost | $100 | |
| Beg Inv. | 0 | | | | | |

| Qtr | Demand | Production | Inventory | Wkers Needed | Wkers Hired | Wkers Fired | Demand Constraint | Production Constraint | Wkforce Constraint |
|---|---|---|---|---|---|---|---|---|---|
| 1 | 80,000 | 80,000 | 0 | 80 | 0 | 20 | 80,000 | 80,000 | 80 |
| 2 | 50,000 | 80,000 | 30,000 | 80 | 0 | 0 | 50,000 | 80,000 | 80 |
| 3 | 120,000 | 90,000 | 0 | 90 | 10 | 0 | 120,000 | 90,000 | 90 |
| 4 | 150,000 | 150,000 | 0 | 150 | 60 | 0 | 150,000 | 150,000 | 150 |
| Total | 400,000 | 400,000 | 30,000 | | 70 | 20 | | | |

Exhibit 13.3b

**The LP Solution**

## APP BY THE TRANSPORTATION METHOD

For cases in which the decision to change the size of the workforce has already been made or is prohibited, the transportation method of linear programming can be used to develop an aggregate production plan. (See Supplement 10 for an introduction to the transportation method.) The transportation method gathers all the cost information into one matrix and plans production based on the lowest-cost alternatives. Table 13.1 shows a blank transportation tableau with *i* for inventory, *h* for holding cost, *r* for regular production cost, *o* for overtime, *s* for subcontracting, and *b* for backordering. The capital letters indicate individual capacities or demand. The periods of production, along with the pro-

Use the transportation method when hiring and firing is not an option.

Table 13.1

**Transportation Tableau for Aggregate Production Planning**

| Period of Production | | Period of Use 1 | 2 | 3 | 4 | Unused Capacity | Capacity |
|---|---|---|---|---|---|---|---|
| | Beginning Inventory | 0 | $h$ | $2h$ | $3h$ | | $I$ |
| 1 | Regular | $r$ | $r+h$ | $r+2h$ | $r+3h$ | | $R_1$ |
| | Overtime | $o$ | $o+h$ | $o+2h$ | $o+3h$ | | $O_1$ |
| | Subcontract | $s$ | $s+h$ | $s+2h$ | $s+3h$ | | $S_1$ |
| 2 | Regular | $r+b$ | $r$ | $r+h$ | $r+2h$ | | $R_2$ |
| | Overtime | $o+b$ | $o$ | $o+h$ | $o+2h$ | | $O_2$ |
| | Subcontract | $s+b$ | $s$ | $s+h$ | $s+2h$ | | $S_2$ |
| 3 | Regular | $r+2b$ | $r+b$ | $r$ | $r+h$ | | $R_3$ |
| | Overtime | $o+2b$ | $o+b$ | $o$ | $o+h$ | | $O_3$ |
| | Subcontract | $s+2b$ | $s+b$ | $s$ | $s+h$ | | $S_3$ |
| 4 | Regular | $r+3b$ | $r+2b$ | $r+b$ | $r$ | | $R_4$ |
| | Overtime | $o+3b$ | $o+2b$ | $o+b$ | $o$ | | $O_4$ |
| | Subcontract | $s+3b$ | $s+2b$ | $s+b$ | $s$ | | $S_4$ |
| | Demand | $D_1$ | $D_2$ | $D_3$ | $D_4$ | | |

$h$ = holding cost per unit
$r$ = regular production cost per unit
$o$ = overtime cost per unit
$s$ = subcontracting cost per unit
$b$ = backordering cost per unit
$D$ = demand
$I$ = beginning inventory
$R$ = regular capacity
$O$ = overtime capacity
$S$ = subcontracting capacity

duction options, appear in the first column. The periods of use (regardless of when the items are produced) appear across the top row. Cost entries in the period-of-use columns differ by the cost of holding the item in inventory before its use.

Example 13.4 illustrates the transportation method of aggregate planning. A blank transportation tableau and an Excel file of Example 13.4 are available online.

Example 13.4

**The Transportation Method of Aggregate Planning**

Burruss Manufacturing Company uses overtime, inventory, and subcontracting to absorb fluctuations in demand. An aggregate production plan is devised annually and updated quarterly. Cost data, expected demand, and available capacities in units for the next four quarters are given here. Demand must be satisfied in the period it occurs; that is, no backordering is allowed. Design a production plan that will satisfy demand at minimum cost.

| Quarter | Expected Demand | Regular Capacity | Overtime Capacity | Subcontract Capacity |
|---|---|---|---|---|
| 1 | 900 | 1000 | 100 | 500 |
| 2 | 1500 | 1200 | 150 | 500 |
| 3 | 1600 | 1300 | 200 | 500 |
| 4 | 3000 | 1300 | 200 | 500 |

| | |
|---|---|
| Regular production cost per unit | \$20 |
| Overtime production cost per unit | \$25 |
| Subcontracting cost per unit | \$28 |
| Inventory holding cost per unit per period | \$ 3 |
| Beginning inventory | 300 units |

*Solution*

The problem is solved using the transportation tableau shown in Table 13.2. The tableau is a worksheet that is completed as follows:

Rim Requirements

- To set up the tableau, demand requirements for each quarter are listed on the bottom row, and capacity constraints for each type of production (i.e., regular, overtime, or subcontracting) are placed in the far right column.

Beginning Inventory

- Next, cost figures are entered into the small square at the corner of each cell. Starting with the beginning inventory row, inventory on hand in period 1 that is used in period 1 incurs zero cost. Inventory on hand in period 1 that is not used until period 2 incurs a \$3 holding cost. Inventory held until period 3, costs \$3 more, or \$6. Similarly, inventory held until period 4 costs an additional \$3, or \$9.

Table 13.2

| | Period of Production | Period of Use 1 | 2 | 3 | 4 | Unused Capacity | Capacity |
|---|---|---|---|---|---|---|---|
| | Beginning inventory | 300 (0) | — (3) | — (6) | — (9) | | 300 |
| 1 | Regular | 600 (20) | 300 (23) | 100 (26) | — (29) | | 1000 |
| | Overtime | (25) | (28) | (31) | 100 (34) | | 100 |
| | Subcontract | (28) | (31) | (34) | (37) | | 500 |
| 2 | Regular | | 1200 (20) | — (23) | — (26) | | 1200 |
| | Overtime | | (25) | (28) | 150 (31) | | 150 |
| | Subcontract | | (28) | (31) | 250 (34) | 250 | 500 |
| 3 | Regular | | | 1300 (20) | — (23) | | 1300 |
| | Overtime | | | 200 (25) | — (28) | | 200 |
| | Subcontract | | | (28) | 500 (31) | | 500 |
| 4 | Regular | | | | 1300 (20) | | 1300 |
| | Overtime | | | | 200 (25) | | 200 |
| | Subcontract | | | | 500 (28) | | 500 |
| | Demand | 900 | 1500 | 1600 | 3000 | 250 | |

Cost figures

- For regular production, a unit produced in period 1 and used in period 1, costs \$20. A unit produced under regular production in period 1 but not used until period 2, incurs a production cost of \$20 plus an inventory cost of \$3, or \$23. If the unit is held until period 3, it costs \$3 more, or \$26. If held until period 4, it costs \$29. The cost calculations continue for overtime and subcontracting, beginning with production costs of \$25 and \$28, respectively.

No backorders

- The costs for production in periods 2, 3, and 4 are determined in a similar fashion, with one exception. Half of the remaining transportation tableau is blocked out as infeasible. This occurs because no backordering is allowed for this problem, and production cannot take place in one period to satisfy demand for a period that has already passed.

Allocating units to cells:

Period 1

- Now that the tableau is set up, we can begin to allocate units to the cells and develop our production plan. The procedure is to assign units to the lowest-cost cells in a column so that demand requirements for the column are met, yet capacity constraints of each row are not exceeded. Beginning with the first demand column for period 1, we have 300 units of beginning inventory available to us at no cost. If we use all 300 units in period 1, there is no inventory left for use in later periods. We indicate this fact by putting a dash in the remaining cells of the beginning inventory row. We can satisfy the remaining 600 units of demand for period 1 with regular production at a cost of \$20 per unit.

Period 2

- In period 2, the lowest-cost alternative is regular production in period 2. We assign 1200 units to that cell and, in the process, use up all the capacity for that row. Dashes are placed in the remaining cells of the row to indicate that they are no longer feasible choices. The remaining units needed to meet demand in period 2 are taken from regular production in period 1 that is inventoried until period 2, at a cost of \$23 per unit. We assign 300 units to that cell.

Period 3

- Continuing to the third period's demand of 1600 units, we fully utilize the 1300 units available from regular production in the same period and 200 units of overtime production. The remaining 100 units are produced with regular production in period 1 and held until period 3, at a cost of $26 per unit. As noted by the dashed line, period 1's regular production has reached its capacity and is no longer an alternative source of production.

Period 4

- Of the fourth period's demand of 3000 units, 1300 units come from regular production, 200 from overtime, and 500 from subcontracting in the same period. One hundred fifty more units can be provided at a cost of $31 per unit from overtime production in period 2 and 500 from subcontracting in period 3. The next-lowest alternative is $34 from overtime in period 1 or subcontracting in period 2. At this point, we can make a judgment call as to whether our workers want overtime or whether it would be easier to subcontract out the entire amount. As shown in Table 13.2, we decide to use overtime to its full capacity of 100 units and fill the remaining demand of 250 from subcontracting.

Unused capacity

- The unused capacity column is filled in last. In period 2, 250 units of subcontracting capacity are available but unused. This information is valuable because it tells us the flexibility the company has to accept additional orders.

The Production Plan

The optimal production plan, derived from the transportation tableau, is given in Table 13.3.[3] The values in the production plan are taken from the transportation tableau one row at a time. For example, the 1000 units of a regular production for period 1 is the sum of 600 + 300 + 100 from the second row of the transportation tableau. Ending inventory is calculated by summing beginning inventory, and all forms of production for that period and then subtracting demand. For example, the ending inventory for period 1 is

$$\begin{aligned}&(\text{Beginning inventory} + \text{Regular production}\\&+ \text{Overtime production} + \text{Subcontracting}) - \text{Demand}\\&= (300 + 1000 + 100 + 0) - 900 = 500\end{aligned}$$

Cost of the plan

The cost of the production plan can be determined directly from the transportation tableau by multiplying the units in each cell times the cost in the corner of the cell and summing them. Alternatively, the cost can be determined from the production plan by multiplying the total units produced in each production category, or held in inventory, by their respective costs and summing them, as follows:

$$(4800 \times \$20) + (650 \times \$25) + (1250 \times \$28) + (2100 \times \$3) = \$153,550$$

**Table 13.3**
**The Production Plan**

| | | Production Plan | | | |
|---|---|---|---|---|---|
| Period | Demand | Regular Production | Overtime | Subcontract | Ending Inventory |
| 1 | 900 | 1000 | 100 | 0 | 500 |
| 2 | 1500 | 1200 | 150 | 250 | 600 |
| 3 | 1600 | 1300 | 200 | 500 | 1000 |
| 4 | 3000 | 1300 | 200 | 500 | 0 |
| Total | 7000 | 4800 | 650 | 1250 | 2100 |

An Excel solution to this problem is shown in Exhibit 13.4.

[3]For this example, our initial solution to the aggregate production problem happens to be optimal. In other cases, it may be necessary to iterate to additional transportation tableaux before an optimal solution is reached. Students unfamiliar with the transportation method should review the topic in the Supplement to Chapter 10.

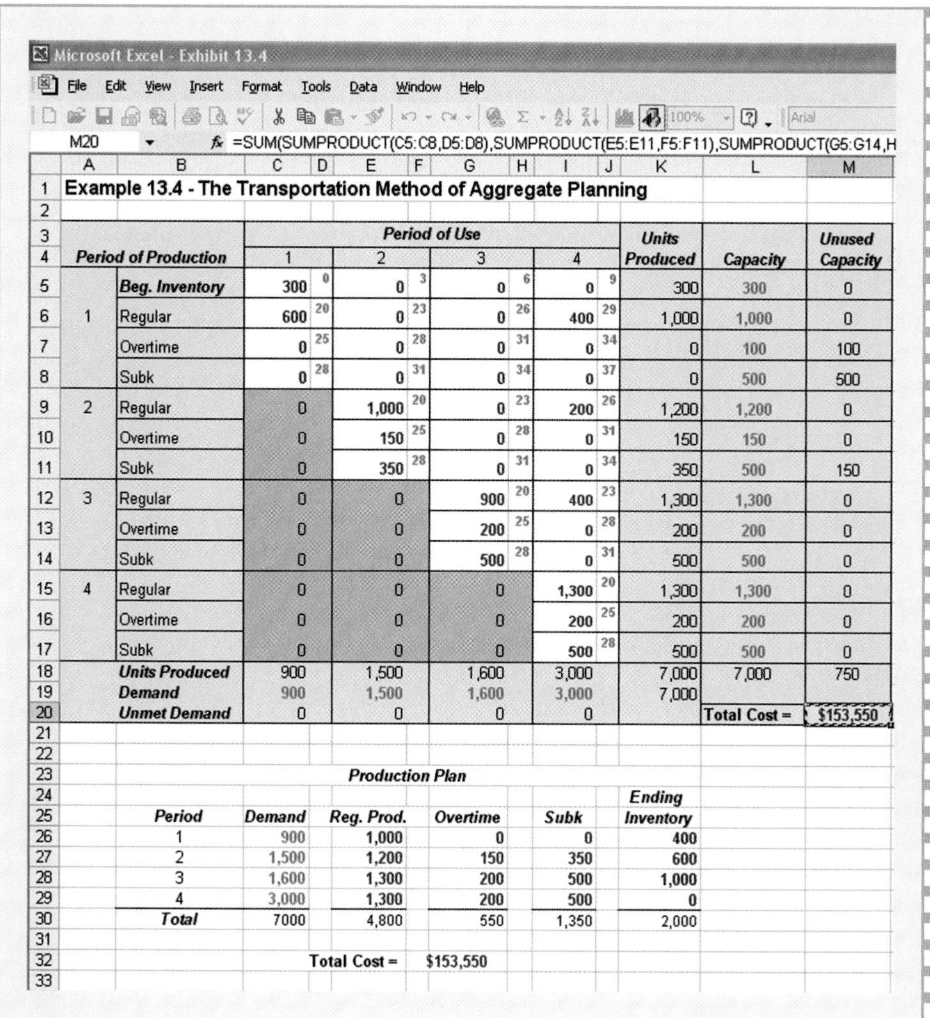

Microsoft Excel - Exhibit 13.4

M20 =SUM(SUMPRODUCT(C5:C8,D5:D8),SUMPRODUCT(E5:E11,F5:F11),SUMPRODUCT(G5:G14,H

**Example 13.4 - The Transportation Method of Aggregate Planning**

| Period of Production | | Period of Use 1 | 2 | 3 | 4 | Units Produced | Capacity | Unused Capacity |
|---|---|---|---|---|---|---|---|---|
| | Beg. Inventory | 300 [0] | 0 [3] | 0 [6] | 0 [9] | 300 | 300 | 0 |
| 1 | Regular | 600 [20] | 0 [23] | 0 [26] | 400 [29] | 1,000 | 1,000 | 0 |
| | Overtime | 0 [25] | 0 [28] | 0 [31] | 0 [34] | 0 | 100 | 100 |
| | Subk | 0 [28] | 0 [31] | 0 [34] | 0 [37] | 0 | 500 | 500 |
| 2 | Regular | 0 | 1,000 [20] | 0 [23] | 200 [26] | 1,200 | 1,200 | 0 |
| | Overtime | 0 | 150 [25] | 0 [28] | 0 [31] | 150 | 150 | 0 |
| | Subk | 0 | 350 [28] | 0 [31] | 0 [34] | 350 | 500 | 150 |
| 3 | Regular | 0 | 0 | 900 [20] | 400 [23] | 1,300 | 1,300 | 0 |
| | Overtime | 0 | 0 | 200 [25] | 0 [28] | 200 | 200 | 0 |
| | Subk | 0 | 0 | 500 [28] | 0 [31] | 500 | 500 | 0 |
| 4 | Regular | 0 | 0 | 0 | 1,300 [20] | 1,300 | 1,300 | 0 |
| | Overtime | 0 | 0 | 0 | 200 [25] | 200 | 200 | 0 |
| | Subk | 0 | 0 | 0 | 500 [28] | 500 | 500 | 0 |
| | Units Produced | 900 | 1,500 | 1,600 | 3,000 | 7,000 | 7,000 | 750 |
| | Demand | 900 | 1,500 | 1,600 | 3,000 | 7,000 | | |
| | Unmet Demand | 0 | 0 | 0 | 0 | | Total Cost = | $153,550 |

**Production Plan**

| Period | Demand | Reg. Prod. | Overtime | Subk | Ending Inventory |
|---|---|---|---|---|---|
| 1 | 900 | 1,000 | 0 | 0 | 400 |
| 2 | 1,500 | 1,200 | 150 | 350 | 600 |
| 3 | 1,600 | 1,300 | 200 | 500 | 1,000 |
| 4 | 3,000 | 1,300 | 200 | 500 | 0 |
| Total | 7000 | 4,800 | 550 | 1,350 | 2,000 |

Total Cost = $153,550

Exhibit 13.4

**Using Excel for the Transportation Method of Aggregate Planning**

## OTHER QUANTITATIVE TECHNIQUES

Although linear programming models will yield an optimal solution to the aggregate planning problem, there are some limitations. The relationships among variables must be linear, the model is deterministic, and only one objective is allowed (usually minimizing cost).

The linear decision rule, search decision rule, and management coefficients model use different types of cost functions to solve aggregate planning problems. The *linear decision rule (LDR)* is an optimizing technique originally developed for aggregate planning in a paint factory. It solves a set of four quadratic equations that describe the major capacity-related costs in the factory: payroll costs, hiring and firing, overtime and undertime, and inventory costs. The results yield the optimal workforce level and production rate.

The *search decision rule (SDR)* is a pattern search algorithm that tries to find the minimum cost combination of various workforce levels and production rates. Any type of cost function can be used. The search is performed by computer and may involve the evaluation of thousands of possible solutions, but an optimal solution is not guaranteed. The *management coefficients model* uses regression analysis to improve the consistency of planning decisions. Techniques like SDR and management coefficients are often embedded in commercial decision support systems or expert systems for aggregate planning.

## THE HIERARCHICAL NATURE OF PLANNING

Planning involves a hierarchy of decisions. By determining a strategy for meeting and managing demand, aggregate planning provides a framework within which shorter term production and capacity decisions can be made. The levels of production and capacity planning are shown in Figure 13.3. In production planning, the next level of detail is a *master production schedule*, in which weekly (not monthly or quarterly) production plans are specified by individual final product (not product line). At another level of detail, *material requirements planning* plans the production of the components that go into the final products. *Shop floor scheduling* schedules the manufacturing operations required to make each component.

In capacity planning, we might develop a *resource requirements plan*, to verify that an aggregate production plan is doable, and a *rough-cut capacity plan* as a quick check to see if the master production schedule is feasible. One level down, we would develop a much more detailed *capacity requirements plan* that matches the factory's machine and labor resources to the material requirements plan. Finally, we would use *input/output control* to monitor the production that takes place at individual machines or work centers.

**Disaggregation:** the process of breaking an aggregate plan into more detailed plans.

At each level, decisions are made within the parameters set by the higher-level decisions. The process of moving from the aggregate plan to the next level down is called **disaggregation**. We examine this process more thoroughly in Chapter 14. In the next section, we discuss two important tools for planning in an e-business environment: collaborative planning and available-to-promise.

## COLLABORATIVE PLANNING

**Collaborative planning:** sharing information and synchronizing production across the supply chain.

**Collaborative planning** is part of the supply chain process of CPFR (collaborative planning, forecasting, and replenishment) presented in Chapter 11. In terms of production, CPFR involves selecting the products to be jointly managed, creating a single forecast of customer demand, and synchronizing production across the supply chain. Consensus among partners is reached first on the sales forecast, then on the production plan. Although the process differs by software vendor, basically each partner has access to an Internet-enabled planning book in which forecasts, customer orders, and production plans are visible for specific items. Partners agree on the level of aggregation to be used. Events trigger responses by partners. Alerts warn partners of conditions that require special action or changes to the plan.

One example of an event that requires collaboration among trading partners is quoting available-to-promise dates for customers.

Figure 13.3
**Hierarchical Planning**

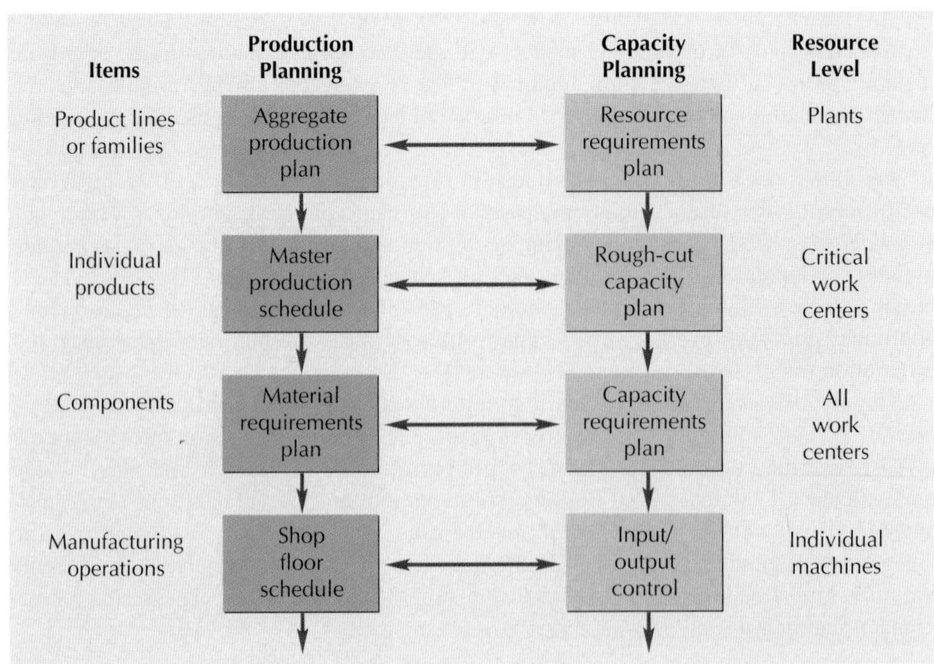

## AVAILABLE-TO-PROMISE

In the current business environment of outsourcing and build-to-order products, companies must be able to provide the customer with accurate promise dates. Recall that the aggregate plan is the company's *game plan* for matching supply and demand. As the time horizon grows shorter and more information becomes available, we develop and execute more detailed plans of action. For example, we convert the aggregate production plan for product families into a master schedule for individual products based on best estimates of future demand. As customer orders come in *consuming the forecast*, the remaining quantities are **available-to-promise** to future customers. Example 13.5 illustrates the process.

**Available-to-promise (ATP):** the quantity of items that can be promised to the customer; the difference between planned production and customer orders already received.

Available-to-promise is the difference between customer orders and planned production. In the first period of the planning horizon, available-to-promise is calculated by summing the on-hand quantity and planned production, then subtracting customer orders up until the next period of planned production. In subsequent periods, the ATP is simply planned production minus customer orders. No on-hand quantities are used. However, if customer orders exceed production, units can be taken from the ATP of previous periods.

ATP in period 1 = (On-hand quantity + MPS in period 1) − (CO until the next period of planned production)

ATP in period $n$ = (MPS in period $n$) − (CO until the next period of planned production)

**Example 13.5**
**Available-to-Promise**

East Coast Bicycle Company has recently begun to accept customer orders over the Internet. The company uses both an aggregate production plan for product families and a master production schedule for individual products. Now East Coast wants to add available-to-promise functionality to the planning process. Using the information given below, determine how many girls 26″ bikes are available-to-promise in April, May, and June.

**Aggregate Production Plan**

| | Quarter | | | |
|---|---|---|---|---|
| **Product Family** | *1* | *2* | *3* | *4* |
| Juvenile Bikes | 800 | 1000 | 1500 | 4000 |

**Master Production Schedule**

| | April | May | June | Total |
|---|---|---|---|---|
| Boys 26″ | 150 | 100 | 150 | 400 |
| Girls 26″ | 100 | 100 | 100 | 300 |
| Boys 20″ | 30 | 20 | 50 | 100 |
| Girls 20″ | 40 | 20 | 140 | 200 |
| Total | 320 | 240 | 440 | 1000 |

**Available-to-Promise for Girls 26″ Bike**

| **On Hand = 10** | **April** | **May** | **June** | **Total** |
|---|---|---|---|---|
| Forecast | 50 | 100 | 150 | 300 |
| Customer Orders | | | | |
| Master Production Schedule | 100 | 100 | 100 | 300 |
| Available-to-Promise | | | | |

| **On Hand = 10** | **April** | **May** | **June** | **Total** |
|---|---|---|---|---|
| Forecast | 50 | 100 | 150 | 300 |
| Customer Orders | **70** | **110** | **50** | **230** |
| Master Production Schedule | 100 | 100 | 100 | 300 |
| Available-to-Promise | | | | |

*Solution*

The first available-to-promise table shows a master production schedule (MPS) determined from forecasts of demand. The second table shows customer orders that have been received to date. The available-to-promise (ATP) row is calculated by summing the on-hand quantity with the scheduled production units and subtracting the customer orders up until the next period of planned production.

| On Hand = 10 | April | May | June | Total |
|---|---|---|---|---|
| Forecast | 50 | 100 | 150 | 300 |
| Customer Orders | **70** | **110** | **50** | **230** |
| Master Production Schedule | 100 | 100 | 100 | 300 |
| Available-to-Promise | **30** | **0** | **50** | **80** |

ATP in April = (10 + 100) − 70 = ~~40~~ 30
ATP in May = 100 − 110 = −~~10~~ 0 Take excess units from April
ATP in June = 100 − 50 = 50

**Capable-to-promise:** the quantity of items that can be produced and made available at a later date.

As companies venture beyond their boundaries to complete customer orders, so available-to-promise inquiries extend beyond a particular plant or distribution center to a network of plants and supplier's plants worldwide. ATP may also involve drilling down beyond the end item level to check the availability of critical components. Supply chain and enterprise planning software vendors such as SAP and i2 have available-to-promise modules that execute a series of rules when assessing product availability, and alert the planner when customer orders exceed or fall short of forecasts. The rules prescribe product substitutions, alternative sources, and allocation procedures as shown in Figure 13.4. When the product is not available, the system proposes a **capable-to-promise** date that is subject to customer approval.

**Figure 13.4**
**Rules-Based ATP**

*Source:* Adapted from SAP AG, "Global Available-to-Promise," http://www.sap.com/solutions/scm/apo/pdf/atp.pdf.

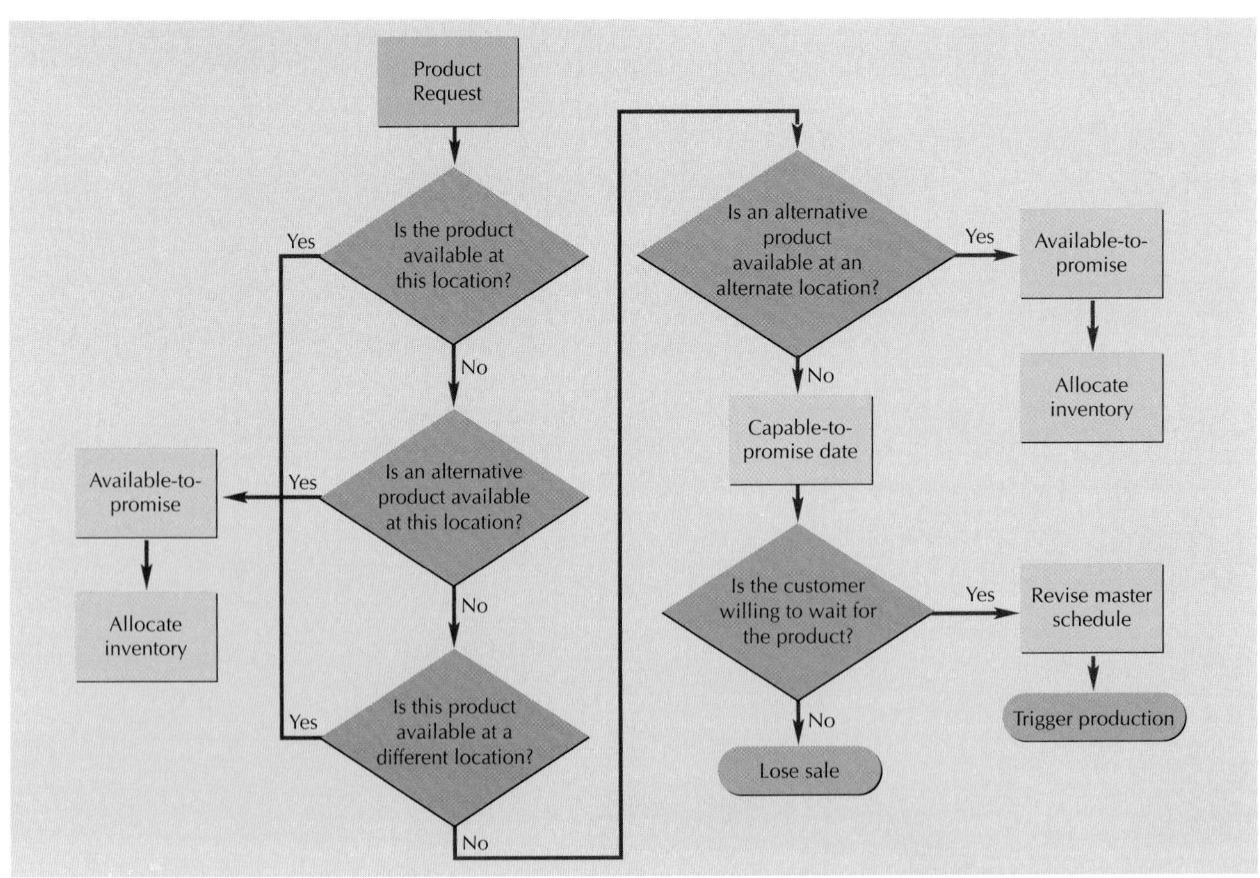

## AGGREGATE PLANNING FOR SERVICES

The aggregate planning process is different for services in the following ways:

1. ***Most services cannot be inventoried.*** It is impossible to store an airline seat, hotel room, or hair appointment for use later when demand may be higher. When the goods that accompany a service can be inventoried, they typically have a very short life. Newspapers are good for only a day; flowers, at most a week; and cooked hamburgers, only 10 minutes.
2. ***Demand for services is difficult to predict.*** Demand variations occur frequently and are often severe. The exponential distribution is commonly used to simulate the erratic demand for services—high-demand peaks over short periods of time with long periods of low demand in between. *Customer service levels* established by management express the percentage of demand that must be met and, sometimes, how quickly demand must be met. This is an important input to aggregate planning for services.
3. ***Capacity is also difficult to predict.*** The variety of services offered and the individualized nature of services make capacity difficult to predict. The "capacity" of a bank teller depends on the number and type of transactions requested by the customer. Units of capacity can also vary. Should a hospital define capacity in terms of number of beds, number of patients, size of the nursing or medical staff, or number of patient hours?
4. ***Service capacity must be provided at the appropriate place and time.*** Many services have branches or outlets widely dispersed over a geographic region. Determining the range of services and staff levels at each location is part of aggregate planning.
5. ***Labor is usually the most constraining resource for services.*** This is an advantage in aggregate planning because labor is very flexible. Variations in demand can be handled by hiring temporary workers, using part-time workers, or using overtime. Summer recreation programs and theme parks hire teenagers out of school for the summer. Federal Express staffs its peak hours of midnight to 2 A.M. with area college students. McDonald's, Wal-Mart, and other retail establishments woo senior citizens as reliable part-time workers. Workers can also be cross-trained to perform a variety of jobs and can be called upon as needed. A common example is the sales clerk who also stocks inventory. Less common are police officers who are cross-trained as firefighters and paramedics.

**Characteristics of aggregate planning for services**

There are several services that have unique aggregate planning problems. Doctors, lawyers, and other professionals have emergency or priority calls for their service that must be meshed with regular appointments. Hotels and airlines routinely *overbook* their capacity in anticipation of customers who do not show up. Airlines design complex pricing structures for different routes and classes of customers. Planners incorporate these decisions in a process called *yield management* or *revenue management*.

## YIELD MANAGEMENT

**Yield management** seeks to maximize yield or profit from time-sensitive products and services. It is used in industries with inflexible and expensive capacity, perishable products or services, segmented markets, advanced sales, and uncertain demand. The types of problems addressed by yield management include overbooking, partitioning demand into fare classes, and single order quantities.

**Yield management:** maximizes the yield of time sensitive products and services.

### Overbooking

Services with reservation systems can lose money when customers fail to show up, or cancel reservations at the last minute. It is not unusual for no-shows to account for 10 to 30% of an aircraft's available seats. Thus, hotels, airlines, and restaurants routinely overbook their capacity. Managers who underestimate the number of no-shows must then compensate a customer who has been "bumped" by providing the service free of charge at another time or place.

### Fare Classes

Hotels, airlines, stadiums, and theaters typically offer different ticket prices for certain classes of seats or customers. Planners must determine the number of seats or rooms to allocate to these different fare classes. Too many high-priced seats can lose customers, while too few high-priced seats can lower profits. Sabre estimates that airlines make more profits from the 3% of customers who are "business travelers" than the rest of customers who have discounted fares.

## Single Order Quantities

The useful life for products such as newspapers, flowers, baked goods, and seasonal items is so short that in many instances only one order for production can take place. Determining the size of that single order can be difficult.

Table 13.4 shows the various types of yield management problems with cost descriptions. In each of these problems, the cost of overestimating demand (times the probability that it will occur) must be balanced with the cost of underestimating demand and its probability of occurrence.

The optimum probability is where the cost of underestimating demand is equal to or *just* greater than the cost of overestimating demand. The derivation of the formula is shown below, followed by an example.

$$\text{Cost of underestimating demand} \geq \text{Cost of overestimating demand}$$

$$P(N \geq X)C_u \geq P(N < X)C_o$$

$$[1 - P(N < X)]C_u \geq P(N < X)C_o$$

$$P(N < X) \leq \frac{C_u}{C_u + C_o}$$

where

$C_o$ = cost of overestimating demand or no-shows

$C_u$ = cost of underestimating demand or no-shows

$P(N < X)$ = probability of overestimating demand or no-shows

$P(N \geq X)$ = probability of underestimating demand or no-shows

$N$ = number of no-shows or units demanded

$X$ = units ordered or overbooked

**Table 13.4**
**Yield Management**

| Type of Problem | Type of Business | Probability of Overestimating Demand or No-Shows, $P(N < X)$ | Optimal Probability of Demand or No-Shows $\frac{C_u}{(C_u + C_o)}$ | Cost Description |
|---|---|---|---|---|
| Overbooking | Hotel, airlines, restaurants | $N$ = number of no-shows<br>$X$ = number of overbooked rooms or seats | $C_o$ = cost of overbooking<br>$C_u$ = cost of underbooking | Replacement cost<br>Lost profit |
| Fare Classes | Airlines, cruise ships, passenger trains, extended stay hotels | $N$ = number of full-fare tickets that can be sold<br>$X$ = seats reserved for full fare passengers | $C_o$ = cost of overestimating full fare passengers<br>$C_u$ = cost of underestimating full fare passengers | Lost full-fare (Full-Fare − discounted fare) |
| Premium Seats | Stadiums, theaters | $N$ = no. of premium tickets that can be sold<br>$X$ = seats reserved for premium ticket holders | $C_o$ = cost of overestimating premium ticket sales<br>$C_u$ = cost of underestimating premium ticket sales | Lost regular revenue<br>(Premium ticket − regular ticket revenue) |
| Single Order Quantities | Newspapers, magazines, florists, nurseries, bakeries, sale items | $N$ = number of items that can be sold<br>$X$ = number of items ordered | $C_o$ = cost of overestimating demand<br>$C_u$ = cost of underestimating demand | (Cost − salvage value)<br>Lost profit |

Given cost information and a distribution of demand or no-shows from past data, we can now match our planning policy with the optimum probability of overestimating demand. Example 13.6 illustrates the procedure for overbooking. A single order quantity problem is included in the solved problems at the end of this chapter.

**Example 13.6**

**Yield Management**

Lauren Lacy, manager of the Lucky Traveler Inn in Las Vegas, is tired of customers who make reservations and then don't show up. Rooms rent for $100 a night and cost $25 to maintain per day. Overflow customers can be sent to the Motel 7 for $70 a night. Lauren's records of no-shows over the past six months are given below. Should the Lucky Traveler start overbooking? If so, how many rooms should be overbooked?

| No-Shows | Probability |
|---|---|
| 0 | 0.15 |
| 1 | 0.25 |
| 2 | 0.30 |
| 3 | 0.30 |

*Solution*

$$C_o = \$70$$

$$C_u = \$100 - \$25 = \$75$$

$$P(N < X) \leq \frac{C_u}{C_u + C_o} = \frac{75}{75 + 70} = 0.517$$

Adding a cumulative probability column of no-shows being less than expected gives us:

| No-Shows | Probability | $P(N < X)$ | |
|---|---|---|---|
| 0 | 0.15 | 0.00 | |
| 1 | 0.25 | 0.15 | |
| 2 | 0.30 | 0.40 | **←0.517** |
| 3 | 0.30 | 0.70 | |

The optimal probability of no-shows falls between 0.40 and 0.70. Since we are concerned with no-shows *less than or equal to* 0.517 we choose the next lowest value, or 0.40. Following across the table, the Lucky Traveler should overbook by two rooms.

## SUMMARY

*Aggregate planning* does the following:

- Determines the resource capacity needed to meet demand
- Matches market demand to company resources
- Plans production 6 to 12 months in advance
- Expresses demand, resources, and capacity in general terms
- Develops a strategy for economically meeting demand
- Establishes a company-wide game plan for allocating resources

Aggregate planning is critical for companies with seasonal demand patterns and for services. Variations in demand can be met by *adjusting capacity* or *managing demand*. There are several mathematical techniques for aggregate planning, including linear programming, linear decision rule, search decision rule, and management coefficient model.

Production and capacity plans are developed at several levels of detail. The process of deriving more detailed production and capacity plans from the aggregate plan is called *disaggregation*. Collaborative planning sets production plans in concert with suppliers and trading partners. *Available-to-promise* often involves collaboration along a supply chain.

Aggregate planning for services is somewhat different from that for manufacturing because the variation in demand is usually more severe and occurs over shorter time frames. Fortunately, the constraining resource in most services is labor, which is quite flexible. Services use part-time workers, overtime, and undertime. *Yield management* is a special aggregate planning tool for industries with time-sensitive products and segmented customer classes.

## SUMMARY OF KEY TERMS

**aggregate planning** the process of determining the quantity and timing of production over an intermediate time frame.

**available-to-promise** the quantity of items that can be promised to the customer; the difference between planned production and customer orders already received.

**backlog** accumulated customer orders to be completed at a later date.

**backordering** ordering an item that is temporarily out-of-stock.

**capable-to-promise** the quantity of items that can be produced and made available at a later date.

**chase demand** an aggregate planning strategy that schedules production to match demand and absorbs variations in demand by adjusting the size of the workforce.

**collaborative planning** sharing information and synchronizing production plans across the supply chain.

**disaggregation** the process of breaking down the aggregate plan into more detailed plans.

**level production** an aggregate planning strategy that produces units at a constant rate and uses inventory to absorb variations in demand.

**linear decision rule (LDR)** a mathematical technique that solves a set of four quadratic equations to determine the optimal workforce size and production rate.

**lost sales** forfeited sales for out-of-stock items

**management coefficients model** an aggregate planning technique that uses regression analysis to improve the consistency of production planning decisions.

**mixed strategy** an aggregate planning strategy that varies two or more capacity factors to determine a feasible production plan.

**peak demand** staffing for high levels of customer service.

**pure strategy** an aggregate planning strategy that varies only one capacity factor in determining a feasible production plan.

**search decision rule (SDR)** a pattern search algorithm for aggregate planning.

**yield management** the process of determining the percentage of seats or rooms to be allocated to different fare classes.

## SOLVED PROBLEMS

**1.** Fabulous Fit Fibers produces a line of sweatclothes that exhibits a varying demand pattern. Given the following demand forecasts, production costs, and constraints, design a production plan for Fabulous Fit using the transportation method of LP. Also, calculate the cost of the production plan.

| Period | Demand |
|---|---|
| September | 100 |
| October | 130 |
| November | 200 |
| December | 300 |

| | |
|---|---|
| Maximum regular production | 100 units/month |
| Maximum overtime production | 50 units/month |
| Maximum subcontracting | 50 units/month |
| Regular production costs | $10/unit |
| Overtime production costs | $25/unit |
| Subcontracting costs | $35/unit |
| Inventory holding costs | $5/unit/month |
| Beginning inventory | 0 |

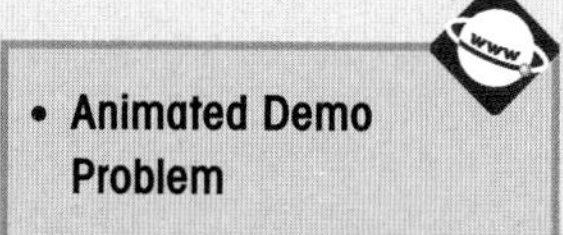


### SOLUTION

Period of Use (unit costs shown in brackets)

| Period of Production | | 1 | 2 | 3 | 4 | *Unused Capacity* | *Capacity* |
|---|---|---|---|---|---|---|---|
| | Beginning inventory | — [0] | — [5] | — [10] | — [15] | | 0 |
| 1 | Regular | 100 [10] | — [15] | — [20] | — [25] | | 100 |
| | Overtime | [25] | [30] | [35] | 50 [40] | | 50 |
| | Subcontract | [35] | [40] | [45] | [50] | 50 | 50 |
| 2 | Regular | | 100 [10] | — [15] | — [20] | | 100 |
| | Overtime | | 30 [25] | 20 [30] | — [35] | | 50 |
| | Subcontract | | [35] | [40] | 30 [45] | 20 | 50 |
| 3 | Regular | | | 100 [10] | — [15] | | 100 |
| | Overtime | | | 50 [25] | — [30] | | 50 |
| | Subcontract | | | 30 [35] | 20 [40] | | 50 |
| 4 | Regular | | | | 100 [10] | | 100 |
| | Overtime | | | | 50 [25] | | 50 |
| | Subcontract | | | | 50 [35] | | 50 |
| | *Demand* | 100 | 130 | 200 | 300 | | |

| Period | Demand | Regular Production | Overtime | Subcontract | Ending Inventory |
|---|---|---|---|---|---|
| Sept | 100 | 100 | 50 | 0 | 50 |
| Oct | 130 | 100 | 50 | 30 | 100 |
| Nov | 200 | 100 | 50 | 50 | 100 |
| Dec | 300 | 100 | 50 | 50 | 0 |
| Total | 730 | 400 | 200 | 130 | 250 |

(Production Plan)

$$\text{Cost} = (400 \times \$10) + (200 \times \$25) + (130 \times \$35) + (250 \times \$5)$$
$$= 4000 + 5000 + 4550 + 1250$$
$$= \$14{,}800$$

2. Calculate the available-to-promise for periods 1, 3, and 5.

| On Hand = 50 | 1 | 2 | 3 | 4 | 5 | 6 |
|---|---|---|---|---|---|---|
| Forecast | 100 | 100 | 100 | 100 | 100 | 100 |
| Customer orders | 90 | 120 | 130 | 70 | 20 | 10 |
| Master production schedule | 200 | | 200 | | 200 | |
| Available-to-promise | | | | | | |

(Period)

**SOLUTION**

| On Hand = 50 | 1 | 2 | 3 | 4 | 5 | 6 |
|---|---|---|---|---|---|---|
| Forecast | 100 | 100 | 100 | 100 | 100 | 100 |
| Customer orders | 90 | 120 | 130 | 70 | 20 | 10 |
| Master production schedule | 200 | | 200 | | 200 | |
| Available-to-promise | 40 | | 0 | | 170 | |

(Period)

ATP in period 1 = (50 + 200) − (90 + 120) = 40

ATP in period 3 = 200 − (130 + 70) = 0

ATP in period 5 = 200 − (20 + 10) = 170

3. Doughman Bakery bakes a variety of pastries, but none is more popular than its jumbo doughnuts. Doughnuts are made fresh every morning at 4:00 A.M. and sold throughout the day. Leftover doughnuts are put in a grab bag and sold at 75% discount the next day. Fresh doughnuts are sold for $1.20 each. The cost to make each doughnut is $0.45. The bakery has recorded first-day sales data for the last 200 days. Determine how many doughnuts Doughman Bakery should bake in the morning.

| Dozens of Doughnuts | Frequency |
|---|---|
| 2 | 14 |
| 3 | 18 |
| 4 | 26 |
| 5 | 32 |
| 6 | 30 |
| 7 | 26 |
| 8 | 20 |
| 9 | 18 |
| 10 | 12 |
| 11 | 2 |
| 12 | 2 |

**SOLUTION**

| Dozens of Doughnuts | Frequency | Probability | $P(N < X)$ | |
|---|---|---|---|---|
| 2 | 14 | 0.07 | 0.00 | |
| 3 | 18 | 0.09 | 0.07 | |
| 4 | 26 | 0.13 | 0.16 | |
| 5 | 32 | 0.16 | 0.29 | |
| 6 | 30 | 0.15 | 0.45 | |
| 7 | 26 | 0.13 | 0.60 | |
| 8 | 20 | 0.10 | 0.73 | |
| 9 | 18 | 0.09 | 0.83 | ← 0.833 |
| 10 | 12 | 0.06 | 0.92 | |
| 11 | 2 | 0.01 | 0.98 | |
| 12 | 2 | 0.01 | 0.99 | |
| Total | 200 | 1.00 | | |

$$C_u = \$1.20 - \$0.45 = \$0.75$$
$$C_o = \$0.45 - \$0.30 = \$0.15$$
$$P(N < X) \leq \frac{C_u}{C_u + C_o} = \frac{0.75}{0.75 + 0.15} = 0.833$$

Doughman should make 9 dozen doughnuts.

# QUESTIONS

**13-1.** What is the purpose of aggregate production planning? When is aggregate production planning most useful?

**13-2.** List several alternatives for adjusting capacity. List several alternatives for managing demand.

**13-3.** Describe the output of aggregate production planning.

**13-4.** How do linear programming, the linear decision rule, the search decision rule, and the management coefficients model differ in terms of cost functions and output?

**13-5.** Identify several industries that have highly variable demand patterns. Explore how they adjust capacity.

**13-6.** What options are available for altering the capacity of (a) an elementary school, (b) a prison, and (c) an airline?

**13-7.** Discuss the advantages and disadvantages of using part-time workers, subcontracting work, and building up inventory as strategies for meeting demand.

**13-8.** Describe the levels of production and capacity planning in the hierarchical planning process.

13-9. Explain the process of collaborative planning. How is available-to-promise involved?

13-10. Access a major vendor of business software, such as SAP or Oracle. Read about their demand management, available-to-promise, and production planning products. What kinds of capabilities do these systems have?

13-11. How is the aggregate planning process different when used for services rather than for manufacturing?

13-12. What does yield management entail? What types of businesses, besides hotels and airlines, would benefit from yield management? As a consumer, how do you view the practice?

## PROBLEMS

13-1. Bioway, Inc., a manufacturer of medical supplies, uses aggregate planning to set labor and inventory levels for the year. While a variety of items are produced, a standard kit composed of basic supplies is used for planning purposes. Demand varies with seasonal illnesses and the quarterly ordering policies of hospitals. The average worker at Bioway can produce 1000 kits a month at a cost of $9 per kit during regular production hours and $10 a kit during overtime production. Completed kits can also be purchased from outside suppliers at $12 each. Inventory carrying costs are $2 per kit per month. Overtime is limited to regular production, but subcontracting is unlimited. Due to high quality standards and extensive training, hiring and firing costs are $1500 per worker. Bioway currently employs 25 workers. Given the demand forecast below, develop a six-month aggregate production plan for Bioway using (a) a pure strategy, and (b) a mixed strategy.

| Month | Demand |
|---|---|
| April | 60,000 |
| May | 22,000 |
| June | 15,000 |
| July | 46,000 |
| August | 80,000 |
| September | 15,000 |

13-2. Paul's Produce ships fresh fruit from its Florida distribution center to households across the country. Demand varies significantly during the year with peaks in the fall and winter months when local fruits and vegetables are typically not available. The average demand for fruit is 1000 cases in the spring, 3500 cases during the summer months, 4500 cases in the fall, and 9250 cases in the winter. No inventory is held since fruit is highly perishable. Paul needs to know how many workers he should hire, how much overtime he should use, and how many units he should subcontract. He has gathered the following information to help in the analysis: Each worker can pack an average of 100 boxes per period at a cost of $0.50 per box under regular production. Overtime production costs $0.70 per box and is limited to regular production. Subcontracting is unlimited at $1.00 per box. The cost to hire or fire a worker is $50. Paul currently employs 10 workers.

a. Design a fulfillment plan for Paul and calculate the cost of the plan.
b. How would the plan change if hiring and firing costs increased to $300?

13-3. Rowley Apparel, manufacturer of the famous "Race-A-Rama" swimwear line, needs help planning production for next year. Demand for swimwear follows a seasonal pattern, as shown here. Given the following costs and demand forecasts, test these four strategies for meeting demand: (a) level production with overtime and subcontracting, as needed, (b) level production with backorders as needed, (c) chase demand, and (d) 3000 units regular production from April through September and as much regular, overtime, and subcontracting production in the other months as needed to meet annual demand. Determine the cost of each strategy. Which strategy would you recommend?

| Month | Demand Forecast |
|---|---|
| January | 1000 |
| February | 500 |
| March | 500 |
| April | 2000 |
| May | 3000 |
| June | 4000 |
| July | 5000 |
| August | 3000 |
| September | 1000 |
| October | 500 |
| November | 500 |
| December | 3000 |

| | |
|---|---|
| Beginning workforce | 8 workers |
| Subcontracting capacity | unlimited |
| Overtime capacity | 2000 units/month |
| Production rate per worker | 250 units/month |
| Regular wage rate | $15 per unit |
| Overtime wage rate | $25 per unit |
| Subcontracting cost | $30 per unit |
| Hiring cost | $100 per worker |
| Firing cost | $200 per worker |
| Holding cost | $0.50 per unit/month |
| Backordering cost | $10 per unit/month |

13-4. Mama's Stuffin' is a popular food item during the fall and winter months, but it is marginal in the spring and summer. Use the following demand forecasts and costs to determine which of the following production planning strategies is best for Mama's Stuffin':

a. Level production over the 12 months.
b. Produce to meet demand each month. Absorb variations in demand by changing the size of the workforce.

c. Keep the workforce at its current level. Supplement with overtime and subcontracting as necessary.

| Month | Demand Forecast |
|---|---|
| March | 2000 |
| April | 1000 |
| May | 1000 |
| June | 1000 |
| July | 1000 |
| August | 1500 |
| September | 2500 |
| October | 3000 |
| November | 9000 |
| December | 7000 |
| January | 4000 |
| February | 3000 |

| | |
|---|---|
| Overtime capacity per month | regular production |
| Subcontracting capacity per month | unlimited |
| Regular production cost | $30 per pallet |
| Overtime production cost | $40 per pallet |
| Subcontracting cost | $50 per pallet |
| Holding cost | $2 per pallet |
| Beginning workforce | 10 workers |
| Production rate | 200 pallets per worker per month |
| Hiring cost | $5000 per worker |
| Firing cost | $8000 per worker |

**13-5.** FansForYou is a small, privately owned company that manufactures fans. Large variations in demand due to seasonality have contributed to high costs for the company. FansForYou currently uses a level production strategy because it prefers not to hire and fire employees. However, if there is enough cost justification, the company will consider alternative production plans.

a. What is the cost of the current production plan?
b. How much would FansForYou save by using a chase demand strategy?
c. How much would FansForYou save by keeping a steady workforce of 20 workers and supplementing with overtime and subcontracting as needed?

| Month | Demand |
|---|---|
| Sep | 1500 |
| Oct | 1000 |
| Nov | 600 |
| Dec | 600 |
| Jan | 600 |
| Feb | 800 |
| Mar | 1000 |
| Apr | 1000 |
| May | 4000 |
| Jun | 6500 |
| Jul | 6000 |
| Aug | 4000 |

| | |
|---|---|
| Beginning inventory | 0 |
| Beginning workforce | 25 workers |
| Production rate | 100 fans per worker per month |
| Regular production cost | $40 per fan |
| Overtime production cost | $60 per fan |
| Subcontracting cost | $70 per fan |
| Overtime capacity | Not to exceed regular production |
| Subcontracting capacity | Unlimited |
| Holding cost | $8 per fan |
| Hiring cost | $2000 |
| Firing cost | $3000 |

**13-6.** Slopes & Sleds (S&S) makes skis, snowboards, and high-end sledding equipment. As shown below, the demand for its products is highly seasonal. The company employs 10 workers who can each produce 200 units of various equipment per month. The cost of regular production is $8 per unit, overtime $12, and subcontracting $16. Overtime is limited to regular production each period. Hiring and firing costs are $500 per worker. Inventory holding costs are $2 per unit per month. Given the estimates of demand below, create an aggregate production plan for Slopes & Sleds using:

a. the current workforce level (supplemented with overtime and subcontracting as needed),
b. chase demand.

| Month | Demand |
|---|---|
| Jan | 6400 |
| Feb | 7000 |
| Mar | 1500 |
| Apr | 500 |
| May | 600 |
| Jun | 1400 |
| July | 1600 |
| Aug | 2000 |
| Sept | 1400 |
| Oct | 1500 |
| Nov | 5200 |
| Dec | 6900 |

**13-7.** Sawyer Furniture is one of the few remaining domestic manufacturers of wood furniture. In the current competitive environment, cost containment is the key to its continued survival. Demand for furniture follows a seasonal demand pattern with increased sales in the summer and fall months, culminating with peak demand in November.

a. The cost of production is $16 per unit for regular production, $24 for overtime, and $33 for subcontracting. Hiring and firing costs are $500 per worker. Inventory holding costs are $20 per unit per month. There is no beginning inventory. Ten workers are currently employed. Each worker can produce 50 pieces of furniture per month. Overtime cannot exceed regular production. Given the following demand data, design an aggregate production plan for Sawyer Furniture that will meet demand at the lowest possible cost.

b. In an attempt to stem the flow of jobs overseas, the local labor union has negotiated a penalty clause for layoffs. The new contract increases the firing cost per worker to $2500. Create a revised aggregate plan with these new cost figures. Assuming any subcontracting is, in fact, foreign production, does the penalty work? Why or why not?

| Month | Demand |
|---|---|
| Jan | 500 |
| Feb | 500 |
| Mar | 1000 |
| Apr | 1200 |
| May | 2000 |
| Jun | 400 |
| July | 400 |
| Aug | 1000 |
| Sept | 1000 |
| Oct | 1500 |
| Nov | 7000 |
| Dec | 500 |

**13-8.** Midlife Shoes, Inc. is a manufacturer of sensible shoes for aging baby-boomers. The company is having great success, and although demand is seasonal, it is expected to increase steadily over the next few years. The company is purchasing a new facility to accommodate the increase in demand, but the facility will not open until 13 months from now. The current facility can only accommodate 15 workers. Hiring and firing costs are negligible. Using the information below, help Midlife manage this transition year by deriving a production plan that will meet demand at the lowest cost.

| Month | Demand |
|---|---|
| Jan | 1000 |
| Feb | 1200 |
| Mar | 1200 |
| Apr | 3000 |
| May | 3000 |
| Jun | 3000 |
| Jul | 2200 |
| Aug | 2200 |
| Sep | 4000 |
| Oct | 4000 |
| Nov | 2200 |
| Dec | 3000 |

| | |
|---|---|
| Beginning inventory | 0 units |
| Beginning workforce | 8 workers |
| Production rate | 100 units per worker per month |
| Regular capacity | Maximum of 15 workers |
| Overtime capacity | Half of regular production |
| Subcontracting capacity | 1000 units |
| Regular production cost | $36 per unit |
| Overtime production cost | $54 per unit |
| Subcontracting cost | $70 per unit |
| Inventory holding cost | $10 per unit |

**13-9.** Design a production plan for Rowley Apparel in Problem 13-3 using linear programming and Excel Solver.

**13-10.** Design a production plan for Mama's Stuffin' in Problem 13-4 using linear programming and Excel Solver.

**13-11.** Design a production plan for FansForYou in Problem 13-5 using linear programming and Excel Solver.

**13-12.** Design a production plan for Slopes and Sleds in Problem 13-6 using linear programming and Excel Solver.

**13-13.** The global sourcing department of Slopes and Sleds (see Problems 13-6 and 13-12) has located a company in China that can make S&S products for $9 a unit. Revise the production plan using Solver. How much money can be saved by outsourcing to China? What other factors should be considered in the outsourcing decision?

**13-14.** The Wetski Water Ski Company is the world's largest producer of water skis. As you might suspect, water skis exhibit a highly seasonal demand pattern, with peaks during the summer months and valleys during the winter months. Given the following costs and quarterly sales forecasts, use the transportation method to design a production plan that will economically meet demand. What is the cost of the plan?

| Quarter | Sales Forecast |
|---|---|
| 1 | 50,000 |
| 2 | 150,000 |
| 3 | 200,000 |
| 4 | 52,000 |

| | |
|---|---|
| Inventory carrying cost | $3.00 per pair of skis per quarter |
| Production per employee | 1000 pairs of skis per quarter |
| Regular workforce | 50 workers |
| Overtime capacity | 50,000 pairs of skis |
| Subcontracting capacity | 40,000 pairs of skis |
| Cost of regular production | $50 per pair of skis |
| Cost of overtime production | $75 per pair of skis |
| Cost of subcontracting | $85 per pair of skis |

**13-15.** College Press publishes textbooks for the college market. The demand for college textbooks is high during the beginning of each semester and then tapers off during the semester. The unavailability of books can cause a professor to switch adoptions, but the cost of storing books and their rapid obsolescence must also be considered. Given the demand and cost factors shown here, use the transportation method to design an aggregate production plan for College Press that will economically meet demand. What is the cost of the production plan?

| Months | Demand Forecast |
|---|---|
| February–April | 5,000 |
| May–July | 10,000 |
| August–October | 30,000 |
| November–January | 25,000 |

| | |
|---|---|
| Regular capacity per quarter | 10,000 books |
| Overtime capacity per quarter | 5,000 books |
| Subcontracting capacity per qtr | 10,000 books |
| Regular production rate | $20 per book |
| Overtime wage rate | $30 per book |
| Subcontracting cost | $35 per book |
| Holding cost | $2.00 per book |

**13-16.** Bits and Pieces uses overtime, inventory, and subcontracting to absorb fluctuations in demand. An annual production plan is devised and updated quarterly. Expected demand over the next four quarters is 600, 800, 1600, and 1900 units, respectively. The capacity for regular production is 1000 units per quarter with an overtime capacity of 100 units a quarter. Subcontracting is limited to 500 units a quarter. Regular production costs $20 per unit, overtime $25 per unit, and subcontracting $30 per unit. Inventory holding costs are assessed at $3 per unit per period. There is no beginning inventory. Design a production plan that will satisfy demand at minimum cost.

**13-17.** GF Incorporated, a manufacturer of power systems, uses overtime, inventory, and subcontracting to absorb fluctuations in demand. An annual production plan is devised and updated quarterly. The expected demand and available capacities for the next four quarters are as follows:

| Period | Demand | Regular Capacity | Overtime Capacity | Subcontracting Capacity |
|---|---|---|---|---|
| 1 | 2000 | 1000 | 1000 | 5000 |
| 2 | 4500 | 1000 | 1000 | 5000 |
| 3 | 7500 | 1000 | 1000 | 5000 |
| 4 | 3000 | 1000 | 1000 | 5000 |

Relevant cost data are as follows:

| | |
|---|---|
| Regular production cost per unit | $20 |
| Overtime production cost per unit | $25 |
| Subcontracting cost per unit | $30 |
| Inventory holding cost per unit per period | $3 |
| Beginning inventory | 0 |

Design a production plan that will satisfy demand at minimum cost.

**13-18.** Fashion Apparel Direct (FAD) outsources production of its line of women's wear to three major suppliers. The aggregate planning process at FAD consists of purchasing capacity at each supplier and submitting specific orders during the year to utilize the capacity. Costs and available capacity differ by supplier and time of year. Garments may be produced in advance of need, but their value decreases by 25% each month. (*Hint*: consider the decrease a holding cost.) Demand for September through December is 3500, 2000, 2500, and 5000 units, respectively. Use the demand and cost information given below to design an aggregate plan for FAD.

| | Supplier 1 | | Supplier 2 | | Supplier 3 | |
|---|---|---|---|---|---|---|
| **Month** | *Capacity* | *Cost* | *Capacity* | *Cost* | *Capacity* | *Cost* |
| September | 1000 | $12 | 2000 | $20 | 1500 | $12 |
| October | 1000 | $16 | 500 | $20 | 2000 | $12 |
| November | 1000 | $28 | 500 | $20 | 2500 | $20 |
| December | 1000 | $28 | 500 | $20 | 3000 | $28 |

**13-19.** How many units are available-to-promise in period 1? period 4?

| | Period | | | | | |
|---|---|---|---|---|---|---|
| **On hand = 60** | 1 | 2 | 3 | 4 | 5 | 6 |
| Forecast | 50 | 100 | 100 | 100 | 100 | 50 |
| Customer Orders | 85 | 125 | 95 | 85 | 45 | 15 |
| Master Production Schedule | 250 | | | 250 | | |
| Available to Promise | | | | | | |

**13-20.** Complete the available-to-promise table below.

| | Period | | | | | |
|---|---|---|---|---|---|---|
| **On hand = 10** | 1 | 2 | 3 | 4 | 5 | 6 |
| Forecast | 50 | 50 | 50 | 50 | 50 | 50 |
| Customer Orders | 56 | 17 | 75 | 50 | 16 | 14 |
| Master Production Schedule | 100 | | 100 | | 100 | |
| Available to Promise | | | | | | |

**13-21.** Complete the available-to-promise table below.

| | Period | | | | | |
|---|---|---|---|---|---|---|
| **On hand = 30** | 1 | 2 | 3 | 4 | 5 | 6 |
| Forecast | 100 | 50 | 100 | 50 | 100 | 50 |
| Customer Orders | 75 | 50 | 116 | 73 | 45 | 23 |
| Master Production Schedule | 100 | 50 | 100 | 50 | 100 | 50 |
| Available-to-Promise | | | | | | |

**13-22.** Calculate the available-to-promise row in the following matrix.

| | Period | | | | | |
|---|---|---|---|---|---|---|
| **On Hand = 10** | 1 | 2 | 3 | 4 | 5 | 6 |
| Forecast | 50 | 100 | 50 | 100 | 50 | 100 |
| Customer Orders | 50 | 125 | 75 | 175 | 45 | 15 |
| Master Production Schedule | 200 | | | 200 | | |
| Available-to-Promise | | | | | | |

**13-23.** How many B's are available-to-promise in week 2? How soon could you fill an order for 250 B's?

| | Period | | | | | |
|---|---|---|---|---|---|---|
| **B's on hand = 10** | 1 | 2 | 3 | 4 | 5 | 6 |
| Forecast | 100 | 100 | 100 | 100 | 100 | 100 |
| Customer orders | 25 | 50 | 137 | 72 | 23 | 5 |
| Master production schedule | 100 | 100 | 100 | 100 | 100 | 100 |
| Available-to-promise | | | | | | |

**13-24.** Managers at the Dew Drop Inn are concerned about the increasing number of guests who make reservations but fail to show up. They have decided to institute a policy of overbooking like larger hotel chains. The profit from a paying guest averages $50 per room per night. The cost of putting up a guest at another hotel is $100 per room per night. Records show the following number of no-shows over the past three months:

| No-Shows | Frequency |
|---|---|
| 0 | 18 |
| 1 | 36 |
| 2 | 27 |
| 3 | 9 |

How many rooms should Dew Drop overbook?

**13-25.** Atlanta Airlines routinely overbooks its flight from Atlanta to Boston. Overbooking discounted seats can be expensive because providing a bumped passenger with a last-minute flight on a competing carrier can cost $450. A 120-passenger jet costs about $6000 to operate from Atlanta to Boston. The average ticket price is $300.

a. Given the frequency of no-shows in the following table, how many seats should be overbooked?
b. Atlanta Air offers special rates on its Atlanta/Boston route for the holidays. How would a $200 ticket price affect the number of seats overbooked?

| No. of No-Shows | Frequency |
|---|---|
| 1 | 15 |
| 2 | 10 |
| 3 | 10 |
| 4 | 5 |
| 5 | 3 |
| 6 | 5 |

**13-26.** The Blue Roof Inn overbooks two rooms a night. Room rates run $100 a night but cost only $30 to maintain. Bumped customers are sent to a nearby hotel for $80 a night. What is the cost of overbooking? What is the cost of underbooking? Given the following distribution of no-shows, should Blue Roof continue its current policy?

| No-Shows | Probability |
|---|---|
| 0 | 0.30 |
| 1 | 0.20 |
| 2 | 0.10 |
| 3 | 0.30 |
| 4 | 0.10 |

**13-27.** FlyUs Airlines is unhappy with the number of empty seats on its New York to Philadelphia flight. To remedy the problem, the airline is offering a special discounted rate of $89 instead of the normal $169, but only for 7-day advance purchases and for a limited number of seats per flight. The aircraft flown from NY to Philly holds 100 passengers. Last month's distribution of full-fare passengers is shown below. How many seats should FlyUs reserve for full-fare passengers?

| Full-Fare | Frequency |
|---|---|
| 50 | 15 |
| 55 | 20 |
| 60 | 35 |
| 65 | 20 |
| 70 | 10 |

**13-28.** NorthStar Airlines runs daily commuter flights from Washington, D.C., to Chicago. The planes hold 60 passengers and cater to the business traveler with comparable business rates. The recent economic downturn has reduced the occupancy rate of flights to such an extent that NorthStar would like to offer a set number of seats at discount rates to gain more passengers. The board of directors is worried that discounted seats will cut into profit margins and will upset the regular business traveler. The ticket price for a business traveler is $350. Discounted tickets would sell for $120. Assuming that empty seats can be sold if discounted, use the following data gathered from 100 flights to determine how many seats should be discounted.

| No. of Full-Fare Passengers | Frequency |
|---|---|
| 10 | 15 |
| 20 | 25 |
| 30 | 25 |
| 40 | 20 |
| 50 | 10 |
| 60 | 5 |

**13-29.** The Forestry Club sells Christmas trees each year to raise money for club activities. The trees cost $10 to cut and are sold for $25. Unused trees are stripped of their limbs and sold as firewood for $1 apiece. Data on past sales appear below. How many trees should the forestry club cut this year?

| No. of Trees Sold | Frequency |
|---|---|
| 10 | 6 |
| 15 | 3 |
| 20 | 6 |
| 25 | 3 |
| 30 | 2 |

**13-30.** Pizza Pie runs the pizza concessions at the University basketball games. Personal size pizzas are assembled two hours prior to the game and cooked throughout the night in a mobile oven outside of the coliseum. Pizza sells for $5 and costs approximately $2 to make. Unsold pizzas at the end of the game are given to nearby dormitory students for a nominal $1 per pizza. Having sold out of pizza during the past two games, Pizza Pie is reevaluating its planning policy. Use the past demand data given below to determine how many pizzas should be made for each game.

| No. of Pizzas Sold | Frequency |
|---|---|
| 25 | 15 |
| 50 | 15 |
| 75 | 30 |
| 100 | 20 |
| 125 | 10 |
| 150 | 10 |

## CASE PROBLEM 13.1

### *Have a Seat, Bloke*

Blokie State's football program has risen to the ranks of the elite with postseason bowl games in each of the past 10 years, including a national championship game. The Blokes (as the fans are called) fill the stadium each game. Season tickets are increasingly difficult to find. In response to the outstanding fan support, Blokie State has decided to use its bowl revenues to expand the stadium to 75,000 seats.

The administration is confident that all 75,000 seats can be sold at the normal price of $40 per game ticket; however, Frank Pinto's job, as athletic director, is to get as much revenue out of the stadium expansion as possible. In addition to stadium boxes for the truly endowed, Frank would like to take this opportunity to repurpose existing seats. A certain number of seats (yet to be determined) would be set aside for premium ticket holders who would pay $200 per ticket for the privilege of 50-yard line seats with chair backs and access to indoor concessions. The question is, how many fans would be willing to pay such a premium? If too many seats are designated in the premium sections, they could remain vacant. Too few premium seats would lose potential revenue for the program.

Frank has decided that if the plan has any chance of success, unsold premium seats should be sold at reduced rates. It would be better to donate them to local charities instead. Gathering data from his cohorts at peer institutions, Frank has put together the following probability distribution of premium ticket holders. The data begin with 1000 tickets since Frank already has requests for 999 tickets from alumni donors. He is asking for your help in performing the analysis.

| NO. OF PREMIUM TICKETS | PROBABILITY |
|---|---|
| 1,000 | 0.10 |
| 5,000 | 0.30 |
| 10,000 | 0.24 |
| 15,000 | 0.15 |
| 20,000 | 0.10 |
| 25,000 | 0.06 |
| 30,000 | 0.05 |

**a.** Using yield management, determine how many seats should be reserved for premium ticket holders.

**b.** Considering your answer to part (a) and the possible outcomes listed above, how much total revenue (i.e., regular and premium) can be expected from ticket sales?

**c.** The administration is unsure about Frank's plan. The VP of Finance thinks an expected value of the number of premium seats would produce better results. How would the number of premium seats change using expected value? Considering the possible outcomes, which approach yields the most potential revenue?

## CASE PROBLEM 13.2

### *Erin's Energy Plan*

The discussion was getting heated. A brightly colored chart at the front of the room told the story all too well. At Waylan Industries sales were up, profits down.

"Larry, there's no way we can hit our profit objective with your high cost of production. You've got to cut back."

"Why pick on me? We're running bare bones as it is. Last winter's energy prices really killed us. How can you cut costs with a 250% increase in energy prices?"

Everyone stared at Erin. Erin swallowed hard and spoke up. "You know, we've never had to stockpile fuel before and I'm not sure how far we can go in managing demand, but I've been collecting data on purchase options. . . ."

"Well, let's see it then."

"Although it's not how we purchase energy, I've converted the prices to millions of BTUs for comparison. Coal costs $8 per million BTUs, but we can only burn 500 million per quarter to stay within our environmental air standards. Natural gas costs $32 per million BTUs, and petroleum $46. We can burn 1000 million BTUs of each per quarter. Coal and natural gas can be stored for later use at a holding cost of 30 percent of purchase price per quarter. The holding cost for petroleum is 20 percent. Electricity cannot be stored, but it can be reserved in advance. The cost of electricity also varies considerably by season of the year, as do our energy needs. The cost of electricity from the local utility is $20 per million BTUs in the spring, $40 in the summer, $24 in the fall, and $70 in the winter. These are averages from last year. A nearby utility quotes slightly higher prices at $22, $44, $26, and $75 for spring, summer, fall, and winter. As far as availability is concerned, 4000 million BTUs of electricity are available in the spring and fall, 5000 in the summer and winter. We can save some money by contracting with the utilities in advance of the season. I've summarized the options in the table here, along with our energy needs. What I need now is some help analyzing the data. Larry, could you . . ."

Before Erin could finish, Tom spoke up. "Yes, Larry—you and Erin work up an energy plan—like those aggregate production plans you're always bringing in. And have it ready by Thursday."

*Source:* This case was developed with the help of Richard Hirsh, Professor of Science and Technology at Virginia Tech.

| | USED IN | | | | | | | |
|---|---|---|---|---|---|---|---|---|
| | *Spring* | | *Summer* | | *Fall* | | *Winter* | |
| **PURCHASED IN** | *Utility A* | *Utility B* | *Utility A* | *Utility B* | *Utility A* | *Utility B* | *Utility A* | *Utility B* |
| Spring | $20 | $22 | $40 | $44 | $20 | $22 | $45 | $50 |
| Summer | | | $40 | $44 | $22 | $24 | $50 | $60 |
| Fall | | | | | $24 | $26 | $60 | $65 |
| Winter | | | | | | | $70 | $75 |
| Demand | 1500 | | 5000 | | 5000 | | 10,000 | |

Use Erin's data to develop an aggregate energy plan for Waylan Industries.

## REFERENCES

Bowman, E. H. "Production Planning by the Transportation Method of Linear Programming." *Journal of Operations Research Society* (February 1956), pp. 100–103.

Bowman, E. H. "Consistency and Optimality in Managerial Decision Making." *Management Science* (January 1963), pp. 310–321.

Buffa, E. S., and J. G. Miller. *Production-Inventory Systems: Planning and Control*, 3rd ed. Homewood, IL: Irwin, 1979.

Correll, J., and N. Edson. *Gaining Control*. New York: Wiley, 1998.

Haksever, C., B. Render, and R. Russell and R. Murdick. *Service Operations and Management*. Upper Saddle River, NJ: Prentice Hall, 2000.

Holt, C., F. Modigliani, J. Muth, and H. Simon. *Planning Production, Inventories and Work Force*. Englewood Cliffs, NJ: Prentice Hall, 1960.

Palmatier, G. E. and C. Crum. *Enterprise Sales and Operations Planning*. Boca Raton: J. Ross Publishers, 2003.

SAP AG. "Global Available to Promise." December 1999. SAP AG 2000, APO ATP 3.0. http://www.sap.com/solutions/scm/apo/pdf/atp.pdf.

Taubert, W. "A Search Decision Rule for the Aggregate Scheduling Problem." *Management Science* (February 1968), pp. B343–359.

Tersine, R. *Production/Operations Management: Concepts, Structure, and Analysis*. New York: Elsevier-North Holland, 1985.

Vollmann, T., W. Berry, and D. C. Whybark. *Manufacturing Planning and Control Systems*, 4th ed. Homewood, IL: Irwin, 1997.

Wallace, T. *Sales and Operations Planning—The How-to Handbook*. Columbus, OH: T. F. Wallace & Co., 2000.

# Operational Decision-Making Tools: Linear Programming SUPPLEMENT 13

## CHAPTER OUTLINE

In this supplement, you will learn about . . .

- Model Formulation
- Graphical Solution Method
- Linear Programming Model Solution
- Solving Linear Programming Problems with Excel
- Sensitivity Analysis

**Linear programming:** a model consisting of linear relationships representing a firm's objective and resource constraints.

One of the quantitative techniques used in Chapter 13 for aggregate production planning and in Chapter 16 for scheduling is linear programming. Linear programming is one of the most widely used and powerful quantitative tools in operations management. It can be applied to a wide variety of different operational problems. Some of the more popular model types and their specific OM applications are described in Table S13.1.

**Linear programming** is a mathematical modeling technique used to determine a level of operational activity in order to achieve an objective, subject to restrictions called constraints. Many decisions faced by an operations manager are centered around the best way to achieve the objectives of the firm subject to the constraints of the operating environ-

Table S13.1
**Types of Linear Programming Models and Applications**

| Linear Programming Model Type | OM Application |
|---|---|
| Aggregate Production Planning | Determines the resource capacity needed to meet demand over an immediate time horizon, including units produced, workers hired and fired and inventory. (See Chapter 13.) |
| Product Mix | Mix of different products to produce that will maximize profit or minimize cost given resource constraints such as material, labor, budget, etc. |
| Transportation | Logistical flow of items (goods or services) from sources to destinations, for example, truckloads of goods from plants to warehouses. (See Supplement 10.) |
| Transshipment | Flow of items from sources to destinations with intermediate points, for example, shipping from plant to distribution center and then to stores. (See Supplement 10.) |
| Assignment | Assigns work to limited resources, called "Loading," for example, assigning jobs or workers to different machines. (See Chapter 16.) |
| Multiperiod Scheduling | Schedules regular and overtime production, plus inventory to carry over, to meet demand in future periods. |
| Blend | Determines "recipe" requirements, for example, how to blend different petroleum components to produce different grades of gasoline and other petroleum products. |
| Diet | Menu of food items that meets nutritional or other requirements, for example, hospital or school cafeteria menus. |
| Investment/Capital Budgeting | Financial model that determines amount to invest in different alternatives given return objectives and constraints for risk, diversity, etc., for example, how much to invest in new plant, facilities or equipment. |
| Data Envelopment Analysis (DEA) | Compares service units of the same type—banks, hospitals, schools—based on their resources and outputs to see which units are less productive or inefficient. |
| Shortest Route | Shortest routes from sources to destinations, for example, the shortest highway truck route from coast to coast. |
| Maximal Flow | Maximizes the amount of flow from sources to destinations, for example, the flow of work-in process through an assembly operation. |
| Trim-Loss | Determines patterns to cut sheet items to minimize waste, for example, cutting lumber, film, cloth, glass, etc. |
| Facility Location | Selects facility locations based on constraints such as fixed, operating, and shipping costs, production capacity, etc. |
| Set Covering | Selection of facilities that can service a set of other facilities, for example, the selection of distribution hubs that will be able to deliver packages to a set of cities. |

ment. These constraints can be limited resources, such as time, labor, energy, materials, or money, or they can be restrictive guidelines, such as a recipe for making cereal, engineering specifications, or a blend for gasoline. The most frequent objective of business firms is to *maximize profit*—whereas the objective of individual operational units within a firm (such as a production or packaging department) is often to *minimize cost.*

A common linear programming problem is to determine the number of units to produce to maximize profit subject to resource constraints such as labor and materials. All these components of the decision situation—the decisions, objectives, and constraints—are expressed as mathematically linear relationships that together form a model.

## MODEL FORMULATION

A linear programming model consists of decision variables, an objective function, and model constraints. **Decision variables** are mathematical symbols that represent levels of activity of an operation. For example, an electrical manufacturing firm wants to produce radios, toasters, and clocks. The number of each item to produce is represented by symbols, $x_1$, $x_2$, and $x_3$. Thus, $x_1$ = the number of radios, $x_2$ = the number of toasters, and $x_3$ = the number of clocks. The final values of $x_1$, $x_2$, and $x_3$, as determined by the firm, constitute a *decision* (e.g., $x_1 = 10$ radios is a decision by the firm to produce 10 radios).

**Decision variables:** mathematical symbols representing levels of activity of an operation.

The **objective function** is a linear mathematical relationship that describes the objective of an operation in terms of the decision variables. The objective function always either *maximizes* or *minimizes* some value (e.g., maximizing the profit or minimizing the cost of producing radios). For example, if the profit from a radio is \$6, the profit from a toaster is \$4, and the profit from a clock is \$2, then the total profit, Z, is $Z = \$6x_1 + 4x_2 + 2x_3$.

**Objective function:** a linear relationship reflecting the objective of an operation.

The model **constraints** are also linear relationships of the decision variables; they represent the restrictions placed on the decision situation by the operating environment. The restrictions can be in the form of limited resources or restrictive guidelines. For example, if it requires 2 hours of labor to produce a radio, 1 hour to produce a toaster, and 1.5 hours to produce a clock, and only 40 hours of labor are available, the constraint reflecting this is $2x_1 + 1x_2 + 1.5x_3 \le 40$.

**Constraint:** a linear relationship representing a restriction on decision making.

The general structure of a linear programming model is as follows:

$$\text{Maximize (or minimize) } Z = c_1x_1 + c_2x_2 + \cdots + c_nx_n$$

subject to

$$\begin{aligned} a_{11}x_1 + a_{12}x_2 + \cdots + a_{1n}x_n &(\le, =, \ge) b_1 \\ a_{21}x_1 + a_{22}x_2 + \cdots + a_{2n}x_n &(\le, =, \ge) b_2 \\ &\vdots \\ a_{n1}x_1 + a_{n2}x_2 + \cdots + a_{nn}x_n &(\le, =, \ge) b_n \\ x_i &\ge 0 \end{aligned}$$

where

$x_i$ = decision variables
$b_i$ = constraint levels
$c_j$ = objective function coefficients
$a_{ij}$ = constraint coefficients

**Example S13.1**

**Linear Programming Model Formulation**

The Highlands Craft Store is a small craft operation that employs local artisans to produce clay bowls and mugs based on designs and colors from the 1700s and 1800s. The two primary resources used by the company are special pottery clay and skilled labor. Given these limited resources, the company wants to know how many bowls and mugs to produce each day to maximize profit.

The two products have the following resource requirements for production and selling price per item produced (i.e., the model parameters):

| | Resource Requirements | | |
|---|---|---|---|
| **Product** | *Labor (hr/unit)* | *Clay (lb/unit)* | *Revenue ($/unit)* |
| Bowl | 1 | 4 | 40 |
| Mug | 2 | 3 | 50 |

There are 40 hours of labor and 120 pounds of clay available each day. Formulate this problem as a linear programming model.

*Solution*

Management's decision is how many bowls and mugs to produce represented by the following decision variables.

$$x_1 = \text{number of bowls to produce}$$
$$x_2 = \text{number of mugs to produce}$$

The objective of the company is to maximize total revenue computed as the sum of the individual profits gained from each bowl and mug:

$$\text{Maximize } Z = \$40x_1 + 50x_2$$

The model contains the constraints for labor and clay, which are

$$x_1 + 2x_2 \leq 40 \text{ hr}$$
$$4x_1 + 3x_2 \leq 120 \text{ lb}$$

The less than or equal to inequality ($\leq$) is used instead of an equality ($=$) because 40 hours of labor is a maximum that *can be used*, not an amount that *must be used*. However, constraints can be equalities ($=$), greater than or equal to inequalities ($\geq$), or less than or equal to inequalities ($\leq$).

The complete linear programming model for this problem can now be summarized as follows:

$$\text{Maximize } Z = \$40x_1 + \$50x_2$$

subject to

$$1x_1 + 2x_2 \leq 40$$
$$4x_1 + 3x_2 \leq 120$$
$$x_1, x_2 \geq 0$$

The solution of this model will result in numerical values for $x_1$ and $x_2$ that maximize total profit, Z, without violating the constraints. The solution that achieves this objective is $x_1 = 24$ bowls and $x_2 = 8$ mugs, with a corresponding revenue of $1360. We will discuss how we determined these values next.

## GRAPHICAL SOLUTION METHOD

**A picture of how a solution is obtained for a linear programming model**

The linear programming model in the previous section has characteristics common to all linear programming models. The mathematical relationships are additive; the model parameters are assumed to be known with certainty; the variable values are continuous (not restricted to integers); and the relationships are linear. Because of linearity, models with two decision variables (corresponding to two dimensions) can be solved graphically. Although graphical solution is cumbersome, it is useful in that it provides a picture of how a solution is derived.

The basic steps in the **graphical solution method** are to plot the model constraints on a set of coordinates in a plane and identify the area on the graph that satisfies all the constraints simultaneously. The point on the boundary of this space that maximizes (or minimizes) the objective function is the solution. The following example illustrates these steps.

**Graphical solution method:** a method for solving a linear programming problem using a graph.

Example S13.2

**Graphical Solution**

Determine the solution for Highlands Craft Store in Example S13.1:

$$\text{Maximize } Z = \$40x_1 + \$50x_2$$

subject to

$$x_1 + 2x_2 \leq 40$$
$$4x_1 + 3x_2 \leq 120$$
$$x_1, x_2 \geq 0$$

*Solution*

The graph of the model constraints is shown in the following figure of the feasible solution space. The graph is produced in the positive quadrant since both decision variables must be positive or zero; that is, $x_1, x_2 \geq 0$:

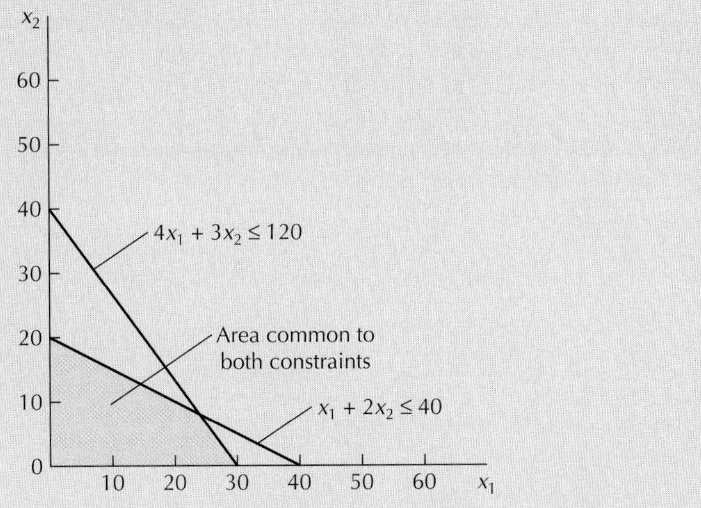


The first step is to plot the constraints on the graph. This is done by treating both constraints as equations (or straight lines) and plotting each line on the graph. A simple way to plot a line is to determine where it intersects the horizontal and vertical axes and draw a straight line connecting the points. The shaded area in the preceding figure is the area that is common to both model constraints. Therefore, this is the only area on the graph that contains points (i.e., values for $x_1$ and $x_2$) that will satisfy both constraints simultaneously. This area is the **feasible solution space**, because it is the only area that contains values for the variables that are feasible, or do not violate the constraints.

**Feasible solution space:** an area that satisfies all constraints in a linear programming model simultaneously.

The second step in the graphical solution method is to locate the point in the feasible solution area that represents the greatest total revenue. We will plot the objective function line for an *arbitrarily* selected level of revenue. For example, if revenue, Z, is \$800, the objective function is

$$\$800 = 40x_1 + 50x_2$$

Plotting this line just as we plotted the constraint lines results in the graph showing the determination of the optimal point in the following figure. Every point on this line is in the feasible solution area and will result in a revenue of \$800 (i.e., every combination of $x_1$ and $x_2$ on this line will give a $Z$ value of \$800). As the value of $Z$ increases, the objective function line moves out through the feasible solution space away from the origin until it reaches the last feasible point on the boundary of the solution space and then leaves the solution space.

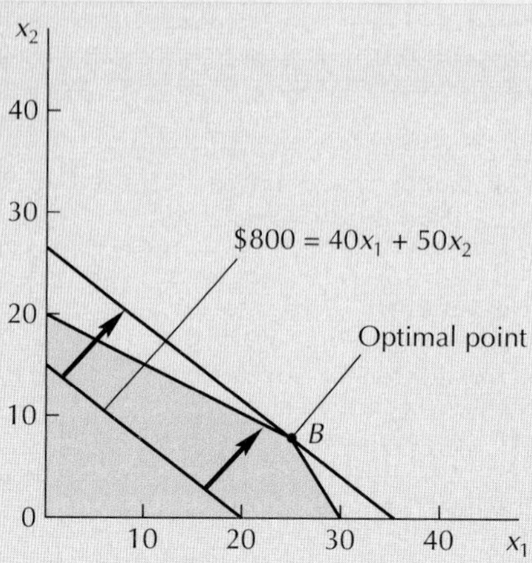


The solution point is always on this boundary, because the boundary contains the points farthest from the origin (i.e., the points corresponding to the greatest profit). Moreover, the solution point will not only be on the boundary of the feasible solution area, but it will be at one of the *corners* of the boundary where two constraint lines intersect. These corners (labeled *A*, *B*, and *C* in the following figure) are protrusions called **extreme points**. It has been proven mathematically that the optimal solution in a linear programming model will always occur at an extreme point. Therefore, in our example problem, the possible solution points are limited to the three extreme points *A*, *B*, and *C*. The **optimal**, or "one best," **solution** point is *B*, since the objective function touches it last before it leaves the feasible solution area.

**Extreme points:** corner points on the boundary of the feasible solution space.

**Optimal solution:** the single best solution to a problem.

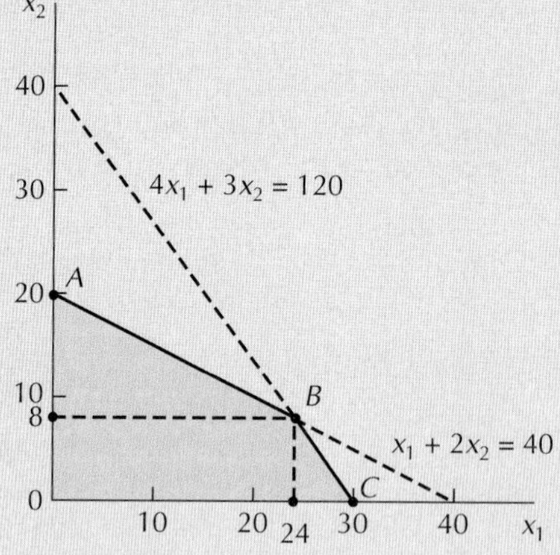


Because point *B* is formed by the intersection of two constraint lines, these two lines are *equal* at point *B*. Thus, the values of $x_1$ and $x_2$ at that intersection can be found by solving the two equations *simultaneously*:

$$\begin{aligned} x_1 + 2x_2 &= 40 \\ 4x_1 + 3x_2 &= 120 \\ \hline 4x_1 + 8x_2 &= 160 \\ -4x_1 - 3x_2 &= -120 \\ \hline 5x_2 &= 40 \\ x_2 &= 8 \end{aligned}$$

Thus,

$$x_1 + 2(8) = 40$$
$$x_1 = 24$$

The optimal solution at point *B* in the preceding figure is $x_1 = 24$ bowls and $x_2 = 8$ mugs. Substituting these values into the objective function gives the maximum revenue,

$$Z = \$40(24) + \$50(8)$$
$$= \$1360$$

Given that the optimal solution will be at one of the extreme corner points *A*, *B*, or *C*, you can find the solution by testing each of the three points to see which results in the greatest revenue rather than by graphing the objective function and seeing which point it last touches as it moves out of the feasible solution area. The following figure shows the solution values for all three points *A*, *B*, and *C* and the amount of revenue, *Z*, at each point:

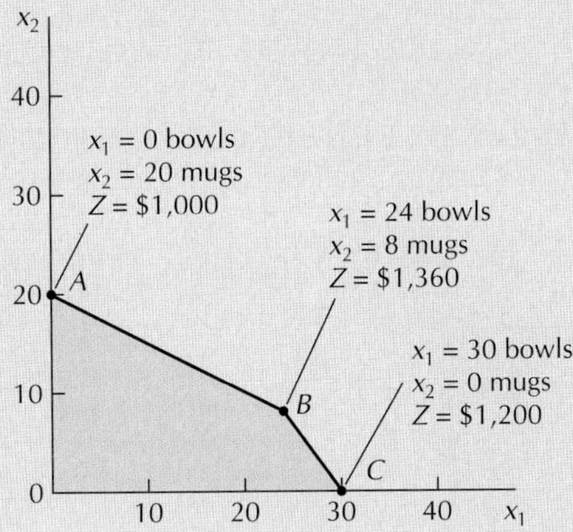


The objective function determines which extreme point is optimal, because the objective function designates the revenue that will accrue from each combination of $x_1$ and $x_2$ values at the extreme points. If the objective function had had different coefficients (i.e., different $x_1$ and $x_2$ profit values), one of the extreme points other than *B* might have been optimal.

Assume for a moment that the revenue for a bowl is \$70 instead of \$40 and the revenue for a mug is \$20 instead of \$50. These values result in a new objective function, $Z = \$70x_1 + 20x_2$. If the model constraints for labor or clay are not changed, the feasible solution area remains the same, as shown in the following figure. However, the location of the objective function in this figure is different from that of the original objective function in the previous figure because the new profit coefficients give the linear objective function a new *slope*. Point *C* becomes optimal, with $Z = \$2100$. This demonstrates one of the useful functions of linear programming—and model analysis in general—called *sensitivity analysis*: the testing of changes in the model parameters reflecting different operating environments to analyze the impact on the solution.

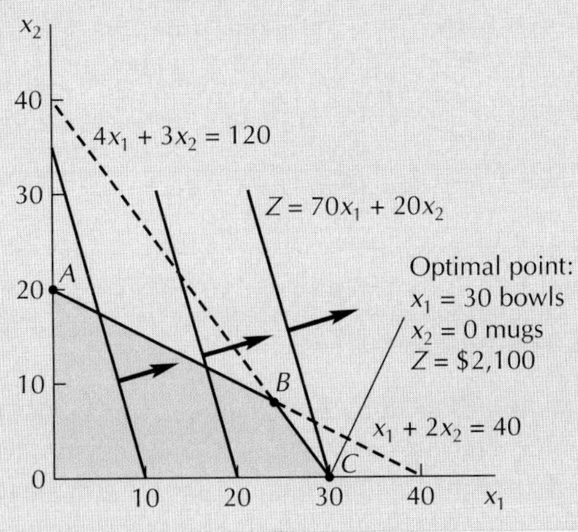

**Example S13.3**

**A Minimization Linear Programming Model**

The Farmer's Hardware and Feed Store is preparing a fertilizer mix for a farmer who is preparing a field to plant a crop. The store will use two brands of fertilizer, Gro-Plus and Crop-Fast, to make the proper mix for the farmer. Each brand yields a specific amount of nitrogen and phosphate, as follows:

| | **Chemical Contribution** | |
|---|---|---|
| **Brand** | *Nitrogen (lb/bag)* | *Phosphate (lb/bag)* |
| Gro-Plus | 2 | 4 |
| Crop-Fast | 4 | 3 |

The farmer's field requires at least 16 pounds of nitrogen and 24 pounds of phosphate. Gro-Plus costs \$6 per bag, and Crop-Fast costs \$3. The store wants to know how many bags of each brand to purchase to minimize the total cost of fertilizing.

Formulate a linear programming model for this problem, and solve it using the graphical method.

*Solution*

This problem is formulated as follows:

$$\text{Minimize } Z = \$6x_1 + 3x_2$$

subject to

$$2x_1 + 4x_2 \geq 16 \text{ lb of nitrogen}$$
$$4x_1 + 3x_2 \geq 24 \text{ lb of phosphate}$$
$$x_1, x_2 \geq 0$$

The graphical solution of the problem is shown in the following figure. Notice that the optimal solution, point *A*, occurs at the last extreme point the objective function touches as it moves toward the origin (point 0,0).

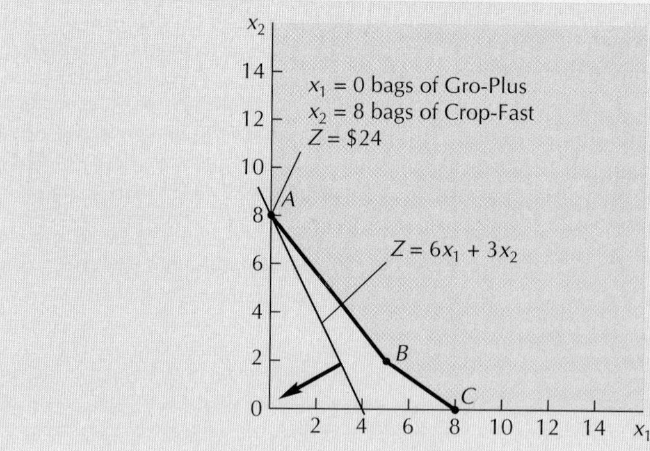


## LINEAR PROGRAMMING MODEL SOLUTION

**Simplex method:** a mathematical procedure for solving a linear programming problem according to a set of steps.

### THE SIMPLEX METHOD

Graphically determining the solution to a linear programming model can provide insight into how a solution is derived, but it is not generally effective or efficient. The traditional mathematical approach for solving a linear programming problem is a mathematical procedure called the **simplex method**. In the simplex method, the model is put into the form of a table, and then a number of mathematical steps are performed on the

THE COMPETITIVE EDGE

## Operational Cost Control at Kellogg's

Kellogg's is the world's largest cereal producer and a leading producer of convenience foods with worldwide sales in 1999 of almost $7 billion. The company started with a single product, Kellogg's Corn Flakes, in 1906 and over the years developed a product line of other cereals including Rice Krispies and Corn Pops, and convenience foods such as Pop-Tarts and Nutri-Grain Cereal bars. Kellogg's operates five plants in the United States and Canada and seven distribution centers, and it contracts with 15 co-packers to produce or pack some of Kellogg's products. Kellogg's must coordinate the production, packaging, inventory, and distribution of roughly 80 cereal products alone at these various facilities.

For more than a decade, Kellogg's has been using a large-scale linear programming model called the Kellogg Planning System (KPS) to plan its weekly production, inventory, and distribution decisions. The model decision variables include the amount of each product produced in a production process at each plant, the units of product packaged, the amount of inventory held, and the shipments of products to other plants and distribution centers. Model constraints include production processing time, packaging capacity, balancing constraints that make sure that all products produced are also packaged during the week, inventory balancing constraints, and inventory safety stock requirements. The model objective is cost minimization. Kellogg's has also developed a tactical version of this basic operational linear programming model for long-range planning for 12 to 24 months into the future. The KPS model is credited with saving Kellogg's $4.5 million in reduced production, inventory, and distribution costs in 1995, and it is estimated that KPS has saved Kellogg's many more millions since the mid-1990s. The tactical version of KPS recently helped the company consolidate production capacity with estimated projected savings of almost $40 million.

*Source:* G. Brown, J. Keegan, B. Vigus, and K. Wood, "The Kellogg Company Optimizes Production, Inventory, and Distribution," *Interfaces* 31, no. 6 (November–December 2001), pp. 1–15.

table. These mathematical steps are the same as moving from one extreme point on the solution boundary to another. However, unlike the graphical method, in which we simply searched through *all* the solution points to find the best one, the simplex method moves from one *better* solution to another until the best one is found.

The simplex method for solving linear programming problems is based, at least partially, on the solution of simultaneous equations and matrix algebra. In this supplement on linear programming, we are not going to provide a detailed presentation of the simplex method. It is a mathematically cumbersome approach that is very time-consuming even for very small problems of two or three variables and a few constraints. It includes a number of mathematical steps and requires numerous arithmetic computations, which frequently result in simple arithmetic errors when done by hand. Instead, we will demonstrate how linear programming problems are solved on the computer. Depending on the software used, the computer solution to a linear programming problem may be in the same form as a simplex solution. As such, we will review the procedures for setting up a linear programming model in the simplex format for solution.

## SLACK AND SURPLUS VARIABLES

Recall that the solution to a linear programming problem occurs at an extreme point where constraint equation lines intersect with each other or with the axis. Thus, the model constraints must all be in the form of *equations* (=) rather than inequalities ($\geq$ or $\leq$).

The procedure for transforming $\leq$ inequality constraints into equations is by adding a new variable, called a **slack variable**, to each constraint. For the Beaver Creek Pottery Company, the addition of a unique slack variable ($s_i$) to each of the constraint inequalities results in the following equations:

**Slack variable:** a variable representing unused resources added to a $\leq$ constraint to make it an equality.

$$x_1 + 2x_2 + s_1 = 40 \text{ hours of labor}$$
$$4x_1 + 3x_2 + s_2 = 120 \text{ lb of clay}$$

The slack variables, $s_1$ and $s_2$, will take on any value necessary to make the left-hand side of the equation equal to the right-hand side. If slack variables have a value in the solution, they generally represent unused resources. Since unused resources would contribute nothing to total revenue, they have a coefficient of zero in the objective function:

$$\text{Maximize } Z = \$40x_1 + 50x_2 + 0s_1 + 0s_2$$

Figure S13.1
**Solution Points with Slack Variables**

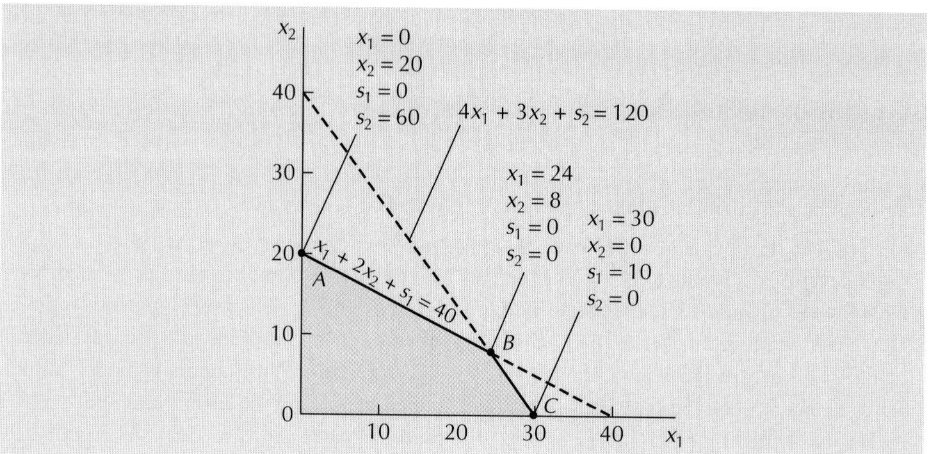


Figure S13.2
**Solution Points with Surplus Variables**

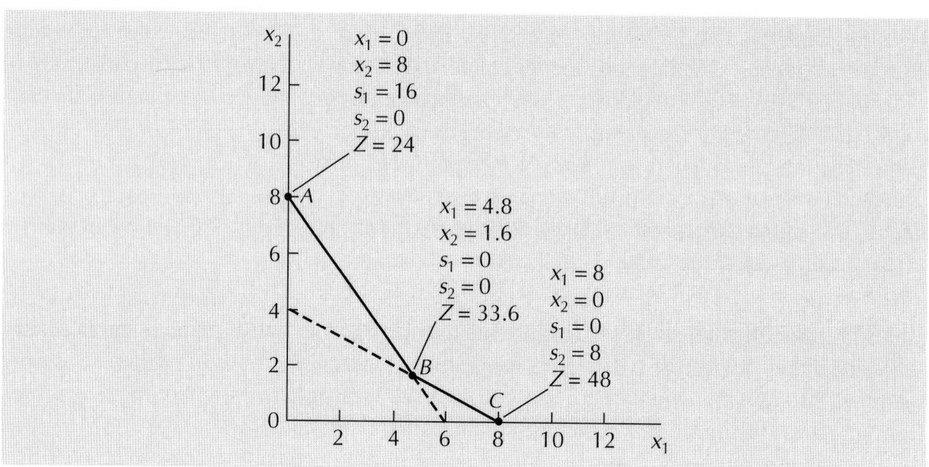


The graph in Figure S13.1 shows all the solution points in our Beaver Creek Pottery Company example with the values for decision *and* slack variables.

This example is a maximization problem with all $\leq$ constraints. A minimization problem with $\geq$ constraints requires a different adjustment. With a $\geq$ constraint, instead of adding a slack variable, we subtract a **surplus variable**. Whereas a slack variable is added and reflects unused resources, a surplus variable is subtracted and reflects the excess above a minimum resource-requirement level. Like the slack variable, a surplus variable is represented symbolically by $s_i$ and must be nonnegative. For example, consider the following constraint from our fertilizer mix problem in Example S13.3:

**Surplus variable:** a variable representing an excess above a resource requirement that is subtracted from a $\geq$ constraint to make it an equality.

$$2x_1 + 4x_2 \geq 16$$

Subtracting a surplus variable results in

$$2x_1 + 4x_2 - s_1 = 16$$

The graph in Figure S13.2 shows all the solution points with the values for decision *and* surplus variables for the minimization problem in Example S13.3.

## SOLVING LINEAR PROGRAMMING PROBLEMS WITH EXCEL

In this section we will demonstrate how to use Excel to solve the Highlands Craft Store model from Example S13.1.

Exhibit S13.1 shows the Excel spreadsheet screen for Example S13.1 for the Highlands Craft Store. The values for bowls, mugs, and maximum profit are contained in cells B10, B11, and B12. They are currently empty since the problem has not yet been solved.

Exhibit S13.1

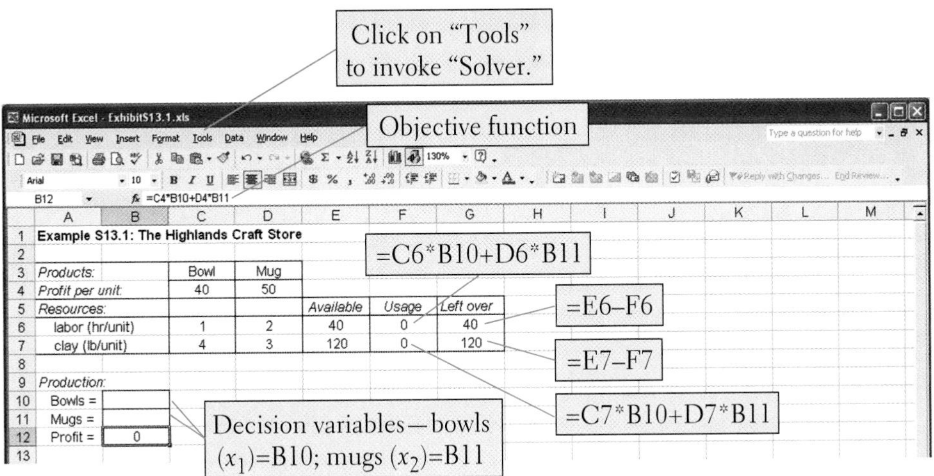


The objective function for profit embedded in cell B12 is shown on the formula bar on the top of the screen. Similar formulas for the constraints for labor and clay are embedded in cells F6 and F7.

To solve this problem, first bring down the "Tools" window from the toolbar at the top of the screen and then select "Solver" from the list of menu items. (If Solver is not shown on the Tools menu, it can be activated by clicking on "Add-ins" on the Tools menu and then "Solver." If Solver is not available from the Add-ins menu, it must be installed on the Add-ins menu directly from the Office or Excel software.) The window for "Solver Parameters" will appear as shown in Exhibit S13.2. Initially all the windows on this screen are blank, and we must input the objective function cell, the cells representing the decision variables, and the cells that make up the model constraints.

Exhibit S13.2

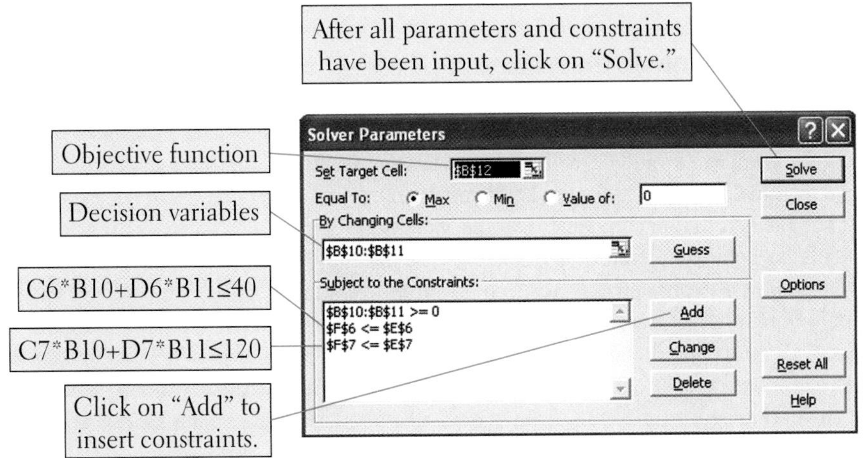


When inputting the solver parameters as shown in Exhibit S13.2, we would first input the "target cell" that contains our objective function, which is B12 for our example. (Excel automatically inserts the "$" sign next to cell addresses; you should not type it in.) Next we indicate that we want to maximize the target cell by clicking on "Max." We achieve our objective "By Changing Cells" B10 and B11, which represent our model decision variables. The designation "B10:B11" means all the cells between B10 and B11 inclusive. We next input our model constraints by clicking on "Add," which will access a window for adding constraints.

After all the constraints have been added, there is one more necessary step before proceeding to solve the problem. Select "Options" from the "Solver Parameters" screen and then when the "Options" screen appears, click on "Assume Linear Models," then "OK." You can also click on "Assume Non-negative" to establish the non-negativity condition for the decision variables. This will allow you to eliminate the constraints, B10:B11>=0. Once the complete model is input, click on "Solve" in the upper right-hand corner of the

**Exhibit S13.3**

B12 =C4*B10+D4*B11

| | A | B | C | D | E | F | G |
|---|---|---|---|---|---|---|---|
| 1 | **Example S13.1: The Highlands Craft Store** | | | | | | |
| 2 | | | | | | | |
| 3 | *Products:* | | Bowl | Mug | | | |
| 4 | *Profit per unit:* | | 40 | 50 | | | |
| 5 | *Resources:* | | | | *Available* | *Usage* | *Left over* |
| 6 | labor (hr/unit) | | 1 | 2 | 40 | 40 | 0 |
| 7 | clay (lb/unit) | | 4 | 3 | 120 | 120 | 0 |
| 8 | | | | | | | |
| 9 | *Production:* | | | | | | |
| 10 | Bowls = | 24 | | | | | |
| 11 | Mugs = | 8 | | | | | |
| 12 | Profit = | 1360 | | | | | |
| 13 | | | | | | | |

"Solver Parameters" screen. First, a screen will appear entitled "Solver Results," which will provide you with the opportunity to select several different reports and then by clicking on "OK" the solution screen shown in Exhibit S13.3 will appear.

If there had been any slack left over for labor or clay, it would have appeared in column G on our spreadsheet under the heading "Left Over." In this case there are no slack resources left over.

We can also generate several reports that summarize the model results. When you click on "OK" from the "Solver" screen, an intermediate screen will appear before the original spreadsheet with the solution results. This screen is entitled "Solver Results" and it provides an opportunity for you to select several reports, including an "Answer" report. This report provides a summary of the solution results.

## SENSITIVITY ANALYSIS

The Excel solution also provides an additional useful piece of information called the "sensitivity report" as shown in Exhibit S13.4.

Notice the values 16 and 6 under the column labeled "Shadow Price" for the rows labeled "Labor usage" and "Clay usage." These values are the *marginal values* (also referred to as *Shadow prices* and *dual values*) of labor and clay in our problem. The marginal value is the amount the company would be willing to pay for one additional unit of a resource. For example, the marginal value of 16 for the labor constraint means that if one additional hour of labor could be obtained by the company, it would increase profit by $6. Likewise, if one additional pound of clay could be obtained, it would increase profit by $6. Sixteen dollars and $16 are the marginal values of labor and clay, respectively, for the company. The marginal value is not the original selling price of a resource; it is how much the company should pay to get more of the resource. The store should not be willing to pay more than $16 for an hour of labor because if it gets one more hour, profit will increase by only $16. The marginal value is helpful to the company in pricing resources and making decisions about securing additional resources.

**Exhibit S13.4**

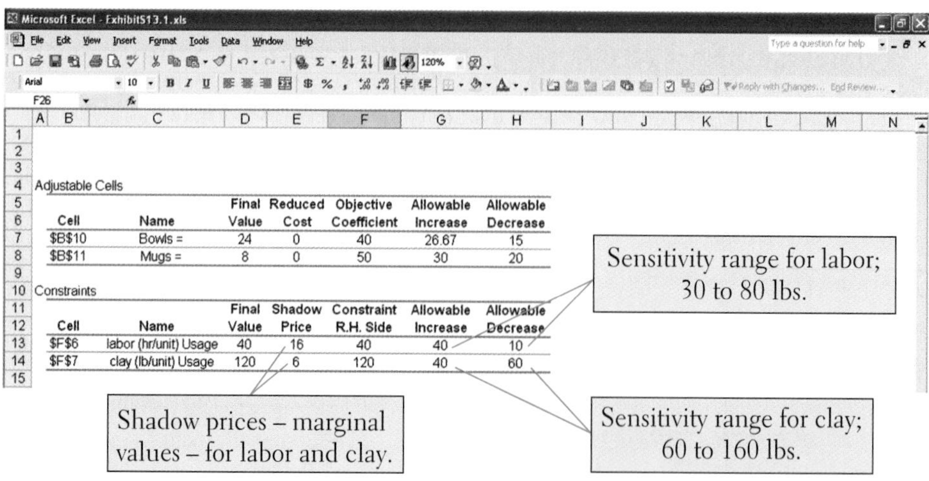

Adjustable Cells

| Cell | Name | Final Value | Reduced Cost | Objective Coefficient | Allowable Increase | Allowable Decrease |
|---|---|---|---|---|---|---|
| $B$10 | Bowls = | 24 | 0 | 40 | 26.67 | 15 |
| $B$11 | Mugs = | 8 | 0 | 50 | 30 | 20 |

Constraints

| Cell | Name | Final Value | Shadow Price | Constraint R.H. Side | Allowable Increase | Allowable Decrease |
|---|---|---|---|---|---|---|
| $F$6 | labor (hr/unit) Usage | 40 | 16 | 40 | 40 | 10 |
| $F$7 | clay (lb/unit) Usage | 120 | 6 | 120 | 40 | 60 |

## SENSITIVITY RANGES

The marginal, or dual values do not hold for an unlimited supply of labor and clay. As the store increases (or reduces) the amount of labor or clay it has, the constraints change, which will eventually change the solution to a new point. Thus, the dual values are only good within a range of consistent values. These ranges are given under the column labeled "Allowable Increase" and "Allowable Decrease" in Exhibit S13.4. For example, the original amount of labor available is 40 hours. The dual value of \$16 for one hour of labor holds if the available labor is between 30 and 80 hours. If there are more than 80 hours of labor, then a new solution point occurs and the dual value of \$16 is no longer valid. The problem would have to be solved again to see what the new solution is and the new dual value.

This can be observed graphically in Figure S13.3. If the labor hours are increased from 40 to 80 hours, the constraint line moves out and up. The new solution space is $OA'C$, and a new solution variable mix occurs at $A'$, as shown in Figure S13.3*a*. At the original optimal point, $B$, both $x_1$ and $x_2$ are in the solution; however, at the new optimal point, $A'$, only $x_2$ is produced (i.e., $x_1 = 0$, $x_2 = 40$, $s_1 = 0$, $s_2 = 0$).

Thus, the upper limit of the sensitivity range for the labor constraint is 80 hours. At this value the solution mix changes such that bowls are no longer produced. Furthermore, as labor increases past 80 hours, $s_1$ increases (i.e., slack hours are created). Similarly, if labor hours are decreased to 30 hours, the constraint line moves down and in. The new feasible solution space is $OA'C$, as shown in Figure S13.3*b*. The new optimal point is at $C$, where no mugs ($x_2$) are produced. The new solution is $x_1 = 30$, $x_2 = 0$, $s_1 = 0$, $s_2 = 0$, and $Z = \$1200$. Again, the variable mix is changed. Summarizing, the sensitivity range for the constraint quantity value for labor hours is between 30 and 80 hours as shown in the Excel spreadsheet in Exhibit S13.4.

A similar range of values exist for the clay constraint. The solution values are good for down to 60 lb and up to 160 lb as shown in Exhibit S13.4.

There are also sensitivity ranges for the objective function coefficients: "\$40" for bowls and "\$50" for mugs. The optimal solution point will remain the same if the profit for a bowl remains within \$25 and \$66.67, or if the profit for mugs remains between \$30 and \$80, as shown in the Excel spreadsheet in Exhibit S13.4. This can also be observed graphically in Figure S13.4.

If the profit for a bowl increases from \$40 to \$66.67, the objective function line rotates to a new location where it is parallel with the constraint line for clay as shown in Figure S13.4*a*. (At this new location, the objective function line and the constraint line for clay have the same slope). Both points $B$ and $C$ are now optimal. If the profit for bowls is increased greater than \$66.67, then only point $C$ will be optimal and we will have a new solution mix. Similarly, if the profit for a bowl is decreased to \$25 as shown in Figure S13.4*b*, points $A$ and $B$ are both optimal. If the profit for a bowl is decreased to less than \$25, only point $A$ will be optimal and a new solution exists. Thus, the range for the profit

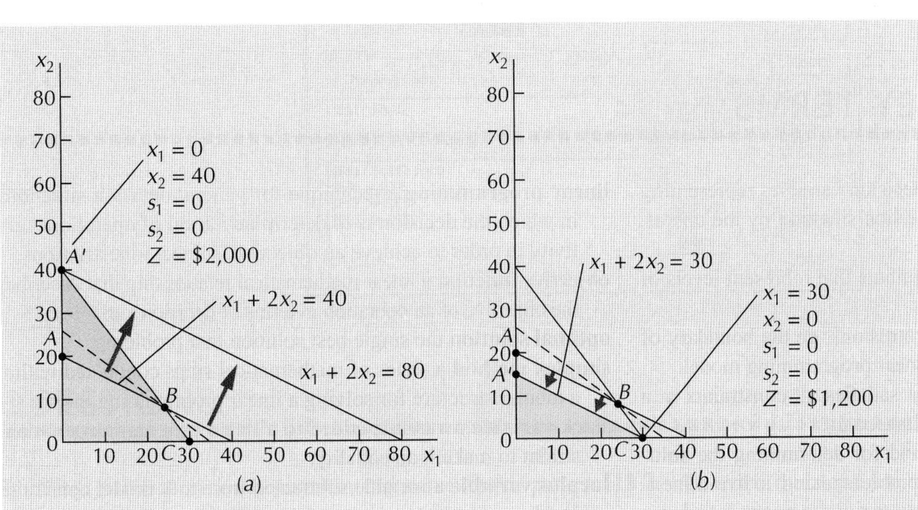


**Figure S13.3** **The Sensitivity Range for Labor Hours**

**S13-10.** The Home Improvement Building Supply Company has received the following order for boards in three lengths:

| Length | Order (quantity) |
|---|---|
| 7 feet | 700 boards |
| 9 feet | 1200 boards |
| 10 feet | 500 boards |

The company has 25-foot standard-length boards in stock. Therefore, the standard-length boards must be cut into the lengths necessary to meet order requirements. Naturally, the company wishes to minimize the number of standard-length boards used. The company must, therefore, determine how to cut up the 25-foot boards in order to meet the order requirements and minimize the number of standard-length boards used.

a. Formulate and solve a linear programming model for this problem.
b. When a board is cut in a specific pattern, the amount of board left over is referred to as *trim loss*. Reformulate and solve the linear programming model for this problem, assuming that the objective is to minimize trim loss rather than to minimize the total number of boards used.

**S13-11.** IT Computer Services assembles its own brand of personal computers from component parts it purchases overseas and domestically. IT sells most of its computers locally to different departments at State University as well as to individuals and businesses in the immediate geographic region.

IT has enough regular production capacity to produce 160 computers per week. It can produce an additional 50 computers with overtime. The cost of assembly, inspecting, and packaging a computer during regular time is \$190. Overtime production of a computer costs \$260. Further, it costs \$5 per computer per week to hold a computer in inventory for future delivery. IT wants to be able to meet all customer orders with no shortages in order to provide quality service. IT's order schedule for the next 6 weeks is as follows:

| Week | Computer orders |
|---|---|
| 1 | 105 |
| 2 | 170 |
| 3 | 230 |
| 4 | 180 |
| 5 | 150 |
| 6 | 250 |

IT Computers wants to determine a schedule that will indicate how much regular and overtime production it will need each week in order to meet its orders at the minimum cost. The company wants no inventory left over at the end of the six-week period. Formulate and solve a linear programming model for this problem.

**S13-12.** The manager of Biggs Department Store has four employees available to assign to three departments in the store: lamps, sporting goods, and linen. The manager wants each of these departments to have at least one employee but not more than two. Therefore, two departments will be assigned one employee, and one department will be assigned two. Each employee has different areas of expertise, which are reflected in the following average daily sales record for each employee from previous experience in each department:

| Employee | Department | | |
|---|---|---|---|
| | *Lamps* | *Sporting Goods* | *Linen* |
| 1 | \$130 | \$190 | \$ 90 |
| 2 | 275 | 300 | 100 |
| 3 | 180 | 225 | 140 |
| 4 | 200 | 120 | 160 |

The manager wishes to know which employee(s) to assign to each department in order to maximize expected sales. Formulate and solve a linear programming model for this problem.

**S13-13.** Dr. Beth McKenzie, the head administrator at Washington County Regional Hospital, must determine a schedule for nurses to make sure there are enough nurses on duty throughout the day. During the day, the demand for nurses varies. Beth has broken the day into twelve 2-hour periods. The slowest time of the day encompasses the three periods from 12:00 A.M. to 6:00 A.M., which, beginning at midnight, require a minimum of 30, 20, and 40 nurses, respectively. The demand for nurses steadily increases during the next four daytime periods. Beginning with the 6:00 A.M.–8:00 A.M. period, a minimum of 50, 60, 80, and 90 nurses are required for these four periods, respectively. After 2:00 P.M., the demand for nurses decreases during the afternoon and evening hours. For the five 2-hour periods beginning at 2:00 P.M., and ending at midnight, 70, 70, 60, 50, and 40 nurses are required, respectively. A nurse reports for duty at the beginning of one of the 2-hour periods and works 8 consecutive hours (which is required in the nurses' contract). Dr. McKenzie wants to determine a nursing schedule that will meet the hospital's minimum requirements throughout the day while using the minimum number of nurses. Formulate and solve a linear programming model for this problem.

**S13-14.** Grass Unlimited is a lawn care and maintenance company. One of its services is to seed new lawns as well as bare areas or damaged areas in established lawns. The company uses three basic grass seed mixes it calls Home 1, Home 2, and Commercial 3. It uses three kinds of grass seed—tall fescue, mustang fescue, and bluegrass. The requirements for each grass mix are as follows:

| Mix | Mix Requirements |
|---|---|
| Home 1 | No more than 50% tall fescue |
| | At least 20% mustang fescue |
| Home 2 | At least 30% bluegrass |
| | At least 30% mustang fescue |
| | No more than 20% tall fescue |
| Commercial 3 | At least 50% but no more than 70% tall fescue |
| | At least 10% bluegrass |

The company believes it needs to have at least 1500 pounds of Home 1 mix, 900 pounds of Home 2 mix, and 2400 pounds of Commercial 3 seed mix on hand. A pound of tall fescue costs the company \$1.70, a pound of mustang fescue costs \$2.80, and a pound of bluegrass costs \$3.25. The company wants to know how many pounds of each type of grass seed to purchase in order to minimize cost. Formulate a linear programming model for this problem.

**S13-15.** A jewelry store makes necklaces and bracelets from gold and platinum. The store has developed the following linear programming model for determining the number of necklaces and bracelets ($x_1$ and $x_2$) to make in order to maximize profit:

$$\text{Maximize } Z = 300x_1 + 400x_2 \text{ (profit, \$)}$$

subject to

$$3x_1 + 2x_2 \leq 18 \quad \text{(gold, oz)}$$
$$2x_1 + 4x_2 \leq 20 \quad \text{(platinum, oz)}$$
$$x_2 \leq 4 \quad \text{(demand, bracelets)}$$
$$x_1, x_2 \geq 0$$

a. Solve this model graphically.
b. The maximum demand for bracelets is 4. If the store produces the optimal number of bracelets and necklaces, will the maximum demand for bracelets be met? If not, by how much will it be missed?
c. What profit for a necklace would result in no bracelets being produced, and what would be the optimal solution for this problem?

**S13-16.** The Copperfield Mining Company owns two mines, which produce three grades of ore: high, medium, and low. The company has a contract to supply a smelting company with 12 tons of high-grade ore, 8 tons of medium-grade ore, and 24 tons of low-grade ore. Each mine produces a certain amount of each type of ore each hour it is in operation. The company has developed the following linear programming model to determine the number of hours to operate each mine ($x_1$ and $x_2$) so that contracted obligations can be met at the lowest cost:

$$\text{Minimize } Z = 200x_1 + 160x_2 \text{ (cost, \$)}$$

subject to

$$6x_1 + 2x_2 \geq 12 \quad \text{(high-grade ore, tons)}$$
$$2x_1 + 2x_2 \geq 8 \quad \text{(medium-grade ore, tons)}$$
$$4x_1 + 12x_2 \geq 24 \quad \text{(low-grade ore, tons)}$$
$$x_1, x_2 \geq 0$$

a. Solve this model graphically.
b. Solve the model using Excel.

**S13-17.** A manufacturing firm produces two products. Each product must go through an assembly process and a finishing process. The product is then transferred to the warehouse, which has space for only a limited number of items. The following linear programming model has been developed for determining the quantity of each product to produce in order to maximize profit:

$$\text{Maximize } Z = 30x_1 + 70x_2 \text{ (profit, \$)}$$

subject to

$$4x_1 + 10x_2 \leq 80 \quad \text{(assembly, hours)}$$
$$14x_1 + 8x_2 \leq 112 \quad \text{(finishing, hours)}$$
$$x_1 + x_2 \leq 10 \quad \text{(inventory, units)}$$
$$x_1, x_2 \geq 0$$

a. Solve this model graphically.
b. Assume that the objective function has been changed to $Z = 90x_1 + 70x_2$. Determine the slope of each objective function and discuss what effect these slopes have on the optimal solution.

**S13-18.** The Admissions Office at Tech wants to determine how many in-state and out-of-state students to accept for next fall's entering freshman class. Tuition for an in-state student is \$7600 per year while out-of-state tuition is \$22,500 per year. A total of 12,800 in-state and 8100 out-of-state freshman have applied for next fall, and Tech does not want to accept more than 3500 students. However, since Tech is a state institution, the state mandates that it can accept no more than 40% out-of-state students. From past experience the admissions office knows that 12% of in-state students and 24% of out-of-state students will drop out during their first year. Tech wants to maximize total tuition while limiting the total attrition to 600 first-year students.

a. Formulate a linear programming model for this problem.
b. Solve this model using graphical analysis.
c. Solve this problem using Excel.

**S13-19.** Janet Lopez is establishing an investment portfolio that will include stock and bond funds. She has \$720,000 to invest, and she does not want the portfolio to include more than 65% stocks. The average annual return for the stock fund she plans to invest in is 18%, while the average annual return for the bond fund is 6%. She further estimates that the most she could lose in the next year in the stock fund is 22%, while the most she could lose in the bond fund is 5%. To reduce her risk she wants to limit her potential maximum losses to \$100,000.

a. Formulate a linear programming model for this problem.
b. Solve this model using graphical analysis.
c. Solve this problem using Excel.

**S13-20.** Breathtakers, a health and fitness center, operates a morning fitness program for senior citizens. The program includes aerobic exercise, either swimming or step exercise, followed by a healthy breakfast in its dining room. The dietitian of Breathtakers wants to develop a breakfast that will be high in calories, calcium, protein, and fiber, which are especially important to senior citizens, but low in fat and cholesterol. She also wants to minimize cost. She has selected the following possible food items, with individual nutrient contributions and cost from which to develop a standard breakfast menu.

| Breakfast Food | Calories | Fat (g) | Cholesterol (mg) | Iron (mg) | Calcium (mg) | Protein (g) | Fiber (g) | Cost (\$) |
|---|---|---|---|---|---|---|---|---|
| 1. Bran cereal (cup) | 90 | 0 | 0 | 6 | 20 | 3 | 5 | 0.18 |
| 2. Dry cereal (cup) | 110 | 2 | 0 | 4 | 48 | 4 | 2 | 0.22 |
| 3. Oatmeal (cup) | 100 | 2 | 0 | 2 | 12 | 5 | 3 | 0.10 |
| 4. Oat bran (cup) | 90 | 2 | 0 | 3 | 8 | 6 | 4 | 0.12 |
| 5. Egg | 75 | 5 | 270 | 1 | 30 | 7 | 0 | 0.10 |
| 6. Bacon (slice) | 35 | 3 | 8 | 0 | 0 | 2 | 0 | 0.09 |
| 7. Orange | 65 | 0 | 0 | 1 | 52 | 1 | 1 | 0.40 |
| 8. Milk—2% (cup) | 100 | 4 | 12 | 0 | 250 | 9 | 0 | 0.16 |
| 9. Orange juice (cup) | 120 | 0 | 0 | 0 | 3 | 1 | 0 | 0.50 |
| 10. Wheat toast (slice) | 65 | 1 | 0 | 1 | 26 | 3 | 3 | 0.07 |

sheets come back from the cleaners and are put on the beds, 20% are taken off and thrown away.

At the beginning of the summer, the camp has no sheets available, so initially sheets must be purchased. Sheets are thrown away at the end of the summer.

Mary's major at State is operations management, and she wants to develop a plan for purchasing and cleaning sheets using linear programming. Help Mary formulate a linear programming model for this problem, and solve it using Excel.

## CASE PROBLEM S13.3

### *Spring Garden Tools*

The Spring family has owned and operated a garden tool and implements manufacturing company since 1952. The company sells garden tools to distributors and also directly to hardware stores and home improvement discount chains. The Spring Company's four most popular small garden tools are a trowel, a hoe, a rake, and a shovel. Each of these tools is made from durable steel and has a wooden handle. The Spring family prides itself on its high-quality tools.

The manufacturing process encompasses two stages. The first stage includes two operations—stamping out the metal tool heads and drilling screw holes in them. The completed tool heads then flow to the second stage. The second stage includes an assembly operation, in which the handles are attached to the tool heads, a finishing step, and finally packaging. The processing times per tool for each operation are provided in the following table:

| | Tool (Hours/Unit) | | | | Total Hours Available |
|---|---|---|---|---|---|
| **Operation** | *Trowel* | *Hoe* | *Rake* | *Shovel* | **Per Month** |
| Stamping | 0.04 | 0.17 | 0.06 | 0.12 | 500 |
| Drilling | 0.05 | 0.14 | — | 0.14 | 400 |
| Assembly | 0.06 | 0.13 | 0.05 | 0.10 | 600 |
| Finishing | 0.05 | 0.21 | 0.02 | 0.10 | 550 |
| Packaging | 0.03 | 0.15 | 0.04 | 0.15 | 500 |

The steel the company uses is ordered from an iron and steel works in Japan. The company has 10,000 square feet of sheet steel available each month. The metal required for each tool and the monthly contracted production volume per tool are provided in the following table:

| | Sheet Metal (FT2) | Monthly Contracted Sales |
|---|---|---|
| Trowel | 1.2 | 1800 |
| Hoe | 1.6 | 1400 |
| Rake | 2.1 | 1600 |
| Shovel | 2.4 | 1800 |

The reasons the company has prospered are its ability to meet customer demand on time and its high quality. As a result, the Spring Company will produce on an overtime basis in order to meet its sales requirements, and it also has a longstanding arrangement with a local tool and die company to manufacture its tool heads. The Spring Company feels comfortable subcontracting the first-stage operations, since it is easier to detect defects prior to assembly and finishing. For the same reason, the company will not subcontract for the entire tool, since defects would be particularly hard to detect after the tool is finished and packaged. However, the company does have 100 hours of overtime available each month for each operation in both stages. The regular production and overtime costs per tool for both stages are provided in the following table:

| | Stage 1 | | Stage 2 | |
|---|---|---|---|---|
| | *Regular Cost ($)* | *Overtime Cost ($)* | *Regular Cost ($)* | *Overtime Cost ($)* |
| Trowel | 6.00 | 6.20 | 3.00 | 3.10 |
| Hoe | 10.00 | 10.70 | 5.00 | 5.40 |
| Rake | 8.00 | 8.50 | 4.00 | 4.30 |
| Shovel | 10.00 | 10.70 | 5.00 | 5.40 |

The cost of subcontracting in stage 1 adds 20% to the regular production cost.

The Spring Company wants to establish a production schedule for regular and overtime production in each stage and for the number of tool heads subcontracted, at the minimum cost. Formulate a linear programming model for this problem and solve the model using Excel. Which resources appear to be most critical in the production process?

## CASE PROBLEM S13.4

### *Walsh's Juice Company*

Walsh's Juice Company produces three products from unprocessed grape juice—bottled juice, frozen juice concentrate, and jelly. It purchases grape juice from three vineyards near the Great Lakes. The climate in this area is good for growing the concord grapes necessary to produce grape juice products. The grapes are harvested at the vineyards and immediately converted into juice at plants at the vineyard sites and stored in refrigerated tanks. The juice is then transported to four different plants in Virginia, Michigan, Tennessee, and Indiana, where it is processed into bottled grape juice, frozen concentrated juice, and jelly. Vineyard output typically differs each month in the harvesting season and the plants have different processing capacity.

In a particular month the vineyard in New York has 1400 tons of unprocessed grape juice available, while the vineyard in Ohio has 1700 tons and the vineyard in Pennsylvania has 1100 tons. The processing capacity per month is 1200 tons of unprocessed juice at the plant in Virginia, 1100 tons of juice at the plant in Michigan, 1400 tons at the plant in Tennessee, and 1400 tons at the plant in Indiana. The cost per ton of transporting unprocessed juice from the vineyards to the plant is as follows:

| | Plant | | | |
|---|---|---|---|---|
| **Vineyard** | *Virginia* | *Michigan* | *Tennessee* | *Indiana* |
| New York | $850 | 720 | 910 | 750 |
| Pennsylvania | 970 | 790 | 1050 | 880 |
| Ohio | 900 | 830 | 780 | 820 |

The plants are different ages, have different equipment, and have different wage rates; thus, the cost of processing each product at each plant ($/ton) differs as follows:

| | Plant | | | |
|---|---|---|---|---|
| **Product** | *Virginia* | *Michigan* | *Tennessee* | *Indiana* |
| Juice | $2100 | 2350 | 2200 | 1900 |
| Concentrate | 4100 | 4300 | 3950 | 3900 |
| Jelly | 2600 | 2300 | 2500 | 2800 |

This month the company needs to process a total of 1200 tons of bottled juice, 900 tons of frozen concentrate, and 700 tons of jelly at the four plants combined. However, the production process for frozen concentrate results in some juice dehydration, and the process for jelly includes a cooking stage that evaporates water content. To process 1 ton of frozen concentrate requires 2 tons of unprocessed juice; a ton of jelly requires 1.5 tons of unprocessed juice; and a ton of bottled juice requires 1 ton of unprocessed juice.

Walsh's management wants to determine how many tons of grape juice to ship from each of the vineyards to each of the plants, and the number of tons of each product to process at each plant. Thus, management needs a model that includes both the logistical aspects of this problem and the production processing aspects. It wants a solution that will minimize total costs, including the cost of transporting grape juice from the vineyards to the plants and the product processing costs. Help Walsh's solve this problem by formulating a linear programming model and solve it using Excel.

## CASE PROBLEM S13.5

### *Julia's Food Booth*

Julia Robertson is a senior at Tech, and she's investigating different ways to finance her final year at school. In her first three years at school she worked a part-time job at a local bar, but she wants more free time during the week in her senior year to interview for jobs after she graduates, to work on some senior projects, and to have some fun with her friends. She is considering leasing a food booth outside the stadium at the Tech home football games which Tech allows for selected students and student groups. Tech sells out every home game, and she knows from going to the games herself that everyone eats a lot of food. She has to pay $1000 per game for a booth and the booths are not very large. Vendors can sell only food or drinks on Tech property but not both. Only the Tech athletic department concession stands can sell both inside the stadium. She thinks slices of cheese pizza, hot dogs, and barbecue sandwiches are the most popular food items among fans, so these are the items she would sell.

Most food items are sold during the hour before the game starts and during half time; thus, it will not be possible for Julia to prepare the food while she is selling it. She must prepare the food ahead of time and then store it in a warming oven. She can lease a warming oven for the home season, which includes six games, for $600. The oven has 16 shelves, and each shelf is 3 ft by 4 ft. She plans to fill the oven with the three food items before the game and before half time.

Julia has negotiated with a local pizza delivery company to deliver 14-inch cheese pizzas twice each game; two hours before the game and right after the opening kickoff. Each pizza will cost her $6 and will include eight slices. She estimates it will cost her $0.45 for each hot dog and $0.90 for each barbecue sandwich if she makes the barbecue herself the night before. She measured a hot dog and found it takes up about 16 in.$^2$ of space, while a barbecue sandwich takes up about 25 in.$^2$ She plans to sell a slice of pizza and a hot dog for $1.50 apiece and a barbecue sandwich for $2.25. She has $1500 in cash available to purchase and prepare the food items for the first home game; for the remaining five games she will purchase her ingredients with money she has made from the previous game.

Julia has talked to some students and vendors who have sold food at previous football games at Tech as well as at other universities. From this she has discovered that she can expect to sell at least as many slices of pizza as hot dogs and barbecue sandwiches combined. She also anticipates that she will probably sell at least twice as many hot dogs as barbecue sandwiches. She believes that she will sell everything she can stock and develop a customer base for the season if she follows these general guidelines for demand.

If Julia clears at least $1000 in profit for each game after paying all her expenses, she believes it will be worth leasing the booth.

**a.** Formulate and solve a linear programming model for Julia that will help you advise her if she should lease the booth.

**b.** If Julia can borrow some more money from a friend before the first game to purchase more ingredients, could she increase her profit? If so, how much should she borrow and how much additional profit would she make? What factor constrains her from borrowing even more money than this amount (indicated in your answer to the previous question)?

**c.** When Julia looked at the solution in (a), she realized that it would be physically difficult for her to prepare all the hot dogs and barbecue sandwiches indicated in this solution. She believes she can hire a friend of hers to help her for $100 per game. Based on the results in (a) and (b), is this something you think she could reasonably do and should do?

**d.** Julia seems to be basing her analysis on "certain" assumptions that everything will go as she plans. What are some of the uncertain factors in the model that could go wrong and adversely affect Julia's analysis? Given these uncertainties and the results in (a), (b), and (c), what do you recommend that Julia do?

## REFERENCES

Charnes, A., and W. W. Cooper. *Management Models and Industrial Applications of Linear Programming*. New York: John Wiley & Sons, 1961.

Dantzig, G. B. *Linear Programming and Extensions*. Princeton, NJ: Princeton University, 1963.

Gass, S. *Linear Programming*, 4th ed. New York: McGraw-Hill, 1975.

Moore, L. J., S. M. Lee, and B. W. Taylor. *Management Science*, 4th ed. Needham heights, MA: Allyn and Bacon, 1993.

Taylor, B. W. *Introduction to Management Science*, 6th ed. Upper Saddle River, NJ: Prentice Hall, 1999.

Wagner, A. M. *Principles of Operations Research*, 2nd ed. Upper Saddle River, NJ: Prentice Hall, 1975.

# Resource Planning

CHAPTER 14

Web resources for this chapter include

- Internet Exercises
- Online Practice Quizzes
- Virtual Tours
- Excel Worksheets
- Company and Resource Weblinks
- Animated Demo Problems
- Microsoft Project Exhibits

www.wiley.com/college/russell

## CHAPTER OUTLINE

In this chapter, you will learn about . . .

- Material Requirements Planning (MRP)
- Capacity Requirements Planning (CRP)
- Enterprise Resource Planning (ERP)
- Customer Relationship Management (CRM)
- Supply Chain Management (SCM)
- Collaborative Product Commerce (CPC)

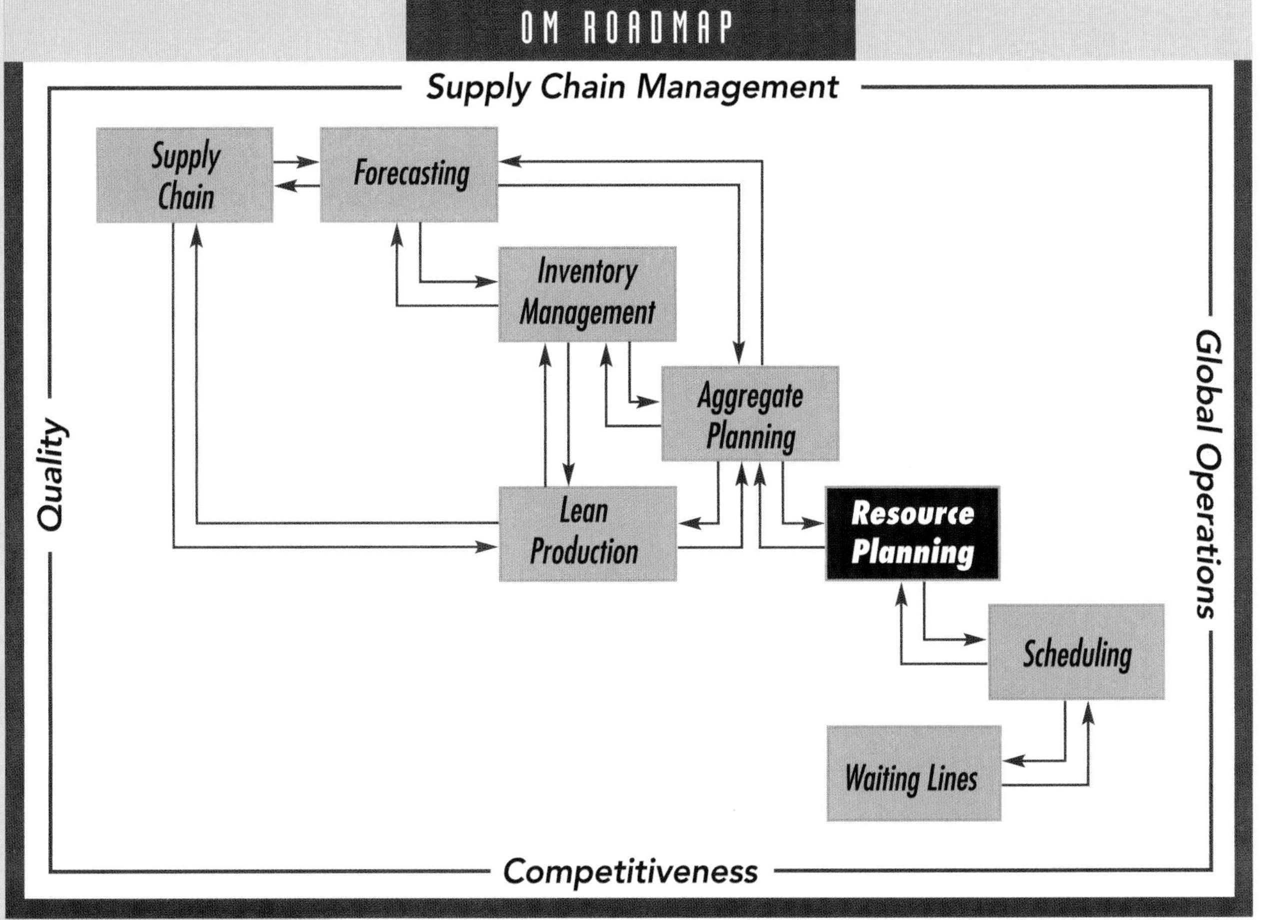

## ENTERPRISE RESOURCE PLANNING AT CYBEX

Cybex, an $80 million producer of high-end exercise equipment, ships more than 200 different products to 250 distributors and thousands of customers around the world. Treadmills and bikes are built to stock; weight training equipment is built to order. Until recently, Cybex's three factories were run by different software systems that had trouble communicating. Now they're all integrated with PeopleSoft's enterprise software. From a customer portal fitness dealers and sales reps can order in-stock items, configure customized pieces of equipment, order spare parts, and track orders. The customer order triggers a series of events internally. The financial system performs a credit check. The order management system sends an order to the manufacturing plant for custom-built items and to the warehouse for in-stock items. Manufacturing responds with an available-to-promise date, and customers are notified of estimated delivery times. Removing an item from stock triggers a purchase requisition for replacement stock. A shipment triggers an invoice and online tracking through the customer's preferred carrier. Finally, the event management system notifies dealers, customers, and sales reps when items are shipped or when scheduled shipping dates change. These automated processes are part of enterprise resource planning, or ERP, at Cybex.

Cybex has recently added customer relationship management (CRM) capabilities to its ERP system. A corporate Web site handles customer inquiries concerning the operation, maintenance, and repair of its products. Responses are enhanced by a Cybex database that contains a complete history of each customer and piece of equipment. Takeup of the new system has been brisk, especially for international customers. Half of Cybex's customers use the Web site at least three times a week. With ERP and CRM, Cybex has completed the buy-self-service cycle for its customers.

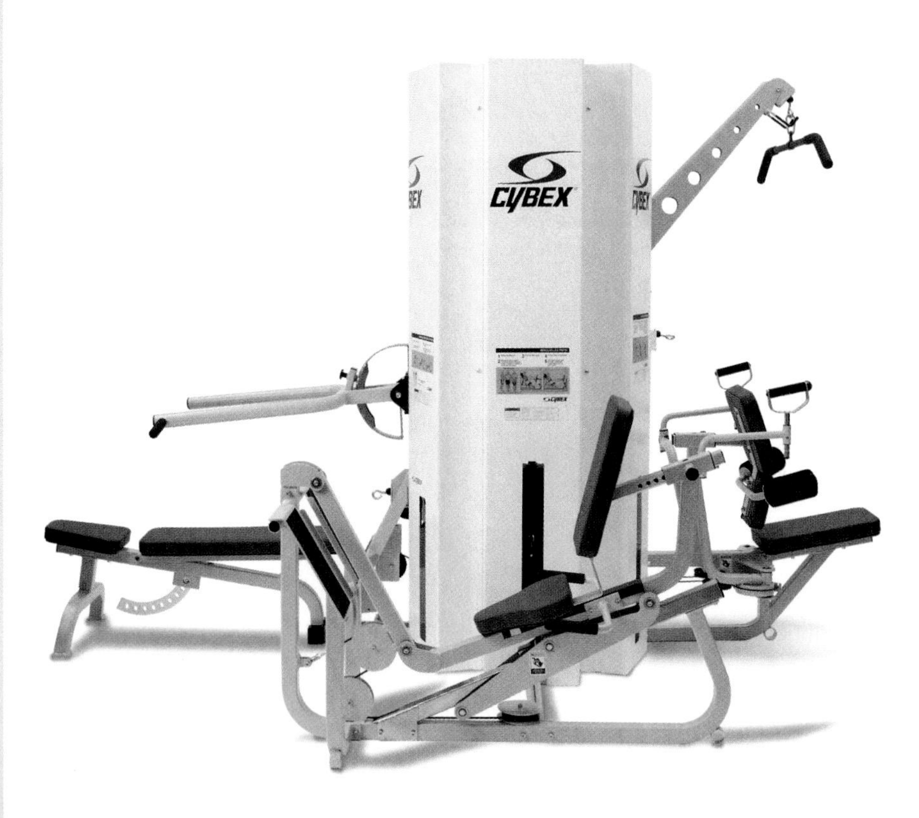


*Customers can order customized weight training equipment from Cybex online. An ERP system handles the back office activities required to fill the order.*

*Source: Adapted from "Taking the Pulse of ERP," Modern Materials Management (February 1, 2001). http://www.manufacturing.net/mmh1, and Malcolm Wheatley, "Suite as it sounds?" MSI (March 2003).*

As seen in the opening vignette for this chapter, an enterprise planning system (ERP) provides the information infrastructure for today's corporations. It brings functions, processes, and resources together to meet customer needs and provide value to shareholders. ERP evolved from more modest versions of manufacturing resource planning aimed at providing material resources and machine/labor resources to support production plans. We begin this chapter by describing the resource planning systems of material requirements planning (MRP) and capacity requirements planning (CRP), and we end with a discussion of the scope and impact of more elaborate ERP systems, with extensions to customer and suppliers.

As a framework for discussion, Figure 14.1 shows the resource planning process from the aggregate production plan to manufacture. Recall that the *aggregate production plan* is for families of items and the *master production schedule* is for individual products. The *material requirements plan* (MRP) translates the master production schedule into requirements for components, subassemblies, and raw materials. The *capacity requirements plan* converts the material plan into labor and machine requirements. Once the plans have been approved, purchase orders are released to suppliers and work orders are released to the shop. Purchased parts and manufactured parts are assembled in manufacture.

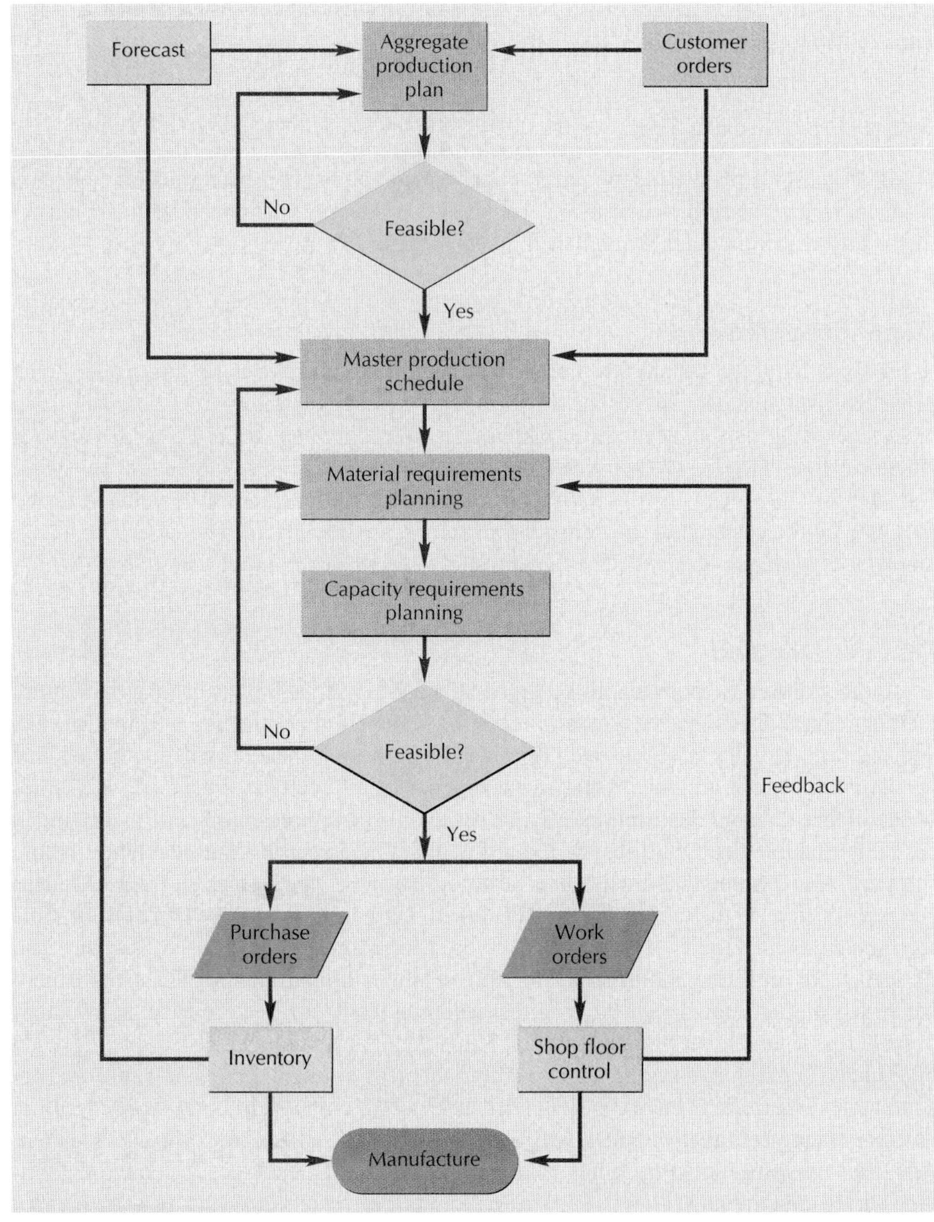


**Figure 14.1**
**Resource Planning for Manufacturing**

## MATERIAL REQUIREMENTS PLANNING (MRP)

**Material requirements planning:**
a computerized inventory control and production planning system.

**Material requirements planning** is a computerized inventory control and production planning system. The main objective of any inventory system is to ensure that material is available when needed—which can easily lead to a tremendous investment of funds in unnecessary inventory. One objective of MRP is to maintain the lowest possible level of inventory. MRP does this by determining *when* component items are needed and scheduling them to be ready at that time, no earlier and no later.

MRP was the first inventory system to recognize that inventories of raw materials, components, and finished goods may need to be handled differently. In the process of planning inventory levels for these various types of goods, the system also planned purchasing activities (for raw materials and purchased components), manufacturing activities (for component parts and assemblies), and delivery schedules (for finished products). Thus, the system was more than an inventory control system; it became a production scheduling system as well.

One of the few certainties in a manufacturing environment is that things rarely go as planned—orders arrive late, machines break down, workers are absent, designs are changed, and so on. With its computerized database, MRP is able to keep track of the relationship of job orders so that if a delay in one aspect of production is unavoidable, other related activities can be rescheduled, too. MRP systems have the ability to keep schedules valid and up to date.

### WHEN TO USE MRP

MRP is useful for dependent and discrete demand items, complex products, job shop production, and assemble-to-order environments. Managing component demand inventory is different from managing finished goods inventory.

#### Dependent Demand

For one thing, the demand for component parts does not have to be forecasted; it can be derived from the demand for the finished product. For example, suppose demand for a table, consisting of four legs and a tabletop, is 100 units per week. Then, demand for tabletops would also be 100 per week, and demand for table legs would be 400 per week. Demand for table legs is totally *dependent* on the demand for tables. The demand for tables may be forecasted, but the demand for table legs is calculated. The tables are an example of *independent demand*. The tabletop and table legs exhibit *dependent demand*.

#### Discrete Demand

Another difference between finished products and component parts is the continuity of their demand. For the inventory-control systems in the previous chapter, we assumed that demand occurred at a constant rate. The inventory systems were designed to keep some inventory on hand at all times, enough, we hoped, to meet each day's demand. With component items, demand does not necessarily occur on a continuous basis. Let us assume in our table example that table legs are the last items to be assembled onto the tables before shipping. Also assume that it takes one week to make a batch of tables and that table legs are assembled onto the tabletops every Friday. If we were to graph the demand for table legs, as shown in Figure 14.2, it would be zero for Monday, Tuesday, Wednesday, and Thursday, but on Friday the demand for table legs would jump to 400. The same pattern would repeat the following week. With this scenario, we do not need to keep an inventory of table legs available on Monday through Thursday of any week. We need table legs only on Fridays. Looking at our graph, demand for table legs occurs in *lumps*; it is *discrete*, not continuous. Using an inventory system such as EOQ for component items would result in inventory being held that we know will not be needed until a later date. The excess inventory takes up space, soaks up funds, and requires additional resources for counting, sorting, storing, and moving.

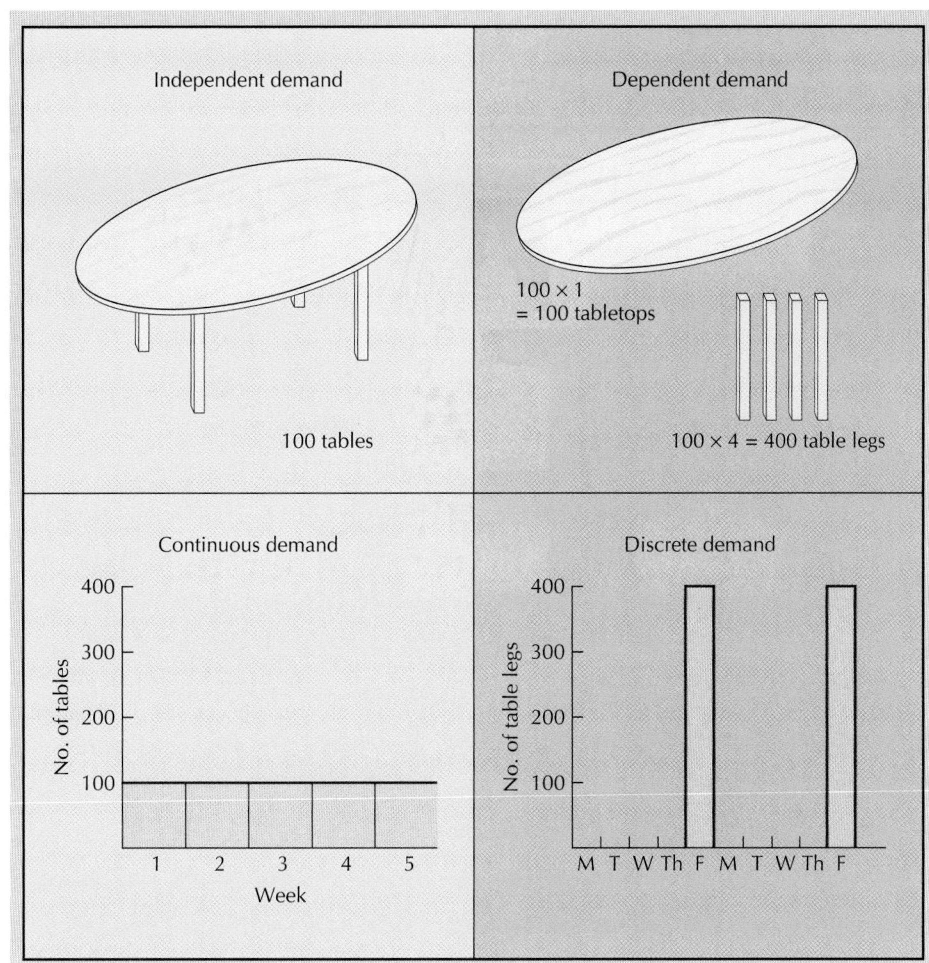


Figure 14.2
**Demand Characteristics for Finished Products and Their Components**

## Complex Products

Industries that manufacture complex products, requiring the coordination of component production, find MRP especially useful. A complex product may have hundreds of component parts, dozens of assemblies, and several levels of assembly. MRP tries to ensure that multiple components of an assembly are ready at the same time so that they can be assembled together. Products with simple structures do not need MRP to plan production or monitor inventory levels.

## Erratic Orders

The advantages of MRP are more evident when the manufacturing environment is complex and uncertain. Manufacturing environments in which customer orders are erratic, each job takes a different path through the system, lead time is uncertain, and due dates vary need an information system such as MRP to keep track of the different jobs and coordinate their schedules. The type of environment we are describing is characteristic of *batch*, or *job shop*, processes.[1] Although MRP is currently available for continuous and repetitive manufacturing, it was designed primarily for systems that produce goods in batches.

## Assemble-to-Order

Finally, MRP systems are very useful in industries in which the customer is allowed to choose among many different options. These products have many common components that are inventoried in some form before the customer order is received. For example, customers of a well-known electronics firm routinely expect delivery in six weeks on goods that

[1]For a more thorough discussion of types of processes, see Chapter 6.

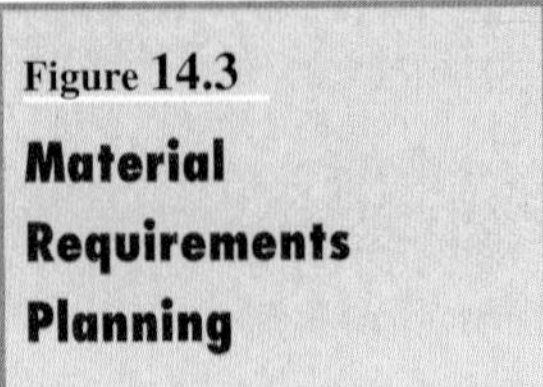

Figure 14.3
**Material Requirements Planning**

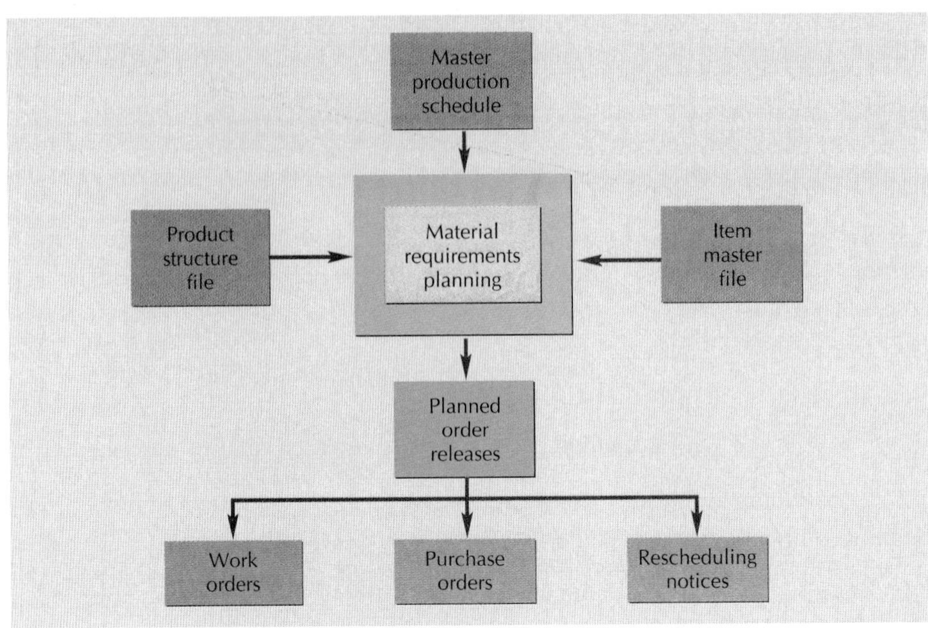


take 28 weeks to manufacture. The manufacturer copes with this seemingly unrealistic demand by producing major assemblies and subassemblies in advance of the customer order and then completing the product on receipt of the order. This type of operation is called **assemble-to-order** or *build-to-order*.

**Assemble-to-order:** a manufacturing environment in which previously completed subassemblies are configured to order.

Figure 14.3 shows the inputs to and outputs from the MRP process. There are three major inputs:

- Master production schedule,
- Product structure file, and
- Item master file.

## MASTER PRODUCTION SCHEDULE

**Master production schedule:** a schedule of finished products that drives the MRP process.

The **master production schedule (MPS)**, also called the *master schedule*, specifies which end items or finished products a firm is to produce, how many are needed, and when they are needed. Recall that aggregate production planning creates a similar schedule for product lines or families, given by months or quarters of a year. The master production schedule works within the constraints of the production plan but produces a more specific schedule by individual products. The time frame is more specific, too. An MPS is usually expressed in days or weeks and may extend over several months to cover the complete manufacture of the items contained in the MPS. The total length of time required to manufacture a product is called its **cumulative lead time**.

**Cumulative lead time:** the total length of time needed to manufacture a product.

The master production schedule drives the MRP process. The schedule of finished products provided by the master schedule is needed before the MRP system can do its job of generating production schedules for component items. Table 14.1 shows a sample master production schedule consisting of four end items produced by a manufacturer of specialty writing accessories.

Table 14.1
**Master Production Schedule (MPS)**

| | Period | | | | |
|---|---|---|---|---|---|
| MPS Item | 1 | 2 | 3 | 4 | 5 |
| Pencil case | 125 | 125 | 125 | 125 | 125 |
| Clipboard | 85 | 95 | 120 | 100 | 100 |
| Lapboard | 75 | 120 | 47 | 20 | 17 |
| Lapdesk | 0 | 60 | 0 | 60 | 0 |

Several comments should be made concerning the quantities contained in the MPS:

- ***The quantities represent production, not demand.*** As we saw in Chapter 13, production does not necessarily have to match demand. Strategy decisions made in the aggregate planning stage filter down to the master production schedule. Common strategies are chase demand, level production, and batching. In Table 14.1, pencil cases are following a level production strategy, clipboards and lapboards a chase demand strategy, and lapdesks a batching strategy.
- ***The quantities may consist of a combination of customer orders and demand forecasts.*** Some figures in the MPS are confirmed, but others are predictions. As might be expected, the quantities in the more recent time periods are more firm, whereas the forecasted quantities further in the future may need to be revised several times before the schedule is completed. Some companies set a **time fence**, within which no more changes to the master schedule are allowed. This helps to stabilize the production environment.

  The MPS for clipboards and lapboards shown in Table 14.1 illustrates two approaches to future scheduling. For clipboards, production beyond period 3 is based on demand forecasts of an even 100 units per period. Projecting these requirements now based on past demand data helps in planning for the availability of resources. For lapboards, production beyond period 3 appears sparse, probably because it is based on actual customer orders received. We can expect those numbers to increase as the future time periods draw nearer.
- ***The quantities represent what needs to be produced, not what can be produced.*** Because the MPS is derived from the aggregate production plan, its requirements are probably "doable," but until the MRP system considers the specific resource needs and the timing of those needs, the feasibility of the MPS cannot be guaranteed. Thus, the MRP system is often used to *simulate* production to verify that the MPS is feasible or to confirm that a particular order can be completed by a certain date before the quote is given to the customer.
- ***The quantities represent end items that may or may not be finished products.*** The level of master scheduling can differ by type of production system. In make-to-stock companies, the MPS consists of finished products. In assemble-to-order companies, the MPS usually represents major subassemblies or modules. In make-to-order companies, the master schedule can consist of critical components, hard to get materials, and service parts. Separate final assembly schedules are then used for the finished product or customer order. As Figure 14.4 shows, companies usually master schedule at the smallest part of the product structure. To simplify discussions, we assume in this chapter that an end item is, in fact, the finished product.

**Time fence:** a management-specified date within which no changes in the master schedule are allowed.

## PRODUCT STRUCTURE FILE

Once the MPS is set, the MRP system accesses the **product structure file** to determine which component items need to be scheduled. The product structure file contains a **bill of material (BOM)** for every item produced. The bill of material for a product lists the items that go into the product, includes a brief description of each item, and specifies when and in what quantity each item is needed in the assembly process.

**Product structure file:** a file that contains a computerized **bill of material** for every item produced.

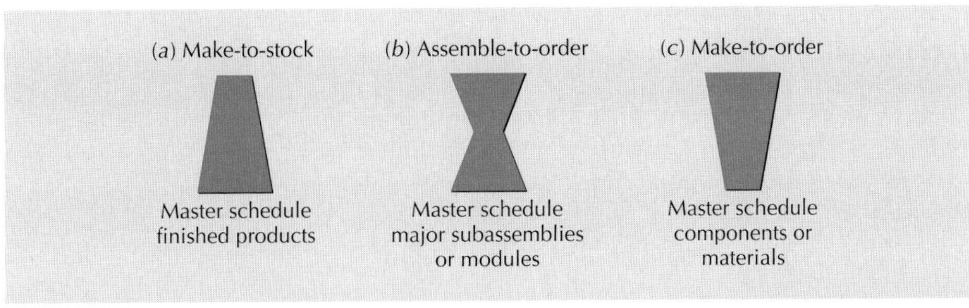


Figure 14.4 **Levels of Master Production Scheduling (Master schedule at the smallest part of the product structure)**

Figure 14.5
**Product Structure Diagram for a Clipboard**

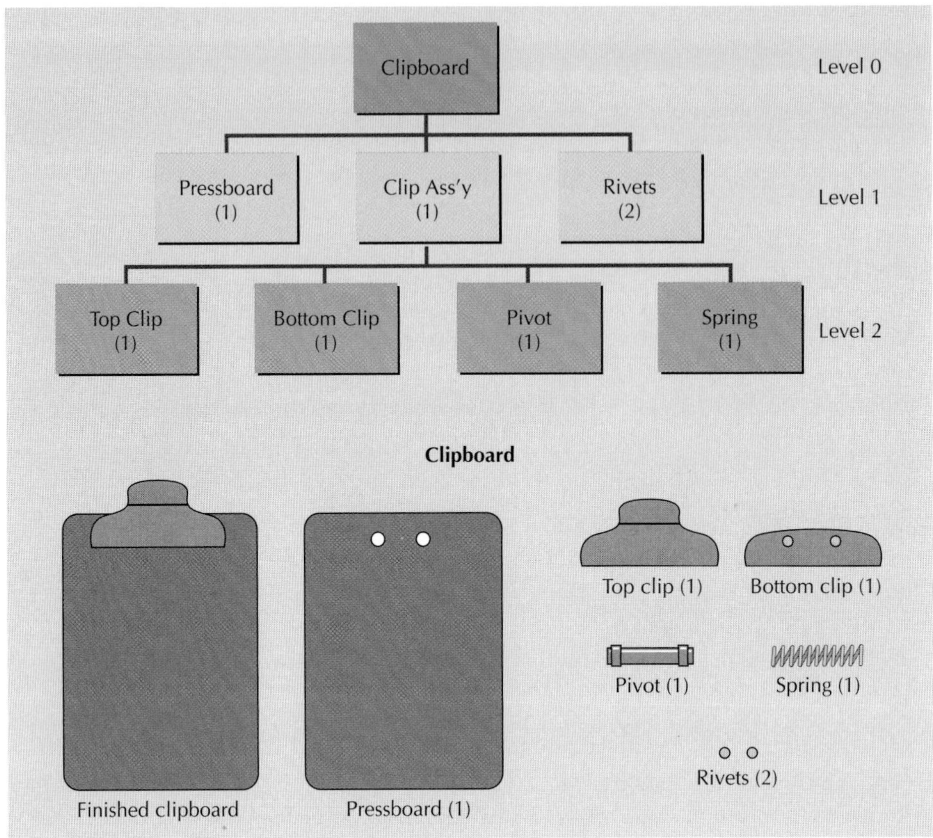


*When* each item is needed can best be described in the form of a product structure diagram, shown in Figure 14.5 for a clipboard. An assembled item is sometimes referred to as a *parent*, and a component as a *child*. The number in parentheses with each item is the quantity of a given component needed to make *one* parent. Thus, one clip assembly, two rivets, and one pressboard are needed to make each clipboard. The clip assembly, rivets, and board appear at the same level of the product structure because they are to be assembled together.

A diagram can be converted to a computerized bill of material by labeling the levels in the product structure. The final product or end item at the top of the structure—in this case, the clipboard—is labeled level 0. The level number increases as we move down the product structure. The clipboard has three levels of assembly. The bill of material for the clipboard, listed in Table 14.2, shows some levels indented underneath others. This specifies which components belong to which parents and can easily be matched to the product structure diagram.

Several specialized bills of material have been designed to simplify information requirements, clarify relationships, and reduce computer processing time. They include phantom bills, K-bills, and modular bills.

Table 14.2
**Multilevel Indented Bill of Material**

| Level | Item | Unit of Measure | Quantity |
|---|---|---|---|
| 0– – – – | Clipboard | ea | 1 |
| –1– – – | Clip assembly | ea | 1 |
| – –2– – | Top clip | ea | 1 |
| – –2– – | Bottom clip | ea | 1 |
| – –2– – | Pivot | ea | 1 |
| – –2– – | Spring | ea | 1 |
| –1– – – | Rivet | ea | 2 |
| –1– – – | Pressboard | ea | 1 |

## Phantom Bills

*Phantom bills* are used for transient subassemblies that never see a stockroom because they are immediately consumed in the next stage of manufacture. These items have a lead time of zero and a special code so that no orders for them will be released. Phantom bills are becoming more common as companies adopt lean manufacturing concepts that speed products through the manufacturing and assembly process.

Phantom bills, K-bills, and modular bills simplify planning.

## K-Bills

*K-bills* or kit numbers, group small, loose parts such as fasteners, nuts, and bolts together under one pseudo-item number. In this way, requirements for the items are processed only once (for the group), rather than for each individual item. K-bills reduce the paperwork, processing time, and file space required in generating orders for small, inexpensive items that are usually ordered infrequently in large quantities.

## Modular Bills

**Modular bills of material** are appropriate when the product is manufactured in major subassemblies or modules that are later assembled into the final product with customer-designated options. With this approach, the end item in the master production schedule is not a finished product, but a major option or module. This reduces the number of bills of material that need to be input, maintained, and processed by the MRP system.

**Modular bills of material:** bills used to plan the production of products with many optional features.

Consider the options available on the X10 automobile, partially diagrammed in Figure 14.6. The customer has a choice between three engine types, eight exterior colors, three interiors, eight interior colors, and four car bodies. Thus, there are $3 \times 8 \times 3 \times 8 \times 4 =$ 2304 possible model configurations—and the same number of bills of material—unless modular bills are used. By establishing a bill of material for each option rather than each combination of options, the entire range of options can be accounted for by $3 + 8 + 3 + 8 + 4 = 26$ modular bills of material.

Modular bills of material also simplify forecasting and planning. The quantity per assembly for an option is given as a decimal figure, interpreted as a percentage of the requirements for the parent item. For example, from Figure 14.6, in preparation for an anticipated demand of 1000 X10 automobiles, 1000 engines are needed. Of those 1000 engines, the master production schedule would generate requirements for 400 four-cylinder engines, 500 six-cylinder engines, and 100 eight-cylinder engines.

**Figure 14.6 Modular Bills of Material**

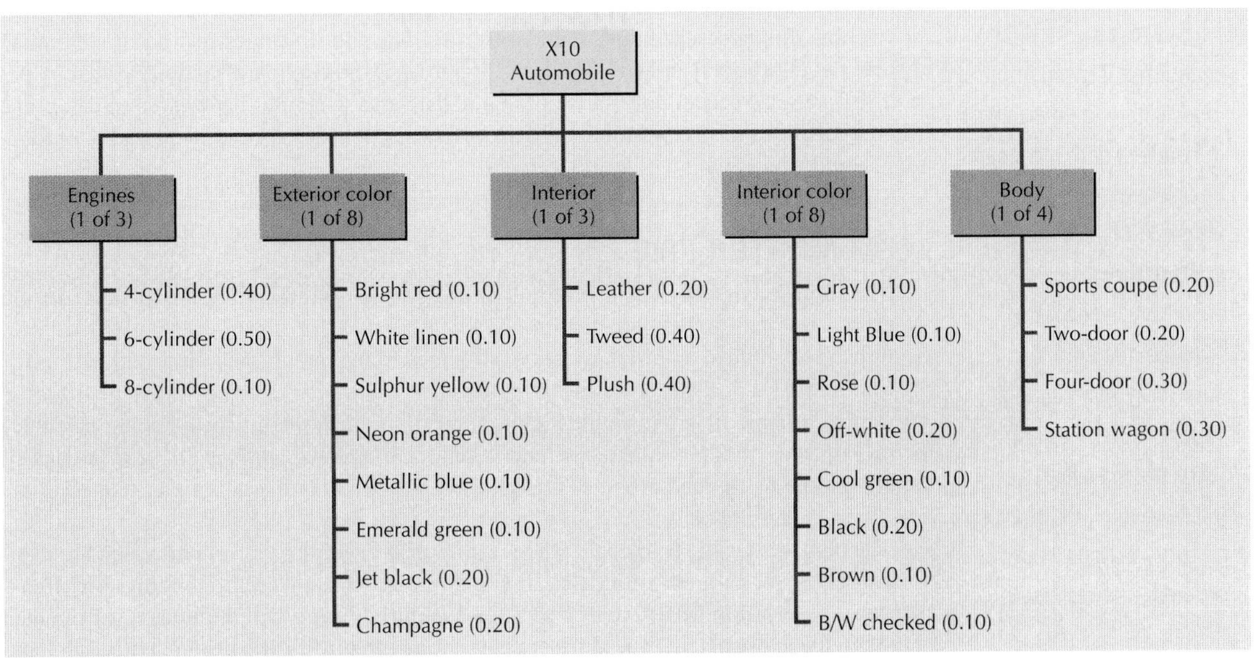

**Figure 14.7**
**Time-Phased Assembly Chart**

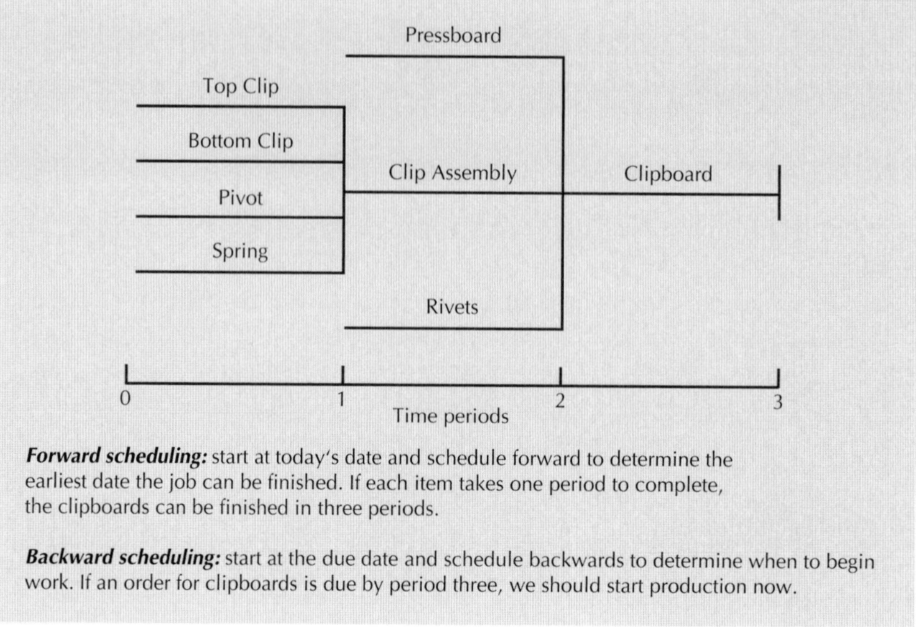


The creation of a product structure file can take a considerable amount of time. Accurate bills of material are essential to an effective MRP system. The bill of material must specify how a product is actually manufactured rather than how it was *designed* to be manufactured. Redundant or obsolete part numbers must be purged from the system. This may not seem like a big task, but in some companies every time a part is purchased from a different supplier, it is assigned a different part number. One firm in the process of implementing MRP was able to eliminate 6000 extra part numbers from its database and dispose of thousands of dollars of obsolete inventory that had not previously been identified as such.

## TIME-PHASED BILLS

**Time-phased bill of material:** an assembly chart shown against a time scale.

**Forward scheduling:** scheduling forward from today's date to determine the earliest date a job can be finished.

**Backward scheduling:** scheduling backwards from the due date to determine when to begin work.

**Item master file:** a database of information on every item produced, ordered, or inventoried.

A **time-phased bill of material**, also known as a *time-phased assembly chart*, is basically a horizontal product structure diagram that graphically shows the lead time required to purchase or manufacture an item. Assuming the lead time for each item in the bill of material for a clipboard is one week, Figure 14.7 shows how long it will take to assemble a clipboard from scratch. An MRP system can **forward schedule** or **backward schedule** production. Forward scheduling starts at today's date and schedules forward to determine the earliest date a job can be finished. In Figure 14.7, the clipboard can be finished by period 3. Backward scheduling starts at the due date and schedules backwards to determine when to begin work. In our example, if an order for clipboards is due by period 3, production should begin now.

## ITEM MASTER FILE

The **item master file**, or inventory file, contains an extensive amount of information on every item that is produced, ordered, or inventoried in the system. It includes such data as on-hand quantities, on-order quantities, lot sizes, safety stock, lead time, and past usage figures. Table 14.3 displays the item master file of the pressboard component from the clipboard example. It provides a detailed description of the item, specifies the inventory policy, updates the physical inventory count, summarizes the item's year-to-date or month-to-date usage, and provides internal codes to link this file with other related information in the MRP database.

The item master file is updated whenever items are withdrawn from or added to inventory or whenever an order is released, revised, or completed. Accuracy of inventory transactions is essential to MRP's ability to keep inventory levels at a minimum. It is estimated that 95% inventory accuracy is a prerequisite for an effective MRP system. Although tech-

**Table 14.3**
**Item Master File**

| Description | | Inventory Policy | |
|---|---|---|---|
| Item | Pressboard | Lead time | 1 |
| Item no. | 7341 | Annual demand | 5000 |
| Item type | Purch | Holding cost | 1 |
| Product/sales class | Comp | Ordering/setup cost | 50 |
| Value class | B | Safety stock | 0 |
| Buyer/planner | RSR | Reorder point | 39 |
| Vendor/drawing | 07142 | EOQ | 316 |
| Phantom code | N | Minimum order qty. | 100 |
| Unit price/cost | 1.25 | Maximum order qty. | 500 |
| Pegging | Y | Multiple order qty. | 1 |
| LLC | 1 | Policy code | 3 |
| **Physical Inventory** | | **Usage/Sales** | |
| On hand | 150 | YTD usage/sales | 1100 |
| Location | W142 | MTD usage/sales | 75 |
| On order | 100 | YTD receipts | 1200 |
| Allocated | 75 | MTD receipts | 0 |
| Cycle | 3 | Last receipt | 8/25 |
| Last count | 9/5 | Last issue | 10/5 |
| Difference | −2 | | |
| | | **Codes** | |
| | | Cost acct. | 00754 |
| | | Routing | 00326 |
| | | Engr. | 07142 |

nologies such as bar codes, voice-activated systems, and automated "picking" equipment can improve inventory accuracy considerably, a general overhaul of inventory procedures is often needed. This involves (1) maintaining orderly stockrooms; (2) establishing and enforcing procedures for inventory withdrawal; (3) ensuring prompt and accurate entry of inventory transactions; (4) taking physical inventory count on a regular basis; and (5) reconciling inventory discrepancies in a timely manner.

## THE COMPETITIVE EDGE

### Five Million Possibilities at Hubbell Lighting

Hubbell Lighting manufactures industrial lighting products for a diverse group of customers, including schools, shopping malls, amusement parks, football franchises, and NASA. The work is specialized for each customer, involves little automation, and can generally be described as a "glorified job shop." Its complexity is derived from the sheer size of the manufacturing task—the hundreds of different products produced, the thousands of parts needed to make up a typical product, the tremendous number of scheduling decisions required on a day-to-day basis, and the vast amount of information that is necessary to support those decisions. For example, one of Hubbell's factories, which employs about 425 workers, develops an aggregate production plan for 63 product families and weekly schedules for the production of 3200 end items. These end items consist of 15,000 components that may be assembled into 5 million possible final product configurations. The factory (and the company as a whole) uses MRP to help plan and coordinate the various stages of production. Without an MRP system, a factory of this type simply could not function. Prior to MRP, the factory completed less than 75% of its orders on time. After MRP, on-time delivery rose to 97%, with an additional 2% completed within one or two days of promised completion.

*Source:* Hubbell Lighting, Christiansburg, VA.

If you have ever taken part in an end-of-year inventory count, you can verify the wide discrepancies that are commonly found between what the records say is in inventory and what is physically there. Unfortunately, by the time the errors are discovered, it is too late to correct them or find out why they occurred. The slate is merely cleaned for next year's record, with the hope or promise that next time will be better.

**Cycle counting:** taking physical count of inventory at various cycles during the year.

**Cycle counting** involves taking physical count of at least some inventory items daily and reconciling differences as they occur. The system specifies which items are to be counted each day on a computer printout and may tie the frequency of the count to the frequency of orders for the item within the MRP system. Thus, items that are used more often are counted more often. The cycle counting system may also be related to the *ABC classification system* discussed in Chapter 12. *A* items would be counted more often than *B* items, perhaps weekly. *B* items would be counted monthly, and *C* items may still be counted only once a year. Approved cycle counting systems are accepted by the accounting standards board as valid replacements for end-of-year physical inventories.

## THE MRP PROCESS

The MRP system is responsible for scheduling the production of all items beneath the end item level. It recommends the release of work orders and purchase orders, and issues rescheduling notices when necessary.

**Netting:** the process of subtracting on-hand quantities and scheduled receipts from gross requirements to produce net requirements.

The MRP process consists of four basic steps: (1) exploding the bill of material, (2) **netting** out inventory, (3) lot sizing, and (4) time-phasing requirements. The process is performed again and again, moving down the product structure until all items have been scheduled. An MRP matrix, as shown in Table 14.4, is completed for each item starting with level zero items. Identifying information at the top of the matrix includes the item name or number, the lowest level at which the item appears in the product structure (called *low level code* or LLC), the time required to make or purchase an item (called *lead time* or LT), and the quantities in which an item is usually made or purchased (called *lot size*).

Entries in the matrix include gross requirements, scheduled receipts, projected on hand, net requirements, planned order receipts, and planned order releases. *Gross requirements* begin the MRP process. They are given in the master production schedule (MPS) for end items and derived from the parent for component items. *Scheduled receipts* are items on order that are scheduled to arrive in future time periods. *Projected on hand* is inventory currently on hand or projected to be on hand at the end of each time period as a result of the MRP schedule. *Net requirements* are what actually needs to be produced after on-hand and on-order quantities have been taken into account. *Planned order receipts* represent the quantities that will be ordered and when they must be received. These quantities differ from net requirements by **lot sizing** rules when production or purchasing is made in predetermined batches or lots. Common lot sizing rules include ordering in minimum or multiple quantities, using an EOQ or periodic order quantity, or ordering the exact quantities needed (called *lot-for-lot* or L4L). We discuss these techniques later in the chapter.

**Lot sizing:** determining the quantities in which items are usually made or purchased.

**Table 14.4**
**The MRP Matrix**

| Item<br>Lot Size | LLC<br>LT | Period 1 | 2 | 3 | 4 | 5 |
|---|---|---|---|---|---|---|
| Gross Requirements | | *Derived from MPS or planned order releases of the parent* | | | | |
| Scheduled Receipts | | *On order and scheduled to be received* | | | | |
| Projected on Hand | Beg Inv | *Anticipated quantity on hand at the end of the period* | | | | |
| Net Requirements | | *Gross requirements net of inventory and scheduled receipts* | | | | |
| Planned Order Receipts | | *When orders need to be received* | | | | |
| Planned Order Releases | | *When orders need to be placed to be received on time* | | | | |

The last row of the matrix, *planned order releases*, determines when orders should be placed (i.e., released) so that they are received when needed. This involves offsetting or **time phasing** the planned order receipts by the item's lead time. Planned order releases at one level of a product structure generate gross requirements at the next lower level. When the MRP process is complete, the planned order releases are compiled in a planned order report.

**Time phasing:** subtracting an item's lead time from its due date to determine when to order an item.

**Example 12.1**
**School Mate Products**

School Mate offers a number of standard products to encourage writing outside of the classroom, including clipboards, lapdesks, lapboards, and pencil boxes. Rising costs and inventory levels have prompted the company to install a computerized planning and control system called MRP. The MPS and bill of material modules are up and running. Sample output is shown in Tables 14.1 and 14.2 and Figure 14.5. Before going live with the MRP module, School Mate has asked for a manual demonstration. Since manual calculations can be quite tedious, you have decided to prepare MRP matrices for only three items—the clipboard and lapdesk, and a common component, pressboard. The master production schedule, abbreviated product structure diagrams, and inventory information are given below.

**Master Production Schedule**

| | 1 | 2 | 3 | 4 | 5 |
|---|---|---|---|---|---|
| Clipboard | 85 | 95 | 120 | 100 | 100 |
| Lapdesk | 0 | 60 | 0 | 60 | 0 |

**Item Master File**

| | Clipboard | Lapdesk | Pressboard |
|---|---|---|---|
| On hand | 25 | 20 | 150 |
| On order (sch receipt) | 175 (period 1) | 0 | 0 |
| LLC | 0 | 0 | 1 |
| Lot size | L4L | Mult 50 | Min 100 |
| Lead time | 1 | 1 | 1 |

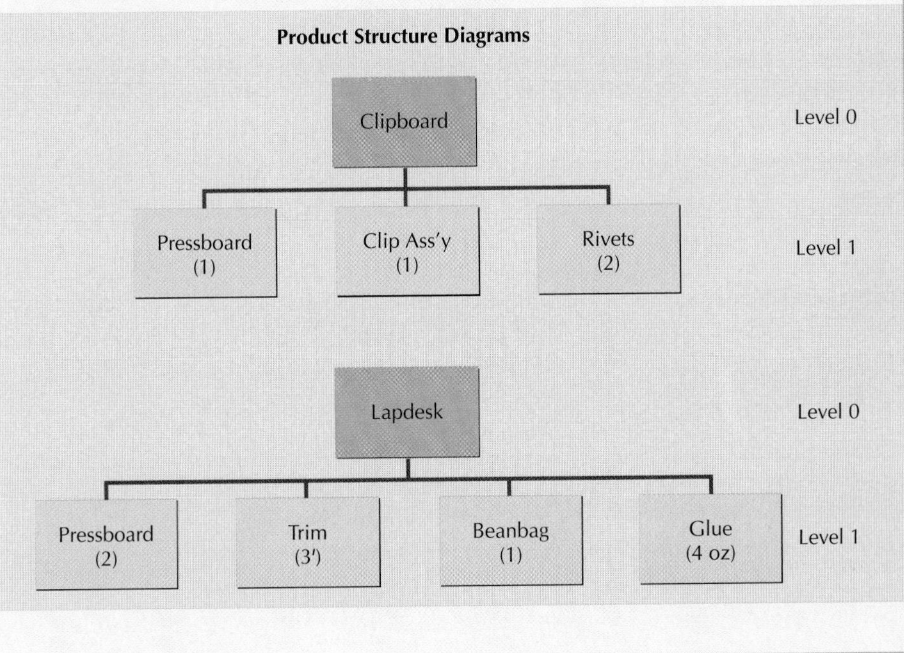

*Solution*

We begin with the level 0 items, the clipboard and lapdesk. Since these are finished products, the *gross requirements* row is simply copied from the master production schedule for those items. We'll begin with the clipboard.

| Item: Clipboard | LLC: 0 | Period | | | | |
|---|---|---|---|---|---|---|
| Lot Size: L4L | LT: 1 | 1 | 2 | 3 | 4 | 5 |
| Gross Requirements | | 85 | 95 | 120 | 100 | 100 |
| Scheduled Receipts | | 175 | | | | |
| Projected on Hand | 25 | 115 | 20 | 0 | 0 | 0 |
| Net Requirements | | 0 | 0 | 100 | 100 | 100 |
| Planned Order Receipts | | | | 100 | 100 | 100 |
| Planned Order Releases | | | 100 | 100 | 100 | |

In period 1 we have 25 units on hand and 175 scheduled to be received. That gives us (25 + 175) = 200 units available. We use 85 of them to satisfy demand, leaving (200 − 85) = 115 units in inventory at the end of period 1. In period 2, we can meet demand from stock, leaving (115 − 95) = 20 units in inventory at the end of the period. In period 3, the 20 units on hand is not enough to cover our demand of 120 units. We need to make 100 more. Thus, our *net requirements* are 100 units. Since our lot sizing rule is lot-for-lot, we order exactly what we need, 100 units. Recall that our lead time is one week. If we wish to *receive* our order for 100 units in period 3, we must *place* the order one week in advance, in period 2. To meet demand in periods 4 and 5, we order 100 units in weeks 3 and 4, one week in advance of when we need them.

The MRP matrix for lapdesks appears below. To meet our demand for 60 units in period 2, we'll use the 20 units in stock and make 40 more. Before we release our work order for production, we check our lot sizing rule. It says we should make 50 lapdesks at a time. If the 50 desks are to be ready by week 2, we need to start production in week 1. When the desks are completed, we'll use 40 of them to meet demand and place 10 back in inventory. Those 10 remain in inventory until period 4 when we use them to partially satisfy the demand for 60 desks. We'll need to make 50 more, and since 50 is our lot size quantity, that's what we make. If the desks are to be completed by week 4, we need to start production in week 3.

| Item: Lapdesk | LLC: 0 | Period | | | | |
|---|---|---|---|---|---|---|
| Lot Size: Mult 50 | LT: 1 | 1 | 2 | 3 | 4 | 5 |
| Gross Requirements | | 0 | 60 | 0 | 60 | 0 |
| Scheduled Receipts | | | | | | |
| Projected on Hand | 20 | 20 | 10 | 10 | 0 | 0 |
| Net Requirements | | | 40 | | 50 | |
| Planned Order Receipts | | | 50 | | 50 | |
| Planned Order Releases | | 50 | | 50 | | |

Pressboard is a purchased component cut to size and used in both the clipboard and the lapdesk. As shown below, its gross requirements are calculated by multiplying the planned order releases of each parent times the quantity per assembly contained in the bill of material. This process is called **explosion**. Since one pressboard is needed for every clipboard and two for every lapdesk, period 1 gross requirements are (50 × 2) = 100; period 2, (100 × 1 = 100); period 3, (100 × 1) + (50 × 2) = 200; and period 4, (100 × 1) = 100.

**Explosion:** the process of determining requirements for lower-level items.

| **Item: Clipboard** | **LLC: 0** | | | **Period** | | |
|---|---|---|---|---|---|---|
| **Lot Size: L4L** | **LT: 1** | *1* | *2* | *3* | *4* | *5* |
| Planned Order Releases | | | 100 | 100 | 100 | |

**100 × 1**

| **Item: Lapdesk** | **LLC: 0** | | | **Period** | | |
|---|---|---|---|---|---|---|
| **Lot Size: Mult 50** | **LT: 1** | *1* | *2* | *3* | *4* | *5* |
| Planned Order Releases | | 50 | | 50 | | |

**50 × 2** **50 × 2** **100 × 1** **100 × 1**

| **Item: Pressboard** | **LLC: 1** | | | **Period** | | |
|---|---|---|---|---|---|---|
| **Lot Size: Min 100** | **LT: 1** | *1* | *2* | *3* | *4* | *5* |
| Gross Requirements | | 100 | 100 | 200 | 100 | 0 |
| Scheduled Receipts | | | | | | |
| Projected on Hand | 150 | 50 | 50 | 0 | 0 | 0 |
| Net Requirements | | | 50 | 150 | 100 | |
| Planned Order Receipts | | | 100 | 150 | 100 | |
| Planned Order Releases | | 100 | 150 | 100 | | |

With 150 units on hand, we can satisfy the demand in period 1 with 50 units left over. For period 2, we use the 50 in inventory and need 50 more. Because our lot sizing rule says we must order *at least* 100 units and it takes 1 week to process an order, we place an order for 100 pressboards in week 1. When the 100 boards come in, we use 50 of them and put 50 back in stock. To meet our demand in period 3, we use the 50 boards in stock and order 150 more. The order is placed in week 2 to arrive in week 3. To meet period 4's demand, we order 100 boards in week 3, one week in advance of delivery.

We have now completed the MRP calculations. To summarize the results, we construct a *planned order report* from the planned order release row of each matrix, as follows:

**Planned Order Report**

| | | | **Period** | | |
|---|---|---|---|---|---|
| **Item** | *1* | *2* | *3* | *4* | *5* |
| Clipboard | | 100 | 100 | 100 | |
| Lapdesk | 50 | | 50 | | |
| Pressboard | 100 | 150 | 100 | | |

An Excel solution for Example 14.1 is shown in Exhibit 14.1. The file is available for you on the text Web site.

## LOT SIZING IN MRP SYSTEMS

Example 14.1 illustrated the use of minimum order quantities, multiple order quantities, and lot-for-lot lot sizing rules. Although the lot-for-lot (L4L) approach is most consistent with the objectives of MRP, in some circumstances it is useful to order an amount different from what is needed. For example, *minimum order quantities* are typically used to take advantage of purchasing or shipping discounts, or to conform to vendor requirements, *maximum order quantities* are used for large or expensive items when space or funds are limited, and *multiple order quantities* accommodate packaging restrictions (such as a set number in a box, gallon containers, bundles, or pallet loads). Several additional lot sizing techniques are available with most MRP systems. These include economic order quantity (EOQ) and **periodic order quantity** (POQ).

**Periodic order quantity:** a lot sizing technique that orders at set time intervals.

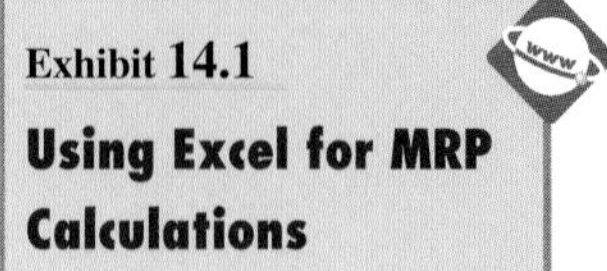


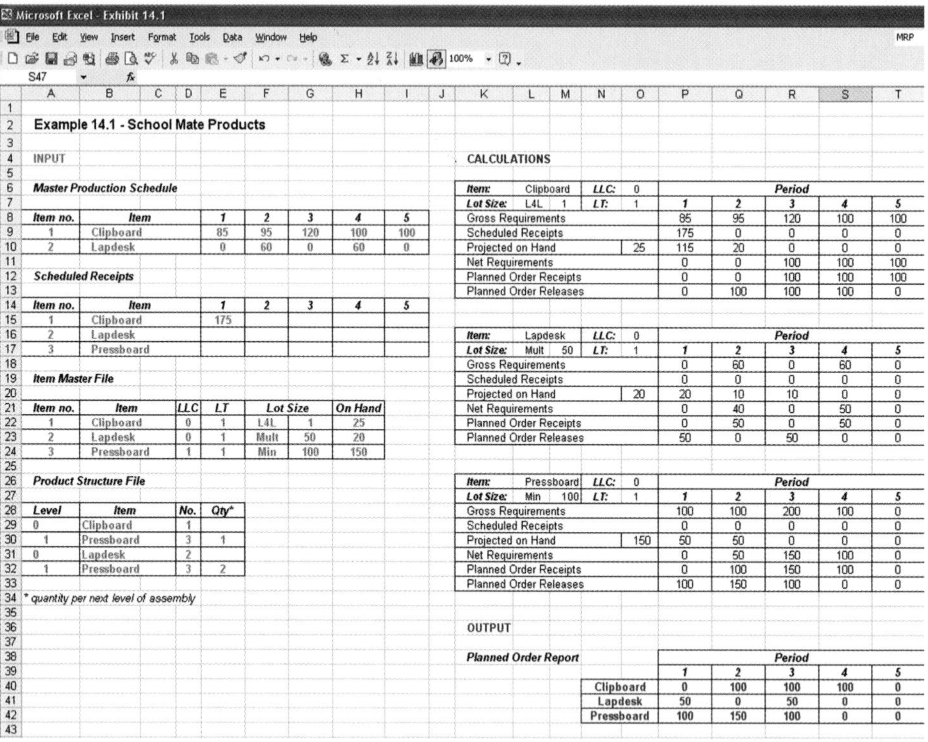

Microsoft Excel - Exhibit 14.1

**Example 14.1 - School Mate Products**

INPUT

***Master Production Schedule***

| Item no. | Item | 1 | 2 | 3 | 4 | 5 |
|---|---|---|---|---|---|---|
| 1 | Clipboard | 85 | 95 | 120 | 100 | 100 |
| 2 | Lapdesk | 0 | 60 | 0 | 60 | 0 |

***Scheduled Receipts***

| Item no. | Item | 1 | 2 | 3 | 4 | 5 |
|---|---|---|---|---|---|---|
| 1 | Clipboard | 175 | | | | |
| 2 | Lapdesk | | | | | |
| 3 | Pressboard | | | | | |

***Item Master File***

| Item no. | Item | LLC | LT | Lot Size | | On Hand |
|---|---|---|---|---|---|---|
| 1 | Clipboard | 0 | 1 | L4L | 1 | 25 |
| 2 | Lapdesk | 0 | 1 | Mult | 50 | 20 |
| 3 | Pressboard | 1 | 1 | Min | 100 | 150 |

***Product Structure File***

| Level | Item | No. | Qty* |
|---|---|---|---|
| 0 | Clipboard | 1 | |
| 1 | Pressboard | 3 | 1 |
| 0 | Lapdesk | 2 | |
| 1 | Pressboard | 3 | 2 |

* quantity per next level of assembly

CALCULATIONS

| Item: Clipboard | LLC: 0 | Period | | | | |
|---|---|---|---|---|---|---|
| Lot Size: L4L 1 | LT: 1 | 1 | 2 | 3 | 4 | 5 |
| Gross Requirements | | 85 | 95 | 120 | 100 | 100 |
| Scheduled Receipts | | 175 | 0 | 0 | 0 | 0 |
| Projected on Hand | 25 | 115 | 20 | 0 | 0 | 0 |
| Net Requirements | | 0 | 0 | 100 | 100 | 100 |
| Planned Order Receipts | | 0 | 0 | 100 | 100 | 100 |
| Planned Order Releases | | 0 | 100 | 100 | 100 | 0 |

| Item: Lapdesk | LLC: 0 | Period | | | | |
|---|---|---|---|---|---|---|
| Lot Size: Mult 50 | LT: 1 | 1 | 2 | 3 | 4 | 5 |
| Gross Requirements | | 0 | 60 | 0 | 60 | 0 |
| Scheduled Receipts | | 0 | 0 | 0 | 0 | 0 |
| Projected on Hand | 20 | 20 | 10 | 10 | 0 | 0 |
| Net Requirements | | 0 | 40 | 0 | 50 | 0 |
| Planned Order Receipts | | 0 | 50 | 0 | 50 | 0 |
| Planned Order Releases | | 50 | 0 | 50 | 0 | 0 |

| Item: Pressboard | LLC: 0 | Period | | | | |
|---|---|---|---|---|---|---|
| Lot Size: Min 100 | LT: 1 | 1 | 2 | 3 | 4 | 5 |
| Gross Requirements | | 100 | 100 | 200 | 100 | 0 |
| Scheduled Receipts | | 0 | 0 | 0 | 0 | 0 |
| Projected on Hand | 150 | 50 | 50 | 0 | 0 | 0 |
| Net Requirements | | 0 | 50 | 150 | 100 | 0 |
| Planned Order Receipts | | 0 | 100 | 150 | 100 | 0 |
| Planned Order Releases | | 100 | 150 | 100 | 0 | 0 |

OUTPUT

***Planned Order Report***

| | Period | | | | |
|---|---|---|---|---|---|
| | 1 | 2 | 3 | 4 | 5 |
| Clipboard | 0 | 100 | 100 | 100 | 0 |
| Lapdesk | 50 | 0 | 50 | 0 | 0 |
| Pressboard | 100 | 150 | 100 | 0 | 0 |

## Economic Order Quantity

We discussed the economic order quantity for independent demand items in Chapter 12. The EOQ can be adapted for use with MRP if it is treated as a minimum order quantity. In addition, annual demand, $D$, is replaced with average demand per period, $d$, and carrying cost, $C_c$, is converted to a per-period amount. The EOQ is used only sparingly, usually at the finished product or raw material level, and does not perform well when demand is highly variable.

*MRP systems can be used for services, too. In renovating hotel rooms, Marriot develops a bill of material and a bill of labor for each room type and then "explodes" the bill throughout the facility to summarize its furniture and decorating needs. Menus in restaurants can be thought of as master schedules. Demand for menu items is forecasted and then multiplied by a bill of ingredients to ensure sufficient "material" is on hand for the chef to prepare what the customer orders. The bill of ingredients can also be used to accurately price menu items.*

## Periodic Order Quantity

The periodic order quantity (POQ) was created as a variation of the EOQ more suited to variable demand. POQ is calculated by dividing the EOQ by average demand. It represents the number of demand periods covered by each order. Thus, if the POQ were three, an order would be placed for three weeks worth of demand.

Example 14.2 compares the L4L, EOQ, and POQ, lot sizing techniques.

**Example 14.2**

**Advanced Lot Sizing Rules**

The Lifetime Sports Company has been using MRP to manufacture sports equipment for a number of years. Recently, Bob Sage, the operations manager, decided to investigate the use of lot sizing for MRP-generated orders. As a test case, Bob selected a typical product in their line of fishing rods and gathered weekly data over a month's time. Ordering costs are \$60 per order, and carrying costs are \$1 per unit per week. The beginning inventory is 30 units, and lead time is one week. Help Bob determine whether the L4L, EOQ or POQ lot sizing technique is more appropriate.

| Period | 1 | 2 | 3 | 4 | 5 |
|---|---|---|---|---|---|
| Gross Requirements | 30 | 50 | 20 | 10 | 40 |

$$C_o = \$60$$
$$C_c = \$1$$
$$\bar{d} = (30 + 50 + 20 + 10 + 40)/5 = 30$$

a. With L4L ordering, orders would be placed in periods 2, 3, 4, and 5 for the exact amount needed. Total cost is calculated as (number of orders × ordering cost) + (projected on hand × carrying cost).

| **Item: Rod** | **LLC: 0** | **Period** | | | | |
|---|---|---|---|---|---|---|
| **Lot Size: L4L** | **LT: 1** | *1* | 2 | 3 | 4 | 5 |
| Gross Requirements | | 30 | 50 | 20 | 10 | 40 |
| Scheduled Receipts | | | | | | |
| Projected on hand | 30 | 0 | 0 | 0 | 0 | 0 |
| Net Requirements | | | 50 | 20 | 10 | 40 |
| Planned Order Receipts | | | 50 | 20 | 10 | 40 |
| Planned Order Releases | | 50 | 20 | 10 | 40 | |

Total cost of L4L = (4 × \$60) + (0 × \$1) = \$240

b. $\text{EOQ} = \sqrt{\dfrac{2(30)(60)}{1}} = 60$ minimum order quantity

| **Item: Rod** | **LLC: 0** | **Period** | | | | |
|---|---|---|---|---|---|---|
| **Lot Size: EOQ 60** | **LT: 1** | *1* | 2 | 3 | 4 | 5 |
| Gross Requirements | | 30 | 50 | 20 | 10 | 40 |
| Scheduled Receipts | | | | | | |
| Projected on hand | 30 | 0 | 10 | 50 | 40 | 0 |
| Net Requirements | | | 50 | 10 | | |
| Planned Order Receipts | | | 60 | 60 | | |
| Planned Order Releases | | 60 | 60 | | | |

Total cost of EOQ = (2 × \$60) + [(10 + 50 + 40) × \$1)] = \$220

c. POQ = $Q/\bar{d}$ = 60/30 = 2 periods worth of requirements

| Item: Rod | LLC: 0 | Period | | | | |
|---|---|---|---|---|---|---|
| Lot Size: POQ 2 | LT: 1 | 1 | 2 | 3 | 4 | 5 |
| Gross Requirements | | 30 | 50 | 20 | 10 | 40 |
| Scheduled Receipts | | | | | | |
| Projected on hand | 30 | 0 | 20 | 0 | 40 | 0 |
| Net Requirements | | | 50 | | 10 | |
| Planned Order Receipts | | | 70 | | 50 | |
| Planned Order Releases | | 70 | | 50 | | |

Total cost of POQ = (2 × \$60) + [(20 + 40) × \$1] = \$180

## MRP OUTPUTS

The outputs of the MRP process are planned orders from the planned order release row of the MRP matrix. As shown in Figure 14.4, these can represent *work orders* to be released to the shop floor for in-house production or *purchase orders* to be sent to outside suppliers. MRP output can also recommend changes in previous plans or existing schedules. These *action notices*, or *rescheduling notices*, are issued for items that are no longer needed as soon as planned or for quantities that may have changed. One of the advantages of the MRP system is its ability to show the effect of change in one part of the production process on the rest of the system. It simulates the ordering, receiving, and use of raw materials, components, and assemblies into future time periods and issues warnings to the MRP planner of impending stockouts or missed due dates.

Table 14.5 shows a monthly *planned order report* for an individual item, in this case, item #2740. The report maps out the material orders planned and released orders scheduled to be completed in anticipation of demand. Notice that safety stock is treated as a quantity not to be used and that a problem exists on 10-01, when projected on hand first goes negative. To correct this, the system suggests that the scheduled receipt of 200 units due on 10-08 be moved forward to 10-01. The MRP system will not generate a new order

**Table 14.5**
**Planned Order Report**

| Item | #2740 | | | Date | 9-25-05 |
|---|---|---|---|---|---|
| On hand | 100 | | | Lead time | 2 weeks |
| On order | 200 | | | Lot size | 200 |
| Allocated | 50 | | | Safety stock | 50 |

| Date | Order No. | Gross Reqs. | Scheduled Receipts | Projected On Hand | Action |
|---|---|---|---|---|---|
| | | | | 50 | |
| 9–26 | AL 4416 | 25 | | 25 | |
| 9–30 | AL 4174 | 25 | | 0 | |
| 10–01 | GR 6470 | 50 | | −50 | |
| 10–08 | SR 7542 | | 200 | 150 | Expedite SR 10–01 |
| 10–10 | CO 4471 | 75 | | 75 | |
| 10–15 | GR 6471 | 50 | | 25 | |
| 10–23 | GR 6471 | 25 | | 0 | |
| 10–27 | GR 6473 | 50 | | −50 | Release PO 10–13 |

Key: AL = allocated; CO = customer order; PO = purchase order; WO = work order; SR = scheduled receipt; GR = gross requirement

**Table 14.6**
**MRP Action Report**

Current date: 9-25-02

| Item | Date | Order No. | Qty. | Action | | |
|---|---|---|---|---|---|---|
| #2740 | 10-08 | 7542 | 200 | Expedite | SR | 10-01 |
| #3616 | 10-09 | | | Move forward | PO | 10-07 |
| #2412 | 10-10 | | | Move forward | PO | 10-05 |
| #3427 | 10-15 | | | Move backward | PO | 10-25 |
| #2516 | 10-20 | 7648 | 100 | De-expedite | SR | 10-30 |
| #2740 | 10-27 | | 200 | Release | PO | 10-13 |
| #3666 | 10-31 | | 50 | Release | WO | 10-24 |

if a deficit can be solved by expediting existing orders. It is up to the MRP planner to assess the feasibility of expediting the scheduled receipt and to take appropriate action.

Table 14.6 shows an *MRP action report* for a family of items for which a particular MRP planner is responsible. It summarizes the action messages that have been compiled for individual items. On 10-08, we see the action message for item #2740 that appeared on the previous report. Notice the variety of action messages listed. Some suggest that planned orders be moved forward or backward. Others suggest that scheduled receipts be expedited or de-expedited.

It is the planner's job to respond to the actions contained in the action report. If a planner decides to **expedite** an order—that is, have it completed in less than its normal lead time—he or she might call up a supplier or a shop supervisor and ask for priority treatment. Giving one job higher priority may involve reducing the priority of other jobs. This is possible if the MRP action report indicates that some jobs are not needed as early as anticipated. The process of moving some jobs *forward* in the schedule (expediting) and moving other jobs *backward* (de-expediting) allows the material planner, with the aid of the MRP system, to fine-tune the material plan. Temporary lead time adjustments through overtime or outside purchases of material can also fix a timing problem in the MRP plan, but at a cost. An MRP action report that is exceedingly long or does not strike a balance between speeding up some orders and slowing down others can signify trouble. Action messages that recommend only the expediting of orders indicate an overloaded master schedule and an ineffective MRP system.

**Expedite:**
to speed up an order so it is completed in less than its normal lead time.

The MRP system, as the name implies, ensures that *material* requirements are met. However, material is not the only resource necessary to produce goods—a certain amount of labor and machine hours are also required. Thus, the next step in the planning process is to verify that the MRP plan is "feasible" by checking for the availability of labor and/or machine hours. This process is called *capacity requirements planning* and is similar to MRP.

## CAPACITY REQUIREMENTS PLANNING

**Capacity requirements planning (CRP)** is a computerized system that projects the load from a given material plan onto the capacity of a system and identifies underloads and overloads. It is then up to the MRP planner to *level the load*—smooth out the resource requirements so that capacity constraints are not violated. This can be accomplished by shifting requirements, reducing requirements, or temporarily expanding capacity.

**CRP:**
creates a load profile that identifies underloads and overloads.

There are three major inputs to CRP, as shown in Figure 14.8:

- The *planned order* releases from the MRP process;
- A *routing file*, which specifies which machines or workers are required to complete an order from the MRP plan, in what order the operations are to be conducted, and the length of time each operation should take; and
- an *open orders file*, which contains information on the status of jobs that have already been released but have not yet been completed.

**Figure 14.8**
**Capacity Requirements Planning**

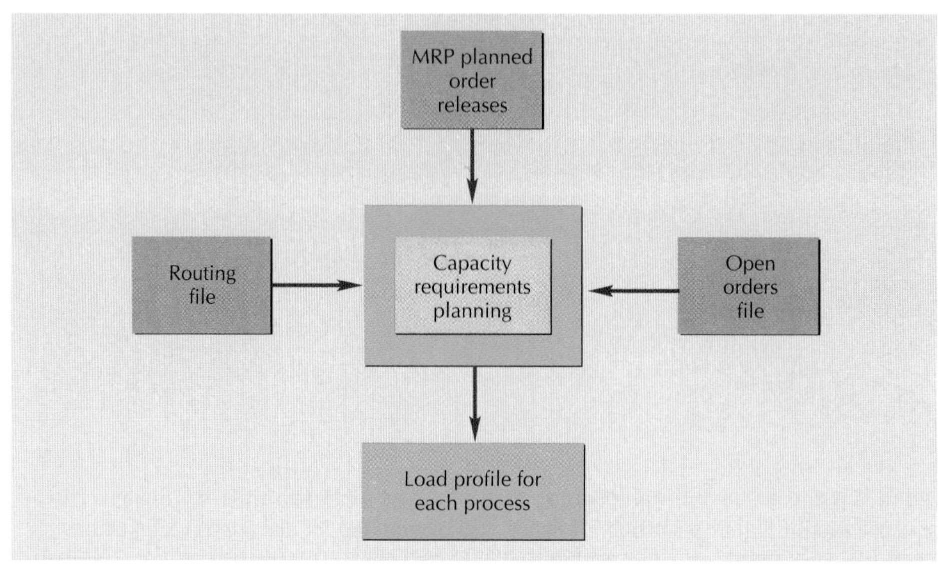


**Load profile:** a graphical comparison of load versus capacity.

With this information, CRP can produce a **load profile** for each process or work center in the shop. The load profile compares released orders and planned orders with work center capacity.

Load profiles can be displayed graphically, as shown in Figure 14.9. The normal capacity of Department A is 40 hours per week. We can see that the machine is *underloaded* in periods 1, 5, and 6, and *overloaded* in periods 2, 3, and 4.

Underloaded conditions can be leveled by:

1. Acquiring more work;
2. *Pulling work ahead* that is scheduled for later periods; or
3. Reducing normal capacity.

Additional work can be acquired by transferring similar work from other machines in the same shop that are near or over capacity, by making components in-house that are normally purchased from outside suppliers, or by seeking work from outside sources. Pulling work ahead seems like a quick and easy alternative to alleviate both underloads and overloads. However, we must remember that the MRP plan was devised based on an interrelated product structure, so the feasibility of scheduling work in an earlier time period is contingent on the availability of required materials or components. In addition, work completed prior to its due date must be stored in inventory and thus incurs a holding cost.

**Figure 14.9**
**Initial Load Profile for Department A**

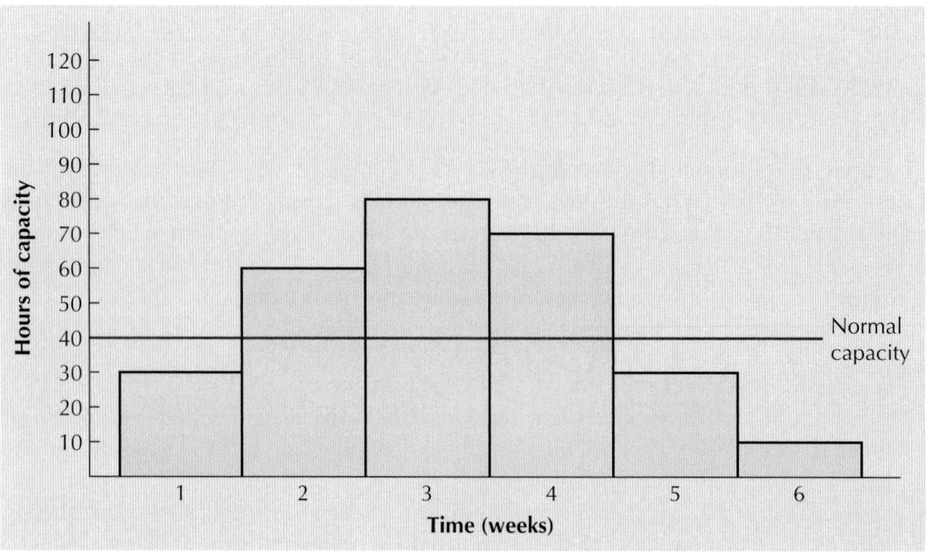

When work is shifted to other time periods, the MRP plan should be rerun to check the feasibility of the proposed schedule.

If an underloaded condition continues for some time, reducing the size of the workforce may be necessary. Smaller underloads can be handled by reducing the length of the working day or workweek, by scheduling idled workers for training sessions or vacations, or by transferring workers to other positions at machine centers or processes where overloads are occurring.

## OVERLOADS

Overloaded conditions are the primary concern of the MRP planner because an overloaded schedule left unchecked cannot possibly be completed as planned. Overloads can be reduced by:

1. Eliminating unnecessary requirements;
2. Rerouting jobs to alternative machines, workers, or work centers;
3. Splitting lots between two or more machines;
4. Increasing normal capacity;
5. Subcontracting;
6. Increasing the efficiency of the operation;
7. Pushing work back to later time periods; or
8. Revising the master schedule.

Some capacity problems are generated from an MRP plan that includes lot sizes, safety stock and unsubstantiated requirements for service parts or forecasted demand. To verify that a capacity overload is caused by "real" need, the planner might examine the MRP matrices of the items assigned to a machine center during an overloaded period as well as the matrices of the parents of those items processed, all the way up the product structure to the master schedule. Or, the MRP system could be rerun with lot sizes temporarily set to one and safety stock to zero to see if the capacity problem is eliminated.

MRP systems assume that an entire lot of goods is processed by one machine or operator. Given the job shop environment in which most MRP systems are installed, there are usually several machines that can perform the same job (although perhaps not as efficiently). With CRP, load profiles are determined with jobs assigned to the preferred machine first, but when capacity problems occur, jobs can certainly be reassigned to alternate machines. In addition, if two or more similar machines are available at the same time, it may be possible to *split* a batch—that is, assign part of an order to one machine and the remainder to another machine.

Reduce overloads by increasing normal capacity, improving efficiency, or postponing work.

Normal capacity can be increased by adding extra hours to the work day, extra days to the work week, or extra shifts. Temporary overloads are usually handled with overtime. More extensive overloads may require hiring additional workers. Work can also be outsourced.

Improving the efficiency of an operation increases its capacity. Assigning the most efficient workers to an overloaded machine, improving the operating procedures or tools, or decreasing the percentage of items that need to be reworked or scrapped increases efficiency and allows more items to be processed in the same amount of time. Because output increases with the same amount of input, *productivity* increases. This is especially useful for alleviating chronic overloads at bottleneck operations, but it does take time to put into effect.

If later time periods are underloaded, it may be possible to push work back to those periods so that the work is completed but later than originally scheduled. There are two problems with this approach. First, postponing some jobs could throw the entire schedule off, meaning customers will not receive the goods when promised. This could involve a penalty for late delivery, loss of an order, or loss of a customer. Second, filling up the later time periods may preclude accepting new orders during those periods. It is normal for time periods further in the future to be underloaded. As these periods draw nearer, customer orders accelerate and begin taking up more of the system's capacity.

If all the preceding approaches to remedying overloads have been tried, but an overload still exists, the only option is to revise the master schedule. That means some customer will not receive goods as previously promised. The planner, in conjunction with someone from marketing, should determine which customers have the lowest priority and whether their orders should be postponed or canceled.

There are cost consequences associated with each of these alternatives, but there is usually no attempt to derive an optimal solution. More than likely, the MRP planner will use the options that produce a feasible solution quickly. In many manufacturing environments, new customer orders arrive daily, and feasible MRP plans can become infeasible overnight.

## LOAD LEVELING

Figure 14.10 shows one possible remedy for the overloads shown in Figure 14.9. Ten hours of work are pulled ahead from period 2 to period 1. Ten hours of overtime are assigned in period 2. An entire 40-hour shift is added in period 3. Ten hours of work from period 4 are pushed back to period 5, and 20 hours are pushed back to period 6. This process of balancing underloads and overloads is called **load leveling**.

**Load leveling:** the process of balancing underloads and overloads.

CRP *identifies* capacity problems, but the planner *solves* the problems. With experience, the task of shifting work and leveling loads is not as formidable as it appears. However, it is helpful if the initial load profile is as accurate as possible and if previous planning stages (i.e., aggregate production planning and master production scheduling) have considered capacity constraints. Some companies formalize capacity planning at each stage of production planning. *Resource requirements planning* is associated with an aggregate production plan, and *rough-cut capacity planning* is performed prior to the approval of a master schedule. Capacity requirements planning may still be performed on the material requirements plan, but its role is to fine-tune existing resources rather than to find or develop new resources.

Once the feasibility of an MRP plan has been verified by CRP, the plan can be executed by releasing orders in the time periods indicated. Normally, the ERP system automatically releases the orders. Work orders sent to the shop enter a shop floor control system, where daily scheduling and monitoring take place. When received, purchase orders are logged through the inventory system electronically before moving to manufacturing. Refer back to Figure 14.1 shown on page 645. The figure shows the entire MRP process from the aggregate production plan to manufacture as a *closed-loop* system. The term is used to describe the numerous feedback loops between plans for production and available capacity.

## RELAXING MRP ASSUMPTIONS

The MRP process described in the previous sections and depicted in Figure 14.1 makes certain assumptions about production resources and how they should be allocated.

**Figure 14.10**
**Adjusted Load Profile for Department A**

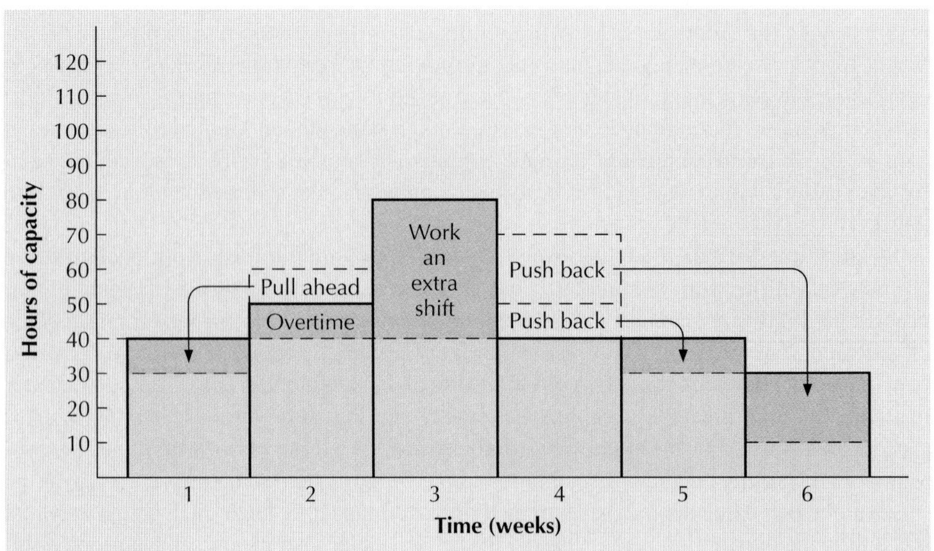

Today's ERP technology allows us to relax some of the more restrictive assumptions of MRP. For example, we have learned the following:

- ***Material is not always the most constraining resource.*** The iterative procedure described in the previous section for determining material availability first, then verifying capacity may not be relevant to some industries. If there are particular processes that constrain the system or other capacity constraints that are difficult to relax, then they should drive the schedule rather than the availability of materials. Similarly, a bill of material may not be as important as a *bill of labor*, a *bill of resources*, a *bill of distribution*, or a *bill of information*.
- ***Lead times can vary.*** Fixed lead times assume that either lot sizes will continue unchanged or that they have no bearing on lead time. Under this assumption, the lead time necessary to process an order would remain the same whether that order consists of 1 unit or 100 units, and whether the shop is operating empty or at capacity. ERP processors today are able to handle variable lead times, but users must determine how sensitive the system should be to parameters that change.
- ***Not every transaction needs to be recorded.*** MRP tries to keep track of the status of all jobs in the system and reschedules jobs as problems occur. In a manufacturing environment of speed and small lot sizes, this is cumbersome. It might take as long to *record* the processing of an item at a workstation as it does to process the item. Managers must assess how much processing detail is really needed in the common database and how much control is enough.
- ***The shop floor may require a more sophisticated scheduling system.*** Dynamic scheduling environments require a level of sophistication not present in most MRP systems. Chapter 16 introduces more advanced planning and control techniques for detailed scheduling.
- ***Scheduling in advance may not be appropriate for on-demand production.*** Many companies today produce products on-demand from customers. The just-in-time or lean production environment, discussed in the next chapter, may produce better results under those circumstances. Whereas the master scheduling and bill-of-material explosion aspects of MRP are used in virtually all manufacturing environments, the MRP and CRP processes are unnecessary in repetitive manufacturing driven by customer orders.

## ENTERPRISE RESOURCE PLANNING (ERP)

**Enterprise Resource Planning (ERP)** is software that organizes and manages a company's business processes by sharing information across functional areas. It transforms transactional data like sales into useful information that supports business decisions in other parts of the company, such as manufacturing, inventory, procurement, invoicing, distribution, and accounting. In addition to managing all sorts of back-office functions, ERP connects with supply chain and customer management applications, helping businesses share information both inside and outside the company. Thus, ERP serves as the backbone for an organization's information needs, as well as its e-business initiatives.

**ERP:** software that organizes and manages a company's business processes by sharing information across functional areas.

Prior to ERP, most companies supported a full staff of program developers, who wrote their business applications from scratch or developed complicated interfaces to allow prepackaged applications from several vendors to pass data back and forth as necessary to complete business transactions throughout the enterprise. This process was costly, time-consuming, and error-prone. Communication among various areas of the business was difficult, and managers could not get a comprehensive view of how the business was doing at any point in time.

ERP integrates business processes.

SAP AG, a German software company, created a generic ERP software package to integrate all business processes together for use by any business in the world. Established first in a mainframe version, the software was updated to client server architecture just as companies began replacing their old legacy systems in preparation for the Y2K problem. Sales were robust, and with essentially one product SAP became the third largest software company in the world.

With ERP, companies could integrate their accounting, sales, distribution, manufacturing, planning, purchasing, human resources, and other transactions into one application software. This enabled transactions to be synchronized throughout the entire system. For example, a customer order entered into an ERP system would ripple through the company, adjusting inventory, parts supplies, accounting entries, production schedules, shipping schedules, and balance sheets.

ERP systems facilitate customer interaction.

ERP systems help companies manage their resources efficiently and, at the same time, better serve their customers. Owens Corning replaced over 200 legacy systems with one ERP system. By coordinating customer orders, financial reporting, and global procurement, the company was able to save over $65 million. IBM Storage Systems reduced the time required to reprice its line of products from 5 days to 5 minutes, the time to ship a replacement part from 22 days to 3 days, and the time to complete a credit check from 20 minutes to 3 seconds. Microsoft saved $12 million annually just in early-payment discounts from vendors when its ERP system went live. Monsanto cut its production planning from 6 weeks to 3, reduced working capital, and enhanced its bargaining position with suppliers, saving the company an estimated $200 million a year.

Global companies benefit the most from ERP.

Global companies and those that share data regularly benefit the most from ERP. Nation-specific laws, currencies, and business practices embedded in the system enable it to translate sales transactions smoothly between business units in different countries—for example, a company in Taiwan and its customer in Brazil.

ERP simplifies customer interaction and speeds production with its configure-to-order capabilities. Customers ordering online or through a sales rep can quickly choose from a variety of options, for which a bill of material is automatically generated and sent to production. National Park Service employees log onto a special segment of Vanity Fair's Web site to purchase their uniforms. Vanity Fair's ERP system makes sure the items selected are approved and automatically debits their clothing allowance. Wal-Mart's 5000 suppliers can link directly to the data warehouse to see how its products are selling and decide when to replenish the stock.

Data entered once into an ERP system, say from manufacturing, need not be reconciled with accounting or warehouse records because the records are all the same. With broader, more timely access to operating and financial data, ERP systems encourage flatter organizational structures and more decentralized decision making. At the same time, they centralize control over information and standardize processes. Standardized transactions make businesses more efficient; shared data makes them more creative.

## ERP MODULES

ERP systems consist of a series of application modules that can be used alone or in concert. The modules are fully integrated, use a common database, and support processes that extend across functional areas. Transactions in one module are immediately available to all other modules at all relevant sites—corporate headquarters, manufacturing plants, suppliers, sales offices, and subsidiaries.

Although ERP modules differ by vendor, they are typically grouped into four main categories: (1) finance and accounting, (2) sales and marketing, (3) production and materials management, and (4) human resources. Figure 14.11 shows the type of information that flows between customers, suppliers, and these various functional areas.

## FINANCE/ACCOUNTING

The *finance and accounting module* encompasses financial accounting, investment management, cost control, treasury management, asset management, and enterprise controlling. Included are cost centers, profit centers, activity-based costing, capital budgeting, and profitability analysis, as well as enterprise measures of performance. The finance module provides consistent financial data that is updated in real time and that links operational results with the financial effects of those results. For every physical transaction, the financial result is shown.

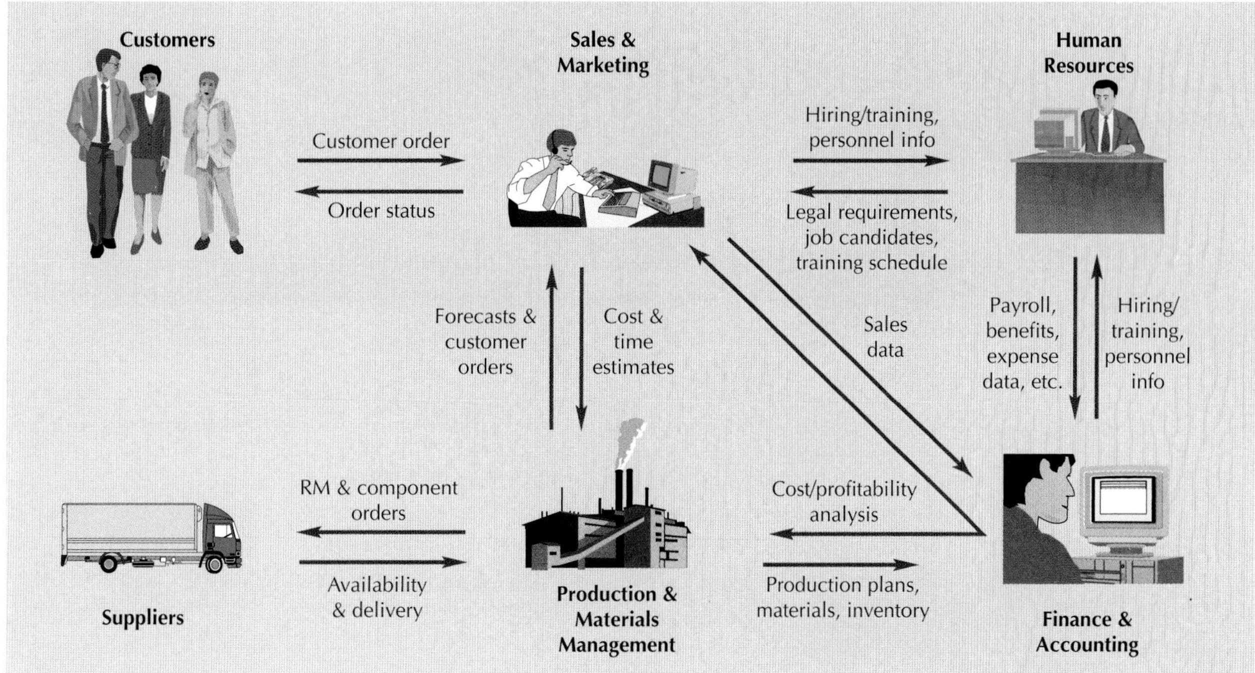


**Figure 14.11**
**Organizational Data Flows**

*Source:* Adapted from Joseph Brady, Ellen Monk, and Bret Wagner, *Concepts in Enterprise Resource Planning* (Boston: Course Technology, 2001), pp. 7–12.

*Note:* The flow between HR and Production is similar to that between HR and Sales. It was eliminated from the figure to simplify the diagram.

## Sales/Marketing

The *sales and marketing module* supports customer-related activities such as order processing, product configuration, and delivery quotations. Pricing, promotions, availability, and shipping options are determined as sales orders are entered. The sales module allows for profitability analyses based on different pricing designs with discounts and rebates, and the projection of accurate delivery dates. It can also look into the company's finished goods and work-in-process inventories as well as material availability to determine how quickly an order can be filled. Managers can reserve inventory for specific customers, request certain supplier options, and customize orders. Distribution requirements, transportation management, shipping schedules, and export controls are included in the module, as are billing, invoicing, rebate processing, product registrations, and customer complaints. Distribution is coordinated more closely with manufacturing and sales in order to maintain customer delivery schedules.

## Production/Materials Management

The *production and materials management module* is set up to handle all types of manufacturing processes—make-to-order, assemble-to-order, repetitive, and continuous. The module interfaces with CAD programs; performs process planning, bill-of-material processing, and product costing; processes engineering change orders; plans material requirements (MRP); allocates resources; and schedules and monitors production. Kanbans, Gantt charts, master schedules, and available-to-promise are all supported. It links sales and distribution to materials management, production planning, and financial effects in real time. Inventory is adjusted instantly and resource planning is done on a daily basis. Materials management refers to supply chain related activities such as purchasing, inventory and warehouse functions, supplier evaluations, JIT deliveries, and invoice verification.

## Human Resources

The *human resources* module covers all personnel management tasks, including workforce planning, employee scheduling, training and development, payroll and benefits, travel expense reimbursement, applicant data, job descriptions, organization charts, and workflow analysis. It provides a database of personnel, maintains salary and benefits structures, and does payroll accounting as well.

**Figure 14.12**
**ERP's Central Database**

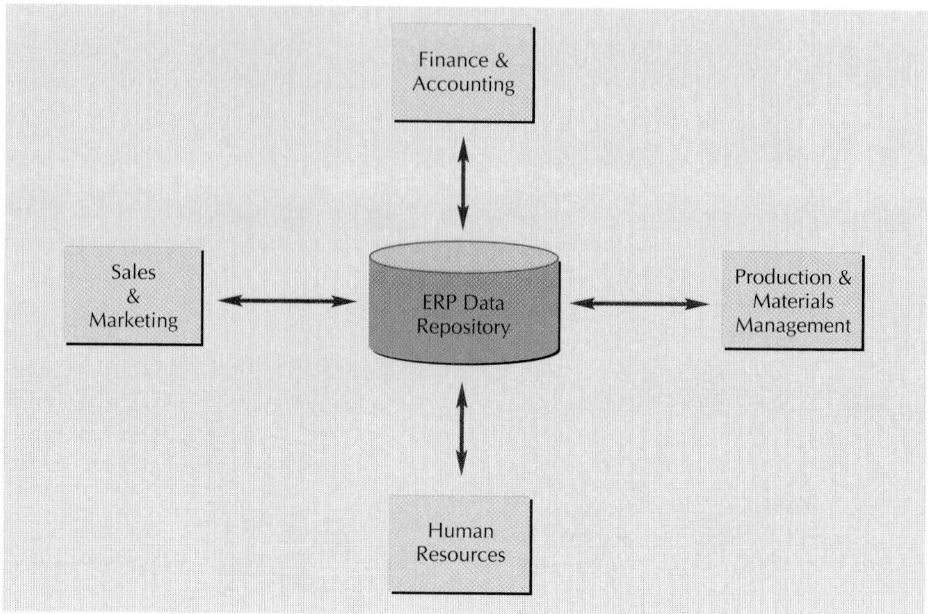


Together, these modules form an integrated information technology strategy for effectively managing the entire enterprise. ERP connects processes that belong together, giving every employee fast, convenient access to the information required for their jobs. As shown in Figure 14.12, ERP creates a central depository for the company's data, which enables the company to perform various business analyses. A company can quickly access data in real time related to forecasting and planning, purchasing and materials management, product distribution, and accounting and financial management, so that it can deploy its resources quickly and efficiently. It can help schedule its production capacity to meet demand and reduce inventory levels. By consolidating information from sales the company can better negotiate contracts and product prices, and determine their effect on the company's financial position. These types of decisions often require advanced analytical capabilities collectively called *business intelligence*.

*Business intelligence* sifts through data to find patterns and predict behavior.

Both the scope and detail of ERP systems are impressive. In addition to the four major modules in an ERP system, there are hundreds of functional support modules. Many of the systems are table-driven, with over 8000 tables to configure. As might be expected, these systems require considerable time and skill to implement. In the next section, we discuss issues in implementation.

***Vignesh Ramachandran,***
***Systems Auditor for a Big Four Accounting Firm***

In today's regulatory environment, audits go far beyond the scope of traditional financial and regulatory compliance. With the Sarbanes-Oxley Act, PATRIOT Act, and revised Financial Modernization Act, it has become a requirement for all public corporations to document their business processes and verify them by external auditors. As a financial auditor and now a systems auditor, I interview various personnel at different stages of the production or service process, compare their activities with those documented, and point out inconsistencies, as well as inefficiencies. It takes about two months to thoroughly understand a process and about two weeks to audit it.

Corporations nowadays have complicated enterprise planning systems whose methods of operation are not always evident to the people using the systems. These systems, though technologically advanced, rely on basic concepts in operations management. As an auditor, a complete understanding of the various processes and methodologies is very important, and my study of operations management has provided the groundwork for such knowledge.

## THE COMPETITIVE EDGE

### Best-of-Breed at Best Buy

The mantra at electronics retailer Best Buy is "the first three-quarters of the year are for practice, and the last one is real." As with many retailers, the fourth quarter accounts for 60% of Best Buy's annual revenue. Coordinating activities between its 750 affiliated stores in North America, 8 distribution centers, 14 delivery centers, 2 consolidation/deconsolidation centers, and 2 return centers is critical to a profitable season. Retailers, in general, are focusing on collaborative planning between themselves and manufacturers, with retailers sharing point-of-sale, forecasting, and promotion data, and manufacturers providing access to production schedules and expediting costs.

Best Buy goes one step further by creating collaborative transportation management for its 20 top vendors who supply approximately 80% of its products. In the new system, Best Buy and its vendors use customer-profile-modeling technology to ship specific products to specific distribution centers based on regional factors, rather than shipping identical products to all stores. With proper coordination, Best Buy can update inventories within 30 minutes.

To accomplish all of this, Best Buy uses a best-of-breed approach to its enterprise software. Oracle implements its back office, i2 Technologies handles it transportation management and supply chain event management, and Retek provides an inventory management system that coordinates stock counts and replenishment cycles between stores and headquarters.

*Source:* Adapted from Beth Bacheldor, "Steady Supply," *InformationWeek*, November 24, 2003.

## ERP IMPLEMENTATION

ERP implementation has a checkered history of mammoth projects over budget and out of control. Dow Chemical spent half a billion dollars and seven years implementing an ERP system that it is now overhauling. Hershey spent $100 million on its ERP system and saw a 19% drop in profits when its candy failed to reach stores in time for Halloween sales. FoxMeyer Drug claims that ERP implementation sent it into bankruptcy.

ERP vendors and their customers have learned from these debacles, and the second-generation ERP systems (dubbed by some as ERP II) are substantially different from the first generation. New ERP offerings sport stand-alone modules and open architecture. Companies can pick and choose the modules they want to install and can even choose a collection of modules from different vendors—the **best-of-breed** approach. While single-source ERP systems are easier to integrate, best-of-breed systems may provide a better match with organizational needs. Table 14.7 lists several enterprise software vendors and their area of expertise. ERP implementation involves: (1) analyzing business processes, (2) choosing the modules to implement, (3) aligning the level of sophistication, (4) finalizing delivery and access, and (5) linking with external partners.

**Best of breed:** refers to the selection of ERP modules from different vendors.

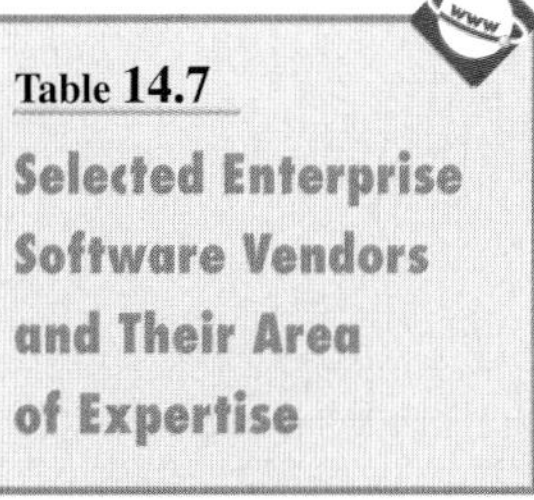

Table 14.7 **Selected Enterprise Software Vendors and Their Area of Expertise**

| Vendor | Specialty |
|---|---|
| **1.** SAP ERP, SCM | Large enterprise discrete manufacturing |
| **2.** Oracle Corp. | Large enterprise discrete manufacturing and services |
| **3.** Invensys Software Systems | Electronics industry |
| **4.** PeopleSoft, Inc. | Employee and customer relationship management |
| **5.** Siebel Systems | Customer relationship management |
| **6.** i2 Technologies | Supply chain management |
| **7.** PTC, EDS, Dassault Systems | Collaborative product commerce |
| **8.** Siemens Energy & Automation | Manufacturing execution systems |
| **9.** SCT | Process industry; education; energy |
| **10.** QAD | Multinational midmarket manufacturing |

*Source:* "The Top 100 Software Vendors," *MSI* (2003); note these are not listed by rank; various company Web sites.

## Analyze Business Processes

Analyzing business processes is the first step in implementation. Since ERP is an integrated technology that pervades and connects all parts of a company, it usually alters the way a company makes decisions; thus, its implementation typically requires major changes in a company's organizational structure and business processes. Companies that have had success with ERP have taken the time to think about how their processes work and how they can best be integrated before "automating" them. To guide companies in this massive project, ERP vendors have designed their software around best practices for specific industries. Solution maps and stories of successful implementations are available for such industries as aerospace and defense, apparel, automotive, chemicals, consumer products, engineering and construction, health care, high-tech industries, insurance, media, oil and gas, pharmaceuticals, the public sector, real estate, retail, telecommunications, and utilities. Companies can either use the software as a blueprint for how their processes should operate and adjust their processes, or they can map out their own business processes and customize the software accordingly. Most companies try a combination of these approaches.

## Choose Modules to Implement

Determining which ERP modules to implement and how they should be configured is a process-oriented (rather than technology-oriented) decision. The decision should be guided by questions such as: (1) Which processes have the biggest impact on customer relations? (2) Which processes would benefit the most from cross-functional or interorganizational integration? (3) Which processes should be standardized throughout the organization and which should be allowed to vary?

Small-market and midsize-market companies with time and budget constraints have an especially hard time implementing ERP. In response, software vendors like SAP have created a fast-track approach to ERP implementation. Based on the processes and applications that have proved most successful in the past, SAP has created 11 industry-specific best-practices templates designed to maximize efficiency and minimize customization. Plain vanilla, template-based modules chosen by the client are provided at a fixed price and implemented over a fixed timetable. The results are impressive. eCompany installed fully functional ERP modules for materials management, function planning, finance, and online retailing in three weeks for less than $200,000. Interactive Apparel implemented SAP's materials management, sales and distribution, warehouse management, and financial modules in nine weeks for less than $150,000.

## Align Level of Sophistication

Knowing the level of sophistication needed for your business is also key to effective ERP implementation. QAD (for quality, application, delivery) offers MFG/PRO and eQ software to manufacturing companies and international clients. QAD software can be directed with instructions much simpler than those of larger ERP vendors. Instead of deploying a single system to manage all of a company's plants, QAD tailors its software to individual plants, then links them with corporate financial, distribution, and support functions. Since 65% of QAD's customers are international, its software incorporates different countries' methods for invoicing, accounting, and amortization. For example, eQ uses a model to decide how an incoming order from a trading partner should be handled. It can automatically process transactions across enterprises, languages, and customs. QAD is known for both its ease of implementation (weeks instead of months) and ease of use.

## Finalize Delivery and Access

The Internet provides another aid to implementation. ERP vendors, including Oracle, PeopleSoft, and SAP, now offer their products through portals. The vendor hosts the application, which the customer accesses over the Internet with their browser. Portals are less expensive, so they give midsize market and smaller clients access to the same services as larger corporations. ERP services can also be accessed through third-party application service providers (ASPs). Redback Networks, for example, uses Qwest CyberSolutions to

Enterprise systems tend to add complexity with their own jargon.

access Oracle's suite of enterprise solutions, including finance, order management, human resources, manufacturing, shipping, and inventory systems.

## Link with External Partners

The value of e-business relies on a company's ability to integrate its internal processes with external suppliers, customers, and companies. First-generation ERP systems lacked the ability to interact outside the organization with other ERP systems, with e-businesses, or directly with customers. By the second generation of ERP, vendors had learned to create Web-centric systems by consolidating data and allowing dynamic access from various clients. Called ERP II, extended ERP, or XRP, these more advanced versions are Web-enabled, collaborative, and in some cases, wireless.

ERP systems provide vast amounts of data for analysis. Software vendors have developed powerful new analytic tools and applications that capitalize on ERP's infrastructure. Examples of such software systems are customer relationship management (CRM), supply chain management (SCM), and collaborative product commerce (CPC).

## THE COMPETITIVE EDGE

### Operational Excellence at Nike

Nike is the world's leading brand name, designer, and marketer of athletic goods. In 1999, the company began a five-year journey with SAP to implement an integrated ERP system. The ERP system includes modules for production planning, supply chain management, customer relationship management, business process improvement, inventory control, and others.

Business at Nike is very complex. Nike has 120,000 stock-keeping units (SKUs) (in comparison to Dell, for example, with 1200 SKUs), 304 seasonal product cycles during the year, and 350 factory partners who produce 90% of their total output. Any ERP system for Nike would have to handle supply chain management as well. Nike chose to implement a single instance of SAP R/3, with a single planning engine and centralized demand management to manage its global distribution network and coordinate with its global suppliers. Initial goals for the project included greater responsiveness, more integrated systems, and improved cash flows.

Nike's VP of Supply Chains, Shelley Davis, says that SAP has allowed (1) integrated, constraint-based planning, (2) a larger window for consumers to place orders, (3) a better understanding of customer requirements, (4) a better match of supply chain and go-to-market strategies, and (5) better tracking of in-bound shipments. ERP implementation began with Canada going live in the fall of 2000, the United States in the fall of 2001 (called "the big bang"), followed by Europe in 2002 and Asia in 2004. The U.S. implementation alone involved more than 100,000 hours of training. Currently, the system is installed in 23 countries using 13 currencies and 18 languages. Over 4000 users and 5 billion businesses access the ERP system.

Keys to implementation success include starting with a business vision, partnering business units with IT functions, insisting on clarity in translation of vision to requirements, involving key executives, and building an implementation team with a clear focus.

With 80% of global rollout complete, Nike expects a \$3 million increase in cash flow due to inventory reductions and streamlined accounts payable. Return on invested capital is running at 20%. Operational performance is the best it's been in 10 years, gross margins are up, business processes are being integrated, and information visibility has improved dramatically. So what's next for Nike? Nike will continue with worldwide deployment while adding more functionality and capabilities to the system. In essence, Nike will keep up its pace. As one Nike executive put it, "There is no finish line when it comes to operational excellence."

*Source:* "Learn What Nike Knows," MSI Executive Series Broadcast (March 31, 2004), www.msimag.com.

## CUSTOMER RELATIONSHIP MANAGEMENT (CRM)

**CRM:** software that plans and executes business processes involving customer interaction, such as sales, marketing, fulfillment, and customer service.

Perhaps no new application reinforces the changing focus of ERP better than customer relationship management. **Customer relationship management (CRM)** software plans and executes business processes that involve customer interaction, such as marketing, sales, fulfillment, and service. CRM changes the focus from managing products to managing customers. With the advent of e-commerce, companies have the opportunity to sell directly to the customer. Marketing can be personalized to individual preferences and behaviors. A wealth of data on customer buying behavior is available from records of purchases and analysis of clickstreams. Special events, such as holidays or product promotions, can trigger customer purchases. Point-of-sale data from physical stores, mail-order purchases, and online purchases are monitored. All of these data go into a data warehouse, where they are analyzed for patterns (called *data mining*) and from which predictions of future behavior are made.

Prospect information, customer profiles, sales-force automation, and campaign modules for direct mail and special sales promotions are managed with CRM. In addition to collecting and analyzing customer data, CRM provides decision support for forecasting demand, demand management, pricing products and services, quoting order delivery dates, and planning for customer service needs. Customer service includes tracking and tracing orders, returns, repairs, service, and warranty management. CRM interacts with supply chain management (SCM) software and ERP to ensure prompt and accurate order fulfillment, and to plan for future requirements.

## SUPPLY CHAIN MANAGEMENT (SCM)

**SCM:** software that plans and executes business processes related to supply chains.

As discussed in Chapter 9, **supply chain management** software includes supply chain planning, supply chain execution, and supplier relationship management. *Planning* involves designing the supply chain network, demand planning, and collaborative production planning. *Execution* involves fulfillment, manufacturing, and delivery. *Relationship management* handles all the interactions with suppliers from supplier certification to quality assurance, contracts, and agreements.

From the above list you can see that the distinction between business software applications has become increasingly blurred as ERP vendors are adding more SCM functions, and SCM vendors are encroaching on ERP. SAP AG, whose ERP application, R/3, runs most *Fortune* 500 companies, is now concentrating on e-business with its mySAP suite of products. mySAP includes supply chain management (SCM), customer relationship management (CRM), and product life cycle management (PLM). i2 technologies, a leader in supply chain management software, has incorporated ERP functions into its TradeMatrix software. Oracle, a leader in e-business software and databases, emphasizes CRM, B2B, and business intelligence.

## COLLABORATIVE PRODUCT COMMERCE (CPC)

**CPC:** software that manages the product development process, product life cycles, and design collaboration with suppliers and customers.

A new entry into business application software is collaborative product commerce (CPC). As introduced in Chapter 5, **collaborative product commerce** is concerned with new product design and development, as well as product life cycle management. CPC manages product data through the life of the product, coordinates product and processes redesign, and collaborates with suppliers and customers in the design process.

CPC, CRM, ERP, and SCM make a powerful combination. Figure 14.13 shows how these types of software systems can work together. Customer and supplier collaboration on design with CPC can reduce time to market for new products and services. Similarly, customer and supplier collaboration in manufacturing via ERP helps speed the product to the customer. Design and manufacture collaborate in the DFMA (design for manufacture and assembly) process discussed in Chapter 5.

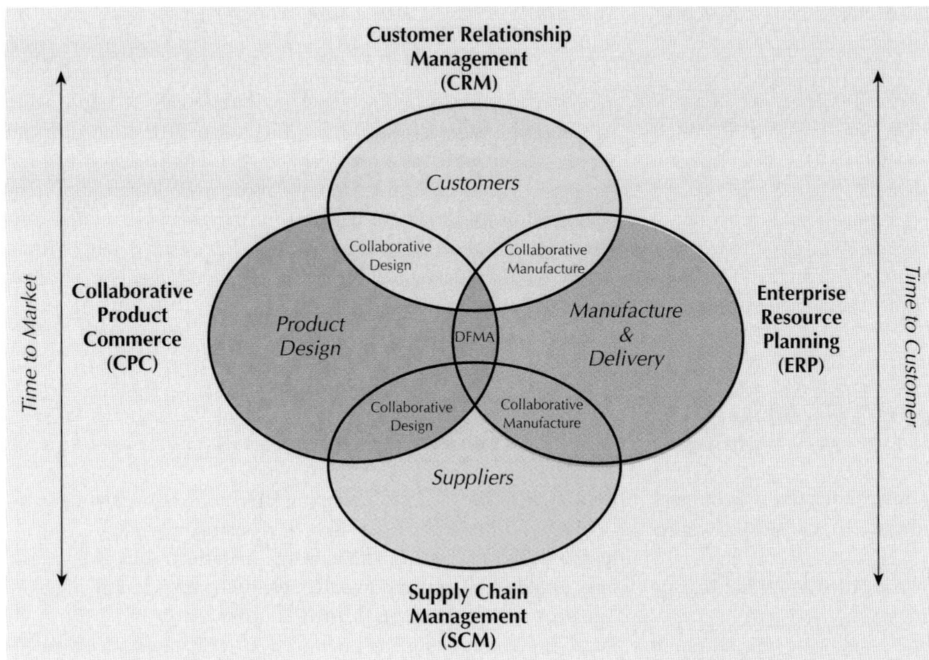


**Figure 14.13**

**ERP and Related Software Systems**

*Source:* Adapted from George Shaw, "Building the Lean Enterprise: Reducing Time to Market." *Industry Week* (Webcast, June 14, 2001), http://www.industryweek.com/Events/TimeToMarket/pent0614.html.

## CONNECTIVITY

Getting ERP, CPC, CRM, and SCM systems talking to each other within a company is difficult. Getting them to communicate across hundreds of different companies and vendors is a daunting task. Using the same suite of products from one vendor facilitates integration, but most companies prefer a best-of-breed approach, buying the products or modules that best fit their business from a variety of vendors. It is common for e-business applications to come with application programming interfaces (APIs) that give other programs well-defined ways of speaking to them. But APIs that allow communication between application A and application B are overwhelmed when applications C, D, and E are added to the exchange. Enter third-party vendors that offer enterprise application integration (EAI). This software breaks down a complex business process into a series of transactions between applications. It then brokers those transactions in language each application can understand. That language is most likely **XML** (for extensible markup language); newer software uses XML extensively.

**XML:** the business language of the Internet.

Electronic data interchange (EDI) used to be the language of business-to-business communication. While EDI is good at transmitting orders and invoices, it cannot change product descriptions, transmit product drawings, update in real time, or easily communicate with ERP systems. XML, on the other hand, was built for the Internet. Instead of downloading data from one system and reentering it into another, XML tags each chunk of data—such as part number, price, and delivery date—before sending it to a trading partner. The receiving XML-run system picks out the data by its tag and inserts it into the proper place in its ERP system. Thus, Web sites can communicate with Web sites, computers with computers.

Connectivity and integration will continue to be an issue as new technologies emerge. IBM estimates that 70% of all code written today consists of interfaces, protocols, and other procedures to establish linkages among various systems.

## SUMMARY

Material requirements planning (MRP) is a computerized inventory control and production planning system. It has enjoyed widespread use in U.S. industry, primarily for batch manufacturing, as an information system that improves manufacturing decision making. MRP began as a system for ensuring that sufficient *material* was available when needed. However, in application, it became clear that material was not the only resource in short supply. Planning capabilities for machine and labor resources were added to the system in the form of *capacity requirements planning* (CRP).

MRP requires input from other functional areas of a firm, such as marketing and finance. As these areas began to see the power of a common database system, they encouraged the expansion of MRP into areas such as demand forecasting, demand management, customer order entry, accounts payable, accounts receivable, budgets, and cash flow analysis. Clearly, this enhanced version was more powerful than the original MRP system that ordered material and scheduled production. It provided a common database that the entire company could use. Its what if? capability proved invaluable in evaluating tradeoffs, and the easy access to information encouraged more sophisticated planning. Thus, MRP evolved into a more comprehensive *enterprise resource planning system*, or ERP.

ERP is a powerful software system that organizes and manages business processes across functional areas. In addition to managing all sorts of back-office functions, ERP connects with supply chain and customer management applications, helping businesses share information both inside and outside the company. ERP is essential to e-business initiatives and to related software systems, such as customer relationship management (CRM), supply chain management (SCM), and collaborative product commerce (CPC).

## SUMMARY OF KEY TERMS

**assemble-to-order** a manufacturing environment in which major subassemblies are produced in advance of a customer's order and are then *configured to order*.

**backward scheduling** scheduling backward from a due date to determine when to begin a job.

**best-of-breed** the selection of ERP modules from different vendors.

**bill of material (BOM)** a list of all the materials, parts, and assemblies that make up a product, including quantities, parent–component relationships, and order of assembly.

**capacity requirements planning (CRP)** a computerized system that projects the load from a given material plan onto the capacity of a system and identifies underloads and overloads.

**collaborative product commerce (CPC)** software that manages the product development process, product life cycles, and design collaboration with suppliers and customers.

**cumulative lead time** the total length of time required to manufacture a product; also, the longest path through a product structure.

**customer relationship management (CRM)** software that plans and executes business processes that involve customer interaction, such as sales, marketing, fulfillment, and customer service.

**cycle counting** a method for auditing inventory accuracy that counts inventory and reconciles errors on a cyclical schedule rather than once a year.

**enterprise resource planning (ERP)** software that organizes and manages a company's business processes by sharing information across functional areas.

**expedite** to speed up orders so that they are completed in less than their normal lead time.

**explosion** the process of determining requirements for lower-level items by multiplying the planned orders of parent items by the quantity per assembly of component items.

**forward scheduling** scheduling forward from today's date to determine the earliest time a job can be completed.

**item master file** a file that contains inventory status and descriptive information on every item in inventory.

**load leveling** the process of balancing underloads and overloads.

**load profile** a chart that compares released orders and planned orders with capacity of a facility.

**lot sizing** determining the quantities in which items are usually made or purchased.

**master production schedule (MPS)** a schedule for the production of end items (usually final products). It drives the MRP process that schedules the production of component parts.

**material requirements planning (MRP)** a computerized inventory control and production planning system for generating purchase orders and work orders of materials, components, and assemblies.

**modular bill of material** a special bill of material used to plan the production of products with many optional features.

**netting** the process of subtracting on-hand quantities and scheduled receipts from gross requirements to produce net requirements.

**periodic order quantity** a lot sizing technique that orders at set time invervals.

**product structure file** a file that contains computerized bills of material for all products.

**supply chain management (SCM)** software that plans and executes business processes related to supply chains.

**time fence** a date specified by management beyond which no changes in the master schedule are allowed.

**time-phased bill of material** an assembly chart shown against a time scale.

**time phasing** the process of subtracting an item's lead time from its due date to determine when an order should be released.

**XML** extensible markup language; used to help different ERP systems communicate over the Internet.

## QUESTIONS

**14-1.** Describe a production environment in which MRP would be useful. Describe a production environment in which MRP would *not* be useful.

**14-2.** Explain with an example the difference between dependent and independent demand.

**14-3.** What are the objectives, inputs, and outputs of an MRP system?

**14-4.** How is a master production schedule created, and how is it used?

**14-5.** What is the purpose of phantom bills, K-bills, and modular bills of material?

**14-6.** What type of information is included in the item master file?

**14-7.** Describe cycle counting. How does it improve inventory performance?

**14-8.** Describe the MRP process, including netting, explosion, and time phasing.

**14-9.** What are the inputs to capacity requirements planning? Discuss several alternatives for leveling the load on a facility.

**14-10.** Discuss several assumptions of MRP and how they are being relaxed with new technology.

**14-11.** Explain how MRP could be applied to (a) the surgery suite of a hospital, (b) scheduling university classes, (c) a chain of restaurants, and (d) hotel renovations.

**14-12.** How does MRP differ from ERP? Find a description of an MRP module from a software vendor.

**14-13.** Access the Web site of an ERP vendor such as Oracle, SAP, PeopleSoft, i2 Technologies or QAD. Make a list of the modules available. Choose one module to describe in detail.

**14-14.** What are the capabilities of customer relationship management (CRM) software? How do ERP and CRM relate?

**14-15.** What are the capabilities of supply chain management software? How do ERP and SCM relate?

**14-16.** Compare the ERP/CRM/SCM offerings of two different software vendors.

**14-17.** What is collaborative product commerce (CPC)? How does it relate to other business software?

**14-18.** Describe how the ERP systems from two different companies can converse.

**14-19.** Choose an industry solution map from the SAP Web site to explore. Drill down to more detailed solutions. Compare the map with that of one other industry. How do they differ?

**14-20.** Discuss the scope of ERP and difficulties in implementation.

**14-21.** Interview managers at three companies in your area about their use of ERP. How have their experiences been similar? What accounts for the similarities and differences?

**14-22.** Find out if there is a local APICS chapter in your area. Attend a meeting and write a summary of the speaker's comments.

**14-23.** From articles in recent business magazines, describe the newest trends in e-business software.

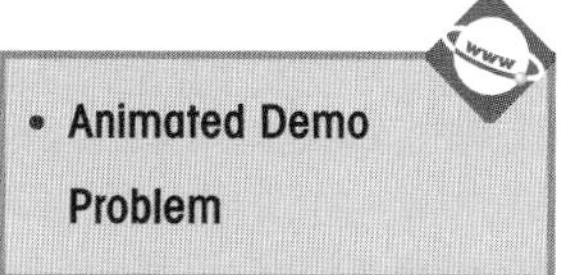


## SOLVED PROBLEM

Complete the following MRP matrix for item X.

| ITEM: X | LLC: 0 | PERIOD | | | | | | | |
|---|---|---|---|---|---|---|---|---|---|
| LOT SIZE: MIN 50 | LT: 2 | 1 | 2 | 3 | 4 | 5 | 6 | 7 | 8 |
| Gross Requirements | | 20 | 30 | 50 | 50 | 60 | 90 | 40 | 60 |
| Scheduled Receipts | | | 50 | | | | | | |
| Projected on Hand | 40 | | | | | | | | |
| Net Requirements | | | | | | | | | |
| Planned Order Receipts | | | | | | | | | |
| Planned Order Releases | | | | | | | | | |

a. In what periods should orders be released, and what should be the size of those orders?

b. How would your answer change if the cost of ordering item X were \$100, the cost of carrying were \$2 a week, and the POQ lot sizing technique were used?

c. Which lot sizing technique yields the lowest total cost?

### SOLUTION

a.

| ITEM: X | LLC: 0 | PERIOD | | | | | | | |
|---|---|---|---|---|---|---|---|---|---|
| LOT SIZE: MIN 50 | LT: 2 | 1 | 2 | 3 | 4 | 5 | 6 | 7 | 8 |
| Gross Requirements | | 20 | 30 | 50 | 50 | 60 | 90 | 40 | 60 |
| Scheduled Receipts | | | 50 | | | | | | |
| Projected on Hand | 40 | 20 | 40 | 40 | 40 | 30 | 0 | 10 | 0 |
| Net Requirements | | | | 10 | 10 | 20 | 60 | 40 | 50 |
| Planned Order Receipts | | | | 50 | 50 | 50 | 60 | 50 | 50 |
| Planned Order Releases | | 50 | 50 | 50 | 60 | 50 | 50 | | |

b. $\bar{d} = 50$ $\qquad Q = \sqrt{\dfrac{2(50)(100)}{2}} = 70.711$

$C_o = \$100$

$C_c = \$2$

$$POQ = Q/\bar{d} = 1.41 \text{ or } 2 \text{ periods}$$

| ITEM: X | LLC: 0 | PERIOD | | | | | | | |
|---|---|---|---|---|---|---|---|---|---|
| LOT SIZE: POQ 2 | LT: 2 | 1 | 2 | 3 | 4 | 5 | 6 | 7 | 8 |
| Gross Requirements | | 20 | 30 | 50 | 50 | 60 | 90 | 40 | 60 |
| Scheduled Receipts | | | 50 | | | | | | |
| Projected on Hand | 40 | 20 | 40 | 50 | 0 | 90 | 0 | 60 | 0 |
| Net Requirements | | | | 10 | | 60 | | 40 | |
| Planned Order Receipts | | | | 60 | | 150 | | 100 | |
| Planned Order Releases | | 60 | | 150 | | 100 | | | |

c. $TC_{MIN50} = (6 \times \$100) + (180 \times \$2) = \$960$

$TC_{POQ2} = (3 \times \$100) + (260 \times \$2) = \$820$

Choose the POQ lot sizing technique.

## PROBLEMS

**14-1.** Referring to the product structure diagram for product A determine:

a. how many K's are needed for each A.
b. how many E's are needed for each A.
c. the low-level code for item E.

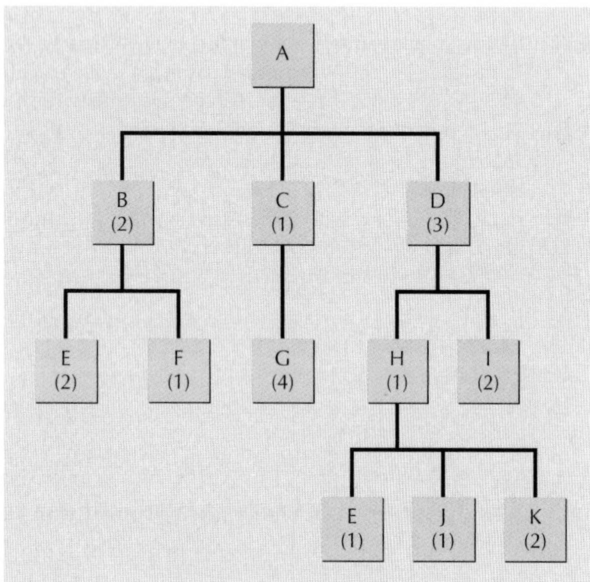


**14-2.** Construct a multilevel bill of material for product Z. How many Us are needed to make each Z? How many Ws are needed to make each Z?

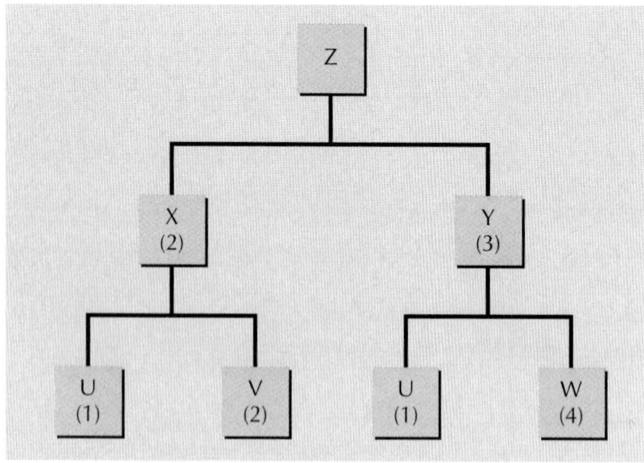


**14-3.** The classic One-Step step stool shown below is assembled from a prefabricated seat (with bolts attached), one bottom leg, one top leg, five nuts, and four leg tips. Construct a product structure diagram for the One-Step step stool. Be sure to include subassemblies that are formed as part of the assembly process.

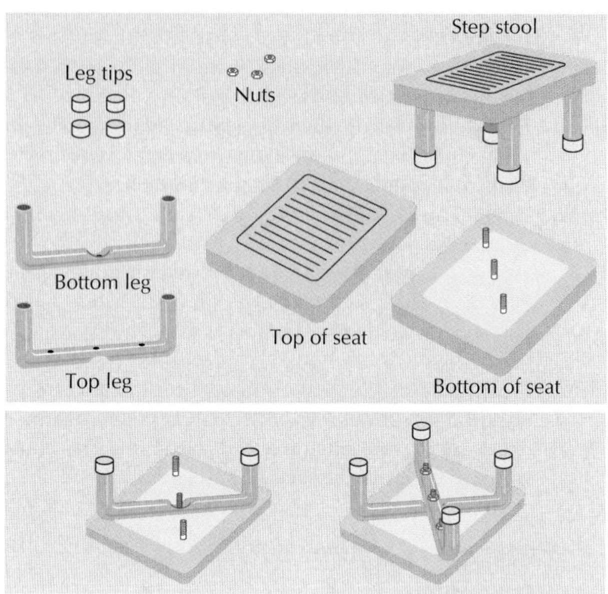


**14-4.** Construct a multilevel bill of material from Item A's product structure diagram shown below. Assume all quantities are one. What is the low-level code for item E?

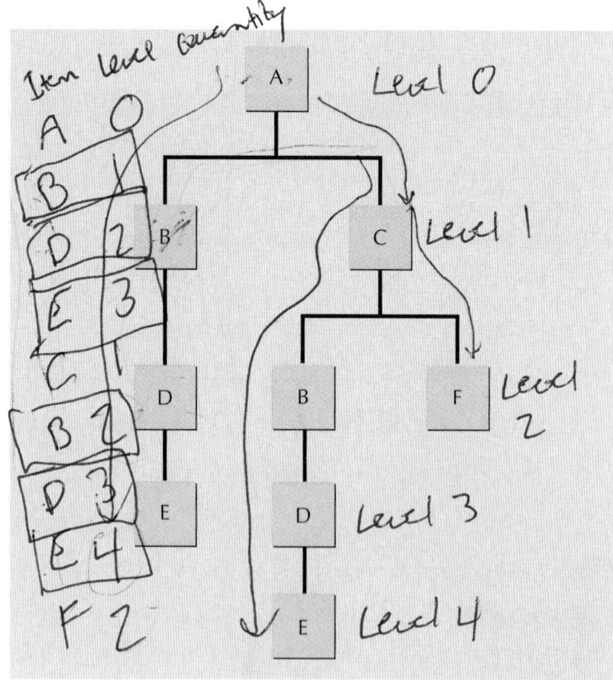


**14-5.** Product A is assembled from two units of S1 and three units of S2. S1 is made of one unit of C1, four units of C2, and one unit of C3. S2 is made of three units of C2 and two units of C3.

a. Draw a product structure diagram for product A.
b. How many C3's are needed to fill an order for 100 A's?
c. Assume no inventory on hand, products take one day to assemble, subassemblies take two days and components take three days. When should an order be released for C3 if the 100 A's are needed by day 7?

**14-6.** The popular Racer Scooter comes in a variety of colors with lots of options. The customer can choose one of four color wheels, one of three sizes (small, medium, or large), and whether or not to have shocks, a wheelie bar, foam handles, racing stripes, lights, sound effects, a carrying strap, or a carrying bag.

How many different scooters can be made from the various options? Construct a modular bill of material for the Racer Scooter. How many items are in the modular bill? What are the pros and cons of giving the customer so many choices?

**14-7.** Draw a product structure diagram from the bill of material for an Xavier skateboard shown below. Assuming a 10% profit margin, how should the Xavier be priced?

| Level | Item | Quantity | Price |
|---|---|---|---|
| 0 | Skateboard | 1 | |
| –1 | Deck | 1 | $54.90 |
| –1 | Grip tape | 1 | $ 4.95 |
| –1 | Wheel assembly | 2 | — |
| – –2 | Wheels | 2 | $ 8.95 |
| – –2 | Bearings | 4 | $ 4.95 |
| – –2 | Truck | 1 | $33.90 |
| –1 | Nuts and Bolts | 4 | $ 1.99 |
| –1 | Riser | 2 | $ 3.95 |

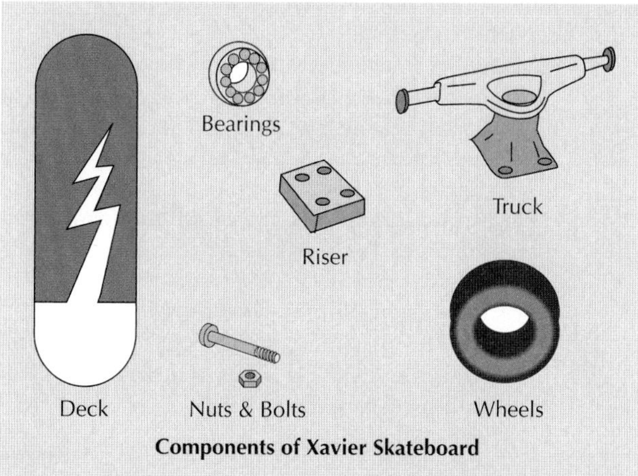

**Components of Xavier Skateboard**

**14-8.** The Best Wheels Bicycle Company produces bicycles in different styles for boys and girls, in heights of 26 inches or 20 inches, and with 10 speeds, 3 speeds, or 1 speed.

a. How many different kinds of bicycles does Best Wheels make?

b. Construct a modular bill of material for Best Wheels (one level). Assume that bike sales are equally split between boys and girls, 26-inch bikes are preferred two-to-one to 20-inch bikes, and 3-speed bikes account for only 20% of sales. The remaining sales are divided equally between 10-speed and 1-speed bikes.

c. If bicycle sales are expected to reach 10,000 over the holiday shopping season, how many 26-inch bikes should Best Wheels plan to produce? How many 10-speed bikes?

**14-9.** From the product structure diagram for item X shown at the top of the next column, determine how many of each lower-level items (B through I) are needed to fill an order for 50 X's.

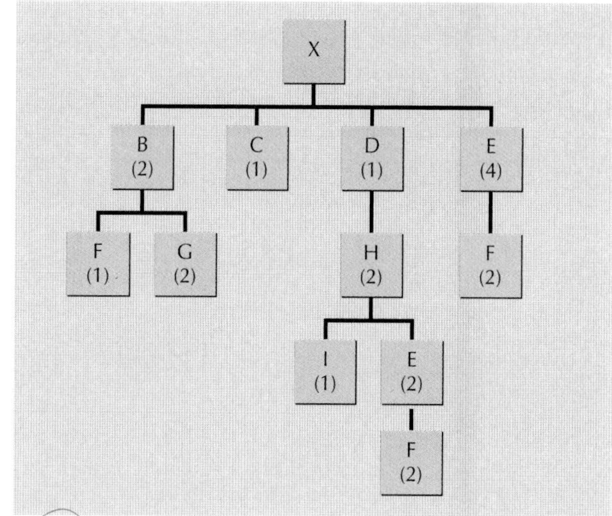


**14-10.** The Alpha Beta Company produces two products; A and B, that are made from components C and D. Given the following product structures, master scheduling requirements, and inventory information, determine when orders should be released for A, B, C, and D and the size of those orders.

| | On Hand | Scheduled Receipts | Lot Size | MPS |
|---|---|---|---|---|
| A | 10 | 0 | L4L | 100, period 8 |
| B | 5 | 0 | L4L | 200, period 6 |
| C | 140 | 0 | Min 150 | — |
| D | 200 | 250, period 2 | Mult 250 | — |

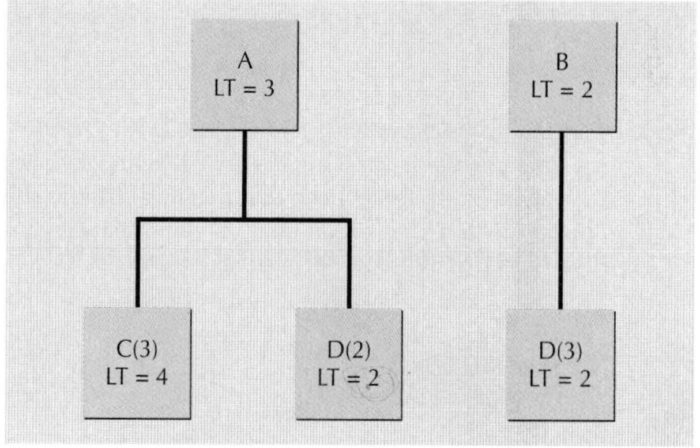


**14-11.** Kid's World sells outdoor play equipment for children. One of its most popular items is a 5-foot by 7-foot wooden sandbox shown below. General assembly instructions follow.

*Assembly Instructions:* The wood pieces for the sandbox are ordered precut and treated. Kid's World sands the wood, drills several holes in each piece as required for assembly, and coats each piece with 2 ounces of water sealer. The sides are then assembled one corner at a time by attaching a 1-foot wood strip cater-corner between a 5-foot and 7-foot side. Four bolts are inserted through the predrilled holes and secured with nuts. After the left and right corners of the sandbox have been assembled, the two pieces are joined in a similar manner to form the box assembly. A triangular-shaped wooden seat is attached to each corner of the box assembly with four flat-headed nails for each seat. The sandbox is now complete.

Construct a multilevel bill of material for the sandbox.

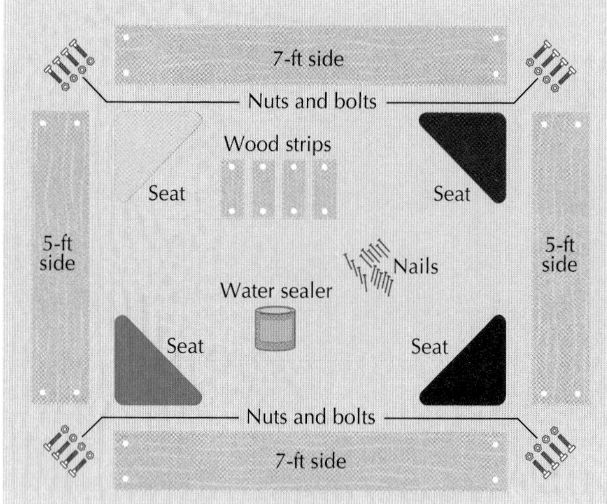


**14-12.** Complete the following MRP matrix for item A:

| Item: A | LLC: 1 | Period | | | | | | | |
|---|---|---|---|---|---|---|---|---|---|
| Lot Size: Mult 25 | LT: 2 | 1 | 2 | 3 | 4 | 5 | 6 | 7 | 8 |
| Gross Requirements | | 10 | 15 | 25 | 75 | 60 | 85 | 45 | 60 |
| Scheduled Receipts | | | | | | | | | |
| Projected on Hand | 50 | | | | | | | | |
| Net Requirements | | | | | | | | | |
| Planned Order Receipts | | | | | | | | | |
| Planned Order Releases | | | | | | | | | |

**14-13.** Camp's Inc. produces two products, X and Z, with product structures as shown. An order for 200 units of X, and 350 units of Z has been received for period 8. An inquiry of available stock reveals 25 units of X on hand, 40 units of Z, 90 of T, 120 of U, 150 of V, and 160 of W. For economy reasons, U is never made in quantities under 100. Similarly, V and W have multiple order quantities of 100 and 500, respectively.

Determine what orders should be released to satisfy demand for X and Z.

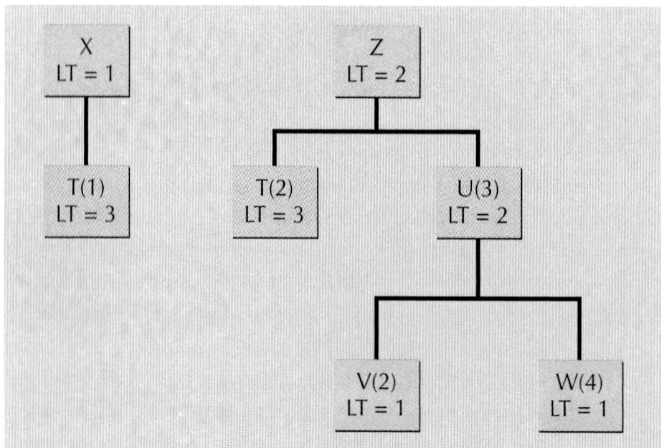


**14-14.** Files and More, Inc. (F&M), a manufacturer of office equipment, uses MRP to schedule its production. Because of the current recession and the need to cut costs, F&M has targeted inventory as a prime area for cost reduction. However, the company does not want to reduce its customer service level in the process. Demand and inventory data for a two-drawer file cabinet are given in the following table. Complete an MRP matrix for the file cabinet using: (a) L4L, (b) EOQ, and (c) POQ lot sizing. Which lot-sizing rule do you recommend?

| Period | 1 | 2 | 3 | 4 | 5 |
|---|---|---|---|---|---|
| Demand | 20 | 40 | 30 | 10 | 45 |

Ordering cost = \$100 per order

Holding cost = \$1 per cabinet per period

Lead time = 1 period

Beginning inventory = 25

**14-15.** F&M's best-selling item is a standard office desk. The desk consists of four legs, one top, one drawer, two side panels, one back panel, and two drawer guides, as shown below. Each side is assembled from a side panel, two legs, and a drawer guide. The base is formed from the back panel and two sides. In final assembly, the top is attached to the base and the drawer is slid into place. Lead times are two days for purchased items and one day for assembled items:

a. Construct a time-phased assembly chart for the desk.
b. With no inventory on hand, how long would it take to complete a customer order?
c. The desk sides, back, and drawer are metal. The top is woodgrain. F&M is considering making the desk top in its own factory. The top would take four days to manufacture. Would making the desk top in-house affect the time required to fill a customer order?
d. F&M's customers like the desk and its price, but would like to be able to get desks in three days. Which items should F&M keep in inventory to fill an order in three days?

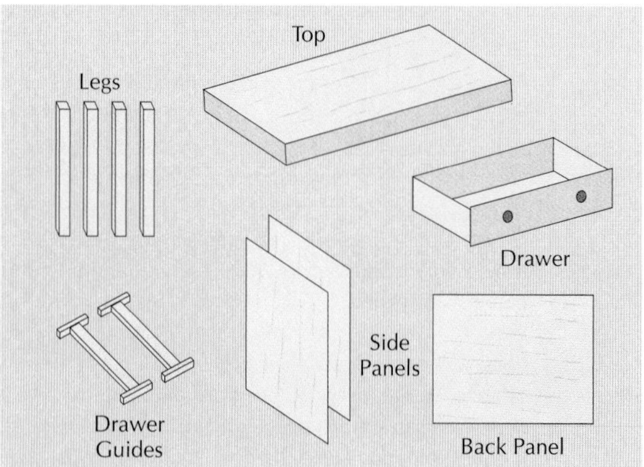


**14-16.** Given 150 units of beginning inventory, a lead time of one period, an ordering cost of \$400 per order, and a holding cost of \$2 per unit per period, determine which lot sizing technique would result in the lowest total cost for the following demand data.

| Period | 1 | 2 | 3 | 4 | 5 | 6 | 7 | 8 |
|---|---|---|---|---|---|---|---|---|
| Gross Requirements | 100 | 90 | 85 | 70 | 150 | 200 | 300 | 250 |

**14-17.** Given an ordering cost of \$200, a holding cost of \$2 per unit, and a negligible lead time, examine the following demand patterns and predict which lot sizing technique would result in the lowest total cost. Verify your predictions.

a.

| Period | 1 | 2 | 3 | 4 |
|---|---|---|---|---|
| Gross Requirements | 50 | 50 | 50 | 50 |

b.

| Period | 1 | 2 | 3 | 4 |
|---|---|---|---|---|
| Gross Requirements | 50 | 10 | 50 | 10 |

c.

| Period | 1 | 2 | 3 | 4 |
|---|---|---|---|---|
| Gross Requirements | 50 | 50 | 10 | 10 |

d.

| Period | 1 | 2 | 3 | 4 |
|---|---|---|---|---|
| Gross Requirements | 50 | 10 | 10 | 50 |

**14-18.** Daily demand for an item is shown here. Assume a holding cost of \$0.50 per unit per day, a setup cost of \$100 per setup, a lead time of one day and 70 units on hand. Determine when a work order should be released for the item and the size of the order using the L4L, EOQ, and POQ lot sizing techniques. Which technique produces the lowest total cost?

| Period | 1 | 2 | 3 | 4 | 5 | 6 | 7 | 8 | 9 | 10 |
|---|---|---|---|---|---|---|---|---|---|---|
| Gross Requirements | 50 | 30 | 25 | 35 | 40 | 50 | 35 | 45 | 70 | 75 |

**14-19.** Product A is assembled from one B and two C's. Each item requires one or more operations, as indicated by the circles in the product structure diagram. Assume lead time is negligible. From the information given:

a. Develop a load profile chart for each of the three work centers.

b. Level the loads. Discuss possible consequences of shifting work to other periods.

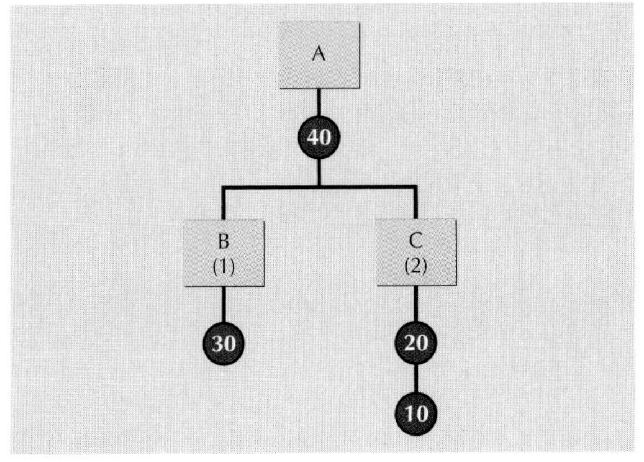


**Master Production Schedule**

| Period | 1 | 2 | 3 | 4 | 5 | 6 |
|---|---|---|---|---|---|---|
| Product A | 100 | 150 | 100 | 200 | 100 | 100 |

**Routing and Work Standards File**

| Operation | Item | Work Center | Standard Time per Unit (hr) |
|---|---|---|---|
| 10 | C | Machining | 0.50 |
| 20 | C | Heat treat | 2.00 |
| 30 | B | Machining | 1.00 |
| 40 | A | Assembly | 0.40 |

**14-20.** Sitting on Maggie Brumfield's desk is the latest planned order report from the company's MRP system. Maggie's job is to determine if there is enough capacity to handle the workload and to level the load if it's uneven. She gathers the latest cost figures and gets to work. Subcontracting and hiring extra workers are not options at this point, but overtime, pulling work ahead, and postponing work are. Regular production costs \$10 an hour and is limited to 40 hours a week. Overtime costs \$15 an hour and cannot exceed 40 extra hours (i.e., a double shift). An inventory cost of \$3 per period is assessed for each hour's worth of work performed in advance. Postponing work costs \$20 per item per period.

Use the following information to construct an initial load summary chart. Level the loads. Then create a revised chart that meets demand at the least possible cost. How much money is saved by economically leveling the load?

**Planned Order Report**

| | Week | | | |
|---|---|---|---|---|
| Item | 1 | 2 | 3 | 4 |
| A | 90 | | | |
| B | 100 | | 250 | |
| C | | 600 | | 160 |
| D | 60 | | | |

**Processing Times**

| Item | Setup Time (min) | Run Time (min per unit) |
|---|---|---|
| A | 15 | 3 |
| B | 30 | 15 |
| C | 50 | 10 |
| D | 45 | 4 |

## CASE PROBLEM 14.1

### *Hosuki*

Hosuki, a small car maker, competes with larger manufacturers by building cars to order. The company has invested heavily in technology and close partnerships with suppliers. Customers enter their orders and choose their options on the company Web site. Hosuki's ERP system responds with an estimated cost and completion date. After the customer approves the order, Hosuki sets to work.

Quick response for Hosuki is dependent on collaborative manufacturing with its trading partners. A virtual bill of material for a typical car appears below. Notice each item is color-coded to the supplier who is responsible for providing that item. Hosuki has full visibility into its suppliers' ERP systems to check on-hand quantities and order progress. These data are essential in quoting accurate due dates. Most of the car's components are purchased. Hosuki makes the body of the car, assembles the main components, and takes care of final inspection and testing. The machine that stamps out body parts operates eight hours a day.

Since the suppliers produce in high volume, the lead time for an order is the same regardless of the quantity of the order. In contrast, with limited sales volume and limited space, Hosuki assembles its cars in batches of 10. Each assembly process takes half a day. The setup times and run times per unit for the body stamping machine are given below.

Hosuki has just received its first corporate order—for 10 midsized vehicles. The company would like delivery as soon as possible.

1. Create a time-phased assembly chart to determine when the 10 cars can be delivered.
2. What adjustments are needed in inventory levels, lead times, and batch sizes to fill an additional customer order for five custom cars in five days?

**Virtual Bill of Material**

| Item | Qty |
|---|---|
| Midsize car | 1 |
| Frame Ass'y | 1 |
| Chassis | 1 |
| Engine | 1 |
| Engine Block | 1 |
| Transmission | 1 |
| Radiator | 1 |
| Battery | 1 |
| Suspension | 1 |
| Shocks | 2 |
| Brakes | 1 |
| Body | 1 |
| Windshield | 1 |
| Seats | 4 |
| Tire Ass'y | 4 |
| Wheels | 1 |
| Rims | 1 |
| Tires | 1 |

**Supplier**

| A | B | C | D | E | F | Hosuki |
|---|---|---|---|---|---|---|

**Supplier lead time is given in days.**

| Supplier A | OH | LT |
|---|---|---|
| Shocks | 20 | 1 |
| Brakes | 2 | 4 |

| Supplier B | OH | LT |
|---|---|---|
| Seats | 6 | 2 |

| Supplier C | OH | LT |
|---|---|---|
| Wheels | 20 | 1 |
| Rims | 2 | 4 |
| Tires | 10 | 5 |

| Supplier D | OH | LT |
|---|---|---|
| Chassis | 10 | 2 |
| Windshield | 5 | 4 |

| Supplier E | OH | LT |
|---|---|---|
| Engine Block | 5 | 5 |
| Transmission | 10 | 6 |

| Supplier F | OH | LT |
|---|---|---|
| Radiator | 10 | 1 |
| Battery | 5 | 3 |

**Body Stamping Machine**

| | Qty | Setup (hrs) | Runtime (hrs/unit) |
|---|---|---|---|
| Qrtr Panel | 4 | 2 | 0.5 |
| Hood | 1 | 1 | 0.3 |
| Fender | 2 | 2 | 0.3 |
| Roof | 1 | 2 | 0.2 |
| Doors | 4 | 2 | 0.2 |

## REFERENCES


Bancroft, N., H. Seip, and A. Spungel. *Implementing SAP R/3* Greenwich, CT: Manning, 1998.

Bond, B., Y. Genovese, et al. "ERP Is Dead—Long live ERP II." *Gartner Advisory Research Note* (October 4, 2000) http://www.gartner.com.

Brady, J., E. Monk, and B. Wagner. *Concepts in Enterprise Resource Planning*. Boston: Course Technology, 2001.

Bylinsky, G. "Heroes of U.S. Manufacturing." *Fortune* (March 19, 2001). http://www.fortune.com.

Curran, T., and G. Keller. *SAP/3 Business Blueprint*. Upper Saddle River, NJ: Prentice Hall, 1998.

Davenport, T. "Putting the Enterprise into the Enterprise System." *Harvard Business Review* (July/August 1998), pp. 121–131.

Davenport, T. *Mission Critical: Realizing the Promise of Enterprise Systems*. Boston: Harvard Business School Press, 2000.

Kerstetter, J. "When Machines Chat." *Business Week* (July 23, 2001), pp. 76–77.

Michel, R. "ERP Gets Redefined." *MSI Magazine* (February 1, 2001). http://www.manufacturingsystems.com.

Miller, D. "Tying It All Together." *The Industry Standard Magazine* (July 2, 2001). http://www.thestandard.net.

Orlicky, J. *Material Requirements Planning*. New York: McGraw-Hill, 1975.

Palitza, K. "SAP Lets ERP Fall Behind, Focuses on B2B." http://www.computerwire.com. Accessed October 29, 2001.

Pender, L. "Faster, Cheaper ERP." *CIO Magazine* (May 15, 2001). http://www.cio.com.

Peterson, K., K. Brant, et al. "Manufacturing Imperatives in Collaborative Commerce." *Gartner Advisory Research Note* (July 31, 2000). http://www.gartner.com.

Ptak, Carol. *ERP: Tools, Techniques and Applications for Integrating the Supply Chain.* Boca Raton, FL: St. Lucie Press, 2000.

"Taking the Pulse of ERP." *Modern Materials Handling* (February 1, 2001). http://www.manufacturing.net/mmh.

Vollman, T. E., W. L. Berry, and D. C. Whybark. *Manufacturing Planning and Control Systems,* 3rd ed. Homewood, IL: Irwin, 1992.

Wight, O. *Production Planning and Inventory Control in the Computer Age.* Boston: Cahners Books International, 1974.

ERP software vendors: www.sap.com, www.i2.com, www.oracle.com, www.QAD.com

# Lean Production

CHAPTER **15**

Web resources for this chapter include

- Internet Exercises
- Online Practice Quizzes
- Virtual Tours
- Excel Worksheets
- Company and Resource Weblinks
- Animated Demo Problems
- Microsoft Project Exhibits

www.wiley.com/college/russell

## CHAPTER OUTLINE

In this chapter, you will learn about . . .

- Basic Elements of Lean Production
- Benefits of Lean Production
- Implementing Lean Production
- Lean Services

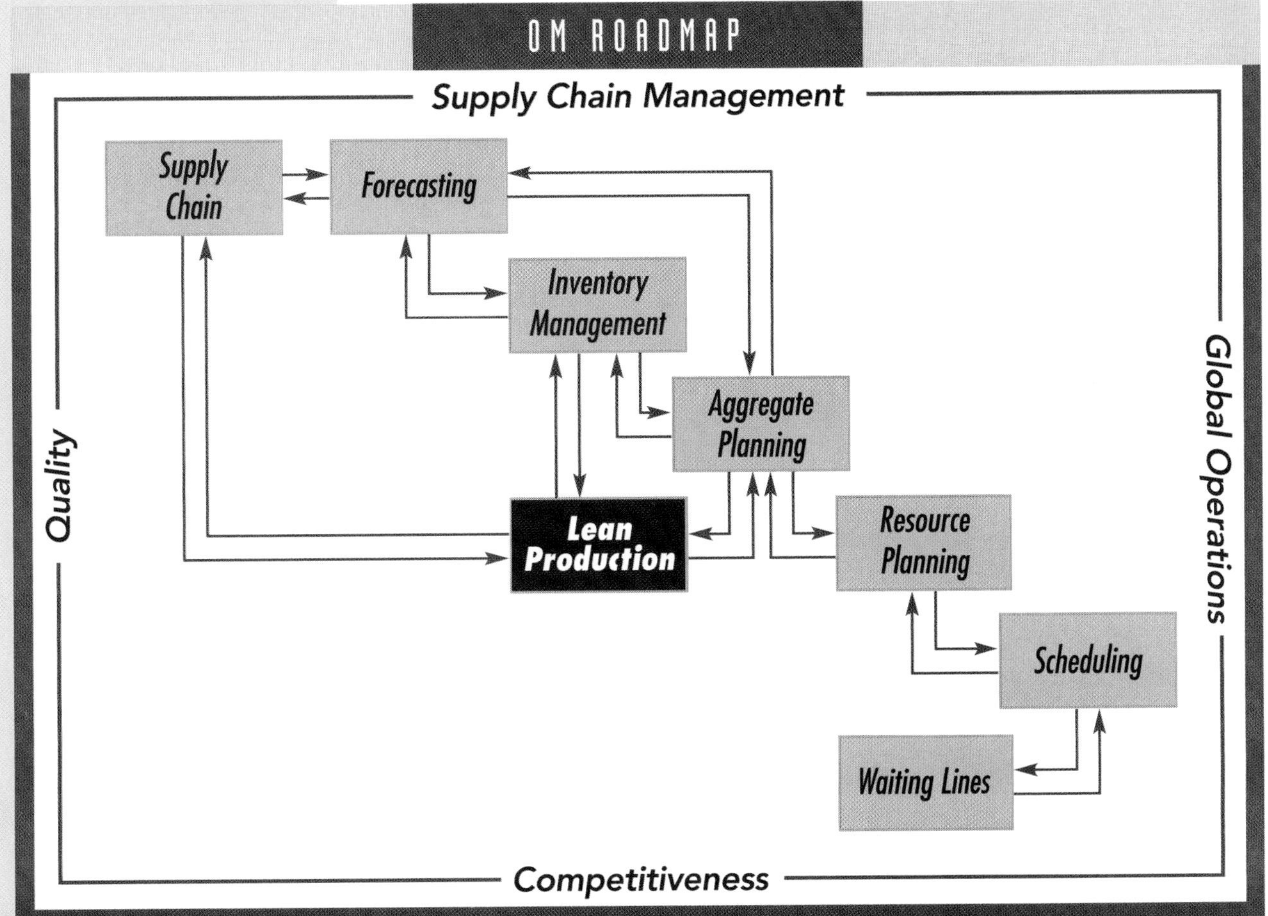

## KAIZEN AT SOLECTRON

Solectron Corporation is a leading electronics manufacturing services company, offering a full range of integrated supply chain solutions for the world's leading electronics original equipment manufacturers. The company, based in Milpitas, California, employs more than 60,000 associates in 20 countries worldwide. Solectron has received more than 400 quality customer and community service awards, and is the first two-time winner of the Malcolm Baldrige National Quality Award for manufacturing.

Solectron believes that in order to maintain its position as an industry leader, it must always work to improve its business and processes. Under Solectron's quality umbrella are continuous improvement methods such as *six sigma* for reducing variation and *lean manufacturing* for reducing waste within processes. In combination, the company has many success stories. One of the more powerful lean manufacturing tools applied at Solectron is kaizen.

Kaizen is a Japanese term that means "change for the good of all." With this improvement tool, a cross-functional team dedicates a week's worth of their time to plan and deliver quick low-cost improvements to a critical process. A kaizen quickly changes the way the product is produced and eliminates activities that have no value. Its key building blocks are waste elimination, workplace organization (5S), standardized work, and total productive maintenance. (*We'll discuss all these topics later in this chapter.*)

*Team members are energized by the rapid pace of change in a kaizen project.*

Prior to the kaizen project kickoff, a leadership team is established consisting of a Project Champion from upper-level management, two co-leaders, a facilitator, and a liaison. The co-leaders support the champion and ensure that he or she understands the process and issues faced by the team. Facilitators provide structure to the team process, document team activities, and track and record progress toward target objectives. A liaison is the point of contact with support personnel needed during the kaizen process. The leadership team develops a project charter, selects six to eight people from various functional areas as team members, records the baseline condition of the target area, and determines the achievable goals and objectives for the week. The leadership team conducts its own process analysis to fully understand the process's value stream and communication loops.

Team members are expected to understand the current process, identify improvement actions, be active, implement change, check results, and standardize the process. A typical kaizen is conducted over a five-day time period as follows.

- Day 1 is spent introducing the team to kaizen and lean manufacturing techniques, reviewing expectations of team members, touring the process in question, and developing process maps.
- Days 2 and 3 are spent gathering and analyzing data, identifying waste (called *muda* walks), conducting gripe interviews, performing 5S activities, examining the value stream, and analyzing cycle time. At the end of each day the team meets to go over their progress and set goals for the next day.
- Day 4 involves testing suggested improvements; creating postprocess maps and postvalue streams; documenting visual controls and procedures; and devising a 30-day action plan.
- On Day 5, kaizen results are presented to management and the team celebrates its success.

After the kaizen week, the leadership team establishes a Relentless Improvement Team (RIT) to make sure that the changes are sustained and to continue with incremental improvements within the process. A recent kaizen reduced process changeover times from 2.7 hours to less than 1 hour. As a result, without purchasing any additional capital equipment, Solectron was able to handle an additional $6 million of business.

Shortened product life cycles, demanding customers, globalization and e-commerce have placed intense pressure on companies for quicker response and shorter cycle times. One way to ensure a quick turnaround is by holding inventory. But inventory costs can easily become prohibitive, especially when product obsolescence is considered. A wiser approach is to make your operating system lean and agile, able to adapt to changing customer demands. We have talked extensively in this book about supply chains. Collaboration along a supply chain can work only if the participants coordinate their production and operate under the same rhythm. Companies have found this rhythm in a well-respected but difficult to implement philosophy called lean production.

**Lean production** means doing more with less—less inventory, fewer workers, less space. The term was coined by James Womack and Daniel Jones[1] to describe the Toyota Production System, widely recognized as the most efficient manufacturing system in the world.

**Lean production:** an integrated management system that emphasizes the elimination of waste and the continuous improvement of operations.

The Toyota Production System evolved slowly over a span of 15 years. Initially known as **JIT (just-in-time)**, it emphasized minimizing inventory and smoothing the flow of materials so that material arrived just as it was needed or "just-in-time." As the concept widened in scope, the term *lean production* became more prevalent. Now the terms are often used interchangeably.

**Just-in-time (JIT):** smoothing the *flow* of material to arrive just as it is needed.

Taiichi Ohno, a former shop manager and later vice president of Toyota Motor Company, is the individual generally credited with the development of lean production. The idea of producing only what you need when you need it hardly seems the basis of a revolution in manufacturing, but the concept is deceptively simple. If you produce only what you need when you need it, there is no room for error. For lean production to work well, many fundamental elements must be in place—steady production, flexible resources, extremely high quality, reliable equipment, reliable suppliers, quick setups, and lots of discipline to maintain the other elements.

In this chapter, we explore the elements of lean production and try to discover how they became part of Ohno's integrated management system, known as the *Toyota Production System*. We also explore the benefits and drawbacks of lean production and its implementation. We conclude with a discussion of lean services.

## THE BASIC ELEMENTS OF LEAN PRODUCTION

In the 1950s, the entire Japanese automobile industry produced 30,000 vehicles, fewer than a half day's production for U.S. automakers. With such low levels of demand, the principles of mass production that worked so well for U.S. manufacturers could not be applied in Japan. Furthermore, the Japanese were short on capital and storage space. So it seems natural that efforts to improve performance (and stay solvent) would center on reducing the asset that soaks up both funds and space—inventory. What is significant is that a system originally designed to reduce inventory levels eventually became a system for continually improving all aspects of operations. The stage was set for this evolution by the president of Toyota, Eiji Toyoda, who gave a mandate to his people to "eliminate waste." Waste, or **muda**, was defined as "anything other than the minimum amount of equipment, materials, parts, space, and time which are absolutely essential to add value to the product."[2] Examples of waste in operations are shown in Figure 15.1.

Lean's mandate: *Eliminate waste.*

**Muda:** waste, anything other than that which adds value to the product or service.

Lean production is the result of the mandate to eliminate waste. It is composed of ten elements:

Basic elements of lean production:

1. Flexible resources
2. Cellular layouts
3. Pull system
4. Kanbans
5. Small lots
6. Quick setups
7. Uniform production levels
8. Quality at the source
9. Total productive maintenance
10. Supplier networks

These elements can be loosely organized into three phases, as shown in Figure 5.2. Let's explore each of these elements and determine how they work in concert.[3]

[1]J. Womack and D. Jones, *The Machine that Changed the World* (New York: Macmillan, 1990).

[2]Ibid., pp. 8–9.

[3]Much of the material in these sections is adapted from Chapter 5 in Michael Cusomano's book, *The Japanese Automobile Industry* (Cambridge, MA: Harvard University Press), 1985.

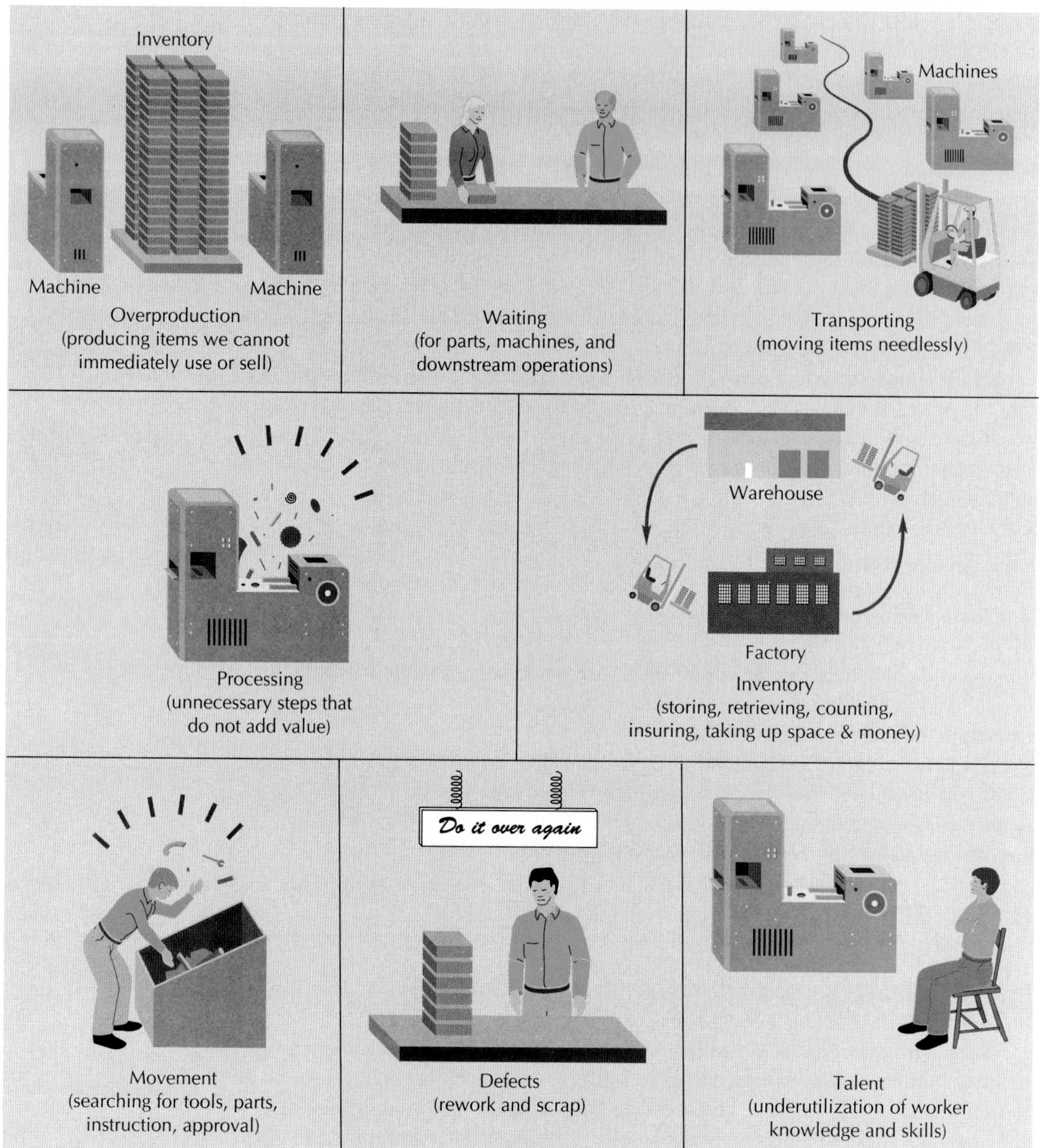


**Figure 15.1**
**Waste in Operations**

**Multifunctional workers:** perform more than one job; **general-purpose machines** perform several basic functions.

## FLEXIBLE RESOURCES

The concept of flexible resources, in the form of **multifunctional workers** and **general-purpose machines**, is recognized as a key element of lean production, but most people do not realize that it was the first element to fall into place. Taiichi Ohno had transferred to Toyota from Toyoda textile mills with no knowledge of (or preconceived notions about) automobile manufacturing. His first attempt to eliminate waste (not unlike U.S. managers) concentrated on worker productivity. Borrowing heavily from U.S. time and motion studies, he set out to analyze every job and every machine in his shop. He quickly noted a distinction between the operating time of a machine and the operating time of the worker. Initially, he asked each worker to operate two machines rather than one. To make this possible, he located the machines in parallel lines or in L-formations. After a time, he asked workers to operate three or four machines arranged in a U-shape. The machines were no longer of the same type (as in a process layout) but represented a series of different processes common to a group of parts (i.e., a cellular layout).

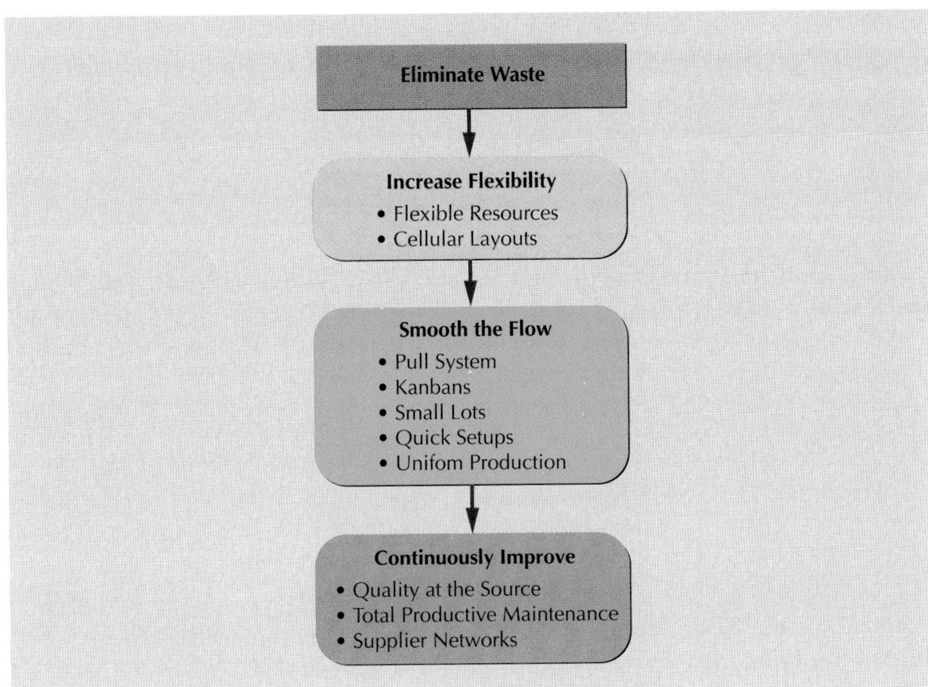


**Figure 15.2**
**Elements of Lean Production**

The operation of different, multiple machines required additional training for workers and specific rotation schedules. Figure 15.3 shows a standard operating routine for an individual worker. The solid lines represent operator processing time (e.g., loading, unloading, or setting up a machine), the dashed lines represent machine processing time, and the squiggly lines represent walking time for the operator from machine to machine. The time required for the worker to complete one pass through the operations assigned is called the operator *cycle time*.

Closely related to the concept of cycle time is *takt time*. "Takt" is the German word for baton, such as an orchestra leader would use to signal the timing at which musicians play. **Takt time**, then, is the pace at which production should take place to match the rate of customer demand. An operator's cycle time is coordinated with the takt time of the product or service being produced.

**Takt time:** the pace at which production should take place to match customer demand.

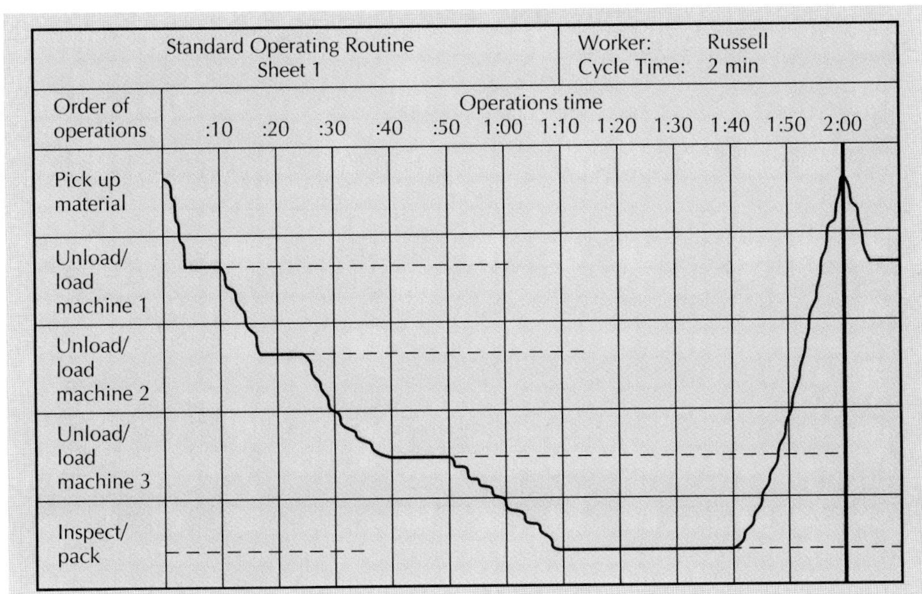


**Figure 15.3**
**Standard Operating Routine for a Worker**

With single workers operating multiple machines, the machines themselves also required some adjustments. Limit switches were installed to turn off machines automatically after each operation was completed. Changes in jigs and fixtures allowed machines to hold a workpiece in place, rather than rely on the presence of an operator. Extra tools and fixtures were purchased and placed at their point of use so that operators did not have to leave their stations to retrieve them when needed. By the time Ohno was finished with this phase of his improvement efforts, it was possible for one worker to operate as many as 17 machines (the average was 5 to 10).

The flexibility of labor brought about by Ohno's changes prompted a switch to more flexible machines. Thus, although other manufacturers were interested in purchasing more specialized automated equipment, Toyota preferred small, general-purpose machines. A general-purpose lathe, for example, might be used to bore holes in an engine block and then do other drilling, milling, and threading operations at the same station. The waste of movement to other machines, setting up other machines, and waiting at other machines was eliminated.

## CELLULAR LAYOUTS

**Manufacturing cells:** dissimilar machines brought together to manufacture a family of parts.

While it is true that Ohno first reorganized his shop into **manufacturing cells** to use labor more efficiently, the flexibility of the new layout proved to be fundamental to the effectiveness of the system as a whole. The concept of cellular layouts did not originate with Ohno. It was first described by a U.S. engineer in the 1920s, but it was Ohno's inspired application of the idea that brought it to the attention of the world. We discussed cellular layouts (and the concept of group technology on which it is based) in Chapter 7. Let us review some of that material here.

*Cells* group dissimilar machines together to process a family of parts with similar shapes or processing requirements. The layout of machines within the cell resembles a small assembly line and is usually U-shaped. Work is moved within the cell, ideally one unit at a time, from one process to the next by a worker as he or she walks around the cell in a prescribed path. Figure 15.4 shows a typical manufacturing cell with worker routes.

Cycle time is adjusted to match takt time by changing worker paths.

Work normally flows through the cell in one direction and experiences little waiting. In a one-person cell, the cycle time of the cell is determined by the time it takes for the

**Figure 15.4**
**Cells with Worker Routes**

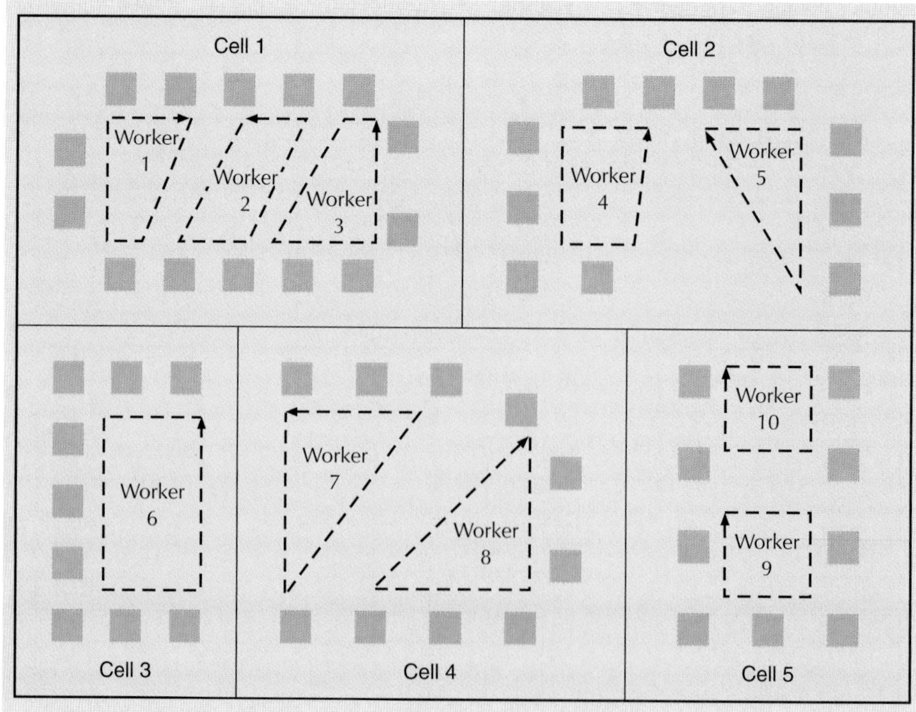

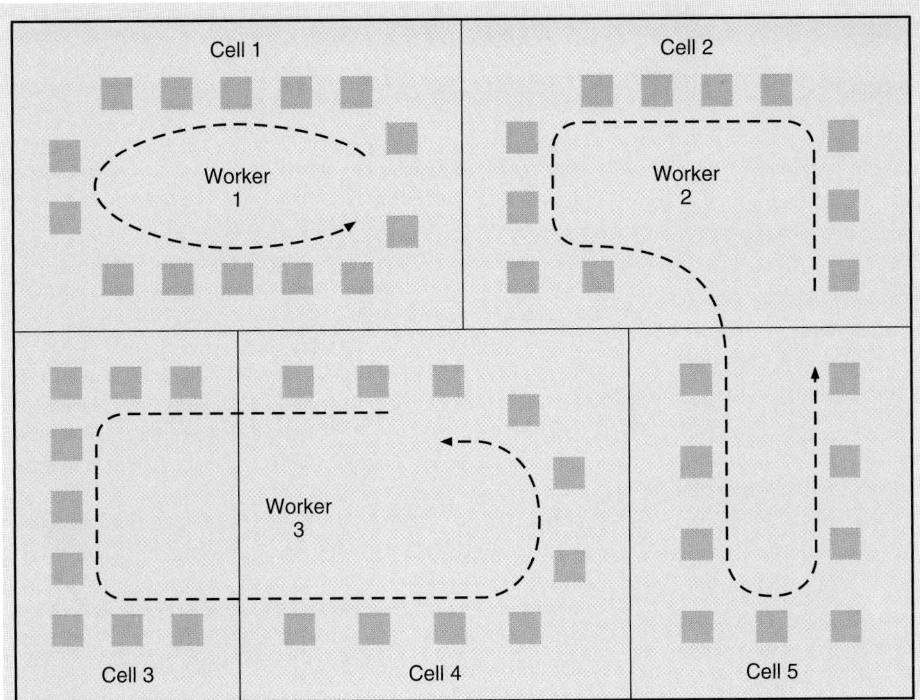


Figure 15.5
**Worker Routes Lengthen as Volume Decreases**

worker to complete his or her path through the cell. This means that, although different items produced in the cell may take different amounts of time to complete, the time between successive items leaving the cell remains virtually the same because the worker's path remains the same. Thus, changes of product mix within the cell are easy to accommodate. Changes in volume or takt time can be handled by adding workers to or subtracting workers from the cell and adjusting their walking routes accordingly as shown in Figure 15.5.

Because cells produce similar items, setup time requirements are low and lot sizes can be reduced. Movement of output from the cells to subassembly or assembly lines occurs in small lots and is controlled by kanbans (which we discuss later). Cellular layouts, because of their manageable size, workflow, and flexibility, facilitate another element of lean production, the *pull system*.

## THE PULL SYSTEM

A major problem in automobile manufacturing is coordinating the production and delivery of materials and parts with the production of subassemblies and the requirements of the final assembly line. It is a complicated process, not because of the technology, but because of the thousands of large and small components produced by thousands of workers for a single automobile. Traditionally, inventory has been used to cushion against lapses in coordination, and these inventories can be quite large. Ohno struggled for five years trying to come up with a system to improve the coordination between processes and thereby eliminate the need for large amounts of inventory. He finally got the idea for his *pull* system from another American classic, the supermarket. Ohno read (and later observed) that Americans do not keep large stocks of food at home. Instead, they make frequent visits to nearby supermarkets to purchase items as they need them. The supermarkets, in turn, carefully control their inventory by replenishing items on their shelves only as they are removed. Customers actually "pull through" the system the items they need, and supermarkets do not order more items than can be sold.

Applying this concept to manufacturing requires a reversal of the normal process/information flow, called a *push* system. In a **push system**, a schedule is prepared in advance for a series of workstations, and each workstation pushes its completed work to the next

## THE COMPETITIVE EDGE

### Lean Service at Jefferson Pilot

Jefferson Pilot Financial (JPF) is a full-service life insurance and annuities company. Over the past 10 years, rising customer expectations have led to a proliferation of more specialized and more complex insurance products that are more costly to administer. Competition has accelerated from smaller niche players offering lower premiums and faster service. Jefferson Pilot knew it had to improve service *and* streamline costs, so it turned to a philosophy and practice that has helped manufacturing companies regain their competitiveness, *lean production*.

Like assembling an automobile, an insurance policy goes through a series of steps from initial application to underwriting to issuing the policy. Just as excess inventory in a factory can hide defects and delay production, so can piles of documents waiting to be processed in a service firm. Jefferson Pilot tested the idea of processing policies in a line flow rather than in batches in its *model cell*, a microcosm of work where new ideas could be practiced and perfected. A five-person *lean team* was assembled to re-design business processes, and a 10-person model cell was designated in the new Business unit to test the new ideas.

They found the following aspects of lean production most useful in their project:

1. *Co-locate linked processes.* In the old organization, JPF employees were located by function. It could take longer than a day for documents to travel from receiving (on one floor) to sorting (on another floor). Placing receiving next to sorting also helped workers feel like a part of an integrated process instead of focusing only on their tasks.
2. *Standardize procedures.* Employees had been given considerable freedom in doing their work. As a result, it was difficult for another person to "fill-in" their jobs when they were absent. The lean team insisted that all customer files be stored alphabetically in the same drawer in each workstation. The physical workspace for data entry was also standardized so that it was easy to tell at a glance how much work had been completed and how much work was left to be done.
3. *Eliminate loop-backs.* Loop-backs occur when work is returned to a previous step for processing. For example, the person who received the initial application was required to reassemble it once all the sections had been added. Moving this step to the end of the process and assigning it to a new group of workers allowed the receivers to process more incoming policies and keep the flow of work moving along.
4. *Set a common tempo.* The pace at which work is performed should be tracked to customer demand. New Business needed to process 10 applications an hour to keep up with the demand. Thus, each application should take no longer that six minutes to process. Six minutes is the *takt time* of the application process. That means that no individual involved in this process should take longer than six minutes to complete his or her task. The lean team divided each task into work elements, timed them, improved them, and assigned them to workers so that the process proceeded at a common tempo.
5. *Balance the loads.* From the tempo exercise, it became apparent that work should be balanced as evenly as possible among employees. Assigning work alphabetically by the applicant's last name did not follow that principle. The lean team recommended that work be assigned to the next available processor, period.
6. *Segregate complexity.* One of the quickest improvements came from segregating the applications into two groups: those that needed a physician's statement and those that did not. The turnaround for those in the second category decreased by 80%.
7. *Post-performance results.* The model cell's hourly production rates as compared to company goals were posted on a large white board for all employees to see. Another board was used to discuss problems and brainstorm solutions. Although not warmly received at first, the boards became rallying points for improved performance and proof that performance evaluations would be based on objective data rather then personal opinion.

The results from Jefferson Pilot's lean initiative are impressive. Over a two-year period, the company reduced the time to process an application by 50%, reduced labor by 26%, reduced errors by 40%, and increased new annualized life insurance premiums by 60%. Lean production has transformed manufacturing. Jefferson Pilot has proved it can transform services, too.

*Source:* Adapted from Cynthia Swank, "The Lean Service Machine," *Harvard Business Review* (October 2003), pp. 123–131.

**Push systems:** rely on a predetermined schedule.

**Pull systems:** rely on customer requests.

station. With the **pull system**, workers go back to previous stations and take only the parts or materials they need and can process immediately. When their output has been taken, workers at the previous station know it is time to start producing more, and they replenish the exact quantity that the subsequent station just took away. If their output is not taken, workers at the previous station simply stop production; no excess is produced. This system forces operations to work in coordination with one another. It prevents overproduction and underproduction; only necessary quantities are produced. "Necessary" is not defined by a schedule that specifies what ought to be needed; rather, it is defined by the operation of the shop floor, complete with unanticipated occurrences and variations in performance.

Although the concept of pull production seems simple, it can be difficult to implement because it is so different from normal scheduling procedures. After several years of experimenting with the pull system, Ohno found it necessary to introduce *kanbans* to exercise more control over the pull process on the shop floor.

*This supplier kanban attached to a container rotates between Purodenso Manufacturing and a Toyota assembly plant. The part number, description, and quantity per container appear in the center of the card, directly beneath the kanban number. Notice the container holds four air flow meter assemblies. The store address in the upper left-hand corner specifies where the full container is to be delivered. The line side address in the upper right-hand corner specifies where the empty container is to be picked up. The lower left-hand corner identifies the preceding process (the assemblies come from Purodenso), and the lower right-hand corner identifies the subsequent process (N2). Barcoding the information on the card speeds processing and increases the accuracy of production and financial records.*

## KANBANS

**Kanban:** a card that corresponds to a standard quantity of production (usually a container size).

**Kanban** is the Japanese word for card. In the pull system, each kanban corresponds to a standard quantity of production or size of container. A kanban contains basic information such as part number, brief description, type of container, unit load (i.e., quantity per container), preceding station (where it came from), and subsequent station (where it goes to). Sometimes the kanban is color-coded to indicate raw materials or other stages of manufacturing. The information on the kanban does not change during production. The same kanban can rotate back and forth between preceding and subsequent workstations.

Kanbans were derived from the *two-bin* inventory system.

Kanbans are closely associated with the fixed-quantity inventory system we discussed in Chapter 12. Recall that in the fixed-quantity system, a certain quantity, $Q$, is ordered whenever the stock on hand falls below a reorder point. The reorder point is determined so that demand can be met while an order for new material is being processed. Thus, the reorder point corresponds to demand during lead time. A visual fixed-quantity system, called the *two-bin system*, illustrates the concept nicely. Referring to Figure 15.6*a*, two bins are maintained for each item. The first (and usually larger) bin contains the order quantity minus the reorder point, and the second bin contains the reorder point quantity. At the bottom of the first bin is an order card that describes the item and specifies the supplier and the quantity that is to be ordered. When the first bin is empty, the card is removed and sent to the supplier as a new order. While the order is being filled, the quantity in the second bin is used. If everything goes as planned, when the second bin is empty, the new order will arrive and both bins will be filled again.

Ohno looked at this system and liked its simplicity, but he could not understand the purpose of the first bin. As shown in Figure 15.5*b*, by eliminating the first bin and placing the order card (which he called a *kanban*) at the top of the second bin, $(Q - R)$ inventory

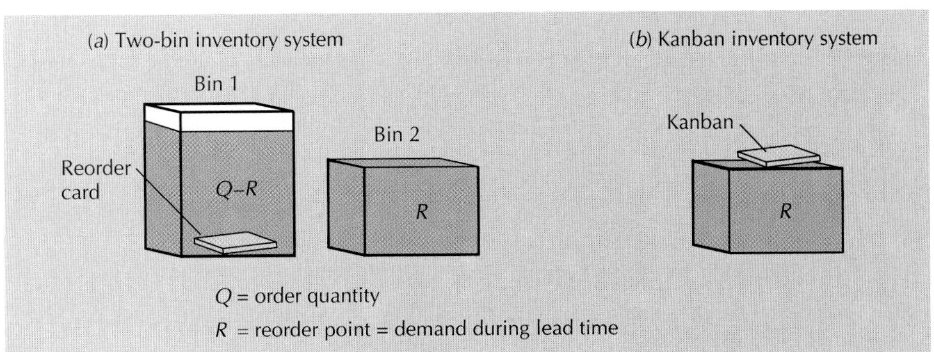


**Figure 15.6**
**The Origin of Kanban**

could be eliminated. In this system, an order is continually in transit. When the new order arrives, the supplier is reissued the same kanban to fill the order again. The only inventory that is maintained is the amount needed to cover usage until the next order can be processed. This concept is the basis for the kanban system.

Kanbans maintain the discipline of pull production.

Kanbans do not make the schedule of production; they maintain the discipline of pull production by authorizing the production and movement of materials. If there is no kanban, there is no production. If there is no kanban, there is no movement of material. There are many different types and variations of kanbans. The most sophisticated is probably the dual kanban system used by Toyota, which uses two types of kanbans: *production kanbans* and *withdrawal kanbans*. As their names imply, a **production kanban** is a card authorizing production of goods, and a **withdrawal kanban** is a card authorizing the movement of goods. Each kanban is physically attached to a container or cart. As shown in Figure 15.7, an empty cart signals production or withdrawal of goods. Kanbans are exchanged between containers as needed to support the pull process.

**Production kanban:** a card authorizing production of goods.

**Withdrawal kanban:** a card authorizing the movement of goods.

The dual kanban approach is used when material is not necessarily moving between two consecutive processes, or when there is more than one input to a process and the inputs are dispersed throughout the facility (as for an assembly process). If the processes are tightly linked, other types of kanbans can be used.

Figure 15.8*a* shows the use of kanban squares placed between successive workstations. A **kanban square** is a marked area that will hold a certain number of output items (usually one or two). If the kanban square following his or her process is empty, the worker knows it is time to begin production again. *Kanban racks*, illustrated in Figure 15.8*b*, can be used in a similar manner. When the allocated slots on a rack are empty, workers know it is time to begin a new round of production to fill up the slots. If the distance between stations prohibits the use of kanban squares or racks, the signal for production can be a colored golf ball rolled down a tube, a flag on a post, a light flashing on a board, or an electronic or verbal message requesting more.

**Kanban square:** a marked area designated to hold items.

**Signal kanbans** are used when inventory between processes is still necessary. It closely resembles the reorder point system. As shown in Figure 15.8*c*, a triangular marker is placed at a certain level of inventory. When the marker is reached (a visual reorder point), it is removed from the stack of goods and placed on an order post, thereby generating a replenishment order for the item. The rectangular-shaped kanban in the diagram is called a **material kanban**. In some cases it is necessary to order the *material* for a process in advance of the initiation of the process.

**Signal kanban:** a triangular kanban used to signal production at the previous workstation.

**Material kanban:** a rectangular kanban used to order material in advance of a process.

Kanbans can also be used outside the factory to order material from suppliers. The supplier brings the order (e.g., a filled container) directly to its point of use in the factory and then picks up an empty container with kanban to fill and return later. It would not be unusual for 5000 to 10,000 of these **supplier kanbans** to rotate between the factory and suppliers. To handle this volume of transactions, a kind of kanban "post office" can be set

**Supplier kanbans:** rotate between the factory and suppliers.

**Figure 15.7**
**Dual Kanbans**

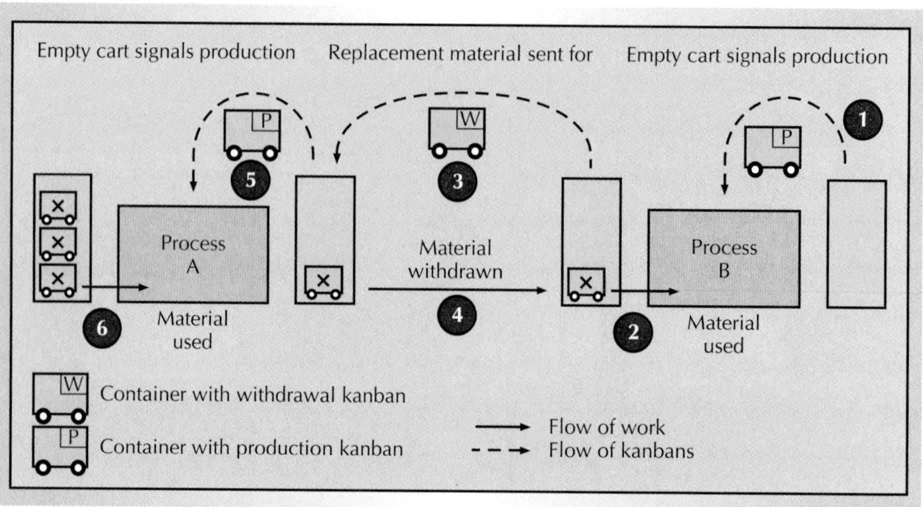

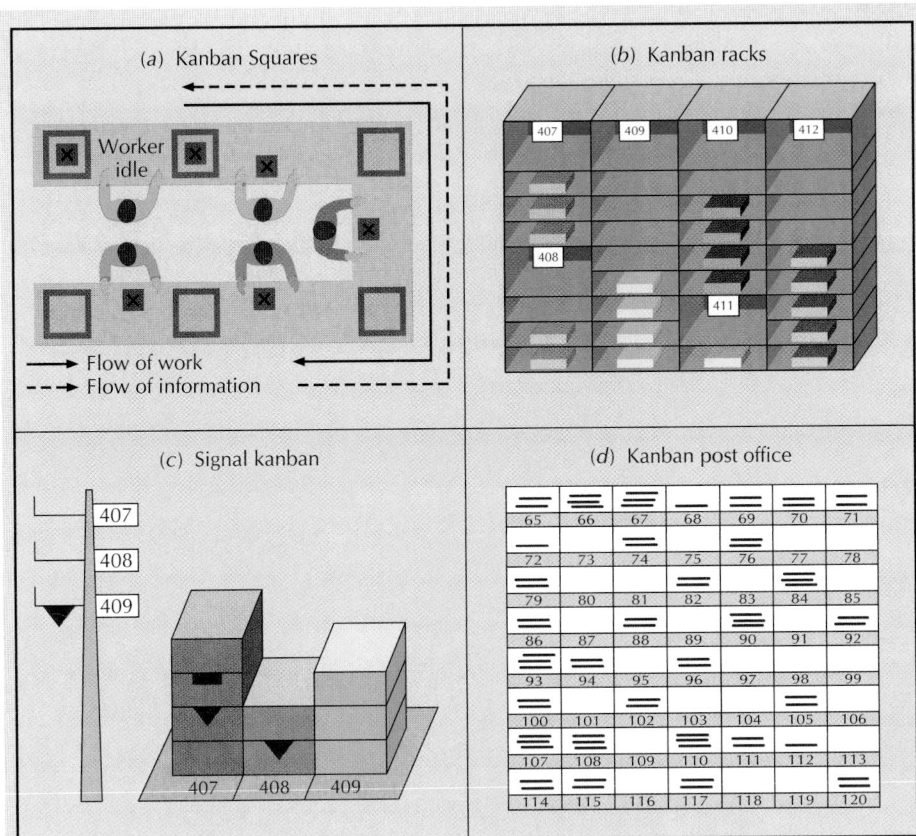


**Figure 15.8**

**Other Types of Kanbans**

up, with the kanbans sorted by supplier, as in Figure 15.8*d*. The supplier then checks his or her "mailbox" to pick up new orders before returning to the factory. Bar-coded kanbans and electronic kanbans can also be used to facilitate communication between customer and supplier.

It is easy to get caught up with the technical aspects of kanbans and lose sight of the objective of the pull system, which is to reduce inventory levels. The kanban system is actually very similar to the reorder point system. The difference is in application. The reorder point system attempts to create a permanent ordering policy, whereas the kanban system encourages the continual reduction of inventory. We can see how that occurs by examining the formula for determining the number of kanbans needed to control the production of a particular item.

The number of kanbans needed can be calculated from demand and lead time information.

$$\text{No. of kanbans} = \frac{\text{average demand during lead time} + \text{safety stock}}{\text{container size}}$$

$$N = \frac{\bar{d}L + S}{C}$$

where

$N$ = number of kanbans or containers

$\bar{d}$ = average number of units demanded over some time period

$L$ = lead time; the time it takes to replenish an order (expressed in the same terms as demand)

$S$ = safety stock; usually given as a percentage of a demand during lead time but can be based on service level and variance of demand during lead time (as in Chapter 12)

$C$ = container size

To force the improvement process, the container size is usually much smaller than the demand during lead time. At Toyota, containers can hold at most 10% of a day's demand.

This allows the number of kanbans (i.e., containers) to be reduced one at a time. The smaller number of kanbans (and corresponding lower level of inventory) causes problems in the system to become visible. Workers and managers then attempt to solve the problems that have been identified.

**Example 15.1**

**Determining the Number of Kanbans**

Julie Hurling works in a cosmetic factory filling, capping, and labeling bottles. She is asked to process an average of 150 bottles per hour through her work cell. If one kanban is attached to every container, a container holds 25 bottles, it takes 30 minutes to receive new bottles from the previous workstation, and the factory uses a safety stock factor of 10%, how many kanbans are needed for the bottling process?

*Solution*

Given:

$$\bar{d} = 150 \text{ bottles per hour}$$
$$L = 30 \text{ minutes} = 0.5 \text{ hour}$$
$$S = 0.10\,(150 \times 0.5) = 7.5$$
$$C = 25 \text{ bottles}$$

Then,

$$N = \frac{dL + S}{C} = \frac{(150 \times 0.5) + 7.5}{25}$$
$$= \frac{75 + 7.5}{25} = 3.3 \text{ kanbans or containers}$$

Round either up or down (three containers would force us to improve operations, and four would allow some slack).

## SMALL LOTS

Small-lot production requires less space and capital investment than systems that incur large inventories. By producing small amounts at a time, processes can be physically moved closer together and transportation between stations can be simplified. In small-lot production, quality problems are easier to detect and workers show less tendency to let poor quality pass (as they might in a system that is producing huge amounts of an item anyway). Lower inventory levels make processes more dependent on each other. This is beneficial because it reveals errors and bottlenecks more quickly and gives workers an opportunity to solve them.

Small-lot production improves quality and reduces lead time.

The analogy of water flowing over a bed of rocks is useful here. As shown in Figure 15.9, the inventory level is like the level of water. It hides problems but allows for smooth sailing. When the inventory level is reduced, the problems (or rocks) are exposed. After the exposed rocks are removed from the river, the boat can again progress, this time more quickly than before.

Although it is true that a company can produce in small lot sizes without using the pull system or kanbans, from experience we know that small-lot production in a push system is difficult to coordinate. Similarly, using large lot sizes with a pull system and kanbans would not be advisable. Let's look more closely at the relationship between small lot sizes, the pull system, and kanbans.

From the kanban formula, it becomes clear that a reduction in the number of kanbans (given a constant container size) requires a corresponding reduction in safety stock or in lead time itself. The need for safety stock can be reduced by making demand and supply more certain. Flexible resources allow the system to adapt more readily to unanticipated changes in demand. Demand fluctuations can also be controlled through closer contact with customers and better forecasting systems. Deficiencies in supply can be controlled through eliminating mistakes, producing only good units, and reducing or eliminating machine breakdowns.

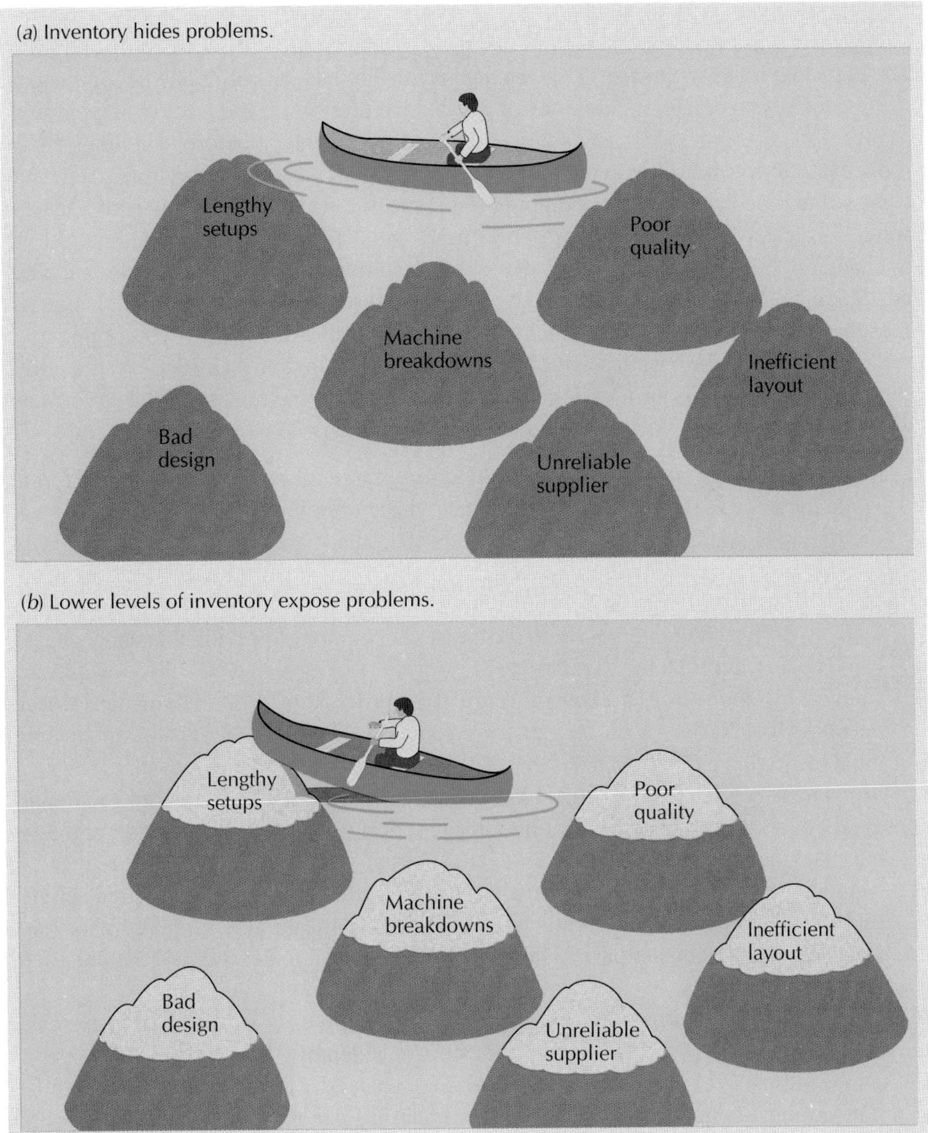


**Figure 15.9**

**Reduced Inventory Makes Problems Visible**

Lead time is typically made up of four components:

- Processing time
- Move time
- Waiting time
- Setup time

*Processing time* can be reduced by reducing the number of items processed and the efficiency or speed of the machine or worker. *Move time* can be decreased if machines are moved closer together, the method of movement is simplified, routings are standardized, or the need for movement is eliminated. *Waiting time* can be reduced through better scheduling of materials, workers, and machines and sufficient capacity. In many companies, however, lengthy *setup times* are the biggest bottleneck. Reduction of setup time is an important part of lean production.

## QUICK SETUPS

Several processes in automobile manufacturing defy production in small lots because of the enormous amount of time required to set up the machines. Stamping is a good example. First, a large roll of sheet steel is run through a blanking press to produce stacks of flat blanks slightly larger than the size of the desired parts. Then, the blanks are inserted into huge stamping presses that contain a matched set of upper and lower dies. When the dies are held together under thousands of pounds of pressure, a three-dimensional shape emerges, such as a car door or fender. Because the dies weigh several tons each and have to be aligned with exact precision, die changes typically take an entire day to complete.

Obviously, manufacturers are reluctant to change dies often. Ford, for example, might produce 500,000 right door panels and store them in inventory before switching dies to produce left door panels. Some manufacturers have found it easier to purchase several sets of presses and dedicate them to stamping out a specific part for months or years. Due to capital constraints, that was not an option for Toyota. Instead, Ohno began simplifying die-changing techniques. Convinced that major improvements could be made, a consultant, Shigeo Shingo, was hired to study die setup systematically, to reduce changeover times further, and to teach these techniques to production workers and Toyota suppliers.

Shingo proved to be a genius at the task. He reduced setup time on a 1000-ton press from 6 hours to 3 minutes using a system he called **SMED** (single-minute exchange of dies). SMED is based on the following principles, which can be applied to any type of setup:

**Internal setup:** setup activities that can be performed only when a process is stopped.

**External setup** setup activities that can be performed in advance.

1. ***Separate internal setup from external setup.*** **Internal setup** has to be performed while the machine is stopped; it cannot take place until the machine has finished with the previous operation. **External setup**, on the other hand, can be performed in advance, while the machine is running. By the time a machine has finished processing its current operation, the worker should have completed the external setup and be ready to perform the internal setup for the next operation. Applying this concept alone can reduce setup time by 30 to 50%.
2. ***Convert internal setup to external setup.*** This process involves making sure that the operating conditions, such as gathering tools and fixtures, preheating an injection mold, centering a die, or standardizing die heights, are prepared in advance.
3. ***Streamline all aspects of setup.*** External setup activities can be reduced by organizing the workplace properly, locating tools and dies near their points of use, and keeping machines and fixtures in good repair. Internal setup activities can be reduced by simplifying or eliminating adjustments. Examples include precoding desired settings, using quick fasteners and locator pins, preventing misalignment, eliminating tools, and making movements easier. Figure 15.10 provides some common analogies for these improvements.
4. ***Perform setup activities in parallel or eliminate them entirely.*** Adding an extra person to the setup team can reduce setup time considerably. In most cases, two people can perform a setup in less than half the time needed by a single person. In addition, standardizing components, parts, and raw materials can reduce and sometimes eliminate setup requirements.

*Reducing setup time requires teamwork, practice, and a careful coordination of activities, not unlike the precision pit crews in auto racing.*

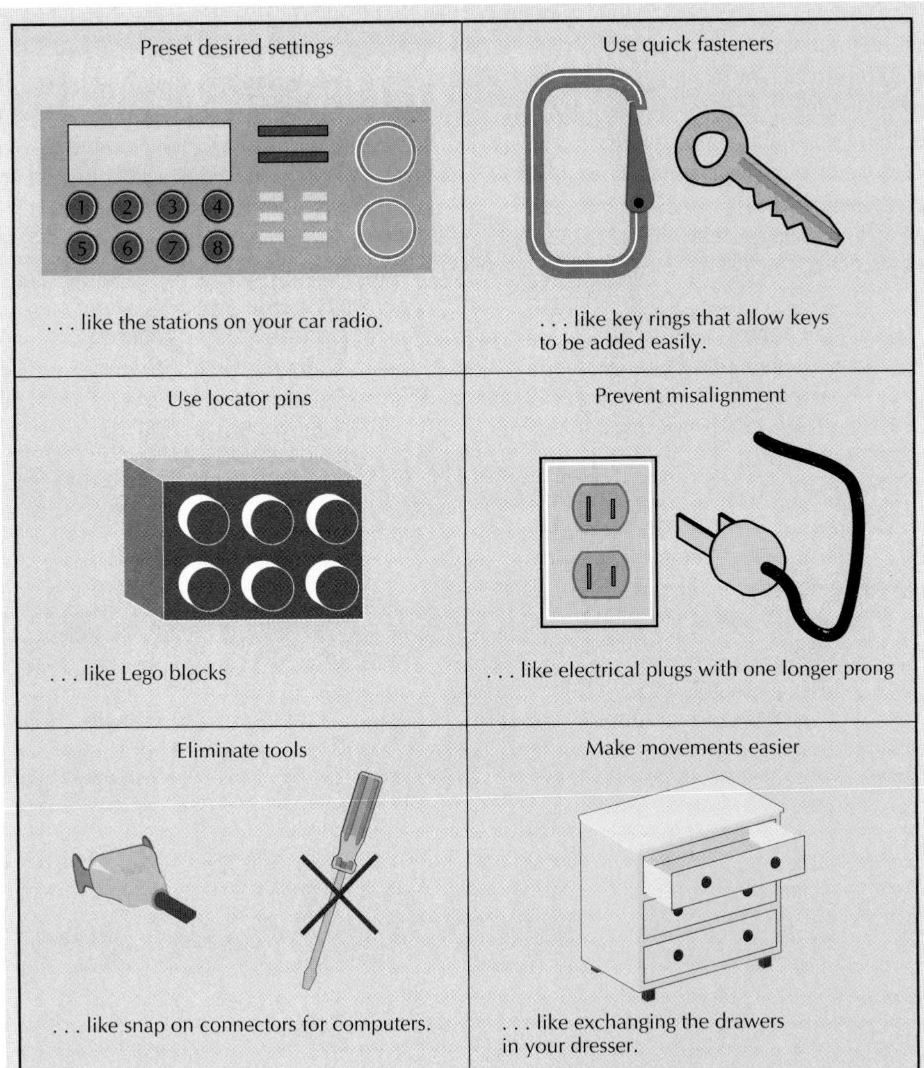


**Figure 15.10**

**Some Common Techniques for Reducing Setup Time**

In order to view the setup process objectively, it is useful to assign the task of setup-time reduction to a team of workers and engineers. Videotaping the setup in progress often helps the team generate ideas for improvement. Time and motion study principles (like those discussed in the Supplement to Chapter 8) can be applied. After the new setup procedures have been agreed on, they need to be practiced until they are perfected. One only has to view the pit crews at the Indy 500 to realize that quick changeovers have to be orchestrated and practiced.

## UNIFORM PRODUCTION LEVELS

The flow of production created by the pull system, kanbans, small lots, and quick setups can only be maintained if production is relatively steady. Lean production systems attempt to maintain **uniform production levels** by smoothing the production requirements on the final assembly line. Changes in final assembly often have dramatic effects on component production upstream. When this happens in a kanban system, kanbans for certain parts will circulate very quickly at some times and very slowly at others. Adjustments of plus or minus 10% in monthly demand can be absorbed by the kanban system, but wider demand fluctuations cannot be handled without substantially increasing inventory levels or scheduling large amounts of overtime.[4]

**Uniform production levels:** the result from smoothing production requirements on the final assembly line.

[4]P. Y. Huang, L. P. Rees, and B. W. Taylor, "A Simulation Analysis of the Just-in-Time Technique (with Kanbans) for a Multiline, Multistage Production System," *Decision Sciences* (July 1983), pp. 326–345.

Reduce variability with more accurate forecasts.

One way to reduce variability in production is to guard against unexpected demand through more accurate forecasts. To accomplish this, the sales division of Toyota takes the lead in production planning. Toyota Motor Sales conducts surveys of tens of thousands of people twice a year to estimate demand for Toyota cars and trucks. Monthly production schedules are drawn up from the forecasts two months in advance. The plans are reviewed one month in advance and then again 10 days in advance. Daily production schedules, which by then include firm orders from dealers, are finalized four days from the start of production. Model mix changes can still be made the evening before or the morning of production. This flexibility is possible because schedule changes are communicated only to the final assembly line. Kanbans take care of dispatching revised orders to the rest of the system.

Reduce variability by smoothing demand.

Another approach to achieving uniform production is to *level* or smooth demand across the planning horizon. Demand is divided into small increments of time and spread out as evenly as possible so that the same amount of each item is produced each day, and item production is *mixed* throughout the day in very small quantities. The mix is controlled by the sequence of models on the final assembly line.

Steady component production with *mixed-model assembly*.

Toyota assembles several different vehicle models on each final assembly line. The assembly lines were initially designed this way because of limited space and resources and lack of sufficient volume to dedicate an entire line to a specific model. However, the mixed-model concept has since become an integral part of lean production systems. Daily production is arranged in the same ratio as monthly demand, and jobs are distributed as evenly as possible across the day's schedule. This means that at least some quantity of every item is produced daily, and the company will always have some quantity of an item available to respond to variations in demand. The mix of assembly also steadies component production, reduces inventory levels, and supports the pull system of production. Let's look at an example of mixed-model sequencing.

**Example 15.2**
**Mixed-Model Sequencing**

Tyrone Motors makes cars, SUVs and vans on a single assembly line at its Cleveland plant. September's sales forecast is for 220 vehicles. SUVs sell at twice the rate of cars and three times the rate of vans. Assuming 20 working days in September, how should the vehicles (S, C, and V) be produced to smooth production as much as possible?

*Solution*

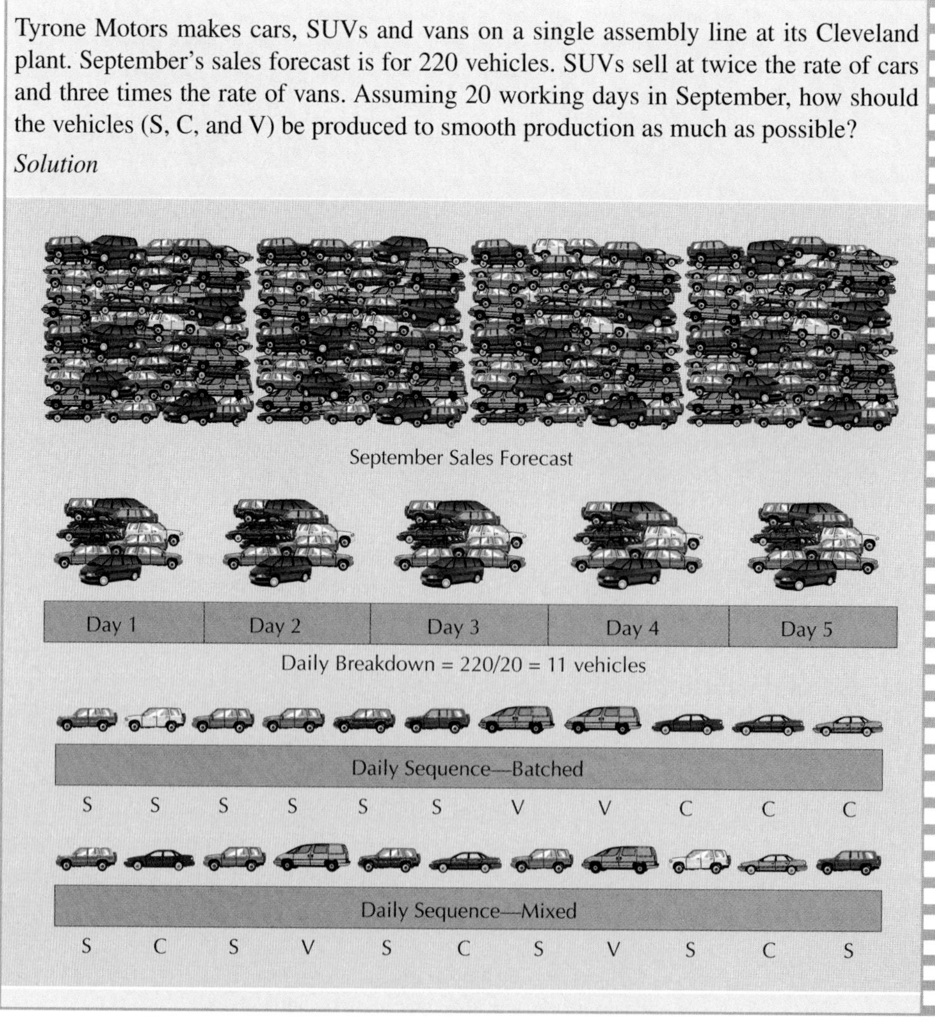

If the preceding example sounds extreme, it is not. Toyota assembles three models in 100 variations on a single assembly line at its Tahara plant, and the mix is jiggled daily with almost no warning. The plant is highly automated, and each model carries with it a small yellow disc that transmits instructions to the next workstation. Cars roll off the final assembly line in what looks like unit production—a black Lexus sedan, a blue Camry, a red Lexus sports coupe, a white Corolla with left-hand drive, and so on.

This is in sharp contrast to the large lots of similar items produced by mass production factories, in which luxury cars might be produced the first week and a half of the month, midsize cars the second week and a half, and small cars the final week. Under mass production, it's difficult to change product mix midway through the month, and small-car customers would have to wait three to four weeks before their order would be available.

## QUALITY AT THE SOURCE

For lean systems to work well, quality has to be extremely high. There is no extra inventory to buffer against defective units. Producing poor-quality items and then having to rework or reject them is a waste that should be eliminated. Producing in smaller lots encourages better quality. Workers can observe quality problems more easily; when problems are detected, they can be traced to their source and remedied without reworking too many units. Also, by inspecting the first and the last unit in a small batch or by having a worker make a part and then use the part, virtually 100% inspection can be achieved.

Smaller lot sizes encourage quality.

### Visual Control

Quality improves when problems are made visible and workers have clear expectations of performance. Production systems designed with quality in mind include visible instructions for worker or machine action, and direct feedback on the results of that action. This is known as **visual control**. Examples include kanbans, standard operation sheets, andons, process control charts, and tool boards. A factory with visual control will look different from other factories. You may find machines or stockpoints in each section painted different colors, material-handling routes marked clearly on the floor, demonstration stands and instructional photographs placed near machines, graphs of quality or performance data displayed at each workstation, and explanations and pictures of recent improvement efforts posted by work teams. Figure 15.11 shows several examples of visual control.

**Visual control:** procedures or mechanisms that make problems visible.

Visual control of quality often leads to what the Japanese call a **poka-yoke**. A poka-yoke is any foolproof device or mechanism that prevents defects from occurring. For example, a dial on which desired ranges are marked in different colors is an example of visual control. A dial that shuts off a machine whenever the instrument needle falls above or below the desired range is a poka-yoke. Machines set to stop after a certain amount of production are poka-yokes, as are sensors that prevent the addition of too many items into a package or the misalignment of components for an assembly.

**Poka-yoke:** a foolproof device that prevents defects from occurring.

Quality in lean systems is based on **kaizen**, the Japanese term for "change for the good of all" or *continuous improvement*. As a practical system for production created from trial-and-error experiences in eliminating waste and simplifying operations, lean production continually looks for ways to reduce inventory, quicken setups, improve quality, and react faster to customer demand. Continuous improvement is not something that can be delegated to a department or a staff of experts. It is a monumental undertaking that requires the participation of every employee at every level. The essence of lean success is the willingness of workers to spot quality problems, halt operations when necessary, generate ideas for improvement, analyze processes, perform different functions, and adjust their working routines. In one year alone workers at Toyota's Georgetown, Kentucky, plant suggested 500 kaizens, 99.8% of which were implemented. Team member ideas helped the plant install the first assembly line shared by a sedan and a minivan.

**Kaizen:** a system of continuous improvement; "change for the good of all."

### Jidoka

It was the idea that workers could identify quality problems at their source, solve them, and never pass on a defective item that led Ohno to believe in zero defects. To that

**Figure 15.11**
**Examples of Visual Control**

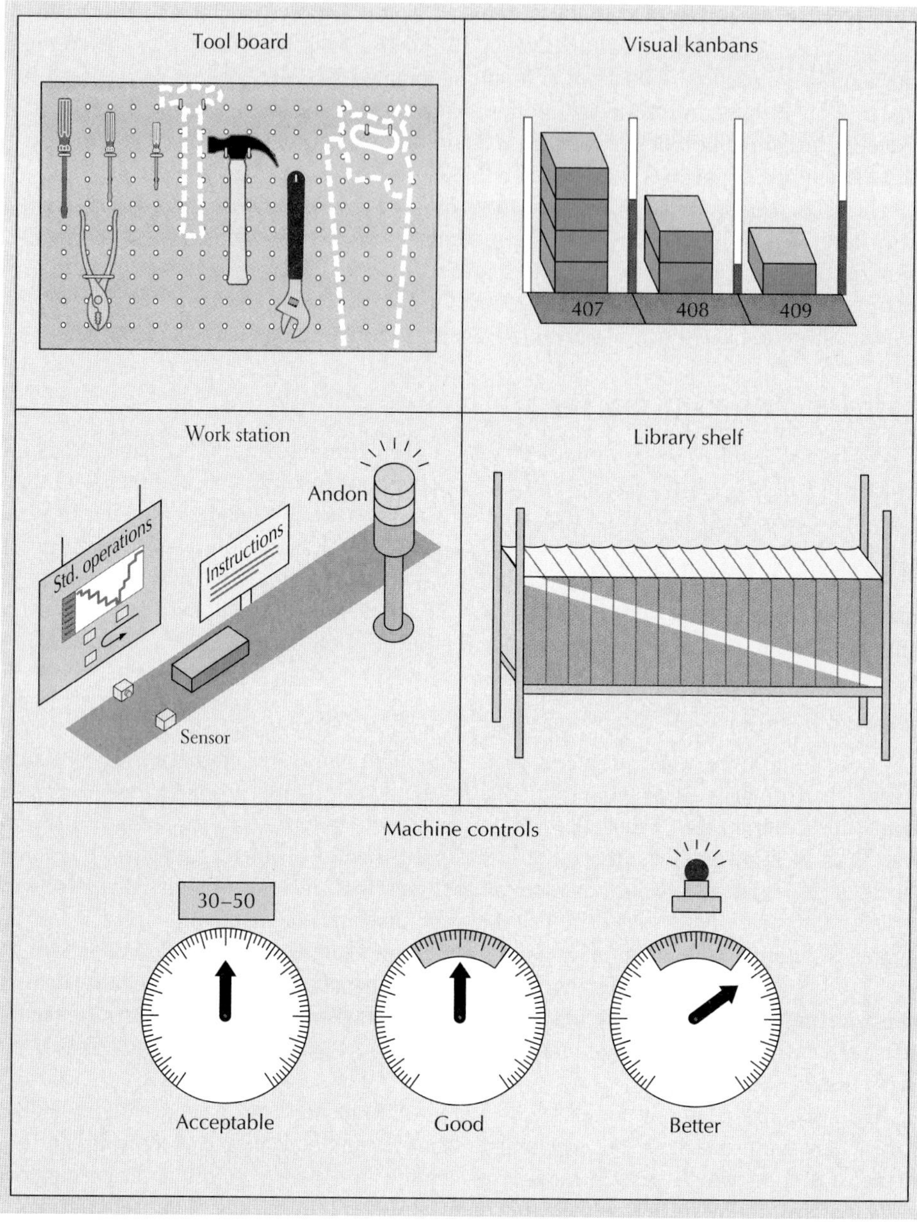


end, Ohno was determined that the workers, not inspectors, should be responsible for product quality. To go along with this responsibility, he also gave workers the unprecedented authority of **jidoka**—the authority to stop the production line if quality problems were encountered.

**Jidoka:** authority to stop the production line.

**Andons:** call lights that signal quality problems.

**Undercapacity scheduling:** extra time built into a schedule for planning, problem solving, and maintenance.

To encourage jidoka, each worker is given access to a switch that can be used to activate call lights or to halt production. The call lights, called **andons**, flash above the workstation and at several andon boards throughout the plant. Green lights indicate normal operation, yellow lights show a call for help, and red lights indicate a line stoppage. Supervisors, maintenance personnel, and engineers are summoned to troubled workstations quickly by flashing lights on the andon board. At Toyota, the assembly line is stopped for an average of 20 minutes a day because of jidoka. Each jidoka drill is recorded on easels kept at the work area. A block of time is reserved at the end of the day for workers to go over the list and work on solving the problems raised. For example, an eight-hour day might consist of seven hours of production and one hour of problem solving.

This concept of allocating extra time to a schedule for nonproductive tasks is called **undercapacity scheduling**. Another example of undercapacity scheduling is producing for two shifts each day and reserving the third shift for preventive maintenance activities.

## THE COMPETITIVE EDGE

### Xerox is Back, Thanks to Lean Six Sigma

Well into the 1990s, Xerox was a leader in quality and innovation, building printers and copiers that combined both high-precision machinery and cutting-edge information systems. But success breeds complacency, or at least impatience, and Xerox ignored its quality roots in pursuit of growth and profits. For example, in 1999 the company sought millions in cost savings by consolidating 36 administrative centers into three, at the same time that it was reorganizing its sales division. The upheaval of two key business units created chaos across the company's billing system, sending invoices to customers for prices they had never agreed to or for equipment they had never ordered. Even worse, the mistakes took months to sort out, resulting in the loss of some longtime customers.

After several failed attempts at fixing the problem, Xerox hired GE Capital Systems to handle its billing process—and got lots of good advice as well. GE showed Xerox a whole new way to diagnose and fix its problems. By omitting superfluous steps from its design, manufacturing, and service processes, and refining those that remained, Xerox could deliver better quality to its customers *and* save costs.

What did GE know that Xerox didn't? Something called ***Lean Six Sigma***, a combination of six sigma and lean production. *Six sigma* (as your learned in Chapter 3) is a data-driven technique for reducing variability and ultimately eliminating defects. *Lean production* eliminates waste and smoothes the flow of operations. In combination, they are a powerful competitive weapon.

Xerox began training its top executives in Lean Six Sigma in late 2002. Since then, the company has launched over 250 improvement projects for savings of about $6 million. Rather than automating complex processes, the focus of these projects is to "lean out" the process by removing unnecessary steps and fixing those that remain. This sounds easy, buy figuring out what steps to replace takes time and skill. The hardest task, however, may be getting employees to accept the idea that how they've always done things may not be the best way.

These days, Xerox has gotten so good at applying Lean Six Sigma that, like GE before, it's helping out its customers. In one case, the mail volume at a customer's document-management unit had grown out of control. Xerox moved in, streamlined the mailroom—with changes as simple as changing the layout—to use half the amount of space and save $180,000. From failing to fix its own operations to improving those of others is a big leap. Says John Laing, Senior VP, "We've moved from being consciously incompetent to consciously competent." Now, Xerox is pushing to become unconsciously competent—the point where quality (*six sigma*) and process (*lean*) are such a natural part of doing business that no one even thinks about them anymore.

*Source:* Faith Arner and Adam Aston, "How Xerox Got up to Speed," *Business Week Online* (May 3, 2004). Special Report on Quality Manufacturing, http://www.businessweek.com/magazine/toc/04_18/B38810418qualman.htm

Making time to plan, train, solve problems, and maintain the work environment is an important part of lean's success.

## TOTAL PRODUCTIVE MAINTENANCE

Machines cannot operate continuously without some attention. Maintenance activities can be performed when a machine breaks down to restore the machine to its original operating condition, or at different times during regular operation of the machine in an attempt to prevent a breakdown from occurring. The first type of activity is referred to as **breakdown maintenance**; the second is called **preventive maintenance**.

**Breakdown maintenance:** repairs needed to make a failed machine operational.

**Preventive maintenance:** a system of periodic inspection and maintenance designed to keep a machine in operation.

Breakdowns seldom occur at convenient times. Lost production, poor quality, and missed deadlines from an inefficient or broken-down machine can represent a significant expense. In addition, the cost of breakdown maintenance is usually much greater than preventive maintenance. (Most of us know that to be true from our own experience at maintaining an automobile. Regular oil changes cost pennies compared to replacing a car engine.) For these reasons, most companies do not find it cost-effective to rely solely on breakdown maintenance. The question then becomes, how much preventive maintenance is necessary and when should it be performed?

With accurate records on the time between breakdowns, the frequency of breakdowns, and the cost of breakdown and preventive maintenance, we can mathematically determine the best preventive maintenance schedule. But even with this degree of precision, breakdowns can still occur. Lean production requires more than preventive maintenance—it requires *total productive maintenance*.

*This lighted board shows where an andon cord has been pulled to signal a problem on the line at Toyota Motor Corp.'s plant in Georgetown, KY. If the issue is not fixed before the car reaches the next stage of assembly, the line stops.*

**Total productive maintenance:** a system that combines the practice of preventive maintenance with the concepts of total quality.

**Total productive maintenance (TPM)** combines the practice of preventive maintenance with the concepts of total quality—employee involvement, decisions based on data, zero defects, and a strategic focus. Machine operators maintain their own machines with daily care, periodic inspections, and preventive repair activities. They compile and interpret maintenance and operating data on their machines, identifying signs of deterioration prior to failure.[5] They also scrupulously clean equipment, tools, and workspaces to make unusual occurrences more noticeable. Oil spots on a clean floor may indicate a machine problem, whereas oil spots on a dirty floor would go unnoticed. In Japan this is known as the 5 S's—*seiri, seiton, seiso, seiketsu*, and *shitsuke*—roughly translated as sort, set, shine, standardize, and sustain. Table 15.1 explains the 5 S's in more detail.

**Table 15.1**
**5S Workplace Scan**

| 5 S's | Goal | Eliminate or Correct |
|---|---|---|
| **1.** Seiri (*sort*) | Keep only what you need | Unneeded equipment, tools, furniture; unneeded items on walls, bulletins; items blocking aisles or stacked in corners; unneeded inventory, supplies, parts; safety hazards |
| **2.** Seiton (*set in order*) | A place for everything and everything in its place | Items not in their correct places; correct places not obvious; aisles, workstations, & equipment locations not indicated; items not put away immediately after use |
| **3.** Seisou (*shine*) | Cleaning, and looking for ways to keep clean and organized | Floors, walls, stairs, equipment, & surfaces not clean; cleaning materials not easily accessible; lines, labels, signs broken or unclean; other cleaning problems |
| **4.** Seiketsu (*standardize*) | Maintaining and monitoring the first three categories | Necessary information not visible; standards not known; checklists missing; quantities and limits not easily recognizable; items can't be located within 30 seconds |
| **5.** Shisuke (*sustain*) | Sticking to the rules | Number of workers without 5 S training; number of daily 5 S inspections not performed; number of personal items not stored; number of times job aids not available or up-to-date |

[5]Maintaining and repairing your own machine is called *autonomous maintenance.* Collecting data and designing maintenance remedies based on the data collected is referred to as *predictive maintenance.*

In addition to operator involvement and attention to detail, TPM requires management to take a broader, strategic view of maintenance. That means:

- Designing products that can easily be produced on existing machines;
- Designing machines for easier operation, changeover, and maintenance;
- Training and retraining workers to operate and maintain machines properly;
- Purchasing machines that maximize productive potential; and
- Designing a preventive maintenance plan that spans the entire life of each machine.

## SUPPLIER NETWORKS

Supplier support is essential to the success of lean production. Not only do suppliers need to be reliable, their production needs to be synchronized to the needs of the customer they are supplying. Toyota understood this and developed strong long-term working relationships with a select group of suppliers. Supplier plants encircled the 50-mile radius around Toyota City, making deliveries several times a day. Bulky parts such as engines and transmissions were delivered every 15 to 30 minutes. Suppliers who met stringent quality standards could forgo inspection of incoming goods. That meant goods could be brought right to the assembly line or area of use without being counted, inspected, tagged, or stocked.

Suppliers who try to meet the increasing demands of a lean customer without being lean themselves are overrun with inventory and exorbitantly high production and distribution costs. Lean supply involves:

1. ***Long-term supplier contracts.*** Suppliers are chosen on the basis of their ability to meet delivery schedules with high quality at a reasonable cost, and their willingness to adapt their production system to meet increasingly stringent customer requirements. Typical contracts are for three to five years, although some companies will choose a supplier for the life of the product.
2. ***Synchronized production.*** With longer term contracts, suppliers are able to concentrate on fewer customers. Guaranteed, steady demand with advanced notice of volume changes allows the supplier to synchronize their production with that of the customer. Engineering and quality management assistance may also be provided to the supplier.
3. ***Supplier certification.*** Suppliers go through several stages before certification. Typically, their products undergo quality tests, their production facilities and quality systems are examined, and statistical measures of quality are sent with each shipment. After six months or so with no complications, a certification is issued that exempts the supplier from incoming quality and quantity inspections. In spite of certification, many companies bill their suppliers for the damage incurred by a defective part, such as the cost of a line shutdown or product recall.
4. ***Mixed loads and frequent deliveries.*** A lean supplier is an extension of the customer's assembly line. Small quantities may be delivered several times a day (or even hourly) directly to their point of use in the customer's factory. This usually involves smaller trucks containing a mixed load of goods. Different suppliers often join together to consolidate deliveries or share local warehouses.
5. ***Precise delivery schedules.*** Delivery windows to specific locations (docks, bays, or areas along an assembly line) can be as short as 15 minutes. Penalties for missing delivery times are high. Chrysler penalizes its suppliers $32,000 for each hour a delivery is late. With such tight schedules, signing for and paying for a shipment at the time of delivery is too-time consuming. Paying at regular intervals for shipments documented with bar codes or RFID[6] tags is more in tune with lean.
6. ***Standardized, sequenced delivery.*** Using standardized containers and exchanging full containers with empty ones upon delivery also speeds the delivery and replenishment process. In some cases, deliveries made directly to the manufacturer are sequenced in the order of assembly. Nissan, for example, receives deliveries of vehicle seats four times an hour and notifies the supplier two hours in advance with the exact sequence (size and color) in which seats are to be unloaded.

[6]RFID tags are radio frequency IDs that can store updated information on an item.

## THE COMPETITIVE EDGE

### As You Like It

Johnson's Controls, Inc. (JCI), assembles seats for Ford's Expedition, Navigator, and Lincoln LS series at its Port Street facility in Plymouth, Michigan. Production of LS seats is particularly taxing because of its leather exterior, power lumbar control, seat heater, side impact airbags, optional left-hand or right-hand seating and multiple headrest configurations. All in all the seat has 124 different build configurations. As Ford's premier automobile, quality must be "consistently flawless" too, a goal JCI has met with zero defects in three out of the last four months.

The assembly or "build" process starts with a broadcast from Ford usually 8 to 12 hours before the seat is needed. The broadcast triggers a build sheet that stays with the seat until it is installed in the vehicle and includes options, color, and other information. This information is important because seats are delivered to Ford in the exact sequence specified.

Seats are assembled entirely of subassembled components—tracks, foam cushions, back frames, leather covers, airbags, wiring harnesses, etc. There are stored line-side in inventories ranging from two to eight hours of supply. That means JCI's 27 suppliers must deliver daily, too. Operators work in cells, which are combinations of the 16 or so discrete steps in assembly. Each cell has a measured *takt time* that ensures the line can run at optimal speed. Right now, the line meets production demand with 45 operators; however, as demand increases, more operators will be added (up to twice the current number). In this way, JCI can adapt production levels to Ford's demand. As more operators are added, work assignments in each cell are changed to reduce takt times. The plant's floor space, conveyors, fixtures, and machinery were designed for maximum capacity.

Seat assembly tasks such as stretching leather and stuffing foam are best suited to manual rather than robotic assembly. But with humans come inherent quality challenges. While there may be an art to getting a seat cover to fit, the proper alignment of a seat back frame with the track and cushion pan needs to be absolute every time. JCI uses fixtures as a *poka-yoke* for every seat component. The fixtures were built and debugged during the initial prototype stage of product design.

Besides fixtures, JCI employs other in-line quality measures. Operators use torque-sensing guns with visual indicators. If fasteners are not attached at the correct torque setting, a light above the line comes on and the line shuts down until an operator corrects the problem. Similarly, the electrical system in the seat is tested as it moves on the conveyor by plugging a machine into the wiring harness. Each of the seats also passes through a color detection machine that verifies that all trim pieces match the color of the seat. At the final assembly stage, an automated fixture moves the seat through a full range of motion to calibrate the power adjustment controls.

Seats for the LS are actually assembled on two lines: one for the simple rear seats and another for the more complicated front seats. The lines converge at the end, where a complete set of seats is palletized and put on a rack for shipment. Three shipments per shift, two shifts per day, are delivered in sequence to Visteon, a company that provides seats for the other Lincolns built at Ford's Wixom, Michigan, assembly plant. All the seats are then blended, again in sequence, for shipment to Wixom.

Seats are in constant use by Ford. Their only storage time is on the delivery truck. When they arrive at the Wixom plant, automated conveyors bring the seats from the truck to the assembly line in perfect style and color sequence. A photo sensor determines when the last seat has been unloaded and when to begin loading empty pallets back on the empty trailer to prepare for the next delivery.

*Source:* Jeff Sabatini, "Seat Time," *Automotive Manufacturing and Production* (January 2000), http://www.automfg.com/articles/010005.html

7. **Locating in close proximity to the customer**. With the increased number of deliveries in lean production, it is imperative that the source of supply be located close to the customer. When geographic distances between supplier and customer prohibit daily deliveries, suppliers may need to establish small warehouses near to the customer or consolidate warehouses with other suppliers. Trucking firms increasingly use consolidation warehouses as load-switching points for JIT delivery to various customers. Maintaining close proximity can mean relocating around the world, as shown by the number of suppliers who have moved to China and other Asian countries in support of their customers.

## THE BENEFITS OF LEAN PRODUCTION

A study of the average benefits accrued to U.S. manufacturers over a five-year period from implementing lean production are impressive: 90% reductions in manufacturing cycle time, 70% reductions in inventory, 50% reductions in labor costs, and 80% reductions in space requirements.

While not every company can achieve results at this level, lean production does provide a wide range of benefits, including:

1. Reduced inventory
2. Improved quality
3. Lower costs
4. Reduced space requirements
5. Shorter lead time
6. Increased productivity
7. Greater flexibility
8. Better relations with suppliers
9. Simplified scheduling and control activities
10. Increased capacity
11. Better use of human resources
12. More product variety

## IMPLEMENTATING LEAN PRODUCTION

Japanese industry embraced lean production in the mid-1970s, after manufacturers observed Toyota's superior ability to withstand the 1973 oil crisis. Many U.S. firms, in turn, adopted lean production in some form in the 1980s. The firms that tried to implement lean by slashing inventory and demanding that their suppliers make frequent deliveries missed the power of the system. Supplier deliveries and kanbans are some of the last elements of lean production to implement. Today, globalization and e-commerce have brought a new generation of manufacturers and suppliers into the lean fold.

The firms that are most successful in implementing lean production understood the breadth and interrelatedness of the concepts and have adapted them to their own particular environment. This makes sense when you consider the essence of lean—eliminate waste, speed up changeovers, work closely with suppliers, streamline the flow of work, use flexible resources, pay attention to quality, expose problems, and use worker teams to solve problems. None of these concepts or techniques are new or particularly revolutionary. How they are applied can differ considerably from company to company. What is unique and remarkable is how the pieces are tied together into a finely tuned operating system and how synchronized that system can be with both the external and internal business environments.

Use lean to finely tune an operating system.

## The Competitive Edge

### TPS, A Learning Organization

It's been 25 years now since the Western world learned of the Toyota Production System (TPS) and the concept of JIT. Toyota has been unusually forthcoming about its philosophy of operations. The company has opened up its manufacturing plants for the world to see, partnered with competitors, and shared its methodologies and skills. Yet, no other company can match the production prowess of Toyota.

Why is it so hard to emulate their success? It's because the crux of JIT (or what we call *lean production*) is continuous improvement, and Toyota managers and employees are rigorous problem-solvers. The result is a moving target. By the time other companies have reached Toyota's level of achievement, Toyota has moved on.

The Toyota principle asks every employee at every level of the organization to follow these steps in performing their tasks:

1. Before you do work, make clear what you expect to happen.
2. Each time you complete a task, see that what you expected has actually occurred.
3. When there is a difference between what actually happened and what was predicted, solve the problem while the information is still fresh.

Everyday work becomes an experiment. Systems are tested with each use. Ideas for improvement are daily occurrences—ideas that are focused on a limited set of objectives.

First, it was superior quality and lower costs; then it was better designs faster; now it's the flexibility of production. Toyota has used a nested, modular structure for its production-design process for years; now the same approach has been applied to designing its production processes.

At Toyota factories, six or more different vehicle models can be produced on one assembly line—including models as different as cars, trucks, SUVs, and minivans. With factories no longer limited to one type of model, production can be switched from one plant to another in different locations around the world. That means new platforms may not require the construction of new facilities—a feat that can save billions.

What makes this possible is the *global body line*. In the past, each different vehicle model required separate tooling to grab the outside body of the vehicle and hold it in place for robots to weld and perform other tasks. The tooling was then redesigned to go inside the car body and hold it in place from the inside out. Thus, the same fixture can be used for all types of cars, trucks, and minivans. With this new technology, factories can be designed to produce customized cars for local markets and still be able to shift production to other models when demand surges somewhere else in the world market.

*Automated assembly is easier on this mixed model line because each different model uses the same type of fixture.*

The technology, of course, can be copied. Ford's flexible assembly system and General Motors' C-flex welding system can also produce different models on the same line with little changeover time, mostly through programmable welding robots, but their implementation is three to four years behind Toyota. And when they do catch up, Toyota will be on to something else.

*Source:* Steven Spear, "Comments on the Second Toyota Paradox," Teaching Note 9-602-035, *Harvard Business School* (March 2003); Brian Bremner and Chester Dawson, "Can Anything Stop Toyota?" *Business Week* (November 17, 2003) pp. 114–118; Christine Tierney, "Big Three Play Catch-Up to Toyota Plant Prowess," *Detroit News* (February 22, 2004); and Stuart Brown, "Toyota's Global Body Shop," *Fortune's Industrial Edition* (February 9, 2004), http://www.fortune.com/fortune/subs/columnist/0,15704,581557,00.html

Lean applications on U.S. soil, whether in Japanese- or U.S.-run plants, differ somewhat from the original Japanese versions. Lean U.S. plants are typically larger, deliveries from suppliers are less frequent, more buffer inventory is held (because of the longer delivery lead times), and kanbans are very simple compared to lean plants in Japan. Worker-designed feedback systems are different, too. Instead of alarms and flashing lights when things go wrong, workers at the Saturn plant hear a recording of "The Pink Panther." At the Nissan plant, workers are reminded to change workstations along an S-shaped assembly line by the changing tempo of piped-in music (from country to rock). Morning calisthenics are out for most U.S. plants, but the placement of ping-pong tables and basketball hoops alongside the assembly line for exercise during worker-designated breaks is popular. The slow pace of continuous improvement is hard to maintain for American workers. Thus, *kaizen blitzes*, intense process improvement over a week's time with immediate results, are easier and more energizing to conduct.

## DRAWBACKS OF LEAN PRODUCTION

Lean production is not appropriate for every type of organization. Professor Rajan Suri, author of *Quick Response Manufacturing*, notes that the key to lean production is creating flow. To do this, lean manufacturers determine takt times, create a level schedule, and use kanbans to control production. This approach starts to have serious deficiencies when applied to companies that have high variability in demand (takt time breaks down), or large variety of low-volume products (too many kanbans in the system), or custom-engineered products (there are no kanbans for something that is yet to be designed).

Nor is lean production the best choice for high-volume repetitive items where mass production is more common. Even Toyota produces high-demand components (typically, small items that require stamping and forging) in lots as large as 10,000 units, sending them to subsequent processes in small batches only when requested.

Lean production can also present problems when unexpected changes in demand or supply occur. For example, a fire at one supplier's brake factory shut down three Toyota plants one year.[7] In the United States, longshoremen strikes have cut off overseas supply and brought hundreds of factories to a halt. Add to that the SARS epidemic, natural disasters, terrorist attacks, and armed conflicts, and being completely lean is not very appealing.

Thus, lean production must be compatible with a company's products, processes, and customers. Companies must also assess risk and uncertainty in their business environment, and adapt lean practices accordingly. Even with these drawbacks, however, we have found that most types of businesses can find some parts or processes that can benefit from lean concepts. That includes service industries.

## LEAN SERVICES

Most people who think of lean production as a system for reducing inventory do not consider the system to be applicable to services. However, you know from reading this chapter that lean production consists of more than low inventory levels. It eliminates waste, streamlines operations, promotes fast changeovers and close supplier relations, and adjusts quickly to changes in demand. As a result, products and services can be provided quickly, at less cost, and in more variety. Thus, we can readily observe the basic elements of lean production in service operations. Think about:

- McDonald's, Domino's, and Federal Express, who compete on speed and still provide their products and services at low cost and with increasing variety;
- Construction firms that coordinate the arrival of materials "just as needed" instead of stockpiling them at the site;
- Multifunctional workers in department stores who work the cash register, stock goods, arrange displays, and make sales;
- Level selling with "everyday low prices" at Wal-Mart and Food Lion;
- Work cells at fast-food restaurants that allow workers to be added during peak times and reduced during slow times;
- "Dollar" stores that price everything the same and simply count the number of items purchased as the customer leaves;
- Process mapping that has streamlined operations and eliminated waste in many services (especially in terms of paper flow and information processing);

[7]V. Reitman, "Toyota Factories in Japan Grind to a Halt," *Wall Street Journal* (February 4, 1997), p. A14.

*The basic concept for JIT began in the supermarket! Japanese factories, trying to duplicate the ease with which goods are replenished in American supermarkets, decided to forgo huge inventory buildups and complex scheduling algorithms in favor of simply replacing items as they are used. This pull system is the basis for lean production.*

- Medical facilities that have the flexibility to fill prescriptions, perform tests, and treat patients without routing them from one end of the building to another;
- Just-in-time publishing that allows professors to choose material from a variety of sources and construct a custom-made book in the same amount of time off-the-shelf books can be ordered and at competitive prices;
- Lens providers, cleaners, and car-repair services that can turn around customer orders in an hour;
- Cleaning teams that follow standard operating routines in quickly performing their tasks;
- Supermarkets that replenish their shelves according to what the customer withdraws; and
- Retailers who introduce dozens of new clothing lines each year in smaller quantities.

In addition to these incidences of lean, entire service systems have been redesigned around lean principles. The most prevalent applications are lean retailing, lean banking, and lean health care.

## Lean Retailing

Retail stores provide customers with more choices faster than ever before. *Lean retailing*, like lean production, involves smaller, more frequent orders and rapid replenishment of stock. For example, Zara, a Spanish fashion chain, ships new products to its stores around the world every few days, not once a season. The company produces over 11,000 different stock items per year, instead of several hundred. Time-to-market (from design to store) is an amazing 10 days. That means Zara can keep up with fashion trends and adjust its merchandise accordingly.[8] While introducing new products at Blockbuster is not as dramatic as it is at Zara, lean principles can be used to simplify the restocking process, streamline new rental displays, and improve customer service. Read "The Competitive Edge" box on Blockbuster and you will be able to identify aspects of lean retailing the next time you rent a movie.

[8]John Tagliabue, "Spanish Clothing Chain Zara Grows by Being Fast and Flexible," *The New York Times* (May 30, 2003). For a similar story, see the H&M "Competitive Edge" box in Chapter 5.

THE COMPETITIVE EDGE

## Lean Retailing at Blockbuster

Blockbuster Inc., one of the world's leading providers of videos, DVDs, and video games, has grown from a single rental store to more than 8500 company-owned and franchised stores in the United States and 28 other countries. Blockbuster stores are everywhere, located with a 10-minute drive of an estimated 64% of the U.S. population and serving an average of 3 million visitors every day.

Yes, everyone knows Blockbuster, but did you know that Blockbuster uses lean manufacturing techniques in its retail operations? With double-digit growth and healthy margins, Blockbuster had focused more on merchandising the stores than efficient operations. As competition increased and the business model changed to include revenue-sharing, DVDs, games, and retail sales, operating the stores became more challenging. The frequency of transactions and the quantity of product increased drastically, but the operations model remained the same.

Project Store was initiated to redesign and standardize business processes across the 8500 retail stores. The project used lean manufacturing techniques to simplify complicated processes, separate time spent with the customer from time spent processing tasks, eliminate nonvalue-added tasks, reallocate time savings to better serve the customer, build the customer experience, and reduce worker stress. Expected financial results from the project include both driving sales and reducing expenses.

The project proceeded as follows:

- *Get the facts.* Sixty different franchise stores were visited where 2000 hours of observation was logged, including 300 step-by-step transactions, 100 customer journeys, and 600 customer exit surveys. The company found that less than 40% of an employee's time was spent with the customer. Project Store's goal is to increase customer contact time to 60% (with a dream goal of 70%).
- *Identify improvement ideas.* In order to increase customer contact time, administrative task times need to be reduced. Tasks that take the most time and have the greatest variation across the stores were targeted for improvement, including checkout, opening and closing, returns-to-shelf, and physical inventories. Brainstorming sessions were held with over 75 store employees. Suggestions were practical. For example, using a loose alpha (by first letter only) to alphabetize items on the new release wall could save several hours a week.

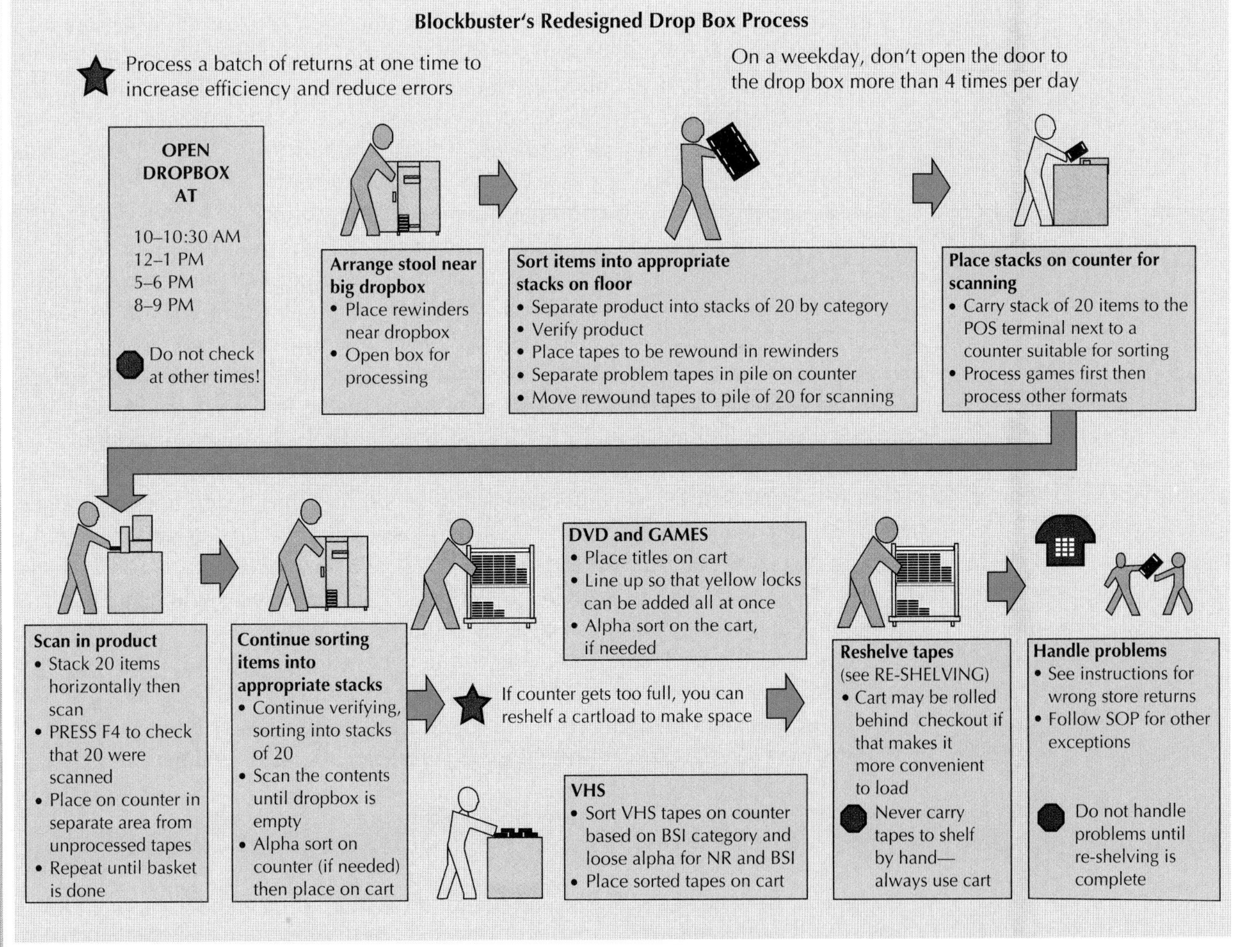

- *Test the ideas.* Selected ideas were tested in laboratory environments, called *learning stores*, where ideas were operationalized and bullet-proofed, allowing store employees to take ownership of the ideas, adapt them, and perfect them. Cost/benefit analyses were conducted, and detailed process improvement flowcharts were developed. An example of the revised drop-box process is shown below.
- *Pilot the ideas.* In pilot stores, the company learned how to roll out the revised processes, train employees, and anticipate problems.
- *National rollout.* The campaign for national rollout was developed and executed, including plans for reassessment and evaluation. Blockbuster found that managing behavioral change was 10 times harder than redesigning the process.

Project Store is continuing its rollout stage, but preliminary results are encouraging. Blockbuster has learned the power of lean retailing—observing customers, listening to employees, separating tasks, simplifying, and standardizing.

*Source:* Dale Dauten, "The Corporate Curmudgeon: Blockbuster Observers Take Big Bite out of Bureaucracy," *Arizona Daily Star* (February 2, 2004); Richard Metters, "Linking Marketing and Operations: An Application at Blockbuster, Inc." *Journal of Service Research* (November 2002), pp. 91–101.

## LEAN BANKING

Lean banking is practiced by Bank of America, Citibank, ING Direct, Jefferson Pilot, and Progressive Insurance, among others. The banking and insurance industries are particularly well suited to lean techniques because of their repetitive processes. Significant savings in both time and money can be achieved through differentiating processes, rationalizing decision approvals, simplifying service offerings, designing services in modules, and standardizing processes. "The Competitive Edge" box on Jefferson Pilot presented earlier in the chapter is a good example of lean banking success.

## LEAN HEALTH CARE

Lean concepts are popular in the health care industry. One reason is the interest of manufacturers in keeping the cost of health care down. Pella Corporation loans its employees to a regional health center for "hot teams" to scrutinize medical operations. Boeing convinced 30 executives from Seattle's Virgnia Mason Medical Center to spend two weeks in Japan studying Toyota's methods. ThedaCare of Wisconsin hired lean production consultants after touring a lean snow blower plant nearby.[9]

In Iowa, a group of manufacturers, including Maytag, formed a task force to facilitate lean best practices in their local health care systems. People from hospitals, health care providers, third-party insurance providers, and manufacturing executives met together to identify waste and map out the way money and information flows through the health care system. The group discovered that every insurance company and employer had specific plans and rules for processing employee health care claims, requiring different information on a multitude of forms. The forms were so confusing that much of the processor's time was spent calling the provider for clarifications and reworking returned claims.

At ThedaCare, a dozen doctors, nurses, and staffers brainstormed ways of cutting a typical 61 minute office visit to 30 minutes or less. They constructed a 25-foot process map of a pneumonia patient's office visit, concluding that 17 steps were useful and 51 were not. At the end of the session, the team concluded that doctor's assistants should be assigned to a pool rather than individual doctors and that lab tests should be performed in examining rooms rather than at a central location.

Waste in health care is rampant—wasted time, wasted money, wasted materials. Blue Cross Blue Shield saved \$3.7 million in 2002 and \$2 million in 2003 by applying Lean Sigma to their operations. With results like that, lean health care is definitely the way of the future. Flowcharts, mistake-proofing, flow management, quick setups, and kaizen are just a few of the lean health care tools.

[9]The material in this section comes from Patricia Panchak, "Lean Health Care? It Works!" *Industry Week* (November 1, 2003), and Bernard Wysocki, "Industrial Strength: To Fix Health Care, Hospitals Take Tips from Factory Floor," *Wall Street Journal* (April 9, 2004), p. A1.

## SUMMARY

Lean production has truly changed the face of manufacturing and transformed the global economy. Originally known as just-in-time (JIT); it began at Toyota Motor Company as an effort to eliminate waste (particularly inventories), but it evolved into a system for the continuous improvement of all aspects of manufacturing operations. *Lean production* is both a philosophy and a collection of management methods and techniques. The main advantage of the system is derived from the integration of the techniques into a focused, smooth-running management system.

In lean systems, workers are multifunctional and are required to perform different tasks, as well as aid in the improvement process. Machines are also multifunctional and are arranged in small, U-shaped work cells that enable parts to be processed in a continuous flow through the cell. Workers produce parts one at a time within the cells and transport parts between cells in small lots as called for by subassembly lines, assembly lines, or other work cells. The environment is kept clean, orderly, and free of waste so that unusual occurrences are visible.

Schedules are prepared only for the final assembly line, in which several different models are assembled on the same line. Requirements for component parts and subassemblies are then pulled through the system with kanbans. The principle of the pull system is not to make anything until requested to do so by the next station. The "pull" system will not work unless production is uniform, setups are quick, and lot sizes are low.

The pull system and kanbans are also used to order materials from outside suppliers. Suppliers are fewer in number and must be very reliable. They may be requested to make multiple deliveries of the same item in the same day, so their manufacturing system must be flexible, too. Deliveries are made directly to the factory floor, eliminating stockrooms and the waste of counting, inspecting, recording, storing, and transporting.

Lean production does not produce in anticipation of need. It produces only necessary items in necessary quantities at necessary times. Inventory is viewed as a waste of resources and an obstacle to improvement. Because there is little buffer inventory between workstations, quality must be extremely high, and every effort is made to prevent machine breakdowns.

When all these elements are in place, lean systems produce high-quality goods, quickly and at low cost. These systems also are able to respond to changes in customer demand. Lean production systems are most effective in repetitive environments, but elements of lean can be applied to almost any operation, including service operations. Lean retailing, lean banking, and lean health care are good examples.

## SUMMARY OF KEY FORMULAS

*Determining the number of kanbans*

$$N = \frac{\bar{d}L + S}{C}$$

## SUMMARY OF KEY TERMS

**andons** call lights installed at workstations to notify management and other workers of a quality problem in production.

**breakdown maintenance** a maintenance activity that involves repairs needed to make a failed machine operational.

**external setup** setup activities that can be performed in advance while the machine is operating.

**general-purpose machines** machines that perform basic functions such as turning, drilling, and milling.

**internal setup** setup activities that can be performed only when the machine is stopped.

**jidoka** authority given to the workers to stop the assembly line when quality problems are encountered.

**just-in-time (JIT)** smoothing the flow of material to arrive just as it is needed; evolved into a system for eliminating waste.

**kaizen** a Japanese term for a system of continuous improvement.

**kanban** a card corresponding to a standard quantity of production (or size container) used in the pull system to authorize the production or withdrawal of goods.

**kanban square** a marked area designated to hold a certain amount of items; an empty square is the signal to produce more items.

**lean production** both a philosophy and an integrated system of management that emphasizes the elimination of waste and the continuous improvement of operations.

**manufacturing cell** a group of dissimilar machines brought together to manufacture a family of parts with similar shapes or processing requirements.

**material kanban** a rectangular-shaped kanban used to order material in advance of a process.

**muda** anything other than the minimum amount of equipment, materials, parts, space, and time that are absolutely essential to add value to the product.

**multifunctional workers** workers who have been trained to perform more than one job or function.

**poka-yoke** any foolproof device or mechanism that prevents defects from occurring.

**preventive maintenance** a system of daily maintenance, periodic inspection, and preventive repairs designed to reduce the probability of machine breakdown.

**production kanban** a card authorizing the production of a container of goods.

**pull system** a production system in which items are manufactured only when called for by the users of those items.

**push system** a production system in which items are manufactured according to a schedule prepared in advance.

**signal kanban** a triangular kanban used as a reorder point to signal production at the previous workstation.

**supplier kanban** a kanban that rotates between a factory and its supplier.

**takt time** the cycle time of an operation paced to the rate of customer demand.

**total productive maintenance (TPM)** an approach to machine maintenance that combines the practice of preventive maintenance with the concepts of total quality and employer involvement.

**undercapacity scheduling** the allocation of extra time in a schedule for nonproductive tasks such as problem solving or maintenance.

**uniform production levels** the result of smoothing production requirements on the final assembly line.

**visual control** procedures and mechanisms for making problems visible.

**withdrawal kanban** a card authorizing the withdrawal and movement of a container of goods.

## QUESTIONS

**15-1.** What is the purpose of lean production?

**15-2.** How did lean production evolve into a system of continuous improvement?

**15-3.** Why are flexible resources essential to lean production?

**15-4.** What does a cellular layout contribute to lean production?

**15-5.** Differentiate between a push and a pull production system.

**15-6.** How was the concept of kanban developed from the two-bin inventory system?

**15-7.** How are the kanban system and the reorder point system similar? How are they different?

**15-8.** Describe how the following kanbans operate:

**a.** Production and withdrawal kanbans
**b.** Kanban squares
**c.** Signal kanbans
**d.** Material kanbans
**e.** Supplier kanbans

**15-9.** What are the advantages of small-lot sizes?

**15-10.** Why do large lot sizes not work well with pull systems?

**15-11.** Why are small-lot sizes not as effective in a push system?

**15-12.** Explain the principles of SMED. What does SMED try to achieve?

**15-13.** Why is uniform production important to JIT? How is it achieved?

**15-14.** What are the advantages of mixed-model sequencing?

**15-15.** How are lean production and quality related?

**15-16.** How can a balance be struck between the cost of breakdown maintenance and the cost of preventive maintenance?

**15-17.** Explain the concept of total productive maintenance (TPM).

**15-18.** What role does the equipment operator play in TPM?

**15-19.** Preventive maintenance can be viewed as the process of maintaining the "health" of a machine. Using health care as an analogy, explain the differences and tradeoffs between breakdown maintenance, preventive maintenance, and total productive maintenance.

**15-20.** How are suppliers affected by lean production?

**15-21.** Suggest several ways that lean requirements can be made easier for suppliers.

**15-22.** Give examples of visual control. How does visual control affect quality?

**15-23.** What is a poka-yoke? Give an example.

**15-24.** Why is worker involvement important to kaizen? Find the Kaizen Institute on the Web and walk through the site. Summarize what you learned.

**15-25.** What are some typical benefits from implementing lean?

**15-26.** Which elements of lean are the most difficult to implement? Why?

**15-27.** In what type of environment is lean production most successful?

**15-28.** Give examples of lean services.

**15-29.** JIT has been applied extensively in the automobile industry. Report on other industries who use lean production.

## PROBLEMS

**15-1.** Demand for the popular water toy Sudsy Soaker has far exceeded expectations. In order to increase the availability of different models of the toy, the manufacturer has decided to begin producing its most popular models as often as possible on its one assembly line. Given monthly requirements of 7200, 3600, and 3600 units for Sudsy Soaker 50, Sudsy Soaker 100, and Sudsy Soaker 200, respectively, determine a model sequence for the final assembly line that will smooth out the production of each model. (Assume 30 working days per month and 8 working hours per day. Also assume that the time required to assemble each model is approximately the same.)

**15-2.** As local developers prepare for an increase in housing starts, they must anticipate their demand for various materials. One such material is tile. Used in bathrooms, kitchens, and for decoration, tiles come in many shapes, colors, and sizes. In order to accommodate the varying needs, the tile manufacturer must schedule its production efficiently. Each month developers order 30,000 boxes of quarry tile, 15,000 boxes of Italian mosaic tile, and 45,000 boxes of 4-inch bathroom tile. Determine a mixed-model sequence that will efficiently meet these needs. Assume 30 days per month.

**15-3.** An assembly station is asked to process 100 circuit boards per hour. It takes 20 minutes to receive the necessary components from the previous workstation. Completed circuit boards are placed in a rack that will hold 10 boards. The rack must be full before it is sent on to the next workstation. If the factory uses a safety factor of 10%, how many kanbans are needed for the circuit board assembly process?

**15-4.** Referring to Problem 15-3, how many kanbans would be needed in each case?

a. Demand is increased to 200 circuit boards per hour.
b. The lead time for components is increased to 30 minutes.
c. The rack size is halved.
d. The safety factor is increased to 20%.

**15-5.** It takes Aaron 15 minutes to produce 10 widgets to fill a container and 5 minutes to transport the container to the next station, where Maria works. Maria's process takes about 30 minutes. The factory uses a safety factor of 20%. Currently, five kanbans rotate between Aaron and Maria's stations. What is the approximate demand for widgets?

**15-6.** Stan Weakly can sort a bin of 100 letters in 10 minutes. He typically receives 600 letters an hour. A truck arrives with more bins every 30 minutes. The office uses a safety factor of 10%. How many kanbans are needed for the letter-sorting process?

**15-7.** The office administrator wishes to decrease the number of kanbans in the letter-sorting process described in Problem 15-6. Which of the following alternatives has the greatest effect on reducing the number of kanbans?

a. Eliminating the safety factor.
b. Receiving truck deliveries every 15 minutes
c. Increasing the bin capacity to 300 letters

What is the effect on inventory levels of decreasing the number of kanbans?

**15-8.** Sandy is asked to produce 250 squidgets an hour. It takes 30 minutes to receive the necessary material from the previous workstation. Each output container holds 25 squidgets. The factory currently works with a safety factor of 10%. How many kanbans should be circulating between Sandy's process and the previous process?

**15-9.** Referring to Problem 15-8, what happens to the number of kanbans and to inventory levels in each case?

a. The time required to receive material is increased to 45 minutes.
b. Output expectations decrease to 125 squidgets an hour.
c. The size of the container is cut to 10 squidgets.

**15-10.** In a large microelectronics plant, the assembly cell for circuit boards has a demand for 200 units an hour. Two feeder cells supply parts A and B to the assembly cell (one A and one B for each board). Standard containers that look like divided trays are used. A container will hold 20 As or 10 Bs. It takes 10 minutes to fill up a container with As and 20 minutes to fill up a container with Bs. Transit time to the assembly cell is 5 minutes for both A and B. No safety factor is used. Set up a kanban control system for the assembly process.

# CASE PROBLEM 15.1

## *The Blitz Is On*

Tina Rossi looked at the pile of papers in front of her and sighed. She had been preparing material for her company's first Kaizen Blitz and wondered if she had thought of everything. The process they had chosen to kaizen had been the subject of numerous customer complaints and employee grumblings. Tina's list of reported problems, goals for the kaizen process, and team objectives were stated in the team charter. Tina had planned for the group to review the charter first, then tour the process, measure overall cycle time, and complete a process map. From there the team would break up into four subgroups to perform a muda walk and 5 S scan, conduct gripe interviews, and analyze process flow. Tina provided forms for each activity and a digital camera for visually documenting the current process and future improvements.

The second day of the blitz was less directed. Team members would regroup to go over the data collected in the previous day and suggest improvements to be tried out on the third day. This is when Tina would have to prod the team to take action—to transform the process or the layout, to improve quality or safety—to *try something* and analyze the results. On day four, the team would observe the new process in action, review cycle times, identify problems, and make adjustments. After agreeing on the parameters of the new process, the team would record their kaizen results by drawing standard operation sheets, training operators, and establishing visual control tools.

All those things in one week. Tina was ready and anxious to begin.

Use the material Tina has developed (see Kaizen Blitz.xls on the text website) to kaizen a process at your university or place of work. To simulate the Blitz experience, conduct your analysis with a team of four to six people in just five days time.

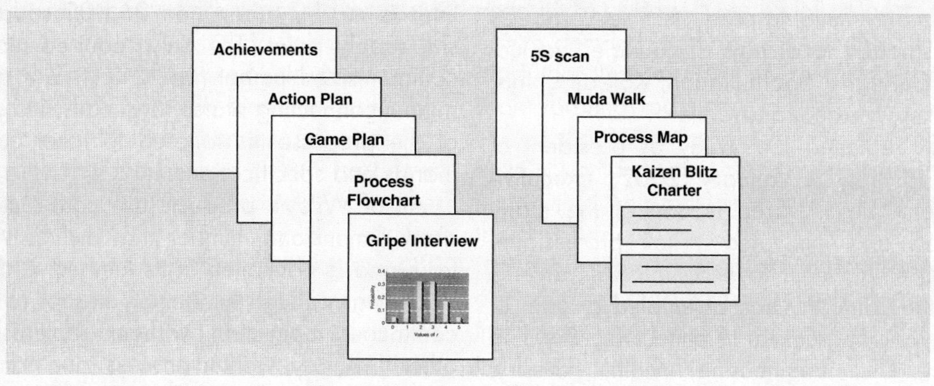

assigned to it. These numbers would be handwritten on the work order, by the individual who loads the cart, before it is given to the plant supervisor to be assigned. There is a chance of multiple carts being needed for the same job, but each cart has its own individual work order and therefore would have its own three-digit identification number and light. This is no deviation from the current process. The assembly workers would walk to the plant control office, retrieve their next job from the bin, type the three-digit code into the keypad, and then find the cart that has the strobe light turned on. This process would eliminate all of the guessing currently required to locate the cart with the raw materials and should reduce the overall average time needed to locate a cart. This would also allow for remote storage of the carts, rather than stacking as many as 30 carts at the top of the assembly line, a hindrance to traffic flow and safety.

**1.** Evaluate the usefulness of the pager suggestion. Have the students and Mr. Alvarez found the root cause of the cart problem?

**2.** Identify waste in the current production process. How would you apply the principles of lean production to improve Wiley's situation?

## REFERENCES

Abernathy, F., J. Dunlap, J. Hammond, and D. Weil. *A Stitch in Time: Lean Retailing and the Transformation of Manufacturing—Lessons from the Apparel and Textile Industries*. Oxford, UK: Oxford University Press, 1999.

Black, J. T. *The Design of the Factory with a Future*. New York: McGraw-Hill, 1991.

Bremner, B. and C. Dawson. "Can Anything Stop Toyota?" *Business Week* (November 17, 2003), pp. 114–118.

Brown, S. "Toyota's Global Body Shop." *Fortune* (February 9, 2004), Industrial Edition, http://www.fortune.com/fortune/subs/columnist/0,15704,581557,00.html.

Bylinsky, G. "Heroes of Manufacturing." *Fortune* (March 20, 2000), pp. 192A–205A.

Cusomano, M. *The Japanese Automobile Industry*. Cambridge, MA: Harvard University Press, 1985.

Hall, R. *Zero Inventories*. Homewood, IL: Dow Jones-Irwin, 1983.

Hirano, H. *JIT Factory Revolution*. Cambridge, MA: Productivity Press, 1988.

Huang, P. Y., L. P. Rees, and B. W. Taylor. "A Simulation Analysis of the Just-in-Time Technique (with Kanbans) for a Multiline, Multistage Production System." *Decision Sciences* (July 1983), pp. 326–345.

Jusko, J. "A Look at Lean." *Industry Week* (December 6, 1999), pp. 88–91.

Kinni, T. *America's Best*. New York: Wiley, 1996.

Liker, J. *Becoming Lean: Inside Stories of U.S. Manufacturers*. Cambridge, MA: Productivity Press, 1998.

Monden, Y., ed. *Applying Just-In-Time: The American/Japanese Experience*. Atlanta: Industrial Engineering and Management Press, 1986.

Monden, Y. *Toyota Production System: An Integrated Approach to Just-in-Time*, 3rd ed. Atlanta: Industrial Engineering and Management Press, 1986.

Panchak, P. "Lean Health Care? It Works!" *Industry Week* (November 1, 2003).

Phillips, T. "Building the Lean Machine." *Advanced Manufacturing* (January 1, 2000). http://www.advancedmanufacturing.com.

Sepehri, M. *Just-in-Time, Not Just in Japan*. Falls Church, VA: American Production and Inventory Control Society, 1986.

Shingo, S. *Modern Approaches to Manufacturing Improvement*. Cambridge, MA: Productivity Press, 1990.

Sobek, D., J. Liker, and A. Ward. "Another Look at How Toyota Integrates Product Development." *Harvard Business Review* July–August 1998, pp. 36–49.

Spear, S. "Comments on the Second Toyota Paradox." Teaching Note 9-602-035, Harvard Business School (March 2003).

Spear, S., and K. Bowen. "Decoding the DNA of the Toyota Production System." *Harvard Business Review* (September–October 1999), pp. 96–106.

Suzaki, K. *The New Manufacturing Challenge*. New York: Free Press, 1985.

Swank, C. "The Lean Service Machine." *Harvard Business Review* (October 2003), pp. 123–131.

Tagliabue, J. "Spanish Clothing Chain Zara Grows by Being Fast and Flexible." *The New York Times* (May 30, 2003).

Tierney, C. "Big Three Play Catch-Up to Toyota Plant Prowess." *Detroit News* (February 22, 2004).

*The Toyota Production System*. Company brochure. Japan: Toyota Motor Corporation, 1998.

Vasilash, G. "Lean Lessons." *Automotive Manufacturing and Production* (March 2001).

Vasilash, G. "Standardized Lean." *Automotive Manufacturing and Production* (February 2000). http://www.automfg.com

Ward, A., J. Liker, J. Cristiano, and Durward Sobek II. "The Second Toyota Paradox: How Delaying Decisions Can Make Better Cars Faster." *Sloan Management Review* (Spring 1995), pp. 43–62.

Womack, J., D. Jones, and D. Roos. *The Machine That Changed the World*. New York: Macmillan, 1990.

Womack, J., and D. Jones. *Lean Thinking*. New York: Simon & Schuster, 1996.

Wysocki, B. "Industrial Strength: To Fix Health Care, Hospitals Take Tips from Factory Floor," *The Wall Street Journal* (April 9, 2004), p. A1.

# Scheduling

CHAPTER **16**

Web resources for this chapter include

- Internet Exercises
- Online Practice Quizzes
- Virtual Tours
- Excel Worksheets
- Company and Resource Weblinks
- Animated Demo Problems
- Microsoft Project Exhibits

www.wiley.com/college/russell

## CHAPTER OUTLINE

In this chapter, you will learn about . . .

- Objectives in Scheduling
- Loading
- Sequencing
- Monitoring
- Advanced Planning and Scheduling Systems
- Theory of Constraints
- Employee Scheduling

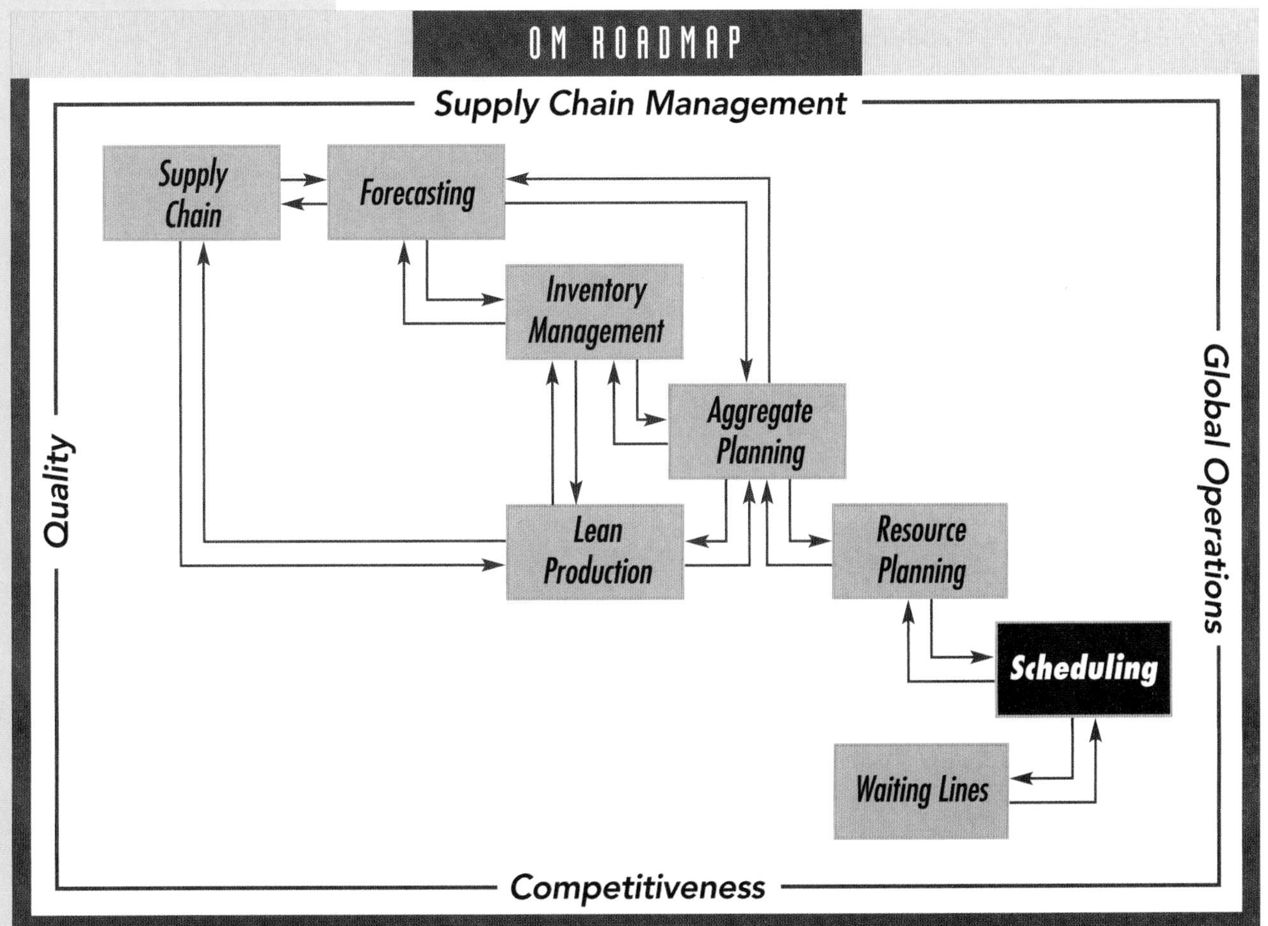

## WHEN GOOD GENES MAKE GOOD SCHEDULES

Deere & Co.'s Moline, Illinois, plant sported the latest machinery, self-managed work teams, and spotless surroundings—and still the plant had trouble meeting deadlines. Deere made parts for seed planters at Moline, which were shipped to dealers and assembled there to customer order. As the product became more complex, dealers couldn't handle the intricate assembly. Now the Moline plant manufactures the parts *and* assembles them.

A planter has a steel frame with 4 to 32 "row units," each holding seeds and fertilizer. Controls can be hydraulic or electronic at various levels of sophistication. With over 300 options, millions of combinations are possible. Deere found that even scheduling the 5000 most likely configurations was unmanageable.

Fabrication work takes considerably longer than assembly. For example, welding an extra-large planter can take an hour or more, creating quite a bottleneck. The sequence in which planters are assembled is important too, as completed machines leave the assembly line and move directly to waiting trucks. Planters going to the same location need to come off the assembly line at approximately the same time. Demand varies so widely that patterns detected one month are no longer valid the next. The Moline plant averaged a 500-order backlog, orders that farmers could cancel at any time.

That's when Deere employees Bill Fulkerson and Dick McKinnon found a solution (or rather a solution method) called *genetic algorithms*. Based on the theory of natural selection, genetic algorithms (GA) change or *mutate* the sequence of items assembled until a satisfactory schedule is determined, then keep experimenting until a good schedule emerges. Details about the production process and factors that make a good schedule are assigned point values that influence their selection in GA. The computer system tries different sequences of orders, observes the results, and learns whether to keep certain characteristics in the "offspring" of the next generation. As the program runs, red, yellow, and blue lights flash on the computer screen—red for trouble, yellow for better, and blue for best. It takes about an hour to generate a two-week schedule that increases output and uses less overtime than the old schedule (which took three days to calculate).

Genetic algorithms now schedule tractors and $200,000 combines at other Deere plants. Companies like GM, GE, Motorola, and Caterpillar use GA, too, to cut inventories, shorten assembly time, and boost yields.

*John Deere's policy of building farm equipment to customer order makes scheduling difficult. For example, customers can choose among 300 options for planter equipment resulting in millions of possible product configurations. If not scheduled properly, configurations that require long processing times can put a strain on resources and clog the flow of work through the system.*

*Source:* Gene Bylinsky, "Heroes of U.S. Manufacturing," *Fortune* (March 19, 2001), http://www.fortune.com, Document ID #200872. 

**Scheduling** specifies *when* labor, equipment and facilities are needed to produce a product or provide a service. It is the last stage of planning before production takes place. The scheduling function differs considerably based on the type of operation:

**Scheduling:** the last stage of planning before production.

- In *process industries*, such as chemicals and pharmaceuticals, scheduling might consist of determining the mix of ingredients that goes into a vat or when the system should stop producing one type of mixture, clean out the vat, and start producing another. Linear programming can find the lowest-cost mix of ingredients, and the production order quantity can determine the optimal length of a production run. These techniques are described in detail in Chapter 13 Supplement and Chapter 12, respectively.
- For *mass production*, the schedule of production is pretty much determined when the assembly line is laid out. Products simply flow down the assembly line from one station to the next in the same prescribed, nondeviating order every time. Day-to-day scheduling decisions consist of determining how fast to feed items into the line and how many hours per day to run the line. On a mixed-model assembly line, the *order* of products assembled also has to be determined. We discuss these issues in Chapters 7 and 15.
- For *projects*, the scheduling decisions are so numerous and interrelated that specialized project-scheduling techniques such as PERT and CPM have been devised. Chapter 8 is devoted to these planning and control tools for project management.
- For *batch* or *job shop production*, scheduling decisions can be quite complex. In previous chapters, we discussed *aggregate planning*, which plans for the production of product lines or families; *master scheduling*, which plans for the production of individual end items or finished goods; and *material requirements planning* (MRP) and *capacity requirements planning* (CRP), which plan for the production of components and assemblies. Scheduling determines to which machine a part will be routed for processing, which worker will operate a machine that produces a part, and the order in which the parts are to be processed. Scheduling also determines which patient to assign to an operating room, which doctors and nurses are to care for a patient during certain hours of the day, the order in which a doctor is to see patients, and when meals should be delivered or medications dispensed.

**The scheduling function differs by type of process.**

What makes scheduling so difficult in a job shop is the variety of jobs (or patients) that are processed, each with distinctive routing and processing requirements. In addition, although the volume of each customer order may be small, there are probably a great number of different orders in the shop at any one time. This necessitates planning for the production of each job as it arrives, scheduling its use of limited resources, and monitoring its progress through the system.

This chapter concentrates on scheduling issues for job shop production. We also examine one of the most difficult scheduling problems for services—employee scheduling.

## OBJECTIVES IN SCHEDULING

There are many possible objectives in constructing a schedule, including

- Meeting customer due dates;
- Minimizing job lateness;
- Minimizing response time;
- Minimizing completion time;
- Minimizing time in the system;
- Minimizing overtime;
- Maximizing machine or labor utilization;
- Minimizing idle time; and
- Minimizing work-in-process inventory.

**Managers have multiple, conflicting scheduling objectives.**

**Shop floor control:** the scheduling and monitoring of day-to-day production in a job shop. It is usually performed by the *production control department*.

**Load leveling:** the process of smoothing out the work assigned.

**Dispatch list:** a shop paper that specifies the sequence in which jobs should be processed.

*Job shop scheduling* is also known as **shop floor control (SFC)**, *production control*, and *production activity control* (PAC). Regardless of their primary scheduling objective, manufacturers typically have a *production control department* whose responsibilities consist of

1. ***Loading**—checking the availability of material, machines, and labor*. The MRP system plans for material availability. CRP converts the material plan into machine and labor requirements, and projects resource overloads and underloads. Production control assigns work to individual workers or machines, and then attempts to smooth out the load to make the MRP schedule "doable." Smoothing the load is called **load leveling**.
2. ***Sequencing**—releasing work orders to the shop and issuing dispatch lists for individual machines*. MRP recommends when orders should be released (hence the name, *planned* order releases). After verifying their feasibility, production control actually releases the orders. When several orders are released to one machine center, they must be prioritized so that the worker will know which ones to do first. The **dispatch list** contains the sequence in which jobs should be processed. This sequence is often based on certain *sequencing rules*.
3. ***Monitoring**—maintaining progress reports on each job until it is completed*. This is important because items may need to be rescheduled as changes occur in the system. In addition to timely data collection, it involves the use of Gantt charts and input/output control charts.

## LOADING

**Loading:** the process of assigning work to limited resources.

**Loading** is the process of assigning work to limited resources. Many times an operation can be performed by various persons, machines, or work centers but with varying efficiencies. If there is enough capacity, each worker should be assigned to the task that he or she performs best, and each job to the machine that can process it most efficiently. In effect, that is what happens when CRP generates a load profile for each machine center. The routing file used by CRP lists the machine that can perform the job most efficiently first. If no overloads appear in the load profile, then production control can proceed to the next task of sequencing the work at each center. However, when resource constraints produce overloads in the load profile, production control must examine the list of jobs initially assigned and decide which jobs to reassign elsewhere. The problem of determining how best to allocate jobs to machines or workers to tasks can be solved with the *assignment method* of linear programming.

### THE ASSIGNMENT METHOD OF LOADING

The *assignment method* of loading is a form of linear programming.

The *assignment method* is a specialized linear programming solution procedure for deciding which worker to assign to a task, or which job to assign to a machine. (See Supplement 13 for linear programming.) Given a table of tasks and resources, the procedure creates an *opportunity cost matrix* and selects the best assignment in consideration of tradeoffs among alternatives. With this technique, only one job may be assigned to each worker or machine. The procedure for a minimization problem is outlined as follows:

1. Perform *row reductions* by subtracting the minimum value in each row from all other row values.
2. Perform *column reductions* by subtracting the minimum value in each column from all other column values.
3. The resulting table is an *opportunity cost matrix*. Cross out all zeros in the matrix using the minimum number of horizontal or vertical lines.
4. If the number of lines equals the number of rows in the matrix, an optimal solution has been reached and assignments can be made where the zeros appear. Otherwise, *modify the matrix* by subtracting the minimum uncrossed value from all other uncrossed values and adding this same amount to all cells where two lines intersect. All other values in the matrix remain unchanged.
5. Repeat steps 3 and 4 until an optimal solution is reached.

Example 16.1

**Assigning Work at WebStar**

WebStar, Inc. has four Web projects to complete and four workers with varying degrees of expertise in Web development for particular industries. Estimates of processing times (in hours) for each project by each worker are shown below. Development time costs an average of $100 an hour. Assign each worker to a project so that cost is minimized.

| Initial Matrix | Project 1 | Project 2 | Project 3 | Project 4 |
|---|---|---|---|---|
| Bryan | 10 | 5 | 6 | 10 |
| Kari | 6 | 2 | 4 | 6 |
| Noah | 7 | 6 | 5 | 6 |
| Chris | 9 | 5 | 4 | 10 |

*Solution*

1. ***Row reduction****—Find the best assignment in each row. Subtract the smallest value in each row from all other row values.* The resulting number is the opportunity cost of assigning a worker to that project. For example, the best assignment for Bryan would be project 2. Thus, its value in the following matrix is zero. However, if Bryan were assigned to project 1 or 4, it would take $(10 - 5) = 5$ hours longer to complete, and if assigned to project 3, one hour longer.

| Row Reduction | Project 1 | Project 2 | Project 3 | Project 4 |
|---|---|---|---|---|
| Bryan | 5 | 0 | 1 | 5 |
| Kari | 4 | 0 | 2 | 4 |
| Noah | 2 | 1 | 0 | 1 |
| Chris | 5 | 1 | 0 | 6 |

2. ***Column reduction****—Find the best assignment in each column. Subtract the smallest value in each column from all other values in the column.* For example, project 1 can be completed the fastest with Noah as project leader, so it has an opportunity cost of zero. Assigning Bryan to project 1 would require 3 more hours of processing; thus, its opportunity cost is 3.

| Column Reduction | Project 1 | Project 2 | Project 3 | Project 4 |
|---|---|---|---|---|
| Bryan | 3 | 0 | 1 | 4 |
| Kari | 2 | 0 | 2 | 3 |
| Noah | 0 | 1 | 0 | 0 |
| Chris | 3 | 1 | 0 | 5 |

3. ***Look for unique assignments****—Examine the matrix and cover all zeroes.* Remember that each person can only be assigned to one project and each project can only have one leader. A problem occurs when project 2 is the best for both Bryan and Kari, and project 3 is best for both Noah and Chris. In the following matrix, rows or columns containing optimal assignments are highlighted. This is called "covering all zeroes." If the number of lines (or highlighting) is less than the number of rows, the matrix needs to be modified.

| Initial Assignment | Project 1 | Project 2 | Project 3 | Project 4 |
|---|---|---|---|---|
| Bryan | 3 | **0** | 1 | 4 |
| Kari | 2 | **0** | 2 | 3 |
| Noah | **0** | 1 | **0** | **0** |
| Chris | 3 | 1 | **0** | 5 |

4. ***Modify the matrix*** *Find the smallest value of the entries that are not highlighted. Subtract that value from all other non-highlighted entries, and add it to the entries where the lines intersect.* Below we have subtracted 2 from the noncovered entries and added it to the intersection points (i.e., Noah's project 2 and project 3 values).

| Modified Matrix | Project 1 | Projecst 2 | Project 3 | Project 4 |
|---|---|---|---|---|
| Bryan | 1 | **0** | 1 | 2 |
| Kari | **0** | **0** | 2 | 1 |
| Noah | **0** | 3 | 2 | **0** |
| Chris | 1 | 1 | **0** | 3 |

5. ***Look for unique assignments*** *Assign each worker to the best project available.* Bryan is assigned to project 2. With project 2 eliminated, Kari is assigned to project 1. Since project 1 has been eliminated, Noah is assigned to project 4. That leaves Chris for project 3.

| Final Assignment | Project 1 | Project 2 | Project 3 | Project 4 |
|---|---|---|---|---|
| Bryan | 1 | **0** | 1 | 2 |
| Kari | **0** | 0 | 2 | 1 |
| Noah | 0 | 3 | 2 | **0** |
| Chris | 1 | 1 | **0** | 3 |

6. ***Calculate performance*** Referring back to the original assignment matrix, the times required to finish each project are given below. At a cost of \$100 hour, the projects will cost $(5 + 6 + 4 + 6) \times \$100 = \$2100$ to complete.

| Final Matrix | Project 1 | Project 2 | Project 3 | Project 4 |
|---|---|---|---|---|
| Bryan | 10 | **5** | 6 | 10 |
| Kari | **6** | 2 | 4 | 6 |
| Noah | 7 | 6 | 5 | **6** |
| Chris | 9 | 5 | **4** | 10 |

Smaller assignment problems, such as our example, are usually solved by hand. Larger ones can be solved in Excel with solver, as shown in Exhibit 16.1. Assignment problems may also involve maximizing profit or customer satisfaction. When solving maximization problems by hand, each entry in the initial matrix should be subtracted from the largest matrix value before proceeding as a minimization problem. When solving with Excel, simply change the solver objective function from min to max.

## SEQUENCING

**Sequencing:** prioritizes jobs that have been assigned to a resource.

When more than one job is assigned to a machine or activity, the operator needs to know the order in which to process the jobs. The process of prioritizing jobs is called **sequencing**. If no particular order is specified, the operator would probably process the job that arrived first. This default sequence is called *first-come, first-served* (FCFS). If jobs are stacked on arrival to a machine, it might be easier to process the job first that arrived last and is now on top of the stack. This is called *last-come, first-served* (LCFS) sequencing.

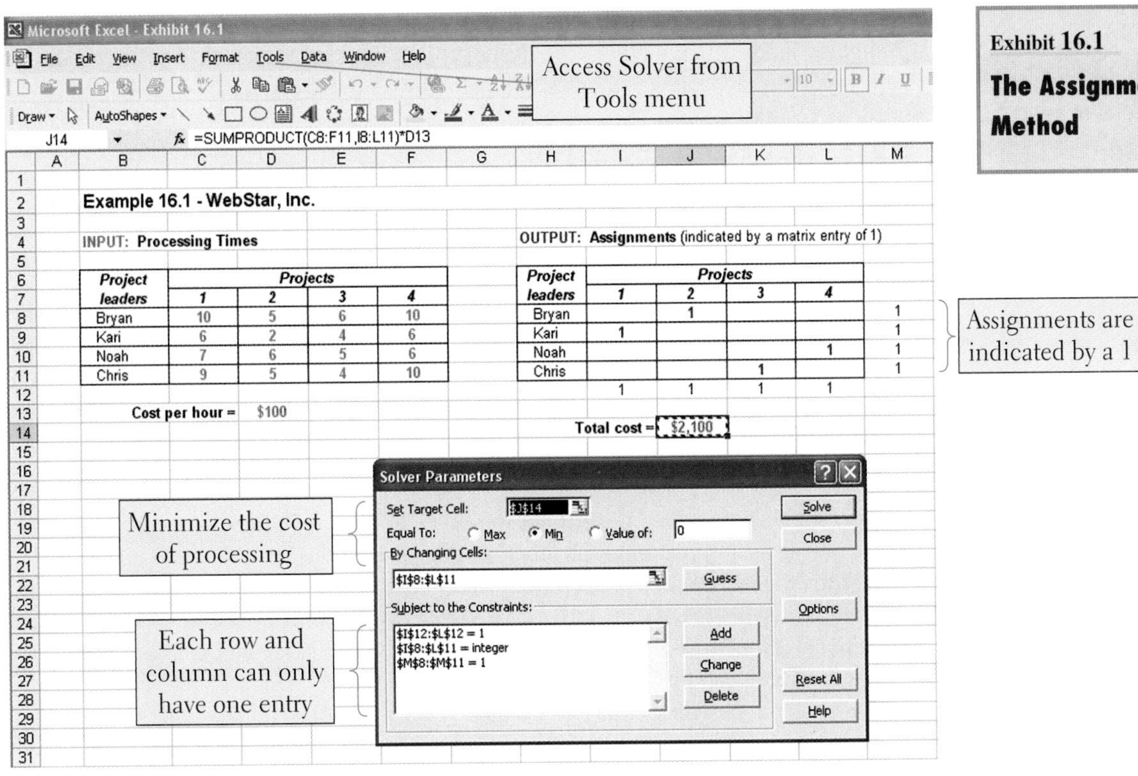


| Project leaders | Projects 1 | 2 | 3 | 4 |
|---|---|---|---|---|
| Bryan | 10 | 5 | 6 | 10 |
| Kari | 6 | 2 | 4 | 6 |
| Noah | 7 | 6 | 5 | 6 |
| Chris | 9 | 5 | 4 | 10 |

| Project leaders | Projects 1 | 2 | 3 | 4 | |
|---|---|---|---|---|---|
| Bryan | | 1 | | | 1 |
| Kari | 1 | | | | 1 |
| Noah | | | | 1 | 1 |
| Chris | | | 1 | | 1 |
| | 1 | 1 | 1 | 1 | |

**Exhibit 16.1**

**The Assignment Method**

Another common approach is to process the job first that is due the soonest or the job that has the highest customer priority. These are known as *earliest due date* (DDATE) and *highest customer priority* (CUSTPR) sequencing. Operators may also look through a stack of jobs to find one with a *similar setup* to the job that is currently being processed (SETUP). That would minimize the downtime of the machine and make the operator's job easier.

A sampling of heuristic sequencing rules.

Variations on the DDATE rule include *minimum slack* (SLACK) and *smallest critical ratio* (CR). SLACK considers the work remaining to be performed on a job as well as the time remaining (until the due date) to perform that work. Jobs are processed first that have the least difference (or slack) between the two, as follows:

$$\text{SLACK} = (\text{due date} - \text{today's date}) - (\text{processing time})$$

The critical ratio uses the same information as SLACK, but recalculates the sequence as processing continues and arranges the information in ratio form. Mathematically, the CR is calculated as follows:

$$\text{CR} = \frac{\text{time remaining}}{\text{work remaining}} = \frac{\text{due date} - \text{today's date}}{\text{remaining processing time}}$$

If the work remaining is greater than the time remaining, the critical ratio will be less than 1. If the time remaining is greater than the work remaining, the critical ratio will be greater than 1. If the time remaining equals work remaining, the critical ratio exactly equals 1. The critical ratio allows us to make the following statements about our schedule:

If CR $> 1$, then the job is *ahead of schedule*

If CR $< 1$, then the job is *behind schedule*

If CR $= 1$, then the job is exactly *on schedule*

Other sequencing rules examine processing time at a particular operation and order the work either by shortest processing time (SPT) or longest processing time (LPT). LPT assumes long jobs are important jobs and is analogous to the strategy of doing larger tasks first to get them out of the way. SPT focuses instead on shorter jobs and is able to complete many more jobs earlier than LPT. With either rule, some jobs may be inordinately late because they are always put at the back of a queue.

**Flow time:** the time it takes a job to flow through the system.

**Makespan:** the time it takes for a group of jobs to be completed.

**Tardiness:** the difference between the late job's due date and its completion time.

All these "rules" for arranging jobs in a certain order for processing seem reasonable. We might wonder which methods are best or if it really matters which jobs are processed first anyway. Perhaps a few examples will help answer those questions.

## SEQUENCING JOBS THROUGH ONE PROCESS

The simplest sequencing problem consists of a queue of jobs at one machine or process. No new jobs arrive to the machine during the analysis, processing times and due dates are fixed, and setup time is considered negligible. For this scenario, the *completion time* (also called **flow time**) of each job will differ depending on its place in the sequence, but the overall completion time for the set of jobs (called the **makespan**) will not change. **Tardiness** is the difference between a late job's due date and its completion time. Even in this simple case, there is no sequencing rule that optimizes both processing efficiency and due date performance. Let's consider an example.

**Example 16.2**

**Simple Sequencing Rules**

Because of the approaching holiday season, Joe Palotty is scheduled to work seven days a week for the next two months. October's work for Joe consists of five jobs, A, B, C, D, and E. Job A takes five days to complete and is due on day 10, job B takes ten days to complete and is due on day 15, job C takes two days to process and is due on day 5, job D takes eight days to process and is due on day 12, and job E, which takes six days to process, is due on day 8.

There are 120 possible sequences for the five jobs. Clearly, enumeration is impossible. Let's try some simple sequencing rules. Sequence the jobs by (a) first-come, first-served (FCFS), (b) earliest due date (DDATE), (c) minimum slack (SLACK), and (d) shortest processing time (SPT). Determine the completion time and tardiness of each job under each sequencing rule. Should Joe process his work as is—first-come, first-served? If not, what sequencing rule would you recommend to Joe?

*Solution*

Prepare a table for each sequencing rule. Start the first job at time 0. (When today's date is not given, assume it is day 0.) Completion time is the sum of the start time and the processing time. The start time of the next job is the completion time of the previous job.

a. FCFS: Process the jobs in order of their arrival, A, B, C, D, E.

| FCFS Sequence | Start Time | Processing Time | Completion Time | Due Date | Tardiness |
|---|---|---|---|---|---|
| A | 0 | 5 | 5 | 10 | 0 |
| B | 5 | 10 | 15 | 15 | 0 |
| C | 15 | 2 | 17 | 5 | 12 |
| D | 17 | 8 | 25 | 12 | 13 |
| E | 25 | 6 | 31 | 8 | 23 |
| Total | | | 93 | | 48 |
| Average | | | 93/5 = 18.60 | | 48/5 = 9.6 |

b. DDATE: Sequence the jobs by earliest due date.

| DDATE Sequence | Start Time | Processing Time | Completion Time | Due Date | Tardiness |
|---|---|---|---|---|---|
| C | 0 | 2 | 2 | 5 | 0 |
| E | 2 | 6 | 8 | 8 | 0 |
| A | 8 | 5 | 13 | 10 | 3 |
| D | 13 | 8 | 21 | 12 | 9 |
| B | 21 | 10 | 31 | 15 | 16 |
| Total | | | 75 | | 28 |
| Average | | | 75/5 = 15.00 | | 28/5 = 5.6 |

c. SLACK: Sequence the jobs by minimum slack. The slack for each job is calculated as: (due date − today's date) − remaining processing time.

| | | |
|---|---|---|
| Job A | (10 − 0) − 5 | = 5* |
| B | (15 − 0) − 10 | = 5* |
| C | (5 − 0) − 2 | = 3 |
| D | (12 − 0) − 8 | = 4 |
| E | (8 − 0) − 6 | = 2 |

*break the tie arbitrarily

| Slack Sequence | Start Time | Processing Time | Completion Time | Due Date | Tardiness |
|---|---|---|---|---|---|
| E | 0 | 6 | 6 | 8 | 0 |
| C | 6 | 2 | 8 | 5 | 3 |
| D | 8 | 8 | 16 | 12 | 4 |
| A | 16 | 5 | 21 | 10 | 11 |
| B | 21 | 10 | 31 | 15 | 16 |
| Total | | | 82 | | 34 |
| Average | | | 82/5 = 16.40 | | 34/5 = 6.8 |

d. SPT: Sequence the jobs by smallest processing time.

| SPT Sequence | Start Time | Processing Time | Completion Time | Due Date | Tardiness |
|---|---|---|---|---|---|
| C | 0 | 2 | 2 | 5 | 0 |
| A | 2 | 5 | 7 | 10 | 0 |
| E | 7 | 6 | 13 | 8 | 5 |
| D | 13 | 8 | 21 | 12 | 9 |
| B | 21 | 10 | 31 | 15 | 16 |
| Total | | | 74 | | 30 |
| Average | | | 74/5 = 14.80 | | 30/5 = 6 |

**Summary**

| Rule | Average Completion Time | Average Tardiness | No. of Jobs Tardy | Maximum Tardiness |
|---|---|---|---|---|
| FCFS | 18.60 | 9.6 | 3* | 23 |
| DDATE | 15.00 | 5.6* | 3* | 16* |
| SLACK | 16.40 | 6.8 | 4 | 16* |
| SPT | 14.80* | 6.0 | 3* | 16* |

*Best Value

All the sequencing rules complete the month's work by day 31, as planned. However, no sequencing rule is able to complete *all* jobs on time. The performance of FCFS is either met or exceeded by DDATE and SPT. Thus, Joe should take the time to sequence this month's work.

Whether Joe sequences his work by DDATE or SPT depends on the objectives of the company for whom he works. The particular jobs that are tardy may also make a difference.

The Excel solution to this problem is shown in Exhibit 16.2.

Exhibit 16.2
**Using Excel for Sequencing Rules**

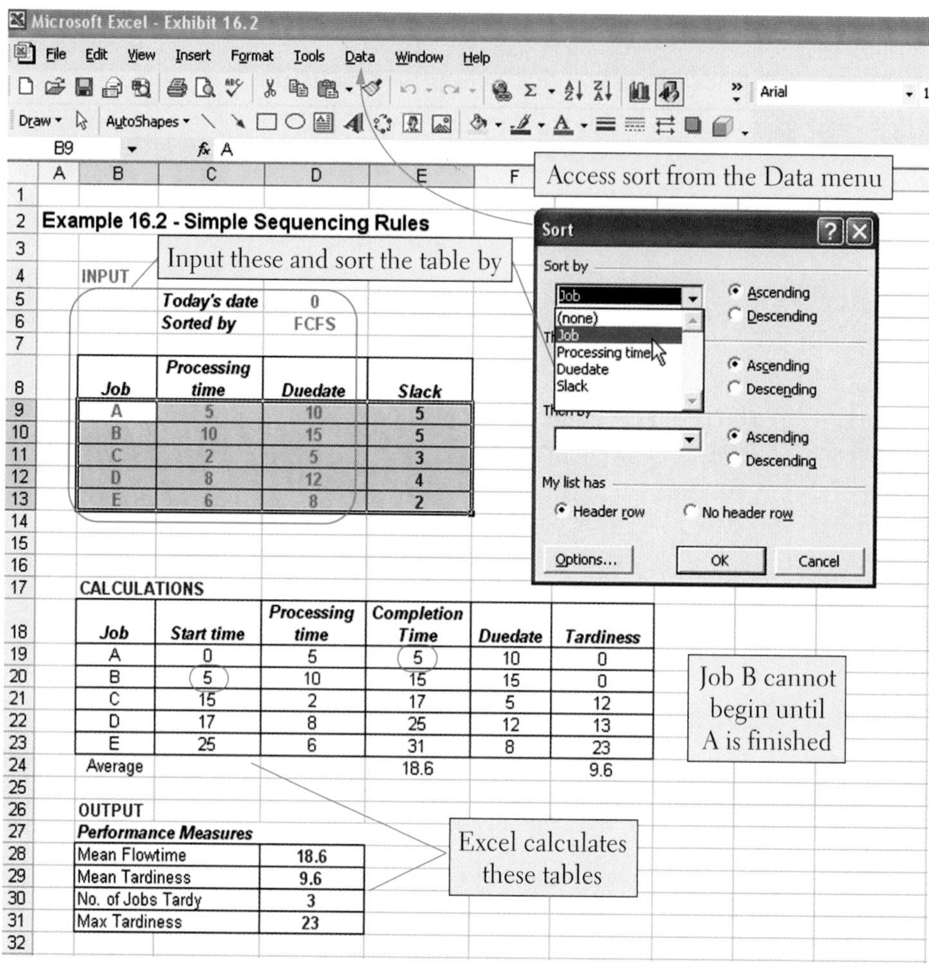


There is no one sequencing rule that optimizes both processing efficiency and due date performance.

Are the preceding results a function of this particular example, or are they indicative of the types of results we will get whenever these rules are applied? Analytically, we can prove that for a set number of jobs to be processed on *one* machine, the SPT sequencing rule will minimize mean job completion time (also known as *flowtime*) and minimize mean number of jobs in the system. On the other hand, the DDATE sequencing rule will minimize mean tardiness. No definitive statements can be made concerning the performance of the other sequencing rules.

## SEQUENCING JOBS THROUGH TWO SERIAL PROCESSES

**Johnson's rule:** gives an optimal sequence for jobs processed serially through two processes.

Since few factories consist of just one process, we might wonder if techniques exist that will produce an optimal sequence for any number of jobs processed through more than one machine or process. **Johnson's rule** finds the fastest way to process a series of jobs through a two-step system in which every job follows the same sequence through two processes. Based on a variation of the SPT rule, it requires that the sequence be "mapped out" to determine the final completion time, or *makespan*, for the set of jobs. The procedure is as follows:

1. List the time required to complete each job at each process. Set up a one-dimensional matrix to represent the desired sequence with the number of slots equal to the number of jobs.
2. Select the smallest processing time at either process. If that time occurs at process 1, put the associated job as near to the *beginning* of the sequence as possible.
3. If the smallest time occurs at process 2, put the associated job as near to the *end* of the sequence as possible.
4. Remove the job from the list.
5. Repeat steps 2–4 until all slots in the matrix have been filled or all jobs have been sequenced.

**Example 16.3**

**Johnson's Rule**

Johnson's Fine Restorations has received a rush order to refinish five carousel animals—an alligator, a bear, a cat, a deer, and an elephant. The restoration involves two major processes: sanding and painting. Mr. Johnson takes care of the sanding; his son does the painting. The time required for each refinishing job differs by the state of disrepair and degree of detail of each animal. Given the following processing times (in hours), determine the order in which the jobs should be processed so that the rush order can be completed as soon as possible.

| Job | Process 1 | Process 2 |
|---|---|---|
| A | 6 | 8 |
| B | 11 | 6 |
| C | 7 | 3 |
| D | 9 | 7 |
| E | 5 | 10 |

*Solution*

The smallest processing time, three hours, occurs at process 2 for job C, so we place job C as near to the end of the sequence as possible. C is now eliminated from the job list.

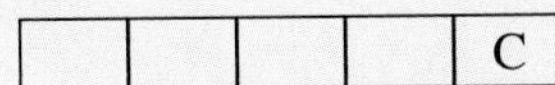


The next smallest time is five hours. It occurs at process 1 for job E, so we place job E as near to the beginning of the sequence as possible. Job E is eliminated from the job list.

| E | | | | C |
|---|---|---|---|---|

The next smallest time is six hours. It occurs at process 1 for job A and at process 2 for job B. Thus, we place job A as near to the beginning of the sequence as possible and job B as near to the end of the sequence as possible. Jobs A and B are eliminated from the job list.

| E | A | | B | C |
|---|---|---|---|---|

The only job remaining is job D. It is placed in the only available slot, in the middle of the sequence.

| E | A | D | B | C |
|---|---|---|---|---|

This sequence will complete these jobs faster than any other sequence. The following bar charts (called *Gantt charts*) are used to determine the makespan or final completion time for the set of five jobs. Notice that the sequence of jobs (E, A, D, B, C) is the same for both processes and that a job cannot begin at process 2 until it has been completed at process 1. Also, a job cannot begin at process 2 if another job is currently in process. Time periods during which a job is being processed are labeled with the job's letter. The gray shaded areas represent idle time.

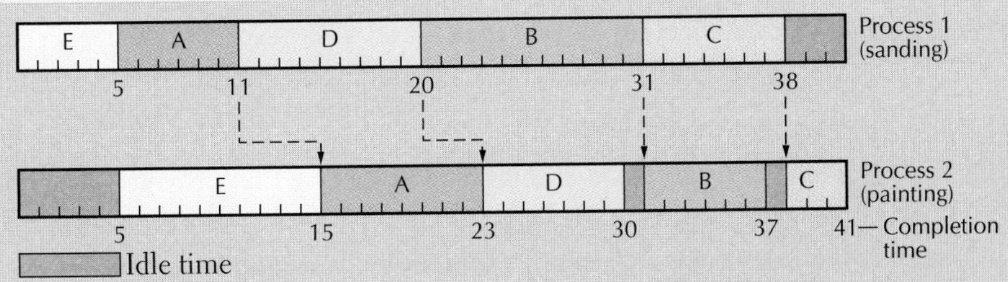


The completion time for the set of five jobs is 41 hours. Note that although Johnson's rule minimizes makespan and idle time, it does not consider job due dates in constructing a sequence, so there is no attempt to minimize job tardiness.

The Excel solution to this problem is shown in Exhibit 16.3.

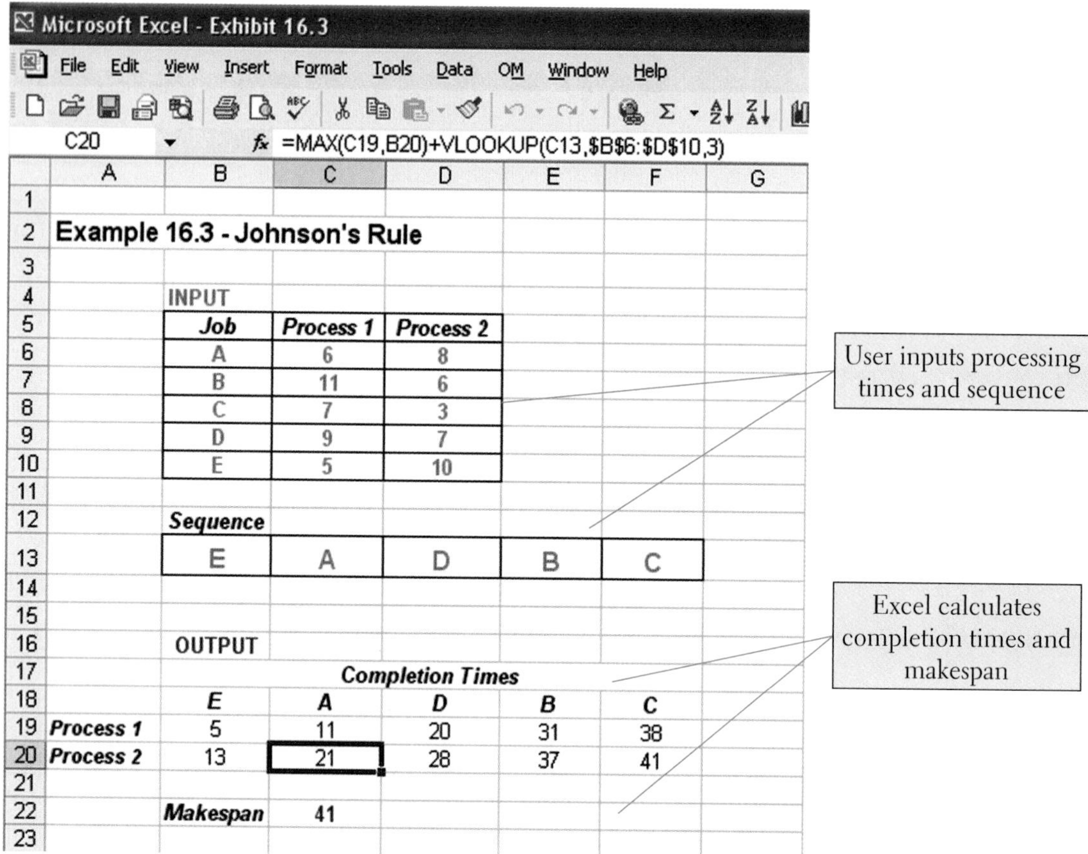


Exhibit 16.3
**Using Excel for Johnson's Rule**

## GUIDELINES FOR SELECTING A SEQUENCING RULE

In a real-world job shop, jobs follow different routes through a facility that consists of many different machine centers or departments. A small job shop may have three or four departments; a large job shop may have 50 or more. From several to several hundred jobs may be circulating the shop at any given time. New jobs are released into the shop daily and placed in competition with existing jobs for priority in processing. Queues form and dissipate as jobs move through the system. A dispatch list that shows the sequence in which jobs are to be processed at a particular machine may be valid at the beginning of a day or week but become outdated as new jobs arrive in the system. Some jobs may have to wait to be assembled with others before continuing to be processed. Delays in completing operations can cause due dates to be revised and schedules changed.

Use simulation to test sequencing rules.

The complexity and dynamic nature of most scheduling environments precludes the use of analytical solution techniques. The most popular form of analysis for these systems is *simulation.* Academia has especially enjoyed creating and testing sequencing rules in simulations of hypothetical job shops. One early simulation study alone examined 92 different sequencing rules. Although no optimal solutions have been identified in these simulation studies, they have produced some general guidelines for *when* certain sequencing rules may be appropriate. Here are a few of their suggestions:

Guidelines for selecting a sequencing rule

1. ***SPT is most useful when the shop is highly congested.*** SPT tends to minimize mean flow time, mean number of jobs in the system (and thus work-in-process inventory), and percent of jobs tardy. By completing more jobs quickly, it theoretically satisfies a greater number of customers than the other rules. However, with SPT some long jobs may be completed *very* late, resulting in a small number of very unsatisfied customers.

   For this reason, when SPT is used in practice, it is usually truncated (or stopped), depending on the amount of time a job has been waiting or the nearness of its due date. For example, many mainframe computer systems process jobs by SPT. Jobs that are submitted are placed in several categories (A, B, or C) based on expected CPU time. The shorter jobs, or A jobs, are processed first, but every couple of hours the system stops processing A jobs and picks the first job from the B stack to run. After the B job is finished, the system returns to the A stack and continues processing. C jobs may be processed only once a day. Other systems that have access to due date information will keep a long job waiting until its SLACK is zero or its due date is within a certain range.

2. ***Use SLACK for periods of normal activity.*** When capacity is not severely restrained, a SLACK-oriented rule that takes into account both due date and processing time will produce good results.
3. ***Use DDATE when only small tardiness values can be tolerated.*** DDATE tends to minimize mean tardiness and maximum tardiness. Although more jobs will be tardy under DDATE than SPT, the degree of tardiness will be much less.
4. ***Use LPT if subcontracting is anticipated*** so that larger jobs are completed in-house, and smaller jobs are sent out as their due date draws near.
5. ***Use FCFS when operating at low-capacity levels.*** FCFS allows the shop to operate essentially without sequencing jobs. When the workload at a facility is light, any sequencing rule will do, and FCFS is certainly the easiest to apply.
6. ***Do not use SPT to sequence jobs that have to be assembled with other jobs at a later date.*** For assembly jobs, a sequencing rule that gives a common priority to the processing of different components in an assembly, such as *assembly DDATE*, produces a more effective schedule.

## MONITORING

In a job shop environment, where jobs follow different paths through the shop, visit many different machine centers, and compete for similar resources, it is not always easy to keep track of the status of a job. When jobs are first released to the shop, it is relatively easy to observe the queue that they join and predict when their initial operations might be completed. As the job progresses, however, or the shop becomes more congested, it becomes increasingly difficult to follow the job through the system. Competition for resources (resulting in long queues), machine breakdowns, quality problems, and setup requirements are just a few of the things that can delay a job's progress.

Shop paperwork, sometimes called a **work package**, travels with a job to specify what work needs to be done at a particular work center and where the item should be routed next. Workers are usually required to sign off on a job, indicating the work they have performed either manually on the work package or electronically through a PC located on the shop floor. Bar code technology and RFID tags have made this task easier by eliminating much of the tedium and errors of entering the information by computer keyboard. In its simplest form, the bar code is attached to the work package, which the worker reads with a wand at the beginning and end of his or her work on the job. In other cases, an RFID tag is attached to the pallet or crate that carries the items from work center to work center. The tag is read automatically as it enters and leaves the work area. The time a worker spends on each job, the results of quality checks or inspections, and the utilization of resources can also be recorded in a similar fashion.

**Work package:** shop paperwork that travels with a job.

For the information gathered at each work center to be valuable, it must be up-to-date, accurate, and accessible to operations personnel. The monitoring function performed by production control takes this information and transforms it into various reports for workers and managers to use. Progress reports can be generated to show the status of individual jobs, the availability or utilization of certain resources, and the performance of individual workers or work centers. Exception reports may be generated to highlight deficiencies in certain areas, such as scrap, rework, shortages, anticipated delays, and unfilled orders. *Hot lists* show which jobs receive the highest priority and must be done immediately. A well-run facility will produce fewer *exception reports* and more *progress reports*. In the next two sections we describe two such progress reports, the Gantt chart and the input/output control chart.

**Figure 16.1**

**A Gantt Chart**

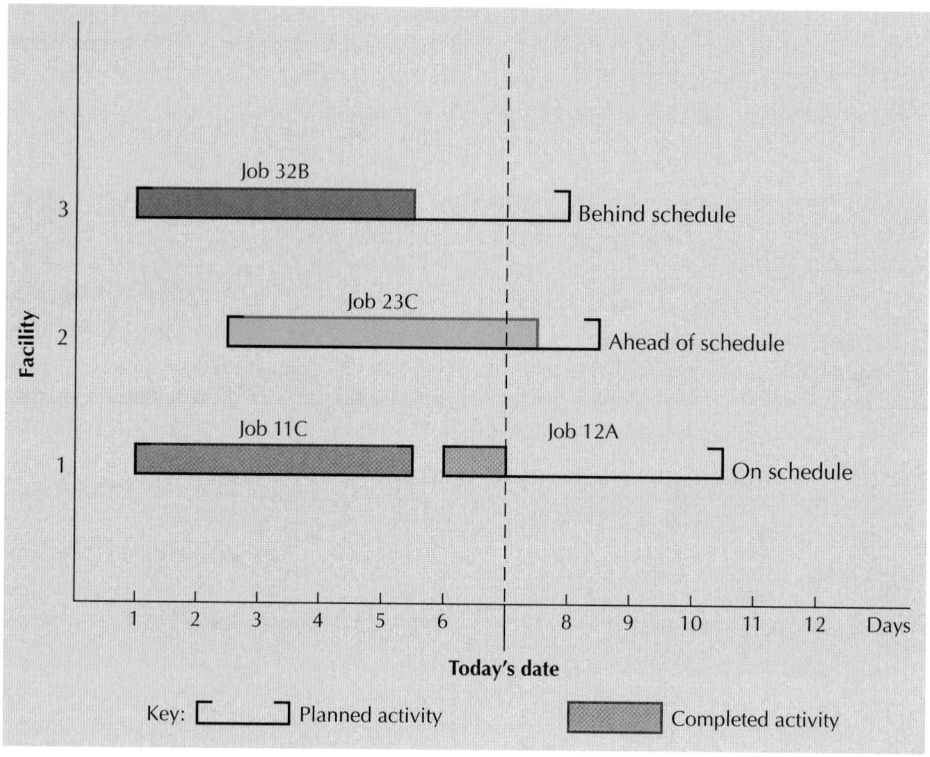


## GANTT CHARTS

**Gantt charts:** show both planned and completed activities against a time scale.

**Gantt charts**, used to plan or map out work activities, can also be used to monitor a job's progress against the plan. As shown in Figure 16.1, Gantt charts can display both planned and completed activities against a time scale. In this figure, the dashed line indicating today's date crosses over the schedules for job 12A, job 23C, and job 32B.

From the chart we can quickly see that job 12A is exactly on schedule because the bar monitoring its completion exactly meets the line for the current date. Job 23C is ahead of schedule and job 32B is behind schedule.

Gantt charts have been used since the early 1900s and are still popular today. They may be created and maintained by computer or by hand. In some facilities, Gantt charts consist of large scheduling boards (the size of several bulletin boards) with magnetic strips, pegs, or string of different colors that mark job schedules and job progress for the benefit of an entire plant. Gantt charts are a common feature of project management software, such as Microsoft Project.

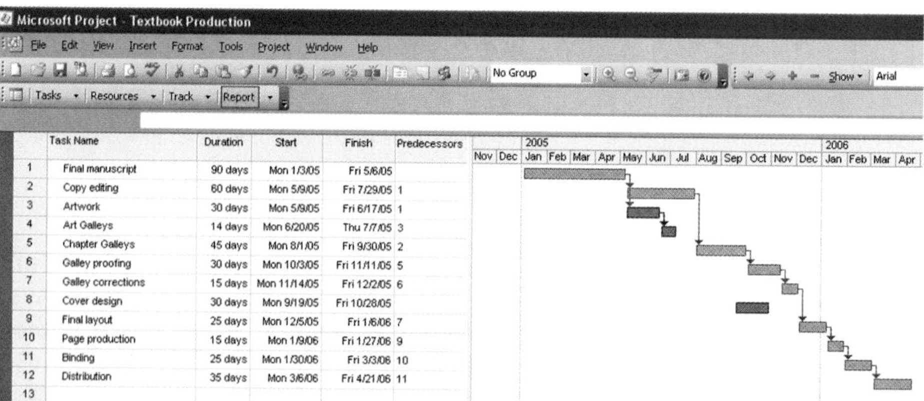


| | Task Name | Duration | Start | Finish | Predecessors |
|---|---|---|---|---|---|
| 1 | Final manuscript | 90 days | Mon 1/3/05 | Fri 5/6/05 | |
| 2 | Copy editing | 60 days | Mon 5/9/05 | Fri 7/29/05 | 1 |
| 3 | Artwork | 30 days | Mon 5/9/05 | Fri 6/17/05 | 1 |
| 4 | Art Galleys | 14 days | Mon 6/20/05 | Thu 7/7/05 | 3 |
| 5 | Chapter Galleys | 45 days | Mon 8/1/05 | Fri 9/30/05 | 2 |
| 6 | Galley proofing | 30 days | Mon 10/3/05 | Fri 11/11/05 | 5 |
| 7 | Galley corrections | 15 days | Mon 11/14/05 | Fri 12/2/05 | 6 |
| 8 | Cover design | 30 days | Mon 9/19/05 | Fri 10/28/05 | |
| 9 | Final layout | 25 days | Mon 12/5/05 | Fri 1/6/06 | 7 |
| 10 | Page production | 15 days | Mon 1/9/06 | Fri 1/27/06 | 9 |
| 11 | Binding | 25 days | Mon 1/30/06 | Fri 3/3/06 | 10 |
| 12 | Distribution | 35 days | Mon 3/6/06 | Fri 4/21/06 | 11 |
| 13 | | | | | |

*Gantt charts have been used for more than 75 years to plan and monitor schedules. Today Gantt charts are more widely used than ever, often as part of the action plan from a quality-improvement team. In some factories, Gantt charts appear on large magnetic boards, displaying the plant's daily progress for everyone to see. Computerized versions chart time, resources, and precedence requirements in an easy-to-read visual format. This Gantt chart is for publishing a textbook.*

## INPUT/OUTPUT CONTROL

**Input/output (I/O) control** monitors the input to and output from each work center. Prior to such analysis, it was common to examine only the output from a work center and to compare the actual output with the output planned in the shop schedule. Using that approach in a job shop environment in which the performance of different work centers is interrelated may result in erroneous conclusions about the source of a problem. Reduced output at one point in the production process may be caused by problems at the current work center, but it may also be caused by problems at previous work centers that *feed* the current work center. Thus, to identify more clearly the source of a problem, the *input* to a work center must be compared with the *planned input*, and the *output* must be compared with the *planned output*. Deviations between planned and actual values are calculated, and their cumulative effects are observed. The resulting backlog or waiting line of work to be completed is monitored to ensure that it stays within a manageable range.

**I/O control:** monitors the input and output from each work center.

The input rate to a work center can be controlled only for the initial operations of a job. These first work centers are often called *gateway* work centers, because the majority of jobs must pass through them before subsequent operations are performed. Input to later operations, performed at *downstream* work centers, is difficult to control because it is a function of how well the rest of the shop is operating—that is, where queues are forming and how smoothly jobs are progressing through the system. The deviation of planned to actual input for downstream work centers can be minimized by controlling the output rates of feeding work centers. The use of input/output reports can best be illustrated with an example.

**Example 16.4**
**Input/Output Control**

Hall Industries has begun input/output planning for its work centers. Below are the planned inputs and outputs for Work Center 5.

a. If production proceeds as planned, what will be the backlog at the end of period 4?
b. If actual input values are 60, 60, 65, 65 for periods 1 through 4, respectively, and output values cannot exceed 75, how much output can be expected from Work Center 5?
c. Is there a problem with production at Work Center 5?

*Input/Output Report for Work Center 5*

| Period | | 1 | 2 | 3 | 4 | Total |
|---|---|---|---|---|---|---|
| Planned input | | 65 | 65 | 70 | 70 | 270 |
| Actual input | | | | | | 0 |
| Deviation | | | | | | 0 |
| Planned output | | 75 | 75 | 75 | 75 | 300 |
| Actual output | | | | | | 0 |
| Deviation | | | | | | 0 |
| Backlog | 30 | | | | | |

*Solution*

a.

| Period | | 1 | 2 | 3 | 4 | Total |
|---|---|---|---|---|---|---|
| Planned input | | 65 | 65 | 70 | 70 | 270 |
| Actual input | | | | | | 0 |
| Deviation | | | | | | 0 |
| Planned output | | 75 | 75 | 75 | 75 | 300 |
| Actual output | | | | | | 0 |
| Deviation | | | | | | 0 |
| Backlog | 30 | 20 | 10 | 5 | 0 | |

If everything goes as planned, the backlog will be zero by period 4.

b.

| Period | | 1 | 2 | 3 | 4 | Total |
|---|---|---|---|---|---|---|
| Planned input | | 65 | 65 | 70 | 70 | 270 |
| Actual input | | 60 | 60 | 65 | 65 | 250 |
| Deviation | | −5 | −5 | −5 | −5 | −20 |
| Planned output | | 75 | 75 | 75 | 75 | 300 |
| Actual output | | 75 | 75 | 65 | 65 | 280 |
| Deviation | | 0 | 0 | −10 | −10 | −20 |
| Backlog | 30 | 15 | 0 | 0 | 0 | |

With the reduced input, the backlog is worked off sooner, but the total production cannot keep pace with what was planned.

c. Although Work Center 5 has produced only 280 units instead of the planned 300, the problem appears to be with the process that feeds Work Center 5. Notice the deviations from planned are the same for both the input and output values. An Excel solution to this example is shown in Exhibit 16.4.

Input/output control provides the information necessary to regulate the flow of work to and from a network of work centers. Increasing the capacity of a work center that is processing all the work available to it will not increase output. The source of the problem needs to be identified. Excessive queues, or *backlogs*, are one indication that *bottlenecks* exist. To alleviate bottleneck work centers, the problem causing the backlog can be worked on, the capacity of the work center can be adjusted, or input to the work center can be reduced. Increasing the input to a bottleneck work center will not increase the center's output. It will merely clog the system further and create longer queues of work-in-process.

Exhibit 16.4

**Using Excel for Input/Output Control**

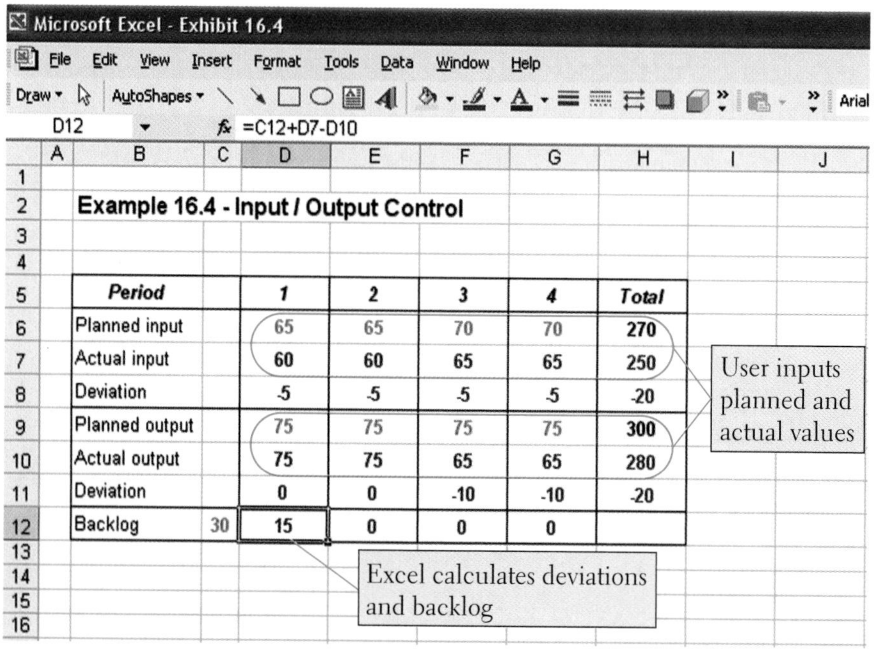

Microsoft Excel - Exhibit 16.4

D12 =C12+D7-D10

Example 16.4 - Input / Output Control

| Period | | 1 | 2 | 3 | 4 | Total |
|---|---|---|---|---|---|---|
| Planned input | | 65 | 65 | 70 | 70 | 270 |
| Actual input | | 60 | 60 | 65 | 65 | 250 |
| Deviation | | -5 | -5 | -5 | -5 | -20 |
| Planned output | | 75 | 75 | 75 | 75 | 300 |
| Actual output | | 75 | 75 | 65 | 65 | 280 |
| Deviation | | 0 | 0 | -10 | -10 | -20 |
| Backlog | 30 | 15 | 0 | 0 | 0 | |

User inputs planned and actual values

Excel calculates deviations and backlog

***Margie Deck***
***Plant Manager***

I began working for a manufacturing company as a third-shift supervisor 15 years ago, straight out of grad school. I had no desire to work in a factory and just took the job to gain what I thought would be useful experience for pursuing a career in Human Resources. But I loved it from the start—manufacturing is fast-paced and exciting. There are deadlines to meet and real work to be done. No sitting behind a computer all day writing reports. Nothing is routine. We are always trying to get work done better or faster or cheaper than before. Our customers are demanding, and so are our stockholders.

We make engine bearings at this plant—lots of them, 88 million bearings a year—for a total of six customers in the automotive and industrial machinery industry. We use so many of the things you learn in an operations class—scheduling, lean production, theory of constraints, and tons of quality tools, like Pareto charts, root cause analysis, process improvement teams, and SPC. Quality and safety are our biggest concerns. You'll hear your professor talk about six sigma quality. Well, *our* defect rate is even better, at 2 parts per million. But if even one bad part goes to a customer's plant, it could cause a line shutdown and we'd be charged $500 a minute until the line is up and running again!

We have a very close relationship with our customers. They each have their own personality and ways of doing business. These are longstanding customers. If we get the bid for an engine program, we have it for the life of the product. The contract might say that we should be capable of producing 100,000 bearings per day. We'll be given a three-month forecast of usage that we use for manpower planning, and a two-week forecast for material planning. But day-to-day usage can vary significantly. Every morning at 2 A.M. our customers send us their orders for the day and tell us when a truck will be arriving to pick them up. We check the EDI system when we get in and start to work putting together the day's schedule. There's always a challenge, always something new.

## ADVANCED PLANNING AND SCHEDULING SYSTEMS

The process for scheduling that we have described thus far in this chapter, loading work into work centers, leveling the load, sequencing the work, and monitoring its progress, is called **infinite scheduling**. The term *infinite* is used because the initial loading process assumes infinite capacity. Leveling and sequencing decisions are made after overloads or underloads have been identified. This iterative process is time-consuming and not very efficient.

**Infinite scheduling:** loads without regard to capacity, then levels the load and sequences the jobs.

An alternative approach to scheduling called **finite scheduling** assumes a fixed maximum capacity and will not load the resource beyond its capacity. Loading and sequencing decisions are made at the same time, so that the first jobs loaded onto a work center are of highest priority. Any jobs remaining after the capacity of the work center or resource has been reached are of lower priority and are scheduled for later time periods. This approach is easier than the infinite scheduling approach, but it will be successful only if the criteria for choosing the work to be performed, as well as capacity limitations, can be expressed accurately and concisely.

**Finite scheduling:** sequences jobs as part of the loading decision. Resources are never loaded beyond capacity.

Finite scheduling systems use a variety of methods to develop their schedules, including mathematical programming, network analysis, simulation, constraint-based programming, genetic algorithms, neural networks, and expert systems. Because the scheduling system, not the human scheduler, makes most of the decisions, considerable time is spent incorporating the special characteristics and requirements of the production system into the database and knowledge base of the scheduling software. While some companies will develop their own finite scheduling software, most will purchase generic or industry-specific scheduling software as an add-on to their ERP system. This class of scheduling software, with libraries of algorithms and heuristics from which to choose, has become known as **advanced planning and scheduling (APS)**. SAP's APS system is called the Advanced Planner and Optimizer (APO), and i2 Technologies' is called Factory Planner. These systems also support collaborative planning and scheduling with trading partners. Both APO and Factory Planner use constraint-based programming and genetic algorithms to develop schedules. Figure 16.2 applies these techniques to sequence a set of jobs so that setup time is minimized.

**APS:** a software system that uses intelligent analytical tools and techniques to develop realistic schedules.

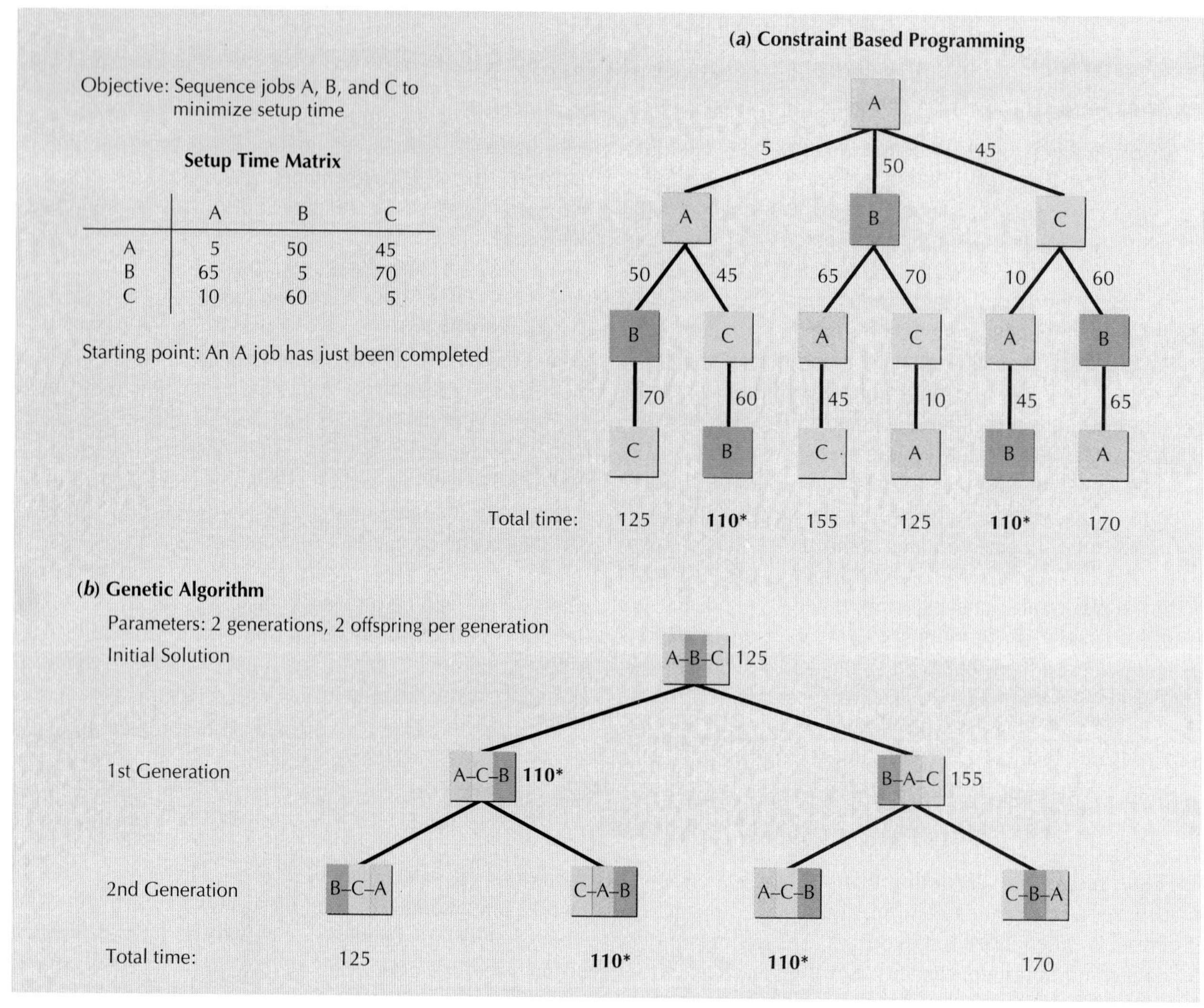


**Figure 16.2**

**Advanced Planning and Scheduling Techniques**

Source: SAP AG, *Advanced Planner and Optimizer*, company brochure, 1999.

**Genetic algorithm:** method that generates possible solutions based on genetic combinations of previous solutions.

**MES:** manufacturing software that monitors operations, collects data, and controls processes on the shop floor.

*Constraint-based programming* (CBP) identifies a solution space and then systematically evaluates possible solutions subject to constraints on the system. In scheduling, when one job or person is assigned, the options for additional job assignments are reduced or further constrained. This cascading effect on the remaining jobs to be scheduled is called *constraint propagation*. In part (a) of Figure 16.2, all possible sequences are evaluated, with A-C-B and C-A-B yielding the best solutions.

**Genetic algorithms** are based on the natural selection properties of genetics. Starting from a feasible solution, alternative solutions or "offspring" are generated with slightly different characteristics. These are evaluated against an objective function and compared to subsequent solutions. The number of generations and number of offspring per generation are specified by the user. In this example, two generations are produced with two offspring per generation. That's more than enough offspring to try all possible combinations. Again, A-C-B and C-A-B are identified as optimal sequences.

As schedules are executed, another type of software, aptly named a **manufacturing execution system** (MES), monitors work status, machine status, material usage and availability, and quality data. Alerts are sent to the APS system that shop conditions have changed and a scheduling revision is required.

Scheduling problems can be enormous in size, especially as the number of product options proliferate and linked schedules along a supply chain are considered. Some relief has come from the availability of more powerful computers and the use of artificial intelligence techniques. But the biggest impact has come from altered views of the production system. By grouping parts or products into families and scheduling bottleneck resources first, the scheduling problem is sufficiently reduced so that sophisticated solutions are feasible. In the next section, we present a common precept of today's scheduling systems, the *theory of constraints*.

## THE COMPETITIVE EDGE

### Scheduling—More Important than Ever

Customer behavior is changing. Build-to-order products, heightened expectations of fast delivery, and changing product designs have prompted an increase in the frequency of customer orders and a decrease in the number of items per order. For manufacturers, that means producing in smaller lots and changing over lines more often. To remain profitable, companies must understand the real constraints and cost tradeoffs of their systems. And scheduling those systems efficiently is more important than ever.

Sauder Woodworking makes ready-to-assemble furniture for large retailers such as Home Depot, Sears, and Wal-Mart. The company used to resolve its scheduling conflicts manually, but now it uses a manufacturing execution system (MES) from SynQuest to identify bottlenecks, monitor orders, and juggle the schedule. For example, in an order for 1500 entertainment centers, cabinet doors must arrive at the packaging station at a certain time. If the doors are delayed, there's a problem. The MES will recommend whether to assemble a limited number of entertainment centers, work on another order, or schedule overtime. It will also slow down production of the shelves that are added after the cabinet doors. Sauder has found that the new scheduling system helps keep the company competitive. In an e-business environment, if Sauder can't meet deadlines, its customers will find someone who will.

Bayliner Yachts assembles 33-foot to 56-foot yachts on seven separate assembly lines. Each yacht takes up to 60 days to assemble. On any given day the shop may have 38 boats in process. Bayliner's scheduling system, from Rockwell Software, coordinates the activities of several hundred people and millions of dollars of material. Hulls, decks, modules, assemblies, and small laminated parts feed each of the seven assembly lines. Two scheduling goals are spreading the workload out over the week and meeting the need for components with minimal inventory. The system also reallocates resources to address absenteeism, problems upstream, and in-process design changes. So far Bayliner has been able to achieve 100 percent on-time delivery with a six-figure reduction in work-in-process inventory.

*Source:* Jim Fulcher, "Inseparable Processes," *Manufacturing Systems* (February 2001), http://www.manufacturingsystems.com.

## THEORY OF CONSTRAINTS

In the 1970s, an Israeli physicist named Eliyahu Goldratt responded to a friend's request for help in scheduling his chicken coop business. Lacking a background in manufacturing or production theory, Dr. Goldratt took a commonsense, intuitive approach to the scheduling problem. He developed a software system that used mathematical programming and simulation to create a schedule that realistically considered the constraints of the manufacturing system. The software produced good schedules quickly and was marketed in the early 1980s in the United States. After more than 100 firms had successfully used the scheduling system (called OPT), the creator sold the rights to the software and began marketing the theory behind the software instead. He called his approach to scheduling the **theory of constraints** (TOC). General Motors and other manufacturers call its application *synchronous manufacturing*.

**Theory of constraints:** a finite scheduling approach that concentrates on scheduling the bottleneck resource.

Decision making in manufacturing is often difficult because of the size and complexity of the problems faced. Dr. Goldratt's first insight into the scheduling problem led him to simplify the number of variables considered. He learned early that manufacturing resources typically are not used evenly. Instead of trying to balance the capacity of the manufacturing system, he decided that most systems are inherently unbalanced and that he would try to balance the *flow* of work through the system instead. He identified resources as bottleneck or nonbottleneck and observed that the flow through the system is controlled by the bottleneck resource. This resource should always have material to work on, should spend as little time as possible on nonproductive activities (e.g., setups, waiting for work), should be fully staffed, and should be the focus of improvement or automation efforts. Goldratt pointed out that an hour's worth of production lost at a bottleneck reduces the output of the system by the same amount of time, whereas an hour lost at a nonbottleneck may have no effect on system output.

From this realization, Goldratt was able to simplify the scheduling problem significantly. He concentrated initially on scheduling production at the bottleneck resource and then scheduling the nonbottleneck resources to support the bottleneck activities. Thus, production is synchronized, or "in sync," with the needs of the bottleneck and the system as a whole.

## DRUM-BUFFER-ROPE

**Drum-buffer-rope:** the *drum* sets the pace for the production, a *buffer* is placed before the bottleneck, and a *rope* communicates changes.

To maintain this synchronization, Goldratt introduced the concept of **drum-buffer-rope (DBR)**. The *drum* is the bottleneck, beating to set the pace of production for the rest of the system. The *buffer* is inventory placed in front of the bottleneck to ensure it is always kept busy. This is necessary because output from the bottleneck determines the output or *throughput* of the system. The *rope* is the communication signal that tells the processes upstream from the bottleneck when they should begin production (similar to a kanban).

This idea of scheduling the bottleneck first and supporting its schedule with production at nonbottleneck operations is the basis for virtually all scheduling software on the market today.

## PROCESS VS. TRANSFER BATCH SIZES

Process batch sizes and transfer batch sizes do not have to match.

Goldratt's second insight into manufacturing concerned the concept of lot sizes or batch sizes. Goldratt saw no reason for fixed lot sizes. He differentiated between the quantity in which items are produced, called the *process batch*, and the quantity in which the items are transported, called the *transfer batch*. Ideally, items should be transferred in lot sizes of one. The process batch size for bottlenecks should be large, to eliminate the need for setups. The process batch size for nonbottlenecks can be small because time spent in setups for nonbottlenecks does not affect the rest of the system.

The TOC scheduling procedure, illustrated in Example 16.5, follows these steps:

1. Identify the bottleneck.
2. Schedule the job first whose lead time to the bottleneck is less than or equal to the bottleneck processing time.
3. Forward schedule the bottleneck machine.
4. Backward schedule the other machines to sustain the bottleneck schedule.
5. Transfer in batch sizes smaller than the process batch size.

**Example 16.5**
**Synchronous Manufacturing**

The following diagram contains the product structure, routing, and processing time information for product A. The process flows from the bottom of the diagram upward. Assume one unit of items B, C, and D are needed to make each A. The manufacture of each item requires three operations at machine centers 1, 2, or 3. Each machine center contains only one machine. A machine setup time of 60 minutes occurs whenever a machine is switched from one operation to another (within the same item or between items).

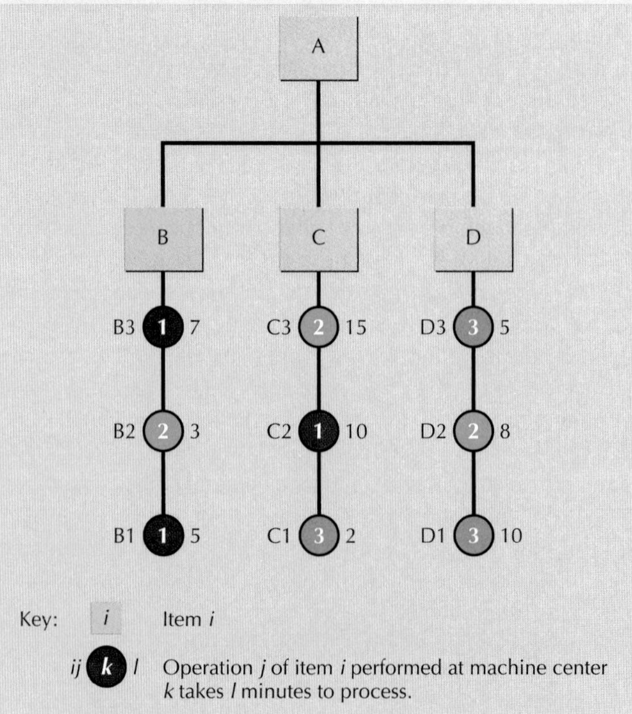

Design a schedule of production for each machine center that will produce 100 A's as quickly as possible. Show the schedule on a Gantt chart of each machine center.

*Solution*

The bottleneck machine is identified by summing the processing times of all operations to be performed at a machine.

| Machine 1 | | Machine 2 | | Machine 3 | |
|---|---|---|---|---|---|
| B1 | 5 | B2 | 3 | C1 | 2 |
| B3 | 7 | C3 | 15 | D3 | 5 |
| C2 | 10 | D2 | 8 | D1 | 10 |
| Sum | 22 | | 26* | | 17 |

*Bottleneck

- Machine 2 is identified as the bottleneck, so we schedule machine 2 first. From the product structure diagram, we see that three operations are performed at machine 2—B2, C3, and D2. If we schedule item B first, B will reach machine 2 every five minutes (since B has to be processed through machine 1 first), but each B takes only three minutes to process at machine 2, so the bottleneck will be idle for two minutes of every five minutes. A similar result occurs if we schedule item D first on machine 2. The bottleneck will be idle for two minutes of every ten until D has finished processing. The best alternative is to schedule item C first. The first C will not reach machine 2 until time 12, but after that the bottleneck machine will remain busy.

Identify the bottleneck.

- We begin our Gantt charts by processing item C through the three machine centers. As shown in Figure 16.3, the Gantt charts look different from our earlier examples because we allow each item to be transferred to the next operation immediately after it is completed at the current operation (i.e., the transfer batch size is 1). We will still process the items in batches of 100 to match our demand requirements. The shaded areas represent idle time between operations due to setup time requirements or because a feeding operation has not yet been completed.

Process in batches of 100; transfer one-at-a-time.

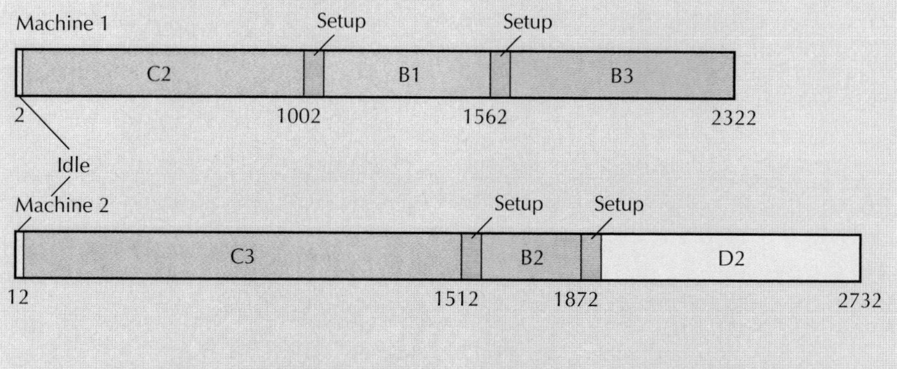


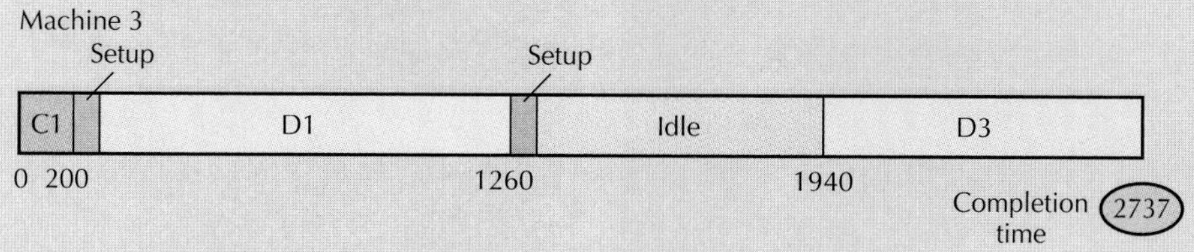


Figure 16.3
**Gantt Chart Solution to Example 16.5**

- C3 is completed at machine center 2 at time 1512. After setup, it is ready for a new item at time 1572. We have a choice between B2 and D2, since both B1 and D1 can be completed by 1572. Completion time at machine center 2 will be the same regardless of whether B2 or D2 is processed first; however, the completion time at the other machine centers (and thus for product A) will be affected by the bottleneck sequence. From the product structure diagram, we note that B3 can be completed more

Sustain the bottleneck.

quickly than D3 because D3 must wait three minutes for D2 to be completed, whereas B3 will always have a queue of items from B2 to work on. Thus, we schedule B2 and then D2 on machine center 2.

Sequence the other machines to support the bottleneck sequence.

- With the bottleneck sequence of C3, B2, D2 established, we can now schedule machine center 1 (C2, B1, B3) and machine center 3 (C1, D1, D3) in the same general order as the bottleneck sequence. The completion time for producing 100 A's is 2737 minutes. The total idle time at the three machine centers is 980 minutes.

## EMPLOYEE SCHEDULING

Employee scheduling has lots of options because labor is a very flexible resource.

Labor is one of the most flexible resources. Workers can be hired and fired more easily than equipment can be purchased or sold. Labor-limited systems can expand capacity through overtime, expanded workweeks, extra shifts, or part-time workers. This flexibility is valuable but it tends to make scheduling difficult. Service firms especially spend an inordinate amount of time developing employee schedules. A supervisor might spend an entire week making up the next month's employee schedule. The task becomes even more daunting for facilities that operate on a 24-hour basis with multiple shifts.

The assignment method of linear programming discussed earlier in this chapter can be used to assign workers with different performance ratings to available jobs. Large-scale linear programming is currently used by McDonald's to schedule its large part-time workforce. American Airlines uses a combination of integer linear programming and expert systems for scheduling ticket agents to coincide with peak and slack demand periods and for the complicated scheduling of flight crews. Although mathematical programming certainly has found application in employee scheduling, most scheduling problems are solved

*Scheduling employees, especially part-time workers, can take considerable time and effort. Most employers develop weekly or monthly schedules by hand, trying to balance the needs of employees, supervisors, and customers. One way to avoid the headaches of employee scheduling and improve customer responsiveness is to automate. That's what the banking industry did with ATMs that operate 24 hours a day. Now maintenance activities must be scheduled to ensure that the facility is available to the customer as promised!*

by heuristics (i.e., rules of thumb) that develop a repeating pattern of work assignments. Often heuristics are imbedded in a decision support system to facilitate their use and increase their flexibility. One such heuristic[1] used for scheduling full-time workers with two days off per week, is given next.

*Employee Scheduling Heuristic*:

1. Let $N$ = no. of workers available
   $D_i$ = demand for workers on day $i$
   X = day working
   O = day off
2. Assign the first $N - D_1$ workers day 1 off. Assign the next $N - D_2$ workers day 2 off. Continue in a similar manner until all days have been scheduled.
3. If the number of workdays for a full-time employee is less than 5, assign the remaining workdays so that consecutive days off are possible or where unmet demand is highest.
4. Assign any remaining work to part-time employees, subject to maximum hour restrictions.
5. If consecutive days off are desired, consider switching schedules among days with the same demand requirements.

**Example 16.6**

**Employee Scheduling**

Diet-Tech employs five workers to operate its weight-reduction facility. Demand for service each week (in terms of minimum number of workers required) is given in the following table. Create an employee schedule that will meet the demand requirements and guarantee each worker two days off per week.

| Day of Week | M | T | W | Th | F | Sa | Su |
|---|---|---|---|---|---|---|---|
| No. of Workers | 3 | 3 | 4 | 3 | 4 | 5 | 3 |
| Taylor | | | | | | | |
| Smith | | | | | | | |
| Simpson | | | | | | | |
| Allen | | | | | | | |
| Dickerson | | | | | | | |

*Solution*

The completed employee schedule matrix is shown next.

| Day of Week | M | T | W | Th | F | Sa | Su |
|---|---|---|---|---|---|---|---|
| No. of Workers | 3 | 3 | 4 | 3 | 4 | 5 | 3 |
| Taylor | O | X | X | O | X | X | X |
| Smith | O | X | X | O | X | X | X |
| Simpson | X | O | X | X | O | X | X |
| Allen | X | O | X | X | X | X | O |
| Dickerson | X | X | O | X | X | X | O |

Following the heuristic, the first (5 − 3) = 2 workers, Taylor and Smith, are assigned Monday off. The next (5 − 3) = 2 workers, Simpson and Allen, are assigned Tuesday off. The next (5 − 4) = 1 worker, Dickerson, is assigned Wednesday off. Returning to the top of the roster, the next (5 − 3) = 2 workers, Taylor and Smith, are assigned Thursday off. The next (5 − 4) = 1 worker, Simpson, is assigned Friday off. Everyone works on Saturday, and the next (5 − 3) = 2 workers, Allen and Dickerson, get Sunday off.

[1] Kenneth R. Baker and Michael J. Magazine, "Workforce Scheduling with Cyclic Demands and Days-off Constraints." *Management Science* 24(2; October 1977), pp. 161–167.

The resulting schedule meets demand and has every employee working 5 days a week with 2 days off. Unfortunately, none of the days off are consecutive. By switching the initial schedules for Tuesday and Thursday (both with a demand of 3) and the schedules for Wednesday and Friday (both with a demand of 4), the following schedule results:

| Day of Week | M | T | W | Th | F | Sa | Su |
|---|---|---|---|---|---|---|---|
| **No. of Workers** | **3** | **3** | **4** | **3** | **4** | **5** | **3** |
| Taylor | O | O | X | X | X | X | X |
| Smith | O | O | X | X | X | X | X |
| Simpson | X | X | O | O | X | X | X |
| Allen | X | X | X | O | X | X | O |
| Dickerson | X | X | X | X | O | X | O |

In this revised schedule, the first three workers have consecutive days off. The last two workers have one weekend day off and one day off during the week.

The heuristic just illustrated can be adapted to ensure that the two days off per week are consecutive. Other heuristics schedule workers two weeks at a time, with every other weekend off.

## AUTOMATED SCHEDULING SYSTEMS

Scheduling large numbers of workers at numerous locations requires a computerized scheduling system. Sophisticated employee scheduling software is available as a stand-alone system or as part of an ERP package. These systems usually provide:[2]

- **Staff Scheduling** assigns qualified workers to standardize shift patterns taking into account leave requests and scheduling conflicts. The solutions include social constraints such as labor laws for minors, overtime payment regulations, and holidays or religious holidays that may differ by global location.
- **Schedule Bidding** puts certain shift positions or schedule assignments up for bid by workers; allows workers to post and trade schedules with others as long as coverage and skill criteria are met.
- **Schedule Optimization** creates demand-driven forecasts of labor requirements and assigns workers to variable schedules (in some cases, as small as 15 minutes blocks of time) that change dynamically with demand. Uses mathematical programming and artificial intelligence techniques.

## SUMMARY

Scheduling techniques vary by type of production process. Scheduling in a job shop environment is difficult because jobs arrive at varying time intervals, require different resources and sequences of operations, and are due at different times. This lowest level of scheduling is referred to as *shop floor control* or *production control*. It involves assigning jobs to machines or workers (called loading), specifying the order in which operations are to be performed, and monitoring the work as it progresses. Techniques such as the assignment method are used for *loading*, various rules whose performance varies according to the scheduling objective are used for *sequencing*, and Gantt charts and input/output control charts are used for *monitoring*.

Realistic schedules must reflect capacity limitations. *Infinite scheduling* initially assumes infinite capacity and then manually "levels the load" of resources that have exceeded capacity. *Finite scheduling* loads jobs in priority order and delays those jobs for which current capacity is exceeded. The *theory of constraints* is a finite scheduling approach that schedules bottleneck resources first and then schedules other resources to support the bottleneck schedule. It also allows items to be transferred between resources in lot sizes that differ from the lot size in which the item is produced. Other advanced planning and scheduling techniques include mathematical programming, genetic algorithms, and simulation.

Employee scheduling is often difficult because of the variety of options available and the special requirements for individual workers. Scheduling heuristics are typically used to develop patterns of worker assignment. Automated workforce scheduling systems are becoming more commonplace.

[2]These examples are from Workbrain, an enterprise workforce management system. See www.workbrain.com.

## SUMMARY OF KEY FORMULAS

*Minimum Slack*

SLACK = (due date − today's date) − (processing time)

*Critical Ratio*

$$CR = \frac{\text{time remaining}}{\text{work remaining}} = \frac{\text{due date} - \text{today's date}}{\text{remaining processing time}}$$

## SUMMARY OF KEY TERMS

**advanced planning and scheduling (APS)** a software system that uses intelligent analytical tools and techniques to develop realistic schedules.

**dispatch list** a shop paper that specifies the sequence in which jobs should be processed; it is often derived from specific sequencing rules.

**drum-buffer-rope** a concept in theory of constraints where the *drum* sets the pace of production, *buffer* is placed in front of the bottleneck, and *rope* communicates changes.

**finite scheduling** an approach to scheduling that loads jobs in priority order and delays those jobs for which current capacity is exceeded.

**flow time** the time that it takes for a job to "flow" through the system; that is, its completion time.

**Gantt chart** a bar chart that shows a job's progress graphically or compares actual against planned performance.

**genetic algorithms** a method that generates possible solutions based on genetic combinations of previous solutions.

**infinite scheduling** an approach to scheduling that initially assumes infinite capacity and then manually "levels the load" of resources that have exceeded capacity.

**input/output (I/O) control** a procedure for monitoring the input to and output from a work center to regulate the flow of work through a system.

**Johnson's rule** an algorithm for sequencing any number of jobs through two serial operations to minimize makespan.

**load leveling** the process of smoothing out the work assigned across time and the available resources.

**loading** the process of assigning work to individual workers or machines.

**makespan** the time that it takes for a group of jobs to be completed—that is, the completion time of the last job in a group.

**manufacturing execution systems (MES)** manufacturing software that monitors operations, collects data, and controls processes on the shop floor.

**scheduling** the determination of *when* labor, equipment, and facilities are needed to produce a product or provide a service.

**sequencing** the process of assigning priorities to jobs so that they are processed in a particular order.

**shop floor control (SFC)** scheduling and monitoring day-to-day production in a job shop; also known as production control or production activity control.

**tardiness** the difference between a job's due date and its completion time for jobs completed after their due date.

**theory of constraints** a finite scheduling approach that differentiates between bottleneck and nonbottleneck resources and between transfer batches and process batches.

**work package** shop paperwork that travels with a job to specify what work needs to be done at a particular machine center and where the item should be routed next.

## SOLVED PROBLEMS

### 1. ASSIGNMENT PROBLEM

Wilkerson Printing has four jobs waiting to be run this morning. Fortunately, they have four printing presses available. However, the presses are of different vintage and operate at different speeds. The approximate times (in minutes) required to process each job on each press are given next. Assign jobs to presses to minimize the press running times.

| | PRESS | | | |
|---|---|---|---|---|
| JOB | *1* | *2* | *3* | *4* |
| A | 20 | 90 | 40 | 10 |
| B | 40 | 45 | 50 | 35 |
| C | 30 | 70 | 35 | 25 |
| D | 60 | 45 | 70 | 40 |

### SOLUTION

Row reduction:

| | | | |
|---|---|---|---|
| 10 | 80 | 30 | 0 |
| 5 | 10 | 15 | 0 |
| 5 | 45 | 10 | 0 |
| 20 | 5 | 30 | 0 |

Column reduction:

| | | | |
|---|---|---|---|
| 5 | 75 | 20 | 0 |
| 0 | 5 | 5 | 0 |
| 0 | 40 | 0 | 0 |
| 15 | 0 | 20 | 0 |

Cover all zeroes:

| | | | |
|---|---|---|---|
| 5 | 75 | 20 | 0 |
| 0 | 5 | 5 | 0 |
| 0 | 40 | 0 | 0 |
| 15 | 0 | 20 | 0 |

The number of lines equals the number of rows, so this is the final solution. Make assignments:

| | | | |
|---|---|---|---|
| 5 | 75 | 20 | **0** |
| **0** | 5 | 5 | 0 |
| 0 | 40 | **0** | 0 |
| 15 | **0** | 20 | 0 |

Assign job A to press 4, job B to press 1, job C to press 3, and job D to press 2. Refer to the original matrix for actual processing times. The total machining time required is $(10 + 40 + 35 + 45) = 130$ minutes.

### 2. JOHNSON'S RULE

Clean and Shine Car Service has five cars waiting to be washed and waxed. The time required (in minutes) for each activity is given next. In what order should the cars be processed through the facility? When will the batch of cars be completed?

| CAR | WASH | WAX |
|---|---|---|
| 1 | 5 | 10 |
| 2 | 7 | 2 |
| 3 | 10 | 5 |
| 4 | 8 | 6 |
| 5 | 3 | 5 |

**SOLUTION**

Use Johnson's rule to sequence the cars. The lowest processing time is two minutes for waxing car 2. Since waxing is the second operation, we place car 2 as near to the end of the sequence as possible, in last place. The next-lowest time is three minutes for washing car 5. Since washing is the first operation, we place car 5 as near to the front of the sequence as possible, in first place. The next-lowest time is five minutes for washing car 1 and waxing car 3. Car 1 is scheduled in second place, and car 3 is put in next-to-last place (i.e., fourth). That leaves car 4 for third place.

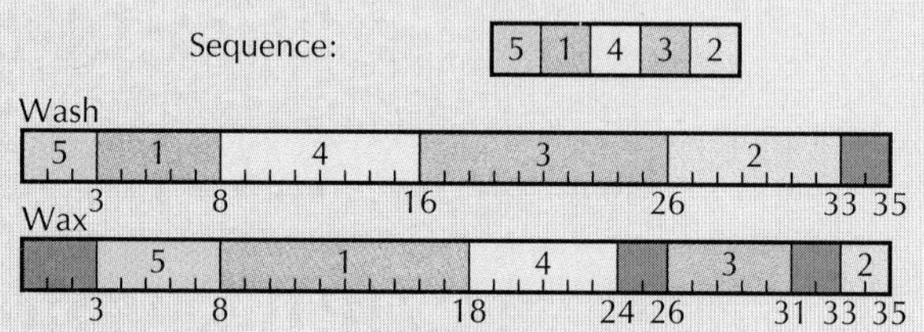


The completion time for washing and waxing the five cars is 35 minutes. The washing facility is idle for two minutes at the end of the cycle. The waxing facility is idle for three minutes at the beginning of the cycle and four minutes during the cycle.

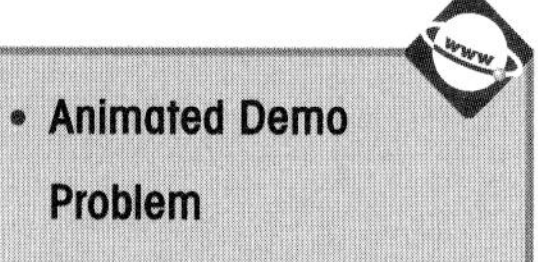


## QUESTIONS

**16-1.** How do scheduling activities differ for projects, mass production, and process industries?

**16-2.** Why is scheduling a job shop so difficult?

**16-3.** What three functions are typically performed by a production control department?

**16-4.** Give examples of four types of operations (manufacturing or service) and suggest which scheduling objectives might be appropriate for each.

**16-5.** How can the success of a scheduling system be measured?

**16-6.** Describe the process of loading and load leveling. What quantitative techniques are available to help in this process?

**16-7.** What is the purpose of dispatch lists? How are they usually constructed?

**16-8.** When should the following sequencing rules be used? (a) SPT; (b) Johnson's rule; (c) DDATE; (d) FCFS.

**16-9.** Give examples of sequencing rules you use to prioritize work.

**16-10.** What information is provided by the critical ratio sequencing rule? How does it differ from SLACK?

**16-11.** How are work packages, hot lists, and exception reports used in a job shop?

**16-12.** What are Gantt charts, and why are they used so often?

**16-13.** Explain the concept behind input/output control. Describe how gateway work centers, downstream work centers, and backlogs affect shop performance.

**16-14.** Explain the difference between infinite and finite scheduling.

**16-15.** How does theory of constraints differ from traditional scheduling? How should bottleneck resources and nonbottleneck resources be scheduled? Why should transfer batches and process batches be treated differently?

**16-16.** Explain the drum-buffer-rope concept.

**16-17.** Discuss the similarities and differences between theory of constraints and lean production.

**16-18.** What are some typical issues involved in employee scheduling?

**16-19.** What quantitative techniques are available to help develop employee schedules? What quantitative techniques are available for advanced planning and scheduling systems?

**16-20.** Look for advanced planning and scheduling software on the Internet. Write a summary of the techniques presented.

## PROBLEMS

**16-1.** At Valley Hospital, nurses beginning a new shift report to a central area to receive their primary patient assignments. Not every nurse is as efficient as another with particular kinds of patients. Given the following patient roster, care levels, and time estimates, assign nurses to patients to optimize efficiency. Also, determine how long it will take for the nurses to complete their routine tasks on this shift.

| | | Time Required (Hours) to Complete Routine Tasks | | | |
|---|---|---|---|---|---|
| **Patient** | **Care Level** | *Nurse 1* | *Nurse 2* | *Nurse 3* | *Nurse 4* |
| A. Jones | A2 | 3 | 5 | 4 | 3 |
| B. Hathaway | B2 | 2 | 1 | 3 | 2 |
| C. Bryant | B1 | 3 | 4 | 2 | 2 |
| D. Sweeney | A1 | 4 | 3 | 3 | 4 |

**16-2.** Valley Hospital (from Problem 16-1) wants to focus on customer perceptions of quality, so it has asked its patients to evaluate the nursing staff and indicate preferences for assignment. Reassign the nursing staff to obtain the highest customer approval rating possible (a perfect score is 100).

| | Rating | | | |
|---|---|---|---|---|
| **Patient** | *Nurse 1* | *Nurse 2* | *Nurse 3* | *Nurse 4* |
| A. Jones | 89 | 95 | 83 | 84 |
| B. Hathaway | 88 | 80 | 96 | 85 |
| C. Bryant | 87 | 92 | 82 | 84 |
| D. Sweeney | 93 | 82 | 86 | 94 |

Compare the results with those from Problem 16-1. What is the average rating of the assignment? What other criteria could be used to assign nurses?

**16-3.** Fibrous Incorporated makes products from rough tree fibers. Its product line consists of five items processed through one of five machines. The machines are not identical, and some products are better suited to some machines. Given the following production time in minutes per unit, determine an optimal assignment of product to machine:

| | Machine | | | | |
|---|---|---|---|---|---|
| **Product** | *A* | *B* | *C* | *D* | *E* |
| 1 | 17 | 10 | 15 | 16 | 20 |
| 2 | 12 | 9 | 16 | 9 | 14 |
| 3 | 11 | 16 | 14 | 15 | 12 |
| 4 | 14 | 10 | 10 | 18 | 17 |
| 5 | 13 | 12 | 9 | 15 | 11 |

**16-4.** Sunshine House received a contract this year as a supplier of Girl Scout cookies. Sunshine currently has five production lines, each of which will be dedicated to a particular kind of cookie. The production lines differ by sophistication of machines, site, and experience of personnel. Given the following estimates of processing times (in hours), assign cookies to lines to minimize the sum of completion times:

| | Production Line | | | | |
|---|---|---|---|---|---|
| **Cookies** | *1* | *2* | *3* | *4* | *5* |
| Chocolate Mint | 30 | 18 | 26 | 17 | 15 |
| Peanut Butter | 23 | 22 | 32 | 25 | 30 |
| Shortbread | 17 | 31 | 24 | 22 | 29 |
| Fudge Delight | 28 | 19 | 13 | 18 | 23 |
| Macaroons | 23 | 14 | 16 | 20 | 27 |

**16-5.** Karina Nieto works for New Products Inc., and one of her many tasks is assigning new workers to departments. The company recently hired six new employees and would like each one to be assigned to a different department. The employees have completed a two month training session in each of the six departments from which they received the evaluations shown below (higher numbers are better). Determine how the new employees should be assigned to departments so that overall performance is maximized.

| | Departments | | | | | |
|---|---|---|---|---|---|---|
| **Employees** | **Sales** | **Finance** | **Logistics** | **Marketing Research** | **Production** | **Customer Service** |
| Albertson | 18 | 17 | 14 | 19 | 19 | 18 |
| Bunch | 17 | 15 | 12 | 14 | 20 | 17 |
| Carson | 15 | 15 | 13 | 17 | 20 | 18 |
| Denali | 19 | 16 | 18 | 18 | 18 | 20 |
| Ebersole | 18 | 15 | 12 | 17 | 19 | 17 |
| Finch | 16 | 16 | 16 | 18 | 20 | 17 |

**16-6.** Evan Schwartz has six jobs waiting to be processed through his machine. Processing time (in days) and due date information for each job are as follows:

| Job | Processing Time | Due Date |
|---|---|---|
| A | 2 | 3 |
| B | 1 | 2 |
| C | 4 | 12 |
| D | 3 | 4 |
| E | 4 | 8 |
| F | 5 | 10 |

Sequence the jobs by FCFS, SPT, SLACK, and DDATE. Calculate the mean flow time and mean tardiness of the six jobs under each sequencing rule. Which rule would you recommend?

**16-7.** College students always have a lot of work to do, but this semester, Katie Lawrence is overwhelmed. Following are the assignments she faces, the estimated completion times (in days), and due dates:

| Assignment | Estimated Completion Time | Due Date |
|---|---|---|
| 1. Management case | 5 | 11-20 |
| 2. Marketing survey | 10 | 12-3 |
| 3. Financial analysis | 4 | 11-25 |
| 4. Term project | 21 | 12-15 |
| 5. Computer program | 14 | 12-2 |

Help Katie prioritize her work so that she completes as many assignments on time as possible. Today is November 2. How would your sequence of assignments change if Katie were interested in minimizing the mean tardiness of her assignments?

**16-8.** Today is day 4 of the planning cycle. Sequence the following jobs by FCFS, SPT, SLACK, and DDATE. Calculate the mean flow time and mean tardiness for each sequencing rule. Which rule would you recommend?

| Job | Processing Time (in days) | Due Date |
|---|---|---|
| A | 3 | 10 |
| B | 10 | 12 |
| C | 2 | 25 |
| D | 4 | 8 |
| E | 5 | 15 |
| F | 8 | 18 |
| G | 7 | 20 |

**16-9.** Alice's Alterations has eight jobs to be completed and only one sewing machine (and sewing machine operator). Given the processing times and due dates as shown here, prioritize the jobs by SPT, DDATE, and SLACK. Today is day 5.

| Task | Processing Time (in days) | Due Date |
|---|---|---|
| A | 5 | 10 |
| B | 8 | 15 |
| C | 6 | 15 |
| D | 3 | 20 |
| E | 10 | 25 |
| F | 14 | 40 |
| G | 7 | 45 |
| H | 3 | 50 |

Calculate mean flow time, mean tardiness, maximum tardiness, and number of jobs tardy for each sequence. Which sequencing rule would you recommend? Why?

**16-10.** Jobs A, B, C, and D must be processed through the same machine center. Sequence the following jobs by (a) SPT and (b) SLACK. Calculate mean flow time, mean tardiness, and maximum tardiness. Which sequencing rule would you recommend? Why?

| Job | Processing Time | Due Date |
|---|---|---|
| A | 20 | 20 |
| B | 10 | 15 |
| C | 30 | 50 |
| D | 15 | 30 |

**16-11.** Sequence the following jobs by (a) SPT, (b) DDATE, and (c) SLACK. Calculate mean flow time, mean tardiness, and maximum tardiness. Which sequencing rule would you recommend? Why?

| Job | Processing Time | Due Date |
|---|---|---|
| A | 5 | 8 |
| B | 3 | 5 |
| C | 9 | 18 |
| D | 6 | 7 |

**16-12.** Claims received by Healthwise Insurance Company are entered into the database at one station, and sent to another station for review. The processing time (in minutes) required for each general type of claim is shown here. Currently, Bill Frazier has 10 claims to be reviewed. In what order should he process the claims so that the entire batch can get into the system as soon as possible? How long will it take to process the 10 claims completely?

| Classification | Processing Time | |
|---|---|---|
| | Data Entry | Review |
| 1. Medicare I | 8 | 6 |
| 2. Physician 24 | 15 | 9 |
| 3. Medicare II | 6 | 5 |
| 4. Physician 4 | 5 | 10 |
| 5. HMO I | 17 | 15 |
| 6. Physician 17 | 9 | 10 |
| 7. Emergency II | 5 | 3 |
| 8. HMO II | 4 | 15 |
| 9. Physician 37 | 12 | 10 |
| 10. Emergency I | 20 | 4 |

**16-13.** Jobs processed through Percy's machine shop pass through three operations: milling, grinding, and turning. The hours required for each of these operations is as follows:

| Job | Milling | Grinding | Turning |
|---|---|---|---|
| A | 5 | 1 | 4 |
| B | 2 | 2 | 5 |
| C | 3 | 2 | 1 |
| D | 1 | 3 | 0 |
| E | 4 | 1 | 2 |

Sequence the job by (a) FCFS and (b) shortest processing time (SPT). Make a Gantt chart for each machine and each rule. Which sequencing rule would you recommend?

**16-14.** Given that all the jobs listed below must be machined first, then polished, determine a sequence that will minimize the time required to process all six jobs. Chart the schedule on a Gantt chart and indicate the makespan.

| Jobs | Machining | Polishing |
|---|---|---|
| A | 5.0 | 4.0 |
| B | 7.0 | 3.0 |
| C | 3.0 | 2.0 |
| D | 2.0 | 1.0 |
| E | 2.0 | 3.0 |
| F | 6.0 | 5.0 |

**16-15.** Precision Painters, Inc., has five house painting jobs in one neighborhood. The houses differ in size, state of repair, and painting requirements, but each house must be prepped (cleaned, old paint chipped off, primed) first, then painted. In what sequence should the houses be worked on in order to finish all five houses as soon as possible? Chart out your sequences on Gantt charts and calculate the makespan.

| | Days | |
|---|---|---|
| **Houses** | *Prep* | *Paint* |
| Addison | 4 | 2 |
| Brown | 3 | 6 |
| Clayton | 6 | 4 |
| Daniels | 5 | 6 |
| Ebersole | 1 | 4 |

**16-16.** Sequence the houses in Problem 16-15 by SPT and SLACK. How much time is saved with Johnson's rule?

**16-17.** Tracy has six chapters on her desk that must be typed and proofed as soon as possible. Tracy does the typing; the author does the proofing. Some chapters are easy to type but more difficult to proof. The estimated time (in minutes) for each activity is given here. In what order should Tracy type the chapters so that the entire batch can be finished as soon as possible? When will the chapters be completed?

| Chapter | Typing | Proofing |
|---|---|---|
| 1 | 30 | 20 |
| 2 | 90 | 25 |
| 3 | 60 | 15 |
| 4 | 45 | 30 |
| 5 | 75 | 60 |
| 6 | 20 | 30 |

**16-18.** Sara is throwing a long-awaited graduation party for her friend Claire. She thought it would be fun to have five different cakes to symbolize the different majors Claire has matriculated in over the past seven years. For each cake, Sara must mix and prepare the batter and then bake it in the oven. Using the following processing times below, determine the order in which Sara should prepare and bake the five cakes.

| | | Times (min) | |
|---|---|---|---|
| **College Major** | **Type of Cake** | **Preparing** | **Baking** |
| General Studies | Pound Cake | 15 | 40 |
| Health Care Administration | Carrot Cake | 25 | 45 |
| Hotel & Restaurant Management | Chocolate Mousse | 35 | 20 |
| Physical Education (Gymnastics) | Upside Down Cake | 20 | 30 |
| Theatre | N.Y. Cheese Cake | 30 | 60 |

**16-19.** The following data have been compiled for an input/output report at Work Center 7. Complete the report and analyze the results.

| Period | | 1 | 2 | 3 | 4 | 5 | Total |
|---|---|---|---|---|---|---|---|
| Planned input | | 50 | 55 | 60 | 65 | 65 | |
| Actual input | | 50 | 50 | 55 | 60 | 65 | |
| Deviation | | | | | | | |
| Planned output | | 65 | 65 | 65 | 65 | 65 | |
| Actual output | | 60 | 60 | 60 | 60 | 60 | |
| Deviation | | | | | | | |
| Backlog | 30 | | | | | | |

**16-20.** The input/output report for Work Center 6 is as follows. Complete the report and comment on the results.

| Period | | 1 | 2 | 3 | 4 | 5 | Total |
|---|---|---|---|---|---|---|---|
| Planned input | | 50 | 55 | 60 | 65 | 65 | |
| Actual input | | 40 | 50 | 55 | 60 | 65 | |
| Deviation | | | | | | | |
| Planned output | | 50 | 55 | 60 | 65 | 65 | |
| Actual output | | 50 | 50 | 55 | 60 | 65 | |
| Deviation | | | | | | | |
| Backlog | 10 | | | | | | |

**16-21.** Kim Johnson, R.N., the charge nurse of the antepartum ward of City Hospital in Burtonsville, Maryland, needs help in scheduling the nurse workforce for next week.

a. Create an employee schedule that will meet the demand requirements and guarantee each nurse two days off per week.

b. Revise the schedule so that the two days off are consecutive.

| Days of Week | M | T | W | Th | F | Sa | Su |
|---|---|---|---|---|---|---|---|
| No. of Nurses | 3 | 3 | 4 | 5 | 4 | 3 | 3 |
| Kim Johnson | | | | | | | |
| Tom Swann | | | | | | | |
| Flo Coligny | | | | | | | |
| Shelly Betts | | | | | | | |
| Phuong Truong | | | | | | | |

**16-22.** Rosemary Hanes needs help in scheduling the volunteers working at the local crisis pregnancy center. Create a work schedule that will meet the demand requirements, given that a volunteer will only work four days per week.

| Days of Week | M | T | W | Th | F | Sa | Su |
|---|---|---|---|---|---|---|---|
| Volunteers | 4 | 3 | 2 | 3 | 6 | 4 | 2 |
| Rosemary Hanes | | | | | | | |
| Albert Tagliero | | | | | | | |
| Richard White | | | | | | | |
| Gail Cooke | | | | | | | |
| Shelly Black | | | | | | | |
| Karen Romero | | | | | | | |

**16-23.** Schedule the wait staff at Vincent's Restaurant based on the following estimates of demand. Each employee should have two or more days off per week.

| Days of the Week | M | T | W | Th | F | Sa | Su |
|---|---|---|---|---|---|---|---|
| Employees Needed | 2 | 3 | 4 | 4 | 5 | 5 | 4 |
| Amy Russell | | | | | | | |
| Shannon Hiller | | | | | | | |
| Jessica Jones | | | | | | | |
| Tom Turner | | | | | | | |
| Evalin Trice | | | | | | | |
| Pierre Dubois | | | | | | | |

## CASE PROBLEM 16.1

### *From a Different Perspective*

"And do you have the answer to Problem 6, Pete?" asked Professor Grasso.

"Yes sir, I have the answer according to the textbook, but I'm not sure I get it," replied Pete.

"You don't understand how to get the solution?"

"Oh, I understand the numbers, but I don't know what they're good for. Where I work, nobody ever 'sequences' anything. You don't have time to calculate things like slack and critical ratio. You do what's next in line or on top of the stack, unless you see a red tag on something that needs to be rushed through. Or maybe you run what's most like what you've just finished working on so the machine doesn't have to be changed. Or you run what can get done the fastest because when you produce more you get paid more."

"Pete, it sounds to me like you *are* using sequencing rules—FCFS, highest priority, minimum setup, and SPT."

Pete hesitated. "Maybe you're right, but there's still something that bothers me. If you're going to go to all the trouble to rearrange a stack of jobs, you'd want more information than what we're working with."

"What do you mean?"

"I mean, there's no use rushing a job at one station to let it sit and wait at the next. It's like those maniacs who break their neck to pass you on the road, but they never get anywhere. A few minutes later you're right behind them at a stoplight."

"I see."

"You need some way of looking at the entire job, where it's going next, what resources it's going to use, if it has to be assembled with something else, things like that."

"You've got a point, Pete. Why don't you give us a 'real' example we can work with? You talk, I'll write it on the board."

Pete talked for about 10 more minutes, and when he was finished, Professor Grasso had the following diagram on the board:

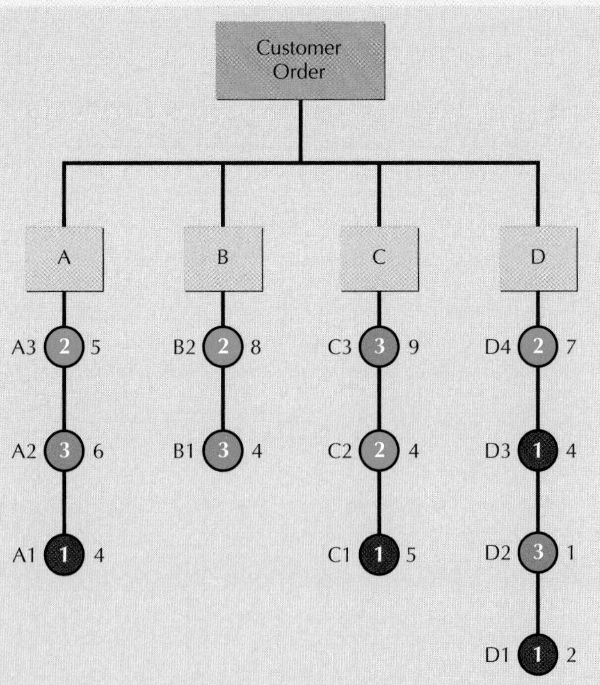


"Okay, class, let's take this home and work on it. A, B, C, and D are products that comprise a customer's order. They must all be completed before the order can be shipped. The circles represent operations that must be performed to make each product. We've labeled them A1 for the first operation of product A, A2 for the second operation, and so on.

The numbers inside the circles are the machines that are used to perform each operation. We have only three machines 1, 2, and 3. Your job is to decide the sequence in which the products should be processed on each machine. There is no setup time between processes, no inventory on hand, and nothing on order. Assume the customer has ordered 50 units of each product. We'll use a process batch of 100 units and a transfer batch of one. Make a Gantt chart for each machine to show us how quickly you can ship the customer's order. Earliest shipment gets 5 extra points on the final exam."

## REFERENCES


Baker, K., and M. Magazine. "Workforce Scheduling with Cyclic Demands and Days-Off Constraints." *Management Science* 24(2; October 1977), pp. 161–167.

Conway, R., W. Maxwell, and L. Miller. *Theory of Scheduling*. Reading, MA: Addison-Wesley, 1967.

Goldratt, E. *What Is This Thing Called Theory of Constraints and How Should It Be Implemented?* Croton-on-Hudson, NY: North River Press, 1990.

Goldratt, E., and J. Cox. *The Goal: Excellence in Manufacturing*. Croton-on-Hudson, NY: North River Press, 1984.

Gupta, J. N. D. "An Excursion in Scheduling Theory." *Production Planning and Control* 13(2; 2002), pp. 105–116.

Huang, P., L. Moore, and R. Russell. "Workload versus Scheduling Policies in a Dual-Resource Constrained Job Shop." *Computers and Operations Research* 11(1; 1984), pp. 37–47.

Langevin, A., D. Riopel, and K. Stecke, "Transfer Batch Sizes in Flexible Manufacturing Systems," *Journal of Manufacturing Systems*, (March–April 1999), p. 140–151.

Pinedo, M., and X. Chao. *Operations Scheduling with Applications in Manufacturing and Services*. New York: Irwin/McGraw-Hill, 1999.

Russell, R., and B. W. Taylor. "An Evaluation of Sequencing Rules for an Assembly Shop." *Decision Sciences* 16(2; 1985), pp. 196–212.

SAP AG. "Production Planning and Detailed Scheduling." Company brochure (December 1999).

Smith, K. A., and J. N. D. Gupta, "Neural Networks in Business." *Computers and Operations Research* 27(1; 2000), pp. 1023–1044.

Umble, M., and M. L. Srikanth. *Synchronous Manufacturing: Principles for World Class Excellence*. Cincinnati: South-Western, 1990.

Vollman, T., W. Berry, and D. C. Whybark. *Manufacturing Planning and Control Systems*. Homewood, IL: Irwin, 1997.

Xudong, H., R. Russell, and J. Dickey. "Workload Analysis Expert System and Optimizer." *Proceedings of the Seventh International Congress of Cybernetics and Systems*, Vol. 1, London (September 1987), pp. 68–72.

# Waiting Line Analysis for Service Improvement

CHAPTER 17

Web resources for this chapter include

- Internet Exercises
- Online Practice Quizzes
- Virtual Tours
- Excel Worksheets
- Company and Resource Weblinks
- Animated Demo Problems
- Microsoft Project Exhibits

www.wiley.com/college/russell

## CHAPTER OUTLINE

In this chapter, you will learn about . . .

- Elements of Waiting Line Analysis
- Waiting Line Analysis and Quality
- Single-Server Models
- Multiple-Server Model

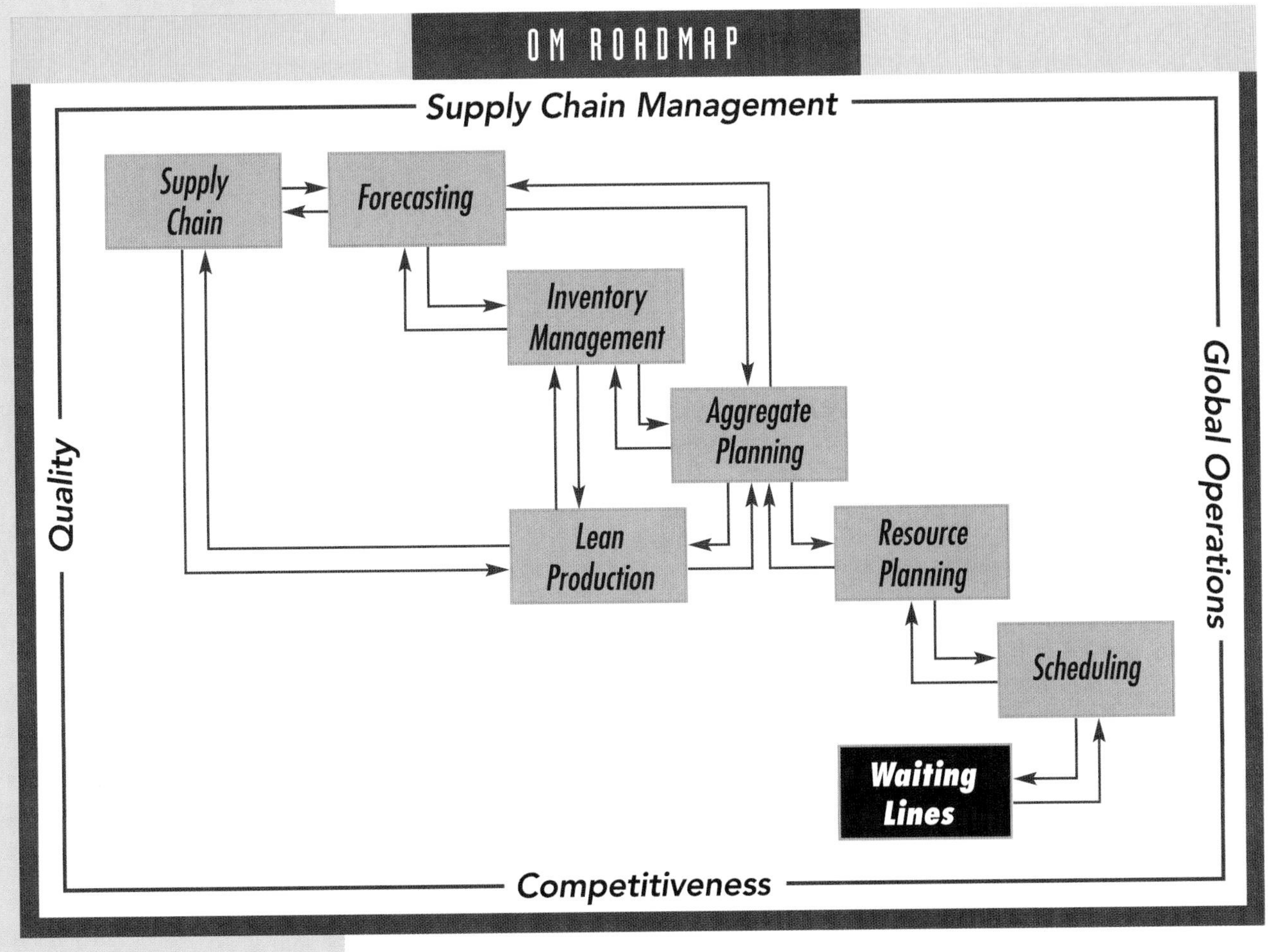

OM ROADMAP

## PROVIDING QUALITY TELEPHONE ORDER SERVICE

The origin of waiting line analysis (also known as queuing theory) is found in telephone congestion problems. A. K. Erlang was a Danish mathematician and scientific advisor to the Copenhagen Telephone Company when in 1917 he published a paper outlining the development of telephone traffic theory. In this groundbreaking paper he was able to determine the probability of the different numbers of calls waiting, and of the waiting time when the system was in equilibrium (i.e., a sufficient number of operators were available to handle the volume of calls without an infinite waiting line growing). Erlang's work formed the basis for the subsequent development of the mathematical analysis of waiting lines.

Today waiting line analysis is still an important tool in analyzing telephone service in one of the largest retail businesses, catalog phone sales. In 2002 one of the country's largest catalogue sales companies, L.L.Bean with over $1 billion in annual sales, received over 12 million customer calls. During the peak holiday season its 3000 customer service representatives took over 140,000 customer calls on its busiest days. Lands' End, the 15th largest mail-order company in the United States, with sales of $1.32 billion handles 15 million phone calls annually. On an average day its almost 300 phone lines handle between 40,000 to 50,000 calls; however, during the weeks prior to Christmas it expands to over 1100 phone lines to handle over 100,000 phone calls daily.

One of the key factors in maintaining a successful catalogue phone order system is providing quality service, in which customer calls are answered promptly and courteously. If customers have to wait too long before connecting to a customer service representative, they are likely to become frustrated, hang up, and perhaps not call back. How do these companies know how many phone lines and customer service representatives they need to prevent long waits, dissatisfied customers (i.e., defects) and lost business? And in today's e-commerce retail environment, how do these companies know how many computer servers and how much computing capacity to have in order that their online customers won't have to wait at a site that is stalled? In many cases they use the mathematical models and principles of waiting line analysis as a basis for answering these questions.

Catalogue companies often use waiting line analysis to make a number of interrelated operational decisions related to order processing. They must determine the number of telephone trunk lines they need for incoming calls during periods of varying call volume, the number of cus-

*Most orders taken by mail-order companies like J. Crew, Eddie Bauer, L.L.Bean, Spiegel, Inc., and Lands' End are by telephone. These telephone ordering systems are, in effect, large-scale waiting line systems in which telephone operators service customers who "wait in line" over the phone for service. To the customer, quality service means knowledgeable, pleasant, and fast service. Fast service in a telephone ordering system is determined by the number of customer calls coming in, the length of the calls, and the number of operators available to answer the calls and take orders.*

tomer service representatives they need to answer calls during normal volume days and peak demand periods, and the maximum number of customers they can put on hold, and for how long, to wait for a service representative. These decisions determine how many customer service representatives need to be hired and trained, how many additional temporary employees need to be hired for peak periods, daily staff schedules, and how many workstations and how much equipment are needed. The basis for all of these decisions is to satisfy customers by providing prompt and effective service, which in turn will reduce costs and increase profits and customer loyalty.

Anyone who goes shopping, to the post office, or to a movie experiences the inconvenience of waiting in line. Not only do people spend time waiting in lines, but parts and products queue up prior to a manufacturing operation and wait to be worked on, machinery waits in line to be serviced or repaired, trucks line up to be loaded or unloaded at a shipping terminal, and planes wait to take off and land. Waiting takes place in virtually every productive process or service. Since the time spent by people and things waiting in line is a valuable resource, the reduction of waiting time is an important aspect of operations management.

Providing quick service is an important aspect of quality customer service and TQM.

Waiting time has also become more important because of the increased emphasis on quality, especially in service-related operations. When customers go into a bank to take out a loan, cash a check, or make a deposit, take their car into a dealer for service or repair, or shop at a grocery store, they equate quality service with quick service. Companies focus on reducing waiting time as part of their quality improvement effort. Companies are able to reduce waiting time and provide faster service by increasing their service capacity, which usually means adding more servers—that is, more tellers, more mechanics, or more checkout clerks. However, increasing service capacity has a monetary cost, and therein lies the basis of waiting line, or queuing, analysis; the trade-off between the cost of improved service and the cost of making customers wait.

Waiting lines are analyzed with a set of mathematical formulas which comprise a field of study called *queuing theory*. Different queuing models and mathematical formulas exist to deal with different types of waiting line systems. Although we discuss several of the most common types of queuing systems, we do not investigate the mathematical derivation of the queuing formulas. They are generally complex and not really pertinent to our understanding of the use of waiting line analysis to improve service.

## ELEMENTS OF WAITING LINE ANALYSIS

Waiting lines form because people or things arrive at the servicing function, or server, faster than they can be served. This does not mean that the service operation is understaffed or does not have the capacity to handle the influx of customers. Most businesses and organizations have sufficient serving capacity available to handle its customers *in the long run*. Waiting lines result because customers do not arrive at a constant, evenly paced rate, nor are they all served in an equal amount of time. Customers arrive at random times, and the time required to serve each individually is not the same. A waiting line is continually increasing and decreasing in length (and is sometimes empty) and in the long run approaches an average length and waiting time. For example, your local bank may have enough tellers to serve an average of 100 customers in an hour, and in a particular hour only 60 customers might arrive. However, at specific points in time during the hour, waiting lines may form because more than an average number of customers arrive and they have transactions that require more than the average amount of time.

**Operating characteristics:** average values for characteristics that describe the performance of a waiting line system.

Decisions about waiting lines and the management of waiting lines are based on these averages for customer arrivals and service times. They are used in queuing formulas or models to compute **operating characteristics** such as the average number of customers waiting in line and the average time a customer must wait in line. Different sets of formulas are used, depending on the type of waiting line system being investigated. A bank drive-up teller window at which one bank clerk serves a single line of customers in cars is

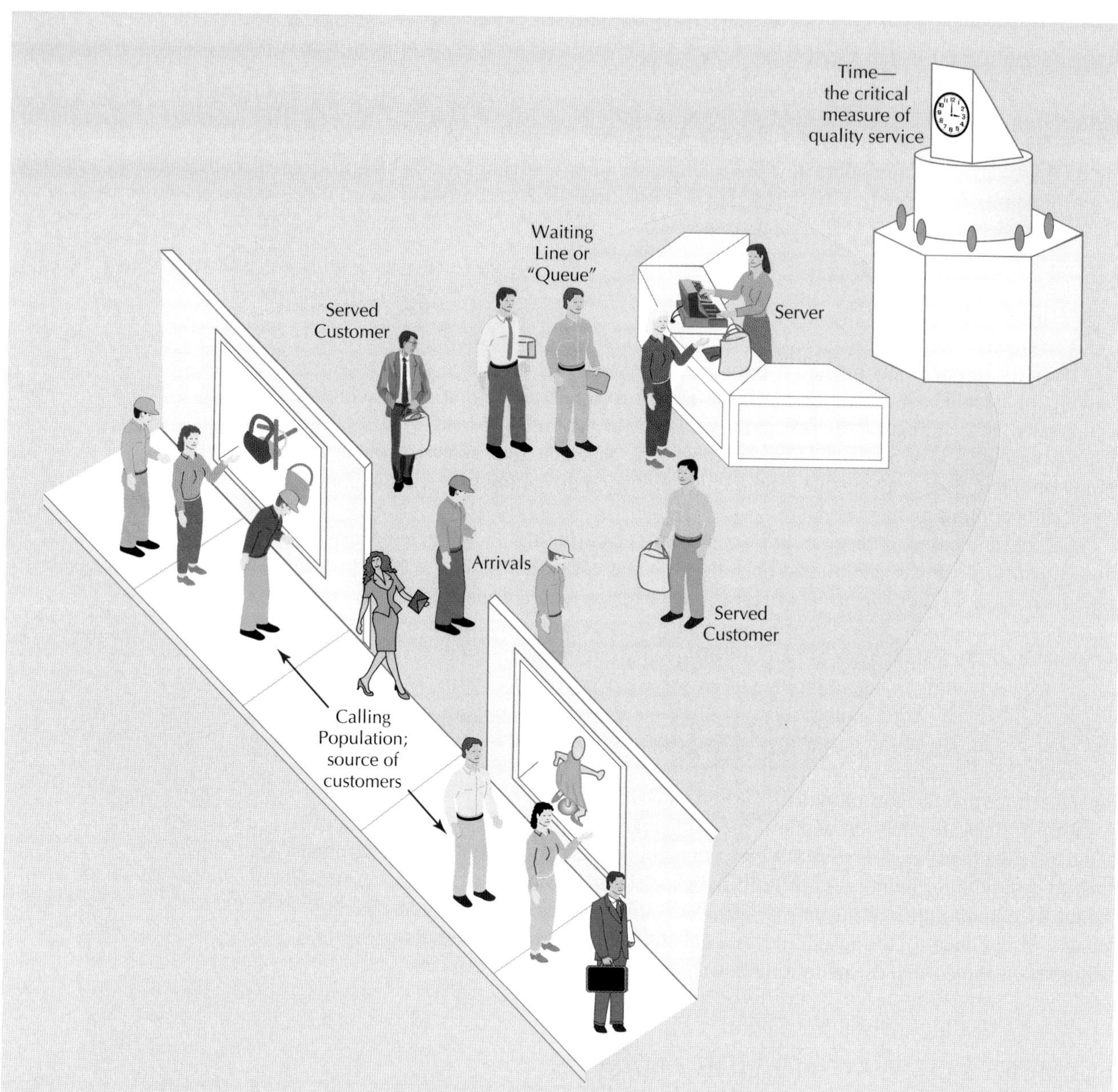


**Figure 17.1**
**Elements of a Waiting Line System**

different from a single line of passengers at an airline ticket counter that are served by three or four airline agents. In this section we present the elements that make up waiting lines before looking at waiting line formulas in the following sections.

## ELEMENTS OF A WAITING LINE

**Queue:** a single waiting line.

*A waiting line system consists of arrivals, servers, and waiting line structure.*

The basic elements of a waiting line, or **queue**, are arrivals, servers, and the waiting line. The relationship between these elements is shown in Figure 17.1 for the simplest type of *waiting line system*, a single server with a single queue. Following is a brief description of each of these waiting line elements.

## THE CALLING POPULATION

**Calling population:** the source of customers; *infinite* or *finite*.

In our discussions of waiting lines, a customer is a person or thing that wants service from an operation. The **calling population** is the source of the customers to the waiting line system, and it can be either *infinite* or *finite*. An infinite calling population assumes such a large number of potential customers that it is always possible for one more customer to arrive to be served. For example, the department store in Figure 17.1, a grocery store, a bank, and a service station are assumed to have infinite calling populations; that is, the whole town or geographic area.

A finite calling population has a specific, countable number of potential customers. All the customers may be waiting in line at the same time; that is, it may occur that there is not one more customer to be served. Examples of a finite calling population are a repair person in a shop, who is responsible for a fixed number of machines to work on, a trucking terminal that services a fleet of ten trucks, or a nurse assigned to attend to only twelve patients.

## THE ARRIVAL RATE

The **arrival rate** is the rate at which customers arrive at the service facility during a specified period. This rate can be estimated from empirical data derived from studying the system or a similar system, or it can be an average of these empirical data. For example, if 100 customers arrive at a store checkout counter during a 10-hour day, we could say the arrival rate averages 10 customers per hour. However, although we might be able to determine a rate for arrivals by counting the number of customers during a specific time period, we would not know exactly when these customers would arrive. It might be that no customers would arrive during one hour and 20 customers would arrive during another hour. Arrivals are assumed to be independent of each other and to vary randomly over time.

**Arrival rate:** the frequency at which customers arrive at a waiting line according to a probability distribution.

The variability of arrivals at a service facility often conform to a probability distribution. Arrivals could be described by many distributions, but it has been determined (through years of research and the practical experience of people in the field of queuing) that the number of arrivals per unit of time at a service facility can frequently be described by a *Poisson distribution*. In queuing, the average arrival rate, or how many customers arrive during a period of time, is signified by $\lambda$.

Arrival rate ($\lambda$) is most frequently described by a Poisson distribution.

In order to use the queuing formulas we will develop in this chapter to analyze different queuing situations, we have to make some other assumptions about customer arrivals. When customers arrive at the service facility, they will join the waiting line and not decide to leave if the line looks to long, which is called *balking*. Another assumption is that customers are *patient*; once they join the waiting line they will not leave, no matter how long they must wait. This is called *reneging*. Finally, a customer in line will not move to another line and then back again; this is called *jockeying*.

## SERVICE TIMES

In waiting line analysis arrivals are described in terms of a *rate*, and service in terms of *time*. **Service times** in a queuing process may also be any one of a large number of different probability distributions. The distribution most commonly assumed for service times is the *negative exponential distribution*. Although this probability distribution is for service *times*, service must be expressed as a *rate* to be compatible with the arrival rate. The average service rate, or how many customers can be served in a period of time is expressed as $\mu$.

**Service time:** the time required to serve a customer, is most frequently described by the negative exponential distribution.

Empirical research has shown that the assumption of negative exponentially distributed service times is not valid as often as is the assumption of Poisson-distributed arrivals. For actual applications of queuing analysis, the assumptions for both arrival rate and service time distribution would have to be carefully checked.

Poisson arrival rate = exponential time between arrivals; exponential service times = Poisson service rate.

Interestingly, if service times are exponentially distributed, then the service rate is Poisson distributed. For example, if the average time to serve a customer is three minutes (and exponentially distributed), then the average service rate is 20 customers per hour (and Poisson distributed). The converse holds true for Poisson arrivals. If the arrival rate is Poisson distributed, then the time between arrivals is exponentially distributed.

## ARRIVAL RATE LESS THAN SERVICE RATE

It is logical to assume that the rate at which service is provided must exceed the arrival rate of customers. If this is not the case, the waiting line will continue to grow infinitely large and there will be no "average" solution. Thus, it is generally assumed that the service rate exceeds the arrival rate, $\lambda < \mu$.

Customers must be served faster than they arrive, or an infinitely large queue will build up; $\lambda < \mu$.

## QUEUE DISCIPLINE AND LENGTH

**Queue discipline:** the order in which customers are served.

The most common service rule is first come, first served.

The **queue discipline** is the order in which waiting customers are served. The most common type of queue discipline is *first come, first served*—the first person or item waiting in line is served first. Other disciplines are possible. For example, a machine operator might stack work-in-process parts beside a machine so that the last part is on top of the stack and will be selected first. This queue discipline is *last in, first out*. Or the machine operator might reach into a box full of parts and select one at random. This queue discipline is *random*. Often customers are scheduled for service according to a predetermined appointment, such as patients at a dentist's office or diners at a restaurant where reservations are required. These customers are taken according to a prearranged schedule regardless of when they arrive at the facility. Another example of the many types of queue disciplines is when customers are processed alphabetically according to their last names, such as at school registration or at job interviews.

In manufacturing operations, sometimes jobs with the shortest expected processing times are selected first in order to get the most jobs processed in the shortest time period. In emergency services like emergency rooms at hospitals, the most critical problem is typically served first.

**Infinite queue:** can be of any length; the length of a **finite queue** is limited.

Queues can be of an infinite or finite size or length. An **infinite queue** can be of any size, with no upper limit, and is the most common queue structure. For example, it is assumed that the waiting line at a movie theater could stretch through the lobby and out the door if necessary. A **finite queue** is limited in size. An example is the driveway at a bank teller window that can accommodate only a limited number of cars, before it backs up to the street.

## BASIC WAITING LINE STRUCTURES

Waiting line processes are generally categorized into four basic structures, according to the nature of the service facilities. In technical terminology they are called single-channel, single-phase; single-channel, multiple-phase; multiple-channel, single-phase; and multiple-channel, multiple-phase processes.

**Channels:** the number of parallel servers for servicing customers.

**Phases:** the number of servers in sequence a customer must go through.

The number of **channels** in a queuing process is the number of parallel servers for servicing arriving customers. The number of **phases**, on the other hand, denotes the number of sequential servers each customer must go through to complete service. An example of a *single-channel, single-phase* queuing operation is a post office with only one postal clerk waiting on a single line of customers. This is more commonly called simply a *single-server* waiting line, and it is illustrated in Figure 17.2*a*. A post office with several postal clerks waiting on a single line of customers is an example of a *multiple-channel, single-phase* process or simply a *multiple-server* waiting line. It is illustrated in Figure 17.2*b*. These are the two basic waiting line structures we will focus on in this chapter.

The other two waiting line structures we mentioned have multiple phases; that is, they have a sequence of servers, one following another. For example, when patients go to a clinic for treatment or check into a hospital, they first wait in a reception room, then they may go to an office to fill out some paperwork. When they get to the treatment room, the patients receive an initial checkup or treatment from a nurse, followed by treatment from a doctor. This arrangement constitutes a *single-channel, multiple-phase* queuing process. If there are several doctors and nurses, the process is a *multiple-channel, multiple-phase process*. Another example of a multiple-phase system is a manufacturing assembly line in which a product is worked on at several sequential machines or by several sequential operators at workstations. These are more complex structures and are beyond the scope of this text.

You may quickly visualize a familiar waiting situation that fits none of these categories of waiting line structures. The four waiting line structures we have described are simply the four basic general categories; but there are many variations, which often require very complex mathematical formulas to analyze. In some cases they can only be analyzed using simulation (the topic of Supplement 12). However, the basic fundamentals of waiting line analysis for the simpler queuing models that we will discuss in this chapter are relevant to the analysis of all queuing problems, regardless of their complexity.

Figure 17.2
**Basic Waiting Line Structures**

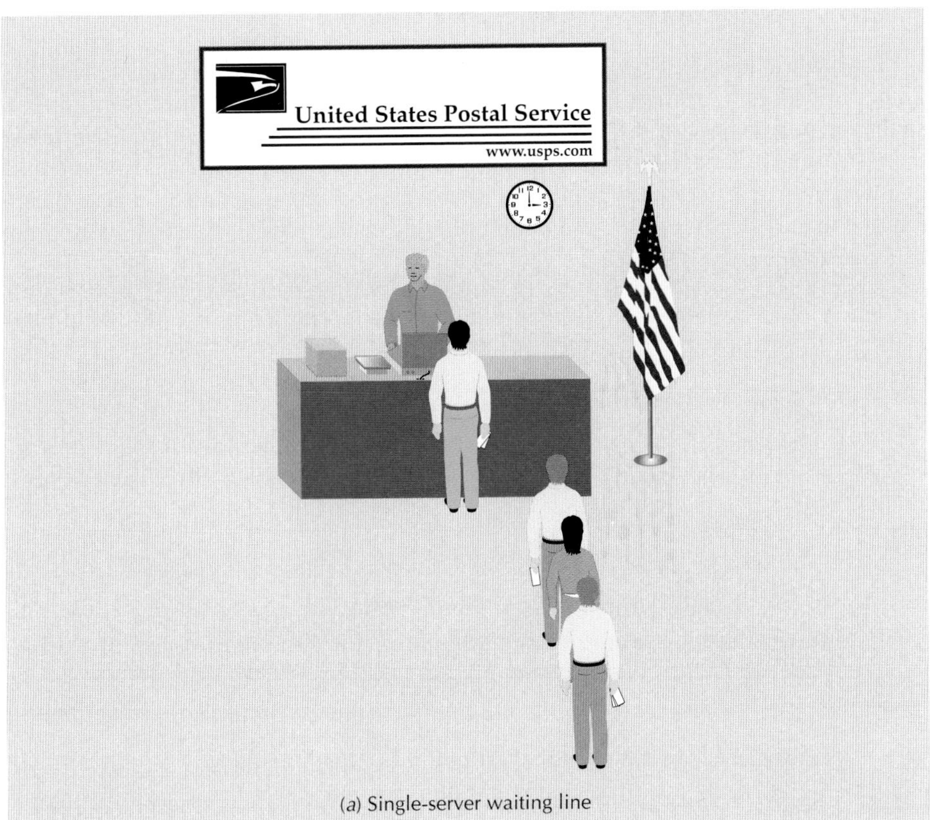


(a) Single-server waiting line

(b) Multiple-server waiting line

## OPERATING CHARACTERISTICS

A *steady state* is a constant, average value for performance characteristics that the system will attain after a long time.

The mathematics used in waiting line analysis do not provide an optimal, or "best," solution. Instead they generate measures referred to as *operating characteristics* that describe the performance of the waiting line system and that management uses to evaluate the system and make decisions. It is assumed these operating characteristics will approach constant, average values after the system has been in operation for a long time, which is referred to as a *steady state*. These basic operating characteristics used in a waiting line analysis are defined in Table 17.1.

**Table 17.1**
**Queuing System Operating Characteristics**

| Notation | Operating Characteristic |
|---|---|
| $L$ | Average number of customers in the system (waiting and being served) |
| $L_q$ | Average number of customers in the waiting line |
| $W$ | Average time a customer spends in the system (waiting and being served) |
| $W_q$ | Average time a customer spends waiting in line |
| $P_0$ | Probability of no (i.e., zero) customers in the system |
| $P_n$ | Probability of $n$ customers in the system |
| $\rho$ | Utilization rate; the proportion of time the system is in use |

# WAITING LINE ANALYSIS AND QUALITY

## THE TRADITIONAL COST RELATIONSHIPS IN WAITING LINE ANALYSIS

As the level of service improves, the cost of service increases.

There is generally an inverse relationship between the cost of providing service and the cost of making customers wait, as reflected in the cost curves in Figure 17.3. As the level of service, reflected by the number of servers, goes up, the cost of service increases, whereas waiting cost decreases. In the traditional view of waiting line analysis, the level of service should coincide with the minimum point on the total cost curve.

Better service requires more servers.

The cost of providing the service is usually reflected in the cost of the servers, such as the cost of the tellers at a bank, postal workers at a post office counter, or the repair crew in a plant or shop. As the number of servers is increased to reduce waiting time, service

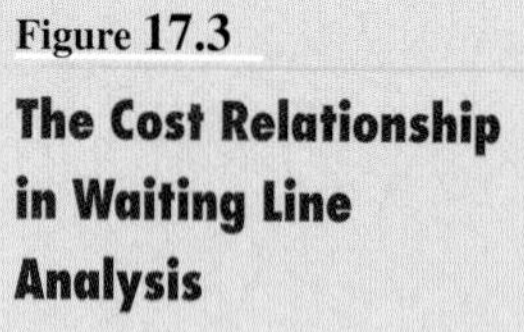
**Figure 17.3**
**The Cost Relationship in Waiting Line Analysis**

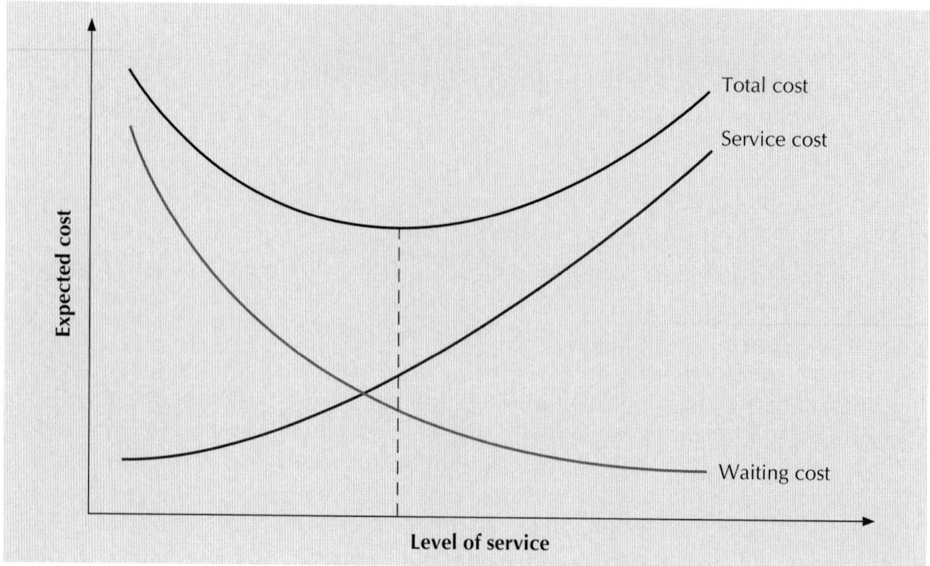

THE COMPETITIVE EDGE

### Improving Waiting Time in England's National Health Service

As part of its 10-year National Health Service plan, the British government has spent billions of pounds to improve service, particularly the reduction of waiting times to see a GP and for accidents and emergencies, and to schedule surgery. At Bridge Lane Medical Centre in Battersea, southwest London, the waiting time for a patient to see a GP has been reduced from between seven to ten days to within 48 hours, the government's goal for waiting time to see a GP. The Medical Centre achieved this waiting time reduction by first hiring a salaried doctor to increase the number of surgeries and having its own GPs work longer hours, until the existing backlog of appointments was eliminated. It then looked for ways to innovate service. One innovation was to create "commuter clinics" in the morning between 8:00 A.M. and 9:00 A.M. and in the evening between 5:30 P.M. and 6:30 P.M. to fit patients' work schedules. Patients who were not as restricted by their work schedules were encouraged to come at other times. Once patients discovered that they could see a doctor quickly, they no longer made unnecessary appointments; the new system also reduced the number of emergency cases that came in without an appointment. Since implementing its improved service, the Medical Centre has achieved 100% patient satisfaction. This is a case where quality service is demanded by the public, even though the cost of the improved service likely far exceeds the financial return since it's in the public domain.

*Source:* N. Timmins, "Extra Funds Fail to Ease Frustrations for Hospitals: Waiting Times Cut by More Than a Week," *FT.com/Financial Times* (October 29, 2002).

cost goes up. Service cost is normally direct and easy to compute. The cost of waiting is not as easy to determine. The major determinant of waiting cost is the loss of business that might result because customers get tired of waiting or frustrated and leave; then, they may purchase the product or service elsewhere. This business loss can be temporary (a single event) or permanent (the customer never comes back). The cost due to a loss of business is especially difficult to determine, since it is not part of normal accounting records, although some trade organizations for businesses and industries occasionally provide such data. Other types of waiting costs include the loss of production time and salary for employees waiting to use machinery or equipment, load or unload vehicles, and so forth.

## WAITING LINE COSTS AND QUALITY SERVICE

The contemporary approach to quality management is to assume that the traditional quality–cost relationship is a short-run perspective that understates the potential long-term loss of business from poor quality service. In the long run, a higher level of quality will gain market share and increase business and thus is more cost effective. Further, as the company focuses on improving service quality, the cost of achieving good quality will be less because of the innovations in processes and work design that will result. This is the philosophy of "zero defects," which in waiting line analysis means "no waiting". This level of better quality, that is quicker service, will in the long run, increase business and be more profitable than the traditional view implies. The increase in revenue (which is not shown in Figure 17.3) resulting from improved service will ultimately increase profit.

**The TQM approach is that absolute quality service will be the most cost effective in the long run.**

## THE PSYCHOLOGY OF WAITING

In some instances, it is not possible to reduce waiting times, or other important issues besides cost may be involved. When these situations occur, the problem of providing quality service often depends more on psychological solutions. In other words, the organization will try to make waiting more palatable. For example, long lines are fairly common at Disney World, especially at certain peak times during the day. Although it is unlikely that any company has analyzed the technical aspects of waiting more than Disney, customers must still wait for long periods of time at certain shows, exhibits, and rides. Given the limited physical capacity of some attractions, the time required for a customer to complete them, and the large flow of customers, it is simply not possible to make the lines shorter or the service quicker without letting fewer people into the park. In these cases Disney

*Disney uses costumed characters like Minnie Mouse to entertain customers waiting in line to distract them from their long wait.*

management attempts to improve service in other ways to reduce customer dissatisfaction. For example, they make use of costumed characters to entertain customers waiting in line and distract them from the long waits. Mobile vendors sell food, drinks, and souvenirs to people in line. The provide accurate wait times, which are more tolerable than vague ones, and they provide frequent updates. For customers who are particularly annoyed by long waits, they sell special passes for a fee that allows customers to go to the front of the line for some attractions and to get into the park early before its normally scheduled opening.

Waiting rooms, such as at a doctor's office, provide magazines and newspapers for customers to read while waiting. Televisions are occasionally available in auto repair waiting areas, in airport terminals, or in bars and lounges of restaurants where customers wait. The "Competitive Edge" box on page 759 describes Bank of America's experiments with using televisions in bank branches to distract customers waiting in line. Mirrors are purposely located near elevators to distract people while they wait. Supermarkets locate magazines and other "impulse-purchase" items at the checkout counter, not only as a diversion while waiting but as potential purchases. All these tactics are designed to improve the quality of service that requires waiting without actually incurring the cost of reducing waiting time.

Some service companies attempt to handle arrivals in a "smarter" way instead of adding cost by using more servers or reducing service time. They might provide selective preferential treatment to good, or certain types of, customers in order to reduce their waiting time. For example, grocery stores have express lanes for customers with only a few purchases. Airlines and car rental agencies issue special cards to frequent-use customers or customers who pay an additional fee that allows them to join special waiting lines at their check-in counters. Some telephone retailers check the phone numbers of incoming calls, and based on a customer's sales history, they are routed to more experienced or specialized salespeople.

For some critical service providers, waiting times of any duration are simply not allowable. A police or fire department must provide sufficient service capacity so that calls for assistance can have quick response. This often results in long periods of underutiliza-

## THE COMPETITIVE EDGE

### The Psychology of Waiting at Bank of America

In a market research study of its customers, the Bank of America discovered that when a person stands in line for more than about three minutes a gap develops between the actual waiting time and the customer's perceived waiting time. For example, if customers wait two minutes, they feel like they've been waiting for two minutes; however, if they have been waiting for five minutes, it may seem more like ten minutes to them. Bank of America also learned from prior studies that long waits have a direct relationship to customer satisfaction. Furthermore, the bank knew from previous psychological studies that if people were distracted from boring activities, time would seem to pass more quickly. As a result, Bank of America undertook a "transaction zone media" experiment to see what would happen if it placed televisions above the tellers in a bank branch lobby to entertain customers waiting in line (i.e., the transaction zone); would it reduce their perceived waiting time? The bank installed television monitors (tuned to CNN) in a typical bank branch and measured actual versus perceived waiting time. The results showed that the amount of waiting times customers overestimated dropped from 32% to 15% when compared to a bank without televisions. To measure the financial impact of these results, the bank employed a customer satisfaction index (based on a customer survey); every one-point improvement in the index results in $1.40 in increased annual revenue per household. The experimental results indicated that the projected reductions in waiting times would result in a 5.9-point increase in the customer satisfaction index. As a result, a bank branch with 10,000 household customers could expect an increase in annual revenue of $82,600. A bank branch with only a few thousand household customers could expect to recoup the estimated $10,000 one-time cost of installing televisions in less than a year.

*Source:* S. Thomke, "R&D Comes to Services: Bank of America's Pathbreaking Experiments," *Harvard Business Review* 81 (April 4, 2003), pp. 70–79.

tion where police officers, or fireman are not doing anything. In these cases cost is not really a factor; that is, there's no cost tradeoff for improved service. In other words, it would not be socially responsible (or acceptable) to reduce the number of fire stations or firemen to reduce cost and incur an "acceptable" increase in waiting time for service.

## SINGLE-SERVER MODELS

The simplest, most basic waiting line structure illustrated in Figure 17.2 is the *single-server* model. We run into this type of waiting line every day. When you buy a cup of coffee at your local Starbucks or convenience store in the morning, when you go to the cable TV office to pay your bill, when you go to a professor's office, when you use the copier in the library, when you buy a ticket to see a movie in the evening, you wait in line to be served by one server.

There are several variations of the single-server waiting line system, and in this section we will present several of the following frequently occurring variations:

Variations of the basic single-server model.

- Poisson arrival rate, exponential service times
- Poisson arrival rate, general (or unknown) distribution of service times
- Poisson arrival rate, constant service times
- Poisson arrival rate, exponential service times with a finite queue
- Poisson arrival rate, exponential service time with a finite calling population

## THE BASIC SINGLE-SERVER MODEL

In the basic single-server model we assume the following:

Assumptions of the basic single-server model.

- Poisson arrival rate
- Exponential service times
- First-come, first-served queue discipline
- Infinite queue length
- Infinite calling population

*"Good" operating characteristics for a waiting line system, and hence good service, are relative and must have some basis for comparison. For example, the waiting time at this McDonald's in Pushkin Square in Moscow averages about 45 minutes. Americans would not accept this level of service. To Muscovites used to waiting in lines that often consume the better part of a day, the waiting time at this McDonald's is amazingly short. It represents good service to them.*

$\lambda$ = mean arrival rate;

$\mu$ = mean service rate.

The basic operating characteristics of this single-server model are computed using the following formulas, where $\lambda$ = mean arrival rate, $\mu$ = mean service rate, and $n$ = the number of customers in the waiting line system, including the customer being served (if any).

The probability that no customers are in the queuing system (either in the queue or being served) is

$$P_0 = \left(1 - \frac{\lambda}{\mu}\right)$$

Basic single-server queuing formulas.

The probability of exactly $n$ customers in the queuing system is

$$P_n = \left(\frac{\lambda}{\mu}\right)^n \cdot P_0$$

$$= \left(\frac{\lambda}{\mu}\right)^n \left(1 - \frac{\lambda}{\mu}\right)$$

The average number of customers in the queuing system (i.e., the customers being serviced and in the waiting line) is

$$L = \frac{\lambda}{\mu - \lambda}$$

The average number of customers in the waiting line is

$$L_q = \frac{\lambda^2}{\mu(\mu - \lambda)}$$

The average time a customer spends in the queuing system (i.e., waiting and being served) is

$$W = \frac{1}{\mu - \lambda}$$

$$= \frac{L}{\lambda}$$

The average time a customer spends waiting in line to be served is

$$W_q = \frac{\lambda}{\mu(\mu - \lambda)}$$

The probability that the server is busy and a customer has to wait, known as the utilization factor, is

$$\rho = \frac{\lambda}{\mu}$$

The probability that the server is idle and a customer can be served is

$$I = 1 - \rho$$
$$= 1 - \frac{\lambda}{\mu} = P_0$$

**Example 17.1**

**A Single-Server Model**

The auxiliary bookstore in the student center at Tech is a small facility that sells school supplies and snacks. It has one checkout counter where one employee operates the cash register. The combination of the cash register and the operator is the server (or service facility) in this waiting line system; the customers who line up at the counter to pay for their selections form the waiting line.

Customers arrive at a rate of 24 per hour according to a Poisson distribution ($\lambda = 24$), and service times are exponentially distributed, with a mean rate of 30 customers per hour ($\mu = 30$). The bookstore manager wants to determine the operating characteristics for this waiting line system.

*Solution*

The operating characteristics are computed using the queuing formulas for the single-server model as follows:

$$P_0 = \left(1 - \frac{\lambda}{\mu}\right)$$
$$= \left(1 - \frac{24}{30}\right)$$
$$= 0.20 \text{ probability of no customers in the system}$$

$$L = \frac{\lambda}{\mu - \lambda}$$
$$= \frac{24}{30 - 24}$$
$$= 4 \text{ customers on the average in the queuing system}$$

$$L_q = \frac{\lambda^2}{\mu(\mu - \lambda)}$$
$$= \frac{(24)^2}{30(30 - 24)}$$
$$= 3.2 \text{ customers on the average in the waiting line}$$

$$W = \frac{1}{\mu - \lambda}$$
$$= \frac{1}{30 - 24}$$
$$= 0.167 \text{ hour (10 minutes) average time in the system per customer}$$

$$W_q = \frac{\lambda}{\mu(\mu - \lambda)}$$
$$= \frac{24}{30(30 - 24)}$$
$$= 0.133 \text{ hour (8 minutes) average time in the waiting line per customer}$$

$$\rho = \frac{\lambda}{\mu}$$
$$= \frac{24}{30}$$
$$= 0.80 \text{ probability that the server will be busy and the customer must wait}$$

$$I = 1 - \rho$$
$$= 1 - 0.80$$
$$= 0.20 \text{ probability that the server will be idle and a customer can be served}$$

Remember that these operating characteristics are averages that result over a period of time; they are not absolutes. In other words, customers who arrive at the bookstore checkout counter will not find 3.2 customers in line. There could be no customers or 1, 2, 3, or 4 customers. The value 3.2 is simply an average over time, as are the other operating characteristics. Notice that there are four customers in the system ($L = 4$) and 3.2 customers in line ($L_q = 3.2$). The difference is only 0.8 customer being served because 20% of the time there is no customer being served ($I = .20$). Also note that the total time in the system of 10 minutes ($W = 10$) is exactly equal to the waiting time of 8 minutes ($W_q = 8$) plus the service time of 2 minutes (i.e., 60/30).

## SERVICE IMPROVEMENT ANALYSIS

The operating characteristics developed from the queuing formulas in Example 17.1 indicate the quality of service at the Tech auxiliary bookstore. The average waiting time of eight minutes is excessive and would likely cause customers to become frustrated and leave without making a purchase. Normally, a waiting time of two to three minutes is the most a customer will comfortably tolerate at a store like this. Thus, the bookstore management could use the operating characteristics to formulate new strategies to improve service and then test these strategies.

For example, the bookstore might consider adding an additional employee to assist the present operator. This would enable more customers to be served in less time, thus increasing the service rate. If the service rate were increased from 30 customers per hour to 40 customers per hour, the waiting time would be reduced to only 2.25 minutes. Management would then have to decide whether the cost of the new employee is worth the reduction in waiting time. Alternatively, the bookstore could be redesigned to add an additional cash register as well as another employee to operate it. This would have the effect of reducing the arrival rate. If exiting customers split evenly between the two cash registers, then the arrival rate at each register would decrease from 24 per hour to 12 per hour with a resulting customer waiting time of 1.33 minutes. Again, management would have to determine whether the reduction in waiting time is worth the cost of a new cash register and employee. This is the crux of waiting line analysis: determining whether the improvement in service is worth the cost to achieve it.

## SOLUTION OF THE SINGLE-SERVER MODEL WITH EXCEL

Excel can be used to solve all of the queuing models in this chapter. The Excel solution screen for the single-server model for the auxiliary bookstore at Tech in Example 17.1 is shown in Exhibit 17.1. Excel files for this exhibit and all other exhibits in this chapter can be downloaded from the text Web site.

Exhibit 17.1

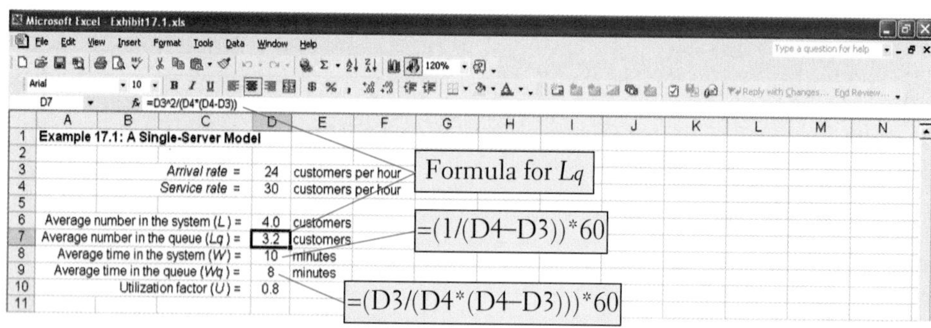


## CONSTANT SERVICE TIMES

*Constant service times* occur with machinery and automated equipment.

The single-server model with Poisson arrivals and *constant service times* is a queuing variation that is of particular interest in operations management, since the most frequent occurrence of constant service times is with automated equipment and machinery as the servers. This type of queuing model has direct application for many manufacturing operations, particularly with robots. You may also experience constant service times when you get a cup of coffee from a vending machine, play a video game in the movie theater lobby,

Figure 17.4
**A Single-Server Waiting Line with a Constant Service Time—An Automated Car Wash**

or get a free automatic car wash with a full tank of gas at a service station, as illustrated in Figure 17.4.

Constant service times are a special case of the single-server model with *undefined* service times.

The constant service time model is actually a special case of a more general variation of the single-server model in which service times cannot be assumed to be exponentially distributed. Service times are said to be *general*, or *undefined*. The basic queuing formulas for the operating characteristics of the undefined service time model are as follows:

$$P_0 = 1 - \frac{\lambda}{\mu}$$

$$L_q = \frac{\lambda^2\sigma^2 + (\lambda/\mu)^2}{2(1 - \lambda/\mu)}$$

$$L = L_q + \frac{\lambda}{\mu}$$

$$W_q = \frac{L_q}{\lambda}$$

$$W = W_q + \frac{1}{\mu}$$

$$\rho = \frac{\lambda}{\mu}$$

The key formula for undefined service times is for $L_q$, the number of customers in the waiting line. In this formula $\mu$ and $\sigma$ are the mean and standard deviation, respectively, for any general probability distribution with independent service times. If we let $\sigma^2 = 1/\mu^2$ in the formula for $L_q$ for undefined service times, it becomes the same as our basic formula with exponential service times. In fact, all the queuing formulas become the same as the basic single-server model.

In the case of constant service times, there is no variability in service times (i.e., service time is the same constant value for each customer); thus, $\sigma = 0$. Substituting $\sigma = 0$ into the undefined service time formula for $L_q$ results in the following formula for constant service times:

$$\begin{aligned} L_q &= \frac{\lambda^2\sigma^2 + (\lambda/\mu)^2}{2(1 - \lambda/\mu)} \\ &= \frac{\lambda^2(0) + (\lambda/\mu)^2}{2(1 - \lambda/\mu)} \\ &= \frac{(\lambda/\mu)^2}{2(1 - \lambda/\mu)} \\ &= \frac{\lambda^2}{2\mu(\mu - \lambda)} \end{aligned}$$

Notice that this new formula for $L_q$ for constant service times is simply the basic single-server formula for $L_q$ divided by 2. The remaining formulas for $L$, $W_q$, and $W$ are the same as the single server formulas using this new formulation for $L_q$.

*A welding operation like this one on an automobile assembly line is an example of a waiting line with a constant service time; i.e., there is no variation in the welding time.*

**Example 17.2**

**A Single-Server Model with Constant Service Times**

The Petrolco Service Station has an automatic car wash, and cars purchasing gas at the station receive a discounted car wash, depending on the number of gallons of gas they buy. The car wash can accommodate one car at a time, and it requires a constant time of 4.5 minutes for a wash. Cars arrive at the car wash at an average rate of 10 per hour (Poisson distributed).

The service station manager wants to determine the average length of the waiting line and the average waiting time at the car wash.

*Solution*

First determine $\lambda$ and $\mu$ such that they are expressed as rates:

$$\lambda = 10 \text{ cars per hour}$$

$$\mu = \frac{60}{4.5} = 13.3 \text{ cars per hour}$$

Substituting $\lambda$ and $\mu$ into the queuing formulas for constant service time gives

$$L_q = \frac{\lambda^2}{2\mu(\mu - \lambda)}$$

$$= \frac{(10)^2}{2(13.3)(13.3 - 10)}$$

$$= 1.14 \text{ cars waiting}$$

$$W_q = \frac{L_q}{\lambda}$$

$$= \frac{1.14}{10}$$

$$= 0.114 \text{ hour, or } 6.84 \text{ minutes, waiting in line}$$

This amount of waiting time may be a little excessive for an automatic car wash. The station owner may want to consider slightly reducing the wash time setting.

## SOLUTION OF THE CONSTANT SERVICE TIME MODEL WITH EXCEL

Excel can be used to solve the single-server model with constant service times. The Excel screen for Example 17.2 is shown in Exhibit 17.2. Notice that the queuing formula for $L_q$ in cell D6 is also shown on the formula bar at the top of the screen.

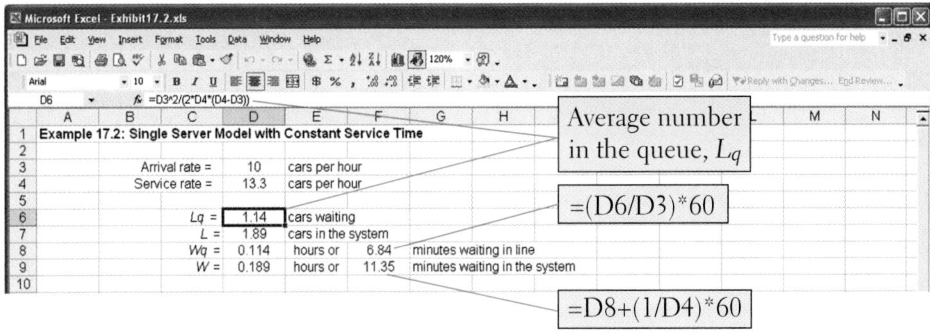

Exhibit 17.2

## FINITE QUEUE LENGTH

For some waiting line systems, the length of the queue may be limited by the physical area in which the queue forms; space may permit only a limited number of customers to enter the queue. Such a waiting line is referred to as a *finite queue*; it results in another variation of the single-phase, single-channel queuing model. For example, the driveway for the bank teller or ATM at your local bank may have only enough space for four cars as shown in Figure 17.5. An auto assembly operation may only have enough space for six cars to wait to be worked on.

The basic single-server model must be modified to consider the finite queuing situation. For this case the service rate does not have to exceed the arrival rate ($\mu > \lambda$) to obtain steady-state conditions. The resultant operating characteristics, where $M$ is the maximum number in the system (being served and waiting), are

$$P_0 = \frac{1 - \lambda/\mu}{1 - (\lambda/\mu)^{M+1}}$$

$$P_n = (P_0)\left(\frac{\lambda}{\mu}\right)^n \text{ for } n \le M$$

$$L = \frac{\lambda/\mu}{1 - \lambda/\mu} - \frac{(M + 1)(\lambda/\mu)^{M+1}}{1 - (\lambda/\mu)^{M+1}}$$

Since $P_n$ is the probability of $n$ units in the system, if we define $M$ as the maximum number allowed in the system, then $P_M$ (the value of $P_n$ for $n = M$) is the probability that the

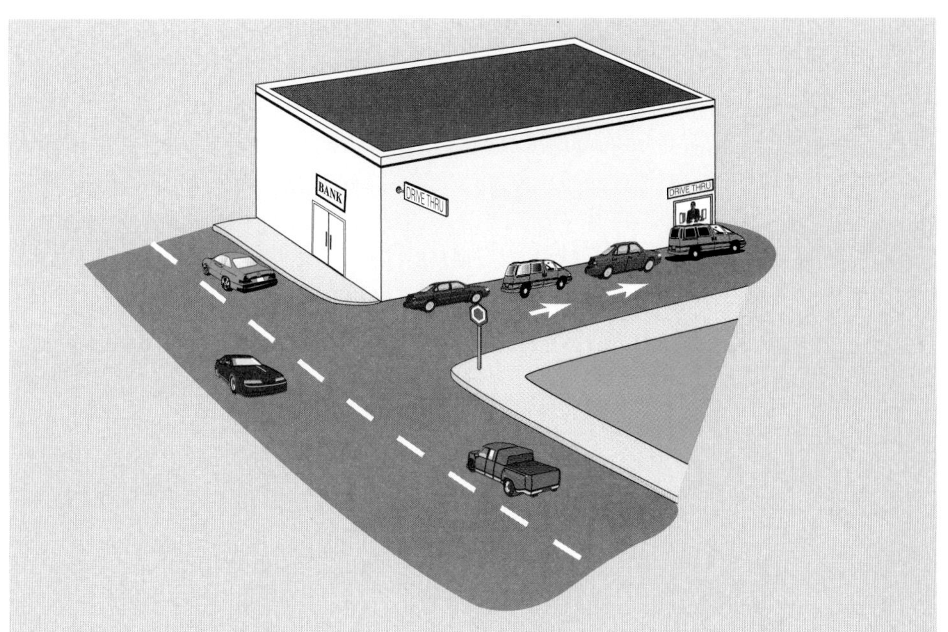


**Figure 17.5 A Finite Waiting Line—A Bank Teller Window**

system is full and that a new customer cannot join the waiting line. The remaining equations are

$$L_q = L - \frac{\lambda(1 - P_M)}{\mu}$$

$$W = \frac{L}{\lambda(1 - P_M)}$$

$$W_q = W - \frac{1}{\mu}$$

**Example 17.3**

**A Single-Server Model with Finite Queue**

The First National Bank has a single-teller drive-in window next to a busy street. The facility has space to serve one customer, at the window and three vehicles lined up to wait for service. There is no space for cars to line up on the busy adjacent street, so if the waiting line is full (three cars), prospective customers must drive on.

The mean time between arrivals for customers seeking service is three minutes. The mean time required by the teller to complete a customer transaction is two minutes. Both the interarrival times and the service times are exponentially distributed (which means their rates are Poisson distributed). The maximum number of vehicles in the system is four. Determine the average waiting time, the average queue length, and the probability that a customer will have to drive on.

*Solution*

$$\lambda = 20$$
$$\mu = 30$$
$$M = 4 \text{ cars}$$

First, we compute the probability that the system is full and the customer must drive on, $P_M$. However, this first requires the determination of $P_0$, as follows:

$$\begin{aligned} P_0 &= \frac{1 - \lambda/\mu}{1 - (\lambda/\mu)^{M+1}} \\ &= \frac{1 - 20/30}{1 - (20/30)^5} \\ &= 0.38 \text{ probability of no cars in the system} \end{aligned}$$

$$\begin{aligned} P_M &= (P_0)\left(\frac{\lambda}{\mu}\right)^{n=M} \\ &= (0.38)\left(\frac{20}{30}\right)^4 \\ &= 0.076 \text{ probability that four cars are in the system,} \\ &\quad \text{it is full (and the customer must drive on)} \end{aligned}$$

Next, to compute the average queue length, $L_q$, the average number of cars in the system, $L$, must be computed as follows:

$$\begin{aligned} L &= \frac{\lambda/\mu}{1 - \lambda/\mu} - \frac{(M + 1)(\lambda/\mu)^{M+1}}{1 - (\lambda/\mu)^{M+1}} \\ &= \frac{20/30}{1 - 20/30} - \frac{(5)(20/30)^5}{1 - (20/30)^5} \\ &= 1.24 \text{ cars in the system} \end{aligned}$$

$$\begin{aligned} L_q &= L - \frac{\lambda(1 - P_M)}{\mu} \\ &= 1.24 - \frac{20(1 - 0.076)}{30} \\ &= 0.62 \text{ cars waiting} \end{aligned}$$

To compute the average waiting time $W_q$, the average time in the system, $W$, must be computed first.

$$W = \frac{L}{\lambda(1 - P_M)}$$
$$= \frac{1.24}{2(1 - 0.076)}$$
$$= 0.067 \text{ hour or } 4.03 \text{ minutes in the system}$$
$$W_q = W - \frac{1}{\mu}$$
$$= 0.067 - \frac{1}{30}$$
$$= 0.033 \text{ hour or } 2.03 \text{ minutes waiting in line}$$

This is a brief waiting time, which would probably be considered good service.

## EXCEL SOLUTION OF THE FINITE QUEUE LENGTH MODEL

Exhibit 17.3 shows the Excel solution screen for the finite queue model in Example 17.3. The formula for $P_0$ is shown on the toolbar at the top of the screen.

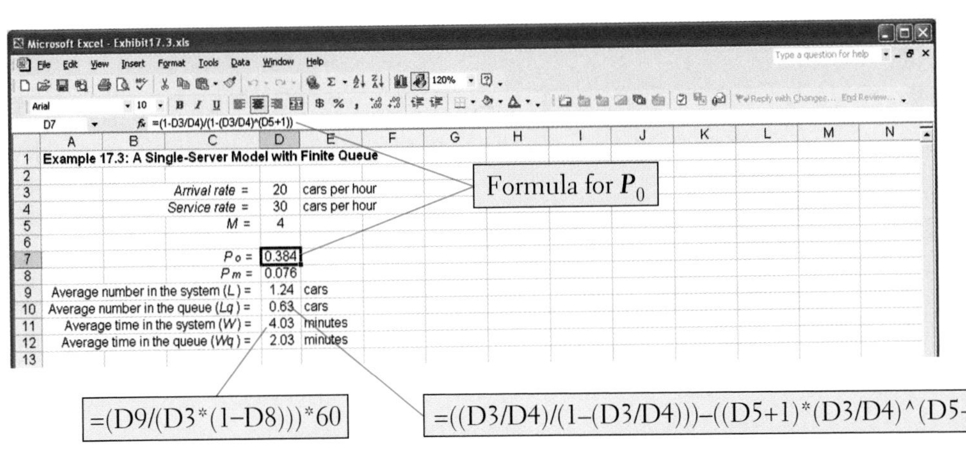


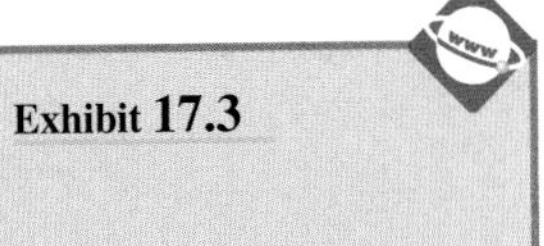

**Exhibit 17.3**

## FINITE CALLING POPULATIONS

The single-server model with a Poisson arrival and exponential service times and a finite calling population has the following set of formulas for determining operating characteristics:

The population of customers from which arrivals originate is limited, such as the number of police cars at a station to answer calls.

$$P_0 = \frac{1}{\sum_{n=0}^{N} \frac{N!}{(N-n)!}\left(\frac{\lambda}{\mu}\right)^n}, \quad \text{where } N = \text{population size}$$

$$P_n = \frac{N!}{(N-n)!}\left(\frac{\lambda}{\mu}\right)^n P_0, \quad \text{where } n = 1, 2, \ldots, N$$

$$L_q = N - \left(\frac{\lambda + \mu}{\lambda}\right)(1 - P_0)$$

$$L = L_q + (1 - P_0)$$

$$W_q = \frac{L_q}{(N - L)\lambda}$$

$$W = W_q + \frac{1}{\mu}$$

In this model $\lambda$ is the **arrival rate** of each member of the population. The formulas for $P_0$ and $P_n$ are both relatively complex and can be cumbersome to compute by hand.

**Arrival rate $\lambda$:** is for each member of the population.

**Figure 17.6**

**A Finite Calling Population Waiting Line—A Finite Group of Machines Broken Down Waiting to be Repaired**

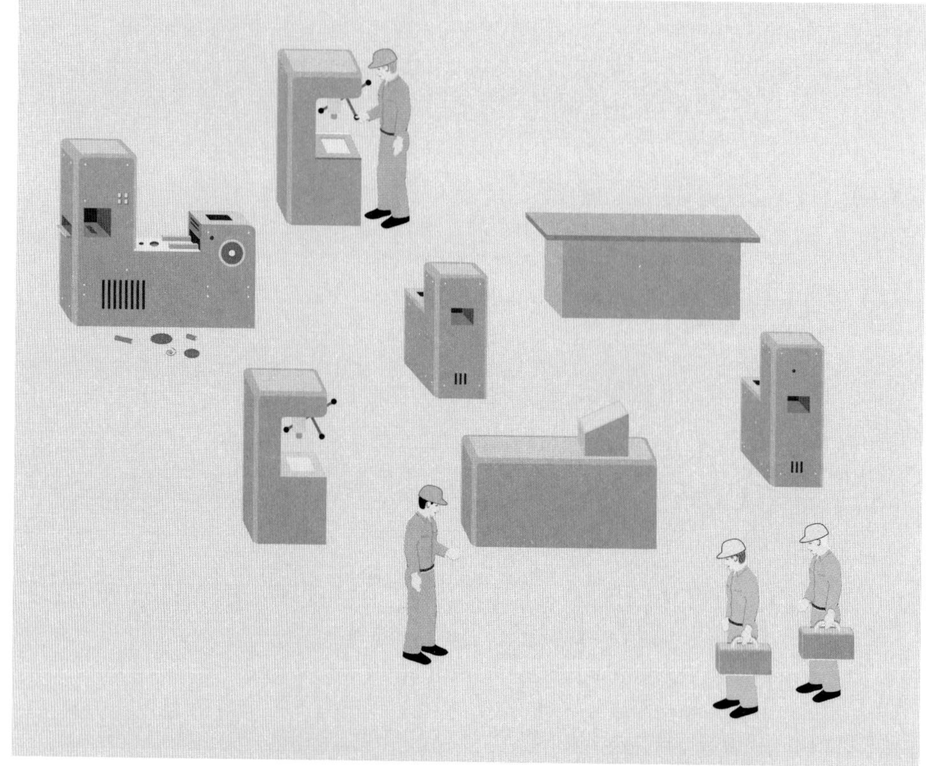

An example of a finite calling population is a maintenance and repair team the services a finite group of machines in a shop as shown in Figure 17.6 or a finite fleet of vehicles, that is, a town's fleet of police cars or garbage trucks. Another example is a student advisor with a finite number of students assigned to her. In each case, the arrival rate is the rate at which the individual items (equipment, cars or people) come to be served.

**Example 17.4**

**A Single-Server Model with Finite Calling Population**

The Wheelco Shipping Company has a fleet of 20 trucks that it uses to ship goods along the east coast from a terminal near Pittsburgh. When a truck needs repair, it is tagged with the date. The company has two mechanics who repair the trucks based on an oldest-date-of-breakdown rule (i.e., a FIFO queue discipline). The mechanics work as a team on one truck at a time. Each truck operates an average of 200 days before needing repair, and the mean repair time is 3.6 days. The breakdown rate is Poisson distributed, and the repair times are exponentially distributed. The company would like an analysis performed of truck idle time due to repair in order to determine if the two mechanics are sufficient.

*Solution*

$$\lambda = \frac{1}{200 \text{ days}} = 0.005 \text{ per day}$$

$$\mu = \frac{1}{3.6 \text{ days}} = 0.2778 \text{ per day}$$

$$N = 20 \text{ trucks}$$

$$P_0 = \frac{1}{\sum_{n=0}^{N} \frac{N!}{(N-n)!}\left(\frac{\lambda}{\mu}\right)^n}$$

$$= \frac{1}{\sum_{n=0}^{20} \frac{20!}{(20-n)!}\left(\frac{0.005}{0.2778}\right)^n}$$

$$= 0.652$$

$$L_q = N - \left(\frac{\lambda + \mu}{\lambda}\right)(1 - P_0)$$
$$= 20 - \frac{0.005 + 0.2778}{0.005}(1 - 0.652)$$
$$= 0.169 \text{ trucks waiting}$$
$$L = L_q + (1 - P_0)$$
$$= 0.169 + (1 - 0.652)$$
$$= 0.520 \text{ trucks in the system}$$
$$W_q = \frac{L_q}{(N - L)\lambda}$$
$$= \frac{0.169}{(20 - 0.520)(0.005)}$$
$$= 1.74 \text{ days waiting for repair}$$
$$W = W_q + \frac{1}{\mu}$$
$$= 1.74 + \frac{1}{0.2778}$$
$$= 5.33 \text{ days time in the system}$$

These results show that the mechanics are busy 35% of the time repairing trucks. Of the 20 trucks, an average of 0.52 or 2.6%, are waiting for repair or under repair. Each truck is idle (broken down waiting for repair or under repair) an average of 5.33 days. The system seems adequate.

This repair system may be adequate but during the 5-plus days (on average) a truck is out of service the company loses revenue. It may also be hindered in its ability to provide quality service to its customers. It would be prudent to investigate the impact of adding more mechanics. Alternatively, the company could explore the possibility and cost of an improved maintenance program to reduce the breakdown (i.e., arrival) rate.

## SOLUTION OF THE FINITE POPULATION MODEL WITH EXCEL

The finite population queuing model can be tedious to solve using an Excel spreadsheet because of the complexity of entering the formula for $P_0$ in the spreadsheet. An array must be created for the $N$ components required by the summation in the denominator of the formula for $P_0$. Exhibit 17.4 shows the Excel spreadsheet for the Wheelco Shipping Company example with this summation array in cells **F4:G26**.

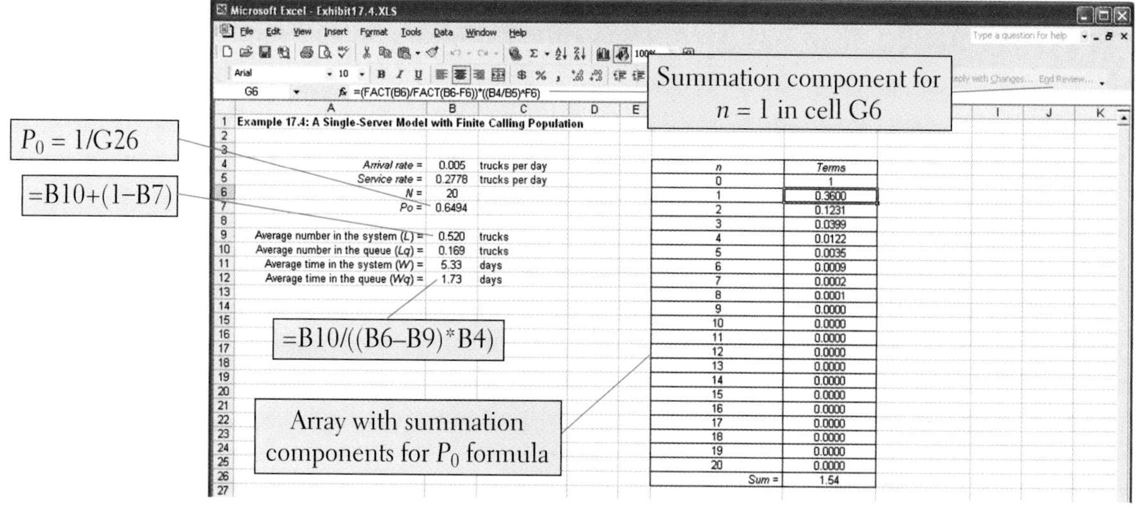

## MULTIPLE-SERVER MODEL

A large number of operational waiting line systems include multiple servers. These models can be very complex, so in this section we present only the most basic multiple-server (or channel) waiting line structure. This system includes a single waiting line and a service facility with several independent servers in parallel, as shown in Figure 17.2*b*. An example of a multiple-server system is an airline ticket and check-in counter, where passengers line up in a roped-off single line waiting for one of several agents for service. The same waiting line structure is found at the post office, where customers in a single line wait for service from several postal clerks, or at a multiplex theater where customers typically line up in a single line to buy movie tickets from one of several ticket sellers.

### THE BASIC MULTIPLE-SERVER MODEL

With *multiple-server models*, two or more independent servers in parallel serve a single waiting line.

$s\mu > \lambda$: The total number of servers must be able to serve customers faster than they arrive.

The formulas for determining the operating characteristics for the multiple-server model are based on the same assumptions as the single-server model—Poisson arrival rate, exponential service times, infinite calling population and queue length, and FIFO queue discipline. Also, recall that in the single-server model, $\mu > \lambda$; however, in the multiple-server model, $s\mu > \lambda$, where $s$ is the number of servers. The operating characteristics formulas are as follows.

The probability that there are no customers in the system (all servers are idle) is

$$P_0 = \frac{1}{\left[\sum_{n=0}^{n=s-1} \frac{1}{n!}\left(\frac{\lambda}{\mu}\right)^n\right] + \frac{1}{s!}\left(\frac{\lambda}{\mu}\right)^s\left(\frac{s\mu}{s\mu - \lambda}\right)}$$

The probability of $n$ customers in the queuing system is

$$P_n = \begin{cases} \dfrac{1}{s!s^{n-s}}\left(\dfrac{\lambda}{\mu}\right)^n P_0, & \text{for } n > s \\ \dfrac{1}{n!}\left(\dfrac{\lambda}{\mu}\right)^n P_0, & \text{for } n \leq s \end{cases}$$

The probability that a customer arriving in the system must wait for service (i.e., the probability that all the servers are busy) is

$$P_w = \frac{1}{s!}\left(\frac{\lambda}{\mu}\right)^s \frac{s\mu}{s\mu - \lambda} P_0$$

$$L = \frac{\lambda\mu(\lambda/\mu)^s}{(s-1)!(s\mu - \lambda)^2} P_0 + \frac{\lambda}{\mu}$$

$$W = \frac{L}{\lambda}$$

$$L_q = L - \frac{\lambda}{\mu}$$

$$W_q = W - \frac{1}{\mu}$$

$$= \frac{L_q}{\lambda}$$

$$\rho = \frac{\lambda}{s\mu}$$

The key formula in this set is for $P_0$, which can be time-consuming to compute manually. Table 17.2 provides values for $P_0$ for selected values of the server utilization factor, $\rho$, and the number of servers, $s$.

| $\rho = \lambda / s\mu$ | Number of Channels: $s$ | | | | | | | | |
|---|---|---|---|---|---|---|---|---|---|
| $\rho$ | 2 | 3 | 4 | 5 | 6 | 7 | 8 | 9 | 10 | 15 |
| 0.02 | 0.96079 | 0.94177 | 0.92312 | 0.90484 | 0.88692 | 0.86936 | 0.85215 | 0.83527 | 0.81873 | 0.74082 |
| 0.04 | 0.92308 | 0.88692 | 0.85215 | 0.81873 | 0.78663 | 0.75578 | 0.72615 | 0.69768 | 0.67032 | 0.54881 |
| 0.06 | 0.88679 | 0.83526 | 0.78663 | 0.74082 | 0.69768 | 0.65705 | 0.61878 | 0.58275 | 0.54881 | 0.40657 |
| 0.08 | 0.85185 | 0.78659 | 0.72615 | 0.67032 | 0.61878 | 0.57121 | 0.52729 | 0.48675 | 0.44983 | 0.30119 |
| 0.10 | 0.81818 | 0.74074 | 0.67031 | 0.60653 | 0.54881 | 0.49659 | 0.44933 | 0.40657 | 0.36788 | 0.22313 |
| 0.12 | 0.78571 | 0.69753 | 0.61876 | 0.54881 | 0.48675 | 0.43171 | 0.38289 | 0.33960 | 0.30119 | 0.16530 |
| 0.14 | 0.75439 | 0.65679 | 0.57116 | 0.49657 | 0.43171 | 0.37531 | 0.72628 | 0.28365 | 0.24660 | 0.12246 |
| 0.16 | 0.72414 | 0.61838 | 0.52720 | 0.44931 | 0.38289 | 0.32628 | 0.27804 | 0.23693 | 0.20190 | 0.09072 |
| 0.18 | 0.69492 | 0.58214 | 0.48660 | 0.40653 | 0.33959 | 0.28365 | 0.23693 | 0.19790 | 0.16530 | 0.06721 |
| 0.20 | 0.66667 | 0.54795 | 0.44910 | 0.36782 | 0.30118 | 0.24659 | 0.20189 | 0.16530 | 0.13534 | 0.04979 |
| 0.22 | 0.63934 | 0.51567 | 0.41445 | 0.33277 | 0.26711 | 0.21437 | 0.17204 | 0.13807 | 0.11080 | 0.03688 |
| 0.24 | 0.61290 | 0.48519 | 0.38244 | 0.30105 | 0.23688 | 0.18636 | 0.14660 | 0.11532 | 0.09072 | 0.02732 |
| 0.26 | 0.58730 | 0.45640 | 0.35284 | 0.27233 | 0.21007 | 0.16200 | 0.12492 | 0.09632 | 0.07427 | 0.02024 |
| 0.28 | 0.56250 | 0.42918 | 0.32548 | 0.24633 | 0.18628 | 0.14082 | 0.10645 | 0.08045 | 0.06081 | 0.01500 |
| 0.30 | 0.53846 | 0.40346 | 0.30017 | 0.22277 | 0.16517 | 0.12241 | 0.09070 | 0.06720 | 0.04978 | 0.01111 |
| 0.32 | 0.51515 | 0.37913 | 0.27676 | 0.20144 | 0.14644 | 0.10639 | 0.07728 | 0.05612 | 0.04076 | 0.00823 |
| 0.34 | 0.49254 | 0.35610 | 0.25510 | 0.18211 | 0.12981 | 0.09247 | 0.06584 | 0.04687 | 0.03337 | 0.00610 |
| 0.36 | 0.47059 | 0.33431 | 0.23505 | 0.16460 | 0.11505 | 0.08035 | 0.05609 | 0.03915 | 0.02732 | 0.00452 |
| 0.38 | 0.44928 | 0.31367 | 0.21649 | 0.14872 | 0.10195 | 0.06981 | 0.04778 | 0.03269 | 0.02236 | 0.00335 |
| 0.40 | 0.42857 | 0.29412 | 0.19929 | 0.13433 | 0.09032 | 0.06065 | 0.04069 | 0.02729 | 0.01830 | 0.00248 |
| 0.42 | 0.40845 | 0.27559 | 0.18336 | 0.12128 | 0.07998 | 0.05627 | 0.03465 | 0.02279 | 0.01498 | 0.00184 |
| 0.44 | 0.38889 | 0.25802 | 0.16860 | 0.10944 | 0.07080 | 0.04573 | 0.02950 | 0.01902 | 0.01225 | 0.00136 |
| 0.46 | 0.36986 | 0.24135 | 0.15491 | 0.09870 | 0.02650 | 0.03968 | 0.02511 | 0.01587 | 0.01003 | 0.00101 |
| 0.48 | 0.35135 | 0.22554 | 0.14221 | 0.08895 | 0.05540 | 0.03442 | 0.02136 | 0.01324 | 0.00826 | 0.00075 |
| 0.50 | 0.33330 | 0.21053 | 0.13043 | 0.08010 | 0.04896 | 0.02984 | 0.01816 | 0.01104 | 0.00671 | 0.00055 |
| 0.52 | 0.31579 | 0.19627 | 0.11951 | 0.07207 | 0.04323 | 0.02586 | 0.01544 | 0.00920 | 0.00548 | 0.00041 |
| 0.54 | 0.29870 | 0.18273 | 0.10936 | 0.06477 | 0.03814 | 0.02239 | 0.01313 | 0.00767 | 0.00448 | 0.00030 |
| 0.56 | 0.28205 | 0.16986 | 0.09994 | 0.05814 | 0.03362 | 0.01936 | 0.01113 | 0.00638 | 0.00366 | 0.00022 |
| 0.58 | 0.26582 | 0.15762 | 0.09119 | 0.05212 | 0.02959 | 0.01673 | 0.00943 | 0.00531 | 0.00298 | 0.00017 |
| 0.60 | 0.25000 | 0.14599 | 0.08306 | 0.04665 | 0.02601 | 0.01443 | 0.00799 | 0.00441 | 0.00243 | 0.00012 |
| 0.62 | 0.23457 | 0.13491 | 0.07550 | 0.04167 | 0.02282 | 0.01243 | 0.00675 | 0.00366 | 0.00198 | 0.00009 |
| 0.64 | 0.21951 | 0.12438 | 0.06847 | 0.03715 | 0.01999 | 0.01069 | 0.00570 | 0.00303 | 0.00161 | 0.00007 |
| 0.66 | 0.20482 | 0.11435 | 0.06194 | 0.03304 | 0.01746 | 0.00918 | 0.00480 | 0.00251 | 0.00131 | 0.00005 |
| 0.68 | 0.19048 | 0.10479 | 0.05587 | 0.02930 | 0.01522 | 0.00786 | 0.00404 | 0.00207 | 0.00106 | 0.00004 |
| 0.70 | 0.17647 | 0.09569 | 0.05021 | 0.02590 | 0.01322 | 0.00670 | 0.00338 | 0.00170 | 0.00085 | 0.00003 |
| 0.72 | 0.16279 | 0.08702 | 0.04495 | 0.02280 | 0.01144 | 0.00570 | 0.00283 | 0.00140 | 0.00069 | 0.00002 |
| 0.74 | 0.14943 | 0.07875 | 0.04006 | 0.01999 | 0.00986 | 0.00483 | 0.00235 | 0.00114 | 0.00055 | 0.00001 |
| 0.76 | 0.13636 | 0.07087 | 0.03550 | 0.01743 | 0.00847 | 0.00407 | 0.00195 | 0.00093 | 0.00044 | 0.00001 |
| 0.78 | 0.12360 | 0.06335 | 0.03125 | 0.01510 | 0.00721 | 0.00341 | 0.00160 | 0.00075 | 0.00035 | 0.00001 |
| 0.80 | 0.11111 | 0.05618 | 0.02730 | 0.01299 | 0.00610 | 0.00284 | 0.00131 | 0.00060 | 0.00028 | 0.00001 |
| 0.82 | 0.09890 | 0.04933 | 0.02362 | 0.01106 | 0.00511 | 0.00234 | 0.00106 | 0.00048 | 0.00022 | 0.00000 |
| 0.84 | 0.08696 | 0.04280 | 0.02019 | 0.00931 | 0.00423 | 0.00190 | 0.00085 | 0.00038 | 0.00017 | 0.00000 |
| 0.86 | 0.07527 | 0.03656 | 0.01700 | 0.00772 | 0.00345 | 0.00153 | 0.00067 | 0.00029 | 0.00013 | 0.00000 |
| 0.88 | 0.06383 | 0.03060 | 0.01403 | 0.00627 | 0.00276 | 0.00120 | 0.00052 | 0.00022 | 0.00010 | 0.00000 |
| 0.90 | 0.05263 | 0.02491 | 0.01126 | 0.00496 | 0.00215 | 0.00092 | 0.00039 | 0.00017 | 0.00007 | 0.00000 |
| 0.92 | 0.04167 | 0.01947 | 0.00867 | 0.00377 | 0.00161 | 0.00068 | 0.00028 | 0.00012 | 0.00005 | 0.00000 |
| 0.94 | 0.03093 | 0.01427 | 0.00627 | 0.00268 | 0.00113 | 0.00047 | 0.00019 | 0.00008 | 0.00003 | 0.00000 |
| 0.96 | 0.02041 | 0.00930 | 0.00403 | 0.00170 | 0.00070 | 0.00029 | 0.00012 | 0.00005 | 0.00002 | 0.00000 |
| 0.98 | 0.01010 | 0.00454 | 0.00194 | 0.00081 | 0.00033 | 0.00013 | 0.00005 | 0.00002 | 0.00001 | 0.00000 |

**Table 17.2**

**Selected Values of $P_0$ for the Multiple-Server Model**

*These passengers waiting in line to purchase tickets or check baggage and get a boarding pass at LAX are part of a waiting line system multiple servers. Passengers are cordoned into a single line to wait for one of several airline agents to serve them. The number of agents scheduled for duty at the check-in counter is determined by waiting line operating characteristics based on different passenger arrival rates during the day and for different days.*

**Example 17.5**

**A Multiple-Server Waiting Line System**

The student health service at Tech has a waiting room in which chairs are placed along a wall, forming a single waiting line. Some students have health problems that only require a nurse. The students are served by three nurses, each located in a separate room. Students are treated on a first-come, first-served basis.

The health service administrator wants to analyze this queuing system because excessive waiting times can make students angry and they complain. Students have a medical problem and thus are impatient anyway. Waiting increases their impatience.

A study of the health service for a six-month period shows that an average of 10 students arrive per hour (according to a Poisson distribution), and an average of four students can be served per hour by a nurse (Poisson distributed).

*Solution*

$$\lambda = 10 \text{ students per hour}$$
$$\mu = 4 \text{ students per hour per service representative}$$
$$s = 3 \text{ service representatives}$$
$$s\mu = (3)(4) = 12 \qquad (> \lambda = 10)$$

Using the multiple-server model formulas, we can compute the following operating characteristics for the service department:

$$P_0 = \frac{1}{\left[\sum_{n=0}^{n=s-1} \frac{1}{n!}\left(\frac{\lambda}{\mu}\right)^n\right] + \frac{1}{s!}\left(\frac{\lambda}{\mu}\right)^s\left(\frac{s\mu}{s\mu - \lambda}\right)}$$

$$= \frac{1}{\left[\frac{0}{0!}\left(\frac{10}{4}\right)^0 + \frac{1}{1!}\left(\frac{10}{4}\right)^1 + \frac{1}{2!}\left(\frac{10}{4}\right)^2\right] + \frac{1}{3!}\left(\frac{10}{4}\right)^3 \frac{3(4)}{3(4) - 10}}$$

$= 0.045$ probability that no customers are in the health service.

Notice that this value could have been estimated from Table 17.2 using $\rho = 0.833$ (i.e., $\rho = \lambda/s\mu = 10/12 = 0.833$) and $s = 3$. $\rho$ is read from the left-hand column and $s$ across the top.

$$L = \frac{\lambda\mu(\lambda/\mu)^s}{(s-1)!(s\mu - \lambda)^2} P_0 + \frac{\lambda}{\mu}$$

$$= \frac{(10)(4)(10/4)^3}{(3-1)![3(4) - 10]^2}(0.045) + \frac{10}{4}$$

$= 6$ students in the health service

$$W = \frac{L}{\lambda}$$
$$= \frac{6}{10}$$
$$= 0.60 \text{ hour or 36 minutes in the health service}$$

$$L_q = L - \frac{\lambda}{\mu}$$
$$= 6 - \frac{10}{4}$$
$$= 3.5 \text{ students waiting to be served}$$

$$W_q = \frac{L_q}{\lambda}$$
$$= \frac{3.5}{10}$$
$$= 0.35 \text{ hour or 21 minutes waiting in line}$$

$$P_w = \frac{1}{s!}\left(\frac{\lambda}{\mu}\right)^s \frac{s\mu}{s\mu - \lambda} P_0$$
$$= \frac{1}{3!}\left(\frac{10}{4}\right)^3 \frac{3(4)}{3(4) - (10)} (0.045)$$
$$= 0.703 \text{ probability that a student must wait for service}$$
(i.e., that there are three or more students in the system)

The health service administrator has observed that students are frustrated by the waiting time of 21 minutes and the 0.703 probability of waiting. To try to improve matters, the administrator is considering adding another nurse. The operating characteristics for this system must be recomputed with $s = 4$ nurses.

Substituting $s = 4$ along with $\lambda$ and $\mu$ in the queuing formulas results in the following operating characteristics:

$P_0 = 0.073$ probability that no students are in the health service
$L = 3.0$ students in the health service
$W = 0.30$ hour, or 18 minutes, in the health service
$L_q = 0.5$ students waiting to be served
$W_q = 0.05$ hour, or 3 minutes, waiting in line
$P_w = 0.31$ probability that a student must wait for service

These results are significantly better; waiting time is reduced from 21 minutes to 3 minutes. This improvement in the quality of the service would have to be compared to the cost of adding an extra nurse.

## SOLUTION OF THE MULTIPLE-SERVER MODEL WITH EXCEL

The multiple-server model is somewhat cumbersome to set up in a spreadsheet format because of the necessity to enter some of the complex queuing formulas for this model into spreadsheet cells. Exhibit 17.5 shows an Excel spreadsheet set up for our Tech Health Service multiple-server example.

The formula for $P_0$ in cell D7 is shown on the formula bar at the top of the spreadsheet. As you can see, it is somewhat complex. The specific summation terms in $P_0$ for our example are entered directly into the formula. Thus, for a larger problem with a larger number of servers, additional summation terms would have to be entered. The term "FACT()" takes the factorial of a number or numbers in a cell. For example, FACT(1) is 1! Notice also that two of the other more complex formulas in this model for $P_w$ and $L$ are shown in boxes attached to Exhibit 17.5.

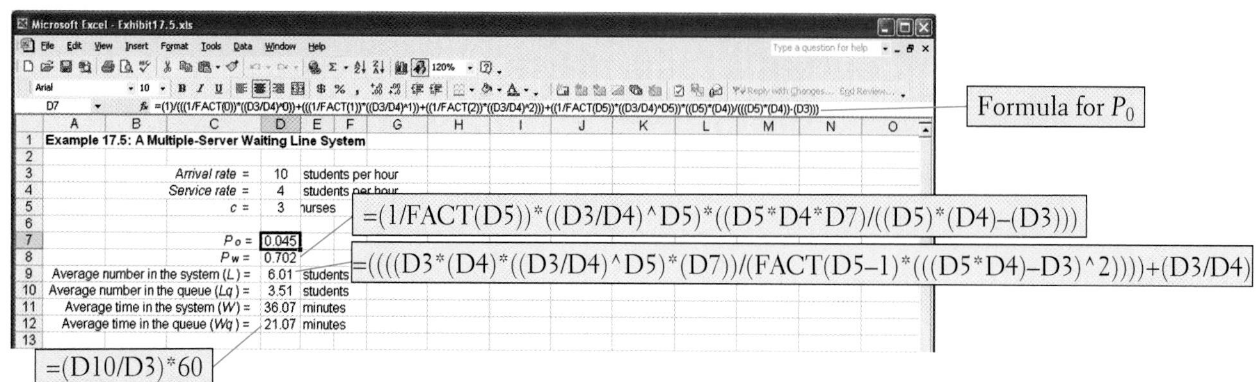

Exhibit 17.5

## SUMMARY

Since waiting is an integral part of many service-related operations, it is an important area of analysis, especially relative to achieving improved-quality service. The mathematical formulas for analyzing a variety of waiting line structures provide operating characteristics that are the basis for designing and improving waiting line systems.

However, although the queuing models presented in this chapter describe a wide variety of realistic waiting line systems, the number of conceivable waiting line structures is almost infinite, and many are so complex that no specific queuing model or formula is directly applicable. Examples of such complex queuing systems include a network of queues in which the leaving customers from several queuing systems provide the arrivals for succeeding queuing systems. A manufacturing system in which the process output from several production areas or production lines is the input to subsequent production areas or lines is an example of such a network. For such complex systems, a specific analytical model, such as those presented in this chapter, is not available, and simulation is the only alternative.

## SUMMARY OF KEY FORMULAS

*Single-Server Model*

$$P_0 = 1 - \frac{\lambda}{\mu} \qquad W = \frac{1}{\mu - \lambda}$$

$$P_n = \left(\frac{\lambda}{\mu}\right)^n \left(\frac{1-\lambda}{\mu}\right) \qquad W_q = \frac{\lambda}{\mu(\mu - \lambda)}$$

$$L = \frac{\lambda}{\mu - \lambda} \qquad \rho = \frac{\lambda}{\mu}$$

$$L_q = \frac{\lambda^2}{\mu(\mu - \lambda)} \qquad I = 1 - \frac{\lambda}{\mu}$$

*Single-Server Model with Undefined Service Times*

$$P_0 = 1 - \frac{\lambda}{\mu} \qquad W_q = \frac{L_q}{\lambda}$$

$$L_q = \frac{\lambda^2\sigma^2 + (\lambda/\mu)^2}{2(1 - \lambda/\mu)} \qquad W = W_q + \frac{1}{\mu}$$

$$L = L_q + \frac{\lambda}{\mu} \qquad \rho = \frac{\lambda}{\mu}$$

*Single-Server Model with Constant Service Times*

$$P_0 = 1 - \frac{\lambda}{\mu} \qquad W_q = \frac{L_q}{\lambda}$$

$$L_q = \frac{\lambda^2}{2\mu(\mu - \lambda)} \qquad W = W_q + \frac{1}{\mu}$$

$$L = L_q + \frac{\lambda}{\mu} \qquad \rho = \frac{\lambda}{\mu}$$

*Single-Server Model with Finite Queue*

$$P_0 = \frac{1 - \lambda/\mu}{1 - (\lambda/\mu)^{M+1}} \qquad W = \frac{L}{\lambda(1 - P_M)}$$

$$P_n = (P_0)(\lambda/\mu)^n, \quad n \le M \qquad W_q = W - \frac{1}{\mu}$$

$$L = \frac{\lambda/\mu}{1 - \lambda/\mu} - \frac{(M+1)(\lambda/\mu)^{M+1}}{1 - (\lambda/\mu)^{M+1}}$$

$$L_q = L - \frac{\lambda(1 - P_M)}{\mu}$$

*Single-Server Model with Finite Calling Population*

$$P_0 = \frac{1}{\sum_{n=0}^{N} \frac{N!}{(N-n)!}\left(\frac{\lambda}{\mu}\right)^n} \qquad W_q = \frac{L_q}{(N-L)\lambda}$$

$$L_q = N - \left(\frac{\lambda+\mu}{\lambda}\right)(1-P_0) \qquad W = W_q + \frac{1}{\mu}$$

$$L = L_q + (1-P_0) \qquad P_n = \frac{N!}{(N-n)!}\left(\frac{\lambda}{\mu}\right)^n P_0$$

*Multiple-Server Model*

$$P_0 = \frac{1}{\left[\sum_{n=0}^{n=s-1} \frac{1}{n!}\left(\frac{\lambda}{\mu}\right)^n\right] + \frac{1}{s!}\left(\frac{\lambda}{\mu}\right)^s\left(\frac{s\mu}{s\mu-\lambda}\right)}$$

$$P_n = \begin{cases} \frac{1}{s!s^{n-s}}\left(\frac{\lambda}{\mu}\right)^n P_0, & \text{for } n > s \\ \frac{1}{n!}\left(\frac{\lambda}{\mu}\right)^n P_0, & \text{for } n \le s \end{cases}$$

$$P_w = \frac{1}{s!}\left(\frac{\lambda}{\mu}\right)^s \frac{s\mu}{s\mu-\lambda} P_0$$

$$L = \frac{\lambda\mu(\lambda/\mu)^s}{(s-1)!(s\mu-\lambda)^2} P_0 + \frac{\lambda}{\mu}$$

$$W = \frac{L}{\lambda}$$

$$L_q = L - \frac{\lambda}{\mu}$$

$$W_q = W - \frac{1}{\mu}$$

## SUMMARY OF KEY TERMS

**arrival rate** the rate ($\lambda$) at which customers arrive at a service facility during a specified period.

**calling population** the source of customers to a waiting line.

**channels** the number of parallel servers.

**finite queue** a waiting line that has a limited capacity.

**infinite queue** a waiting line that grows to any length.

**operating characteristics** measures of waiting line performance expressed as averages.

**phases** the number of sequential servers a customer must go through to receive service.

**queue** a single waiting line that forms in front of a service facility.

**queue discipline** the order in which customers are served.

**service time** the time required to serve a customer; the time period divided by service time yields the service rate ($\mu$).

**utilization factor ($\rho$)** the probability the server is busy and the customer must wait.

## SOLVED PROBLEMS

### 1. SINGLE-SERVER MODEL

The new-accounts officer at the Citizens Northern Savings Bank enrolls all new customers in checking accounts. During the three-week period in August encompassing the beginning of the new school year at State University, the bank opens a lot of new accounts for students. The bank estimates that the arrival rate during this period will be Poisson distributed with an average of four customers per hour. The service time is exponentially distributed with an average of 12 minutes per customer to set up a new account. The bank wants to determine the operating characteristics for this system to determine if the current person is sufficient to handle the increased traffic.

#### SOLUTION

Determine operating characteristics for the single-server system:

$\lambda = 4$ customers per hour arrive

$\mu = 5$ customers per hour are served

$$P_0 = \left(1 - \frac{\lambda}{\mu}\right) = \left(1 - \frac{4}{5}\right)$$

= 0.20 probability of no customers in the system

$$L = \frac{\lambda}{\mu-\lambda} = \frac{4}{5-4}$$

= 4 customers on average in the queuing system

$$L_q = \frac{\lambda^2}{\mu(\mu-\lambda)} = \frac{4^2}{5(5-4)}$$

= 3.2 customers on average waiting

$$W = \frac{1}{\mu-\lambda} = \frac{1}{5-4}$$

= 1 hour average time in the system

$$W_q = \frac{\lambda}{\mu(\mu-\lambda)} = \frac{4}{5(5-4)}$$

= 0.80 hour (48 minutes) average time waiting

$$P_w = \frac{\lambda}{\mu} = \frac{4}{5}$$

= 0.80 probability that the new-accounts officer will be busy and that a customer must wait

The average waiting time of 48 minutes and the average time in the system are excessive, and the bank needs to add an extra employee during the busy period.

### 2. MULTIPLE-SERVER MODEL

The Citizens Northern Bank wants to compute the operating characteristics if an extra employee was added to assist with new-accounts enrollments.

**SOLUTION**

Determine the operating characteristics for the multiple-server system:

$\lambda = 4$ customers per hour arrive

$\mu = 5$ customers per hour are served

$s = 2$ servers

$$P_0 = \frac{1}{\left[\sum_{n=0}^{n=s-1} \frac{1}{n!}\left(\frac{\lambda}{\mu}\right)^n\right] + \frac{1}{s!}\left(\frac{\lambda}{\mu}\right)^s\left(\frac{s\mu}{s\mu - \lambda}\right)}$$

$$= \frac{1}{\left[\frac{1}{0!}\left(\frac{4}{5}\right)^0 + \frac{1}{1!}\left(\frac{4}{5}\right)^1\right] + \frac{1}{2!}\left(\frac{4}{5}\right)^2 \frac{(2)(5)}{(2)(5) - 4}}$$

$= 0.429$ probability that no customers are in the system

$$L = \frac{\lambda\mu(\lambda/\mu)^s}{(s-1)!(s\mu - \lambda)^2} P_0 + \frac{\lambda}{\mu}$$

$$= \frac{(4)(5)(4/5)^2}{1![(2)(5) - 4]^2}(0.429) + \frac{4}{5}$$

$= 0.952$ customer on average in the system

$$L_q = L - \frac{\lambda}{\mu} = 0.952 - \frac{4}{5}$$

$= 0.152$ customer on average waiting to be served

$$W = \frac{L}{\lambda} = \frac{0.952}{4}$$

$= 0.238$ hour (14.3 minutes) average time in the system

$$W_q = \frac{L_q}{\lambda} = \frac{0.152}{4}$$

$= 0.038$ hour (2.3 minutes) average time spent waiting in line

$$P_w = \frac{1}{s!}\left(\frac{\lambda}{\mu}\right)^s \frac{s\mu}{s\mu - \lambda} P_0$$

$$= \frac{1}{2!}\left(\frac{4}{5}\right)^2 \frac{(2)(5)}{(2)(5) - 4}(0.429)$$

$= 0.229$ probability that a customer must wait for service

The waiting time with the multiple-server model is 2.3 minutes, which is a significant improvement over the previous system; thus, the bank should add the second new-accounts officer.

# QUESTIONS

**17-1.** Identify 10 real-life examples of queuing systems with which you are familiar.

**17-2.** Why must the utilization factor in a single-server model be less than 1?

**17-3.** Give five examples of real-world queuing systems with finite calling populations.

**17-4.** List the elements that define a queuing system.

**17-5.** How can the results of queuing analysis be used by a decision maker for making decisions?

**17-6.** What is the mean effective service rate in a multiple-server model, and what must be its relationship to the arrival rate?

**17-7.** For each of the following queuing systems, indicate if it is a single- or multiple-server model, the queue discipline, and if its calling population is infinite or finite:

**a.** Hair salon
**b.** Bank
**c.** Laundromat
**d.** Doctor's office
**e.** Adviser's office
**f.** Airport runway
**g.** Service station
**h.** Copy center
**i.** Team trainer
**j.** Mainframe computer

**17-8.** For Example 17.1 in this chapter, discuss why the multiple-server model would or would not be appropriate as an alternative to reduce waiting time?

**17-9.** Discuss briefly the relationship between waiting line analysis and quality improvement.

**17-10.** Define the four basic waiting line structures and give an example of each.

**17-11.** Describe the traditional cost relationship in waiting line analysis.

**17-12.** **a.** Is the following statement true or false? The single-phase, single-channel model with Poisson arrivals and undefined service times will always have larger (i.e., greater) operating characteristic values (i.e., $W$, $W_q$, $L$, $L_q$) than the same model with exponentially distributed service times. Explain your answer.

**b.** Is the following statement true or false? The single-phase, single-channel model with Poisson arrivals and constant service times will always have smaller (i.e., lower) operating characteristic values (i.e., $W$, $W_q$, $L$, $L_q$) than the same model with exponentially distributed service times. Explain your answer.

**17-13.** Under what conditions can the basic single-server and multiple-server models be used to analyze a multiple-phase waiting line system?

**17-14.** Why do waiting lines form at a service facility even though there may be more than enough service capacity to meet normal demand in the long run?

**17-15.** Provide an example of when a first-in, first-out (FIFO) rule for queue discipline would not be appropriate.

**17-16.** Under what conditions will the single-channel, single-phase queuing model with Poisson arrivals and undefined service times provide the same operating characteristics as the basic model with exponentially distributed service times?

**17-17.** What types of waiting line systems have constant service times?

## PROBLEMS

**17-1.** McBurger's fast-food restaurant has a drive-through window with a single server who takes orders from an intercom and also is the cashier. The window operator is assisted by other employees who prepare the orders. Customers arrive at the ordering station prior to the drive-through window every 3.6 minutes (exponentially distributed) and the service time is 2.4 minutes (exponentially distributed). Determine the average length of the waiting line and the waiting time. Discuss the quality implications of your results. If you decide that the quality of the service could be improved, indicate what things you might do to improve quality.

**17-2.** The ticket booth on the Tech campus is operated by one person, who is selling tickets for the annual Tech versus State football game on Saturday. The ticket seller can serve an average of 12 customers per hour (Poisson distributed); on average, 18 customers arrive to purchase tickets each hour (Poisson distributed). Determine the average time a ticket buyer must wait and the portion of time the ticket seller is busy.

**17-3.** The Minute Stop Market has one pump for gasoline, which can service 10 customers per hour (Poisson distributed). Cars arrive at the pump at a rate of 5 per hour (Poisson distributed).

a. Determine the average queue length, the average time a car is in the system, and the average time a car must wait.

b. If, during the period from 4:00 P.M. to 5:00 P.M., the arrival rate increases to 12 cars per hour, what will be the effect on the average queue length?

**17-4.** The Universal Manufacturing Company produces a particular product in an assembly-line operation. One of the machines on the line is a drill press that has a single assembly line feeding into it. A partially completed unit arrives at the press to be worked on every 8 minutes, on average, according to an exponential distribution. The machine operator can process an average of 10 parts per hour (Poisson distributed). Determine the average number of parts waiting to be worked on, the percentage of time the operator is working, and the percentage of time the machine is idle.

**17-5.** The management of Universal Manufacturing Company (Problem 17-4) likes to have its operators working 90% of the time. What must the assembly line arrival rate be in order for the operators to be as busy as management would like?

**17-6.** The Peachtree Airport in Atlanta serves light aircraft. It has a single runway and one air traffic controller to land planes. It takes an airplane 8 minutes to land and clear the runway (exponentially distributed). Planes arrive at the airport at the rate of 5 per hour (Poisson distributed).

a. Determine the average number of planes that will stack up waiting to land.

b. Find the average time a plane must wait in line before it can land.

c. Calculate the average time it takes a plane to clear the runway once it has notified the airport that it is in the vicinity and wants to land.

d. The FAA has a rule that an air traffic controller can, on the average, land planes a maximum of 45 minutes out of every hour. There must be 15 minutes of idle time available to relieve the tension. Will this airport have to hire an extra air traffic controller?

**17-7.** The National Bank of Union City currently has one outside drive-up teller. It takes the teller an average of three minutes (exponentially distributed) to serve a bank customer. Customers arrive at the drive-up window at the rate of 12 per hour (Poisson distributed). The bank operations officer is currently analyzing the possibility of adding a second drive-up window at an annual cost of $20,000. It is assumed that arriving cars would be equally divided between both windows. The operations officer estimates that each minute's reduction in customer waiting time would increase the bank's revenue by $2000 annually. Should the second drive-up window be installed? What other factors should be considered in the decision besides cost?

**17-8.** During registration at Tech every quarter, students in the Department of Management must have their courses approved by the departmental advisor. It takes the advisor an average of five minutes (exponentially distributed) to approve each schedule, and students arrive at the adviser's office at the rate of 10 per hour (Poisson distributed). Compute $L$, $L_q$, $W$, $W_q$, and $\rho$. What do you think about this system? How would you change it?

**17-9.** All trucks traveling on Interstate 40 between Albuquerque and Amarillo are required to stop at a weigh station. Trucks arrive at the weigh station at a rate of 120 per eight-hour day (Poisson distributed), and the station can weigh, on the average, 140 trucks per day (Poisson distributed).

a. Determine the average number of trucks waiting, the average time spent at the weigh station by each truck, and the average waiting time before being weighed for each truck.

b. If the truck drivers find out they must remain at the weigh station longer than 15 minutes on the average, they will start taking a different route or traveling at night, thus depriving the state of taxes. The state of New Mexico estimates it loses $10,000 in taxes per year for each extra minute (over 15) that trucks must remain at the weigh station. A new set of scales would have the same service capacity as the present set of scales, and it is assumed that arriving trucks would line up equally behind the two sets of scales. It would cost $50,000 per year to operate the new scales. Should the state install the new set of scales?

**17-10.** In Problem 17-9(a), suppose arriving truck drivers look to see how many trucks are waiting to be weighed at the weigh station. If they see four or more trucks in line, they will pass by the station and risk being caught and ticketed. What is the probability that a truck will pass by the station?

**17-11.** In Problem 17-8, the head of the Management Department at Tech is considering the addition of a second advisor in the college advising office to serve students waiting to have their schedules approved. This new advisor could serve the same number of students per hour as the present advisor. Determine $L$, $L_q$, $W$, and $W_q$ for this altered advising system. As a student, would you recommend adding the advisor?

**17-12.** Annie Campbell is a nurse on the evening shift from 10:00 P.M. to 6:00 A.M. at Community Hospital. She is responsible for 15 patients in her area. She averages two calls from each of her patients every evening (Poisson distributed), and she must spend an average of 10 minutes (negative exponential distribution) with each patient who calls. Nurse Smith has indicated to her shift supervisor that although she has not kept records she believes her patients must wait about 10 minutes on average for her to respond and she has requested that her supervisor assign a second nurse to her area. The supervisor believes 10 minutes is too long to wait, but she does not want her nurses to be idle more than 40% of the time. Determine what the supervisor should do.

**17-13.** Wallace Publishers has a large number of employees who use the company's single fax machine. Employees arrive randomly to use the fax machine at an average rate of 20 per hour. This arrival process is approximated by a Poisson distribution. Employees spend an average of two minutes using the fax machine, either transmitting or receiving items. The time spent using the machine is distributed according to a negative exponential distribution. Employees line up in single file to use the machine, and they obtain access to it on a first-come, first-served basis. There is no defined limit to the number who can line up to use the machine.

Management has determined that by assigning an operator to the fax machine rather than allowing the employees to operate the machine themselves, it can reduce the average service time from the current 2 minutes to 1.5 minutes. However, the fax operator's salary is $8 per hour, which must be paid 8 hours per day even if there are no employees wishing to use the fax machine part of the time. Management has estimated the cost of employee time spent waiting in line and at the fax machine during service to be 17¢ per minute (based on an average salary of $10.20 per hour per employee). Should the firm assign an operator to the fax machine?

**17-14.** The Universal Manufacturing Company has a single assembly line that feeds two drill presses in parallel. As partially completed products come off the line, they are lined up to be worked on as drill presses become available. The units arrive at the workstation (containing both presses) at the rate of 90 per hour (Poisson distributed). Each press operator can process an average of 60 units per hour (Poisson distributed). Compute $L$, $L_q$, $W$, and $W_q$.

**17-15.** The Escargot is a small French restaurant with 6 waiters and waitresses. The average service time at the restaurant for a table (of any size) is 80 minutes (exponentially distributed). The restaurant does not take reservations and parties arrive for dinner (and stay and wait) every 16 minutes (Poisson distributed). The restaurant is concerned that a lengthy waiting time might hurt its business in the long run. What is the current waiting time and queue length for the restaurant? Discuss the quality implications of the current waiting time and any actions the restaurant might take.

**17-16.** Cakes baked by the Freshfood Bakery are transported from the ovens to be packaged by one of three wrappers. Each wrapper can wrap an average of 120 cakes per hour (Poisson distributed). The cakes are brought to the wrappers at the rate of 300 per hour (Poisson distributed). If a cake sits longer than 5 minutes before being wrapped, it will not be fresh enough to meet the bakery's quality control standards. Does the bakery need to hire another wrapper?

**17-17.** The Draper Clinic has two general practitioners who see patients daily. An average of 6.5 patients arrive at the clinic per hour (Poisson distributed). Each doctor spends an average of 15 minutes (exponentially distributed) with a patient. The patients wait in a waiting area until one of the two doctors is able to see them. However, since patients typically do not feel well when they come to the clinic, the doctors do not believe it is good practice to have a patient wait longer than an average of 20 minutes. Should this clinic add a third doctor, and, if so, will this alleviate the waiting problem?

**17-18.** The Wearever Shoe Company is going to open a new branch at a mall, and company managers are attempting to determine how many salespeople to hire. Based on an analysis of mall traffic, the company estimates that customers will arrive at the store at the rate of 9 per hour (Poisson distributed), and from past experience at its other branches, the company knows that salespeople can serve an average of 6 customers per hour (Poisson distributed). How many salespeople should the company hire in order to maintain a company policy that on average a customer should have to wait for service no more than 30% of the time?

**17-19.** When customers arrive at Gilley's Ice Cream Shop, they take a number and wait to be called to purchase ice cream from one of the counter servers. From experience in past summers, the store's staff knows that customers arrive at the rate of 35 per hour (Poisson distributed) on summer days between 3:00 P.M. and 10:00 P.M. and a server can serve 15 customers per hour on average (Poisson distributed). Gilley's wants to make sure that customers wait no longer than 5 minutes for service. Gilley's is contemplating keeping three servers behind the ice cream counter during the peak summer hours. Will this number be adequate to meet the waiting time policy?

**17-20.** Huang's television-repair service receives an average of four TV sets per eight-hour day to be repaired. The service manager would like to be able to tell customers that they can expect their TV back in 3 days. What average repair time per set will the repair shop have to achieve to provide 3-day service on the average? (Assume that the arrival rate is Poisson distributed and repair times are exponentially distributed.)

**17-21.** Partially completed products arrive at a workstation in a manufacturing operation at a mean rate of 40 per hour (Poisson distributed). The processing time at the workstation averages 1.2 minutes per unit (exponentially distributed). The manufacturing company estimates that each unit of in-process inventory at the workstation costs $31 per day (on the average). However, the company can add extra employees and reduce the processing time to 0.90 minute per unit at a cost of $52 per day. Determine whether the company should continue the present operation or add extra employees.

**17-22.** The Seaboard Shipping Company has a warehouse terminal in Spartanburg, South Carolina. The capacity of each terminal dock is three trucks. As trucks enter the terminal, the drivers receive numbers, and when one of the three dock spaces becomes available, the truck with the lowest number enters the vacant dock. Truck arrivals are Poisson distributed, and the unloading and loading times (service times) are exponentially distributed. The average arrival rate at the terminal is five trucks per hour, and the average service rate per dock is two trucks per hour (30 minutes per truck).

a. Compute $L$, $L_q$, $W$, and $W_q$.
b. The management of the shipping company is considering adding extra employees and equipment to improve the average service time per terminal dock to 25 minutes per truck. It would cost the company $18,000 per year to achieve this improved service. Management estimates that it will increase its profit by $750 per year for each minute it is able to reduce a truck's waiting time. Determine whether management should make the investment.
c. Now suppose that the managers of the shipping company have decided that truck waiting time is excessive and they want to reduce the waiting time. They have determined that there are two alternatives available for reducing the waiting time. They can add a fourth dock, or they can add extra employees and equipment at the existing docks, which will reduce the average service time per location from the original 30 minutes per truck to 23 minutes per truck. The costs of these alternatives are approximately equal. Management desires to implement the alternative that reduces waiting time by the greatest amount. Which alternative should be selected?

**17-23.** Drivers who come to get their licenses at the department of motor vehicles have their photograph taken by an automated machine that develops the photograph onto the license card and laminates the complete license. The machine requires a constant time of 4.5 minutes to develop a completed license. If drivers arrive at the machine at the mean rate of 11 per hour (Poisson distributed), determine the average length of the waiting line and the average waiting time.

**17-24.** A vending machine at Municipal Airport dispenses hot coffee, hot chocolate, or hot tea in a constant service time of 30 seconds. Customers arrive at the vending machine at a mean rate of 50 per hour, Poisson distributed. Determine the average length of the waiting line and the average time a customer must wait.

**17-25.** In Problem 17-20 suppose that Huang's television-repair service cannot accommodate more than 10 TV sets at a time (under repair and waiting for service). What is the probability that the number of TV sets on hand will exceed the shop capacity?

**17-26.** Norfolk, Virginia, a major seaport on the East Coast, has a ship coal-loading facility. Currently, coal trucks filled with coal arrive at the port facility at the mean rate of 149 per day (Poisson distributed). The facility operates 24 hours a day. The coal trucks are unloaded one at a time on a first-come, first-served basis by automated mechanical equipment that empties the trucks in a constant time of eight minutes per truck, regardless of truck size. The port authority is negotiating with a coal company for an additional 30 trucks per day. However, the coal company will not use this port facility unless the port authority can assure them that their coal trucks will not have to wait to be unloaded at the port facility for more than 12 hours per truck on the average. Can the port authority provide this assurance?

**17-27.** The Waterfall Buffet in the lower level of the National Art Gallery serves food cafeteria-style daily to visitors and employees. The buffet is self-service. From 7:00 A.M. to 9:00 A.M. customers arrive at the buffet at a rate of eight per minute; from 9:00 A.M. to noon, at four per minute; from noon to 2:00, at 14 per minute; and from 2:00 P.M. to closing at 5:00 P.M., at eight per minute (Poisson distributed). All the customers take about the same amount of time to serve themselves and proceed to the buffet. Once a customer goes through the buffet, it takes an average of 0.4 minute (exponentially distributed) to pay the cashier. The gallery does not want a customer to have to wait longer than four minutes to pay. How many cashiers should be working at each of the four times during the day?

**17-28.** The Hair Port is a hair-styling salon at Riverside Mall. Four stylists are always available to serve customers on a first-come, first-served basis. Customers arrive at an average rate of four per hour (Poisson distributed), and the stylists spend an average of 45 minutes (exponentially distributed) on each customer.

a. Determine the average number of customers in the salon, the average time a customer must wait, and the average number waiting to be served.
b. The salon manager is considering adding a fifth stylist. Would this have a significant impact on waiting time?

**17-29.** The Riverton Police Department has eight patrol cars that are on constant call 24 hours per day. A patrol car requires repairs every 30 days, on average, according to an exponential distribution. When a patrol car is in need of repair it is driven into the motor pool, which has a repairperson on duty at all times. The average time required to repair a patrol car is 12 hours (exponentially distributed). Determine the average time a patrol car is not available for use and the average number of patrol cars out of service at any one time, and indicate if the repair service seems adequate.

**17-30.** The Crosstown Cab Company has four cabs on duty during normal business hours. The cab company dispatcher receives requests for service every seven minutes, on average, according to an exponential distribution. The average time to complete a trip is 20 minutes (exponentially distributed). Determine the average number of customers waiting for service and the average time a customer must wait for a cab.

**17-31.** A retail catalogue operation employs a bank of six telephone operators, who process orders using computer terminals. When a terminal breaks down, it must be disconnected and taken to a nearby electronics repair shop, where it is repaired. The mean time between terminal breakdowns is six working days, and the mean time required to repair a terminal is two working days (both exponentially distributed). As a result of lost sales, it costs the mail-order operation an estimated $50 per day in lost profits each day a terminal is out for repair. The company pays the electronics repair shop $3000 per year on a service agreement to repair the terminals. The company is considering the possibility of signing a new service agreement with another electronics repair shop that will provide substitute terminals while the broken ones are at the repair shop. However, the new service agreement would cost the mail-order operation $15,000 per year. Assuming that there are 250 working days in a year, determine what the mail-order operation should do.

**17-32.** The Baytown Post Office has four stations for service. Customers line up in single file for service on an FIFO basis. The mean arrival rate is 40 per hour, Poisson distributed, and the mean service time per server is five minutes, exponentially distributed. Compute the operating characteristics for this operation. Does the operation appear to be satisfactory in terms of: (a) postal workers' (servers') idle time; (b) customer waiting time and/or the number waiting for service; and (c) the percentage of the time a customer can walk in and get served without waiting at all?

**17-33.** Andromeda Books is a small independent publisher of fiction and nonfiction books. Each week the publisher receives an average of eight unsolicited manuscripts to review (Poisson distributed). The publisher has 12 freelance reviewers in the area who read and evaluate manuscripts. It takes a reviewer an average of 10 days (exponentially distributed) to read a manuscript and write a brief synopsis. (Reviewers work on their own, seven days a week). Determine how long the publisher must wait on average to receive a reviewer's manuscript evaluation, how many manuscripts are waiting to be reviewed, and how busy the reviewers are.

**17-34.** Amanda Fall is starting up a new house painting business, Fall Colors. She has been advertising in the local newspaper for several months, and based on inquiries and informal surveys of the local housing market she anticipates that she will get painting jobs at the rate of four per week (Poisson distributed). Amanda has also determined that it will take a four-person team of painters an average of 0.7 week (exponentially distributed) for a typical painting job.

a. Determine the number of teams of painters Amanda needs to hire so that customers will have to wait no longer than two weeks to get their houses painted.
b. If the average price for a painting job is $1700 and Amanda pays a team of painters $500 per week, will she make any money?

**17-35.** The Associate Dean in the College of Business at Tech is attempting to determine which of two copiers he should lease for the college's administrative suite. A regular copier leases for $8 per hour and it takes an employee an average of six minutes (exponentially distributed) to complete a copying job. A deluxe, high-speed copier leases for $16 per hour, and it requires an average of three minutes to complete a copying job. Employees arrive at the copying machine at the rate of seven per hour (Poisson distributed) and an employee's time is valued at $10 per hour. Determine which copier the college should lease.

**17-36.** The Corner Cleaners 24-hour laundromat has 16 washing machines. A machine breaks down every 20 days (exponentially distributed). The repair service the laundromat contracts takes an average of one day to repair a machine (exponentially distributed). A washing machine averages $5 per hour in revenue. The laundromat is considering a new repair service that guarantees repairs in 0.50 day, but they charge $10 more per hour than the current repair service. Should the laundromat switch to the new repair service?

**17-37.** The Ritz Hotel has enough space for six taxicabs to load passengers, line up, and wait for guests at its entrance. Cabs arrive at the hotel every 10 minutes and if a taxi drives by the hotel and the line is full it must drive on. Hotel guests require taxis every five minutes on average and then it takes a cab driver an average of 3.5 minutes to load passengers and luggage and leave the hotel (exponentially distributed).

a. What is the average time a cab must wait for a fare?
b. What is the probability that the line will be full when a cab drives by and it must drive on?

**17-38.** The local Quick Burger fast food restaurant has a drive-through window. Customers in cars arrive at the window at the rate of 10 per hour (Poisson distributed). It requires an average of four minutes (exponentially distributed) to take and fill an order. The restaurant chain has a service goal of an average waiting time of three minutes.

a. Will the current system meet the restaurant's service goal?
b. If the restaurant is not meeting its service goal, it can add a second drive-in window that will reduce the service time per customer to 2.5 minutes. Will the additional window enable the restaurant to meet its service goal?
c. During the two-hour lunch period the arrival rate of drive-in customers increases to 20 per hour. Will the two-window system be able to achieve the restaurant's service goal during the rush period?

**17-39.** From 3:00 P.M. to 8:00 P.M. the local Big-W Supermarket has a steady arrival of customers. Customers finish shopping and arrive at the checkout area at the rate of 80 per hour (Poisson distributed). It is assumed that when customers arrive at the cash registers they will divide themselves relatively evenly so that all the checkout lines are even. The average checkout time at a register is seven minutes (exponentially distributed). The store manager's service goal is for customers to be out of the store within 12 minutes (on average) after they complete their shopping and arrive at the cash register. How many cash registers must the store have open in order to achieve the manager's service goal?

**17-40.** Customers arrive at the lobby of the exclusive and expensive Ritz Hotel at the rate of 40 per hour (Poisson distributed) to check in. The hotel normally has three clerks available at the desk to check guests in. The average time for a clerk to check in a guest is four minutes (exponentially distributed). Clerks at the Regency are paid $12 per hour and the hotel assigns a goodwill cost of $2 per minute for the time a guest must wait in line. Determine if the present check-in system is cost effective; if it is not, recommend what hotel management should do.

**17-41.** The Delacroix Inn in Alexandria is a small exclusive hotel with 20 rooms. Guests can call housekeeping from 8:00 A.M. to midnight for any of their service needs. Housekeeping keeps one person on duty during this time to respond to guest calls. Each room averages 0.7 call per day to housekeeping (Poisson distributed), and a guest request requires an average response time of 30 minutes (exponentially distributed) from the staff person. Determine the portion of time the staff person is busy and how long a guest must wait for his or her request to be addressed. Does the housekeeping system seem adequate?

**17-42.** Jim Carter builds custom furniture, primarily cabinets, bookcases, small tables, and chairs. He only works on one piece of furniture for a customer at a time. It takes him an average of five weeks (exponentially distributed) to build a piece of furniture. An average of 14 customers approach Jim to order pieces of furniture each year (Poisson distributed): however, Jim will only take a maximum of eight advance orders. Determine the average time a customer must wait to receive a furniture order once it is placed and how busy Jim is. What is the probability that a customer will be able to place an order with Jim?

**17-43.** Judith Lewis is a doctoral student at State University, and she also works full time as an academic tutor for 10 scholarship student athletes. She took the job hoping it would leave her free time between tutoring to devote to her own studies. An athlete visits her for tutoring an average of every 16 hours (exponentially distributed), and she spends an average 1.5 hours (exponentially distributed) with the athlete. She is able to tutor only one athlete at a time, and athletes study while they are waiting.

a. Determine how long a player must wait to see her and the percentage of time Judith is busy. Does the job seem to meet Judith's expectations, and does the system seem adequate to meet the athlete's needs?
b. If the results in part (a) indicate that the tutoring arrangement is ineffective, suggest an adjustment that could make it better for both the athletes and Judith.

## CASE PROBLEM 17.1

### *The College of Business Copy Center*

The copy center in the College of Business at State University has become an increasingly contentious item among the college administrators. The department heads have complained to the associate dean about the long lines and waiting times for their secretaries at the copy center. They claim that it is a waste of scarce resources for the secretaries to wait in line talking when they could be doing more productive work in the office. Hanford Burris, the associate dean, says the limited operating budget will not allow the college to purchase a new copier or copiers to relieve the problem. This standoff has been going on for several years.

To make her case for improved copying facilities, Lauren Moore, a teacher in Operations Management, assigned students in her class to gather some information about the copy center as a class project. The students were to record the arrivals at the center and the length of time it took to do a copy job once the secretary actually reached a copy machine. In addition, the students were to describe how the copy center system worked.

When the students completed the project, they turned in a report to Professor Moore. The report described the copy center as containing two machines. When secretaries arrive for a copy job, they join a queue, which looked more like milling around to the students, but they acknowledged that each secretary knew when it was his or her turn, and, in effect, the secretaries formed a single queue for the first available copy machine. Also, since copy jobs are assigned tasks, secretaries always stayed to do the job no matter how long the line was or how long they had to wait. They never left the queue.

From the data the students gathered, Professor Moore was able to determine that secretaries arrived every eight minutes for a copy job and that the arrival rate was Poisson distributed. Furthermore, she was able to determine that the average time it takes to complete a job was 12 minutes, and this is exponentially distributed.

Using her department's personnel records and data from the university personnel office, Dr. Moore determined that a secretary's average salary is $8.50 per hour. From her academic calendar she added up the actual days in the year when the college and departmental offices were open and found there were 247. However, as she added up working days, it occurred to her that during the summer months the workload is much less, and the copy center would probably get less traffic. The summer included about 70 days, during which she expected the copy center traffic would be about half of what it is during the normal year, but she speculated that the average time of a copying job would remain about the same.

Professor Moore next called a local office supply firm to check the prices on copiers. A new copier of the type in the copy center now would cost $36,000. It would also require $8000 per year for maintenance and would have a normal useful life of 6 years.

Do you think Dr. Moore will be able to convince the associate dean that a new copy machine will be cost effective?

## CASE PROBLEM 17.2

### *Northwoods Backpackers*

Bob and Carol Packer operate a successful outdoor wear store in Vermont called Northwoods Backpackers. They stock mostly cold-weather outdoor items such as hiking and backpacking clothes, gear, and accessories. They established an excellent reputation throughout New England for quality products and service. Eventually, Bob and Carol noticed that more and more of their sales were from customers who did not live in the immediate vicinity but were calling in orders on the telephone. As a result, the Packers decided to distribute a catalog and establish a phone-order service. The order department consisted of five operators working eight hours per day from 10:00 A.M. to 6:00 P.M., Monday through Friday. For a few years the mail-order service was only moderately successful; the Packers just about broke even on their investment. However, during the holiday season of the third year of the catalog order service, they were overwhelmed with phone orders. Although they made a substantial profit, they were concerned about the large number of lost sales they estimated they incurred. Based on information provided by the telephone company regarding call volume and complaints from customers, the Packers estimated they lost sales of approximately $100,000. Also they felt they had lost a substantial number of old and potentially new customers because of the poor service of the catalog order department.

Prior to the next holiday season, the Packers explored several alternatives for improving the catalog order service. The current system includes the five original operators with computer terminals who work eight-hour days, five days per week. The Packers have hired a consultant to study this system, and she reported that the time for an operator to take a customer order is exponentially distributed with a mean of 3.6 minutes. Calls are expected to arrive at the telephone center during the six-week holiday season according to a Poisson distribution with a mean rate of 175 calls per hour. When all operators are busy, callers are put on hold, listening to music until an operator can answer. Waiting calls are answered on a first-in, first-out basis. Based on her experience with other catalog telephone order operations and data from Northwoods Backpackers, the consultant has determined that if Northwoods Backpackers can reduce customer call waiting time to approximately one-half minute or less, the company will save $135,000 in lost sales during the coming holiday season.

Therefore, the Packers have adopted this level of call service as their goal. However, in addition to simply avoiding lost sales, the Packers believe it is important to reduce waiting time to maintain their reputation for good customer service. Thus, they would like about 70% of their callers to receive immediate service.

The Packers can maintain the same number of workstations/computer terminals they currently have and increase their service to 16 hours per day with two operator shifts running from 8:00 A.M. to midnight. The Packers believe when customers become aware of their extended hours the calls will spread out uniformly, resulting in a new call average arrival rate of 87.5 calls per hour (still Poisson distributed). This schedule change would cost Northwoods Backpackers approximately $11,500 for the six-week holiday season.

Another alternative for reducing customer waiting times is to offer weekend service. However, the Packers believe that if they do offer weekend service, it must coincide with whatever service they offer during the week. In other words, if they have phone order service eight hours per day during the week, they must have the same service during the weekend; the same is true with 16-hours-per-day service. They feel that if weekend hours differ from weekday hours it will confuse customers. If eight-hour service is offered seven days per week, the new call arrival rate will be reduced to 125 calls per hour at a cost of $3600. If Northwoods offers 16-hour service, the mean call arrival rate will be reduced to 62.5 calls per hour, at a cost of $7300.

Still another possibility is to add more operator stations. Each station includes a desk, an operator, a phone, and a computer terminal. An additional station that is in operation five days per week, eight hours per day, will cost $2900 for the holiday season. For a 16-hour day the cost per new station is $4700. For seven-day service, the cost of an additional station for eight-hour per-day service is $3800; for 16-hour-per-day service the cost is $6300.

The facility Northwoods Backpackers uses to house its operators can accommodate a maximum of 10 stations. Additional operators in excess of 10 would require the Packers to lease, remodel, and wire a new facility, which is a capital expenditure they do not want to undertake this holiday season. Alternatively, the Packers do not want to reduce their current number of operator stations.

Determine what order service configuration the Packers should use to achieve their goals, and explain your recommendation.

## REFERENCES

Cooper, R. B. *Introduction to Queuing Theory*, 2nd ed. New York: North Holland, 1981.

Gross, D., and C. Harris. *Fundamentals of Queuing Theory*, 2nd ed. New York: Wiley, 1985.

Hillier, F. S., and O. S. Yu. *Queuing Tables and Graphics*. New York: North Holland, 1981.

Kleinrock, L. *Queuing Systems*, vols. 1 and 2. New York: Wiley, 1975.

Lee, A. *Applied Queuing Theory*. New York: St. Martin's Press, 1966.

Morse, P. M. *Queues, Inventories, and Maintenance*. New York: Wiley, 1958.

Saaty, T. L. *Elements of Queuing Theory with Applications*. New York: Dover, 1983.

Solomon, S. L. *Simulation of Waiting Line Systems*. Upper Saddle River, NJ: Prentice Hall, 1983.

White, J. A., J. W. Schmidt, and G. K. Bennett. *Analysis of Queuing Systems*. New York: Academic Press, 1975.

# Epilogue: Change

The single most pervasive factor that has affected the field of operations management—and business in general—during the past two decades is change. Information technology and the Internet represent just one manifestation of the rapid, mind-boggling changes that have occurred since the late 1970s. As the 1980s approached, we were keypunching cards for mainframe computers and the PC was only in planning steps at IBM. When one thought of Honda, it was in terms of motorcycles or boxlike little cars that people jokingly said were run by lawnmower engines. VCRs and DVDs were unimaginable to most people, and televisions were made in America. JIT was the way they pronounced *jet* in Texas, not an approach to inventory management; and strategic planning at many companies was nothing more than next year's "management by objectives (MBO)" plan. Robots were in science fiction movies, not on assembly lines, and good stereo speakers were only slightly smaller than a closet door. Quality was something most U.S. consumers thought they could not afford, or didn't think about at all.

Although technology progressed at a steady pace, markets remained parochial and were certainly not international. The changes in products often tended to be cosmetic rather than substantive. Cars looked different in 1970 from what they did in 1940; but to our parents the only real difference was that they were higher-priced, came in colors other than black, broke down more frequently, and cost more to repair. They had the same basic features, traveled at the same speed, got the same gas mileage, and were about as comfortable. Basic operational principles and functions remained relatively consistent. Manufacturing was dominated by the assembly line, and workers and jobs conformed to norms that had gained credence at the beginning of the last century. The field of operations management was static, sustaining the basic principles and techniques of scheduling, inventory control, purchasing, and job design throughout much of the twentieth century. There was little need for change, because consumer demands and tastes seemed to remain the same.

During the period between the end of World War I and the late 1970s, the pace of change in manufacturing was slow and deliberate, almost creeping in comparison to the change of the past 20 years. A friend who worked at a textile mill that was a major manufacturer of denim in the early 1970s recounts that some of the machines in the plant dated back to just after the Civil War. Parts were replaced as they wore out, but the basic technology and products remained the same. Visiting the plant a decade later, he found it was unrecognizable. It not only had undergone a technological metamorphosis, but it was clean and safe. Unable to compete with foreign competitors under the old ground rules, the textile company adapted to change.

When change came in the late 1970s, it seemed to start with a low rumble, recognizable to only a few seers and visionaries. Then it gained momentum, like a snowball, going downhill fast through the 1980s and 1990s hurtling into the twenty-first century. Change became both the diagnosis for the failure of hundreds of businesses and enterprises and the prescription for success for many others. Technological change, change in modes of transportation, changes in communication, and, most importantly, the development of information and computer technology and microelectronics resulted in a new and expanded international market environment and new products to drive it. Consumer tastes and expectations, once static, undemanding and parochial, suddenly became eclectic, diverse, and discriminating.

If there is one consistent theme that seems to run through all the success stories reported in the media and described in this book, it is recognition of the need to adapt to change. Companies that have survived in this changing environment—so far—point to their ability to adapt to changes as the key to their success. However, they are also quick to point out that their future depends on their ability to recognize changes in the future before they are overwhelmed by them and to react to them as rapidly as possible. Employers demand that employees be willing to accept change and to retrain and adapt or lose their jobs. Likewise, employees now look to companies for a commitment to invest in their training and education to help them withstand the onslaught of change in the future. There is a renewed commitment to research and new product development and to changing the way companies operate.

How has this affected the field of operations management and its teaching? Initially caught napping, OM educators and academicians are now riding the whirlwind and, like others, are reeducating themselves so they can teach a new generation of students the latest methods and techniques in OM. This book has attempted to reflect this era of change and provide a contemporary, up-to-date perspective on OM. This need explains why we have focused on change agents like information technology and the Internet.

In our opinion computers, information technology, and the Internet are the most pervasive and important change in operations management in this new century, and strategy or strategic planning is the most important means for coping with change now and in the future, in order to remain competitive. Unfortunately, parts of this book will probably be outdated by the time it reaches students and teachers. The interval between the time we started revising this edition and the time when it was published was approximately two years, plenty of time for significant changes to occur. So we apologize in advance for our omissions and deficiencies and assure you that they did not result from a lack of trying.

Yet as we speak of change, we are also reminded of a popular song of the 1970s, "Everything Old Is New Again." A number of the most important reactions to change have been the rediscovery of things that worked in the past. We have recounted how the basic principles of TQM, W. E. Deming's 14 points, and statistical process control are not new but are simply rediscovered philosophies and tools from an earlier era. Worker empowerment seems like a throwback to the era before F. W. Taylor at the turn of the century. It does not appear that Harley-Davidson's machinists, who control their own work centers, deal with vendors, and are responsible for product quality, are much different from the skilled craftspeople/machinists of the early 1900s. They likewise controlled their own workplaces and were not subject to supervisory management. We hear our grandparents reminisce about this era: products were made to last and workers took pride in what they made—not so much different than today's emerging "new" philosophy of the workplace. Adapting to change means not only trying the new, but also discovering the best of the old.

What change does the new century hold? We are no more able to predict the changes of the next decade now than businesspeople and academicians were in the 1970s. However, it is certain that change will occur, and it is likely to be as rapid and powerful—even more so—than the changes we have just experienced. The lesson of the recent past is that to be successful in the future, companies must be ready, able, and willing to adapt to change. Similarly, to secure and retain jobs in the future, employees and students must be willing to retrain and educate themselves to adapt to change.

January 2005<br>
Roberta S. Russell<br>
Bernard W. Taylor III

# Appendix A: Normal Curve Areas

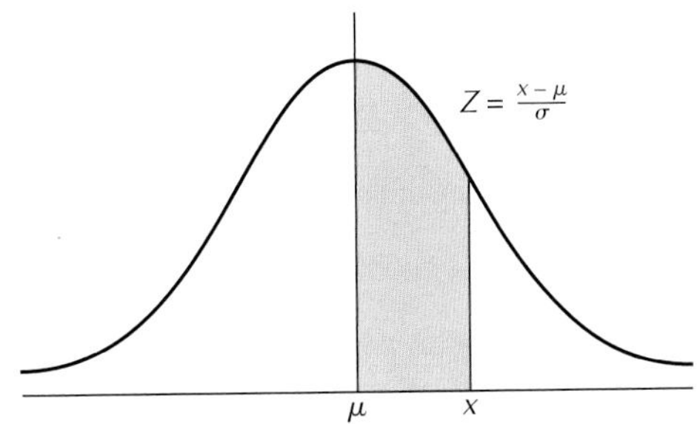


**TABLE A.1 Normal Curve Areas**

| Z | 0.00 | 0.01 | 0.02 | 0.03 | 0.04 | 0.05 | 0.06 | 0.07 | 0.08 | 0.09 |
|---|---|---|---|---|---|---|---|---|---|---|
| 0.0 | 0.0000 | 0.0040 | 0.0080 | 0.0120 | 0.0160 | 0.0199 | 0.0239 | 0.0279 | 0.0319 | 0.0359 |
| 0.1 | 0.0398 | 0.0438 | 0.0478 | 0.0517 | 0.0557 | 0.0596 | 0.0636 | 0.0675 | 0.0714 | 0.0753 |
| 0.2 | 0.0793 | 0.0832 | 0.0871 | 0.0910 | 0.0948 | 0.0987 | 0.1026 | 0.1064 | 0.1103 | 0.1141 |
| 0.3 | 0.1179 | 0.1217 | 0.1255 | 0.1293 | 0.1331 | 0.1368 | 0.1406 | 0.1443 | 0.1480 | 0.1517 |
| 0.4 | 0.1554 | 0.1591 | 0.1628 | 0.1664 | 0.1700 | 0.1736 | 0.1772 | 0.1808 | 0.1844 | 0.1879 |
| 0.5 | 0.1915 | 0.1950 | 0.1985 | 0.2019 | 0.2054 | 0.2088 | 0.2123 | 0.2157 | 0.2190 | 0.2224 |
| 0.6 | 0.2257 | 0.2291 | 0.2324 | 0.2357 | 0.2389 | 0.2422 | 0.2454 | 0.2486 | 0.2517 | 0.2549 |
| 0.7 | 0.2580 | 0.2611 | 0.2642 | 0.2673 | 0.2704 | 0.2734 | 0.2764 | 0.2794 | 0.2823 | 0.2852 |
| 0.8 | 0.2881 | 0.2910 | 0.2939 | 0.2967 | 0.2995 | 0.3023 | 0.3051 | 0.3078 | 0.3106 | 0.3133 |
| 0.9 | 0.3159 | 0.3186 | 0.3212 | 0.3238 | 0.3264 | 0.3289 | 0.3315 | 0.3340 | 0.3365 | 0.3389 |
| 1.0 | 0.3413 | 0.3438 | 0.3461 | 0.3485 | 0.3508 | 0.3531 | 0.3554 | 0.3577 | 0.3599 | 0.3621 |
| 1.1 | 0.3643 | 0.3665 | 0.3686 | 0.3708 | 0.3729 | 0.3749 | 0.3770 | 0.3790 | 0.3810 | 0.3830 |
| 1.2 | 0.3849 | 0.3869 | 0.3888 | 0.3907 | 0.3925 | 0.3944 | 0.3962 | 0.3980 | 0.3997 | 0.4015 |
| 1.3 | 0.4032 | 0.4049 | 0.4066 | 0.4082 | 0.4099 | 0.4115 | 0.4131 | 0.4147 | 0.4162 | 0.4177 |
| 1.4 | 0.4192 | 0.4207 | 0.4222 | 0.4236 | 0.4251 | 0.4265 | 0.4279 | 0.4292 | 0.4306 | 0.4319 |
| 1.5 | 0.4332 | 0.4345 | 0.4357 | 0.4370 | 0.4382 | 0.4394 | 0.4406 | 0.4418 | 0.4429 | 0.4441 |
| 1.6 | 0.4452 | 0.4463 | 0.4474 | 0.4484 | 0.4495 | 0.4505 | 0.4515 | 0.4525 | 0.4535 | 0.4545 |
| 1.7 | 0.4554 | 0.4564 | 0.4573 | 0.4582 | 0.4591 | 0.4599 | 0.4608 | 0.4616 | 0.4625 | 0.4633 |
| 1.8 | 0.4641 | 0.4649 | 0.4656 | 0.4664 | 0.4671 | 0.4678 | 0.4686 | 0.4693 | 0.4699 | 0.4706 |
| 1.9 | 0.4713 | 0.4719 | 0.4726 | 0.4732 | 0.4738 | 0.4744 | 0.4750 | 0.4756 | 0.4761 | 0.4767 |
| 2.0 | 0.4772 | 0.4778 | 0.4783 | 0.4788 | 0.4793 | 0.4798 | 0.4803 | 0.4808 | 0.4812 | 0.4817 |
| 2.1 | 0.4821 | 0.4826 | 0.4830 | 0.4834 | 0.4838 | 0.4842 | 0.4846 | 0.4850 | 0.4854 | 0.4857 |
| 2.2 | 0.4861 | 0.4864 | 0.4868 | 0.4871 | 0.4875 | 0.4878 | 0.4881 | 0.4884 | 0.4887 | 0.4890 |
| 2.3 | 0.4893 | 0.4896 | 0.4898 | 0.4901 | 0.4904 | 0.4906 | 0.4909 | 0.4911 | 0.4913 | 0.4916 |
| 2.4 | 0.4918 | 0.4920 | 0.4922 | 0.4925 | 0.4927 | 0.4929 | 0.4931 | 0.4932 | 0.4934 | 0.4936 |
| 2.5 | 0.4938 | 0.4940 | 0.4941 | 0.4943 | 0.4945 | 0.4946 | 0.4948 | 0.4949 | 0.4951 | 0.4952 |
| 2.6 | 0.4953 | 0.4955 | 0.4956 | 0.4957 | 0.4959 | 0.4960 | 0.4961 | 0.4962 | 0.4963 | 0.4964 |
| 2.7 | 0.4965 | 0.4966 | 0.4967 | 0.4968 | 0.4969 | 0.4970 | 0.4971 | 0.4972 | 0.4973 | 0.4974 |
| 2.8 | 0.4974 | 0.4975 | 0.4976 | 0.4977 | 0.4977 | 0.4978 | 0.4979 | 0.4979 | 0.4980 | 0.4981 |
| 2.9 | 0.4981 | 0.4982 | 0.4982 | 0.4983 | 0.4984 | 0.4984 | 0.4985 | 0.4985 | 0.4986 | 0.4986 |
| 3.0 | 0.4987 | 0.4987 | 0.4987 | 0.4988 | 0.4988 | 0.4989 | 0.4989 | 0.4989 | 0.4990 | 0.4990 |

# SOLUTIONS TO SELECTED ODD-NUMBERED PROBLEMS

## Chapter 1

1. Blacksburg
3. last year; yes
5. U.S.
7. Hall; Dayne
9. a. 15.38, 26.67, 40.54; b. decreases; c. no

## Supplement 2

1. a. Mexico; b. China; c. Taiwan; d. Taiwan
3. a. office building; b. parking lot; c. parking lot or shopping mall; d. parking lot
5. a. risk fund; b. savings bond; c. bond fund; d. bond fund
7. a. Widget; b. EVPI = \$24,000; c. maximax-widget, maximin-nimnot, regret-widget, equal likelihood-widget
9. a. stock 28 boxes, \$53.50; b. EV = \$54.90, EVPI = \$1.60
11. press, EV = \$10,800
13. a. Gordon; b. Jackson; c. Gordon; d. Jackson
15. Do not install power generator; EV = \$552,000
17. oil change and sample; \$400
19. settle; EV = \$600,000
21. grower B; EV = \$39,830

## Chapter 3

1. a. 2000: 84.24%, 2001: 80.22%, 2002: 72.28%, 2003: 65.6%, 2004: 58.3%, decreasing trend; b. 2000: 1.71% and 14.05%, 2001: 5.3% and 14.48%, 2002: 13.32% and 14.4%, 2003: 21.97% and 12.43%, 2004. 29.96% and 11.74%; c. 2000: 6.93 and 44.48, 2001: 7.50 and 47.64, 2002: 7.85 and 50.04, 2003: 6.90 and 44.46, 2004: 5.79 and 38.32
3. a. 139.8; b. good = 91.67%
5. 2002: \$10.54, 2003: \$9.74, 2004: \$9.34; 2002–03: −8.21%, 2003–04: −4.22%
7. a. alternative 2, 204; b. alternative 2
9. a. 5.11; b. 5.11; c. 5.58; d. 5.24
11. a. 6.39; b. \$31,982

## Chapter 4

1. $\bar{p} = 0.151$, UCL = 0.258, LCL = 0.044; out of control
3. $\bar{p} = 0.053$, UCL = 0.100, LCL = 0.005; in control
5. $\bar{c} = 24.73$, UCL = 39.65, LCL = 9.81; out of control
7. $\bar{c} = 10.67$, UCL = 17.20, LCL = 4.14; in control
9. $\bar{c} = 12.75$, UCL = 23.46, LCL = 2.04; in control
11. $\bar{R} = 3.17$, UCL = 6.69, LCL = 0; $\bar{\bar{x}} = 3.00$, UCL = 4.83, LCL = 1.18; in control
13. $\bar{R} = 0.57$, UCL = 1.21, LCL = 0; in control
15. a. $\bar{R} = 2$, UCL = 4.56, LCL = 0; b. out of control
17. $\bar{\bar{x}} = 39.7$, UCL = 43.31, LCL = 36.12; out of control
19. no pattern
21. pattern may exist
23. patterns exist
25. $\bar{\bar{x}} = 3.25$, UCL = 5.50, LCL = 1.00; in control
27. $\bar{c} = 16.3$, UCL = 28.41, LCL = 4.19; in control
29. $\bar{p} = .22$, UCL = .45, LCL = 0; in control
31. $\bar{\bar{x}} = 3.17$, UCL = 5.04, LCL = 1.29; in control
33. $\bar{\bar{x}} = 7.28$, $\bar{R} = 4.25$, $C_p = .81$, $C_{pk} = .52$
35. $C_p = 1.27$, $C_{pk} = .82$
37. process mean = 1125 hr, UCL = 1230, LCL = 1020
39. $\bar{\bar{x}} = 145.06$, $\bar{R} = 6.1$, $C_p$, = .99, $C_{pk} = .86$
41. $\bar{\bar{x}} = 9.42$, $\bar{R} = 8.48$, $C_p = .61$, $C_{pk} = .52$

43. a. $\overline{R} = 3.107$, UCL $= 6.21$, LCL $= 0$; $\overline{\overline{x}} = 5.23$, UCL $= 6.73$, LCL:$= 3.74$; in control;
b. $C_p = .67$, $C_{pk} = .51$; process not capable of producing within specifications, will generate defects.

## Supplement 4

1. a. $n = 131$, $c = 5$, $\alpha = .0049$, $\beta = .095$
3. no; $n = 208$, $c \leq 18$
5. $n = 131$, $c = 5$

## Chapter 5

3. 0.934
5. 0.944
7. a. no; b. 0.9919
9. a. professional; b. standard
11. 80.65%
13. Airway

## Chapter 6

3. 500; $7500
5. 625; $31,250
7. a. 18,118; b. 363 days, 91 days; c. 84 days, yes
9. choose supplier if demand <800; choose process B if demand >2000; choose process A otherwise
11. a. >187 min; b. >226 min
13. choose provider 1 if claims >10; choose provider 2 if claims <5; otherwise, choose provider 3
15. choose labor-intensive if units <6667; choose fully automated if units >41,666; otherwise, choose automated
17. choose A if demand <2400; choose C if demand >20,000; otherwise, choose B
19. choose A if rent <20 movies; choose C if rent >40 movies; choose B otherwise
21. a. 3.53 hr; b. 162.74%

## Chapter 7

1.

| 3 | 1 | 2 |
|---|---|---|
| 4 | 6 | 5 |

3.

| 1 | 3 | 2 |
|---|---|---|
| | 5 | 4 |

5.

| 2 | 1 | 3 |
|---|---|---|
| 4 | 5 | |

7. a. 135; b. 70; c. switch 4 and 5, or 1 and 3
9.

| 1 | 3 | 2 |
|---|---|---|
| 4 | 5 | 6 |

; 90 nonadjacent loads

11.

B A C
E D F

13. A, B → D → C, E ; 85.19%, 53.33

15. a. A → B, C, D → E, F, G → H, I, J (multiple solutions); 4 workers; 77.5%;
b. A, B, C, D → E, F, G → H, I, J ; 3 workers, 93.94% (multiple solutions)

17. $C_d = 4$ min; N = 4; A, E → B, C → D → F ; 100%

19. 4 students; | A, B | → | C | → | D, E | → | F |; no, students would have to work more than 5 days a week (multiple solutions)
21. | A, B, C, D, E | → | F, G, H | → | I, J | → | K |; (multiple solutions); 75%
23. Multiple solutions; | A, B, D | → | E, F, C | → | G, H, I | → | J, K |; 34 beds;
or | A, B, D | → | E, F, H | → | G, I, J | → | C, K |; 36 beds
25. | A, D, F | → | E, H | → | B, C, G | → | I, J, K |; 95.8%; 40 units
27.

| | | | |
|---|---|---|---|
| 1 | 7 | 8 | 9 |
| 2 | 6 | 10 | 11 |
| 3 | 4 | 5 | 12 |

## Supplement 7

1. Mall 1 = 62.75, mall 2 = 73.50, mall 3 = 79.50, mall 4 = 67.00; select mall 3
3. South = 73.80, West A = 74.50, West B = 67.25, East = 73.90; select East
5. C = 76, E = 75, D = 74, B = 70, A = 69; select E
7. $x = 19.68$, $y = 19.26$
9. LD(A) = 22,549.4, LD(B) = 20,505.1, LD(C) = 19,640.5; site C
11. $x = 1{,}665.4$, $y = 1{,}562.9$
13. a. $x = 78.8$, $y = 106.0$; b. Seagrove closest, Ashboro better
15. $x = 265.33$, $y = 363.84$

## Chapter 8

1. $t_{100} = 20.5$ min; 16,424.1 min per week
3. $t_{60} = 48.89$ hr, $t_{120} = 44.98$ hr
5. 0.9024
7. $t_{80} = 45.1$ sec
9. $t_{136{,}000} = 3$ min per line; 250 lines

## Supplement 8

1. 4.163 min
3. a. 2.39 min; b. avg. = $4.52/hr, subject = $4.82/hr
5. a. 4.52 min; b. $n = 31$
7. $n = 12.2$ or 13 cycles
9. a. 1.383 min; b. $n = 7.7$ or 8 cycles; c. poorer quality
11. $n = 683$
13. a. 88.8%; b. 151 more observations
15. 3.946 min
17. a. $n = 271$
19. a. 347 additional observations; b. 69%

## Chapter 9

1. Time = 10 weeks
3. a. 23 weeks; $s_1 = 0$, $s_2 = 1$, $s_3 = 0$, $s_4 = 10$, $s_5 = 1$, $s_6 = 0$, $s_7 = 9$, $s_8 = 0$, $s_9 = 11$; b. 1-3-6-8
5. 1: ES =0, EF = 7, LS = 2, LF = 9, S = 2; 2: ES = 0, EF = 10, LS = 0, LF = 10, S = 0; 3: ES = 7, EF = 13, LS = 9, LF = 15, S = 2; 4: ES = 10, EF = 15, LS = 10, LF = 15, S = 0; 5: ES = 10, EF = 14, LS = 14, LF = 18, S = 4; 6: ES = 15, EF = 18, LS = 15, LF = 18, S = 0; 7: ES = 18, EF = 20, LS = 18, LF = 20, S = 0; CP = 2-4-6-7
7. 1: ES = 0, EF = 10, LS = 0, LF = 10, S = 0; 2: ES = 0, EF = 7, LS = 5, LF = 12, S = 5; 4: ES = 10, EF = 14, LS = 14, LF = 18, S = 4; 3: ES = 10, EF = 25, LS = 10, LF = 25, S = 0; 5: ES = 7, EF = 13, LS = 12, LF = 18, S = 5; 6: ES = 7, EF = 19, LS = 13, LF = 25, S = 6; 7: ES = 14, EF = 21, LS = 18, LF = 25, S = 4; 8: ES = 25, EF = 34, LS = 25, LF = 34, S = 0; CP = 1-3-8 = 34
9. CP = 1-3-7-8-10-12 = 15 days
11. CP = a-b-f-h = 15 wk

13. CP = a-d-g-k = 33 wk, $\sigma = 3.87$, $P(x \leq 40) = .9649$
15. e. CP = 1-3-7-8-10-12; f. 18 months
17. c. CP = b-f-j-k; d. 28.17 wk; e. 0.0113
19. 57.33 days; $P(x \leq 67) = .9535$
21. CP = a-c-d-h-l-o-q = 118.67; $P(x \leq 120) = .59$
23. crash cost = $23,250
25. CP = a-d-g-k, crashing cost = $5100
27. CP = a-e-f-g-j-o-p = 91.667; $P(x \leq 101) = .9976$
29. CP = a-h-l-m-n-o-s-w = 126.67 days; $P(x \leq 150) = .9979$

## Chapter 10

1. Inventory turns = 14.2; days of supply = 25.94
3. Inventory turns = 18.4; weeks of supply = 2.7
5. (a) year 1: inventory turns = 8, days of supply = 45.7; year 2: inventory turns = 8.3, days of supply = 44.1; year 3: inventory turns = 11.1, days of supply = 32.8; year 4: inventory turns = 12, days of supply = 30.5. (b) marginally improved
7. $\bar{c} = 7.3$, UCL = 15.41, LCL = 0, in control
9. $\bar{p} = 0.421$, UCL = .069, LCL = .015; out of control
11. $\bar{\bar{x}} = 3.17$, UCL = 5.04, LCL = 1.29; $\bar{R} = 3.25$, UCL = 6.86, LCL = 0; out of control

## Supplement 10

1. Bethlehem − Detroit = 130, Bethlehem − St. Louis = 50, Birmingham − Detroit = 30, Birmingham − Norfolk = 220, Gary − St. Louis = 70, Gary − Chicago = 170; $84,100.
3. T − NY = 160, T − C = 130, M − P = 140, F − P = 70, F − B = 180; $6220
5. P − L = 10, S − L = 5, St.L. − C = 15, D − G = 10, D − C = 5; $215,000
7. A − B = 25, A − P = 25, St.L. − B = 25, St.L. − D = 90; $10,500
9. No change
11. Alternative 1 = $28,920, alternative 2 = $25,600; select 2
13. 1 − 1 = 27, 1 − 2 = 5, 1 − 4 = 10, 2 − 2 = 21, 3 − 3 = 18, 4 − 4 = 23, 5 − 4 = 4, 5 − 5 = 31, 6 − 3 = 4, 6 − 4 = 7, 6 − 6 = 16; 467 miles
15. A − 3 = 1, C − 1 = 1, D − 1 = 1, E − 3 = 1, F − 2 = 1, G − 2 = 1, H − 1 = 1; 1070
17. N − Addison = 270, S − Beeks = 120, S − Canfield = 190, E − Addison = 130, E − Canfield = 190, W − Daley = 220, C − Beeks = 280; 20,550 minutes
19. A − 3, = 8, A − 4 = 18, B − 3 = 13, B − 5 = 27, D − 3 = 5, D − 6 = 35, E − 1 = 25, E − 2 = 15, E − 3 = 4; $1528
21. 1 − E = 8, 2 − C = 12, 3 − E = 2, 4 − D = 8, 5 − A = 9, 6 − B = 6; 1,236 hrs.
23. Sac. − St Paul = 15, Sac. − Topeka = 1, Bak. − Denver = 10, S.A. − Topeka = 12, Mont. − Denver = 10, Jack. − Akron = 15, Jack. − Topeka = 7, Ocala − Louisville = 15; $276,200
25. L.A. − Singapore = 150, L.A. − Taipei = 300, Savannah − H.K. = 400, Savannah − Taipei = 200, Galv. − Singapore = 350, Shortages − H.K. = 200; $723,500; penalties = $160,000
27. Mexico − Houston = 18, P.R. − Miami = 11, Haiti − Miami = 23, Miami − NY = 20, Miami − St.L. = 12, Miami − L.A. = 2, Houston − L.A. = 18; $479,000
29. 1 − C = 70, 2 − B = 80, 3 − A = 50, B − A = 10, C − B = 6 ; 30; $14,900

## Chapter 11

1. a. Apr = 8.67, May = 8.33, Jun = 8.33, Jul = 9.00, Aug = 9.67, Sep = 11.0, Oct = 11.00, Nov = 11.00, Dec = 12.00, Jan = 13.33; b. Jun = 8.20, Jul = 8.80, Aug = 9.40, Sep = 9.60, Oct = 10.40, Nov = 11.00, Dec = 11.40, Jan = 12.60; c. MAD(3) = 1.89, MAD(5) = 2.43
3. a. $F_4 = 116.00$, $F_5 = 121.33$, $F_6 = 118.00$, $F_7 = 143.67$, $F_8 = 138.33$, $F_9 = 141.67$, $F_{10} = 135.00$, $F_{11} = 156.67$, $F_{12} = 143.33$, $F_{13} = 136.67$; b. $F_6 = 121.80$, $F_7 = 134.80$, $F_8 = 125.80$, $F_9 = 137.20$, $F_{10} = 143.00$, $F_{11} = 149.00$, $F_{12} = 137.00$, $F_{13} = 142.00$; c. $F_4 = 113.95$, $F_5 = 116.69$, $F_6 = 125.74$, $F_7 = 151.77$, $F_8 = 132.4$, $F_9 = 138.55$; $F_{10} = 142.35$, $F_{11} = 160.00$, $F_{12} = 136.69$, $F_{13} = 130.20$; d. 3-qtr MA: $E = 32.0$, 5-qtr MA: $E = 36.4$, weighted MA: $E = 28.05$
5. a. $F_4 = 276.67$, $F_5 = 283.32$, $F_6 = 303.33$, $F_7 = 356.67$, $F_8 = 393.33$, $F_9 = 420.00$; b. $F_2 = 270.00$, $F_3 = 278.00$, $F_4 = 272.40$, $F_5 = 275.92$, $F_6 = 294.74$, $F_7 = 317.79$, $F_8 = 334.23$, $F_9 = 357.38$; c. 3-sem MAD = 61.33, exp. smooth MAD = 70.42
7. $F_{11}$ (exp. smooth) = 68.6, $F_{11}$ (adjusted) = 69.17, $F_{11}$ (linear trend) = 70.22; exp. smooth: $E = 14.75$, MAD = 1.89; adjusted: $E = 10.73$, MAD = 1.72; linear trend: MAD = 1.09
9. a. MAD = 3.12; b. MAD = 2.98; c. MAD = 2.87

11. $F_{13} = 631.22$, $\bar{E} = 26.30$, $E = 289.33$, biased low
13. $F_1 = 155.6$, $F_2 = 192.9$, $F_3 = 118.2$, $F_4 = 155.6$
15. $F_9$ (adjusted) $= 3{,}313.19$, $F_9$ (linear trend) $= 2{,}785.00$; adjusted: MAD $= 431.71$, $E = -2{,}522$; linear trend: MAD $= 166.25$
17. $y = 195.55 + 2.39x$; fall $= 44.61$ winter $= 40.13$, spring $= 52.38$, summer $= 70.34$
19. $E = 86.00$, $\bar{E} = 8.60$, MAD $= 15.00$, MAPD $= 0.08$
21. UCL $= 718.14$, LCL $= -718.84$, no apparent bias
23. a. $\bar{E} = 10.73$, MAD $= 16.76$, MAPD $= 0.1038$, $E = 75.10$; b. $\bar{E} = 8.00$, MAD $= 12.67$, MAPD $= 0.08$, $E = 39.99$; c. biased low
25. MAD $= 1.78$, $E = 12.36$, biased high; MAD (linear trend) $= 0.688$
27. a. $y = 0.51 + 0.403x$, $y(x = 25) = 10.57$; b. R $= .914$
29. 0.694
31. $y = 15.864 - 0.575x$; $r^2 = 0.616$; $y(23) = 2.64\%$
33. $y = 6253.33 - 183.606x$; a. MAD (linear regression) $= 310$, MAD (linear trend) $= 256$; b. $-0.850$
35. a. $y = 380.93 + 16.03x$ ($y = 557.26$); b. $y = -22.07 + 41x$ ($y = 594.10$): (c) "b" best
37. a. $SF_1 = 62.78$, $SF_2 = 68.53$, $SF_3 = 82.89$, $SF_4 = 71.40$; b. Q1 $= 64.64$, Q2 $= 66.06$, Q3 $= 80.82$, Q4 $= 69.27$
39. Exponential smoothing models appear to be most accurate
41. (a) $y = 37.72 + 247x$, 65.15%; (b) $y(11) = 64.54\%$
45. a. $y = 608.795 + 0.215x_1 - 0.985x_2$; b. $r^2 = 0.766$; c. $y = 635.79$

## Chapter 12

1. a. $Q = 120.1$; b. TC $= \$15{,}612.49$; c. 12.49 orders; d. 29.14 days
3. a. $Q = 292.5$; b. TC $= \$7{,}897.47$; c. 56.41 orders; d. 5.67 days
5. a. $Q = 278{,}971.3$; b. TC $= \$22{,}317.71$; c. 5.07 orders; d. 72 days
7. a. $Q = 79$, TC $= \$5{,}924.53$
9. a. $Q = 1{,}264.9$; b. TC $= \$632.46$; c. $R = 54.79$
11. $Q = 20{,}263.88$; TC $= \$486{,}333.22$
13. a. $Q = 2{,}529.8$; b. TC $= \$12{,}648$; c. 4 orders; d. 42.2 days
15. $Q = 90{,}137.52$; TC $= \$3{,}020.45$
17. a. $Q = 9.1$; TC $= \$1{,}095.45$; b. $Q = 6$, TC $= \$1{,}193.33$
19. $Q = 70{,}000$; TC $= \$56{,}000$; 4 orders
21. $Q = 5{,}000$; TC $= \$68{,}725$
23. $Q = 500$; TC $= \$64{,}704$
25. $Q = 6{,}000$; TC $= \$87{,}030.33$
27. $Q = 20{,}000$; TC $= \$893{,}368$
29. $R = 30{,}603.42$; safety stock $= 2{,}603.42$
31. $R = 83{,}016.7$
33. $R = 259.2$; safety stock $= 46.67$
35. $R = 32.38$
37. $Q = 122$ pizzas, 117 pizzas
41. $R = 9.22$

## Supplement 12

1. b. $\mu = 3.48$, EV $= 3.65$, not enough simulations; c. 21 calls, no, repeat simulation
3. $\mu = \$251$
5. reorder at 5-car level
7. avg. waiting time $= 22$ min
11. avg. rating of Salem dates: 2.92

## Chapter 13

1. a. \$2,457,000; b. \$2,367,000 (answers will vary)
3. a. \$448,000; b. \$443,250; c. \$367,600; d. \$388,400; choose chase demand
5. a. \$1,638,800; b. \$284,800; c. \$61,400
7. a. \$381,600; b. \$432,900; no, more work is subcontracted
9. \$367,000
11. \$1,308,900
13. \$314,000
15. \$1,800,000
17. \$451,500
19. 5; 105

21. 16, 0, 0, 0, 55, 27
23. 85, 13, 0, 28, 77, 95; 6 weeks
25. 2 seats; 1 seat
27. 55 seats
29. 20 trees

## Supplement 13

1. a. Maximize $Z = \$2.25x_1 + 3.10x_2$; s.t. $5.0x_1 + 7.5x_2 \le 6500$, $3.0x_1 + 3.2x_2 \le 3000$, $x_2 \le 510$, $x_1 \ge 0$, $x_2 \ge 0$; b. and c. $x_1 = 456$, $x_2 = 510$, $Z = \$2,607$
3. Maximize $Z = 1,800x_{1a} + 2,100x_{1b} + 1,600x_{1c} + 1,000x_{2a} + 700x_{2b} + 900x_{2c} + 1,400x_{3a} + 800x_{3b} + 2,200x_{3c}$; s.t. $x_{1a} + x_{1b} + x_{1c} = 40$, $x_{2a} + x_{2b} + x_{2c} = 40$, $x_{3a} + x_{3b} + x_{3c} = 40$, $x_{1a} + x_{2a} + x_{3a} \le 40$, $x_{1b} + x_{2b} + x_{3b} \le 60$, $x_{1c} + x_{2c} + x_{3c} \le 50$, $x_{ij} \ge 0$; $x_{1b} = 40$, $x_{2a} = 40$, $x_{3c} = 40$, $Z = \$212,000$
5. Maximize $Z = 4.5x_{bs} + 3.75x_{os} + 3.60x_{cs} + 4.8x_{ms} + 3.25x_{bd} + 2.5x_{od} + 2.35x_{cd} + 3.55x_{md} + 1.75x_{br} + 1.00x_{or} + 0.85x_{cr} + 2.05x_{mr}$; s.t. $0.6x_{cs} - 0.4x_{bs} - 0.4x_{os} - 0.4x_{ms} \ge 0$, $-0.3x_{bs} + 0.7x_{os} - 0.3x_{cs} - 0.3x_{ms} \ge 0$, $0.4x_{bd} - 0.6x_{od} - 0.6x_{cd} - 0.6x_{md} \ge 0$, $-0.1x_{bd} - 0.1x_{od} - 0.1x_{cd} + 0.9x_{md} \le 0$, $-0.6x_{br} - 0.6x_{or} - 0.6x_{cr} + 0.4x_{mr} \le 0$, $0.7x_{br} - 0.3x_{or} - 0.3x_{cr} - 0.3x_{mr} \ge 0$, $x_{bs} + x_{bd} + x_{br} \le 110$, $x_{os} + x_{od} + x_{or} \le 80$, $x_{cs} + x_{cd} + x_{cr} \le 70$, $x_{ms} + x_{md} + x_{mr} \le 150$, $x_{ij} \ge 0$
   b. $x_{os} = 52.5$, $x_{cs} = 70$, $x_{ms} = 52.5$, $x_{bd} = 52.2$, $x_{md} = 8.7$, $x_{br} = 57.8$, $x_{or} = 1.4$, $x_{mr} = 88.8$, $x_{od} = 26.1$, $Z = \$1,251$
7. a. Maximize $Z = 8x_1 + 10x_2$; s.t. $x_1 + x_2 \ge 400$, $x_1 \ge 0.4\,(x_1 + x_2)$, $x_2 \le 250$, $x_1 = 2x_2$, $x_1 + x_2 \le 500$, $x_i \ge 0$; b. $x_1 = 333.3$, $x_2 = 166.6$, $Z = 4332.4$
9. Maximize $Z = 3x_{1s} + 5x_{2s} + 6x_{4s} + 9x_{1P} + 11x_{2P} + 6x_{3P} + 12x_{4P} + 1x_{1R} + 3x_{2R} + 4x_{4R} - 2x_{3R}$; s.t. $x_{1S} + x_{2S} + x_{3S} + x_{4S} \ge 3000$, $x_{1P} + x_{2P} + x_{3P} + x_{4P} \ge 3000$, $x_{1R} + x_{2R} + x_{3R} + x_{4R} \ge 4000$, $x_{1S} + x_{1P} + x_{1R} \le 5000$, $x_{2S} + x_{2P} + x_{2R} \le 2400$, $x_{3S} + x_{3P} + x_{3R} \le 4000$, $x_{4S} + x_{4P} + x_{4R} \le 1500$, $0.6x_{1S} - 0.4x_{2S} - 0.4x_{3S} - 0.4x_{4S} \ge 0$, $-0.2x_{1S} + 0.8x_{2S} - 0.2x_{3S} - 0.2x_{4S} \le 0$, $-0.3x_{1S} - 0.3x_{2S} + 0.7x_{3S} - 0.3x_{4S} \ge 0$, $-0.4x_{1P} - 0.4x_{2P} + 0.6x_{3P} - 0.4x_{4P} \ge 0$, $-0.5x_{1R} + 0.5x_{2R} - 0.5x_{3R} - 0.5x_{4R} \le 0$, $0.9x_{1R} - 0.1x_{2R} - 0.1x_{3R} - 0.1x_{4R} \ge 0$, $x_{ij} \ge 0$; $x_{1S} = 1200$, $x_{1R} = 3800$, $x_{2P} = 2200$, $x_{2R} = 200$, $x_{3S} = 900$, $x_{3P} = 3100$, $x_{4S} = 900$, $x_{4P} = 600$, $Z = \$63,400$
11. Minimize $Z = 190\,\Sigma r_j + 260\,\Sigma O_j + 5\,\Sigma i_j$; s.t. $r_j \le 160$, $O_j \le 50$, $r_1 + O_1 - i_1 \ge 105$, $r_2 + O_2 + i_1 - i_2 \ge 170$, $r_3 + O_3 + i_2 - i_3 \ge 230$, $r_4 + O_4 + i_3 - i_4 \ge 180$, $r_5 + O_5 + i_4 - i_5 \ge 150$, $r_6 + O_6 + i_5 \ge 250$, $Z = \$215,600$
13. $x_1 = 12$ A.M. $- 2$ A.M. $= 40$, $x_4 = 20$, $x_5 = 40$, $x_6 = 20$, $x_7 = 10$, $x_9 = 40$, $x_{10} = 10$, $Z = 180$
15. $x_{t1} = 750$, $x_{t2} = 180$, $x_{t3} = 1,680$, $x_{m1} = 750$, $x_{m2} = 450$, $x_{m3} = 480$, $x_{b2} = 270$, $x_{b3} = 240$, $Z = 10,798.50$
17. $x_1 = 3.3$, $x_2 = 6.7$, $Z = 566.67$
19. $x_1 = 376,470.59$; $x_2 = 343,526.41$; $Z = 88,376.47$
21. b. $x_{11} = 65.385$, $x_{14} = 384.615$, $x_{22} = 400$, $x_{23} = 170$, $x_{31} = 150.3$, $x_{33} = 169.7$; $Z = \$11,738.28$
23. $x_{13} = 25,000$, $x_{14} = 8,000$, $x_{16} = 2,000$, $x_{24} = 4,000$, $x_{25} = 8,000$, $x_{34} = 5,000$, $Z = \$59,100$; b. $Z = \$52,000$
25. a. $x_{14} = 20$, $x_{44} = 40$, $x_{35} = 20$, $x_{55} = 60$, $x_{66} = 90$, $x_{17} = 20$, $x_{27} = 30$, $x_{77} = 50$, $y_5 = 5$, $y_6 = 10$, $y_7 = 20$, $Z = \$31,500$; b. $x_{34} = 20$, $x_{44} = 40$, $x_{25} = 5$, $x_{35} = 20$, $x_{55} = 60$, $x_{26} = 10$, $x_{66} = 90$, $x_{17} = 40$, $x_{27} = 25$, $x_{77} = 50$, $y_7 = 5$, $Z = \$26,000$
27. $x_l = 6$, $x_n = 0$, $x_s = 6$, $x_w = 6$, $y_l = 14.44$, $y_n = 10$, $y_s = 7.56$, $y_w = 10$, $Z = \$15,600$
29. $x_1 = 54$, $x_2 = 108$, $x_3 = 162$, $Z = \$253.80$; a. \$0.78; b. \$0; c. $x_1 = 108$, $x_2 = 104$, $x_3 = 162$, $Z = \$249.48$
31. $x_1 = 1,000$, $x_2 = 800$, $x_3 = 200$, $Z = \$760$; a. \$38; b. $x_1 = 1,000$, $x_2 = 1,000$, $Z = \$770$; c. $x_1 = 1,600$, $x_2 = 200$, $x_3 = 200$
33. $x_{A3} = 400$, $x_{A4} = 50$, $x_{B4} = 250$, $x_{B5} = 350$, $x_{C4} = 175$, $x_{C7} = 274.1$, $x_{C8} = 50.93$, $x_{D2} = 131.7$, $x_{D7} = 15.93$, $x_{E1} = 208.33$, $x_{E8} = 149.07$, $x_{F1} = 291.67$, $x_{F2} = 108.3$, $x_{F6} = 460$; $Z = 12,853.33$
35. $x_{12} = x_{13} = x_{14} = x_{15} = 37,000$; $x_{26} = x_{36} = x_{46} = x_{56} = 12,000$; $x_{27} = x_{37} = x_{47} = x_{57} = 6,000$; $x_{28} = x_{38} = x_{48} = x_{58} = 19,000$; $x_{69} = 5,000$; $x_{79} = 6,000$; $x_{89} = 3,000$; $x_{810} = 16,000$; $x_{611} = 7,000$; $x_{912} = 14,000$; $x_{1012} = 16,000$; $x_{1112} = 7,000$; $Z = \$40,680$

## Chapter 14

1. a. 6; b. 7; c. 3
5. b. 800; c. day 1

7. $240.80
9. 100 B's, 50 C's, 50 D's, 400 E's, 900 F's, 200 G's, 100 H's, 100 I's
13.

| Period | 3 | 4 | 5 | 6 | 7 | 8 |
|---|---|---|---|---|---|---|
| X | | | | | 175 | |
| Z | | | | 310 | | |
| T | 530 | 175 | | | | |
| U | | 810 | | | | |
| V | 1500 | | | | | |
| W | 3500 | | | | | |

15. b. 5 days; c. no; d. back panel, side panel, legs, drawer guide
17. a. POQ or EOQ; b. POQ; c. POQ; d. POQ
19. a. Machining 250 hours; Heat treat 500 hours; Assembly 50 hours

## Chapter 15

1. SS50—SS100—SS50—SS200
3. 4 (these answers are rounded up)
5. 125/hr
7. c; decreases
9. a. 9 kanbans, inventory increases; b. 3 kanbans, inventory halved; c. 14 kanbans, no change in inventory

## Chapter 16

1. Jones to Nurse 1, Hathaway to Nurse 2, Sweeney to Nurse 3, Bryant to Nurse 4
3. Product 1 to machine B, product 2 to machine D, product 3 to machine A, product 4 to machine C, product 5 to machine E
5. A to Finance, B to Production, C to Customer Service, D to Logistics, E to Sales, F to Marketing Research
7. FCFS; DDATE or SLACK; Point value of assignment, grade in class, major
9. SPT: 23.88, 9.75, 22, 5; DDATE: 30.75, 8.25, 13, 7; SLACK: 3.63, 9.13, 17, 7; depends on criteria
11. a. 12, 3, 7; b. 12.25, 3.25, 6; c. 13, 3.75, 6; depends on criteria
13. a. 18 hours, b. 20 hours; FCFS
15. E, B, D, C, A; 23
17. 6, 5, 4, 2, 1, 3; 5 hr 35 min
19. Backlog = 20, 10, 5, 5, 10
21. b.

| | M | T | W | Th | F | Sa | Sn |
|---|---|---|---|---|---|---|---|
| K.J. | 0 | x | x | x | x | x | 0 |
| T.S. | 0 | 0 | x | x | x | x | x |
| F.C. | x | x | x | x | 0 | 0 | x |
| S.B. | x | x | x | x | x | 0 | 0 |
| P.T. | x | 0 | 0 | x | x | x | x |

23.

| | M | T | W | Th | F | Sa | Sn |
|---|---|---|---|---|---|---|---|
| A.R. | 0 | 0 | x | x | x | 0 | x |
| S.H. | 0 | x | 0 | x | x | x | 0 |
| J.J. | 0 | x | 0 | x | x | x | 0 |
| T.T. | 0 | x | x | 0 | x | x | x |
| E.T. | x | 0 | x | 0 | x | x | x |
| P.D. | x | 0 | x | x | 0 | x | x |

## Chapter 17

1. $L_q = 1.33$, $W_q = 4.80$ min; not good service
3. a. $L_q = 0.5$, $W = 0.20$ hr, $W_q = 0.10$ hr; b. $\lambda > \mu$
5. $\lambda = 9$/hr
7. no
9. a. $L_q = 5.14$ trucks, $W = 0.05$ day, $W_q = 0.03$ day; b. yes
11. $L = 1.01$, $L_q = 0.177$, $W = 0.101$ hr, $W_q = .0175$ hr; yes
13. Yes, assign an operator
15. $P_0 = 0.005$, $L = 7.94$, $L_q = 2.938$, $W_q = .783$, $W = 2.11$
17. Yes, hire a third doctor
19. 3 servers should be sufficient
21. Add more employees; expected savings = $25.50/day
23. $L_q = 1.94$, $W_q = 0.176$ hr
25. $P_{n \geq 10} = 0.4182$

27. 7:00 A.M. − 9:00 A.M. = 4, 9:00 A.M. − noon = 2, noon − 2:00 P.M. = 6, 2:00 P.M. − 5:00 P.M. = 4
29. $L = 0.1476$ car out of service, $W = 13.52$ hr.
31. Select new service agreement, savings = \$1813.50
33. $L_q = 16.35$ manuscripts, $L = 27.78$ manuscripts, $W_q = 2.09$ weeks, $w = 3.47$ weeks, $U = 0.952$
35. high-speed copier
37. a. $W_q = 17.34$ min.; b. $P(x \geq 6) = 0.0006$
39. 4 registers
41. $W_q = 0.31$ hr, $W = .81$ hr, system adequate
43. a. $L_q = 1.177$, $W_q = 2.33$ hr, $W = 3.82$ hr, $U = 0.7551$; not effective; reduce athletes to 6.

# Index